CHARLENE FEMMININO

Comprehensive Compound Interest Tables

Newly Revised and Updated Edition

Michael Sherman, Ph.D.

CONTEMPORARY
BOOKS, INC.
CHICAGO • NEW YORK

Acknowledgments

Computer Analyst: Thomas Locke

Copyright © 1986, 1982 by Delphi Information Sciences Corporation
All rights reserved
Published by Contemporary Books, Inc.
180 North Michigan Avenue, Chicago, Illinois 60601
Manufactured in the United States of America
International Standard Book Number: 0-8092-4875-1

Published simultaneously in Canada by Beaverbooks, Ltd.
195 Allstate Parkway, Valleywood Business Park
Markham, Ontario L3R 4T8 Canada

This edition published by arrangement with Delphi Information Sciences
    Corporation

CONTENTS

INTRODUCTION..1
SECTION 1: FUTURE VALUE OF $1
   Instructions..4
   Monthly Compounding...8
   Quarterly Compounding...20
   Semiannual Compounding......................................30
   Annual Compounding..38
SECTION 2: FUTURE VALUE OF $1 PER PERIOD
   Instructions..50
   Monthly Compounding...54
   Quarterly Compounding...66
   Semiannual Compounding......................................76
   Annual Compounding..84
SECTION 3: SINKING FUND OF $1
   Instructions..96
   Monthly Compounding...100
   Quarterly Compounding...112
   Semiannual Compounding......................................122
   Annual Compounding..130
SECTION 4: PRESENT VALUE OF $1
   Instructions..142
   Monthly Compounding...146
   Quarterly Compounding...158
   Semiannual Compounding......................................168
   Annual Compounding..176

SECTION 5: PRESENT VALUE OF $1 PER PERIOD

Instructions..188
Monthly Compounding.....................................192
Quarterly Compounding..................................204
Semiannual Compounding................................214
Annual Compounding.....................................222

SECTION 6: PARTIAL PAYMENT TO AMORTIZE $1

Instructions..234
Monthly Compounding.....................................238
Quarterly Compounding..................................250
Semiannual Compounding................................260
Annual Compounding.....................................268

DEPRECIATION TABLES

Instructions..280
Depreciation Tables.......................................281

INTRODUCTION

The purpose of this book is to show how time affects the value of invested money. The tables and explanations are appropriate for people in business, finance, real estate, or any other field that requires analysis of investments. This handy pocket guide is also useful to students in the investment field. No advanced mathematical skills are required to understand these tables. You need only the ability to read and follow directions.

SCOPE

The main virtue of this pocket edition is that it contains the most comprehensive range of interest rates and terms ever published in a book of this size. Each of the six compound interest functions is represented in a separate section. Within each section, four different compounding periods are displayed: monthly, quarterly, semiannual, and annual. Each section contains the following ranges of interest rates and terms:

- **Monthly Compounding:** Nominal interest rates from 5.25% to 22% by 0.25% increments, then to 24% by 0.50% increments. Terms to 360 months (30 years).
- **Quarterly Compounding:** Nominal interest rates from 5.25% to 16% by 0.25% increments, then to 24% by 0.50% increments. Terms to 120 quarters (30 years).
- **Semiannual Compounding:** Nominal interest rates from 5.25% to 10% by 0.25% increments, then to 24% by 0.50% increments. Terms to 80 half-years (40 years).
- **Annual Compounding:** Nominal interest rates from 5.25% to 22% by 0.25% increments, then to 24% by 0.50% increments. Terms to 50 years.

METHOD

General Principles. To use these tables correctly, your first and most important job is to select the appropriate section for analyzing your financial mathematical problem. The examples in each section are intended to simplify this task. Most of the examples are designed to

1

use only the tables for the applicable section. Complex problems may require the use of more than one compound interest function.

Keep in mind a number of general points when you solve any problem:

- Break down a complicated problem into a few easier problems.
- Remember that all column headings are for *nominal annual rates* of interest. The nominal annual rate is the usual stated rate for any situation involving the repayment of debts or the growth of an investment.
- All tabular entries are based on one dollar as the simplest monetary factor for the calculation of a value. Usually, you will find an answer with only a simple multiplication.

The compounding of interest represents interest on principal plus interest. Interest is earned for a *period*, then it is added to the principal and begins to earn interest. The period is the compounding period. Remember that all tabular entries represent values per period. You must establish the compounding period before you attempt to solve a problem. For you to use the tables directly, a series of payments, deposits, withdrawals, etc., must correspond with the compounding period. If they do not, you must convert them to an equivalent series.

The overriding principle of these tables is the *time value of money*. Money has a certain value today, was worth less yesterday, and will be worth more tomorrow. When you compare two monetary values, it is essential that you compare them at the same moment in time.

Finally, remember the general character of all problems in financial mathematics. They each have the following components: How much was borrowed or invested? How much will be paid back or received? How much time will elapse before the payback or receipt? What is the interest rate *per period*?

Interpolation. The examples in this book have all been written to fit the tables exactly. However, you may find yourself with a problem that has values between those in the tables. All of the tables consist of entries in columns by nominal annual interest rate, and in rows by period (months, quarters, half-years, or years). To find a value that falls between two entries, use interpolation.

Interpolation problems are like simple algebra problems. For example, if 6 pounds of apples cost 18 cents, and 9 pounds cost 27 cents, how much do 7 pounds cost? Intuitively, you can see that the answer lies between 18 and 27 cents. To get a more precise answer, you can use the following equation:

2

$$\text{new cost} = \text{cost}_1 + \frac{\text{new weight} - \text{weight}_1}{\text{weight}_2 - \text{weight}_1} \times (\text{cost}_2 - \text{cost}_1)$$

$$\text{new cost} = 18 + \frac{7 - 6}{9 - 6} \times (27 - 18)$$

new cost = 21 cents

You can use the same kind of equation to apply interpolation to the tables:

$$\text{new entry} = \text{entry}_1 + \frac{\text{new rate} - \text{rate}_1}{\text{rate}_2 - \text{rate}_1} \times (\text{entry}_2 - \text{entry}_1)$$

Hint: Use the smaller entry for entry $_1$

Let's say that you deposited $1,000 in an account that paid interest at the nominal rate of 10.2% compounded monthly. You wish to find how much you will have accumulated in the account at the end of 12 months. In this problem, you use the tables in Section 1, Future Value. Turn to page 11 to find a 10.2% annual rate. There is no column labeled 10.2%. Find the two nearest annual rates that bracket the desired annual rate. In the table on page 11, the annual rates nearest to 10.2% are 10.00% and 10.25%. Look down these two columns to the row for 12 months. The values for 10.00% and 10.25% at 12 months are 1.104713 and 1.107455. Construct a table of these values as follows:

Annual Rate	12-Months Entry
10.00%	1.104713
10.25%	1.107455

To find the entry for 10.2%, use the proportional relationship as shown here:

$$\text{entry} = 1.104713 + \frac{(10.20 - 10.00)}{(10.25 - 10.00)} \times (1.107455 - 1.104713)$$

$$\text{entry} = 1.104713 + \frac{0.20}{0.25} \times 0.002742$$

entry = 1.106907

Thus, the account will grow from $1,000 to $1,106.91 after 12 months. Whenever you complete an interpolation, always check to be sure that the interpolated value falls between the two table entries. In the example, 1.106907 does fall between 1.104713 and 1.107455, which is a clue that you interpolated correctly.

SECTION 1
FUTURE VALUE
OF $1

Future value is the basic compound interest function for a single investment or deposit. You make an investment at the start of a period, interest is earned on the investment, and after each compounding period, interest begins to be earned on the interest as well.

USE OF FUTURE VALUE

Future value is the amount you will have in the future if you start with $1 today. The assumptions are:

- No additional interim investments are made.
- All interest earned is left in the investment to begin earning interest on interest.
- The investment earns interest at a uniform rate throughout the term of the investment.

The tables in this section are used to solve the following types of problems:

1. How much will an investment today be worth in the future?
2. How long will it take for an investment today to grow to a certain value in the future?

4

3. What rate must an investment earn today to be worth a certain value at a certain time in the future?

EXAMPLES

Future Value of an Investment. You have $1,250 to invest today in an account that pays an 8% annual rate compounded monthly. What will the investment be worth in 20 years (240 months)?

Turn to page 9 in the monthly compounding section and locate the column labeled 8.00%. Move down the column to the 20-year row and find the entry 4.926803. Multiply $1,250 by 4.926803 to get $6,158.50, the future value of the investment.

Time to Reach a Future Value. How long will it take you to double your money in an investment that pays a 9% annual rate compounded annually?

Turn to page 40 in the annual compounding section and locate the column labeled 9%. Move down the column and find the entry that is closest to 2. The entry is 1.992563. Move left across the row to the column indicating the number of years. You are in the row corresponding to 8 years. It takes slightly more than 8 years for money to double at 9% interest.

This example demonstrates the "Rule of 72." To estimate how many years it takes for money to double, simply divide 72 by the annual rate of the investment. In the example, 72 divided by 9 equals 8 years. This rule of thumb works very well for most interest rates.

Desired Rate of Interest. What rate of interest must you earn on a $5,000 investment today for it to be worth $7,000 in 36 months? Assume the interest is compounded monthly.

First divide the future investment value by today's value to get the future value factor: $7,000 divided by $5,000 equals 1.4. Turn to the first page of the monthly compounding section and find the row labeled 36 months. Scan across this row until you find the entry that is closest to 1.4. You may have to look at more than one page. On page 12, find the table entry 1.399238. Look at the top of the column to find 11.25%, the annual rate. Your $5,000 must earn slightly more than 11.25% per year to achieve the investment goal. If you wish more precise results, use the interpolation technique discussed in the Introduction.

Comparing Returns. An investor has been offered a choice of two investments. One pays 14% compounded *monthly* for 4 years (48 months); the other pays 14.5% compounded *annually* for 4 years. Which investment will provide the investor with the greater return?

First turn to page 13 in the monthly compounding section and find the column labeled 14%. Move down the column to the 4-year row and read the table entry: 1.745007. Next turn to page 44 in the annual compounding section and find the column labeled 14.50%. Move down the column to the 4-year row and read the table entry: 1.718787. The size of the entry is in proportion to the size of the return. Since the entry for 14.5% compounded annually is smaller, the investor will receive a greater return at 14% compounded monthly.

Change in Interest Rates. An investor placed $6,000 in a savings account that paid 8.5% compounded quarterly. At the end of 3 years (12 quarters), the interest rate was changed to 8% compounded quarterly. The investor maintained the account for an additional 4 years (16 quarters). What will the $6,000 be worth after 7 years?

First find the value of the account after the first 3 years. Turn to page 22 in the quarterly compounding section and find the column labeled 8.50%. Move down the column to the row for the 12th quarter (3rd year) and read the table entry: 1.287019. Multiply $6,000 by 1.287019 to get $7,722.11, the value of the account after the first 3 years.

Next find what this amount grew to during the next 4 years. Turn to page 21 in the quarterly compounding section and find the column labeled 8.00%. Move down the column to the row for the 16th quarter and read the table entry: 1.372786. Multiply $7,722.11 by 1.372786 to get $10,600.80, the value of the account after the full 7 years.

This example demonstrates how one problem is broken into two simpler problems to find the solution.

Partial Withdrawal. An investor deposited $4,000 in an account paying 10% interest compounded monthly. After 48 months he withdrew $1,000. How much will he have accumulated in 10 years? Remember, he withdrew part of the original investment.

First find how much was in the account at the time of the investor's withdrawal. Turn to page 11 of the monthly compounding section and find the column labeled 10.00%. Move down the column to the 4-year row and read the table entry: 1.489354. Multiply $4,000 by 1.489354 to get $5,957.42, the amount accumulated after 4 years.

Now find the amount accumulated after 10 years. Subtract the $1,000 withdrawal made after 4 years to get $4,957.42, the residual value of the account. Return to the 10.00% column on page 11 and move to the 6-year row because the residual value earned interest for 6 more years. Read the table entry: 1.817594. Multiply $4,957.42 by

1.817594 to get $9,010.58, the value of the account after a full 10 years.

THE FORMULA FOR FUTURE VALUE

The symbol S is the widely accepted notation for future value. The formula for figuring future value table entries is:

$$S = (1 + i)^n$$

where:

   i = interest rate per period
   n = number of compounding periods

Note that i is the interest rate *per period*, not the nominal annual rate. You can easily find the interest rate per period by dividing the annual rate by the number of compounding periods per year. For example, a nominal annual rate of 12% compounded monthly converts to 1% per month (12% ÷ 12 months per year).

MOS	5.25% ANNUAL RATE	5.50% ANNUAL RATE	5.75% ANNUAL RATE	6.00% ANNUAL RATE	6.25% ANNUAL RATE	6.50% ANNUAL RATE	MOS
1	1.004 375	1.004 583	1.004 792	1.005 000	1.005 208	1.005 417	1
2	1.008 769	1.009 188	1.009 606	1.010 025	1.010 444	1.010 863	2
3	1.013 183	1.013 813	1.014 444	1.015 075	1.015 707	1.016 338	3
4	1.017 615	1.018 460	1.019 305	1.020 151	1.020 997	1.021 843	4
5	1.022 067	1.023 128	1.024 189	1.025 251	1.026 314	1.027 378	5
6	1.026 539	1.027 817	1.029 097	1.030 378	1.031 660	1.032 943	6
7	1.031 030	1.032 528	1.034 028	1.035 529	1.037 033	1.038 538	7
8	1.035 541	1.037 260	1.038 982	1.040 707	1.042 434	1.044 164	8
9	1.040 071	1.042 014	1.043 961	1.045 911	1.047 864	1.049 820	9
10	1.044 621	1.046 790	1.048 963	1.051 140	1.053 321	1.055 506	10
11	1.049 192	1.051 588	1.053 989	1.056 396	1.058 807	1.061 224	11
12	1.053 782	1.056 408	1.059 040	1.061 678	1.064 322	1.066 972	12
13	1.058 392	1.061 250	1.064 114	1.066 986	1.069 865	1.072 751	13
14	1.063 023	1.066 114	1.069 213	1.072 321	1.075 437	1.078 562	14
15	1.067 673	1.071 000	1.074 337	1.077 683	1.081 039	1.084 404	15
16	1.072 344	1.075 909	1.079 484	1.083 071	1.086 669	1.090 278	16
17	1.077 036	1.080 840	1.084 657	1.088 487	1.092 329	1.096 184	17
18	1.081 748	1.085 794	1.089 854	1.093 929	1.098 018	1.102 121	18
19	1.086 481	1.090 771	1.095 077	1.099 399	1.103 737	1.108 091	19
20	1.091 234	1.095 770	1.100 324	1.104 896	1.109 485	1.114 093	20
21	1.096 008	1.100 792	1.105 596	1.110 420	1.115 264	1.120 128	21
22	1.100 803	1.105 837	1.110 894	1.115 972	1.121 073	1.126 195	22
23	1.105 619	1.110 906	1.116 217	1.121 552	1.126 912	1.132 296	23
24	1.110 456	1.115 998	1.121 565	1.127 160	1.132 781	1.138 429	24
25	1.115 315	1.121 113	1.126 940	1.132 796	1.138 681	1.144 595	25
26	1.120 194	1.126 251	1.132 339	1.138 460	1.144 611	1.150 795	26
27	1.125 095	1.131 413	1.137 765	1.144 152	1.150 573	1.157 029	27
28	1.130 017	1.136 599	1.143 217	1.149 873	1.156 566	1.163 296	28
29	1.134 961	1.141 808	1.148 695	1.155 622	1.162 589	1.169 597	29
30	1.139 926	1.147 041	1.154 199	1.161 400	1.168 644	1.175 933	30
31	1.144 914	1.152 299	1.159 730	1.167 207	1.174 731	1.182 302	31
32	1.149 923	1.157 580	1.165 287	1.173 043	1.180 850	1.188 706	32
33	1.154 954	1.162 886	1.170 870	1.178 908	1.187 000	1.195 145	33
34	1.160 006	1.168 215	1.176 481	1.184 803	1.193 182	1.201 619	34
35	1.165 081	1.173 570	1.182 118	1.190 727	1.199 397	1.208 128	35
36	1.170 179	1.178 949	1.187 782	1.196 681	1.205 643	1.214 672	36
37	1.175 298	1.184 352	1.193 474	1.202 664	1.211 923	1.221 251	37
38	1.180 440	1.189 780	1.199 193	1.208 677	1.218 235	1.227 866	38
39	1.185 605	1.195 234	1.204 939	1.214 721	1.224 580	1.234 517	39
40	1.190 792	1.200 712	1.210 712	1.220 794	1.230 958	1.241 204	40
41	1.196 001	1.206 215	1.216 514	1.226 898	1.237 369	1.247 927	41
42	1.201 234	1.211 743	1.222 343	1.233 033	1.243 814	1.254 687	42
43	1.206 489	1.217 297	1.228 200	1.239 198	1.250 292	1.261 483	43
44	1.211 768	1.222 877	1.234 085	1.245 394	1.256 804	1.268 316	44
45	1.217 069	1.228 481	1.239 998	1.251 621	1.263 350	1.275 186	45
46	1.222 394	1.234 112	1.245 940	1.257 879	1.269 930	1.282 093	46
47	1.227 742	1.239 768	1.251 910	1.264 168	1.276 544	1.289 038	47

YRS							
4	1.233 113	1.245 451	1.257 909	1.270 489	1.283 193	1.296 020	48
5	1.299 432	1.315 704	1.332 176	1.348 850	1.365 730	1.382 817	60
6	1.369 318	1.389 920	1.410 827	1.432 044	1.453 576	1.475 427	72
7	1.442 963	1.468 322	1.494 122	1.520 370	1.547 073	1.574 239	84
8	1.520 568	1.551 147	1.582 335	1.614 143	1.646 583	1.679 669	96
9	1.602 347	1.638 644	1.675 755	1.713 699	1.752 495	1.792 160	108
10	1.688 524	1.731 076	1.774 692	1.819 397	1.865 218	1.912 184	120
11	1.779 336	1.828 723	1.879 469	1.931 613	1.985 192	2.040 246	132
12	1.875 032	1.931 877	1.990 433	2.050 751	2.112 884	2.176 885	144
13	1.975 875	2.040 850	2.107 948	2.177 237	2.248 788	2.322 675	156
14	2.082 141	2.155 970	2.232 401	2.311 524	2.393 434	2.478 229	168
15	2.194 123	2.277 584	2.364 201	2.454 094	2.547 384	2.644 201	180
16	2.312 127	2.406 057	2.503 783	2.605 457	2.711 237	2.821 288	192
17	2.436 477	2.541 778	2.651 606	2.766 156	2.885 628	3.010 235	204
18	2.567 516	2.685 154	2.808 156	2.936 766	3.071 237	3.211 836	216
19	2.705 602	2.836 618	2.973 950	3.117 899	3.268 785	3.426 938	228
20	2.851 114	2.996 626	3.149 531	3.310 204	3.479 039	3.656 447	240
21	3.004 452	3.165 659	3.335 479	3.514 371	3.702 817	3.901 326	252
22	3.166 037	3.344 227	3.532 405	3.731 129	3.940 989	4.162 605	264
23	3.336 313	3.532 868	3.740 958	3.961 257	4.194 480	4.441 382	276
24	3.515 746	3.732 149	3.961 823	4.205 579	4.464 277	4.738 830	288
25	3.704 830	3.942 672	4.195 728	4.464 970	4.751 427	5.056 198	300
26	3.904 082	4.165 069	4.443 443	4.740 359	5.057 048	5.394 821	312
27	4.114 051	4.400 012	4.705 784	5.032 734	5.382 326	5.756 122	324
28	4.335 313	4.648 207	4.983 612	5.343 142	5.728 527	6.141 620	336
29	4.568 474	4.910 403	5.277 844	5.672 696	6.096 997	6.552 936	348
30	4.814 175	5.187 388	5.589 447	6.022 575	6.489 166	6.991 798	360

8

FUTURE VALUE

MONTHLY COMPOUNDING

MOS	6.75% ANNUAL RATE	7.00% ANNUAL RATE	7.25% ANNUAL RATE	7.50% ANNUAL RATE	7.75% ANNUAL RATE	8.00% ANNUAL RATE	MOS
1	1.005 625	1.005 833	1.006 042	1.006 250	1.006 458	1.006 667	1
2	1.011 282	1.011 701	1.012 120	1.012 539	1.012 958	1.013 378	2
3	1.016 970	1.017 602	1.018 235	1.018 867	1.019 500	1.020 134	3
4	1.022 691	1.023 538	1.024 387	1.025 235	1.026 085	1.026 935	4
5	1.028 443	1.029 509	1.030 576	1.031 643	1.032 711	1.033 781	5
6	1.034 228	1.035 514	1.036 802	1.038 091	1.039 381	1.040 673	6
7	1.040 046	1.041 555	1.043 066	1.044 579	1.046 094	1.047 610	7
8	1.045 896	1.047 631	1.049 368	1.051 108	1.052 850	1.054 595	8
9	1.051 779	1.053 742	1.055 708	1.057 677	1.059 649	1.061 625	9
10	1.057 695	1.059 889	1.062 086	1.064 287	1.066 493	1.068 703	10
11	1.063 645	1.066 071	1.068 503	1.070 939	1.073 381	1.075 827	11
12	1.069 628	1.072 290	1.074 958	1.077 633	1.080 313	1.083 000	12
13	1.075 645	1.078 545	1.081 453	1.084 368	1.087 290	1.090 220	13
14	1.081 695	1.084 837	1.087 987	1.091 145	1.094 312	1.097 488	14
15	1.087 780	1.091 165	1.094 560	1.097 965	1.101 380	1.104 804	15
16	1.093 898	1.097 530	1.101 173	1.104 827	1.108 493	1.112 170	16
17	1.100 052	1.103 932	1.107 826	1.111 732	1.115 652	1.119 584	17
18	1.106 239	1.110 372	1.114 519	1.118 681	1.122 857	1.127 048	18
19	1.112 462	1.116 849	1.121 252	1.125 672	1.130 109	1.134 562	19
20	1.118 720	1.123 364	1.128 027	1.132 708	1.137 407	1.142 125	20
21	1.125 012	1.129 917	1.134 842	1.139 787	1.144 753	1.149 740	21
22	1.131 341	1.136 508	1.141 698	1.146 911	1.152 146	1.157 404	22
23	1.137 704	1.143 138	1.148 596	1.154 079	1.159 587	1.165 120	23
24	1.144 104	1.149 806	1.155 535	1.161 292	1.167 076	1.172 888	24
25	1.150 540	1.156 513	1.162 517	1.168 550	1.174 614	1.180 707	25
26	1.157 011	1.163 260	1.169 540	1.175 854	1.182 200	1.188 579	26
27	1.163 519	1.170 045	1.176 606	1.183 203	1.189 835	1.196 502	27
28	1.170 064	1.176 870	1.183 715	1.190 598	1.197 519	1.204 479	28
29	1.176 646	1.183 736	1.190 866	1.198 039	1.205 253	1.212 509	29
30	1.183 265	1.190 641	1.198 061	1.205 527	1.213 037	1.220 592	30
31	1.189 920	1.197 586	1.205 300	1.213 061	1.220 871	1.228 730	31
32	1.196 614	1.204 572	1.212 582	1.220 643	1.228 756	1.236 921	32
33	1.203 345	1.211 599	1.219 908	1.228 272	1.236 692	1.245 167	33
34	1.210 113	1.218 666	1.227 278	1.235 949	1.244 679	1.253 468	34
35	1.216 920	1.225 775	1.234 693	1.243 673	1.252 717	1.261 825	35
36	1.223 766	1.232 926	1.242 152	1.251 446	1.260 808	1.270 237	36
37	1.230 649	1.240 118	1.249 657	1.259 268	1.268 950	1.278 705	37
38	1.237 572	1.247 352	1.257 207	1.267 138	1.277 146	1.287 230	38
39	1.244 533	1.254 628	1.264 803	1.275 058	1.285 394	1.295 812	39
40	1.251 533	1.261 947	1.272 444	1.283 027	1.293 695	1.304 450	40
41	1.258 573	1.269 308	1.280 132	1.291 046	1.302 050	1.313 147	41
42	1.265 653	1.276 712	1.287 866	1.299 115	1.310 460	1.321 901	42
43	1.272 772	1.284 160	1.295 647	1.307 234	1.318 923	1.330 714	43
44	1.279 931	1.291 651	1.303 475	1.315 404	1.327 441	1.339 585	44
45	1.287 131	1.299 185	1.311 350	1.323 626	1.336 014	1.348 516	45
46	1.294 371	1.306 764	1.319 273	1.331 898	1.344 642	1.357 506	46
47	1.301 652	1.314 387	1.327 243	1.340 223	1.353 327	1.366 556	47

YRS							
4	1.308 974	1.322 054	1.335 262	1.348 599	1.362 067	1.375 666	48
5	1.400 115	1.417 625	1.435 351	1.453 294	1.471 458	1.489 846	60
6	1.497 602	1.520 106	1.542 942	1.566 117	1.589 636	1.613 502	72
7	1.601 877	1.629 994	1.658 599	1.687 699	1.717 304	1.747 422	84
8	1.713 412	1.747 826	1.782 924	1.818 720	1.855 226	1.892 457	96
9	1.832 714	1.874 177	1.916 569	1.959 912	2.004 225	2.049 530	108
10	1.960 322	2.009 661	2.060 232	2.112 065	2.165 190	2.219 640	120
11	2.096 815	2.154 940	2.214 664	2.276 030	2.339 083	2.403 869	132
12	2.242 812	2.310 721	2.380 671	2.452 724	2.526 942	2.603 389	144
13	2.398 974	2.477 763	2.559 122	2.643 135	2.729 888	2.819 469	156
14	2.566 010	2.656 881	2.750 950	2.848 329	2.949 133	3.053 484	168
15	2.744 676	2.848 947	2.957 156	3.069 452	3.185 987	3.306 921	180
16	2.935 782	3.054 897	3.178 819	3.307 741	3.441 863	3.581 394	192
17	3.140 194	3.275 736	3.417 098	3.564 530	3.718 290	3.878 648	204
18	3.358 840	3.512 539	3.673 238	3.841 254	4.016 917	4.200 574	216
19	3.592 709	3.766 461	3.948 578	4.139 460	4.339 527	4.549 220	228
20	3.842 862	4.038 739	4.244 557	4.460 817	4.688 048	4.926 803	240
21	4.110 432	4.330 700	4.562 721	4.807 122	5.064 559	5.335 725	252
22	4.396 633	4.643 766	4.904 735	5.180 311	5.471 309	5.778 588	264
23	4.702 762	4.979 464	5.272 386	5.582 472	5.910 726	6.258 207	276
24	5.030 205	5.339 430	5.667 595	6.015 854	6.385 434	6.777 636	288
25	5.380 448	5.725 418	6.092 428	6.482 880	6.898 268	7.340 176	300
26	5.755 077	6.139 309	6.549 106	6.986 163	7.452 288	7.949 407	312
27	6.155 792	6.583 120	7.040 016	7.528 517	8.050 804	8.609 204	324
28	6.584 407	7.059 015	7.567 724	8.112 976	8.697 388	9.323 763	336
29	7.042 865	7.569 311	8.134 987	8.742 807	9.395 901	10.097 631	348
30	7.533 245	8.116 497	8.744 772	9.421 534	10.150 514	10.935 730	360

FUTURE VALUE

MONTHLY COMPOUNDING

MOS	8.25% ANNUAL RATE	8.50% ANNUAL RATE	8.75% ANNUAL RATE	9.00% ANNUAL RATE	9.25% ANNUAL RATE	9.50% ANNUAL RATE	MOS
1	1.006 875	1.007 083	1.007 292	1.007 500	1.007 708	1.007 917	1
2	1.013 797	1.014 217	1.014 637	1.015 056	1.015 476	1.015 896	2
3	1.020 767	1.021 401	1.022 035	1.022 669	1.023 304	1.023 939	3
4	1.027 785	1.028 636	1.029 487	1.030 339	1.031 192	1.032 045	4
5	1.034 851	1.035 922	1.036 994	1.038 067	1.039 140	1.040 215	5
6	1.041 966	1.043 260	1.044 555	1.045 852	1.047 150	1.048 450	6
7	1.049 129	1.050 650	1.052 172	1.053 696	1.055 222	1.056 750	7
8	1.056 342	1.058 092	1.059 844	1.061 599	1.063 356	1.065 116	8
9	1.063 604	1.065 586	1.067 572	1.069 561	1.071 553	1.073 548	9
10	1.070 916	1.073 134	1.075 356	1.077 583	1.079 813	1.082 047	10
11	1.078 279	1.080 736	1.083 198	1.085 664	1.088 136	1.090 614	11
12	1.085 692	1.088 391	1.091 096	1.093 807	1.096 524	1.099 248	12
13	1.093 156	1.096 100	1.099 052	1.102 010	1.104 977	1.107 950	13
14	1.100 672	1.103 864	1.107 066	1.110 276	1.113 494	1.116 721	14
15	1.108 239	1.111 683	1.115 138	1.118 603	1.122 077	1.125 562	15
16	1.115 858	1.119 558	1.123 269	1.126 992	1.130 727	1.134 473	16
17	1.123 530	1.127 488	1.131 460	1.135 445	1.139 443	1.143 454	17
18	1.131 254	1.135 474	1.139 710	1.143 960	1.148 226	1.152 506	18
19	1.139 031	1.143 517	1.148 020	1.152 540	1.157 077	1.161 630	19
20	1.146 862	1.151 617	1.156 391	1.161 184	1.165 996	1.170 826	20
21	1.154 747	1.159 775	1.164 823	1.169 893	1.174 984	1.180 096	21
22	1.162 686	1.167 990	1.173 317	1.178 667	1.184 041	1.189 438	22
23	1.170 679	1.176 263	1.181 872	1.187 507	1.193 168	1.198 854	23
24	1.178 727	1.184 595	1.190 490	1.196 414	1.202 365	1.208 345	24
25	1.186 831	1.192 986	1.199 171	1.205 387	1.211 633	1.217 911	25
26	1.194 991	1.201 436	1.207 915	1.214 427	1.220 973	1.227 553	26
27	1.203 206	1.209 946	1.216 722	1.223 535	1.230 385	1.237 271	27
28	1.211 478	1.218 517	1.225 594	1.232 712	1.239 869	1.247 066	28
29	1.219 807	1.227 148	1.234 531	1.241 957	1.249 426	1.256 939	29
30	1.228 193	1.235 840	1.243 533	1.251 272	1.259 057	1.266 890	30
31	1.236 637	1.244 594	1.252 600	1.260 656	1.268 763	1.276 919	31
32	1.245 139	1.253 410	1.261 734	1.270 111	1.278 543	1.287 028	32
33	1.253 699	1.262 288	1.270 934	1.279 637	1.288 398	1.297 217	33
34	1.262 319	1.271 229	1.280 201	1.289 234	1.298 329	1.307 487	34
35	1.270 997	1.280 234	1.289 536	1.298 904	1.308 337	1.317 838	35
36	1.279 735	1.289 302	1.298 939	1.308 645	1.318 422	1.328 271	36
37	1.288 533	1.298 435	1.308 410	1.318 460	1.328 585	1.338 786	37
38	1.297 392	1.307 632	1.317 951	1.328 349	1.338 827	1.349 385	38
39	1.306 312	1.316 894	1.327 561	1.338 311	1.349 147	1.360 067	39
40	1.315 292	1.326 222	1.337 241	1.348 349	1.359 546	1.370 835	40
41	1.324 335	1.335 616	1.346 992	1.358 461	1.370 026	1.381 687	41
42	1.333 440	1.345 077	1.356 813	1.368 650	1.380 587	1.392 625	42
43	1.342 607	1.354 605	1.366 707	1.378 915	1.391 229	1.403 650	43
44	1.351 838	1.364 200	1.376 672	1.389 256	1.401 953	1.414 763	44
45	1.361 132	1.373 863	1.386 711	1.399 676	1.412 760	1.425 963	45
46	1.370 489	1.383 594	1.396 822	1.410 173	1.423 650	1.437 252	46
47	1.379 911	1.393 395	1.407 007	1.420 750	1.434 624	1.448 630	47

YRS							
4	1.389 398	1.403 265	1.417 267	1.431 405	1.445 682	1.460 098	48
5	1.508 459	1.527 301	1.546 374	1.565 681	1.585 225	1.605 009	60
6	1.637 722	1.662 300	1.687 242	1.712 553	1.738 238	1.764 303	72
7	1.778 062	1.809 232	1.840 943	1.873 202	1.906 020	1.939 406	84
8	1.930 428	1.969 152	2.008 645	2.048 921	2.089 997	2.131 887	96
9	2.095 850	2.143 207	2.191 624	2.241 124	2.291 732	2.343 472	108
10	2.275 448	2.332 647	2.391 272	2.451 357	2.512 939	2.576 055	120
11	2.470 436	2.538 832	2.609 107	2.681 311	2.755 499	2.831 723	132
12	2.682 133	2.763 242	2.846 785	2.932 837	3.021 471	3.112 744	144
13	2.911 971	3.007 487	3.106 116	3.207 957	3.313 116	3.421 699	156
14	3.161 504	3.273 321	3.389 070	3.508 886	3.632 911	3.761 294	168
15	3.432 420	3.562 653	3.697 800	3.838 043	3.983 575	4.134 593	180
16	3.726 551	3.877 559	4.034 654	4.198 078	4.368 086	4.544 942	192
17	4.045 887	4.220 300	4.402 194	4.591 887	4.789 712	4.996 016	204
18	4.392 588	4.593 337	4.803 215	5.022 638	5.252 035	5.491 859	216
19	4.768 998	4.999 346	5.240 768	5.493 796	5.758 983	6.036 912	228
20	5.177 664	5.441 243	5.718 180	6.009 152	6.314 864	6.636 061	240
21	5.621 349	5.922 199	6.239 083	6.572 851	6.924 401	7.294 674	252
22	6.103 055	6.445 667	6.807 437	7.189 430	7.592 773	8.018 653	264
23	6.626 038	7.015 406	7.427 566	7.863 848	8.325 659	8.814 485	276
24	7.193 838	7.635 504	8.104 186	8.601 532	9.129 286	9.689 302	288
25	7.810 293	8.310 413	8.842 444	9.408 415	10.010 482	10.650 941	300
26	8.479 574	9.044 978	9.647 954	10.290 989	10.976 736	11.708 022	312
27	9.206 207	9.844 472	10.526 842	11.256 354	12.036 256	12.870 014	324
28	9.995 106	10.714 634	11.485 793	12.312 278	13.198 045	14.147 332	336
29	10.851 608	11.661 710	12.532 101	13.467 255	14.471 975	15.551 421	348
30	11.781 506	12.692 499	13.673 723	14.730 576	15.868 870	17.094 862	360

FUTURE VALUE

MONTHLY COMPOUNDING

MOS	9.75% ANNUAL RATE	10.00% ANNUAL RATE	10.25% ANNUAL RATE	10.50% ANNUAL RATE	10.75% ANNUAL RATE	11.00% ANNUAL RATE	MOS
1	1.008 125	1.008 333	1.008 542	1.008 750	1.008 958	1.009 167	1
2	1.016 316	1.016 736	1.017 156	1.017 577	1.017 997	1.018 417	2
3	1.024 574	1.025 209	1.025 845	1.026 480	1.027 116	1.027 753	3
4	1.032 898	1.033 752	1.034 607	1.035 462	1.036 318	1.037 174	4
5	1.041 291	1.042 367	1.043 444	1.044 522	1.045 601	1.046 681	5
6	1.049 751	1.051 053	1.052 357	1.053 662	1.054 968	1.056 276	6
7	1.058 280	1.059 812	1.061 346	1.062 881	1.064 419	1.065 958	7
8	1.066 879	1.068 644	1.070 411	1.072 182	1.073 954	1.075 730	8
9	1.075 547	1.077 549	1.079 555	1.081 563	1.083 575	1.085 591	9
10	1.084 286	1.086 529	1.088 776	1.091 027	1.093 282	1.095 542	10
11	1.093 096	1.095 583	1.098 076	1.100 573	1.103 076	1.105 584	11
12	1.101 977	1.104 713	1.107 455	1.110 203	1.112 958	1.115 719	12
13	1.110 931	1.113 919	1.116 915	1.119 918	1.122 928	1.125 946	13
14	1.119 957	1.123 202	1.126 455	1.129 717	1.132 988	1.136 267	14
15	1.129 057	1.132 562	1.136 077	1.139 602	1.143 138	1.146 683	15
16	1.138 230	1.142 000	1.145 781	1.149 574	1.153 378	1.157 194	16
17	1.147 478	1.151 516	1.155 568	1.159 632	1.163 710	1.167 802	17
18	1.156 802	1.161 112	1.165 438	1.169 779	1.174 135	1.178 507	18
19	1.166 201	1.170 788	1.175 393	1.180 015	1.184 654	1.189 310	19
20	1.175 676	1.180 545	1.185 433	1.190 340	1.195 266	1.200 212	20
21	1.185 228	1.190 383	1.195 558	1.200 755	1.205 974	1.211 214	21
22	1.194 858	1.200 303	1.205 770	1.211 262	1.216 777	1.222 317	22
23	1.204 567	1.210 305	1.216 070	1.221 860	1.227 678	1.233 521	23
24	1.214 354	1.220 391	1.226 457	1.232 552	1.238 676	1.244 829	24
25	1.224 220	1.230 561	1.236 933	1.243 337	1.249 772	1.256 239	25
26	1.234 167	1.240 816	1.247 498	1.254 216	1.260 968	1.267 755	26
27	1.244 195	1.251 156	1.258 154	1.265 190	1.272 264	1.279 376	27
28	1.254 304	1.261 582	1.268 901	1.276 261	1.283 661	1.291 104	28
29	1.264 495	1.272 095	1.279 739	1.287 428	1.295 161	1.302 939	29
30	1.274 769	1.282 696	1.290 670	1.298 693	1.306 763	1.314 882	30
31	1.285 127	1.293 385	1.301 695	1.310 056	1.318 470	1.326 935	31
32	1.295 568	1.304 163	1.312 814	1.321 519	1.330 281	1.339 099	32
33	1.306 095	1.315 031	1.324 027	1.333 083	1.342 198	1.351 374	33
34	1.316 707	1.325 990	1.335 337	1.344 747	1.354 222	1.363 762	34
35	1.327 405	1.337 040	1.346 743	1.356 514	1.366 354	1.376 263	35
36	1.338 190	1.348 182	1.358 246	1.368 383	1.378 594	1.388 879	36
37	1.349 063	1.359 417	1.369 848	1.380 357	1.390 944	1.401 610	37
38	1.360 024	1.370 745	1.381 548	1.392 435	1.403 404	1.414 458	38
39	1.371 074	1.382 168	1.393 349	1.404 618	1.415 976	1.427 424	39
40	1.382 214	1.393 686	1.405 251	1.416 909	1.428 661	1.440 509	40
41	1.393 445	1.405 300	1.417 254	1.429 307	1.441 460	1.453 713	41
42	1.404 767	1.417 011	1.429 360	1.441 813	1.454 373	1.467 039	42
43	1.416 180	1.428 819	1.441 569	1.454 429	1.467 402	1.480 487	43
44	1.427 687	1.440 726	1.453 882	1.467 155	1.480 547	1.494 058	44
45	1.439 287	1.452 732	1.466 301	1.479 993	1.493 810	1.507 754	45
46	1.450 981	1.464 838	1.478 825	1.492 943	1.507 192	1.521 575	46
47	1.462 770	1.477 045	1.491 457	1.506 006	1.520 694	1.535 522	47
YRS							
4	1.474 655	1.489 354	1.504 196	1.519 184	1.534 317	1.549 598	48
5	1.625 036	1.645 309	1.665 830	1.686 603	1.707 630	1.728 916	60
6	1.790 753	1.817 594	1.844 832	1.872 472	1.900 521	1.928 984	72
7	1.973 369	2.007 920	2.043 069	2.078 825	2.115 200	2.152 204	84
8	2.174 608	2.218 176	2.262 607	2.307 919	2.354 129	2.401 254	96
9	2.396 368	2.450 448	2.505 736	2.562 260	2.620 047	2.679 124	108
10	2.640 743	2.707 041	2.774 990	2.844 630	2.916 002	2.989 150	120
11	2.910 039	2.990 504	3.073 177	3.158 118	3.245 388	3.335 051	132
12	3.206 797	3.303 649	3.403 406	3.506 153	3.611 980	3.720 979	144
13	3.533 817	3.649 584	3.769 119	3.892 543	4.019 982	4.151 566	156
14	3.894 185	4.031 743	4.174 130	4.321 515	4.474 072	4.631 980	168
15	4.291 304	4.453 920	4.622 662	4.797 761	4.979 454	5.167 988	180
16	4.728 919	4.920 303	5.119 391	5.326 491	5.541 923	5.766 021	192
17	5.211 161	5.435 523	5.669 496	5.913 488	6.167 928	6.433 259	204
18	5.742 581	6.004 693	6.278 712	6.565 175	6.864 644	7.177 708	216
19	6.328 193	6.633 463	6.953 392	7.288 680	7.640 061	8.008 304	228
20	6.973 525	7.328 074	7.700 570	8.091 918	8.503 067	8.935 015	240
21	7.684 665	8.095 419	8.528 036	8.983 675	9.463 557	9.968 865	252
22	8.468 326	8.943 115	9.444 417	9.973 707	10.532 541	11.122 562	264
23	9.331 902	9.879 576	10.459 268	11.072 844	11.722 276	12.409 652	276
24	10.283 544	10.914 097	11.583 170	12.293 109	13.046 401	13.845 682	288
25	11.332 231	12.056 945	12.827 841	13.647 852	14.520 096	15.447 889	300
26	12.487 860	13.319 465	14.206 259	15.151 893	16.160 258	17.235 500	312
27	13.761 338	14.714 187	15.732 794	16.821 684	17.985 688	19.229 972	324
28	15.164 681	16.254 954	17.423 364	18.675 491	20.017 316	21.455 242	336
29	16.711 133	17.957 060	19.295 594	20.733 595	22.278 432	23.938 018	348
30	18.415 288	19.837 399	21.369 005	23.018 509	24.794 959	26.708 098	360

MOS	11.25% ANNUAL RATE	11.50% ANNUAL RATE	11.75% ANNUAL RATE	12.00% ANNUAL RATE	12.25% ANNUAL RATE	12.50% ANNUAL RATE	MOS
1	1.009 375	1.009 583	1.009 792	1.010 000	1.010 208	1.010 417	1
2	1.018 838	1.019 259	1.019 679	1.020 100	1.020 521	1.020 942	2
3	1.028 389	1.029 026	1.029 664	1.030 301	1.030 939	1.031 577	3
4	1.038 031	1.038 888	1.039 746	1.040 604	1.041 463	1.042 322	4
5	1.047 762	1.048 844	1.049 927	1.051 010	1.052 094	1.053 180	5
6	1.057 585	1.058 895	1.060 207	1.061 520	1.062 835	1.064 150	6
7	1.067 500	1.069 043	1.070 588	1.072 135	1.073 684	1.075 235	7
8	1.077 508	1.079 288	1.081 071	1.082 857	1.084 645	1.086 436	8
9	1.087 609	1.089 631	1.091 657	1.093 685	1.095 717	1.097 753	9
10	1.097 806	1.100 074	1.102 346	1.104 622	1.106 903	1.109 188	10
11	1.108 098	1.110 616	1.113 140	1.115 668	1.118 202	1.120 742	11
12	1.118 486	1.121 259	1.124 039	1.126 825	1.129 617	1.132 416	12
13	1.128 972	1.132 005	1.135 045	1.138 093	1.141 149	1.144 212	13
14	1.139 556	1.142 853	1.146 159	1.149 474	1.152 798	1.156 131	14
15	1.150 239	1.153 805	1.157 382	1.160 969	1.164 566	1.168 174	15
16	1.161 023	1.164 863	1.168 715	1.172 579	1.176 455	1.180 342	16
17	1.171 907	1.176 026	1.180 158	1.184 304	1.188 464	1.192 638	17
18	1.182 894	1.187 296	1.191 714	1.196 147	1.200 596	1.205 061	18
19	1.193 984	1.198 675	1.203 383	1.208 109	1.212 853	1.217 614	19
20	1.205 177	1.210 162	1.215 166	1.220 190	1.225 234	1.230 297	20
21	1.216 476	1.221 759	1.227 065	1.232 392	1.237 741	1.243 113	21
22	1.227 880	1.233 468	1.239 080	1.244 716	1.250 377	1.256 062	22
23	1.239 391	1.245 288	1.251 212	1.257 163	1.263 141	1.269 146	23
24	1.251 011	1.257 222	1.263 464	1.269 735	1.276 035	1.282 366	24
25	1.262 739	1.269 271	1.275 835	1.282 432	1.289 062	1.295 724	25
26	1.274 577	1.281 435	1.288 328	1.295 256	1.302 221	1.309 221	26
27	1.286 526	1.293 715	1.300 943	1.308 209	1.315 514	1.322 859	27
28	1.298 588	1.306 113	1.313 681	1.321 291	1.328 943	1.336 639	28
29	1.310 762	1.318 630	1.326 544	1.334 504	1.342 510	1.350 562	29
30	1.323 050	1.331 267	1.339 533	1.347 849	1.356 215	1.364 630	30
31	1.335 454	1.344 025	1.352 649	1.361 327	1.370 059	1.378 845	31
32	1.347 974	1.356 905	1.365 894	1.374 941	1.384 045	1.393 208	32
33	1.360 611	1.369 909	1.379 268	1.388 690	1.398 174	1.407 721	33
34	1.373 367	1.383 037	1.392 774	1.402 577	1.412 447	1.422 385	34
35	1.386 242	1.396 291	1.406 411	1.416 603	1.426 866	1.437 201	35
36	1.399 238	1.409 672	1.420 183	1.430 769	1.441 432	1.452 172	36
37	1.412 356	1.423 182	1.434 088	1.445 076	1.456 146	1.467 299	37
38	1.425 597	1.436 821	1.448 131	1.459 527	1.471 011	1.482 583	38
39	1.438 962	1.450 590	1.462 310	1.474 123	1.486 028	1.498 027	39
40	1.452 452	1.464 492	1.476 629	1.488 864	1.501 198	1.513 631	40
41	1.466 069	1.478 526	1.491 087	1.503 752	1.516 522	1.529 398	41
42	1.479 813	1.492 696	1.505 688	1.518 790	1.532 004	1.545 329	42
43	1.493 686	1.507 001	1.520 431	1.533 978	1.547 643	1.561 427	43
44	1.507 690	1.521 443	1.535 318	1.549 318	1.563 442	1.577 691	44
45	1.521 824	1.536 023	1.550 352	1.564 811	1.579 402	1.594 126	45
46	1.536 091	1.550 743	1.565 532	1.580 459	1.595 525	1.610 731	46
47	1.550 492	1.565 605	1.580 861	1.596 263	1.611 812	1.627 510	47

YRS							
4	1.565 028	1.580 608	1.596 341	1.612 226	1.628 266	1.644 463	48
5	1.750 462	1.772 272	1.794 349	1.816 697	1.839 318	1.862 216	60
6	1.957 867	1.987 176	2.016 918	2.047 099	2.077 725	2.108 803	72
7	2.189 847	2.228 140	2.267 095	2.306 723	2.347 035	2.388 043	84
8	2.449 313	2.498 323	2.548 303	2.599 273	2.651 251	2.704 258	96
9	2.739 522	2.801 268	2.864 392	2.928 926	2.994 899	3.062 345	108
10	3.064 117	3.140 948	3.219 689	3.300 387	3.383 090	3.467 849	120
11	3.427 171	3.521 817	3.619 056	3.718 959	3.821 598	3.927 048	132
12	3.833 243	3.948 870	4.067 960	4.190 616	4.316 943	4.447 052	144
13	4.287 428	4.427 707	4.572 546	4.722 091	4.876 494	5.035 913	156
14	4.795 428	4.964 608	5.139 720	5.320 970	5.508 572	5.702 748	168
15	5.363 619	5.566 613	5.777 245	5.995 802	6.222 579	6.457 884	180
16	5.999 132	6.241 617	6.493 849	6.756 220	7.029 133	7.313 011	192
17	6.709 945	6.998 471	7.299 340	7.613 078	7.940 231	8.281 371	204
18	7.504 979	7.847 101	8.204 743	8.578 606	8.969 423	9.377 958	216
19	8.394 214	8.798 635	9.222 451	9.666 588	10.132 016	10.619 750	228
20	9.388 810	9.865 552	10.366 395	10.892 554	11.445 301	12.025 975	240
21	10.501 252	11.061 842	11.652 233	12.274 002	12.928 811	13.618 407	252
22	11.745 503	12.403 194	13.097 564	13.830 653	14.604 609	15.421 703	264
23	13.137 180	13.907 196	14.722 173	15.584 726	16.497 620	17.463 783	276
24	14.693 751	15.593 574	16.548 297	17.561 259	18.635 998	19.776 269	288
25	16.434 754	17.484 440	18.600 932	19.788 466	21.051 547	22.394 964	300
26	18.382 041	19.604 591	20.908 173	22.298 139	23.780 193	25.360 417	312
27	20.560 054	21.981 831	23.501 603	25.126 101	26.862 519	28.718 543	324
28	22.996 132	24.647 333	26.416 719	28.312 720	30.344 369	32.521 339	336
29	25.720 850	27.636 052	29.693 422	31.903 481	34.277 526	36.827 686	348
30	28.768 409	30.987 181	33.376 565	35.949 641	38.720 488	41.704 262	360

FUTURE VALUE

MONTHLY COMPOUNDING

MOS	12.75% ANNUAL RATE	13.00% ANNUAL RATE	13.25% ANNUAL RATE	13.50% ANNUAL RATE	13.75% ANNUAL RATE	14.00% ANNUAL RATE	MOS
1	1.010 625	1.010 833	1.011 042	1.011 250	1.011 458	1.011 667	1
2	1.021 363	1.021 784	1.022 205	1.022 627	1.023 048	1.023 469	2
3	1.032 215	1.032 853	1.033 492	1.034 131	1.034 770	1.035 410	3
4	1.043 182	1.044 043	1.044 904	1.045 765	1.046 627	1.047 490	4
5	1.054 266	1.055 353	1.056 441	1.057 530	1.058 620	1.059 710	5
6	1.065 468	1.066 786	1.068 106	1.069 427	1.070 750	1.072 074	6
7	1.076 788	1.078 343	1.079 900	1.081 458	1.083 019	1.084 581	7
8	1.088 229	1.090 025	1.091 823	1.093 625	1.095 428	1.097 235	8
9	1.099 791	1.101 834	1.103 879	1.105 928	1.107 980	1.110 036	9
10	1.111 477	1.113 770	1.116 068	1.118 370	1.120 676	1.122 986	10
11	1.123 286	1.125 836	1.128 391	1.130 951	1.133 517	1.136 088	11
12	1.135 221	1.138 032	1.140 850	1.143 674	1.146 505	1.149 342	12
13	1.147 283	1.150 361	1.153 447	1.156 541	1.159 642	1.162 751	13
14	1.159 473	1.162 823	1.166 183	1.169 552	1.172 930	1.176 316	14
15	1.171 792	1.175 421	1.179 060	1.182 709	1.186 369	1.190 040	15
16	1.184 242	1.188 154	1.192 079	1.196 015	1.199 963	1.203 924	16
17	1.196 825	1.201 026	1.205 241	1.209 470	1.213 713	1.217 970	17
18	1.209 541	1.214 037	1.218 549	1.223 077	1.227 620	1.232 179	18
19	1.222 393	1.227 189	1.232 004	1.236 836	1.241 686	1.246 555	19
20	1.235 381	1.240 484	1.245 607	1.250 751	1.255 914	1.261 098	20
21	1.248 506	1.253 922	1.259 361	1.264 821	1.270 305	1.275 811	21
22	1.261 772	1.267 507	1.273 266	1.279 051	1.284 860	1.290 695	22
23	1.275 178	1.281 238	1.287 325	1.293 440	1.299 583	1.305 753	23
24	1.288 727	1.295 118	1.301 539	1.307 991	1.314 474	1.320 987	24
25	1.302 420	1.309 148	1.315 910	1.322 706	1.329 535	1.336 399	25
26	1.316 258	1.323 331	1.330 440	1.337 587	1.344 770	1.351 990	26
27	1.330 243	1.337 667	1.345 131	1.352 634	1.360 179	1.367 763	27
28	1.344 377	1.352 158	1.359 983	1.367 852	1.375 764	1.383 720	28
29	1.358 661	1.366 807	1.375 000	1.383 240	1.391 528	1.399 864	29
30	1.373 097	1.381 614	1.390 182	1.398 801	1.407 472	1.416 196	30
31	1.387 686	1.396 581	1.405 532	1.414 538	1.423 600	1.432 718	31
32	1.402 430	1.411 711	1.421 051	1.430 451	1.439 912	1.449 433	32
33	1.417 331	1.427 004	1.436 742	1.446 544	1.456 411	1.466 343	33
34	1.432 390	1.442 464	1.452 606	1.462 818	1.473 099	1.483 450	34
35	1.447 609	1.458 090	1.468 645	1.479 274	1.489 978	1.500 757	35
36	1.462 990	1.473 886	1.484 861	1.495 916	1.507 051	1.518 266	36
37	1.478 534	1.489 853	1.501 257	1.512 745	1.524 319	1.535 979	37
38	1.494 244	1.505 993	1.517 833	1.529 764	1.541 785	1.553 899	38
39	1.510 120	1.522 308	1.534 593	1.546 973	1.559 452	1.572 028	39
40	1.526 165	1.538 800	1.551 537	1.564 377	1.577 320	1.590 368	40
41	1.542 381	1.555 470	1.568 669	1.581 976	1.595 394	1.608 922	41
42	1.558 768	1.572 321	1.585 989	1.599 773	1.613 674	1.627 693	42
43	1.575 330	1.589 355	1.603 501	1.617 771	1.632 164	1.646 683	43
44	1.592 068	1.606 573	1.621 207	1.635 971	1.650 866	1.665 894	44
45	1.608 984	1.623 977	1.639 107	1.654 375	1.669 782	1.685 330	45
46	1.626 079	1.641 570	1.657 206	1.672 987	1.688 915	1.704 992	46
47	1.643 356	1.659 354	1.675 504	1.691 808	1.708 267	1.724 883	47

YRS							
4	1.660 817	1.677 330	1.694 005	1.710 841	1.727 841	1.745 007	48
5	1.885 394	1.908 857	1.932 606	1.956 645	1.980 979	2.005 610	60
6	2.140 340	2.172 341	2.204 814	2.237 765	2.271 202	2.305 132	72
7	2.429 759	2.472 194	2.515 362	2.559 275	2.603 945	2.649 385	84
8	2.758 313	2.813 437	2.869 652	2.926 977	2.985 436	3.045 049	96
9	3.131 295	3.201 783	3.273 843	3.347 509	3.422 817	3.499 803	108
10	3.554 712	3.643 733	3.734 964	3.828 460	3.924 277	4.022 471	120
11	4.035 384	4.146 687	4.261 035	4.378 512	4.499 203	4.623 195	132
12	4.581 054	4.719 064	4.861 203	5.007 593	5.158 359	5.313 632	144
13	5.200 509	5.370 448	5.545 905	5.727 056	5.914 084	6.107 180	156
14	5.903 727	6.111 745	6.327 047	6.549 887	6.780 527	7.019 239	168
15	6.702 035	6.955 364	7.218 213	7.490 939	7.773 909	8.067 507	180
16	7.608 292	7.915 430	8.234 901	8.567 195	8.912 825	9.272 324	192
17	8.637 093	9.008 017	9.394 788	9.798 082	10.218 599	10.657 072	204
18	9.805 010	10.251 416	10.718 047	11.205 816	11.715 675	12.248 621	216
19	11.130 854	11.666 444	12.227 687	12.815 805	13.432 081	14.077 855	228
20	12.635 980	13.276 792	13.949 959	14.657 109	15.399 948	16.180 270	240
21	14.344 631	15.109 421	15.914 815	16.762 961	17.656 118	18.596 664	252
22	16.284 328	17.195 012	18.156 421	19.171 370	20.242 827	21.373 928	264
23	18.486 312	19.568 482	20.713 757	21.925 805	23.208 503	24.565 954	276
24	20.986 051	22.269 568	23.631 296	25.075 983	26.608 666	28.234 683	288
25	23.823 808	25.343 491	26.959 770	28.678 761	30.506 969	32.451 308	300
26	27.045 289	28.841 716	30.757 061	32.799 166	34.976 393	37.297 652	312
27	30.702 382	32.822 810	35.089 201	37.511 568	40.100 611	42.867 759	324
28	34.853 991	37.353 424	40.031 524	42.901 021	45.975 552	49.269 718	336
29	39.566 985	42.509 410	45.669 975	49.064 802	52.711 201	56.627 757	348
30	44.917 276	48.377 089	52.102 603	56.114 160	60.433 657	65.084 661	360

FUTURE VALUE

MONTHLY COMPOUNDING

MOS	14.25% ANNUAL RATE	14.50% ANNUAL RATE	14.75% ANNUAL RATE	15.00% ANNUAL RATE	15.25% ANNUAL RATE	15.50% ANNUAL RATE	MOS
1	1.011 875	1.012 083	1.012 292	1.012 500	1.012 708	1.012 917	1
2	1.023 891	1.024 313	1.024 734	1.025 156	1.025 578	1.026 000	2
3	1.036 050	1.036 690	1.037 330	1.037 971	1.038 612	1.039 253	3
4	1.048 353	1.049 216	1.050 081	1.050 945	1.051 811	1.052 676	4
5	1.060 802	1.061 894	1.062 988	1.064 082	1.065 177	1.066 273	5
6	1.073 399	1.074 726	1.076 054	1.077 383	1.078 714	1.080 046	6
7	1.086 146	1.087 712	1.089 280	1.090 850	1.092 423	1.093 997	7
8	1.099 044	1.100 855	1.102 669	1.104 486	1.106 305	1.108 128	8
9	1.112 095	1.114 157	1.116 223	1.118 292	1.120 365	1.122 441	9
10	1.125 301	1.127 620	1.129 943	1.132 271	1.134 603	1.136 939	10
11	1.138 664	1.141 245	1.143 832	1.146 424	1.149 022	1.151 624	11
12	1.152 185	1.155 035	1.157 892	1.160 755	1.163 624	1.166 500	12
13	1.165 868	1.168 992	1.172 124	1.175 264	1.178 412	1.181 567	13
14	1.179 712	1.183 117	1.186 531	1.189 955	1.193 387	1.196 829	14
15	1.193 721	1.197 413	1.201 116	1.204 829	1.208 553	1.212 288	15
16	1.207 897	1.211 882	1.215 880	1.219 890	1.223 912	1.227 947	16
17	1.222 241	1.226 526	1.230 825	1.235 138	1.239 466	1.243 808	17
18	1.236 755	1.241 346	1.245 954	1.250 577	1.255 217	1.259 873	18
19	1.251 441	1.256 346	1.261 269	1.266 210	1.271 169	1.276 147	19
20	1.266 302	1.271 527	1.276 772	1.282 037	1.287 323	1.292 630	20
21	1.281 339	1.286 891	1.292 465	1.298 063	1.303 683	1.309 327	21
22	1.296 555	1.302 441	1.308 352	1.314 288	1.320 251	1.326 239	22
23	1.311 952	1.318 179	1.324 434	1.330 717	1.337 029	1.343 370	23
24	1.327 531	1.334 107	1.340 713	1.347 351	1.354 020	1.360 721	24
25	1.343 296	1.350 227	1.357 193	1.364 193	1.371 228	1.378 297	25
26	1.359 247	1.366 542	1.373 875	1.381 245	1.388 654	1.396 100	26
27	1.375 388	1.383 055	1.390 762	1.398 511	1.406 301	1.414 133	27
28	1.391 721	1.399 767	1.407 857	1.415 992	1.424 173	1.432 399	28
29	1.408 248	1.416 681	1.425 162	1.433 692	1.442 272	1.450 901	29
30	1.424 971	1.433 799	1.442 679	1.451 613	1.460 601	1.469 642	30
31	1.441 892	1.451 124	1.460 412	1.469 759	1.479 163	1.488 625	31
32	1.459 015	1.468 658	1.478 363	1.488 131	1.497 960	1.507 853	32
33	1.476 341	1.486 405	1.496 535	1.506 732	1.516 997	1.527 329	33
34	1.493 872	1.504 365	1.514 930	1.525 566	1.536 275	1.547 057	34
35	1.511 612	1.522 543	1.533 551	1.544 636	1.555 799	1.567 040	35
36	1.529 562	1.540 940	1.552 401	1.563 944	1.575 570	1.587 281	36
37	1.547 726	1.559 560	1.571 482	1.583 493	1.595 593	1.607 783	37
38	1.566 105	1.578 405	1.590 798	1.603 287	1.615 871	1.628 551	38
39	1.584 703	1.597 477	1.610 352	1.623 328	1.636 406	1.649 586	39
40	1.603 521	1.616 780	1.630 146	1.643 619	1.657 202	1.670 893	40
41	1.622 563	1.636 316	1.650 183	1.664 165	1.678 262	1.692 476	41
42	1.641 831	1.656 088	1.670 467	1.684 967	1.699 590	1.714 337	42
43	1.661 327	1.676 099	1.690 999	1.706 029	1.721 189	1.736 480	43
44	1.681 056	1.696 352	1.711 785	1.727 354	1.743 062	1.758 910	44
45	1.701 018	1.716 850	1.732 825	1.748 946	1.765 214	1.781 629	45
46	1.721 218	1.737 595	1.754 125	1.770 808	1.787 647	1.804 642	46
47	1.741 657	1.758 591	1.775 686	1.792 943	1.810 365	1.827 952	47
YRS							
4	1.762 339	1.779 841	1.797 512	1.815 355	1.833 371	1.851 563	48
5	2.030 542	2.055 779	2.081 324	2.107 181	2.133 354	2.159 847	60
6	2.339 561	2.374 497	2.409 948	2.445 920	2.482 422	2.519 461	72
7	2.695 608	2.742 628	2.790 459	2.839 113	2.888 605	2.938 950	84
8	3.105 840	3.167 833	3.231 049	3.295 513	3.361 250	3.428 284	96
9	3.578 504	3.658 959	3.741 205	3.825 282	3.911 231	3.999 093	108
10	4.123 101	4.226 227	4.331 910	4.440 213	4.551 201	4.664 940	120
11	4.750 577	4.881 441	5.015 882	5.153 998	5.295 886	5.441 651	132
12	5.473 545	5.638 237	5.807 849	5.982 526	6.162 419	6.347 684	144
13	6.306 539	6.512 363	6.724 860	6.944 244	7.170 738	7.404 571	156
14	7.266 303	7.522 010	7.786 659	8.060 563	8.344 042	8.637 429	168
15	8.372 129	8.688 187	9.016 108	9.356 334	9.709 326	10.075 557	180
16	9.646 245	10.035 163	10.439 677	10.860 408	11.298 003	11.753 134	192
17	11.114 263	11.590 968	12.088 015	12.606 267	13.146 625	13.710 027	204
18	12.805 693	13.387 978	13.996 612	14.632 781	15.297 726	15.992 741	216
19	14.754 533	15.463 588	16.206 561	16.985 067	17.800 798	18.655 526	228
20	16.999 959	17.860 991	18.765 442	19.715 494	20.713 433	21.761 665	240
21	19.587 105	20.630 076	21.728 350	22.884 848	24.102 644	25.384 974	252
22	22.567 978	23.828 467	25.159 076	26.563 691	28.046 411	29.611 562	264
23	26.002 496	27.522 721	29.131 485	30.833 924	32.635 472	34.541 877	276
24	29.959 698	31.789 716	33.731 105	35.790 617	37.975 413	40.293 008	288
25	34.519 129	36.718 246	39.056 966	41.544 120	44.189 095	47.001 870	300
26	39.772 439	42.410 872	45.223 737	48.222 525	51.419 484	54.827 664	312
27	45.825 226	48.986 057	52.364 190	55.974 514	59.832 937	63.956 450	324
28	52.799 159	56.580 627	60.632 060	64.972 670	69.623 030	74.605 175	336
29	60.834 424	65.352 625	70.205 359	75.417 320	81.015 017	87.026 910	348
30	70.092 540	75.484 592	81.290 203	87.540 995	94.271 004	101.516 858	360

FUTURE VALUE

MOS	15.75% ANNUAL RATE	16.00% ANNUAL RATE	16.25% ANNUAL RATE	16.50% ANNUAL RATE	16.75% ANNUAL RATE	17.00% ANNUAL RATE	MOS
1	1.013 125	1.013 333	1.013 542	1.013 750	1.013 958	1.014 167	1
2	1.026 422	1.026 844	1.027 267	1.027 689	1.028 112	1.028 534	2
3	1.039 894	1.040 536	1.041 178	1.041 820	1.042 462	1.043 105	3
4	1.053 543	1.054 410	1.055 277	1.056 145	1.057 013	1.057 882	4
5	1.067 370	1.068 468	1.069 567	1.070 667	1.071 767	1.072 869	5
6	1.081 380	1.082 715	1.084 051	1.085 388	1.086 727	1.088 068	6
7	1.095 573	1.097 151	1.098 731	1.100 313	1.101 896	1.103 482	7
8	1.109 952	1.111 779	1.113 609	1.115 442	1.117 277	1.119 115	8
9	1.124 520	1.126 603	1.128 689	1.130 779	1.132 872	1.134 969	9
10	1.139 280	1.141 625	1.143 974	1.146 327	1.148 685	1.151 048	10
11	1.154 233	1.156 846	1.159 465	1.162 089	1.164 719	1.167 354	11
12	1.169 382	1.172 271	1.175 166	1.178 068	1.180 977	1.183 892	12
13	1.184 730	1.187 901	1.191 080	1.194 267	1.197 461	1.200 664	13
14	1.200 280	1.203 740	1.207 209	1.210 688	1.214 176	1.217 673	14
15	1.216 033	1.219 790	1.223 557	1.227 335	1.231 124	1.234 923	15
16	1.231 994	1.236 053	1.240 126	1.244 211	1.248 308	1.252 418	16
17	1.248 164	1.252 534	1.256 919	1.261 318	1.265 732	1.270 161	17
18	1.264 546	1.269 235	1.273 940	1.278 662	1.283 400	1.288 155	18
19	1.281 143	1.286 158	1.291 191	1.296 243	1.301 314	1.306 403	19
20	1.297 958	1.303 307	1.308 676	1.314 067	1.319 478	1.324 911	20
21	1.314 994	1.320 684	1.326 398	1.332 135	1.337 896	1.343 680	21
22	1.332 253	1.338 293	1.344 359	1.350 452	1.356 571	1.362 716	22
23	1.349 739	1.356 137	1.362 564	1.369 020	1.375 506	1.382 021	23
24	1.367 454	1.374 219	1.381 016	1.387 845	1.394 706	1.401 600	24
25	1.385 402	1.392 542	1.399 717	1.406 927	1.414 174	1.421 456	25
26	1.403 585	1.411 109	1.418 671	1.426 273	1.433 913	1.441 593	26
27	1.422 007	1.429 924	1.437 882	1.445 884	1.453 928	1.462 015	27
28	1.440 671	1.448 989	1.457 354	1.465 765	1.474 223	1.482 727	28
29	1.459 580	1.468 309	1.477 089	1.485 919	1.494 800	1.503 733	29
30	1.478 737	1.487 887	1.497 091	1.506 350	1.515 665	1.525 036	30
31	1.498 146	1.507 725	1.517 364	1.527 063	1.536 821	1.546 640	31
32	1.517 809	1.527 828	1.537 912	1.548 060	1.558 273	1.568 551	32
33	1.537 730	1.548 199	1.558 738	1.569 346	1.580 024	1.590 772	33
34	1.557 913	1.568 842	1.579 846	1.590 924	1.602 078	1.613 308	34
35	1.578 360	1.589 760	1.601 239	1.612 799	1.624 441	1.636 163	35
36	1.599 076	1.610 957	1.622 923	1.634 975	1.647 115	1.659 342	36
37	1.620 064	1.632 436	1.644 900	1.657 455	1.670 106	1.682 850	37
38	1.641 327	1.654 202	1.667 175	1.680 246	1.693 418	1.706 690	38
39	1.662 870	1.676 258	1.689 751	1.703 350	1.717 055	1.730 868	39
40	1.684 695	1.698 608	1.712 633	1.726 771	1.741 022	1.755 389	40
41	1.706 807	1.721 256	1.735 825	1.750 514	1.765 324	1.780 257	41
42	1.729 208	1.744 206	1.759 331	1.774 583	1.789 965	1.805 477	42
43	1.751 904	1.767 462	1.783 155	1.798 984	1.814 950	1.831 055	43
44	1.774 898	1.791 028	1.807 302	1.823 720	1.840 284	1.856 994	44
45	1.798 194	1.814 909	1.831 776	1.848 796	1.865 971	1.883 302	45
46	1.821 795	1.839 108	1.856 581	1.874 217	1.892 017	1.909 982	46
47	1.845 706	1.863 629	1.881 722	1.899 988	1.918 426	1.937 040	47

YRS							
4	1.869 931	1.888 477	1.907 204	1.926 112	1.945 204	1.964 482	48
5	2.186 663	2.213 807	2.241 282	2.269 092	2.297 241	2.325 733	60
6	2.557 045	2.595 181	2.633 878	2.673 145	2.712 988	2.753 417	72
7	2.990 162	3.042 255	3.095 245	3.149 146	3.203 975	3.259 747	84
8	3.496 641	3.566 347	3.637 427	3.709 909	3.783 820	3.859 188	96
9	4.088 909	4.180 724	4.274 581	4.370 526	4.468 603	4.568 860	108
10	4.781 497	4.900 941	5.023 343	5.148 777	5.277 316	5.409 036	120
11	5.591 396	5.745 230	5.903 263	6.065 610	6.232 386	6.403 713	132
12	6.538 478	6.734 965	6.937 315	7.145 702	7.360 303	7.581 303	144
13	7.645 978	7.895 203	8.152 499	8.418 123	8.692 346	8.975 441	156
14	8.941 068	9.255 316	9.580 541	9.917 123	10.265 457	10.625 951	168
15	10.455 524	10.849 737	11.258 727	11.683 046	12.123 265	12.579 975	180
16	12.226 501	12.718 830	13.230 876	13.763 425	14.317 293	14.893 329	192
17	14.297 449	14.909 912	15.548 478	16.214 252	16.908 388	17.632 089	204
18	16.719 179	17.478 455	18.272 045	19.101 493	19.968 411	20.874 484	216
19	19.551 106	20.489 482	21.472 690	22.502 860	23.582 227	24.713 129	228
20	22.862 711	24.019 222	25.233 979	26.509 903	27.850 060	29.257 669	240
21	26.735 242	28.157 032	29.654 119	31.230 471	32.890 270	34.637 912	252
22	31.263 709	33.007 667	34.848 518	36.791 623	38.842 640	41.007 538	264
23	36.559 217	38.693 924	40.952 800	43.343 038	45.872 251	48.548 485	276
24	42.751 688	45.359 757	48.126 345	51.061 052	54.174 056	57.476 150	288
25	49.993 053	53.173 919	56.556 454	60.153 398	63.978 295	68.045 538	300
26	58.460 974	62.334 232	66.463 232	70.864 801	75.556 871	80.558 550	312
27	68.363 207	73.072 600	78.105 343	83.483 564	89.230 900	95.372 601	324
28	79.942 701	85.660 875	91.786 758	98.349 325	105.379 608	112.910 833	336
29	93.483 551	100.417 742	107.864 694	115.862 206	124.450 855	133.674 202	348
30	109.317 978	117.716 787	126.758 941	136.493 572	146.973 553	158.255 782	360

SECTION 1

MOS	17.25% ANNUAL RATE	17.50% ANNUAL RATE	17.75% ANNUAL RATE	18.00% ANNUAL RATE	18.25% ANNUAL RATE	18.50% ANNUAL RATE	MOS
1	1.014 375	1.014 583	1.014 792	1.015 000	1.015 208	1.015 417	1
2	1.028 957	1.029 379	1.029 802	1.030 225	1.030 648	1.031 071	2
3	1.043 748	1.044 391	1.045 035	1.045 678	1.046 322	1.046 967	3
4	1.058 752	1.059 622	1.060 492	1.061 364	1.062 235	1.063 107	4
5	1.073 971	1.075 075	1.076 179	1.077 284	1.078 390	1.079 497	5
6	1.089 410	1.090 753	1.092 097	1.093 443	1.094 791	1.096 139	6
7	1.105 070	1.106 660	1.108 251	1.109 845	1.111 440	1.113 038	7
8	1.120 955	1.122 798	1.124 644	1.126 493	1.128 344	1.130 197	8
9	1.137 069	1.139 173	1.141 280	1.143 390	1.145 504	1.147 621	9
10	1.153 414	1.155 785	1.158 161	1.160 541	1.162 925	1.165 314	10
11	1.169 995	1.172 641	1.175 292	1.177 949	1.180 611	1.183 279	11
12	1.186 813	1.189 742	1.192 677	1.195 618	1.198 566	1.201 521	12
13	1.203 874	1.207 092	1.210 318	1.213 552	1.216 795	1.220 045	13
14	1.221 180	1.224 696	1.228 221	1.231 756	1.235 300	1.238 854	14
15	1.238 734	1.242 556	1.246 388	1.250 232	1.254 087	1.257 953	15
16	1.256 541	1.260 676	1.264 825	1.268 986	1.273 159	1.277 346	16
17	1.274 604	1.279 061	1.283 533	1.288 020	1.292 522	1.297 039	17
18	1.292 926	1.297 714	1.302 519	1.307 341	1.312 179	1.317 035	18
19	1.311 512	1.316 639	1.321 785	1.326 951	1.332 135	1.337 339	19
20	1.330 365	1.335 840	1.341 337	1.346 855	1.352 395	1.357 956	20
21	1.349 489	1.355 321	1.361 177	1.367 058	1.372 962	1.378 891	21
22	1.368 888	1.375 086	1.381 312	1.387 564	1.393 843	1.400 149	22
23	1.388 565	1.395 140	1.401 743	1.408 377	1.415 041	1.421 735	23
24	1.408 526	1.415 485	1.422 478	1.429 503	1.436 561	1.443 653	24
25	1.428 774	1.436 128	1.443 518	1.450 945	1.458 409	1.465 910	25
26	1.449 312	1.457 071	1.464 870	1.472 710	1.480 589	1.488 509	26
27	1.470 146	1.478 320	1.486 538	1.494 800	1.503 106	1.511 457	27
28	1.491 279	1.499 879	1.508 527	1.517 222	1.525 966	1.534 759	28
29	1.512 717	1.521 752	1.530 840	1.539 981	1.549 173	1.558 419	29
30	1.534 462	1.543 945	1.553 484	1.563 080	1.572 734	1.582 445	30
31	1.556 520	1.566 460	1.576 463	1.586 526	1.596 652	1.606 841	31
32	1.578 895	1.589 305	1.599 781	1.610 324	1.620 935	1.631 613	32
33	1.601 591	1.612 482	1.623 444	1.634 479	1.645 587	1.656 767	33
34	1.624 614	1.635 997	1.647 458	1.658 996	1.670 613	1.682 309	34
35	1.647 968	1.659 856	1.671 827	1.683 881	1.696 020	1.708 245	35
36	1.671 658	1.684 062	1.696 556	1.709 140	1.721 814	1.734 580	36
37	1.695 688	1.708 621	1.721 651	1.734 777	1.748 000	1.761 322	37
38	1.720 063	1.733 539	1.747 117	1.760 798	1.774 584	1.788 475	38
39	1.744 789	1.758 819	1.772 959	1.787 210	1.801 573	1.816 048	39
40	1.769 870	1.784 469	1.799 184	1.814 018	1.828 972	1.844 045	40
41	1.795 312	1.810 492	1.825 797	1.841 229	1.856 787	1.872 474	41
42	1.821 120	1.836 895	1.852 804	1.868 847	1.885 026	1.901 341	42
43	1.847 299	1.863 683	1.880 210	1.896 880	1.913 694	1.930 654	43
44	1.873 854	1.890 862	1.908 021	1.925 333	1.942 798	1.960 418	44
45	1.900 790	1.918 437	1.936 244	1.954 213	1.972 345	1.990 641	45
46	1.928 114	1.946 414	1.964 885	1.983 526	2.002 341	2.021 330	46
47	1.955 831	1.974 800	1.993 948	2.013 279	2.032 793	2.052 492	47
YRS							
4	1.983 946	2.003 599	2.023 442	2.043 478	2.063 708	2.084 135	48
5	2.354 573	2.383 765	2.413 312	2.443 220	2.473 492	2.504 132	60
6	2.794 439	2.836 065	2.878 301	2.921 158	2.964 644	3.008 768	72
7	3.316 478	3.374 184	3.432 883	3.492 590	3.553 322	3.615 099	84
8	3.936 041	4.014 408	4.094 319	4.175 804	4.258 893	4.343 618	96
9	4.671 346	4.776 108	4.883 198	4.992 667	5.104 566	5.218 949	108
10	5.544 016	5.682 335	5.824 076	5.969 323	6.118 161	6.270 678	120
11	6.579 712	6.760 511	6.946 240	7.137 031	7.333 022	7.534 353	132
12	7.808 891	8.043 262	8.284 618	8.533 164	8.789 113	9.052 685	144
13	9.267 696	9.569 405	9.880 870	10.202 406	10.534 335	10.876 993	156
14	10.999 026	11.385 120	11.784 683	12.198 182	12.626 100	13.068 938	168
15	13.053 792	13.545 352	14.055 315	14.584 368	15.133 219	15.702 606	180
16	15.492 416	16.115 470	16.763 446	17.437 335	18.138 168	18.867 015	192
17	18.386 607	19.173 247	19.993 370	20.848 395	21.739 798	22.669 119	204
18	21.821 471	22.811 211	23.845 625	24.926 719	26.056 590	27.237 428	216
19	25.898 015	27.139 450	28.440 120	29.802 839	31.230 553	32.726 348	228
20	30.736 111	32.288 935	33.919 866	35.632 816	37.431 890	39.321 402	240
21	36.478 029	38.415 493	40.455 431	42.603 242	44.864 605	47.245 499	252
22	43.292 614	45.704 514	48.250 247	50.937 210	53.773 207	56.766 471	264
23	51.380 255	54.376 566	57.546 941	60.901 454	64.450 757	68.206 120	276
24	60.978 776	64.694 069	68.634 892	72.814 885	77.248 510	81.951 101	288
25	72.370 840	76.969 232	81.859 231	87.058 800	92.587 467	98.465 988	300
26	85.890 197	91.573 505	97.631 591	104.089 083	110.972 224	118.308 975	312
27	101.935 637	108.948 818	116.442 916	124.450 799	133.007 576	142.150 745	324
28	120.978 582	129.620 953	138.878 743	148.795 637	159.418 407	170.797 139	336
29	143.579 004	154.215 454	165.637 430	177.902 767	191.073 542	205.216 389	348
30	170.401 487	183.476 557	197.551 891	212.703 781	229.014 322	246.571 848	360

FUTURE VALUE

MOS	18.75% ANNUAL RATE	19.00% ANNUAL RATE	19.25% ANNUAL RATE	19.50% ANNUAL RATE	19.75% ANNUAL RATE	20.00% ANNUAL RATE	MOS
1	1.015 625	1.015 833	1.016 042	1.016 250	1.016 458	1.016 667	1
2	1.031 494	1.031 917	1.032 341	1.032 764	1.033 188	1.033 611	2
3	1.047 611	1.048 256	1.048 901	1.049 546	1.050 192	1.050 838	3
4	1.063 980	1.064 853	1.065 727	1.066 602	1.067 476	1.068 352	4
5	1.080 605	1.081 714	1.082 823	1.083 934	1.085 045	1.086 158	5
6	1.097 489	1.098 841	1.100 194	1.101 548	1.102 903	1.104 260	6
7	1.114 638	1.116 239	1.117 843	1.119 448	1.121 055	1.122 665	7
8	1.132 054	1.133 913	1.135 775	1.137 639	1.139 506	1.141 376	8
9	1.149 742	1.151 866	1.153 994	1.156 126	1.158 260	1.160 399	9
10	1.167 707	1.170 104	1.172 506	1.174 913	1.177 323	1.179 739	10
11	1.185 952	1.188 631	1.191 315	1.194 005	1.196 700	1.199 401	11
12	1.204 483	1.207 451	1.210 426	1.213 408	1.216 396	1.219 391	12
13	1.223 303	1.226 569	1.229 843	1.233 125	1.236 416	1.239 714	13
14	1.242 417	1.245 990	1.249 572	1.253 164	1.256 765	1.260 376	14
15	1.261 830	1.265 718	1.269 617	1.273 528	1.277 449	1.281 382	15
16	1.281 546	1.285 758	1.289 984	1.294 222	1.298 474	1.302 739	16
17	1.301 570	1.306 116	1.310 677	1.315 254	1.319 845	1.324 451	17
18	1.321 907	1.326 796	1.331 703	1.336 626	1.341 567	1.346 525	18
19	1.342 562	1.347 804	1.353 066	1.358 347	1.363 647	1.368 967	19
20	1.363 539	1.369 144	1.374 771	1.380 420	1.386 091	1.391 784	20
21	1.384 845	1.390 822	1.396 825	1.402 852	1.408 903	1.414 980	21
22	1.406 483	1.412 844	1.419 232	1.425 648	1.432 092	1.438 563	22
23	1.428 459	1.435 214	1.441 999	1.448 815	1.455 661	1.462 539	23
24	1.450 779	1.457 938	1.465 131	1.472 358	1.479 619	1.486 915	24
25	1.473 447	1.481 022	1.488 634	1.496 284	1.503 971	1.511 697	25
26	1.496 470	1.504 471	1.512 514	1.520 598	1.528 724	1.536 891	26
27	1.519 852	1.528 292	1.536 777	1.545 308	1.553 884	1.562 506	27
28	1.543 600	1.552 490	1.561 430	1.570 419	1.579 459	1.588 548	28
29	1.567 719	1.577 071	1.586 478	1.595 939	1.605 454	1.615 024	29
30	1.592 214	1.602 042	1.611 928	1.621 873	1.631 877	1.641 941	30
31	1.617 092	1.627 407	1.637 786	1.648 228	1.658 735	1.669 307	31
32	1.642 360	1.653 175	1.664 058	1.675 012	1.686 035	1.697 128	32
33	1.668 021	1.679 350	1.690 753	1.702 231	1.713 784	1.725 414	33
34	1.694 084	1.705 940	1.717 875	1.729 892	1.741 990	1.754 171	34
35	1.720 554	1.732 950	1.745 433	1.758 003	1.770 661	1.783 407	35
36	1.747 438	1.760 389	1.773 432	1.786 570	1.799 803	1.813 130	36
37	1.774 742	1.788 261	1.801 881	1.815 602	1.829 424	1.843 349	37
38	1.802 472	1.816 576	1.830 786	1.845 106	1.859 534	1.874 072	38
39	1.830 636	1.845 338	1.860 155	1.875 089	1.890 139	1.905 306	39
40	1.859 239	1.874 556	1.889 995	1.905 559	1.921 247	1.937 061	40
41	1.888 290	1.904 236	1.920 314	1.936 524	1.952 868	1.969 346	41
42	1.917 795	1.934 387	1.951 119	1.967 993	1.985 009	2.002 168	42
43	1.947 760	1.965 015	1.982 418	1.999 972	2.017 679	2.035 538	43
44	1.978 194	1.996 127	2.014 220	2.032 472	2.050 886	2.069 463	44
45	2.009 103	2.027 733	2.046 531	2.065 500	2.084 640	2.103 954	45
46	2.040 495	2.059 838	2.079 361	2.099 064	2.118 950	2.139 020	46
47	2.072 378	2.092 452	2.112 717	2.133 174	2.153 824	2.174 671	47

YRS							MOS
4	2.104 759	2.125 583	2.146 609	2.167 838	2.189 273	2.210 915	48
5	2.535 146	2.566 537	2.598 311	2.630 471	2.663 023	2.695 970	60
6	3.053 540	3.098 968	3.145 063	3.191 833	3.239 290	3.287 442	72
7	3.677 936	3.741 852	3.806 865	3.872 995	3.940 259	4.008 677	84
8	4.430 010	4.518 103	4.607 929	4.699 521	4.792 915	4.888 145	96
9	5.335 871	5.455 388	5.577 556	5.702 435	5.830 083	5.960 561	108
10	6.426 965	6.587 114	6.751 219	6.919 378	7.091 689	7.268 255	120
11	7.741 168	7.953 617	8.171 850	8.396 025	8.626 302	8.862 845	132
12	9.324 104	9.603 603	9.891 420	10.187 801	10.492 999	10.807 275	144
13	11.230 722	11.595 879	11.972 831	12.361 955	12.763 641	13.178 294	156
14	13.527 212	14.001 456	14.492 225	15.000 089	15.525 642	16.069 495	168
15	16.293 293	16.906 072	17.541 765	18.201 222	18.885 328	19.594 998	180
16	19.624 991	20.413 254	21.233 007	22.085 501	22.972 037	23.893 966	192
17	23.637 964	24.648 004	25.700 982	26.798 714	27.943 093	29.136 090	204
18	28.471 520	29.761 257	31.109 135	32.517 763	33.989 865	35.528 288	216
19	34.293 455	35.935 259	37.655 304	39.457 300	41.345 134	43.322 878	228
20	41.305 876	43.390 065	45.578 956	47.877 787	50.292 054	52.827 531	240
21	49.752 216	52.391 377	55.169 950	58.095 269	61.175 052	64.417 420	252
22	59.925 687	63.260 020	66.779 138	70.493 240	74.413 086	78.550 028	264
23	72.179 458	76.383 375	80.831 200	85.537 031	90.515 777	95.783 203	276
24	86.938 913	92.229 182	97.840 181	103.791 282	110.103 025	116.797 184	288
25	104.716 423	111.362 218	118.428 292	125.941 129	133.928 875	142.421 445	300
26	126.129 127	134.464 421	143.348 675	152.817 920	162.910 542	173.667 440	312
27	151.920 360	162.359 199	173.512 953	185.430 422	198.163 726	211.768 529	324
28	182.985 456	196.040 777	210.024 578	225.002 680	241.045 555	258.228 656	336
29	220.402 829	236.709 632	254.219 195	273.019 957	293.206 839	314.881 721	348
30	265.471 410	285.815 282	307.713 505	331.284 485	356.655 615	383.963 963	360

SECTION 1

MOS	20.25% ANNUAL RATE	20.50% ANNUAL RATE	20.75% ANNUAL RATE	21.00% ANNUAL RATE	21.25% ANNUAL RATE	21.50% ANNUAL RATE	MOS
1	1.016 875	1.017 083	1.017 292	1.017 500	1.017 708	1.017 917	1
2	1.034 035	1.034 459	1.034 882	1.035 306	1.035 730	1.036 154	2
3	1.051 484	1.052 131	1.052 777	1.053 424	1.054 071	1.054 719	3
4	1.069 228	1.070 104	1.070 981	1.071 859	1.072 737	1.073 616	4
5	1.087 271	1.088 385	1.089 501	1.090 617	1.091 734	1.092 851	5
6	1.105 619	1.106 979	1.108 340	1.109 702	1.111 066	1.112 432	6
7	1.124 276	1.125 889	1.127 505	1.129 122	1.130 741	1.132 363	7
8	1.143 248	1.145 123	1.147 001	1.148 882	1.150 765	1.152 651	8
9	1.162 541	1.164 686	1.166 835	1.168 987	1.171 143	1.173 303	9
10	1.182 158	1.184 583	1.187 011	1.189 444	1.191 882	1.194 324	10
11	1.202 107	1.204 819	1.207 537	1.210 260	1.212 988	1.215 723	11
12	1.222 393	1.225 402	1.228 417	1.231 439	1.234 468	1.237 504	12
13	1.243 021	1.246 336	1.249 658	1.252 990	1.256 329	1.259 676	13
14	1.263 997	1.267 627	1.271 267	1.274 917	1.278 576	1.282 245	14
15	1.285 327	1.289 282	1.293 249	1.297 228	1.301 218	1.305 219	15
16	1.307 017	1.311 308	1.315 612	1.319 929	1.324 260	1.328 604	16
17	1.329 073	1.333 709	1.338 361	1.343 028	1.347 711	1.352 408	17
18	1.351 501	1.356 493	1.361 504	1.366 531	1.371 576	1.376 639	18
19	1.374 307	1.379 667	1.385 046	1.390 445	1.395 865	1.401 304	19
20	1.397 499	1.403 236	1.408 996	1.414 778	1.420 583	1.426 410	20
21	1.421 081	1.427 208	1.433 360	1.439 537	1.445 739	1.451 967	21
22	1.445 062	1.451 590	1.458 145	1.464 729	1.471 341	1.477 981	22
23	1.469 448	1.476 388	1.483 359	1.490 361	1.497 396	1.504 462	23
24	1.494 245	1.501 609	1.509 008	1.516 443	1.523 912	1.531 417	24
25	1.519 460	1.527 262	1.535 102	1.542 981	1.550 898	1.558 855	25
26	1.545 101	1.553 352	1.561 646	1.569 983	1.578 362	1.586 784	26
27	1.571 174	1.579 889	1.588 650	1.597 457	1.606 312	1.615 214	27
28	1.597 688	1.606 879	1.616 120	1.625 413	1.634 757	1.644 153	28
29	1.624 649	1.634 329	1.644 066	1.653 858	1.663 706	1.673 611	29
30	1.652 065	1.662 249	1.672 494	1.682 800	1.693 167	1.703 597	30
31	1.679 944	1.690 646	1.701 414	1.712 249	1.723 151	1.734 119	31
32	1.708 293	1.719 528	1.730 835	1.742 213	1.753 665	1.765 189	32
33	1.737 120	1.748 903	1.760 764	1.772 702	1.784 719	1.796 815	33
34	1.766 434	1.778 780	1.791 210	1.803 725	1.816 324	1.829 008	34
35	1.796 242	1.809 168	1.822 183	1.835 290	1.848 488	1.861 778	35
36	1.826 554	1.840 074	1.853 692	1.867 407	1.881 221	1.895 135	36
37	1.857 377	1.871 509	1.885 745	1.900 087	1.914 535	1.929 089	37
38	1.888 720	1.903 481	1.918 353	1.933 338	1.948 438	1.963 652	38
39	1.920 593	1.935 998	1.951 524	1.967 172	1.982 941	1.998 834	39
40	1.953 003	1.969 072	1.985 270	2.001 597	2.018 056	2.034 647	40
41	1.985 959	2.002 710	2.019 598	2.036 625	2.053 792	2.071 101	41
42	2.019 473	2.036 923	2.054 520	2.072 266	2.090 162	2.108 208	42
43	2.053 551	2.071 720	2.090 046	2.108 531	2.127 175	2.145 980	43
44	2.088 205	2.107 112	2.126 187	2.145 430	2.164 844	2.184 429	44
45	2.123 443	2.143 109	2.162 952	2.182 975	2.203 179	2.223 567	45
46	2.159 276	2.179 720	2.200 353	2.221 177	2.242 194	2.263 405	46
47	2.195 714	2.216 957	2.238 401	2.260 048	2.281 900	2.303 958	47

YRS	20.25%	20.50%	20.75%	21.00%	21.25%	21.50%	MOS
4	2.232 767	2.254 830	2.277 107	2.299 599	2.322 308	2.345 237	48
5	2.729 318	2.763 072	2.797 237	2.831 816	2.866 816	2.902 241	60
6	3.336 300	3.385 873	3.436 173	3.487 210	3.538 994	3.591 536	72
7	4.078 269	4.149 055	4.221 054	4.294 287	4.368 776	4.444 541	84
8	4.985 248	5.084 258	5.185 215	5.288 154	5.393 116	5.500 138	96
9	6.093 932	6.230 259	6.369 606	6.512 041	6.657 631	6.806 445	108
10	7.449 179	7.634 569	7.824 533	8.019 183	8.218 635	8.423 004	120
11	9.105 825	9.355 413	9.611 790	9.875 138	10.145 645	10.423 504	132
12	11.130 896	11.464 139	11.807 287	12.160 633	12.524 478	12.899 131	144
13	13.606 329	14.048 174	14.504 273	14.975 081	15.461 071	15.962 729	156
14	16.632 281	17.214 655	17.817 296	18.440 904	19.086 204	19.753 945	168
15	20.331 183	21.094 867	21.887 071	22.708 854	23.561 315	24.445 591	180
16	24.852 695	25.849 684	26.886 451	27.964 576	29.085 698	30.251 523	192
17	30.379 760	31.676 245	33.027 776	34.436 678	35.905 374	37.436 389	204
18	37.136 005	38.816 122	40.571 884	42.406 679	44.324 049	46.327 691	216
19	45.394 791	47.565 339	49.839 195	52.221 252	54.716 637	57.330 715	228
20	55.490 274	58.286 644	61.223 317	64.307 303	67.545 958	70.947 004	240
21	67.830 921	71.424 548	75.207 768	79.190 541	83.383 348	87.797 220	252
22	82.916 040	87.523 758	92.386 506	97.518 346	102.934 107	108.649 434	264
23	101.355 985	107.251 755	113.489 161	120.087 925	127.068 899	134.454 138	276
24	123.896 843	131.426 475	139.412 023	147.880 992	156.862 537	166.387 569	288
25	151.450 630	161.050 216	171.256 109	182.106 467	193.641 841	205.905 325	300
26	185.132 185	197.351 197	210.373 928	224.253 063	239.044 729	254.808 717	312
27	226.304 282	241.834 477	258.426 924	276.154 038	295.093 158	315.326 874	324
28	276.632 763	296.344 362	317.456 045	340.066 940	364.283 171	390.218 350	336
29	338.153 945	363.140 863	389.968 425	418.771 800	449.696 054	482.896 871	348
30	413.357 004	444.993 404	479.043 870	515.692 058	555.135 556	597.586 935	360

18

FUTURE VALUE

MONTHLY COMPOUNDING

MOS	21.75% ANNUAL RATE	22.00% ANNUAL RATE	22.50% ANNUAL RATE	23.00% ANNUAL RATE	23.50% ANNUAL RATE	24.00% ANNUAL RATE	MOS
1	1.018 125	1.018 333	1.018 750	1.019 167	1.019 583	1.020 000	1
2	1.036 579	1.037 003	1.037 852	1.038 701	1.039 550	1.040 400	2
3	1.055 367	1.056 014	1.057 311	1.058 609	1.059 908	1.061 208	3
4	1.074 495	1.075 375	1.077 136	1.078 899	1.080 665	1.082 432	4
5	1.093 970	1.095 090	1.097 332	1.099 578	1.101 828	1.104 081	5
6	1.113 798	1.115 167	1.117 907	1.120 653	1.123 405	1.126 162	6
7	1.133 986	1.135 611	1.138 868	1.142 132	1.145 405	1.148 686	7
8	1.154 540	1.156 431	1.160 222	1.164 023	1.167 836	1.171 659	8
9	1.175 466	1.177 632	1.181 976	1.186 334	1.190 706	1.195 093	9
10	1.196 771	1.199 222	1.204 138	1.209 072	1.214 024	1.218 994	10
11	1.218 462	1.221 208	1.226 715	1.232 246	1.237 799	1.243 374	11
12	1.240 547	1.243 597	1.249 716	1.255 864	1.262 039	1.268 242	12
13	1.263 032	1.266 396	1.273 149	1.279 934	1.286 754	1.293 607	13
14	1.285 924	1.289 613	1.297 020	1.304 467	1.311 953	1.319 479	14
15	1.309 232	1.313 256	1.321 339	1.329 469	1.337 645	1.345 868	15
16	1.332 962	1.337 332	1.346 114	1.354 950	1.363 841	1.372 786	16
17	1.357 121	1.361 850	1.371 354	1.380 920	1.390 549	1.400 241	17
18	1.381 719	1.386 817	1.397 067	1.407 388	1.417 781	1.428 246	18
19	1.406 763	1.412 242	1.423 262	1.434 363	1.445 546	1.456 811	19
20	1.432 261	1.438 133	1.449 948	1.461 855	1.473 854	1.485 947	20
21	1.458 220	1.464 499	1.477 135	1.489 874	1.502 717	1.515 666	21
22	1.484 651	1.491 348	1.504 831	1.518 430	1.532 145	1.545 980	22
23	1.511 560	1.518 690	1.533 046	1.547 533	1.562 150	1.576 899	23
24	1.538 957	1.546 532	1.561 791	1.577 194	1.592 742	1.608 437	24
25	1.566 850	1.574 886	1.591 075	1.607 423	1.623 933	1.640 606	25
26	1.595 250	1.603 758	1.620 907	1.638 232	1.655 735	1.673 418	26
27	1.624 163	1.633 161	1.651 299	1.669 632	1.688 160	1.706 886	27
28	1.653 601	1.663 102	1.682 261	1.701 633	1.721 220	1.741 024	28
29	1.683 573	1.693 592	1.713 804	1.734 248	1.754 927	1.775 845	29
30	1.714 088	1.724 641	1.745 937	1.767 487	1.789 295	1.811 362	30
31	1.745 156	1.756 260	1.778 674	1.801 364	1.824 335	1.847 589	31
32	1.776 787	1.788 458	1.812 024	1.835 890	1.860 061	1.884 541	32
33	1.808 991	1.821 246	1.845 999	1.871 078	1.896 488	1.922 231	33
34	1.841 779	1.854 636	1.880 612	1.906 941	1.933 627	1.960 676	34
35	1.875 161	1.888 637	1.915 873	1.943 490	1.971 494	1.999 890	35
36	1.909 148	1.923 262	1.951 796	1.980 741	2.010 102	2.039 887	36
37	1.943 752	1.958 522	1.988 392	2.018 705	2.049 467	2.080 685	37
38	1.978 982	1.994 429	2.025 674	2.057 397	2.089 602	2.122 299	38
39	2.014 851	2.030 993	2.063 656	2.096 830	2.130 524	2.164 745	39
40	2.051 370	2.068 228	2.102 349	2.137 019	2.172 246	2.208 040	40
41	2.088 551	2.106 145	2.141 768	2.177 979	2.214 786	2.252 200	41
42	2.126 406	2.144 758	2.181 926	2.219 723	2.258 159	2.297 244	42
43	2.164 948	2.184 079	2.222 838	2.262 268	2.302 382	2.343 189	43
44	2.204 187	2.224 120	2.264 516	2.305 628	2.347 470	2.390 053	44
45	2.244 138	2.264 896	2.306 975	2.349 819	2.393 441	2.437 854	45
46	2.284 813	2.306 419	2.350 231	2.394 858	2.440 313	2.486 611	46
47	2.326 225	2.348 703	2.394 298	2.440 759	2.488 102	2.536 344	47

YRS

4	2.368 388	2.391 763	2.439 191	2.487 540	2.536 827	2.587 070	48
5	2.938 097	2.974 388	3.048 297	3.124 012	3.201 575	3.281 031	60
6	3.644 847	3.698 938	3.809 507	3.923 333	4.040 512	4.161 140	72
7	4.521 604	4.599 987	4.760 803	4.927 172	5.099 283	5.277 332	84
8	5.609 262	5.720 528	5.949 654	6.187 857	6.435 493	6.692 933	96
9	6.958 554	7.114 030	7.435 380	7.771 105	8.121 843	8.488 258	108
10	8.632 413	8.846 983	9.292 116	9.759 449	10.250 081	10.765 163	120
11	10.708 914	11.002 078	11.612 509	12.256 539	12.936 001	13.652 830	132
12	13.284 911	13.682 146	14.512 343	15.392 543	16.325 736	17.315 089	144
13	16.480 556	17.015 070	18.136 313	19.330 937	20.603 714	21.959 720	156
14	20.444 904	21.159 883	22.665 247	24.277 024	26.002 688	27.850 234	168
15	25.362 864	26.314 358	28.325 130	30.488 635	32.816 403	35.320 831	180
16	31.463 825	32.724 445	35.398 379	38.289 572	41.415 576	44.795 355	192
17	39.032 353	40.696 008	44.237 934	48.086 486	52.268 067	56.811 341	204
18	48.421 469	50.609 416	55.284 871	60.390 076	65.964 332	72.050 517	216
19	60.069 107	62.937 697	69.090 408	75.841 706	83.249 551	91.377 477	228
20	74.518 550	78.269 105	86.343 415	95.246 853	105.064 170	115.888 735	240
21	92.443 763	97.335 191	107.904 779	119.617 072	132.595 066	146.974 937	252
22	114.680 832	121.045 710	134.850 370	150.222 748	167.340 128	186.399 758	264
23	142.266 962	150.532 031	168.524 715	188.659 306	211.189 746	236.399 964	276
24	176.488 851	187.201 119	210.608 097	236.930 388	266.529 669	299.812 315	288
25	218.942 713	232.802 670	263.200 388	297.552 290	336.370 803	380.234 508	300
26	271.608 724	289.512 604	328.925 835	373.685 140	424.513 029	482.229 295	312
27	336.943 386	360.036 884	411.064 002	469.297 629	535.751 944	611.583 346	324
28	417.994 103	447.740 637	513.713 415	589.373 890	676.139 779	775.635 561	336
29	518.541 327	556.808 724	641.996 068	740.173 316	853.314 683	983.693 435	348
30	643.274 884	692.445 423	802.313 000	929.556 851	1076.916 300	1247.561 128	360

QUARTERLY COMPOUNDING

SECTION 1

QTRS	5.25% ANNUAL RATE	5.50% ANNUAL RATE	5.75% ANNUAL RATE	6.00% ANNUAL RATE	6.25% ANNUAL RATE	6.50% ANNUAL RATE	QTRS
1	1.013 125	1.013 750	1.014 375	1.015 000	1.015 625	1.016 250	1
2	1.026 422	1.027 689	1.028 957	1.030 225	1.031 494	1.032 764	2
3	1.039 894	1.041 820	1.043 748	1.045 678	1.047 611	1.049 546	3
4	1.053 543	1.056 145	1.058 752	1.061 364	1.063 980	1.066 602	4
5	1.067 370	1.070 667	1.073 971	1.077 284	1.080 605	1.083 934	5
6	1.081 380	1.085 388	1.089 410	1.093 443	1.097 489	1.101 548	6
7	1.095 573	1.100 313	1.105 070	1.109 845	1.114 638	1.119 448	7
8	1.109 952	1.115 442	1.120 955	1.126 493	1.132 054	1.137 639	8
9	1.124 520	1.130 779	1.137 069	1.143 390	1.149 742	1.156 126	9
10	1.139 280	1.146 327	1.153 414	1.160 541	1.167 707	1.174 913	10
11	1.154 233	1.162 089	1.169 995	1.177 949	1.185 952	1.194 005	11
12	1.169 382	1.178 068	1.186 813	1.195 618	1.204 483	1.213 408	12
13	1.184 730	1.194 267	1.203 874	1.213 552	1.223 303	1.233 125	13
14	1.200 280	1.210 688	1.221 180	1.231 756	1.242 417	1.253 164	14
15	1.216 033	1.227 335	1.238 734	1.250 232	1.261 830	1.273 528	15
16	1.231 994	1.244 211	1.256 541	1.268 986	1.281 546	1.294 222	16
17	1.248 164	1.261 318	1.274 604	1.288 020	1.301 570	1.315 254	17
18	1.264 546	1.278 662	1.292 926	1.307 341	1.321 907	1.336 626	18
19	1.281 143	1.296 243	1.311 512	1.326 951	1.342 562	1.358 347	19
20	1.297 958	1.314 067	1.330 365	1.346 855	1.363 539	1.380 420	20
21	1.314 994	1.332 135	1.349 489	1.367 058	1.384 845	1.402 852	21
22	1.332 253	1.350 452	1.368 888	1.387 564	1.406 483	1.425 648	22
23	1.349 739	1.369 020	1.388 565	1.408 377	1.428 459	1.448 815	23
24	1.367 454	1.387 845	1.408 526	1.429 503	1.450 779	1.472 358	24
25	1.385 402	1.406 927	1.428 774	1.450 945	1.473 447	1.496 284	25
26	1.403 585	1.426 273	1.449 312	1.472 710	1.496 470	1.520 598	26
27	1.422 007	1.445 884	1.470 146	1.494 800	1.519 852	1.545 308	27
28	1.440 671	1.465 765	1.491 279	1.517 222	1.543 600	1.570 419	28
29	1.459 580	1.485 919	1.512 717	1.539 981	1.567 719	1.595 939	29
30	1.478 737	1.506 350	1.534 462	1.563 080	1.592 214	1.621 873	30
31	1.498 146	1.527 063	1.556 520	1.586 526	1.617 092	1.648 228	31
32	1.517 809	1.548 060	1.578 895	1.610 324	1.642 360	1.675 012	32
33	1.537 730	1.569 346	1.601 591	1.634 479	1.668 021	1.702 231	33
34	1.557 913	1.590 924	1.624 614	1.658 996	1.694 084	1.729 892	34
35	1.578 360	1.612 799	1.647 968	1.683 881	1.720 554	1.758 003	35
36	1.599 076	1.634 975	1.671 658	1.709 140	1.747 438	1.786 570	36
37	1.620 064	1.657 456	1.695 688	1.734 777	1.774 742	1.815 602	37
38	1.641 327	1.680 246	1.720 063	1.760 798	1.802 472	1.845 106	38
39	1.662 870	1.703 350	1.744 789	1.787 210	1.830 636	1.875 089	39
40	1.684 695	1.726 771	1.769 870	1.814 018	1.859 239	1.905 559	40
41	1.706 807	1.750 514	1.795 312	1.841 229	1.888 290	1.936 524	41
42	1.729 208	1.774 583	1.821 120	1.868 847	1.917 795	1.967 993	42
43	1.751 904	1.798 984	1.847 299	1.896 880	1.947 760	1.999 972	43
44	1.774 898	1.823 720	1.873 854	1.925 333	1.978 194	2.032 472	44
45	1.798 194	1.848 796	1.900 790	1.954 213	2.009 103	2.065 500	45
46	1.821 795	1.874 217	1.928 114	1.983 526	2.040 495	2.099 064	46
47	1.845 706	1.899 988	1.955 831	2.013 279	2.072 378	2.133 174	47
48	1.869 931	1.926 112	1.983 946	2.043 478	2.104 759	2.167 838	48
49	1.894 474	1.952 596	2.012 465	2.074 130	2.137 646	2.203 065	49
50	1.919 339	1.979 445	2.041 394	2.105 242	2.171 047	2.238 865	50
51	1.944 530	2.006 662	2.070 739	2.136 821	2.204 969	2.275 247	51
52	1.970 052	2.034 254	2.100 506	2.168 873	2.239 422	2.312 219	52
53	1.995 909	2.062 225	2.130 701	2.201 406	2.274 413	2.349 793	53
54	2.022 105	2.090 580	2.161 330	2.234 428	2.309 950	2.387 977	54
55	2.048 645	2.119 326	2.192 399	2.267 944	2.346 043	2.426 782	55
YRS							
14	2.075 534	2.148 466	2.223 914	2.301 963	2.382 700	2.466 217	56
15	2.186 663	2.269 092	2.354 573	2.443 220	2.535 146	2.630 471	60
16	2.303 743	2.396 489	2.492 909	2.593 144	2.697 345	2.805 665	64
17	2.427 092	2.531 040	2.639 372	2.752 269	2.869 922	2.992 526	68
18	2.557 045	2.673 145	2.794 439	2.921 158	3.053 540	3.191 833	72
19	2.693 956	2.823 228	2.958 618	3.100 411	3.248 906	3.404 415	76
20	2.838 197	2.981 737	3.132 442	3.290 663	3.456 771	3.631 154	80
21	2.990 162	3.149 146	3.316 478	3.492 590	3.677 936	3.872 995	84
22	3.150 263	3.325 955	3.511 327	3.706 907	3.913 251	4.130 943	88
23	3.318 937	3.512 690	3.717 624	3.934 376	4.163 621	4.406 070	92
24	3.496 641	3.709 909	3.936 041	4.175 804	4.430 010	4.699 521	96
25	3.683 861	3.918 201	4.167 290	4.432 046	4.713 443	5.012 517	100
26	3.881 105	4.138 188	4.412 126	4.704 012	5.015 010	5.346 359	104
27	4.088 909	4.370 526	4.671 346	4.992 667	5.335 871	5.702 435	108
28	4.307 840	4.615 908	4.945 796	5.299 034	5.677 261	6.082 226	112
29	4.538 494	4.875 067	5.236 370	5.624 202	6.040 493	6.487 312	116
30	4.781 497	5.148 777	5.544 016	5.969 323	6.426 965	6.919 378	120

FUTURE VALUE

QTRS	6.75% ANNUAL RATE	7.00% ANNUAL RATE	7.25% ANNUAL RATE	7.50% ANNUAL RATE	7.75% ANNUAL RATE	8.00% ANNUAL RATE	QTRS
1	1.016 875	1.017 500	1.018 125	1.018 750	1.019 375	1.020 000	1
2	1.034 035	1.035 306	1.036 579	1.037 852	1.039 125	1.040 400	2
3	1.051 484	1.053 424	1.055 367	1.057 311	1.059 258	1.061 208	3
4	1.069 228	1.071 859	1.074 495	1.077 136	1.079 782	1.082 432	4
5	1.087 271	1.090 617	1.093 970	1.097 332	1.100 702	1.104 081	5
6	1.105 619	1.109 702	1.113 798	1.117 907	1.122 028	1.126 162	6
7	1.124 276	1.129 122	1.133 986	1.138 868	1.143 768	1.148 686	7
8	1.143 248	1.148 882	1.154 540	1.160 222	1.165 928	1.171 659	8
9	1.162 541	1.168 987	1.175 466	1.181 976	1.188 518	1.195 093	9
10	1.182 158	1.189 444	1.196 771	1.204 138	1.211 546	1.218 994	10
11	1.202 107	1.210 260	1.218 462	1.226 715	1.235 019	1.243 374	11
12	1.222 393	1.231 439	1.240 547	1.249 716	1.258 948	1.268 242	12
13	1.243 021	1.252 990	1.263 032	1.273 149	1.283 340	1.293 607	13
14	1.263 997	1.274 917	1.285 924	1.297 020	1.308 205	1.319 479	14
15	1.285 327	1.297 228	1.309 232	1.321 339	1.333 551	1.345 868	15
16	1.307 017	1.319 929	1.332 962	1.346 114	1.359 389	1.372 786	16
17	1.329 073	1.343 028	1.357 121	1.371 354	1.385 727	1.400 241	17
18	1.351 501	1.366 531	1.381 719	1.397 067	1.412 575	1.428 246	18
19	1.374 307	1.390 445	1.406 763	1.423 262	1.439 944	1.456 811	19
20	1.397 499	1.414 778	1.432 261	1.449 948	1.467 843	1.485 947	20
21	1.421 081	1.439 537	1.458 220	1.477 135	1.496 282	1.515 666	21
22	1.445 062	1.464 729	1.484 651	1.504 831	1.525 273	1.545 980	22
23	1.469 448	1.490 361	1.511 560	1.533 046	1.554 825	1.576 899	23
24	1.494 245	1.516 443	1.538 957	1.561 791	1.584 950	1.608 437	24
25	1.519 460	1.542 981	1.566 850	1.591 075	1.615 658	1.640 606	25
26	1.545 101	1.569 983	1.595 250	1.620 907	1.646 961	1.673 418	26
27	1.571 174	1.597 457	1.624 163	1.651 299	1.678 871	1.706 886	27
28	1.597 688	1.625 413	1.653 601	1.682 261	1.711 399	1.741 024	28
29	1.624 649	1.653 858	1.683 573	1.713 804	1.744 558	1.775 845	29
30	1.652 065	1.682 800	1.714 088	1.745 937	1.778 359	1.811 362	30
31	1.679 944	1.712 249	1.745 156	1.778 674	1.812 814	1.847 589	31
32	1.708 293	1.742 213	1.776 787	1.812 024	1.847 938	1.884 541	32
33	1.737 120	1.772 702	1.808 991	1.845 999	1.883 741	1.922 231	33
34	1.766 434	1.803 725	1.841 779	1.880 612	1.920 239	1.960 676	34
35	1.796 242	1.835 290	1.875 161	1.915 873	1.957 444	1.999 890	35
36	1.826 554	1.867 407	1.909 148	1.951 796	1.995 369	2.039 887	36
37	1.857 377	1.900 087	1.943 752	1.988 392	2.034 029	2.080 685	37
38	1.888 720	1.933 338	1.978 982	2.025 674	2.073 439	2.122 299	38
39	1.920 593	1.967 172	2.014 851	2.063 656	2.113 611	2.164 745	39
40	1.953 003	2.001 597	2.051 370	2.102 349	2.154 563	2.208 040	40
41	1.985 959	2.036 625	2.088 551	2.141 768	2.196 307	2.252 200	41
42	2.019 473	2.072 266	2.126 406	2.181 926	2.238 861	2.297 244	42
43	2.053 551	2.108 531	2.164 948	2.222 838	2.282 239	2.343 189	43
44	2.088 205	2.145 430	2.204 187	2.264 516	2.326 457	2.390 053	44
45	2.123 443	2.182 975	2.244 138	2.306 975	2.371 532	2.437 854	45
46	2.159 276	2.221 177	2.284 813	2.350 231	2.417 481	2.486 611	46
47	2.195 714	2.260 048	2.326 225	2.394 298	2.464 319	2.536 344	47
48	2.232 767	2.299 599	2.368 388	2.439 191	2.512 066	2.587 070	48
49	2.270 445	2.339 842	2.411 315	2.484 926	2.560 737	2.638 812	49
50	2.308 759	2.380 789	2.455 020	2.531 518	2.610 351	2.691 588	50
51	2.347 719	2.422 453	2.499 518	2.578 984	2.660 927	2.745 420	51
52	2.387 337	2.464 846	2.544 821	2.627 340	2.712 482	2.800 328	52
53	2.427 623	2.507 980	2.590 946	2.676 603	2.765 036	2.856 335	53
54	2.468 589	2.551 870	2.637 907	2.726 789	2.818 609	2.913 461	54
55	2.510 246	2.596 528	2.685 719	2.777 917	2.873 220	2.971 731	55
YRS							
14	2.552 607	2.641 967	2.734 398	2.830 002	2.928 888	3.031 165	56
15	2.729 318	2.831 816	2.938 097	3.048 297	3.162 559	3.281 031	60
16	2.918 263	3.035 308	3.156 970	3.283 430	3.414 873	3.551 493	64
17	3.120 289	3.253 422	3.392 149	3.536 700	3.687 317	3.844 251	68
18	3.336 300	3.487 210	3.644 847	3.809 507	3.981 497	4.161 140	72
19	3.567 265	3.737 797	3.916 370	4.103 357	4.299 148	4.504 152	76
20	3.814 219	4.006 392	4.208 120	4.419 872	4.642 140	4.875 439	80
21	4.078 269	4.294 287	4.521 604	4.760 864	5.012 498	5.277 332	84
22	4.360 599	4.602 871	4.858 441	5.128 032	5.412 403	5.712 354	88
23	4.662 474	4.933 629	5.220 371	5.523 587	5.844 213	6.183 236	92
24	4.985 248	5.288 154	5.609 262	5.949 654	6.310 473	6.692 933	96
25	5.330 366	5.668 156	6.027 125	6.408 585	6.813 933	7.244 646	100
26	5.699 376	6.075 464	6.476 115	6.902 917	7.357 559	7.841 838	104
27	6.093 932	6.512 041	6.958 554	7.435 380	7.944 557	8.488 258	108
28	6.515 802	6.979 990	7.476 931	8.008 914	8.578 386	9.187 963	112
29	6.966 877	7.481 565	8.033 925	8.626 689	9.262 783	9.945 347	116
30	7.449 179	8.019 183	8.632 413	9.292 116	10.001 783	10.765 163	120

QTRS	8.25% ANNUAL RATE	8.50% ANNUAL RATE	8.75% ANNUAL RATE	9.00% ANNUAL RATE	9.25% ANNUAL RATE	9.50% ANNUAL RATE	QTRS
1	1.020 625	1.021 250	1.021 875	1.022 500	1.023 125	1.023 750	1
2	1.041 675	1.042 952	1.044 229	1.045 506	1.046 785	1.048 064	2
3	1.063 160	1.065 114	1.067 071	1.069 030	1.070 992	1.072 956	3
4	1.085 088	1.087 748	1.090 413	1.093 083	1.095 758	1.098 438	4
5	1.107 468	1.110 863	1.114 266	1.117 678	1.121 098	1.124 526	5
6	1.130 309	1.134 468	1.138 641	1.142 825	1.147 023	1.151 234	6
7	1.153 622	1.158 576	1.163 548	1.168 539	1.173 548	1.178 575	7
8	1.177 415	1.183 196	1.189 001	1.194 831	1.200 686	1.206 567	8
9	1.201 699	1.208 339	1.215 010	1.221 715	1.228 452	1.235 223	9
10	1.226 484	1.234 016	1.241 589	1.249 203	1.256 860	1.264 559	10
11	1.251 781	1.260 239	1.268 748	1.277 311	1.285 925	1.294 592	11
12	1.277 599	1.287 019	1.296 502	1.306 050	1.315 662	1.325 339	12
13	1.303 949	1.314 368	1.324 863	1.335 436	1.346 087	1.356 816	13
14	1.330 843	1.342 298	1.353 845	1.365 483	1.377 215	1.389 040	14
15	1.358 292	1.370 822	1.383 460	1.396 207	1.409 063	1.422 030	15
16	1.386 306	1.399 952	1.413 723	1.427 621	1.441 648	1.455 803	16
17	1.414 899	1.429 701	1.444 648	1.459 743	1.474 986	1.490 378	17
18	1.444 081	1.460 082	1.476 250	1.492 587	1.509 095	1.525 775	18
19	1.473 865	1.491 109	1.508 543	1.526 170	1.543 993	1.562 012	19
20	1.504 264	1.522 795	1.541 542	1.560 509	1.579 698	1.599 110	20
21	1.535 289	1.555 154	1.575 264	1.595 621	1.616 228	1.637 089	21
22	1.566 955	1.588 201	1.609 723	1.631 522	1.653 603	1.675 970	22
23	1.599 273	1.621 951	1.644 935	1.668 231	1.691 843	1.715 774	23
24	1.632 258	1.656 417	1.680 918	1.705 767	1.730 967	1.756 523	24
25	1.665 923	1.691 616	1.717 688	1.744 146	1.770 995	1.798 241	25
26	1.700 283	1.727 563	1.755 263	1.783 390	1.811 950	1.840 949	26
27	1.735 352	1.764 273	1.793 659	1.823 516	1.853 851	1.884 672	27
28	1.771 143	1.801 764	1.832 895	1.864 545	1.896 721	1.929 433	28
29	1.807 673	1.840 052	1.872 990	1.906 497	1.940 583	1.975 257	29
30	1.844 956	1.879 153	1.913 962	1.949 393	1.985 459	2.022 169	30
31	1.883 008	1.919 085	1.955 830	1.993 255	2.031 373	2.070 195	31
32	1.921 845	1.959 865	1.998 613	2.038 103	2.078 348	2.119 363	32
33	1.961 484	2.001 512	2.042 333	2.083 960	2.126 410	2.169 697	33
34	2.001 939	2.044 045	2.087 009	2.130 849	2.175 583	2.221 228	34
35	2.043 229	2.087 481	2.132 662	2.178 794	2.225 894	2.273 982	35
36	2.085 371	2.131 839	2.179 314	2.227 816	2.277 367	2.327 989	36
37	2.128 382	2.177 141	2.226 987	2.277 942	2.330 031	2.383 279	37
38	2.172 279	2.223 405	2.275 702	2.329 196	2.383 913	2.439 882	38
39	2.217 083	2.270 653	2.325 483	2.381 603	2.439 041	2.497 829	39
40	2.262 810	2.318 904	2.376 353	2.435 189	2.495 444	2.557 152	40
41	2.309 480	2.368 181	2.428 336	2.489 981	2.553 151	2.617 885	41
42	2.357 113	2.418 505	2.481 456	2.546 005	2.612 193	2.680 059	42
43	2.405 729	2.469 898	2.535 738	2.603 290	2.672 600	2.743 711	43
44	2.455 347	2.522 383	2.591 207	2.661 864	2.734 404	2.808 874	44
45	2.505 989	2.575 984	2.647 889	2.721 756	2.797 637	2.875 585	45
46	2.557 675	2.630 723	2.705 812	2.782 996	2.862 332	2.943 880	46
47	2.610 427	2.686 626	2.765 002	2.845 613	2.928 524	3.013 797	47
48	2.664 267	2.743 717	2.825 486	2.909 640	2.996 246	3.085 375	48
49	2.719 217	2.802 021	2.887 294	2.975 107	3.065 534	3.158 652	49
50	2.775 301	2.861 564	2.950 453	3.042 046	3.136 425	3.233 670	50
51	2.832 542	2.922 372	3.014 994	3.110 492	3.208 954	3.310 470	51
52	2.890 963	2.984 473	3.080 947	3.180 479	3.283 161	3.389 094	52
53	2.950 589	3.047 893	3.148 343	3.252 039	3.359 084	3.469 585	53
54	3.011 445	3.112 661	3.217 213	3.325 210	3.436 763	3.551 987	54
55	3.073 556	3.178 805	3.287 590	3.400 027	3.516 238	3.636 347	55
YRS							
14	3.136 948	3.246 354	3.359 506	3.476 528	3.597 551	3.722 710	56
15	3.403 863	3.531 215	3.663 249	3.800 135	3.942 047	4.089 167	60
16	3.693 490	3.841 072	3.994 455	4.153 864	4.319 531	4.491 698	64
17	4.007 760	4.178 118	4.355 607	4.540 519	4.733 162	4.933 853	68
18	4.348 771	4.544 740	4.749 411	4.963 166	5.186 402	5.419 533	72
19	4.718 798	4.943 531	5.178 820	5.425 154	5.683 043	5.953 022	76
20	5.120 309	5.377 316	5.647 054	5.930 145	6.227 242	6.539 028	80
21	5.555 984	5.849 165	6.157 622	6.482 143	6.823 552	7.182 718	84
22	6.028 729	6.362 417	6.714 353	7.085 522	7.476 964	7.889 773	88
23	6.541 700	6.920 706	7.321 419	7.745 066	8.192 946	8.666 429	92
24	7.098 317	7.527 984	7.983 371	8.466 003	8.977 489	9.519 537	96
25	7.702 296	8.188 549	8.705 174	9.254 046	9.837 159	10.456 624	100
26	8.357 666	8.907 078	9.492 236	10.115 444	10.779 149	11.485 956	104
27	9.068 800	9.688 655	10.350 459	11.057 023	11.811 342	12.616 613	108
28	9.840 443	10.538 815	11.286 278	12.086 247	12.942 377	13.858 571	112
29	10.677 742	11.463 575	12.306 706	13.211 275	14.181 717	15.222 785	116
30	11.586 286	12.469 480	13.419 395	14.441 024	15.539 735	16.721 290	120

FUTURE VALUE

QUARTERLY COMPOUNDING

QTRS	9.75% ANNUAL RATE	10.00% ANNUAL RATE	10.25% ANNUAL RATE	10.50% ANNUAL RATE	10.75% ANNUAL RATE	11.00% ANNUAL RATE	QTRS
1	1.024 375	1.025 000	1.025 625	1.026 250	1.026 875	1.027 500	1
2	1.049 344	1.050 625	1.051 907	1.053 189	1.054 472	1.055 756	2
3	1.074 922	1.076 891	1.078 862	1.080 835	1.082 811	1.084 790	3
4	1.101 123	1.103 813	1.106 508	1.109 207	1.111 912	1.114 621	4
5	1.127 963	1.131 408	1.134 862	1.138 324	1.141 794	1.145 273	5
6	1.155 457	1.159 693	1.163 943	1.168 205	1.172 480	1.176 768	6
7	1.183 621	1.188 686	1.193 769	1.198 870	1.203 991	1.209 129	7
8	1.212 472	1.218 403	1.224 359	1.230 341	1.236 348	1.242 381	8
9	1.242 026	1.248 863	1.255 733	1.262 637	1.269 575	1.276 546	9
10	1.272 301	1.280 085	1.287 911	1.295 781	1.303 694	1.311 651	10
11	1.303 313	1.312 087	1.320 914	1.329 796	1.338 731	1.347 721	11
12	1.335 081	1.344 889	1.354 763	1.364 703	1.374 710	1.384 784	12
13	1.367 624	1.378 511	1.389 478	1.400 526	1.411 655	1.422 865	13
14	1.400 960	1.412 974	1.425 084	1.437 290	1.449 593	1.461 994	14
15	1.435 108	1.448 298	1.461 601	1.475 019	1.488 551	1.502 199	15
16	1.470 089	1.484 506	1.499 055	1.513 738	1.528 556	1.543 509	16
17	1.505 922	1.521 618	1.537 468	1.553 474	1.569 636	1.585 956	17
18	1.542 629	1.559 659	1.576 866	1.594 252	1.611 820	1.629 570	18
19	1.580 231	1.598 650	1.617 273	1.636 101	1.655 137	1.674 383	19
20	1.618 749	1.638 616	1.658 716	1.679 049	1.699 619	1.720 428	20
21	1.658 206	1.679 582	1.701 220	1.723 124	1.745 296	1.767 740	21
22	1.698 624	1.721 571	1.744 814	1.768 356	1.792 201	1.816 353	22
23	1.740 028	1.764 611	1.789 525	1.814 776	1.840 367	1.866 303	23
24	1.782 442	1.808 726	1.835 382	1.862 413	1.889 827	1.917 626	24
25	1.825 889	1.853 944	1.882 413	1.911 302	1.940 616	1.970 361	25
26	1.870 395	1.900 293	1.930 650	1.961 473	1.992 770	2.024 546	26
27	1.915 985	1.947 800	1.980 123	2.012 962	2.046 325	2.080 221	27
28	1.962 688	1.996 495	2.030 864	2.065 802	2.101 320	2.137 427	28
29	2.010 528	2.046 407	2.082 904	2.120 030	2.157 793	2.196 206	29
30	2.059 535	2.097 568	2.136 279	2.175 680	2.215 784	2.256 602	30
31	2.109 736	2.150 007	2.191 021	2.232 792	2.275 333	2.318 658	31
32	2.161 161	2.203 757	2.247 166	2.291 403	2.336 483	2.382 421	32
33	2.213 839	2.258 851	2.304 750	2.351 552	2.399 276	2.447 938	33
34	2.267 801	2.315 322	2.363 809	2.413 280	2.463 756	2.515 256	34
35	2.323 079	2.373 205	2.424 381	2.476 629	2.529 970	2.584 426	35
36	2.379 704	2.432 535	2.486 506	2.541 641	2.597 963	2.655 498	36
37	2.437 709	2.493 349	2.550 223	2.608 359	2.667 783	2.728 524	37
38	2.497 129	2.555 682	2.615 572	2.676 828	2.739 480	2.803 558	38
39	2.557 996	2.619 574	2.682 596	2.747 095	2.813 103	2.880 656	39
40	2.620 347	2.685 064	2.751 338	2.819 206	2.888 705	2.959 874	40
41	2.684 218	2.752 190	2.821 841	2.893 210	2.966 339	3.041 271	41
42	2.749 646	2.820 995	2.894 151	2.969 157	3.046 060	3.124 905	42
43	2.816 669	2.891 520	2.968 313	3.047 097	3.127 922	3.210 840	43
44	2.885 325	2.963 808	3.044 376	3.127 084	3.211 985	3.299 138	44
45	2.955 655	3.037 903	3.122 388	3.209 169	3.298 307	3.389 865	45
46	3.027 699	3.113 851	3.202 400	3.293 410	3.386 949	3.483 086	46
47	3.101 499	3.191 697	3.284 461	3.379 862	3.477 974	3.578 871	47
48	3.177 098	3.271 490	3.368 625	3.468 584	3.571 444	3.677 290	48
49	3.254 540	3.353 277	3.454 946	3.559 634	3.667 427	3.778 415	49
50	3.333 869	3.437 109	3.543 479	3.653 074	3.765 989	3.882 322	50
51	3.415 132	3.523 036	3.634 281	3.748 968	3.867 200	3.989 086	51
52	3.498 376	3.611 112	3.727 410	3.847 378	3.971 131	4.098 785	52
53	3.583 649	3.701 390	3.822 924	3.948 372	4.077 855	4.211 502	53
54	3.671 000	3.793 925	3.920 887	4.052 016	4.187 447	4.327 318	54
55	3.760 481	3.888 773	4.021 360	4.158 382	4.299 985	4.446 320	55

YRS							
14	3.852 143	3.985 992	4.124 407	4.267 539	4.415 547	4.568 593	56
15	4.241 683	4.399 790	4.563 688	4.733 585	4.909 699	5.092 251	60
16	4.670 616	4.856 545	5.049 755	5.250 527	5.459 152	5.675 932	64
17	5.142 923	5.360 717	5.587 592	5.823 922	6.070 095	6.326 514	68
18	5.662 991	5.917 228	6.182 713	6.459 937	6.749 410	7.051 667	72
19	6.235 651	6.531 513	6.841 219	7.165 408	7.504 748	7.859 938	76
20	6.866 219	7.209 568	7.569 860	7.947 922	8.344 618	8.760 854	80
21	7.560 553	7.958 014	8.376 108	8.815 893	9.278 479	9.765 034	84
22	8.325 100	8.784 158	9.268 227	9.778 652	10.316 850	10.884 315	88
23	9.166 960	9.696 067	10.255 363	10.846 551	11.471 427	12.131 889	92
24	10.093 951	10.702 644	11.347 637	12.031 072	12.755 214	13.522 461	96
25	11.114 683	11.813 716	12.556 247	13.344 952	14.182 673	15.072 422	100
26	12.238 635	13.040 132	13.893 582	14.802 317	15.769 880	16.800 042	104
27	13.476 244	14.393 866	15.373 354	16.418 836	17.534 716	18.725 684	108
28	14.839 004	15.888 135	17.010 733	18.211 892	19.497 056	20.872 046	112
29	16.339 570	17.537 528	18.822 505	20.200 761	21.679 006	23.264 426	116
30	17.991 879	19.358 150	20.827 244	22.406 830	24.105 142	25.931 024	120

SECTION 1

QTRS	11.25% ANNUAL RATE	11.50% ANNUAL RATE	11.75% ANNUAL RATE	12.00% ANNUAL RATE	12.25% ANNUAL RATE	12.50% ANNUAL RATE	QTRS
1	1.028 125	1.028 750	1.029 375	1.030 000	1.030 625	1.031 250	1
2	1.057 041	1.058 327	1.059 613	1.060 900	1.062 188	1.063 477	2
3	1.086 770	1.088 753	1.090 739	1.092 727	1.094 717	1.096 710	3
4	1.117 336	1.120 055	1.122 779	1.125 509	1.128 243	1.130 982	4
5	1.148 761	1.152 257	1.155 761	1.159 274	1.162 796	1.166 326	5
6	1.181 070	1.185 384	1.189 712	1.194 052	1.198 406	1.202 773	6
7	1.214 287	1.219 464	1.224 659	1.229 874	1.235 107	1.240 360	7
8	1.248 439	1.254 523	1.260 634	1.266 770	1.272 933	1.279 121	8
9	1.283 551	1.290 591	1.297 665	1.304 773	1.311 916	1.319 094	9
10	1.319 651	1.327 695	1.335 784	1.343 916	1.352 094	1.360 315	10
11	1.356 767	1.365 867	1.375 022	1.384 234	1.393 501	1.402 825	11
12	1.394 926	1.405 135	1.415 414	1.425 761	1.436 177	1.446 664	12
13	1.434 158	1.445 533	1.456 991	1.468 534	1.480 160	1.491 872	13
14	1.474 494	1.487 092	1.499 791	1.512 590	1.525 490	1.538 493	14
15	1.515 964	1.529 846	1.543 847	1.557 967	1.572 208	1.586 571	15
16	1.558 600	1.573 829	1.589 197	1.604 706	1.620 357	1.636 151	16
17	1.602 436	1.619 077	1.635 880	1.652 848	1.669 981	1.687 281	17
18	1.647 504	1.665 625	1.683 934	1.702 433	1.721 124	1.740 008	18
19	1.693 840	1.713 512	1.733 400	1.753 506	1.773 833	1.794 384	19
20	1.741 480	1.762 775	1.784 318	1.806 111	1.828 157	1.850 458	20
21	1.790 459	1.813 455	1.836 733	1.860 295	1.884 144	1.908 285	21
22	1.840 815	1.865 592	1.890 687	1.916 103	1.941 846	1.967 919	22
23	1.892 588	1.919 228	1.946 226	1.973 587	2.001 315	2.029 416	23
24	1.945 817	1.974 406	2.003 396	2.032 794	2.062 605	2.092 835	24
25	2.000 543	2.031 170	2.062 246	2.093 778	2.125 773	2.158 237	25
26	2.056 809	2.089 566	2.122 824	2.156 591	2.190 874	2.225 681	26
27	2.114 656	2.149 641	2.185 182	2.221 289	2.257 970	2.295 234	27
28	2.174 131	2.211 443	2.249 372	2.287 928	2.327 120	2.366 960	28
29	2.235 279	2.275 022	2.315 447	2.356 566	2.398 388	2.440 928	29
30	2.298 146	2.340 429	2.383 463	2.427 262	2.471 839	2.517 207	30
31	2.362 781	2.407 716	2.453 478	2.500 080	2.547 539	2.595 869	31
32	2.429 234	2.476 938	2.525 549	2.575 083	2.625 558	2.676 990	32
33	2.497 557	2.548 150	2.599 737	2.652 335	2.705 965	2.760 646	33
34	2.567 800	2.621 409	2.676 104	2.731 905	2.788 835	2.846 916	34
35	2.640 020	2.696 775	2.754 714	2.813 862	2.874 243	2.935 882	35
36	2.714 270	2.774 307	2.835 634	2.898 278	2.962 267	3.027 629	36
37	2.790 609	2.854 068	2.918 931	2.985 227	3.052 987	3.122 242	37
38	2.869 095	2.936 123	3.004 674	3.074 783	3.146 484	3.219 812	38
39	2.949 788	3.020 536	3.092 937	3.167 027	3.242 845	3.320 431	39
40	3.032 751	3.107 377	3.183 792	3.262 038	3.342 158	3.424 195	40
41	3.118 047	3.196 714	3.277 316	3.359 899	3.444 511	3.531 201	41
42	3.205 742	3.288 619	3.373 587	3.460 696	3.549 999	3.641 551	42
43	3.295 904	3.383 167	3.472 686	3.564 517	3.658 718	3.755 349	43
44	3.388 601	3.480 433	3.574 696	3.671 452	3.770 766	3.872 704	44
45	3.483 906	3.580 496	3.679 703	3.781 596	3.886 246	3.993 726	45
46	3.581 890	3.683 435	3.787 794	3.895 044	4.005 262	4.118 530	46
47	3.682 631	3.789 334	3.899 061	4.011 895	4.127 923	4.247 234	47
48	3.786 205	3.898 277	4.013 595	4.132 252	4.254 341	4.379 960	48
49	3.892 692	4.010 353	4.131 495	4.256 219	4.384 630	4.516 834	49
50	4.002 174	4.125 650	4.252 857	4.383 906	4.518 910	4.657 985	50
51	4.114 735	4.244 263	4.377 785	4.515 423	4.657 301	4.803 547	51
52	4.230 462	4.366 285	4.506 383	4.650 886	4.799 931	4.953 658	52
53	4.349 444	4.491 816	4.638 758	4.790 412	4.946 929	5.108 460	53
54	4.471 772	4.620 956	4.775 021	4.934 125	5.098 429	5.268 099	54
55	4.597 541	4.753 808	4.915 287	5.082 149	5.254 568	5.432 727	55

YRS	11.25% ANNUAL RATE	11.50% ANNUAL RATE	11.75% ANNUAL RATE	12.00% ANNUAL RATE	12.25% ANNUAL RATE	12.50% ANNUAL RATE	QTRS
14	4.726 847	4.890 480	5.059 674	5.234 613	5.415 489	5.602 500	56
15	5.281 474	5.477 607	5.680 898	5.891 603	6.109 988	6.336 329	60
16	5.901 180	6.135 222	6.378 396	6.631 051	6.893 552	7.166 276	64
17	6.593 599	6.871 787	7.161 532	7.463 307	7.777 603	8.104 532	68
18	7.367 264	7.696 780	8.040 821	8.400 017	8.775 027	9.166 536	72
19	8.231 707	8.620 818	9.028 069	9.454 293	9.900 364	10.367 190	76
20	9.197 580	9.655 791	10.136 530	10.640 891	11.170 017	11.725 110	80
21	10.276 784	10.815 018	11.381 088	11.976 416	12.602 495	13.260 893	84
22	11.482 618	12.113 416	12.778 452	13.479 562	14.218 678	14.997 837	88
23	12.829 939	13.567 694	14.347 384	15.171 366	16.042 126	16.962 289	92
24	14.335 349	15.196 565	16.108 948	17.075 506	18.099 418	19.184 051	96
25	16.017 398	17.200 607	18.086 796	19.218 632	20.420 544	21.696 823	100
26	17.896 811	19.064 447	20.307 484	21.630 740	23.039 338	24.538 725	104
27	19.996 746	21.353 231	22.800 826	24.345 588	25.993 974	27.752 867	108
28	22.343 078	23.916 796	25.600 300	27.401 174	29.327 522	31.388 004	112
29	24.964 719	26.788 130	28.743 491	30.840 262	33.088 575	35.499 280	116
30	27.893 972	30.004 182	32.272 602	34.710 987	37.331 957	40.149 060	120

FUTURE VALUE

QTRS	12.75% ANNUAL RATE	13.00% ANNUAL RATE	13.25% ANNUAL RATE	13.50% ANNUAL RATE	13.75% ANNUAL RATE	14.00% ANNUAL RATE	QTRS
1	1.031 875	1.032 500	1.033 125	1.033 750	1.034 375	1.035 000	1
2	1.064 766	1.066 056	1.067 347	1.068 639	1.069 932	1.071 225	2
3	1.098 705	1.100 703	1.102 703	1.104 706	1.106 711	1.108 718	3
4	1.133 727	1.136 476	1.139 230	1.141 989	1.144 754	1.147 523	4
5	1.169 864	1.173 411	1.176 967	1.180 532	1.184 105	1.187 686	5
6	1.207 154	1.211 547	1.215 954	1.220 375	1.224 808	1.229 255	6
7	1.245 632	1.250 923	1.256 233	1.261 562	1.266 911	1.272 279	7
8	1.285 336	1.291 578	1.297 845	1.304 140	1.310 461	1.316 809	8
9	1.326 306	1.333 554	1.340 837	1.348 155	1.355 508	1.362 897	9
10	1.368 582	1.376 894	1.385 252	1.393 655	1.402 104	1.410 599	10
11	1.412 206	1.421 643	1.431 138	1.440 691	1.450 301	1.459 970	11
12	1.457 220	1.467 847	1.478 545	1.489 314	1.500 155	1.511 069	12
13	1.503 669	1.515 552	1.527 521	1.539 578	1.551 723	1.563 956	13
14	1.551 598	1.564 807	1.578 121	1.591 539	1.605 063	1.618 695	14
15	1.601 055	1.615 663	1.630 396	1.645 254	1.660 238	1.675 349	15
16	1.652 089	1.668 173	1.684 403	1.700 781	1.717 308	1.733 986	16
17	1.704 749	1.722 388	1.740 199	1.758 182	1.776 341	1.794 676	17
18	1.759 088	1.778 366	1.797 843	1.817 521	1.837 402	1.857 489	18
19	1.815 159	1.836 163	1.857 396	1.878 862	1.900 563	1.922 501	19
20	1.873 017	1.895 838	1.918 922	1.942 274	1.965 895	1.989 789	20
21	1.932 720	1.957 453	1.982 487	2.007 826	2.033 473	2.059 431	21
22	1.994 325	2.021 070	2.048 157	2.075 590	2.103 373	2.131 512	22
23	2.057 894	2.086 755	2.116 002	2.145 641	2.175 677	2.206 114	23
24	2.123 490	2.154 574	2.186 094	2.218 056	2.250 466	2.283 328	24
25	2.191 176	2.224 598	2.258 509	2.292 916	2.327 825	2.363 245	25
26	2.261 020	2.296 897	2.333 322	2.370 301	2.407 844	2.445 959	26
27	2.333 090	2.371 546	2.410 613	2.450 299	2.490 614	2.531 567	27
28	2.407 457	2.448 622	2.490 465	2.532 997	2.576 229	2.620 172	28
29	2.484 195	2.528 202	2.572 961	2.618 485	2.664 787	2.711 878	29
30	2.563 378	2.610 368	2.658 191	2.706 859	2.756 389	2.806 794	30
31	2.645 086	2.695 205	2.746 243	2.798 216	2.851 140	2.905 031	31
32	2.729 398	2.782 800	2.837 213	2.892 656	2.949 148	3.006 708	32
33	2.816 398	2.873 241	2.931 195	2.990 283	3.050 524	3.111 942	33
34	2.906 170	2.966 621	3.028 291	3.091 205	3.155 386	3.220 860	34
35	2.998 805	3.063 036	3.128 603	3.195 533	3.263 853	3.333 590	35
36	3.094 392	3.162 585	3.232 238	3.303 382	3.376 048	3.450 266	36
37	3.193 025	3.265 369	3.339 306	3.414 871	3.492 099	3.571 025	37
38	3.294 803	3.371 493	3.449 921	3.530 123	3.612 140	3.696 011	38
39	3.399 825	3.481 067	3.564 199	3.649 265	3.736 307	3.825 372	39
40	3.508 194	3.594 201	3.682 263	3.772 428	3.864 743	3.959 260	40
41	3.620 018	3.711 013	3.804 238	3.899 747	3.997 594	4.097 834	41
42	3.735 406	3.831 621	3.930 254	4.031 363	4.135 011	4.241 258	42
43	3.854 472	3.956 149	4.060 443	4.167 422	4.277 152	4.389 702	43
44	3.977 333	4.084 723	4.194 945	4.308 072	4.424 179	4.543 342	44
45	4.104 111	4.217 477	4.333 903	4.453 470	4.576 260	4.702 359	45
46	4.234 929	4.354 545	4.477 464	4.603 774	4.733 569	4.866 941	46
47	4.369 918	4.496 068	4.625 780	4.759 152	4.896 285	5.037 284	47
48	4.509 209	4.642 190	4.779 009	4.919 773	5.064 595	5.213 589	48
49	4.652 940	4.793 061	4.937 313	5.085 816	5.238 691	5.396 065	49
50	4.801 252	4.948 835	5.100 862	5.257 462	5.418 771	5.584 927	50
51	4.954 292	5.109 673	5.269 828	5.434 901	5.605 041	5.780 399	51
52	5.112 210	5.275 737	5.444 391	5.618 329	5.797 714	5.982 713	52
53	5.275 162	5.447 198	5.624 736	5.807 948	5.997 011	6.192 108	53
54	5.443 308	5.624 232	5.811 056	6.003 966	6.203 158	6.408 832	54
55	5.616 813	5.807 020	6.003 547	6.206 600	6.416 391	6.633 141	55

YRS	12.75%	13.00%	13.25%	13.50%	13.75%	14.00%	QTRS
14	5.795 849	5.995 748	6.202 414	6.416 073	6.636 955	6.865 301	56
15	6.570 909	6.814 023	7.065 978	7.327 087	7.597 679	7.878 091	60
16	7.449 614	7.743 974	8.049 775	8.367 456	8.697 471	9.040 291	64
17	8.445 827	8.800 840	9.170 547	9.555 547	9.956 462	10.373 941	68
18	9.575 259	10.001 942	10.447 364	10.912 333	11.397 697	11.904 336	72
19	10.855 726	11.366 967	11.901 952	12.461 770	13.047 556	13.660 500	76
20	12.307 426	12.918 284	13.559 063	14.231 209	14.936 238	15.675 738	80
21	13.953 258	14.681 319	15.446 894	16.251 891	17.098 314	17.988 269	84
22	15.819 180	16.684 965	17.597 568	18.559 488	19.573 359	20.641 953	88
23	17.934 626	18.962 061	20.047 680	21.194 739	22.406 675	23.687 116	92
24	20.332 964	21.549 926	22.838 922	24.204 168	25.650 125	27.181 510	96
25	23.052 024	24.490 973	26.018 790	27.640 905	29.363 076	31.191 408	100
26	26.134 694	27.833 401	29.641 391	31.565 622	33.613 490	35.792 858	104
27	29.629 600	31.631 990	33.768 367	36.047 607	38.479 168	41.073 128	108
28	33.591 867	35.948 995	38.469 943	41.165 986	44.049 170	47.132 359	112
29	38.083 996	40.855 168	43.826 120	47.011 122	50.425 451	54.085 466	116
30	43.176 842	46.430 915	49.928 039	53.686 205	57.724 723	62.064 316	120

QTRS	14.25% ANNUAL RATE	14.50% ANNUAL RATE	14.75% ANNUAL RATE	15.00% ANNUAL RATE	15.25% ANNUAL RATE	15.50% ANNUAL RATE	QTRS
1	1.035 625	1.036 250	1.036 875	1.037 500	1.038 125	1.038 750	1
2	1.072 519	1.073 814	1.075 110	1.076 406	1.077 704	1.079 002	2
3	1.110 728	1.112 740	1.114 754	1.116 771	1.118 791	1.120 813	3
4	1.150 297	1.153 077	1.155 861	1.158 650	1.161 445	1.164 244	4
5	1.191 277	1.194 876	1.198 483	1.202 100	1.205 725	1.209 359	5
6	1.233 716	1.238 190	1.242 677	1.247 179	1.251 693	1.256 221	6
7	1.277 667	1.283 074	1.288 501	1.293 948	1.299 414	1.304 900	7
8	1.323 184	1.329 586	1.336 015	1.342 471	1.348 954	1.355 465	8
9	1.370 322	1.377 783	1.385 280	1.392 813	1.400 383	1.407 989	9
10	1.419 140	1.427 728	1.436 362	1.445 044	1.453 773	1.462 549	10
11	1.469 697	1.479 483	1.489 328	1.499 233	1.509 198	1.519 223	11
12	1.522 055	1.533 114	1.544 247	1.555 454	1.566 736	1.578 092	12
13	1.576 278	1.588 690	1.601 191	1.613 784	1.626 468	1.639 244	13
14	1.632 433	1.646 280	1.660 235	1.674 301	1.688 477	1.702 764	14
15	1.690 588	1.705 957	1.721 456	1.737 087	1.752 850	1.768 746	15
16	1.750 816	1.767 798	1.784 935	1.802 228	1.819 677	1.837 285	16
17	1.813 188	1.831 881	1.850 755	1.869 811	1.889 053	1.908 480	17
18	1.877 783	1.898 287	1.919 001	1.939 929	1.961 073	1.982 434	18
19	1.944 679	1.967 099	1.989 764	2.012 677	2.035 839	2.059 253	19
20	2.013 958	2.038 407	2.063 137	2.088 152	2.113 455	2.139 049	20
21	2.085 706	2.112 299	2.139 215	2.166 458	2.194 030	2.221 937	21
22	2.160 009	2.188 870	2.218 099	2.247 700	2.277 678	2.308 037	22
23	2.236 959	2.268 216	2.299 891	2.331 989	2.364 514	2.397 474	23
24	2.316 651	2.350 439	2.384 700	2.419 438	2.454 661	2.490 376	24
25	2.399 182	2.435 643	2.472 635	2.510 167	2.548 245	2.586 878	25
26	2.484 653	2.523 935	2.563 814	2.604 298	2.645 397	2.687 119	26
27	2.573 168	2.615 427	2.658 354	2.701 960	2.746 253	2.791 245	27
28	2.664 837	2.710 237	2.756 381	2.803 283	2.850 954	2.899 406	28
29	2.759 772	2.808 483	2.858 023	2.908 406	2.959 647	3.011 758	29
30	2.858 089	2.910 290	2.963 412	3.017 471	3.072 483	3.128 464	30
31	2.959 909	3.015 788	3.072 688	3.130 627	3.189 621	3.249 692	31
32	3.065 355	3.125 111	3.185 994	3.248 025	3.311 226	3.375 617	32
33	3.174 559	3.238 396	3.303 477	3.369 826	3.437 466	3.506 422	33
34	3.287 652	3.355 788	3.425 293	3.496 194	3.568 520	3.642 296	34
35	3.404 775	3.477 435	3.551 601	3.627 302	3.704 569	3.783 435	35
36	3.526 070	3.603 492	3.682 566	3.763 326	3.845 806	3.930 043	36
37	3.651 686	3.734 119	3.818 360	3.904 450	3.992 428	4.082 332	37
38	3.781 778	3.869 480	3.959 163	4.050 867	4.144 639	4.240 523	38
39	3.916 503	4.009 749	4.105 157	4.202 775	4.302 653	4.404 843	39
40	4.056 029	4.155 103	4.256 534	4.360 379	4.466 692	4.575 531	40
41	4.200 525	4.305 725	4.413 494	4.523 893	4.636 984	4.752 832	41
42	4.350 169	4.461 808	4.576 242	4.693 539	4.813 770	4.937 005	42
43	4.505 143	4.623 548	4.744 990	4.869 547	4.997 294	5.128 314	43
44	4.665 639	4.791 152	4.919 962	5.052 155	5.187 816	5.327 036	44
45	4.831 852	4.964 831	5.101 386	5.241 610	5.385 602	5.533 458	45
46	5.003 987	5.144 806	5.289 499	5.438 171	5.590 928	5.747 880	46
47	5.182 254	5.331 305	5.484 549	5.642 102	5.804 082	5.970 610	47
48	5.366 872	5.524 565	5.686 792	5.853 681	6.025 363	6.201 971	48
49	5.558 067	5.724 831	5.896 493	6.073 194	6.255 080	6.442 298	49
50	5.756 073	5.932 356	6.113 926	6.300 939	6.493 554	6.691 937	50
51	5.961 133	6.147 404	6.339 377	6.537 224	6.741 121	6.951 249	51
52	6.173 498	6.370 247	6.573 141	6.782 370	6.998 127	7.220 610	52
53	6.393 429	6.601 168	6.815 526	7.036 709	7.264 930	7.500 409	53
54	6.621 195	6.840 461	7.066 849	7.300 585	7.541 906	7.791 050	54
55	6.857 075	7.088 427	7.327 439	7.574 357	7.829 441	8.092 953	55

YRS

YRS	14.25%	14.50%	14.75%	15.00%	15.25%	15.50%	QTRS
14	7.101 359	7.345 383	7.597 638	7.858 396	8.127 938	8.406 555	56
15	8.168 674	8.469 789	8.781 813	9.105 134	9.440 152	9.787 284	60
16	9.396 403	9.766 316	10.150 556	10.549 667	10.964 216	11.394 791	64
17	10.808 657	11.261 311	11.732 631	12.223 376	12.734 333	13.266 321	68
18	12.433 170	12.985 155	13.561 291	14.162 620	14.790 225	15.445 240	72
19	14.301 841	14.972 879	15.674 968	16.409 525	17.178 031	17.982 033	76
20	16.451 370	17.264 877	18.118 084	19.012 903	19.951 336	20.935 481	80
21	18.923 966	19.907 726	20.941 987	22.029 308	23.172 377	24.374 016	84
22	21.768 187	22.955 134	24.206 026	25.524 267	26.913 438	28.377 311	88
23	25.039 887	26.469 029	27.978 802	29.573 702	31.258 475	33.038 124	92
24	28.803 315	30.520 819	32.339 606	34.265 582	36.304 995	38.464 450	96
25	33.132 376	35.192 843	37.380 089	39.701 831	42.166 250	44.782 020	100
26	38.112 082	40.580 046	43.206 188	46.000 543	48.973 775	52.137 215	104
27	43.840 226	46.791 903	49.940 348	53.298 548	56.880 339	60.700 459	108
28	50.429 294	53.954 650	57.724 101	61.754 385	66.063 378	70.670 168	112
29	58.008 681	62.213 846	66.721 037	71.551 744	76.728 971	82.277 345	116
30	66.727 229	71.737 333	77.120 246	82.903 458	89.116 470	95.790 936	120

QTRS	15.75% ANNUAL RATE	16.00% ANNUAL RATE	16.50% ANNUAL RATE	17.00% ANNUAL RATE	17.50% ANNUAL RATE	18.00% ANNUAL RATE	QTRS
1	1.039 375	1.040 000	1.041 250	1.042 500	1.043 750	1.045 000	1
2	1.080 300	1.081 600	1.084 202	1.086 806	1.089 414	1.092 025	2
3	1.122 837	1.124 864	1.128 925	1.132 996	1.137 076	1.141 166	3
4	1.167 049	1.169 859	1.175 493	1.181 148	1.186 823	1.192 519	4
5	1.213 001	1.216 653	1.223 982	1.231 347	1.238 747	1.246 182	5
6	1.260 763	1.265 319	1.274 471	1.283 679	1.292 942	1.302 260	6
7	1.310 406	1.315 932	1.327 043	1.338 235	1.349 508	1.360 862	7
8	1.362 003	1.368 569	1.381 784	1.395 110	1.408 549	1.422 101	8
9	1.415 632	1.423 312	1.438 782	1.454 402	1.470 173	1.486 095	9
10	1.471 373	1.480 244	1.498 132	1.516 214	1.534 493	1.552 969	10
11	1.529 308	1.539 454	1.559 930	1.580 654	1.601 627	1.622 853	11
12	1.589 524	1.601 032	1.624 277	1.647 831	1.671 698	1.695 881	12
13	1.652 112	1.665 074	1.691 279	1.717 864	1.744 835	1.772 196	13
14	1.717 164	1.731 676	1.761 044	1.790 873	1.821 171	1.851 945	14
15	1.784 777	1.800 944	1.833 687	1.866 986	1.900 848	1.935 282	15
16	1.855 053	1.872 981	1.909 327	1.946 332	1.984 010	2.022 370	16
17	1.928 095	1.947 900	1.988 086	2.029 052	2.070 810	2.113 377	17
18	2.004 014	2.025 817	2.070 095	2.115 286	2.161 408	2.208 479	18
19	2.082 922	2.106 849	2.155 486	2.205 186	2.255 970	2.307 860	19
20	2.164 937	2.191 123	2.244 400	2.298 906	2.354 668	2.411 714	20
21	2.250 182	2.278 768	2.336 982	2.396 610	2.457 685	2.520 241	21
22	2.338 783	2.369 919	2.433 382	2.498 466	2.565 209	2.633 652	22
23	2.430 872	2.464 716	2.533 759	2.604 651	2.677 437	2.752 166	23
24	2.526 588	2.563 304	2.638 277	2.715 348	2.794 575	2.876 014	24
25	2.626 072	2.665 836	2.747 106	2.830 750	2.916 837	3.005 434	25
26	2.729 474	2.772 470	2.860 424	2.951 057	3.044 449	3.140 679	26
27	2.836 947	2.883 369	2.978 416	3.076 477	3.177 644	3.282 010	27
28	2.948 652	2.998 703	3.101 276	3.207 228	3.316 666	3.429 700	28
29	3.064 755	3.118 651	3.229 204	3.343 535	3.461 770	3.584 036	29
30	3.185 429	3.243 398	3.362 408	3.485 635	3.613 222	3.745 318	30
31	3.310 856	3.373 133	3.501 108	3.633 775	3.771 301	3.913 857	31
32	3.441 221	3.508 059	3.645 528	3.788 210	3.936 295	4.089 981	32
33	3.576 719	3.648 381	3.795 906	3.949 209	4.108 508	4.274 030	33
34	3.717 552	3.794 316	3.952 487	4.117 050	4.288 255	4.466 362	34
35	3.863 931	3.946 089	4.115 527	4.292 025	4.475 866	4.667 348	35
36	4.016 073	4.103 933	4.285 293	4.474 436	4.671 685	4.877 378	36
37	4.174 206	4.268 090	4.462 061	4.664 599	4.876 072	5.096 860	37
38	4.338 565	4.438 813	4.646 121	4.862 845	5.089 400	5.326 219	38
39	4.509 396	4.616 366	4.837 774	5.069 516	5.312 061	5.565 899	39
40	4.686 954	4.801 021	5.037 332	5.284 970	5.544 464	5.816 365	40
41	4.871 502	4.993 061	5.245 122	5.509 581	5.787 034	6.078 101	41
42	5.063 318	5.192 784	5.461 483	5.743 739	6.040 217	6.351 615	42
43	5.262 686	5.400 495	5.686 769	5.987 848	6.304 476	6.637 438	43
44	5.469 904	5.616 515	5.921 349	6.242 331	6.580 297	6.936 123	44
45	5.685 282	5.841 176	6.165 604	6.507 630	6.868 185	7.248 248	45
46	5.909 140	6.074 823	6.419 935	6.784 204	7.168 668	7.574 420	46
47	6.141 812	6.317 816	6.684 758	7.072 533	7.482 297	7.915 268	47
48	6.383 646	6.570 528	6.960 504	7.373 116	7.809 648	8.271 456	48
49	6.635 002	6.833 349	7.247 625	7.686 473	8.151 320	8.643 671	49
50	6.896 255	7.106 683	7.546 589	8.013 148	8.507 940	9.032 636	50
51	7.167 795	7.390 951	7.857 886	8.353 707	8.880 162	9.439 105	51
52	7.450 027	7.686 589	8.182 024	8.708 740	9.268 670	9.863 865	52
53	7.743 372	7.994 052	8.519 533	9.078 861	9.674 174	10.307 739	53
54	8.048 267	8.313 814	8.870 963	9.464 713	10.097 419	10.771 587	54
55	8.365 168	8.646 367	9.236 890	9.866 963	10.539 181	11.256 308	55
YRS							
14	8.694 546	8.992 222	9.617 912	10.286 309	11.000 270	11.762 842	56
15	10.146 961	10.519 627	11.305 789	12.149 651	13.055 374	14.027 408	60
16	11.842 000	12.306 476	13.289 876	14.350 534	15.494 418	16.727 945	64
17	13.820 194	14.396 836	15.622 156	16.950 102	18.389 131	19.948 385	68
18	16.128 842	16.842 262	18.363 736	20.020 577	21.824 644	23.788 821	72
19	18.823 148	19.703 065	21.586 444	23.647 261	25.901 990	28.368 611	76
20	21.967 535	23.049 799	25.374 714	27.930 910	30.741 077	33.830 096	80
21	25.637 188	26.965 005	29.827 799	32.990 534	36.484 217	40.343 019	84
22	29.919 853	31.545 242	35.062 370	38.966 698	43.300 308	48.109 801	88
23	34.917 933	36.903 471	41.215 571	46.025 430	51.389 802	57.371 832	92
24	40.750 936	43.171 841	48.448 617	54.362 837	60.990 599	68.416 977	96
25	47.558 337	50.504 948	56.951 011	64.210 746	72.385 045	81.588 518	100
26	55.502 906	59.083 646	66.945 517	75.842 147	85.908 236	97.295 825	104
27	64.774 607	69.119 509	78.693 988	89.580 787	101.957 871	116.027 081	108
28	75.595 136	80.860 049	92.504 235	105.808 152	121.005 946	138.364 453	112
29	88.223 223	94.594 821	108.738 083	124.975 068	143.612 640	165.002 184	116
30	102.960 819	110.662 561	127.820 858	147.614 030	170.442 784	196.768 173	120

27

SECTION 1

QTRS	18.50% ANNUAL RATE	19.00% ANNUAL RATE	19.50% ANNUAL RATE	20.00% ANNUAL RATE	20.50% ANNUAL RATE	21.00% ANNUAL RATE	QTRS
1	1.046 250	1.047 500	1.048 750	1.050 000	1.051 250	1.052 500	1
2	1.094 639	1.097 256	1.099 877	1.102 500	1.105 127	1.107 756	2
3	1.145 266	1.149 376	1.153 496	1.157 625	1.161 764	1.165 913	3
4	1.198 235	1.203 971	1.209 728	1.215 506	1.221 305	1.227 124	4
5	1.253 653	1.261 160	1.268 703	1.276 282	1.283 897	1.291 548	5
6	1.311 634	1.321 065	1.330 552	1.340 096	1.349 696	1.359 354	6
7	1.372 298	1.383 816	1.395 416	1.407 100	1.418 868	1.430 720	7
8	1.435 766	1.449 547	1.463 443	1.477 455	1.491 585	1.505 833	8
9	1.502 171	1.518 400	1.534 786	1.551 328	1.568 029	1.584 889	9
10	1.571 646	1.590 524	1.609 607	1.628 895	1.648 390	1.668 096	10
11	1.644 335	1.666 074	1.688 075	1.710 339	1.732 870	1.755 671	11
12	1.720 385	1.745 213	1.770 369	1.795 856	1.821 680	1.847 844	12
13	1.799 953	1.828 110	1.856 674	1.885 649	1.915 041	1.944 856	13
14	1.883 201	1.914 946	1.947 187	1.979 932	2.013 187	2.046 961	14
15	1.970 299	2.005 906	2.042 112	2.078 928	2.116 363	2.154 426	15
16	2.061 425	2.101 186	2.141 665	2.182 875	2.224 826	2.267 533	16
17	2.156 766	2.200 992	2.246 071	2.292 018	2.338 849	2.386 579	17
18	2.256 516	2.305 540	2.355 567	2.406 619	2.458 715	2.511 874	18
19	2.360 880	2.415 053	2.470 401	2.526 950	2.584 724	2.643 748	19
20	2.470 071	2.529 768	2.590 833	2.653 298	2.717 191	2.782 544	20
21	2.584 312	2.649 932	2.717 136	2.785 963	2.856 447	2.928 628	21
22	2.703 836	2.775 803	2.849 597	2.925 261	3.002 840	3.082 381	22
23	2.828 889	2.907 654	2.988 519	3.071 524	3.156 736	3.244 206	23
24	2.959 725	3.045 768	3.134 205	3.225 100	3.318 518	3.414 527	24
25	3.096 612	3.190 442	3.286 997	3.386 355	3.488 592	3.593 789	25
26	3.239 830	3.341 988	3.447 238	3.555 673	3.667 383	3.782 463	26
27	3.389 672	3.500 732	3.615 291	3.733 456	3.855 336	3.981 043	27
28	3.546 445	3.667 017	3.791 537	3.920 129	4.052 922	4.190 047	28
29	3.710 468	3.841 200	3.976 374	4.116 136	4.260 634	4.410 025	29
30	3.882 077	4.023 657	4.170 222	4.321 942	4.478 992	4.641 551	30
31	4.061 623	4.214 781	4.373 521	4.538 039	4.708 540	4.885 233	31
32	4.249 473	4.414 983	4.586 730	4.764 941	4.949 853	5.141 707	32
33	4.446 011	4.624 694	4.810 333	5.003 189	5.203 533	5.411 647	33
34	4.651 639	4.844 367	5.044 837	5.253 348	5.470 214	5.695 758	34
35	4.866 777	5.074 475	5.290 772	5.516 015	5.750 562	5.994 786	35
36	5.091 866	5.315 512	5.548 698	5.791 816	6.045 279	6.309 512	36
37	5.327 365	5.567 999	5.819 197	6.081 407	6.355 099	6.640 761	37
38	5.573 755	5.832 479	6.102 882	6.385 477	6.680 798	6.989 401	38
39	5.831 541	6.109 522	6.400 398	6.704 751	7.023 189	7.356 345	39
40	6.101 250	6.399 724	6.712 417	7.039 989	7.383 127	7.742 553	40
41	6.383 433	6.703 711	7.039 648	7.391 988	7.761 512	8.149 037	41
42	6.678 667	7.022 137	7.382 831	7.761 588	8.159 290	8.576 861	42
43	6.987 555	7.355 689	7.742 744	8.149 667	8.577 454	9.027 147	43
44	7.310 730	7.705 084	8.120 202	8.557 150	9.017 048	9.501 072	44
45	7.648 851	8.071 076	8.516 062	8.985 008	9.479 172	9.999 878	45
46	8.002 610	8.454 452	8.931 220	9.434 258	9.964 979	10.524 872	46
47	8.372 731	8.856 038	9.366 617	9.905 971	10.475 685	11.077 427	47
48	8.759 970	9.276 700	9.823 240	10.401 270	11.012 563	11.658 992	48
49	9.165 118	9.717 343	10.302 123	10.921 333	11.576 957	12.271 089	49
50	9.589 005	10.178 917	10.804 351	11.467 400	12.170 276	12.915 322	50
51	10.032 497	10.662 416	11.331 063	12.040 770	12.794 003	13.593 376	51
52	10.496 500	11.168 881	11.883 453	12.642 808	13.449 696	14.307 028	52
53	10.981 963	11.699 402	12.462 771	13.274 949	14.138 993	15.058 147	53
54	11.489 878	12.255 124	13.070 331	13.938 696	14.863 616	15.848 700	54
55	12.021 285	12.837 242	13.707 510	14.635 631	15.625 376	16.680 757	55
YRS							
14	12.577 270	13.447 011	14.375 751	15.367 412	16.426 177	17.556 496	56
15	15.070 521	16.189 815	17.390 755	18.679 186	20.061 367	21.543 997	60
16	18.058 021	19.492 073	21.038 091	22.704 667	24.501 042	26.437 153	64
17	21.637 746	23.467 896	25.450 377	27.597 665	29.923 239	32.441 663	68
18	25.927 098	28.254 673	30.788 045	33.545 134	36.545 393	39.809 940	72
19	31.066 748	34.017 814	37.245 174	40.774 320	44.633 061	48.851 729	76
20	37.225 255	40.956 471	45.056 547	49.561 441	54.510 568	59.947 125	80
21	44.604 591	49.310 415	54.506 187	60.242 241	66.574 013	73.562 551	84
22	53.446 768	59.368 323	65.937 685	73.224 821	81.307 157	90.270 365	88
23	64.041 771	71.477 756	79.766 694	89.005 227	99.300 814	110.772 923	92
24	76.737 071	86.057 165	96.496 039	108.186 410	121.276 553	135.932 102	96
25	91.949 019	103.610 356	116.734 004	131.501 258	148.115 627	166.805 532	100
26	110.176 503	124.743 892	141.216 447	159.840 601	180.894 314	204.691 057	104
27	132.017 307	150.188 063	170.833 553	194.287 249	220.927 079	251.181 290	108
28	158.187 715	180.822 114	206.662 210	236.157 366	269.819 284	308.230 567	112
29	189.546 005	217.704 632	250.005 156	287.050 754	329.531 565	378.237 098	116
30	227.120 597	262.110 124	302.438 350	348.911 986	402.458 456	464.143 787	120

FUTURE VALUE

QTRS	21.50% ANNUAL RATE	22.00% ANNUAL RATE	22.50% ANNUAL RATE	23.00% ANNUAL RATE	23.50% ANNUAL RATE	24.00% ANNUAL RATE	QTRS
1	1.053 750	1.055 000	1.056 250	1.057 500	1.058 750	1.060 000	1
2	1.110 389	1.113 025	1.115 664	1.118 306	1.120 952	1.123 600	2
3	1.170 072	1.174 241	1.178 420	1.182 609	1.186 807	1.191 016	3
4	1.232 964	1.238 825	1.244 706	1.250 609	1.256 532	1.262 477	4
5	1.299 236	1.306 960	1.314 721	1.322 519	1.330 354	1.338 226	5
6	1.369 070	1.378 843	1.388 674	1.398 564	1.408 512	1.418 519	6
7	1.442 657	1.454 679	1.466 787	1.478 981	1.491 262	1.503 630	7
8	1.520 200	1.534 687	1.549 294	1.564 023	1.578 874	1.593 848	8
9	1.601 911	1.619 094	1.636 442	1.653 954	1.671 633	1.689 479	9
10	1.688 013	1.708 144	1.728 491	1.749 056	1.769 841	1.790 848	10
11	1.778 744	1.802 092	1.825 719	1.849 627	1.873 819	1.898 299	11
12	1.874 352	1.901 207	1.928 416	1.955 980	1.983 906	2.012 196	12
13	1.975 098	2.005 774	2.036 889	2.068 449	2.100 460	2.132 928	13
14	2.081 259	2.116 091	2.151 464	2.187 385	2.223 862	2.260 904	14
15	2.193 127	2.232 476	2.272 484	2.313 160	2.354 514	2.396 558	15
16	2.311 008	2.355 263	2.400 311	2.446 167	2.492 842	2.540 352	16
17	2.435 224	2.484 802	2.535 329	2.586 821	2.639 297	2.692 773	17
18	2.566 118	2.621 466	2.677 941	2.735 563	2.794 355	2.854 339	18
19	2.704 047	2.765 647	2.828 575	2.892 858	2.958 524	3.025 600	19
20	2.849 389	2.917 757	2.987 682	3.059 198	3.132 337	3.207 135	20
21	3.002 544	3.078 234	3.155 740	3.235 101	3.316 362	3.399 564	21
22	3.163 930	3.247 537	3.333 250	3.421 120	3.511 198	3.603 537	22
23	3.333 992	3.426 152	3.520 745	3.617 834	3.717 481	3.819 750	23
24	3.513 194	3.614 590	3.718 787	3.825 860	3.935 883	4.048 935	24
25	3.702 028	3.813 392	3.927 969	4.045 846	4.167 116	4.291 871	25
26	3.901 012	4.023 129	4.148 917	4.278 483	4.411 934	4.549 383	26
27	4.110 691	4.244 401	4.382 294	4.524 495	4.671 135	4.822 346	27
28	4.331 641	4.477 843	4.628 798	4.784 654	4.945 564	5.111 687	28
29	4.564 467	4.724 124	4.889 168	5.059 772	5.236 116	5.418 388	29
30	4.809 807	4.983 951	5.164 183	5.350 708	5.543 738	5.743 491	30
31	5.068 334	5.258 069	5.454 669	5.658 374	5.869 433	6.088 101	31
32	5.340 757	5.547 262	5.761 494	5.983 731	6.214 262	6.453 387	32
33	5.627 823	5.852 362	6.085 578	6.327 795	6.579 350	6.840 590	33
34	5.930 318	6.174 242	6.427 892	6.691 643	6.965 886	7.251 025	34
35	6.249 073	6.513 825	6.789 461	7.076 413	7.375 132	7.686 087	35
36	6.584 960	6.872 085	7.171 368	7.483 307	7.808 421	8.147 252	36
37	6.938 902	7.250 050	7.574 757	7.913 597	8.267 166	8.636 087	37
38	7.311 868	7.648 803	8.000 837	8.368 629	8.752 862	9.154 252	38
39	7.704 881	8.069 487	8.450 884	8.849 825	9.267 093	9.703 507	39
40	8.119 018	8.513 309	8.926 247	9.358 690	9.811 534	10.285 718	40
41	8.555 415	8.981 541	9.428 348	9.896 814	10.387 962	10.902 861	41
42	9.015 269	9.475 525	9.958 692	10.465 881	10.998 255	11.557 033	42
43	9.499 840	9.996 679	10.518 869	11.067 669	11.644 402	12.250 455	43
44	10.010 456	10.546 497	11.110 555	11.704 060	12.328 511	12.985 482	44
45	10.548 518	11.126 554	11.735 524	12.377 044	13.052 811	13.764 611	45
46	11.115 501	11.738 515	12.395 647	13.088 724	13.819 664	14.590 487	46
47	11.712 959	12.384 133	13.092 902	13.841 325	14.631 569	15.465 917	47
48	12.342 530	13.065 260	13.829 378	14.637 201	15.491 174	16.393 872	48
49	13.005 941	13.783 849	14.607 281	15.478 841	16.401 280	17.377 504	49
50	13.705 011	14.541 961	15.428 940	16.368 874	17.364 855	18.420 154	50
51	14.441 655	15.341 769	16.296 818	17.310 084	18.385 040	19.525 364	51
52	15.217 894	16.185 566	17.213 514	18.305 414	19.465 162	20.696 885	52
53	16.035 856	17.075 773	18.181 774	19.357 975	20.608 740	21.938 698	53
54	16.897 783	18.014 940	19.204 499	20.471 059	21.819 503	23.255 020	54
55	17.806 039	19.005 762	20.284 752	21.648 145	23.101 399	24.650 322	55
YRS							
14	18.763 114	20.051 079	21.425 770	22.892 913	24.458 606	26.129 341	56
15	23.134 241	24.839 770	26.668 790	28.630 080	30.733 031	32.987 691	60
16	28.523 683	30.772 120	33.194 811	35.805 032	38.617 050	41.646 200	64
17	35.168 671	38.121 261	41.317 791	44.778 091	48.523 575	52.577 368	68
18	43.361 701	47.225 558	51.428 515	55.999 877	60.971 444	66.377 715	72
19	53.463 411	58.504 185	64.013 396	70.033 943	76.612 595	83.800 336	76
20	65.918 454	72.476 426	79.677 878	87.585 070	96.266 208	105.795 993	80
21	81.275 072	89.785 583	99.175 556	109.534 666	120.961 611	133.565 004	84
22	100.209 227	111.228 594	123.444 440	136.985 025	151.992 183	168.622 741	88
23	123.564 356	137.792 724	153.652 072	171.314 687	190.983 104	212.882 325	92
24	152.338 057	170.701 023	191.251 702	214.247 667	239.976 459	268.759 030	96
25	187.827 321	211.468 636	238.052 198	267.940 032	301.538 197	339.302 084	100
26	231.584 300	261.972 559	296.305 071	335.088 180	378.892 516	428.361 063	104
27	285.535 075	324.538 064	368.812 788	419.064 250	476.090 725	540.795 972	108
28	352.054 431	402.045 753	459.063 601	524.085 468	598.223 424	682.742 455	112
29	434.070 394	498.064 190	571.399 357	655.425 934	751.687 117	861.946 619	116
30	535.193 113	617.014 196	711.224 379	819.681 486	944.519 222	1088.187 748	120

FUTURE VALUE

SEMIANNUAL COMPOUNDING

HALF YRS	5.25% ANNUAL RATE	5.50% ANNUAL RATE	5.75% ANNUAL RATE	6.00% ANNUAL RATE	6.25% ANNUAL RATE	6.50% ANNUAL RATE	HALF YRS
1	1.026 250	1.027 500	1.028 750	1.030 000	1.031 250	1.032 500	1
2	1.053 189	1.055 756	1.058 327	1.060 900	1.063 477	1.066 056	2
3	1.080 835	1.084 790	1.088 753	1.092 727	1.096 710	1.100 703	3
4	1.109 207	1.114 621	1.120 055	1.125 509	1.130 982	1.136 476	4
5	1.138 324	1.145 273	1.152 257	1.159 274	1.166 326	1.173 411	5
6	1.168 205	1.176 768	1.185 384	1.194 052	1.202 773	1.211 547	6
7	1.198 870	1.209 129	1.219 464	1.229 874	1.240 360	1.250 923	7
8	1.230 341	1.242 381	1.254 523	1.266 770	1.279 121	1.291 578	8
9	1.262 637	1.276 546	1.290 591	1.304 773	1.319 094	1.333 554	9
10	1.295 781	1.311 651	1.327 695	1.343 916	1.360 315	1.376 894	10
11	1.329 796	1.347 721	1.365 867	1.384 234	1.402 825	1.421 643	11
12	1.364 703	1.384 784	1.405 135	1.425 761	1.446 664	1.467 847	12
13	1.400 526	1.422 865	1.445 533	1.468 534	1.491 872	1.515 552	13
14	1.437 290	1.461 994	1.487 092	1.512 590	1.538 493	1.564 807	14
15	1.475 019	1.502 199	1.529 846	1.557 967	1.586 571	1.615 663	15
16	1.513 738	1.543 509	1.573 829	1.604 706	1.636 151	1.668 173	16
17	1.553 474	1.585 956	1.619 077	1.652 848	1.687 281	1.722 388	17
18	1.594 252	1.629 570	1.665 625	1.702 433	1.740 008	1.778 366	18
19	1.636 101	1.674 383	1.713 512	1.753 506	1.794 384	1.836 163	19
20	1.679 049	1.720 428	1.762 775	1.806 111	1.850 458	1.895 838	20
21	1.723 124	1.767 740	1.813 455	1.860 295	1.908 285	1.957 453	21
22	1.768 356	1.816 353	1.865 592	1.916 103	1.967 919	2.021 070	22
23	1.814 776	1.866 303	1.919 228	1.973 587	2.029 416	2.086 755	23
24	1.862 413	1.917 626	1.974 406	2.032 794	2.092 835	2.154 574	24
25	1.911 302	1.970 361	2.031 170	2.093 778	2.158 237	2.224 598	25
26	1.961 473	2.024 546	2.089 566	2.156 591	2.225 681	2.296 897	26
27	2.012 962	2.080 221	2.149 641	2.221 289	2.295 234	2.371 546	27
28	2.065 802	2.137 427	2.211 443	2.287 928	2.366 960	2.448 622	28
29	2.120 030	2.196 206	2.275 022	2.356 566	2.440 928	2.528 202	29
30	2.175 680	2.256 602	2.340 429	2.427 262	2.517 207	2.610 368	30
31	2.232 792	2.318 658	2.407 716	2.500 080	2.595 869	2.695 205	31
32	2.291 403	2.382 421	2.476 938	2.575 083	2.676 990	2.782 800	32
33	2.351 552	2.447 938	2.548 150	2.652 335	2.760 646	2.873 241	33
34	2.413 280	2.515 256	2.621 409	2.731 905	2.846 916	2.966 621	34
35	2.476 629	2.584 426	2.696 775	2.813 862	2.935 882	3.063 036	35
36	2.541 641	2.655 498	2.774 307	2.898 278	3.027 629	3.162 585	36
37	2.608 359	2.728 524	2.854 068	2.985 227	3.122 242	3.265 369	37
38	2.676 828	2.803 558	2.936 123	3.074 783	3.219 812	3.371 493	38
39	2.747 095	2.880 656	3.020 536	3.167 027	3.320 431	3.481 067	39
40	2.819 206	2.959 874	3.107 377	3.262 038	3.424 195	3.594 201	40
41	2.893 210	3.041 271	3.196 714	3.359 899	3.531 201	3.711 013	41
42	2.969 157	3.124 905	3.288 619	3.460 696	3.641 551	3.831 621	42
43	3.047 097	3.210 840	3.383 167	3.564 517	3.755 349	3.956 149	43
44	3.127 084	3.299 138	3.480 433	3.671 452	3.872 704	4.084 723	44
45	3.209 169	3.389 865	3.580 496	3.781 596	3.993 726	4.217 477	45
46	3.293 410	3.483 086	3.683 435	3.895 044	4.118 530	4.354 545	46
47	3.379 862	3.578 871	3.789 334	4.011 895	4.247 234	4.496 068	47
48	3.468 58	3.677 290	3.898 277	4.132 252	4.379 960	4.642 190	48
49	3.559 634	3.778 415	4.010 353	4.256 219	4.516 834	4.793 061	49
50	3.653 074	3.882 322	4.125 650	4.383 906	4.657 985	4.948 835	50
51	3.748 968	3.989 086	4.244 263	4.515 423	4.803 547	5.109 673	51
5?	3.847 378	4.098 785	4.366 285	4.650 886	4.953 658	5.275 737	52
53	3.948 372	4.211 502	4.491 816	4.790 412	5.108 460	5.447 198	53
54	4.052 016	4.327 318	4.620 956	4.934 125	5.268 099	5.624 232	54
55	4.158 382	4.446 320	4.753 808	5.082 149	5.432 727	5.807 020	55
56	4.267 539	4.568 593	4.890 480	5.234 613	5.602 500	5.995 748	56
57	4.379 562	4.694 230	5.031 081	5.391 651	5.777 578	6.190 610	57
58	4.494 526	4.823 321	5.175 725	5.553 401	5.958 127	6.391 805	58
59	4.612 507	4.955 962	5.324 527	5.720 003	6.144 319	6.599 538	59

YRS	5.25%	5.50%	5.75%	6.00%	6.25%	6.50%	
30	4.733 585	5.092 251	5.477 607	5.891 603	6.336 329	6.814 023	60
31	4.985 360	5.376 176	5.797 097	6.250 402	6.738 537	7.264 132	62
32	5.250 527	5.675 932	6.135 222	6.631 051	7.166 276	7.743 974	64
33	5.529 798	5.992 400	6.493 068	7.034 882	7.621 167	8.255 511	66
34	5.823 922	6.326 514	6.871 787	7.463 307	8.104 932	8.800 840	68
35	6.133 691	6.679 257	7.272 595	7.917 822	8.619 405	9.382 190	70
36	6.459 937	7.051 667	7.696 780	8.400 017	9.166 536	10.001 942	72
37	6.803 534	7.444 842	8.145 707	8.911 578	9.748 396	10.662 633	74
38	7.165 408	7.859 938	8.620 818	9.454 293	10.367 190	11.366 967	76
39	7.546 529	8.298 179	9.123 640	10.030 060	11.025 264	12.117 826	78
40	7.947 922	8.760 854	9.655 791	10.640 891	11.725 110	12.918 284	80

FUTURE VALUE

HALF YRS	6.75% ANNUAL RATE	7.00% ANNUAL RATE	7.25% ANNUAL RATE	7.50% ANNUAL RATE	7.75% ANNUAL RATE	8.00% ANNUAL RATE	HALF YRS
1	1.033 750	1.035 000	1.036 250	1.037 500	1.038 750	1.040 000	1
2	1.068 639	1.071 225	1.073 814	1.076 406	1.079 002	1.081 600	2
3	1.104 706	1.108 718	1.112 740	1.116 771	1.120 813	1.124 864	3
4	1.141 989	1.147 523	1.153 077	1.158 650	1.164 244	1.169 859	4
5	1.180 532	1.187 686	1.194 876	1.202 100	1.209 359	1.216 653	5
6	1.220 375	1.229 255	1.238 190	1.247 179	1.256 221	1.265 319	6
7	1.261 562	1.272 279	1.283 074	1.293 948	1.304 900	1.315 932	7
8	1.304 140	1.316 809	1.329 586	1.342 471	1.355 465	1.368 569	8
9	1.348 155	1.362 897	1.377 783	1.392 813	1.407 989	1.423 312	9
10	1.393 655	1.410 599	1.427 728	1.445 044	1.462 549	1.480 244	10
11	1.440 691	1.459 970	1.479 483	1.499 233	1.519 223	1.539 454	11
12	1.489 314	1.511 069	1.533 114	1.555 454	1.578 092	1.601 032	12
13	1.539 578	1.563 956	1.588 690	1.613 784	1.639 244	1.665 074	13
14	1.591 539	1.618 695	1.646 280	1.674 301	1.702 764	1.731 676	14
15	1.645 254	1.675 349	1.705 957	1.737 087	1.768 746	1.800 944	15
16	1.700 781	1.733 986	1.767 798	1.802 228	1.837 285	1.872 981	16
17	1.758 182	1.794 676	1.831 881	1.869 811	1.908 480	1.947 900	17
18	1.817 521	1.857 489	1.898 287	1.939 929	1.982 434	2.025 817	18
19	1.878 862	1.922 501	1.967 099	2.012 677	2.059 253	2.106 849	19
20	1.942 274	1.989 789	2.038 407	2.088 152	2.139 049	2.191 123	20
21	2.007 826	2.059 431	2.112 299	2.166 458	2.221 937	2.278 768	21
22	2.075 590	2.131 512	2.188 870	2.247 700	2.308 037	2.369 919	22
23	2.145 641	2.206 114	2.268 216	2.331 989	2.397 474	2.464 716	23
24	2.218 056	2.283 328	2.350 439	2.419 438	2.490 376	2.563 304	24
25	2.292 916	2.363 245	2.435 643	2.510 167	2.586 878	2.665 836	25
26	2.370 301	2.445 959	2.523 935	2.604 298	2.687 119	2.772 470	26
27	2.450 299	2.531 567	2.615 427	2.701 960	2.791 245	2.883 369	27
28	2.532 997	2.620 172	2.710 237	2.803 283	2.899 406	2.998 703	28
29	2.618 485	2.711 878	2.808 483	2.908 406	3.011 758	3.118 651	29
30	2.706 859	2.806 794	2.910 290	3.017 471	3.128 464	3.243 398	30
31	2.798 216	2.905 031	3.015 788	3.130 627	3.249 692	3.373 133	31
32	2.892 656	3.006 708	3.125 111	3.248 025	3.375 617	3.508 059	32
33	2.990 283	3.111 942	3.238 396	3.369 826	3.506 422	3.648 381	33
34	3.091 205	3.220 860	3.355 788	3.496 194	3.642 296	3.794 316	34
35	3.195 533	3.333 590	3.477 435	3.627 302	3.783 435	3.946 089	35
36	3.303 382	3.450 266	3.603 492	3.763 326	3.930 043	4.103 933	36
37	3.414 871	3.571 025	3.734 119	3.904 450	4.082 332	4.268 090	37
38	3.530 123	3.696 011	3.869 480	4.050 867	4.240 523	4.438 813	38
39	3.649 265	3.825 372	4.009 749	4.202 775	4.404 843	4.616 366	39
40	3.772 428	3.959 260	4.155 103	4.360 379	4.575 531	4.801 021	40
41	3.899 747	4.097 834	4.305 725	4.523 893	4.752 832	4.993 061	41
42	4.031 363	4.241 258	4.461 808	4.693 539	4.937 005	5.192 784	42
43	4.167 422	4.389 702	4.623 548	4.869 547	5.128 314	5.400 495	43
44	4.308 072	4.543 342	4.791 152	5.052 155	5.327 036	5.616 515	44
45	4.453 470	4.702 359	4.964 831	5.241 610	5.533 458	5.841 176	45
46	4.603 774	4.866 941	5.144 806	5.438 171	5.747 880	6.074 823	46
47	4.759 152	5.037 284	5.331 305	5.642 102	5.970 610	6.317 816	47
48	4.919 773	5.213 589	5.524 565	5.853 681	6.201 971	6.570 528	48
49	5.085 816	5.396 065	5.724 831	6.073 194	6.442 298	6.833 349	49
50	5.257 462	5.584 927	5.932 356	6.300 939	6.691 937	7.106 683	50
51	5.434 901	5.780 399	6.147 404	6.537 224	6.951 249	7.390 951	51
52	5.618 329	5.982 713	6.370 247	6.782 370	7.220 610	7.686 589	52
53	5.807 948	6.192 108	6.601 168	7.036 709	7.500 409	7.994 052	53
54	6.003 966	6.408 832	6.840 461	7.300 585	7.791 050	8.313 814	54
55	6.206 600	6.633 141	7.088 427	7.574 357	8.092 953	8.646 367	55
56	6.416 073	6.865 301	7.345 383	7.858 396	8.406 555	8.992 222	56
57	6.632 615	7.105 587	7.611 653	8.153 086	8.732 309	9.351 910	57
58	6.856 466	7.354 282	7.887 575	8.458 826	9.070 686	9.725 987	58
59	7.087 871	7.611 682	8.173 500	8.776 032	9.422 175	10.115 026	59

YRS							
30	7.327 087	7.878 091	8.469 789	9.105 134	9.787 284	10.519 627	60
31	7.830 011	8.439 208	9.094 979	9.800 823	10.560 495	11.378 029	62
32	8.367 456	9.040 291	9.766 316	10.549 667	11.394 791	12.306 476	64
33	8.941 790	9.684 185	10.487 208	11.355 727	12.294 997	13.310 685	66
34	9.555 547	10.373 941	11.261 311	12.223 376	13.266 321	14.396 836	68
35	10.211 430	11.112 825	12.092 554	13.157 318	14.314 381	15.571 618	70
36	10.912 333	11.904 336	12.985 155	14.162 620	15.445 240	16.842 262	72
37	11.661 346	12.752 223	13.943 642	15.244 732	16.665 438	18.216 591	74
38	12.461 770	13.660 500	14.972 879	16.409 525	17.982 033	19.703 065	76
39	13.317 134	14.633 469	16.078 088	17.663 315	19.402 642	21.310 835	78
40	14.231 209	15.675 738	17.264 877	19.012 903	20.935 481	23.049 799	80

31

SECTION 1

	8.25% ANNUAL RATE	8.50% ANNUAL RATE	8.75% ANNUAL RATE	9.00% ANNUAL RATE	9.25% ANNUAL RATE	9.50% ANNUAL RATE	
HALF YRS							**HALF YRS**
1	1.041 250	1.042 500	1.043 750	1.045 000	1.046 250	1.047 500	1
2	1.084 202	1.086 806	1.089 414	1.092 025	1.094 639	1.097 256	2
3	1.128 925	1.132 996	1.137 076	1.141 166	1.145 266	1.149 376	3
4	1.175 493	1.181 148	1.186 823	1.192 519	1.198 235	1.203 971	4
5	1.223 982	1.231 347	1.238 747	1.246 182	1.253 653	1.261 160	5
6	1.274 471	1.283 679	1.292 942	1.302 260	1.311 634	1.321 065	6
7	1.327 043	1.338 235	1.349 508	1.360 862	1.372 298	1.383 816	7
8	1.381 784	1.395 110	1.408 549	1.422 101	1.435 766	1.449 547	8
9	1.438 782	1.454 402	1.470 173	1.486 095	1.502 171	1.518 400	9
10	1.498 132	1.516 214	1.534 493	1.552 969	1.571 646	1.590 524	10
11	1.559 930	1.580 654	1.601 627	1.622 853	1.644 335	1.666 074	11
12	1.624 277	1.647 831	1.671 698	1.695 881	1.720 385	1.745 213	12
13	1.691 279	1.717 864	1.744 835	1.772 196	1.799 953	1.828 110	13
14	1.761 044	1.790 873	1.821 171	1.851 945	1.883 201	1.914 946	14
15	1.833 687	1.866 986	1.900 848	1.935 282	1.970 299	2.005 906	15
16	1.909 327	1.946 332	1.984 010	2.022 370	2.061 425	2.101 186	16
17	1.988 086	2.029 052	2.070 810	2.113 377	2.156 766	2.200 992	17
18	2.070 095	2.115 286	2.161 408	2.208 479	2.256 516	2.305 540	18
19	2.155 486	2.205 186	2.255 970	2.307 860	2.360 880	2.415 053	19
20	2.244 400	2.298 906	2.354 668	2.411 714	2.470 071	2.529 768	20
21	2.336 982	2.396 610	2.457 685	2.520 241	2.584 312	2.649 932	21
22	2.433 382	2.498 466	2.565 209	2.633 652	2.703 836	2.775 803	22
23	2.533 759	2.604 651	2.677 437	2.752 166	2.828 889	2.907 654	23
24	2.638 277	2.715 348	2.794 575	2.876 014	2.959 725	3.045 768	24
25	2.747 106	2.830 750	2.916 837	3.005 434	3.096 612	3.190 442	25
26	2.860 424	2.951 057	3.044 449	3.140 679	3.239 830	3.341 988	26
27	2.978 416	3.076 477	3.177 644	3.282 010	3.389 672	3.500 732	27
28	3.101 276	3.207 228	3.316 666	3.429 700	3.546 445	3.667 017	28
29	3.229 204	3.343 535	3.461 770	3.584 036	3.710 468	3.841 200	29
30	3.362 408	3.485 635	3.613 222	3.745 318	3.882 077	4.023 657	30
31	3.501 108	3.633 775	3.771 301	3.913 857	4.061 623	4.214 781	31
32	3.645 528	3.788 210	3.936 295	4.089 981	4.249 473	4.414 983	32
33	3.795 906	3.949 209	4.108 508	4.274 030	4.446 011	4.624 694	33
34	3.952 487	4.117 050	4.288 255	4.466 362	4.651 639	4.844 367	34
35	4.115 527	4.292 025	4.475 866	4.667 348	4.866 777	5.074 475	35
36	4.285 293	4.474 436	4.671 685	4.877 378	5.091 866	5.315 512	36
37	4.462 061	4.664 599	4.876 072	5.096 860	5.327 365	5.567 594	37
38	4.646 121	4.862 845	5.089 400	5.326 219	5.573 755	5.832 479	38
39	4.837 774	5.069 516	5.312 061	5.565 899	5.831 541	6.109 522	39
40	5.037 332	5.284 970	5.544 464	5.816 365	6.101 250	6.399 724	40
41	5.245 122	5.509 581	5.787 034	6.078 101	6.383 433	6.703 711	41
42	5.461 483	5.743 739	6.040 217	6.351 615	6.678 667	7.022 137	42
43	5.686 769	5.987 848	6.304 476	6.637 438	6.987 555	7.355 689	43
44	5.921 349	6.242 331	6.580 297	6.936 123	7.310 730	7.705 084	44
45	6.165 604	6.507 630	6.868 185	7.248 248	7.648 851	8.071 076	45
46	6.419 935	6.784 204	7.168 668	7.574 420	8.002 610	8.454 452	46
47	6.684 758	7.072 533	7.482 297	7.915 268	8.372 731	8.856 038	47
48	6.960 504	7.373 116	7.809 648	8.271 456	8.759 970	9.276 700	48
49	7.247 625	7.686 473	8.151 320	8.643 671	9.165 118	9.717 343	49
50	7.546 589	8.013 148	8.507 940	9.032 636	9.589 005	10.178 917	50
51	7.857 886	8.353 707	8.880 162	9.439 105	10.032 497	10.662 416	51
52	8.182 024	8.708 740	9.268 670	9.863 865	10.496 500	11.168 881	52
53	8.519 533	9.078 861	9.674 174	10.307 739	10.981 963	11.699 402	53
54	8.870 963	9.464 713	10.097 419	10.771 587	11.489 878	12.255 124	54
55	9.236 890	9.866 963	10.539 181	11.256 308	12.021 285	12.837 242	55
56	9.617 912	10.286 309	11.000 270	11.762 842	12.577 270	13.447 011	56
57	10.014 651	10.723 477	11.481 532	12.292 170	13.158 968	14.085 744	57
58	10.427 755	11.179 225	11.983 849	12.845 318	13.767 571	14.754 817	58
59	10.857 900	11.654 342	12.508 143	13.423 357	14.404 321	15.455 671	59
YRS							
30	11.305 789	12.149 651	13.055 374	14.027 408	15.070 521	16.189 815	60
31	12.257 754	13.204 317	14.222 708	15.318 280	16.496 781	17.764 376	62
32	13.289 876	14.350 534	15.494 418	16.727 945	18.058 021	19.492 073	64
33	14.408 904	15.596 250	16.879 837	18.267 334	19.767 015	21.387 799	66
34	15.622 156	16.950 102	18.389 131	19.948 385	21.637 746	23.467 896	68
35	16.937 566	18.421 477	20.033 378	21.784 136	23.685 523	25.750 295	70
36	18.363 736	20.020 577	21.824 644	23.788 821	25.927 098	28.254 673	72
37	19.909 991	21.758 488	23.776 074	25.977 987	28.380 814	31.002 616	74
38	21.586 444	23.647 261	25.901 990	28.368 611	31.066 748	34.017 874	76
39	23.404 056	25.699 991	28.217 992	30.979 233	34.006 876	37.326 259	78
40	25.374 714	27.930 910	30.741 077	33.830 096	37.225 255	40.956 471	80

32

HALF YRS	9.75% ANNUAL RATE	10.00% ANNUAL RATE	10.50% ANNUAL RATE	11.00% ANNUAL RATE	11.50% ANNUAL RATE	12.00% ANNUAL RATE	HALF YRS
1	1.048 750	1.050 000	1.052 500	1.055 000	1.057 500	1.060 000	1
2	1.099 877	1.102 500	1.107 756	1.113 025	1.118 306	1.123 600	2
3	1.153 496	1.157 625	1.165 913	1.174 241	1.182 609	1.191 016	3
4	1.209 728	1.215 506	1.227 124	1.238 825	1.250 609	1.262 477	4
5	1.268 703	1.276 282	1.291 548	1.306 960	1.322 519	1.338 226	5
6	1.330 552	1.340 096	1.359 354	1.378 843	1.398 564	1.418 519	6
7	1.395 416	1.407 100	1.430 720	1.454 679	1.478 981	1.503 630	7
8	1.463 443	1.477 455	1.505 833	1.534 687	1.564 023	1.593 848	8
9	1.534 786	1.551 328	1.584 889	1.619 094	1.653 954	1.689 479	9
10	1.609 607	1.628 895	1.668 096	1.708 144	1.749 056	1.790 848	10
11	1.688 075	1.710 339	1.755 671	1.802 092	1.849 627	1.898 299	11
12	1.770 369	1.795 856	1.847 844	1.901 207	1.955 980	2.012 196	12
13	1.856 674	1.885 649	1.944 856	2.005 774	2.068 449	2.132 928	13
14	1.947 187	1.979 932	2.046 961	2.116 091	2.187 385	2.260 904	14
15	2.042 112	2.078 928	2.154 426	2.232 476	2.313 160	2.396 558	15
16	2.141 665	2.182 875	2.267 533	2.355 263	2.446 167	2.540 352	16
17	2.246 071	2.292 018	2.386 579	2.484 802	2.586 821	2.692 773	17
18	2.355 567	2.406 619	2.511 874	2.621 466	2.735 563	2.854 339	18
19	2.470 401	2.526 950	2.643 748	2.765 647	2.892 858	3.025 600	19
20	2.590 833	2.653 298	2.782 544	2.917 757	3.059 198	3.207 135	20
21	2.717 136	2.785 963	2.928 628	3.078 234	3.235 101	3.399 564	21
22	2.849 597	2.925 261	3.082 381	3.247 537	3.421 120	3.603 537	22
23	2.988 515	3.071 524	3.244 206	3.426 152	3.617 834	3.819 750	23
24	3.134 205	3.225 100	3.414 527	3.614 590	3.825 860	4.048 935	24
25	3.286 997	3.386 355	3.593 789	3.813 392	4.045 846	4.291 871	25
26	3.447 238	3.555 673	3.782 463	4.023 129	4.278 483	4.549 383	26
27	3.615 291	3.733 456	3.981 043	4.244 401	4.524 495	4.822 346	27
28	3.791 537	3.920 129	4.190 047	4.477 843	4.784 654	5.111 687	28
29	3.976 374	4.116 136	4.410 025	4.724 124	5.059 772	5.418 388	29
30	4.170 222	4.321 942	4.641 551	4.983 951	5.350 708	5.743 491	30
31	4.373 521	4.538 039	4.885 233	5.258 069	5.658 374	6.088 101	31
32	4.586 730	4.764 941	5.141 707	5.547 262	5.983 731	6.453 387	32
33	4.810 333	5.003 189	5.411 647	5.852 362	6.327 795	6.840 590	33
34	5.044 837	5.253 348	5.695 758	6.174 242	6.691 643	7.251 025	34
35	5.290 772	5.516 015	5.994 786	6.513 825	7.076 413	7.686 087	35
36	5.548 698	5.791 816	6.309 512	6.872 085	7.483 307	8.147 252	36
37	5.819 197	6.081 407	6.640 761	7.250 050	7.913 597	8.636 087	37
38	6.102 882	6.385 477	6.989 401	7.648 803	8.368 629	9.154 252	38
39	6.400 398	6.704 751	7.356 345	8.069 487	8.849 825	9.703 507	39
40	6.712 417	7.039 989	7.742 553	8.513 309	9.358 690	10.285 718	40
41	7.039 648	7.391 988	8.149 037	8.981 541	9.896 814	10.902 861	41
42	7.382 831	7.761 588	8.576 861	9.475 525	10.465 881	11.557 033	42
43	7.742 744	8.149 667	9.027 147	9.996 679	11.067 669	12.250 455	43
44	8.120 202	8.557 150	9.501 072	10.546 497	11.704 060	12.985 482	44
45	8.516 062	8.985 008	9.999 878	11.126 554	12.377 044	13.764 611	45
46	8.931 220	9.434 258	10.524 872	11.738 515	13.088 724	14.590 487	46
47	9.366 617	9.905 971	11.077 427	12.384 133	13.841 325	15.465 917	47
48	9.823 240	10.401 270	11.658 992	13.065 260	14.637 201	16.393 872	48
49	10.302 123	10.921 333	12.271 089	13.783 849	15.478 841	17.377 504	49
50	10.804 351	11.467 400	12.915 322	14.541 961	16.368 874	18.420 154	50
51	11.331 063	12.040 770	13.593 376	15.341 769	17.310 084	19.525 364	51
52	11.883 453	12.642 808	14.307 028	16.185 566	18.305 414	20.696 885	52
53	12.462 771	13.274 949	15.058 147	17.075 773	19.357 975	21.938 698	53
54	13.070 331	13.938 696	15.848 700	18.014 940	20.471 059	23.255 020	54
55	13.707 510	14.635 631	16.680 757	19.005 762	21.648 145	24.650 322	55
56	14.375 751	15.367 412	17.556 496	20.051 079	22.892 913	26.129 341	56
57	15.076 569	16.135 783	18.478 212	21.153 888	24.209 256	27.697 101	57
58	15.811 551	16.942 572	19.448 319	22.317 352	25.601 288	29.358 927	58
59	16.582 364	17.789 701	20.469 355	23.544 806	27.073 362	31.120 463	59
YRS							
30	17.390 755	18.679 186	21.543 997	24.839 770	28.630 080	32.987 691	60
31	19.127 684	20.593 802	23.865 497	27.647 285	32.017 197	37.064 969	62
32	21.038 091	22.704 667	26.437 153	30.772 120	35.805 032	41.646 200	64
33	23.139 303	25.031 896	29.285 922	34.250 139	40.040 991	46.793 670	66
34	25.450 377	27.597 665	32.441 663	38.121 261	44.778 091	52.577 368	68
35	27.992 273	30.426 426	35.937 455	42.429 916	50.075 619	59.075 930	70
36	30.788 045	33.545 134	39.809 940	47.225 558	55.999 877	66.377 715	72
37	33.863 049	36.983 510	44.099 710	52.563 226	62.625 013	74.582 001	74
38	37.245 174	40.774 320	48.851 729	58.504 185	70.033 943	83.800 336	76
39	40.965 094	44.953 688	54.115 809	65.116 620	78.319 396	94.158 058	78
40	45.056 547	49.561 441	59.947 125	72.476 426	87.585 070	105.795 993	80

HALF YRS	12.50% ANNUAL RATE	13.00% ANNUAL RATE	13.50% ANNUAL RATE	14.00% ANNUAL RATE	14.50% ANNUAL RATE	15.00% ANNUAL RATE	HALF YRS
1	1.062 500	1.065 000	1.067 500	1.070 000	1.072 500	1.075 000	1
2	1.128 906	1.134 225	1.139 556	1.144 900	1.150 256	1.155 625	2
3	1.199 463	1.207 950	1.216 476	1.225 043	1.233 650	1.242 297	3
4	1.274 429	1.286 466	1.298 588	1.310 796	1.323 089	1.335 469	4
5	1.354 081	1.370 087	1.386 243	1.402 552	1.419 013	1.435 629	5
6	1.438 711	1.459 142	1.479 815	1.500 730	1.521 892	1.543 302	6
7	1.528 631	1.553 987	1.579 702	1.605 781	1.632 229	1.659 049	7
8	1.624 170	1.654 996	1.686 332	1.718 186	1.750 566	1.783 478	8
9	1.725 681	1.762 570	1.800 159	1.838 459	1.877 482	1.917 239	9
10	1.833 536	1.877 137	1.921 670	1.967 151	2.013 599	2.061 032	10
11	1.948 132	1.999 151	2.051 383	2.104 852	2.159 585	2.215 609	11
12	2.069 890	2.129 096	2.189 851	2.252 192	2.316 155	2.381 780	12
13	2.199 258	2.267 487	2.337 666	2.409 845	2.484 076	2.560 413	13
14	2.336 712	2.414 874	2.495 459	2.578 534	2.664 172	2.752 444	14
15	2.482 756	2.571 841	2.663 902	2.759 032	2.857 324	2.958 877	15
16	2.637 928	2.739 011	2.843 715	2.952 164	3.064 480	3.180 793	16
17	2.802 799	2.917 046	3.035 666	3.158 815	3.286 655	3.419 353	17
18	2.977 974	3.106 654	3.240 574	3.379 932	3.524 937	3.675 804	18
19	3.164 097	3.308 587	3.459 312	3.616 528	3.780 495	3.951 489	19
20	3.361 853	3.523 645	3.692 816	3.869 684	4.054 581	4.247 851	20
21	3.571 969	3.752 682	3.942 081	4.140 562	4.348 538	4.566 440	21
22	3.795 217	3.996 606	4.208 172	4.430 402	4.663 808	4.908 923	22
23	4.032 418	4.256 386	4.492 223	4.740 530	5.001 934	5.277 092	23
24	4.284 445	4.533 051	4.795 448	5.072 367	5.364 574	5.672 874	24
25	4.552 222	4.827 699	5.119 141	5.427 433	5.753 505	6.098 340	25
26	4.836 736	5.141 500	5.464 683	5.807 353	6.170 634	6.555 715	26
27	5.139 032	5.475 697	5.833 549	6.213 868	6.618 005	7.047 394	27
28	5.460 222	5.831 617	6.227 314	6.648 838	7.097 811	7.575 948	28
29	5.801 486	6.210 672	6.647 657	7.114 257	7.612 402	8.144 144	29
30	6.164 079	6.614 366	7.096 374	7.612 255	8.164 301	8.754 955	30
31	6.549 333	7.044 300	7.575 380	8.145 113	8.756 213	9.411 577	31
32	6.958 667	7.502 179	8.086 718	8.715 271	9.391 039	10.117 445	32
33	7.393 583	7.989 821	8.632 571	9.325 340	10.071 889	10.876 253	33
34	7.855 682	8.509 159	9.215 270	9.978 114	10.802 101	11.691 972	34
35	8.346 663	9.062 255	9.837 300	10.676 581	11.585 253	12.568 870	35
36	8.868 329	9.651 301	10.501 318	11.423 942	12.425 184	13.511 536	36
37	9.422 600	10.278 636	11.210 157	12.223 618	13.326 010	14.524 901	37
38	10.011 512	10.946 747	11.966 843	13.079 271	14.292 146	15.614 268	38
39	10.637 231	11.658 286	12.774 605	13.994 820	15.328 326	16.785 339	39
40	11.302 058	12.416 075	13.636 890	14.974 458	16.439 630	18.044 239	40
41	12.008 437	13.223 119	14.557 380	16.022 670	17.631 503	19.397 557	41
42	12.758 964	14.082 622	15.540 004	17.144 257	18.909 787	20.852 374	42
43	13.556 400	14.997 993	16.588 954	18.344 355	20.280 747	22.416 302	43
44	14.403 675	15.972 862	17.708 708	19.628 460	21.751 101	24.097 524	44
45	15.303 904	17.011 098	18.904 046	21.002 052	23.328 055	25.904 839	45
46	16.260 398	18.116 820	20.180 069	22.472 623	25.019 339	27.847 702	46
47	17.276 673	19.294 413	21.542 224	24.045 707	26.833 242	29.936 279	47
48	18.356 465	20.548 550	22.996 324	25.728 907	28.778 652	32.181 500	48
49	19.503 744	21.884 205	24.548 576	27.529 930	30.865 104	34.595 113	49
50	20.722 728	23.306 679	26.205 605	29.457 025	33.102 824	37.189 746	50
51	22.017 899	24.821 613	27.974 483	31.519 017	35.502 779	39.978 977	51
52	23.394 018	26.435 018	29.862 761	33.725 348	38.076 730	42.977 400	52
53	24.856 144	28.153 294	31.878 497	36.086 122	40.837 293	46.200 705	53
54	26.409 653	29.983 258	34.030 295	38.612 151	43.797 997	49.665 758	54
55	28.060 256	31.932 170	36.327 340	41.315 001	46.973 351	53.390 690	55
56	29.814 022	34.007 761	38.779 436	44.207 052	50.378 919	57.394 992	56
57	31.677 398	36.218 265	41.397 048	47.301 545	54.031 391	61.699 616	57
58	33.657 236	38.572 452	44.191 349	50.612 653	57.948 667	66.327 087	58
59	35.760 813	41.079 662	47.174 265	54.155 539	62.149 945	71.301 619	59

YRS							
30	37.995 864	43.749 840	50.358 527	57.946 427	66.655 816	76.649 240	60
31	42.893 768	49.622 162	57.386 375	66.342 864	76.671 269	88.577 778	62
32	48.423 043	56.282 697	65.395 002	75.955 945	88.191 607	102.362 695	64
33	54.665 076	63.837 242	74.521 283	86.961 962	101.442 947	118.292 890	66
34	61.711 746	72.405 795	84.921 194	99.562 750	116.685 384	136.702 221	68
35	69.666 776	82.124 463	96.772 477	113.989 392	134.218 092	157.976 504	70
36	78.647 258	93.147 619	110.277 681	130.506 455	154.385 199	182.561 597	72
37	88.785 382	105.650 359	125.667 621	149.416 840	177.582 540	210.972 746	74
38	100.230 372	119.831 278	143.205 323	171.067 341	204.265 426	243.805 379	76
39	113.150 694	135.915 631	163.190 521	195.854 998	234.957 583	281.747 591	78
40	127.736 525	154.158 907	185.964 778	224.234 388	270.261 429	325.594 560	80

34

FUTURE VALUE

SEMIANNUAL COMPOUNDING

HALF YRS	15.50% ANNUAL RATE	16.00% ANNUAL RATE	16.50% ANNUAL RATE	17.00% ANNUAL RATE	17.50% ANNUAL RATE	18.00% ANNUAL RATE	HALF YRS
1	1.077 500	1.080 000	1.082 500	1.085 000	1.087 500	1.090 000	1
2	1.161 006	1.166 400	1.171 806	1.177 225	1.182 656	1.188 100	2
3	1.250 984	1.259 712	1.268 480	1.277 289	1.286 139	1.295 029	3
4	1.347 936	1.360 489	1.373 130	1.385 859	1.398 676	1.411 582	4
5	1.452 401	1.469 328	1.486 413	1.503 657	1.521 060	1.538 624	5
6	1.564 962	1.586 874	1.609 042	1.631 468	1.654 153	1.677 100	6
7	1.686 246	1.713 824	1.741 788	1.770 142	1.798 891	1.828 039	7
8	1.816 930	1.850 930	1.885 486	1.920 604	1.956 294	1.992 563	8
9	1.957 742	1.999 005	2.041 038	2.083 856	2.127 470	2.171 893	9
10	2.109 467	2.158 925	2.209 424	2.260 983	2.313 623	2.367 364	10
11	2.272 951	2.331 639	2.391 701	2.453 167	2.516 065	2.580 426	11
12	2.449 105	2.518 170	2.589 017	2.661 686	2.736 221	2.812 665	12
13	2.638 910	2.719 624	2.802 611	2.887 930	2.975 640	3.065 805	13
14	2.843 426	2.937 194	3.033 826	3.133 404	3.236 009	3.341 727	14
15	3.063 791	3.172 169	3.284 117	3.399 743	3.519 160	3.642 482	15
16	3.301 235	3.425 943	3.555 056	3.688 721	3.827 086	3.970 306	16
17	3.557 081	3.700 018	3.848 348	4.002 262	4.161 956	4.327 633	17
18	3.832 755	3.996 019	4.165 837	4.342 445	4.526 127	4.717 120	18
19	4.129 793	4.315 701	4.509 519	4.711 563	4.922 164	5.141 661	19
20	4.449 852	4.660 957	4.881 554	5.112 046	5.352 853	5.604 411	20
21	4.794 716	5.033 834	5.284 282	5.546 570	5.821 228	6.108 808	21
22	5.166 306	5.436 540	5.720 236	6.018 028	6.330 585	6.658 600	22
23	5.566 695	5.871 464	6.192 155	6.529 561	6.884 511	7.257 874	23
24	5.998 114	6.341 181	6.703 008	7.084 574	7.486 906	7.911 083	24
25	6.462 967	6.848 475	7.256 006	7.686 762	8.142 010	8.623 081	25
26	6.963 847	7.396 353	7.854 626	8.340 137	8.854 436	9.399 158	26
27	7.503 546	7.988 061	8.502 633	9.049 049	9.629 199	10.245 082	27
28	8.085 070	8.627 106	9.204 100	9.818 218	10.471 754	11.167 140	28
29	8.711 663	9.317 275	9.963 439	10.652 766	11.388 033	12.172 182	29
30	9.386 817	10.062 657	10.785 422	11.558 252	12.384 485	13.267 678	30
31	10.114 296	10.867 669	11.675 220	12.540 703	13.468 128	14.461 770	31
32	10.898 154	11.737 083	12.638 425	13.606 663	14.646 589	15.763 329	32
33	11.742 760	12.676 050	13.681 095	14.763 229	15.928 166	17.182 028	33
34	12.652 824	13.690 134	14.809 786	16.018 104	17.321 880	18.728 411	34
35	13.633 418	14.785 344	16.031 593	17.379 642	18.837 545	20.413 968	35
36	14.690 008	15.968 172	17.354 199	18.856 912	20.485 830	22.251 225	36
37	15.828 484	17.245 626	18.785 921	20.459 750	22.278 340	24.253 835	37
38	17.055 191	18.625 276	20.335 759	22.198 828	24.227 695	26.436 680	38
39	18.376 969	20.115 298	22.013 459	24.085 729	26.347 618	28.815 982	39
40	19.801 184	21.724 521	23.829 570	26.133 016	28.653 035	31.409 420	40
41	21.335 775	23.462 483	25.795 509	28.354 322	31.160 175	34.236 268	41
42	22.989 298	25.339 482	27.923 639	30.764 439	33.886 691	37.317 532	42
43	24.770 969	27.366 640	30.227 339	33.379 417	36.851 776	40.676 110	43
44	26.690 719	29.555 972	32.721 094	36.216 667	40.076 306	44.336 960	44
45	28.759 249	31.920 449	35.420 585	39.295 084	43.582 983	48.327 286	45
46	30.988 091	34.474 085	38.342 783	42.635 166	47.396 494	52.676 742	46
47	33.389 668	37.232 012	41.506 063	46.259 155	51.543 687	57.417 649	47
48	35.977 368	40.210 573	44.930 313	50.191 183	56.053 760	62.585 237	48
49	38.765 614	43.427 419	48.637 064	54.457 434	60.958 464	68.217 908	49
50	41.769 949	46.901 613	52.649 621	59.086 316	66.292 330	74.357 520	50
51	45.007 120	50.653 742	56.993 215	64.108 652	72.092 909	81.049 699	51
52	48.495 171	54.706 041	61.695 155	69.557 888	78.401 038	88.344 170	52
53	52.253 547	59.082 524	66.785 006	75.470 308	85.261 129	96.295 145	53
54	56.303 197	63.809 126	72.294 768	81.885 284	92.721 478	104.961 708	54
55	60.666 695	68.913 856	78.259 087	88.845 534	100.834 607	114.408 262	55
56	65.368 364	74.426 965	84.715 462	96.397 404	109.657 635	124.705 005	56
57	70.434 412	80.381 122	91.704 487	104.591 183	119.252 678	135.928 456	57
58	75.893 079	86.811 612	99.270 107	113.481 434	129.687 287	148.162 017	58
59	81.774 793	93.756 540	107.459 891	123.127 356	141.034 925	161.496 598	59

YRS							YRS
30	88.112 339	101.257 064	116.325 332	133.593 181	153.375 481	176.031 292	60
31	102.298 976	118.106 239	136.310 751	157.269 233	181.390 471	209.142 778	62
32	118.769 751	137.759 117	159.729 790	185.141 272	214.522 574	248.482 535	64
33	137.892 423	160.682 234	187.172 367	217.952 934	253.706 463	295.222 099	66
34	160.093 965	187.419 758	219.329 749	256.579 643	300.047 535	350.753 376	68
35	185.870 094	218.606 406	257.011 971	302.051 970	354.853 092	416.730 086	70
36	215.796 341	254.982 512	301.168 234	355.583 131	419.669 227	495.117 015	72
37	250.540 900	297.411 602	352.910 818	418.601 351	496.324 434	588.248 526	74
38	290.879 551	346.900 892	413.543 103	492.787 975	586.981 194	698.898 074	76
39	337.712 977	404.625 201	484.592 393	580.122 324	694.196 978	830.360 801	78
40	392.086 877	471.954 834	567.848 394	682.934 503	820.996 395	986.551 668	80

FUTURE VALUE

SEMIANNUAL COMPOUNDING

HALF YRS	18.50% ANNUAL RATE	19.00% ANNUAL RATE	19.50% ANNUAL RATE	20.00% ANNUAL RATE	20.50% ANNUAL RATE	21.00% ANNUAL RATE	HALF YRS
1	1.092 500	1.095 000	1.097 500	1.100 000	1.102 500	1.105 000	1
2	1.193 556	1.199 025	1.204 506	1.210 000	1.215 506	1.221 025	2
3	1.303 960	1.312 932	1.321 946	1.331 000	1.340 096	1.349 233	3
4	1.424 577	1.437 661	1.450 835	1.464 100	1.477 455	1.490 902	4
5	1.556 350	1.574 239	1.592 292	1.610 510	1.628 895	1.647 447	5
6	1.700 312	1.723 791	1.747 540	1.771 561	1.795 856	1.820 429	6
7	1.857 591	1.887 552	1.917 925	1.948 717	1.979 932	2.011 574	7
8	2.029 418	2.066 869	2.104 923	2.143 589	2.182 875	2.222 789	8
9	2.217 139	2.263 222	2.310 153	2.357 948	2.406 619	2.456 182	9
10	2.422 225	2.478 228	2.535 393	2.593 742	2.653 298	2.714 081	10
11	2.646 281	2.713 659	2.782 594	2.853 117	2.925 261	2.999 059	11
12	2.891 062	2.971 457	3.053 897	3.138 428	3.225 100	3.313 961	12
13	3.158 485	3.253 745	3.351 652	3.452 271	3.555 673	3.661 926	13
14	3.450 645	3.562 851	3.678 438	3.797 498	3.920 129	4.046 429	14
15	3.769 829	3.901 322	4.037 085	4.177 248	4.321 942	4.471 304	15
16	4.118 539	4.271 948	4.430 701	4.594 973	4.764 941	4.940 791	16
17	4.499 503	4.677 783	4.862 695	5.054 470	5.253 348	5.459 574	17
18	4.915 707	5.122 172	5.336 807	5.559 917	5.791 816	6.032 829	18
19	5.370 410	5.608 778	5.857 146	6.115 909	6.385 477	6.666 276	19
20	5.867 173	6.141 612	6.428 218	6.727 500	7.039 989	7.366 235	20
21	6.409 887	6.725 065	7.054 969	7.400 250	7.761 588	8.139 690	21
22	7.002 801	7.363 946	7.742 828	8.140 275	8.557 150	8.994 357	22
23	7.650 560	8.063 521	8.497 754	8.954 302	9.434 258	9.938 764	23
24	8.358 237	8.829 556	9.326 285	9.849 733	10.401 270	10.982 335	24
25	9.131 374	9.668 364	10.235 598	10.834 706	11.467 400	12.135 480	25
26	9.976 026	10.586 858	11.233 569	11.918 177	12.642 808	13.409 705	26
27	10.898 809	11.592 610	12.328 842	13.109 994	13.938 696	14.817 724	27
28	11.906 949	12.693 908	13.530 904	14.420 994	15.367 412	16.373 585	28
29	13.008 341	13.899 829	14.850 167	15.863 093	16.942 572	18.092 812	29
30	14.211 613	15.220 313	16.298 058	17.449 402	18.679 186	19.992 557	30
31	15.526 187	16.666 242	17.887 119	19.194 342	20.593 802	22.091 775	31
32	16.962 359	18.249 535	19.631 113	21.113 777	22.704 667	24.411 412	32
33	18.531 378	19.983 241	21.545 147	23.225 154	25.031 896	26.974 610	33
34	20.245 530	21.881 649	23.645 798	25.547 670	27.597 665	29.806 944	34
35	22.118 242	23.960 406	25.951 264	28.102 437	30.426 426	32.936 673	35
36	24.164 179	26.236 644	28.481 512	30.912 681	33.545 134	36.395 024	36
37	26.399 365	28.729 126	31.258 459	34.003 949	36.983 510	40.216 501	37
38	28.841 307	31.458 393	34.306 159	37.404 343	40.774 320	44.439 234	38
39	31.509 128	34.446 940	37.651 010	41.144 778	44.953 688	49.105 354	39
40	34.423 722	37.719 399	41.321 983	45.259 256	49.561 441	54.261 416	40
41	37.607 916	41.302 742	45.350 877	49.785 181	54.641 489	59.958 864	41
42	41.086 649	45.226 503	49.772 587	54.763 699	60.242 241	66.254 545	42
43	44.887 164	49.523 020	54.625 414	60.240 069	66.417 071	73.211 272	43
44	49.039 226	54.227 707	59.951 392	66.264 076	73.224 821	80.898 456	44
45	53.575 355	59.379 340	65.796 653	72.890 484	80.730 365	89.392 794	45
46	58.531 075	65.020 377	72.211 827	80.179 532	89.005 227	98.779 037	46
47	63.945 199	71.197 313	79.252 480	88.197 485	98.128 263	109.150 836	47
48	69.860 130	77.961 057	86.979 596	97.017 234	108.186 410	120.611 674	48
49	76.322 192	85.367 358	95.460 107	106.718 957	119.275 517	133.275 900	49
50	83.381 995	93.477 257	104.767 467	117.390 853	131.501 258	147.269 869	50
51	91.094 830	102.357 596	114.982 295	129.129 938	144.980 137	162.733 205	51
52	99.521 101	112.081 568	126.193 069	142.042 932	159.840 601	179.820 192	52
53	108.726 803	122.729 317	138.496 894	156.247 225	176.224 262	198.701 312	53
54	118.784 033	134.388 602	152.000 341	171.871 948	194.287 249	219.564 950	54
55	129.771 556	147.155 519	166.820 374	189.059 142	214.201 692	242.619 270	55
56	141.775 424	161.135 293	183.085 360	207.965 057	236.157 366	268.094 293	56
57	154.889 651	176.443 146	200.936 183	228.761 562	260.363 496	296.244 194	57
58	169.216 944	193.205 245	220.527 461	251.637 719	287.050 754	327.349 834	58
59	184.869 511	211.559 743	242.028 888	276.801 490	316.473 456	361.721 567	59

YRS							YRS
30	201.969 941	231.657 919	265.626 705	304.481 640	348.911 986	399.702 331	60
31	241.062 485	277.763 636	319.949 026	368.422 784	424.104 699	488.046 539	62
32	287.721 636	333.045 544	385.380 602	445.791 568	515.501 913	595.917 025	64
33	343.411 957	399.329 933	464.193 343	539.407 798	626.595 797	727.629 586	66
34	409.881 488	478.806 573	559.123 783	652.683 435	761.631 107	888.453 915	68
35	489.216 611	574.101 052	673.468 092	789.746 957	925.767 371	1084.824 442	70
36	583.907 544	688.361 513	811.196 525	955.593 818	1125.276 025	1324.597 764	72
37	696.926 498	825.362 664	977.091 285	1156.268 519	1367.780 042	1617.366 985	74
38	831.820 978	989.630 468	1176.912 559	1399.084 909	1662.545 189	1974.845 522	76
39	992.825 127	1186.591 671	1417.598 534	1692.892 739	2020.834 069	2411.335 754	78
40	1184.992 636	1422.753 079	1707.506 294	2048.400 215	2456.336 441	2944.301 239	80

FUTURE VALUE

SEMIANNUAL COMPOUNDING

HALF YRS	21.50% ANNUAL RATE	22.00% ANNUAL RATE	22.50% ANNUAL RATE	23.00% ANNUAL RATE	23.50% ANNUAL RATE	24.00% ANNUAL RATE	HALF YRS
1	1.107 500	1.110 000	1.112 500	1.115 000	1.117 500	1.120 000	1
2	1.226 556	1.232 100	1.237 656	1.243 225	1.248 806	1.254 400	2
3	1.358 411	1.367 631	1.376 893	1.386 196	1.395 541	1.404 928	3
4	1.504 440	1.518 070	1.531 793	1.545 608	1.559 517	1.573 519	4
5	1.666 168	1.685 058	1.704 120	1.723 353	1.742 760	1.762 342	5
6	1.845 281	1.870 415	1.895 833	1.921 539	1.947 535	1.973 823	6
7	2.043 648	2.076 160	2.109 114	2.142 516	2.176 370	2.210 681	7
8	2.263 340	2.304 538	2.346 390	2.388 905	2.432 093	2.475 963	8
9	2.506 650	2.558 037	2.610 359	2.663 629	2.717 864	2.773 079	9
10	2.776 114	2.839 421	2.904 024	2.969 947	3.037 213	3.105 848	10
11	3.074 547	3.151 757	3.230 727	3.311 491	3.394 086	3.478 550	11
12	3.405 060	3.498 451	3.594 183	3.692 312	3.792 891	3.895 976	12
13	3.771 104	3.883 280	3.998 529	4.116 928	4.238 556	4.363 493	13
14	4.176 498	4.310 441	4.448 364	4.590 375	4.736 586	4.887 112	14
15	4.625 472	4.784 589	4.948 804	5.118 268	5.293 135	5.473 566	15
16	5.122 710	5.310 894	5.505 545	5.706 869	5.915 078	6.130 394	16
17	5.673 401	5.895 093	6.124 919	6.363 159	6.610 100	6.866 041	17
18	6.283 292	6.543 553	6.813 972	7.094 922	7.386 787	7.689 966	18
19	6.958 746	7.263 344	7.580 544	7.910 838	8.254 734	8.612 762	19
20	7.706 811	8.062 312	8.433 355	8.820 584	9.224 666	9.646 293	20
21	8.535 293	8.949 166	9.382 108	9.834 951	10.308 564	10.803 848	21
22	9.452 837	9.933 574	10.437 595	10.965 971	11.519 820	12.100 310	22
23	10.469 017	11.026 267	11.611 824	12.227 057	12.873 399	13.552 347	23
24	11.594 436	12.239 157	12.918 154	13.633 169	14.386 023	15.178 629	24
25	12.840 838	13.585 464	14.371 447	15.200 983	16.076 381	17.000 064	25
26	14.221 228	15.079 865	15.988 235	16.949 096	17.965 356	19.040 072	26
27	15.750 010	16.738 650	17.786 911	18.898 243	20.076 285	21.324 881	27
28	17.443 136	18.579 901	19.787 938	21.071 540	22.435 249	23.883 866	28
29	19.318 274	20.623 691	22.014 081	23.494 768	25.071 391	26.749 930	29
30	21.394 988	22.892 297	24.490 666	26.196 666	28.017 279	29.959 922	30
31	23.694 949	25.410 449	27.245 866	29.209 282	31.309 309	33.555 113	31
32	26.242 156	28.205 599	30.311 025	32.568 350	34.988 153	37.581 726	32
33	29.063 188	31.308 214	33.721 016	36.313 710	39.099 261	42.091 533	33
34	32.187 481	34.752 118	37.514 630	40.489 787	43.693 424	47.142 517	34
35	35.647 635	38.574 851	41.735 026	45.146 112	48.827 402	52.799 620	35
36	39.479 756	42.818 085	46.430 216	50.337 915	54.564 621	59.135 574	36
37	43.723 829	47.528 074	51.653 616	56.126 776	60.975 964	66.231 843	37
38	48.424 141	52.756 162	57.464 647	62.581 355	68.140 640	74.179 664	38
39	53.629 736	58.559 340	63.929 420	69.778 211	76.147 165	83.081 224	39
40	59.394 933	65.000 867	71.121 480	77.802 705	85.094 457	93.050 970	40
41	65.779 888	72.150 963	79.122 647	86.750 016	95.093 056	104.217 087	41
42	72.851 226	80.087 569	88.023 944	96.726 268	106.266 490	116.723 137	42
43	80.682 733	88.897 201	97.926 638	107.849 788	118.752 803	130.729 914	43
44	89.356 127	98.675 893	108.943 385	120.252 514	132.706 257	146.417 503	44
45	98.961 910	109.530 242	121.199 516	134.081 553	148.299 242	163.987 604	45
46	109.600 316	121.578 568	134.834 461	149.500 932	165.724 403	183.666 116	46
47	121.382 350	134.952 211	150.003 338	166.693 539	185.197 020	205.706 050	47
48	134.430 952	149.796 954	166.878 714	185.863 296	206.957 670	230.390 776	48
49	148.882 280	166.274 619	185.652 569	207.237 575	231.275 196	258.037 669	49
50	164.887 125	184.564 827	206.538 483	231.069 896	258.450 032	289.002 190	50
51	182.612 491	204.866 958	229.774 062	257.642 934	288.817 911	323.682 453	51
52	202.243 333	227.402 323	255.623 644	287.271 872	322.754 015	362.524 347	52
53	223.984 492	252.416 579	284.381 304	320.308 137	360.677 612	406.027 269	53
54	248.062 824	280.182 402	316.374 201	357.143 573	403.057 231	454.750 541	54
55	274.729 578	311.002 466	351.966 299	398.215 084	450.416 456	509.320 606	55
56	304.263 008	345.212 738	391.562 507	444.009 818	503.340 390	570.439 078	56
57	336.971 281	383.186 139	435.613 289	495.070 947	562.482 885	638.891 768	57
58	373.195 694	425.336 614	484.619 784	552.004 106	628.574 625	715.558 780	58
59	413.314 231	472.123 642	539.139 510	615.484 578	702.432 143	801.425 833	59
YRS							
30	457.745 511	524.057 242	599.792 705	686.265 305	784.967 920	897.596 933	60
31	561.450 617	645.690 928	742.337 190	853.182 184	980.272 844	1125.945 593	62
32	688.650 763	795.555 793	918.758 263	1060.697 420	1224.170 855	1412.386 152	64
33	844.668 898	980.204 292	1137.106 906	1318.685 550	1528.752 214	1771.697 189	66
34	1036.033 916	1207.709 708	1407.347 469	1639.422 843	1909.115 320	2222.416 954	68
35	1270.753 875	1488.019 132	1741.812 391	2038.171 464	2384.115 143	2787.799 828	70
36	1558.651 107	1833.388 372	2155.764 992	2533.905 719	2977.297 892	3497.016 104	72
37	1911.773 257	2258.917 813	2668.096 016	3150.214 937	3718.068 215	4386.657 001	74
38	2344.897 437	2783.212 638	3302.185 710	3916.425 965	4643.146 825	5502.622 542	76
39	2876.148 607	3429.196 291	4086.970 782	4868.998 671	5798.390 775	6902.489 716	78
40	3527.758 050	4225.112 750	5058.264 932	6053.260 872	7241.066 640	8658.483 100	80

FUTURE VALUE

ANNUAL COMPOUNDING

YRS	5.25% ANNUAL RATE	5.50% ANNUAL RATE	5.75% ANNUAL RATE	6.00% ANNUAL RATE	6.25% ANNUAL RATE	6.50% ANNUAL RATE	YRS
1	1.052 500	1.055 000	1.057 500	1.060 000	1.062 500	1.065 000	1
2	1.107 756	1.113 025	1.118 306	1.123 600	1.128 906	1.134 225	2
3	1.165 913	1.174 241	1.182 609	1.191 016	1.199 463	1.207 950	3
4	1.227 124	1.238 825	1.250 609	1.262 477	1.274 429	1.286 466	4
5	1.291 548	1.306 960	1.322 519	1.338 226	1.354 081	1.370 087	5
6	1.359 354	1.378 843	1.398 564	1.418 519	1.438 711	1.459 142	6
7	1.430 720	1.454 679	1.478 981	1.503 630	1.528 631	1.553 987	7
8	1.505 833	1.534 687	1.564 023	1.593 848	1.624 170	1.654 996	8
9	1.584 889	1.619 094	1.653 954	1.689 479	1.725 681	1.762 570	9
10	1.668 096	1.708 144	1.749 056	1.790 848	1.833 536	1.877 137	10
11	1.755 671	1.802 092	1.849 627	1.898 299	1.948 132	1.999 151	11
12	1.847 844	1.901 207	1.955 980	2.012 196	2.069 890	2.129 096	12
13	1.944 856	2.005 774	2.068 449	2.132 928	2.199 258	2.267 487	13
14	2.046 961	2.116 091	2.187 385	2.260 904	2.336 712	2.414 874	14
15	2.154 426	2.232 476	2.313 160	2.396 558	2.482 756	2.571 841	15
16	2.267 533	2.355 263	2.446 167	2.540 352	2.637 928	2.739 011	16
17	2.386 579	2.484 802	2.586 821	2.692 773	2.802 799	2.917 046	17
18	2.511 874	2.621 466	2.735 563	2.854 339	2.977 974	3.106 654	18
19	2.643 748	2.765 647	2.892 858	3.025 600	3.164 097	3.308 587	19
20	2.782 544	2.917 757	3.059 198	3.207 135	3.361 853	3.523 645	20
21	2.928 628	3.078 234	3.235 101	3.399 564	3.571 969	3.752 682	21
22	3.082 381	3.247 537	3.421 120	3.603 537	3.795 217	3.996 606	22
23	3.244 206	3.426 152	3.617 834	3.819 750	4.032 418	4.256 386	23
24	3.414 527	3.614 590	3.825 860	4.048 935	4.284 445	4.533 051	24
25	3.593 789	3.813 392	4.045 846	4.291 871	4.552 222	4.827 699	25
26	3.782 463	4.023 129	4.278 483	4.549 383	4.836 736	5.141 500	26
27	3.981 043	4.244 401	4.524 495	4.822 346	5.139 032	5.475 697	27
28	4.190 047	4.477 843	4.784 654	5.111 687	5.460 222	5.831 617	28
29	4.410 025	4.724 124	5.059 772	5.418 388	5.801 486	6.210 672	29
30	4.641 551	4.983 951	5.350 708	5.743 491	6.164 079	6.614 366	30
31	4.885 233	5.258 069	5.658 374	6.088 101	6.549 333	7.044 300	31
32	5.141 707	5.547 262	5.983 731	6.453 387	6.958 667	7.502 179	32
33	5.411 647	5.852 362	6.327 795	6.840 590	7.393 583	7.989 821	33
34	5.695 758	6.174 242	6.691 643	7.251 025	7.855 682	8.509 159	34
35	5.994 786	6.513 825	7.076 413	7.686 087	8.346 663	9.062 255	35
36	6.309 512	6.872 085	7.483 307	8.147 252	8.868 329	9.651 301	36
37	6.640 761	7.250 050	7.913 597	8.636 087	9.422 600	10.278 636	37
38	6.989 401	7.648 803	8.368 629	9.154 252	10.011 512	10.946 747	38
39	7.356 345	8.069 487	8.849 825	9.703 507	10.637 231	11.658 286	39
40	7.742 553	8.513 309	9.358 690	10.285 718	11.302 058	12.416 075	40
41	8.149 037	8.981 541	9.896 814	10.902 861	12.008 437	13.223 119	41
42	8.576 861	9.475 525	10.465 881	11.557 033	12.758 964	14.082 622	42
43	9.027 147	9.996 679	11.067 669	12.250 455	13.556 400	14.997 993	43
44	9.501 072	10.546 497	11.704 060	12.985 482	14.403 675	15.972 862	44
45	9.999 878	11.126 554	12.377 044	13.764 611	15.303 904	17.011 098	45
46	10.524 872	11.738 515	13.088 724	14.590 487	16.260 398	18.116 820	46
47	11.077 427	12.384 133	13.841 325	15.465 917	17.276 673	19.294 413	47
48	11.658 992	13.065 260	14.637 201	16.393 872	18.356 465	20.548 550	48
49	12.271 089	13.783 849	15.478 841	17.377 504	19.503 744	21.884 205	49
50	12.915 322	14.541 961	16.368 874	18.420 154	20.722 728	23.306 679	50

FUTURE VALUE

YRS	6.75% ANNUAL RATE	7.00% ANNUAL RATE	7.25% ANNUAL RATE	7.50% ANNUAL RATE	7.75% ANNUAL RATE	8.00% ANNUAL RATE	YRS
1	1.067 500	1.070 000	1.072 500	1.075 000	1.077 500	1.080 000	1
2	1.139 556	1.144 900	1.150 256	1.155 625	1.161 006	1.166 400	2
3	1.216 476	1.225 043	1.233 650	1.242 297	1.250 984	1.259 712	3
4	1.298 588	1.310 796	1.323 089	1.335 469	1.347 936	1.360 489	4
5	1.386 243	1.402 552	1.419 013	1.435 629	1.452 401	1.469 328	5
6	1.479 815	1.500 730	1.521 892	1.543 302	1.564 962	1.586 874	6
7	1.579 702	1.605 781	1.632 229	1.659 049	1.686 246	1.713 824	7
8	1.686 332	1.718 186	1.750 566	1.783 478	1.816 930	1.850 930	8
9	1.800 159	1.838 459	1.877 482	1.917 239	1.957 742	1.999 005	9
10	1.921 670	1.967 151	2.013 599	2.061 032	2.109 467	2.158 925	10
11	2.051 383	2.104 852	2.159 585	2.215 609	2.272 951	2.331 639	11
12	2.189 851	2.252 192	2.316 155	2.381 780	2.449 105	2.518 170	12
13	2.337 666	2.409 845	2.484 076	2.560 413	2.638 910	2.719 624	13
14	2.495 459	2.578 534	2.664 172	2.752 444	2.843 426	2.937 194	14
15	2.663 902	2.759 032	2.857 324	2.958 877	3.063 791	3.172 169	15
16	2.843 715	2.952 164	3.064 480	3.180 793	3.301 235	3.425 943	16
17	3.035 666	3.158 815	3.286 655	3.419 353	3.557 081	3.700 018	17
18	3.240 574	3.379 932	3.524 937	3.675 804	3.832 755	3.996 019	18
19	3.459 312	3.616 528	3.780 495	3.951 489	4.129 793	4.315 701	19
20	3.692 816	3.869 684	4.054 581	4.247 851	4.449 852	4.660 957	20
21	3.942 081	4.140 562	4.348 538	4.566 440	4.794 716	5.033 834	21
22	4.208 172	4.430 402	4.663 808	4.908 923	5.166 306	5.436 540	22
23	4.492 223	4.740 530	5.001 934	5.277 092	5.566 695	5.871 464	23
24	4.795 448	5.072 367	5.364 574	5.672 874	5.998 114	6.341 181	24
25	5.119 141	5.427 433	5.753 505	6.098 340	6.462 967	6.848 475	25
26	5.464 683	5.807 353	6.170 634	6.555 715	6.963 847	7.396 353	26
27	5.833 549	6.213 868	6.618 005	7.047 394	7.503 546	7.988 061	27
28	6.227 314	6.648 838	7.097 811	7.575 948	8.085 070	8.627 106	28
29	6.647 657	7.114 257	7.612 402	8.144 144	8.711 663	9.317 275	29
30	7.096 374	7.612 255	8.164 301	8.754 955	9.386 817	10.062 657	30
31	7.575 380	8.145 113	8.756 213	9.411 577	10.114 296	10.867 669	31
32	8.086 718	8.715 271	9.391 039	10.117 445	10.898 154	11.737 083	32
33	8.632 571	9.325 340	10.071 889	10.876 253	11.742 760	12.676 050	33
34	9.215 270	9.978 114	10.802 101	11.691 972	12.652 824	13.690 134	34
35	9.837 300	10.676 581	11.585 253	12.568 870	13.633 418	14.785 344	35
36	10.501 318	11.423 942	12.425 184	13.511 536	14.690 008	15.968 172	36
37	11.210 157	12.223 618	13.326 010	14.524 901	15.828 484	17.245 626	37
38	11.966 843	13.079 271	14.292 146	15.614 268	17.055 191	18.625 276	38
39	12.774 605	13.994 820	15.328 326	16.785 339	18.376 969	20.115 298	39
40	13.636 890	14.974 458	16.439 630	18.044 239	19.801 184	21.724 521	40
41	14.557 380	16.022 670	17.631 503	19.397 557	21.335 775	23.462 483	41
42	15.540 004	17.144 257	18.909 787	20.852 374	22.989 298	25.339 482	42
43	16.588 954	18.344 355	20.280 747	22.416 302	24.770 969	27.366 640	43
44	17.708 708	19.628 460	21.751 101	24.097 524	26.690 719	29.555 972	44
45	18.904 046	21.002 452	23.328 055	25.904 839	28.759 249	31.920 449	45
46	20.180 069	22.472 623	25.019 339	27.847 702	30.988 091	34.474 085	46
47	21.542 224	24.045 707	26.833 242	29.936 279	33.389 668	37.232 012	47
48	22.996 324	25.728 907	28.778 652	32.181 500	35.977 368	40.210 573	48
49	24.548 576	27.529 930	30.865 104	34.595 113	38.765 614	43.427 419	49
50	26.205 605	29.457 025	33.102 824	37.189 746	41.769 949	46.901 613	50

FUTURE VALUE

ANNUAL COMPOUNDING

YRS	8.25% ANNUAL RATE	8.50% ANNUAL RATE	8.75% ANNUAL RATE	9.00% ANNUAL RATE	9.25% ANNUAL RATE	9.50% ANNUAL RATE	YRS
1	1.082 500	1.085 000	1.087 500	1.090 000	1.092 500	1.095 000	1
2	1.171 806	1.177 225	1.182 656	1.188 100	1.193 556	1.199 025	2
3	1.268 480	1.277 289	1.286 139	1.295 029	1.303 960	1.312 932	3
4	1.373 130	1.385 859	1.398 676	1.411 582	1.424 577	1.437 661	4
5	1.486 413	1.503 657	1.521 060	1.538 624	1.556 350	1.574 239	5
6	1.609 042	1.631 468	1.654 153	1.677 100	1.700 312	1.723 791	6
7	1.741 788	1.770 142	1.798 891	1.828 039	1.857 591	1.887 552	7
8	1.885 486	1.920 604	1.956 294	1.992 563	2.029 418	2.066 869	8
9	2.041 038	2.083 856	2.127 470	2.171 893	2.217 139	2.263 222	9
10	2.209 424	2.260 983	2.313 623	2.367 364	2.422 225	2.478 228	10
11	2.391 701	2.453 167	2.516 065	2.580 426	2.646 281	2.713 659	11
12	2.589 017	2.661 686	2.736 221	2.812 665	2.891 062	2.971 457	12
13	2.802 611	2.887 930	2.975 640	3.065 805	3.158 485	3.253 745	13
14	3.033 826	3.133 404	3.236 009	3.341 727	3.450 645	3.562 851	14
15	3.284 117	3.399 743	3.519 160	3.642 482	3.769 829	3.901 322	15
16	3.555 056	3.688 721	3.827 086	3.970 306	4.118 539	4.271 948	16
17	3.848 348	4.002 262	4.161 956	4.327 633	4.499 503	4.677 783	17
18	4.165 837	4.342 455	4.526 127	4.717 120	4.915 707	5.122 172	18
19	4.509 519	4.711 563	4.922 164	5.141 661	5.370 410	5.608 778	19
20	4.881 554	5.112 046	5.352 853	5.604 411	5.867 173	6.141 612	20
21	5.284 282	5.546 570	5.821 228	6.108 808	6.409 887	6.725 065	21
22	5.720 236	6.018 028	6.330 585	6.658 600	7.002 801	7.363 946	22
23	6.192 155	6.529 561	6.884 511	7.257 874	7.650 560	8.063 521	23
24	6.703 008	7.084 574	7.486 906	7.911 083	8.358 237	8.829 556	24
25	7.256 006	7.686 762	8.142 010	8.623 081	9.131 374	9.668 364	25
26	7.854 626	8.340 137	8.854 436	9.399 158	9.976 026	10.586 858	26
27	8.502 633	9.049 049	9.629 199	10.245 082	10.898 809	11.592 610	27
28	9.204 100	9.818 218	10.471 754	11.167 140	11.906 949	12.693 908	28
29	9.963 439	10.652 766	11.388 033	12.172 182	13.008 341	13.899 829	29
30	10.785 422	11.558 252	12.384 485	13.267 678	14.211 613	15.220 313	30
31	11.675 220	12.540 703	13.468 128	14.461 770	15.526 187	16.666 242	31
32	12.638 425	13.606 663	14.646 589	15.763 329	16.962 359	18.249 535	32
33	13.681 095	14.763 229	15.928 166	17.182 028	18.531 378	19.983 241	33
34	14.809 786	16.018 104	17.321 880	18.728 411	20.245 530	21.881 649	34
35	16.031 593	17.379 642	18.837 545	20.413 968	22.118 242	23.960 406	35
36	17.354 199	18.856 912	20.485 830	22.251 225	24.164 179	26.236 644	36
37	18.785 921	20.459 750	22.278 340	24.253 835	26.399 365	28.729 126	37
38	20.335 759	22.198 828	24.227 695	26.436 680	28.841 307	31.458 393	38
39	22.013 459	24.085 729	26.347 618	28.815 982	31.509 128	34.446 940	39
40	23.829 570	26.133 016	28.653 035	31.409 420	34.423 722	37.719 399	40
41	25.795 509	28.354 322	31.160 175	34.236 268	37.607 916	41.302 742	41
42	27.923 639	30.764 439	33.886 691	37.317 532	41.086 649	45.226 503	42
43	30.227 339	33.379 417	36.851 776	40.676 110	44.887 164	49.523 020	43
44	32.721 094	36.216 667	40.076 306	44.336 960	49.039 226	54.227 707	44
45	35.420 585	39.295 084	43.582 983	48.327 286	53.575 355	59.379 340	45
46	38.342 783	42.635 166	47.396 494	52.676 742	58.531 075	65.020 377	46
47	41.506 063	46.259 155	51.543 687	57.417 649	63.945 199	71.197 313	47
48	44.930 313	50.191 183	56.053 760	62.585 237	69.860 130	77.961 057	48
49	48.637 064	54.457 434	60.958 464	68.217 908	76.322 192	85.367 358	49
50	52.649 621	59.086 316	66.292 330	74.357 520	83.381 995	93.477 257	50

FUTURE VALUE

YRS	9.75% ANNUAL RATE	10.00% ANNUAL RATE	10.25% ANNUAL RATE	10.50% ANNUAL RATE	10.75% ANNUAL RATE	11.00% ANNUAL RATE	YRS
1	1.097 500	1.100 000	1.102 500	1.105 000	1.107 500	1.110 000	1
2	1.204 506	1.210 000	1.215 506	1.221 025	1.226 556	1.232 100	2
3	1.321 946	1.331 000	1.340 096	1.349 233	1.358 411	1.367 631	3
4	1.450 835	1.464 100	1.477 455	1.490 902	1.504 440	1.518 070	4
5	1.592 292	1.610 510	1.628 895	1.647 447	1.666 168	1.685 058	5
6	1.747 540	1.771 561	1.795 856	1.820 429	1.845 281	1.870 415	6
7	1.917 925	1.948 717	1.979 932	2.011 574	2.043 648	2.076 160	7
8	2.104 923	2.143 589	2.182 875	2.222 789	2.263 340	2.304 538	8
9	2.310 153	2.357 948	2.406 619	2.456 182	2.506 650	2.558 037	9
10	2.535 393	2.593 742	2.653 298	2.714 081	2.776 114	2.839 421	10
11	2.782 594	2.853 117	2.925 261	2.999 059	3.074 547	3.151 757	11
12	3.053 897	3.138 428	3.225 100	3.313 961	3.405 060	3.498 451	12
13	3.351 652	3.452 271	3.555 673	3.661 926	3.771 104	3.883 280	13
14	3.678 438	3.797 498	3.920 129	4.046 429	4.176 498	4.310 441	14
15	4.037 085	4.177 248	4.321 942	4.471 304	4.625 472	4.784 589	15
16	4.430 701	4.594 973	4.764 941	4.940 791	5.122 710	5.310 894	16
17	4.862 695	5.054 470	5.253 348	5.459 574	5.673 401	5.895 093	17
18	5.336 807	5.559 917	5.791 816	6.032 829	6.283 292	6.543 553	18
19	5.857 146	6.115 909	6.385 477	6.666 276	6.958 746	7.263 344	19
20	6.428 218	6.727 500	7.039 989	7.366 235	7.706 811	8.062 312	20
21	7.054 969	7.400 250	7.761 588	8.139 690	8.535 293	8.949 166	21
22	7.742 828	8.140 275	8.557 150	8.994 357	9.452 837	9.933 574	22
23	8.497 754	8.954 302	9.434 258	9.938 764	10.469 017	11.026 267	23
24	9.326 285	9.849 733	10.401 270	10.982 335	11.594 436	12.239 157	24
25	10.235 598	10.834 706	11.467 400	12.135 480	12.840 838	13.585 464	25
26	11.233 569	11.918 177	12.642 808	13.409 705	14.221 228	15.079 865	26
27	12.328 842	13.109 994	13.938 696	14.817 724	15.750 010	16.738 650	27
28	13.530 904	14.420 994	15.367 412	16.373 585	17.443 136	18.579 901	28
29	14.850 167	15.863 093	16.942 572	18.092 812	19.318 274	20.623 691	29
30	16.298 058	17.449 402	18.679 186	19.992 557	21.394 988	22.892 297	30
31	17.887 119	19.194 342	20.593 802	22.091 775	23.694 949	25.410 449	31
32	19.631 113	21.113 777	22.704 667	24.411 412	26.242 156	28.205 599	32
33	21.545 147	23.225 154	25.031 896	26.974 610	29.063 188	31.308 214	33
34	23.645 798	25.547 670	27.597 665	29.806 944	32.187 481	34.752 118	34
35	25.951 264	28.102 437	30.426 426	32.936 673	35.647 635	38.574 851	35
36	28.481 512	30.912 681	33.545 134	36.395 024	39.479 756	42.818 085	36
37	31.258 459	34.003 949	36.983 510	40.216 501	43.723 829	47.528 074	37
38	34.306 159	37.404 343	40.774 320	44.439 234	48.424 141	52.756 162	38
39	37.651 010	41.144 778	44.953 688	49.105 354	53.629 736	58.559 340	39
40	41.321 983	45.259 256	49.561 441	54.261 416	59.394 933	65.000 867	40
41	45.350 877	49.785 181	54.641 489	59.958 864	65.779 888	72.150 963	41
42	49.772 587	54.763 699	60.242 241	66.254 545	72.851 226	80.087 569	42
43	54.625 414	60.240 069	66.417 071	73.211 272	80.682 733	88.897 201	43
44	59.951 392	66.264 076	73.224 821	80.898 456	89.356 127	98.675 893	44
45	65.796 653	72.890 484	80.730 365	89.392 794	98.961 910	109.530 242	45
46	72.211 827	80.179 532	89.005 227	98.779 037	109.600 316	121.578 568	46
47	79.252 480	88.197 485	98.128 263	109.150 836	121.382 350	134.952 211	47
48	86.979 596	97.017 234	108.186 410	120.611 674	134.430 952	149.796 954	48
49	95.460 107	106.718 957	119.275 517	133.275 900	148.882 280	166.274 619	49
50	104.767 467	117.390 853	131.501 258	147.269 869	164.887 125	184.564 827	50

SECTION 1

YRS	11.25% ANNUAL RATE	11.50% ANNUAL RATE	11.75% ANNUAL RATE	12.00% ANNUAL RATE	12.25% ANNUAL RATE	12.50% ANNUAL RATE	YRS
1	1.112 500	1.115 000	1.117 500	1.120 000	1.122 500	1.125 000	1
2	1.237 656	1.243 225	1.248 806	1.254 400	1.260 006	1.265 625	2
3	1.376 893	1.386 196	1.395 541	1.404 928	1.414 357	1.423 828	3
4	1.531 793	1.545 608	1.559 517	1.573 519	1.587 616	1.601 807	4
5	1.704 120	1.723 353	1.742 760	1.762 342	1.782 099	1.802 032	5
6	1.895 833	1.921 539	1.947 535	1.973 823	2.000 406	2.027 287	6
7	2.109 114	2.142 516	2.176 370	2.210 681	2.245 455	2.280 697	7
8	2.346 390	2.388 905	2.432 093	2.475 963	2.520 524	2.565 785	8
9	2.610 359	2.663 629	2.717 864	2.773 079	2.829 288	2.886 508	9
10	2.904 024	2.969 947	3.037 213	3.105 848	3.175 876	3.247 321	10
11	3.230 727	3.311 491	3.394 086	3.478 550	3.564 920	3.653 236	11
12	3.594 183	3.692 312	3.792 891	3.895 976	4.001 623	4.109 891	12
13	3.998 529	4.116 928	4.238 556	4.363 493	4.491 822	4.623 627	13
14	4.448 364	4.590 375	4.736 586	4.887 112	5.042 070	5.201 580	14
15	4.948 804	5.118 268	5.293 135	5.473 566	5.659 724	5.851 778	15
16	5.505 545	5.706 869	5.915 078	6.130 394	6.353 040	6.583 250	16
17	6.124 919	6.363 159	6.610 100	6.866 041	7.131 287	7.406 156	17
18	6.813 972	7.094 922	7.386 787	7.689 966	8.004 870	8.331 926	18
19	7.580 544	7.910 838	8.254 734	8.612 762	8.985 467	9.373 417	19
20	8.433 355	8.820 584	9.224 666	9.646 293	10.086 186	10.545 094	20
21	9.382 108	9.834 951	10.308 564	10.803 848	11.321 744	11.863 231	21
22	10.437 595	10.965 971	11.519 820	12.100 310	12.708 658	13.346 134	22
23	11.611 824	12.227 057	12.873 399	13.552 347	14.265 469	15.014 401	23
24	12.918 154	13.633 169	14.386 023	15.178 629	16.012 989	16.891 201	24
25	14.371 447	15.200 983	16.076 381	17.000 064	17.974 580	19.002 602	25
26	15.988 235	16.949 096	17.965 356	19.040 072	20.176 466	21.377 927	26
27	17.786 911	18.898 243	20.076 285	21.324 881	22.648 083	24.050 168	27
28	19.787 938	21.071 540	22.435 249	23.883 866	25.422 473	27.056 438	28
29	22.014 081	23.494 768	25.071 391	26.749 930	28.536 726	30.438 493	29
30	24.490 666	26.196 666	28.017 279	29.959 922	32.032 475	34.243 305	30
31	27.245 866	29.209 282	31.309 309	33.555 113	35.956 453	38.523 718	31
32	30.311 025	32.568 350	34.988 153	37.581 726	40.361 118	43.339 183	32
33	33.721 016	36.313 710	39.099 261	42.091 533	45.305 355	48.756 581	33
34	37.514 630	40.489 787	43.693 424	47.142 517	50.855 261	54.851 153	34
35	41.735 026	45.146 112	48.827 402	52.799 620	57.085 031	61.707 547	35
36	46.430 216	50.337 915	54.564 621	59.135 574	64.077 947	69.420 991	36
37	51.653 616	56.126 776	60.975 964	66.231 843	71.927 495	78.098 615	37
38	57.464 647	62.581 355	68.140 640	74.179 664	80.738 614	87.860 942	38
39	63.929 420	69.778 211	76.147 165	83.081 224	90.629 094	98.843 559	39
40	71.121 480	77.802 705	85.094 457	93.050 970	101.731 158	111.199 004	40
41	79.122 647	86.750 016	95.093 056	104.217 087	114.193 225	125.098 880	41
42	88.023 944	96.726 268	106.266 490	116.723 137	128.181 895	140.736 240	42
43	97.926 638	107.849 788	118.752 803	130.729 914	143.884 177	158.328 270	43
44	108.943 385	120.252 514	132.706 257	146.417 503	161.509 988	178.119 303	44
45	121.199 516	134.081 553	148.299 242	163.987 604	181.294 962	200.384 216	45
46	134.834 461	149.500 932	165.724 403	183.666 116	203.503 595	225.432 243	46
47	150.003 338	166.693 539	185.197 020	205.706 050	228.432 785	253.611 274	47
48	166.878 714	185.863 296	206.957 670	230.390 776	256.415 801	285.312 683	48
49	185.652 569	207.237 575	231.275 196	258.037 669	287.826 737	320.976 768	49
50	206.538 483	231.069 896	258.450 032	289.002 190	323.085 512	361.098 864	50

FUTURE VALUE

ANNUAL COMPOUNDING

YRS	12.75% ANNUAL RATE	13.00% ANNUAL RATE	13.25% ANNUAL RATE	13.50% ANNUAL RATE	13.75% ANNUAL RATE	14.00% ANNUAL RATE	YRS
1	1.127 500	1.130 000	1.132 500	1.135 000	1.137 500	1.140 000	1
2	1.271 256	1.276 900	1.282 556	1.288 225	1.293 906	1.299 600	2
3	1.433 341	1.442 897	1.452 495	1.462 135	1.471 818	1.481 544	3
4	1.616 092	1.630 474	1.644 951	1.659 524	1.674 193	1.688 960	4
5	1.822 144	1.842 435	1.862 906	1.883 559	1.904 395	1.925 415	5
6	2.054 468	2.081 952	2.109 742	2.137 840	2.166 249	2.194 973	6
7	2.316 412	2.352 605	2.389 282	2.426 448	2.464 109	2.502 269	7
8	2.611 755	2.658 444	2.705 862	2.754 019	2.802 923	2.852 586	8
9	2.944 754	3.004 042	3.064 389	3.125 811	3.188 325	3.251 949	9
10	3.320 210	3.394 567	3.470 421	3.547 796	3.626 720	3.707 221	10
11	3.743 536	3.835 861	3.930 251	4.026 748	4.125 394	4.226 232	11
12	4.220 837	4.334 523	4.451 010	4.570 359	4.692 636	4.817 905	12
13	4.758 994	4.898 011	5.040 768	5.187 358	5.337 873	5.492 411	13
14	5.365 766	5.534 753	5.708 670	5.887 651	6.071 831	6.261 349	14
15	6.049 901	6.254 270	6.465 069	6.682 484	6.906 708	7.137 938	15
16	6.821 263	7.067 326	7.321 691	7.584 619	7.856 380	8.137 249	16
17	7.690 974	7.986 078	8.291 815	8.608 543	8.936 632	9.276 464	17
18	8.671 574	9.024 268	9.390 480	9.770 696	10.165 419	10.575 169	18
19	9.777 199	10.197 423	10.634 719	11.089 740	11.563 164	12.055 693	19
20	11.023 792	11.523 088	12.043 819	12.586 855	13.153 100	13.743 490	20
21	12.429 326	13.021 089	13.639 625	14.286 080	14.961 651	15.667 578	21
22	14.014 065	14.713 831	15.446 875	16.214 701	17.018 878	17.861 039	22
23	15.800 858	16.626 629	17.493 586	18.403 686	19.358 973	20.361 585	23
24	17.815 467	18.788 091	19.811 486	20.888 184	22.020 832	23.212 207	24
25	20.086 939	21.230 542	22.436 508	23.708 088	25.048 697	26.461 916	25
26	22.648 024	23.990 513	25.409 345	26.908 680	28.492 892	30.166 584	26
27	25.535 647	27.109 279	28.776 084	30.541 352	32.410 665	34.389 906	27
28	28.791 442	30.633 486	32.588 915	34.664 435	36.867 132	39.204 493	28
29	32.462 351	34.615 839	36.906 946	39.344 133	41.936 362	44.693 122	29
30	36.601 300	39.115 898	41.797 116	44.655 591	47.702 612	50.950 159	30
31	41.267 966	44.200 965	47.335 234	50.684 096	54.261 721	58.083 181	31
32	46.529 632	49.947 090	53.607 153	57.526 449	61.722 708	66.214 826	32
33	52.462 160	56.440 212	60.710 101	65.292 520	70.209 580	75.484 902	33
34	59.151 085	63.777 439	68.754 189	74.107 010	79.863 397	86.052 788	34
35	66.692 849	72.068 506	77.864 119	84.111 457	90.844 615	98.100 178	35
36	75.196 187	81.437 412	88.181 115	95.466 503	103.335 749	111.834 203	36
37	84.783 701	92.024 276	99.865 112	108.354 481	117.544 415	127.490 992	37
38	95.593 623	103.987 432	113.097 240	122.982 336	133.706 772	145.339 731	38
39	107.781 810	117.505 798	128.082 624	139.584 951	152.091 453	165.687 293	39
40	121.523 990	132.781 552	145.053 572	158.428 920	173.004 027	188.883 514	40
41	137.018 299	150.043 153	164.273 170	179.816 824	196.792 081	215.327 206	41
42	154.488 132	169.548 763	186.039 365	204.092 095	223.850 992	245.473 015	42
43	174.185 369	191.590 103	210.689 581	231.644 528	254.630 504	279.839 237	43
44	196.394 004	216.496 816	238.605 950	262.916 539	289.642 198	319.016 730	44
45	221.434 239	244.641 402	270.221 239	298.410 272	329.468 000	363.679 072	45
46	249.667 105	276.444 784	306.025 553	338.695 659	374.769 850	414.594 142	46
47	281.499 661	312.382 606	346.573 939	384.419 573	426.300 705	472.637 322	47
48	317.390 868	352.992 345	392.494 986	436.316 215	484.917 051	538.806 547	48
49	357.858 203	398.881 350	444.500 571	495.218 904	551.593 146	614.239 464	49
50	403.485 124	450.735 925	503.396 897	562.073 456	627.437 204	700.232 988	50

YRS	14.25% ANNUAL RATE	14.50% ANNUAL RATE	14.75% ANNUAL RATE	15.00% ANNUAL RATE	15.25% ANNUAL RATE	15.50% ANNUAL RATE	YRS
1	1.142 500	1.145 000	1.147 500	1.150 000	1.152 500	1.155 000	1
2	1.305 306	1.311 025	1.316 756	1.322 500	1.328 256	1.334 025	2
3	1.491 312	1.501 124	1.510 978	1.520 875	1.530 815	1.540 799	3
4	1.703 824	1.718 787	1.733 847	1.749 006	1.764 265	1.779 623	4
5	1.946 619	1.968 011	1.989 589	2.011 357	2.033 315	2.055 464	5
6	2.224 013	2.253 372	2.283 054	2.313 061	2.343 396	2.374 061	6
7	2.540 934	2.580 111	2.619 804	2.660 020	2.700 763	2.742 041	7
8	2.903 018	2.954 227	3.006 225	3.059 023	3.112 630	3.167 057	8
9	3.316 698	3.382 590	3.449 644	3.517 876	3.587 306	3.657 951	9
10	3.789 327	3.873 066	3.958 466	4.045 558	4.134 370	4.224 933	10
11	4.329 306	4.434 660	4.542 340	4.652 391	4.764 861	4.879 798	11
12	4.946 232	5.077 686	5.212 335	5.350 250	5.491 503	5.636 166	12
13	5.651 070	5.813 950	5.981 155	6.152 788	6.328 957	6.509 772	13
14	6.456 348	6.656 973	6.863 375	7.075 706	7.294 123	7.518 787	14
15	7.376 377	7.622 234	7.875 723	8.137 062	8.406 477	8.684 199	15
16	8.427 511	8.727 458	9.037 392	9.357 621	9.688 464	10.030 250	16
17	9.628 432	9.992 940	10.370 407	10.761 264	11.165 955	11.584 938	17
18	11.000 483	11.441 916	11.900 042	12.375 454	12.868 763	13.380 604	18
19	12.568 052	13.100 994	13.655 298	14.231 772	14.831 250	15.454 598	19
20	14.358 999	15.000 638	15.669 455	16.366 537	17.093 015	17.850 060	20
21	16.405 157	17.175 731	17.980 699	18.821 518	19.699 700	20.616 820	21
22	18.742 892	19.666 212	20.632 852	21.644 746	22.703 904	23.812 427	22
23	21.413 754	22.517 812	23.676 198	24.891 458	26.166 250	27.503 353	23
24	24.465 213	25.782 895	27.168 437	28.625 176	30.156 603	31.766 372	24
25	27.951 506	29.521 415	31.175 782	32.918 953	34.755 485	36.690 160	25
26	31.934 596	33.802 020	35.774 210	37.856 796	40.055 696	42.377 135	26
27	36.485 276	38.703 313	41.050 906	43.535 315	46.164 190	48.945 591	27
28	41.684 428	44.315 293	47.105 914	50.065 612	53.204 229	56.532 157	28
29	47.624 459	50.741 011	54.054 037	57.575 454	61.317 874	65.294 642	29
30	54.410 944	58.098 457	62.027 007	66.211 772	70.668 850	75.415 311	30
31	62.164 504	66.522 734	71.175 991	76.143 538	81.445 849	87.104 684	31
32	71.022 946	76.168 530	81.674 449	87.565 068	93.866 341	100.605 910	32
33	81.143 715	87.212 967	93.721 431	100.699 829	108.180 958	116.199 826	33
34	92.706 695	99.858 847	107.545 342	115.804 803	124.678 554	134.210 800	34
35	105.917 399	114.338 380	123.408 279	133.175 523	143.692 034	155.013 474	35
36	121.010 628	130.917 445	141.611 001	153.151 852	165.605 069	179.040 562	36
37	138.254 642	149.900 474	162.498 623	176.124 630	190.859 842	206.791 849	37
38	157.955 929	171.636 043	186.467 170	202.543 324	219.965 968	238.844 586	38
39	180.464 649	196.523 269	213.971 078	232.924 823	253.510 778	275.865 496	39
40	206.180 861	225.019 143	245.531 812	267.863 546	292.171 172	318.624 648	40
41	235.561 634	257.646 919	281.747 754	308.043 078	336.727 276	368.011 469	41
42	269.129 167	295.005 722	323.305 548	354.249 540	388.078 185	425.053 246	42
43	307.480 073	337.781 552	370.993 116	407.386 971	447.260 108	490.936 500	43
44	351.295 984	386.759 877	425.714 601	468.495 017	515.467 275	567.031 657	44
45	401.355 661	442.840 059	488.507 504	538.769 269	594.076 034	654.921 564	45
46	458.548 843	507.051 868	560.562 361	619.584 659	684.672 629	756.434 406	46
47	523.892 053	580.574 389	643.245 309	712.522 358	789.085 205	873.681 739	47
48	598.546 671	664.757 675	738.123 992	819.400 712	909.420 699	1009.102 409	48
49	683.839 572	761.147 538	846.997 281	942.310 819	1048.107 356	1165.513 282	49
50	781.286 710	871.513 931	971.929 380	1083.657 442	1207.943 728	1346.167 841	50

FUTURE VALUE

YRS	15.75% ANNUAL RATE	16.00% ANNUAL RATE	16.25% ANNUAL RATE	16.50% ANNUAL RATE	16.75% ANNUAL RATE	17.00% ANNUAL RATE	YRS
1	1.157 500	1.160 000	1.162 500	1.165 000	1.167 500	1.170 000	1
2	1.339 806	1.345 600	1.351 406	1.357 225	1.363 056	1.368 900	2
3	1.550 826	1.560 896	1.571 010	1.581 167	1.591 368	1.601 613	3
4	1.795 081	1.810 639	1.826 299	1.842 060	1.857 922	1.873 887	4
5	2.077 806	2.100 342	2.123 072	2.146 000	2.169 124	2.192 448	5
6	2.405 060	2.436 396	2.468 072	2.500 089	2.532 453	2.565 164	6
7	2.783 857	2.826 220	2.869 133	2.912 604	2.956 638	3.001 242	7
8	3.222 315	3.278 415	3.335 367	3.393 184	3.451 875	3.511 453	8
9	3.729 830	3.802 961	3.877 365	3.953 059	4.030 065	4.108 400	9
10	4.317 278	4.411 435	4.507 436	4.605 314	4.705 100	4.806 828	10
11	4.997 249	5.117 265	5.239 895	5.365 191	5.493 205	5.623 989	11
12	5.784 316	5.936 027	6.091 378	6.250 447	6.413 316	6.580 067	12
13	6.695 346	6.885 791	7.081 227	7.281 771	7.487 547	7.698 679	13
14	7.749 862	7.987 518	8.231 926	8.483 263	8.741 711	9.007 454	14
15	8.970 466	9.265 521	9.569 614	9.883 002	10.205 948	10.538 721	15
16	10.383 314	10.748 004	11.124 676	11.513 697	11.915 444	12.330 304	16
17	12.018 686	12.467 685	12.932 436	13.413 457	13.911 281	14.426 456	17
18	13.911 629	14.462 514	15.033 957	15.626 678	16.241 420	16.878 953	18
19	16.102 711	16.776 517	17.476 975	18.205 080	18.961 858	19.748 375	19
20	18.638 888	19.460 759	20.316 984	21.208 918	22.137 969	23.105 599	20
21	21.574 513	22.574 481	23.618 494	24.708 389	25.846 079	27.033 551	21
22	24.972 498	26.186 398	27.456 499	28.785 273	30.175 298	31.629 255	22
23	28.905 667	30.376 222	31.918 180	33.534 843	35.229 660	37.006 228	23
24	33.458 309	35.236 417	37.104 884	39.068 093	41.130 628	43.297 287	24
25	38.727 993	40.874 244	43.134 428	45.514 328	48.020 008	50.657 826	25
26	44.827 652	47.414 123	50.143 772	53.024 192	56.063 360	59.269 656	26
27	51.888 007	55.000 382	58.292 135	61.773 184	65.453 972	69.345 497	27
28	60.060 368	63.800 444	67.764 607	71.965 759	76.417 513	81.134 232	28
29	69.519 876	74.008 515	78.776 356	83.840 109	89.217 446	94.927 051	29
30	80.469 257	85.849 877	91.577 513	97.673 727	104.161 369	111.064 650	30
31	93.143 165	99.585 857	106.458 859	113.789 892	121.608 398	129.945 641	31
32	107.813 213	115.519 594	123.758 424	132.565 224	141.977 804	152.036 399	32
33	124.793 794	134.002 729	143.869 168	154.438 487	165.759 087	177.882 587	33
34	144.448 817	155.443 166	167.247 908	179.920 837	193.523 734	208.122 627	34
35	167.199 506	180.314 073	194.425 693	209.607 775	225.938 959	243.503 474	35
36	193.533 428	209.164 324	226.019 868	244.193 058	263.783 735	284.899 064	36
37	224.014 943	242.630 616	262.748 096	284.484 912	307.967 510	333.331 905	37
38	259.297 296	281.451 515	305.444 662	331.424 923	359.552 068	389.998 329	38
39	300.136 620	326.483 757	355.079 419	386.110 035	419.777 039	456.298 045	39
40	347.408 138	378.721 158	412.779 825	449.818 191	490.089 694	533.868 713	40
41	402.124 920	439.316 544	479.856 546	524.038 192	572.179 717	624.626 394	41
42	465.459 595	509.607 191	557.833 235	610.504 494	668.019 820	730.812 881	42
43	538.769 481	591.144 341	648.481 136	711.237 736	779.913 140	855.051 071	43
44	623.625 674	685.727 436	753.859 321	828.591 962	910.548 591	1000.409 753	44
45	721.846 718	795.443 826	876.361 460	965.309 636	1063.065 480	1170.479 411	45
46	835.537 576	922.714 838	1018.770 197	1124.585 725	1241.128 947	1369.460 910	46
47	967.134 744	1070.349 212	1184.320 355	1310.142 370	1449.018 046	1602.269 265	47
48	1119.458 466	1241.605 086	1376.772 412	1526.315 861	1691.728 569	1874.655 040	48
49	1295.773 175	1440.261 900	1600.497 929	1778.157 978	1975.093 104	2193.346 397	49
50	1499.857 450	1670.703 804	1860.578 843	2071.554 045	2305.921 199	2566.215 284	50

FUTURE VALUE

ANNUAL COMPOUNDING

YRS	17.25% ANNUAL RATE	17.50% ANNUAL RATE	17.75% ANNUAL RATE	18.00% ANNUAL RATE	18.25% ANNUAL RATE	18.50% ANNUAL RATE	YRS
1	1.172 500	1.175 000	1.177 500	1.180 000	1.182 500	1.185 000	1
2	1.374 756	1.380 625	1.386 506	1.392 400	1.398 306	1.404 225	2
3	1.611 902	1.622 234	1.632 611	1.643 032	1.653 497	1.664 007	3
4	1.889 955	1.906 125	1.922 400	1.938 778	1.955 260	1.971 848	4
5	2.215 972	2.239 697	2.263 626	2.287 758	2.312 095	2.336 640	5
6	2.598 227	2.631 644	2.665 419	2.699 554	2.734 053	2.768 918	6
7	3.046 421	3.092 182	3.138 531	3.185 474	3.233 017	3.281 168	7
8	3.571 929	3.633 314	3.695 620	3.758 859	3.823 043	3.888 184	8
9	4.188 087	4.269 144	4.351 593	4.435 454	4.520 748	4.607 498	9
10	4.910 532	5.016 244	5.124 000	5.233 836	5.345 785	5.459 885	10
11	5.757 598	5.894 087	6.033 511	6.175 926	6.321 391	6.469 964	11
12	6.750 784	6.925 552	7.104 459	7.287 593	7.475 045	7.666 907	12
13	7.915 294	8.137 524	8.365 500	8.599 359	8.839 240	9.085 285	13
14	9.280 683	9.561 590	9.850 376	10.147 244	10.452 402	10.766 063	14
15	10.881 600	11.234 869	11.598 818	11.973 748	12.359 965	12.757 784	15
16	12.758 676	13.200 971	13.657 608	14.129 023	14.615 659	15.117 974	16
17	14.959 548	15.511 141	16.081 834	16.672 247	17.283 016	17.914 800	17
18	17.540 070	18.225 590	18.936 359	19.673 251	20.437 167	21.229 038	18
19	20.565 732	21.415 068	22.297 563	23.214 436	24.166 950	25.156 410	19
20	24.113 321	25.162 705	26.255 380	27.393 035	28.577 418	29.810 345	20
21	28.272 869	29.566 179	30.915 710	32.323 781	33.792 797	35.325 259	21
22	33.149 939	34.740 260	36.403 249	38.142 061	39.959 982	41.860 432	22
23	38.868 303	40.819 806	42.864 826	45.007 632	47.252 679	49.604 612	23
24	45.573 086	47.963 272	50.473 332	53.109 006	55.876 293	58.781 465	24
25	53.434 443	56.356 844	59.432 349	62.668 627	66.073 716	69.656 036	25
26	62.651 884	66.219 292	69.981 591	73.948 980	78.132 170	82.542 403	26
27	73.459 334	77.807 668	82.403 323	87.259 797	92.391 291	97.812 748	27
28	86.131 069	91.424 010	97.029 913	102.966 560	109.252 701	115.908 106	28
29	100.988 679	107.423 211	114.252 723	121.500 541	129.191 319	137.351 106	29
30	118.409 226	126.222 273	134.532 581	143.370 638	152.768 735	162.761 060	30
31	138.834 817	148.311 171	158.412 114	169.177 353	180.649 029	192.871 856	31
32	162.783 823	174.265 626	186.530 264	199.629 277	213.617 477	228.553 150	32
33	190.864 033	204.762 111	219.639 386	235.562 547	252.602 666	270.835 483	33
34	223.788 078	240.595 480	258.625 377	277.963 805	298.702 653	320.940 047	34
35	262.391 522	282.699 689	304.531 382	327.997 290	353.215 887	380.313 956	35
36	307.654 059	332.172 135	358.585 702	387.036 802	417.677 787	450.672 037	36
37	360.724 385	390.302 259	422.234 664	456.703 427	493.903 983	534.046 364	37
38	422.949 341	458.605 154	497.181 317	538.910 044	584.041 459	632.844 942	38
39	495.908 102	538.861 056	585.431 001	635.913 852	690.629 026	749.921 256	39
40	581.452 250	633.161 741	689.345 003	750.378 345	816.668 823	888.656 688	40
41	681.752 763	743.965 045	811.703 742	885.446 447	965.710 883	1053.058 176	41
42	799.355 115	874.158 928	955.781 156	1044.826 807	1141.953 119	1247.873 938	42
43	937.243 872	1027.136 740	1125.432 311	1232.895 633	1350.359 564	1478.730 617	43
44	1098.918 440	1206.885 670	1325.196 546	1454.816 847	1596.800 184	1752.295 781	44
45	1288.481 871	1418.090 662	1560.418 933	1716.683 879	1888.216 218	2076.470 500	45
46	1510.744 994	1666.256 528	1837.393 293	2025.686 977	2232.815 678	2460.617 543	46
47	1771.348 505	1957.851 421	2163.530 603	2390.310 633	2640.304 539	2915.831 788	47
48	2076.906 122	2300.475 419	2547.557 285	2820.566 547	3122.160 117	3455.260 669	48
49	2435.172 429	2703.058 610	2999.748 703	3328.268 525	3691.954 338	4094.483 893	49
50	2855.239 673	3176.093 866	3532.204 098	3927.356 860	4365.736 005	4851.963 413	50

FUTURE VALUE

ANNUAL COMPOUNDING

YRS	18.75% ANNUAL RATE	19.00% ANNUAL RATE	19.25% ANNUAL RATE	19.50% ANNUAL RATE	19.75% ANNUAL RATE	20.00% ANNUAL RATE	YRS
1	1.187 500	1.190 000	1.192 500	1.195 000	1.197 500	1.200 000	1
2	1.410 156	1.416 100	1.422 056	1.428 025	1.434 006	1.440 000	2
3	1.674 561	1.685 159	1.695 802	1.706 490	1.717 222	1.728 000	3
4	1.988 541	2.005 339	2.022 244	2.039 255	2.056 374	2.073 600	4
5	2.361 392	2.386 354	2.411 526	2.436 910	2.462 508	2.488 320	5
6	2.804 153	2.839 761	2.875 745	2.912 108	2.948 853	2.985 984	6
7	3.329 932	3.379 315	3.429 326	3.479 969	3.531 252	3.583 181	7
8	3.954 294	4.021 385	4.089 471	4.158 563	4.228 674	4.299 817	8
9	4.695 724	4.785 449	4.876 694	4.969 482	5.063 837	5.159 780	9
10	5.576 172	5.694 684	5.815 457	5.938 531	6.063 945	6.191 736	10
11	6.621 705	6.776 674	6.934 933	7.096 545	7.261 574	7.430 084	11
12	7.863 274	8.064 242	8.269 908	8.480 371	8.695 734	8.916 100	12
13	9.337 638	9.596 448	9.861 865	10.134 044	10.413 142	10.699 321	13
14	11.088 445	11.419 773	11.760 274	12.110 182	12.469 737	12.839 185	14
15	13.167 529	13.589 530	14.024 126	14.471 668	14.932 511	15.407 022	15
16	15.636 440	16.171 540	16.723 771	17.293 643	17.881 681	18.488 426	16
17	18.568 273	19.244 133	19.943 097	20.665 903	21.413 314	22.186 111	17
18	22.049 824	22.900 518	23.782 143	24.695 754	25.642 443	26.623 333	18
19	26.184 166	27.251 616	28.360 205	29.511 426	30.706 825	31.948 000	19
20	31.093 697	32.429 423	33.819 545	35.266 154	36.771 423	38.337 600	20
21	36.923 766	38.591 014	40.329 807	42.143 055	44.033 780	46.005 120	21
22	43.846 972	45.923 307	48.093 295	50.360 950	52.730 451	55.206 144	22
23	52.068 279	54.648 735	57.351 254	60.181 336	63.144 715	66.247 373	23
24	61.831 081	65.031 994	68.391 370	71.916 696	75.615 796	79.496 847	24
25	73.424 409	77.388 073	81.556 709	85.940 452	90.549 916	95.396 217	25
26	87.191 485	92.091 807	97.256 376	102.698 840	108.433 525	114.475 460	26
27	103.539 889	109.589 251	115.978 228	122.725 114	129.849 146	137.370 552	27
28	122.953 618	130.411 208	138.304 037	146.656 511	155.494 352	164.844 662	28
29	146.007 421	155.189 338	164.927 564	175.254 530	186.204 486	197.813 595	29
30	173.383 813	184.675 312	196.676 120	209.429 164	222.979 872	237.376 314	30
31	205.893 278	219.763 621	234.536 273	250.267 851	267.018 397	284.851 577	31
32	244.498 267	261.518 710	279.684 505	299.070 082	319.754 531	341.821 892	32
33	290.341 692	311.207 264	333.523 773	357.388 747	382.906 050	410.186 270	33
34	344.780 760	370.336 645	397.727 099	427.079 553	458.529 995	492.223 524	34
35	409.427 152	440.700 607	474.289 565	510.360 066	549.089 670	590.668 229	35
36	486.194 743	524.433 722	565.590 307	609.880 279	657.534 879	708.801 875	36
37	577.356 257	624.076 130	674.466 441	728.806 933	787.398 018	850.562 250	37
38	685.610 556	742.650 594	804.301 230	870.924 285	942.909 126	1020.674 700	38
39	814.162 535	883.754 207	959.129 217	1040.754 521	1129.133 679	1224.809 640	39
40	966.818 010	1051.667 507	1143.761 592	1243.701 652	1352.137 580	1469.771 568	40
41	1148.096 387	1251.484 333	1363.935 698	1486.223 475	1619.184 753	1763.725 882	41
42	1363.364 459	1489.266 356	1626.493 320	1776.037 052	1938.973 741	2116.471 058	42
43	1618.995 295	1772.226 964	1939.593 284	2122.364 277	2321.921 055	2539.765 269	43
44	1922.556 913	2108.950 087	2312.964 991	2536.225 312	2780.500 464	3047.718 323	44
45	2283.036 335	2509.650 603	2758.210 752	3030.789 247	3329.649 305	3657.261 988	45
46	2711.105 647	2986.484 218	3289.166 321	3621.793 151	3987.255 043	4388.714 386	46
47	3219.437 956	3553.916 219	3922.330 838	4328.042 815	4774.737 914	5266.457 263	47
48	3823.082 573	4229.160 301	4677.379 525	5172.011 164	5717.748 652	6319.748 715	48
49	4539.910 555	5032.700 758	5577.775 083	6180.553 341	6847.004 010	7583.698 458	49
50	5391.143 785	5988.913 902	6651.496 787	7385.761 242	8199.287 303	9100.438 150	50

FUTURE VALUE

ANNUAL COMPOUNDING

YRS	20.25% ANNUAL RATE	20.50% ANNUAL RATE	20.75% ANNUAL RATE	21.00% ANNUAL RATE	21.25% ANNUAL RATE	21.50% ANNUAL RATE	YRS
1	1.202 500	1.205 000	1.207 500	1.210 000	1.212 500	1.215 000	1
2	1.446 006	1.452 025	1.458 056	1.464 100	1.470 156	1.476 225	2
3	1.738 823	1.749 690	1.760 603	1.771 561	1.782 564	1.793 613	3
4	2.090 934	2.108 377	2.125 928	2.143 589	2.161 359	2.179 240	4
5	2.514 348	2.540 594	2.567 058	2.593 742	2.620 648	2.647 777	5
6	3.023 504	3.061 416	3.099 723	3.138 428	3.177 536	3.217 049	6
7	3.635 763	3.689 006	3.742 915	3.797 498	3.852 762	3.908 714	7
8	4.372 005	4.445 252	4.519 570	4.594 973	4.671 474	4.749 088	8
9	5.257 336	5.356 529	5.457 381	5.559 917	5.664 163	5.770 142	9
10	6.321 947	6.454 617	6.589 787	6.727 500	6.867 797	7.010 723	10
11	7.602 141	7.777 813	7.957 168	8.140 275	8.327 204	8.518 028	11
12	9.141 575	9.372 265	9.608 280	9.849 733	10.096 735	10.349 404	12
13	10.992 744	11.293 579	11.601 999	11.918 177	12.242 291	12.574 526	13
14	13.218 774	13.608 763	14.009 413	14.420 994	14.843 778	15.278 049	14
15	15.895 576	16.398 560	16.916 367	17.449 402	17.998 081	18.562 829	15
16	19.114 430	19.760 264	20.426 513	21.113 777	21.822 674	22.553 837	16
17	22.985 103	23.811 119	24.665 014	25.547 670	26.459 992	27.402 913	17
18	27.639 586	28.692 398	29.783 005	30.912 681	32.082 740	33.294 539	18
19	33.236 602	34.574 339	35.962 978	37.404 343	38.900 322	40.452 865	19
20	39.967 014	41.662 079	43.425 296	45.259 256	47.166 641	49.150 230	20
21	48.060 334	50.202 805	52.436 045	54.763 699	57.189 552	59.717 530	21
22	57.792 552	60.494 380	63.316 524	66.264 076	69.342 332	72.556 799	22
23	69.495 544	72.895 728	76.454 703	80.179 532	84.077 577	88.156 511	23
24	83.568 391	87.839 353	92.319 054	97.017 234	101.944 062	107.110 161	24
25	100.490 990	105.846 420	111.475 258	117.390 853	123.607 175	130.138 845	25
26	120.840 416	127.544 936	134.606 374	142.042 932	149.873 700	158.118 697	26
27	145.310 600	153.691 648	162.537 196	171.871 948	181.721 861	192.114 217	27
28	174.735 997	185.198 435	196.263 665	207.965 057	220.337 757	233.418 773	28
29	210.120 036	223.164 115	236.988 375	251.637 719	267.159 530	283.603 809	29
30	252.669 343	268.912 758	286.163 463	304.481 640	323.930 930	344.578 628	30
31	303.834 885	324.039 874	345.542 382	368.422 784	392.766 253	418.663 034	31
32	365.361 449	390.468 048	417.242 426	445.791 568	476.229 082	508.675 586	32
33	439.347 143	470.513 998	503.820 229	539.407 798	577.427 762	618.040 837	33
34	528.314 939	566.969 367	608.362 927	652.683 435	700.131 161	750.919 617	34
35	635.298 715	683.198 087	734.598 234	789.746 957	848.909 033	912.367 334	35
36	763.946 704	823.253 695	887.027 367	955.593 818	1029.302 202	1108.526 311	36
37	918.645 912	992.020 703	1071.085 546	1156.268 519	1248.028 920	1346.859 468	37
38	1104.671 709	1195.384 947	1293.335 797	1399.084 909	1513.235 065	1636.434 254	38
39	1328.367 730	1440.438 861	1561.702 975	1692.892 739	1834.797 517	1988.267 618	39
40	1597.362 195	1735.728 828	1885.756 342	2048.400 215	2224.691 989	2415.745 156	40
41	1920.828 040	2091.553 237	2277.050 783	2478.564 260	2697.439 037	2935.130 365	41
42	2309.795 718	2520.321 651	2749.538 820	2999.062 754	3270.644 832	3566.183 393	42
43	2777.529 351	3036.987 589	3320.068 125	3628.865 933	3965.656 859	4332.912 822	43
44	3339.979 045	3659.570 045	4008.982 261	4390.927 778	4808.358 942	5264.489 079	44
45	4016.324 801	4409.781 904	4840.846 081	5313.022 612	5830.135 217	6396.354 231	45
46	4829.630 573	5313.787 195	5845.321 643	6428.757 360	7069.038 950	7771.570 391	46
47	5807.630 765	6403.113 570	7058.225 883	7778.796 406	8571.209 727	9442.458 025	47
48	6983.675 994	7715.751 851	8522.807 754	9412.343 651	10392.591 794	11472.586 500	48
49	8397.870 383	9297.480 981	10291.290 363	11388.935 818	12601.017 550	13939.192 598	49
50	10098.439 136	11203.464 582	12426.733 113	13780.612 340	15278.733 780	16936.119 006	50

FUTURE VALUE

YRS	21.75% ANNUAL RATE	22.00% ANNUAL RATE	22.50% ANNUAL RATE	23.00% ANNUAL RATE	23.50% ANNUAL RATE	24.00% ANNUAL RATE	YRS
1	1.217 500	1.220 000	1.225 000	1.230 000	1.235 000	1.240 000	1
2	1.482 306	1.488 400	1.500 625	1.512 900	1.525 225	1.537 600	2
3	1.804 708	1.815 848	1.838 266	1.860 867	1.883 653	1.906 624	3
4	2.197 232	2.215 335	2.251 875	2.288 866	2.326 311	2.364 214	4
5	2.675 130	2.702 708	2.758 547	2.815 306	2.872 994	2.931 625	5
6	3.256 970	3.297 304	3.379 221	3.462 826	3.548 148	3.635 215	6
7	3.965 362	4.022 711	4.139 545	4.259 276	4.381 963	4.507 667	7
8	4.827 828	4.907 707	5.070 943	5.238 909	5.411 724	5.589 507	8
9	5.877 880	5.987 403	6.211 905	6.443 859	6.683 479	6.930 988	9
10	7.156 319	7.304 631	7.609 584	7.925 946	8.254 097	8.594 426	10
11	8.712 819	8.911 650	9.321 740	9.748 914	10.193 810	10.657 088	11
12	10.607 857	10.872 213	11.419 131	11.991 164	12.589 355	13.214 789	12
13	12.915 065	13.264 100	13.988 436	14.749 132	15.547 854	16.386 338	13
14	15.724 092	16.182 202	17.135 834	18.141 432	19.201 599	20.319 059	14
15	19.144 082	19.742 287	20.991 396	22.313 961	23.713 975	25.195 633	15
16	23.307 920	24.085 590	25.714 461	27.446 172	29.286 760	31.242 585	16
17	28.377 393	29.384 420	31.500 214	33.758 792	36.169 148	38.740 806	17
18	34.549 475	35.848 992	38.587 762	41.523 314	44.668 898	48.038 599	18
19	42.063 986	43.735 771	47.270 009	51.073 676	55.166 089	59.567 863	19
20	51.212 903	53.357 640	57.905 761	62.820 622	68.130 120	73.864 150	20
21	62.351 710	65.096 321	70.934 557	77.269 364	84.140 698	91.591 546	21
22	75.913 207	79.417 512	86.894 833	95.041 318	103.913 762	113.573 517	22
23	92.424 329	96.889 364	106.446 170	116.900 822	128.333 496	140.831 161	23
24	112.526 621	118.205 024	130.396 558	143.788 010	158.491 867	174.630 639	24
25	137.001 161	144.210 130	159.735 784	176.859 253	195.737 456	216.541 993	25
26	166.798 913	175.936 358	195.676 335	217.536 881	241.735 758	268.512 071	26
27	203.077 677	214.642 357	239.703 511	267.570 364	298.543 662	332.954 968	27
28	247.247 072	261.863 675	293.636 801	329.111 547	368.701 422	412.864 160	28
29	301.023 310	319.473 684	359.705 081	404.807 203	455.346 256	511.951 559	29
30	366.495 880	389.757 894	440.638 724	497.912 860	562.352 626	634.819 933	30
31	446.208 734	475.504 631	539.782 437	612.432 818	694.505 494	787.176 717	31
32	543.259 133	580.115 650	661.233 485	753.292 366	857.714 285	976.099 129	32
33	661.417 995	707.741 093	810.011 019	926.549 610	1059.277 142	1210.362 920	33
34	805.276 409	863.444 133	992.263 499	1139.656 020	1308.207 270	1500.850 021	34
35	980.424 027	1053.401 842	1215.522 786	1401.776 905	1615.635 978	1861.054 026	35
36	1193.666 253	1285.150 248	1489.015 413	1724.185 593	1995.310 433	2307.706 992	36
37	1453.288 663	1567.883 302	1824.043 881	2120.748 279	2464.208 385	2861.556 670	37
38	1769.378 948	1912.817 629	2234.453 754	2608.520 383	3043.297 356	3548.330 270	38
39	2154.218 869	2333.637 507	2737.205 849	3208.480 071	3758.472 234	4399.929 535	39
40	2622.761 473	2847.037 759	3353.077 165	3946.430 488	4641.713 209	5455.912 624	40
41	3193.212 093	3473.386 066	4107.519 527	4854.109 500	5732.515 813	6765.331 653	41
42	3887.735 724	4237.531 000	5031.711 420	5970.554 685	7079.657 030	8389.011 250	42
43	4733.318 243	5169.787 820	6163.846 490	7343.782 263	8743.376 431	10402.373 950	43
44	5762.814 961	6307.141 140	7550.711 950	9032.852 183	10798.069 893	12898.943 698	44
45	7016.227 215	7694.712 191	9249.622 139	11110.408 185	13335.616 318	15994.690 186	45
46	8542.256 635	9387.548 873	11330.787 120	13665.802 068	16469.486 152	19833.415 831	46
47	10400.197 453	11452.809 626	13880.214 223	16808.936 543	20339.815 398	24593.435 630	47
48	12662.240 399	13972.427 743	17003.262 423	20674.991 948	25119.672 017	30495.860 181	48
49	15416.277 686	17046.361 847	20828.996 468	25430.240 096	31022.794 941	37814.866 624	49
50	18769.318 082	20796.561 453	25515.520 673	31279.195 318	38313.151 752	46890.434 614	50

SECTION 2
FUTURE VALUE
OF $1 PER PERIOD

Future value per period is the basic compound interest function for a series of repeated investments or deposits. By convention, it is assumed that each investment is made at the end of each compounding period. Interest is earned on each investment as it is made, and interest begins to earn on the interest after each period.

Because the first investment is made at the *end* of the first period, no interest is earned for the first period. You can check this with a quick glance at the first row of any column in this section. The entry in the first row is always 1; multiplying this entry by the amount of the investment doesn't increase the total at all.

USE OF FUTURE VALUE PER PERIOD

Future value per period is the amount you will have in the future if you make a $1 deposit at the end of each compounding period. The assumptions are:

- The deposits are uniform and repeat at a regular interval.
- All interest earned is left in the investment to begin earning interest on interest.
- The deposits earn interest at a uniform rate throughout the term of the investment.

The tables in this section are used to solve the following types of problems:

1. How much will a series of repeated deposits be worth in the future?
2. How long will it take for a series of repeated deposits to grow to a certain value in the future?
3. What rate must be earned for a series of repeated deposits to be worth a certain value in the future?

EXAMPLES

Deposits Made at the End of Each Period. You plan to invest $150 at the end of each month in an IRA account that pays a 12% annual rate compounded monthly. What will your account be worth in 3 years (36 months)?

Turn to page 58 in the monthly compounding section and locate the column labeled 12.00%. Move down the column to the row for 36 months and find the entry: 43.076878. Multiply $150 by 43.076878 to get $6,461.53, the future value of the series of deposits.

The next three examples involve variations of this investment.

Deposits Made at the Beginning of Each Period. What will the account be worth if you made the $150 deposits at the start of each month rather than at the end? If you subtract 1 from the future value per period table entry, the entry becomes equivalent to deposits made at the beginning of a month, albeit one deposit less. Therefore to find the value of 36 deposits made at the beginning of the month, simply look up the table entry for 37 months and subtract 1. Find the 37-month factor 44.507647 and subtract 1 to get 43.507647. Multiply 43.507647 by $150 to get $6,526.15, the future value of the series of deposits made at the beginning of each month.

If there is no table entry for one period more than the applicable number of deposits, you can solve the problem as follows. Each deposit made at the beginning of a month has the time to earn one month's more interest than the deposit made at the end of a month. To find the growth of a single deposit after one month, turn to the 12.00% column on page 12 of the future value tables. The entry in the first row, for 1 month, is 1.01. Multiply 1.01 by the accumulated amount found for deposits made at the end of each month, $6,461.53. The answer is $6,526.15, the accumulated amount for deposits made at the start of each month.

Deposits More Frequent Than the Compounding Plan. How much will the $150 IRA deposits be worth after 36 months if you made the deposits at the end of the month into an account where the interest was compounded quarterly rather than monthly? In this example, the deposit period is shorter than the compounding period.

To solve this problem, you must refigure the deposits as equivalent deposits for the compounding period. You must figure what $150 per month will grow to at the end of one quarter at 12% simple interest. The first month's deposit earns two months' interest, the second month's deposit earns one month's interest, and the third month's deposit earns no interest to the end of one quarter. Thus the total interest earned in one quarter for the three deposits is 3 months' simple interest at 12% annual interest, or 3% on a $150 deposit. Simply multiply the rate by the principal amount (3% times $150). This equals $4.50, which when combined with 3 monthly deposits of $150, gives a total equivalent quarterly deposit of $454.50.

Next, turn to page 70 in the quarterly compounding section and locate the column labeled 12.00%. Move down the column and find the entry at the 12-quarter (3-year) row: 14.192030. Multiply 14.192030 by the equivalent quarterly deposit of $454.50 to get $6,450.28, the accumulated amount for monthly deposits compounded quarterly.

Compounding More Frequent Than Deposits. How much will your IRA deposits be worth after 36 months if you deposited $450 at the end of every quarter in an account that compounds monthly? In this situation, the compounding period is shorter than the deposit period.

To solve this problem, you must find the equivalent monthly deposit that will grow to $450 at the end of one quarter. Turn to page 58 in the monthly compounding section and locate the column labeled 12.00%. Move down the column to the 3-month row and find the entry: 3.030100. Divide $450 by 3.030100 to get $148.51, the equivalent monthly deposit.

On the same page of the tables, move down the 12.00% column to the 36-month row. The entry is 43.076878. Multiply $148.51 by 43.076878 to get $6,397.35, the accumulated amount for quarterly deposits of $450 compounded monthly.

Length of Time to Desired Future Value. You deposit $500 at the end of each quarter into an account that pays 11% compounded quarterly. How long will it take to accumulate to $50,000?

First find the factor for the future value per period. Divide $50,000 by $500 to get 100 as the desired factor. Turn to page 69 in the quarterly compounding section and locate the column labeled 11.00%. Move down the column until you find the first entry that exceeds 100. Find 101.033285 and read across to find 49 quarters (12 years and 3 months). It will take slightly less than 49 quarters to accumulate the desired amount.

Rate of Interest for Desired Future Value. You can save $200 each month for the next 48 months, and you need to accumulate $12,000 at the end of 4 years (48 months). If interest is compounded monthly, what rate of interest must you earn to achieve your goal?

First find the factor for the future value per period. Divide $12,000 by $200 to get 60. Starting at the first page of the monthly compounding section, begin to scan across the 4-year row until you find the first entry that exceeds 60. The correct entry is 60.269654, on page 58. Move up the column to find 11.25%. Your account must earn slightly less than 11.25% interest compounded monthly to accumulate the desired amount. If you wish more precise results, use the interpolation technique discussed in the Introduction.

The sinking fund tables (Section 3) are the reciprocal tables to future value per period. The investment growth examples presented in Section 3 are useful supplements to the examples in this section.

THE FORMULA FOR FUTURE VALUE PER PERIOD

The symbol $S_{\overline{n}|}$ is the widely accepted notation for future value per period. The formula for figuring future value per period table entries is:

$$S_{\overline{n}|} = \frac{(1 + i)^n - 1}{i}$$

where:

i = interest rate per period
n = number of compounding periods

Note that i is the interest rate *per period*, not the nominal annual rate. You can easily find the interest rate per period by dividing the annual rate by the number of compounding periods per year. For example, a nominal annual rate of 12% compounded monthly converts to 1% per month (12%÷12 months per year).

53

FUTURE VALUE PER PERIOD

MONTHLY COMPOUNDING

MOS	5.25% ANNUAL RATE	5.50% ANNUAL RATE	5.75% ANNUAL RATE	6.00% ANNUAL RATE	6.25% ANNUAL RATE	6.50% ANNUAL RATE	MOS
1	1.000 000	1.000 000	1.000 000	1.000 000	1.000 000	1.000 000	1
2	2.004 375	2.004 583	2.004 792	2.005 000	2.005 208	2.005 417	2
3	3.013 144	3.013 771	3.014 398	3.015 025	3.015 652	3.016 279	3
4	4.026 327	4.027 584	4.028 842	4.030 100	4.031 359	4.032 618	4
5	5.043 942	5.046 044	5.048 147	5.050 251	5.052 355	5.054 461	5
6	6.066 009	6.069 172	6.072 336	6.075 502	6.078 670	6.081 839	6
7	7.092 548	7.096 989	7.101 432	7.105 879	7.110 329	7.114 782	7
8	8.123 578	8.129 516	8.135 460	8.141 409	8.147 362	8.153 321	8
9	9.159 118	9.166 777	9.174 443	9.182 116	9.189 797	9.197 485	9
10	10.199 190	10.208 791	10.218 403	10.228 026	10.237 660	10.247 304	10
11	11.243 811	11.255 581	11.267 367	11.279 167	11.290 981	11.302 811	11
12	12.293 003	12.307 170	12.321 356	12.335 562	12.349 788	12.364 034	12
13	13.346 785	13.363 577	13.380 396	13.397 240	13.414 110	13.431 006	13
14	14.405 177	14.424 827	14.444 510	14.464 226	14.483 975	14.503 757	14
15	15.468 199	15.490 941	15.513 724	15.536 548	15.559 413	15.582 319	15
16	16.535 873	16.561 941	16.588 060	16.614 230	16.640 451	16.666 724	16
17	17.608 217	17.637 850	17.667 545	17.697 301	17.727 120	17.757 002	17
18	18.685 253	18.718 690	18.752 202	18.785 788	18.819 449	18.853 185	18
19	19.767 001	19.804 484	19.842 056	19.879 717	19.917 467	19.955 307	19
20	20.853 692	20.895 255	20.937 132	20.979 115	21.021 204	21.063 398	20
21	21.944 716	21.991 025	22.037 456	22.084 011	22.130 689	22.177 492	21
22	23.040 724	23.091 817	23.143 052	23.194 431	23.245 953	23.297 620	22
23	24.141 527	24.197 654	24.253 946	24.310 403	24.367 026	24.423 815	23
24	25.247 146	25.308 560	25.370 163	25.431 955	25.493 938	25.556 111	24
25	26.357 603	26.424 558	26.491 728	26.559 115	26.626 719	26.694 540	25
26	27.472 917	27.545 670	27.618 668	27.691 911	27.765 399	27.839 135	26
27	28.593 111	28.671 921	28.751 007	28.830 370	28.910 011	28.989 930	27
28	29.718 206	29.803 334	29.888 773	29.974 522	30.060 584	30.146 959	28
29	30.848 223	30.939 933	31.031 990	31.124 395	31.217 149	31.310 255	29
30	31.983 184	32.081 741	32.180 685	32.280 017	32.379 739	32.479 852	30
31	33.123 110	33.228 782	33.334 884	33.441 417	33.548 383	33.655 785	31
32	34.268 024	34.381 081	34.494 613	34.608 624	34.723 114	34.838 087	32
33	35.417 947	35.538 661	35.659 900	35.781 667	35.903 964	36.026 793	33
34	36.572 900	36.701 546	36.830 770	36.960 575	37.090 964	37.221 939	34
35	37.732 907	37.869 762	38.007 251	38.145 378	38.284 146	38.423 557	35
36	38.897 988	39.043 331	39.189 369	39.336 105	39.483 542	39.631 685	36
37	40.068 167	40.222 280	40.377 152	40.532 785	40.689 186	40.846 357	37
38	41.243 465	41.406 632	41.570 625	41.735 449	41.901 109	42.067 608	38
39	42.423 905	42.596 413	42.769 818	42.944 127	43.119 344	43.295 474	39
40	43.609 510	43.791 646	43.974 757	44.158 847	44.343 923	44.529 991	40
41	44.800 301	44.992 358	45.185 469	45.379 642	45.574 881	45.771 195	41
42	45.996 303	46.198 573	46.401 983	46.606 540	46.812 251	47.019 122	42
43	47.197 536	47.410 316	47.624 326	47.839 572	48.056 064	48.273 809	43
44	48.404 026	48.627 614	48.852 526	49.078 770	49.306 356	49.535 293	44
45	49.615 793	49.850 490	50.086 611	50.324 164	50.563 160	50.803 609	45
46	50.832 862	51.078 972	51.326 609	51.575 785	51.826 510	52.078 795	46
47	52.055 256	52.313 083	52.572 549	52.833 664	53.096 440	53.360 888	47

YRS	5.25%	5.50%	5.75%	6.00%	6.25%	6.50%	MOS
4	53.282 998	53.552 852	53.824 459	54.097 832	54.372 984	54.649 927	48
5	68.441 661	68.880 823	69.323 602	69.770 031	70.220 141	70.673 968	60
6	84.415 585	85.073 412	85.737 812	86.408 856	87.086 617	87.771 168	72
7	101.248 617	102.179 391	103.121 114	104.073 927	105.037 914	106.013 400	84
8	118.986 962	120.250 282	121.530 723	122.828 542	124.143 996	125.477 348	96
9	137.679 308	139.340 512	141.027 233	142.739 900	144.478 951	146.244 833	108
10	157.376 963	159.507 582	161.674 813	163.879 347	166.121 888	168.403 154	120
11	178.133 996	180.812 233	183.541 423	186.322 629	189.156 938	192.045 460	132
12	200.007 381	203.318 634	206.699 033	210.150 163	213.673 643	217.271 134	144
13	223.057 158	227.094 572	231.223 866	235.447 328	239.767 308	244.186 218	156
14	247.346 595	252.211 661	257.196 640	262.304 766	267.539 365	272.903 856	168
15	272.942 365	278.745 550	284.702 842	290.818 712	297.097 771	303.544 767	180
16	299.914 723	306.776 160	313.833 006	321.091 337	328.557 427	336.237 756	192
17	328.337 705	336.387 916	344.683 010	353.231 110	362.040 625	371.120 256	204
18	358.289 329	367.670 008	377.354 392	387.353 194	397.677 524	408.338 901	216
19	389.851 808	400.716 657	411.954 688	423.579 854	435.606 652	448.050 147	228
20	423.111 776	435.627 395	448.597 780	462.040 895	475.975 451	490.420 930	240
21	458.160 528	472.507 374	487.404 273	502.874 129	518.940 844	535.629 362	252
22	495.094 269	511.467 674	528.501 895	546.225 867	564.669 849	583.865 486	264
23	534.014 375	552.625 640	572.025 914	592.251 446	613.340 227	635.332 073	276
24	575.027 679	596.105 240	618.119 583	641.115 782	665.141 172	690.245 473	288
25	618.246 755	642.037 430	666.934 615	692.993 962	720.274 047	748.836 525	300
26	663.790 234	690.560 558	718.631 679	748.071 876	778.953 169	811.351 528	312
27	711.783 128	741.820 771	773.380 928	806.546 975	841.406 639	878.053 277	324
28	762.357 171	795.972 463	831.362 563	868.628 484	907.877 229	949.222 165	336
29	815.651 180	853.178 736	892.767 425	934.539 150	978.623 328	1025.157 366	348
30	871.811 442	913.611 893	957.797 619	1004.515 042	1053.919 945	1106.178 087	360

FUTURE VALUE PER PERIOD

MONTHLY COMPOUNDING

MOS	6.75% ANNUAL RATE	7.00% ANNUAL RATE	7.25% ANNUAL RATE	7.50% ANNUAL RATE	7.75% ANNUAL RATE	8.00% ANNUAL RATE	MOS
1	1.000 000	1.000 000	1.000 000	1.000 000	1.000 000	1.000 000	1
2	2.005 625	2.005 833	2.006 042	2.006 250	2.006 458	2.006 667	2
3	3.016 907	3.017 534	3.018 162	3.018 789	3.019 417	3.020 044	3
4	4.033 877	4.035 136	4.036 396	4.037 656	4.038 917	4.040 178	4
5	5.056 567	5.058 675	5.060 783	5.062 892	5.065 002	5.067 113	5
6	6.085 010	6.088 184	6.091 358	6.094 535	6.097 713	6.100 893	6
7	7.119 239	7.123 698	7.128 160	7.132 626	7.137 094	7.141 566	7
8	8.159 284	8.165 253	8.171 226	8.177 205	8.183 188	8.189 176	8
9	9.205 180	9.212 883	9.220 594	9.228 312	9.236 038	9.243 771	9
10	10.256 960	10.266 625	10.276 302	10.285 989	10.295 687	10.305 396	10
11	11.314 655	11.326 514	11.338 388	11.350 277	11.362 180	11.374 099	11
12	12.378 300	12.392 585	12.406 891	12.421 216	12.435 561	12.449 926	12
13	13.447 928	13.464 875	13.481 849	13.498 848	13.515 874	13.532 926	13
14	14.523 572	14.543 420	14.563 302	14.583 216	14.603 164	14.623 145	14
15	15.605 267	15.628 257	15.651 288	15.674 361	15.697 476	15.720 633	15
16	16.693 047	16.719 422	16.745 848	16.772 326	16.798 856	16.825 437	16
17	17.786 945	17.816 952	17.847 021	17.877 153	17.907 348	17.937 606	17
18	18.886 997	18.920 884	18.954 847	18.988 885	19.023 000	19.057 191	18
19	19.993 236	20.031 256	20.069 366	20.107 566	20.145 857	20.184 238	19
20	21.105 698	21.148 105	21.190 618	21.233 238	21.275 965	21.318 800	20
21	22.224 418	22.271 469	22.318 645	22.365 946	22.413 373	22.460 925	21
22	23.349 430	23.401 386	23.453 487	23.505 733	23.558 126	23.610 665	22
23	24.480 771	24.537 894	24.595 185	24.652 644	24.710 272	24.768 069	23
24	25.618 475	25.681 032	25.743 781	25.806 723	25.869 859	25.933 190	24
25	26.762 579	26.830 838	26.899 316	26.968 015	27.036 935	27.106 078	25
26	27.913 119	27.987 351	28.061 833	28.136 565	28.211 549	28.286 785	26
27	29.070 130	29.150 610	29.231 373	29.312 419	29.393 748	29.475 363	27
28	30.233 649	30.320 656	30.407 979	30.495 621	30.583 583	30.671 866	28
29	31.403 714	31.497 526	31.591 694	31.686 219	31.781 102	31.876 345	29
30	32.580 360	32.681 262	32.782 560	32.884 258	32.986 355	33.088 854	30
31	33.763 624	33.871 902	33.980 622	34.089 784	34.199 392	34.309 446	31
32	34.953 544	35.069 488	35.185 921	35.302 845	35.420 263	35.538 176	32
33	36.150 158	36.274 060	36.398 503	36.523 488	36.649 019	36.775 097	33
34	37.353 503	37.485 659	37.618 411	37.751 760	37.885 710	38.020 264	34
35	38.563 616	38.704 325	38.845 688	38.987 709	39.130 389	39.273 733	35
36	39.780 537	39.930 101	40.080 381	40.231 382	40.383 106	40.535 558	36
37	41.004 302	41.163 026	41.322 533	41.482 828	41.643 914	41.805 795	37
38	42.234 951	42.403 144	42.572 190	42.742 095	42.912 864	43.084 500	38
39	43.472 523	43.650 496	43.829 397	44.009 234	44.190 009	44.371 730	39
40	44.717 056	44.905 124	45.094 200	45.284 291	45.475 403	45.667 542	40
41	45.968 589	46.167 070	46.366 644	46.567 318	46.769 098	46.971 992	41
42	47.227 163	47.436 378	47.646 776	47.858 364	48.071 149	48.285 139	42
43	48.492 815	48.713 090	48.934 642	49.157 479	49.381 608	49.607 039	43
44	49.765 587	49.997 250	50.230 289	50.464 713	50.700 531	50.937 753	44
45	51.045 519	51.288 900	51.533 763	51.780 117	52.027 972	52.277 338	45
46	52.332 650	52.588 086	52.845 113	53.103 743	53.363 986	53.625 854	46
47	53.627 021	53.894 850	54.164 386	54.435 641	54.708 629	54.983 359	47

YRS							
4	54.928 673	55.209 236	55.491 629	55.775 864	56.061 955	56.349 915	48
5	71.131 543	71.592 902	72.058 078	72.527 105	73.000 020	73.476 856	60
6	88.462 585	89.160 944	89.866 319	90.578 789	91.298 431	92.025 325	72
7	107.000 353	107.998 981	109.009 436	110.031 871	111.066 443	112.113 308	84
8	126.828 866	128.198 821	129.587 488	130.995 147	132.422 083	133.868 583	96
9	148.037 998	149.858 909	151.708 036	153.585 857	155.492 858	157.429 535	108
10	170.723 878	173.084 807	175.486 703	177.930 342	180.416 517	182.946 035	120
11	194.989 330	197.989 707	201.047 778	204.164 753	207.341 869	210.580 392	132
12	220.944 334	224.694 985	228.524 868	232.435 809	236.429 677	240.508 387	144
13	248.706 532	253.330 789	258.061 593	262.901 620	267.853 614	272.920 390	156
14	278.401 755	284.036 677	289.812 342	295.732 572	301.801 302	308.022 574	168
15	310.164 594	316.962 297	323.943 072	331.112 276	338.475 430	346.038 222	180
16	344.139 015	352.268 112	360.632 184	369.238 599	378.094 967	387.209 149	192
17	380.479 004	390.126 188	400.071 449	410.324 767	420.896 468	431.797 244	204
18	419.349 272	430.721 027	442.467 014	454.600 560	467.135 486	480.086 128	216
19	460.925 996	474.250 470	488.040 479	502.313 599	517.088 099	532.382 966	228
20	505.397 622	520.926 660	537.030 053	553.730 725	571.052 555	589.020 416	240
21	552.965 715	570.977 075	589.691 802	609.139 496	629.351 059	650.358 746	252
22	603.845 877	624.645 640	646.300 986	668.849 794	692.331 690	716.788 127	264
23	658.268 719	682.193 909	707.153 498	733.195 558	760.370 484	788.731 114	276
24	716.480 912	743.902 347	772.567 411	802.536 650	833.873 678	866.645 333	288
25	778.746 299	810.071 693	842.884 639	877.260 872	913.280 134	951.026 395	300
26	845.347 097	881.024 427	918.472 727	957.786 129	999.063 960	1042.411 042	312
27	916.585 171	957.106 339	999.726 770	1044.562 771	1091.737 343	1141.380 571	324
28	992.783 404	1038.688 219	1087.071 477	1138.076 109	1191.853 602	1248.564 521	336
29	1074.287 164	1126.167 659	1180.963 395	1238.849 131	1300.010 499	1364.644 687	348
30	1161.465 863	1219.970 996	1281.893 291	1347.445 425	1416.853 800	1490.359 449	360

MONTHLY COMPOUNDING

SECTION 2

MOS	8.25% ANNUAL RATE	8.50% ANNUAL RATE	8.75% ANNUAL RATE	9.00% ANNUAL RATE	9.25% ANNUAL RATE	9.50% ANNUAL RATE	MOS
1	1.000 000	1.000 000	1.000 000	1.000 000	1.000 000	1.000 000	1
2	2.006 875	2.007 083	2.007 292	2.007 500	2.007 708	2.007 917	2
3	3.020 672	3.021 300	3.021 928	3.022 556	3.023 184	3.023 813	3
4	4.041 439	4.042 701	4.043 963	4.045 225	4.046 488	4.047 751	4
5	5.069 224	5.071 337	5.073 450	5.075 565	5.077 680	5.079 796	5
6	6.104 075	6.107 259	6.110 444	6.113 631	6.116 820	6.120 011	6
7	7.146 041	7.150 519	7.155 000	7.159 484	7.163 971	7.168 461	7
8	8.195 170	8.201 168	8.207 171	8.213 180	8.219 193	8.225 211	8
9	9.251 512	9.259 260	9.267 015	9.274 779	9.282 549	9.290 328	9
10	10.315 116	10.324 846	10.334 587	10.344 339	10.354 102	10.363 876	10
11	11.386 032	11.397 980	11.409 944	11.421 922	11.433 915	11.445 923	11
12	12.464 311	12.478 716	12.493 141	12.507 586	12.522 052	12.536 537	12
13	13.550 003	13.567 107	13.584 237	13.601 393	13.618 576	13.635 785	13
14	14.643 159	14.663 207	14.683 289	14.703 404	14.723 552	14.743 734	14
15	15.743 831	15.767 072	15.790 354	15.813 679	15.837 046	15.860 456	15
16	16.852 070	16.878 755	16.905 492	16.932 282	16.959 124	16.986 018	16
17	17.967 928	17.998 313	18.028 762	18.059 274	18.089 850	18.120 490	17
18	19.091 458	19.125 801	19.160 221	19.194 718	19.229 293	19.263 944	18
19	20.222 711	20.261 276	20.299 931	20.338 679	20.377 519	20.416 450	19
20	21.361 742	21.404 793	21.447 952	21.491 219	21.534 595	21.578 081	20
21	22.508 604	22.556 410	22.604 343	22.652 403	22.700 591	22.748 907	21
22	23.663 351	23.716 185	23.769 166	23.822 296	23.875 575	23.929 003	22
23	24.826 037	24.884 174	24.942 483	25.000 963	25.059 616	25.118 441	23
24	25.996 716	26.060 437	26.124 355	26.188 471	26.252 784	26.317 295	24
25	27.175 443	27.245 032	27.314 845	27.384 884	27.455 149	27.525 640	25
26	28.362 274	28.438 018	28.514 016	28.590 271	28.666 782	28.743 551	26
27	29.557 265	29.639 454	29.721 931	29.804 698	29.887 755	29.971 105	27
28	30.760 471	30.849 400	30.938 653	31.028 233	31.118 140	31.208 376	28
29	31.971 949	32.067 916	32.164 248	32.260 945	32.358 009	32.455 442	29
30	33.191 756	33.295 064	33.398 779	33.502 902	33.607 435	33.712 381	30
31	34.419 950	34.530 904	34.642 311	34.754 174	34.866 493	34.979 271	31
32	35.656 587	35.775 498	35.894 912	36.014 830	36.135 255	36.256 190	32
33	36.901 726	37.028 908	37.156 645	37.284 941	37.413 798	37.543 218	33
34	38.155 425	38.291 196	38.427 579	38.564 578	38.702 196	38.840 435	34
35	39.417 744	39.562 425	39.707 780	39.853 813	40.000 525	40.147 922	35
36	40.688 741	40.842 659	40.997 316	41.152 716	41.308 863	41.465 760	36
37	41.968 476	42.131 961	42.296 255	42.461 361	42.627 285	42.794 030	37
38	43.257 009	43.430 396	43.604 665	43.779 822	43.955 870	44.132 816	38
39	44.554 401	44.738 028	44.922 616	45.108 170	45.294 697	45.482 201	39
40	45.860 713	46.054 922	46.250 177	46.446 482	46.643 844	46.842 269	40
41	47.176 005	47.381 145	47.587 417	47.794 830	48.003 390	48.213 103	41
42	48.500 340	48.716 761	48.934 409	49.153 291	49.373 416	49.594 790	42
43	49.833 780	50.061 838	50.291 222	50.521 941	50.754 003	50.987 416	43
44	51.176 387	51.416 443	51.657 929	51.900 856	52.145 232	52.391 066	44
45	52.528 225	52.780 643	53.034 602	53.290 112	53.547 184	53.805 829	45
46	53.889 356	54.154 506	54.421 312	54.689 788	54.959 944	55.231 792	46
47	55.259 846	55.538 100	55.818 134	56.099 961	56.383 593	56.669 043	47

YRS	8.25%	8.50%	8.75%	9.00%	9.25%	9.50%	MOS
4	56.639 757	56.931 495	57.225 142	57.520 711	57.818 217	58.117 673	48
5	73.957 650	74.442 437	74.931 254	75.424 137	75.921 123	76.422 249	60
6	92.759 550	93.501 188	94.250 319	95.007 028	95.771 396	96.543 509	72
7	113.172 626	114.244 559	115.329 271	116.426 928	117.537 700	118.661 756	84
8	135.334 941	136.821 455	138.328 427	139.856 164	141.404 978	142.975 186	96
9	159.396 393	161.393 943	163.422 710	165.483 223	167.576 024	169.701 665	108
10	185.519 722	188.138 416	190.802 977	193.514 277	196.273 209	199.080 682	120
11	213.881 614	217.246 858	220.677 472	224.174 837	227.740 365	231.375 495	132
12	244.673 898	248.928 220	253.273 409	257.711 570	262.244 861	266.875 491	144
13	278.104 839	283.409 927	288.838 699	294.394 279	300.079 874	305.898 776	156
14	314.400 549	320.939 504	327.643 839	334.518 079	341.566 880	348.795 027	168
15	353.806 515	361.786 353	369.983 965	378.405 769	387.058 383	395.948 628	180
16	396.589 263	406.243 693	416.181 099	426.410 427	436.940 915	447.782 110	192
17	443.038 156	454.630 657	466.586 599	478.918 252	491.638 316	504.759 939	204
18	493.467 354	507.294 589	521.583 830	536.351 674	551.615 338	567.392 681	216
19	548.217 938	564.613 533	581.591 078	599.172 747	617.381 589	636.241 570	228
20	607.660 217	626.998 591	647.064 737	667.886 870	689.495 873	711.923 546	240
21	672.196 232	694.898 672	718.502 772	743.046 852	768.570 926	795.116 775	252
22	742.262 475	768.800 112	796.448 513	825.257 358	855.278 631	886.566 731	264
23	818.332 845	849.233 766	881.494 785	915.179 777	950.355 723	987.092 874	276
24	900.921 848	936.777 024	974.288 418	1013.537 539	1054.610 051	1097.595 994	288
25	990.588 079	1032.058 310	1075.535 163	1121.121 937	1168.927 439	1219.066 282	300
26	1087.938 001	1135.761 595	1186.005 063	1238.798 495	1294.279 215	1352.592 202	312
27	1193.630 046	1248.631 307	1306.538 310	1367.513 924	1431.730 465	1499.370 247	324
28	1308.379 069	1371.477 676	1438.051 632	1508.303 750	1582.449 079	1660.715 659	336
29	1432.961 180	1505.182 546	1581.545 267	1662.300 631	1747.715 679	1838.074 212	348
30	1568.218 999	1650.705 711	1738.110 574	1830.743 483	1928.934 497	2033.035 174	360

MOS	9.75% ANNUAL RATE	10.00% ANNUAL RATE	10.25% ANNUAL RATE	10.50% ANNUAL RATE	10.75% ANNUAL RATE	11.00% ANNUAL RATE	MOS
1	1.000 000	1.000 000	1.000 000	1.000 000	1.000 000	1.000 000	1
2	2.008 125	2.008 333	2.008 542	2.008 750	2.008 958	2.009 167	2
3	3.024 441	3.025 069	3.025 698	3.026 327	3.026 955	3.027 584	3
4	4.049 015	4.050 278	4.051 542	4.052 807	4.054 072	4.055 337	4
5	5.081 913	5.084 031	5.086 149	5.088 269	5.090 389	5.092 511	5
6	6.123 203	6.126 398	6.129 594	6.132 791	6.135 991	6.139 192	6
7	7.172 954	7.177 451	7.181 951	7.186 453	7.190 959	7.195 468	7
8	8.231 235	8.237 263	8.243 296	8.249 335	8.255 378	8.261 427	8
9	9.298 113	9.305 907	9.313 708	9.321 516	9.329 333	9.337 156	9
10	10.373 661	10.383 456	10.393 262	10.403 080	10.412 908	10.422 747	10
11	11.457 947	11.469 985	11.482 038	11.494 107	11.506 190	11.518 289	11
12	12.551 042	12.565 568	12.580 114	12.594 680	12.609 266	12.623 873	12
13	13.653 020	13.670 281	13.687 569	13.704 884	13.722 224	13.739 592	13
14	14.763 950	14.784 200	14.804 484	14.824 801	14.845 153	14.865 538	14
15	15.883 908	15.907 402	15.930 939	15.954 518	15.978 141	16.001 806	15
16	17.012 964	17.039 964	17.067 015	17.094 120	17.121 278	17.148 489	16
17	18.151 195	18.181 963	18.212 796	18.243 694	18.274 656	18.305 683	17
18	19.298 673	19.333 480	19.368 364	19.403 326	19.438 367	19.473 485	18
19	20.455 475	20.494 592	20.533 802	20.573 105	20.612 502	20.651 992	19
20	21.621 676	21.665 380	21.709 195	21.753 120	21.797 156	21.841 302	20
21	22.797 352	22.845 925	22.894 628	22.943 460	22.992 422	23.041 514	21
22	23.982 580	24.036 308	24.090 186	24.144 215	24.198 396	24.252 728	22
23	25.177 439	25.236 610	25.295 956	25.355 477	25.415 173	25.475 045	23
24	26.382 005	26.446 915	26.512 026	26.577 337	26.642 850	26.708 566	24
25	27.596 359	27.667 306	27.738 483	27.809 889	27.881 526	27.953 394	25
26	28.820 579	28.897 867	28.975 416	29.053 226	29.131 298	29.209 634	26
27	30.054 747	30.138 683	30.222 914	30.307 441	30.392 266	30.477 389	27
28	31.298 942	31.389 838	31.481 068	31.572 631	31.664 530	31.756 765	28
29	32.553 245	32.651 420	32.749 969	32.848 892	32.948 191	33.047 869	29
30	33.817 741	33.923 516	34.029 708	34.136 320	34.243 352	34.350 807	30
31	35.092 510	35.206 212	35.320 379	35.435 012	35.550 116	35.665 690	31
32	36.377 636	36.499 597	36.622 073	36.745 069	36.868 585	36.992 625	32
33	37.673 205	37.803 760	37.934 887	38.066 588	38.198 866	38.331 724	33
34	38.979 299	39.118 791	39.258 914	39.399 671	39.541 065	39.683 099	34
35	40.296 006	40.444 781	40.594 251	40.744 418	40.895 287	41.046 860	35
36	41.623 411	41.781 821	41.940 993	42.100 932	42.261 640	42.423 123	36
37	42.961 601	43.130 003	43.299 239	43.469 315	43.640 234	43.812 002	37
38	44.310 664	44.489 420	44.669 087	44.849 671	45.031 178	45.213 612	38
39	45.670 689	45.860 165	46.050 635	46.242 106	46.434 582	46.628 070	39
40	47.041 763	47.242 333	47.443 985	47.646 724	47.850 559	48.055 494	40
41	48.423 977	48.636 019	48.849 235	49.063 633	49.279 220	49.496 003	41
42	49.817 422	50.041 319	50.266 489	50.492 940	50.720 680	50.949 716	42
43	51.222 189	51.458 330	51.695 849	51.934 753	52.175 052	52.416 755	43
44	52.638 369	52.887 150	53.137 417	53.389 182	53.642 454	53.897 242	44
45	54.066 056	54.327 876	54.591 300	54.856 338	55.123 001	55.391 300	45
46	55.505 342	55.780 608	56.057 600	56.336 331	56.616 811	56.899 054	46
47	56.956 323	57.245 446	57.536 426	57.829 273	58.124 003	58.420 628	47

YRS							
4	58.419 093	58.722 492	59.027 882	59.335 280	59.644 698	59.956 151	48
5	76.927 553	77.437 072	77.950 846	78.468 912	78.991 310	79.518 080	60
6	97.323 453	98.111 314	98.907 179	99.711 137	100.523 278	101.343 692	72
7	119.799 271	120.950 418	122.115 378	123.294 329	124.487 454	125.694 940	84
8	144.567 109	146.181 076	147.817 417	149.476 469	151.158 576	152.864 085	96
9	171.860 704	174.053 713	176.281 272	178.543 972	180.842 414	183.177 212	108
10	201.937 623	204.844 979	207.803 714	210.814 814	213.879 280	216.998 139	120
11	235.081 703	238.860 493	242.713 406	246.642 013	250.647 925	254.732 784	132
12	271.605 724	276.437 876	281.374 322	286.417 494	291.569 882	296.834 038	144
13	311.854 363	317.950 102	324.189 554	330.576 371	337.114 303	343.807 200	156
14	356.207 446	363.809 201	371.605 502	379.601 707	387.803 331	396.216 042	168
15	405.083 533	414.470 346	424.116 537	434.029 805	444.218 090	454.689 575	180
16	458.943 868	470.436 376	482.270 153	494.456 068	507.005 349	519.929 596	192
17	518.296 730	532.262 780	546.672 673	561.541 512	576.884 931	592.719 117	204
18	583.702 232	600.563 216	617.995 576	636.020 005	654.657 972	673.931 757	216
19	655.777 606	676.015 601	696.982 491	718.706 284	741.216 102	764.542 228	228
20	735.203 025	759.368 836	784.456 956	810.504 876	837.551 665	865.638 038	240
21	822.728 028	851.450 244	881.331 002	912.419 990	944.769 102	978.432 537	252
22	919.178 587	953.173 779	988.614 662	1025.566 501	1064.097 607	1104.279 485	264
23	1025.464 906	1065.549 097	1107.426 503	1151.182 148	1196.905 224	1244.689 295	276
24	1142.590 009	1189.691 580	1239.005 287	1290.641 073	1344.714 524	1401.347 165	288
25	1271.659 204	1326.833 403	1384.722 888	1445.468 853	1509.220 069	1576.133 301	300
26	1413.890 516	1478.335 767	1546.098 594	1617.359 188	1692.307 834	1771.145 485	312
27	1570.626 183	1645.702 407	1724.814 949	1808.192 431	1896.076 828	1988.724 252	324
28	1743.345 316	1830.594 523	1922.735 295	2020.056 156	2122.863 162	2231.480 981	336
29	1933.677 867	2034.847 258	2141.923 199	2255.267 995	2375.266 830	2502.329 236	348
30	2143.420 002	2260.487 925	2384.663 970	2516.400 990	2656.181 515	2804.519 736	360

MOS	11.25% ANNUAL RATE	11.50% ANNUAL RATE	11.75% ANNUAL RATE	12.00% ANNUAL RATE	12.25% ANNUAL RATE	12.50% ANNUAL RATE	MOS
1	1.000 000	1.000 000	1.000 000	1.000 000	1.000 000	1.000 000	1
2	2.009 375	2.009 583	2.009 792	2.010 000	2.010 208	2.010 417	2
3	3.028 213	3.028 842	3.029 471	3.030 100	3.030 729	3.031 359	3
4	4.056 602	4.057 868	4.059 134	4.060 401	4.061 668	4.062 935	4
5	5.094 633	5.096 756	5.098 880	5.101 005	5.103 131	5.105 257	5
6	6.142 395	6.145 600	6.148 807	6.152 015	6.155 225	6.158 437	6
7	7.199 980	7.204 495	7.209 014	7.213 535	7.218 060	7.222 588	7
8	8.267 480	8.273 538	8.279 602	8.285 671	8.291 744	8.297 823	8
9	9.344 988	9.352 827	9.360 673	9.368 527	9.376 389	9.384 258	9
10	10.432 597	10.442 458	10.452 330	10.462 213	10.472 106	10.482 011	10
11	11.530 402	11.542 531	11.554 675	11.566 835	11.579 009	11.591 199	11
12	12.638 500	12.653 147	12.667 815	12.682 503	12.697 212	12.711 940	12
13	13.756 986	13.774 407	13.791 854	13.809 328	13.826 829	13.844 357	13
14	14.885 958	14.906 411	14.926 899	14.947 421	14.967 978	14.988 569	14
15	16.025 514	16.049 264	16.073 058	16.096 896	16.120 776	16.144 699	15
16	17.175 753	17.203 070	17.230 440	17.257 864	17.285 342	17.312 873	16
17	18.336 775	18.367 933	18.399 155	18.430 443	18.461 797	18.493 216	17
18	19.508 683	19.543 959	19.579 314	19.614 748	19.650 261	19.685 854	18
19	20.691 577	20.731 255	20.771 028	20.810 895	20.850 857	20.890 914	19
20	21.885 560	21.929 929	21.974 411	22.019 004	22.063 710	22.108 528	20
21	23.090 737	23.140 091	23.189 577	23.239 194	23.288 943	23.338 825	21
22	24.307 213	24.361 861	24.416 641	24.471 586	24.526 685	24.581 938	22
23	25.535 093	25.595 318	25.655 721	25.716 302	25.777 061	25.838 000	23
24	26.774 484	26.840 607	26.906 933	26.973 465	27.040 202	27.107 146	24
25	28.025 495	28.097 829	28.170 397	28.243 200	28.316 238	28.389 512	25
26	29.288 234	29.367 100	29.446 232	29.525 631	29.605 299	29.685 236	26
27	30.562 812	30.648 535	30.734 560	30.820 888	30.907 520	30.994 457	27
28	31.849 338	31.942 250	32.035 502	32.129 097	32.223 034	32.317 316	28
29	33.147 925	33.248 363	33.349 183	33.450 388	33.551 978	33.653 955	29
30	34.458 687	34.566 993	34.675 727	34.784 892	34.894 487	35.004 517	30
31	35.781 737	35.898 260	36.015 261	36.132 740	36.250 702	36.369 147	31
32	37.117 191	37.242 285	37.367 910	37.494 068	37.620 761	37.747 993	32
33	38.465 165	38.599 191	38.733 804	38.869 009	39.004 806	39.141 201	33
34	39.825 776	39.969 099	40.113 073	40.257 699	40.402 981	40.548 922	34
35	41.199 142	41.352 137	41.505 846	41.660 276	41.815 428	41.971 306	35
36	42.585 384	42.748 428	42.912 258	43.076 878	43.242 293	43.408 507	36
37	43.984 622	44.158 100	44.332 440	44.507 647	44.683 725	44.860 679	37
38	45.396 978	45.581 282	45.766 529	45.952 724	46.139 872	46.327 978	38
39	46.822 575	47.018 103	47.214 659	47.412 251	47.610 883	47.810 561	39
40	48.261 537	48.468 693	48.676 970	48.886 373	49.096 911	49.308 588	40
41	49.713 988	49.933 185	50.153 598	50.375 237	50.598 108	50.822 219	41
42	51.180 057	51.411 711	51.644 686	51.878 989	52.114 631	52.351 617	42
43	52.659 870	52.904 406	53.150 373	53.397 779	53.646 634	53.896 946	43
44	54.153 560	54.411 407	54.670 804	54.931 757	55.194 277	55.458 373	44
45	55.661 246	55.932 850	56.206 122	56.481 075	56.757 718	57.036 064	45
46	57.183 070	57.468 873	57.756 474	58.045 885	58.337 120	58.630 190	46
47	58.719 161	59.019 616	59.322 006	59.626 344	59.932 645	60.240 921	47

YRS	11.25%	11.50%	11.75%	12.00%	12.25%	12.50%	MOS
4	60.269 654	60.585 221	60.902 867	61.222 608	61.544 457	61.868 431	48
5	80.049 260	80.584 891	81.125 014	81.669 670	82.218 899	82.772 744	60
6	102.172 472	103.009 708	103.855 497	104.709 931	105.573 108	106.445 124	72
7	126.916 973	128.153 744	129.405 446	130.672 274	131.954 428	133.252 107	84
8	154.593 349	156.346 728	158.124 586	159.927 293	161.755 225	163.608 765	96
9	185.548 987	187.958 374	190.406 019	192.892 579	195.418 723	197.985 131	108
10	220.172 433	223.403 228	226.691 611	230.038 689	233.445 595	236.913 480	120
11	258.898 270	263.146 100	267.478 031	271.895 856	276.401 410	280.996 567	132
12	302.212 574	307.708 167	313.323 559	319.061 559	324.925 044	330.916 961	144
13	350.659 014	357.673 800	364.855 722	372.209 054	379.738 185	387.447 618	156
14	404.845 676	413.698 232	422.779 884	432.096 982	441.656 060	451.463 840	168
15	465.452 695	476.516 149	487.888 901	499.580 198	511.599 567	523.956 837	180
16	533.240 794	546.951 324	561.073 976	575.621 974	590.608 968	606.049 070	192
17	609.060 830	625.927 421	643.336 860	661.307 751	679.859 359	699.011 633	204
18	693.864 473	714.480 107	735.803 550	757.860 630	780.678 151	804.283 930	216
19	788.716 155	813.770 632	839.739 717	866.658 830	894.564 809	923.495 968	228
20	894.806 428	925.101 060	956.568 025	989.255 365	1023.213 156	1058.493 594	240
21	1013.466 907	1049.931 340	1087.887 601	1127.400 210	1168.536 564	1211.367 071	252
22	1146.186 983	1189.898 456	1235.495 930	1283.065 279	1332.696 468	1384.483 450	264
23	1294.632 522	1346.837 891	1401.413 451	1458.472 574	1518.134 220	1580.523 215	276
24	1460.666 770	1522.807 696	1587.911 219	1656.125 905	1727.607 992	1802.521 791	288
25	1646.373 742	1720.115 481	1797.541 987	1878.846 626	1964.233 204	2053.956 131	300
26	1854.084 378	1941.348 676	2033.175 151	2129.813 909	2231.529 152	2338.599 989	312
27	2086.405 804	2189.408 459	2298.036 022	2412.610 125	2533.471 298	2660.980 094	324
28	2346.254 051	2467.547 806	2595.749 977	2731.217 980	2874.550 389	3026.048 499	336
29	2636.890 662	2779.414 142	2930.392 078	3090.348 134	3259.839 255	3439.457 817	348
30	2961.963 624	3129.097 181	3306.542 859	3494.964 133	3695.068 249	3907.609 164	360

58

FUTURE VALUE PER PERIOD

MOS	12.75% ANNUAL RATE	13.00% ANNUAL RATE	13.25% ANNUAL RATE	13.50% ANNUAL RATE	13.75% ANNUAL RATE	14.00% ANNUAL RATE	MOS
1	1.000 000	1.000 000	1.000 000	1.000 000	1.000 000	1.000 000	1
2	2.010 625	2.010 833	2.011 042	2.011 250	2.011 458	2.011 667	2
3	3.031 988	3.032 617	3.033 247	3.033 877	3.034 506	3.035 136	3
4	4.064 203	4.065 471	4.066 739	4.068 008	4.069 277	4.070 546	4
5	5.107 385	5.109 513	5.111 643	5.113 773	5.115 904	5.118 036	5
6	6.161 651	6.164 866	6.168 084	6.171 303	6.174 524	6.177 746	6
7	7.227 118	7.231 652	7.236 190	7.240 730	7.245 273	7.249 820	7
8	8.303 907	8.309 995	8.316 089	8.322 188	8.328 292	8.334 401	8
9	9.392 136	9.400 020	9.407 913	9.415 813	9.423 720	9.431 636	9
10	10.491 927	10.501 854	10.511 792	10.521 741	10.531 701	10.541 672	10
11	11.603 404	11.615 624	11.627 859	11.640 110	11.652 376	11.664 658	11
12	12.726 690	12.741 460	12.756 250	12.771 061	12.785 893	12.800 745	12
13	13.861 911	13.879 492	13.897 101	13.914 736	13.932 398	13.950 087	13
14	15.009 194	15.029 853	15.050 548	15.071 277	15.092 040	15.112 838	14
15	16.168 666	16.192 677	16.216 731	16.240 828	16.264 970	16.289 155	15
16	17.340 459	17.368 098	17.395 791	17.423 538	17.451 339	17.479 195	16
17	18.524 701	18.556 252	18.587 869	18.619 553	18.651 302	18.683 119	17
18	19.721 526	19.757 278	19.793 110	19.829 023	19.865 015	19.901 089	18
19	20.931 067	20.971 315	21.011 659	21.052 099	21.092 635	21.133 268	19
20	22.153 460	22.198 504	22.243 663	22.288 935	22.334 322	22.379 823	20
21	23.388 840	23.438 988	23.489 270	23.539 686	23.590 236	23.640 921	21
22	24.637 347	24.692 911	24.748 631	24.804 507	24.860 541	24.916 731	22
23	25.899 118	25.960 417	26.021 897	26.083 558	26.145 401	26.207 427	23
24	27.174 297	27.241 655	27.309 222	27.376 998	27.444 984	27.513 180	24
25	28.463 023	28.536 773	28.610 761	28.684 989	28.759 457	28.834 167	25
26	29.765 443	29.845 921	29.926 672	30.007 695	30.088 993	30.170 566	26
27	31.081 701	31.169 252	31.257 112	31.345 282	31.433 763	31.522 556	27
28	32.411 944	32.506 919	32.602 243	32.697 916	32.793 941	32.890 319	28
29	33.756 321	33.859 077	33.962 226	34.065 768	34.169 705	34.274 039	29
30	35.114 982	35.225 884	35.337 225	35.449 008	35.561 233	35.673 903	30
31	36.488 078	36.607 498	36.727 407	36.847 809	36.968 705	37.090 099	31
32	37.875 764	38.004 079	38.132 939	38.262 347	38.392 305	38.522 816	32
33	39.278 194	39.415 790	39.553 990	39.692 798	39.832 217	39.972 249	33
34	40.695 525	40.842 794	40.990 732	41.139 342	41.288 628	41.438 592	34
35	42.127 915	42.285 258	42.443 338	42.602 160	42.761 727	42.922 042	35
36	43.575 524	43.743 348	43.911 983	44.081 434	44.251 705	44.422 800	36
37	45.038 514	45.217 234	45.396 845	45.577 350	45.758 756	45.941 065	37
38	46.517 048	46.707 088	46.898 102	47.090 095	47.283 075	47.477 045	38
39	48.011 292	48.213 081	48.415 935	48.619 859	48.824 860	49.030 943	39
40	49.521 412	49.735 390	49.950 527	50.166 832	50.384 311	50.602 971	40
41	51.047 577	51.274 190	51.502 065	51.731 209	51.961 632	52.193 339	41
42	52.589 957	52.829 660	53.070 733	53.313 185	53.557 025	53.802 261	42
43	54.148 726	54.401 981	54.656 723	54.912 959	55.170 700	55.429 954	43
44	55.724 056	55.991 336	56.260 224	56.530 730	56.802 864	57.076 637	44
45	57.316 124	57.597 909	57.881 430	58.166 700	58.453 730	58.742 531	45
46	58.925 108	59.221 886	59.520 538	59.821 076	60.123 512	60.427 861	46
47	60.551 187	60.863 457	61.177 744	61.494 063	61.812 428	62.132 853	47

YRS	12.75%	13.00%	13.25%	13.50%	13.75%	14.00%	
4	62.194 543	62.522 811	62.853 248	63.185 871	63.520 695	63.857 736	48
5	83.331 247	83.894 449	84.462 395	85.035 127	85.612 689	86.195 125	60
6	107.326 078	108.216 068	109.115 196	110.023 563	110.941 271	111.868 425	72
7	134.565 516	135.894 861	137.240 351	138.602 198	139.980 618	141.375 828	84
8	165.488 300	167.394 225	169.326 941	171.286 853	173.274 375	175.289 927	96
9	200.592 497	203.241 525	205.932 935	208.667 457	211.445 835	214.268 826	108
10	240.443 521	244.036 917	247.694 894	251.418 698	255.209 605	259.068 912	120
11	285.683 243	290.463 399	295.339 035	300.312 201	305.384 987	310.559 534	132
12	337.040 330	343.298 242	349.693 867	356.230 450	362.911 316	369.739 871	144
13	395.341 977	403.426 010	411.704 591	420.182 722	428.865 540	437.758 319	156
14	461.527 236	471.853 363	482.449 541	493.323 301	504.482 389	515.934 780	168
15	536.662 137	549.725 914	563.158 937	576.972 311	591.177 487	605.786 272	180
16	621.956 861	638.347 406	655.236 272	672.639 547	690.573 853	709.056 369	192
17	718.785 230	739.201 542	760.282 725	782.051 719	804.532 285	827.749 031	204
18	828.706 835	853.976 825	880.124 998	907.183 624	935.186 201	964.167 496	216
19	953.492 158	984.594 826	1016.847 086	1050.293 785	1084.981 571	1120.958 972	228
20	1095.151 087	1133.242 353	1172.826 517	1213.965 218	1256.722 716	1301.166 005	240
21	1255.965 290	1302.408 067	1350.775 692	1401.152 054	1453.624 802	1508.285 522	252
22	1438.524 963	1494.924 144	1553.789 056	1615.232 853	1679.374 032	1746.336 688	264
23	1645.770 552	1714.013 694	1785.396 905	1860.071 591	1938.196 659	2019.938 898	276
24	1881.040 113	1963.344 717	2049.626 781	2140.087 398	2234.938 102	2334.401 417	288
25	2148.123 079	2247.091 520	2351.073 504	2460.334 319	2575.153 657	2695.826 407	300
26	2451.321 292	2570.004 599	2694.979 079	2826.592 538	2965.212 500	3111.227 338	312
27	2795.518 294	2937.490 172	3087.323 844	3245.472 702	3412.416 924	3588.665 088	324
28	3186.257 987	3355.700 690	3534.930 473	3724.535 238	3925.139 043	4137.404 359	336
29	3629.833 924	3831.637 843	4045.582 614	4272.426 817	4512.977 528	4768.093 467	348
30	4133.390 677	4373.269 783	4628.160 244	4899.036 412	5186.937 305	5492.970 967	360

FUTURE VALUE PER PERIOD

MONTHLY COMPOUNDING

MOS	14.25% ANNUAL RATE	14.50% ANNUAL RATE	14.75% ANNUAL RATE	15.00% ANNUAL RATE	15.25% ANNUAL RATE	15.50% ANNUAL RATE	MOS
1	1.000 000	1.000 000	1.000 000	1.000 000	1.000 000	1.000 000	1
2	2.011 875	2.012 083	2.012 292	2.012 500	2.012 708	2.012 917	2
3	3.035 766	3.036 396	3.037 026	3.037 656	3.038 287	3.038 917	3
4	4.071 816	4.073 086	4.074 356	4.075 627	4.076 898	4.078 170	4
5	5.120 169	5.122 302	5.124 437	5.126 572	5.128 709	5.130 846	5
6	6.180 971	6.184 197	6.187 425	6.190 654	6.193 886	6.197 119	6
7	7.254 370	7.258 922	7.263 478	7.268 038	7.272 600	7.277 165	7
8	8.340 515	8.346 634	8.352 759	8.358 888	8.365 023	8.371 162	8
9	9.439 559	9.447 490	9.455 428	9.463 374	9.471 328	9.479 290	9
10	10.551 654	10.561 647	10.571 651	10.581 666	10.591 693	10.601 730	10
11	11.676 954	11.689 267	11.701 594	11.713 937	11.726 296	11.738 669	11
12	12.815 618	12.830 512	12.845 426	12.860 361	12.875 317	12.890 294	12
13	13.967 804	13.985 547	14.003 318	14.021 116	14.038 941	14.056 794	13
14	15.133 671	15.154 539	15.175 442	15.196 380	15.217 353	15.238 361	14
15	16.313 384	16.337 657	16.361 974	16.386 335	16.410 740	16.435 189	15
16	17.507 105	17.535 070	17.563 090	17.591 164	17.619 293	17.647 477	16
17	18.715 002	18.746 952	18.778 969	18.811 053	18.843 205	18.875 424	17
18	19.937 243	19.973 478	20.009 794	20.046 192	20.082 671	20.119 231	18
19	21.173 998	21.214 824	21.255 748	21.296 769	21.337 888	21.379 105	19
20	22.425 439	22.471 170	22.517 016	22.562 979	22.609 057	22.655 252	20
21	23.691 741	23.742 696	23.793 788	23.845 016	23.896 380	23.947 882	21
22	24.973 080	25.029 587	25.086 253	25.143 078	25.200 063	25.257 209	22
23	26.269 636	26.332 028	26.394 605	26.457 367	26.520 314	26.583 448	23
24	27.581 587	27.650 207	27.719 039	27.788 084	27.857 343	27.926 817	24
25	28.909 119	28.984 314	29.059 752	29.135 435	29.211 364	29.287 539	25
26	30.252 415	30.334 541	30.416 945	30.499 628	30.582 591	30.665 836	26
27	31.611 662	31.701 083	31.790 820	31.880 873	31.971 245	32.061 936	27
28	32.987 051	33.084 138	33.181 582	33.279 384	33.377 546	33.476 070	28
29	34.378 772	34.483 904	34.589 439	34.695 377	34.801 719	34.908 469	29
30	35.787 020	35.900 585	36.014 601	36.129 069	36.243 991	36.359 370	30
31	37.211 991	37.334 384	37.457 280	37.580 682	37.704 592	37.829 012	31
32	38.653 883	38.785 507	38.917 693	39.050 441	39.183 754	39.317 637	32
33	40.112 898	40.254 166	40.396 056	40.538 571	40.681 715	40.825 489	33
34	41.589 238	41.740 570	41.892 591	42.045 303	42.198 711	42.352 819	34
35	43.083 111	43.244 935	43.407 520	43.570 870	43.734 987	43.899 876	35
36	44.594 723	44.767 478	44.941 071	45.115 505	45.290 786	45.466 916	36
37	46.124 285	46.308 419	46.493 472	46.679 449	46.866 356	47.054 197	37
38	47.672 011	47.867 979	48.064 954	48.262 942	48.461 949	48.661 980	38
39	49.238 116	49.446 384	49.655 753	49.866 229	50.077 820	50.290 531	39
40	50.822 819	51.043 861	51.266 105	51.489 557	51.714 225	51.940 117	40
41	52.426 340	52.660 641	52.896 250	53.133 177	53.371 427	53.611 010	41
42	54.048 902	54.296 957	54.546 433	54.797 341	55.049 689	55.303 486	42
43	55.690 733	55.953 045	56.216 900	56.482 308	56.749 279	57.017 822	43
44	57.352 060	57.629 144	57.907 899	58.188 337	58.470 468	58.754 302	44
45	59.033 116	59.325 496	59.619 684	59.915 691	60.213 530	60.513 212	45
46	60.734 134	61.042 346	61.352 509	61.664 637	61.978 743	62.294 841	46
47	62.455 352	62.779 941	63.106 634	63.435 445	63.766 390	64.099 483	47
YRS							
4	64.197 010	64.538 532	64.882 320	65.228 388	65.576 754	65.927 435	48
5	86.782 480	87.374 798	87.972 126	88.574 508	89.181 991	89.794 622	60
6	112.805 130	113.751 493	114.707 620	115.673 621	116.649 607	117.635 687	72
7	142.788 050	144.217 508	145.664 428	147.129 040	148.611 579	150.112 280	84
8	177.333 935	179.406 832	181.509 058	183.641 059	185.803 291	187.996 213	96
9	217.137 201	220.051 745	223.013 257	226.022 551	229.080 453	232.187 807	108
10	262.997 946	266.998 057	271.070 626	275.217 058	279.438 790	283.737 285	120
11	315.838 029	321.222 707	326.715 854	332.319 805	338.036 951	343.869 732	132
12	376.719 606	383.854 095	391.147 001	398.602 077	406.223 167	414.014 209	144
13	446.866 473	456.195 562	465.751 291	475.539 523	485.566 272	495.837 716	156
14	527.688 675	539.752 513	552.134 980	564.845 011	577.891 799	591.284 807	168
15	620.810 841	636.263 747	652.157 936	668.506 759	685.323 883	702.623 803	180
16	728.104 847	747.737 633	767.973 687	788.832 603	810.334 631	832.500 700	192
17	851.727 442	876.493 913	902.075 783	928.501 369	955.799 999	984.002 053	204
18	994.163 599	1025.211 968	1057.351 487	1090.622 520	1125.066 967	1160.728 325	216
19	1158.276 469	1196.986 579	1237.143 935	1278.805 378	1322.030 043	1366.879 457	228
20	1347.364 934	1395.392 327	1445.324 119	1497.239 481	1551.220 972	1607.354 675	240
21	1565.229 914	1624.557 981	1686.374 225	1750.787 854	1817.912 996	1887.868 929	252
22	1816.250 779	1889.252 413	1965.484 142	2045.095 372	2128.242 190	2215.088 702	264
23	2105.473 371	2194.983 839	2288.663 198	2386.713 938	2489.348 633	2596.790 447	276
24	2438.711 438	2548.114 445	2662.869 543	2783.249 347	2909.540 692	3042.045 391	288
25	2822.663 497	2955.992 779	3096.159 965	3243.529 615	3398.486 184	3561.435 118	300
26	3265.047 479	3427.106 674	3597.863 346	3777.802 015	3967.434 806	4167.303 044	312
27	3774.755 874	3971.259 878	4178.781 527	4397.961 118	4629.476 978	4874.047 755	324
28	4362.034 480	4599.776 067	4851.421 866	5117.813 598	5399.845 021	5698.465 199	336
29	5038.688 355	5325.734 484	5630.266 531	5953.385 616	6296.263 629	6660.147 843	348
30	5818.319 116	6164.242 121	6532.084 302	6923.279 611	7339.357 678	7781.950 293	360

FUTURE VALUE PER PERIOD

MOS	15.75% ANNUAL RATE	16.00% ANNUAL RATE	16.25% ANNUAL RATE	16.50% ANNUAL RATE	16.75% ANNUAL RATE	17.00% ANNUAL RATE	MOS
1	1.000 000	1.000 000	1.000 000	1.000 000	1.000 000	1.000 000	1
2	2.013 125	2.013 333	2.013 542	2.013 750	2.013 958	2.014 167	2
3	3.039 547	3.040 178	3.040 808	3.041 439	3.042 070	3.042 701	3
4	4.079 441	4.080 713	4.081 986	4.083 259	4.084 532	4.085 806	4
5	5.132 984	5.135 123	5.137 263	5.139 404	5.141 545	5.143 688	5
6	6.200 354	6.203 591	6.206 830	6.210 070	6.213 313	6.216 557	6
7	7.281 734	7.286 306	7.290 881	7.295 459	7.300 040	7.304 625	7
8	8.377 307	8.383 457	8.389 611	8.395 771	8.401 937	8.408 107	8
9	9.487 259	9.495 236	9.503 221	9.511 213	9.519 214	9.527 222	9
10	10.611 779	10.621 839	10.631 910	10.641 993	10.652 086	10.662 191	10
11	11.751 059	11.763 464	11.775 884	11.788 320	11.800 771	11.813 238	11
12	12.905 291	12.920 310	12.935 349	12.950 409	12.965 490	12.980 593	12
13	14.074 673	14.092 581	14.110 515	14.128 477	14.146 467	14.164 484	13
14	15.259 404	15.280 482	15.301 595	15.322 744	15.343 928	15.365 148	14
15	16.459 683	16.484 221	16.508 804	16.533 432	16.558 104	16.582 821	15
16	17.675 717	17.704 011	17.732 361	17.760 766	17.789 227	17.817 744	16
17	18.907 710	18.940 065	18.972 487	19.004 977	19.037 535	19.070 162	17
18	20.155 874	20.192 599	20.229 406	20.266 295	20.303 268	20.340 323	18
19	21.420 420	21.461 833	21.503 346	21.544 957	21.586 667	21.628 477	19
20	22.701 563	22.747 991	22.794 537	22.841 200	22.887 981	22.934 881	20
21	23.999 521	24.051 298	24.103 213	24.155 267	24.207 459	24.259 792	21
22	25.314 515	25.371 982	25.429 611	25.487 402	25.545 355	25.603 472	22
23	26.646 768	26.710 275	26.773 970	26.837 853	26.901 926	26.966 188	23
24	27.996 506	28.066 412	28.136 534	28.206 874	28.277 432	28.348 209	24
25	29.363 961	29.440 631	29.517 550	29.594 718	29.672 138	29.749 808	25
26	30.749 363	30.833 172	30.917 266	31.001 646	31.086 311	31.171 264	26
27	32.152 948	32.244 281	32.335 938	32.427 918	32.520 224	32.612 857	27
28	33.574 955	33.674 205	33.773 820	33.873 802	33.974 152	34.074 872	28
29	35.015 027	35.123 195	35.231 174	35.339 567	35.448 375	35.557 600	29
30	36.475 207	36.591 504	36.708 263	36.825 486	36.943 175	37.061 332	30
31	37.953 944	38.079 390	38.205 354	38.331 836	38.458 840	38.586 368	31
32	39.452 089	39.587 116	39.722 718	39.858 899	39.995 662	40.133 008	32
33	40.969 898	41.114 944	41.260 630	41.406 959	41.553 934	41.701 559	33
34	42.507 628	42.663 143	42.819 368	42.976 305	43.133 958	43.292 331	34
35	44.065 541	44.231 985	44.399 213	44.567 229	44.736 036	44.905 639	35
36	45.643 901	45.821 745	46.000 453	46.180 028	46.360 477	46.541 802	36
37	47.242 977	47.432 701	47.623 375	47.815 004	48.007 592	48.201 145	37
38	48.863 041	49.065 137	49.268 275	49.472 460	49.677 698	49.883 994	38
39	50.504 368	50.719 339	50.935 450	51.152 706	51.371 116	51.590 684	39
40	52.167 238	52.395 597	52.625 201	52.856 056	53.088 171	53.321 552	40
41	53.851 933	54.094 205	54.337 834	54.582 827	54.829 193	55.076 941	41
42	55.558 740	55.815 461	56.073 658	56.333 341	56.594 517	56.857 197	42
43	57.287 948	57.559 667	57.832 989	58.107 924	58.384 482	58.662 674	43
44	59.039 853	59.327 130	59.616 144	59.906 908	60.199 433	60.493 729	44
45	60.814 751	61.118 158	61.423 446	61.730 628	62.039 716	62.350 723	45
46	62.612 944	62.933 067	63.255 222	63.579 424	63.905 687	64.234 025	46
47	64.434 739	64.772 174	65.111 803	65.453 641	65.797 704	66.144 007	47

YRS							
4	66.280 445	66.635 803	66.993 526	67.353 629	67.716 130	68.081 048	48
5	90.412 448	91.035 516	91.663 875	92.297 573	92.936 659	93.581 182	60
6	118.631 976	119.638 587	120.655 636	121.683 238	122.721 513	123.770 579	72
7	151.631 383	153.169 132	154.725 772	156.301 554	157.896 730	159.511 558	84
8	190.220 294	192.476 010	194.763 845	197.084 288	199.437 840	201.825 006	96
9	235.345 470	238.554 316	241.815 234	245.129 128	248.496 920	251.919 548	108
10	288.114 310	292.570 569	297.108 435	301.729 222	306.434 548	311.226 062	120
11	349.820 646	355.892 244	362.087 136	368.407 990	374.857 532	381.438 553	132
12	421.397 844	430.122 395	438.447 908	446.960 120	455.663 476	464.562 540	144
13	506.360 199	517.140 233	528.184 505	539.499 881	551.093 414	562.972 341	156
14	605.033 769	619.148 703	633.639 919	648.518 025	663.793 937	679.478 890	168
15	720.420 860	738.730 255	757.567 556	776.948 825	796.890 622	817.410 030	180
16	855.352 443	878.912 215	903.203 125	928.249 057	954.074 698	980.705 566	192
17	1013.139 000	1043.243 434	1074.349 121	1106.491 039	1139.705 420	1174.029 800	204
18	1197.651 751	1235.884 123	1275.474 109	1316.472 236	1358.930 965	1402.904 761	216
19	1413.417 633	1461.711 177	1511.829 393	1563.844 393	1617.831 213	1673.867 935	228
20	1665.730 360	1726.441 638	1789.586 131	1855.265 646	1923.586 357	1994.658 995	240
21	1960.780 310	2036.777 427	2115.996 458	2198.579 736	2284.676 038	2374.440 878	252
22	2305.806 395	2400.575 011	2499.582 837	2603.027 124	2711.114 516	2824.061 507	264
23	2709.273 672	2827.044 294	2950.360 579	3079.493 701	3214.728 397	3356.363 651	276
24	3181.081 024	3326.981 781	3480.099 338	3640.803 789	3809.484 623	3986.551 756	288
25	3732.804 025	3913.043 898	4102.630 416	4302.065 315	4511.877 883	4732.626 240	300
26	4377.978 944	4600.067 404	4834.207 889	5081.076 442	5341.387 803	5615.897 651	312
27	5132.434 850	5405.444 997	5693.932 997	5998.804 623	6321.019 699	6661.595 368	324
28	6014.681 969	6349.565 632	6704.252 874	7079.950 943	7477.942 081	7899.588 246	336
29	7046.365 826	7456.330 682	7891.546 631	8353.614 965	8844.240 387	9365.237 774	348
30	8252.798 308	8753.759 030	9286.814 107	9854.077 955	10457.806 766	11100.408 126	360

61

MOS	17.25% ANNUAL RATE	17.50% ANNUAL RATE	17.75% ANNUAL RATE	18.00% ANNUAL RATE	18.25% ANNUAL RATE	18.50% ANNUAL RATE	MOS
1	1.000 000	1.000 000	1.000 000	1.000 000	1.000 000	1.000 000	1
2	2.014 375	2.014 583	2.014 792	2.015 000	2.015 208	2.015 417	2
3	3.043 332	3.043 963	3.044 594	3.045 225	3.045 856	3.046 488	3
4	4.087 080	4.088 354	4.089 628	4.090 903	4.092 179	4.093 454	4
5	5.145 831	5.147 976	5.150 121	5.152 267	5.154 414	5.156 562	5
6	6.219 803	6.223 050	6.226 300	6.229 551	6.232 804	6.236 059	6
7	7.309 212	7.313 803	7.318 397	7.322 994	7.327 595	7.332 198	7
8	8.414 282	8.420 463	8.426 648	8.432 839	8.439 035	8.445 236	8
9	9.535 238	9.543 261	9.551 293	9.559 332	9.567 379	9.575 433	9
10	10.672 307	10.682 434	10.692 572	10.702 722	10.712 883	10.723 055	10
11	11.825 721	11.838 219	11.850 733	11.863 262	11.875 808	11.888 368	11
12	12.995 716	13.010 860	13.026 025	13.041 211	13.056 419	13.071 647	12
13	14.182 529	14.200 602	14.218 702	14.236 830	14.254 985	14.273 169	13
14	15.386 403	15.407 694	15.429 020	15.450 382	15.471 780	15.493 213	14
15	16.607 583	16.632 389	16.657 241	16.682 138	16.707 080	16.732 067	15
16	17.846 317	17.874 945	17.903 629	17.932 370	17.961 167	17.990 020	16
17	19.102 857	19.135 621	19.168 454	19.201 355	19.234 326	19.267 366	17
18	20.377 461	20.414 682	20.451 987	20.489 376	20.526 848	20.564 405	18
19	21.670 387	21.712 396	21.754 506	21.796 716	21.839 027	21.881 439	19
20	22.981 899	23.029 036	23.076 292	23.123 667	23.171 162	23.218 778	20
21	24.312 263	24.364 876	24.417 628	24.470 522	24.523 557	24.576 734	21
22	25.661 752	25.720 197	25.778 806	25.837 580	25.896 520	25.955 625	22
23	27.030 640	27.095 283	27.160 117	27.225 144	27.290 363	27.355 775	23
24	28.419 205	28.490 422	28.561 861	28.633 521	28.705 403	28.777 510	24
25	29.827 732	29.905 908	29.984 338	30.063 024	30.141 965	30.221 163	25
26	31.256 505	31.342 036	31.427 857	31.513 969	31.600 374	31.687 072	26
27	32.705 817	32.799 107	32.892 727	32.986 678	33.080 963	33.175 581	27
28	34.175 964	34.277 427	34.379 265	34.481 479	34.584 069	34.687 038	28
29	35.667 243	35.777 306	35.887 792	35.998 701	36.110 035	36.221 797	29
30	37.179 960	37.299 059	37.418 632	37.538 681	37.659 209	37.780 216	30
31	38.714 422	38.843 003	38.972 116	39.101 762	39.231 943	39.362 661	31
32	40.270 941	40.409 464	40.548 579	40.688 288	40.828 595	40.969 502	32
33	41.849 836	41.998 769	42.148 360	42.298 612	42.449 530	42.601 115	33
34	43.451 428	43.611 251	43.771 804	43.933 092	44.095 116	44.257 883	34
35	45.076 042	45.247 248	45.419 262	45.592 088	45.765 730	45.940 192	35
36	46.724 010	46.907 104	47.091 089	47.275 969	47.461 750	47.648 436	36
37	48.395 668	48.591 166	48.787 644	48.985 109	49.183 564	49.383 016	37
38	50.091 355	50.299 787	50.509 295	50.719 885	50.931 564	51.144 338	38
39	51.811 418	52.033 325	52.256 412	52.480 684	52.706 149	52.932 813	39
40	53.556 208	53.792 145	54.029 371	54.267 894	54.507 721	54.748 860	40
41	55.326 078	55.576 614	55.828 555	56.081 912	56.336 693	56.592 905	41
42	57.121 390	57.387 106	57.654 353	57.923 141	58.193 480	58.465 379	42
43	58.942 510	59.224 001	59.507 157	59.791 988	60.078 506	60.366 721	43
44	60.789 809	61.087 684	61.387 367	61.688 868	61.992 200	62.297 374	44
45	62.663 663	62.978 546	63.295 388	63.614 201	63.934 998	64.257 792	45
46	64.564 453	64.896 984	65.231 633	65.568 414	65.907 343	66.248 433	46
47	66.492 567	66.843 398	67.196 517	67.551 940	67.909 683	68.269 763	47

YRS	17.25%	17.50%	17.75%	18.00%	18.25%	18.50%	MOS
4	68.448 397	68.818 198	69.190 466	69.565 219	69.942 477	70.322 255	48
5	94.231 192	94.886 740	95.547 876	96.214 652	96.887 119	97.565 330	60
6	124.830 558	125.901 571	126.983 743	128.077 197	129.182 062	130.298 463	72
7	161.146 296	162.801 210	164.476 566	166.172 636	167.889 694	169.628 018	84
8	204.246 302	206.702 250	209.193 381	211.720 235	214.283 360	216.883 312	96
9	255.397 966	258.933 147	262.526 080	266.177 771	269.889 247	273.661 552	108
10	316.105 448	321.074 424	326.134 743	331.288 191	336.536 595	341.881 813	120
11	388.153 901	395.006 493	401.999 308	409.135 393	416.417 864	423.849 905	132
12	473.661 972	482.966 559	492.481 202	502.210 922	512.160 866	522.336 307	144
13	575.144 008	587.616 318	600.396 841	613.493 716	626.915 210	640.669 811	156
14	695.584 446	712.122 501	729.105 301	746.545 446	764.455 906	782.850 028	168
15	838.524 666	860.252 699	882.612 872	905.624 513	929.307 560	953.682 578	180
16	1008.168 036	1036.489 374	1065.697 763	1095.822 335	1126.893 208	1158.941 514	192
17	1209.503 064	1246.165 497	1284.058 832	1323.226 308	1363.712 721	1405.564 483	204
18	1448.450 176	1495.625 924	1544.492 974	1595.114 630	1647.556 626	1701.887 217	216
19	1732.035 813	1792.419 399	1855.106 687	1920.189 249	1987.762 384	2057.925 274	228
20	2068.599 050	2145.526 975	2225.568 401	2308.854 370	2395.521 565	2485.712 559	240
21	2468.036 816	2565.633 784	2667.409 426	2773.549 452	2884.248 007	2999.708 064	252
22	2942.094 913	3065.452 376	3194.382 887	3329.147 335	3470.019 084	3617.284 577	264
23	3504.713 421	3660.107 401	3822.891 814	3993.430 261	4172.104 598	4359.315 869	276
24	4172.436 614	4367.593 285	4572.499 718	4787.658 998	5013.600 685	5250.882 223	288
25	4964.899 455	5209.318 748	5466.535 540	5737.253 308	6022.189 595	6322.118 126	300
26	5905.404 985	6210.754 636	6532.839 934	6872.605 521	7231.050 344	7609.230 808	312
27	7021.609 563	7402.204 679	7804.591 485	8230.053 258	8679.950 185	9155.724 025	324
28	8346.336 128	8819.722 487	9321.379 828	9853.042 439	10416.552 809	11013.868 459	336
29	9918.539 384	10506.202 542	11130.417 824	11793.517 795	12497.986 313	13246.468 450	348
30	11784.451 297	12512.678 200	13288.015 149	14113.585 393	14992.722 513	15928.984 743	360

FUTURE VALUE PER PERIOD

MONTHLY COMPOUNDING

MOS	18.75% ANNUAL RATE	19.00% ANNUAL RATE	19.25% ANNUAL RATE	19.50% ANNUAL RATE	19.75% ANNUAL RATE	20.00% ANNUAL RATE	MOS
1	1.000 000	1.000 000	1.000 000	1.000 000	1.000 000	1.000 000	1
2	2.015 625	2.015 833	2.016 042	2.016 250	2.016 458	2.016 667	2
3	3.047 119	3.047 751	3.048 382	3.049 014	3.049 646	3.050 278	3
4	4.094 730	4.096 007	4.097 283	4.098 561	4.099 838	4.101 116	4
5	5.158 711	5.160 860	5.163 011	5.165 162	5.167 314	5.169 468	5
6	6.239 315	6.242 574	6.245 834	6.249 096	6.252 360	6.255 625	6
7	7.336 805	7.341 415	7.346 028	7.350 644	7.355 263	7.359 886	7
8	8.451 442	8.457 654	8.463 870	8.470 092	8.476 319	8.482 551	8
9	9.583 496	9.591 566	9.599 645	9.607 731	9.615 825	9.623 926	9
10	10.733 238	10.743 238	10.753 639	10.763 856	10.774 085	10.784 325	10
11	11.900 945	11.913 537	11.926 145	11.938 769	11.951 409	11.964 064	11
12	13.086 897	13.102 168	13.117 461	13.132 774	13.148 109	13.163 465	12
13	14.291 380	14.309 619	14.327 886	14.346 182	14.364 505	14.382 856	13
14	15.514 683	15.536 188	15.557 730	15.579 307	15.600 921	15.622 570	14
15	16.757 100	16.782 178	16.807 302	16.832 471	16.857 686	16.882 947	15
16	18.018 929	18.047 896	18.076 919	18.105 999	18.135 135	18.164 329	16
17	19.300 475	19.333 654	19.366 903	19.400 221	19.433 609	19.467 068	17
18	20.602 045	20.639 770	20.677 580	20.715 475	20.753 454	20.791 519	18
19	21.923 952	21.966 567	22.009 283	22.052 101	22.095 021	22.138 044	19
20	23.266 514	23.314 371	23.362 348	23.410 448	23.458 669	23.507 012	20
21	24.630 053	24.683 515	24.737 119	24.790 867	24.844 759	24.898 795	21
22	26.014 898	26.074 337	26.133 944	26.193 719	26.253 663	26.313 775	22
23	27.421 381	27.487 181	27.553 176	27.619 367	27.685 754	27.752 338	23
24	28.849 840	28.922 394	28.995 175	29.068 182	29.141 415	29.214 877	24
25	30.300 618	30.380 332	30.460 306	30.540 540	30.621 035	30.701 792	25
26	31.774 066	31.861 354	31.948 940	32.036 823	32.125 006	32.213 488	26
27	33.270 535	33.365 826	33.461 454	33.557 422	33.653 730	33.750 380	27
28	34.790 387	34.894 118	34.998 232	35.102 730	35.207 614	35.312 886	28
29	36.333 987	36.446 608	36.559 662	36.673 149	36.787 073	36.901 434	29
30	37.901 706	38.023 680	38.146 140	38.269 088	38.392 527	38.516 458	30
31	39.493 920	39.625 721	39.758 067	39.890 961	40.024 404	40.158 399	31
32	41.111 012	41.253 128	41.395 853	41.539 189	41.683 139	41.827 706	32
33	42.753 372	42.906 303	43.059 911	43.214 201	43.369 174	43.524 834	33
34	44.421 393	44.585 653	44.750 664	44.916 431	45.082 958	45.250 248	34
35	46.115 478	46.291 592	46.468 539	46.646 323	46.824 948	47.004 419	35
36	47.836 032	48.024 542	48.213 972	48.404 326	48.595 609	48.787 826	36
37	49.583 470	49.784 931	49.987 405	50.190 896	50.395 412	50.600 956	37
38	51.358 212	51.573 192	51.789 286	52.006 498	52.224 836	52.444 305	38
39	53.160 684	53.389 768	53.620 072	53.851 604	54.084 370	54.318 377	39
40	54.991 319	55.235 106	55.480 228	55.726 693	55.974 509	56.223 683	40
41	56.850 559	57.109 662	57.370 223	57.632 251	57.895 756	58.160 745	41
42	58.738 849	59.013 898	59.290 537	59.568 775	59.848 623	60.130 091	42
43	60.656 643	60.948 285	61.241 656	61.536 768	61.833 632	62.132 259	43
44	62.604 403	62.913 299	63.224 074	63.536 741	63.851 310	64.167 796	44
45	64.582 597	64.909 427	65.238 294	65.569 213	65.902 197	66.237 260	45
46	66.591 700	66.937 159	67.284 825	67.634 712	67.986 837	68.341 214	46
47	68.632 196	68.996 998	69.364 185	69.733 776	70.105 787	70.480 234	47

YRS							MOS
4	70.704 574	71.089 450	71.476 903	71.866 950	72.259 611	72.654 905	48
5	98.249 338	98.939 196	99.634 957	100.336 676	101.044 408	101.758 208	60
6	131.426 532	132.566 399	133.718 196	134.882 057	136.058 119	137.246 517	72
7	171.387 891	173.169 599	174.973 432	176.799 685	178.648 655	180.520 645	84
8	219.520 659	222.195 973	224.909 840	227.662 852	230.455 611	233.288 730	96
9	277.495 748	281.392 918	285.354 163	289.380 604	293.473 383	297.633 662	108
10	347.325 745	352.870 328	358.517 538	364.269 392	370.127 946	376.095 300	120
11	431.434 773	439.175 798	447.076 385	455.140 015	463.370 247	471.770 720	132
12	532.742 648	543.385 424	554.270 310	565.403 117	576.789 805	588.436 476	144
13	654.766 237	669.213 441	684.020 615	699.197 202	714.752 897	730.697 658	156
14	801.741 549	821.144 606	841.073 750	861.543 958	882.570 645	904.169 675	168
15	978.770 779	1004.594 042	1031.174 936	1058.536 743	1086.703 475	1115.699 905	180
16	1191.999 436	1226.100 247	1261.278 342	1297.569 280	1335.009 825	1373.637 983	192
17	1448.829 680	1493.558 135	1539.801 470	1587.613 173	1637.048 666	1688.165 376	204
18	1758.177 284	1816.500 430	1876.933 087	1939.554 631	2004.447 491	2071.697 274	216
19	2130.781 143	2206.437 425	2285.005 937	2366.603 063	2451.349 938	2539.372 652	228
20	2579.576 071	2677.267 240	2778.947 897	2884.786 867	2994.960 268	3109.651 838	240
21	3120.141 830	3245.771 169	3376.828 052	3513.555 022	3656.205 678	3805.045 193	252
22	3771.243 971	3932.211 806	4100.517 696	4276.507 066	4460.541 922	4653.001 652	264
23	4555.485 283	4761.055 238	4976.490 405	5202.278 860	5438.933 280	5686.992 197	276
24	5500.090 431	5761.843 068	6036.790 486	6325.617 371	6629.044 574	6947.831 050	288
25	6637.851 055	6970.445 332	7320.205 198	7688.684 833	8076.691 143	8485.286 707	300
26	8008.264 125	8429.331 851	8873.683 644	9342.641 223	9837.602 581	10360.046 428	312
27	9658.903 054	10191.107 326	10754.054 236	11349.564 442	11979.568 138	12646.111 719	324
28	11647.069 205	12318.364 881	13030.103 558	13784.780 285	14585.046 388	15433.719 354	336
29	14041.781 078	14886.924 139	15785.092 675	16739.689 647	17754.339 603	18832.903 252	348
30	16926.170 269	17988.333 579	19119.802 939	20325.199 061	21609.455 063	22977.837 794	360

FUTURE VALUE PER PERIOD

MOS	20.25% ANNUAL RATE	20.50% ANNUAL RATE	20.75% ANNUAL RATE	21.00% ANNUAL RATE	21.25% ANNUAL RATE	21.50% ANNUAL RATE	MOS
1	1.000 000	1.000 000	1.000 000	1.000 000	1.000 000	1.000 000	1
2	2.016 875	2.017 083	2.017 292	2.017 500	2.017 708	2.017 917	2
3	3.050 910	3.051 542	3.052 174	3.052 806	3.053 439	3.054 052	3
4	4.102 394	4.103 672	4.104 951	4.106 230	4.107 510	4.108 790	4
5	5.171 622	5.173 777	5.175 933	5.178 089	5.180 247	5.182 406	5
6	6.258 893	6.262 162	6.265 433	6.268 706	6.271 981	6.275 257	6
7	7.364 512	7.369 141	7.373 773	7.378 408	7.383 047	7.387 689	7
8	8.488 788	8.495 030	8.501 278	8.507 530	8.513 788	8.520 051	8
9	9.632 036	9.640 154	9.648 279	9.656 412	9.664 553	9.672 702	9
10	10.794 577	10.804 840	10.815 114	10.825 399	10.835 697	10.846 005	10
11	11.976 735	11.989 422	12.002 125	12.014 844	12.027 579	12.040 329	11
12	13.178 843	13.194 242	13.209 662	13.225 104	13.240 567	13.256 052	12
13	14.401 236	14.419 643	14.438 079	14.456 543	14.475 035	14.493 556	13
14	15.644 256	15.665 979	15.687 737	15.709 533	15.731 364	15.753 232	14
15	16.908 253	16.933 606	16.959 005	16.984 449	17.009 940	17.035 478	15
16	18.193 580	18.222 888	18.252 254	18.281 677	18.311 158	18.340 697	16
17	19.500 597	19.534 196	19.567 866	19.601 607	19.635 418	19.669 301	17
18	20.829 669	20.867 905	20.906 227	20.944 635	20.983 129	21.021 709	18
19	22.181 170	22.224 399	22.267 730	22.311 166	22.354 705	22.398 348	19
20	23.555 477	23.604 065	23.652 777	23.701 611	23.750 569	23.799 652	20
21	24.952 976	25.007 301	25.061 773	25.116 389	25.171 152	25.226 062	21
22	26.374 057	26.434 510	26.495 132	26.555 926	26.616 892	26.678 029	22
23	27.819 120	27.886 099	27.953 277	28.020 655	28.088 232	28.156 011	23
24	29.288 567	29.362 487	29.436 636	29.511 016	29.585 628	29.660 472	24
25	30.782 812	30.864 096	30.945 645	31.027 459	31.109 540	31.191 889	25
26	32.302 272	32.391 357	32.480 746	32.570 440	32.660 438	32.750 744	26
27	33.847 373	33.944 710	34.042 393	34.140 422	34.238 800	34.337 528	27
28	35.418 547	35.524 599	35.631 042	35.737 880	35.845 113	35.952 742	28
29	37.016 235	37.131 477	37.247 162	37.363 293	37.479 870	37.596 895	29
30	38.640 884	38.765 807	38.891 228	39.017 150	39.143 576	39.270 506	30
31	40.292 949	40.428 056	40.563 722	40.699 950	40.836 743	40.974 103	31
32	41.972 892	42.118 702	42.265 136	42.412 200	42.559 894	42.708 222	32
33	43.681 185	43.838 229	43.995 971	44.154 413	44.313 559	44.473 411	33
34	45.418 305	45.587 133	45.756 735	45.927 115	46.098 278	46.270 227	34
35	47.184 739	47.365 913	47.547 945	47.730 840	47.914 602	48.099 235	35
36	48.980 981	49.175 080	49.370 128	49.566 129	49.763 089	49.961 013	36
37	50.807 514	51.015 155	51.223 820	51.433 537	51.644 311	51.856 148	37
38	52.664 912	52.886 664	53.109 565	53.333 624	53.558 845	53.785 237	38
39	54.553 633	54.790 144	55.027 918	55.266 962	55.507 283	55.748 889	39
40	56.474 225	56.726 142	56.979 443	57.234 134	57.490 225	57.747 723	40
41	58.427 228	58.695 214	58.964 712	59.235 731	59.508 281	59.782 370	41
42	60.413 187	60.697 924	60.984 310	61.272 357	61.562 073	61.853 471	42
43	62.432 660	62.734 847	63.038 831	63.344 623	63.652 235	63.961 679	43
44	64.486 211	64.806 567	65.128 877	65.453 154	65.779 410	66.107 659	44
45	66.574 416	66.913 679	67.255 064	67.598 584	67.944 254	68.292 088	45
46	68.697 859	69.056 788	69.418 016	69.781 559	70.147 433	70.515 654	46
47	70.857 136	71.236 508	71.618 369	72.002 736	72.389 627	72.779 060	47
YRS							
4	73.052 850	73.453 465	73.856 770	74.262 784	74.671 527	75.083 018	48
5	102.478 133	103.204 237	103.936 579	104.675 216	105.420 206	106.171 607	60
6	138.447 391	139.660 882	140.887 130	142.126 280	143.378 477	144.643 867	72
7	182.415 960	184.334 913	186.277 817	188.244 992	190.236 762	192.253 454	84
8	236.162 830	239.078 544	242.036 513	245.037 388	248.081 833	251.170 521	96
9	301.862 626	306.161 478	310.531 446	314.973 777	319.489 744	324.080 641	108
10	382.173 594	388.365 015	394.671 791	401.096 196	407.640 552	414.307 227	120
11	480.345 157	489.097 362	498.031 227	507.150 729	516.459 937	525.963 010	132
12	600.349 386	612.534 945	624.999 722	637.750 450	650.794 025	664.137 518	144
13	747.041 711	763.795 559	780.969 990	798.576 080	816.625 209	835.129 061	156
14	926.357 378	949.150 562	972.566 529	996.623 085	1021.338 561	1046.731 823	168
15	1145.551 588	1176.284 885	1207.926 988	1240.505 953	1274.050 719	1308.591 144	180
16	1413.493 050	1454.615 652	1497.047 794	1540.832 905	1586.015 887	1632.643 169	192
17	1741.022 809	1795.682 628	1852.208 728	1910.667 320	1971.127 020	2033.658 931	204
18	2141.392 884	2213.626 655	2288.494 481	2366.095 959	2446.534 534	2529.917 645	216
19	2630.802 449	2725.775 945	2824.435 348	2926.928 691	3033.410 075	3144.039 919	228
20	3229.053 260	3353.364 518	3482.794 258	3617.560 166	3757.889 370	3904.018 849	240
21	3960.350 845	4122.412 577	4291.533 581	4468.030 916	4652.236 147	4844.496 015	252
22	4854.283 872	5064.805 318	5285.002 771	5515.334 034	5756.278 959	6008.340 515	264
23	5947.021 319	6219.614 917	6505.397 283	6805.024 269	7119.184 893	7448.603 043	276
24	7282.775 892	7634.720 477	8004.550 735	8393.199 527	8801.649 166	9230.934 059	288
25	8915.592 890	9368.793 133	9846.136 426	10348.940 980	10878.598 101	11436.576 288	300
26	10911.536 909	11493.728 585	12108.371 726	12757.317 895	13442.525 876	14166.067 944	312
27	13351.364 844	14097.627 945	14887.340 185	15723.087 912	16607.613 626	17543.825 501	324
28	16333.793 360	17288.450 456	18301.072 479	19375.253 711	20514.814 356	21723.814 872	336
29	19979.493 008	21198.489 552	22494.559 503	23872.674 261	25338.130 087	26896.569 531	348
30	24435.970 627	25989.857 819	27645.910 548	29410.974 741	31292.360 814	33297.875 465	360

FUTURE VALUE PER PERIOD

MOS	21.75% ANNUAL RATE	22.00% ANNUAL RATE	22.50% ANNUAL RATE	23.00% ANNUAL RATE	23.50% ANNUAL RATE	24.00% ANNUAL RATE	MOS
1	1.000 000	1.000 000	1.000 000	1.000 000	1.000 000	1.000 000	1
2	2.018 125	2.018 333	2.018 750	2.019 167	2.019 583	2.020 000	2
3	3.054 704	3.055 336	3.056 602	3.057 867	3.059 134	3.060 400	3
4	4.110 070	4.111 351	4.113 913	4.116 476	4.119 042	4.121 608	4
5	5.184 565	5.186 725	5.191 049	5.195 376	5.199 706	5.204 040	5
6	6.278 535	6.281 815	6.288 381	6.294 954	6.301 534	6.308 121	6
7	7.392 334	7.396 982	7.406 288	7.415 607	7.424 939	7.434 283	7
8	8.526 320	8.532 593	8.545 156	8.557 739	8.570 344	8.582 969	8
9	9.680 859	9.689 024	9.705 378	9.721 763	9.738 180	9.754 628	9
10	10.856 325	10.866 656	10.887 353	10.908 097	10.928 886	10.949 721	10
11	12.053 096	12.065 878	12.091 491	12.117 168	12.142 910	12.168 715	11
12	13.271 558	13.287 086	13.318 207	13.349 414	13.380 708	13.412 090	12
13	14.512 105	14.530 683	14.567 923	14.605 278	14.642 747	14.680 332	13
14	15.775 137	15.797 078	15.841 072	15.885 212	15.929 501	15.973 938	14
15	17.061 061	17.086 692	17.138 092	17.189 679	17.241 454	17.293 417	15
16	18.370 293	18.399 948	18.459 431	18.519 148	18.579 099	18.639 285	16
17	19.703 255	19.737 280	19.805 545	19.874 098	19.942 940	20.012 071	17
18	21.060 376	21.099 130	21.176 899	21.255 018	21.333 489	21.412 312	18
19	22.442 096	22.485 948	22.573 966	22.662 406	22.751 270	22.840 559	19
20	23.848 858	23.898 190	23.997 228	24.096 769	24.196 815	24.297 370	20
21	25.281 119	25.336 323	25.447 176	25.558 624	25.670 670	25.783 317	21
22	26.739 339	26.800 823	26.924 311	27.048 497	27.173 387	27.298 984	22
23	28.223 990	28.292 171	28.429 141	28.566 927	28.705 532	28.844 963	23
24	29.735 550	29.810 861	29.962 188	30.114 460	30.267 682	30.421 862	24
25	31.274 507	31.357 393	31.523 979	31.691 653	31.860 425	32.030 300	25
26	32.841 357	32.932 279	33.115 053	33.299 077	33.484 358	33.670 906	26
27	34.436 607	34.536 037	34.735 961	34.937 309	35.140 093	35.344 324	27
28	36.060 770	36.169 198	36.387 260	36.606 941	36.828 253	37.051 210	28
29	37.714 371	37.832 300	38.069 521	38.308 574	38.549 473	38.792 235	29
30	39.397 944	39.525 892	39.783 325	40.042 822	40.304 400	40.568 079	30
31	41.112 032	41.250 533	41.529 262	41.810 309	42.093 695	42.379 441	31
32	42.857 188	43.006 793	43.307 936	43.611 673	43.918 030	44.227 030	32
33	44.633 974	44.795 251	45.119 959	45.447 564	45.778 091	46.111 570	33
34	46.442 965	46.616 497	46.965 999	47.318 642	47.674 579	48.033 802	34
35	48.284 744	48.471 133	48.846 570	49.225 583	49.608 206	49.994 478	35
36	50.159 905	50.359 771	50.762 444	51.169 073	51.579 700	51.994 367	36
37	52.069 053	52.283 033	52.714 239	53.149 813	53.589 803	54.034 255	37
38	54.012 805	54.241 555	54.702 631	55.168 518	55.639 270	56.114 940	38
39	55.991 787	56.235 984	56.728 306	57.225 915	57.728 872	58.237 238	39
40	58.006 638	58.266 977	58.791 961	59.322 745	59.859 396	60.401 983	40
41	60.058 008	60.335 205	60.894 311	61.459 764	62.031 642	62.610 023	41
42	62.146 560	62.441 350	63.036 079	63.637 743	64.246 428	64.862 223	42
43	64.272 966	64.586 108	65.218 006	65.857 466	66.504 588	67.159 468	43
44	66.437 914	66.770 187	67.440 843	68.119 734	68.806 969	69.502 657	44
45	68.642 101	68.994 307	69.705 359	70.425 363	71.154 439	71.892 710	45
46	70.886 239	71.259 203	72.012 334	72.775 182	73.547 880	74.330 564	46
47	73.171 052	73.565 621	74.362 566	75.170 040	75.988 193	76.817 176	47

YRS

YRS							MOS
4	75.497 277	75.914 324	76.756 864	77.610 799	78.476 295	79.353 519	48
5	106.929 478	107.693 880	109.242 516	110.818 005	112.420 843	114.051 539	60
6	145.922 601	147.214 827	149.840 369	152.521 731	155.260 182	158.057 019	72
7	194.295 401	196.362 941	200.576 169	204.895 930	209.325 093	213.866 607	84
8	254.304 134	257.483 368	263.981 530	270.670 790	277.557 113	284.646 659	96
9	328.747 786	333.492 521	343.220 248	353.275 053	363.668 574	374.412 879	108
10	421.098 305	428.017 244	442.246 172	457.014 754	472.344 585	488.258 152	120
11	535.664 203	545.567 866	566.000 490	587.297 686	609.497 936	632.641 484	132
12	677.788 174	691.753 417	720.658 289	750.915 300	782.590 795	815.754 461	144
13	854.099 638	873.549 268	913.936 672	956.396 733	1001.040 713	1047.985 991	156
14	1072.822 295	1099.629 967	1155.479 833	1214.453 422	1276.733 000	1342.511 724	168
15	1344.158 028	1380.783 150	1457.340 277	1538.537 467	1624.667 383	1716.041 568	180
16	1680.762 756	1730.424 286	1834.580 217	1945.542 878	2063.774 099	2189.767 727	192
17	2098.336 739	2165.236 806	2306.023 148	2456.686 228	2617.943 844	2790.567 042	204
18	2616.356 886	2705.968 169	2895.193 100	3098.612 642	3317.327 603	3552.525 843	216
19	3258.985 222	3378.419 841	3631.488 437	3904.784 769	4199.977 093	4518.873 840	228
20	4056.195 871	4214.678 439	4551.648 778	4917.227 136	5313.915 060	5744.436 758	240
21	5045.173 142	5254.646 770	5701.588 225	6188.716 824	6719.748 075	7298.746 872	252
22	6272.045 921	6547.947 827	7138.686 385	7785.534 657	8493.963 986	9269.987 921	264
23	7794.039 256	8156.292 597	8934.651 489	9790.920 321	10733.093 433	11769.998 206	276
24	9682.143 509	10156.424 648	11179.098 493	12309.411 522	13558.961 834	14940.615 736	288
25	12024.425 558	12643.782 022	13984.020 033	15472.293 377	17125.317 603	18961.725 403	300
26	14930.136 509	15737.051 142	17489.377 848	19444.442 108	21626.197 213	24061.464 743	312
27	18534.807 486	19583.830 033	21870.080 120	24432.919 789	27306.482 237	30529.167 325	324
28	23006.571 222	24367.671 098	27344.715 492	30697.768 177	34475.222 740	38731.778 032	336
29	28554.004 271	30316.839 476	34186.456 971	38565.564 293	43522.451 915	49134.671 768	348
30	35435.855 651	37715.204 912	42736.693 342	48446.444 386	54940.406 816	62328.056 387	360

65

FUTURE VALUE PER PERIOD

QTRS	5.25% ANNUAL RATE	5.50% ANNUAL RATE	5.75% ANNUAL RATE	6.00% ANNUAL RATE	6.25% ANNUAL RATE	6.50% ANNUAL RATE	QTRS
1	1.000 000	1.000 000	1.000 000	1.000 000	1.000 000	1.000 000	1
2	2.013 125	2.013 750	2.014 375	2.015 000	2.015 625	2.016 250	2
3	3.039 547	3.041 439	3.043 332	3.045 225	3.047 119	3.049 014	3
4	4.079 441	4.083 259	4.087 080	4.090 903	4.094 730	4.098 561	4
5	5.132 984	5.139 404	5.145 831	5.152 267	5.158 711	5.165 162	5
6	6.200 354	6.210 070	6.219 803	6.229 551	6.239 315	6.249 096	6
7	7.281 734	7.295 459	7.309 212	7.322 994	7.336 805	7.350 644	7
8	8.377 307	8.395 771	8.414 282	8.432 839	8.451 442	8.470 092	8
9	9.487 259	9.511 213	9.535 238	9.559 332	9.583 496	9.607 731	9
10	10.611 779	10.641 993	10.672 307	10.702 722	10.733 238	10.763 856	10
11	11.751 059	11.788 320	11.825 721	11.863 262	11.900 945	11.938 769	11
12	12.905 291	12.950 409	12.995 716	13.041 211	13.086 897	13.132 774	12
13	14.074 673	14.128 477	14.182 529	14.236 830	14.291 380	14.346 182	13
14	15.259 404	15.322 744	15.386 403	15.450 382	15.514 683	15.579 307	14
15	16.459 683	16.533 432	16.607 583	16.682 138	16.757 100	16.832 471	15
16	17.675 717	17.760 766	17.846 317	17.932 370	18.018 929	18.105 999	16
17	18.907 710	19.004 977	19.102 857	19.201 355	19.300 475	19.400 221	17
18	20.155 874	20.266 295	20.377 461	20.489 376	20.602 045	20.715 475	18
19	21.420 420	21.544 957	21.670 387	21.796 716	21.923 952	22.052 101	19
20	22.701 563	22.841 200	22.981 899	23.123 667	23.266 514	23.410 448	20
21	23.999 521	24.155 267	24.312 263	24.470 522	24.630 053	24.790 867	21
22	25.314 515	25.487 402	25.661 752	25.837 580	26.014 898	26.193 719	22
23	26.646 768	26.837 853	27.030 640	27.225 144	27.421 381	27.619 367	23
24	27.996 506	28.206 874	28.419 205	28.633 521	28.849 840	29.068 182	24
25	29.363 961	29.594 718	29.827 732	30.063 024	30.300 618	30.540 540	25
26	30.749 363	31.001 646	31.256 505	31.513 969	31.774 066	32.036 823	26
27	32.152 948	32.427 918	32.705 817	32.986 678	33.270 535	33.557 422	27
28	33.574 955	33.873 802	34.175 964	34.481 479	34.790 387	35.102 730	28
29	35.015 627	35.339 567	35.667 243	35.998 701	36.333 987	36.673 149	29
30	36.475 207	36.825 486	37.179 960	37.538 681	37.901 706	38.269 088	30
31	37.953 944	38.331 836	38.714 422	39.101 762	39.493 920	39.890 961	31
32	39.452 089	39.858 899	40.270 941	40.688 288	41.111 012	41.539 189	32
33	40.969 898	41.406 959	41.849 836	42.298 612	42.753 372	43.214 201	33
34	42.507 628	42.976 305	43.451 428	43.933 092	44.421 393	44.916 431	34
35	44.065 541	44.567 229	45.076 042	45.592 088	46.115 478	46.646 323	35
36	45.643 901	46.180 028	46.724 010	47.275 969	47.836 032	48.404 326	36
37	47.242 977	47.815 004	48.395 668	48.985 109	49.583 470	50.190 896	37
38	48.863 041	49.472 460	50.091 355	50.719 885	51.358 212	52.006 498	38
39	50.504 368	51.152 706	51.811 418	52.480 684	53.160 684	53.851 604	39
40	52.167 238	52.856 056	53.556 208	54.267 894	54.991 319	55.726 693	40
41	53.851 933	54.582 827	55.326 078	56.081 912	56.850 559	57.632 251	41
42	55.558 740	56.333 341	57.121 390	57.923 141	58.738 849	59.568 775	42
43	57.287 948	58.107 924	58.942 510	59.791 988	60.656 643	61.536 768	43
44	59.039 853	59.906 908	60.789 809	61.688 868	62.604 403	63.536 741	44
45	60.814 751	61.730 628	62.663 663	63.614 201	64.582 597	65.569 213	45
46	62.612 944	63.579 424	64.564 453	65.568 414	66.591 700	67.634 712	46
47	64.434 739	65.453 641	66.492 567	67.551 940	68.632 196	69.733 776	47
48	66.280 445	67.353 629	68.448 397	69.565 219	70.704 574	71.866 950	48
49	68.150 376	69.279 741	70.432 343	71.608 698	72.809 333	74.034 788	49
50	70.044 850	71.232 338	72.444 808	73.682 828	74.946 978	76.237 853	50
51	71.964 188	73.211 782	74.486 202	75.788 070	77.118 025	78.476 719	51
52	73.908 718	75.218 444	76.556 941	77.924 892	79.322 994	80.751 965	52
53	75.878 770	77.252 698	78.657 447	80.093 765	81.562 416	83.064 185	53
54	77.874 679	79.314 923	80.788 148	82.295 171	83.836 829	85.413 978	54
55	79.896 784	81.405 503	82.949 478	84.529 599	86.146 779	87.801 955	55

YRS							
14	81.945 430	83.524 828	85.141 877	86.797 543	88.492 823	90.228 737	56
15	90.412 448	92.297 573	94.231 192	96.214 652	98.249 338	100.336 676	60
16	99.332 813	101.562 861	103.854 521	106.209 628	108.630 077	111.117 821	64
17	108.730 798	111.348 348	114.043 237	116.817 931	119.674 977	122.617 007	68
18	118.631 976	121.683 238	124.830 558	128.077 197	131.426 532	134.882 057	72
19	129.063 290	132.598 379	136.251 654	140.027 372	143.929 953	147.963 980	76
20	140.053 124	144.126 349	148.343 759	152.710 852	157.233 345	161.917 180	80
21	151.631 383	156.301 554	161.146 296	166.172 636	171.387 891	176.799 685	84
22	163.829 573	169.160 334	174.701 006	180.460 482	186.448 046	192.673 389	88
23	176.680 887	182.741 067	189.052 078	195.625 082	202.471 753	209.604 307	92
24	190.220 294	197.084 288	204.246 302	211.720 235	219.520 659	227.662 852	96
25	204.484 637	212.232 807	220.333 213	228.803 043	237.660 356	246.924 124	100
26	219.512 732	228.231 836	237.365 258	246.934 114	256.960 635	267.468 229	104
27	235.345 470	245.129 128	255.397 966	266.177 771	277.495 748	289.380 604	108
28	252.025 936	262.975 115	274.490 128	286.602 288	299.344 702	312.752 378	112
29	269.599 518	281.823 062	294.703 988	308.280 125	322.591 555	337.680 750	116
30	288.114 037	301.729 222	316.105 448	331.288 191	347.325 745	364.269 392	120

66

FUTURE VALUE PER PERIOD

QUARTERLY COMPOUNDING

	6.75% ANNUAL RATE	7.00% ANNUAL RATE	7.25% ANNUAL RATE	7.50% ANNUAL RATE	7.75% ANNUAL RATE	8.00% ANNUAL RATE	
QTRS							QTRS
1	1.000 000	1.000 000	1.000 000	1.000 000	1.000 000	1.000 000	1
2	2.016 875	2.017 500	2.018 125	2.018 750	2.019 375	2.020 000	2
3	3.050 910	3.052 806	3.054 704	3.056 602	3.058 500	3.060 400	3
4	4.102 394	4.106 230	4.110 070	4.113 913	4.117 759	4.121 608	4
5	5.171 622	5.178 089	5.184 565	5.191 049	5.197 540	5.204 040	5
6	6.258 893	6.268 706	6.278 535	6.288 381	6.298 243	6.308 121	6
7	7.364 512	7.378 408	7.392 334	7.406 288	7.420 271	7.434 283	7
8	8.488 788	8.507 530	8.526 320	8.545 156	8.564 039	8.582 969	8
9	9.632 036	9.656 412	9.680 859	9.705 378	9.729 967	9.754 628	9
10	10.794 577	10.825 399	10.856 325	10.887 353	10.918 485	10.949 721	10
11	11.976 735	12.014 844	12.053 096	12.091 491	12.130 031	12.168 715	11
12	13.178 843	13.225 104	13.271 558	13.318 207	13.365 050	13.412 090	12
13	14.401 236	14.456 543	14.512 105	14.567 923	14.623 998	14.680 332	13
14	15.644 256	15.709 533	15.775 137	15.841 072	15.907 338	15.973 938	14
15	16.908 253	16.984 449	17.061 061	17.138 092	17.215 543	17.293 417	15
16	18.193 580	18.281 677	18.370 293	18.459 431	18.549 094	18.639 285	16
17	19.500 597	19.601 607	19.703 255	19.805 545	19.908 483	20.012 071	17
18	20.829 669	20.944 635	21.060 376	21.176 899	21.294 210	21.412 312	18
19	22.181 170	22.311 166	22.442 096	22.573 966	22.706 785	22.840 559	19
20	23.555 477	23.701 611	23.848 858	23.997 228	24.146 729	24.297 370	20
21	24.952 976	25.116 389	25.281 119	25.447 176	25.614 572	25.783 317	21
22	26.374 057	26.555 926	26.739 339	26.924 311	27.110 854	27.298 984	22
23	27.819 120	28.020 655	28.223 990	28.429 141	28.636 127	28.844 963	23
24	29.288 567	29.511 016	29.735 550	29.962 188	30.190 952	30.421 862	24
25	30.782 812	31.027 459	31.274 507	31.523 979	31.775 901	32.030 300	25
26	32.302 272	32.570 440	32.841 357	33.115 053	33.391 560	33.670 906	26
27	33.847 373	34.140 422	34.436 607	34.735 961	35.038 521	35.344 324	27
28	35.418 547	35.737 880	36.060 770	36.387 260	36.717 392	37.051 210	28
29	37.016 235	37.363 293	37.714 371	38.069 521	38.428 792	38.792 235	29
30	38.640 884	39.017 150	39.397 944	39.783 325	40.173 350	40.568 079	30
31	40.292 949	40.699 950	41.112 032	41.529 262	41.951 708	42.379 441	31
32	41.972 892	42.412 200	42.857 188	43.307 936	43.764 523	44.227 030	32
33	43.681 185	44.154 413	44.633 974	45.119 959	45.612 460	46.111 570	33
34	45.418 305	45.927 115	46.442 965	46.965 959	47.496 202	48.033 802	34
35	47.184 739	47.730 840	48.284 744	48.846 570	49.416 441	49.994 478	35
36	48.980 981	49.566 129	50.159 905	50.762 444	51.373 884	51.994 367	36
37	50.807 535	51.433 537	52.069 053	52.714 239	53.369 253	54.034 255	37
38	52.664 912	53.333 624	54.012 805	54.702 631	55.403 282	56.114 940	38
39	54.553 633	55.266 963	55.991 787	56.728 306	57.476 721	58.237 238	39
40	56.474 225	57.234 134	58.006 638	58.791 961	59.590 332	60.401 983	40
41	58.427 228	59.235 731	60.058 008	60.894 311	61.744 895	62.610 023	41
42	60.413 187	61.272 357	62.146 560	63.036 079	63.941 203	64.862 223	42
43	62.432 660	63.344 623	64.272 966	65.218 006	66.180 063	67.159 468	43
44	64.486 211	65.453 154	66.437 914	67.440 843	68.462 302	69.502 657	44
45	66.574 416	67.598 584	68.642 101	69.705 359	70.788 759	71.892 710	45
46	68.697 859	69.781 559	70.886 239	72.012 334	73.160 291	74.330 564	46
47	70.857 136	72.002 736	73.171 052	74.362 566	75.577 772	76.817 176	47
48	73.052 850	74.262 784	75.497 277	76.756 864	78.042 091	79.353 519	48
49	75.285 617	76.562 383	77.865 665	79.196 055	80.554 157	81.940 590	49
50	77.556 061	78.902 225	80.276 981	81.680 981	83.114 894	84.579 401	50
51	79.864 820	81.283 014	82.732 001	84.212 499	85.725 245	87.270 989	51
52	82.212 539	83.705 466	85.231 518	86.791 484	88.386 171	90.016 409	52
53	84.599 875	86.170 312	87.776 340	89.418 824	91.098 653	92.816 737	53
54	87.027 498	88.678 292	90.367 286	92.095 427	93.863 690	95.673 072	54
55	89.496 087	91.230 163	93.005 193	94.822 216	96.682 299	98.586 534	55
YRS							
14	92.006 334	93.826 690	95.690 912	97.600 133	99.555 518	101.558 264	56
15	102.478 133	104.675 216	106.929 478	109.242 516	111.615 973	114.051 539	60
16	113.674 872	116.303 306	119.005 262	121.782 945	124.638 631	127.574 662	64
17	125.646 738	128.766 979	131.980 631	135.290 691	138.700 256	142.212 525	68
18	138.447 391	142.126 280	145.922 601	149.840 369	153.883 740	158.057 019	72
19	152.134 207	156.445 567	160.903 178	165.512 348	170.278 587	175.207 608	76
20	166.768 532	171.793 824	176.999 733	182.393 199	187.981 440	193.771 958	80
21	182.415 960	188.244 992	194.295 401	200.576 169	207.096 654	213.866 607	84
22	199.146 626	205.878 326	212.879 511	220.161 699	227.736 911	235.617 701	88
23	217.035 524	224.778 773	232.848 044	241.257 975	250.023 880	259.161 785	92
24	236.162 830	245.037 388	254.304 134	263.981 530	274.088 938	284.646 659	96
25	256.614 280	266.751 768	277.358 595	288.457 887	300.073 945	312.232 306	100
26	278.481 541	290.026 522	302.130 499	314.822 249	328.132 076	342.091 897	104
27	301.862 626	314.973 777	328.747 786	343.220 248	358.428 730	374.412 879	108
28	326.862 334	341.713 718	357.347 929	373.808 752	391.142 498	409.398 150	112
29	353.592 720	370.375 165	388.078 640	406.756 727	426.466 222	447.267 331	116
30	382.173 594	401.096 196	421.098 635	442.246 172	464.608 129	488.258 152	120

QTRS	8.25% ANNUAL RATE	8.50% ANNUAL RATE	8.75% ANNUAL RATE	9.00% ANNUAL RATE	9.25% ANNUAL RATE	9.50% ANNUAL RATE	QTRS
1	1.000 000	1.000 000	1.000 000	1.000 000	1.000 000	1.000 000	1
2	2.020 625	2.021 250	2.021 875	2.022 500	2.023 125	2.023 750	2
3	3.062 300	3.064 202	3.066 104	3.068 006	3.069 910	3.071 814	3
4	4.125 460	4.129 316	4.133 175	4.137 036	4.140 901	4.144 770	4
5	5.210 548	5.217 064	5.223 588	5.230 120	5.236 660	5.243 208	5
6	6.318 016	6.327 926	6.337 854	6.347 797	6.357 758	6.367 734	6
7	7.448 325	7.462 395	7.476 494	7.490 623	7.504 781	7.518 968	7
8	8.601 946	8.620 971	8.640 043	8.659 162	8.678 329	8.697 543	8
9	9.779 361	9.804 166	9.829 043	9.853 993	9.879 015	9.904 110	9
10	10.981 061	11.012 505	11.044 054	11.075 708	11.107 467	11.139 333	10
11	12.207 545	12.246 521	12.285 643	12.324 911	12.364 327	12.403 892	11
12	13.459 326	13.506 759	13.554 391	13.602 222	13.650 253	13.698 484	12
13	14.736 924	14.793 778	14.850 893	14.908 272	14.965 915	15.023 823	13
14	16.040 873	16.108 146	16.175 757	16.243 708	16.312 001	16.380 639	14
15	17.371 716	17.450 444	17.529 601	17.609 191	17.689 216	17.769 679	15
16	18.730 008	18.821 266	18.913 061	19.005 398	19.098 280	19.191 709	16
17	20.116 314	20.221 218	20.326 784	20.433 020	20.539 927	20.647 512	17
18	21.531 213	21.650 918	21.771 433	21.892 763	22.014 913	22.137 890	18
19	22.975 295	23.111 000	23.247 683	23.385 350	23.524 008	23.663 665	19
20	24.449 160	24.602 109	24.756 226	24.911 520	25.068 001	25.225 677	20
21	25.953 424	26.124 904	26.297 768	26.472 029	26.647 698	26.824 787	21
22	27.488 713	27.680 058	27.873 032	28.067 650	28.263 926	28.461 876	22
23	29.055 668	29.268 259	29.482 755	29.699 172	29.917 530	30.137 846	23
24	30.654 941	30.890 210	31.127 690	31.367 403	31.609 372	31.853 619	24
25	32.287 200	32.546 627	32.808 608	33.073 170	33.340 339	33.610 143	25
26	33.953 123	34.238 243	34.526 296	34.817 316	35.111 334	35.408 384	26
27	35.653 406	35.965 805	36.281 559	36.600 706	36.923 284	37.249 333	27
28	37.388 758	37.730 079	38.075 218	38.424 222	38.777 135	39.134 004	28
29	39.159 901	39.531 843	39.908 114	40.288 767	40.673 856	41.063 437	29
30	40.967 514	41.371 895	41.781 104	42.195 264	42.614 439	43.038 694	30
31	42.812 530	43.251 047	43.695 065	44.144 657	44.599 898	45.060 863	31
32	44.695 538	45.170 132	45.650 895	46.137 912	46.631 271	47.131 058	32
33	46.617 384	47.129 997	47.649 508	48.176 015	48.709 619	49.250 421	33
34	48.578 867	49.131 510	49.691 841	50.259 976	50.836 029	51.420 118	34
35	50.580 807	51.175 554	51.778 850	52.390 825	53.011 612	53.641 346	35
36	52.624 036	53.263 035	53.911 513	54.569 619	55.237 505	55.915 328	36
37	54.709 406	55.394 874	56.090 827	56.797 435	57.514 873	58.243 317	37
38	56.837 788	57.572 016	58.317 814	59.075 377	59.844 904	60.626 596	38
39	59.010 067	59.795 421	60.593 516	61.404 573	62.228 818	63.066 478	39
40	61.227 150	62.066 074	62.918 999	63.786 176	64.667 859	65.564 306	40
41	63.489 960	64.384 978	65.295 352	66.221 365	67.163 303	68.121 459	41
42	65.799 440	66.753 158	67.723 688	68.711 346	69.716 455	70.739 343	42
43	68.156 554	69.171 663	70.205 144	71.257 351	72.328 648	73.419 403	43
44	70.562 283	71.641 561	72.740 881	73.860 642	75.001 248	76.163 114	44
45	73.017 630	74.163 944	75.332 088	76.522 506	77.735 652	78.971 987	45
46	75.523 618	76.739 928	77.979 977	79.244 262	80.533 288	81.847 572	46
47	78.081 293	79.370 651	80.685 789	82.027 258	83.395 621	84.791 452	47
48	80.691 720	82.057 278	83.450 791	84.872 872	86.324 144	87.805 249	48
49	83.355 986	84.800 995	86.276 277	87.782 511	89.320 390	90.890 624	49
50	86.075 204	87.603 016	89.163 571	90.757 618	92.385 924	94.049 276	50
51	88.850 505	90.464 580	92.114 024	93.799 664	95.522 349	97.282 946	51
52	91.683 046	93.386 952	95.129 018	96.910 157	98.731 303	100.593 416	52
53	94.574 009	96.371 425	98.209 965	100.090 635	102.014 465	103.982 510	53
54	97.524 598	99.419 318	101.358 308	103.342 674	105.373 549	107.452 094	54
55	100.536 043	102.531 978	104.575 521	106.667 885	108.810 312	111.004 082	55

YRS							
14	103.609 599	105.710 783	107.863 111	110.067 912	112.326 551	114.640 429	56
15	116.550 953	119.116 005	121.748 534	124.450 435	127.223 657	130.070 205	60
16	130.593 457	133.697 507	136.889 382	140.171 731	143.547 285	147.018 862	64
17	145.830 804	149.558 507	153.399 162	157.356 417	161.434 037	165.635 915	68
18	162.364 660	166.811 276	171.401 645	176.140 711	181.033 595	186.085 599	72
19	180.305 343	185.577 942	191.031 790	196.673 509	202.509 974	208.548 315	76
20	199.772 555	205.991 344	212.436 758	219.117 569	226.042 839	233.222 222	80
21	220.896 187	228.195 980	235.777 018	243.650 796	251.829 291	260.324 986	84
22	243.817 178	252.349 028	261.227 546	270.467 657	280.084 948	290.095 699	88
23	268.688 461	278.621 457	288.979 137	299.780 720	311.046 321	322.796 990	92
24	295.675 983	307.199 238	319.239 838	331.822 341	344.972 503	358.717 340	96
25	324.959 809	338.284 660	352.238 505	366.846 502	382.147 401	398.173 627	100
26	356.735 326	372.097 766	388.216 507	405.130 828	422.882 105	441.513 923	104
27	391.214 546	408.877 902	427.449 575	446.978 787	467.517 498	489.120 564	108
28	428.627 521	448.885 420	470.229 831	492.722 092	516.427 101	541.413 520	112
29	469.223 876	492.403 517	516.877 986	542.723 336	570.020 207	598.854 105	116
30	513.274 479	539.740 238	567.743 749	597.378 862	628.745 301	661.949 042	120

FUTURE VALUE PER PERIOD

QTRS	9.75% ANNUAL RATE	10.00% ANNUAL RATE	10.25% ANNUAL RATE	10.50% ANNUAL RATE	10.75% ANNUAL RATE	11.00% ANNUAL RATE	QTRS
1	1.000 000	1.000 000	1.000 000	1.000 000	1.000 000	1.000 000	1
2	2.024 375	2.025 000	2.025 625	2.026 250	2.026 875	2.027 500	2
3	3.073 719	3.075 625	3.077 532	3.079 439	3.081 347	3.083 256	3
4	4.148 641	4.152 516	4.156 393	4.160 274	4.164 158	4.168 046	4
5	5.249 764	5.256 329	5.262 901	5.269 482	5.276 070	5.282 667	5
6	6.377 727	6.387 737	6.397 763	6.407 805	6.417 865	6.427 940	6
7	7.533 184	7.547 430	7.561 705	7.576 010	7.590 345	7.604 709	7
8	8.716 806	8.736 116	8.755 474	8.774 881	8.794 335	8.813 838	8
9	9.929 278	9.954 519	9.979 833	10.005 221	10.030 683	10.056 219	9
10	11.171 304	11.203 382	11.235 566	11.267 858	11.300 258	11.332 765	10
11	12.443 604	12.483 466	12.523 478	12.563 640	12.603 952	12.644 416	11
12	13.746 917	13.795 553	13.844 392	13.893 435	13.942 683	13.992 137	12
13	15.081 998	15.140 442	15.199 154	15.258 138	15.317 393	15.376 921	13
14	16.449 622	16.518 953	16.588 633	16.658 664	16.729 048	16.799 786	14
15	17.850 582	17.931 927	18.013 717	18.095 954	18.178 641	18.261 781	15
16	19.285 690	19.380 225	19.475 318	19.570 973	19.667 192	19.763 979	16
17	20.755 778	20.864 730	20.974 373	21.084 711	21.195 748	21.307 489	17
18	22.261 700	22.386 349	22.511 841	22.638 184	22.765 383	22.893 445	18
19	23.804 329	23.946 007	24.088 707	24.232 437	24.377 203	24.523 015	19
20	25.384 560	25.544 658	25.705 980	25.868 538	26.032 340	26.197 398	20
21	27.003 309	27.183 274	27.364 696	27.547 587	27.731 960	27.917 826	21
22	28.661 514	28.862 856	29.065 917	29.270 711	29.477 256	29.685 566	22
23	30.360 139	30.584 427	30.810 731	31.039 068	31.269 457	31.501 919	23
24	32.100 167	32.349 038	32.600 256	32.853 843	33.109 824	33.368 222	24
25	33.882 609	34.157 764	34.435 637	34.716 256	34.999 650	35.285 848	25
26	35.708 497	36.011 708	36.318 050	36.627 558	36.940 266	37.256 209	26
27	37.578 892	37.912 001	38.248 700	38.589 032	38.933 036	39.280 755	27
28	39.494 877	39.859 801	40.228 823	40.601 994	40.979 361	41.360 975	28
29	41.457 565	41.856 296	42.259 687	42.667 796	43.080 681	43.498 402	29
30	43.468 093	43.902 703	44.342 591	44.787 826	45.238 475	45.694 608	30
31	45.527 628	46.000 271	46.478 870	46.963 506	47.454 259	47.951 210	31
32	47.637 364	48.150 278	48.669 891	49.196 298	49.729 592	50.269 868	32
33	49.798 524	50.354 034	50.917 057	51.487 701	52.066 075	52.652 290	33
34	52.012 363	52.612 885	53.221 807	53.839 253	54.465 350	55.100 228	34
35	54.280 165	54.928 207	55.585 616	56.252 533	56.929 107	57.615 484	35
36	56.603 244	57.301 413	58.009 997	58.729 162	59.459 076	60.199 910	36
37	58.982 948	59.733 948	60.496 503	61.270 803	62.057 039	62.855 407	37
38	61.420 657	62.227 297	63.046 726	63.879 162	64.724 822	65.583 931	38
39	63.917 786	64.782 979	65.662 299	66.555 990	67.464 302	68.387 489	39
40	66.475 782	67.402 554	68.344 895	69.303 084	70.277 405	71.268 145	40
41	69.096 129	70.087 617	71.096 233	72.122 290	73.166 110	74.228 019	41
42	71.780 347	72.839 808	73.918 074	75.015 500	76.132 449	77.269 289	42
43	74.529 993	75.660 803	76.812 224	77.984 657	79.178 509	80.394 195	43
44	77.346 662	78.552 323	79.780 538	81.031 754	82.306 431	83.605 035	44
45	80.231 987	81.516 131	82.824 914	84.158 838	85.518 417	86.904 174	45
46	83.187 641	84.554 034	85.947 302	87.368 008	88.816 724	90.294 039	46
47	86.215 340	87.667 885	89.149 702	90.661 418	92.203 673	93.777 125	47
48	89.316 839	90.859 582	92.434 163	94.041 280	95.681 647	97.355 996	48
49	92.493 937	94.131 072	95.802 789	97.509 864	99.253 091	101.033 285	49
50	95.748 476	97.484 349	99.257 735	101.069 497	102.920 518	104.811 701	50
51	99.082 346	100.921 458	102.801 215	104.722 572	106.686 507	108.694 023	51
52	102.497 478	104.444 494	106.435 496	108.471 539	110.553 707	112.683 108	52
53	105.995 854	108.055 606	110.162 905	112.318 917	114.524 838	116.781 894	53
54	109.579 503	111.756 996	113.985 830	116.267 289	118.602 693	120.993 396	54
55	113.250 503	115.550 921	117.906 717	120.319 305	122.790 140	125.320 714	55

YRS							
14	117.010 984	119.439 694	121.928 076	124.477 687	127.090 125	129.767 034	56
15	132.992 142	135.991 590	139.070 734	142.231 821	145.477 163	148.809 140	60
16	150.589 364	154.261 786	158.039 215	161.924 834	165.921 927	170.033 877	64
17	169.966 072	174.428 663	179.027 983	183.768 467	188.654 700	193.691 420	68
18	191.302 213	196.689 122	202.252 213	207.997 581	213.931 538	220.060 621	72
19	214.795 932	221.260 504	227.950 001	234.872 689	242.037 151	249.452 292	76
20	240.665 409	248.382 713	256.384 797	264.682 753	273.288 113	282.212 873	80
21	269.150 888	278.320 556	287.848 115	297.748 290	308.036 425	318.728 514	84
22	300.516 909	311.366 333	322.662 514	334.424 821	346.673 482	359.429 624	88
23	335.054 759	347.842 687	361.184 912	375.106 694	389.634 479	404.795 946	92
24	373.085 184	388.105 758	403.810 236	420.231 321	437.403 318	455.362 213	96
25	414.961 365	432.548 654	450.975 481	470.283 882	490.518 051	511.724 449	100
26	461.072 196	481.605 296	503.164 181	525.802 543	549.576 947	574.546 995	104
27	511.845 699	535.754 649	560.911 374	587.384 241	615.245 228	644.570 341	108
28	567.753 997	595.525 404	624.809 081	655.691 105	688.262 563	722.619 851	112
29	629.315 697	661.501 133	695.512 378	731.457 570	769.451 395	809.615 495	116
30	697.102 708	734.325 993	773.746 112	815.498 278	859.726 213	906.582 688	120

FUTURE VALUE PER PERIOD

QUARTERLY COMPOUNDING

QTRS	11.25% ANNUAL RATE	11.50% ANNUAL RATE	11.75% ANNUAL RATE	12.00% ANNUAL RATE	12.25% ANNUAL RATE	12.50% ANNUAL RATE	QTRS
1	1.000 000	1.000 000	1.000 000	1.000 000	1.000 000	1.000 000	1
2	2.028 125	2.028 750	2.029 375	2.030 000	2.030 625	2.031 250	2
3	3.085 166	3.087 077	3.088 988	3.090 900	3.092 813	3.094 727	3
4	4.171 936	4.175 830	4.179 727	4.183 627	4.187 530	4.191 437	4
5	5.289 272	5.295 885	5.302 506	5.309 136	5.315 773	5.322 419	5
6	6.438 033	6.448 142	6.458 268	6.468 410	6.478 569	6.488 745	6
7	7.619 102	7.633 526	7.647 979	7.662 462	7.676 975	7.691 518	7
8	8.833 390	8.852 990	8.872 639	8.892 336	8.912 082	8.931 878	8
9	10.081 829	10.107 513	10.133 272	10.159 106	10.185 015	10.210 999	9
10	11.365 380	11.398 104	11.430 937	11.463 879	11.496 931	11.530 093	10
11	12.685 032	12.725 800	12.766 721	12.807 796	12.849 025	12.890 408	11
12	14.041 798	14.091 666	14.141 743	14.192 030	14.242 526	14.293 234	12
13	15.436 724	15.496 802	15.557 157	15.617 790	15.678 703	15.739 897	13
14	16.870 882	16.942 335	17.014 149	17.086 324	17.158 864	17.231 769	14
15	18.345 375	18.429 427	18.513 939	18.598 914	18.684 354	18.770 262	15
16	19.861 339	19.959 273	20.057 786	20.156 881	20.256 562	20.356 832	16
17	21.419 939	21.533 102	21.646 984	21.761 588	21.876 919	21.992 983	17
18	23.022 375	23.152 179	23.282 864	23.414 435	23.546 900	23.680 264	18
19	24.669 879	24.817 804	24.966 798	25.116 868	25.268 024	25.420 272	19
20	26.363 719	26.531 316	26.700 198	26.870 374	27.041 857	27.214 656	20
21	28.105 199	28.294 091	28.484 516	28.676 486	28.870 014	29.065 114	21
22	29.895 658	30.107 546	30.321 248	30.536 780	30.754 158	30.973 399	22
23	31.736 473	31.973 138	32.211 935	32.452 884	32.696 004	32.941 317	23
24	33.629 061	33.892 366	34.158 161	34.426 470	34.697 319	34.970 734	24
25	35.574 879	35.866 772	36.161 557	36.459 264	36.759 925	37.063 569	25
26	37.575 422	37.897 941	38.223 802	38.553 042	38.885 697	39.221 805	26
27	39.632 231	39.987 507	40.346 627	40.709 634	41.076 572	41.447 487	27
28	41.746 887	42.137 148	42.531 809	42.930 923	43.334 542	43.742 721	28
29	43.921 019	44.348 591	44.781 181	45.218 850	45.661 662	46.109 681	29
30	46.156 297	46.623 613	47.096 628	47.575 416	48.060 051	48.550 608	30
31	48.454 443	48.964 042	49.480 091	50.002 678	50.531 890	51.067 815	31
32	50.817 224	51.371 758	51.933 569	52.502 759	53.079 429	53.663 684	32
33	53.246 459	53.848 696	54.459 118	55.077 841	55.704 986	56.340 674	33
34	55.744 015	56.396 846	57.058 854	57.730 177	58.410 952	59.101 320	34
35	58.311 816	59.018 255	59.734 958	60.462 082	61.199 787	61.948 237	35
36	60.951 836	61.715 030	62.489 672	63.275 944	64.074 031	64.884 119	36
37	63.666 106	64.489 337	65.325 307	66.174 223	67.036 298	67.911 748	37
38	66.456 715	67.343 406	68.244 237	69.159 449	70.089 284	71.033 990	38
39	69.325 810	70.279 529	71.248 912	72.234 233	73.235 769	74.253 802	39
40	72.275 599	73.300 065	74.341 849	75.401 260	76.478 614	77.574 233	40
41	75.308 350	76.407 442	77.525 640	78.663 298	79.820 772	80.998 428	41
42	78.426 397	79.604 156	80.802 956	82.023 196	83.265 283	84.529 629	42
43	81.632 140	82.892 775	84.176 543	85.483 892	86.815 282	88.171 180	43
44	84.928 044	86.275 943	87.649 229	89.048 409	90.474 000	91.926 529	44
45	88.316 645	89.756 376	91.223 925	92.719 861	94.244 766	95.799 233	45
46	91.800 550	93.336 872	94.903 628	96.501 457	98.131 012	99.792 959	46
47	95.382 441	97.020 307	98.691 422	100.396 501	102.136 275	103.911 489	47
48	99.065 072	100.809 641	102.590 482	104.408 396	106.264 198	108.158 723	48
49	102.851 277	104.707 918	106.604 078	108.540 648	110.518 539	112.538 683	49
50	106.743 969	108.718 271	110.735 573	112.796 867	114.903 169	117.055 517	50
51	110.746 144	112.843 921	114.988 430	117.180 773	119.422 079	121.713 502	51
52	114.860 879	117.088 184	119.366 215	121.696 197	124.079 380	126.517 049	52
53	119.091 341	121.454 469	123.872 598	126.347 082	128.879 311	131.470 707	53
54	123.440 785	125.946 285	128.511 355	131.137 495	133.826 240	136.579 167	54
55	127.912 557	130.567 240	133.286 376	136.071 620	138.924 668	141.847 266	55

YRS							
14	132.510 098	135.321 049	138.201 664	141.153 768	144.179 236	147.279 993	56
15	152.230 200	155.742 862	159.349 719	163.053 437	166.856 761	170.762 516	60
16	174.264 175	178.616 419	183.094 321	187.701 707	192.442 522	197.320 837	64
17	198.883 522	204.236 064	209.754 273	215.443 551	221.309 481	227.357 830	68
18	226.391 597	232.931 477	239.687 520	246.667 242	253.878 429	261.329 141	72
19	257.127 352	265.071 922	273.295 956	281.809 781	290.624 119	299.750 096	76
20	291.469 508	301.070 992	311.030 817	321.363 019	332.082 192	343.203 519	80
21	329.841 226	341.391 934	353.398 746	365.880 536	378.856 977	392.348 576	84
22	372.715 316	386.553 611	400.968 586	415.985 393	431.630 306	447.930 771	88
23	420.620 069	437.137 178	454.379 027	472.378 852	491.171 451	510.793 254	92
24	474.145 759	493.793 562	514.347 173	535.850 186	558.348 339	581.889 617	96
25	533.951 924	557.251 834	581.678 178	607.287 733	634.140 199	662.298 352	100
26	600.775 487	628.328 595	657.276 047	687.691 320	719.651 844	753.239 215	104
27	675.439 841	707.938 486	742.155 784	778.186 267	816.129 768	856.091 731	108
28	758.864 990	797.105 951	837.457 011	880.039 126	924.980 322	972.416 117	112
29	852.078 888	896.978 426	944.459 273	994.675 416	1047.790 210	1103.976 950	116
30	956.230 104	1008.841 102	1064.599 216	1123.699 571	1186.349 621	1252.769 936	120

FUTURE VALUE PER PERIOD

QTRS	12.75% ANNUAL RATE	13.00% ANNUAL RATE	13.25% ANNUAL RATE	13.50% ANNUAL RATE	13.75% ANNUAL RATE	14.00% ANNUAL RATE	QTRS
1	1.000 000	1.000 000	1.000 000	1.000 000	1.000 000	1.000 000	1
2	2.031 875	2.032 500	2.033 125	2.033 750	2.034 375	2.035 000	2
3	3.096 641	3.098 556	3.100 472	3.102 389	3.104 307	3.106 225	3
4	4.195 346	4.199 259	4.203 175	4.207 095	4.211 017	4.214 943	4
5	5.329 073	5.335 735	5.342 406	5.349 084	5.355 771	5.362 466	5
6	6.498 937	6.509 147	6.519 373	6.529 616	6.539 876	6.550 152	6
7	7.706 091	7.720 694	7.735 327	7.749 990	7.764 684	7.779 408	7
8	8.951 723	8.971 616	8.991 560	9.011 552	9.031 595	9.051 687	8
9	10.237 059	10.263 194	10.289 405	10.315 692	10.342 056	10.368 496	9
10	11.563 365	11.596 748	11.630 242	11.663 847	11.697 564	11.731 393	10
11	12.931 947	12.973 642	13.015 493	13.057 502	13.099 668	13.141 992	11
12	14.344 153	14.395 285	14.446 632	14.498 192	14.549 969	14.601 962	12
13	15.801 373	15.863 132	15.925 176	15.987 506	16.050 124	16.113 030	13
14	17.305 042	17.378 684	17.452 698	17.527 085	17.601 847	17.676 986	14
15	18.856 640	18.943 491	19.030 818	19.118 624	19.206 911	19.295 681	15
16	20.457 695	20.559 155	20.661 214	20.763 877	20.867 148	20.971 030	16
17	22.109 784	22.227 327	22.345 617	22.464 658	22.584 456	22.705 016	17
18	23.814 534	23.949 715	24.085 816	24.222 841	24.360 797	24.499 691	18
19	25.573 622	25.728 081	25.883 658	26.040 361	26.198 199	26.357 180	19
20	27.388 781	27.564 244	27.741 054	27.919 224	28.098 762	28.279 682	20
21	29.261 799	29.460 082	29.659 977	29.861 497	30.064 657	30.269 471	21
22	31.194 518	31.417 534	31.642 464	31.869 323	32.098 130	32.328 902	22
23	33.188 844	33.438 604	33.690 620	33.944 913	34.201 503	34.460 414	23
24	35.246 738	35.525 359	35.806 622	36.090 553	36.377 180	36.666 528	24
25	37.370 228	37.679 933	37.992 716	38.308 610	38.627 645	38.949 857	25
26	39.561 404	39.904 531	40.251 225	40.601 525	40.955 471	41.313 102	26
27	41.822 424	42.201 428	42.584 547	42.971 827	43.363 315	43.759 060	27
28	44.155 513	44.572 975	44.995 160	45.422 126	45.853 929	46.290 627	28
29	46.562 970	47.021 596	47.485 625	47.955 123	48.430 158	48.910 799	29
30	49.047 165	49.549 798	50.058 586	50.573 608	51.094 945	51.622 677	30
31	51.610 543	52.160 167	52.716 777	53.280 467	53.851 333	54.429 471	31
32	54.255 630	54.855 372	55.463 020	56.078 683	56.702 473	57.334 502	32
33	56.985 028	57.638 172	58.300 232	58.971 338	59.651 620	60.341 210	33
34	59.801 425	60.511 412	61.231 428	61.961 621	62.702 145	63.453 152	34
35	62.707 596	63.478 033	64.259 719	65.052 826	65.857 531	66.674 013	35
36	65.706 401	66.541 069	67.388 322	68.248 359	69.121 384	70.007 603	36
37	68.800 792	69.703 654	70.620 560	71.551 741	72.497 431	73.457 869	37
38	71.993 817	72.969 023	73.959 866	74.966 612	75.989 530	77.028 895	38
39	75.288 620	76.340 516	77.409 787	78.496 735	79.601 670	80.724 906	39
40	78.688 445	79.821 583	80.973 986	82.146 000	83.337 978	84.550 278	40
41	82.196 639	83.415 784	84.656 249	85.918 428	87.202 721	88.509 537	41
42	85.816 657	87.126 797	88.460 487	89.818 175	91.200 314	92.607 371	42
43	89.552 063	90.958 418	92.390 741	93.849 538	95.335 325	96.848 629	43
44	93.406 535	94.914 566	96.451 184	98.016 960	99.612 477	101.238 331	44
45	97.383 268	98.999 290	100.646 130	102.325 032	104.036 656	105.781 673	45
46	101.487 979	103.216 767	104.980 033	106.778 502	108.612 916	110.484 031	46
47	105.722 908	107.571 312	109.457 496	111.382 276	113.346 485	115.350 973	47
48	110.092 826	112.067 379	114.083 276	116.141 428	118.242 770	120.388 257	48
49	114.602 035	116.709 569	118.862 284	121.061 202	123.307 366	125.601 846	49
50	119.254 975	121.502 630	123.799 597	126.147 017	128.546 056	130.997 910	50
51	124.056 227	126.451 466	128.900 459	131.404 479	133.964 827	136.582 837	51
52	129.010 519	131.561 138	134.170 287	136.839 380	139.569 868	142.363 236	52
53	134.122 730	136.836 875	139.614 678	142.457 709	145.367 582	148.345 950	53
54	139.397 892	142.284 074	145.239 414	148.265 657	151.364 593	154.538 058	54
55	144.841 200	147.908 306	151.050 469	154.269 623	157.567 751	160.946 890	55
YRS							
14	150.458 013	153.715 326	157.054 016	160.476 223	163.984 142	167.580 031	56
15	174.773 608	178.893 027	183.123 851	187.469 247	191.932 473	196.516 883	60
16	202.340 847	207.506 879	212.823 395	218.294 996	223.926 429	229.722 586	64
17	233.594 560	240.025 832	246.658 011	253.497 677	260.551 629	267.826 894	68
18	269.027 729	276.982 839	285.203 427	293.698 766	302.478 462	311.552 464	72
19	309.199 257	318.983 589	329.115 528	339.607 986	350.474 361	361.728 561	76
20	354.742 790	366.716 429	379.141 519	392.035 830	405.417 844	419.306 787	80
21	406.376 708	420.963 654	436.132 639	451.907 875	468.314 600	485.379 125	84
22	464.915 457	482.614 318	501.058 643	520.281 119	540.315 896	561.198 653	88
23	531.282 399	552.678 815	575.024 306	598.362 641	622.739 647	648.203 305	92
24	606.524 370	632.305 428	659.288 222	687.530 915	717.094 542	748.043 145	96
25	691.828 200	722.799 158	755.284 219	789.360 144	825.107 658	862.611 657	100
26	788.559 426	825.643 103	864.645 756	905.648 048	948.756 075	994.081 659	104
27	898.183 523	942.522 771	989.233 720	1038.447 607	1090.303 059	1144.946 512	108
28	1022.489 959	1075.353 700	1131.168 090	1190.103 302	1252.339 495	1318.067 399	112
29	1163.419 481	1226.312 854	1292.864 008	1363.292 505	1437.831 308	1516.727 600	116
30	1323.195 038	1397.874 298	1477.072 879	1561.072 748	1650.173 749	1744.694 750	120

FUTURE VALUE PER PERIOD

QUARTERLY COMPOUNDING

QTRS	14.25% ANNUAL RATE	14.50% ANNUAL RATE	14.75% ANNUAL RATE	15.00% ANNUAL RATE	15.25% ANNUAL RATE	15.50% ANNUAL RATE	QTRS
1	1.000 000	1.000 000	1.000 000	1.000 000	1.000 000	1.000 000	1
2	2.035 625	2.036 250	2.036 875	2.037 500	2.038 125	2.038 750	2
3	3.108 144	3.110 064	3.111 985	3.113 906	3.115 829	3.117 752	3
4	4.218 872	4.222 804	4.226 739	4.230 678	4.234 619	4.238 564	4
5	5.369 169	5.375 881	5.382 600	5.389 328	5.396 064	5.402 809	5
6	6.560 446	6.570 756	6.581 084	6.591 428	6.601 789	6.612 168	6
7	7.794 162	7.808 946	7.823 761	7.838 607	7.853 483	7.868 389	7
8	9.071 829	9.092 020	9.112 262	9.132 554	9.152 897	9.173 289	8
9	10.395 013	10.421 606	10.448 277	10.475 025	10.501 851	10.528 754	9
10	11.765 335	11.799 389	11.833 557	11.867 838	11.902 234	11.936 743	10
11	13.184 475	13.227 117	13.269 920	13.312 882	13.356 006	13.399 292	11
12	14.654 172	14.706 600	14.759 248	14.812 116	14.865 204	14.918 515	12
13	16.176 227	16.239 714	16.303 495	16.367 570	16.431 940	16.496 607	13
14	17.752 505	17.828 404	17.904 686	17.981 354	18.058 408	18.135 851	14
15	19.384 938	19.474 684	19.564 922	19.655 654	19.746 885	19.838 615	15
16	21.075 526	21.180 641	21.286 378	21.392 742	21.499 735	21.607 361	16
17	22.826 342	22.948 439	23.071 313	23.194 969	23.319 412	23.444 647	17
18	24.639 530	24.780 320	24.922 068	25.064 781	25.208 465	25.353 127	18
19	26.517 313	26.678 607	26.841 069	27.004 710	27.169 537	27.335 560	19
20	28.461 993	28.645 706	28.830 834	29.017 387	29.205 376	29.394 813	20
21	30.475 951	30.684 113	30.893 971	31.105 539	31.318 831	31.533 862	21
22	32.561 657	32.796 412	33.033 186	33.271 996	33.512 861	33.755 799	22
23	34.721 666	34.985 282	35.251 285	35.519 696	35.790 539	36.063 837	23
24	36.958 625	37.253 499	37.551 176	37.851 685	38.155 053	38.461 310	24
25	39.275 276	39.603 938	39.935 875	40.271 123	40.609 715	40.951 686	25
26	41.674 458	42.039 581	42.408 511	42.781 290	43.157 960	43.538 564	26
27	44.159 111	44.563 516	44.972 325	45.385 588	45.803 357	46.225 683	27
28	46.732 279	47.178 943	47.630 679	48.087 548	48.549 610	49.016 928	28
29	49.397 116	49.889 180	50.387 061	50.890 831	51.400 564	51.916 334	29
30	52.156 889	52.697 663	53.245 083	53.799 237	54.360 211	54.928 092	30
31	55.014 978	55.607 953	56.208 496	56.816 709	57.432 694	58.056 556	31
32	57.974 886	58.623 741	59.281 184	59.947 335	60.622 315	61.306 248	32
33	61.040 242	61.748 852	62.467 178	63.195 360	63.933 541	64.681 865	33
34	64.214 800	64.987 248	65.770 655	66.565 186	67.371 007	68.188 287	34
35	67.502 453	68.343 035	69.195 948	70.061 381	70.939 527	71.830 583	35
36	70.907 228	71.820 470	72.747 548	73.688 682	74.644 096	75.614 018	36
37	74.433 298	75.423 962	76.430 114	77.452 008	78.489 903	79.544 061	37
38	78.084 984	79.158 081	80.248 475	81.356 458	82.482 330	83.626 394	38
39	81.866 761	83.027 561	84.207 637	85.407 326	86.626 969	87.866 916	39
40	85.783 265	87.037 311	88.312 794	89.610 100	90.929 622	92.271 759	40
41	89.839 293	91.192 413	92.569 328	93.970 479	95.396 314	96.847 290	41
42	94.039 818	95.498 138	96.982 822	98.494 372	100.033 299	101.600 123	42
43	98.389 987	99.959 946	101.559 064	103.187 911	104.847 068	106.537 127	43
44	102.895 130	104.583 494	106.304 054	108.057 458	109.844 362	111.665 441	44
45	107.560 769	109.374 645	111.224 016	113.109 612	115.032 179	116.992 477	45
46	112.392 622	114.339 476	116.325 402	118.351 223	120.417 781	122.525 935	46
47	117.396 609	119.484 282	121.614 901	123.789 394	126.008 709	128.273 815	47
48	122.578 863	124.815 587	127.099 450	129.431 496	131.812 791	134.244 426	48
49	127.945 735	130.340 152	132.786 243	135.285 177	137.838 153	140.446 397	49
50	133.503 802	136.064 983	138.682 735	141.358 371	144.093 233	146.888 695	50
51	139.259 875	141.997 338	144.796 661	147.659 310	150.586 787	153.580 632	51
52	145.221 008	148.144 742	151.136 038	154.196 534	157.327 909	160.531 882	52
53	151.394 506	154.514 989	157.709 180	160.978 904	164.326 035	167.752 492	53
54	157.787 935	161.116 157	164.524 706	168.015 613	171.590 965	175.252 901	54
55	164.409 130	167.956 618	171.591 554	175.316 198	179.132 871	183.043 951	55

YRS

	14.25%	14.50%	14.75%	15.00%	15.25%	15.50%	
14	171.266 206	175.045 045	178.918 993	182.890 556	186.962 311	191.136 904	56
15	201.225 927	206.063 157	211.032 226	216.136 896	221.381 036	226.768 629	60
16	235.688 514	241.829 416	248.150 661	254.657 782	261.356 488	268.252 665	64
17	275.330 734	283.070 655	291.054 412	299.290 023	307.785 771	316.550 220	68
18	320.931 074	330.624 964	340.645 186	351.003 187	361.710 824	372.780 376	72
19	373.385 022	385.458 727	397.965 227	410.920 666	424.341 799	438.246 019	76
20	433.722 657	448.686 258	464.219 228	480.344 078	497.084 224	514.464 026	80
21	503.128 876	521.592 447	540.799 644	560.781 543	581.570 540	603.200 411	84
22	582.966 663	605.658 870	629.315 961	653.980 443	679.696 739	706.511 248	88
23	674.803 855	702.593 899	731.648 520	761.965 392	793.664 908	826.790 309	92
24	780.443 929	814.367 417	849.887 618	887.082 195	926.032 654	966.824 528	96
25	901.961 421	943.250 850	986.578 698	1032.048 832	1079.770 492	1129.858 580	100
26	1041.742 665	1091.863 325	1144.574 588	1200.014 485	1258.328 516	1319.670 057	104
27	1202.532 654	1263.224 899	1327.195 876	1394.627 959	1465.713 816	1540.657 001	108
28	1387.488 946	1460.817 927	1538.280 703	1620.116 941	1706.580 409	1797.939 807	112
29	1600.243 670	1688.657 832	1782.265 423	1881.379 844	1986.333 676	2097.479 865	116
30	1844.974 855	1951.374 705	2064.277 848	2184.092 215	2311.251 673	2446.217 693	120

FUTURE VALUE PER PERIOD

QUARTERLY COMPOUNDING

QTRS	15.75% ANNUAL RATE	16.00% ANNUAL RATE	16.50% ANNUAL RATE	17.00% ANNUAL RATE	17.50% ANNUAL RATE	18.00% ANNUAL RATE	QTRS
1	1.000 000	1.000 000	1.000 000	1.000 000	1.000 000	1.000 000	1
2	2.039 375	2.040 000	2.041 250	2.042 500	2.043 750	2.045 000	2
3	3.119 675	3.121 600	3.125 452	3.129 306	3.133 164	3.137 025	3
4	4.242 513	4.246 464	4.254 376	4.262 302	4.270 240	4.278 191	4
5	5.409 562	5.416 323	5.429 869	5.443 450	5.457 063	5.470 710	5
6	6.622 563	6.632 975	6.653 852	6.674 796	6.695 809	6.716 892	6
7	7.883 326	7.898 294	7.928 323	7.958 475	7.988 751	8.019 152	7
8	9.193 732	9.214 226	9.255 366	9.296 710	9.338 259	9.380 014	8
9	10.555 736	10.582 795	10.637 150	10.691 820	10.746 808	10.802 114	9
10	11.971 368	12.006 107	12.075 933	12.146 223	12.216 981	12.288 209	10
11	13.442 740	13.486 351	13.574 065	13.662 437	13.751 474	13.841 179	11
12	14.972 048	15.025 805	15.133 995	15.243 091	15.353 101	15.464 032	12
13	16.561 573	16.626 838	16.758 272	16.890 922	17.024 799	17.159 913	13
14	18.213 685	18.291 911	18.449 551	18.608 786	18.769 634	18.932 109	14
15	19.930 848	20.023 588	20.210 595	20.399 660	20.590 805	20.784 054	15
16	21.715 626	21.824 531	22.044 282	22.266 645	22.491 653	22.719 337	16
17	23.570 678	23.697 512	23.953 609	24.212 978	24.475 663	24.741 707	17
18	25.498 774	25.645 413	25.941 695	26.242 029	26.546 473	26.855 084	18
19	27.502 788	27.671 229	28.011 790	28.357 316	28.707 881	29.063 562	19
20	29.585 710	29.778 079	30.167 276	30.562 501	30.963 851	31.371 423	20
21	31.750 648	31.969 202	32.411 676	32.861 408	33.318 519	33.783 137	21
22	34.000 829	34.247 970	34.748 658	35.258 018	35.776 205	36.303 378	22
23	36.339 612	36.617 889	37.182 040	37.756 483	38.341 414	38.937 030	23
24	38.770 484	39.082 604	39.715 799	40.361 134	41.018 850	41.689 196	24
25	41.297 072	41.645 908	42.354 076	43.076 482	43.813 425	44.565 210	25
26	43.923 144	44.311 745	45.101 182	45.907 233	46.730 262	47.570 645	26
27	46.652 618	47.084 214	47.961 605	48.858 290	49.774 711	50.711 324	27
28	49.489 565	49.967 583	50.940 022	51.934 767	52.952 355	53.993 333	28
29	52.438 217	52.966 286	54.041 298	55.141 995	56.269 021	57.423 033	29
30	55.502 971	56.084 938	57.270 501	58.485 530	59.730 790	61.007 070	30
31	58.688 401	59.328 335	60.632 909	61.971 165	63.344 012	64.752 388	31
32	61.999 257	62.701 469	64.134 017	65.604 939	67.115 313	68.666 245	32
33	65.440 477	66.209 527	67.779 545	69.393 149	71.051 608	72.756 226	33
34	69.017 196	69.857 909	71.575 451	73.342 358	75.160 116	77.030 256	34
35	72.734 748	73.652 225	75.527 939	77.459 408	79.448 371	81.496 618	35
36	76.598 679	77.598 314	79.643 466	81.751 433	83.924 237	86.163 966	36
37	80.614 752	81.702 246	83.928 759	86.225 869	88.595 922	91.041 344	37
38	84.788 958	85.970 336	88.390 820	90.890 468	93.471 994	96.138 205	38
39	89.127 523	90.409 150	93.036 942	95.753 313	98.561 394	101.464 424	39
40	93.636 919	95.025 516	97.874 716	100.822 829	103.873 455	107.030 323	40
41	98.323 873	99.826 536	102.912 048	106.107 799	109.417 918	112.846 688	41
42	103.195 375	104.819 598	108.157 170	111.617 381	115.204 952	118.924 789	42
43	108.258 693	110.012 382	113.618 653	117.361 119	121.245 169	125.276 404	43
44	113.521 379	115.412 877	119.305 422	123.348 967	127.549 645	131.913 842	44
45	118.991 284	121.029 392	125.226 771	129.591 298	134.129 942	138.849 965	45
46	124.676 565	126.870 568	131.392 375	136.098 928	140.998 127	146.098 214	46
47	130.585 705	132.945 390	137.812 311	142.883 133	148.166 795	153.672 633	47
48	136.727 517	139.263 206	144.497 068	149.955 666	155.649 092	161.587 902	48
49	143.111 163	145.833 734	151.457 572	157.328 782	163.458 740	169.859 357	49
50	149.746 165	152.667 084	158.705 197	165.015 255	171.610 060	178.503 028	50
51	156.642 421	159.773 767	166.251 787	173.028 403	180.118 000	187.535 665	51
52	163.810 216	167.164 718	174.109 673	181.382 110	188.998 162	196.974 769	52
53	171.260 243	174.851 306	182.291 697	190.090 850	198.266 832	206.838 634	53
54	179.003 615	182.845 359	190.811 229	199.169 711	207.941 006	217.146 373	54
55	187.051 883	191.159 173	199.682 193	208.634 424	218.038 425	227.917 959	55

YRS							
14	195.417 050	199.805 540	208.919 083	218.501 387	228.577 606	239.174 268	56
15	232.303 773	237.990 685	249.837 302	262.344 740	275.551 400	289.497 954	60
16	275.352 383	282.661 904	297.936 383	314.130 221	331.300 979	349.509 886	64
17	325.592 218	334.920 912	354.476 518	375.296 529	397.465 862	421.075 231	68
18	384.224 563	396.056 560	420.939 052	447.542 980	475.991 866	506.418 237	72
19	452.651 380	467.576 621	499.065 297	532.876 720	569.188 335	608.191 358	76
20	532.508 823	551.244 977	590.902 154	633.668 480	679.796 047	729.557 699	80
21	625.706 367	649.125 119	698.855 738	752.718 449	811.067 823	874.289 317	84
22	734.472 461	763.631 041	825.754 424	893.334 060	966.864 187	1046.884 464	88
23	861.407 815	897.586 774	974.922 945	1059.421 884	1151.766 894	1252.707 387	92
24	1009.547 585	1054.296 034	1150.269 502	1255.596 156	1371.213 680	1498.155 051	96
25	1182.433 945	1237.623 705	1356.388 156	1487.306 971	1631.658 173	1790.855 956	100
26	1384.200 788	1452.091 149	1598.679 197	1760.991 695	1940.759 687	2139.907 230	104
27	1619.672 567	1702.987 724	1883.490 627	2084.253 813	2307.608 473	2556.157 367	108
28	1894.479 655	1996.501 231	2218.284 477	2466.074 159	2742.993 050	3052.543 397	112
29	2215.192 975	2339.870 519	2611.832 314	2917.060 432	3259.717 480	3644.492 971	116
30	2589.481 112	2741.564 020	3074.445 052	3449.741 886	3872.977 917	4350.403 849	120

73

FUTURE VALUE PER PERIOD

QUARTERLY COMPOUNDING

QTRS	18.50% ANNUAL RATE	19.00% ANNUAL RATE	19.50% ANNUAL RATE	20.00% ANNUAL RATE	20.50% ANNUAL RATE	21.00% ANNUAL RATE	QTRS
1	1.000 000	1.000 000	1.000 000	1.000 000	1.000 000	1.000 000	1
2	2.046 250	2.047 500	2.048 750	2.050 000	2.051 250	2.052 500	2
3	3.140 889	3.144 756	3.148 627	3.152 500	3.156 377	3.160 256	3
4	4.286 155	4.294 132	4.302 122	4.310 125	4.318 141	4.326 170	4
5	5.484 390	5.498 103	5.511 851	5.525 631	5.539 446	5.553 294	5
6	6.738 043	6.759 263	6.780 553	6.801 913	6.823 342	6.844 842	6
7	8.049 677	8.080 328	8.111 105	8.142 008	8.173 038	8.204 196	7
8	9.421 975	9.464 144	9.506 522	9.549 109	9.591 907	9.634 916	8
9	10.857 741	10.913 691	10.969 965	11.026 564	11.083 492	11.140 749	9
10	12.359 912	12.432 091	12.504 750	12.577 893	12.651 521	12.725 638	10
11	13.931 558	14.022 615	14.114 357	14.206 787	14.299 911	14.393 734	11
12	15.575 892	15.688 690	15.802 432	15.917 127	16.032 782	16.149 405	12
13	17.296 277	17.433 902	17.572 800	17.712 983	17.854 462	17.997 249	13
14	19.096 230	19.262 013	19.429 474	19.598 632	19.769 503	19.942 105	14
15	20.979 431	21.176 958	21.376 661	21.578 564	21.782 690	21.989 065	15
16	22.949 729	23.182 864	23.418 773	23.657 492	23.899 053	24.143 491	16
17	25.011 154	25.284 050	25.560 439	25.840 366	26.123 879	26.411 025	17
18	27.167 920	27.485 042	27.806 510	28.132 385	28.462 728	28.797 603	18
19	29.424 437	29.790 582	30.162 077	30.539 004	30.921 443	31.309 478	19
20	31.785 317	32.205 635	32.632 479	33.065 954	33.506 167	33.953 225	20
21	34.255 388	34.735 402	35.223 312	35.719 252	36.223 358	36.735 769	21
22	36.839 699	37.385 334	37.940 449	38.505 214	39.079 805	39.664 397	22
23	39.543 536	40.161 137	40.790 045	41.430 475	42.082 645	42.746 778	23
24	42.372 424	43.068 791	43.778 560	44.501 999	45.239 381	45.990 984	24
25	45.332 149	46.114 559	46.912 765	47.727 099	48.557 899	49.405 511	25
26	48.428 761	49.305 000	50.199 762	51.113 454	52.046 491	52.999 300	26
27	51.668 591	52.646 988	53.647 001	54.669 126	55.713 874	56.781 763	27
28	55.058 263	56.147 720	57.262 292	58.402 583	59.569 210	60.762 806	28
29	58.604 708	59.814 736	61.053 829	62.322 712	63.622 132	64.952 853	29
30	62.315 175	63.655 936	65.030 203	66.438 848	67.882 766	69.362 878	30
31	66.197 252	67.679 593	69.200 425	70.760 790	72.361 758	74.004 429	31
32	70.258 875	71.894 374	73.573 946	75.298 829	77.070 298	78.889 662	32
33	74.508 348	76.309 357	78.160 676	80.063 771	82.020 151	84.031 369	33
34	78.954 359	80.934 051	82.971 009	85.066 959	87.223 684	89.443 016	34
35	83.605 998	85.778 419	88.015 845	90.320 307	92.693 897	95.138 774	35
36	88.472 776	90.852 894	93.306 618	95.836 323	98.444 460	101.133 560	36
37	93.564 642	96.168 406	98.855 315	101.628 139	104.489 738	107.443 071	37
38	98.892 006	101.736 405	104.674 512	107.709 546	110.844 837	114.083 833	38
39	104.465 762	107.568 884	110.777 395	114.095 023	117.525 635	121.073 234	39
40	110.297 303	113.678 406	117.177 792	120.799 774	124.548 824	128.429 579	40
41	116.398 553	120.078 131	123.890 210	127.839 763	131.931 951	136.172 132	41
42	122.781 987	126.781 842	130.929 858	135.231 751	139.693 464	144.321 169	42
43	129.460 653	133.803 980	138.312 688	142.993 339	147.852 754	152.898 030	43
44	136.448 209	141.159 669	146.055 432	151.143 006	156.430 207	161.925 176	44
45	143.758 938	148.864 753	154.175 634	159.700 156	165.447 255	171.426 248	45
46	151.407 789	156.935 829	162.691 696	168.685 164	174.926 427	181.426 126	46
47	159.410 399	165.390 280	171.622 916	178.119 422	184.891 407	191.950 998	47
48	167.783 130	174.246 319	180.989 534	188.025 393	195.367 091	203.028 425	48
49	176.543 100	183.523 019	190.812 773	198.426 663	206.379 655	214.687 418	49
50	185.708 219	193.240 362	201.114 896	209.347 996	217.956 612	226.958 507	50
51	195.297 224	203.419 279	211.919 247	220.815 396	230.126 888	239.873 829	51
52	205.329 720	214.081 695	223.250 310	232.856 165	242.920 891	253.467 205	52
53	215.826 220	225.250 576	235.133 763	245.498 974	256.370 587	267.774 233	53
54	226.808 183	236.949 978	247.596 534	258.773 922	270.509 580	282.832 380	54
55	238.298 061	249.205 102	260.666 865	272.712 618	285.373 196	298.681 080	55
YRS							
14	250.319 346	262.042 344	274.374 375	287.348 249	300.998 572	315.361 837	56
15	304.227 476	319.785 589	336.220 610	353.583 718	371.929 117	391.314 220	60
16	368.822 067	389.306 796	411.037 760	434.093 344	458.556 927	484.517 205	64
17	446.221 546	473.008 333	501.546 196	531.953 298	564.355 880	598.888 816	68
18	538.964 285	573.782 579	611.036 826	650.902 683	693.568 640	739.236 955	72
19	650.091 851	695.111 877	743.490 756	795.486 404	851.376 794	911.461 512	76
20	783.248 754	841.188 868	903.724 044	971.228 821	1044.108 637	1122.802 384	80
21	942.801 973	1017.061 368	1097.562 811	1184.844 828	1279.492 946	1382.143 820	84
22	1133.984 173	1228.806 808	1332.055 084	1444.496 418	1566.968 914	1700.387 898	88
23	1363.065 315	1483.742 235	1615.727 057	1760.104 549	1918.064 671	2090.912 814	92
24	1637.558 283	1790.677 168	1958.893 115	2143.728 205	2346.859 575	2570.135 276	96
25	1966.465 276	2160.218 011	2374.030 860	2610.025 157	2870.548 814	3158.200 618	100
26	2360.573 040	2605.134 571	2876.234 801	3176.812 016	3510.132 954	3879.829 659	104
27	2832.806 630	3140.801 332	3483.765 197	3865.744 985	4291.260 083	4765.357 908	108
28	3398.653 292	3785.728 726	4218.712 004	4703.147 316	5245.254 331	5852.010 796	112
29	4076.670 386	4562.202 786	5107.798 067	5721.015 082	6410.372 009	7185.468 535	116
30	4889.093 979	5497.055 251	6183.350 775	6958.239 713	7833.335 727	8821.786 410	120

SECTION 2

QTRS	21.50% ANNUAL RATE	22.00% ANNUAL RATE	22.50% ANNUAL RATE	23.00% ANNUAL RATE	23.50% ANNUAL RATE	24.00% ANNUAL RATE	QTRS
1	1.000 000	1.000 000	1.000 000	1.000 000	1.000 000	1.000 000	1
2	2.053 750	2.055 000	2.056 250	2.057 500	2.058 750	2.060 000	2
3	3.164 139	3.168 025	3.171 914	3.175 806	3.179 702	3.183 600	3
4	4.334 212	4.342 266	4.350 334	4.358 415	4.366 509	4.374 616	4
5	5.567 175	5.581 091	5.595 041	5.609 024	5.623 041	5.637 093	5
6	6.866 411	6.888 051	6.909 762	6.931 543	6.953 395	6.975 319	6
7	8.235 481	8.266 894	8.298 436	8.330 107	8.361 907	8.393 838	7
8	9.678 138	9.721 573	9.765 223	9.809 088	9.853 169	9.897 468	8
9	11.198 338	11.256 260	11.314 516	11.373 110	11.432 043	11.491 316	9
10	12.800 248	12.875 354	12.950 958	13.027 064	13.103 675	13.180 795	10
11	14.488 262	14.583 498	14.679 449	14.776 120	14.873 516	14.971 643	11
12	16.267 006	16.385 591	16.505 168	16.625 747	16.747 335	16.869 941	12
13	18.141 357	18.286 798	18.433 584	18.581 728	18.731 241	18.882 138	13
14	20.116 455	20.292 572	20.470 473	20.650 177	20.831 702	21.015 066	14
15	22.197 715	22.408 663	22.621 937	22.837 562	23.055 564	23.275 970	15
16	24.390 842	24.641 140	24.894 421	25.150 722	25.410 079	25.672 528	16
17	26.701 850	26.996 403	27.294 733	27.596 888	27.902 921	28.212 880	17
18	29.137 074	29.481 205	29.830 061	30.183 710	30.542 217	30.905 653	18
19	31.703 192	32.102 671	32.508 002	32.919 273	33.336 573	33.759 992	19
20	34.407 238	34.868 318	35.336 577	35.812 131	36.295 096	36.785 591	20
21	37.256 627	37.786 076	38.324 260	38.871 329	39.427 433	39.992 727	21
22	40.259 171	40.864 310	41.479 999	42.106 430	42.743 795	43.392 290	22
23	43.423 102	44.111 847	44.813 249	45.527 550	46.254 993	46.995 828	23
24	46.757 093	47.537 998	48.333 995	49.145 384	49.972 474	50.815 577	24
25	50.270 287	51.152 588	52.052 782	52.971 243	53.908 356	54.864 512	25
26	53.972 315	54.965 981	55.980 751	57.017 090	58.075 472	59.156 383	26
27	57.873 327	58.989 109	60.129 668	61.295 573	62.487 406	63.705 766	27
28	61.984 018	63.233 510	64.511 962	65.820 068	67.158 541	68.528 112	28
29	66.315 659	67.711 354	69.140 760	70.604 722	72.104 106	73.639 798	29
30	70.880 126	72.435 478	74.029 927	75.664 493	77.340 222	79.058 186	30
31	75.689 933	77.419 429	79.194 111	81.015 202	82.883 960	84.801 677	31
32	80.758 267	82.677 498	84.648 780	86.673 576	88.753 393	90.889 778	32
33	86.099 023	88.224 760	90.410 273	92.657 307	94.967 654	97.343 165	33
34	91.726 846	94.077 122	96.495 851	98.985 102	101.547 004	104.183 755	34
35	97.657 164	100.251 364	102.923 743	105.676 745	108.512 891	111.434 780	35
36	103.906 236	106.765 189	109.713 203	112.753 158	115.888 023	119.120 867	36
37	110.491 197	113.637 274	116.884 571	120.236 464	123.696 444	127.268 119	37
38	117.430 098	120.887 324	124.459 328	128.150 061	131.963 610	135.904 206	38
39	124.741 966	128.536 127	132.460 165	136.518 690	140.716 473	145.058 458	39
40	132.446 847	136.605 614	140.911 050	145.368 514	149.983 565	154.761 966	40
41	140.565 865	145.118 923	149.837 296	154.727 204	159.795 100	165.047 684	41
42	149.121 280	154.100 464	159.265 644	164.624 018	170.183 062	175.950 545	42
43	158.136 549	163.575 989	169.224 337	175.089 899	181.181 317	187.507 577	43
44	167.636 388	173.572 669	179.743 206	186.157 568	192.825 719	199.758 032	44
45	177.646 844	184.119 165	190.853 761	197.861 628	205.154 230	212.743 514	45
46	188.195 362	195.245 719	202.589 285	210.238 672	218.207 041	226.508 125	46
47	199.310 863	206.984 234	214.984 932	223.327 396	232.026 705	241.098 612	47
48	211.023 822	219.368 367	228.077 835	237.168 721	246.658 274	256.564 529	48
49	223.366 352	232.433 627	241.907 213	251.805 922	262.149 447	272.958 401	49
50	236.372 294	246.217 476	256.514 494	267.284 763	278.550 727	290.335 905	50
51	250.077 304	260.759 438	271.943 434	283.653 637	295.915 583	308.756 059	51
52	264.518 960	276.101 207	288.240 252	300.963 721	314.300 623	328.281 422	52
53	279.736 854	292.286 773	305.453 766	319.269 135	333.765 785	348.978 308	53
54	295.772 710	309.362 546	323.635 541	338.627 110	354.374 524	370.917 006	54
55	312.670 493	327.377 486	342.840 040	359.098 169	376.194 028	394.172 027	55

YRS

YRS	21.50%	22.00%	22.50%	23.00%	23.50%	24.00%	QTRS
14	330.476 532	346.383 247	363.124 792	380.746 314	399.295 427	418.822 348	56
15	411.799 835	433.450 372	456.334 051	480.523 132	506.094 152	533.128 181	60
16	512.068 530	541.311 272	572.352 202	605.304 906	640.290 212	677.436 661	64
17	635.696 208	674.932 013	716.760 727	761.358 098	808.911 909	859.622 792	68
18	788.124 668	840.464 682	896.506 926	956.519 605	1020.790 536	1089.628 586	72
19	976.063 452	1045.530 633	1120.238 154	1200.590 316	1287.022 896	1380.005 601	76
20	1207.785 183	1299.571 387	1398.717 822	1505.827 313	1621.552 485	1746.599 891	80
21	1493.489 706	1614.283 336	1745.343 220	1887.559 407	2041.899 753	2209.416 737	84
22	1845.753 059	2004.156 256	2176.790 036	2364.956 950	2570.079 718	2793.712 342	88
23	2280.081 046	2487.140 140	2713.814 607	2961.994 551	3233.754 959	3531.372 080	92
24	2815.591 763	3085.473 153	3382.252 474	3708.655 070	4067.684 406	4462.650 505	96
25	3475.857 128	3826.702 467	4214.261 298	4642.435 337	5115.543 781	5638.368 059	100
26	4289.940 468	4744.955 613	5249.867 923	5810.229 220	6432.213 041	7122.684 382	104
27	5293.675 813	5882.510 246	6538.894 014	7270.682 608	8086.650 634	8996.599 542	108
28	6531.245 229	7291.740 906	8143.352 910	9097.138 567	10165.505 082	11362.374 256	112
29	8057.123 606	9037.530 721	10140.433 008	11381.320 587	12777.653 063	14349.110 325	116
30	9938.476 515	11200.258 105	12626.211 187	14237.938 880	16059.901 649	18119.795 797	120

	5.25%	5.50%	5.75%	6.00%	6.25%	6.50%	
HALF YRS	ANNUAL RATE	ANNUAL RATE	ANNUAL RATE	ANNUAL RATE	ANNUAL RATE	ANNUAL RATE	HALF YRS
1	1.000 000	1.000 000	1.000 000	1.000 000	1.000 000	1.000 000	1
2	2.026 250	2.027 500	2.028 750	2.030 000	2.031 250	2.032 500	2
3	3.079 439	3.083 256	3.087 077	3.090 900	3.094 727	3.098 556	3
4	4.160 274	4.168 046	4.175 830	4.183 627	4.191 437	4.199 259	4
5	5.269 482	5.282 667	5.295 885	5.309 136	5.322 419	5.335 735	5
6	6.407 805	6.427 940	6.448 142	6.468 410	6.488 745	6.509 147	6
7	7.576 010	7.604 709	7.633 526	7.662 462	7.691 518	7.720 694	7
8	8.774 881	8.813 838	8.852 990	8.892 336	8.931 878	8.971 616	8
9	10.005 221	10.056 219	10.107 513	10.159 106	10.210 999	10.263 194	9
10	11.267 858	11.332 765	11.398 104	11.463 879	11.530 093	11.596 748	10
11	12.563 640	12.644 416	12.725 800	12.807 796	12.890 408	12.973 642	11
12	13.893 435	13.992 137	14.091 666	14.192 030	14.293 234	14.395 285	12
13	15.258 138	15.376 921	15.496 802	15.617 790	15.739 897	15.863 132	13
14	16.658 664	16.799 786	16.942 335	17.086 324	17.231 769	17.378 684	14
15	18.095 954	18.261 781	18.429 427	18.598 914	18.770 262	18.943 491	15
16	19.570 973	19.763 979	19.959 273	20.156 881	20.356 832	20.559 155	16
17	21.084 711	21.307 489	21.533 102	21.761 588	21.992 983	22.227 327	17
18	22.638 184	22.893 445	23.152 179	23.414 435	23.680 264	23.949 715	18
19	24.232 437	24.523 015	24.817 804	25.116 868	25.420 272	25.728 081	19
20	25.868 538	26.197 398	26.531 316	26.870 374	27.214 656	27.564 244	20
21	27.547 587	27.917 826	28.294 091	28.676 486	29.065 114	29.460 082	21
22	29.270 711	29.685 566	30.107 546	30.536 780	30.973 399	31.417 534	22
23	31.039 068	31.501 919	31.973 138	32.452 884	32.941 317	33.438 604	23
24	32.853 843	33.368 222	33.892 366	34.426 470	34.970 734	35.525 359	24
25	34.716 256	35.285 848	35.866 772	36.459 264	37.063 569	37.679 933	25
26	36.627 558	37.256 209	37.897 941	38.553 042	39.221 805	39.904 531	26
27	38.589 032	39.280 755	39.987 507	40.709 634	41.447 487	42.201 428	27
28	40.601 994	41.360 975	42.137 148	42.930 923	43.742 721	44.572 975	28
29	42.667 796	43.498 402	44.348 591	45.218 850	46.109 681	47.021 596	29
30	44.787 826	45.694 608	46.623 613	47.575 416	48.550 608	49.549 798	30
31	46.963 506	47.951 210	48.964 042	50.002 678	51.067 815	52.160 167	31
32	49.196 298	50.269 868	51.371 758	52.502 759	53.663 684	54.855 372	32
33	51.487 701	52.652 290	53.848 696	55.077 841	56.340 674	57.638 172	33
34	53.839 253	55.100 228	56.396 846	57.730 177	59.101 320	60.511 412	34
35	56.252 533	57.615 484	59.018 255	60.462 082	61.948 237	63.478 033	35
36	58.729 162	60.199 910	61.715 030	63.275 944	64.884 119	66.541 069	36
37	61.270 803	62.855 407	64.489 337	66.174 223	67.911 748	69.703 654	37
38	63.879 162	65.583 931	67.343 406	69.159 449	71.033 990	72.969 023	38
39	66.555 990	68.387 489	70.279 529	72.234 233	74.253 802	76.340 516	39
40	69.303 084	71.268 145	73.300 065	75.401 260	77.574 233	79.821 583	40
41	72.122 290	74.228 019	76.407 442	78.663 298	80.998 428	83.415 784	41
42	75.015 500	77.269 289	79.604 156	82.023 196	84.529 629	87.126 797	42
43	77.984 657	80.394 195	82.892 775	85.483 892	88.171 180	90.958 418	43
44	81.031 754	83.605 035	86.275 943	89.048 409	91.926 529	94.914 566	44
45	84.158 838	86.904 174	89.756 376	92.719 861	95.799 233	98.999 299	45
46	87.368 008	90.294 039	93.336 872	96.501 457	99.792 959	103.216 767	46
47	90.661 418	93.777 125	97.020 307	100.396 501	103.911 489	107.571 312	47
48	94.041 280	97.355 996	100.809 641	104.408 396	108.158 723	112.067 379	48
49	97.509 864	101.033 285	104.707 918	108.540 648	112.538 683	116.709 569	49
50	101.069 497	104.811 701	108.718 271	112.796 867	117.055 517	121.502 630	50
51	104.722 572	108.694 023	112.843 921	117.180 773	121.713 502	126.451 466	51
52	108.471 539	112.683 108	117.088 184	121.696 197	126.517 049	131.561 138	52
53	112.318 917	116.781 894	121.454 469	126.347 082	131.470 707	136.836 875	53
54	116.267 289	120.993 396	125.946 285	131.137 495	136.579 167	142.284 074	54
55	120.319 305	125.320 714	130.567 240	136.071 620	141.847 266	147.908 306	55
56	124.477 687	129.767 034	135.321 049	141.153 768	147.279 993	153.715 326	56
57	128.745 226	134.335 627	140.211 529	146.388 381	152.882 492	159.711 074	57
58	133.124 788	139.029 857	145.242 610	151.780 033	158.660 070	165.901 684	58
59	137.619 314	143.853 178	150.418 335	157.333 434	164.618 197	172.293 489	59
YRS							
30	142.231 821	148.809 140	155.742 862	163.053 437	170.762 516	178.893 027	60
31	151.823 248	159.133 680	166.855 558	175.013 391	183.633 184	192.742 530	62
32	161.924 834	170.033 877	178.616 419	187.701 707	197.320 837	207.506 879	64
33	172.563 715	181.541 829	191.063 251	201.162 741	211.877 335	223.246 505	66
34	183.768 467	193.691 420	204.236 064	215.443 551	227.357 830	240.025 832	68
35	195.569 189	206.518 427	218.177 201	230.594 064	243.820 974	257.913 538	70
36	207.997 581	220.060 621	232.931 477	246.667 242	261.329 141	276.982 839	72
37	221.087 027	234.357 876	248.546 320	263.719 277	279.948 667	297.311 787	74
38	234.872 689	249.452 292	265.071 922	281.809 781	299.750 096	318.983 589	76
39	249.391 597	265.388 316	282.561 406	301.001 997	320.808 451	342.086 948	78
40	264.682 753	282.212 873	301.070 992	321.363 019	343.203 519	366.716 429	80

FUTURE VALUE PER PERIOD

HALF YRS	6.75% ANNUAL RATE	7.00% ANNUAL RATE	7.25% ANNUAL RATE	7.50% ANNUAL RATE	7.75% ANNUAL RATE	8.00% ANNUAL RATE	HALF YRS
1	1.000 000	1.000 000	1.000 000	1.000 000	1.000 000	1.000 000	1
2	2.033 750	2.035 000	2.036 250	2.037 500	2.038 750	2.040 000	2
3	3.102 389	3.106 225	3.110 064	3.113 906	3.117 752	3.121 600	3
4	4.207 095	4.214 943	4.222 804	4.230 678	4.238 564	4.246 464	4
5	5.349 084	5.362 466	5.375 881	5.389 328	5.402 809	5.416 323	5
6	6.529 616	6.550 152	6.570 756	6.591 428	6.612 168	6.632 975	6
7	7.749 990	7.779 408	7.808 946	7.838 607	7.868 389	7.898 294	7
8	9.011 552	9.051 687	9.092 020	9.132 554	9.173 289	9.214 226	8
9	10.315 692	10.368 496	10.421 606	10.475 025	10.528 754	10.582 795	9
10	11.663 847	11.731 393	11.799 389	11.867 838	11.936 743	12.006 107	10
11	13.057 502	13.141 992	13.227 117	13.312 882	13.399 292	13.486 351	11
12	14.498 192	14.601 962	14.706 600	14.812 116	14.918 515	15.025 805	12
13	15.987 506	16.113 030	16.239 714	16.367 570	16.496 607	16.626 838	13
14	17.527 085	17.676 986	17.828 404	17.981 354	18.135 851	18.291 911	14
15	19.118 624	19.295 681	19.474 684	19.655 654	19.838 615	20.023 588	15
16	20.763 877	20.971 030	21.180 641	21.392 742	21.607 361	21.824 531	16
17	22.464 658	22.705 016	22.948 439	23.194 969	23.444 647	23.697 512	17
18	24.222 841	24.499 691	24.780 320	25.064 781	25.353 127	25.645 413	18
19	26.040 361	26.357 180	26.678 607	27.004 710	27.335 560	27.671 229	19
20	27.919 224	28.279 682	28.645 706	29.017 387	29.394 813	29.778 079	20
21	29.861 497	30.269 471	30.684 113	31.105 539	31.533 862	31.969 202	21
22	31.869 323	32.328 902	32.796 412	33.271 996	33.755 799	34.247 970	22
23	33.944 913	34.460 414	34.985 282	35.519 696	36.063 837	36.617 889	23
24	36.090 553	36.666 528	37.253 499	37.851 685	38.461 310	39.082 604	24
25	38.308 610	38.949 857	39.603 938	40.271 123	40.951 686	41.645 908	25
26	40.601 525	41.313 102	42.039 581	42.781 290	43.538 564	44.311 745	26
27	42.971 827	43.759 060	44.563 516	45.385 588	46.225 683	47.084 214	27
28	45.422 126	46.290 627	47.178 943	48.087 548	49.016 928	49.967 583	28
29	47.955 123	48.910 799	49.889 180	50.890 831	51.916 334	52.966 286	29
30	50.573 608	51.622 677	52.697 663	53.799 237	54.928 092	56.084 938	30
31	53.280 467	54.429 471	55.607 953	56.816 709	58.056 556	59.328 335	31
32	56.078 683	57.334 502	58.623 741	59.947 335	61.306 248	62.701 469	32
33	58.971 338	60.341 210	61.748 852	63.195 360	64.681 865	66.209 527	33
34	61.961 621	63.453 152	64.987 248	66.565 186	68.188 287	69.857 909	34
35	65.052 826	66.674 013	68.343 035	70.061 381	71.830 583	73.652 225	35
36	68.248 359	70.007 603	71.820 470	73.688 682	75.614 018	77.598 314	36
37	71.551 741	73.457 869	75.423 962	77.452 008	79.544 061	81.702 246	37
38	74.966 612	77.028 895	79.158 081	81.356 458	83.626 394	85.970 336	38
39	78.496 735	80.724 906	83.027 561	85.407 326	87.866 916	90.409 150	39
40	82.146 000	84.550 278	87.037 311	89.610 100	92.271 759	95.025 516	40
41	85.918 428	88.509 537	91.192 413	93.970 479	96.847 290	99.826 536	41
42	89.818 175	92.607 371	95.498 138	98.494 372	101.600 123	104.819 598	42
43	93.849 538	96.848 629	99.959 946	103.187 911	106.537 127	110.012 382	43
44	98.016 960	101.238 331	104.583 494	108.057 458	111.665 441	115.412 877	44
45	102.325 032	105.781 673	109.374 645	113.109 612	116.992 477	121.029 392	45
46	106.778 502	110.484 031	114.339 476	118.351 223	122.525 935	126.870 568	46
47	111.382 276	115.350 973	119.484 282	123.789 394	128.273 815	132.945 390	47
48	116.141 428	120.388 257	124.815 587	129.431 496	134.244 426	139.263 206	48
49	121.061 202	125.601 846	130.340 152	135.285 177	140.446 397	145.833 734	49
50	126.147 017	130.997 910	136.064 983	141.358 371	146.888 695	152.667 084	50
51	131.404 479	136.582 837	141.997 338	147.659 310	153.580 632	159.773 767	51
52	136.839 380	142.363 236	148.144 742	154.196 534	160.531 882	167.164 718	52
53	142.457 709	148.345 950	154.514 989	160.978 904	167.752 492	174.851 306	53
54	148.265 657	154.538 058	161.116 157	168.015 613	175.252 901	182.845 359	54
55	154.269 623	160.946 890	167.956 618	175.316 198	183.043 951	191.159 173	55
56	160.476 223	167.580 031	175.045 045	182.890 556	191.136 904	199.805 540	56
57	166.892 295	174.445 332	182.390 428	190.748 952	199.543 459	208.797 762	57
58	173.524 910	181.550 919	190.002 081	198.902 037	208.275 768	218.149 672	58
59	180.381 376	188.905 201	197.889 657	207.360 864	217.346 454	227.875 659	59

YRS

YRS	6.75%	7.00%	7.25%	7.50%	7.75%	8.00%	
30	187.469 247	196.516 883	206.063 157	216.136 896	226.768 629	237.990 685	60
31	202.370 710	212.548 798	223.309 766	234.688 606	246.722 435	259.450 725	62
32	218.294 996	229.722 586	241.829 416	254.657 782	268.252 665	282.661 904	64
33	235.312 310	248.119 577	261.716 078	276.152 728	291.483 794	307.767 116	66
34	253.497 677	267.826 894	283.070 655	299.290 023	316.550 220	334.920 912	68
35	272.931 269	288.937 865	306.001 500	324.195 151	343.596 932	364.290 459	70
36	293.698 766	311.552 464	330.624 964	351.003 187	372.780 376	396.056 560	72
37	315.891 724	335.777 788	357.065 986	379.859 524	404.269 358	430.414 770	74
38	339.607 986	361.728 561	385.458 727	410.920 666	438.246 019	467.576 621	76
39	364.952 109	389.527 678	415.947 251	444.355 073	474.906 889	507.770 873	78
40	392.035 830	419.306 787	448.686 258	480.344 078	514.464 026	551.244 977	80

SECTION 2

HALF YRS	8.25% ANNUAL RATE	8.50% ANNUAL RATE	8.75% ANNUAL RATE	9.00% ANNUAL RATE	9.25% ANNUAL RATE	9.50% ANNUAL RATE	HALF YRS
1	1.000 000	1.000 000	1.000 000	1.000 000	1.000 000	1.000 000	1
2	2.041 250	2.042 500	2.043 750	2.045 000	2.046 250	2.047 500	2
3	3.125 452	3.129 306	3.133 164	3.137 025	3.140 889	3.144 756	3
4	4.254 376	4.262 302	4.270 240	4.278 191	4.286 155	4.294 132	4
5	5.429 869	5.443 450	5.457 063	5.470 710	5.484 390	5.498 103	5
6	6.653 852	6.674 796	6.695 809	6.716 892	6.738 043	6.759 263	6
7	7.928 323	7.958 475	7.988 751	8.019 152	8.049 677	8.080 328	7
8	9.255 366	9.296 710	9.338 259	9.380 014	9.421 975	9.464 144	8
9	10.637 150	10.691 820	10.746 808	10.802 114	10.857 741	10.913 691	9
10	12.075 933	12.146 223	12.216 981	12.288 209	12.359 912	12.432 091	10
11	13.574 065	13.662 437	13.751 474	13.841 179	13.931 558	14.022 615	11
12	15.133 995	15.243 091	15.353 101	15.464 032	15.575 892	15.688 690	12
13	16.758 272	16.890 922	17.024 799	17.159 913	17.296 277	17.433 902	13
14	18.449 551	18.608 786	18.769 634	18.932 109	19.096 230	19.262 013	14
15	20.210 595	20.399 660	20.590 805	20.784 054	20.979 431	21.176 958	15
16	22.044 282	22.266 645	22.491 653	22.719 337	22.949 729	23.182 864	16
17	23.953 609	24.212 978	24.475 663	24.741 707	25.011 154	25.284 050	17
18	25.941 695	26.242 023	26.546 473	26.855 084	27.167 920	27.485 042	18
19	28.011 790	28.357 316	28.707 881	29.063 562	29.424 437	29.790 582	19
20	30.167 276	30.562 501	30.963 851	31.371 423	31.785 317	32.205 635	20
21	32.411 676	32.861 408	33.318 519	33.783 137	34.255 388	34.735 402	21
22	34.748 658	35.258 018	35.776 205	36.303 378	36.839 699	37.385 334	22
23	37.182 040	37.756 483	38.341 414	38.937 030	39.543 536	40.161 137	23
24	39.715 799	40.361 134	41.018 850	41.689 196	42.372 424	43.068 791	24
25	42.354 076	43.076 482	43.813 425	44.565 210	45.332 149	46.114 559	25
26	45.101 182	45.907 233	46.730 262	47.570 645	48.428 761	49.305 000	26
27	47.961 605	48.858 290	49.774 711	50.711 324	51.668 591	52.646 988	27
28	50.940 022	51.934 767	52.952 355	53.993 333	55.058 263	56.147 720	28
29	54.041 298	55.141 995	56.269 021	57.423 033	58.604 708	59.814 736	29
30	57.270 501	58.485 530	59.730 790	61.007 070	62.315 175	63.655 936	30
31	60.632 909	61.971 165	63.344 012	64.752 388	66.197 252	67.679 593	31
32	64.134 017	65.604 939	67.115 313	68.666 245	70.258 875	71.894 374	32
33	67.779 545	69.393 149	71.051 608	72.756 226	74.508 348	76.309 357	33
34	71.575 451	73.342 358	75.160 116	77.030 256	78.954 359	80.934 051	34
35	75.527 939	77.459 408	79.448 371	81.496 618	83.605 998	85.778 419	35
36	79.643 466	81.751 433	83.924 237	86.163 966	88.472 776	90.852 894	36
37	83.928 759	86.225 869	88.595 922	91.041 344	93.564 642	96.168 406	37
38	88.390 820	90.890 468	93.471 994	96.138 205	98.892 006	101.736 405	38
39	93.036 942	95.753 313	98.561 394	101.464 424	104.465 762	107.568 884	39
40	97.874 716	100.822 829	103.873 455	107.030 323	110.297 303	113.678 406	40
41	102.912 048	106.107 799	109.417 918	112.846 688	116.398 533	120.078 131	41
42	108.157 170	111.617 381	115.204 952	118.924 789	122.781 987	126.781 842	42
43	113.618 653	117.361 119	121.245 169	125.276 404	129.460 653	133.803 980	43
44	119.305 422	123.348 967	127.549 645	131.913 842	136.448 209	141.159 669	44
45	125.226 771	129.591 298	134.129 942	138.849 965	143.758 938	148.864 753	45
46	131.392 373	136.098 928	140.998 127	146.098 214	151.407 789	156.935 829	46
47	137.812 311	142.883 133	148.166 795	153.672 633	159.410 399	165.390 280	47
48	144.497 068	149.955 666	155.649 092	161.587 902	167.783 130	174.246 319	48
49	151.457 572	157.328 782	163.458 740	169.859 357	176.543 100	183.523 019	49
50	158.705 197	165.015 255	171.610 060	178.503 028	185.708 219	193.240 362	50
51	166.251 787	173.028 403	180.118 000	187.535 665	195.297 224	203.419 279	51
52	174.109 673	181.382 110	188.998 162	196.974 769	205.329 720	214.081 695	52
53	182.291 697	190.090 850	198.266 832	206.838 634	215.826 220	225.250 576	53
54	190.811 229	199.169 711	207.941 006	217.146 373	226.808 183	236.949 978	54
55	199.682 193	208.634 424	218.038 425	227.917 959	238.298 061	249.205 102	55
56	208.919 083	218.501 387	228.577 606	239.174 268	250.319 346	262.042 344	56
57	218.536 995	228.787 696	239.577 876	250.937 110	262.896 616	275.489 356	57
58	228.551 646	239.511 173	251.059 408	263.229 280	276.055 585	289.575 100	58
59	238.979 402	250.690 398	263.043 258	276.074 597	289.823 155	304.329 917	59

YRS

YRS	8.25%	8.50%	8.75%	9.00%	9.25%	9.50%	HALF YRS
30	249.837 302	262.344 740	275.551 400	289.497 954	304.227 476	319.785 589	60
31	272.915 243	287.160 403	302.233 320	318.184 003	335.065 529	352.934 236	62
32	297.936 383	314.130 221	331.300 979	349.509 886	368.822 067	389.306 796	64
33	325.064 342	343.441 187	362.967 696	383.718 533	405.773 292	429.216 815	66
34	354.476 518	375.296 529	397.465 862	421.075 231	446.221 546	473.008 333	68
35	386.365 244	409.917 113	435.048 649	461.869 680	490.497 784	521.058 849	70
36	420.939 502	447.542 980	475.991 866	506.418 237	538.964 285	573.782 579	72
37	458.424 028	488.435 008	520.595 983	555.066 375	592.017 609	631.634 021	74
38	499.065 297	532.876 702	569.188 335	608.191 358	650.091 811	695.111 877	76
39	543.128 625	581.176 249	622.125 526	666.205 168	713.662 184	764.763 352	78
40	590.902 154	633.668 480	679.796 047	729.557 699	783.248 754	841.188 868	80

FUTURE VALUE PER PERIOD

SEMIANNUAL COMPOUNDING

HALF YRS	9.75% ANNUAL RATE	10.00% ANNUAL RATE	10.50% ANNUAL RATE	11.00% ANNUAL RATE	11.50% ANNUAL RATE	12.00% ANNUAL RATE	HALF YRS
1	1.000 000	1.000 000	1.000 000	1.000 000	1.000 000	1.000 000	1
2	2.048 750	2.050 000	2.052 500	2.055 000	2.057 500	2.060 000	2
3	3.148 627	3.152 500	3.160 256	3.168 025	3.175 806	3.183 600	3
4	4.302 122	4.310 125	4.326 170	4.342 266	4.358 415	4.374 616	4
5	5.511 851	5.525 631	5.553 294	5.581 091	5.609 024	5.637 093	5
6	6.780 553	6.801 913	6.844 842	6.888 051	6.931 543	6.975 319	6
7	8.111 105	8.142 008	8.204 196	8.266 894	8.330 107	8.393 838	7
8	9.506 522	9.549 109	9.634 916	9.721 573	9.809 088	9.897 468	8
9	10.969 965	11.026 564	11.140 749	11.256 260	11.373 110	11.491 316	9
10	12.504 750	12.577 893	12.725 638	12.875 354	13.027 064	13.180 795	10
11	14.114 357	14.206 787	14.393 734	14.583 498	14.776 120	14.971 643	11
12	15.802 432	15.917 127	16.149 405	16.385 591	16.625 747	16.869 941	12
13	17.572 800	17.712 983	17.997 249	18.286 798	18.581 728	18.882 138	13
14	19.429 474	19.598 632	19.942 105	20.292 572	20.650 177	21.015 066	14
15	21.376 661	21.578 564	21.989 065	22.408 663	22.837 562	23.275 970	15
16	23.418 773	23.657 492	24.143 491	24.641 140	25.150 722	25.672 528	16
17	25.560 439	25.840 366	26.411 025	26.996 403	27.596 888	28.212 880	17
18	27.806 510	28.132 385	28.797 603	29.481 205	30.183 710	30.905 653	18
19	30.162 077	30.539 004	31.309 478	32.102 671	32.919 273	33.759 992	19
20	32.632 479	33.065 954	33.953 225	34.868 318	35.812 131	36.785 591	20
21	35.223 312	35.719 252	36.735 769	37.786 076	38.871 329	39.992 727	21
22	37.940 449	38.505 214	39.664 397	40.864 310	42.106 430	43.392 290	22
23	40.790 045	41.430 475	42.746 778	44.111 847	45.527 550	46.995 828	23
24	43.778 560	44.501 999	45.990 984	47.537 998	49.145 384	50.815 577	24
25	46.912 765	47.727 099	49.405 511	51.152 588	52.971 243	54.864 512	25
26	50.199 762	51.113 454	52.999 300	54.965 981	57.017 090	59.156 383	26
27	53.647 001	54.669 126	56.781 763	58.989 109	61.295 573	63.705 766	27
28	57.262 292	58.402 583	60.762 806	63.233 510	65.820 068	68.528 112	28
29	61.053 829	62.322 712	64.952 853	67.711 354	70.604 722	73.639 798	29
30	65.030 203	66.438 848	69.362 878	72.435 478	75.664 493	79.058 186	30
31	69.200 425	70.760 790	74.004 429	77.419 429	81.015 202	84.801 677	31
32	73.573 946	75.298 829	78.889 662	82.677 498	86.673 576	90.889 778	32
33	78.160 676	80.063 771	84.031 369	88.224 760	92.657 307	97.343 165	33
34	82.971 009	85.066 959	89.443 016	94.077 122	98.985 102	104.183 755	34
35	88.015 845	90.320 307	95.138 774	100.251 364	105.676 745	111.434 780	35
36	93.306 618	95.836 323	101.133 560	106.765 189	112.753 158	119.120 867	36
37	98.855 315	101.628 139	107.443 071	113.637 274	120.236 464	127.268 119	37
38	104.674 512	107.709 546	114.083 833	120.887 324	128.150 061	135.904 206	38
39	110.777 395	114.095 023	121.073 234	128.536 127	136.518 690	145.058 458	39
40	117.177 792	120.799 774	128.429 579	136.605 614	145.368 514	154.761 966	40
41	123.890 210	127.839 763	136.172 132	145.118 923	154.727 204	165.047 684	41
42	130.929 858	135.231 751	144.321 169	154.100 464	164.624 018	175.950 545	42
43	138.312 688	142.993 339	152.898 030	163.575 989	175.089 899	187.507 577	43
44	146.055 432	151.143 006	161.925 176	173.572 669	186.157 568	199.758 032	44
45	154.175 634	159.700 156	171.426 248	184.119 165	197.861 628	212.743 514	45
46	162.691 696	168.685 164	181.426 126	195.245 719	210.238 672	226.508 125	46
47	171.622 916	178.119 422	191.950 998	206.984 234	223.327 396	241.098 612	47
48	180.989 534	188.025 393	203.028 425	219.368 367	237.168 721	256.564 529	48
49	190.812 773	198.426 663	214.687 418	232.433 627	251.805 922	272.958 401	49
50	201.114 896	209.347 996	226.958 507	246.217 476	267.284 763	290.335 905	50
51	211.919 247	220.815 396	239.873 829	260.759 438	283.653 637	308.756 059	51
52	223.250 310	232.856 165	253.467 205	276.101 207	300.963 721	328.281 422	52
53	235.133 763	245.498 974	267.774 233	292.286 773	319.269 135	348.978 308	53
54	247.596 534	258.773 922	282.832 380	309.362 546	338.627 110	370.917 006	54
55	260.666 865	272.712 618	298.681 080	327.377 486	359.098 169	394.172 027	55
56	274.374 375	287.348 249	315.361 837	346.383 247	380.746 314	418.822 348	56
57	288.750 126	302.715 662	332.918 333	366.434 326	403.639 227	444.951 689	57
58	303.826 694	318.851 445	351.396 546	387.588 214	427.848 482	472.648 790	58
59	319.638 245	335.794 017	370.844 864	409.905 566	453.449 770	502.007 718	59

YRS

YRS							HALF YRS
30	336.220 610	353.583 718	391.314 220	433.450 372	480.523 132	533.128 181	60
31	371.849 919	391.876 049	435.533 273	484.496 100	539.429 522	601.082 824	62
32	411.037 760	434.093 344	484.517 205	541.311 272	605.304 906	677.436 661	64
33	454.139 549	480.637 912	538.779 462	604.547 978	678.973 759	763.227 832	66
34	501.546 196	531.953 298	598.888 816	674.932 013	761.358 098	859.622 792	68
35	553.687 656	588.528 511	665.475 329	753.271 204	853.489 020	967.932 170	70
36	611.036 826	650.902 683	739.236 955	840.464 682	956.519 605	1089.628 586	72
37	674.113 833	719.670 208	820.946 857	937.513 203	1071.739 353	1226.366 679	74
38	743.490 756	795.486 404	911.461 637	1045.530 633	1200.590 316	1380.005 601	76
39	819.796 807	879.073 761	1011.729 687	1165.756 732	1344.685 155	1552.634 293	78
40	903.724 044	971.228 821	1122.802 384	1299.571 387	1505.827 313	1746.599 891	80

79

HALF YRS	12.50% ANNUAL RATE	13.00% ANNUAL RATE	13.50% ANNUAL RATE	14.00% ANNUAL RATE	14.50% ANNUAL RATE	15.00% ANNUAL RATE	HALF YRS
1	1.000 000	1.000 000	1.000 000	1.000 000	1.000 000	1.000 000	1
2	2.062 500	2.065 000	2.067 500	2.070 000	2.072 500	2.075 000	2
3	3.191 406	3.199 225	3.207 056	3.214 900	3.222 756	3.230 625	3
4	4.390 869	4.407 175	4.423 533	4.439 943	4.456 406	4.472 922	4
5	5.665 298	5.693 641	5.722 121	5.750 739	5.779 496	5.808 391	5
6	7.019 380	7.063 728	7.108 364	7.153 291	7.198 509	7.244 020	6
7	8.458 091	8.522 870	8.588 179	8.654 021	8.720 401	8.787 322	7
8	9.986 722	10.076 856	10.167 881	10.259 803	10.352 630	10.446 371	8
9	11.610 892	11.731 852	11.854 213	11.977 989	12.103 196	12.229 849	9
10	13.336 572	13.494 423	13.654 372	13.816 448	13.980 677	14.147 087	10
11	15.170 108	15.371 560	15.576 042	15.783 599	15.994 276	16.208 119	11
12	17.118 240	17.370 711	17.627 425	17.888 451	18.153 861	18.423 728	12
13	19.188 130	19.499 808	19.817 276	20.140 643	20.470 016	20.805 508	13
14	21.387 388	21.767 295	22.154 942	22.550 488	22.954 093	23.365 921	14
15	23.724 100	24.182 169	24.650 401	25.129 022	25.618 264	26.118 365	15
16	26.206 856	26.754 010	27.314 303	27.888 054	28.475 588	29.077 242	16
17	28.844 784	29.493 021	30.158 019	30.840 217	31.540 069	32.258 035	17
18	31.647 585	32.410 067	33.193 685	33.999 033	34.826 724	35.677 388	18
19	34.625 557	35.516 722	36.434 259	37.378 965	38.351 661	39.353 192	19
20	37.789 655	38.825 309	39.893 571	40.995 492	42.132 156	43.304 681	20
21	41.151 508	42.348 954	43.586 387	44.865 177	46.186 738	47.552 532	21
22	44.723 477	46.101 636	47.528 468	49.005 739	50.535 276	52.118 972	22
23	48.518 695	50.098 242	51.736 640	53.436 141	55.199 084	57.027 895	23
24	52.551 113	54.354 628	56.228 863	58.176 671	60.201 017	62.304 987	24
25	56.835 558	58.887 679	61.024 311	63.249 038	65.565 591	67.977 862	25
26	61.387 780	63.715 378	66.143 452	68.676 470	71.319 096	74.076 201	26
27	66.224 516	68.856 877	71.608 135	74.483 823	77.489 731	80.631 916	27
28	71.363 549	74.332 574	77.441 684	80.697 691	84.107 736	87.679 310	28
29	76.823 771	80.164 192	83.668 998	87.346 529	91.205 547	95.255 258	29
30	82.625 256	86.374 864	90.316 655	94.460 786	98.817 949	103.399 403	30
31	88.789 335	92.989 230	97.413 030	102.073 041	106.982 251	112.154 358	31
32	95.338 668	100.033 530	104.988 409	110.218 154	115.738 464	121.565 935	32
33	102.297 335	107.535 710	113.075 127	118.933 425	125.129 503	131.683 380	33
34	109.690 918	115.525 531	121.707 698	128.258 765	135.201 392	142.559 633	34
35	117.546 601	124.034 690	130.922 967	138.236 878	146.003 492	154.251 606	35
36	125.893 263	133.096 945	140.760 268	148.913 460	157.588 746	166.820 476	36
37	134.761 592	142.748 247	151.261 586	160.337 402	170.013 930	180.332 012	37
38	144.184 192	153.026 883	162.471 743	172.561 020	183.339 940	194.856 913	38
39	154.195 704	163.973 630	174.438 586	185.640 292	197.632 085	210.471 181	39
40	164.832 935	175.631 916	187.213 190	199.635 112	212.960 411	227.256 520	40
41	176.134 994	188.047 990	200.850 080	214.609 570	229.400 041	245.500 759	41
42	188.143 431	201.271 110	215.407 461	230.632 240	247.031 544	264.698 315	42
43	200.902 395	215.353 732	230.947 464	247.776 496	265.941 331	285.550 689	43
44	214.458 795	230.351 725	247.536 418	266.120 851	286.222 078	307.966 991	44
45	228.862 470	246.324 587	265.245 127	285.749 311	307.973 178	332.064 515	45
46	244.166 364	263.335 685	284.149 173	306.751 763	331.301 234	357.969 354	46
47	260.426 772	281.452 504	304.329 242	329.224 386	356.320 573	385.817 055	47
48	277.703 445	300.746 917	325.871 466	353.270 093	383.153 815	415.753 334	48
49	296.059 911	321.295 467	348.867 789	378.999 000	411.932 466	447.934 835	49
50	315.563 655	343.179 672	373.416 365	406.528 929	442.797 570	482.529 947	50
51	336.286 384	366.486 351	399.621 970	435.985 955	475.900 394	519.719 693	51
52	358.304 283	391.307 963	427.596 453	467.504 971	511.403 173	559.698 670	52
53	381.698 300	417.742 981	457.459 213	501.230 319	549.479 903	602.676 070	53
54	406.554 444	445.896 275	489.337 710	537.316 442	590.317 195	648.876 776	54
55	432.964 097	475.879 533	523.368 006	575.928 593	634.115 192	698.542 534	55
56	461.024 353	507.811 702	559.695 346	617.243 594	681.088 544	751.933 224	56
57	490.838 375	541.819 463	598.474 782	661.450 646	731.467 463	809.328 216	57
58	522.515 773	578.037 728	639.871 830	708.752 191	785.498 854	871.027 832	58
59	556.173 009	616.610 180	684.063 178	759.364 844	843.447 521	937.354 919	59

YRS							
30	591.933 822	657.689 842	731.237 443	813.520 383	905.597 466	1008.656 538	60
31	670.300 292	748.033 261	835.353 698	933.469 487	1043.741 646	1167.703 712	62
32	758.768 689	850.503 026	954.000 028	1070.799 216	1202.642 851	1351.502 602	64
33	858.641 215	966.726 794	1089.204 194	1228.028 022	1385.419 956	1563.905 195	66
34	971.387 934	1098.550 698	1243.276 947	1408.039 282	1595.660 463	1809.362 940	68
35	1098.668 410	1248.068 666	1418.851 516	1614.134 174	1837.490 921	2093.020 048	70
36	1242.356 135	1417.655 682	1618.928 612	1850.092 216	2115.657 916	2420.821 293	72
37	1404.566 105	1610.005 516	1846.567 719	2120.240 578	2435.621 241	2799.636 607	74
38	1587.685 954	1828.173 507	2106.745 125	2429.533 438	2803.661 055	3237.405 054	76
39	1794.411 097	2075.625 096	2402.822 530	2783.642 833	3227.001 151	3743.301 215	78
40	2027.784 403	2356.290 874	2740.218 932	3189.062 680	3713.950 743	4327.927 467	80

80

SECTION 2

HALF YRS	15.50% ANNUAL RATE	16.00% ANNUAL RATE	16.50% ANNUAL RATE	17.00% ANNUAL RATE	17.50% ANNUAL RATE	18.00% ANNUAL RATE	HALF YRS
1	1.000 000	1.000 000	1.000 000	1.000 000	1.000 000	1.000 000	1
2	2.077 500	2.080 000	2.082 500	2.085 000	2.087 500	2.090 000	2
3	3.238 506	3.246 400	3.254 306	3.262 225	3.270 156	3.278 100	3
4	4.489 490	4.506 112	4.522 787	4.539 514	4.556 295	4.573 129	4
5	5.837 426	5.866 601	5.895 916	5.925 373	5.954 971	5.984 711	5
6	7.289 827	7.335 929	7.382 330	7.429 030	7.476 031	7.523 335	6
7	8.854 788	8.922 803	8.991 372	9.060 497	9.130 183	9.200 435	7
8	10.541 034	10.636 628	10.733 160	10.830 639	10.929 074	11.028 474	8
9	12.357 964	12.487 558	12.618 646	12.751 244	12.885 368	13.021 036	9
10	14.315 707	14.486 562	14.659 684	14.835 099	15.012 838	15.192 930	10
11	16.425 174	16.645 487	16.869 108	17.096 083	17.326 461	17.560 293	11
12	18.698 125	18.977 126	19.260 809	19.549 250	19.842 527	20.140 720	12
13	21.147 229	21.495 297	21.849 826	22.210 936	22.578 748	22.953 385	13
14	23.786 140	24.214 920	24.652 436	25.098 866	25.554 388	26.019 189	14
15	26.629 566	27.152 114	27.686 262	28.232 269	28.790 397	29.360 916	15
16	29.693 357	30.324 283	30.970 379	31.632 012	32.309 557	33.003 399	16
17	32.994 592	33.750 226	34.525 435	35.320 733	36.136 643	36.973 705	17
18	36.551 673	37.450 244	38.373 784	39.322 995	40.298 600	41.301 338	18
19	40.384 428	41.446 263	42.539 621	43.665 450	44.824 727	46.018 458	19
20	44.514 221	45.761 964	47.049 140	48.377 013	49.746 891	51.160 120	20
21	48.964 073	50.422 921	51.930 694	53.489 059	55.099 744	56.764 530	21
22	53.758 788	55.456 755	57.214 976	59.035 629	60.920 971	62.873 338	22
23	58.925 095	60.893 296	62.935 212	65.053 658	67.251 556	69.531 939	23
24	64.491 789	66.764 759	69.127 366	71.583 219	74.136 067	76.789 813	24
25	70.489 903	73.105 940	75.830 374	78.667 792	81.622 973	84.700 896	25
26	76.952 870	79.954 415	83.086 380	86.354 555	89.764 984	93.323 977	26
27	83.916 718	87.350 768	90.941 006	94.694 692	98.619 420	102.723 135	27
28	91.420 264	95.338 830	99.443 639	103.743 741	108.248 619	112.968 217	28
29	99.505 334	103.965 936	108.647 740	113.561 959	118.720 373	124.135 356	29
30	108.216 997	113.283 211	118.611 178	124.214 725	130.108 406	136.307 539	30
31	117.603 815	123.345 868	129.396 600	135.772 977	142.492 891	149.575 217	31
32	127.718 110	134.213 537	141.071 820	148.313 680	155.961 019	164.036 987	32
33	138.616 264	145.950 620	153.710 245	161.920 343	170.607 608	179.800 315	33
34	150.359 024	158.626 670	167.391 340	176.683 572	186.535 774	196.982 344	34
35	163.011 849	172.316 804	182.201 126	192.701 675	203.857 654	215.710 755	35
36	176.645 267	187.102 148	198.232 719	210.081 318	222.695 199	236.124 723	36
37	191.335 275	203.070 320	215.586 918	228.938 230	243.181 029	258.375 948	37
38	207.163 759	220.315 945	234.372 839	249.397 979	265.459 369	282.629 783	38
39	224.218 950	238.941 221	254.708 598	271.596 808	289.687 064	309.066 463	39
40	242.595 919	259.056 519	276.722 058	295.682 536	316.034 682	337.882 445	40
41	262.397 103	280.781 040	300.551 627	321.815 552	344.687 716	369.291 865	41
42	283.732 878	304.243 523	326.347 137	350.169 874	375.847 892	403.528 133	42
43	306.722 176	329.583 005	354.270 775	380.934 313	409.734 582	440.845 665	43
44	331.493 145	356.949 646	384.498 114	414.313 730	446.586 358	481.521 775	44
45	358.183 864	386.505 617	417.219 209	450.530 397	486.662 664	525.858 734	45
46	386.943 113	418.426 067	452.639 793	489.825 480	530.245 648	574.186 021	46
47	417.931 204	452.900 152	490.982 576	532.460 646	577.642 142	626.862 762	47
48	451.320 873	490.132 164	532.488 639	578.719 801	629.185 829	684.280 411	48
49	487.298 240	530.342 737	577.418 952	628.910 984	685.239 589	746.865 648	49
50	526.063 834	573.770 156	626.056 015	683.368 418	746.198 053	815.083 556	50
51	567.833 803	620.671 769	678.705 636	742.454 733	812.490 383	889.441 076	51
52	612.840 922	671.325 510	735.698 851	806.563 386	884.583 291	970.490 773	52
53	661.336 094	726.031 551	797.394 007	876.121 273	962.984 329	1058.834 943	53
54	713.589 641	785.114 075	864.179 012	951.591 582	1048.245 458	1155.130 088	54
55	769.892 838	848.923 201	936.473 781	1033.476 866	1140.966 936	1260.091 796	55
56	830.559 533	917.837 058	1014.732 868	1122.322 400	1241.801 543	1374.500 057	56
57	895.927 897	992.264 022	1099.448 329	1218.719 804	1351.459 178	1499.205 063	57
58	966.362 309	1072.645 144	1191.152 816	1323.310 987	1470.711 856	1635.133 518	58
59	1042.255 388	1159.456 755	1290.422 924	1436.792 421	1600.399 143	1783.295 535	59
YRS							
30	1124.030 180	1253.213 296	1397.882 815	1559.919 777	1741.434 068	1944.792 133	60
31	1307.083 565	1463.827 988	1640.130 319	1838.461 559	2061.605 385	2312.697 533	62
32	1519.609 688	1709.498 966	1923.997 459	2166.367 909	2440.257 993	2749.805 939	64
33	1766.353 845	1996.027 929	2256.634 747	2552.387 462	2888.073 867	3269.134 436	66
34	2052.825 354	2330.246 977	2646.421 201	3006.819 330	3417.686 109	3886.148 624	68
35	2385.420 566	2720.080 074	3103.175 403	3541.787 885	4044.035 338	4619.223 180	70
36	2771.565 686	3174.781 398	3638.402 832	4171.566 243	4784.791 168	5490.189 060	72
37	3219.882 584	3705.145 023	4265.585 679	4912.957 071	5660.850 679	6524.983 622	74
38	3740.381 304	4323.761 154	5000.522 698	5785.740 887	6696.927 936	7754.423 041	76
39	4344.683 572	5045.135 011	5861.725 970	6813.203 816	7922.251 179	9215.120 015	78
40	5046.282 281	5886.935 428	6870.889 627	8022.758 863	9371.387 371	10950.574 090	80

FUTURE VALUE PER PERIOD

SEMIANNUAL COMPOUNDING

HALF YRS	18.50% ANNUAL RATE	19.00% ANNUAL RATE	19.50% ANNUAL RATE	20.00% ANNUAL RATE	20.50% ANNUAL RATE	21.00% ANNUAL RATE	HALF YRS
1	1.000 000	1.000 000	1.000 000	1.000 000	1.000 000	1.000 000	1
2	2.092 500	2.095 000	2.097 500	2.100 000	2.102 500	2.105 000	2
3	3.286 056	3.294 025	3.302 006	3.310 000	3.318 006	3.326 025	3
4	4.590 016	4.606 957	4.623 952	4.641 000	4.658 102	4.675 258	4
5	6.014 593	6.044 618	6.074 787	6.105 100	6.135 557	6.166 160	5
6	7.570 943	7.618 857	7.667 079	7.715 610	7.764 452	7.813 606	6
7	9.271 255	9.342 648	9.414 619	9.487 171	9.560 308	9.634 035	7
8	11.128 846	11.230 200	11.332 544	11.435 888	11.540 240	11.645 609	8
9	13.158 264	13.297 069	13.437 468	13.579 477	13.723 114	13.868 398	9
10	15.375 404	15.560 291	15.747 621	15.937 425	16.129 734	16.324 579	10
11	17.797 629	18.038 518	18.283 014	18.531 167	18.783 031	19.038 660	11
12	20.443 909	20.752 178	21.065 607	21.384 284	21.708 292	22.037 720	12
13	23.334 971	23.723 634	24.119 504	24.522 712	24.933 392	25.351 680	13
14	26.493 456	26.977 380	27.471 156	27.974 983	28.489 065	29.013 607	14
15	29.944 100	30.540 231	31.149 594	31.772 482	32.409 194	33.060 035	15
16	33.713 930	34.441 553	35.186 679	35.949 730	36.731 136	37.531 339	16
17	37.832 468	38.713 500	39.617 380	40.544 703	41.496 078	42.472 130	17
18	42.331 972	43.391 283	44.480 075	45.599 173	46.749 426	47.931 703	18
19	47.247 679	48.513 454	49.816 882	51.159 090	52.541 242	53.964 532	19
20	52.618 089	54.122 233	55.674 028	57.274 999	58.926 719	60.630 808	20
21	58.485 262	60.263 845	62.102 246	64.002 499	65.966 708	67.997 043	21
22	64.895 149	66.988 910	69.157 215	71.402 749	73.728 295	76.136 732	22
23	71.897 951	74.352 856	76.900 043	79.543 024	82.285 446	85.131 089	23
24	79.548 511	82.416 378	85.397 797	88.497 327	91.719 704	95.069 854	24
25	87.906 748	91.245 934	94.724 083	98.347 059	102.120 974	106.052 188	25
26	97.038 122	100.914 297	104.959 681	109.181 765	113.588 373	118.187 668	26
27	107.014 149	111.501 156	116.193 249	121.099 942	126.231 182	131.597 373	27
28	117.912 958	123.093 766	128.522 091	134.209 936	140.169 878	146.415 097	28
29	129.819 906	135.787 673	142.052 995	148.630 930	155.537 290	162.788 683	29
30	142.828 247	149.687 502	156.903 162	164.494 023	172.479 862	180.881 494	30
31	157.039 860	164.907 815	173.201 221	181.943 425	191.159 048	200.874 051	31
32	172.566 047	181.574 057	191.088 340	201.137 767	211.752 851	222.965 827	32
33	189.528 407	199.823 593	210.719 453	222.251 544	234.457 518	247.377 238	33
34	208.059 784	219.806 834	232.264 599	245.476 699	259.489 414	274.351 848	34
35	228.305 315	241.688 483	255.910 398	271.024 368	287.087 078	304.158 792	35
36	250.423 556	265.648 889	281.861 661	299.126 805	317.513 504	337.095 466	36
37	274.587 735	291.885 534	310.343 173	330.039 486	351.058 638	373.490 489	37
38	300.987 101	320.614 659	341.601 633	364.043 434	388.042 148	413.706 991	38
39	329.828 407	352.073 052	375.907 792	401.447 778	428.816 469	458.146 225	39
40	361.337 535	386.519 992	413.558 802	442.592 556	473.770 157	507.251 579	40
41	395.761 257	424.239 391	454.880 785	487.851 811	523.331 598	561.512 994	41
42	433.369 173	465.542 133	500.231 662	537.636 992	577.973 087	621.471 859	42
43	474.455 822	510.768 636	550.004 249	592.400 692	638.215 328	687.726 404	43
44	519.342 985	560.291 656	604.629 663	652.640 761	704.632 399	760.937 676	44
45	568.382 212	614.519 364	664.581 055	718.904 837	777.857 220	841.836 132	45
46	621.957 566	673.898 703	730.377 708	791.795 321	858.587 585	931.228 926	46
47	680.488 641	738.919 080	802.589 534	871.974 853	947.592 813	1030.007 963	47
48	744.433 840	810.116 993	881.842 014	960.172 338	1045.721 076	1139.158 800	48
49	814.293 970	888.077 450	968.821 610	1057.189 572	1153.907 486	1259.770 473	49
50	890.616 163	973.444 808	1064.281 717	1163.908 529	1273.183 003	1393.046 373	50
51	973.998 158	1066.922 065	1169.049 185	1281.299 382	1404.684 261	1540.316 242	51
52	1065.092 987	1169.279 661	1284.031 480	1410.429 320	1549.664 398	1703.049 448	52
53	1164.614 089	1281.361 229	1410.224 549	1552.472 252	1709.504 999	1882.869 640	53
54	1273.340 892	1404.090 545	1548.721 443	1708.719 477	1885.729 261	2081.570 952	54
55	1392.124 924	1538.479 147	1700.721 784	1880.591 425	2080.016 510	2301.135 902	55
56	1521.896 480	1685.634 666	1867.542 158	2069.650 567	2294.218 203	2543.755 172	56
57	1663.671 904	1846.769 959	2050.627 518	2277.615 624	2530.375 569	2811.849 465	57
58	1818.561 555	2023.213 106	2251.563 701	2506.377 186	2790.739 064	3108.093 659	58
59	1987.778 499	2216.418 351	2472.091 162	2758.014 905	3077.789 818	3435.443 493	59
YRS							
30	2172.648 011	2427.978 094	2714.120 050	3034.816 395	3394.263 275	3797.165 059	60
31	2595.270 112	2913.301 434	3271.272 064	3674.227 838	4127.850 725	4638.538 467	62
32	3099.693 363	3495.216 252	3942.365 146	4447.915 685	5019.530 865	5665.876 431	64
33	3701.750 886	4192.946 666	4750.700 958	5384.077 978	6103.373 626	6920.281 770	66
34	4420.340 406	5029.542 877	5724.346 496	6516.834 354	7420.791 289	8451.942 048	68
35	5278.017 419	6032.642 648	6897.108 632	7887.469 568	9022.120 691	10322.137 539	70
36	6301.703 178	7235.384 351	8309.707 954	9545.938 177	10968.546 589	12605.692 988	72
37	7523.529 713	8677.501 721	10011.192 666	11552.685 195	13334.439 432	15393.971 281	74
38	8981.848 411	10406.636 501	12060.641 636	13980.849 085	16210.196 970	18798.528 783	76
39	10722.433 808	12479.912 331	14529.215 729	16918.927 393	19705.698 230	22955.578 608	78
40	12799.920 387	14965.821 882	17502.628 654	20474.002 146	23954.501 860	28031.440 370	80

82

FUTURE VALUE PER PERIOD

SEMIANNUAL COMPOUNDING

HALF YRS	21.50% ANNUAL RATE	22.00% ANNUAL RATE	22.50% ANNUAL RATE	23.00% ANNUAL RATE	23.50% ANNUAL RATE	24.00% ANNUAL RATE	HALF YRS
1	1.000 000	1.000 000	1.000 000	1.000 000	1.000 000	1.000 000	1
2	2.107 500	2.110 000	2.112 500	2.115 000	2.117 500	2.120 000	2
3	3.334 056	3.342 100	3.350 156	3.358 225	3.366 306	3.374 400	3
4	4.692 467	4.709 731	4.727 049	4.744 421	4.761 847	4.779 328	4
5	6.196 908	6.227 801	6.258 842	6.290 029	6.321 364	6.352 847	5
6	7.863 075	7.912 860	7.962 962	8.013 383	8.064 125	8.115 189	6
7	9.708 356	9.783 274	9.858 795	9.934 922	10.011 659	10.089 012	7
8	11.752 004	11.859 434	11.967 909	12.077 438	12.188 029	12.299 693	8
9	14.015 344	14.163 972	14.314 299	14.466 343	14.620 123	14.775 656	9
10	16.521 994	16.722 009	16.924 657	17.129 972	17.337 987	17.548 735	10
11	19.298 108	19.561 430	19.828 681	20.099 919	20.375 200	20.654 583	11
12	22.372 655	22.713 187	23.059 408	23.411 410	23.769 287	24.133 133	12
13	25.777 715	26.211 638	26.653 592	27.103 722	27.562 178	28.029 109	13
14	29.548 820	30.094 918	30.652 121	31.220 650	31.800 734	32.392 602	14
15	33.725 318	34.405 359	35.100 484	35.811 025	36.537 320	37.279 715	15
16	38.350 789	39.189 948	40.049 289	40.929 293	41.830 455	42.753 280	16
17	43.473 499	44.500 843	45.554 834	46.636 161	47.745 533	48.883 674	17
18	49.146 900	50.395 936	51.679 752	52.999 320	54.355 634	55.749 715	18
19	55.430 192	56.939 488	58.493 725	60.094 242	61.742 420	63.439 681	19
20	62.388 938	64.202 832	66.074 269	68.005 080	69.997 155	72.052 442	20
21	70.095 749	72.265 144	74.507 624	76.825 664	79.221 821	81.698 736	21
22	78.631 042	81.214 309	83.889 731	86.660 615	89.530 384	92.502 584	22
23	88.083 879	91.147 884	94.327 326	97.626 586	101.050 205	104.602 894	23
24	98.552 895	102.174 151	105.939 150	109.853 643	113.923 604	118.155 241	24
25	110.147 332	114.413 307	118.857 305	123.486 812	128.309 627	133.333 870	25
26	122.988 170	127.998 771	133.228 752	138.687 796	144.386 008	150.333 934	26
27	137.209 398	143.078 636	149.216 966	155.636 892	162.351 364	169.374 007	27
28	152.959 408	159.817 286	167.003 897	174.535 135	182.427 650	190.698 887	28
29	170.402 545	178.397 187	186.791 836	195.606 675	204.862 898	214.582 754	29
30	189.720 818	199.020 878	208.805 917	219.101 443	229.934 289	241.332 684	30
31	211.115 806	221.913 174	233.296 583	245.298 109	257.951 568	271.292 606	31
32	234.810 756	247.323 624	260.542 448	274.507 391	289.260 877	304.847 719	32
33	261.052 912	275.529 222	290.853 474	307.075 741	324.249 030	342.429 446	33
34	290.116 100	306.837 437	324.574 489	343.389 451	363.348 291	384.520 979	34
35	322.303 581	341.589 555	362.089 120	383.879 238	407.041 715	431.663 496	35
36	357.951 215	380.164 406	403.824 145	429.025 351	455.869 117	484.463 116	36
37	397.430 971	422.982 490	450.254 362	479.363 266	510.433 738	543.598 690	37
38	441.154 801	470.510 564	501.907 978	535.490 042	571.409 702	609.830 533	38
39	489.578 942	523.266 726	559.372 625	598.071 396	639.550 343	684.010 197	39
40	543.208 678	581.826 066	623.302 045	667.849 607	715.697 508	767.091 420	40
41	602.603 611	646.826 934	694.423 525	745.652 312	800.791 965	860.142 391	41
42	668.383 499	718.977 896	773.546 172	832.402 327	895.885 021	964.359 478	42
43	741.234 725	799.065 465	861.570 116	929.128 595	1002.151 511	1081.082 615	43
44	821.917 458	887.962 666	959.496 755	1036.978 384	1120.904 313	1211.812 529	44
45	911.273 585	986.638 559	1068.440 139	1157.230 898	1253.610 570	1358.230 032	45
46	1010.235 495	1096.168 801	1189.639 655	1291.312 451	1401.909 812	1522.217 636	46
47	1119.835 811	1217.747 369	1324.474 116	1440.813 383	1567.634 215	1705.883 752	47
48	1241.218 160	1352.699 580	1474.477 454	1607.506 922	1752.831 235	1911.589 803	48
49	1375.649 113	1502.496 533	1641.356 168	1793.370 218	1959.788 905	2141.980 579	49
50	1524.531 392	1668.771 152	1827.008 737	2000.607 793	2191.064 102	2400.018 249	50
51	1689.418 517	1853.335 979	2033.547 220	2231.677 689	2449.514 134	2689.020 438	51
52	1872.031 007	2058.202 937	2263.321 282	2489.320 623	2738.332 044	3012.702 891	52
53	2074.274 341	2285.605 260	2518.944 926	2776.592 495	3061.086 060	3375.227 238	53
54	2298.258 832	2538.021 838	2803.326 230	3096.900 632	3421.763 672	3781.254 506	54
55	2546.321 657	2818.204 240	3119.700 431	3454.044 205	3824.820 903	4236.005 047	55
56	2821.051 235	3129.206 707	3471.666 730	3852.259 288	4275.237 359	4745.325 653	56
57	3125.314 243	3474.419 445	3863.229 237	4296.269 106	4778.577 749	5315.764 731	57
58	3462.285 524	3857.605 583	4298.842 526	4791.340 053	5341.060 634	5954.656 499	58
59	3835.481 218	4282.942 198	4783.462 310	5343.344 159	5969.635 259	6670.215 279	59

YRS							
30	4248.795 449	4755.065 839	5322.601 820	5958.828 738	6672.067 402	7471.641 112	60
31	5213.494 112	5860.826 621	6589.663 909	7410.279 858	8334.236 972	9374.546 611	62
32	6396.751 288	7223.234 479	8157.851 223	9214.760 176	10409.964 719	11761.551 269	64
33	7848.082 772	8901.857 202	10098.728 052	11458.145 220	13000.541 514	14755.809 912	66
34	9628.222 474	10970.088 259	12500.866 391	14247.155 159	16239.279 317	18511.807 954	68
35	11811.663 952	13518.355 744	15473.887 919	17714.534 472	20281.831 007	23223.331 897	70
36	14489.777 744	16658.076 112	19153.466 595	22025.267 119	25330.194 823	29133.467 532	72
37	17774.463 952	20526.525 577	23707.520 140	27384.477 714	31634.623 109	36547.141 672	74
38	21803.697 092	25292.842 164	29343.872 974	34047.182 306	39493.620 547	45846.854 514	76
39	26745.568 442	31165.420 830	36319.740 285	42330.423 222	49339.495 957	57512.414 302	78
40	32807.051 632	38401.025 004	44953.466 062	52628.355 411	61617.588 423	72145.692 501	80

ANNUAL COMPOUNDING

SECTION 2

YRS	5.25% ANNUAL RATE	5.50% ANNUAL RATE	5.75% ANNUAL RATE	6.00% ANNUAL RATE	6.25% ANNUAL RATE	6.50% ANNUAL RATE	YRS
1	1.000 000	1.000 000	1.000 000	1.000 000	1.000 000	1.000 000	1
2	2.052 500	2.055 000	2.057 500	2.060 000	2.062 500	2.065 000	2
3	3.160 256	3.168 025	3.175 806	3.183 600	3.191 406	3.199 225	3
4	4.326 170	4.342 266	4.358 415	4.374 616	4.390 869	4.407 175	4
5	5.553 294	5.581 091	5.609 024	5.637 093	5.665 298	5.693 641	5
6	6.844 842	6.888 051	6.931 543	6.975 319	7.019 380	7.063 728	6
7	8.204 196	8.266 894	8.330 107	8.393 838	8.458 091	8.522 870	7
8	9.634 916	9.721 573	9.809 088	9.897 468	9.986 722	10.076 856	8
9	11.140 749	11.256 260	11.373 110	11.491 316	11.610 892	11.731 852	9
10	12.725 638	12.875 354	13.027 064	13.180 795	13.336 572	13.494 423	10
11	14.393 734	14.583 498	14.776 120	14.971 643	15.170 108	15.371 560	11
12	16.149 405	16.385 591	16.625 747	16.869 941	17.118 240	17.370 711	12
13	17.997 249	18.286 798	18.581 728	18.882 138	19.188 130	19.499 808	13
14	19.942 105	20.292 572	20.650 177	21.015 066	21.387 388	21.767 295	14
15	21.989 065	22.408 663	22.837 562	23.275 970	23.724 100	24.182 169	15
16	24.143 491	24.641 140	25.150 722	25.672 528	26.206 856	26.754 010	16
17	26.411 025	26.996 403	27.596 888	28.212 880	28.844 784	29.493 021	17
18	28.797 603	29.481 205	30.183 710	30.905 653	31.647 583	32.410 067	18
19	31.309 478	32.102 671	32.919 273	33.759 992	34.625 557	35.516 722	19
20	33.953 225	34.868 318	35.812 131	36.785 591	37.789 655	38.825 309	20
21	36.735 769	37.786 076	38.871 329	39.992 727	41.151 508	42.348 954	21
22	39.664 397	40.864 310	42.106 430	43.392 290	44.723 477	46.101 636	22
23	42.746 778	44.111 847	45.527 550	46.995 828	48.518 695	50.098 242	23
24	45.990 984	47.537 998	49.145 384	50.815 577	52.551 113	54.354 628	24
25	49.405 511	51.152 588	52.971 243	54.864 512	56.835 558	58.887 679	25
26	52.999 300	54.965 981	57.017 090	59.156 383	61.387 780	63.715 378	26
27	56.781 763	58.989 109	61.295 573	63.705 766	66.224 516	68.856 877	27
28	60.762 806	63.233 510	65.820 068	68.528 112	71.363 549	74.332 574	28
29	64.952 853	67.711 354	70.604 722	73.639 798	76.823 771	80.164 192	29
30	69.362 878	72.435 478	75.664 493	79.058 186	82.625 256	86.374 864	30
31	74.004 429	77.419 429	81.015 202	84.801 677	88.789 335	92.989 230	31
32	78.889 662	82.677 498	86.673 576	90.889 778	95.338 668	100.033 530	32
33	84.031 369	88.224 760	92.657 307	97.343 165	102.297 335	107.535 710	33
34	89.443 016	94.077 122	98.985 102	104.183 755	109.690 918	115.525 531	34
35	95.138 774	100.251 364	105.676 745	111.434 780	117.546 601	124.034 690	35
36	101.133 560	106.765 189	112.753 158	119.120 867	125.893 263	133.096 945	36
37	107.443 071	113.637 274	120.236 464	127.268 119	134.761 592	142.748 247	37
38	114.083 833	120.887 324	128.150 061	135.904 206	144.184 192	153.026 883	38
39	121.073 234	128.536 127	136.518 690	145.058 458	154.195 704	163.973 630	39
40	128.429 579	136.605 614	145.368 514	154.761 966	164.832 935	175.631 916	40
41	136.172 132	145.118 923	154.727 204	165.047 684	176.134 994	188.047 990	41
42	144.321 169	154.100 464	164.624 018	175.950 545	188.143 431	201.271 110	42
43	152.898 030	163.575 989	175.089 899	187.507 577	200.902 395	215.353 732	43
44	161.925 176	173.572 669	186.157 568	199.758 032	214.458 795	230.351 725	44
45	171.426 248	184.119 165	197.861 628	212.743 514	228.862 470	246.324 587	45
46	181.426 126	195.245 719	210.238 672	226.508 125	244.166 374	263.335 685	46
47	191.950 998	206.984 234	223.327 396	241.098 612	260.426 772	281.452 504	47
48	203.028 425	219.368 367	237.168 721	256.564 529	277.703 445	300.746 917	48
49	214.687 418	232.433 627	251.805 922	272.958 401	296.059 911	321.295 467	49
50	226.958 507	246.217 476	267.284 763	290.335 905	315.563 655	343.179 672	50

84

YRS	6.75% ANNUAL RATE	7.00% ANNUAL RATE	7.25% ANNUAL RATE	7.50% ANNUAL RATE	7.75% ANNUAL RATE	8.00% ANNUAL RATE	YRS
1	1.000 000	1.000 000	1.000 000	1.000 000	1.000 000	1.000 000	1
2	2.067 500	2.070 000	2.072 500	2.075 000	2.077 500	2.080 000	2
3	3.207 056	3.214 900	3.222 756	3.230 625	3.238 506	3.246 400	3
4	4.423 533	4.439 943	4.456 406	4.472 922	4.489 490	4.506 112	4
5	5.722 121	5.750 739	5.779 496	5.808 391	5.837 426	5.866 601	5
6	7.108 364	7.153 291	7.198 509	7.244 020	7.289 827	7.335 929	6
7	8.588 179	8.654 021	8.720 401	8.787 322	8.854 788	8.922 803	7
8	10.167 881	10.259 803	10.352 630	10.446 371	10.541 034	10.636 628	8
9	11.854 213	11.977 989	12.103 196	12.229 849	12.357 964	12.487 558	9
10	13.654 372	13.816 448	13.980 677	14.147 087	14.315 707	14.486 562	10
11	15.576 042	15.783 599	15.994 276	16.208 119	16.425 174	16.645 487	11
12	17.627 425	17.888 451	18.153 861	18.423 728	18.698 125	18.977 126	12
13	19.817 276	20.140 643	20.470 016	20.805 508	21.147 229	21.495 297	13
14	22.154 942	22.550 488	22.954 093	23.365 921	23.786 140	24.214 920	14
15	24.650 401	25.129 022	25.618 264	26.118 365	26.629 566	27.152 114	15
16	27.314 303	27.888 054	28.475 588	29.077 242	29.693 357	30.324 283	16
17	30.158 019	30.840 217	31.540 069	32.258 035	32.994 592	33.750 226	17
18	33.193 685	33.999 033	34.826 724	35.677 388	36.551 673	37.450 244	18
19	36.434 259	37.378 965	38.351 661	39.353 192	40.384 428	41.446 263	19
20	39.893 571	40.995 492	42.132 156	43.304 681	44.514 221	45.761 964	20
21	43.586 387	44.865 177	46.186 738	47.552 532	48.964 073	50.422 921	21
22	47.528 468	49.005 739	50.535 276	52.118 972	53.758 788	55.456 755	22
23	51.736 640	53.436 141	55.199 084	57.027 895	58.925 095	60.893 296	23
24	56.228 863	58.176 671	60.201 017	62.304 987	64.491 789	66.764 759	24
25	61.024 311	63.249 038	65.565 591	67.977 862	70.489 903	73.105 940	25
26	66.143 452	68.676 470	71.319 096	74.076 201	76.952 870	79.954 415	26
27	71.608 135	74.483 823	77.489 731	80.631 916	83.916 718	87.350 768	27
28	77.441 684	80.697 691	84.107 736	87.679 310	91.420 264	95.338 830	28
29	83.668 998	87.346 529	91.205 547	95.255 258	99.505 334	103.965 936	29
30	90.316 655	94.460 786	98.817 949	103.399 403	108.216 997	113.283 211	30
31	97.413 030	102.073 041	106.982 251	112.154 358	117.603 815	123.345 868	31
32	104.988 409	110.218 154	115.738 464	121.565 935	127.718 110	134.213 537	32
33	113.075 127	118.933 425	125.129 503	131.683 380	138.616 264	145.950 620	33
34	121.707 698	128.258 765	135.201 392	142.559 633	150.359 024	158.626 670	34
35	130.922 967	138.236 878	146.003 492	154.251 606	163.011 849	172.316 804	35
36	140.760 268	148.913 460	157.588 746	166.820 476	176.645 267	187.102 148	36
37	151.261 586	160.337 402	170.013 930	180.332 012	191.335 275	203.070 320	37
38	162.471 743	172.561 020	183.339 940	194.856 913	207.163 759	220.315 945	38
39	174.438 586	185.640 292	197.632 085	210.471 181	224.218 950	238.941 221	39
40	187.213 190	199.635 112	212.960 411	227.256 520	242.595 919	259.056 519	40
41	200.850 080	214.609 570	229.400 041	245.300 759	262.397 103	280.781 040	41
42	215.407 461	230.632 240	247.031 544	264.698 315	283.732 878	304.243 523	42
43	230.947 464	247.776 496	265.941 331	285.550 689	306.722 176	329.583 005	43
44	247.536 418	266.120 851	286.222 078	307.966 991	331.493 145	356.949 646	44
45	265.245 127	285.749 311	307.973 178	332.064 515	358.183 864	386.505 617	45
46	284.149 173	306.751 763	331.301 234	357.969 354	386.943 113	418.426 067	46
47	304.329 242	329.224 386	356.320 573	385.817 055	417.931 204	452.900 152	47
48	325.871 466	353.270 093	383.153 815	415.753 334	451.320 873	490.132 164	48
49	348.867 789	378.999 000	411.932 466	447.934 835	487.298 240	530.342 737	49
50	373.416 365	406.528 929	442.797 570	482.529 947	526.063 854	573.770 156	50

YRS	8.25% ANNUAL RATE	8.50% ANNUAL RATE	8.75% ANNUAL RATE	9.00% ANNUAL RATE	9.25% ANNUAL RATE	9.50% ANNUAL RATE	YRS
1	1.000 000	1.000 000	1.000 000	1.000 000	1.000 000	1.000 000	1
2	2.082 500	2.085 000	2.087 500	2.090 000	2.092 500	2.095 000	2
3	3.254 306	3.262 225	3.270 156	3.278 100	3.286 056	3.294 025	3
4	4.522 787	4.539 514	4.556 295	4.573 129	4.590 016	4.606 957	4
5	5.895 916	5.925 373	5.954 971	5.984 711	6.014 593	6.044 618	5
6	7.382 330	7.429 030	7.476 031	7.523 335	7.570 943	7.618 857	6
7	8.991 372	9.060 497	9.130 183	9.200 435	9.271 255	9.342 648	7
8	10.733 160	10.830 639	10.929 074	11.028 474	11.128 846	11.230 200	8
9	12.618 646	12.751 244	12.885 368	13.021 036	13.158 264	13.297 069	9
10	14.659 684	14.835 099	15.012 838	15.192 930	15.375 404	15.560 291	10
11	16.869 108	17.096 083	17.326 461	17.560 293	17.797 629	18.038 518	11
12	19.260 809	19.549 250	19.842 527	20.140 720	20.443 909	20.752 178	12
13	21.849 826	22.210 936	22.578 748	22.953 385	23.334 971	23.723 634	13
14	24.652 436	25.098 866	25.554 388	26.019 189	26.493 456	26.977 380	14
15	27.686 262	28.232 269	28.790 397	29.360 916	29.944 100	30.540 231	15
16	30.970 379	31.632 012	32.309 557	33.003 399	33.713 930	34.441 553	16
17	34.525 435	35.320 733	36.136 643	36.973 705	37.832 468	38.713 500	17
18	38.373 784	39.322 995	40.298 600	41.301 338	42.331 972	43.391 283	18
19	42.539 621	43.665 450	44.824 727	46.018 458	47.247 679	48.513 454	19
20	47.049 140	48.377 013	49.746 891	51.160 120	52.618 089	54.122 233	20
21	51.930 694	53.489 059	55.099 744	56.764 530	58.485 262	60.263 845	21
22	57.214 976	59.035 629	60.920 971	62.873 338	64.895 149	66.988 910	22
23	62.935 212	65.053 658	67.251 556	69.531 939	71.897 951	74.352 856	23
24	69.127 366	71.583 219	74.136 067	76.789 813	79.548 511	82.416 378	24
25	75.830 374	78.667 792	81.622 973	84.700 896	87.906 748	91.245 934	25
26	83.086 380	86.354 555	89.764 984	93.323 977	97.038 122	100.914 297	26
27	90.941 006	94.694 692	98.619 420	102.723 135	107.014 149	111.501 156	27
28	99.443 639	103.743 741	108.248 619	112.968 217	117.912 958	123.093 766	28
29	108.647 740	113.561 959	118.720 373	124.135 356	129.819 906	135.787 673	29
30	118.611 178	124.214 725	130.108 406	136.307 539	142.828 247	149.687 502	30
31	129.396 600	135.772 977	142.492 891	149.575 217	157.039 860	164.907 815	31
32	141.071 820	148.313 680	155.961 019	164.036 987	172.566 047	181.574 057	32
33	153.710 245	161.920 343	170.607 608	179.800 315	189.528 407	199.823 593	33
34	167.391 340	176.683 572	186.535 774	196.982 344	208.059 784	219.806 834	34
35	182.201 126	192.701 675	203.857 654	215.710 755	228.305 315	241.688 483	35
36	198.232 719	210.081 318	222.695 199	236.124 723	250.423 556	265.648 889	36
37	215.586 918	228.938 230	243.181 029	258.375 948	274.587 735	291.885 534	37
38	234.372 839	249.397 979	265.459 369	282.629 783	300.987 101	320.614 659	38
39	254.708 598	271.596 808	289.687 064	309.066 463	329.828 407	352.073 052	39
40	276.722 058	295.682 536	316.034 682	337.882 445	361.337 535	386.519 992	40
41	300.551 627	321.815 552	344.687 716	369.291 865	395.761 257	424.239 391	41
42	326.347 137	350.169 874	375.847 892	403.528 133	433.369 173	465.542 133	42
43	354.270 775	380.934 313	409.734 582	440.845 665	474.455 822	510.768 636	43
44	384.498 114	414.313 730	446.586 358	481.521 775	519.342 985	560.291 656	44
45	417.219 209	450.530 397	486.662 664	525.858 734	568.382 212	614.519 364	45
46	452.639 793	489.825 480	530.245 648	574.186 021	621.957 566	673.898 703	46
47	490.982 576	532.460 646	577.642 142	626.862 762	680.488 641	738.919 080	47
48	532.488 639	578.719 801	629.185 829	684.280 411	744.433 840	810.116 393	48
49	577.418 952	628.910 984	685.239 589	746.865 648	814.293 970	888.077 450	49
50	626.056 015	683.368 418	746.198 053	815.083 556	890.616 163	973.444 808	50

SECTION 2

YRS	9.75% ANNUAL RATE	10.00% ANNUAL RATE	10.25% ANNUAL RATE	10.50% ANNUAL RATE	10.75% ANNUAL RATE	11.00% ANNUAL RATE	YRS
1	1.000 000	1.000 000	1.000 000	1.000 000	1.000 000	1.000 000	1
2	2.097 500	2.100 000	2.102 500	2.105 000	2.107 500	2.110 000	2
3	3.302 006	3.310 000	3.318 006	3.326 025	3.334 056	3.342 100	3
4	4.623 952	4.641 000	4.658 102	4.675 258	4.692 467	4.709 731	4
5	6.074 787	6.105 100	6.135 557	6.166 160	6.196 908	6.227 801	5
6	7.667 079	7.715 610	7.764 452	7.813 606	7.863 075	7.912 860	6
7	9.414 619	9.487 171	9.560 308	9.634 035	9.708 356	9.783 274	7
8	11.332 544	11.435 888	11.540 240	11.645 609	11.752 004	11.859 434	8
9	13.437 468	13.579 477	13.723 114	13.868 398	14.015 344	14.163 972	9
10	15.747 621	15.937 425	16.129 734	16.324 579	16.521 994	16.722 009	10
11	18.283 014	18.531 167	18.783 031	19.038 660	19.298 108	19.561 430	11
12	21.065 607	21.384 284	21.708 292	22.037 720	22.372 655	22.713 187	12
13	24.119 504	24.522 712	24.933 392	25.351 680	25.777 715	26.211 638	13
14	27.471 156	27.974 983	28.489 065	29.013 607	29.548 820	30.094 918	14
15	31.149 594	31.772 482	32.409 194	33.060 035	33.725 318	34.405 359	15
16	35.186 679	35.949 730	36.731 136	37.531 339	38.350 789	39.189 948	16
17	39.617 380	40.544 703	41.496 078	42.472 130	43.473 499	44.500 843	17
18	44.480 075	45.599 173	46.749 426	47.931 703	49.146 900	50.395 936	18
19	49.816 882	51.159 090	52.541 242	53.964 532	55.430 192	56.939 488	19
20	55.674 028	57.274 999	58.926 719	60.630 808	62.388 938	64.202 832	20
21	62.102 246	64.002 499	65.966 708	67.997 043	70.095 749	72.265 144	21
22	69.157 215	71.402 749	73.728 295	76.136 732	78.631 042	81.214 309	22
23	76.900 043	79.543 024	82.285 446	85.131 089	88.083 879	91.147 884	23
24	85.397 797	88.497 327	91.719 704	95.069 854	98.552 895	102.174 151	24
25	94.724 083	98.347 059	102.120 974	106.052 188	110.147 332	114.413 307	25
26	104.959 681	109.181 765	113.588 373	118.187 668	122.988 170	127.998 771	26
27	116.193 249	121.099 942	126.231 182	131.597 373	137.209 398	143.078 636	27
28	128.522 091	134.209 936	140.169 878	146.415 097	152.959 408	159.817 286	28
29	142.052 995	148.630 930	155.537 290	162.788 683	170.402 545	178.397 187	29
30	156.903 162	164.494 023	172.479 862	180.881 494	189.720 818	199.020 878	30
31	173.201 221	181.943 425	191.159 048	200.874 051	211.115 806	221.913 174	31
32	191.088 340	201.137 767	211.752 851	222.965 827	234.810 756	247.323 624	32
33	210.719 453	222.251 544	234.457 518	247.377 238	261.052 912	275.529 222	33
34	232.264 599	245.476 699	259.489 414	274.351 848	290.116 100	306.837 437	34
35	255.910 398	271.024 368	287.087 078	304.158 792	322.303 581	341.589 555	35
36	281.861 661	299.126 805	317.513 504	337.095 466	357.951 215	380.164 406	36
37	310.343 173	330.039 486	351.058 638	373.490 489	422.982 490	422.982 490	37
38	341.601 633	364.043 434	388.042 148	413.706 991	441.154 801	470.510 564	38
39	375.907 792	401.447 778	428.816 469	458.146 225	489.578 942	523.266 726	39
40	413.558 802	442.592 556	473.770 157	507.251 579	543.208 678	581.826 066	40
41	454.880 785	487.851 811	523.331 598	561.512 994	602.603 611	646.826 934	41
42	500.231 662	537.636 992	577.973 087	621.471 859	668.383 499	718.977 896	42
43	550.004 249	592.400 692	638.215 328	687.726 404	741.234 725	799.065 465	43
44	604.629 663	652.640 761	704.632 399	760.937 676	821.917 458	887.962 666	44
45	664.581 055	718.904 837	777.857 220	841.836 132	911.273 585	986.638 559	45
46	730.377 708	791.795 321	858.587 585	931.228 926	1010.235 495	1096.168 801	46
47	802.589 534	871.974 853	947.592 813	1030.007 963	1119.835 811	1217.747 369	47
48	881.842 014	960.172 338	1045.721 076	1139.158 800	1241.218 160	1352.699 580	48
49	968.821 610	1057.189 572	1153.907 486	1259.770 473	1375.649 113	1502.496 533	49
50	1064.281 717	1163.908 529	1273.183 003	1393.046 373	1524.531 392	1668.771 152	50

YRS	11.25% ANNUAL RATE	11.50% ANNUAL RATE	11.75% ANNUAL RATE	12.00% ANNUAL RATE	12.25% ANNUAL RATE	12.50% ANNUAL RATE	YRS
1	1.000 000	1.000 000	1.000 000	1.000 000	1.000 000	1.000 000	1
2	2.112 500	2.115 000	2.117 500	2.120 000	2.122 500	2.125 000	2
3	3.350 156	3.358 225	3.366 306	3.374 400	3.382 506	3.390 625	3
4	4.727 049	4.744 421	4.761 847	4.779 328	4.796 863	4.814 453	4
5	6.258 842	6.290 029	6.321 364	6.352 847	6.384 479	6.416 260	5
6	7.962 962	8.013 383	8.064 125	8.115 189	8.166 578	8.218 292	6
7	9.858 795	9.934 922	10.011 659	10.089 012	10.166 983	10.245 579	7
8	11.967 909	12.077 438	12.188 029	12.299 693	12.412 439	12.526 276	8
9	14.314 299	14.466 343	14.620 123	14.775 656	14.932 963	15.092 061	9
10	16.924 657	17.129 972	17.337 987	17.548 735	17.762 251	17.978 568	10
11	19.828 681	20.099 919	20.375 200	20.654 583	20.938 126	21.225 889	11
12	23.059 408	23.411 410	23.769 287	24.133 133	24.503 047	24.879 125	12
13	26.653 592	27.103 722	27.562 178	28.029 109	28.504 670	28.989 016	13
14	30.652 121	31.220 650	31.800 734	32.392 602	32.996 492	33.612 643	14
15	35.100 484	35.811 025	36.537 320	37.279 715	38.038 562	38.814 223	15
16	40.049 289	40.929 293	41.830 455	42.753 280	43.698 286	44.666 001	16
17	45.554 834	46.636 161	47.745 533	48.883 674	50.051 326	51.249 252	17
18	51.679 752	52.999 320	54.355 634	55.749 715	57.182 614	58.655 408	18
19	58.493 725	60.094 242	61.742 420	63.439 681	65.187 484	66.987 334	19
20	66.074 269	68.005 080	69.997 155	72.052 442	74.172 951	76.360 751	20
21	74.507 624	76.825 664	79.221 821	81.698 736	84.259 137	86.905 845	21
22	83.889 731	86.660 615	89.530 384	92.502 584	95.580 882	98.769 075	22
23	94.327 326	97.626 586	101.050 205	104.602 894	108.289 540	112.115 210	23
24	105.939 150	109.853 643	113.923 604	118.155 241	122.555 008	127.129 611	24
25	118.857 305	123.486 812	128.309 627	133.333 870	138.567 997	144.020 812	25
26	133.228 752	138.687 796	144.386 008	150.333 934	156.542 576	163.023 414	26
27	149.216 986	155.636 892	162.351 364	169.374 007	176.719 042	184.401 340	27
28	167.003 897	174.535 135	182.427 650	190.698 887	199.367 125	208.451 508	28
29	186.791 836	195.606 675	204.862 898	214.582 754	224.789 597	235.507 946	29
30	208.805 917	219.101 443	229.934 289	241.332 684	253.326 323	265.946 440	30
31	233.296 583	245.298 109	257.951 568	271.292 606	285.358 798	300.189 745	31
32	260.542 448	274.507 391	289.260 877	304.847 719	321.315 250	338.713 463	32
33	290.853 474	307.075 741	324.249 030	342.429 446	361.676 369	382.052 645	33
34	324.574 489	343.389 451	363.348 291	384.520 979	406.981 724	430.809 226	34
35	362.089 120	383.879 238	407.041 715	431.663 496	457.836 985	485.660 379	35
36	403.824 145	429.025 351	455.869 117	484.463 116	514.922 016	547.367 927	36
37	450.254 362	479.363 266	510.433 738	543.598 690	578.999 963	616.788 918	37
38	501.907 978	535.490 042	571.409 702	609.830 533	650.927 458	694.887 532	38
39	559.372 625	598.071 396	639.550 343	684.010 197	731.666 072	782.748 474	39
40	623.302 045	667.849 607	715.697 508	767.091 420	822.295 165	881.592 033	40
41	694.423 525	745.652 312	800.791 965	860.142 391	924.026 323	992.791 037	41
42	773.546 172	832.402 327	895.885 021	964.359 478	1038.219 548	1117.889 917	42
43	861.570 116	929.128 595	1002.151 511	1081.082 615	1166.401 442	1258.626 157	43
44	959.496 755	1036.978 384	1120.904 313	1211.812 529	1310.285 619	1416.954 426	44
45	1068.440 139	1157.230 898	1253.610 570	1358.230 032	1471.795 607	1595.073 729	45
46	1189.639 655	1291.312 451	1401.909 812	1522.217 636	1653.090 569	1795.457 946	46
47	1324.474 116	1440.813 383	1567.634 215	1705.883 752	1856.594 164	2020.890 189	47
48	1474.477 454	1607.506 922	1752.831 235	1911.589 803	2085.026 949	2274.501 462	48
49	1641.356 168	1793.370 218	1959.788 905	2141.980 579	2341.442 750	2559.814 145	49
50	1827.008 737	2000.607 793	2191.064 102	2400.018 249	2629.269 487	2880.790 913	50

FUTURE VALUE PER PERIOD

YRS	12.75% ANNUAL RATE	13.00% ANNUAL RATE	13.25% ANNUAL RATE	13.50% ANNUAL RATE	13.75% ANNUAL RATE	14.00% ANNUAL RATE	YRS
1	1.000 000	1.000 000	1.000 000	1.000 000	1.000 000	1.000 000	1
2	2.127 500	2.130 000	2.132 500	2.135 000	2.137 500	2.140 000	2
3	3.398 756	3.406 900	3.415 056	3.423 225	3.431 406	3.439 600	3
4	4.832 098	4.849 797	4.867 551	4.885 360	4.903 225	4.921 144	4
5	6.448 190	6.480 271	6.512 502	6.544 884	6.577 418	6.610 104	5
6	8.270 334	8.322 706	8.375 408	8.428 443	8.481 813	8.535 519	6
7	10.324 802	10.404 658	10.485 150	10.566 283	10.648 062	10.730 491	7
8	12.641 214	12.757 263	12.874 432	12.992 731	13.112 171	13.232 760	8
9	15.252 969	15.415 707	15.580 294	15.746 750	15.915 094	16.085 347	9
10	18.197 723	18.419 749	18.644 683	18.872 561	19.103 420	19.337 295	10
11	21.517 932	21.814 317	22.115 104	22.420 357	22.730 140	23.044 516	11
12	25.261 469	25.650 178	26.045 355	26.447 106	26.855 534	27.270 749	12
13	29.482 306	29.984 701	30.496 365	31.017 465	31.548 170	32.088 654	13
14	34.241 300	34.882 712	35.537 133	36.204 823	36.886 044	37.581 065	14
15	39.607 066	40.417 464	41.245 803	42.092 474	42.957 875	43.842 414	15
16	45.656 966	46.671 735	47.710 872	48.774 957	49.864 582	50.980 352	16
17	52.478 230	53.739 060	55.032 563	56.359 577	57.720 962	59.117 601	17
18	60.169 204	61.725 138	63.324 377	64.968 120	66.657 595	68.394 066	18
19	68.840 777	70.749 406	72.714 857	74.738 816	76.823 014	78.969 235	19
20	78.617 977	80.946 829	83.349 576	85.828 556	88.386 178	91.024 928	20
21	89.641 769	92.469 917	95.393 395	98.415 411	101.539 278	104.768 418	21
22	102.071 094	105.491 006	109.033 020	112.701 491	116.500 929	120.435 996	22
23	116.085 159	120.204 837	124.479 895	128.916 193	133.519 806	138.297 035	23
24	131.886 016	136.831 465	141.973 481	147.319 879	152.878 780	158.658 620	24
25	149.701 483	155.619 556	161.784 967	168.208 062	174.899 612	181.870 827	25
26	169.788 423	176.850 098	184.221 475	191.916 151	199.948 309	208.332 743	26
27	192.436 446	200.840 611	209.630 821	218.824 831	228.441 201	238.499 327	27
28	217.972 093	227.949 890	238.406 904	249.366 183	260.851 866	272.889 233	28
29	246.763 535	258.583 376	270.995 819	284.030 618	297.718 998	312.093 725	29
30	279.225 886	293.199 215	307.902 765	323.374 752	339.655 360	356.786 847	30
31	315.827 187	332.315 113	349.699 882	368.030 343	387.357 972	407.737 006	31
32	357.095 153	376.516 078	397.035 116	418.714 439	441.619 693	465.820 186	32
33	403.624 785	426.463 168	450.642 269	476.240 889	503.342 401	532.035 012	33
34	456.086 945	482.903 380	511.352 369	541.533 409	573.551 981	607.519 914	34
35	515.238 030	546.680 819	580.106 558	615.640 419	653.415 378	693.572 702	35
36	581.930 879	618.749 325	657.970 677	699.751 875	744.259 993	791.672 881	36
37	657.127 066	700.186 738	746.151 792	795.218 378	847.595 742	903.507 084	37
38	741.910 767	792.211 014	846.016 904	903.572 859	965.140 157	1030.998 076	38
39	837.504 390	896.198 445	959.114 144	1026.555 195	1098.846 928	1176.337 806	39
40	945.286 200	1013.704 243	1087.196 768	1166.140 147	1250.938 381	1342.025 099	40
41	1066.810 190	1146.485 795	1232.250 340	1324.569 067	1423.942 408	1530.908 613	41
42	1203.828 490	1296.528 948	1396.523 510	1504.385 891	1620.734 489	1746.235 819	42
43	1358.316 622	1466.077 712	1582.562 875	1708.477 986	1844.585 481	1991.708 833	43
44	1532.501 991	1657.667 814	1793.252 456	1940.122 514	2099.215 985	2271.548 070	44
45	1728.895 995	1874.164 630	2031.858 407	2203.039 053	2388.858 183	2590.564 800	45
46	1950.330 235	2118.806 032	2302.079 646	2501.449 326	2718.326 183	2954.243 872	46
47	2199.997 339	2395.250 816	2608.105 199	2840.144 984	3093.096 034	3368.838 014	47
48	2481.497 000	2707.633 422	2954.679 138	3224.564 557	3519.396 738	3841.475 336	48
49	2798.887 868	3060.625 767	3347.174 124	3660.880 773	4004.313 790	4380.281 883	49
50	3156.746 071	3459.507 117	3791.674 695	4156.099 677	4555.906 936	4994.521 346	50

YRS	14.25% ANNUAL RATE	14.50% ANNUAL RATE	14.75% ANNUAL RATE	15.00% ANNUAL RATE	15.25% ANNUAL RATE	15.50% ANNUAL RATE	YRS
1	1.000 000	1.000 000	1.000 000	1.000 000	1.000 000	1.000 000	1
2	2.142 500	2.145 000	2.147 500	2.150 000	2.152 500	2.155 000	2
3	3.447 806	3.456 025	3.464 256	3.472 500	3.480 756	3.489 025	3
4	4.939 119	4.957 149	4.975 234	4.993 375	5.011 572	5.029 824	4
5	6.642 943	6.675 935	6.709 081	6.742 381	6.775 836	6.809 447	5
6	8.589 562	8.643 946	8.698 671	8.753 738	8.809 151	8.864 911	6
7	10.813 575	10.897 318	10.981 724	11.066 799	11.152 547	11.238 972	7
8	13.354 510	13.477 429	13.601 529	13.726 819	13.853 310	13.981 013	8
9	16.257 527	16.431 656	16.607 754	16.785 842	16.965 940	17.148 070	9
10	19.574 225	19.814 246	20.057 398	20.303 718	20.553 246	20.806 020	10
11	23.363 552	23.687 312	24.015 864	24.349 276	24.687 616	25.030 954	11
12	27.692 858	28.121 972	28.558 204	29.001 667	29.452 477	29.910 751	12
13	32.639 090	33.199 658	33.770 539	34.351 917	34.943 980	35.546 918	13
14	38.290 161	39.013 609	39.751 694	40.504 705	41.272 937	42.056 690	14
15	44.746 508	45.670 582	46.615 069	47.580 411	48.567 060	49.575 477	15
16	52.122 886	53.292 816	54.490 791	55.717 472	56.973 537	58.259 676	16
17	60.550 397	62.020 275	63.528 183	65.075 093	66.662 001	68.289 926	17
18	70.178 829	72.013 215	73.898 590	75.836 357	77.827 956	79.874 864	18
19	81.179 312	83.455 131	85.798 632	88.211 811	90.696 719	93.255 468	19
20	93.747 364	96.556 125	99.453 930	102.443 583	105.527 969	108.710 066	20
21	108.106 363	111.556 763	115.123 385	118.810 120	122.620 984	126.560 126	21
22	124.511 520	128.732 494	133.104 084	137.631 638	142.320 685	147.176 945	22
23	143.254 411	148.398 705	153.736 937	159.276 384	165.024 589	170.989 372	23
24	164.668 165	170.916 517	177.413 135	184.167 841	191.190 839	198.492 725	24
25	189.133 378	196.699 412	204.581 573	212.793 017	221.347 442	230.259 097	25
26	217.084 885	226.220 827	235.757 354	245.711 970	256.102 927	266.949 257	26
27	249.019 481	260.022 847	271.531 564	283.568 766	296.158 623	309.326 392	27
28	285.504 757	298.726 160	312.582 470	327.104 080	342.322 813	358.271 982	28
29	327.189 185	343.041 453	359.688 384	377.169 693	395.527 042	414.804 140	29
30	374.813 643	393.782 464	413.742 421	434.745 146	456.844 916	480.098 781	30
31	429.224 588	451.880 921	475.769 428	500.956 918	527.513 765	555.514 092	31
32	491.389 091	518.403 655	546.945 419	577.100 456	608.959 615	642.618 777	32
33	562.412 037	594.572 185	628.619 868	664.665 524	702.825 956	743.224 687	33
34	643.555 752	681.785 151	722.341 299	765.365 353	811.006 914	859.424 513	34
35	736.262 447	781.643 998	829.886 640	881.170 156	935.685 468	993.635 313	35
36	842.179 845	895.982 378	953.294 920	1014.345 680	1079.377 502	1148.648 787	36
37	963.190 473	1026.899 823	1094.905 920	1167.497 532	1244.982 571	1327.689 348	37
38	1101.445 116	1176.800 297	1257.404 543	1343.622 161	1435.842 414	1534.481 197	38
39	1259.401 045	1348.436 340	1443.871 714	1546.165 485	1655.808 382	1773.325 783	39
40	1439.865 694	1544.959 609	1657.842 791	1779.090 308	1909.319 160	2049.191 279	40
41	1646.046 555	1769.978 753	1903.374 603	2046.953 854	2201.490 332	2367.815 928	41
42	1881.608 189	2027.625 672	2185.122 357	2354.996 933	2538.217 607	2735.827 397	42
43	2150.737 356	2322.631 394	2508.427 905	2709.246 473	2926.295 792	3160.880 643	43
44	2458.217 430	2660.412 947	2879.421 020	3116.633 443	3373.555 901	3651.817 143	44
45	2809.513 413	3047.172 824	3305.135 621	3585.128 460	3889.023 176	4218.848 800	45
46	3210.869 075	3490.012 883	3793.643 125	4123.897 729	4483.099 210	4873.770 364	46
47	3669.417 918	3997.064 751	4354.205 486	4743.482 388	5167.771 839	5630.204 770	47
48	4193.309 971	4577.639 140	4997.450 795	5456.004 746	5956.857 045	6503.886 510	48
49	4791.856 642	5242.396 816	5735.574 787	6275.405 458	6866.277 744	7512.988 919	49
50	5475.696 214	6003.544 354	6582.572 069	7217.716 277	7914.385 100	8678.502 201	50

SECTION 2

YRS	15.75% ANNUAL RATE	16.00% ANNUAL RATE	16.25% ANNUAL RATE	16.50% ANNUAL RATE	16.75% ANNUAL RATE	17.00% ANNUAL RATE	YRS
1	1.000 000	1.000 000	1.000 000	1.000 000	1.000 000	1.000 000	1
2	2.157 500	2.160 000	2.162 500	2.165 000	2.167 500	2.170 000	2
3	3.497 306	3.505 600	3.513 906	3.522 225	3.530 556	3.538 900	3
4	5.048 132	5.066 496	5.084 916	5.103 392	5.121 924	5.140 513	4
5	6.843 213	6.877 135	6.911 215	6.945 452	6.979 847	7.014 400	5
6	8.921 019	8.977 477	9.034 287	9.091 451	9.148 971	9.206 848	6
7	11.326 079	11.413 873	11.502 359	11.591 541	11.681 424	11.772 012	7
8	14.109 937	14.240 093	14.371 492	14.504 145	14.638 062	14.773 255	8
9	17.332 252	17.518 508	17.706 860	17.897 329	18.089 938	18.284 708	9
10	21.062 081	21.321 469	21.584 225	21.850 388	22.120 002	22.393 108	10
11	25.379 359	25.732 904	26.091 661	26.455 702	26.825 103	27.199 937	11
12	30.376 608	30.850 169	31.331 556	31.820 893	32.318 307	32.823 926	12
13	36.160 924	36.786 196	37.422 934	38.071 341	38.731 624	39.403 993	13
14	42.856 270	43.671 987	44.504 160	45.353 112	46.219 171	47.102 672	14
15	50.606 132	51.659 505	52.736 087	53.836 375	54.960 882	56.110 126	15
16	59.576 598	60.925 026	62.305 701	63.719 377	65.166 830	66.648 848	16
17	69.959 912	71.673 030	73.430 377	75.233 075	77.082 273	78.979 152	17
18	81.978 598	84.140 715	86.362 813	88.646 532	90.993 554	93.405 608	18
19	95.890 228	98.603 230	101.396 770	104.273 210	107.234 975	110.284 561	19
20	111.992 038	115.379 747	118.873 746	122.478 289	126.196 833	130.032 936	20
21	130.631 826	134.840 506	139.190 729	143.687 207	148.334 802	153.138 535	21
22	152.206 339	157.414 987	162.809 223	168.395 596	174.180 882	180.172 086	22
23	177.178 837	183.601 385	190.265 721	197.180 869	204.356 179	211.801 341	23
24	206.084 504	213.977 607	222.183 901	230.715 713	239.585 839	248.807 569	24
25	239.542 813	249.214 024	259.288 785	269.783 805	280.716 468	292.104 856	25
26	278.270 806	290.088 267	302.423 213	315.298 133	328.736 476	342.762 681	26
27	323.098 458	337.502 390	352.566 985	368.322 325	384.799 836	402.032 337	27
28	374.986 466	392.502 773	410.859 120	430.095 509	450.253 808	471.377 835	28
29	435.046 834	456.303 216	478.623 727	502.061 268	526.671 321	552.512 066	29
30	504.566 710	530.311 731	557.400 082	585.901 377	615.888 767	647.439 118	30
31	585.035 967	616.161 608	648.977 596	683.575 105	720.050 136	758.503 768	31
32	678.179 132	715.747 465	755.436 455	797.364 997	841.658 533	888.449 408	32
33	785.992 345	831.267 059	879.194 879	929.930 221	983.636 338	1040.485 808	33
34	910.786 140	965.269 789	1023.064 047	1084.368 708	1149.395 424	1218.368 395	34
35	1055.234 957	1120.712 955	1190.311 954	1264.289 545	1342.919 158	1426.491 022	35
36	1222.434 462	1301.027 028	1384.737 647	1473.897 320	1568.858 117	1669.994 496	36
37	1415.967 890	1510.191 352	1610.757 515	1718.090 377	1832.641 851	1954.893 560	37
38	1639.982 833	1752.821 968	1873.505 611	2002.575 290	2140.609 362	2288.225 465	38
39	1899.280 129	2034.273 483	2178.950 272	2334.000 212	2500.161 430	2678.223 794	39
40	2199.416 750	2360.757 241	2534.029 692	2720.110 247	2919.938 469	3134.521 839	40
41	2546.824 888	2739.478 399	2946.809 517	3169.928 438	3410.028 163	3668.390 552	41
42	2948.949 807	3178.794 943	3426.666 063	3693.966 630	3982.207 880	4293.016 946	42
43	3414.409 402	3688.402 134	3984.499 298	4304.471 124	4650.227 700	5023.829 827	43
44	3953.178 883	4279.546 475	4632.980 434	5015.708 860	5430.140 839	5878.880 897	44
45	4576.804 557	4965.273 911	5386.839 755	5844.300 822	6340.689 430	6879.290 650	45
46	5298.651 275	5760.717 737	6263.201 215	6809.610 458	7403.754 909	8049.770 061	46
47	6134.188 850	6683.432 575	7281.971 412	7934.196 183	8644.883 857	9419.230 971	47
48	7101.323 594	7753.781 787	8466.291 767	9244.338 553	10093.901 903	11021.500 236	48
49	8220.782 060	8995.386 873	9843.064 179	10770.654 414	11785.630 472	12896.155 276	49
50	9516.555 235	10435.648 773	11443.562 108	12548.812 393	13760.723 576	15089.501 673	50

SECTION 2

YRS	17.25% ANNUAL RATE	17.50% ANNUAL RATE	17.75% ANNUAL RATE	18.00% ANNUAL RATE	18.25% ANNUAL RATE	18.50% ANNUAL RATE	YRS
1	1.000 000	1.000 000	1.000 000	1.000 000	1.000 000	1.000 000	1
2	2.172 500	2.175 000	2.177 500	2.180 000	2.182 500	2.185 000	2
3	3.547 256	3.555 625	3.564 006	3.572 400	3.580 806	3.589 225	3
4	5.159 158	5.177 859	5.196 617	5.215 432	5.234 303	5.253 232	4
5	7.049 113	7.083 985	7.119 017	7.154 210	7.189 564	7.225 079	5
6	9.265 085	9.323 682	9.382 642	9.441 968	9.501 659	9.561 719	6
7	11.863 312	11.955 326	12.048 061	12.141 522	12.235 712	12.330 637	7
8	14.909 733	15.047 509	15.186 592	15.326 996	15.468 729	15.611 805	8
9	18.481 662	18.680 823	18.882 213	19.085 855	19.291 772	19.499 989	9
10	22.669 749	22.949 967	23.233 805	23.521 309	23.812 521	24.107 487	10
11	27.580 280	27.966 211	28.357 806	28.755 144	29.158 306	29.567 372	11
12	33.337 879	33.860 298	34.391 316	34.931 070	35.479 697	36.037 336	12
13	40.088 663	40.785 850	41.495 775	42.218 663	42.954 742	43.704 243	13
14	48.003 957	48.923 373	49.861 275	50.818 022	51.793 982	52.789 528	14
15	57.284 640	58.484 964	59.711 651	60.965 266	62.246 384	63.555 591	15
16	68.166 240	69.719 832	71.310 469	72.939 014	74.606 349	76.313 375	16
17	80.924 916	82.920 803	84.968 078	87.068 036	89.222 007	91.431 350	17
18	95.884 464	98.431 944	101.049 911	103.740 283	106.505 024	109.346 149	18
19	113.424 535	116.657 534	119.986 271	123.413 534	126.942 190	130.575 187	19
20	133.990 267	138.072 602	142.283 834	146.627 970	151.109 140	155.731 596	20
21	158.103 588	163.235 307	168.539 214	174.021 005	179.686 558	185.541 942	21
22	186.376 457	192.801 486	199.454 925	206.344 785	213.479 355	220.867 201	22
23	219.526 395	227.541 746	235.858 174	244.486 847	253.439 337	262.727 633	23
24	258.394 699	268.361 552	278.723 000	289.494 479	300.692 016	312.332 245	24
25	303.967 784	316.324 823	329.196 332	342.603 486	356.568 309	371.113 710	25
26	357.402 227	372.681 667	388.628 681	405.272 113	422.642 026	440.769 747	26
27	420.054 111	438.900 959	458.610 272	479.221 093	500.774 195	523.312 150	27
28	493.513 445	516.708 627	541.013 595	566.480 890	593.165 486	621.124 898	28
29	579.644 514	608.132 637	638.043 508	669.447 450	702.418 187	737.033 004	29
30	680.633 193	715.555 848	752.296 231	790.947 991	831.609 507	874.384 110	30
31	799.042 419	841.778 122	886.828 812	934.318 630	984.378 241	1037.145 170	31
32	937.877 236	990.089 293	1045.240 926	1103.495 983	1165.027 271	1230.017 026	32
33	1100.661 059	1164.354 919	1231.771 190	1303.125 260	1378.644 747	1458.570 176	33
34	1291.525 092	1369.117 030	1451.410 576	1538.687 807	1631.247 414	1729.405 659	34
35	1515.313 171	1609.712 511	1710.035 954	1816.651 612	1929.950 067	2050.345 706	35
36	1777.704 693	1892.412 200	2014.567 335	2144.648 902	2283.165 954	2430.659 662	36
37	2085.358 752	2224.584 335	2373.153 037	2531.685 705	2700.843 741	2881.331 699	37
38	2446.083 137	2614.886 594	2795.387 701	2988.389 132	3194.747 723	3415.378 063	38
39	2869.032 478	3073.491 747	3292.569 018	3527.299 175	3778.789 183	4048.223 005	39
40	3364.940 580	3612.352 803	3878.000 019	4163.213 027	4469.418 209	4798.144 261	40
41	3946.392 830	4245.514 544	4567.345 023	4913.591 372	5286.087 032	5686.800 949	41
42	4628.145 594	4989.479 589	5379.048 764	5799.037 819	6251.797 915	6739.859 125	42
43	5427.500 708	5863.638 517	6334.829 920	6843.864 626	7393.751 034	7987.733 063	43
44	6364.744 581	6890.775 258	7460.262 231	8076.760 259	8744.110 598	9466.463 679	44
45	7463.663 021	8097.660 928	8785.458 777	9531.577 105	10340.910 782	11218.759 460	45
46	8752.144 892	9515.751 590	10345.877 709	11248.260 984	12229.127 000	13295.229 960	46
47	10262.889 886	11182.008 118	12183.271 003	13273.947 961	14461.942 678	15755.847 503	47
48	12034.238 391	13139.859 539	14346.801 606	15664.258 594	17102.247 216	18671.679 201	48
49	14111.144 514	15440.334 958	16894.358 891	18484.825 141	20224.407 333	22126.939 959	49
50	16546.316 942	18143.393 576	19894.107 594	21813.093 666	23916.361 672	26221.423 852	50

SECTION 2

YRS	18.75% ANNUAL RATE	19.00% ANNUAL RATE	19.25% ANNUAL RATE	19.50% ANNUAL RATE	19.75% ANNUAL RATE	20.00% ANNUAL RATE	YRS
1	1.000 000	1.000 000	1.000 000	1.000 000	1.000 000	1.000 000	1
2	2.187 500	2.190 000	2.192 500	2.195 000	2.197 500	2.200 000	2
3	3.597 656	3.606 100	3.614 556	3.623 025	3.631 506	3.640 000	3
4	5.272 217	5.291 259	5.310 358	5.329 515	5.348 729	5.368 000	4
5	7.260 757	7.296 598	7.332 602	7.368 770	7.405 103	7.441 600	5
6	9.622 149	9.682 952	9.744 128	9.805 680	9.867 610	9.929 920	6
7	12.426 302	12.522 713	12.619 873	12.717 788	12.816 463	12.915 904	7
8	15.756 234	15.902 028	16.049 198	16.197 757	16.347 715	16.499 085	8
9	19.710 528	19.923 413	20.138 669	20.356 319	20.576 389	20.798 902	9
10	24.406 252	24.708 862	25.015 363	25.325 802	25.640 226	25.958 682	10
11	29.982 424	30.403 546	30.830 820	31.264 333	31.704 170	32.150 419	11
12	36.604 129	37.180 220	37.765 753	38.360 878	38.965 744	39.580 502	12
13	44.467 403	45.244 461	46.035 661	46.841 249	47.661 478	48.496 603	13
14	53.805 041	54.840 909	55.897 526	56.975 293	58.074 620	59.195 923	14
15	64.893 487	66.260 682	67.657 799	69.085 475	70.544 357	72.035 108	15
16	78.061 015	79.850 211	81.681 926	83.557 143	85.476 868	87.442 129	16
17	93.697 456	96.021 751	98.405 696	100.850 785	103.358 549	105.930 555	17
18	112.265 729	115.265 884	118.348 793	121.516 689	124.771 863	128.116 666	18
19	134.315 553	138.166 402	142.130 935	146.212 443	150.414 306	154.740 000	19
20	160.499 719	165.418 018	170.491 140	175.723 869	181.121 131	186.688 000	20
21	191.593 416	197.847 442	204.310 685	210.990 024	217.892 555	225.025 600	21
22	228.517 182	236.438 456	244.640 492	253.133 078	261.926 334	271.030 719	22
23	272.364 153	282.361 762	292.733 786	303.494 029	314.656 785	326.236 863	23
24	324.432 432	337.010 497	350.085 040	363.675 364	377.801 500	392.484 236	24
25	386.263 513	402.042 491	418.476 411	435.592 060	453.417 297	471.981 083	25
26	459.687 921	479.430 565	500.033 120	521.532 512	543.967 213	567.377 300	26
27	546.879 407	571.522 372	597.289 495	624.231 352	652.400 737	681.852 760	27
28	650.419 295	681.111 623	713.267 723	746.956 465	782.249 883	819.223 312	28
29	773.372 913	811.522 831	851.571 759	893.612 976	937.744 235	984.067 974	29
30	919.380 335	966.712 169	1016.499 323	1068.867 506	1123.948 721	1181.881 569	30
31	1092.764 147	1151.387 481	1213.175 443	1278.296 670	1346.928 593	1419.257 883	31
32	1298.657 425	1371.151 103	1447.711 716	1528.564 521	1613.946 991	1704.109 459	32
33	1543.155 692	1632.669 812	1727.396 221	1827.634 602	1933.701 521	2045.931 351	33
34	1833.497 384	1943.877 077	2060.919 993	2185.023 310	2316.607 572	2456.117 621	34
35	2178.278 144	2314.213 721	2458.647 092	2612.102 903	2775.137 567	2948.341 146	35
36	2587.705 296	2754.914 328	2932.936 657	3122.462 969	3324.227 237	3539.009 375	36
37	3073.900 039	3279.348 051	3498.526 964	3732.343 248	3981.762 116	4247.811 250	37
38	3651.256 296	3903.424 180	4172.993 405	4461.150 181	4769.160 134	5098.373 500	38
39	4336.866 852	4646.074 775	4977.294 635	5332.074 466	5712.069 260	6119.048 200	39
40	5151.029 386	5529.828 982	5936.423 852	6372.828 987	6841.202 939	7343.857 840	40
41	6117.847 396	6581.496 488	7080.185 444	7616.530 640	8193.340 519	8813.629 408	41
42	7265.943 783	7832.980 821	8444.121 142	9102.754 114	9812.525 272	10577.355 289	42
43	8629.308 242	9322.247 177	10070.614 461	10878.791 167	11751.499 013	12693.826 347	43
44	10248.303 538	11094.474 141	12010.207 745	13001.155 444	14073.420 068	15233.591 617	44
45	12170.860 451	13203.424 228	14323.172 736	15537.380 756	16853.920 532	18281.309 940	45
46	14453.896 786	15713.074 831	17081.383 488	18568.170 003	20183.569 837	21938.571 928	46
47	17165.002 433	18699.559 049	20370.549 809	22189.963 154	24170.824 880	26327.286 314	47
48	20384.440 390	22253.475 268	24292.880 647	26518.005 968	28945.562 794	31593.743 576	48
49	24207.522 963	26482.635 569	28970.260 172	31690.017 132	34663.311 445	37913.492 292	49
50	28747.433 518	31515.336 327	34548.035 255	37870.570 473	41510.315 456	45497.190 750	50

SECTION 2

YRS	20.25% ANNUAL RATE	20.50% ANNUAL RATE	20.75% ANNUAL RATE	21.00% ANNUAL RATE	21.25% ANNUAL RATE	21.50% ANNUAL RATE	YRS
1	1.000 000	1.000 000	1.000 000	1.000 000	1.000 000	1.000 000	1
2	2.202 500	2.205 000	2.207 500	2.210 000	2.212 500	2.215 000	2
3	3.648 506	3.657 025	3.665 556	3.674 100	3.682 656	3.691 225	3
4	5.387 329	5.406 025	5.426 159	5.445 661	5.465 221	5.484 838	4
5	7.478 263	7.515 092	7.552 087	7.589 250	7.626 580	7.664 079	5
6	9.992 611	10.055 686	10.119 145	10.182 992	10.247 228	10.311 856	6
7	13.016 115	13.117 101	13.218 868	13.321 421	13.424 764	13.528 904	7
8	16.651 878	16.806 107	16.961 783	17.118 919	17.277 527	17.437 619	8
9	21.023 883	21.251 359	21.481 353	21.713 892	21.949 001	22.186 707	9
10	26.281 220	26.607 887	26.938 734	27.273 809	27.613 164	27.956 849	10
11	32.603 167	33.062 504	33.528 521	34.001 309	34.480 961	34.967 572	11
12	40.205 308	40.840 317	41.485 689	42.141 584	42.808 166	43.485 599	12
13	49.346 883	50.212 582	51.093 970	51.991 317	52.904 901	53.835 003	13
14	60.339 627	61.506 162	62.695 968	63.909 493	65.147 192	66.409 529	14
15	73.558 401	75.114 925	76.705 382	78.330 487	79.990 971	81.687 578	15
16	89.453 977	91.513 485	93.621 748	95.779 889	97.989 052	100.250 407	16
17	108.568 408	111.273 749	114.048 261	116.893 666	119.811 726	122.804 244	17
18	131.553 510	135.084 868	138.713 276	142.441 336	146.271 717	150.207 157	18
19	159.193 096	163.777 266	168.496 280	173.354 016	178.354 457	183.501 696	19
20	192.429 698	198.351 605	204.459 258	210.758 360	217.254 779	223.954 560	20
21	232.396 712	240.013 684	247.884 554	256.017 615	264.421 420	273.104 791	21
22	280.457 046	290.216 489	300.320 599	310.781 315	321.610 972	332.822 321	22
23	338.249 598	350.710 869	363.637 124	377.045 391	390.953 303	405.379 120	23
24	407.745 141	423.606 598	440.091 827	457.224 923	475.030 880	493.535 631	24
25	491.313 532	511.445 950	532.410 881	554.242 157	576.974 942	600.645 791	25
26	591.804 523	617.292 370	643.886 139	671.633 009	700.582 118	730.784 636	26
27	712.644 939	744.837 306	778.492 513	813.675 941	850.455 818	888.903 333	27
28	857.955 539	898.528 954	941.029 709	985.547 889	1032.177 679	1081.017 550	28
29	1032.691 535	1083.727 389	1137.293 374	1193.512 946	1252.515 436	1314.436 323	29
30	1242.811 571	1306.891 504	1374.281 749	1445.150 664	1519.674 966	1598.040 132	30
31	1495.480 914	1575.804 262	1660.445 212	1749.632 304	1843.605 896	1942.618 761	31
32	1799.315 800	1899.844 136	2005.987 594	2118.055 088	2236.372 149	2361.281 794	32
33	2164.677 249	2290.312 184	2423.230 019	2563.846 656	2712.601 231	2869.957 380	33
34	2604.024 392	2760.826 181	2927.050 248	3103.254 454	3290.028 992	3487.998 217	34
35	3132.339 331	3327.795 548	3535.413 175	3755.937 890	3990.160 153	4238.917 834	35
36	3767.638 046	4010.993 636	4270.011 409	4545.684 846	4839.069 186	5151.285 168	36
37	4531.584 750	4834.247 331	5157.038 776	5501.278 664	5868.371 388	6259.811 479	37
38	5450.230 662	5826.268 034	6228.124 322	6657.547 183	7116.400 308	7606.670 947	38
39	6554.902 371	7021.652 981	7521.460 119	8056.632 092	8629.635 373	9243.105 200	39
40	7883.270 101	8462.091 842	9083.163 093	9749.524 831	10464.432 890	11231.372 819	40
41	9480.632 297	10197.820 669	10968.919 435	11797.925 046	12689.124 879	13647.117 975	41
42	11401.460 337	12289.373 907	13245.970 218	14276.489 306	15386.563 916	16582.248 339	42
43	13711.256 055	14809.695 557	15995.509 038	17275.552 060	18657.208 748	20148.431 732	43
44	16488.785 406	17846.683 147	19315.577 164	20904.417 992	22622.865 607	24481.344 554	44
45	19828.764 450	21506.253 192	23324.559 425	25295.345 771	27431.224 549	29745.833 634	45
46	23845.089 252	25916.035 096	28165.405 506	30608.368 383	33261.359 766	36142.187 865	46
47	28674.719 825	31229.822 291	34010.727 149	37037.125 743	40330.398 716	43913.758 256	47
48	34482.350 590	37632.935 861	41068.953 032	44815.922 149	48901.608 443	53356.216 281	48
49	41466.026 584	45348.687 712	49591.760 786	54228.265 800	59294.200 237	64828.802 781	49
50	49863.896 968	54646.168 693	59883.051 149	65617.201 618	71895.217 787	78767.995 379	50

FUTURE VALUE PER PERIOD

ANNUAL COMPOUNDING

YRS	21.75% ANNUAL RATE	22.00% ANNUAL RATE	22.50% ANNUAL RATE	23.00% ANNUAL RATE	23.50% ANNUAL RATE	24.00% ANNUAL RATE	YRS
1	1.000 000	1.000 000	1.000 000	1.000 000	1.000 000	1.000 000	1
2	2.217 500	2.220 000	2.225 000	2.230 000	2.235 000	2.240 000	2
3	3.699 806	3.708 400	3.725 625	3.742 900	3.760 225	3.777 600	3
4	5.504 514	5.524 248	5.563 891	5.603 767	5.643 878	5.684 224	4
5	7.701 746	7.739 583	7.815 766	7.892 633	7.970 189	8.048 438	5
6	10.376 876	10.442 291	10.574 313	10.707 939	10.843 184	10.980 063	6
7	13.633 846	13.739 595	13.953 534	14.170 765	14.391 332	14.615 278	7
8	17.599 208	17.762 306	18.093 079	18.430 041	18.773 295	19.122 945	8
9	22.427 035	22.670 013	23.164 022	23.668 950	24.185 019	24.712 451	9
10	28.304 916	28.657 416	29.375 927	30.112 809	30.868 498	31.643 440	10
11	35.461 235	35.962 047	36.985 510	38.038 755	39.122 596	40.237 865	11
12	44.174 053	44.873 697	46.307 250	47.787 669	49.316 406	50.894 953	12
13	54.781 910	55.745 911	57.726 381	59.778 833	61.905 761	64.109 741	13
14	67.696 975	69.010 011	71.714 817	74.527 964	77.453 615	80.496 079	14
15	83.421 067	85.192 213	88.850 651	92.669 396	96.655 214	100.815 138	15
16	102.565 149	104.934 500	109.842 047	114.983 357	120.369 190	126.010 772	16
17	125.873 069	129.020 090	135.556 508	142.429 529	149.655 949	157.253 357	17
18	154.250 462	158.404 510	167.056 722	176.188 321	185.825 097	195.994 162	18
19	188.799 937	194.253 503	205.644 485	217.711 635	230.493 995	244.032 761	19
20	230.863 924	237.989 273	252.914 494	268.785 311	285.660 084	303.600 624	20
21	282.076 827	291.346 913	310.820 255	331.605 932	353.790 203	377.464 774	21
22	344.428 537	356.443 234	381.754 812	408.875 297	437.930 901	469.056 320	22
23	420.341 744	435.860 746	468.649 645	503.916 615	541.844 663	582.629 836	23
24	512.766 073	532.750 110	575.095 815	620.817 437	670.178 159	723.460 997	24
25	625.292 904	650.955 134	705.492 373	764.605 447	828.670 026	898.091 636	25
26	762.293 855	795.165 264	865.228 157	941.464 700	1024.407 482	1114.633 629	26
27	929.092 768	971.101 622	1060.904 492	1159.001 581	1266.143 241	1383.145 700	27
28	1132.170 445	1185.743 978	1300.608 003	1426.571 945	1564.686 902	1716.100 668	28
29	1379.417 517	1447.607 654	1594.244 804	1755.683 492	1933.388 325	2128.964 828	29
30	1680.440 827	1767.081 337	1953.949 885	2160.490 695	2388.734 581	2640.916 387	30
31	2046.936 706	2156.839 232	2394.588 609	2658.403 555	2951.087 207	3275.736 320	31
32	2493.145 440	2632.343 863	2934.371 046	3270.836 373	3645.592 701	4062.913 037	32
33	3036.404 573	3212.459 512	3595.604 531	4024.128 738	4503.306 986	5039.012 166	33
34	3697.822 568	3920.200 605	4405.615 551	4950.678 348	5562.584 127	6249.375 086	34
35	4503.098 977	4783.644 738	5397.879 049	6090.334 368	6870.791 397	7750.225 106	35
36	5483.523 004	5837.046 581	6613.401 836	7492.111 273	8486.427 376	9611.279 132	36
37	6677.189 257	7122.196 829	8102.417 249	9216.296 866	10481.737 809	11918.986 124	37
38	8130.477 921	8690.080 131	9926.461 130	11337.045 145	12945.946 194	14780.542 793	38
39	9899.856 869	10602.897 760	12160.914 884	13945.565 528	15989.243 550	18328.873 064	39
40	12054.075 738	12936.535 267	14898.120 733	17154.045 599	19747.715 784	22728.802 599	40
41	14676.837 210	15783.573 025	18251.197 897	21100.476 087	24389.428 993	28184.715 222	41
42	17870.049 304	19256.959 091	22358.717 424	25954.585 587	30121.944 807	34950.046 876	42
43	21757.785 027	23494.490 091	27390.428 845	31925.140 272	37201.601 836	43339.058 126	43
44	26491.103 271	28664.277 911	33554.275 335	39268.922 535	45944.978 268	53741.432 076	44
45	32253.918 232	34971.419 051	41104.987 285	48301.774 718	56743.048 160	66640.375 775	45
46	39270.145 448	42666.131 243	50354.609 424	59412.182 903	70078.664 478	82635.065 961	46
47	47812.402 082	52053.680 116	61685.396 545	73077.984 971	86548.150 630	102468.481 791	47
48	58212.599 535	63506.489 742	75565.610 767	89886.921 514	106887.966 029	127061.917 421	48
49	70874.839 934	77478.917 485	92568.873 190	110561.913 462	132007.638 045	157557.777 602	49
50	86291.117 620	94525.279 331	113397.869 658	135992.153 559	163030.432 986	195372.644 226	50

SECTION 3
SINKING FUND
OF $1

The *sinking fund* is the basic compound interest function for a series of repeated investments or deposits. It is the reciprocal of future value per period. By convention, it is assumed that each investment is made at the end of each compounding period. Interest is earned on each investment as it is made, and interest begins to be earned on the interest after each period.

Because the first investment is made at the *end* of the first period, no interest is earned for the first period. You can check this with a quick glance at the first row of any column in this section. The entry in the first row is always 1; multiplying this entry by the amount of the investment doesn't increase the total at all.

USE OF SINKING FUND

The sinking fund is the amount you need to start putting away today in a series of deposits if you wish to accumulate $1 in the future. The assumptions are:

- The deposits are uniform and repeat at a regular interval.
- All interest earned is left in the investment to begin earning interest on interest.
- The deposits earn interest at a uniform rate throughout the term of the investment.

The tables in this section are used to solve the following types of problems:

1. In what amount must repeated deposits be made to meet a future obligation?
2. How long will it take for a series of repeated deposits to meet a future obligation?
3. What rate must be earned for a series of repeated deposits to meet a future obligation?

The future value per period tables (Section 2) are the reciprocal tables to Sinking Fund. The investment growth examples presented in Section 2 are useful supplements to the examples in this section.

EXAMPLES

Size of Deposits Needed to Meet a Future Obligation. A municipality has a $750,000 bond issue coming due in 20 years (240 months). If the controller can earn 7% compounded monthly on deposits, what monthly deposit must she make each month to ensure retirement of the obligation at maturity?

Turn to page 101 in the monthly compounding section and locate the column labeled 7.00%. Move down the column to the 20-year row and find the entry: 0.001920. Multiply $750,000 by 0.001920 to get $1,440, the required monthly deposit.

Time Required to Meet a Future Obligation. You wish to provide a fund for your child's education. You estimate that he will need $30,000. If you can add to an investment account at $750 each quarter, and the account earns interest at 7.5% compounded quarterly, how long will it take to grow to the required amount?

First figure the required sinking fund factor. Divide $750 by $30,000 to get 0.025. Turn to page 113 in the quarterly compounding section and locate the column labeled 7.50%. Move down the column until you find the first entry that is less than 0.025. Find 0.024079 and read across to find 31 quarters (7 years and 9 months). It will take slightly less than 31 quarters to accumulate $30,000.

Interest Rate Needed to Meet a Future Obligation. Fifteen years ago, a corporation began depositing $75,000 at the end of each year into a sinking fund to retire a corporate bond issue. They now have accumulated $2,500,000. What average rate of interest compounded annually have they been earning?

First find the sinking fund factor. Divide $75,000 by $2,500,000 to get 0.03. Start at the first page of the annual compounding section and begin to scan across the 15-year row until you find the first entry that is less than 0.03. On page 133 find 0.029651. Move up the column to find 10.75%. The corporation has been earning slightly less than 10.75% on the sinking fund. If you wish more precise results, use the interpolation technique discussed in the Introduction.

The Influence of Reinvestment on Overall Yield. An investor purchases a $100,000 mortgage that will pay him $1,101.10 each month for 20 years (240 months). His interest rate on the mortgage is 12%. As the mortgage payments are received, he will reinvest them to earn 10% compounded monthly. Of his earnings, he will need $100,000 at the end of 20 years to repay the mortgage principal. What will be his overall yield?

First find the amount that the investor must deposit each month to accumulate $100,000 at the end of 20 years. Turn to page 103 in the monthly compounding section and locate the column labeled 10.00%. Move down the column to the 20-year row and find the entry: 0.001317. Multiply 0.001317 by $100,000 to get $131.70, the required deposit.

His monthly net proceeds are the difference between the $1,101.10 he receives and the $131.70 he deposits to repay the principal, or $969.40. Thus he receives a total of $11,632.80 each year and preserves his $100,000 principal through the establishment of the sinking fund. His yield, including the effect of reinvestment at the lower rate, is $11,632.80 divided by $100,000, or 11.63%.

The Cost of a Loan that Is Paid Off by Share Deposits. You borrow $10,000 from an industrial loan company and agree to pay interest monthly at a 12% nominal annual rate. Simultaneously you purchase $10,000 of shares in the industrial loan company, which you agree to pay for by making 180 monthly deposits to an account that earns 8% compounded quarterly. What is the required deposit? What is the total monthly payment you must make?

To find the monthly deposit, you must first find the quarterly deposit that will accumulate to the amount required to complete the share purchase. Turn to page 113 in the quarterly compounding section and locate the column labeled 8.00%. Move down the column to the 15-year (60-quarter) row and find the entry: 0.008768. Multiply 0.008768 by $10,000 to get $87.68, the required quarterly deposit for the stock.

Next, what monthly deposit will accumulate to $87.68 after one quarter at 8% simple interest? The first month's deposit earns two months' interest, the second month's deposit earns one month's interest, and the third month's deposit earns no interest to the end of the quarter. Thus the total interest earned in one quarter for the three deposits is 3 months' simple interest. At an 8% annual rate, this would be 2% on a monthly deposit. This equals $0.02 on a $1 deposit, which means that depositing a dollar a month is equivalent to depositing $3.02 at the end of each quarter ($0.02 plus 3 deposits of $1). Divide $87.68 by $3.02 to get $29.03, the required monthly deposit.

The interest-only payment at 12% on the $10,000 borrowed is $1,200 per year, or $100 per month. Therefore your total monthly payment consists of the $100 payment and the $29.03 deposit, or $129.03.

THE FORMULA FOR SINKING FUND

The symbol $\dfrac{1}{S_{\overline{n}|}}$ is the widely accepted notation for sinking fund. The formula for figuring sinking fund table entries is:

$$\frac{1}{S_{\overline{n}|}} = \frac{i}{(1 + i)^n - 1}$$

where:

i = interest rate per period
n = number of compounding periods

Note that i is the interest rate *per period*, not the nominal annual rate. You can easily find the interest rate per period by dividing the annual rate by the number of compounding periods per year. For example, a nominal annual rate of 12% compounded monthly converts to 1% per month (12% ÷ 12 months per year).

SINKING FUND

MOS	5.25% ANNUAL RATE	5.50% ANNUAL RATE	5.75% ANNUAL RATE	6.00% ANNUAL RATE	6.25% ANNUAL RATE	6.50% ANNUAL RATE	MOS
1	1.000 000	1.000 000	1.000 000	1.000 000	1.000 000	1.000 000	1
2	0.498 909	0.498 857	0.498 805	0.498 753	0.498 701	0.498 649	2
3	0.331 879	0.331 810	0.331 741	0.331 672	0.331 603	0.331 534	3
4	0.248 365	0.248 288	0.248 210	0.248 133	0.248 055	0.247 978	4
5	0.198 258	0.198 175	0.198 092	0.198 010	0.197 927	0.197 845	5
6	0.164 853	0.164 767	0.164 681	0.164 595	0.164 510	0.164 424	6
7	0.140 993	0.140 905	0.140 817	0.140 729	0.140 640	0.140 552	7
8	0.123 098	0.123 009	0.122 919	0.122 829	0.122 739	0.122 649	8
9	0.109 181	0.109 090	0.108 998	0.108 907	0.108 816	0.108 725	9
10	0.098 047	0.097 955	0.097 863	0.097 771	0.097 679	0.097 587	10
11	0.088 938	0.088 845	0.088 752	0.088 659	0.088 566	0.088 474	11
12	0.081 347	0.081 253	0.081 160	0.081 066	0.080 973	0.080 880	12
13	0.074 924	0.074 830	0.074 736	0.074 642	0.074 548	0.074 455	13
14	0.069 419	0.069 325	0.069 230	0.069 136	0.069 042	0.068 948	14
15	0.064 649	0.064 554	0.064 459	0.064 364	0.064 270	0.064 175	15
16	0.060 475	0.060 379	0.060 284	0.060 189	0.060 095	0.060 000	16
17	0.056 792	0.056 696	0.056 601	0.056 506	0.056 411	0.056 316	17
18	0.053 518	0.053 423	0.053 327	0.053 232	0.053 137	0.053 041	18
19	0.050 589	0.050 494	0.050 398	0.050 303	0.050 207	0.050 112	19
20	0.047 954	0.047 858	0.047 762	0.047 666	0.047 571	0.047 476	20
21	0.045 569	0.045 473	0.045 377	0.045 282	0.045 186	0.045 091	21
22	0.043 401	0.043 305	0.043 210	0.043 114	0.043 018	0.042 923	22
23	0.041 422	0.041 326	0.041 230	0.041 135	0.041 039	0.040 944	23
24	0.039 608	0.039 512	0.039 416	0.039 321	0.039 225	0.039 130	24
25	0.037 940	0.037 844	0.037 748	0.037 652	0.037 556	0.037 461	25
26	0.036 399	0.036 303	0.036 207	0.036 112	0.036 016	0.035 921	26
27	0.034 973	0.034 877	0.034 781	0.034 686	0.034 590	0.034 495	27
28	0.033 649	0.033 553	0.033 457	0.033 362	0.033 266	0.033 171	28
29	0.032 417	0.032 321	0.032 225	0.032 129	0.032 034	0.031 938	29
30	0.031 266	0.031 170	0.031 075	0.030 979	0.030 884	0.030 788	30
31	0.030 190	0.030 094	0.029 999	0.029 903	0.029 808	0.029 713	31
32	0.029 182	0.029 086	0.028 990	0.028 895	0.028 799	0.028 704	32
33	0.028 234	0.028 138	0.028 043	0.027 947	0.027 852	0.027 757	33
34	0.027 343	0.027 247	0.027 151	0.027 056	0.026 961	0.026 866	34
35	0.026 502	0.026 406	0.026 311	0.026 215	0.026 120	0.026 026	35
36	0.025 708	0.025 613	0.025 517	0.025 422	0.025 327	0.025 232	36
37	0.024 957	0.024 862	0.024 766	0.024 671	0.024 577	0.024 482	37
38	0.024 246	0.024 151	0.024 055	0.023 960	0.023 866	0.023 771	38
39	0.023 572	0.023 476	0.023 381	0.023 286	0.023 191	0.023 097	39
40	0.022 931	0.022 835	0.022 740	0.022 646	0.022 551	0.022 457	40
41	0.022 321	0.022 226	0.022 131	0.022 036	0.021 942	0.021 848	41
42	0.021 741	0.021 646	0.021 551	0.021 456	0.021 362	0.021 268	42
43	0.021 188	0.021 092	0.020 998	0.020 903	0.020 809	0.020 715	43
44	0.020 659	0.020 564	0.020 470	0.020 375	0.020 281	0.020 188	44
45	0.020 155	0.020 060	0.019 965	0.019 871	0.019 777	0.019 684	45
46	0.019 672	0.019 578	0.019 483	0.019 389	0.019 295	0.019 202	46
47	0.019 210	0.019 116	0.019 021	0.018 927	0.018 834	0.018 740	47
YRS							
4	0.018 768	0.018 673	0.018 579	0.018 485	0.018 391	0.018 298	48
5	0.014 611	0.014 518	0.014 425	0.014 333	0.014 241	0.014 149	60
6	0.011 846	0.011 755	0.011 663	0.011 573	0.011 483	0.011 393	72
7	0.009 877	0.009 787	0.009 697	0.009 609	0.009 520	0.009 433	84
8	0.008 404	0.008 316	0.008 228	0.008 141	0.008 055	0.007 970	96
9	0.007 263	0.007 177	0.007 091	0.007 006	0.006 921	0.006 838	108
10	0.006 354	0.006 269	0.006 185	0.006 102	0.006 020	0.005 938	120
11	0.005 614	0.005 531	0.005 448	0.005 367	0.005 287	0.005 207	132
12	0.005 000	0.004 918	0.004 838	0.004 759	0.004 680	0.004 603	144
13	0.004 483	0.004 403	0.004 325	0.004 247	0.004 171	0.004 095	156
14	0.004 043	0.003 965	0.003 888	0.003 812	0.003 738	0.003 664	168
15	0.003 664	0.003 588	0.003 512	0.003 439	0.003 366	0.003 294	180
16	0.003 334	0.003 260	0.003 186	0.003 114	0.003 044	0.002 974	192
17	0.003 046	0.002 973	0.002 901	0.002 831	0.002 762	0.002 695	204
18	0.002 791	0.002 720	0.002 650	0.002 582	0.002 515	0.002 449	216
19	0.002 565	0.002 496	0.002 427	0.002 361	0.002 296	0.002 232	228
20	0.002 363	0.002 296	0.002 229	0.002 164	0.002 101	0.002 039	240
21	0.002 183	0.002 116	0.002 052	0.001 989	0.001 927	0.001 867	252
22	0.002 020	0.001 955	0.001 892	0.001 831	0.001 771	0.001 713	264
23	0.001 873	0.001 810	0.001 748	0.001 688	0.001 630	0.001 574	276
24	0.001 739	0.001 678	0.001 618	0.001 560	0.001 503	0.001 449	288
25	0.001 617	0.001 558	0.001 499	0.001 443	0.001 388	0.001 335	300
26	0.001 507	0.001 448	0.001 392	0.001 337	0.001 284	0.001 233	312
27	0.001 405	0.001 348	0.001 293	0.001 240	0.001 188	0.001 139	324
28	0.001 312	0.001 256	0.001 203	0.001 151	0.001 101	0.001 053	336
29	0.001 226	0.001 172	0.001 120	0.001 070	0.001 022	0.000 975	348
30	0.001 147	0.001 095	0.001 044	0.000 996	0.000 949	0.000 904	360

SINKING FUND

	6.75% ANNUAL RATE	7.00% ANNUAL RATE	7.25% ANNUAL RATE	7.50% ANNUAL RATE	7.75% ANNUAL RATE	8.00% ANNUAL RATE	
MOS							MOS
1	1.000 000	1.000 000	1.000 000	1.000 000	1.000 000	1.000 000	1
2	0.498 598	0.498 546	0.498 494	0.498 442	0.498 391	0.498 339	2
3	0.331 465	0.331 396	0.331 328	0.331 259	0.331 190	0.331 121	3
4	0.247 900	0.247 823	0.247 746	0.247 668	0.247 591	0.247 514	4
5	0.197 763	0.197 680	0.197 598	0.197 516	0.197 433	0.197 351	5
6	0.164 338	0.164 253	0.164 167	0.164 081	0.163 996	0.163 910	6
7	0.140 464	0.140 377	0.140 289	0.140 201	0.140 113	0.140 025	7
8	0.122 560	0.122 470	0.122 381	0.122 291	0.122 202	0.122 112	8
9	0.108 634	0.108 544	0.108 453	0.108 362	0.108 272	0.108 181	9
10	0.097 495	0.097 403	0.097 311	0.097 220	0.097 128	0.097 037	10
11	0.088 381	0.088 288	0.088 196	0.088 104	0.088 011	0.087 919	11
12	0.080 787	0.080 693	0.080 600	0.080 507	0.080 415	0.080 322	12
13	0.074 361	0.074 267	0.074 174	0.074 080	0.073 987	0.073 894	13
14	0.068 854	0.068 760	0.068 666	0.068 572	0.068 478	0.068 385	14
15	0.064 081	0.063 987	0.063 893	0.063 798	0.063 705	0.063 611	15
16	0.059 905	0.059 811	0.059 716	0.059 622	0.059 528	0.059 434	16
17	0.056 221	0.056 126	0.056 032	0.055 937	0.055 843	0.055 749	17
18	0.052 946	0.052 852	0.052 757	0.052 662	0.052 568	0.052 474	18
19	0.050 017	0.049 922	0.049 827	0.049 733	0.049 638	0.049 544	19
20	0.047 381	0.047 286	0.047 191	0.047 096	0.047 001	0.046 907	20
21	0.044 996	0.044 900	0.044 806	0.044 711	0.044 616	0.044 522	21
22	0.042 828	0.042 733	0.042 638	0.042 543	0.042 448	0.042 354	22
23	0.040 848	0.040 753	0.040 658	0.040 564	0.040 469	0.040 375	23
24	0.039 034	0.038 939	0.038 844	0.038 750	0.038 655	0.038 561	24
25	0.037 366	0.037 271	0.037 176	0.037 081	0.036 986	0.036 892	25
26	0.035 825	0.035 730	0.035 636	0.035 541	0.035 446	0.035 352	26
27	0.034 400	0.034 305	0.034 210	0.034 115	0.034 021	0.033 927	27
28	0.033 076	0.032 981	0.032 886	0.032 792	0.032 697	0.032 603	28
29	0.031 843	0.031 749	0.031 654	0.031 559	0.031 465	0.031 371	29
30	0.030 693	0.030 599	0.030 504	0.030 410	0.030 316	0.030 222	30
31	0.029 618	0.029 523	0.029 429	0.029 334	0.029 240	0.029 146	31
32	0.028 609	0.028 515	0.028 420	0.028 326	0.028 232	0.028 139	32
33	0.027 662	0.027 568	0.027 474	0.027 380	0.027 286	0.027 192	33
34	0.026 771	0.026 677	0.026 583	0.026 489	0.026 395	0.026 302	34
35	0.025 931	0.025 837	0.025 743	0.025 649	0.025 556	0.025 462	35
36	0.025 138	0.025 044	0.024 950	0.024 856	0.024 763	0.024 670	36
37	0.024 388	0.024 294	0.024 200	0.024 106	0.024 013	0.023 920	37
38	0.023 677	0.023 583	0.023 490	0.023 396	0.023 303	0.023 210	38
39	0.023 003	0.022 909	0.022 816	0.022 723	0.022 630	0.022 537	39
40	0.022 363	0.022 269	0.022 176	0.022 083	0.021 990	0.021 897	40
41	0.021 754	0.021 660	0.021 567	0.021 474	0.021 382	0.021 289	41
42	0.021 174	0.021 081	0.020 988	0.020 895	0.020 802	0.020 710	42
43	0.020 622	0.020 528	0.020 435	0.020 343	0.020 250	0.020 158	43
44	0.020 094	0.020 001	0.019 908	0.019 816	0.019 724	0.019 632	44
45	0.019 590	0.019 497	0.019 405	0.019 312	0.019 220	0.019 129	45
46	0.019 109	0.019 016	0.018 923	0.018 831	0.018 739	0.018 648	46
47	0.018 647	0.018 555	0.018 462	0.018 370	0.018 279	0.018 187	47
YRS							
4	0.018 205	0.018 113	0.018 021	0.017 929	0.017 837	0.017 746	48
5	0.014 058	0.013 968	0.013 878	0.013 788	0.013 699	0.013 610	60
6	0.011 304	0.011 216	0.011 128	0.011 040	0.010 953	0.010 867	72
7	0.009 346	0.009 259	0.009 174	0.009 088	0.009 004	0.008 920	84
8	0.007 885	0.007 800	0.007 717	0.007 634	0.007 552	0.007 470	96
9	0.006 755	0.006 673	0.006 592	0.006 511	0.006 431	0.006 352	108
10	0.005 857	0.005 778	0.005 698	0.005 620	0.005 543	0.005 466	120
11	0.005 128	0.005 051	0.004 974	0.004 898	0.004 823	0.004 749	132
12	0.004 526	0.004 450	0.004 376	0.004 302	0.004 230	0.004 158	144
13	0.004 021	0.003 947	0.003 875	0.003 804	0.003 733	0.003 664	156
14	0.003 592	0.003 521	0.003 451	0.003 381	0.003 313	0.003 247	168
15	0.003 224	0.003 155	0.003 087	0.003 020	0.002 954	0.002 890	180
16	0.002 906	0.002 839	0.002 773	0.002 708	0.002 645	0.002 583	192
17	0.002 628	0.002 563	0.002 500	0.002 437	0.002 376	0.002 316	204
18	0.002 385	0.002 322	0.002 260	0.002 200	0.002 141	0.002 083	216
19	0.002 170	0.002 109	0.002 049	0.001 991	0.001 934	0.001 878	228
20	0.001 979	0.001 920	0.001 862	0.001 806	0.001 751	0.001 698	240
21	0.001 808	0.001 751	0.001 696	0.001 642	0.001 589	0.001 538	252
22	0.001 656	0.001 601	0.001 547	0.001 495	0.001 444	0.001 395	264
23	0.001 519	0.001 466	0.001 414	0.001 364	0.001 315	0.001 268	276
24	0.001 396	0.001 344	0.001 294	0.001 246	0.001 199	0.001 154	288
25	0.001 284	0.001 234	0.001 186	0.001 140	0.001 095	0.001 051	300
26	0.001 183	0.001 135	0.001 089	0.001 044	0.001 001	0.000 959	312
27	0.001 091	0.001 045	0.001 000	0.000 957	0.000 916	0.000 876	324
28	0.001 007	0.000 963	0.000 920	0.000 879	0.000 839	0.000 801	336
29	0.000 931	0.000 888	0.000 847	0.000 807	0.000 769	0.000 733	348
30	0.000 861	0.000 820	0.000 780	0.000 742	0.000 706	0.000 671	360

SECTION 3

MOS	8.25% ANNUAL RATE	8.50% ANNUAL RATE	8.75% ANNUAL RATE	9.00% ANNUAL RATE	9.25% ANNUAL RATE	9.50% ANNUAL RATE	MOS
1	1.000 000	1.000 000	1.000 000	1.000 000	1.000 000	1.000 000	1
2	0.498 287	0.498 235	0.498 184	0.498 132	0.498 080	0.498 029	2
3	0.331 052	0.330 983	0.330 915	0.330 846	0.330 777	0.330 708	3
4	0.247 437	0.247 359	0.247 282	0.247 205	0.247 128	0.247 051	4
5	0.197 269	0.197 187	0.197 105	0.197 022	0.196 940	0.196 858	5
6	0.163 825	0.163 740	0.163 654	0.163 569	0.163 484	0.163 398	6
7	0.139 938	0.139 850	0.139 762	0.139 675	0.139 587	0.139 500	7
8	0.122 023	0.121 934	0.121 845	0.121 756	0.121 666	0.121 577	8
9	0.108 090	0.108 000	0.107 910	0.107 819	0.107 729	0.107 639	9
10	0.096 945	0.096 854	0.096 762	0.096 671	0.096 580	0.096 489	10
11	0.087 827	0.087 735	0.087 643	0.087 551	0.087 459	0.087 367	11
12	0.080 229	0.080 136	0.080 044	0.079 951	0.079 859	0.079 767	12
13	0.073 801	0.073 708	0.073 615	0.073 522	0.073 429	0.073 336	13
14	0.068 291	0.068 198	0.068 105	0.068 011	0.067 918	0.067 825	14
15	0.063 517	0.063 423	0.063 330	0.063 236	0.063 143	0.063 050	15
16	0.059 340	0.059 246	0.059 152	0.059 059	0.058 965	0.058 872	16
17	0.055 655	0.055 561	0.055 467	0.055 373	0.055 280	0.055 186	17
18	0.052 379	0.052 285	0.052 191	0.052 098	0.052 004	0.051 910	18
19	0.049 449	0.049 355	0.049 261	0.049 167	0.049 074	0.048 980	19
20	0.046 813	0.046 719	0.046 624	0.046 531	0.046 437	0.046 343	20
21	0.044 427	0.044 333	0.044 239	0.044 145	0.044 052	0.043 958	21
22	0.042 259	0.042 165	0.042 071	0.041 977	0.041 884	0.041 790	22
23	0.040 280	0.040 186	0.040 092	0.039 998	0.039 905	0.039 811	23
24	0.038 466	0.038 372	0.038 278	0.038 185	0.038 091	0.037 998	24
25	0.036 798	0.036 704	0.036 610	0.036 516	0.036 423	0.036 330	25
26	0.035 258	0.035 164	0.035 070	0.034 977	0.034 884	0.034 790	26
27	0.033 833	0.033 739	0.033 645	0.033 552	0.033 459	0.033 365	27
28	0.032 509	0.032 416	0.032 322	0.032 229	0.032 136	0.032 043	28
29	0.031 277	0.031 184	0.031 090	0.030 997	0.030 904	0.030 811	29
30	0.030 128	0.030 034	0.029 941	0.029 848	0.029 755	0.029 663	30
31	0.029 053	0.028 960	0.028 866	0.028 774	0.028 681	0.028 588	31
32	0.028 045	0.027 952	0.027 859	0.027 766	0.027 674	0.027 581	32
33	0.027 099	0.027 006	0.026 913	0.026 820	0.026 728	0.026 636	33
34	0.026 209	0.026 116	0.026 023	0.025 931	0.025 838	0.025 746	34
35	0.025 369	0.025 277	0.025 184	0.025 092	0.025 000	0.024 908	35
36	0.024 577	0.024 484	0.024 392	0.024 300	0.024 208	0.024 116	36
37	0.023 827	0.023 735	0.023 643	0.023 551	0.023 459	0.023 368	37
38	0.023 118	0.023 025	0.022 933	0.022 842	0.022 750	0.022 659	38
39	0.022 444	0.022 352	0.022 261	0.022 169	0.022 078	0.021 987	39
40	0.021 805	0.021 713	0.021 622	0.021 530	0.021 439	0.021 348	40
41	0.021 197	0.021 105	0.021 014	0.020 923	0.020 832	0.020 741	41
42	0.020 618	0.020 527	0.020 436	0.020 345	0.020 254	0.020 163	42
43	0.020 067	0.019 975	0.019 884	0.019 793	0.019 703	0.019 613	43
44	0.019 540	0.019 449	0.019 358	0.019 268	0.019 177	0.019 087	44
45	0.019 037	0.018 946	0.018 856	0.018 765	0.018 675	0.018 585	45
46	0.018 557	0.018 466	0.018 375	0.018 285	0.018 195	0.018 106	46
47	0.018 096	0.018 006	0.017 915	0.017 825	0.017 736	0.017 646	47
YRS							
4	0.017 655	0.017 565	0.017 475	0.017 385	0.017 296	0.017 206	48
5	0.013 521	0.013 433	0.013 346	0.013 258	0.013 172	0.013 085	60
6	0.010 781	0.010 695	0.010 610	0.010 526	0.010 442	0.010 358	72
7	0.008 836	0.008 753	0.008 671	0.008 589	0.008 508	0.008 427	84
8	0.007 389	0.007 309	0.007 229	0.007 150	0.007 072	0.006 994	96
9	0.006 274	0.006 196	0.006 119	0.006 043	0.005 967	0.005 893	108
10	0.005 390	0.005 315	0.005 241	0.005 168	0.005 095	0.005 023	120
11	0.004 675	0.004 603	0.004 532	0.004 461	0.004 391	0.004 322	132
12	0.004 087	0.004 017	0.003 948	0.003 880	0.003 813	0.003 747	144
13	0.003 596	0.003 528	0.003 462	0.003 397	0.003 332	0.003 269	156
14	0.003 181	0.003 116	0.003 052	0.002 989	0.002 928	0.002 867	168
15	0.002 826	0.002 764	0.002 703	0.002 643	0.002 584	0.002 526	180
16	0.002 522	0.002 462	0.002 403	0.002 345	0.002 289	0.002 233	192
17	0.002 257	0.002 200	0.002 143	0.002 088	0.002 034	0.001 981	204
18	0.002 026	0.001 971	0.001 917	0.001 864	0.001 813	0.001 762	216
19	0.001 824	0.001 771	0.001 719	0.001 669	0.001 620	0.001 572	228
20	0.001 646	0.001 595	0.001 545	0.001 497	0.001 450	0.001 405	240
21	0.001 488	0.001 439	0.001 392	0.001 346	0.001 301	0.001 258	252
22	0.001 347	0.001 301	0.001 256	0.001 212	0.001 169	0.001 128	264
23	0.001 222	0.001 178	0.001 134	0.001 093	0.001 052	0.001 013	276
24	0.001 110	0.001 067	0.001 026	0.000 987	0.000 948	0.000 911	288
25	0.001 010	0.000 969	0.000 930	0.000 892	0.000 855	0.000 820	300
26	0.000 919	0.000 880	0.000 843	0.000 807	0.000 773	0.000 739	312
27	0.000 838	0.000 801	0.000 765	0.000 731	0.000 698	0.000 667	324
28	0.000 764	0.000 729	0.000 695	0.000 663	0.000 632	0.000 602	336
29	0.000 698	0.000 664	0.000 632	0.000 602	0.000 572	0.000 544	348
30	0.000 638	0.000 606	0.000 575	0.000 546	0.000 518	0.000 492	360

MOS	9.75% ANNUAL RATE	10.00% ANNUAL RATE	10.25% ANNUAL RATE	10.50% ANNUAL RATE	10.75% ANNUAL RATE	11.00% ANNUAL RATE	MOS
1	1.000 000	1.000 000	1.000 000	1.000 000	1.000 000	1.000 000	1
2	0.497 977	0.497 925	0.497 874	0.497 822	0.497 770	0.497 719	2
3	0.330 640	0.330 571	0.330 502	0.330 434	0.330 365	0.330 296	3
4	0.246 974	0.246 897	0.246 820	0.246 743	0.246 666	0.246 589	4
5	0.196 776	0.196 694	0.196 612	0.196 530	0.196 449	0.196 367	5
6	0.163 313	0.163 228	0.163 143	0.163 058	0.162 973	0.162 888	6
7	0.139 413	0.139 325	0.139 238	0.139 151	0.139 064	0.138 976	7
8	0.121 488	0.121 400	0.121 311	0.121 222	0.121 133	0.121 044	8
9	0.107 549	0.107 459	0.107 369	0.107 279	0.107 189	0.107 099	9
10	0.096 398	0.096 307	0.096 216	0.096 125	0.096 035	0.095 944	10
11	0.087 276	0.087 184	0.087 093	0.087 001	0.086 910	0.086 818	11
12	0.079 675	0.079 583	0.079 491	0.079 399	0.079 307	0.079 215	12
13	0.073 244	0.073 151	0.073 059	0.072 967	0.072 874	0.072 782	13
14	0.067 733	0.067 640	0.067 547	0.067 455	0.067 362	0.067 270	14
15	0.062 957	0.062 864	0.062 771	0.062 678	0.062 586	0.062 493	15
16	0.058 779	0.058 686	0.058 593	0.058 500	0.058 407	0.058 314	16
17	0.055 093	0.055 000	0.054 906	0.054 813	0.054 721	0.054 628	17
18	0.051 817	0.051 724	0.051 631	0.051 538	0.051 445	0.051 352	18
19	0.048 887	0.048 793	0.048 700	0.048 607	0.048 514	0.048 421	19
20	0.046 250	0.046 157	0.046 063	0.045 970	0.045 878	0.045 785	20
21	0.043 865	0.043 771	0.043 678	0.043 585	0.043 493	0.043 400	21
22	0.041 697	0.041 604	0.041 511	0.041 418	0.041 325	0.041 232	22
23	0.039 718	0.039 625	0.039 532	0.039 439	0.039 347	0.039 254	23
24	0.037 905	0.037 812	0.037 719	0.037 626	0.037 534	0.037 441	24
25	0.036 237	0.036 144	0.036 051	0.035 958	0.035 866	0.035 774	25
26	0.034 697	0.034 605	0.034 512	0.034 420	0.034 327	0.034 235	26
27	0.033 273	0.033 180	0.033 087	0.032 995	0.032 903	0.032 811	27
28	0.031 950	0.031 857	0.031 765	0.031 673	0.031 581	0.031 489	28
29	0.030 719	0.030 627	0.030 534	0.030 442	0.030 351	0.030 259	29
30	0.029 570	0.029 478	0.029 386	0.029 294	0.029 203	0.029 111	30
31	0.028 496	0.028 404	0.028 312	0.028 221	0.028 129	0.028 038	31
32	0.027 489	0.027 398	0.027 306	0.027 215	0.027 123	0.027 032	32
33	0.026 544	0.026 452	0.026 361	0.026 270	0.026 179	0.026 088	33
34	0.025 655	0.025 563	0.025 472	0.025 381	0.025 290	0.025 200	34
35	0.024 816	0.024 725	0.024 634	0.024 543	0.024 453	0.024 362	35
36	0.024 025	0.023 934	0.023 843	0.023 752	0.023 662	0.023 572	36
37	0.023 277	0.023 186	0.023 095	0.023 005	0.022 915	0.022 825	37
38	0.022 568	0.022 477	0.022 387	0.022 297	0.022 207	0.022 117	38
39	0.021 896	0.021 805	0.021 715	0.021 625	0.021 536	0.021 446	39
40	0.021 258	0.021 167	0.021 077	0.020 988	0.020 898	0.020 809	40
41	0.020 651	0.020 561	0.020 471	0.020 382	0.020 293	0.020 204	41
42	0.020 073	0.019 983	0.019 894	0.019 805	0.019 716	0.019 627	42
43	0.019 523	0.019 433	0.019 344	0.019 255	0.019 166	0.019 078	43
44	0.018 998	0.018 908	0.018 819	0.018 730	0.018 642	0.018 554	44
45	0.018 496	0.018 407	0.018 318	0.018 229	0.018 141	0.018 053	45
46	0.018 016	0.017 927	0.017 839	0.017 751	0.017 663	0.017 575	46
47	0.017 557	0.017 469	0.017 380	0.017 292	0.017 205	0.017 117	47
YRS							
4	0.017 118	0.017 029	0.016 941	0.016 853	0.016 766	0.016 679	48
5	0.012 999	0.012 914	0.012 829	0.012 744	0.012 660	0.012 576	60
6	0.010 275	0.010 193	0.010 110	0.010 029	0.009 948	0.009 867	72
7	0.008 347	0.008 268	0.008 189	0.008 111	0.008 033	0.007 956	84
8	0.006 917	0.006 841	0.006 765	0.006 690	0.006 616	0.006 542	96
9	0.005 819	0.005 745	0.005 673	0.005 601	0.005 530	0.005 459	108
10	0.004 952	0.004 882	0.004 812	0.004 743	0.004 676	0.004 608	120
11	0.004 254	0.004 187	0.004 120	0.004 054	0.003 990	0.003 926	132
12	0.003 682	0.003 617	0.003 554	0.003 491	0.003 430	0.003 369	144
13	0.003 207	0.003 145	0.003 085	0.003 025	0.002 966	0.002 909	156
14	0.002 807	0.002 749	0.002 691	0.002 634	0.002 579	0.002 524	168
15	0.002 469	0.002 413	0.002 358	0.002 304	0.002 251	0.002 199	180
16	0.002 179	0.002 126	0.002 074	0.002 022	0.001 972	0.001 923	192
17	0.001 929	0.001 879	0.001 829	0.001 781	0.001 733	0.001 687	204
18	0.001 713	0.001 665	0.001 618	0.001 572	0.001 528	0.001 484	216
19	0.001 525	0.001 479	0.001 435	0.001 391	0.001 349	0.001 308	228
20	0.001 360	0.001 317	0.001 275	0.001 234	0.001 194	0.001 155	240
21	0.001 215	0.001 174	0.001 135	0.001 096	0.001 058	0.001 022	252
22	0.001 088	0.001 049	0.001 012	0.000 975	0.000 940	0.000 906	264
23	0.000 975	0.000 938	0.000 903	0.000 869	0.000 835	0.000 803	276
24	0.000 875	0.000 841	0.000 807	0.000 775	0.000 744	0.000 714	288
25	0.000 786	0.000 754	0.000 722	0.000 692	0.000 663	0.000 634	300
26	0.000 707	0.000 676	0.000 647	0.000 618	0.000 591	0.000 565	312
27	0.000 637	0.000 608	0.000 580	0.000 553	0.000 527	0.000 503	324
28	0.000 574	0.000 546	0.000 520	0.000 495	0.000 471	0.000 448	336
29	0.000 517	0.000 491	0.000 467	0.000 443	0.000 421	0.000 400	348
30	0.000 467	0.000 442	0.000 419	0.000 397	0.000 376	0.000 357	360

SINKING FUND

MOS	11.25% ANNUAL RATE	11.50% ANNUAL RATE	11.75% ANNUAL RATE	12.00% ANNUAL RATE	12.25% ANNUAL RATE	12.50% ANNUAL RATE	MOS
1	1.000 000	1.000 000	1.000 000	1.000 000	1.000 000	1.000 000	1
2	0.497 667	0.497 616	0.497 564	0.497 512	0.497 461	0.497 409	2
3	0.330 228	0.330 159	0.330 091	0.330 022	0.329 954	0.329 885	3
4	C.246 512	0.246 435	0.246 358	0.246 281	0.246 204	0.246 127	4
5	0.196 285	0.196 203	0.196 121	0.196 040	0.195 958	0.195 877	5
6	0.162 803	0.162 718	0.162 633	0.162 548	0.162 464	0.162 379	6
7	0.138 889	0.138 802	0.138 715	0.138 628	0.138 541	0.138 455	7
8	0.120 956	0.120 867	0.120 779	0.120 690	0.120 602	0.120 514	8
9	0.107 009	0.106 920	0.106 830	0.106 740	0.106 651	0.106 561	9
10	0.095 853	0.095 763	0.095 672	0.095 582	0.095 492	0.095 402	10
11	0.086 727	0.086 636	0.086 545	0.086 454	0.086 363	0.086 272	11
12	0.079 123	0.079 032	0.078 940	0.078 849	0.078 757	0.078 666	12
13	0.072 690	0.072 598	0.072 507	0.072 415	0.072 323	0.072 232	13
14	0.067 177	0.067 085	0.066 993	0.066 901	0.066 809	0.066 718	14
15	0.062 400	0.062 308	0.062 216	0.062 124	0.062 032	0.061 940	15
16	0.058 222	0.058 129	0.058 037	0.057 945	0.057 852	0.057 760	16
17	0.054 535	0.054 443	0.054 350	0.054 258	0.054 166	0.054 074	17
18	0.051 259	0.051 167	0.051 074	0.050 982	0.050 890	0.050 798	18
19	0.048 329	0.048 236	0.048 144	0.048 052	0.047 960	0.047 868	19
20	0.045 692	0.045 600	0.045 507	0.045 415	0.045 323	0.045 231	20
21	0.043 307	0.043 215	0.043 123	0.043 031	0.042 939	0.042 847	21
22	0.041 140	0.041 048	0.040 956	0.040 864	0.040 772	0.040 680	22
23	0.039 162	0.039 070	0.038 978	0.038 886	0.038 794	0.038 703	23
24	0.037 349	0.037 257	0.037 165	0.037 073	0.036 982	0.036 891	24
25	0.035 682	0.035 590	0.035 498	0.035 407	0.035 315	0.035 224	25
26	0.034 143	0.034 052	0.033 960	0.033 869	0.033 778	0.033 687	26
27	0.032 720	0.032 628	0.032 537	0.032 446	0.032 355	0.032 264	27
28	0.031 398	0.031 306	0.031 215	0.031 124	0.031 034	0.030 943	28
29	0.030 168	0.030 077	0.029 986	0.029 895	0.029 805	0.029 714	29
30	0.029 020	0.028 929	0.028 839	0.028 748	0.028 658	0.028 568	30
31	0.027 947	0.027 857	0.027 766	0.027 676	0.027 586	0.027 496	31
32	0.026 942	0.026 851	0.026 761	0.026 671	0.026 581	0.026 491	32
33	0.025 998	0.025 907	0.025 817	0.025 727	0.025 638	0.025 549	33
34	0.025 109	0.025 019	0.024 930	0.024 840	0.024 751	0.024 662	34
35	0.024 272	0.024 183	0.024 093	0.024 004	0.023 915	0.023 826	35
36	0.023 482	0.023 393	0.023 303	0.023 214	0.023 126	0.023 037	36
37	0.022 735	0.022 646	0.022 557	0.022 468	0.022 380	0.022 291	37
38	0.022 028	0.021 939	0.021 850	0.021 761	0.021 673	0.021 585	38
39	0.021 357	0.021 268	0.021 180	0.021 092	0.021 004	0.020 916	39
40	0.020 720	0.020 632	0.020 544	0.020 456	0.020 368	0.020 280	40
41	0.020 115	0.020 027	0.019 939	0.019 851	0.019 764	0.019 676	41
42	0.019 539	0.019 451	0.019 363	0.019 276	0.019 188	0.019 102	42
43	0.018 990	0.018 902	0.018 815	0.018 727	0.018 640	0.018 554	43
44	0.018 466	0.018 378	0.018 291	0.018 204	0.018 118	0.018 032	44
45	0.017 966	0.017 879	0.017 792	0.017 705	0.017 619	0.017 533	45
46	0.017 488	0.017 401	0.017 314	0.017 228	0.017 142	0.017 056	46
47	0.017 030	0.016 944	0.016 857	0.016 771	0.016 685	0.016 600	47
YRS							
4	0.016 592	0.016 506	0.016 420	0.016 334	0.016 248	0.016 163	48
5	0.012 492	0.012 409	0.012 327	0.012 244	0.012 163	0.012 081	60
6	0.009 787	0.009 708	0.009 629	0.009 550	0.009 472	0.009 395	72
7	0.007 879	0.007 803	0.007 728	0.007 653	0.007 578	0.007 505	84
8	0.006 469	0.006 396	0.006 324	0.006 253	0.006 182	0.006 112	96
9	0.005 389	0.005 320	0.005 252	0.005 184	0.005 117	0.005 051	108
10	0.004 542	0.004 476	0.004 411	0.004 347	0.004 284	0.004 221	120
11	0.003 863	0.003 800	0.003 739	0.003 678	0.003 618	0.003 559	132
12	0.003 309	0.003 250	0.003 192	0.003 134	0.003 078	0.003 022	144
13	0.002 852	0.002 796	0.002 741	0.002 687	0.002 633	0.002 581	156
14	0.002 470	0.002 417	0.002 365	0.002 314	0.002 264	0.002 215	168
15	0.002 148	0.002 099	0.002 050	0.002 002	0.001 955	0.001 909	180
16	0.001 875	0.001 828	0.001 782	0.001 737	0.001 693	0.001 650	192
17	0.001 642	0.001 598	0.001 554	0.001 512	0.001 471	0.001 431	204
18	0.001 441	0.001 400	0.001 359	0.001 320	0.001 281	0.001 243	216
19	0.001 268	0.001 229	0.001 191	0.001 154	0.001 118	0.001 083	228
20	0.001 118	0.001 081	0.001 045	0.001 011	0.000 977	0.000 945	240
21	0.000 987	0.000 952	0.000 919	0.000 887	0.000 856	0.000 826	252
22	0.000 872	0.000 840	0.000 809	0.000 779	0.000 750	0.000 722	264
23	0.000 772	0.000 742	0.000 714	0.000 686	0.000 659	0.000 633	276
24	0.000 685	0.000 657	0.000 630	0.000 604	0.000 579	0.000 555	288
25	0.000 607	0.000 581	0.000 556	0.000 532	0.000 509	0.000 487	300
26	0.000 539	0.000 515	0.000 492	0.000 470	0.000 448	0.000 428	312
27	0.000 479	0.000 457	0.000 435	0.000 414	0.000 395	0.000 376	324
28	0.000 426	0.000 405	0.000 385	0.000 366	0.000 348	0.000 330	336
29	0.000 379	0.000 360	0.000 341	0.000 324	0.000 307	0.000 291	348
30	0.000 338	0.000 320	0.000 302	0.000 286	0.000 271	0.000 256	360

SINKING FUND

MOS	12.75% ANNUAL RATE	13.00% ANNUAL RATE	13.25% ANNUAL RATE	13.50% ANNUAL RATE	13.75% ANNUAL RATE	14.00% ANNUAL RATE	MOS
1	1.000 000	1.000 000	1.000 000	1.000 000	1.000 000	1.000 000	1
2	0.497 358	0.497 306	0.497 255	0.497 203	0.497 152	0.497 100	2
3	0.329 817	0.329 748	0.329 680	0.329 611	0.329 543	0.329 475	3
4	0.246 051	0.245 974	0.245 897	0.245 821	0.245 744	0.245 667	4
5	0.195 795	0.195 713	0.195 632	0.195 550	0.195 469	0.195 387	5
6	0.162 294	0.162 210	0.162 125	0.162 040	0.161 956	0.161 871	6
7	0.138 368	0.138 281	0.138 194	0.138 108	0.138 021	0.137 934	7
8	0.120 425	0.120 337	0.120 249	0.120 161	0.120 073	0.119 985	8
9	0.106 472	0.106 383	0.106 294	0.106 204	0.106 115	0.106 026	9
10	0.095 311	0.095 221	0.095 131	0.095 041	0.094 951	0.094 862	10
11	0.086 182	0.086 091	0.086 000	0.085 910	0.085 819	0.085 729	11
12	0.078 575	0.078 484	0.078 393	0.078 302	0.078 211	0.078 120	12
13	0.072 140	0.072 049	0.071 957	0.071 866	0.071 775	0.071 684	13
14	0.066 626	0.066 534	0.066 443	0.066 351	0.066 260	0.066 169	14
15	0.061 848	0.061 756	0.061 665	0.061 573	0.061 482	0.061 391	15
16	0.057 669	0.057 577	0.057 485	0.057 394	0.057 302	0.057 211	16
17	0.053 982	0.053 890	0.053 799	0.053 707	0.053 616	0.053 524	17
18	0.050 706	0.050 614	0.050 523	0.050 431	0.050 340	0.050 249	18
19	0.047 776	0.047 684	0.047 593	0.047 501	0.047 410	0.047 319	19
20	0.045 140	0.045 048	0.044 957	0.044 865	0.044 774	0.044 683	20
21	0.042 755	0.042 664	0.042 573	0.042 481	0.042 390	0.042 300	21
22	0.040 589	0.040 497	0.040 406	0.040 315	0.040 224	0.040 134	22
23	0.038 611	0.038 520	0.038 429	0.038 338	0.038 248	0.038 157	23
24	0.036 799	0.036 708	0.036 618	0.036 527	0.036 437	0.036 346	24
25	0.035 133	0.035 043	0.034 952	0.034 861	0.034 771	0.034 681	25
26	0.033 596	0.033 505	0.033 415	0.033 325	0.033 235	0.033 145	26
27	0.032 173	0.032 083	0.031 993	0.031 903	0.031 813	0.031 723	27
28	0.030 853	0.030 763	0.030 673	0.030 583	0.030 493	0.030 404	28
29	0.029 624	0.029 534	0.029 444	0.029 355	0.029 266	0.029 177	29
30	0.028 478	0.028 388	0.028 299	0.028 210	0.028 121	0.028 032	30
31	0.027 406	0.027 317	0.027 228	0.027 139	0.027 050	0.026 961	31
32	0.026 402	0.026 313	0.026 224	0.026 135	0.026 047	0.025 959	32
33	0.025 459	0.025 371	0.025 282	0.025 193	0.025 105	0.025 017	33
34	0.024 573	0.024 484	0.024 396	0.024 308	0.024 220	0.024 132	34
35	0.023 737	0.023 649	0.023 561	0.023 473	0.023 385	0.023 298	35
36	0.022 949	0.022 861	0.022 773	0.022 685	0.022 598	0.022 511	36
37	0.022 203	0.022 115	0.022 028	0.021 941	0.021 854	0.021 767	37
38	0.021 497	0.021 410	0.021 323	0.021 236	0.021 149	0.021 063	38
39	0.020 828	0.020 741	0.020 654	0.020 568	0.020 481	0.020 395	39
40	0.020 193	0.020 106	0.020 020	0.019 933	0.019 847	0.019 762	40
41	0.019 590	0.019 503	0.019 417	0.019 331	0.019 245	0.019 160	41
42	0.019 015	0.018 929	0.018 843	0.018 757	0.018 672	0.018 587	42
43	0.018 468	0.018 382	0.018 296	0.018 211	0.018 126	0.018 041	43
44	0.017 946	0.017 860	0.017 775	0.017 689	0.017 605	0.017 520	44
45	0.017 447	0.017 362	0.017 277	0.017 192	0.017 108	0.017 023	45
46	0.016 971	0.016 886	0.016 801	0.016 717	0.016 632	0.016 549	46
47	0.016 515	0.016 430	0.016 346	0.016 262	0.016 178	0.016 095	47

YRS							
4	0.016 079	0.015 994	0.015 910	0.015 826	0.015 743	0.015 660	48
5	0.012 000	0.011 920	0.011 840	0.011 760	0.011 681	0.011 602	60
6	0.009 317	0.009 241	0.009 165	0.009 089	0.009 014	0.008 939	72
7	0.007 431	0.007 359	0.007 286	0.007 215	0.007 144	0.007 073	84
8	0.006 043	0.005 974	0.005 906	0.005 838	0.005 771	0.005 705	96
9	0.004 985	0.004 920	0.004 856	0.004 792	0.004 729	0.004 667	108
10	0.004 159	0.004 098	0.004 037	0.003 977	0.003 918	0.003 860	120
11	0.003 500	0.003 443	0.003 386	0.003 330	0.003 275	0.003 220	132
12	0.002 967	0.002 913	0.002 860	0.002 807	0.002 755	0.002 705	144
13	0.002 529	0.002 479	0.002 429	0.002 380	0.002 332	0.002 284	156
14	0.002 167	0.002 119	0.002 073	0.002 027	0.001 982	0.001 938	168
15	0.001 863	0.001 819	0.001 776	0.001 733	0.001 692	0.001 651	180
16	0.001 608	0.001 567	0.001 526	0.001 487	0.001 448	0.001 410	192
17	0.001 391	0.001 353	0.001 315	0.001 279	0.001 243	0.001 208	204
18	0.001 207	0.001 171	0.001 136	0.001 102	0.001 069	0.001 037	216
19	0.001 049	0.001 016	0.000 983	0.000 952	0.000 922	0.000 892	228
20	0.000 913	0.000 882	0.000 853	0.000 824	0.000 796	0.000 769	240
21	0.000 796	0.000 768	0.000 740	0.000 714	0.000 688	0.000 663	252
22	0.000 695	0.000 669	0.000 644	0.000 619	0.000 595	0.000 573	264
23	0.000 608	0.000 583	0.000 560	0.000 538	0.000 516	0.000 495	276
24	0.000 532	0.000 509	0.000 488	0.000 467	0.000 447	0.000 428	288
25	0.000 466	0.000 445	0.000 425	0.000 406	0.000 388	0.000 371	300
26	0.000 408	0.000 389	0.000 371	0.000 354	0.000 337	0.000 321	312
27	0.000 358	0.000 340	0.000 324	0.000 308	0.000 293	0.000 279	324
28	0.000 314	0.000 298	0.000 283	0.000 268	0.000 255	0.000 242	336
29	0.000 275	0.000 261	0.000 247	0.000 234	0.000 222	0.000 210	348
30	0.000 242	0.000 229	0.000 216	0.000 204	0.000 193	0.000 182	360

SINKING FUND

MOS	14.25% ANNUAL RATE	14.50% ANNUAL RATE	14.75% ANNUAL RATE	15.00% ANNUAL RATE	15.25% ANNUAL RATE	15.50% ANNUAL RATE	MOS
1	1.000 000	1.000 000	1.000 000	1.000 000	1.000 000	1.000 000	1
2	0.497 049	0.496 997	0.496 946	0.496 894	0.496 843	0.496 792	2
3	0.329 406	0.329 338	0.329 269	0.329 201	0.329 133	0.329 065	3
4	0.245 591	0.245 514	0.245 438	0.245 361	0.245 285	0.245 208	4
5	0.195 306	0.195 225	0.195 143	0.195 062	0.194 981	0.194 900	5
6	0.161 787	0.161 702	0.161 618	0.161 534	0.161 450	0.161 365	6
7	0.137 848	0.137 761	0.137 675	0.137 589	0.137 502	0.137 416	7
8	0.119 897	0.119 809	0.119 721	0.119 633	0.119 545	0.119 458	8
9	0.105 937	0.105 848	0.105 759	0.105 671	0.105 582	0.105 493	9
10	0.094 772	0.094 682	0.094 593	0.094 503	0.094 414	0.094 324	10
11	0.085 639	0.085 549	0.085 458	0.085 368	0.085 278	0.085 189	11
12	0.078 030	0.077 939	0.077 849	0.077 758	0.077 668	0.077 578	12
13	0.071 593	0.071 502	0.071 412	0.071 321	0.071 230	0.071 140	13
14	0.066 078	0.065 987	0.065 896	0.065 805	0.065 714	0.065 624	14
15	0.061 299	0.061 208	0.061 117	0.061 026	0.060 936	0.060 845	15
16	0.057 120	0.057 029	0.056 938	0.056 847	0.056 756	0.056 665	16
17	0.053 433	0.053 342	0.053 251	0.053 160	0.053 070	0.052 979	17
18	0.050 157	0.050 066	0.049 976	0.049 885	0.049 794	0.049 704	18
19	0.047 228	0.047 137	0.047 046	0.046 955	0.046 865	0.046 775	19
20	0.044 592	0.044 501	0.044 411	0.044 320	0.044 230	0.044 140	20
21	0.042 209	0.042 118	0.042 028	0.041 937	0.041 847	0.041 757	21
22	0.040 043	0.039 953	0.039 862	0.039 772	0.039 682	0.039 593	22
23	0.038 067	0.037 977	0.037 887	0.037 797	0.037 707	0.037 617	23
24	0.036 256	0.036 166	0.036 076	0.035 987	0.035 897	0.035 808	24
25	0.034 591	0.034 501	0.034 412	0.034 322	0.034 233	0.034 144	25
26	0.033 055	0.032 966	0.032 876	0.032 787	0.032 698	0.032 610	26
27	0.031 634	0.031 545	0.031 456	0.031 367	0.031 278	0.031 190	27
28	0.030 315	0.030 226	0.030 137	0.030 049	0.029 960	0.029 872	28
29	0.029 088	0.028 999	0.028 911	0.028 822	0.028 734	0.028 646	29
30	0.027 943	0.027 855	0.027 767	0.027 679	0.027 591	0.027 503	30
31	0.026 873	0.026 785	0.026 697	0.026 609	0.026 522	0.026 435	31
32	0.025 871	0.025 783	0.025 695	0.025 608	0.025 521	0.025 434	32
33	0.024 930	0.024 842	0.024 755	0.024 668	0.024 581	0.024 495	33
34	0.024 045	0.023 958	0.023 871	0.023 784	0.023 697	0.023 611	34
35	0.023 211	0.023 124	0.023 037	0.022 951	0.022 865	0.022 779	35
36	0.022 424	0.022 338	0.022 251	0.022 165	0.022 080	0.021 994	36
37	0.021 681	0.021 594	0.021 508	0.021 423	0.021 337	0.021 252	37
38	0.020 977	0.020 891	0.020 805	0.020 720	0.020 635	0.020 550	38
39	0.020 309	0.020 224	0.020 139	0.020 054	0.019 969	0.019 884	39
40	0.019 676	0.019 591	0.019 506	0.019 421	0.019 337	0.019 253	40
41	0.019 074	0.018 990	0.018 905	0.018 821	0.018 737	0.018 653	41
42	0.018 502	0.018 417	0.018 333	0.018 249	0.018 165	0.018 082	42
43	0.017 956	0.017 872	0.017 788	0.017 705	0.017 621	0.017 538	43
44	0.017 436	0.017 352	0.017 269	0.017 186	0.017 103	0.017 020	44
45	0.016 940	0.016 856	0.016 773	0.016 690	0.016 608	0.016 525	45
46	0.016 465	0.016 382	0.016 299	0.016 217	0.016 135	0.016 053	46
47	0.016 011	0.015 929	0.015 846	0.015 764	0.015 682	0.015 601	47
YRS							
4	0.015 577	0.015 495	0.015 413	0.015 331	0.015 249	0.015 168	48
5	0.011 523	0.011 445	0.011 367	0.011 290	0.011 213	0.011 137	60
6	0.008 865	0.008 791	0.008 718	0.008 645	0.008 573	0.008 501	72
7	0.007 003	0.006 934	0.006 865	0.006 797	0.006 729	0.006 662	84
8	0.005 639	0.005 574	0.005 509	0.005 445	0.005 382	0.005 319	96
9	0.004 605	0.004 544	0.004 484	0.004 424	0.004 365	0.004 307	108
10	0.003 802	0.003 745	0.003 689	0.003 633	0.003 579	0.003 524	120
11	0.003 166	0.003 113	0.003 061	0.003 009	0.002 958	0.002 908	132
12	0.002 654	0.002 605	0.002 557	0.002 509	0.002 462	0.002 415	144
13	0.002 238	0.002 192	0.002 147	0.002 103	0.002 059	0.002 017	156
14	0.001 895	0.001 853	0.001 811	0.001 770	0.001 730	0.001 691	168
15	0.001 611	0.001 572	0.001 533	0.001 496	0.001 459	0.001 423	180
16	0.001 373	0.001 337	0.001 302	0.001 268	0.001 234	0.001 201	192
17	0.001 174	0.001 141	0.001 109	0.001 077	0.001 046	0.001 016	204
18	0.001 006	0.000 975	0.000 946	0.000 917	0.000 889	0.000 862	216
19	0.000 863	0.000 835	0.000 808	0.000 782	0.000 756	0.000 732	228
20	0.000 742	0.000 717	0.000 692	0.000 668	0.000 645	0.000 622	240
21	0.000 639	0.000 616	0.000 593	0.000 571	0.000 550	0.000 530	252
22	0.000 551	0.000 529	0.000 509	0.000 489	0.000 470	0.000 451	264
23	0.000 475	0.000 456	0.000 437	0.000 419	0.000 402	0.000 385	276
24	0.000 410	0.000 392	0.000 376	0.000 359	0.000 344	0.000 329	288
25	0.000 354	0.000 338	0.000 323	0.000 308	0.000 294	0.000 281	300
26	0.000 306	0.000 292	0.000 278	0.000 265	0.000 252	0.000 240	312
27	0.000 265	0.000 252	0.000 239	0.000 227	0.000 216	0.000 205	324
28	0.000 229	0.000 217	0.000 206	0.000 195	0.000 185	0.000 175	336
29	0.000 198	0.000 188	0.000 178	0.000 168	0.000 159	0.000 150	348
30	0.000 172	0.000 162	0.000 153	0.000 144	0.000 136	0.000 129	360

SINKING FUND

MOS	15.75% ANNUAL RATE	16.00% ANNUAL RATE	16.25% ANNUAL RATE	16.50% ANNUAL RATE	16.75% ANNUAL RATE	17.00% ANNUAL RATE	MOS
1	1.000 000	1.000 000	1.000 000	1.000 000	1.000 000	1.000 000	1
2	0.496 740	0.496 689	0.496 637	0.496 586	0.496 535	0.496 483	2
3	0.328 996	0.328 928	0.328 860	0.328 792	0.328 724	0.328 655	3
4	0.245 132	0.245 055	0.244 979	0.244 902	0.244 826	0.244 750	4
5	0.194 818	0.194 737	0.194 656	0.194 575	0.194 494	0.194 413	5
6	0.161 281	0.161 197	0.161 113	0.161 029	0.160 945	0.160 861	6
7	0.137 330	0.137 244	0.137 158	0.137 072	0.136 986	0.136 900	7
8	0.119 370	0.119 283	0.119 195	0.119 108	0.119 020	0.118 933	8
9	0.105 405	0.105 316	0.105 227	0.105 139	0.105 051	0.104 962	9
10	0.094 235	0.094 146	0.094 056	0.093 967	0.093 878	0.093 789	10
11	0.085 099	0.085 009	0.084 919	0.084 830	0.084 740	0.084 651	11
12	0.077 488	0.077 398	0.077 308	0.077 218	0.077 128	0.077 038	12
13	0.071 050	0.070 959	0.070 869	0.070 779	0.070 689	0.070 599	13
14	0.065 533	0.065 443	0.065 353	0.065 262	0.065 172	0.065 082	14
15	0.060 755	0.060 664	0.060 574	0.060 484	0.060 393	0.060 303	15
16	0.056 575	0.056 484	0.056 394	0.056 304	0.056 214	0.056 124	16
17	0.052 888	0.052 798	0.052 708	0.052 618	0.052 528	0.052 438	17
18	0.049 613	0.049 523	0.049 433	0.049 343	0.049 253	0.049 163	18
19	0.046 684	0.046 594	0.046 504	0.046 415	0.046 325	0.046 235	19
20	0.044 050	0.043 960	0.043 870	0.043 781	0.043 691	0.043 602	20
21	0.041 667	0.041 578	0.041 488	0.041 399	0.041 310	0.041 220	21
22	0.039 503	0.039 414	0.039 324	0.039 235	0.039 146	0.039 057	22
23	0.037 528	0.037 439	0.037 350	0.037 261	0.037 172	0.037 083	23
24	0.035 719	0.035 630	0.035 541	0.035 452	0.035 364	0.035 276	24
25	0.034 055	0.033 967	0.033 878	0.033 790	0.033 702	0.033 614	25
26	0.032 521	0.032 433	0.032 344	0.032 256	0.032 169	0.032 081	26
27	0.031 101	0.031 013	0.030 925	0.030 838	0.030 750	0.030 663	27
28	0.029 784	0.029 696	0.029 609	0.029 521	0.029 434	0.029 347	28
29	0.028 559	0.028 471	0.028 384	0.028 297	0.028 210	0.028 123	29
30	0.027 416	0.027 329	0.027 242	0.027 155	0.027 069	0.026 982	30
31	0.026 348	0.026 261	0.026 174	0.026 088	0.026 002	0.025 916	31
32	0.025 347	0.025 261	0.025 175	0.025 089	0.025 003	0.024 917	32
33	0.024 408	0.024 322	0.024 236	0.024 151	0.024 065	0.023 980	33
34	0.023 525	0.023 439	0.023 354	0.023 269	0.023 184	0.023 099	34
35	0.022 693	0.022 608	0.022 523	0.022 438	0.022 353	0.022 269	35
36	0.021 909	0.021 824	0.021 739	0.021 654	0.021 570	0.021 486	36
37	0.021 167	0.021 083	0.020 998	0.020 914	0.020 830	0.020 746	37
38	0.020 465	0.020 381	0.020 297	0.020 213	0.020 130	0.020 047	38
39	0.019 800	0.019 716	0.019 633	0.019 549	0.019 466	0.019 383	39
40	0.019 169	0.019 086	0.019 002	0.018 919	0.018 837	0.018 754	40
41	0.018 569	0.018 486	0.018 403	0.018 321	0.018 238	0.018 156	41
42	0.017 999	0.017 916	0.017 834	0.017 751	0.017 670	0.017 588	42
43	0.017 456	0.017 373	0.017 291	0.017 209	0.017 128	0.017 047	43
44	0.016 938	0.016 856	0.016 774	0.016 693	0.016 611	0.016 531	44
45	0.016 443	0.016 362	0.016 280	0.016 199	0.016 119	0.016 038	45
46	0.015 971	0.015 890	0.015 809	0.015 728	0.015 648	0.015 568	46
47	0.015 520	0.015 439	0.015 358	0.015 278	0.015 198	0.015 119	47
YRS							
4	0.015 087	0.015 007	0.014 927	0.014 847	0.014 768	0.014 688	48
5	0.011 060	0.010 985	0.010 909	0.010 835	0.010 760	0.010 686	60
6	0.008 429	0.008 359	0.008 288	0.008 218	0.008 149	0.008 079	72
7	0.006 595	0.006 529	0.006 463	0.006 398	0.006 333	0.006 269	84
8	0.005 257	0.005 195	0.005 134	0.005 074	0.005 014	0.004 955	96
9	0.004 249	0.004 192	0.004 135	0.004 079	0.004 024	0.003 970	108
10	0.003 471	0.003 418	0.003 366	0.003 314	0.003 263	0.003 213	120
11	0.002 859	0.002 810	0.002 762	0.002 714	0.002 668	0.002 622	132
12	0.002 370	0.002 325	0.002 281	0.002 237	0.002 195	0.002 153	144
13	0.001 975	0.001 934	0.001 893	0.001 854	0.001 815	0.001 776	156
14	0.001 653	0.001 615	0.001 578	0.001 542	0.001 506	0.001 472	168
15	0.001 388	0.001 354	0.001 320	0.001 287	0.001 255	0.001 223	180
16	0.001 169	0.001 138	0.001 107	0.001 077	0.001 048	0.001 020	192
17	0.000 987	0.000 959	0.000 931	0.000 904	0.000 877	0.000 852	204
18	0.000 835	0.000 809	0.000 784	0.000 760	0.000 736	0.000 713	216
19	0.000 708	0.000 684	0.000 661	0.000 639	0.000 618	0.000 597	228
20	0.000 600	0.000 579	0.000 559	0.000 539	0.000 520	0.000 501	240
21	0.000 510	0.000 491	0.000 473	0.000 455	0.000 438	0.000 421	252
22	0.000 434	0.000 417	0.000 400	0.000 384	0.000 369	0.000 354	264
23	0.000 369	0.000 354	0.000 339	0.000 325	0.000 311	0.000 298	276
24	0.000 314	0.000 301	0.000 287	0.000 275	0.000 263	0.000 251	288
25	0.000 268	0.000 256	0.000 244	0.000 232	0.000 222	0.000 211	300
26	0.000 228	0.000 217	0.000 207	0.000 197	0.000 187	0.000 178	312
27	0.000 195	0.000 185	0.000 176	0.000 167	0.000 158	0.000 150	324
28	0.000 166	0.000 157	0.000 149	0.000 141	0.000 134	0.000 127	336
29	0.000 142	0.000 134	0.000 127	0.000 120	0.000 113	0.000 107	348
30	0.000 121	0.000 114	0.000 108	0.000 101	0.000 096	0.000 090	360

MONTHLY COMPOUNDING

SECTION 3

MOS	17.25% ANNUAL RATE	17.50% ANNUAL RATE	17.75% ANNUAL RATE	18.00% ANNUAL RATE	18.25% ANNUAL RATE	18.50% ANNUAL RATE	MOS
1	1.000 000	1.000 000	1.000 000	1.000 000	1.000 000	1.000 000	1
2	0.496 432	0.496 381	0.496 329	0.496 278	0.496 227	0.496 175	2
3	0.328 587	0.328 519	0.328 451	0.328 383	0.328 315	0.328 247	3
4	0.244 673	0.244 597	0.244 521	0.244 445	0.244 369	0.244 292	4
5	0.194 332	0.194 251	0.194 170	0.194 089	0.194 008	0.193 928	5
6	0.160 777	0.160 693	0.160 609	0.160 525	0.160 441	0.160 358	6
7	0.136 814	0.136 728	0.136 642	0.136 556	0.136 470	0.136 385	7
8	0.118 846	0.118 758	0.118 671	0.118 584	0.118 497	0.118 410	8
9	0.104 874	0.104 786	0.104 698	0.104 610	0.104 522	0.104 434	9
10	0.093 700	0.093 612	0.093 523	0.093 434	0.093 346	0.093 257	10
11	0.084 561	0.084 472	0.084 383	0.084 294	0.084 205	0.084 116	11
12	0.076 948	0.076 859	0.076 769	0.076 680	0.076 591	0.076 501	12
13	0.070 509	0.070 420	0.070 330	0.070 240	0.070 151	0.070 062	13
14	0.064 992	0.064 903	0.064 813	0.064 723	0.064 634	0.064 544	14
15	0.060 213	0.060 124	0.060 034	0.059 944	0.059 855	0.059 765	15
16	0.056 034	0.055 944	0.055 855	0.055 765	0.055 676	0.055 586	16
17	0.052 348	0.052 259	0.052 169	0.052 080	0.051 990	0.051 901	17
18	0.049 074	0.048 984	0.048 895	0.048 806	0.048 717	0.048 628	18
19	0.046 146	0.046 057	0.045 967	0.045 878	0.045 790	0.045 701	19
20	0.043 513	0.043 423	0.043 335	0.043 246	0.043 157	0.043 069	20
21	0.041 132	0.041 043	0.040 954	0.040 865	0.040 777	0.040 689	21
22	0.038 969	0.038 880	0.038 792	0.038 703	0.038 615	0.038 527	22
23	0.036 995	0.036 907	0.036 819	0.036 731	0.036 643	0.036 555	23
24	0.035 187	0.035 100	0.035 012	0.034 924	0.034 837	0.034 749	24
25	0.033 526	0.033 438	0.033 351	0.033 263	0.033 176	0.033 089	25
26	0.031 993	0.031 906	0.031 819	0.031 732	0.031 645	0.031 559	26
27	0.030 576	0.030 489	0.030 402	0.030 315	0.030 229	0.030 143	27
28	0.029 260	0.029 174	0.029 087	0.029 001	0.028 915	0.028 829	28
29	0.028 037	0.027 951	0.027 865	0.027 779	0.027 693	0.027 608	29
30	0.026 896	0.026 810	0.026 725	0.026 639	0.026 554	0.026 469	30
31	0.025 830	0.025 745	0.025 659	0.025 574	0.025 489	0.025 405	31
32	0.024 832	0.024 747	0.024 662	0.024 577	0.024 493	0.024 408	32
33	0.023 895	0.023 810	0.023 726	0.023 641	0.023 557	0.023 474	33
34	0.023 014	0.022 930	0.022 846	0.022 762	0.022 678	0.022 595	34
35	0.022 185	0.022 101	0.022 017	0.021 934	0.021 850	0.021 767	35
36	0.021 402	0.021 319	0.021 235	0.021 152	0.021 070	0.020 987	36
37	0.020 663	0.020 580	0.020 497	0.020 414	0.020 332	0.020 250	37
38	0.019 964	0.019 881	0.019 798	0.019 716	0.019 634	0.019 553	38
39	0.019 301	0.019 218	0.019 136	0.019 055	0.018 973	0.018 892	39
40	0.018 672	0.018 590	0.018 508	0.018 427	0.018 346	0.018 265	40
41	0.018 075	0.017 993	0.017 912	0.017 831	0.017 750	0.017 670	41
42	0.017 507	0.017 426	0.017 345	0.017 264	0.017 184	0.017 104	42
43	0.016 966	0.016 885	0.016 805	0.016 725	0.016 645	0.016 565	43
44	0.016 450	0.016 370	0.016 290	0.016 210	0.016 131	0.016 052	44
45	0.015 958	0.015 878	0.015 799	0.015 720	0.015 641	0.015 562	45
46	0.015 488	0.015 409	0.015 330	0.015 251	0.015 173	0.015 095	46
47	0.015 039	0.014 960	0.014 882	0.014 803	0.014 725	0.014 648	47

YRS	17.25%	17.50%	17.75%	18.00%	18.25%	18.50%	MOS
4	0.014 610	0.014 531	0.014 453	0.014 375	0.014 297	0.014 220	48
5	0.010 612	0.010 539	0.010 466	0.010 393	0.010 321	0.010 250	60
6	0.008 011	0.007 943	0.007 875	0.007 808	0.007 741	0.007 675	72
7	0.006 206	0.006 142	0.006 080	0.006 018	0.005 956	0.005 895	84
8	0.004 896	0.004 838	0.004 780	0.004 723	0.004 667	0.004 611	96
9	0.003 915	0.003 862	0.003 809	0.003 757	0.003 705	0.003 654	108
10	0.003 164	0.003 115	0.003 066	0.003 019	0.002 971	0.002 925	120
11	0.002 576	0.002 532	0.002 488	0.002 444	0.002 401	0.002 359	132
12	0.002 111	0.002 071	0.002 031	0.001 991	0.001 953	0.001 914	144
13	0.001 739	0.001 702	0.001 666	0.001 630	0.001 595	0.001 561	156
14	0.001 438	0.001 404	0.001 372	0.001 340	0.001 308	0.001 277	168
15	0.001 193	0.001 162	0.001 133	0.001 104	0.001 076	0.001 049	180
16	0.000 992	0.000 965	0.000 938	0.000 913	0.000 887	0.000 863	192
17	0.000 827	0.000 802	0.000 779	0.000 756	0.000 733	0.000 711	204
18	0.000 690	0.000 669	0.000 647	0.000 627	0.000 607	0.000 588	216
19	0.000 577	0.000 558	0.000 539	0.000 521	0.000 503	0.000 486	228
20	0.000 483	0.000 466	0.000 449	0.000 433	0.000 417	0.000 402	240
21	0.000 405	0.000 390	0.000 375	0.000 361	0.000 347	0.000 333	252
22	0.000 340	0.000 326	0.000 313	0.000 300	0.000 288	0.000 276	264
23	0.000 285	0.000 273	0.000 262	0.000 250	0.000 240	0.000 229	276
24	0.000 240	0.000 229	0.000 219	0.000 209	0.000 199	0.000 190	288
25	0.000 201	0.000 192	0.000 183	0.000 174	0.000 166	0.000 158	300
26	0.000 169	0.000 161	0.000 153	0.000 146	0.000 138	0.000 131	312
27	0.000 142	0.000 135	0.000 128	0.000 122	0.000 115	0.000 109	324
28	0.000 120	0.000 113	0.000 107	0.000 101	0.000 096	0.000 091	336
29	0.000 101	0.000 095	0.000 090	0.000 085	0.000 080	0.000 075	348
30	0.000 085	0.000 080	0.000 075	0.000 071	0.000 067	0.000 063	360

SINKING FUND

MOS	18.75% ANNUAL RATE	19.00% ANNUAL RATE	19.25% ANNUAL RATE	19.50% ANNUAL RATE	19.75% ANNUAL RATE	20.00% ANNUAL RATE	MOS
1	1.000 000	1.000 000	1.000 000	1.000 000	1.000 000	1.000 000	1
2	0.496 124	0.496 073	0.496 021	0.495 970	0.495 919	0.495 868	2
3	0.328 179	0.328 111	0.328 043	0.327 975	0.327 907	0.327 839	3
4	0.244 216	0.244 140	0.244 064	0.243 988	0.243 912	0.243 836	4
5	0.193 847	0.193 766	0.193 685	0.193 605	0.193 524	0.193 444	5
6	0.160 274	0.160 190	0.160 107	0.160 023	0.159 940	0.159 856	6
7	0.136 299	0.136 214	0.136 128	0.136 043	0.135 957	0.135 872	7
8	0.118 323	0.118 236	0.118 149	0.118 062	0.117 976	0.117 889	8
9	0.104 346	0.104 258	0.104 171	0.104 083	0.103 995	0.103 908	9
10	0.093 169	0.093 080	0.092 992	0.092 904	0.092 815	0.092 727	10
11	0.084 027	0.083 938	0.083 849	0.083 761	0.083 672	0.083 584	11
12	0.076 412	0.076 323	0.076 234	0.076 145	0.076 057	0.075 968	12
13	0.069 972	0.069 883	0.069 794	0.069 705	0.069 616	0.069 527	13
14	0.064 455	0.064 366	0.064 277	0.064 188	0.064 099	0.064 010	14
15	0.059 676	0.059 587	0.059 498	0.059 409	0.059 320	0.059 231	15
16	0.055 497	0.055 408	0.055 319	0.055 230	0.055 142	0.055 053	16
17	0.051 812	0.051 723	0.051 634	0.051 546	0.051 457	0.051 369	17
18	0.048 539	0.048 450	0.048 362	0.048 273	0.048 185	0.048 097	18
19	0.045 612	0.045 524	0.045 435	0.045 347	0.045 259	0.045 171	19
20	0.042 980	0.042 892	0.042 804	0.042 716	0.042 628	0.042 540	20
21	0.040 601	0.040 513	0.040 425	0.040 337	0.040 250	0.040 163	21
22	0.038 440	0.038 352	0.038 264	0.038 177	0.038 090	0.038 003	22
23	0.036 468	0.036 381	0.036 293	0.036 206	0.036 120	0.036 033	23
24	0.034 662	0.034 575	0.034 488	0.034 402	0.034 315	0.034 229	24
25	0.033 003	0.032 916	0.032 830	0.032 743	0.032 657	0.032 571	25
26	0.031 472	0.031 386	0.031 300	0.031 214	0.031 128	0.031 043	26
27	0.030 057	0.029 971	0.029 885	0.029 800	0.029 714	0.029 629	27
28	0.028 744	0.028 658	0.028 573	0.028 488	0.028 403	0.028 318	28
29	0.027 522	0.027 437	0.027 353	0.027 268	0.027 183	0.027 099	29
30	0.026 384	0.026 299	0.026 215	0.026 131	0.026 047	0.025 963	30
31	0.025 320	0.025 236	0.025 152	0.025 068	0.024 985	0.024 901	31
32	0.024 324	0.024 241	0.024 157	0.024 074	0.023 991	0.023 908	32
33	0.023 390	0.023 307	0.023 223	0.023 141	0.023 058	0.022 975	33
34	0.022 512	0.022 429	0.022 346	0.022 264	0.022 181	0.022 099	34
35	0.021 685	0.021 602	0.021 520	0.021 438	0.021 356	0.021 275	35
36	0.020 905	0.020 823	0.020 741	0.020 659	0.020 578	0.020 497	36
37	0.020 168	0.020 086	0.020 005	0.019 924	0.019 843	0.019 762	37
38	0.019 471	0.019 390	0.019 309	0.019 228	0.019 148	0.019 068	38
39	0.018 811	0.018 730	0.018 650	0.018 570	0.018 490	0.018 410	39
40	0.018 185	0.018 104	0.018 024	0.017 945	0.017 865	0.017 786	40
41	0.017 590	0.017 510	0.017 431	0.017 351	0.017 272	0.017 194	41
42	0.017 025	0.016 945	0.016 866	0.016 787	0.016 709	0.016 631	42
43	0.016 486	0.016 407	0.016 329	0.016 250	0.016 172	0.016 095	43
44	0.015 973	0.015 895	0.015 817	0.015 739	0.015 661	0.015 584	44
45	0.015 484	0.015 406	0.015 328	0.015 251	0.015 174	0.015 097	45
46	0.015 017	0.014 939	0.014 862	0.014 785	0.014 709	0.014 632	46
47	0.014 570	0.014 493	0.014 417	0.014 340	0.014 264	0.014 188	47

YRS							
4	0.014 143	0.014 067	0.013 991	0.013 915	0.013 839	0.013 764	48
5	0.010 178	0.010 107	0.010 037	0.009 966	0.009 897	0.009 827	60
6	0.007 609	0.007 543	0.007 478	0.007 414	0.007 350	0.007 286	72
7	0.005 835	0.005 775	0.005 715	0.005 656	0.005 598	0.005 540	84
8	0.004 555	0.004 501	0.004 446	0.004 392	0.004 339	0.004 287	96
9	0.003 604	0.003 554	0.003 504	0.003 456	0.003 407	0.003 360	108
10	0.002 879	0.002 834	0.002 789	0.002 745	0.002 702	0.002 659	120
11	0.002 318	0.002 277	0.002 237	0.002 197	0.002 158	0.002 120	132
12	0.001 877	0.001 840	0.001 804	0.001 769	0.001 734	0.001 699	144
13	0.001 527	0.001 494	0.001 462	0.001 430	0.001 399	0.001 369	156
14	0.001 247	0.001 218	0.001 189	0.001 161	0.001 133	0.001 106	168
15	0.001 022	0.000 995	0.000 970	0.000 945	0.000 920	0.000 896	180
16	0.000 839	0.000 816	0.000 793	0.000 771	0.000 749	0.000 728	192
17	0.000 690	0.000 670	0.000 649	0.000 630	0.000 611	0.000 592	204
18	0.000 569	0.000 551	0.000 533	0.000 516	0.000 499	0.000 483	216
19	0.000 469	0.000 453	0.000 438	0.000 423	0.000 408	0.000 394	228
20	0.000 388	0.000 374	0.000 360	0.000 347	0.000 334	0.000 322	240
21	0.000 320	0.000 308	0.000 296	0.000 285	0.000 274	0.000 263	252
22	0.000 265	0.000 254	0.000 244	0.000 234	0.000 224	0.000 215	264
23	0.000 220	0.000 210	0.000 201	0.000 192	0.000 184	0.000 176	276
24	0.000 182	0.000 174	0.000 166	0.000 158	0.000 151	0.000 144	288
25	0.000 151	0.000 143	0.000 137	0.000 130	0.000 124	0.000 118	300
26	0.000 125	0.000 119	0.000 113	0.000 107	0.000 102	0.000 097	312
27	0.000 104	0.000 098	0.000 093	0.000 088	0.000 083	0.000 079	324
28	0.000 086	0.000 081	0.000 077	0.000 073	0.000 069	0.000 065	336
29	0.000 071	0.000 067	0.000 063	0.000 060	0.000 056	0.000 053	348
30	0.000 059	0.000 056	0.000 052	0.000 049	0.000 046	0.000 044	360

SINKING FUND

MOS	20.25% ANNUAL RATE	20.50% ANNUAL RATE	20.75% ANNUAL RATE	21.00% ANNUAL RATE	21.25% ANNUAL RATE	21.50% ANNUAL RATE	MOS
1	1.000 000	1.000 000	1.000 000	1.000 000	1.000 000	1.000 000	1
2	0.495 817	0.495 765	0.495 714	0.495 663	0.495 612	0.495 561	2
3	0.327 771	0.327 703	0.327 635	0.327 567	0.327 500	0.327 432	3
4	0.243 760	0.243 684	0.243 608	0.243 532	0.243 457	0.243 381	4
5	0.193 363	0.193 282	0.193 202	0.193 121	0.193 041	0.192 961	5
6	0.159 773	0.159 689	0.159 606	0.159 523	0.159 439	0.159 356	6
7	0.135 786	0.135 701	0.135 616	0.135 531	0.135 445	0.135 360	7
8	0.117 802	0.117 716	0.117 629	0.117 543	0.117 457	0.117 370	8
9	0.103 820	0.103 733	0.103 645	0.103 558	0.103 471	0.103 384	9
10	0.092 639	0.092 551	0.092 463	0.092 375	0.092 288	0.092 200	10
11	0.083 495	0.083 407	0.083 319	0.083 230	0.083 142	0.083 054	11
12	0.075 879	0.075 791	0.075 702	0.075 614	0.075 525	0.075 437	12
13	0.069 438	0.069 350	0.069 261	0.069 173	0.069 084	0.068 996	13
14	0.063 921	0.063 833	0.063 744	0.063 656	0.063 567	0.063 479	14
15	0.059 143	0.059 054	0.058 966	0.058 877	0.058 789	0.058 701	15
16	0.054 964	0.054 876	0.054 788	0.054 700	0.054 612	0.054 524	16
17	0.051 280	0.051 192	0.051 104	0.051 016	0.050 928	0.050 841	17
18	0.048 008	0.047 920	0.047 833	0.047 745	0.047 657	0.047 570	18
19	0.045 083	0.044 996	0.044 908	0.044 821	0.044 733	0.044 646	19
20	0.042 453	0.042 366	0.042 278	0.042 191	0.042 104	0.042 017	20
21	0.040 075	0.039 988	0.039 901	0.039 815	0.039 728	0.039 642	21
22	0.037 916	0.037 829	0.037 743	0.037 656	0.037 570	0.037 484	22
23	0.035 947	0.035 860	0.035 774	0.035 688	0.035 602	0.035 516	23
24	0.034 143	0.034 057	0.033 971	0.033 886	0.033 800	0.033 715	24
25	0.032 486	0.032 400	0.032 315	0.032 230	0.032 144	0.032 060	25
26	0.030 958	0.030 872	0.030 787	0.030 703	0.030 618	0.030 534	26
27	0.029 544	0.029 460	0.029 375	0.029 291	0.029 207	0.029 123	27
28	0.028 234	0.028 150	0.028 065	0.027 982	0.027 898	0.027 814	28
29	0.027 015	0.026 931	0.026 848	0.026 764	0.026 681	0.026 598	29
30	0.025 879	0.025 796	0.025 713	0.025 630	0.025 547	0.025 464	30
31	0.024 818	0.024 735	0.024 653	0.024 570	0.024 488	0.024 406	31
32	0.023 825	0.023 742	0.023 660	0.023 578	0.023 496	0.023 415	32
33	0.022 893	0.022 811	0.022 729	0.022 648	0.022 566	0.022 485	33
34	0.022 018	0.021 936	0.021 855	0.021 774	0.021 693	0.021 612	34
35	0.021 193	0.021 112	0.021 031	0.020 951	0.020 870	0.020 790	35
36	0.020 416	0.020 336	0.020 255	0.020 175	0.020 095	0.020 016	36
37	0.019 682	0.019 602	0.019 522	0.019 443	0.019 363	0.019 284	37
38	0.018 988	0.018 908	0.018 829	0.018 750	0.018 671	0.018 592	38
39	0.018 331	0.018 251	0.018 173	0.018 094	0.018 016	0.017 938	39
40	0.017 707	0.017 629	0.017 550	0.017 472	0.017 394	0.017 317	40
41	0.017 115	0.017 037	0.016 959	0.016 882	0.016 804	0.016 727	41
42	0.016 553	0.016 475	0.016 398	0.016 321	0.016 244	0.016 167	42
43	0.016 017	0.015 940	0.015 863	0.015 787	0.015 710	0.015 634	43
44	0.015 507	0.015 431	0.015 354	0.015 278	0.015 202	0.015 127	44
45	0.015 021	0.014 945	0.014 869	0.014 793	0.014 718	0.014 643	45
46	0.014 556	0.014 481	0.014 405	0.014 330	0.014 256	0.014 181	46
47	0.014 113	0.014 038	0.013 963	0.013 888	0.013 814	0.013 740	47

YRS

YRS							MOS
4	0.013 689	0.013 614	0.013 540	0.013 466	0.013 392	0.013 319	48
5	0.009 758	0.009 690	0.009 621	0.009 553	0.009 486	0.009 419	60
6	0.007 223	0.007 160	0.007 098	0.007 036	0.006 975	0.006 914	72
7	0.005 482	0.005 425	0.005 368	0.005 312	0.005 257	0.005 201	84
8	0.004 234	0.004 183	0.004 132	0.004 081	0.004 031	0.003 981	96
9	0.003 313	0.003 266	0.003 220	0.003 175	0.003 130	0.003 086	108
10	0.002 617	0.002 575	0.002 534	0.002 493	0.002 453	0.002 414	120
11	0.002 082	0.002 045	0.002 008	0.001 972	0.001 936	0.001 901	132
12	0.001 666	0.001 633	0.001 600	0.001 568	0.001 537	0.001 506	144
13	0.001 339	0.001 309	0.001 280	0.001 252	0.001 225	0.001 197	156
14	0.001 079	0.001 054	0.001 028	0.001 003	0.000 979	0.000 955	168
15	0.000 873	0.000 850	0.000 828	0.000 806	0.000 785	0.000 764	180
16	0.000 707	0.000 687	0.000 668	0.000 649	0.000 631	0.000 613	192
17	0.000 574	0.000 557	0.000 540	0.000 523	0.000 507	0.000 492	204
18	0.000 467	0.000 452	0.000 437	0.000 423	0.000 409	0.000 395	216
19	0.000 380	0.000 367	0.000 354	0.000 342	0.000 330	0.000 318	228
20	0.000 310	0.000 298	0.000 287	0.000 276	0.000 266	0.000 256	240
21	0.000 253	0.000 243	0.000 233	0.000 224	0.000 215	0.000 206	252
22	0.000 206	0.000 197	0.000 189	0.000 181	0.000 174	0.000 166	264
23	0.000 168	0.000 161	0.000 154	0.000 147	0.000 140	0.000 134	276
24	0.000 137	0.000 131	0.000 125	0.000 119	0.000 114	0.000 108	288
25	0.000 112	0.000 107	0.000 102	0.000 097	0.000 092	0.000 087	300
26	0.000 092	0.000 087	0.000 083	0.000 078	0.000 074	0.000 071	312
27	0.000 075	0.000 071	0.000 067	0.000 064	0.000 060	0.000 057	324
28	0.000 061	0.000 058	0.000 055	0.000 052	0.000 049	0.000 046	336
29	0.000 050	0.000 047	0.000 044	0.000 042	0.000 039	0.000 037	348
30	0.000 041	0.000 038	0.000 036	0.000 034	0.000 032	0.000 030	360

MOS	21.75% ANNUAL RATE	22.00% ANNUAL RATE	22.50% ANNUAL RATE	23.00% ANNUAL RATE	23.50% ANNUAL RATE	24.00% ANNUAL RATE	MOS
1	1.000 000	1.000 000	1.000 000	1.000 000	1.000 000	1.000 000	1
2	0.495 509	0.495 458	0.495 356	0.495 254	0.495 152	0.495 050	2
3	0.327 364	0.327 296	0.327 161	0.327 025	0.326 890	0.326 755	3
4	0.243 305	0.243 229	0.243 078	0.242 926	0.242 775	0.242 624	4
5	0.192 880	0.192 800	0.192 639	0.192 479	0.192 319	0.192 158	5
6	0.159 273	0.159 190	0.159 023	0.158 857	0.158 692	0.158 526	6
7	0.135 275	0.135 190	0.135 020	0.134 851	0.134 681	0.134 512	7
8	0.117 284	0.117 198	0.117 025	0.116 853	0.116 681	0.116 510	8
9	0.103 297	0.103 210	0.103 036	0.102 862	0.102 689	0.102 515	9
10	0.092 112	0.092 025	0.091 850	0.091 675	0.091 501	0.091 327	10
11	0.082 966	0.082 878	0.082 703	0.082 528	0.082 353	0.082 178	11
12	0.075 349	0.075 261	0.075 085	0.074 910	0.074 734	0.074 560	12
13	0.068 908	0.068 820	0.068 644	0.068 468	0.068 293	0.068 118	13
14	0.063 391	0.063 303	0.063 127	0.062 952	0.062 777	0.062 602	14
15	0.058 613	0.058 525	0.058 350	0.058 174	0.058 000	0.057 825	15
16	0.054 436	0.054 348	0.054 173	0.053 998	0.053 824	0.053 650	16
17	0.050 753	0.050 666	0.050 491	0.050 317	0.050 143	0.049 970	17
18	0.047 483	0.047 395	0.047 221	0.047 048	0.046 875	0.046 702	18
19	0.044 559	0.044 472	0.044 299	0.044 126	0.043 954	0.043 782	19
20	0.041 931	0.041 844	0.041 671	0.041 499	0.041 328	0.041 157	20
21	0.039 555	0.039 469	0.039 297	0.039 126	0.038 955	0.038 785	21
22	0.037 398	0.037 312	0.037 141	0.036 971	0.036 801	0.036 631	22
23	0.035 431	0.035 345	0.035 175	0.035 006	0.034 836	0.034 668	23
24	0.033 630	0.033 545	0.033 375	0.033 207	0.033 039	0.032 871	24
25	0.031 975	0.031 890	0.031 722	0.031 554	0.031 387	0.031 220	25
26	0.030 449	0.030 365	0.030 198	0.030 031	0.029 865	0.029 699	26
27	0.029 039	0.028 955	0.028 789	0.028 623	0.028 458	0.028 293	27
28	0.027 731	0.027 648	0.027 482	0.027 317	0.027 153	0.026 990	28
29	0.026 515	0.026 432	0.026 268	0.026 104	0.025 941	0.025 778	29
30	0.025 382	0.025 300	0.025 136	0.024 973	0.024 811	0.024 650	30
31	0.024 324	0.024 242	0.024 079	0.023 918	0.023 757	0.023 596	31
32	0.023 333	0.023 252	0.023 090	0.022 930	0.022 770	0.022 611	32
33	0.022 404	0.022 324	0.022 163	0.022 003	0.021 845	0.021 687	33
34	0.021 532	0.021 452	0.021 292	0.021 133	0.020 976	0.020 819	34
35	0.020 710	0.020 631	0.020 472	0.020 315	0.020 158	0.020 002	35
36	0.019 936	0.019 857	0.019 700	0.019 543	0.019 387	0.019 233	36
37	0.019 205	0.019 127	0.018 970	0.018 815	0.018 660	0.018 507	37
38	0.018 514	0.018 436	0.018 281	0.018 126	0.017 973	0.017 821	38
39	0.017 860	0.017 782	0.017 628	0.017 475	0.017 322	0.017 171	39
40	0.017 239	0.017 162	0.017 009	0.016 857	0.016 706	0.016 556	40
41	0.016 651	0.016 574	0.016 422	0.016 271	0.016 121	0.015 972	41
42	0.016 091	0.016 015	0.015 864	0.015 714	0.015 565	0.015 417	42
43	0.015 559	0.015 483	0.015 333	0.015 184	0.015 037	0.014 890	43
44	0.015 052	0.014 977	0.014 828	0.014 680	0.014 533	0.014 388	44
45	0.014 568	0.014 494	0.014 346	0.014 199	0.014 054	0.013 910	45
46	0.014 107	0.014 033	0.013 887	0.013 741	0.013 597	0.013 453	46
47	0.013 667	0.013 593	0.013 448	0.013 303	0.013 160	0.013 018	47

YRS							
4	0.013 246	0.013 173	0.013 028	0.012 885	0.012 743	0.012 602	48
5	0.009 352	0.009 286	0.009 154	0.009 024	0.008 895	0.008 768	60
6	0.006 853	0.006 793	0.006 673	0.006 556	0.006 441	0.006 327	72
7	0.005 147	0.005 093	0.004 986	0.004 881	0.004 777	0.004 676	84
8	0.003 932	0.003 884	0.003 788	0.003 695	0.003 603	0.003 513	96
9	0.003 042	0.002 999	0.002 914	0.002 831	0.002 750	0.002 671	108
10	0.002 375	0.002 336	0.002 261	0.002 188	0.002 117	0.002 048	120
11	0.001 867	0.001 833	0.001 767	0.001 703	0.001 641	0.001 581	132
12	0.001 475	0.001 446	0.001 388	0.001 332	0.001 278	0.001 226	144
13	0.001 171	0.001 145	0.001 094	0.001 046	0.000 999	0.000 954	156
14	0.000 932	0.000 909	0.000 865	0.000 823	0.000 783	0.000 745	168
15	0.000 744	0.000 724	0.000 686	0.000 650	0.000 616	0.000 583	180
16	0.000 595	0.000 578	0.000 545	0.000 514	0.000 485	0.000 457	192
17	0.000 477	0.000 462	0.000 434	0.000 407	0.000 382	0.000 358	204
18	0.000 382	0.000 370	0.000 345	0.000 323	0.000 301	0.000 281	216
19	0.000 307	0.000 296	0.000 275	0.000 256	0.000 238	0.000 221	228
20	0.000 247	0.000 237	0.000 220	0.000 203	0.000 188	0.000 174	240
21	0.000 198	0.000 190	0.000 175	0.000 162	0.000 149	0.000 137	252
22	0.000 159	0.000 153	0.000 140	0.000 128	0.000 118	0.000 108	264
23	0.000 128	0.000 123	0.000 112	0.000 102	0.000 093	0.000 085	276
24	0.000 103	0.000 098	0.000 089	0.000 081	0.000 074	0.000 067	288
25	0.000 083	0.000 079	0.000 072	0.000 065	0.000 058	0.000 053	300
26	0.000 067	0.000 064	0.000 057	0.000 051	0.000 046	0.000 042	312
27	0.000 054	0.000 051	0.000 046	0.000 041	0.000 037	0.000 033	324
28	0.000 043	0.000 041	0.000 037	0.000 033	0.000 029	0.000 026	336
29	0.000 035	0.000 033	0.000 029	0.000 026	0.000 023	0.000 020	348
30	0.000 028	0.000 027	0.000 023	0.000 021	0.000 018	0.000 016	360

SINKING FUND

QUARTERLY COMPOUNDING

	5.25% ANNUAL RATE	5.50% ANNUAL RATE	5.75% ANNUAL RATE	6.00% ANNUAL RATE	6.25% ANNUAL RATE	6.50% ANNUAL RATE	
QTRS							QTRS
1	1.000 000	1.000 000	1.000 000	1.000 000	1.000 000	1.000 000	1
2	0.496 740	0.496 586	0.496 432	0.496 278	0.496 124	0.495 970	2
3	0.328 996	0.328 792	0.328 587	0.328 383	0.328 179	0.327 975	3
4	0.245 132	0.244 902	0.244 673	0.244 445	0.244 216	0.243 988	4
5	0.194 818	0.194 575	0.194 332	0.194 089	0.193 847	0.193 605	5
6	0.161 281	0.161 029	0.160 777	0.160 525	0.160 274	0.160 023	6
7	0.137 330	0.137 072	0.136 814	0.136 556	0.136 299	0.136 043	7
8	0.119 370	0.119 108	0.118 846	0.118 584	0.118 323	0.118 062	8
9	0.105 405	0.105 139	0.104 874	0.104 610	0.104 346	0.104 083	9
10	0.094 235	0.093 967	0.093 700	0.093 434	0.093 169	0.092 904	10
11	0.085 099	0.084 830	0.084 561	0.084 294	0.084 027	0.083 761	11
12	0.077 488	0.077 218	0.076 948	0.076 680	0.076 412	0.076 145	12
13	0.071 050	0.070 779	0.070 509	0.070 240	0.069 972	0.069 705	13
14	0.065 533	0.065 262	0.064 992	0.064 723	0.064 455	0.064 188	14
15	0.060 755	0.060 484	0.060 213	0.059 944	0.059 676	0.059 409	15
16	0.056 575	0.056 304	0.056 034	0.055 765	0.055 497	0.055 230	16
17	0.052 888	0.052 618	0.052 348	0.052 080	0.051 812	0.051 546	17
18	0.049 613	0.049 343	0.049 074	0.048 806	0.048 539	0.048 273	18
19	0.046 684	0.046 415	0.046 146	0.045 878	0.045 612	0.045 347	19
20	0.044 050	0.043 781	0.043 513	0.043 246	0.042 980	0.042 716	20
21	0.041 667	0.041 399	0.041 132	0.040 865	0.040 601	0.040 337	21
22	0.039 503	0.039 235	0.038 969	0.038 703	0.038 440	0.038 177	22
23	0.037 528	0.037 261	0.036 995	0.036 731	0.036 468	0.036 206	23
24	0.035 719	0.035 452	0.035 187	0.034 924	0.034 662	0.034 402	24
25	0.034 055	0.033 790	0.033 526	0.033 263	0.033 003	0.032 743	25
26	0.032 521	0.032 256	0.031 993	0.031 732	0.031 472	0.031 214	26
27	0.031 101	0.030 838	0.030 576	0.030 315	0.030 057	0.029 800	27
28	0.029 784	0.029 521	0.029 260	0.029 001	0.028 744	0.028 488	28
29	0.028 559	0.028 297	0.028 037	0.027 779	0.027 522	0.027 268	29
30	0.027 416	0.027 155	0.026 896	0.026 639	0.026 384	0.026 131	30
31	0.026 348	0.026 088	0.025 830	0.025 574	0.025 320	0.025 068	31
32	0.025 347	0.025 089	0.024 832	0.024 577	0.024 324	0.024 074	32
33	0.024 408	0.024 151	0.023 895	0.023 641	0.023 390	0.023 141	33
34	0.023 525	0.023 269	0.023 014	0.022 762	0.022 512	0.022 264	34
35	0.022 693	0.022 438	0.022 185	0.021 934	0.021 685	0.021 438	35
36	0.021 909	0.021 654	0.021 402	0.021 152	0.020 905	0.020 659	36
37	0.021 167	0.020 914	0.020 663	0.020 414	0.020 168	0.019 924	37
38	0.020 465	0.020 213	0.019 964	0.019 716	0.019 471	0.019 228	38
39	0.019 800	0.019 549	0.019 301	0.019 055	0.018 811	0.018 570	39
40	0.019 169	0.018 919	0.018 672	0.018 427	0.018 185	0.017 945	40
41	0.018 569	0.018 321	0.018 075	0.017 831	0.017 590	0.017 351	41
42	0.017 999	0.017 751	0.017 507	0.017 264	0.017 025	0.016 787	42
43	0.017 456	0.017 209	0.016 966	0.016 725	0.016 486	0.016 250	43
44	0.016 938	0.016 693	0.016 450	0.016 210	0.015 973	0.015 739	44
45	0.016 443	0.016 199	0.015 958	0.015 720	0.015 484	0.015 251	45
46	0.015 971	0.015 728	0.015 488	0.015 251	0.015 017	0.014 785	46
47	0.015 520	0.015 278	0.015 039	0.014 803	0.014 570	0.014 340	47
48	0.015 087	0.014 847	0.014 610	0.014 375	0.014 143	0.013 915	48
49	0.014 673	0.014 434	0.014 198	0.013 965	0.013 735	0.013 507	49
50	0.014 277	0.014 039	0.013 804	0.013 572	0.013 343	0.013 117	50
51	0.013 896	0.013 659	0.013 425	0.013 195	0.012 967	0.012 743	51
52	0.013 530	0.013 295	0.013 062	0.012 833	0.012 607	0.012 384	52
53	0.013 179	0.012 945	0.012 713	0.012 485	0.012 261	0.012 039	53
54	0.012 841	0.012 608	0.012 378	0.012 151	0.011 928	0.011 708	54
55	0.012 516	0.012 284	0.012 056	0.011 830	0.011 608	0.011 389	55
YRS							
14	0.012 203	0.011 972	0.011 745	0.011 521	0.011 300	0.011 083	56
15	0.011 060	0.010 835	0.010 612	0.010 393	0.010 178	0.009 966	60
16	0.010 067	0.009 846	0.009 629	0.009 415	0.009 206	0.008 999	64
17	0.009 197	0.008 981	0.008 769	0.008 560	0.008 356	0.008 155	68
18	0.008 429	0.008 218	0.008 011	0.007 808	0.007 609	0.007 414	72
19	0.007 748	0.007 542	0.007 339	0.007 141	0.006 948	0.006 758	76
20	0.007 140	0.006 938	0.006 741	0.006 548	0.006 360	0.006 176	80
21	0.006 595	0.006 398	0.006 206	0.006 018	0.005 835	0.005 656	84
22	0.006 104	0.005 912	0.005 724	0.005 541	0.005 363	0.005 190	88
23	0.005 660	0.005 472	0.005 290	0.005 112	0.004 939	0.004 771	92
24	0.005 257	0.005 074	0.004 896	0.004 723	0.004 555	0.004 392	96
25	0.004 890	0.004 712	0.004 539	0.004 371	0.004 208	0.004 050	100
26	0.004 556	0.004 382	0.004 213	0.004 050	0.003 892	0.003 739	104
27	0.004 249	0.004 079	0.003 915	0.003 757	0.003 604	0.003 456	108
28	0.003 968	0.003 803	0.003 643	0.003 489	0.003 341	0.003 197	112
29	0.003 709	0.003 548	0.003 393	0.003 244	0.003 100	0.002 961	116
30	0.003 471	0.003 314	0.003 164	0.003 019	0.002 879	0.002 745	120

	6.75% ANNUAL RATE	7.00% ANNUAL RATE	7.25% ANNUAL RATE	7.50% ANNUAL RATE	7.75% ANNUAL RATE	8.00% ANNUAL RATE	
QTRS							QTRS
1	1.000 000	1.000 000	1.000 000	1.000 000	1.000 000	1.000 000	1
2	0.495 817	0.495 663	0.495 509	0.495 356	0.495 203	0.495 050	2
3	0.327 771	0.327 567	0.327 364	0.327 161	0.326 958	0.326 755	3
4	0.243 760	0.243 532	0.243 305	0.243 078	0.242 851	0.242 624	4
5	0.193 363	0.193 121	0.192 880	0.192 639	0.192 399	0.192 158	5
6	0.159 773	0.159 523	0.159 273	0.159 023	0.158 774	0.158 526	6
7	0.135 786	0.135 531	0.135 275	0.135 020	0.134 766	0.134 512	7
8	0.117 802	0.117 543	0.117 284	0.117 025	0.116 767	0.116 510	8
9	0.103 820	0.103 558	0.103 297	0.103 036	0.102 775	0.102 515	9
10	0.092 639	0.092 375	0.092 112	0.091 850	0.091 588	0.091 327	10
11	0.083 495	0.083 230	0.082 966	0.082 703	0.082 440	0.082 178	11
12	0.075 879	0.075 614	0.075 349	0.075 085	0.074 822	0.074 560	12
13	0.069 438	0.069 173	0.068 908	0.068 644	0.068 381	0.068 118	13
14	0.063 921	0.063 656	0.063 391	0.063 127	0.062 864	0.062 602	14
15	0.059 143	0.058 877	0.058 613	0.058 350	0.058 087	0.057 825	15
16	0.054 964	0.054 700	0.054 436	0.054 173	0.053 911	0.053 650	16
17	0.051 280	0.051 016	0.050 753	0.050 491	0.050 230	0.049 970	17
18	0.048 008	0.047 745	0.047 483	0.047 221	0.046 961	0.046 702	18
19	0.045 083	0.044 821	0.044 559	0.044 299	0.044 040	0.043 782	19
20	0.042 453	0.042 191	0.041 931	0.041 671	0.041 413	0.041 157	20
21	0.040 075	0.039 815	0.039 555	0.039 297	0.039 040	0.038 785	21
22	0.037 916	0.037 656	0.037 398	0.037 141	0.036 886	0.036 631	22
23	0.035 947	0.035 688	0.035 431	0.035 175	0.034 921	0.034 668	23
24	0.034 143	0.033 886	0.033 630	0.033 375	0.033 123	0.032 871	24
25	0.032 486	0.032 230	0.031 975	0.031 722	0.031 470	0.031 220	25
26	0.030 958	0.030 703	0.030 449	0.030 198	0.029 948	0.029 699	26
27	0.029 544	0.029 291	0.029 039	0.028 789	0.028 540	0.028 293	27
28	0.028 234	0.027 982	0.027 731	0.027 482	0.027 235	0.026 990	28
29	0.027 015	0.026 764	0.026 515	0.026 268	0.026 022	0.025 778	29
30	0.025 879	0.025 630	0.025 382	0.025 136	0.024 892	0.024 650	30
31	0.024 818	0.024 570	0.024 324	0.024 079	0.023 837	0.023 596	31
32	0.023 825	0.023 578	0.023 333	0.023 090	0.022 850	0.022 611	32
33	0.022 893	0.022 648	0.022 404	0.022 163	0.021 924	0.021 687	33
34	0.022 018	0.021 774	0.021 532	0.021 292	0.021 054	0.020 819	34
35	0.021 193	0.020 951	0.020 710	0.020 472	0.020 236	0.020 002	35
36	0.020 416	0.020 175	0.019 936	0.019 700	0.019 465	0.019 233	36
37	0.019 682	0.019 443	0.019 205	0.018 970	0.018 737	0.018 507	37
38	0.018 988	0.018 750	0.018 514	0.018 281	0.018 049	0.017 821	38
39	0.018 331	0.018 094	0.017 860	0.017 628	0.017 398	0.017 171	39
40	0.017 707	0.017 472	0.017 239	0.017 009	0.016 781	0.016 556	40
41	0.017 115	0.016 882	0.016 651	0.016 422	0.016 196	0.015 972	41
42	0.016 553	0.016 321	0.016 091	0.015 864	0.015 639	0.015 417	42
43	0.016 017	0.015 787	0.015 559	0.015 333	0.015 110	0.014 890	43
44	0.015 507	0.015 278	0.015 052	0.014 828	0.014 607	0.014 388	44
45	0.015 021	0.014 793	0.014 568	0.014 346	0.014 127	0.013 910	45
46	0.014 556	0.014 330	0.014 107	0.013 887	0.013 669	0.013 453	46
47	0.014 113	0.013 888	0.013 667	0.013 448	0.013 231	0.013 018	47
48	0.013 689	0.013 466	0.013 246	0.013 028	0.012 814	0.012 602	48
49	0.013 283	0.013 061	0.012 843	0.012 627	0.012 414	0.012 204	49
50	0.012 894	0.012 674	0.012 457	0.012 243	0.012 032	0.011 823	50
51	0.012 521	0.012 303	0.012 087	0.011 875	0.011 665	0.011 459	51
52	0.012 164	0.011 947	0.011 733	0.011 522	0.011 314	0.011 109	52
53	0.011 820	0.011 605	0.011 393	0.011 183	0.010 977	0.010 774	53
54	0.011 491	0.011 277	0.011 066	0.010 858	0.010 654	0.010 452	54
55	0.011 174	0.010 961	0.010 752	0.010 546	0.010 343	0.010 143	55
YRS							
14	0.010 869	0.010 658	0.010 450	0.010 246	0.010 045	0.009 847	56
15	0.009 758	0.009 553	0.009 352	0.009 154	0.008 959	0.008 768	60
16	0.008 797	0.008 598	0.008 403	0.008 211	0.008 023	0.007 839	64
17	0.007 959	0.007 766	0.007 577	0.007 391	0.007 210	0.007 032	68
18	0.007 223	0.007 036	0.006 853	0.006 674	0.006 498	0.006 327	72
19	0.006 573	0.006 392	0.006 215	0.006 042	0.005 873	0.005 708	76
20	0.005 996	0.005 821	0.005 650	0.005 483	0.005 320	0.005 161	80
21	0.005 482	0.005 312	0.005 147	0.004 986	0.004 829	0.004 676	84
22	0.005 021	0.004 857	0.004 697	0.004 542	0.004 391	0.004 244	88
23	0.004 608	0.004 449	0.004 295	0.004 145	0.004 000	0.003 859	92
24	0.004 234	0.004 081	0.003 932	0.003 788	0.003 648	0.003 513	96
25	0.003 897	0.003 749	0.003 605	0.003 467	0.003 333	0.003 203	100
26	0.003 591	0.003 448	0.003 310	0.003 176	0.003 048	0.002 923	104
27	0.003 313	0.003 175	0.003 042	0.002 914	0.002 790	0.002 671	108
28	0.003 059	0.002 926	0.002 798	0.002 675	0.002 557	0.002 443	112
29	0.002 828	0.002 700	0.002 577	0.002 458	0.002 345	0.002 236	116
30	0.002 617	0.002 493	0.002 375	0.002 261	0.002 152	0.002 048	120

QTRS	8.25% ANNUAL RATE	8.50% ANNUAL RATE	8.75% ANNUAL RATE	9.00% ANNUAL RATE	9.25% ANNUAL RATE	9.50% ANNUAL RATE	QTRS
1	1.000 000	1.000 000	1.000 000	1.000 000	1.000 000	1.000 000	1
2	0.494 896	0.494 743	0.494 590	0.494 438	0.494 285	0.494 132	2
3	0.326 552	0.326 349	0.326 147	0.325 945	0.325 742	0.325 541	3
4	0.242 397	0.242 171	0.241 945	0.241 719	0.241 493	0.241 268	4
5	0.191 918	0.191 679	0.191 439	0.191 200	0.190 961	0.190 723	5
6	0.158 278	0.158 030	0.157 782	0.157 535	0.157 288	0.157 042	6
7	0.134 258	0.134 005	0.133 753	0.133 500	0.133 248	0.132 997	7
8	0.116 253	0.115 996	0.115 740	0.115 485	0.115 230	0.114 975	8
9	0.102 256	0.101 997	0.101 739	0.101 482	0.101 225	0.100 968	9
10	0.091 066	0.090 806	0.090 546	0.090 288	0.090 030	0.089 772	10
11	0.081 917	0.081 656	0.081 396	0.081 136	0.080 878	0.080 620	11
12	0.074 298	0.074 037	0.073 777	0.073 517	0.073 259	0.073 001	12
13	0.067 857	0.067 596	0.067 336	0.067 077	0.066 819	0.066 561	13
14	0.062 341	0.062 080	0.061 821	0.061 562	0.061 305	0.061 048	14
15	0.057 565	0.057 305	0.057 046	0.056 789	0.056 532	0.056 276	15
16	0.053 390	0.053 131	0.052 874	0.052 617	0.052 361	0.052 106	16
17	0.049 711	0.049 453	0.049 196	0.048 940	0.048 686	0.048 432	17
18	0.046 444	0.046 187	0.045 932	0.045 677	0.045 424	0.045 171	18
19	0.043 525	0.043 269	0.043 015	0.042 762	0.042 510	0.042 259	19
20	0.040 901	0.040 647	0.040 394	0.040 142	0.039 891	0.039 642	20
21	0.038 531	0.038 278	0.038 026	0.037 776	0.037 527	0.037 279	21
22	0.036 379	0.036 127	0.035 877	0.035 628	0.035 381	0.035 135	22
23	0.034 417	0.034 167	0.033 918	0.033 671	0.033 425	0.033 181	23
24	0.032 621	0.032 373	0.032 126	0.031 880	0.031 636	0.031 394	24
25	0.030 972	0.030 725	0.030 480	0.030 236	0.029 994	0.029 753	25
26	0.029 452	0.029 207	0.028 963	0.028 721	0.028 481	0.028 242	26
27	0.028 048	0.027 804	0.027 562	0.027 322	0.027 083	0.026 846	27
28	0.026 746	0.026 504	0.026 264	0.026 025	0.025 788	0.025 553	28
29	0.025 536	0.025 296	0.025 058	0.024 821	0.024 586	0.024 353	29
30	0.024 410	0.024 171	0.023 934	0.023 699	0.023 466	0.023 235	30
31	0.023 358	0.023 121	0.022 886	0.022 653	0.022 422	0.022 192	31
32	0.022 374	0.022 139	0.021 905	0.021 674	0.021 445	0.021 217	32
33	0.021 451	0.021 218	0.020 987	0.020 757	0.020 530	0.020 304	33
34	0.020 585	0.020 354	0.020 124	0.019 897	0.019 671	0.019 448	34
35	0.019 770	0.019 541	0.019 313	0.019 087	0.018 864	0.018 642	35
36	0.019 003	0.018 775	0.018 549	0.018 325	0.018 104	0.017 884	36
37	0.018 278	0.018 052	0.017 828	0.017 606	0.017 387	0.017 169	37
38	0.017 594	0.017 370	0.017 147	0.016 928	0.016 710	0.016 494	38
39	0.016 946	0.016 724	0.016 503	0.016 285	0.016 070	0.015 856	39
40	0.016 333	0.016 112	0.015 893	0.015 677	0.015 464	0.015 252	40
41	0.015 751	0.015 532	0.015 315	0.015 101	0.014 889	0.014 680	41
42	0.015 198	0.014 981	0.014 766	0.014 554	0.014 344	0.014 136	42
43	0.014 672	0.014 457	0.014 244	0.014 034	0.013 826	0.013 620	43
44	0.014 172	0.013 958	0.013 747	0.013 539	0.013 333	0.013 130	44
45	0.013 695	0.013 484	0.013 275	0.013 068	0.012 864	0.012 663	45
46	0.013 241	0.013 031	0.012 824	0.012 619	0.012 417	0.012 218	46
47	0.012 807	0.012 599	0.012 394	0.012 191	0.011 991	0.011 794	47
48	0.012 393	0.012 187	0.011 983	0.011 782	0.011 584	0.011 389	48
49	0.011 997	0.011 792	0.011 591	0.011 392	0.011 196	0.011 002	49
50	0.011 618	0.011 415	0.011 215	0.011 018	0.010 824	0.010 633	50
51	0.011 255	0.011 054	0.010 856	0.010 661	0.010 469	0.010 279	51
52	0.010 907	0.010 708	0.010 512	0.010 319	0.010 129	0.009 941	52
53	0.010 574	0.010 377	0.010 182	0.009 991	0.009 803	0.009 617	53
54	0.010 254	0.010 058	0.009 866	0.009 677	0.009 490	0.009 306	54
55	0.009 947	0.009 753	0.009 562	0.009 375	0.009 190	0.009 009	55

YRS							
14	0.009 652	0.009 460	0.009 271	0.009 085	0.008 903	0.008 723	56
15	0.008 580	0.008 395	0.008 214	0.008 035	0.007 860	0.007 688	60
16	0.007 657	0.007 480	0.007 305	0.007 134	0.006 966	0.006 802	64
17	0.006 857	0.006 686	0.006 519	0.006 355	0.006 194	0.006 037	68
18	0.006 159	0.005 995	0.005 834	0.005 677	0.005 524	0.005 374	72
19	0.005 546	0.005 389	0.005 235	0.005 085	0.004 938	0.004 795	76
20	0.005 006	0.004 855	0.004 707	0.004 564	0.004 424	0.004 288	80
21	0.004 527	0.004 382	0.004 241	0.004 104	0.003 971	0.003 841	84
22	0.004 101	0.003 963	0.003 828	0.003 697	0.003 570	0.003 447	88
23	0.003 722	0.003 589	0.003 460	0.003 336	0.003 215	0.003 098	92
24	0.003 382	0.003 255	0.003 132	0.003 014	0.002 899	0.002 788	96
25	0.003 077	0.002 956	0.002 839	0.002 726	0.002 617	0.002 511	100
26	0.002 803	0.002 687	0.002 576	0.002 468	0.002 365	0.002 265	104
27	0.002 556	0.002 446	0.002 339	0.002 237	0.002 139	0.002 044	108
28	0.002 333	0.002 228	0.002 127	0.002 030	0.001 936	0.001 847	112
29	0.002 131	0.002 031	0.001 935	0.001 843	0.001 754	0.001 670	116
30	0.001 948	0.001 853	0.001 761	0.001 674	0.001 590	0.001 511	120

SINKING FUND

QTRS	9.75% ANNUAL RATE	10.00% ANNUAL RATE	10.25% ANNUAL RATE	10.50% ANNUAL RATE	10.75% ANNUAL RATE	11.00% ANNUAL RATE	QTRS
1	1.000 000	1.000 000	1.000 000	1.000 000	1.000 000	1.000 000	1
2	0.493 980	0.493 827	0.493 675	0.493 523	0.493 370	0.493 218	2
3	0.325 339	0.325 137	0.324 936	0.324 734	0.324 533	0.324 332	3
4	0.241 043	0.240 818	0.240 593	0.240 369	0.240 145	0.239 921	4
5	0.190 485	0.190 247	0.190 009	0.189 772	0.189 535	0.189 298	5
6	0.156 796	0.156 550	0.156 305	0.156 060	0.155 815	0.155 571	6
7	0.132 746	0.132 495	0.132 245	0.131 996	0.131 746	0.131 497	7
8	0.114 721	0.114 467	0.114 214	0.113 962	0.113 710	0.113 458	8
9	0.100 712	0.100 457	0.100 202	0.099 948	0.099 694	0.099 441	9
10	0.089 515	0.089 259	0.089 003	0.088 748	0.088 494	0.088 240	10
11	0.080 363	0.080 106	0.079 850	0.079 595	0.079 340	0.079 086	11
12	0.072 744	0.072 487	0.072 231	0.071 976	0.071 722	0.071 469	12
13	0.066 304	0.066 048	0.065 793	0.065 539	0.065 285	0.065 033	13
14	0.060 792	0.060 537	0.060 282	0.060 029	0.059 776	0.059 525	14
15	0.056 021	0.055 766	0.055 513	0.055 261	0.055 010	0.054 759	15
16	0.051 852	0.051 599	0.051 347	0.051 096	0.050 846	0.050 597	16
17	0.048 179	0.047 928	0.047 677	0.047 428	0.047 179	0.046 932	17
18	0.044 920	0.044 670	0.044 421	0.044 173	0.043 926	0.043 681	18
19	0.042 009	0.041 761	0.041 513	0.041 267	0.041 022	0.040 778	19
20	0.039 394	0.039 147	0.038 901	0.038 657	0.038 414	0.038 172	20
21	0.037 032	0.036 787	0.036 543	0.036 301	0.036 059	0.035 819	21
22	0.034 890	0.034 647	0.034 405	0.034 164	0.033 924	0.033 686	22
23	0.032 938	0.032 696	0.032 456	0.032 217	0.031 980	0.031 744	23
24	0.031 152	0.030 913	0.030 675	0.030 438	0.030 203	0.029 969	24
25	0.029 514	0.029 276	0.029 040	0.028 805	0.028 572	0.028 340	25
26	0.028 005	0.027 769	0.027 535	0.027 302	0.027 071	0.026 841	26
27	0.026 611	0.026 377	0.026 145	0.025 914	0.025 685	0.025 458	27
28	0.025 320	0.025 088	0.024 858	0.024 629	0.024 403	0.024 177	28
29	0.024 121	0.023 891	0.023 663	0.023 437	0.023 212	0.022 989	29
30	0.023 005	0.022 778	0.022 552	0.022 327	0.022 105	0.021 884	30
31	0.021 965	0.021 739	0.021 515	0.021 293	0.021 073	0.020 855	31
32	0.020 992	0.020 768	0.020 547	0.020 327	0.020 109	0.019 893	32
33	0.020 081	0.019 859	0.019 640	0.019 422	0.019 206	0.018 993	33
34	0.019 226	0.019 007	0.018 789	0.018 574	0.018 360	0.018 149	34
35	0.018 423	0.018 206	0.017 990	0.017 777	0.017 566	0.017 356	35
36	0.017 667	0.017 452	0.017 238	0.017 027	0.016 818	0.016 611	36
37	0.016 954	0.016 741	0.016 530	0.016 321	0.016 114	0.015 910	37
38	0.016 281	0.016 070	0.015 861	0.015 655	0.015 450	0.015 248	38
39	0.015 645	0.015 436	0.015 229	0.015 025	0.014 823	0.014 623	39
40	0.015 043	0.014 836	0.014 632	0.014 429	0.014 229	0.014 032	40
41	0.014 473	0.014 268	0.014 065	0.013 865	0.013 668	0.013 472	41
42	0.013 931	0.013 729	0.013 528	0.013 331	0.013 135	0.012 942	42
43	0.013 417	0.013 217	0.013 019	0.012 823	0.012 630	0.012 439	43
44	0.012 929	0.012 730	0.012 534	0.012 341	0.012 150	0.011 961	44
45	0.012 464	0.012 268	0.012 074	0.011 882	0.011 693	0.011 507	45
46	0.012 021	0.011 827	0.011 635	0.011 446	0.011 259	0.011 075	46
47	0.011 599	0.011 407	0.011 217	0.011 030	0.010 846	0.010 664	47
48	0.011 196	0.011 006	0.010 819	0.010 634	0.010 451	0.010 272	48
49	0.010 812	0.010 623	0.010 438	0.010 255	0.010 075	0.009 898	49
50	0.010 444	0.010 258	0.010 075	0.009 894	0.009 716	0.009 541	50
51	0.010 093	0.009 909	0.009 728	0.009 549	0.009 373	0.009 200	51
52	0.009 756	0.009 574	0.009 395	0.009 219	0.009 045	0.008 874	52
53	0.009 434	0.009 254	0.009 077	0.008 903	0.008 732	0.008 563	53
54	0.009 126	0.008 948	0.008 773	0.008 601	0.008 432	0.008 265	54
55	0.008 830	0.008 654	0.008 481	0.008 311	0.008 144	0.007 980	55

YRS

YRS							QTRS
14	0.008 546	0.008 372	0.008 202	0.008 034	0.007 868	0.007 706	56
15	0.007 519	0.007 353	0.007 191	0.007 031	0.006 874	0.006 720	60
16	0.006 641	0.006 482	0.006 328	0.006 176	0.006 027	0.005 881	64
17	0.005 884	0.005 733	0.005 586	0.005 442	0.005 301	0.005 163	68
18	0.005 227	0.005 084	0.004 944	0.004 808	0.004 674	0.004 544	72
19	0.004 656	0.004 520	0.004 387	0.004 258	0.004 132	0.004 009	76
20	0.004 155	0.004 026	0.003 900	0.003 778	0.003 659	0.003 543	80
21	0.003 715	0.003 593	0.003 474	0.003 359	0.003 246	0.003 137	84
22	0.003 328	0.003 212	0.003 099	0.002 990	0.002 885	0.002 782	88
23	0.002 985	0.002 875	0.002 769	0.002 666	0.002 567	0.002 470	92
24	0.002 680	0.002 577	0.002 476	0.002 380	0.002 286	0.002 196	96
25	0.002 410	0.002 312	0.002 217	0.002 126	0.002 039	0.001 954	100
26	0.002 169	0.002 076	0.001 987	0.001 902	0.001 820	0.001 741	104
27	0.001 954	0.001 867	0.001 783	0.001 702	0.001 625	0.001 551	108
28	0.001 761	0.001 679	0.001 600	0.001 525	0.001 453	0.001 384	112
29	0.001 589	0.001 512	0.001 438	0.001 367	0.001 300	0.001 235	116
30	0.001 435	0.001 362	0.001 292	0.001 226	0.001 163	0.001 103	120

SINKING FUND

	11.25%	11.50%	11.75%	12.00%	12.25%	12.50%	
	ANNUAL RATE	ANNUAL RATE	ANNUAL RATE	ANNUAL RATE	ANNUAL RATE	ANNUAL RATE	
QTRS							QTRS
1	1.000 000	1.000 000	1.000 000	1.000 000	1.000 000	1.000 000	1
2	0.493 066	0.492 914	0.492 763	0.492 611	0.492 459	0.492 308	2
3	0.324 132	0.323 931	0.323 731	0.323 530	0.323 330	0.323 130	3
4	0.239 697	0.239 473	0.239 250	0.239 027	0.238 804	0.238 582	4
5	0.189 062	0.188 826	0.188 590	0.188 355	0.188 119	0.187 884	5
6	0.155 327	0.155 083	0.154 840	0.154 598	0.154 355	0.154 113	6
7	0.131 249	0.131 001	0.130 753	0.130 506	0.130 260	0.130 013	7
8	0.113 207	0.112 956	0.112 706	0.112 456	0.112 207	0.111 959	8
9	0.099 188	0.098 936	0.098 685	0.098 434	0.098 183	0.097 934	9
10	0.087 986	0.087 734	0.087 482	0.087 231	0.086 980	0.086 730	10
11	0.078 833	0.078 581	0.078 329	0.078 077	0.077 827	0.077 577	11
12	0.071 216	0.070 964	0.070 713	0.070 462	0.070 212	0.069 963	12
13	0.064 781	0.064 529	0.064 279	0.064 030	0.063 781	0.063 533	13
14	0.059 274	0.059 024	0.058 775	0.058 526	0.058 279	0.058 032	14
15	0.054 510	0.054 261	0.054 013	0.053 767	0.053 521	0.053 276	15
16	0.050 349	0.050 102	0.049 856	0.049 611	0.049 367	0.049 124	16
17	0.046 685	0.046 440	0.046 196	0.045 953	0.045 710	0.045 469	17
18	0.043 436	0.043 192	0.042 950	0.042 709	0.042 468	0.042 229	18
19	0.040 535	0.040 294	0.040 053	0.039 814	0.039 576	0.039 339	19
20	0.037 931	0.037 691	0.037 453	0.037 216	0.036 980	0.036 745	20
21	0.035 581	0.035 343	0.035 107	0.034 872	0.034 638	0.034 406	21
22	0.033 450	0.033 214	0.032 980	0.032 747	0.032 516	0.032 286	22
23	0.031 509	0.031 276	0.031 044	0.030 814	0.030 585	0.030 357	23
24	0.029 736	0.029 505	0.029 276	0.029 047	0.028 821	0.028 595	24
25	0.028 110	0.027 881	0.027 654	0.027 428	0.027 204	0.026 981	25
26	0.026 613	0.026 387	0.026 162	0.025 938	0.025 716	0.025 496	26
27	0.025 232	0.025 008	0.024 785	0.024 564	0.024 345	0.024 127	27
28	0.023 954	0.023 732	0.023 512	0.023 293	0.023 076	0.022 861	28
29	0.022 768	0.022 549	0.022 331	0.022 115	0.021 900	0.021 687	29
30	0.021 666	0.021 448	0.021 233	0.021 019	0.020 807	0.020 597	30
31	0.020 638	0.020 423	0.020 210	0.019 999	0.019 789	0.019 582	31
32	0.019 678	0.019 466	0.019 255	0.019 047	0.018 840	0.018 635	32
33	0.018 781	0.018 571	0.018 362	0.018 156	0.017 952	0.017 749	33
34	0.017 939	0.017 731	0.017 526	0.017 322	0.017 120	0.016 920	34
35	0.017 149	0.016 944	0.016 741	0.016 539	0.016 340	0.016 143	35
36	0.016 406	0.016 204	0.016 003	0.015 804	0.015 607	0.015 412	36
37	0.015 707	0.015 506	0.015 308	0.015 112	0.014 917	0.014 725	37
38	0.015 047	0.014 849	0.014 653	0.014 459	0.014 268	0.014 078	38
39	0.014 425	0.014 229	0.014 035	0.013 844	0.013 655	0.013 467	39
40	0.013 836	0.013 643	0.013 451	0.013 262	0.013 076	0.012 891	40
41	0.013 279	0.013 088	0.012 899	0.012 712	0.012 528	0.012 346	41
42	0.012 751	0.012 562	0.012 376	0.012 192	0.012 010	0.011 830	42
43	0.012 250	0.012 064	0.011 880	0.011 698	0.011 519	0.011 342	43
44	0.011 775	0.011 591	0.011 409	0.011 230	0.011 053	0.010 878	44
45	0.011 323	0.011 141	0.010 962	0.010 785	0.010 611	0.010 438	45
46	0.010 893	0.010 714	0.010 537	0.010 363	0.010 190	0.010 021	46
47	0.010 484	0.010 307	0.010 133	0.009 961	0.009 791	0.009 624	47
48	0.010 094	0.009 920	0.009 747	0.009 578	0.009 411	0.009 246	48
49	0.009 723	0.009 550	0.009 381	0.009 213	0.009 048	0.008 886	49
50	0.009 368	0.009 198	0.009 031	0.008 865	0.008 703	0.008 543	50
51	0.009 030	0.008 862	0.008 697	0.008 534	0.008 374	0.008 216	51
52	0.008 706	0.008 541	0.008 378	0.008 217	0.008 059	0.007 904	52
53	0.008 397	0.008 234	0.008 073	0.007 915	0.007 759	0.007 606	53
54	0.008 101	0.007 940	0.007 781	0.007 626	0.007 472	0.007 322	54
55	0.007 818	0.007 659	0.007 503	0.007 349	0.007 198	0.007 050	55
YRS							
14	0.007 547	0.007 390	0.007 236	0.007 084	0.006 936	0.006 790	56
15	0.006 569	0.006 421	0.006 276	0.006 133	0.005 993	0.005 856	60
16	0.005 738	0.005 599	0.005 462	0.005 328	0.005 196	0.005 068	64
17	0.005 028	0.004 896	0.004 767	0.004 642	0.004 519	0.004 398	68
18	0.004 417	0.004 293	0.004 172	0.004 054	0.003 939	0.003 827	72
19	0.003 889	0.003 773	0.003 659	0.003 548	0.003 441	0.003 336	76
20	0.003 431	0.003 321	0.003 215	0.003 112	0.003 011	0.002 914	80
21	0.003 032	0.002 929	0.002 830	0.002 733	0.002 640	0.002 549	84
22	0.002 683	0.002 587	0.002 494	0.002 404	0.002 317	0.002 232	88
23	0.002 377	0.002 288	0.002 201	0.002 117	0.002 036	0.001 958	92
24	0.002 109	0.002 025	0.001 944	0.001 866	0.001 791	0.001 719	96
25	0.001 873	0.001 795	0.001 719	0.001 647	0.001 577	0.001 510	100
26	0.001 665	0.001 592	0.001 521	0.001 454	0.001 390	0.001 328	104
27	0.001 481	0.001 413	0.001 347	0.001 285	0.001 225	0.001 168	108
28	0.001 318	0.001 255	0.001 194	0.001 136	0.001 081	0.001 028	112
29	0.001 174	0.001 115	0.001 059	0.001 005	0.000 954	0.000 906	116
30	0.001 046	0.000 991	0.000 939	0.000 890	0.000 843	0.000 798	120

SINKING FUND

QTRS	12.75% ANNUAL RATE	13.00% ANNUAL RATE	13.25% ANNUAL RATE	13.50% ANNUAL RATE	13.75% ANNUAL RATE	14.00% ANNUAL RATE	QTRS
1	1.000 000	1.000 000	1.000 000	1.000 000	1.000 000	1.000 000	1
2	0.492 156	0.492 005	0.491 854	0.491 703	0.491 551	0.491 400	2
3	0.322 931	0.322 731	0.322 532	0.322 332	0.322 133	0.321 934	3
4	0.238 359	0.238 137	0.237 915	0.237 694	0.237 472	0.237 251	4
5	0.187 650	0.187 416	0.187 182	0.186 948	0.186 714	0.186 481	5
6	0.153 871	0.153 630	0.153 389	0.153 148	0.152 908	0.152 668	6
7	0.129 767	0.129 522	0.129 277	0.129 032	0.128 788	0.128 544	7
8	0.111 710	0.111 463	0.111 215	0.110 969	0.110 722	0.110 477	8
9	0.097 684	0.097 436	0.097 187	0.096 940	0.096 693	0.096 446	9
10	0.086 480	0.086 231	0.085 983	0.085 735	0.085 488	0.085 241	10
11	0.077 328	0.077 079	0.076 832	0.076 584	0.076 338	0.076 092	11
12	0.069 715	0.069 467	0.069 220	0.068 974	0.068 729	0.068 484	12
13	0.063 286	0.063 039	0.062 794	0.062 549	0.062 305	0.062 062	13
14	0.057 787	0.057 542	0.057 298	0.057 055	0.056 812	0.056 571	14
15	0.053 032	0.052 789	0.052 546	0.052 305	0.052 065	0.051 825	15
16	0.048 881	0.048 640	0.048 400	0.048 161	0.047 922	0.047 685	16
17	0.045 229	0.044 990	0.044 752	0.044 514	0.044 278	0.044 043	17
18	0.041 991	0.041 754	0.041 518	0.041 283	0.041 050	0.040 817	18
19	0.039 103	0.038 868	0.038 634	0.038 402	0.038 171	0.037 940	19
20	0.036 511	0.036 279	0.036 048	0.035 818	0.035 589	0.035 361	20
21	0.034 174	0.033 944	0.033 715	0.033 488	0.033 262	0.033 037	21
22	0.032 057	0.031 829	0.031 603	0.031 378	0.031 154	0.030 932	22
23	0.030 131	0.029 906	0.029 682	0.029 459	0.029 238	0.029 019	23
24	0.028 371	0.028 149	0.027 928	0.027 708	0.027 490	0.027 273	24
25	0.026 759	0.026 539	0.026 321	0.026 104	0.025 888	0.025 674	25
26	0.025 277	0.025 060	0.024 844	0.024 630	0.024 417	0.024 205	26
27	0.023 911	0.023 696	0.023 483	0.023 271	0.023 061	0.022 852	27
28	0.022 647	0.022 435	0.022 225	0.022 016	0.021 808	0.021 603	28
29	0.021 476	0.021 267	0.021 059	0.020 853	0.020 648	0.020 445	29
30	0.020 389	0.020 182	0.019 977	0.019 773	0.019 571	0.019 371	30
31	0.019 376	0.019 172	0.018 969	0.018 769	0.018 570	0.018 372	31
32	0.018 431	0.018 230	0.018 030	0.017 832	0.017 636	0.017 442	32
33	0.017 548	0.017 350	0.017 153	0.016 957	0.016 764	0.016 572	33
34	0.016 722	0.016 526	0.016 331	0.016 139	0.015 948	0.015 760	34
35	0.015 947	0.015 753	0.015 562	0.015 372	0.015 184	0.014 998	35
36	0.015 219	0.015 028	0.014 839	0.014 652	0.014 467	0.014 284	36
37	0.014 535	0.014 346	0.014 160	0.013 976	0.013 794	0.013 613	37
38	0.013 890	0.013 704	0.013 521	0.013 339	0.013 160	0.012 982	38
39	0.013 282	0.013 099	0.012 918	0.012 739	0.012 563	0.012 388	39
40	0.012 708	0.012 528	0.012 350	0.012 173	0.011 999	0.011 827	40
41	0.012 166	0.011 988	0.011 812	0.011 639	0.011 468	0.011 298	41
42	0.011 653	0.011 478	0.011 304	0.011 134	0.010 965	0.010 798	42
43	0.011 167	0.010 994	0.010 824	0.010 655	0.010 489	0.010 325	43
44	0.010 706	0.010 536	0.010 368	0.010 202	0.010 039	0.009 878	44
45	0.010 269	0.010 101	0.009 936	0.009 773	0.009 612	0.009 453	45
46	0.009 853	0.009 688	0.009 526	0.009 365	0.009 207	0.009 051	46
47	0.009 459	0.009 296	0.009 136	0.008 978	0.008 823	0.008 669	47
48	0.009 083	0.008 923	0.008 766	0.008 610	0.008 457	0.008 306	48
49	0.008 726	0.008 568	0.008 413	0.008 260	0.008 110	0.007 962	49
50	0.008 385	0.008 230	0.008 078	0.007 927	0.007 779	0.007 634	50
51	0.008 061	0.007 908	0.007 758	0.007 610	0.007 465	0.007 322	51
52	0.007 751	0.007 601	0.007 453	0.007 308	0.007 165	0.007 024	52
53	0.007 456	0.007 308	0.007 163	0.007 020	0.006 879	0.006 741	53
54	0.007 174	0.007 028	0.006 885	0.006 745	0.006 607	0.006 471	54
55	0.006 904	0.006 761	0.006 620	0.006 482	0.006 346	0.006 213	55

YRS							
14	0.006 646	0.006 506	0.006 367	0.006 231	0.006 098	0.005 967	56
15	0.005 722	0.005 590	0.005 461	0.005 334	0.005 210	0.005 089	60
16	0.004 942	0.004 819	0.004 699	0.004 581	0.004 466	0.004 353	64
17	0.004 281	0.004 166	0.004 054	0.003 945	0.003 838	0.003 734	68
18	0.003 717	0.003 610	0.003 506	0.003 405	0.003 306	0.003 210	72
19	0.003 234	0.003 135	0.003 038	0.002 945	0.002 853	0.002 765	76
20	0.002 819	0.002 727	0.002 638	0.002 551	0.002 467	0.002 385	80
21	0.002 461	0.002 376	0.002 293	0.002 213	0.002 135	0.002 060	84
22	0.002 151	0.002 072	0.001 996	0.001 922	0.001 851	0.001 782	88
23	0.001 882	0.001 809	0.001 739	0.001 671	0.001 606	0.001 543	92
24	0.001 649	0.001 582	0.001 517	0.001 454	0.001 395	0.001 337	96
25	0.001 445	0.001 384	0.001 324	0.001 267	0.001 212	0.001 159	100
26	0.001 268	0.001 211	0.001 157	0.001 104	0.001 054	0.001 006	104
27	0.001 113	0.001 061	0.001 011	0.000 963	0.000 917	0.000 873	108
28	0.000 978	0.000 930	0.000 884	0.000 840	0.000 799	0.000 759	112
29	0.000 860	0.000 815	0.000 773	0.000 734	0.000 695	0.000 659	116
30	0.000 756	0.000 715	0.000 677	0.000 641	0.000 606	0.000 573	120

SINKING FUND

QTRS	14.25% ANNUAL RATE	14.50% ANNUAL RATE	14.75% ANNUAL RATE	15.00% ANNUAL RATE	15.25% ANNUAL RATE	15.50% ANNUAL RATE	QTRS
1	1.000 000	1.000 000	1.000 000	1.000 000	1.000 000	1.000 000	1
2	0.491 250	0.491 099	0.490 948	0.490 798	0.490 647	0.490 497	2
3	0.321 735	0.321 537	0.321 338	0.321 140	0.320 942	0.320 744	3
4	0.237 030	0.236 809	0.236 589	0.236 369	0.236 149	0.235 929	4
5	0.186 249	0.186 016	0.185 784	0.185 552	0.185 320	0.185 089	5
6	0.152 429	0.152 189	0.151 951	0.151 712	0.151 474	0.151 236	6
7	0.128 301	0.128 058	0.127 816	0.127 574	0.127 332	0.127 091	7
8	0.110 231	0.109 987	0.109 742	0.109 498	0.109 255	0.109 012	8
9	0.096 200	0.095 954	0.095 710	0.095 465	0.095 221	0.094 978	9
10	0.084 995	0.084 750	0.084 505	0.084 261	0.084 018	0.083 775	10
11	0.075 847	0.075 602	0.075 358	0.075 115	0.074 873	0.074 631	11
12	0.068 240	0.067 997	0.067 754	0.067 512	0.067 271	0.067 031	12
13	0.061 819	0.061 577	0.061 337	0.061 096	0.060 857	0.060 619	13
14	0.056 330	0.056 090	0.055 851	0.055 613	0.055 376	0.055 139	14
15	0.051 586	0.051 349	0.051 112	0.050 876	0.050 641	0.050 407	15
16	0.047 448	0.047 213	0.046 978	0.046 745	0.046 512	0.046 281	16
17	0.043 809	0.043 576	0.043 344	0.043 113	0.042 883	0.042 654	17
18	0.040 585	0.040 355	0.040 125	0.039 897	0.039 669	0.039 443	18
19	0.037 711	0.037 483	0.037 256	0.037 031	0.036 806	0.036 582	19
20	0.035 135	0.034 909	0.034 685	0.034 462	0.034 240	0.034 020	20
21	0.032 813	0.032 590	0.032 369	0.032 149	0.031 930	0.031 712	21
22	0.030 711	0.030 491	0.030 273	0.030 055	0.029 839	0.029 625	22
23	0.028 800	0.028 583	0.028 368	0.028 153	0.027 940	0.027 729	23
24	0.027 057	0.026 843	0.026 630	0.026 419	0.026 209	0.026 000	24
25	0.025 461	0.025 250	0.025 040	0.024 832	0.024 625	0.024 419	25
26	0.023 996	0.023 787	0.023 580	0.023 375	0.023 171	0.022 968	26
27	0.022 645	0.022 440	0.022 236	0.022 033	0.021 832	0.021 633	27
28	0.021 398	0.021 196	0.020 995	0.020 795	0.020 597	0.020 401	28
29	0.020 244	0.020 044	0.019 846	0.019 650	0.019 455	0.019 262	29
30	0.019 173	0.018 976	0.018 781	0.018 588	0.018 396	0.018 206	30
31	0.018 177	0.017 983	0.017 791	0.017 600	0.017 412	0.017 225	31
32	0.017 249	0.017 058	0.016 869	0.016 681	0.016 496	0.016 312	32
33	0.016 383	0.016 195	0.016 008	0.015 824	0.015 641	0.015 460	33
34	0.015 573	0.015 388	0.015 204	0.015 023	0.014 843	0.014 665	34
35	0.014 814	0.014 632	0.014 452	0.014 273	0.014 097	0.013 922	35
36	0.014 103	0.013 924	0.013 746	0.013 571	0.013 397	0.013 225	36
37	0.013 435	0.013 258	0.013 084	0.012 911	0.012 740	0.012 572	37
38	0.012 807	0.012 633	0.012 461	0.012 292	0.012 124	0.011 958	38
39	0.012 215	0.012 044	0.011 875	0.011 709	0.011 544	0.011 381	39
40	0.011 657	0.011 489	0.011 323	0.011 159	0.010 998	0.010 838	40
41	0.011 131	0.010 966	0.010 803	0.010 642	0.010 483	0.010 326	41
42	0.010 634	0.010 471	0.010 311	0.010 153	0.009 997	0.009 843	42
43	0.010 164	0.010 004	0.009 846	0.009 691	0.009 538	0.009 386	43
44	0.009 719	0.009 562	0.009 407	0.009 254	0.009 104	0.008 955	44
45	0.009 297	0.009 143	0.008 991	0.008 841	0.008 693	0.008 548	45
46	0.008 897	0.008 746	0.008 597	0.008 449	0.008 304	0.008 162	46
47	0.008 518	0.008 369	0.008 223	0.008 078	0.007 936	0.007 796	47
48	0.008 158	0.008 012	0.007 868	0.007 726	0.007 587	0.007 449	48
49	0.007 816	0.007 672	0.007 531	0.007 392	0.007 255	0.007 120	49
50	0.007 490	0.007 349	0.007 211	0.007 074	0.006 940	0.006 808	50
51	0.007 181	0.007 042	0.006 906	0.006 772	0.006 641	0.006 511	51
52	0.006 886	0.006 750	0.006 617	0.006 485	0.006 356	0.006 229	52
53	0.006 605	0.006 472	0.006 341	0.006 212	0.006 085	0.005 961	53
54	0.006 338	0.006 207	0.006 078	0.005 952	0.005 828	0.005 706	54
55	0.006 082	0.005 954	0.005 828	0.005 704	0.005 582	0.005 463	55

YRS							
14	0.005 839	0.005 713	0.005 589	0.005 468	0.005 349	0.005 232	56
15	0.004 970	0.004 853	0.004 739	0.004 627	0.004 517	0.004 410	60
16	0.004 243	0.004 135	0.004 030	0.003 927	0.003 826	0.003 728	64
17	0.003 632	0.003 533	0.003 436	0.003 341	0.003 249	0.003 159	68
18	0.003 116	0.003 025	0.002 936	0.002 849	0.002 765	0.002 683	72
19	0.002 678	0.002 594	0.002 513	0.002 434	0.002 357	0.002 282	76
20	0.002 306	0.002 229	0.002 154	0.002 082	0.002 012	0.001 944	80
21	0.001 988	0.001 917	0.001 849	0.001 783	0.001 719	0.001 658	84
22	0.001 715	0.001 651	0.001 589	0.001 529	0.001 471	0.001 415	88
23	0.001 482	0.001 423	0.001 367	0.001 312	0.001 260	0.001 209	92
24	0.001 281	0.001 228	0.001 177	0.001 127	0.001 080	0.001 034	96
25	0.001 109	0.001 060	0.001 014	0.000 969	0.000 926	0.000 885	100
26	0.000 960	0.000 916	0.000 874	0.000 833	0.000 795	0.000 758	104
27	0.000 832	0.000 792	0.000 753	0.000 717	0.000 682	0.000 649	108
28	0.000 721	0.000 685	0.000 650	0.000 617	0.000 586	0.000 556	112
29	0.000 625	0.000 592	0.000 561	0.000 532	0.000 503	0.000 477	116
30	0.000 542	0.000 512	0.000 484	0.000 458	0.000 433	0.000 409	120

SINKING FUND

QTRS	15.75% ANNUAL RATE	16.00% ANNUAL RATE	16.50% ANNUAL RATE	17.00% ANNUAL RATE	17.50% ANNUAL RATE	18.00% ANNUAL RATE	QTRS
1	1.000 000	1.000 000	1.000 000	1.000 000	1.000 000	1.000 000	1
2	0.490 346	0.490 196	0.489 896	0.489 596	0.489 297	0.488 998	2
3	0.320 546	0.320 349	0.319 954	0.319 560	0.319 166	0.318 773	3
4	0.235 709	0.235 490	0.235 052	0.234 615	0.234 179	0.233 744	4
5	0.184 858	0.184 627	0.184 166	0.183 707	0.183 249	0.182 792	5
6	0.150 999	0.150 762	0.150 289	0.149 817	0.149 347	0.148 878	6
7	0.126 850	0.126 610	0.126 130	0.125 652	0.125 176	0.124 701	7
8	0.108 770	0.108 528	0.108 045	0.107 565	0.107 086	0.106 610	8
9	0.094 735	0.094 493	0.094 010	0.093 529	0.093 051	0.092 574	9
10	0.083 533	0.083 291	0.082 809	0.082 330	0.081 853	0.081 379	10
11	0.074 390	0.074 149	0.073 670	0.073 193	0.072 719	0.072 248	11
12	0.066 791	0.066 552	0.066 076	0.065 603	0.065 133	0.064 666	12
13	0.060 381	0.060 144	0.059 672	0.059 203	0.058 738	0.058 275	13
14	0.054 904	0.054 669	0.054 202	0.053 738	0.053 278	0.052 820	14
15	0.050 173	0.049 941	0.049 479	0.049 020	0.048 565	0.048 114	15
16	0.046 050	0.045 820	0.045 363	0.044 910	0.044 461	0.044 015	16
17	0.042 426	0.042 199	0.041 747	0.041 300	0.040 857	0.040 418	17
18	0.039 218	0.038 993	0.038 548	0.038 107	0.037 670	0.037 237	18
19	0.036 360	0.036 139	0.035 699	0.035 264	0.034 834	0.034 407	19
20	0.033 800	0.033 582	0.033 149	0.032 720	0.032 296	0.031 876	20
21	0.031 495	0.031 280	0.030 853	0.030 431	0.030 013	0.029 601	21
22	0.029 411	0.029 199	0.028 778	0.028 362	0.027 952	0.027 546	22
23	0.027 518	0.027 309	0.026 895	0.026 486	0.026 081	0.025 682	23
24	0.025 793	0.025 587	0.025 179	0.024 776	0.024 379	0.023 987	24
25	0.024 215	0.024 012	0.023 610	0.023 215	0.022 824	0.022 439	25
26	0.022 767	0.022 567	0.022 172	0.021 783	0.021 399	0.021 021	26
27	0.021 435	0.021 239	0.020 850	0.020 467	0.020 091	0.019 719	27
28	0.020 206	0.020 013	0.019 631	0.019 255	0.018 885	0.018 521	28
29	0.019 070	0.018 880	0.018 504	0.018 135	0.017 772	0.017 415	29
30	0.018 017	0.017 830	0.017 461	0.017 098	0.016 742	0.016 392	30
31	0.017 039	0.016 855	0.016 493	0.016 137	0.015 787	0.015 443	31
32	0.016 129	0.015 949	0.015 592	0.015 243	0.014 900	0.014 563	32
33	0.015 281	0.015 104	0.014 754	0.014 411	0.014 074	0.013 745	33
34	0.014 489	0.014 315	0.013 971	0.013 635	0.013 305	0.012 982	34
35	0.013 749	0.013 577	0.013 240	0.012 910	0.012 587	0.012 270	35
36	0.013 055	0.012 887	0.012 556	0.012 232	0.011 916	0.011 606	36
37	0.012 405	0.012 240	0.011 915	0.011 597	0.011 287	0.010 984	37
38	0.011 794	0.011 632	0.011 313	0.011 002	0.010 698	0.010 402	38
39	0.011 220	0.011 061	0.010 748	0.010 444	0.010 146	0.009 856	39
40	0.010 680	0.010 523	0.010 217	0.009 918	0.009 627	0.009 343	40
41	0.010 170	0.010 017	0.009 717	0.009 424	0.009 139	0.008 862	41
42	0.009 690	0.009 540	0.009 246	0.008 959	0.008 680	0.008 409	42
43	0.009 237	0.009 090	0.008 801	0.008 521	0.008 248	0.007 982	43
44	0.008 809	0.008 665	0.008 382	0.008 107	0.007 840	0.007 581	44
45	0.008 404	0.008 262	0.007 986	0.007 717	0.007 455	0.007 202	45
46	0.008 021	0.007 882	0.007 611	0.007 348	0.007 092	0.006 845	46
47	0.007 658	0.007 522	0.007 256	0.006 999	0.006 749	0.006 507	47
48	0.007 314	0.007 181	0.006 921	0.006 669	0.006 425	0.006 189	48
49	0.006 988	0.006 857	0.006 603	0.006 356	0.006 118	0.005 887	49
50	0.006 678	0.006 550	0.006 301	0.006 060	0.005 827	0.005 602	50
51	0.006 384	0.006 259	0.006 015	0.005 779	0.005 552	0.005 332	51
52	0.006 105	0.005 982	0.005 744	0.005 513	0.005 291	0.005 077	52
53	0.005 839	0.005 719	0.005 486	0.005 261	0.005 044	0.004 835	53
54	0.005 586	0.005 469	0.005 241	0.005 021	0.004 809	0.004 605	54
55	0.005 346	0.005 231	0.005 008	0.004 793	0.004 586	0.004 388	55

YRS	15.75% ANNUAL RATE	16.00% ANNUAL RATE	16.50% ANNUAL RATE	17.00% ANNUAL RATE	17.50% ANNUAL RATE	18.00% ANNUAL RATE	QTRS
14	0.005 117	0.005 005	0.004 787	0.004 577	0.004 375	0.004 181	56
15	0.004 305	0.004 202	0.004 003	0.003 812	0.003 629	0.003 454	60
16	0.003 632	0.003 538	0.003 356	0.003 183	0.003 018	0.002 861	64
17	0.003 071	0.002 986	0.002 821	0.002 665	0.002 516	0.002 375	68
18	0.002 603	0.002 525	0.002 376	0.002 234	0.002 101	0.001 975	72
19	0.002 209	0.002 139	0.002 004	0.001 877	0.001 757	0.001 644	76
20	0.001 878	0.001 814	0.001 692	0.001 578	0.001 471	0.001 371	80
21	0.001 598	0.001 541	0.001 431	0.001 329	0.001 233	0.001 144	84
22	0.001 362	0.001 310	0.001 211	0.001 119	0.001 034	0.000 955	88
23	0.001 161	0.001 114	0.001 026	0.000 944	0.000 868	0.000 798	92
24	0.000 991	0.000 949	0.000 869	0.000 796	0.000 729	0.000 667	96
25	0.000 846	0.000 808	0.000 737	0.000 672	0.000 613	0.000 558	100
26	0.000 722	0.000 689	0.000 626	0.000 568	0.000 515	0.000 467	104
27	0.000 617	0.000 587	0.000 531	0.000 480	0.000 433	0.000 391	108
28	0.000 528	0.000 501	0.000 451	0.000 406	0.000 365	0.000 328	112
29	0.000 451	0.000 427	0.000 383	0.000 343	0.000 307	0.000 274	116
30	0.000 386	0.000 365	0.000 325	0.000 290	0.000 258	0.000 230	120

QTRS	18.50% ANNUAL RATE	19.00% ANNUAL RATE	19.50% ANNUAL RATE	20.00% ANNUAL RATE	20.50% ANNUAL RATE	21.00% ANNUAL RATE	QTRS
1	1.000 000	1.000 000	1.000 000	1.000 000	1.000 000	1.000 000	1
2	0.488 699	0.488 400	0.488 103	0.487 805	0.487 508	0.487 211	2
3	0.318 381	0.317 990	0.317 599	0.317 209	0.316 819	0.316 430	3
4	0.233 309	0.232 876	0.232 443	0.232 012	0.231 581	0.231 151	4
5	0.182 336	0.181 881	0.181 427	0.180 975	0.180 523	0.180 073	5
6	0.148 411	0.147 945	0.147 481	0.147 017	0.146 556	0.146 095	6
7	0.124 229	0.123 757	0.123 288	0.122 820	0.122 354	0.121 889	7
8	0.106 135	0.105 662	0.105 191	0.104 722	0.104 255	0.103 789	8
9	0.092 100	0.091 628	0.091 158	0.090 690	0.090 224	0.089 761	9
10	0.080 907	0.080 437	0.079 970	0.079 505	0.079 042	0.078 582	10
11	0.071 779	0.071 313	0.070 850	0.070 389	0.069 931	0.069 475	11
12	0.064 202	0.063 740	0.063 281	0.062 825	0.062 372	0.061 922	12
13	0.057 816	0.057 360	0.056 906	0.056 456	0.056 008	0.055 564	13
14	0.052 366	0.051 916	0.051 468	0.051 024	0.050 583	0.050 145	14
15	0.047 666	0.047 221	0.046 780	0.046 342	0.045 908	0.045 477	15
16	0.043 573	0.043 135	0.042 701	0.042 270	0.041 843	0.041 419	16
17	0.039 982	0.039 551	0.039 123	0.038 699	0.038 279	0.037 863	17
18	0.036 808	0.036 383	0.035 963	0.035 546	0.035 134	0.034 725	18
19	0.033 985	0.033 568	0.033 154	0.032 745	0.032 340	0.031 939	19
20	0.031 461	0.031 050	0.030 644	0.030 243	0.029 845	0.029 452	20
21	0.029 192	0.028 789	0.028 390	0.027 996	0.027 606	0.027 221	21
22	0.027 145	0.026 748	0.026 357	0.025 971	0.025 589	0.025 212	22
23	0.025 289	0.024 900	0.024 516	0.024 137	0.023 763	0.023 394	23
24	0.023 600	0.023 219	0.022 842	0.022 471	0.022 105	0.021 743	24
25	0.022 059	0.021 685	0.021 316	0.020 952	0.020 594	0.020 241	25
26	0.020 649	0.020 282	0.019 920	0.019 564	0.019 214	0.018 868	26
27	0.019 354	0.018 994	0.018 640	0.018 292	0.017 949	0.017 611	27
28	0.018 163	0.017 810	0.017 463	0.017 123	0.016 787	0.016 457	28
29	0.017 063	0.016 718	0.016 379	0.016 046	0.015 718	0.015 396	29
30	0.016 047	0.015 709	0.015 377	0.015 051	0.014 731	0.014 417	30
31	0.015 106	0.014 776	0.014 451	0.014 132	0.013 819	0.013 513	31
32	0.014 233	0.013 909	0.013 592	0.013 280	0.012 975	0.012 676	32
33	0.013 421	0.013 105	0.012 794	0.012 490	0.012 192	0.011 900	33
34	0.012 666	0.012 356	0.012 052	0.011 755	0.011 465	0.011 180	34
35	0.011 961	0.011 658	0.011 362	0.011 072	0.010 788	0.010 511	35
36	0.011 303	0.011 007	0.010 717	0.010 434	0.010 158	0.009 888	36
37	0.010 688	0.010 398	0.010 116	0.009 840	0.009 570	0.009 307	37
38	0.010 112	0.009 829	0.009 553	0.009 284	0.009 022	0.008 765	38
39	0.009 573	0.009 296	0.009 027	0.008 765	0.008 509	0.008 259	39
40	0.009 066	0.008 797	0.008 534	0.008 278	0.008 029	0.007 786	40
41	0.008 591	0.008 328	0.008 072	0.007 822	0.007 580	0.007 344	41
42	0.008 145	0.007 888	0.007 638	0.007 395	0.007 159	0.006 929	42
43	0.007 724	0.007 474	0.007 230	0.006 993	0.006 763	0.006 540	43
44	0.007 329	0.007 084	0.006 847	0.006 616	0.006 393	0.006 176	44
45	0.006 956	0.006 718	0.006 486	0.006 262	0.006 044	0.005 833	45
46	0.006 605	0.006 372	0.006 147	0.005 928	0.005 717	0.005 512	46
47	0.006 273	0.006 046	0.005 827	0.005 614	0.005 409	0.005 210	47
48	0.005 960	0.005 739	0.005 525	0.005 318	0.005 119	0.004 925	48
49	0.005 664	0.005 449	0.005 241	0.005 040	0.004 845	0.004 658	49
50	0.005 385	0.005 175	0.004 972	0.004 777	0.004 588	0.004 406	50
51	0.005 120	0.004 916	0.004 719	0.004 529	0.004 345	0.004 169	51
52	0.004 870	0.004 671	0.004 479	0.004 294	0.004 117	0.003 945	52
53	0.004 633	0.004 440	0.004 253	0.004 073	0.003 901	0.003 734	53
54	0.004 409	0.004 220	0.004 039	0.003 864	0.003 697	0.003 536	54
55	0.004 196	0.004 013	0.003 836	0.003 667	0.003 504	0.003 348	55
YRS							
14	0.003 995	0.003 816	0.003 645	0.003 480	0.003 322	0.003 171	56
15	0.003 287	0.003 127	0.002 974	0.002 828	0.002 689	0.002 555	60
16	0.002 711	0.002 569	0.002 433	0.002 304	0.002 181	0.002 064	64
17	0.002 241	0.002 114	0.001 994	0.001 880	0.001 772	0.001 670	68
18	0.001 855	0.001 743	0.001 637	0.001 536	0.001 442	0.001 353	72
19	0.001 538	0.001 439	0.001 345	0.001 257	0.001 175	0.001 097	76
20	0.001 277	0.001 189	0.001 107	0.001 030	0.000 958	0.000 891	80
21	0.001 061	0.000 983	0.000 911	0.000 844	0.000 782	0.000 724	84
22	0.000 882	0.000 814	0.000 751	0.000 692	0.000 638	0.000 588	88
23	0.000 734	0.000 674	0.000 619	0.000 568	0.000 521	0.000 478	92
24	0.000 611	0.000 558	0.000 510	0.000 466	0.000 426	0.000 389	96
25	0.000 509	0.000 463	0.000 421	0.000 383	0.000 348	0.000 317	100
26	0.000 424	0.000 384	0.000 348	0.000 315	0.000 285	0.000 258	104
27	0.000 353	0.000 318	0.000 287	0.000 259	0.000 233	0.000 210	108
28	0.000 294	0.000 264	0.000 237	0.000 213	0.000 191	0.000 171	112
29	0.000 245	0.000 219	0.000 196	0.000 175	0.000 156	0.000 139	116
30	0.000 205	0.000 182	0.000 162	0.000 144	0.000 128	0.000 113	120

SINKING FUND

QTRS	21.50% ANNUAL RATE	22.00% ANNUAL RATE	22.50% ANNUAL RATE	23.00% ANNUAL RATE	23.50% ANNUAL RATE	24.00% ANNUAL RATE	QTRS
1	1.000 000	1.000 000	1.000 000	1.000 000	1.000 000	1.000 000	1
2	0.486 914	0.486 618	0.486 322	0.486 027	0.485 732	0.485 437	2
3	0.316 042	0.315 654	0.315 267	0.314 881	0.314 495	0.314 110	3
4	0.230 722	0.230 294	0.229 867	0.229 441	0.229 016	0.228 591	4
5	0.179 624	0.179 176	0.178 730	0.178 284	0.177 840	0.177 396	5
6	0.145 636	0.145 179	0.144 723	0.144 268	0.143 815	0.143 363	6
7	0.121 426	0.120 964	0.120 505	0.120 046	0.119 590	0.119 135	7
8	0.103 326	0.102 864	0.102 404	0.101 946	0.101 490	0.101 036	8
9	0.089 299	0.088 839	0.088 382	0.087 927	0.087 473	0.087 022	9
10	0.078 123	0.077 668	0.077 214	0.076 763	0.076 314	0.075 868	10
11	0.069 021	0.068 571	0.068 122	0.067 677	0.067 234	0.066 793	11
12	0.061 474	0.061 029	0.060 587	0.060 148	0.059 711	0.059 277	12
13	0.055 123	0.054 684	0.054 249	0.053 816	0.053 387	0.052 960	13
14	0.049 711	0.049 279	0.048 851	0.048 426	0.048 004	0.047 585	14
15	0.045 050	0.044 626	0.044 205	0.043 788	0.043 373	0.042 963	15
16	0.040 999	0.040 583	0.040 170	0.039 760	0.039 354	0.038 952	16
17	0.037 451	0.037 042	0.036 637	0.036 236	0.035 839	0.035 445	17
18	0.034 321	0.033 920	0.033 523	0.033 130	0.032 742	0.032 357	18
19	0.031 543	0.031 150	0.030 762	0.030 377	0.029 997	0.029 621	19
20	0.029 064	0.028 679	0.028 299	0.027 923	0.027 552	0.027 185	20
21	0.026 841	0.026 465	0.026 093	0.025 726	0.025 363	0.025 005	21
22	0.024 839	0.024 471	0.024 108	0.023 749	0.023 395	0.023 046	22
23	0.023 029	0.022 670	0.022 315	0.021 965	0.021 619	0.021 278	23
24	0.021 387	0.021 036	0.020 689	0.020 348	0.020 011	0.019 679	24
25	0.019 892	0.019 549	0.019 211	0.018 878	0.018 550	0.018 227	25
26	0.018 528	0.018 193	0.017 863	0.017 539	0.017 219	0.016 904	26
27	0.017 279	0.016 952	0.016 631	0.016 314	0.016 003	0.015 697	27
28	0.016 133	0.015 814	0.015 501	0.015 193	0.014 890	0.014 593	28
29	0.015 079	0.014 769	0.014 463	0.014 163	0.013 869	0.013 580	29
30	0.014 108	0.013 805	0.013 508	0.013 216	0.012 930	0.012 649	30
31	0.013 212	0.012 917	0.012 627	0.012 343	0.012 065	0.011 792	31
32	0.012 383	0.012 095	0.011 814	0.011 538	0.011 267	0.011 002	32
33	0.011 615	0.011 335	0.011 061	0.010 792	0.010 530	0.010 273	33
34	0.010 902	0.010 630	0.010 363	0.010 103	0.009 848	0.009 598	34
35	0.010 240	0.009 975	0.009 716	0.009 463	0.009 215	0.008 974	35
36	0.009 624	0.009 366	0.009 115	0.008 869	0.008 629	0.008 395	36
37	0.009 050	0.008 800	0.008 555	0.008 317	0.008 084	0.007 857	37
38	0.008 516	0.008 272	0.008 035	0.007 803	0.007 578	0.007 358	38
39	0.008 017	0.007 780	0.007 549	0.007 325	0.007 106	0.006 894	39
40	0.007 550	0.007 320	0.007 097	0.006 879	0.006 667	0.006 462	40
41	0.007 114	0.006 891	0.006 674	0.006 463	0.006 258	0.006 059	41
42	0.006 706	0.006 489	0.006 279	0.006 074	0.005 876	0.005 683	42
43	0.006 324	0.006 113	0.005 909	0.005 711	0.005 519	0.005 333	43
44	0.005 965	0.005 761	0.005 563	0.005 372	0.005 186	0.005 006	44
45	0.005 629	0.005 431	0.005 240	0.005 054	0.004 874	0.004 700	45
46	0.005 314	0.005 122	0.004 936	0.004 756	0.004 583	0.004 415	46
47	0.005 017	0.004 831	0.004 651	0.004 478	0.004 310	0.004 148	47
48	0.004 739	0.004 559	0.004 384	0.004 216	0.004 054	0.003 898	48
49	0.004 477	0.004 302	0.004 134	0.003 971	0.003 815	0.003 664	49
50	0.004 231	0.004 061	0.003 898	0.003 741	0.003 590	0.003 444	50
51	0.003 999	0.003 835	0.003 677	0.003 525	0.003 379	0.003 239	51
52	0.003 780	0.003 622	0.003 469	0.003 323	0.003 182	0.003 046	52
53	0.003 575	0.003 421	0.003 274	0.003 132	0.002 996	0.002 866	53
54	0.003 381	0.003 232	0.003 090	0.002 953	0.002 822	0.002 696	54
55	0.003 198	0.003 055	0.002 917	0.002 785	0.002 658	0.002 537	55

YRS							QTRS
14	0.003 026	0.002 887	0.002 754	0.002 626	0.002 504	0.002 388	56
15	0.002 428	0.002 307	0.002 191	0.002 081	0.001 976	0.001 876	60
16	0.001 953	0.001 847	0.001 747	0.001 652	0.001 562	0.001 476	64
17	0.001 573	0.001 482	0.001 395	0.001 313	0.001 236	0.001 163	68
18	0.001 269	0.001 190	0.001 115	0.001 045	0.000 980	0.000 918	72
19	0.001 025	0.000 956	0.000 893	0.000 833	0.000 777	0.000 725	76
20	0.000 828	0.000 769	0.000 715	0.000 664	0.000 617	0.000 573	80
21	0.000 670	0.000 619	0.000 573	0.000 530	0.000 490	0.000 453	84
22	0.000 542	0.000 499	0.000 459	0.000 423	0.000 389	0.000 358	88
23	0.000 439	0.000 402	0.000 368	0.000 338	0.000 309	0.000 283	92
24	0.000 355	0.000 324	0.000 296	0.000 270	0.000 246	0.000 224	96
25	0.000 288	0.000 261	0.000 237	0.000 215	0.000 195	0.000 177	100
26	0.000 233	0.000 211	0.000 190	0.000 172	0.000 155	0.000 140	104
27	0.000 189	0.000 170	0.000 153	0.000 138	0.000 124	0.000 111	108
28	0.000 153	0.000 137	0.000 123	0.000 110	0.000 098	0.000 088	112
29	0.000 124	0.000 111	0.000 099	0.000 088	0.000 078	0.000 070	116
30	0.000 101	0.000 089	0.000 079	0.000 070	0.000 062	0.000 055	120

SECTION 3

HALF YRS	5.25% ANNUAL RATE	5.50% ANNUAL RATE	5.75% ANNUAL RATE	6.00% ANNUAL RATE	6.25% ANNUAL RATE	6.50% ANNUAL RATE	HALF YRS
1	1.000 000	1.000 000	1.000 000	1.000 000	1.000 000	1.000 000	1
2	0.493 523	0.493 218	0.492 914	0.492 611	0.492 308	0.492 005	2
3	0.324 734	0.324 332	0.323 931	0.323 530	0.323 130	0.322 731	3
4	0.240 369	0.239 921	0.239 473	0.239 027	0.238 582	0.238 137	4
5	0.189 772	0.189 298	0.188 826	0.188 355	0.187 884	0.187 416	5
6	0.156 060	0.155 571	0.155 083	0.154 598	0.154 113	0.153 630	6
7	0.131 996	0.131 497	0.131 001	0.130 506	0.130 013	0.129 522	7
8	0.113 962	0.113 458	0.112 956	0.112 456	0.111 959	0.111 463	8
9	0.099 948	0.099 441	0.098 936	0.098 434	0.097 934	0.097 436	9
10	0.088 748	0.088 240	0.087 734	0.087 231	0.086 730	0.086 231	10
11	0.079 595	0.079 086	0.078 581	0.078 077	0.077 577	0.077 079	11
12	0.071 976	0.071 469	0.070 964	0.070 462	0.069 963	0.069 467	12
13	0.065 539	0.065 033	0.064 529	0.064 030	0.063 533	0.063 039	13
14	0.060 029	0.059 525	0.059 024	0.058 526	0.058 032	0.057 542	14
15	0.055 261	0.054 759	0.054 261	0.053 767	0.053 276	0.052 789	15
16	0.051 096	0.050 597	0.050 102	0.049 611	0.049 124	0.048 640	16
17	0.047 428	0.046 932	0.046 440	0.045 953	0.045 469	0.044 990	17
18	0.044 173	0.043 681	0.043 192	0.042 709	0.042 229	0.041 754	18
19	0.041 267	0.040 778	0.040 294	0.039 814	0.039 339	0.038 868	19
20	0.038 657	0.038 172	0.037 691	0.037 216	0.036 745	0.036 279	20
21	0.036 301	0.035 819	0.035 343	0.034 872	0.034 406	0.033 944	21
22	0.034 164	0.033 686	0.033 214	0.032 747	0.032 286	0.031 829	22
23	0.032 217	0.031 744	0.031 276	0.030 814	0.030 357	0.029 906	23
24	0.030 438	0.029 969	0.029 505	0.029 047	0.028 595	0.028 149	24
25	0.028 805	0.028 340	0.027 881	0.027 428	0.026 981	0.026 539	25
26	0.027 302	0.026 841	0.026 387	0.025 938	0.025 496	0.025 060	26
27	0.025 914	0.025 458	0.025 008	0.024 564	0.024 127	0.023 696	27
28	0.024 629	0.024 177	0.023 732	0.023 293	0.022 861	0.022 435	28
29	0.023 437	0.022 989	0.022 549	0.022 115	0.021 687	0.021 267	29
30	0.022 327	0.021 884	0.021 448	0.021 019	0.020 597	0.020 182	30
31	0.021 293	0.020 855	0.020 423	0.019 999	0.019 582	0.019 172	31
32	0.020 327	0.019 893	0.019 466	0.019 047	0.018 635	0.018 230	32
33	0.019 422	0.018 993	0.018 571	0.018 156	0.017 749	0.017 350	33
34	0.018 574	0.018 149	0.017 731	0.017 322	0.016 920	0.016 526	34
35	0.017 777	0.017 356	0.016 944	0.016 539	0.016 143	0.015 753	35
36	0.017 027	0.016 611	0.016 204	0.015 804	0.015 412	0.015 028	36
37	0.016 321	0.015 910	0.015 506	0.015 112	0.014 725	0.014 346	37
38	0.015 655	0.015 248	0.014 849	0.014 459	0.014 078	0.013 704	38
39	0.015 025	0.014 623	0.014 229	0.013 844	0.013 467	0.013 099	39
40	0.014 429	0.014 032	0.013 643	0.013 262	0.012 891	0.012 528	40
41	0.013 865	0.013 472	0.013 088	0.012 712	0.012 346	0.011 988	41
42	0.013 331	0.012 942	0.012 562	0.012 192	0.011 830	0.011 478	42
43	0.012 823	0.012 439	0.012 064	0.011 698	0.011 342	0.010 994	43
44	0.012 341	0.011 961	0.011 591	0.011 230	0.010 878	0.010 536	44
45	0.011 882	0.011 507	0.011 141	0.010 785	0.010 438	0.010 101	45
46	0.011 446	0.011 075	0.010 714	0.010 363	0.010 021	0.009 688	46
47	0.011 030	0.010 664	0.010 307	0.009 961	0.009 624	0.009 296	47
48	0.010 634	0.010 272	0.009 920	0.009 578	0.009 246	0.008 923	48
49	0.010 255	0.009 898	0.009 550	0.009 213	0.008 886	0.008 568	49
50	0.009 894	0.009 541	0.009 198	0.008 865	0.008 543	0.008 230	50
51	0.009 549	0.009 200	0.008 862	0.008 534	0.008 216	0.007 908	51
52	0.009 219	0.008 874	0.008 541	0.008 217	0.007 904	0.007 601	52
53	0.008 903	0.008 563	0.008 234	0.007 915	0.007 606	0.007 308	53
54	0.008 601	0.008 265	0.007 940	0.007 626	0.007 322	0.007 028	54
55	0.008 311	0.007 980	0.007 659	0.007 349	0.007 050	0.006 761	55
56	0.008 034	0.007 706	0.007 390	0.007 084	0.006 790	0.006 506	56
57	0.007 767	0.007 444	0.007 132	0.006 831	0.006 541	0.006 261	57
58	0.007 512	0.007 193	0.006 885	0.006 588	0.006 303	0.006 028	58
59	0.007 266	0.006 952	0.006 648	0.006 356	0.006 075	0.005 804	59

YRS	5.25% ANNUAL RATE	5.50% ANNUAL RATE	5.75% ANNUAL RATE	6.00% ANNUAL RATE	6.25% ANNUAL RATE	6.50% ANNUAL RATE	HALF YRS
30	0.007 031	0.006 720	0.006 421	0.006 133	0.005 856	0.005 590	60
31	0.006 587	0.006 284	0.005 993	0.005 714	0.005 446	0.005 188	62
32	0.006 176	0.005 881	0.005 599	0.005 328	0.005 068	0.004 819	64
33	0.005 795	0.005 508	0.005 234	0.004 971	0.004 720	0.004 479	66
34	0.005 442	0.005 163	0.004 896	0.004 642	0.004 398	0.004 166	68
35	0.005 113	0.004 842	0.004 583	0.004 337	0.004 101	0.003 877	70
36	0.004 808	0.004 544	0.004 293	0.004 054	0.003 827	0.003 610	72
37	0.004 523	0.004 267	0.004 023	0.003 792	0.003 572	0.003 363	74
38	0.004 258	0.004 009	0.003 773	0.003 548	0.003 336	0.003 135	76
39	0.004 010	0.003 768	0.003 539	0.003 322	0.003 117	0.002 923	78
40	0.003 778	0.003 543	0.003 321	0.003 112	0.002 914	0.002 727	80

SINKING FUND

SEMIANNUAL COMPOUNDING

HALF YRS	6.75% ANNUAL RATE	7.00% ANNUAL RATE	7.25% ANNUAL RATE	7.50% ANNUAL RATE	7.75% ANNUAL RATE	8.00% ANNUAL RATE	HALF YRS
1	1.000 000	1.000 000	1.000 000	1.000 000	1.000 000	1.000 000	1
2	0.491 703	0.491 400	0.491 099	0.490 798	0.490 497	0.490 196	2
3	0.322 332	0.321 934	0.321 537	0.321 140	0.320 744	0.320 349	3
4	0.237 694	0.237 251	0.236 809	0.236 369	0.235 929	0.235 490	4
5	0.186 948	0.186 481	0.186 016	0.185 552	0.185 089	0.184 627	5
6	0.153 148	0.152 668	0.152 189	0.151 712	0.151 236	0.150 762	6
7	0.129 032	0.128 544	0.128 058	0.127 574	0.127 091	0.126 610	7
8	0.110 969	0.110 477	0.109 987	0.109 498	0.109 012	0.108 528	8
9	0.096 940	0.096 446	0.095 954	0.095 465	0.094 978	0.094 493	9
10	0.085 735	0.085 241	0.084 750	0.084 261	0.083 775	0.083 291	10
11	0.076 584	0.076 092	0.075 602	0.075 115	0.074 631	0.074 149	11
12	0.068 974	0.068 484	0.067 997	0.067 512	0.067 031	0.066 552	12
13	0.062 549	0.062 062	0.061 577	0.061 096	0.060 619	0.060 144	13
14	0.057 055	0.056 571	0.056 090	0.055 613	0.055 139	0.054 669	14
15	0.052 305	0.051 825	0.051 349	0.050 876	0.050 407	0.049 941	15
16	0.048 161	0.047 685	0.047 213	0.046 745	0.046 281	0.045 820	16
17	0.044 514	0.044 043	0.043 576	0.043 113	0.042 654	0.042 199	17
18	0.041 283	0.040 817	0.040 355	0.039 897	0.039 443	0.038 993	18
19	0.038 402	0.037 940	0.037 483	0.037 031	0.036 582	0.036 139	19
20	0.035 818	0.035 361	0.034 909	0.034 462	0.034 020	0.033 582	20
21	0.033 488	0.033 037	0.032 590	0.032 149	0.031 712	0.031 280	21
22	0.031 378	0.030 932	0.030 491	0.030 055	0.029 625	0.029 199	22
23	0.029 459	0.029 019	0.028 583	0.028 153	0.027 729	0.027 309	23
24	0.027 708	0.027 273	0.026 843	0.026 419	0.026 000	0.025 587	24
25	0.026 104	0.025 674	0.025 250	0.024 832	0.024 419	0.024 012	25
26	0.024 630	0.024 205	0.023 787	0.023 375	0.022 968	0.022 567	26
27	0.023 271	0.022 852	0.022 440	0.022 033	0.021 633	0.021 239	27
28	0.022 016	0.021 603	0.021 196	0.020 795	0.020 401	0.020 013	28
29	0.020 853	0.020 445	0.020 044	0.019 650	0.019 262	0.018 880	29
30	0.019 773	0.019 371	0.018 976	0.018 588	0.018 206	0.017 830	30
31	0.018 769	0.018 372	0.017 983	0.017 600	0.017 225	0.016 855	31
32	0.017 832	0.017 442	0.017 058	0.016 681	0.016 312	0.015 949	32
33	0.016 957	0.016 572	0.016 195	0.015 824	0.015 460	0.015 104	33
34	0.016 139	0.015 760	0.015 388	0.015 023	0.014 665	0.014 315	34
35	0.015 372	0.014 998	0.014 632	0.014 273	0.013 922	0.013 577	35
36	0.014 652	0.014 284	0.013 924	0.013 571	0.013 225	0.012 887	36
37	0.013 976	0.013 613	0.013 258	0.012 911	0.012 572	0.012 240	37
38	0.013 339	0.012 982	0.012 633	0.012 292	0.011 958	0.011 632	38
39	0.012 739	0.012 388	0.012 044	0.011 709	0.011 381	0.011 061	39
40	0.012 173	0.011 827	0.011 489	0.011 159	0.010 838	0.010 523	40
41	0.011 639	0.011 298	0.010 966	0.010 642	0.010 326	0.010 017	41
42	0.011 134	0.010 798	0.010 471	0.010 153	0.009 843	0.009 540	42
43	0.010 655	0.010 325	0.010 004	0.009 691	0.009 386	0.009 090	43
44	0.010 202	0.009 878	0.009 562	0.009 254	0.008 955	0.008 665	44
45	0.009 773	0.009 453	0.009 143	0.008 841	0.008 548	0.008 262	45
46	0.009 365	0.009 051	0.008 746	0.008 449	0.008 162	0.007 882	46
47	0.008 978	0.008 669	0.008 369	0.008 078	0.007 796	0.007 522	47
48	0.008 610	0.008 306	0.008 012	0.007 726	0.007 449	0.007 181	48
49	0.008 260	0.007 962	0.007 672	0.007 392	0.007 120	0.006 857	49
50	0.007 927	0.007 634	0.007 349	0.007 074	0.006 808	0.006 550	50
51	0.007 610	0.007 322	0.007 042	0.006 772	0.006 511	0.006 259	51
52	0.007 308	0.007 024	0.006 750	0.006 485	0.006 229	0.005 982	52
53	0.007 020	0.006 741	0.006 472	0.006 212	0.005 961	0.005 719	53
54	0.006 745	0.006 471	0.006 207	0.005 952	0.005 706	0.005 469	54
55	0.006 482	0.006 213	0.005 954	0.005 704	0.005 463	0.005 231	55
56	0.006 231	0.005 967	0.005 713	0.005 468	0.005 232	0.005 005	56
57	0.005 992	0.005 732	0.005 483	0.005 242	0.005 011	0.004 789	57
58	0.005 763	0.005 508	0.005 263	0.005 028	0.004 801	0.004 584	58
59	0.005 544	0.005 294	0.005 053	0.004 823	0.004 601	0.004 388	59
YRS							
30	0.005 334	0.005 089	0.004 853	0.004 627	0.004 410	0.004 202	60
31	0.004 941	0.004 705	0.004 478	0.004 261	0.004 053	0.003 854	62
32	0.004 581	0.004 353	0.004 135	0.003 927	0.003 728	0.003 538	64
33	0.004 250	0.004 030	0.003 821	0.003 621	0.003 431	0.003 249	66
34	0.003 945	0.003 734	0.003 533	0.003 341	0.003 159	0.002 986	68
35	0.003 664	0.003 461	0.003 268	0.003 085	0.002 910	0.002 745	70
36	0.003 405	0.003 210	0.003 025	0.002 849	0.002 683	0.002 525	72
37	0.003 166	0.002 978	0.002 801	0.002 633	0.002 474	0.002 323	74
38	0.002 945	0.002 765	0.002 594	0.002 434	0.002 282	0.002 139	76
39	0.002 740	0.002 567	0.002 404	0.002 250	0.002 106	0.001 969	78
40	0.002 551	0.002 385	0.002 229	0.002 082	0.001 944	0.001 814	80

SINKING FUND

SEMIANNUAL
COMPOUNDING

	8.25%	8.50%	8.75%	9.00%	9.25%	9.50%	
	ANNUAL RATE	ANNUAL RATE	ANNUAL RATE	ANNUAL RATE	ANNUAL RATE	ANNUAL RATE	
HALF YRS							HALF YRS
1	1.000 000	1.000 000	1.000 000	1.000 000	1.000 000	1.000 000	1
2	0.489 896	0.489 596	0.489 297	0.488 998	0.488 699	0.488 400	2
3	0.319 954	0.319 560	0.319 166	0.318 773	0.318 381	0.317 990	3
4	0.235 052	0.234 615	0.234 179	0.233 744	0.233 309	0.232 876	4
5	0.184 166	0.183 707	0.183 249	0.182 792	0.182 336	0.181 881	5
6	0.150 289	0.149 817	0.149 347	0.148 878	0.148 411	0.147 945	6
7	0.126 130	0.125 652	0.125 176	0.124 701	0.124 229	0.123 757	7
8	0.108 045	0.107 565	0.107 086	0.106 610	0.106 135	0.105 662	8
9	0.094 010	0.093 529	0.093 051	0.092 574	0.092 100	0.091 628	9
10	0.082 809	0.082 330	0.081 853	0.081 379	0.080 907	0.080 437	10
11	0.073 670	0.073 193	0.072 719	0.072 248	0.071 779	0.071 313	11
12	0.066 076	0.065 603	0.065 133	0.064 666	0.064 202	0.063 740	12
13	0.059 672	0.059 203	0.058 738	0.058 275	0.057 816	0.057 360	13
14	0.054 202	0.053 738	0.053 278	0.052 820	0.052 366	0.051 916	14
15	0.049 479	0.049 020	0.048 565	0.048 114	0.047 666	0.047 221	15
16	0.045 363	0.044 910	0.044 461	0.044 015	0.043 573	0.043 135	16
17	0.041 747	0.041 300	0.040 857	0.040 418	0.039 982	0.039 551	17
18	0.038 548	0.038 107	0.037 670	0.037 237	0.036 808	0.036 383	18
19	0.035 699	0.035 264	0.034 834	0.034 407	0.033 985	0.033 568	19
20	0.033 149	0.032 720	0.032 296	0.031 876	0.031 461	0.031 050	20
21	0.030 853	0.030 431	0.030 013	0.029 601	0.029 192	0.028 789	21
22	0.028 778	0.028 362	0.027 952	0.027 546	0.027 145	0.026 748	22
23	0.026 895	0.026 486	0.026 081	0.025 682	0.025 289	0.024 900	23
24	0.025 179	0.024 776	0.024 379	0.023 987	0.023 600	0.023 219	24
25	0.023 610	0.023 215	0.022 824	0.022 439	0.022 059	0.021 685	25
26	0.022 172	0.021 783	0.021 399	0.021 021	0.020 649	0.020 282	26
27	0.020 850	0.020 467	0.020 091	0.019 719	0.019 354	0.018 994	27
28	0.019 631	0.019 255	0.018 885	0.018 521	0.018 163	0.017 810	28
29	0.018 504	0.018 135	0.017 772	0.017 415	0.017 063	0.016 718	29
30	0.017 461	0.017 098	0.016 742	0.016 392	0.016 047	0.015 709	30
31	0.016 493	0.016 137	0.015 787	0.015 443	0.015 106	0.014 776	31
32	0.015 592	0.015 243	0.014 900	0.014 563	0.014 233	0.013 909	32
33	0.014 754	0.014 411	0.014 074	0.013 745	0.013 421	0.013 105	33
34	0.013 971	0.013 635	0.013 305	0.012 982	0.012 666	0.012 356	34
35	0.013 240	0.012 910	0.012 587	0.012 270	0.011 961	0.011 658	35
36	0.012 556	0.012 232	0.011 916	0.011 606	0.011 303	0.011 007	36
37	0.011 915	0.011 597	0.011 287	0.010 984	0.010 688	0.010 398	37
38	0.011 313	0.011 002	0.010 698	0.010 402	0.010 112	0.009 829	38
39	0.010 748	0.010 444	0.010 146	0.009 856	0.009 573	0.009 296	39
40	0.010 217	0.009 918	0.009 627	0.009 343	0.009 066	0.008 797	40
41	0.009 717	0.009 424	0.009 139	0.008 862	0.008 591	0.008 328	41
42	0.009 246	0.008 959	0.008 680	0.008 409	0.008 145	0.007 888	42
43	0.008 801	0.008 521	0.008 248	0.007 982	0.007 724	0.007 474	43
44	0.008 382	0.008 107	0.007 840	0.007 581	0.007 329	0.007 084	44
45	0.007 986	0.007 717	0.007 455	0.007 202	0.006 956	0.006 718	45
46	0.007 611	0.007 348	0.007 092	0.006 845	0.006 605	0.006 372	46
47	0.007 256	0.006 999	0.006 749	0.006 507	0.006 273	0.006 046	47
48	0.006 921	0.006 669	0.006 425	0.006 189	0.005 960	0.005 739	48
49	0.006 603	0.006 356	0.006 118	0.005 887	0.005 664	0.005 449	49
50	0.006 301	0.006 060	0.005 827	0.005 602	0.005 385	0.005 175	50
51	0.006 015	0.005 779	0.005 552	0.005 332	0.005 120	0.004 916	51
52	0.005 744	0.005 513	0.005 291	0.005 077	0.004 870	0.004 671	52
53	0.005 486	0.005 261	0.005 044	0.004 835	0.004 633	0.004 440	53
54	0.005 241	0.005 021	0.004 809	0.004 605	0.004 409	0.004 220	54
55	0.005 008	0.004 793	0.004 586	0.004 388	0.004 196	0.004 013	55
56	0.004 787	0.004 577	0.004 375	0.004 181	0.003 995	0.003 816	56
57	0.004 576	0.004 371	0.004 174	0.003 985	0.003 804	0.003 630	57
58	0.004 375	0.004 175	0.003 983	0.003 799	0.003 622	0.003 453	58
59	0.004 184	0.003 989	0.003 802	0.003 622	0.003 450	0.003 286	59
YRS							
30	0.004 003	0.003 812	0.003 629	0.003 454	0.003 287	0.003 127	60
31	0.003 664	0.003 482	0.003 309	0.003 143	0.002 984	0.002 833	62
32	0.003 356	0.003 183	0.003 018	0.002 861	0.002 711	0.002 569	64
33	0.003 076	0.002 912	0.002 755	0.002 606	0.002 464	0.002 330	66
34	0.002 821	0.002 665	0.002 516	0.002 375	0.002 241	0.002 114	68
35	0.002 588	0.002 440	0.002 299	0.002 165	0.002 039	0.001 919	70
36	0.002 376	0.002 234	0.002 101	0.001 975	0.001 855	0.001 743	72
37	0.002 181	0.002 047	0.001 921	0.001 802	0.001 689	0.001 583	74
38	0.002 004	0.001 877	0.001 757	0.001 644	0.001 538	0.001 439	76
39	0.001 841	0.001 721	0.001 607	0.001 501	0.001 401	0.001 308	78
40	0.001 692	0.001 578	0.001 471	0.001 371	0.001 277	0.001 189	80

HALF YRS	9.75% ANNUAL RATE	10.00% ANNUAL RATE	10.50% ANNUAL RATE	11.00% ANNUAL RATE	11.50% ANNUAL RATE	12.00% ANNUAL RATE	HALF YRS
1	1.000 000	1.000 000	1.000 000	1.000 000	1.000 000	1.000 000	1
2	0.488 103	0.487 805	0.487 211	0.486 618	0.486 027	0.485 437	2
3	0.317 599	0.317 209	0.316 430	0.315 654	0.314 881	0.314 110	3
4	0.232 443	0.232 012	0.231 151	0.230 294	0.229 441	0.228 591	4
5	0.181 427	0.180 975	0.180 073	0.179 176	0.178 284	0.177 396	5
6	0.147 481	0.147 017	0.146 095	0.145 179	0.144 268	0.143 363	6
7	0.123 288	0.122 820	0.121 889	0.120 964	0.120 046	0.119 135	7
8	0.105 191	0.104 722	0.103 789	0.102 864	0.101 946	0.101 036	8
9	0.091 158	0.090 690	0.089 761	0.088 839	0.087 927	0.087 022	9
10	0.079 970	0.079 505	0.078 582	0.077 668	0.076 763	0.075 868	10
11	0.070 850	0.070 389	0.069 475	0.068 571	0.067 677	0.066 793	11
12	0.063 281	0.062 825	0.061 922	0.061 029	0.060 148	0.059 277	12
13	0.056 906	0.056 456	0.055 564	0.054 684	0.053 816	0.052 960	13
14	0.051 468	0.051 024	0.050 145	0.049 279	0.048 426	0.047 585	14
15	0.046 780	0.046 342	0.045 477	0.044 626	0.043 788	0.042 963	15
16	0.042 701	0.042 270	0.041 419	0.040 583	0.039 760	0.038 952	16
17	0.039 123	0.038 699	0.037 863	0.037 042	0.036 236	0.035 445	17
18	0.035 963	0.035 546	0.034 725	0.033 920	0.033 130	0.032 357	18
19	0.033 154	0.032 745	0.031 939	0.031 150	0.030 377	0.029 621	19
20	0.030 644	0.030 243	0.029 452	0.028 679	0.027 923	0.027 185	20
21	0.028 390	0.027 996	0.027 221	0.026 465	0.025 726	0.025 005	21
22	0.026 357	0.025 971	0.025 212	0.024 471	0.023 749	0.023 046	22
23	0.024 516	0.024 137	0.023 394	0.022 670	0.021 965	0.021 278	23
24	0.022 842	0.022 471	0.021 743	0.021 036	0.020 348	0.019 679	24
25	0.021 316	0.020 952	0.020 241	0.019 549	0.018 878	0.018 227	25
26	0.019 920	0.019 564	0.018 868	0.018 193	0.017 539	0.016 904	26
27	0.018 640	0.018 292	0.017 611	0.016 952	0.016 314	0.015 697	27
28	0.017 463	0.017 123	0.016 457	0.015 814	0.015 193	0.014 593	28
29	0.016 379	0.016 046	0.015 396	0.014 769	0.014 163	0.013 580	29
30	0.015 377	0.015 051	0.014 417	0.013 805	0.013 216	0.012 649	30
31	0.014 451	0.014 132	0.013 513	0.012 917	0.012 343	0.011 792	31
32	0.013 592	0.013 280	0.012 676	0.012 095	0.011 538	0.011 002	32
33	0.012 794	0.012 490	0.011 900	0.011 335	0.010 792	0.010 273	33
34	0.012 052	0.011 755	0.011 180	0.010 630	0.010 103	0.009 598	34
35	0.011 362	0.011 072	0.010 511	0.009 975	0.009 463	0.008 974	35
36	0.010 717	0.010 434	0.009 888	0.009 366	0.008 869	0.008 395	36
37	0.010 116	0.009 840	0.009 307	0.008 800	0.008 317	0.007 857	37
38	0.009 553	0.009 284	0.008 765	0.008 272	0.007 803	0.007 358	38
39	0.009 027	0.008 765	0.008 259	0.007 780	0.007 325	0.006 894	39
40	0.008 534	0.008 278	0.007 786	0.007 320	0.006 879	0.006 462	40
41	0.008 072	0.007 822	0.007 344	0.006 891	0.006 463	0.006 059	41
42	0.007 638	0.007 395	0.006 929	0.006 489	0.006 074	0.005 683	42
43	0.007 230	0.006 993	0.006 540	0.006 113	0.005 711	0.005 333	43
44	0.006 847	0.006 616	0.006 176	0.005 761	0.005 372	0.005 006	44
45	0.006 486	0.006 262	0.005 833	0.005 431	0.005 054	0.004 700	45
46	0.006 147	0.005 928	0.005 512	0.005 122	0.004 756	0.004 415	46
47	0.005 827	0.005 614	0.005 210	0.004 831	0.004 478	0.004 148	47
48	0.005 525	0.005 318	0.004 925	0.004 559	0.004 216	0.003 898	48
49	0.005 241	0.005 040	0.004 658	0.004 302	0.003 971	0.003 664	49
50	0.004 972	0.004 777	0.004 406	0.004 061	0.003 741	0.003 444	50
51	0.004 719	0.004 529	0.004 169	0.003 835	0.003 525	0.003 239	51
52	0.004 479	0.004 294	0.003 945	0.003 622	0.003 323	0.003 046	52
53	0.004 253	0.004 073	0.003 734	0.003 421	0.003 132	0.002 866	53
54	0.004 039	0.003 864	0.003 536	0.003 232	0.002 953	0.002 696	54
55	0.003 836	0.003 667	0.003 348	0.003 055	0.002 785	0.002 537	55
56	0.003 645	0.003 480	0.003 171	0.002 887	0.002 626	0.002 388	56
57	0.003 463	0.003 303	0.003 004	0.002 729	0.002 477	0.002 247	57
58	0.003 291	0.003 136	0.002 846	0.002 580	0.002 337	0.002 116	58
59	0.003 129	0.002 978	0.002 697	0.002 440	0.002 205	0.001 992	59

YRS							
30	0.002 974	0.002 828	0.002 555	0.002 307	0.002 081	0.001 876	60
31	0.002 689	0.002 552	0.002 296	0.002 064	0.001 854	0.001 664	62
32	0.002 433	0.002 304	0.002 064	0.001 847	0.001 652	0.001 476	64
33	0.002 202	0.002 081	0.001 856	0.001 654	0.001 473	0.001 310	66
34	0.001 994	0.001 880	0.001 670	0.001 482	0.001 313	0.001 163	68
35	0.001 806	0.001 699	0.001 503	0.001 328	0.001 172	0.001 033	70
36	0.001 637	0.001 536	0.001 353	0.001 190	0.001 045	0.000 918	72
37	0.001 483	0.001 390	0.001 218	0.001 067	0.000 933	0.000 815	74
38	0.001 345	0.001 257	0.001 097	0.000 956	0.000 833	0.000 725	76
39	0.001 220	0.001 138	0.000 988	0.000 858	0.000 744	0.000 644	78
40	0.001 107	0.001 030	0.000 891	0.000 769	0.000 664	0.000 573	80

SINKING FUND

	12.50%	13.00%	13.50%	14.00%	14.50%	15.00%	
	ANNUAL RATE	ANNUAL RATE	ANNUAL RATE	ANNUAL RATE	ANNUAL RATE	ANNUAL RATE	
HALF YRS							HALF YRS
1	1.000 000	1.000 000	1.000 000	1.000 000	1.000 000	1.000 000	1
2	0.484 848	0.484 262	0.483 676	0.483 092	0.482 509	0.481 928	2
3	0.313 341	0.312 576	0.311 812	0.311 052	0.310 293	0.309 538	3
4	0.227 745	0.226 903	0.226 064	0.225 228	0.224 396	0.223 568	4
5	0.176 513	0.175 635	0.174 760	0.173 891	0.173 025	0.172 165	5
6	0.142 463	0.141 568	0.140 679	0.139 796	0.138 918	0.138 045	6
7	0.118 230	0.117 331	0.116 439	0.115 553	0.114 674	0.113 800	7
8	0.100 133	0.099 237	0.098 349	0.097 468	0.096 594	0.095 727	8
9	0.086 126	0.085 238	0.084 358	0.083 486	0.082 623	0.081 767	9
10	0.074 982	0.074 105	0.073 237	0.072 378	0.071 527	0.070 686	10
11	0.065 919	0.065 055	0.064 201	0.063 357	0.062 522	0.061 697	11
12	0.058 417	0.057 568	0.056 730	0.055 902	0.055 085	0.054 278	12
13	0.052 116	0.051 283	0.050 461	0.049 651	0.048 852	0.048 064	13
14	0.046 757	0.045 940	0.045 137	0.044 345	0.043 565	0.042 797	14
15	0.042 151	0.041 353	0.040 567	0.039 795	0.039 035	0.038 287	15
16	0.038 158	0.037 378	0.036 611	0.035 858	0.035 118	0.034 391	16
17	0.034 668	0.033 906	0.033 159	0.032 425	0.031 706	0.031 000	17
18	0.031 598	0.030 855	0.030 126	0.029 413	0.028 714	0.028 029	18
19	0.028 880	0.028 156	0.027 447	0.026 753	0.026 074	0.025 411	19
20	0.026 462	0.025 756	0.025 067	0.024 393	0.023 735	0.023 092	20
21	0.024 300	0.023 613	0.022 943	0.022 289	0.021 651	0.021 029	21
22	0.022 360	0.021 691	0.021 040	0.020 406	0.019 788	0.019 187	22
23	0.020 611	0.019 961	0.019 329	0.018 714	0.018 116	0.017 535	23
24	0.019 029	0.018 398	0.017 784	0.017 189	0.016 611	0.016 050	24
25	0.017 595	0.016 981	0.016 387	0.015 811	0.015 252	0.014 711	25
26	0.016 290	0.015 695	0.015 119	0.014 561	0.014 021	0.013 500	26
27	0.015 100	0.014 523	0.013 965	0.013 426	0.012 905	0.012 402	27
28	0.014 013	0.013 453	0.012 913	0.012 392	0.011 890	0.011 405	28
29	0.013 017	0.012 474	0.011 952	0.011 449	0.010 964	0.010 498	29
30	0.012 103	0.011 577	0.011 072	0.010 586	0.010 120	0.009 671	30
31	0.011 263	0.010 754	0.010 266	0.009 797	0.009 347	0.008 916	31
32	0.010 489	0.009 997	0.009 525	0.009 073	0.008 640	0.008 226	32
33	0.009 775	0.009 299	0.008 844	0.008 408	0.007 992	0.007 594	33
34	0.009 117	0.008 656	0.008 216	0.007 797	0.007 396	0.007 015	34
35	0.008 507	0.008 062	0.007 638	0.007 234	0.006 849	0.006 483	35
36	0.007 943	0.007 513	0.007 104	0.006 715	0.006 346	0.005 994	36
37	0.007 421	0.007 005	0.006 611	0.006 237	0.005 882	0.005 545	37
38	0.006 936	0.006 535	0.006 155	0.005 795	0.005 454	0.005 132	38
39	0.006 485	0.006 099	0.005 733	0.005 387	0.005 060	0.004 751	39
40	0.006 067	0.005 694	0.005 342	0.005 009	0.004 696	0.004 400	40
41	0.005 677	0.005 318	0.004 979	0.004 660	0.004 359	0.004 077	41
42	0.005 315	0.004 968	0.004 642	0.004 336	0.004 048	0.003 778	42
43	0.004 978	0.004 644	0.004 330	0.004 036	0.003 760	0.003 502	43
44	0.004 663	0.004 341	0.004 040	0.003 758	0.003 494	0.003 247	44
45	0.004 369	0.004 060	0.003 770	0.003 500	0.003 247	0.003 011	45
46	0.004 096	0.003 797	0.003 519	0.003 260	0.003 018	0.002 794	46
47	0.003 840	0.003 553	0.003 286	0.003 037	0.002 806	0.002 592	47
48	0.003 601	0.003 325	0.003 069	0.002 831	0.002 610	0.002 405	48
49	0.003 378	0.003 112	0.002 866	0.002 639	0.002 428	0.002 232	49
50	0.003 169	0.002 914	0.002 678	0.002 460	0.002 258	0.002 072	50
51	0.002 974	0.002 729	0.002 502	0.002 294	0.002 101	0.001 924	51
52	0.002 791	0.002 556	0.002 339	0.002 139	0.001 955	0.001 787	52
53	0.002 620	0.002 394	0.002 186	0.001 995	0.001 820	0.001 659	53
54	0.002 460	0.002 243	0.002 044	0.001 861	0.001 694	0.001 541	54
55	0.002 310	0.002 101	0.001 911	0.001 736	0.001 577	0.001 432	55
56	0.002 169	0.001 969	0.001 787	0.001 620	0.001 468	0.001 330	56
57	0.002 037	0.001 846	0.001 671	0.001 512	0.001 367	0.001 236	57
58	0.001 914	0.001 730	0.001 563	0.001 411	0.001 273	0.001 148	58
59	0.001 798	0.001 622	0.001 462	0.001 317	0.001 186	0.001 067	59
YRS							
30	0.001 689	0.001 520	0.001 368	0.001 229	0.001 104	0.000 991	60
31	0.001 492	0.001 337	0.001 197	0.001 071	0.000 958	0.000 856	62
32	0.001 318	0.001 176	0.001 048	0.000 934	0.000 832	0.000 740	64
33	0.001 165	0.001 034	0.000 918	0.000 814	0.000 722	0.000 639	66
34	0.001 029	0.000 910	0.000 804	0.000 710	0.000 627	0.000 553	68
35	0.000 910	0.000 801	0.000 705	0.000 620	0.000 544	0.000 478	70
36	0.000 805	0.000 705	0.000 618	0.000 541	0.000 473	0.000 413	72
37	0.000 712	0.000 621	0.000 541	0.000 472	0.000 411	0.000 357	74
38	0.000 630	0.000 547	0.000 475	0.000 412	0.000 357	0.000 309	76
39	0.000 557	0.000 482	0.000 416	0.000 359	0.000 310	0.000 267	78
40	0.000 493	0.000 424	0.000 365	0.000 314	0.000 269	0.000 231	80

HALF YRS	15.50% ANNUAL RATE	16.00% ANNUAL RATE	16.50% ANNUAL RATE	17.00% ANNUAL RATE	17.50% ANNUAL RATE	18.00% ANNUAL RATE	HALF YRS
1	1.000 000	1.000 000	1.000 000	1.000 000	1.000 000	1.000 000	1
2	0.481 348	0.480 769	0.480 192	0.479 616	0.479 042	0.478 469	2
3	0.308 784	0.308 034	0.307 285	0.306 539	0.305 796	0.305 055	3
4	0.222 742	0.221 921	0.221 103	0.220 288	0.219 477	0.218 669	4
5	0.171 308	0.170 456	0.169 609	0.168 766	0.167 927	0.167 092	5
6	0.137 177	0.136 315	0.135 459	0.134 607	0.133 761	0.132 920	6
7	0.112 933	0.112 072	0.111 218	0.110 369	0.109 527	0.108 691	7
8	0.094 867	0.094 015	0.093 169	0.092 331	0.091 499	0.090 674	8
9	0.080 919	0.080 080	0.079 248	0.078 424	0.077 607	0.076 799	9
10	0.069 853	0.069 029	0.068 214	0.067 408	0.066 610	0.065 820	10
11	0.060 882	0.060 076	0.059 280	0.058 493	0.057 715	0.056 947	11
12	0.053 481	0.052 695	0.051 919	0.051 153	0.050 397	0.049 651	12
13	0.047 288	0.046 522	0.045 767	0.045 023	0.044 289	0.043 567	13
14	0.042 041	0.041 297	0.040 564	0.039 842	0.039 132	0.038 433	14
15	0.037 552	0.036 830	0.036 119	0.035 420	0.034 734	0.034 059	15
16	0.033 678	0.032 977	0.032 289	0.031 614	0.030 951	0.030 300	16
17	0.030 308	0.029 629	0.028 964	0.028 312	0.027 673	0.027 046	17
18	0.027 359	0.026 702	0.026 059	0.025 430	0.024 815	0.024 212	18
19	0.024 762	0.024 128	0.023 507	0.022 901	0.022 309	0.021 730	19
20	0.022 465	0.021 852	0.021 254	0.020 671	0.020 102	0.019 546	20
21	0.020 423	0.019 832	0.019 256	0.018 695	0.018 149	0.017 617	21
22	0.018 602	0.018 032	0.017 478	0.016 939	0.016 415	0.015 905	22
23	0.016 971	0.016 422	0.015 889	0.015 372	0.014 870	0.014 382	23
24	0.015 506	0.014 978	0.014 466	0.013 970	0.013 489	0.013 023	24
25	0.014 186	0.013 679	0.013 187	0.012 712	0.012 251	0.011 806	25
26	0.012 995	0.012 507	0.012 036	0.011 581	0.011 140	0.010 715	26
27	0.011 917	0.011 448	0.010 996	0.010 560	0.010 140	0.009 735	27
28	0.010 938	0.010 489	0.010 056	0.009 639	0.009 238	0.008 852	28
29	0.010 050	0.009 619	0.009 204	0.008 806	0.008 423	0.008 056	29
30	0.009 241	0.008 827	0.008 431	0.008 051	0.007 686	0.007 336	30
31	0.008 503	0.008 107	0.007 728	0.007 365	0.007 018	0.006 686	31
32	0.007 830	0.007 451	0.007 089	0.006 742	0.006 412	0.006 096	32
33	0.007 214	0.006 852	0.006 506	0.006 176	0.005 861	0.005 562	33
34	0.006 651	0.006 304	0.005 974	0.005 660	0.005 361	0.005 077	34
35	0.006 135	0.005 803	0.005 488	0.005 189	0.004 905	0.004 636	35
36	0.005 661	0.005 345	0.005 045	0.004 760	0.004 490	0.004 235	36
37	0.005 226	0.004 924	0.004 639	0.004 368	0.004 112	0.003 870	37
38	0.004 827	0.004 539	0.004 267	0.004 010	0.003 767	0.003 538	38
39	0.004 460	0.004 185	0.003 926	0.003 682	0.003 452	0.003 236	39
40	0.004 122	0.003 860	0.003 614	0.003 382	0.003 164	0.002 960	40
41	0.003 811	0.003 561	0.003 327	0.003 107	0.002 901	0.002 708	41
42	0.003 524	0.003 287	0.003 064	0.002 856	0.002 661	0.002 478	42
43	0.003 260	0.003 034	0.002 823	0.002 625	0.002 441	0.002 268	43
44	0.003 017	0.002 802	0.002 601	0.002 414	0.002 239	0.002 077	44
45	0.002 792	0.002 587	0.002 397	0.002 220	0.002 055	0.001 902	45
46	0.002 584	0.002 390	0.002 209	0.002 042	0.001 886	0.001 742	46
47	0.002 393	0.002 208	0.002 037	0.001 878	0.001 731	0.001 595	47
48	0.002 216	0.002 040	0.001 878	0.001 728	0.001 589	0.001 461	48
49	0.002 052	0.001 886	0.001 732	0.001 590	0.001 459	0.001 339	49
50	0.001 901	0.001 743	0.001 597	0.001 463	0.001 340	0.001 227	50
51	0.001 761	0.001 611	0.001 473	0.001 347	0.001 231	0.001 124	51
52	0.001 632	0.001 490	0.001 359	0.001 240	0.001 130	0.001 030	52
53	0.001 512	0.001 377	0.001 254	0.001 141	0.001 038	0.000 944	53
54	0.001 401	0.001 274	0.001 157	0.001 051	0.000 954	0.000 866	54
55	0.001 299	0.001 178	0.001 068	0.000 968	0.000 876	0.000 794	55
56	0.001 204	0.001 090	0.000 985	0.000 891	0.000 805	0.000 728	56
57	0.001 116	0.001 008	0.000 910	0.000 821	0.000 740	0.000 667	57
58	0.001 035	0.000 932	0.000 840	0.000 756	0.000 680	0.000 612	58
59	0.000 959	0.000 862	0.000 775	0.000 696	0.000 625	0.000 561	59

YRS							
30	0.000 890	0.000 798	0.000 715	0.000 641	0.000 574	0.000 514	60
31	0.000 765	0.000 683	0.000 610	0.000 544	0.000 485	0.000 432	62
32	0.000 658	0.000 585	0.000 520	0.000 462	0.000 410	0.000 364	64
33	0.000 566	0.000 501	0.000 443	0.000 392	0.000 346	0.000 306	66
34	0.000 487	0.000 429	0.000 378	0.000 333	0.000 293	0.000 257	68
35	0.000 419	0.000 368	0.000 322	0.000 282	0.000 247	0.000 216	70
36	0.000 361	0.000 315	0.000 275	0.000 240	0.000 209	0.000 182	72
37	0.000 311	0.000 270	0.000 234	0.000 204	0.000 177	0.000 153	74
38	0.000 267	0.000 231	0.000 200	0.000 173	0.000 149	0.000 129	76
39	0.000 230	0.000 198	0.000 171	0.000 147	0.000 126	0.000 109	78
40	0.000 198	0.000 170	0.000 146	0.000 125	0.000 107	0.000 091	80

SINKING FUND

	18.50% ANNUAL RATE	19.00% ANNUAL RATE	19.50% ANNUAL RATE	20.00% ANNUAL RATE	20.50% ANNUAL RATE	21.00% ANNUAL RATE	
HALF YRS							HALF YRS
1	1.000 000	1.000 000	1.000 000	1.000 000	1.000 000	1.000 000	1
2	0.477 897	0.477 327	0.476 758	0.476 190	0.475 624	0.475 059	2
3	0.304 316	0.303 580	0.302 846	0.302 115	0.301 386	0.300 659	3
4	0.217 864	0.217 063	0.216 265	0.215 471	0.214 680	0.213 892	4
5	0.166 262	0.165 436	0.164 615	0.163 797	0.162 984	0.162 175	5
6	0.132 084	0.131 253	0.130 428	0.129 607	0.128 792	0.127 982	6
7	0.107 860	0.107 036	0.106 218	0.105 405	0.104 599	0.103 799	7
8	0.089 857	0.089 046	0.088 241	0.087 444	0.086 653	0.085 869	8
9	0.075 998	0.075 205	0.074 419	0.073 641	0.072 870	0.072 106	9
10	0.065 039	0.064 266	0.063 502	0.062 745	0.061 997	0.061 257	10
11	0.056 187	0.055 437	0.054 696	0.053 963	0.053 240	0.052 525	11
12	0.048 914	0.048 188	0.047 471	0.046 763	0.046 065	0.045 377	12
13	0.042 854	0.042 152	0.041 460	0.040 779	0.040 107	0.039 445	13
14	0.037 745	0.037 068	0.036 402	0.035 746	0.035 101	0.034 467	14
15	0.033 396	0.032 744	0.032 103	0.031 474	0.030 855	0.030 248	15
16	0.029 661	0.029 035	0.028 420	0.027 817	0.027 225	0.026 644	16
17	0.026 432	0.025 831	0.025 241	0.024 664	0.024 099	0.023 545	17
18	0.023 623	0.023 046	0.022 482	0.021 930	0.021 391	0.020 863	18
19	0.021 165	0.020 613	0.020 074	0.019 547	0.019 033	0.018 531	19
20	0.019 005	0.018 477	0.017 962	0.017 460	0.016 970	0.016 493	20
21	0.017 098	0.016 594	0.016 102	0.015 624	0.015 159	0.014 707	21
22	0.015 409	0.014 928	0.014 460	0.014 005	0.013 563	0.013 134	22
23	0.013 909	0.013 449	0.013 004	0.012 572	0.012 153	0.011 747	23
24	0.012 571	0.012 134	0.011 710	0.011 300	0.010 903	0.010 519	24
25	0.011 376	0.010 959	0.010 557	0.010 168	0.009 792	0.009 429	25
26	0.010 305	0.009 909	0.009 527	0.009 159	0.008 804	0.008 461	26
27	0.009 345	0.008 969	0.008 606	0.008 258	0.007 922	0.007 599	27
28	0.008 481	0.008 124	0.007 781	0.007 451	0.007 134	0.006 830	28
29	0.007 703	0.007 364	0.007 040	0.006 728	0.006 429	0.006 143	29
30	0.007 001	0.006 681	0.006 373	0.006 079	0.005 798	0.005 528	30
31	0.006 368	0.006 064	0.005 774	0.005 496	0.005 231	0.004 978	31
32	0.005 795	0.005 507	0.005 233	0.004 972	0.004 722	0.004 485	32
33	0.005 276	0.005 004	0.004 746	0.004 499	0.004 265	0.004 042	33
34	0.004 806	0.004 549	0.004 305	0.004 074	0.003 854	0.003 645	34
35	0.004 380	0.004 138	0.003 908	0.003 690	0.003 483	0.003 288	35
36	0.003 993	0.003 764	0.003 548	0.003 343	0.003 149	0.002 967	36
37	0.003 642	0.003 426	0.003 222	0.003 030	0.002 849	0.002 677	37
38	0.003 322	0.003 119	0.002 927	0.002 747	0.002 577	0.002 417	38
39	0.003 032	0.002 840	0.002 660	0.002 491	0.002 332	0.002 183	39
40	0.002 767	0.002 587	0.002 418	0.002 259	0.002 111	0.001 971	40
41	0.002 527	0.002 357	0.002 198	0.002 050	0.001 911	0.001 781	41
42	0.002 308	0.002 148	0.001 999	0.001 860	0.001 730	0.001 609	42
43	0.002 108	0.001 958	0.001 818	0.001 688	0.001 567	0.001 454	43
44	0.001 926	0.001 785	0.001 654	0.001 532	0.001 419	0.001 314	44
45	0.001 759	0.001 627	0.001 505	0.001 391	0.001 286	0.001 188	45
46	0.001 608	0.001 484	0.001 369	0.001 263	0.001 165	0.001 074	46
47	0.001 470	0.001 353	0.001 246	0.001 147	0.001 055	0.000 971	47
48	0.001 343	0.001 234	0.001 134	0.001 041	0.000 956	0.000 878	48
49	0.001 228	0.001 126	0.001 032	0.000 946	0.000 867	0.000 794	49
50	0.001 123	0.001 027	0.000 940	0.000 859	0.000 785	0.000 718	50
51	0.001 027	0.000 937	0.000 855	0.000 780	0.000 712	0.000 649	51
52	0.000 939	0.000 855	0.000 779	0.000 709	0.000 645	0.000 587	52
53	0.000 859	0.000 780	0.000 709	0.000 644	0.000 585	0.000 531	53
54	0.000 785	0.000 712	0.000 646	0.000 585	0.000 530	0.000 480	54
55	0.000 718	0.000 650	0.000 588	0.000 532	0.000 481	0.000 435	55
56	0.000 657	0.000 593	0.000 535	0.000 483	0.000 436	0.000 393	56
57	0.000 601	0.000 541	0.000 488	0.000 439	0.000 395	0.000 356	57
58	0.000 550	0.000 494	0.000 444	0.000 399	0.000 358	0.000 322	58
59	0.000 503	0.000 451	0.000 405	0.000 363	0.000 325	0.000 291	59
YRS							
30	0.000 460	0.000 412	0.000 368	0.000 330	0.000 295	0.000 263	60
31	0.000 385	0.000 343	0.000 306	0.000 272	0.000 242	0.000 216	62
32	0.000 323	0.000 286	0.000 254	0.000 225	0.000 199	0.000 176	64
33	0.000 270	0.000 238	0.000 210	0.000 186	0.000 164	0.000 145	66
34	0.000 226	0.000 199	0.000 175	0.000 153	0.000 135	0.000 118	68
35	0.000 189	0.000 166	0.000 145	0.000 127	0.000 111	0.000 097	70
36	0.000 159	0.000 138	0.000 120	0.000 105	0.000 091	0.000 079	72
37	0.000 133	0.000 115	0.000 100	0.000 087	0.000 075	0.000 065	74
38	0.000 111	0.000 096	0.000 083	0.000 072	0.000 062	0.000 053	76
39	0.000 093	0.000 080	0.000 069	0.000 059	0.000 051	0.000 044	78
40	0.000 078	0.000 067	0.000 057	0.000 049	0.000 042	0.000 036	80

SINKING FUND

SEMIANNUAL
COMPOUNDING

HALF YRS	21.50% ANNUAL RATE	22.00% ANNUAL RATE	22.50% ANNUAL RATE	23.00% ANNUAL RATE	23.50% ANNUAL RATE	24.00% ANNUAL RATE	HALF YRS
1	1.000 000	1.000 000	1.000 000	1.000 000	1.000 000	1.000 000	1
2	0.474 496	0.473 934	0.473 373	0.472 813	0.472 255	0.471 698	2
3	0.299 935	0.299 213	0.298 494	0.297 776	0.297 062	0.296 349	3
4	0.213 108	0.212 326	0.211 548	0.210 774	0.210 003	0.209 234	4
5	0.161 371	0.160 570	0.159 774	0.158 982	0.158 194	0.157 410	5
6	0.127 177	0.126 377	0.125 581	0.124 791	0.124 006	0.123 226	6
7	0.103 004	0.102 215	0.101 432	0.100 655	0.099 884	0.099 118	7
8	0.085 092	0.084 321	0.083 557	0.082 799	0.082 048	0.081 303	8
9	0.071 350	0.070 602	0.069 860	0.069 126	0.068 399	0.067 679	9
10	0.060 525	0.059 801	0.059 085	0.058 377	0.057 677	0.056 984	10
11	0.051 819	0.051 121	0.050 432	0.049 751	0.049 079	0.048 415	11
12	0.044 697	0.044 027	0.043 366	0.042 714	0.042 071	0.041 437	12
13	0.038 793	0.038 151	0.037 518	0.036 895	0.036 282	0.035 677	13
14	0.033 842	0.033 228	0.032 624	0.032 030	0.031 446	0.030 871	14
15	0.029 651	0.029 065	0.028 490	0.027 924	0.027 369	0.026 824	15
16	0.026 075	0.025 517	0.024 969	0.024 432	0.023 906	0.023 390	16
17	0.023 003	0.022 471	0.021 952	0.021 443	0.020 944	0.020 457	17
18	0.020 347	0.019 843	0.019 350	0.018 868	0.018 397	0.017 937	18
19	0.018 041	0.017 563	0.017 096	0.016 641	0.016 196	0.015 763	19
20	0.016 028	0.015 576	0.015 134	0.014 705	0.014 286	0.013 879	20
21	0.014 266	0.013 838	0.013 421	0.013 016	0.012 623	0.012 240	21
22	0.012 718	0.012 313	0.011 920	0.011 539	0.011 169	0.010 811	22
23	0.011 353	0.010 971	0.010 601	0.010 243	0.009 896	0.009 560	23
24	0.010 147	0.009 787	0.009 439	0.009 103	0.008 778	0.008 463	24
25	0.009 079	0.008 740	0.008 413	0.008 098	0.007 794	0.007 500	25
26	0.008 131	0.007 813	0.007 506	0.007 210	0.006 926	0.006 652	26
27	0.007 288	0.006 989	0.006 702	0.006 425	0.006 159	0.005 904	27
28	0.006 538	0.006 257	0.005 988	0.005 730	0.005 482	0.005 244	28
29	0.005 868	0.005 605	0.005 354	0.005 112	0.004 881	0.004 660	29
30	0.005 271	0.005 025	0.004 789	0.004 564	0.004 349	0.004 144	30
31	0.004 737	0.004 506	0.004 286	0.004 077	0.003 877	0.003 686	31
32	0.004 259	0.004 043	0.003 838	0.003 643	0.003 457	0.003 280	32
33	0.003 831	0.003 629	0.003 438	0.003 257	0.003 084	0.002 920	33
34	0.003 447	0.003 259	0.003 081	0.002 912	0.002 752	0.002 601	34
35	0.003 103	0.002 927	0.002 762	0.002 605	0.002 457	0.002 317	35
36	0.002 794	0.002 630	0.002 476	0.002 331	0.002 194	0.002 064	36
37	0.002 516	0.002 364	0.002 221	0.002 086	0.001 959	0.001 840	37
38	0.002 267	0.002 125	0.001 992	0.001 867	0.001 750	0.001 640	38
39	0.002 043	0.001 911	0.001 788	0.001 672	0.001 564	0.001 462	39
40	0.001 841	0.001 719	0.001 604	0.001 497	0.001 397	0.001 304	40
41	0.001 659	0.001 546	0.001 440	0.001 341	0.001 249	0.001 163	41
42	0.001 496	0.001 391	0.001 293	0.001 201	0.001 116	0.001 037	42
43	0.001 349	0.001 251	0.001 161	0.001 076	0.000 998	0.000 925	43
44	0.001 217	0.001 126	0.001 042	0.000 964	0.000 892	0.000 825	44
45	0.001 097	0.001 014	0.000 936	0.000 864	0.000 798	0.000 736	45
46	0.000 990	0.000 912	0.000 841	0.000 774	0.000 713	0.000 657	46
47	0.000 893	0.000 821	0.000 755	0.000 694	0.000 638	0.000 586	47
48	0.000 806	0.000 739	0.000 678	0.000 622	0.000 571	0.000 523	48
49	0.000 727	0.000 666	0.000 609	0.000 558	0.000 510	0.000 467	49
50	0.000 656	0.000 599	0.000 547	0.000 500	0.000 456	0.000 417	50
51	0.000 592	0.000 540	0.000 492	0.000 448	0.000 408	0.000 372	51
52	0.000 534	0.000 486	0.000 442	0.000 402	0.000 365	0.000 332	52
53	0.000 482	0.000 438	0.000 397	0.000 360	0.000 327	0.000 296	53
54	0.000 435	0.000 394	0.000 357	0.000 323	0.000 292	0.000 264	54
55	0.000 393	0.000 355	0.000 321	0.000 290	0.000 261	0.000 236	55
56	0.000 354	0.000 320	0.000 288	0.000 260	0.000 234	0.000 211	56
57	0.000 320	0.000 288	0.000 259	0.000 233	0.000 209	0.000 188	57
58	0.000 289	0.000 259	0.000 233	0.000 209	0.000 187	0.000 168	58
59	0.000 261	0.000 233	0.000 209	0.000 187	0.000 168	0.000 150	59
YRS							
30	0.000 235	0.000 210	0.000 188	0.000 168	0.000 150	0.000 134	60
31	0.000 192	0.000 171	0.000 152	0.000 135	0.000 120	0.000 107	62
32	0.000 156	0.000 138	0.000 123	0.000 109	0.000 096	0.000 085	64
33	0.000 127	0.000 112	0.000 099	0.000 087	0.000 077	0.000 068	66
34	0.000 104	0.000 091	0.000 080	0.000 070	0.000 062	0.000 054	68
35	0.000 085	0.000 074	0.000 065	0.000 056	0.000 049	0.000 043	70
36	0.000 069	0.000 060	0.000 052	0.000 045	0.000 039	0.000 034	72
37	0.000 056	0.000 049	0.000 042	0.000 037	0.000 032	0.000 027	74
38	0.000 046	0.000 040	0.000 034	0.000 029	0.000 025	0.000 022	76
39	0.000 037	0.000 032	0.000 028	0.000 024	0.000 020	0.000 017	78
40	0.000 030	0.000 026	0.000 022	0.000 019	0.000 016	0.000 014	80

SINKING FUND

YRS	5.25% ANNUAL RATE	5.50% ANNUAL RATE	5.75% ANNUAL RATE	6.00% ANNUAL RATE	6.25% ANNUAL RATE	6.50% ANNUAL RATE	YRS
1	1.000 000	1.000 000	1.000 000	1.000 000	1.000 000	1.000 000	1
2	0.487 211	0.486 618	0.486 027	0.485 437	0.484 848	0.484 262	2
3	0.316 430	0.315 654	0.314 881	0.314 110	0.313 341	0.312 576	3
4	0.231 151	0.230 294	0.229 441	0.228 591	0.227 745	0.226 903	4
5	0.180 073	0.179 176	0.178 284	0.177 396	0.176 513	0.175 635	5
6	0.146 095	0.145 179	0.144 268	0.143 363	0.142 463	0.141 568	6
7	0.121 889	0.120 964	0.120 046	0.119 135	0.118 230	0.117 331	7
8	0.103 789	0.102 864	0.101 946	0.101 036	0.100 133	0.099 237	8
9	0.089 761	0.088 839	0.087 927	0.087 022	0.086 126	0.085 238	9
10	0.078 582	0.077 668	0.076 763	0.075 868	0.074 982	0.074 105	10
11	0.069 475	0.068 571	0.067 677	0.066 793	0.065 919	0.065 055	11
12	0.061 922	0.061 029	0.060 148	0.059 277	0.058 417	0.057 568	12
13	0.055 564	0.054 684	0.053 816	0.052 960	0.052 116	0.051 283	13
14	0.050 145	0.049 279	0.048 426	0.047 585	0.046 757	0.045 940	14
15	0.045 477	0.044 626	0.043 788	0.042 963	0.042 151	0.041 353	15
16	0.041 419	0.040 583	0.039 760	0.038 952	0.038 158	0.037 378	16
17	0.037 863	0.037 042	0.036 236	0.035 445	0.034 668	0.033 906	17
18	0.034 725	0.033 920	0.033 130	0.032 357	0.031 598	0.030 855	18
19	0.031 939	0.031 150	0.030 377	0.029 621	0.028 880	0.028 156	19
20	0.029 452	0.028 679	0.027 923	0.027 185	0.026 462	0.025 756	20
21	0.027 221	0.026 465	0.025 726	0.025 005	0.024 300	0.023 613	21
22	0.025 212	0.024 471	0.023 749	0.023 046	0.022 360	0.021 691	22
23	0.023 394	0.022 670	0.021 965	0.021 278	0.020 611	0.019 961	23
24	0.021 743	0.021 036	0.020 348	0.019 679	0.019 029	0.018 398	24
25	0.020 241	0.019 549	0.018 878	0.018 227	0.017 595	0.016 981	25
26	0.018 868	0.018 193	0.017 539	0.016 904	0.016 290	0.015 695	26
27	0.017 611	0.016 952	0.016 314	0.015 697	0.015 100	0.014 523	27
28	0.016 457	0.015 814	0.015 193	0.014 593	0.014 013	0.013 453	28
29	0.015 396	0.014 769	0.014 163	0.013 580	0.013 017	0.012 474	29
30	0.014 417	0.013 805	0.013 216	0.012 649	0.012 103	0.011 577	30
31	0.013 513	0.012 917	0.012 343	0.011 792	0.011 263	0.010 754	31
32	0.012 676	0.012 095	0.011 538	0.011 002	0.010 489	0.009 997	32
33	0.011 900	0.011 335	0.010 792	0.010 273	0.009 775	0.009 299	33
34	0.011 180	0.010 630	0.010 103	0.009 598	0.009 117	0.008 656	34
35	0.010 511	0.009 975	0.009 463	0.008 974	0.008 507	0.008 062	35
36	0.009 888	0.009 366	0.008 869	0.008 395	0.007 943	0.007 513	36
37	0.009 307	0.008 800	0.008 317	0.007 857	0.007 421	0.007 005	37
38	0.008 765	0.008 272	0.007 803	0.007 358	0.006 936	0.006 535	38
39	0.008 259	0.007 780	0.007 325	0.006 894	0.006 485	0.006 099	39
40	0.007 786	0.007 320	0.006 879	0.006 462	0.006 067	0.005 694	40
41	0.007 344	0.006 891	0.006 463	0.006 059	0.005 677	0.005 318	41
42	0.006 929	0.006 489	0.006 074	0.005 683	0.005 315	0.004 968	42
43	0.006 540	0.006 113	0.005 711	0.005 333	0.004 978	0.004 644	43
44	0.006 176	0.005 761	0.005 372	0.005 006	0.004 663	0.004 341	44
45	0.005 833	0.005 431	0.005 054	0.004 700	0.004 369	0.004 060	45
46	0.005 512	0.005 122	0.004 756	0.004 415	0.004 096	0.003 797	46
47	0.005 210	0.004 831	0.004 478	0.004 148	0.003 840	0.003 553	47
48	0.004 925	0.004 559	0.004 216	0.003 898	0.003 601	0.003 325	48
49	0.004 658	0.004 302	0.003 971	0.003 664	0.003 378	0.003 112	49
50	0.004 406	0.004 061	0.003 741	0.003 444	0.003 169	0.002 914	50

SINKING FUND

YRS	6.75% ANNUAL RATE	7.00% ANNUAL RATE	7.25% ANNUAL RATE	7.50% ANNUAL RATE	7.75% ANNUAL RATE	8.00% ANNUAL RATE	YRS
1	1.000 000	1.000 000	1.000 000	1.000 000	1.000 000	1.000 000	1
2	0.483 676	0.483 092	0.482 509	0.481 928	0.481 348	0.480 769	2
3	0.311 812	0.311 052	0.310 293	0.309 538	0.308 784	0.308 034	3
4	0.226 064	0.225 228	0.224 396	0.223 568	0.222 742	0.221 921	4
5	0.174 760	0.173 891	0.173 025	0.172 165	0.171 308	0.170 456	5
6	0.140 679	0.139 796	0.138 918	0.138 045	0.137 177	0.136 315	6
7	0.116 439	0.115 553	0.114 674	0.113 800	0.112 933	0.112 072	7
8	0.098 349	0.097 468	0.096 594	0.095 727	0.094 867	0.094 015	8
9	0.084 358	0.083 486	0.082 623	0.081 767	0.080 919	0.080 080	9
10	0.073 237	0.072 378	0.071 527	0.070 686	0.069 853	0.069 029	10
11	0.064 201	0.063 357	0.062 522	0.061 697	0.060 882	0.060 076	11
12	0.056 730	0.055 902	0.055 085	0.054 278	0.053 481	0.052 695	12
13	0.050 461	0.049 651	0.048 852	0.048 064	0.047 288	0.046 522	13
14	0.045 137	0.044 345	0.043 565	0.042 797	0.042 041	0.041 297	14
15	0.040 567	0.039 795	0.039 035	0.038 287	0.037 552	0.036 830	15
16	0.036 611	0.035 858	0.035 118	0.034 391	0.033 678	0.032 977	16
17	0.033 159	0.032 425	0.031 706	0.031 000	0.030 308	0.029 629	17
18	0.030 126	0.029 413	0.028 714	0.028 029	0.027 359	0.026 702	18
19	0.027 447	0.026 753	0.026 074	0.025 411	0.024 762	0.024 128	19
20	0.025 067	0.024 393	0.023 735	0.023 092	0.022 465	0.021 852	20
21	0.022 943	0.022 289	0.021 651	0.021 029	0.020 423	0.019 832	21
22	0.021 040	0.020 406	0.019 788	0.019 187	0.018 602	0.018 032	22
23	0.019 329	0.018 714	0.018 116	0.017 535	0.016 971	0.016 422	23
24	0.017 784	0.017 189	0.016 611	0.016 050	0.015 506	0.014 978	24
25	0.016 387	0.015 811	0.015 252	0.014 711	0.014 186	0.013 679	25
26	0.015 119	0.014 561	0.014 021	0.013 500	0.012 995	0.012 507	26
27	0.013 965	0.013 426	0.012 905	0.012 402	0.011 917	0.011 448	27
28	0.012 913	0.012 392	0.011 890	0.011 405	0.010 938	0.010 489	28
29	0.011 952	0.011 449	0.010 964	0.010 498	0.010 050	0.009 619	29
30	0.011 072	0.010 586	0.010 120	0.009 671	0.009 241	0.008 827	30
31	0.010 266	0.009 797	0.009 347	0.008 916	0.008 503	0.008 107	31
32	0.009 525	0.009 073	0.008 640	0.008 226	0.007 830	0.007 451	32
33	0.008 844	0.008 408	0.007 992	0.007 594	0.007 214	0.006 852	33
34	0.008 216	0.007 797	0.007 396	0.007 015	0.006 651	0.006 304	34
35	0.007 638	0.007 234	0.006 849	0.006 483	0.006 135	0.005 803	35
36	0.007 104	0.006 715	0.006 346	0.005 994	0.005 661	0.005 345	36
37	0.006 611	0.006 237	0.005 882	0.005 545	0.005 226	0.004 924	37
38	0.006 155	0.005 795	0.005 454	0.005 132	0.004 827	0.004 539	38
39	0.005 733	0.005 387	0.005 060	0.004 751	0.004 460	0.004 185	39
40	0.005 342	0.005 009	0.004 696	0.004 400	0.004 122	0.003 860	40
41	0.004 979	0.004 660	0.004 359	0.004 077	0.003 811	0.003 561	41
42	0.004 642	0.004 336	0.004 048	0.003 778	0.003 524	0.003 287	42
43	0.004 330	0.004 036	0.003 760	0.003 502	0.003 260	0.003 034	43
44	0.004 040	0.003 758	0.003 494	0.003 247	0.003 017	0.002 802	44
45	0.003 770	0.003 500	0.003 247	0.003 011	0.002 792	0.002 587	45
46	0.003 519	0.003 260	0.003 018	0.002 794	0.002 584	0.002 390	46
47	0.003 286	0.003 037	0.002 806	0.002 592	0.002 393	0.002 208	47
48	0.003 069	0.002 831	0.002 610	0.002 405	0.002 216	0.002 040	48
49	0.002 866	0.002 639	0.002 428	0.002 232	0.002 052	0.001 886	49
50	0.002 678	0.002 460	0.002 258	0.002 072	0.001 901	0.001 743	50

SECTION 3

YRS	8.25% ANNUAL RATE	8.50% ANNUAL RATE	8.75% ANNUAL RATE	9.00% ANNUAL RATE	9.25% ANNUAL RATE	9.50% ANNUAL RATE	YRS
1	1.000 000	1.000 000	1.000 000	1.000 000	1.000 000	1.000 000	1
2	0.480 192	0.479 616	0.479 042	0.478 469	0.477 897	0.477 327	2
3	0.307 285	0.306 539	0.305 796	0.305 055	0.304 316	0.303 580	3
4	0.221 103	0.220 288	0.219 477	0.218 669	0.217 864	0.217 063	4
5	0.169 609	0.168 766	0.167 927	0.167 092	0.166 262	0.165 436	5
6	0.135 459	0.134 607	0.133 761	0.132 920	0.132 084	0.131 253	6
7	0.111 218	0.110 369	0.109 527	0.108 691	0.107 860	0.107 036	7
8	0.093 169	0.092 331	0.091 499	0.090 674	0.089 857	0.089 046	8
9	0.079 248	0.078 424	0.077 607	0.076 799	0.075 998	0.075 205	9
10	0.068 214	0.067 408	0.066 610	0.065 820	0.065 039	0.064 266	10
11	0.059 280	0.058 493	0.057 715	0.056 947	0.056 187	0.055 437	11
12	0.051 919	0.051 153	0.050 397	0.049 651	0.048 914	0.048 188	12
13	0.045 767	0.045 023	0.044 289	0.043 567	0.042 854	0.042 152	13
14	0.040 564	0.039 842	0.039 132	0.038 433	0.037 745	0.037 068	14
15	0.036 119	0.035 420	0.034 734	0.034 059	0.033 396	0.032 744	15
16	0.032 289	0.031 614	0.030 951	0.030 300	0.029 661	0.029 035	16
17	0.028 964	0.028 312	0.027 673	0.027 046	0.026 432	0.025 831	17
18	0.026 059	0.025 430	0.024 815	0.024 212	0.023 623	0.023 046	18
19	0.023 507	0.022 901	0.022 309	0.021 730	0.021 165	0.020 613	19
20	0.021 254	0.020 671	0.020 102	0.019 546	0.019 005	0.018 477	20
21	0.019 256	0.018 695	0.018 149	0.017 617	0.017 098	0.016 594	21
22	0.017 478	0.016 939	0.016 415	0.015 905	0.015 409	0.014 928	22
23	0.015 889	0.015 372	0.014 870	0.014 382	0.013 909	0.013 449	23
24	0.014 466	0.013 970	0.013 489	0.013 023	0.012 571	0.012 134	24
25	0.013 187	0.012 712	0.012 251	0.011 806	0.011 376	0.010 959	25
26	0.012 036	0.011 580	0.011 140	0.010 715	0.010 305	0.009 909	26
27	0.010 996	0.010 560	0.010 140	0.009 735	0.009 345	0.008 969	27
28	0.010 056	0.009 639	0.009 238	0.008 852	0.008 481	0.008 124	28
29	0.009 204	0.008 806	0.008 423	0.008 056	0.007 703	0.007 364	29
30	0.008 431	0.008 051	0.007 686	0.007 336	0.007 001	0.006 681	30
31	0.007 728	0.007 365	0.007 018	0.006 686	0.006 368	0.006 064	31
32	0.007 089	0.006 742	0.006 412	0.006 096	0.005 795	0.005 507	32
33	0.006 506	0.006 176	0.005 861	0.005 562	0.005 276	0.005 004	33
34	0.005 974	0.005 660	0.005 361	0.005 077	0.004 806	0.004 549	34
35	0.005 488	0.005 189	0.004 905	0.004 636	0.004 380	0.004 138	35
36	0.005 045	0.004 760	0.004 490	0.004 235	0.003 993	0.003 764	36
37	0.004 639	0.004 368	0.004 112	0.003 870	0.003 642	0.003 426	37
38	0.004 267	0.004 010	0.003 767	0.003 538	0.003 322	0.003 119	38
39	0.003 926	0.003 682	0.003 452	0.003 236	0.003 032	0.002 840	39
40	0.003 614	0.003 382	0.003 164	0.002 960	0.002 767	0.002 587	40
41	0.003 327	0.003 107	0.002 901	0.002 708	0.002 527	0.002 357	41
42	0.003 064	0.002 856	0.002 661	0.002 478	0.002 308	0.002 148	42
43	0.002 823	0.002 625	0.002 441	0.002 268	0.002 108	0.001 958	43
44	0.002 601	0.002 414	0.002 239	0.002 077	0.001 926	0.001 785	44
45	0.002 397	0.002 220	0.002 055	0.001 902	0.001 759	0.001 627	45
46	0.002 209	0.002 042	0.001 886	0.001 742	0.001 608	0.001 484	46
47	0.002 037	0.001 878	0.001 731	0.001 595	0.001 470	0.001 353	47
48	0.001 878	0.001 728	0.001 589	0.001 461	0.001 343	0.001 234	48
49	0.001 732	0.001 590	0.001 459	0.001 339	0.001 228	0.001 126	49
50	0.001 597	0.001 463	0.001 340	0.001 227	0.001 123	0.001 027	50

SECTION 3

YRS	9.75% ANNUAL RATE	10.00% ANNUAL RATE	10.25% ANNUAL RATE	10.50% ANNUAL RATE	10.75% ANNUAL RATE	11.00% ANNUAL RATE	YRS
1	1.000 000	1.000 000	1.000 000	1.000 000	1.000 000	1.000 000	1
2	0.476 758	0.476 190	0.475 624	0.475 059	0.474 496	0.473 934	2
3	0.302 846	0.302 115	0.301 386	0.300 659	0.299 935	0.299 213	3
4	0.216 265	0.215 471	0.214 680	0.213 892	0.213 108	0.212 326	4
5	0.164 615	0.163 797	0.162 984	0.162 175	0.161 371	0.160 570	5
6	0.130 428	0.129 607	0.128 792	0.127 982	0.127 177	0.126 377	6
7	0.106 218	0.105 405	0.104 599	0.103 799	0.103 004	0.102 215	7
8	0.088 241	0.087 444	0.086 653	0.085 869	0.085 092	0.084 321	8
9	0.074 419	0.073 641	0.072 870	0.072 106	0.071 350	0.070 602	9
10	0.063 502	0.062 745	0.061 997	0.061 257	0.060 525	0.059 801	10
11	0.054 696	0.053 963	0.053 240	0.052 525	0.051 819	0.051 121	11
12	0.047 471	0.046 763	0.046 065	0.045 377	0.044 697	0.044 027	12
13	0.041 460	0.040 779	0.040 107	0.039 445	0.038 793	0.038 151	13
14	0.036 402	0.035 746	0.035 101	0.034 467	0.033 842	0.033 228	14
15	0.032 103	0.031 474	0.030 855	0.030 248	0.029 651	0.029 065	15
16	0.028 420	0.027 817	0.027 225	0.026 644	0.026 075	0.025 517	16
17	0.025 241	0.024 664	0.024 099	0.023 545	0.023 003	0.022 471	17
18	0.022 482	0.021 930	0.021 391	0.020 863	0.020 347	0.019 843	18
19	0.020 074	0.019 547	0.019 033	0.018 531	0.018 041	0.017 563	19
20	0.017 962	0.017 460	0.016 970	0.016 493	0.016 028	0.015 576	20
21	0.016 102	0.015 624	0.015 159	0.014 707	0.014 266	0.013 838	21
22	0.014 460	0.014 005	0.013 563	0.013 134	0.012 718	0.012 313	22
23	0.013 004	0.012 572	0.012 153	0.011 747	0.011 353	0.010 971	23
24	0.011 710	0.011 300	0.010 903	0.010 519	0.010 147	0.009 787	24
25	0.010 557	0.010 168	0.009 792	0.009 429	0.009 079	0.008 740	25
26	0.009 527	0.009 159	0.008 804	0.008 461	0.008 131	0.007 813	26
27	0.008 606	0.008 258	0.007 922	0.007 599	0.007 288	0.006 989	27
28	0.007 781	0.007 451	0.007 134	0.006 830	0.006 538	0.006 257	28
29	0.007 040	0.006 728	0.006 429	0.006 143	0.005 868	0.005 605	29
30	0.006 373	0.006 079	0.005 798	0.005 528	0.005 271	0.005 025	30
31	0.005 774	0.005 496	0.005 231	0.004 978	0.004 737	0.004 506	31
32	0.005 233	0.004 972	0.004 722	0.004 485	0.004 259	0.004 043	32
33	0.004 746	0.004 499	0.004 265	0.004 042	0.003 831	0.003 629	33
34	0.004 305	0.004 074	0.003 854	0.003 645	0.003 447	0.003 259	34
35	0.003 908	0.003 690	0.003 483	0.003 288	0.003 103	0.002 927	35
36	0.003 548	0.003 343	0.003 149	0.002 967	0.002 794	0.002 630	36
37	0.003 222	0.003 030	0.002 849	0.002 677	0.002 516	0.002 364	37
38	0.002 927	0.002 747	0.002 577	0.002 417	0.002 267	0.002 125	38
39	0.002 660	0.002 491	0.002 332	0.002 183	0.002 043	0.001 911	39
40	0.002 418	0.002 259	0.002 111	0.001 971	0.001 841	0.001 719	40
41	0.002 198	0.002 050	0.001 911	0.001 781	0.001 659	0.001 546	41
42	0.001 999	0.001 860	0.001 730	0.001 609	0.001 496	0.001 391	42
43	0.001 818	0.001 688	0.001 567	0.001 454	0.001 349	0.001 251	43
44	0.001 654	0.001 532	0.001 419	0.001 314	0.001 217	0.001 126	44
45	0.001 505	0.001 391	0.001 286	0.001 188	0.001 097	0.001 014	45
46	0.001 369	0.001 263	0.001 165	0.001 074	0.000 990	0.000 912	46
47	0.001 246	0.001 147	0.001 055	0.000 971	0.000 893	0.000 821	47
48	0.001 134	0.001 041	0.000 956	0.000 878	0.000 806	0.000 739	48
49	0.001 032	0.000 946	0.000 867	0.000 794	0.000 727	0.000 666	49
50	0.000 940	0.000 859	0.000 785	0.000 718	0.000 656	0.000 599	50

SINKING FUND

YRS	11.25% ANNUAL RATE	11.50% ANNUAL RATE	11.75% ANNUAL RATE	12.00% ANNUAL RATE	12.25% ANNUAL RATE	12.50% ANNUAL RATE	YRS
1	1.000 000	1.000 000	1.000 000	1.000 000	1.000 000	1.000 000	1
2	0.473 373	0.472 813	0.472 255	0.471 698	0.471 143	0.470 588	2
3	0.298 494	0.297 776	0.297 062	0.296 349	0.295 639	0.294 931	3
4	0.211 548	0.210 774	0.210 003	0.209 234	0.208 470	0.207 708	4
5	0.159 774	0.158 982	0.158 194	0.157 410	0.156 630	0.155 854	5
6	0.125 581	0.124 791	0.124 006	0.123 226	0.122 450	0.121 680	6
7	0.101 432	0.100 655	0.099 884	0.099 118	0.098 358	0.097 603	7
8	0.083 557	0.082 799	0.082 048	0.081 303	0.080 564	0.079 832	8
9	0.069 860	0.069 126	0.068 399	0.067 679	0.066 966	0.066 260	9
10	0.059 085	0.058 377	0.057 677	0.056 984	0.056 299	0.055 622	10
11	0.050 432	0.049 751	0.049 079	0.048 415	0.047 760	0.047 112	11
12	0.043 366	0.042 714	0.042 071	0.041 437	0.040 811	0.040 194	12
13	0.037 518	0.036 895	0.036 282	0.035 677	0.035 082	0.034 496	13
14	0.032 624	0.032 030	0.031 446	0.030 871	0.030 306	0.029 751	14
15	0.028 490	0.027 924	0.027 369	0.026 824	0.026 289	0.025 764	15
16	0.024 969	0.024 432	0.023 906	0.023 390	0.022 884	0.022 388	16
17	0.021 952	0.021 443	0.020 944	0.020 457	0.019 979	0.019 512	17
18	0.019 350	0.018 868	0.018 397	0.017 937	0.017 488	0.017 049	18
19	0.017 096	0.016 641	0.016 196	0.015 763	0.015 340	0.014 928	19
20	0.015 134	0.014 705	0.014 286	0.013 879	0.013 482	0.013 096	20
21	0.013 421	0.013 016	0.012 623	0.012 240	0.011 868	0.011 507	21
22	0.011 920	0.011 539	0.011 169	0.010 811	0.010 462	0.010 125	22
23	0.010 601	0.010 243	0.009 896	0.009 560	0.009 235	0.008 919	23
24	0.009 439	0.009 103	0.008 778	0.008 463	0.008 160	0.007 866	24
25	0.008 413	0.008 098	0.007 794	0.007 500	0.007 217	0.006 943	25
26	0.007 506	0.007 210	0.006 926	0.006 652	0.006 388	0.006 134	26
27	0.006 702	0.006 425	0.006 159	0.005 904	0.005 659	0.005 423	27
28	0.005 988	0.005 730	0.005 482	0.005 244	0.005 016	0.004 797	28
29	0.005 354	0.005 112	0.004 881	0.004 660	0.004 449	0.004 246	29
30	0.004 789	0.004 564	0.004 349	0.004 144	0.003 947	0.003 760	30
31	0.004 286	0.004 077	0.003 877	0.003 686	0.003 504	0.003 331	31
32	0.003 838	0.003 643	0.003 457	0.003 280	0.003 112	0.002 952	32
33	0.003 438	0.003 257	0.003 084	0.002 920	0.002 765	0.002 617	33
34	0.003 081	0.002 912	0.002 752	0.002 601	0.002 457	0.002 321	34
35	0.002 762	0.002 605	0.002 457	0.002 317	0.002 184	0.002 059	35
36	0.002 476	0.002 331	0.002 194	0.002 064	0.001 942	0.001 827	36
37	0.002 221	0.002 086	0.001 959	0.001 840	0.001 727	0.001 621	37
38	0.001 992	0.001 867	0.001 750	0.001 640	0.001 536	0.001 439	38
39	0.001 788	0.001 672	0.001 564	0.001 462	0.001 367	0.001 278	39
40	0.001 604	0.001 497	0.001 397	0.001 304	0.001 216	0.001 134	40
41	0.001 440	0.001 341	0.001 249	0.001 163	0.001 082	0.001 007	41
42	0.001 293	0.001 201	0.001 116	0.001 037	0.000 963	0.000 895	42
43	0.001 161	0.001 076	0.000 998	0.000 925	0.000 857	0.000 795	43
44	0.001 042	0.000 964	0.000 892	0.000 825	0.000 763	0.000 706	44
45	0.000 936	0.000 864	0.000 798	0.000 736	0.000 679	0.000 627	45
46	0.000 841	0.000 774	0.000 713	0.000 657	0.000 605	0.000 557	46
47	0.000 755	0.000 694	0.000 638	0.000 586	0.000 539	0.000 495	47
48	0.000 678	0.000 622	0.000 571	0.000 523	0.000 480	0.000 440	48
49	0.000 609	0.000 558	0.000 510	0.000 467	0.000 427	0.000 391	49
50	0.000 547	0.000 500	0.000 456	0.000 417	0.000 380	0.000 347	50

ANNUAL COMPOUNDING

SECTION 3

YRS	12.75% ANNUAL RATE	13.00% ANNUAL RATE	13.25% ANNUAL RATE	13.50% ANNUAL RATE	13.75% ANNUAL RATE	14.00% ANNUAL RATE	YRS
1	1.000 000	1.000 000	1.000 000	1.000 000	1.000 000	1.000 000	1
2	0.470 035	0.469 484	0.468 933	0.468 384	0.467 836	0.467 290	2
3	0.294 225	0.293 522	0.292 821	0.292 122	0.291 426	0.290 731	3
4	0.206 949	0.206 194	0.205 442	0.204 693	0.203 947	0.203 205	4
5	0.155 082	0.154 315	0.153 551	0.152 791	0.152 035	0.151 284	5
6	0.120 914	0.120 163	0.119 397	0.118 646	0.117 899	0.117 157	6
7	0.096 854	0.096 111	0.095 373	0.094 641	0.093 914	0.093 192	7
8	0.079 106	0.078 387	0.077 673	0.076 966	0.076 265	0.075 570	8
9	0.065 561	0.064 869	0.064 184	0.063 505	0.062 833	0.062 168	9
10	0.054 952	0.054 290	0.053 635	0.052 987	0.052 347	0.051 714	10
11	0.046 473	0.045 841	0.045 218	0.044 602	0.043 994	0.043 394	11
12	0.039 586	0.038 986	0.038 395	0.037 811	0.037 236	0.036 669	12
13	0.033 919	0.033 350	0.032 791	0.032 240	0.031 698	0.031 164	13
14	0.029 204	0.028 667	0.028 140	0.027 621	0.027 111	0.026 609	14
15	0.025 248	0.024 742	0.024 245	0.023 757	0.023 279	0.022 809	15
16	0.021 902	0.021 426	0.020 960	0.020 502	0.020 054	0.019 615	16
17	0.019 056	0.018 608	0.018 171	0.017 743	0.017 325	0.016 915	17
18	0.016 620	0.016 201	0.015 792	0.015 392	0.015 002	0.014 621	18
19	0.014 526	0.014 134	0.013 752	0.013 380	0.013 017	0.012 663	19
20	0.012 720	0.012 354	0.011 998	0.011 651	0.011 314	0.010 986	20
21	0.011 156	0.010 814	0.010 483	0.010 161	0.009 848	0.009 545	21
22	0.009 797	0.009 479	0.009 172	0.008 873	0.008 584	0.008 303	22
23	0.008 614	0.008 319	0.008 033	0.007 757	0.007 490	0.007 231	23
24	0.007 582	0.007 308	0.007 044	0.006 788	0.006 541	0.006 303	24
25	0.006 680	0.006 426	0.006 181	0.005 945	0.005 718	0.005 498	25
26	0.005 890	0.005 655	0.005 428	0.005 211	0.005 001	0.004 800	26
27	0.005 197	0.004 979	0.004 770	0.004 570	0.004 377	0.004 193	27
28	0.004 588	0.004 387	0.004 195	0.004 010	0.003 834	0.003 664	28
29	0.004 052	0.003 867	0.003 690	0.003 521	0.003 359	0.003 204	29
30	0.003 581	0.003 411	0.003 248	0.003 092	0.002 944	0.002 803	30
31	0.003 166	0.003 009	0.002 860	0.002 717	0.002 582	0.002 453	31
32	0.002 800	0.002 656	0.002 519	0.002 388	0.002 264	0.002 147	32
33	0.002 478	0.002 345	0.002 219	0.002 100	0.001 987	0.001 880	33
34	0.002 193	0.002 071	0.001 956	0.001 847	0.001 744	0.001 646	34
35	0.001 941	0.001 829	0.001 724	0.001 624	0.001 530	0.001 442	35
36	0.001 718	0.001 616	0.001 520	0.001 429	0.001 344	0.001 263	36
37	0.001 522	0.001 428	0.001 340	0.001 258	0.001 180	0.001 107	37
38	0.001 348	0.001 262	0.001 182	0.001 107	0.001 036	0.000 970	38
39	0.001 194	0.001 116	0.001 043	0.000 974	0.000 910	0.000 850	39
40	0.001 058	0.000 986	0.000 920	0.000 858	0.000 799	0.000 745	40
41	0.000 937	0.000 872	0.000 812	0.000 755	0.000 702	0.000 653	41
42	0.000 831	0.000 771	0.000 716	0.000 665	0.000 617	0.000 573	42
43	0.000 736	0.000 682	0.000 632	0.000 585	0.000 542	0.000 502	43
44	0.000 653	0.000 603	0.000 558	0.000 515	0.000 476	0.000 440	44
45	0.000 578	0.000 534	0.000 492	0.000 454	0.000 419	0.000 386	45
46	0.000 513	0.000 472	0.000 434	0.000 400	0.000 368	0.000 338	46
47	0.000 455	0.000 417	0.000 383	0.000 352	0.000 323	0.000 297	47
48	0.000 403	0.000 369	0.000 338	0.000 310	0.000 284	0.000 260	48
49	0.000 357	0.000 327	0.000 299	0.000 273	0.000 250	0.000 228	49
50	0.000 317	0.000 289	0.000 264	0.000 241	0.000 219	0.000 200	50

ANNUAL COMPOUNDING

SECTION 3

YRS	14.25% ANNUAL RATE	14.50% ANNUAL RATE	14.75% ANNUAL RATE	15.00% ANNUAL RATE	15.25% ANNUAL RATE	15.50% ANNUAL RATE	YRS
1	1.000 000	1.000 000	1.000 000	1.000 000	1.000 000	1.000 000	1
2	0.466 744	0.466 200	0.465 658	0.465 116	0.464 576	0.464 037	2
3	0.290 039	0.289 350	0.288 662	0.287 977	0.287 294	0.286 613	3
4	0.202 465	0.201 729	0.200 996	0.200 265	0.199 538	0.198 814	4
5	0.150 536	0.149 792	0.149 052	0.148 316	0.147 583	0.146 855	5
6	0.116 420	0.115 688	0.114 960	0.114 237	0.113 518	0.112 804	6
7	0.092 476	0.091 766	0.091 060	0.090 360	0.089 666	0.088 976	7
8	0.074 881	0.074 198	0.073 521	0.072 850	0.072 185	0.071 526	8
9	0.061 510	0.060 858	0.060 213	0.059 574	0.058 942	0.058 316	9
10	0.051 088	0.050 469	0.049 857	0.049 252	0.048 654	0.048 063	10
11	0.042 802	0.042 217	0.041 639	0.041 069	0.040 506	0.039 951	11
12	0.036 110	0.035 559	0.035 016	0.034 481	0.033 953	0.033 433	12
13	0.030 638	0.030 121	0.029 612	0.029 110	0.028 617	0.028 132	13
14	0.026 116	0.025 632	0.025 156	0.024 688	0.024 229	0.023 777	14
15	0.022 348	0.021 896	0.021 452	0.021 017	0.020 590	0.020 171	15
16	0.019 185	0.018 764	0.018 352	0.017 948	0.017 552	0.017 165	16
17	0.016 515	0.016 124	0.015 741	0.015 367	0.015 001	0.014 643	17
18	0.014 249	0.013 886	0.013 532	0.013 186	0.012 849	0.012 520	18
19	0.012 318	0.011 982	0.011 655	0.011 336	0.011 026	0.010 723	19
20	0.010 667	0.010 357	0.010 055	0.009 761	0.009 476	0.009 199	20
21	0.009 250	0.008 964	0.008 686	0.008 417	0.008 155	0.007 901	21
22	0.008 031	0.007 768	0.007 513	0.007 266	0.007 026	0.006 795	22
23	0.006 981	0.006 739	0.006 505	0.006 278	0.006 060	0.005 848	23
24	0.006 073	0.005 851	0.005 637	0.005 430	0.005 230	0.005 038	24
25	0.005 287	0.005 084	0.004 888	0.004 699	0.004 518	0.004 343	25
26	0.004 606	0.004 420	0.004 242	0.004 070	0.003 905	0.003 746	26
27	0.004 016	0.003 846	0.003 683	0.003 526	0.003 377	0.003 233	27
28	0.003 503	0.003 348	0.003 199	0.003 057	0.002 921	0.002 791	28
29	0.003 056	0.002 915	0.002 780	0.002 651	0.002 528	0.002 411	29
30	0.002 668	0.002 539	0.002 417	0.002 300	0.002 189	0.002 083	30
31	0.002 330	0.002 213	0.002 102	0.001 996	0.001 896	0.001 800	31
32	0.002 035	0.001 929	0.001 828	0.001 733	0.001 642	0.001 556	32
33	0.001 778	0.001 682	0.001 591	0.001 505	0.001 423	0.001 345	33
34	0.001 554	0.001 467	0.001 384	0.001 307	0.001 233	0.001 164	34
35	0.001 358	0.001 279	0.001 205	0.001 135	0.001 069	0.001 006	35
36	0.001 187	0.001 116	0.001 049	0.000 986	0.000 926	0.000 871	36
37	0.001 038	0.000 974	0.000 913	0.000 857	0.000 803	0.000 753	37
38	0.000 908	0.000 850	0.000 795	0.000 744	0.000 696	0.000 652	38
39	0.000 794	0.000 742	0.000 693	0.000 647	0.000 604	0.000 564	39
40	0.000 695	0.000 647	0.000 603	0.000 562	0.000 524	0.000 488	40
41	0.000 608	0.000 565	0.000 525	0.000 489	0.000 454	0.000 422	41
42	0.000 531	0.000 493	0.000 458	0.000 425	0.000 394	0.000 366	42
43	0.000 465	0.000 431	0.000 399	0.000 369	0.000 342	0.000 316	43
44	0.000 407	0.000 376	0.000 347	0.000 321	0.000 296	0.000 274	44
45	0.000 356	0.000 328	0.000 303	0.000 279	0.000 257	0.000 237	45
46	0.000 311	0.000 287	0.000 264	0.000 242	0.000 223	0.000 205	46
47	0.000 273	0.000 250	0.000 230	0.000 211	0.000 194	0.000 178	47
48	0.000 238	0.000 218	0.000 200	0.000 183	0.000 168	0.000 154	48
49	0.000 209	0.000 191	0.000 174	0.000 159	0.000 146	0.000 133	49
50	0.000 183	0.000 167	0.000 152	0.000 139	0.000 126	0.000 115	50

SINKING FUND

YRS	15.75% ANNUAL RATE	16.00% ANNUAL RATE	16.25% ANNUAL RATE	16.50% ANNUAL RATE	16.75% ANNUAL RATE	17.00% ANNUAL RATE	YRS
1	1.000 000	1.000 000	1.000 000	1.000 000	1.000 000	1.000 000	1
2	0.463 499	0.462 963	0.462 428	0.461 894	0.461 361	0.460 829	2
3	0.285 934	0.285 258	0.284 584	0.283 911	0.283 241	0.282 574	3
4	0.198 093	0.197 375	0.196 660	0.195 948	0.195 239	0.194 533	4
5	0.146 130	0.145 409	0.144 692	0.143 979	0.143 270	0.142 564	5
6	0.112 095	0.111 390	0.110 689	0.109 993	0.109 302	0.108 615	6
7	0.088 292	0.087 613	0.086 939	0.086 270	0.085 606	0.084 947	7
8	0.070 872	0.070 224	0.069 582	0.068 946	0.068 315	0.067 690	8
9	0.057 696	0.057 082	0.056 475	0.055 874	0.055 279	0.054 691	9
10	0.047 479	0.046 901	0.046 330	0.045 766	0.045 208	0.044 657	10
11	0.039 402	0.038 861	0.038 326	0.037 799	0.037 279	0.036 765	11
12	0.032 920	0.032 415	0.031 917	0.031 426	0.030 942	0.030 466	12
13	0.027 654	0.027 184	0.026 722	0.026 266	0.025 819	0.025 378	13
14	0.023 334	0.022 898	0.022 470	0.022 049	0.021 636	0.021 230	14
15	0.019 760	0.019 358	0.018 962	0.018 575	0.018 195	0.017 822	15
16	0.016 785	0.016 414	0.016 050	0.015 694	0.015 345	0.015 004	16
17	0.014 294	0.013 952	0.013 618	0.013 292	0.012 973	0.012 662	17
18	0.012 198	0.011 885	0.011 579	0.011 281	0.010 990	0.010 706	18
19	0.010 429	0.010 142	0.009 862	0.009 590	0.009 325	0.009 067	19
20	0.008 929	0.008 667	0.008 412	0.008 165	0.007 924	0.007 690	20
21	0.007 655	0.007 416	0.007 184	0.006 960	0.006 742	0.006 530	21
22	0.006 570	0.006 353	0.006 142	0.005 938	0.005 741	0.005 550	22
23	0.005 644	0.005 447	0.005 256	0.005 071	0.004 893	0.004 721	23
24	0.004 852	0.004 673	0.004 501	0.004 334	0.004 174	0.004 019	24
25	0.004 175	0.004 013	0.003 857	0.003 707	0.003 562	0.003 423	25
26	0.003 594	0.003 447	0.003 307	0.003 172	0.003 042	0.002 917	26
27	0.003 095	0.002 963	0.002 836	0.002 715	0.002 599	0.002 487	27
28	0.002 667	0.002 548	0.002 434	0.002 325	0.002 221	0.002 121	28
29	0.002 299	0.002 192	0.002 089	0.001 992	0.001 899	0.001 810	29
30	0.001 982	0.001 886	0.001 794	0.001 707	0.001 624	0.001 545	30
31	0.001 709	0.001 623	0.001 541	0.001 463	0.001 389	0.001 318	31
32	0.001 475	0.001 397	0.001 324	0.001 254	0.001 188	0.001 126	32
33	0.001 272	0.001 203	0.001 137	0.001 075	0.001 017	0.000 961	33
34	0.001 098	0.001 036	0.000 977	0.000 922	0.000 870	0.000 821	34
35	0.000 948	0.000 892	0.000 840	0.000 791	0.000 745	0.000 701	35
36	0.000 818	0.000 769	0.000 722	0.000 678	0.000 637	0.000 599	36
37	0.000 706	0.000 662	0.000 621	0.000 582	0.000 546	0.000 512	37
38	0.000 610	0.000 571	0.000 534	0.000 499	0.000 467	0.000 437	38
39	0.000 527	0.000 492	0.000 459	0.000 428	0.000 400	0.000 373	39
40	0.000 455	0.000 424	0.000 395	0.000 368	0.000 342	0.000 319	40
41	0.000 393	0.000 365	0.000 339	0.000 315	0.000 293	0.000 273	41
42	0.000 339	0.000 315	0.000 292	0.000 271	0.000 251	0.000 233	42
43	0.000 293	0.000 271	0.000 251	0.000 232	0.000 215	0.000 199	43
44	0.000 253	0.000 234	0.000 216	0.000 199	0.000 184	0.000 170	44
45	0.000 218	0.000 201	0.000 186	0.000 171	0.000 158	0.000 145	45
46	0.000 189	0.000 174	0.000 160	0.000 147	0.000 135	0.000 124	46
47	0.000 163	0.000 150	0.000 137	0.000 126	0.000 116	0.000 106	47
48	0.000 141	0.000 129	0.000 118	0.000 108	0.000 099	0.000 091	48
49	0.000 122	0.000 111	0.000 102	0.000 093	0.000 085	0.000 078	49
50	0.000 105	0.000 096	0.000 087	0.000 080	0.000 073	0.000 066	50

SINKING FUND

YRS	17.25% ANNUAL RATE	17.50% ANNUAL RATE	17.75% ANNUAL RATE	18.00% ANNUAL RATE	18.25% ANNUAL RATE	18.50% ANNUAL RATE	YRS
1	1.000 000	1.000 000	1.000 000	1.000 000	1.000 000	1.000 000	1
2	0.460 299	0.459 770	0.459 242	0.458 716	0.458 190	0.457 666	2
3	0.281 908	0.281 245	0.280 583	0.279 924	0.279 267	0.278 612	3
4	0.193 830	0.193 130	0.192 433	0.191 739	0.191 047	0.190 359	4
5	0.141 862	0.141 163	0.140 469	0.139 778	0.139 090	0.138 407	5
6	0.107 932	0.107 256	0.106 580	0.105 910	0.105 245	0.104 584	6
7	0.084 293	0.083 645	0.083 001	0.082 362	0.081 728	0.081 099	7
8	0.067 070	0.066 456	0.065 848	0.065 244	0.064 647	0.064 054	8
9	0.054 108	0.053 531	0.052 960	0.052 395	0.051 836	0.051 282	9
10	0.044 112	0.043 573	0.043 041	0.042 515	0.041 995	0.041 481	10
11	0.036 258	0.035 757	0.035 264	0.034 776	0.034 296	0.033 821	11
12	0.029 996	0.029 533	0.029 077	0.028 628	0.028 185	0.027 749	12
13	0.024 945	0.024 518	0.024 099	0.023 686	0.023 280	0.022 881	13
14	0.020 832	0.020 440	0.020 056	0.019 678	0.019 307	0.018 943	14
15	0.017 457	0.017 098	0.016 747	0.016 403	0.016 065	0.015 734	15
16	0.014 670	0.014 343	0.014 023	0.013 710	0.013 404	0.013 104	16
17	0.012 357	0.012 060	0.011 769	0.011 485	0.011 208	0.010 937	17
18	0.010 429	0.010 159	0.009 896	0.009 639	0.009 389	0.009 145	18
19	0.008 816	0.008 572	0.008 334	0.008 103	0.007 878	0.007 658	19
20	0.007 463	0.007 243	0.007 028	0.006 820	0.006 618	0.006 421	20
21	0.006 325	0.006 126	0.005 933	0.005 746	0.005 565	0.005 390	21
22	0.005 365	0.005 187	0.005 014	0.004 846	0.004 684	0.004 528	22
23	0.004 555	0.004 395	0.004 240	0.004 090	0.003 946	0.003 806	23
24	0.003 870	0.003 726	0.003 588	0.003 454	0.003 326	0.003 202	24
25	0.003 290	0.003 161	0.003 038	0.002 919	0.002 805	0.002 695	25
26	0.002 798	0.002 683	0.002 573	0.002 467	0.002 366	0.002 269	26
27	0.002 381	0.002 278	0.002 181	0.002 087	0.001 997	0.001 911	27
28	0.002 026	0.001 935	0.001 848	0.001 765	0.001 686	0.001 610	28
29	0.001 725	0.001 644	0.001 567	0.001 494	0.001 424	0.001 357	29
30	0.001 469	0.001 398	0.001 329	0.001 264	0.001 202	0.001 144	30
31	0.001 251	0.001 188	0.001 128	0.001 070	0.001 016	0.000 964	31
32	0.001 066	0.001 010	0.000 957	0.000 906	0.000 858	0.000 813	32
33	0.000 909	0.000 859	0.000 812	0.000 767	0.000 725	0.000 686	33
34	0.000 774	0.000 730	0.000 689	0.000 650	0.000 613	0.000 578	34
35	0.000 660	0.000 621	0.000 585	0.000 550	0.000 518	0.000 488	35
36	0.000 563	0.000 528	0.000 496	0.000 466	0.000 438	0.000 411	36
37	0.000 480	0.000 450	0.000 421	0.000 395	0.000 370	0.000 347	37
38	0.000 409	0.000 382	0.000 358	0.000 335	0.000 313	0.000 293	38
39	0.000 349	0.000 325	0.000 304	0.000 284	0.000 265	0.000 247	39
40	0.000 297	0.000 277	0.000 258	0.000 240	0.000 224	0.000 208	40
41	0.000 253	0.000 236	0.000 219	0.000 204	0.000 189	0.000 176	41
42	0.000 216	0.000 200	0.000 186	0.000 172	0.000 160	0.000 148	42
43	0.000 184	0.000 171	0.000 158	0.000 146	0.000 135	0.000 125	43
44	0.000 157	0.000 145	0.000 134	0.000 124	0.000 114	0.000 106	44
45	0.000 134	0.000 123	0.000 114	0.000 105	0.000 097	0.000 089	45
46	0.000 114	0.000 105	0.000 097	0.000 089	0.000 082	0.000 075	46
47	0.000 097	0.000 089	0.000 082	0.000 075	0.000 069	0.000 063	47
48	0.000 083	0.000 076	0.000 070	0.000 064	0.000 058	0.000 054	48
49	0.000 071	0.000 065	0.000 059	0.000 054	0.000 049	0.000 045	49
50	0.000 060	0.000 055	0.000 050	0.000 046	0.000 042	0.000 038	50

YRS	18.75% ANNUAL RATE	19.00% ANNUAL RATE	19.25% ANNUAL RATE	19.50% ANNUAL RATE	19.75% ANNUAL RATE	20.00% ANNUAL RATE	YRS
1	1.000 000	1.000 000	1.000 000	1.000 000	1.000 000	1.000 000	1
2	0.457 143	0.456 621	0.456 100	0.455 581	0.455 063	0.454 545	2
3	0.277 959	0.277 308	0.276 659	0.276 012	0.275 368	0.274 725	3
4	0.189 674	0.188 991	0.188 311	0.187 634	0.186 960	0.186 289	4
5	0.137 727	0.137 050	0.136 377	0.135 708	0.135 042	0.134 380	5
6	0.103 927	0.103 274	0.102 626	0.101 982	0.101 342	0.100 706	6
7	0.080 474	0.079 855	0.079 240	0.078 630	0.078 025	0.077 424	7
8	0.063 467	0.062 885	0.062 308	0.061 737	0.061 171	0.060 609	8
9	0.050 734	0.050 192	0.049 656	0.049 125	0.048 599	0.048 079	9
10	0.040 973	0.040 471	0.039 975	0.039 485	0.039 001	0.038 523	10
11	0.033 353	0.032 891	0.032 435	0.031 985	0.031 542	0.031 104	11
12	0.027 319	0.026 896	0.026 479	0.026 068	0.025 664	0.025 265	12
13	0.022 488	0.022 102	0.021 722	0.021 349	0.020 981	0.020 620	13
14	0.018 586	0.018 235	0.017 890	0.017 551	0.017 219	0.016 893	14
15	0.015 410	0.015 092	0.014 780	0.014 475	0.014 175	0.013 882	15
16	0.012 810	0.012 523	0.012 243	0.011 968	0.011 699	0.011 436	16
17	0.010 673	0.010 414	0.010 162	0.009 916	0.009 675	0.009 440	17
18	0.008 907	0.008 676	0.008 450	0.008 229	0.008 015	0.007 805	18
19	0.007 445	0.007 238	0.007 036	0.006 839	0.006 648	0.006 462	19
20	0.006 231	0.006 045	0.005 865	0.005 691	0.005 521	0.005 357	20
21	0.005 219	0.005 054	0.004 895	0.004 740	0.004 589	0.004 444	21
22	0.004 376	0.004 229	0.004 088	0.003 950	0.003 818	0.003 690	22
23	0.003 672	0.003 542	0.003 416	0.003 295	0.003 178	0.003 065	23
24	0.003 082	0.002 967	0.002 856	0.002 750	0.002 647	0.002 548	24
25	0.002 589	0.002 487	0.002 390	0.002 296	0.002 205	0.002 119	25
26	0.002 175	0.002 086	0.002 000	0.001 917	0.001 838	0.001 762	26
27	0.001 829	0.001 750	0.001 674	0.001 602	0.001 533	0.001 467	27
28	0.001 537	0.001 468	0.001 402	0.001 339	0.001 278	0.001 221	28
29	0.001 293	0.001 232	0.001 174	0.001 119	0.001 066	0.001 016	29
30	0.001 088	0.001 034	0.000 984	0.000 936	0.000 890	0.000 846	30
31	0.000 915	0.000 869	0.000 824	0.000 782	0.000 742	0.000 705	31
32	0.000 770	0.000 729	0.000 691	0.000 654	0.000 620	0.000 587	32
33	0.000 648	0.000 612	0.000 579	0.000 547	0.000 517	0.000 489	33
34	0.000 545	0.000 514	0.000 485	0.000 458	0.000 432	0.000 407	34
35	0.000 459	0.000 432	0.000 407	0.000 383	0.000 360	0.000 339	35
36	0.000 386	0.000 363	0.000 341	0.000 320	0.000 301	0.000 283	36
37	0.000 325	0.000 305	0.000 286	0.000 268	0.000 251	0.000 235	37
38	0.000 274	0.000 256	0.000 240	0.000 224	0.000 210	0.000 196	38
39	0.000 231	0.000 215	0.000 201	0.000 188	0.000 175	0.000 163	39
40	0.000 194	0.000 181	0.000 168	0.000 157	0.000 146	0.000 136	40
41	0.000 163	0.000 152	0.000 141	0.000 131	0.000 122	0.000 113	41
42	0.000 138	0.000 128	0.000 118	0.000 110	0.000 102	0.000 095	42
43	0.000 116	0.000 107	0.000 099	0.000 092	0.000 085	0.000 079	43
44	0.000 098	0.000 090	0.000 083	0.000 077	0.000 071	0.000 066	44
45	0.000 082	0.000 076	0.000 070	0.000 064	0.000 059	0.000 055	45
46	0.000 069	0.000 064	0.000 059	0.000 054	0.000 050	0.000 046	46
47	0.000 058	0.000 053	0.000 049	0.000 045	0.000 041	0.000 038	47
48	0.000 049	0.000 045	0.000 041	0.000 038	0.000 035	0.000 032	48
49	0.000 041	0.000 038	0.000 035	0.000 032	0.000 029	0.000 026	49
50	0.000 035	0.000 032	0.000 029	0.000 026	0.000 024	0.000 022	50

SINKING FUND

YRS	20.25% ANNUAL RATE	20.50% ANNUAL RATE	20.75% ANNUAL RATE	21.00% ANNUAL RATE	21.25% ANNUAL RATE	21.50% ANNUAL RATE	YRS
1	1.000 000	1.000 000	1.000 000	1.000 000	1.000 000	1.000 000	1
2	0.454 030	0.453 515	0.453 001	0.452 489	0.451 977	0.451 467	2
3	0.274 085	0.273 446	0.272 810	0.272 175	0.271 543	0.270 913	3
4	0.185 621	0.184 955	0.184 292	0.183 632	0.182 975	0.182 321	4
5	0.133 721	0.133 066	0.132 414	0.131 765	0.131 120	0.130 479	5
6	0.100 074	0.099 446	0.098 823	0.098 203	0.097 587	0.096 976	6
7	0.076 828	0.076 236	0.075 649	0.075 067	0.074 489	0.073 916	7
8	0.060 053	0.059 502	0.058 956	0.058 415	0.057 879	0.057 347	8
9	0.047 565	0.047 056	0.046 552	0.046 053	0.045 560	0.045 072	9
10	0.038 050	0.037 583	0.037 121	0.036 665	0.036 215	0.035 769	10
11	0.030 672	0.030 246	0.029 825	0.029 411	0.029 002	0.028 598	11
12	0.024 872	0.024 486	0.024 105	0.023 730	0.023 360	0.022 996	12
13	0.020 265	0.019 915	0.019 572	0.019 234	0.018 902	0.018 575	13
14	0.016 573	0.016 259	0.015 950	0.015 647	0.015 350	0.015 058	14
15	0.013 595	0.013 313	0.013 037	0.012 766	0.012 501	0.012 242	15
16	0.011 179	0.010 927	0.010 681	0.010 441	0.010 205	0.009 975	16
17	0.009 211	0.008 987	0.008 768	0.008 555	0.008 346	0.008 143	17
18	0.007 601	0.007 403	0.007 209	0.007 020	0.006 837	0.006 657	18
19	0.006 282	0.006 106	0.005 935	0.005 769	0.005 607	0.005 450	19
20	0.005 197	0.005 042	0.004 891	0.004 745	0.004 603	0.004 465	20
21	0.004 303	0.004 166	0.004 034	0.003 906	0.003 782	0.003 662	21
22	0.003 566	0.003 446	0.003 330	0.003 218	0.003 109	0.003 005	22
23	0.002 956	0.002 851	0.002 750	0.002 652	0.002 558	0.002 467	23
24	0.002 453	0.002 361	0.002 272	0.002 187	0.002 105	0.002 026	24
25	0.002 035	0.001 955	0.001 878	0.001 804	0.001 733	0.001 665	25
26	0.001 690	0.001 620	0.001 553	0.001 489	0.001 427	0.001 368	26
27	0.001 403	0.001 343	0.001 285	0.001 229	0.001 176	0.001 125	27
28	0.001 166	0.001 113	0.001 063	0.001 015	0.000 969	0.000 925	28
29	0.000 968	0.000 923	0.000 879	0.000 838	0.000 798	0.000 761	29
30	0.000 805	0.000 765	0.000 728	0.000 692	0.000 658	0.000 626	30
31	0.000 669	0.000 635	0.000 602	0.000 572	0.000 542	0.000 515	31
32	0.000 556	0.000 526	0.000 499	0.000 472	0.000 447	0.000 423	32
33	0.000 462	0.000 437	0.000 413	0.000 390	0.000 369	0.000 348	33
34	0.000 384	0.000 362	0.000 342	0.000 322	0.000 304	0.000 287	34
35	0.000 319	0.000 300	0.000 283	0.000 266	0.000 251	0.000 236	35
36	0.000 265	0.000 249	0.000 234	0.000 220	0.000 207	0.000 194	36
37	0.000 221	0.000 207	0.000 194	0.000 182	0.000 170	0.000 160	37
38	0.000 183	0.000 172	0.000 161	0.000 150	0.000 141	0.000 131	38
39	0.000 153	0.000 142	0.000 133	0.000 124	0.000 116	0.000 108	39
40	0.000 127	0.000 118	0.000 110	0.000 103	0.000 096	0.000 089	40
41	0.000 105	0.000 098	0.000 091	0.000 085	0.000 079	0.000 073	41
42	0.000 088	0.000 081	0.000 075	0.000 070	0.000 065	0.000 060	42
43	0.000 073	0.000 068	0.000 063	0.000 058	0.000 054	0.000 050	43
44	0.000 061	0.000 056	0.000 052	0.000 048	0.000 044	0.000 041	44
45	0.000 050	0.000 046	0.000 043	0.000 040	0.000 036	0.000 034	45
46	0.000 042	0.000 039	0.000 036	0.000 033	0.000 030	0.000 028	46
47	0.000 035	0.000 032	0.000 029	0.000 027	0.000 025	0.000 023	47
48	0.000 029	0.000 027	0.000 024	0.000 022	0.000 020	0.000 019	48
49	0.000 024	0.000 022	0.000 020	0.000 018	0.000 017	0.000 015	49
50	0.000 020	0.000 018	0.000 017	0.000 015	0.000 014	0.000 013	50

SINKING FUND

YRS	21.75% ANNUAL RATE	22.00% ANNUAL RATE	22.50% ANNUAL RATE	23.00% ANNUAL RATE	23.50% ANNUAL RATE	24.00% ANNUAL RATE	YRS
1	1.000 000	1.000 000	1.000 000	1.000 000	1.000 000	1.000 000	1
2	0.450 958	0.450 450	0.449 438	0.448 430	0.447 427	0.446 429	2
3	0.270 284	0.269 658	0.268 411	0.267 173	0.265 942	0.264 718	3
4	0.181 669	0.181 020	0.179 730	0.178 451	0.177 183	0.175 926	4
5	0.129 841	0.129 206	0.127 947	0.126 700	0.125 468	0.124 248	5
6	0.096 368	0.095 764	0.094 569	0.093 389	0.092 224	0.091 074	6
7	0.073 347	0.072 782	0.071 666	0.070 568	0.069 486	0.068 422	7
8	0.056 821	0.056 299	0.055 270	0.054 259	0.053 267	0.052 293	8
9	0.044 589	0.044 111	0.043 170	0.042 249	0.041 348	0.040 465	9
10	0.035 330	0.034 895	0.034 041	0.033 208	0.032 395	0.031 602	10
11	0.028 200	0.027 807	0.027 038	0.026 289	0.025 561	0.024 852	11
12	0.022 638	0.022 285	0.021 595	0.020 926	0.020 277	0.019 648	12
13	0.018 254	0.017 939	0.017 323	0.016 728	0.016 154	0.015 598	13
14	0.014 772	0.014 491	0.013 944	0.013 418	0.012 911	0.012 423	14
15	0.011 987	0.011 738	0.011 255	0.010 791	0.010 346	0.009 919	15
16	0.009 750	0.009 530	0.009 104	0.008 697	0.008 308	0.007 936	16
17	0.007 945	0.007 751	0.007 377	0.007 021	0.006 682	0.006 359	17
18	0.006 483	0.006 313	0.005 986	0.005 676	0.005 381	0.005 102	18
19	0.005 297	0.005 148	0.004 863	0.004 593	0.004 339	0.004 098	19
20	0.004 332	0.004 202	0.003 954	0.003 720	0.003 501	0.003 294	20
21	0.003 545	0.003 432	0.003 217	0.003 016	0.002 827	0.002 649	21
22	0.002 903	0.002 805	0.002 619	0.002 446	0.002 283	0.002 132	22
23	0.002 379	0.002 294	0.002 134	0.001 984	0.001 846	0.001 716	23
24	0.001 950	0.001 877	0.001 739	0.001 611	0.001 492	0.001 382	24
25	0.001 599	0.001 536	0.001 417	0.001 308	0.001 207	0.001 113	25
26	0.001 312	0.001 258	0.001 156	0.001 062	0.000 976	0.000 897	26
27	0.001 076	0.001 030	0.000 943	0.000 863	0.000 790	0.000 723	27
28	0.000 883	0.000 843	0.000 769	0.000 701	0.000 639	0.000 583	28
29	0.000 725	0.000 691	0.000 627	0.000 570	0.000 517	0.000 470	29
30	0.000 595	0.000 566	0.000 512	0.000 463	0.000 419	0.000 379	30
31	0.000 489	0.000 464	0.000 418	0.000 376	0.000 339	0.000 305	31
32	0.000 401	0.000 380	0.000 341	0.000 306	0.000 274	0.000 246	32
33	0.000 329	0.000 311	0.000 278	0.000 249	0.000 222	0.000 198	33
34	0.000 270	0.000 255	0.000 227	0.000 202	0.000 180	0.000 160	34
35	0.000 222	0.000 209	0.000 185	0.000 164	0.000 146	0.000 129	35
36	0.000 182	0.000 171	0.000 151	0.000 133	0.000 118	0.000 104	36
37	0.000 150	0.000 140	0.000 123	0.000 109	0.000 095	0.000 084	37
38	0.000 123	0.000 115	0.000 101	0.000 088	0.000 077	0.000 068	38
39	0.000 101	0.000 094	0.000 082	0.000 072	0.000 063	0.000 055	39
40	0.000 083	0.000 077	0.000 067	0.000 058	0.000 051	0.000 044	40
41	0.000 068	0.000 063	0.000 055	0.000 047	0.000 041	0.000 035	41
42	0.000 056	0.000 052	0.000 045	0.000 039	0.000 033	0.000 029	42
43	0.000 046	0.000 043	0.000 037	0.000 031	0.000 027	0.000 023	43
44	0.000 038	0.000 035	0.000 030	0.000 025	0.000 022	0.000 019	44
45	0.000 031	0.000 029	0.000 024	0.000 021	0.000 018	0.000 015	45
46	0.000 025	0.000 023	0.000 020	0.000 017	0.000 014	0.000 012	46
47	0.000 021	0.000 019	0.000 016	0.000 014	0.000 012	0.000 010	47
48	0.000 017	0.000 016	0.000 013	0.000 011	0.000 009	0.000 008	48
49	0.000 014	0.000 013	0.000 011	0.000 009	0.000 008	0.000 006	49
50	0.000 012	0.000 011	0.000 009	0.000 007	0.000 006	0.000 005	50

SECTION 4
PRESENT VALUE
OF $1

Present value is the basic compound interest function for a single payment or withdrawal. You make an investment at the start of a compounding period, interest is earned on the investment, and after each period interest begins to be earned on the interest.

USE OF PRESENT VALUE

Present value is the amount you must start with today if you wish to have $1 for a payment or withdrawal in the future. The assumptions are:

- No additional interim investments are made.
- All interest earned is left in the investment to begin earning interest on interest.
- The investment earns interest at a uniform rate throughout the term of the investment.

The tables in this section are used to solve the following types of problems:

1. How much is a future payment worth today?
2. How long will it take for an investment today to grow to a certain value in the future?

3. What rate must an investment earn today to be worth a certain value at a certain time in the future?

EXAMPLES

Present Worth of a Future Payment. A zero coupon bond earns a nominal rate of interest of 10% and will be worth $25,000 in 10 years. How much should you pay for it?

The answer is called the compound accreted value. Since coupon bonds normally pay interest semiannually, the investment community uses semiannual compounding to calculate compound accreted value. Turn to page 171 in the semiannual compounding section and locate the column labeled 10.00%. Move down the column to the row for 20 half-years and find the entry: 0.376889. Multiply $25,000 by 0.376889 to get $9,422.23, the present value of the zero coupon bond.

Time Required to Accumulate a Certain Value. You must accumulate $10,000 in an investment that pays 11.5% compounded quarterly. If you have only $4,000 today, how long will it take?

First compute the present value factor. Divide $4,000 by $10,000 to get 0.4. Turn to page 162 in the quarterly compounding section and locate the column labeled 11.50%. Move down the column and find the entry that falls closest to 0.4. The entry is 0.403724. Move across the row to the number-of-quarters column and find 32 quarters. It takes slightly more than 8 years to achieve your desired result.

Interest Rate Required to Achieve a Certain Value. What rate of interest must be earned if a $7,500 payment 36 months from now is worth only $4,500 today? Assume the interest is compounded monthly.

Divide today's value by the future payment value to get the present value factor: $4,500 divided by $7,500 equals 0.6. Turn to the first page of the monthly compounding section and begin scanning across the 36-month row until you find the entry that is closest to 0.6. On page 154 find the entry 0.598209. Read up the column to find the annual rate, 17.25%. One must earn slightly less than 17.25% interest to achieve the future payment goal. If a more accurate answer is desired, use the interpolation technique described in the Introduction.

Change of Interest Rates. An investor needs to withdraw $15,000 after 8 years from an account where interest is compounded monthly. He can earn 10.25% interest for the first 3 years and 11.75% interest for the last 5 years. How much must he deposit today?

This is an example of how to break a more difficult problem into two simpler ones. First, find out how much the account must have after 36 months to withdraw $15,000 after 96 months. Turn to page 150 in the monthly compounding section and find the column labeled 11.75%. Move down the column to the 60-month (5-year) row and read the entry: 0.557305. Multiply $15,000 by 0.557305 to get $8,359.58, the value of the account 5 years (60 months) before it must be worth $15,000.

Next, find the required initial value, the value 3 years before the account is worth $8,359.58. Turn to page 149 in the monthly compounding section and find the column labeled 10.25%. Move down the column to the 36-month row and read the entry: 0.736244. Multiply $8,359.58 by 0.736244 to get $6,154.69, the required initial value of the account.

Deposit Made in the Future. An investor wishes to withdraw $12,000 in 10 years from an account paying 12.75% interest compounded monthly. She expects to be able to make a $2,000 deposit 2 years from today. What deposit must she start with today to achieve her goal?

First find the amount she will need on deposit after 2 years to accumulate $12,000 after 10 years. Turn to page 151 in the monthly compounding section and find the column labeled 12.75%. Move down the column to the 96-month (8-year) row and read the entry: 0.362540. Multiply $12,000 by 0.362540 to get $4,350.48, the amount required in 2 years. But since this amount includes the $2,000 deposit that will be made at that time, only $2,350.48 must accumulate in the account after two years.

Next find the amount that the investor needs to deposit today to accumulate $2,350.48 after two years. Read down the 12.75% column to the 24-month row and read the entry: 0.775960. Multiply $2,350.48 by 0.775960 to get $1,823.88, the deposit required today.

This problem is an example of how to break a problem into its simpler component parts.

THE FORMULA FOR PRESENT VALUE

The symbol V^n is the widely accepted notation for present value. The formula for figuring present value table entries is:

$$V^n = \frac{1}{(1 + i)^n}$$

where:

i = interest rate per period
n = number of compounding periods

Note that i is the interest rate *per period*, not the nominal annual rate. You can easily find the interest rate per period by dividing the annual rate by the number of compounding periods per year. For example, a nominal annual rate of 12% compounded monthly converts to 1% per month (12% ÷ 12 months per year).

SECTION 4

MOS	5.25% ANNUAL RATE	5.50% ANNUAL RATE	5.75% ANNUAL RATE	6.00% ANNUAL RATE	6.25% ANNUAL RATE	6.50% ANNUAL RATE	MOS
1	0.995 644	0.995 438	0.995 231	0.995 025	0.994 819	0.994 613	1
2	0.991 307	0.990 896	0.990 485	0.990 075	0.989 664	0.989 254	2
3	0.986 989	0.986 375	0.985 762	0.985 149	0.984 536	0.983 924	3
4	0.982 690	0.981 875	0.981 061	0.980 248	0.979 435	0.978 624	4
5	0.978 409	0.977 395	0.976 382	0.975 371	0.974 360	0.973 351	5
6	0.974 147	0.972 936	0.971 726	0.970 518	0.969 312	0.968 107	6
7	0.969 904	0.968 497	0.967 092	0.965 690	0.964 290	0.962 892	7
8	0.965 679	0.964 078	0.962 480	0.960 885	0.959 293	0.957 704	8
9	0.961 473	0.959 680	0.957 890	0.956 105	0.954 323	0.952 545	9
10	0.957 285	0.955 301	0.953 322	0.951 348	0.949 378	0.947 413	10
11	0.953 115	0.950 943	0.948 776	0.946 615	0.944 459	0.942 309	11
12	0.948 963	0.946 604	0.944 252	0.941 905	0.939 565	0.937 232	12
13	0.944 829	0.942 285	0.939 749	0.937 219	0.934 697	0.932 183	13
14	0.940 714	0.937 986	0.935 267	0.932 556	0.929 854	0.927 160	14
15	0.936 616	0.933 707	0.930 807	0.927 917	0.925 036	0.922 165	15
16	0.932 536	0.929 447	0.926 368	0.923 300	0.920 243	0.917 197	16
17	0.928 474	0.925 206	0.921 950	0.918 707	0.915 475	0.912 256	17
18	0.924 430	0.920 985	0.917 554	0.914 136	0.910 732	0.907 341	18
19	0.920 403	0.916 783	0.913 178	0.909 588	0.906 013	0.902 453	19
20	0.916 394	0.912 600	0.908 823	0.905 063	0.901 319	0.897 591	20
21	0.912 402	0.908 437	0.904 489	0.900 560	0.896 649	0.892 755	21
22	0.908 428	0.904 292	0.900 176	0.896 080	0.892 003	0.887 945	22
23	0.904 471	0.900 166	0.895 883	0.891 622	0.887 381	0.883 162	23
24	0.900 531	0.896 059	0.891 611	0.887 186	0.882 783	0.878 404	24
25	0.896 608	0.891 971	0.887 359	0.882 772	0.878 209	0.873 671	25
26	0.892 703	0.887 902	0.883 127	0.878 380	0.873 659	0.868 964	26
27	0.888 814	0.883 851	0.878 916	0.874 010	0.869 132	0.864 283	27
28	0.884 942	0.879 818	0.874 725	0.869 662	0.864 629	0.859 626	28
29	0.881 088	0.875 804	0.870 553	0.865 335	0.860 149	0.854 995	29
30	0.877 250	0.871 808	0.866 402	0.861 030	0.855 692	0.850 389	30
31	0.873 428	0.867 831	0.862 270	0.856 746	0.851 259	0.845 807	31
32	0.869 624	0.863 871	0.858 158	0.852 484	0.846 848	0.841 251	32
33	0.865 836	0.859 930	0.854 066	0.848 242	0.842 460	0.836 718	33
34	0.862 064	0.856 007	0.849 993	0.844 022	0.838 095	0.832 211	34
35	0.858 309	0.852 101	0.845 939	0.839 823	0.833 753	0.827 727	35
36	0.854 570	0.848 213	0.841 905	0.835 645	0.829 433	0.823 268	36
37	0.850 848	0.844 343	0.837 890	0.831 487	0.825 135	0.818 832	37
38	0.847 142	0.840 491	0.833 894	0.827 351	0.820 860	0.814 421	38
39	0.843 452	0.836 657	0.829 918	0.823 235	0.816 607	0.810 033	39
40	0.839 778	0.832 839	0.825 960	0.819 139	0.812 375	0.805 669	40
41	0.836 119	0.829 040	0.822 021	0.815 064	0.808 166	0.801 329	41
42	0.832 477	0.825 257	0.818 101	0.811 009	0.803 979	0.797 012	42
43	0.828 851	0.821 492	0.814 200	0.806 974	0.799 813	0.792 718	43
44	0.825 241	0.817 744	0.810 317	0.802 959	0.795 669	0.788 447	44
45	0.821 646	0.814 013	0.806 453	0.798 964	0.791 546	0.784 199	45
46	0.818 067	0.810 299	0.802 607	0.794 989	0.787 445	0.779 974	46
47	0.814 504	0.806 602	0.798 779	0.791 034	0.783 365	0.775 772	47
YRS							
4	0.810 956	0.802 922	0.794 970	0.787 098	0.779 306	0.771 593	48
5	0.769 567	0.760 050	0.750 652	0.741 372	0.732 209	0.723 161	60
6	0.730 290	0.719 466	0.708 804	0.698 302	0.687 958	0.677 770	72
7	0.693 019	0.681 049	0.669 289	0.657 735	0.646 382	0.635 227	84
8	0.657 649	0.644 684	0.631 978	0.619 524	0.607 318	0.595 355	96
9	0.624 085	0.610 261	0.596 746	0.583 533	0.570 615	0.557 986	108
10	0.592 233	0.577 675	0.563 478	0.549 633	0.536 130	0.522 962	120
11	0.562 007	0.546 830	0.532 065	0.517 702	0.503 730	0.490 137	132
12	0.533 324	0.517 631	0.502 403	0.487 626	0.473 287	0.459 372	144
13	0.506 105	0.489 992	0.474 395	0.459 298	0.444 684	0.430 538	156
14	0.480 275	0.463 828	0.447 948	0.432 615	0.417 810	0.403 514	168
15	0.455 763	0.439 062	0.422 976	0.407 482	0.392 560	0.378 186	180
16	0.432 502	0.415 618	0.399 396	0.383 810	0.368 835	0.354 448	192
17	0.410 429	0.393 425	0.377 130	0.361 513	0.346 545	0.332 200	204
18	0.389 482	0.372 418	0.356 106	0.340 511	0.325 602	0.311 348	216
19	0.369 604	0.352 532	0.336 253	0.320 729	0.305 924	0.291 806	228
20	0.350 740	0.333 709	0.317 508	0.302 096	0.287 436	0.273 490	240
21	0.332 839	0.315 890	0.299 807	0.284 546	0.270 065	0.256 323	252
22	0.315 852	0.299 023	0.283 093	0.268 015	0.253 743	0.240 234	264
23	0.299 732	0.283 056	0.267 311	0.252 445	0.238 409	0.225 155	276
24	0.284 435	0.267 942	0.252 409	0.237 779	0.224 000	0.211 023	288
25	0.269 918	0.253 635	0.238 338	0.223 966	0.210 463	0.197 777	300
26	0.256 142	0.240 092	0.225 051	0.210 954	0.197 744	0.185 363	312
27	0.243 069	0.227 272	0.212 504	0.198 699	0.185 793	0.173 728	324
28	0.230 664	0.215 137	0.200 658	0.187 156	0.174 565	0.162 823	336
29	0.218 891	0.203 649	0.189 471	0.176 283	0.164 015	0.152 603	348
30	0.207 720	0.192 775	0.178 909	0.166 042	0.154 103	0.143 025	360

MOS	6.75% ANNUAL RATE	7.00% ANNUAL RATE	7.25% ANNUAL RATE	7.50% ANNUAL RATE	7.75% ANNUAL RATE	8.00% ANNUAL RATE	MOS
1	0.994 406	0.994 200	0.993 995	0.993 789	0.993 583	0.993 377	1
2	0.988 844	0.988 435	0.988 025	0.987 616	0.987 207	0.986 799	2
3	0.983 313	0.982 702	0.982 092	0.981 482	0.980 873	0.980 264	3
4	0.977 813	0.977 003	0.976 194	0.975 386	0.974 578	0.973 772	4
5	0.972 343	0.971 337	0.970 332	0.969 327	0.968 325	0.967 323	5
6	0.966 905	0.965 704	0.964 504	0.963 307	0.962 111	0.960 917	6
7	0.961 496	0.960 103	0.958 712	0.957 324	0.955 937	0.954 553	7
8	0.956 118	0.954 535	0.952 955	0.951 377	0.949 803	0.948 232	8
9	0.950 770	0.948 999	0.947 232	0.945 468	0.943 708	0.941 952	9
10	0.945 452	0.943 495	0.941 543	0.939 596	0.937 653	0.935 714	10
11	0.940 163	0.938 024	0.935 889	0.933 760	0.931 636	0.929 517	11
12	0.934 905	0.932 583	0.930 269	0.927 960	0.925 658	0.923 361	12
13	0.929 675	0.927 175	0.924 682	0.922 196	0.919 718	0.917 246	13
14	0.924 475	0.921 798	0.919 129	0.916 468	0.913 816	0.911 172	14
15	0.919 304	0.916 452	0.913 609	0.910 776	0.907 952	0.905 138	15
16	0.914 162	0.911 137	0.908 123	0.905 119	0.902 126	0.899 143	16
17	0.909 048	0.905 853	0.902 669	0.899 497	0.896 337	0.893 189	17
18	0.903 963	0.900 599	0.897 248	0.893 910	0.890 585	0.887 274	18
19	0.898 907	0.895 376	0.891 860	0.888 358	0.884 871	0.881 398	19
20	0.893 879	0.890 183	0.886 504	0.882 840	0.879 193	0.875 561	20
21	0.888 879	0.885 021	0.881 180	0.877 357	0.873 551	0.869 762	21
22	0.883 907	0.879 888	0.875 888	0.871 907	0.867 945	0.864 002	22
23	0.878 963	0.874 785	0.870 628	0.866 492	0.862 376	0.858 280	23
24	0.874 046	0.869 712	0.865 400	0.861 110	0.856 842	0.852 596	24
25	0.869 157	0.864 668	0.860 203	0.855 761	0.851 344	0.846 950	25
26	0.864 296	0.859 653	0.855 037	0.850 446	0.845 881	0.841 341	26
27	0.859 461	0.854 668	0.849 902	0.845 164	0.840 453	0.835 769	27
28	0.854 654	0.849 711	0.844 798	0.839 914	0.835 060	0.830 234	28
29	0.849 873	0.844 783	0.839 725	0.834 697	0.829 701	0.824 736	29
30	0.845 120	0.839 884	0.834 682	0.829 513	0.824 377	0.819 274	30
31	0.840 392	0.835 013	0.829 669	0.824 361	0.819 087	0.813 849	31
32	0.835 692	0.830 170	0.824 687	0.819 240	0.813 831	0.808 459	32
33	0.831 017	0.825 356	0.819 734	0.814 152	0.808 609	0.803 105	33
34	0.826 369	0.820 569	0.814 811	0.809 095	0.803 420	0.797 786	34
35	0.821 746	0.815 810	0.809 918	0.804 070	0.798 265	0.792 503	35
36	0.817 150	0.811 079	0.805 054	0.799 076	0.793 142	0.787 255	36
37	0.812 579	0.806 375	0.800 220	0.794 112	0.788 053	0.782 041	37
38	0.808 034	0.801 699	0.795 414	0.789 180	0.782 996	0.776 862	38
39	0.803 514	0.797 049	0.790 637	0.784 278	0.777 972	0.771 717	39
40	0.799 020	0.792 427	0.785 889	0.779 407	0.772 980	0.766 606	40
41	0.794 550	0.787 831	0.781 170	0.774 566	0.768 019	0.761 530	41
42	0.790 106	0.783 262	0.776 478	0.769 755	0.763 091	0.756 486	42
43	0.785 687	0.778 719	0.771 815	0.764 974	0.758 194	0.751 477	43
44	0.781 292	0.774 203	0.767 180	0.760 222	0.753 329	0.746 500	44
45	0.776 922	0.769 713	0.762 573	0.755 501	0.748 495	0.741 556	45
46	0.772 576	0.765 249	0.757 993	0.750 808	0.743 692	0.736 645	46
47	0.768 254	0.760 811	0.753 441	0.746 145	0.738 920	0.731 767	47

YRS							
4	0.763 957	0.756 399	0.748 917	0.741 510	0.734 178	0.726 921	48
5	0.714 227	0.705 405	0.696 694	0.688 092	0.679 598	0.671 210	60
6	0.667 734	0.657 849	0.648 112	0.638 522	0.629 075	0.619 770	72
7	0.624 268	0.613 499	0.602 919	0.592 523	0.582 308	0.572 272	84
8	0.583 631	0.572 139	0.560 876	0.549 837	0.539 018	0.528 414	96
9	0.545 639	0.533 568	0.521 766	0.510 227	0.498 946	0.487 917	108
10	0.510 120	0.497 596	0.485 382	0.473 470	0.461 853	0.450 523	120
11	0.476 914	0.464 050	0.451 536	0.439 362	0.427 518	0.415 996	132
12	0.445 869	0.432 765	0.420 050	0.407 710	0.395 735	0.384 115	144
13	0.416 845	0.403 590	0.390 759	0.378 339	0.366 315	0.354 677	156
14	0.389 710	0.376 381	0.363 511	0.351 083	0.339 083	0.327 495	168
15	0.364 342	0.351 007	0.338 163	0.325 791	0.313 874	0.302 396	180
16	0.340 625	0.327 343	0.314 582	0.302 321	0.290 540	0.279 221	192
17	0.318 452	0.305 275	0.292 646	0.280 542	0.268 941	0.257 822	204
18	0.297 722	0.284 694	0.272 239	0.260 332	0.248 947	0.238 063	216
19	0.278 342	0.265 501	0.253 256	0.241 577	0.230 440	0.219 818	228
20	0.260 223	0.247 602	0.235 596	0.224 174	0.213 308	0.202 971	240
21	0.243 283	0.230 910	0.219 167	0.208 025	0.197 451	0.187 416	252
22	0.227 447	0.215 342	0.203 885	0.193 030	0.182 772	0.173 053	264
23	0.212 641	0.200 825	0.189 667	0.179 132	0.169 184	0.159 790	276
24	0.198 799	0.187 286	0.176 442	0.166 227	0.156 606	0.147 544	288
25	0.185 858	0.174 660	0.164 138	0.154 252	0.144 964	0.136 237	300
26	0.173 760	0.162 885	0.152 693	0.143 140	0.134 187	0.125 796	312
27	0.162 449	0.151 904	0.142 045	0.132 828	0.124 211	0.116 155	324
28	0.151 874	0.141 663	0.132 140	0.123 259	0.114 977	0.107 253	336
29	0.141 988	0.132 112	0.122 926	0.114 380	0.106 429	0.099 033	348
30	0.132 745	0.123 206	0.114 354	0.106 140	0.098 517	0.091 443	360

PRESENT VALUE

MOS	8.25% ANNUAL RATE	8.50% ANNUAL RATE	8.75% ANNUAL RATE	9.00% ANNUAL RATE	9.25% ANNUAL RATE	9.50% ANNUAL RATE	MOS
1	0.993 172	0.992 966	0.992 761	0.992 556	0.992 351	0.992 146	1
2	0.986 391	0.985 982	0.985 575	0.985 167	0.984 760	0.984 353	2
3	0.979 655	0.979 048	0.978 440	0.977 833	0.977 227	0.976 621	3
4	0.972 966	0.972 161	0.971 357	0.970 554	0.969 752	0.968 950	4
5	0.966 323	0.965 324	0.964 326	0.963 329	0.962 334	0.961 340	5
6	0.959 725	0.958 534	0.957 345	0.956 158	0.954 973	0.953 789	6
7	0.953 172	0.951 792	0.950 415	0.949 040	0.947 668	0.946 297	7
8	0.946 663	0.945 098	0.943 535	0.941 975	0.940 419	0.938 865	8
9	0.940 199	0.938 450	0.936 705	0.934 963	0.933 225	0.931 490	9
10	0.933 780	0.931 850	0.929 924	0.928 003	0.926 086	0.924 174	10
11	0.927 404	0.925 296	0.923 193	0.921 095	0.919 002	0.916 915	11
12	0.921 071	0.918 788	0.916 510	0.914 238	0.911 973	0.909 713	12
13	0.914 782	0.912 325	0.909 875	0.907 432	0.904 997	0.902 568	13
14	0.908 536	0.905 908	0.903 289	0.900 677	0.898 074	0.895 479	14
15	0.902 333	0.899 537	0.896 750	0.893 973	0.891 204	0.888 445	15
16	0.896 171	0.893 210	0.890 259	0.887 318	0.884 387	0.881 467	16
17	0.890 052	0.886 927	0.883 814	0.880 712	0.877 622	0.874 543	17
18	0.883 975	0.880 689	0.877 416	0.874 156	0.870 909	0.867 674	18
19	0.877 939	0.874 495	0.871 065	0.867 649	0.864 247	0.860 859	19
20	0.871 945	0.868 344	0.864 759	0.861 190	0.857 636	0.854 098	20
21	0.865 991	0.862 237	0.858 499	0.854 779	0.851 076	0.847 389	21
22	0.860 078	0.856 172	0.852 285	0.848 416	0.844 565	0.840 733	22
23	0.854 205	0.850 150	0.846 115	0.842 100	0.838 105	0.834 130	23
24	0.848 373	0.844 171	0.839 990	0.835 831	0.831 694	0.827 578	24
25	0.842 580	0.838 233	0.833 910	0.829 609	0.825 332	0.821 078	25
26	0.836 827	0.832 337	0.827 873	0.823 434	0.819 019	0.814 629	26
27	0.831 113	0.826 483	0.821 880	0.817 304	0.812 754	0.808 230	27
28	0.825 438	0.820 670	0.815 931	0.811 220	0.806 537	0.801 882	28
29	0.819 802	0.814 898	0.810 024	0.805 181	0.800 367	0.795 584	29
30	0.814 204	0.809 166	0.804 161	0.799 187	0.794 245	0.789 335	30
31	0.808 645	0.803 475	0.798 339	0.793 238	0.788 170	0.783 135	31
32	0.803 123	0.797 824	0.792 560	0.787 333	0.782 141	0.776 984	32
33	0.797 639	0.792 212	0.786 823	0.781 472	0.776 158	0.770 881	33
34	0.792 193	0.786 640	0.781 127	0.775 654	0.770 221	0.764 826	34
35	0.786 784	0.781 107	0.775 473	0.769 880	0.764 329	0.758 819	35
36	0.781 412	0.775 613	0.769 859	0.764 149	0.758 482	0.752 859	36
37	0.776 076	0.770 158	0.764 286	0.758 461	0.752 680	0.746 945	37
38	0.770 777	0.764 741	0.758 754	0.752 814	0.746 923	0.741 078	38
39	0.765 514	0.759 362	0.753 261	0.747 210	0.741 209	0.735 258	39
40	0.760 287	0.754 021	0.747 808	0.741 648	0.735 539	0.729 483	40
41	0.755 096	0.748 718	0.742 395	0.736 127	0.729 913	0.723 753	41
42	0.749 940	0.743 452	0.737 021	0.730 647	0.724 330	0.718 068	42
43	0.744 819	0.738 223	0.731 686	0.725 208	0.718 789	0.712 428	43
44	0.739 734	0.733 030	0.726 389	0.719 810	0.713 291	0.706 832	44
45	0.734 683	0.727 875	0.721 131	0.714 451	0.707 835	0.701 281	45
46	0.729 666	0.722 755	0.715 911	0.709 133	0.702 420	0.695 772	46
47	0.724 684	0.717 672	0.710 728	0.703 854	0.697 047	0.690 307	47
YRS							
4	0.719 736	0.712 624	0.705 584	0.698 614	0.691 715	0.684 885	48
5	0.662 928	0.654 750	0.646 674	0.638 700	0.630 825	0.623 049	60
6	0.610 604	0.601 576	0.592 683	0.583 924	0.575 295	0.566 796	72
7	0.562 410	0.552 721	0.543 200	0.533 845	0.524 654	0.515 622	84
8	0.518 020	0.507 833	0.497 848	0.488 062	0.478 470	0.469 068	96
9	0.477 133	0.466 590	0.456 283	0.446 205	0.436 351	0.426 717	108
10	0.439 474	0.428 698	0.418 188	0.407 937	0.397 940	0.388 190	120
11	0.404 787	0.393 882	0.383 273	0.372 952	0.362 911	0.353 142	132
12	0.372 838	0.361 894	0.351 273	0.340 967	0.330 965	0.321 258	144
13	0.343 410	0.332 504	0.321 946	0.311 725	0.301 831	0.292 253	156
14	0.316 305	0.305 500	0.295 066	0.284 991	0.275 261	0.265 866	168
15	0.291 340	0.280 690	0.270 431	0.260 549	0.251 031	0.241 862	180
16	0.268 345	0.257 894	0.247 853	0.238 204	0.228 933	0.220 025	192
17	0.247 165	0.236 950	0.227 159	0.217 775	0.208 781	0.200 159	204
18	0.227 656	0.217 707	0.208 194	0.199 099	0.190 402	0.182 088	216
19	0.209 688	0.200 026	0.190 812	0.182 024	0.173 642	0.165 648	228
20	0.193 137	0.183 782	0.174 881	0.166 413	0.158 357	0.150 692	240
21	0.177 893	0.168 856	0.160 280	0.152 141	0.144 417	0.137 086	252
22	0.163 852	0.155 143	0.146 898	0.139 093	0.131 704	0.124 709	264
23	0.150 920	0.142 543	0.134 634	0.127 164	0.120 111	0.113 450	276
24	0.139 008	0.130 967	0.123 393	0.116 258	0.109 538	0.103 207	288
25	0.128 036	0.120 331	0.113 091	0.106 288	0.099 895	0.093 888	300
26	0.117 930	0.110 559	0.103 649	0.097 172	0.091 102	0.085 412	312
27	0.108 622	0.101 580	0.094 995	0.088 839	0.083 082	0.077 700	324
28	0.100 049	0.093 330	0.087 064	0.081 220	0.075 769	0.070 685	336
29	0.092 152	0.085 751	0.079 795	0.074 254	0.069 099	0.064 303	348
30	0.084 879	0.078 787	0.073 133	0.067 886	0.063 016	0.058 497	360

PRESENT VALUE

MOS	9.75% ANNUAL RATE	10.00% ANNUAL RATE	10.25% ANNUAL RATE	10.50% ANNUAL RATE	10.75% ANNUAL RATE	11.00% ANNUAL RATE	MOS
1	0.991 940	0.991 736	0.991 531	0.991 326	0.991 121	0.990 917	1
2	0.983 946	0.983 539	0.983 133	0.982 727	0.982 321	0.981 916	2
3	0.976 016	0.975 411	0.974 807	0.974 203	0.973 599	0.972 997	3
4	0.968 150	0.967 350	0.966 551	0.965 752	0.964 955	0.964 158	4
5	0.960 347	0.959 355	0.958 365	0.957 375	0.956 387	0.955 401	5
6	0.952 607	0.951 427	0.950 248	0.949 071	0.947 896	0.946 722	6
7	0.944 929	0.943 563	0.942 200	0.940 839	0.939 480	0.938 123	7
8	0.937 314	0.935 765	0.934 220	0.932 678	0.931 138	0.929 602	8
9	0.929 759	0.928 032	0.926 308	0.924 588	0.922 871	0.921 158	9
10	0.922 266	0.920 362	0.918 463	0.916 568	0.914 677	0.912 790	10
11	0.914 833	0.912 756	0.910 684	0.908 617	0.906 556	0.904 499	11
12	0.907 460	0.905 212	0.902 971	0.900 736	0.898 506	0.896 283	12
13	0.900 146	0.897 731	0.895 324	0.892 923	0.890 529	0.888 142	13
14	0.892 891	0.890 312	0.887 741	0.885 177	0.882 622	0.880 075	14
15	0.885 695	0.882 954	0.880 222	0.877 499	0.874 785	0.872 080	15
16	0.878 557	0.875 657	0.872 767	0.869 888	0.867 018	0.864 159	16
17	0.871 476	0.868 420	0.865 376	0.862 342	0.859 320	0.856 309	17
18	0.864 452	0.861 243	0.858 046	0.854 862	0.851 691	0.848 531	18
19	0.857 485	0.854 125	0.850 779	0.847 447	0.844 129	0.840 824	19
20	0.850 574	0.847 067	0.843 574	0.840 096	0.836 634	0.833 186	20
21	0.843 719	0.840 066	0.836 429	0.832 809	0.829 205	0.825 618	21
22	0.836 919	0.833 123	0.829 345	0.825 585	0.821 843	0.818 119	22
23	0.830 174	0.826 238	0.822 321	0.818 424	0.814 546	0.810 687	23
24	0.823 483	0.819 410	0.815 357	0.811 325	0.807 314	0.803 323	24
25	0.816 846	0.812 638	0.808 451	0.804 287	0.800 146	0.796 027	25
26	0.810 263	0.805 922	0.801 604	0.797 311	0.793 042	0.788 796	26
27	0.803 733	0.799 261	0.794 815	0.790 395	0.786 000	0.781 631	27
28	0.797 255	0.792 656	0.788 084	0.783 539	0.779 022	0.774 531	28
29	0.790 829	0.786 105	0.781 409	0.776 743	0.772 105	0.767 496	29
30	0.784 456	0.779 608	0.774 791	0.770 005	0.765 249	0.760 524	30
31	0.778 133	0.773 165	0.768 229	0.763 326	0.758 455	0.753 616	31
32	0.771 862	0.766 775	0.761 723	0.756 705	0.751 721	0.746 771	32
33	0.765 641	0.760 438	0.755 272	0.750 141	0.745 046	0.739 988	33
34	0.759 471	0.754 154	0.748 875	0.743 634	0.738 431	0.733 266	34
35	0.753 350	0.747 921	0.742 532	0.737 184	0.731 875	0.726 605	35
36	0.747 278	0.741 740	0.736 244	0.730 789	0.725 377	0.720 005	36
37	0.741 255	0.735 610	0.730 008	0.724 451	0.718 936	0.713 465	37
38	0.735 281	0.729 530	0.723 826	0.718 167	0.712 553	0.706 985	38
39	0.729 355	0.723 501	0.717 695	0.711 937	0.706 226	0.700 563	39
40	0.723 477	0.717 522	0.711 617	0.705 762	0.699 956	0.694 199	40
41	0.717 646	0.711 592	0.705 590	0.699 640	0.693 741	0.687 894	41
42	0.711 862	0.705 711	0.699 614	0.693 571	0.687 582	0.681 645	42
43	0.706 125	0.699 879	0.693 689	0.687 555	0.681 477	0.675 453	43
44	0.700 434	0.694 094	0.687 814	0.681 591	0.675 426	0.669 318	44
45	0.694 789	0.688 358	0.681 988	0.675 679	0.669 429	0.663 238	45
46	0.689 189	0.682 669	0.676 212	0.669 818	0.663 485	0.657 214	46
47	0.683 634	0.677 027	0.670 485	0.664 008	0.657 594	0.651 244	47
YRS							
4	0.678 125	0.671 432	0.664 807	0.658 248	0.651 756	0.645 329	48
5	0.615 371	0.607 789	0.600 301	0.592 908	0.585 607	0.578 397	60
6	0.558 424	0.550 178	0.542 055	0.534 053	0.526 171	0.518 408	72
7	0.506 748	0.498 028	0.489 460	0.481 041	0.472 769	0.464 640	84
8	0.459 863	0.450 821	0.441 968	0.433 291	0.424 786	0.416 449	96
9	0.417 298	0.408 089	0.399 084	0.390 280	0.381 673	0.373 256	108
10	0.378 681	0.369 407	0.360 362	0.351 540	0.342 935	0.334 543	120
11	0.343 638	0.334 392	0.325 396	0.316 644	0.308 130	0.299 846	132
12	0.311 838	0.302 646	0.293 823	0.285 213	0.276 856	0.268 747	144
13	0.282 980	0.274 004	0.265 314	0.256 901	0.248 757	0.240 873	156
14	0.256 793	0.248 032	0.239 571	0.231 400	0.223 510	0.215 890	168
15	0.233 029	0.224 521	0.216 326	0.208 431	0.200 825	0.193 499	180
16	0.211 465	0.203 240	0.195 336	0.187 741	0.180 443	0.173 430	192
17	0.191 896	0.183 975	0.176 383	0.169 105	0.162 129	0.155 442	204
18	0.174 138	0.166 536	0.159 268	0.152 319	0.145 674	0.139 320	216
19	0.158 023	0.150 751	0.143 815	0.137 199	0.130 889	0.124 870	228
20	0.143 400	0.136 462	0.129 861	0.123 580	0.117 605	0.111 919	240
21	0.130 129	0.123 527	0.117 260	0.111 313	0.105 669	0.100 311	252
22	0.118 087	0.111 818	0.105 883	0.100 264	0.094 944	0.089 907	264
23	0.107 159	0.101 219	0.095 609	0.090 311	0.085 308	0.080 582	276
24	0.097 243	0.091 625	0.086 332	0.081 346	0.076 649	0.072 225	288
25	0.088 244	0.082 940	0.077 955	0.073 272	0.068 870	0.064 734	300
26	0.080 078	0.075 078	0.070 392	0.065 998	0.061 880	0.058 020	312
27	0.072 667	0.067 962	0.063 561	0.059 447	0.055 600	0.052 002	324
28	0.065 943	0.061 520	0.057 394	0.053 546	0.049 957	0.046 609	336
29	0.059 840	0.055 688	0.051 825	0.048 231	0.044 886	0.041 775	348
30	0.054 303	0.050 410	0.046 797	0.043 443	0.040 331	0.037 442	360

PRESENT VALUE

MONTHLY COMPOUNDING

MOS	11.25% ANNUAL RATE	11.50% ANNUAL RATE	11.75% ANNUAL RATE	12.00% ANNUAL RATE	12.25% ANNUAL RATE	12.50% ANNUAL RATE	MOS
1	0.990 712	0.990 508	0.990 303	0.990 099	0.989 895	0.989 691	1
2	0.981 510	0.981 105	0.980 701	0.980 296	0.979 892	0.979 488	2
3	0.972 394	0.971 792	0.971 191	0.970 590	0.969 990	0.969 390	3
4	0.963 363	0.962 568	0.961 774	0.960 980	0.960 188	0.959 396	4
5	0.954 415	0.953 431	0.952 448	0.951 466	0.950 485	0.949 506	5
6	0.945 551	0.944 380	0.943 212	0.942 045	0.940 880	0.939 717	6
7	0.936 768	0.935 416	0.934 066	0.932 718	0.931 372	0.930 029	7
8	0.928 068	0.926 537	0.925 009	0.923 483	0.921 961	0.920 441	8
9	0.919 448	0.917 742	0.916 039	0.914 340	0.912 644	0.910 952	9
10	0.910 908	0.909 030	0.907 156	0.905 287	0.903 422	0.901 561	10
11	0.902 448	0.900 401	0.898 360	0.896 324	0.894 292	0.892 266	11
12	0.894 066	0.891 854	0.889 649	0.887 449	0.885 256	0.883 068	12
13	0.885 762	0.883 389	0.881 022	0.878 663	0.876 310	0.873 964	13
14	0.877 535	0.875 003	0.872 479	0.869 963	0.867 455	0.864 954	14
15	0.869 384	0.866 697	0.864 019	0.861 349	0.858 689	0.856 037	15
16	0.861 310	0.858 470	0.855 641	0.852 821	0.850 012	0.847 212	16
17	0.853 310	0.850 321	0.847 344	0.844 377	0.841 422	0.838 478	17
18	0.845 384	0.842 250	0.839 127	0.836 017	0.832 919	0.829 834	18
19	0.837 532	0.834 255	0.830 991	0.827 740	0.824 503	0.821 279	19
20	0.829 754	0.826 336	0.822 933	0.819 544	0.816 171	0.812 812	20
21	0.822 047	0.818 492	0.814 953	0.811 430	0.807 923	0.804 432	21
22	0.814 412	0.810 722	0.807 051	0.803 396	0.799 759	0.796 139	22
23	0.806 848	0.803 027	0.799 225	0.795 442	0.791 677	0.787 932	23
24	0.799 354	0.795 404	0.791 475	0.787 566	0.783 677	0.779 809	24
25	0.791 929	0.787 854	0.783 800	0.779 768	0.775 758	0.771 769	25
26	0.784 574	0.780 375	0.776 200	0.772 048	0.767 919	0.763 813	26
27	0.777 287	0.772 968	0.768 673	0.764 404	0.760 159	0.755 939	27
28	0.770 067	0.765 630	0.761 220	0.756 836	0.752 477	0.748 145	28
29	0.762 915	0.758 363	0.753 838	0.749 342	0.744 874	0.740 432	29
30	0.755 829	0.751 164	0.746 529	0.741 923	0.737 346	0.732 799	30
31	0.748 809	0.744 034	0.739 290	0.734 577	0.729 895	0.725 245	31
32	0.741 854	0.736 971	0.732 121	0.727 304	0.722 520	0.717 768	32
33	0.734 964	0.729 976	0.725 022	0.720 103	0.715 219	0.710 368	33
34	0.728 138	0.723 046	0.717 992	0.712 973	0.707 991	0.703 045	34
35	0.721 375	0.716 183	0.711 029	0.705 914	0.700 837	0.695 797	35
36	0.714 675	0.709 385	0.704 135	0.698 925	0.693 755	0.688 624	36
37	0.708 037	0.702 651	0.697 307	0.692 005	0.686 744	0.681 524	37
38	0.701 461	0.695 981	0.690 545	0.685 153	0.679 804	0.674 498	38
39	0.694 946	0.689 375	0.683 849	0.678 370	0.672 935	0.667 545	39
40	0.688 491	0.682 831	0.677 218	0.671 653	0.666 135	0.660 663	40
41	0.682 096	0.676 349	0.670 652	0.665 003	0.659 403	0.653 852	41
42	0.675 761	0.669 929	0.664 148	0.658 419	0.652 740	0.647 111	42
43	0.669 485	0.663 570	0.657 708	0.651 900	0.646 144	0.640 440	43
44	0.663 267	0.657 271	0.651 331	0.645 445	0.639 615	0.633 838	44
45	0.657 106	0.651 032	0.645 015	0.639 055	0.633 151	0.627 303	45
46	0.651 003	0.644 852	0.638 760	0.632 728	0.626 753	0.620 836	46
47	0.644 957	0.638 731	0.632 567	0.626 463	0.620 420	0.614 436	47
YRS							
4	0.638 966	0.632 668	0.626 433	0.620 260	0.614 150	0.608 101	48
5	0.571 278	0.564 248	0.557 305	0.550 450	0.543 680	0.536 995	60
6	0.510 760	0.503 227	0.495 806	0.488 496	0.481 296	0.474 203	72
7	0.456 653	0.448 805	0.441 093	0.433 515	0.426 070	0.418 753	84
8	0.408 278	0.400 269	0.392 418	0.384 723	0.377 180	0.369 787	96
9	0.365 027	0.356 981	0.349 114	0.341 422	0.333 901	0.326 547	108
10	0.326 358	0.318 375	0.310 589	0.302 995	0.295 588	0.288 363	120
11	0.291 786	0.283 944	0.276 315	0.268 892	0.261 671	0.254 644	132
12	0.260 876	0.253 237	0.245 823	0.238 628	0.231 645	0.224 868	144
13	0.233 240	0.225 851	0.218 697	0.211 771	0.205 065	0.198 574	156
14	0.208 532	0.201 426	0.194 563	0.187 936	0.181 535	0.175 354	168
15	0.186 441	0.179 642	0.173 093	0.166 783	0.160 705	0.154 849	180
16	0.166 691	0.160 215	0.153 992	0.148 012	0.142 265	0.136 743	192
17	0.149 033	0.142 888	0.136 999	0.131 353	0.125 941	0.120 753	204
18	0.133 245	0.127 436	0.121 881	0.116 569	0.111 490	0.106 633	216
19	0.119 130	0.113 654	0.108 431	0.103 449	0.098 697	0.094 164	228
20	0.106 510	0.101 363	0.096 466	0.091 806	0.087 372	0.083 153	240
21	0.095 227	0.090 401	0.085 820	0.081 473	0.077 347	0.073 430	252
22	0.085 139	0.080 624	0.076 350	0.072 303	0.068 472	0.064 844	264
23	0.076 120	0.071 905	0.067 925	0.064 165	0.060 615	0.057 261	276
24	0.068 056	0.064 129	0.060 429	0.056 944	0.053 660	0.050 566	288
25	0.060 847	0.057 194	0.053 761	0.050 534	0.047 502	0.044 653	300
26	0.054 401	0.051 008	0.047 828	0.044 847	0.042 052	0.039 432	312
27	0.048 638	0.045 492	0.042 550	0.039 799	0.037 227	0.034 821	324
28	0.043 486	0.040 572	0.037 855	0.035 320	0.032 955	0.030 749	336
29	0.038 879	0.036 185	0.033 677	0.031 345	0.029 174	0.027 153	348
30	0.034 760	0.032 271	0.029 961	0.027 817	0.025 826	0.023 978	360

PRESENT VALUE

MOS	12.75% ANNUAL RATE	13.00% ANNUAL RATE	13.25% ANNUAL RATE	13.50% ANNUAL RATE	13.75% ANNUAL RATE	14.00% ANNUAL RATE	MOS
1	0.989 487	0.989 283	0.989 079	0.988 875	0.988 671	0.988 468	1
2	0.979 084	0.978 680	0.978 277	0.977 874	0.977 471	0.977 069	2
3	0.968 791	0.968 192	0.967 593	0.966 995	0.966 398	0.965 801	3
4	0.958 605	0.957 815	0.957 026	0.956 238	0.955 450	0.954 663	4
5	0.948 527	0.947 550	0.946 574	0.945 600	0.944 626	0.943 654	5
6	0.938 555	0.937 395	0.936 237	0.935 080	0.933 925	0.932 772	6
7	0.928 688	0.927 349	0.926 012	0.924 677	0.923 345	0.922 015	7
8	0.918 924	0.917 410	0.915 899	0.914 391	0.912 885	0.911 382	8
9	0.909 263	0.907 578	0.905 896	0.904 218	0.902 543	0.900 872	9
10	0.899 704	0.897 851	0.896 003	0.894 159	0.892 319	0.890 483	10
11	0.890 245	0.888 229	0.886 218	0.884 211	0.882 210	0.880 214	11
12	0.880 886	0.878 710	0.876 539	0.874 375	0.872 216	0.870 063	12
13	0.871 625	0.869 292	0.866 966	0.864 647	0.862 335	0.860 029	13
14	0.862 461	0.859 976	0.857 498	0.855 028	0.852 566	0.850 111	14
15	0.853 394	0.850 759	0.848 133	0.845 516	0.842 908	0.840 308	15
16	0.844 422	0.841 641	0.838 871	0.836 110	0.833 359	0.830 617	16
17	0.835 544	0.832 621	0.829 710	0.826 808	0.823 918	0.821 038	17
18	0.826 760	0.823 698	0.820 648	0.817 610	0.814 584	0.811 570	18
19	0.818 068	0.814 870	0.811 686	0.808 515	0.805 356	0.802 211	19
20	0.809 467	0.806 137	0.802 821	0.799 520	0.796 233	0.792 960	20
21	0.800 957	0.797 498	0.794 054	0.790 625	0.787 213	0.783 815	21
22	0.792 536	0.788 951	0.785 382	0.781 830	0.778 295	0.774 776	22
23	0.784 204	0.780 495	0.776 805	0.773 132	0.769 478	0.765 841	23
24	0.775 960	0.772 130	0.768 321	0.764 531	0.760 761	0.757 010	24
25	0.767 802	0.763 855	0.759 930	0.756 026	0.752 142	0.748 280	25
26	0.759 730	0.755 669	0.751 631	0.747 615	0.743 622	0.739 650	26
27	0.751 742	0.747 570	0.743 422	0.739 298	0.735 198	0.731 121	27
28	0.743 839	0.739 558	0.735 303	0.731 073	0.726 869	0.722 689	28
29	0.736 019	0.731 632	0.727 273	0.722 940	0.718 635	0.714 355	29
30	0.728 281	0.723 791	0.719 330	0.714 898	0.710 493	0.706 117	30
31	0.720 624	0.716 034	0.711 474	0.706 945	0.702 445	0.697 974	31
32	0.713 048	0.708 360	0.703 704	0.699 080	0.694 487	0.689 925	32
33	0.705 552	0.700 769	0.696 019	0.691 303	0.686 619	0.681 969	33
34	0.698 134	0.693 258	0.688 418	0.683 612	0.678 841	0.674 104	34
35	0.690 794	0.685 829	0.680 900	0.676 007	0.671 151	0.666 330	35
36	0.683 532	0.678 478	0.673 463	0.668 487	0.663 548	0.658 646	36
37	0.676 346	0.671 207	0.666 109	0.661 050	0.656 031	0.651 051	37
38	0.669 235	0.664 014	0.658 834	0.653 696	0.648 599	0.643 543	38
39	0.662 199	0.656 897	0.651 639	0.646 424	0.641 251	0.636 121	39
40	0.655 237	0.649 857	0.644 522	0.639 232	0.633 987	0.628 785	40
41	0.648 348	0.642 892	0.637 483	0.632 121	0.626 805	0.621 534	41
42	0.641 532	0.636 002	0.630 521	0.625 089	0.619 704	0.614 366	42
43	0.634 788	0.629 186	0.623 635	0.618 135	0.612 683	0.607 281	43
44	0.628 114	0.622 443	0.616 825	0.611 258	0.605 743	0.600 278	44
45	0.621 510	0.615 772	0.610 088	0.604 458	0.598 880	0.593 356	45
46	0.614 976	0.609 173	0.603 425	0.597 733	0.592 096	0.586 513	46
47	0.608 511	0.602 644	0.596 835	0.591 084	0.585 388	0.579 749	47

YRS							
4	0.602 113	0.596 185	0.590 317	0.584 508	0.578 757	0.573 064	48
5	0.530 393	0.523 874	0.517 436	0.511 079	0.504 801	0.498 601	60
6	0.467 216	0.460 333	0.453 553	0.446 874	0.440 295	0.433 815	72
7	0.411 564	0.404 499	0.397 557	0.390 736	0.384 033	0.377 446	84
8	0.362 540	0.355 437	0.348 474	0.341 649	0.334 960	0.328 402	96
9	0.319 357	0.312 326	0.305 451	0.298 730	0.292 157	0.285 730	108
10	0.281 317	0.274 444	0.267 740	0.261 202	0.254 824	0.248 603	120
11	0.247 808	0.241 156	0.234 685	0.228 388	0.222 262	0.216 301	132
12	0.218 290	0.211 906	0.205 710	0.199 697	0.193 860	0.188 195	144
13	0.192 289	0.186 204	0.180 313	0.174 610	0.169 088	0.163 742	156
14	0.169 385	0.163 619	0.158 052	0.152 674	0.147 481	0.142 466	168
15	0.149 208	0.143 774	0.138 538	0.133 495	0.128 635	0.123 954	180
16	0.131 436	0.126 336	0.121 434	0.116 724	0.112 198	0.107 848	192
17	0.115 780	0.111 012	0.106 442	0.102 061	0.097 861	0.093 834	204
18	0.101 989	0.097 548	0.093 301	0.089 239	0.085 356	0.081 642	216
19	0.089 840	0.085 716	0.081 782	0.078 029	0.074 449	0.071 034	228
20	0.079 139	0.075 319	0.071 685	0.068 226	0.064 935	0.061 804	240
21	0.069 712	0.066 184	0.062 835	0.059 655	0.056 638	0.053 773	252
22	0.061 409	0.058 156	0.055 077	0.052 161	0.049 400	0.046 786	264
23	0.054 094	0.051 103	0.048 277	0.045 608	0.043 088	0.040 707	276
24	0.047 651	0.044 904	0.042 317	0.039 879	0.037 582	0.035 417	288
25	0.041 975	0.039 458	0.037 092	0.034 869	0.032 779	0.030 815	300
26	0.036 975	0.034 672	0.032 513	0.030 489	0.028 591	0.026 811	312
27	0.032 571	0.030 467	0.028 499	0.026 658	0.024 937	0.023 328	324
28	0.028 691	0.026 771	0.024 980	0.023 309	0.021 751	0.020 296	336
29	0.025 274	0.023 524	0.021 896	0.020 381	0.018 971	0.017 659	348
30	0.022 263	0.020 671	0.019 193	0.017 821	0.016 547	0.015 365	360

151

MOS	14.25% ANNUAL RATE	14.50% ANNUAL RATE	14.75% ANNUAL RATE	15.00% ANNUAL RATE	15.25% ANNUAL RATE	15.50% ANNUAL RATE	MOS
1	0.988 264	0.988 061	0.987 858	0.987 654	0.987 451	0.987 248	1
2	0.976 666	0.976 264	0.975 863	0.975 461	0.975 060	0.974 659	2
3	0.965 205	0.964 609	0.964 013	0.963 418	0.962 824	0.962 230	3
4	0.953 877	0.953 092	0.952 308	0.951 524	0.950 742	0.949 960	4
5	0.942 683	0.941 713	0.940 745	0.939 777	0.938 811	0.937 846	5
6	0.931 620	0.930 470	0.929 322	0.928 175	0.927 030	0.925 886	6
7	0.920 687	0.919 361	0.918 037	0.916 716	0.915 397	0.914 080	7
8	0.909 882	0.908 385	0.906 890	0.905 398	0.903 909	0.902 423	8
9	0.899 204	0.897 539	0.895 878	0.894 221	0.892 566	0.890 916	9
10	0.888 651	0.886 824	0.885 000	0.883 181	0.881 366	0.879 555	10
11	0.878 222	0.876 236	0.874 254	0.872 277	0.870 306	0.868 339	11
12	0.867 916	0.865 774	0.863 639	0.861 509	0.859 384	0.857 266	12
13	0.857 730	0.855 438	0.853 152	0.850 873	0.848 600	0.846 334	13
14	0.847 664	0.845 225	0.842 793	0.840 368	0.837 951	0.835 541	14
15	0.837 716	0.835 133	0.832 559	0.829 993	0.827 436	0.824 887	15
16	0.827 885	0.825 163	0.822 450	0.819 746	0.817 052	0.814 368	16
17	0.818 169	0.815 311	0.812 463	0.809 626	0.806 799	0.803 983	17
18	0.808 568	0.805 577	0.802 598	0.799 631	0.796 675	0.793 731	18
19	0.799 079	0.795 959	0.792 853	0.789 759	0.786 677	0.783 609	19
20	0.789 701	0.786 456	0.783 225	0.780 009	0.776 806	0.773 616	20
21	0.780 433	0.777 067	0.773 715	0.770 379	0.767 058	0.763 751	21
22	0.771 274	0.767 789	0.764 320	0.760 868	0.757 432	0.754 012	22
23	0.762 223	0.758 622	0.755 040	0.751 475	0.747 927	0.744 397	23
24	0.753 278	0.749 565	0.745 872	0.742 197	0.738 541	0.734 904	24
25	0.744 438	0.740 616	0.736 815	0.733 034	0.729 273	0.725 533	25
26	0.735 701	0.731 774	0.727 868	0.723 984	0.720 122	0.716 281	26
27	0.727 067	0.723 037	0.719 030	0.715 046	0.711 085	0.707 147	27
28	0.718 535	0.714 405	0.710 299	0.706 219	0.702 162	0.698 129	28
29	0.710 102	0.705 875	0.701 675	0.697 500	0.693 351	0.689 227	29
30	0.701 769	0.697 448	0.693 155	0.688 889	0.684 650	0.680 438	30
31	0.693 533	0.689 121	0.684 738	0.680 384	0.676 058	0.671 761	31
32	0.685 394	0.680 894	0.676 424	0.671 984	0.667 574	0.663 195	32
33	0.677 350	0.672 764	0.668 210	0.663 688	0.659 197	0.654 738	33
34	0.669 401	0.664 732	0.660 097	0.655 494	0.650 925	0.646 388	34
35	0.661 545	0.656 796	0.652 081	0.647 402	0.642 757	0.638 146	35
36	0.653 782	0.648 954	0.644 164	0.639 409	0.634 691	0.630 008	36
37	0.646 109	0.641 206	0.636 342	0.631 515	0.626 726	0.621 974	37
38	0.638 527	0.633 551	0.628 615	0.623 719	0.618 861	0.614 043	38
39	0.631 033	0.625 987	0.620 982	0.616 019	0.611 095	0.606 213	39
40	0.623 628	0.618 513	0.613 442	0.608 413	0.603 427	0.598 482	40
41	0.616 309	0.611 129	0.605 993	0.600 902	0.595 855	0.590 850	41
42	0.609 076	0.603 833	0.598 635	0.593 484	0.588 377	0.583 316	42
43	0.601 928	0.596 623	0.591 366	0.586 157	0.580 994	0.575 878	43
44	0.594 864	0.589 500	0.584 186	0.578 920	0.573 703	0.568 534	44
45	0.587 883	0.582 462	0.577 092	0.571 773	0.566 504	0.561 284	45
46	0.580 984	0.575 508	0.570 085	0.564 714	0.559 395	0.554 127	46
47	0.574 166	0.568 637	0.563 163	0.557 742	0.552 375	0.547 060	47
YRS							
4	0.567 428	0.561 848	0.556 325	0.550 856	0.545 443	0.540 084	48
5	0.492 479	0.486 434	0.480 463	0.474 568	0.468 745	0.462 996	60
6	0.427 431	0.421 142	0.414 947	0.408 844	0.402 832	0.396 910	72
7	0.370 974	0.364 614	0.358 364	0.352 223	0.346 188	0.340 258	84
8	0.321 974	0.315 673	0.309 497	0.303 443	0.297 508	0.291 691	96
9	0.279 446	0.273 302	0.267 294	0.261 419	0.255 674	0.250 057	108
10	0.242 536	0.236 618	0.230 845	0.225 214	0.219 722	0.214 365	120
11	0.210 501	0.204 858	0.199 367	0.194 024	0.188 826	0.183 768	132
12	0.182 697	0.177 360	0.172 181	0.167 153	0.162 274	0.157 538	144
13	0.158 566	0.153 554	0.148 702	0.144 004	0.139 456	0.135 052	156
14	0.137 622	0.132 943	0.128 425	0.124 061	0.119 846	0.115 775	168
15	0.119 444	0.115 099	0.110 913	0.106 879	0.102 994	0.099 250	180
16	0.103 667	0.099 650	0.095 788	0.092 078	0.088 511	0.085 084	192
17	0.089 974	0.086 274	0.082 727	0.079 326	0.076 065	0.072 939	204
18	0.078 090	0.074 694	0.071 446	0.068 340	0.065 369	0.062 528	216
19	0.067 776	0.064 668	0.061 703	0.058 875	0.056 177	0.053 603	228
20	0.058 824	0.055 988	0.053 289	0.050 722	0.048 278	0.045 952	240
21	0.051 054	0.048 473	0.046 023	0.043 697	0.041 489	0.039 393	252
22	0.044 311	0.041 967	0.039 747	0.037 645	0.035 655	0.033 771	264
23	0.038 458	0.036 334	0.034 327	0.032 432	0.030 642	0.028 950	276
24	0.033 378	0.031 457	0.029 646	0.027 940	0.026 333	0.024 818	288
25	0.028 969	0.027 234	0.025 604	0.024 071	0.022 630	0.021 276	300
26	0.025 143	0.023 579	0.022 112	0.020 737	0.019 448	0.018 239	312
27	0.021 822	0.020 414	0.019 097	0.017 865	0.016 713	0.015 636	324
28	0.018 940	0.017 674	0.016 493	0.015 391	0.014 363	0.013 404	336
29	0.016 438	0.015 302	0.014 244	0.013 260	0.012 343	0.011 491	348
30	0.014 267	0.013 248	0.012 302	0.011 423	0.010 608	0.009 851	360

PRESENT VALUE

	15.75%	16.00%	16.25%	16.50%	16.75%	17.00%	
	ANNUAL RATE	ANNUAL RATE	ANNUAL RATE	ANNUAL RATE	ANNUAL RATE	ANNUAL RATE	
MOS							MOS
1	0.987 045	0.986 842	0.986 639	0.986 436	0.986 234	0.986 031	1
2	0.974 258	0.973 857	0.973 457	0.973 057	0.972 657	0.972 258	2
3	0.961 636	0.961 043	0.960 451	0.959 859	0.959 267	0.958 676	3
4	0.949 178	0.948 398	0.947 619	0.946 840	0.946 062	0.945 285	4
5	0.936 882	0.935 919	0.934 958	0.933 997	0.933 038	0.932 080	5
6	0.924 745	0.923 604	0.922 466	0.921 329	0.920 194	0.919 060	6
7	0.912 765	0.911 452	0.910 141	0.908 833	0.907 526	0.906 222	7
8	0.900 940	0.899 459	0.897 981	0.896 506	0.895 033	0.893 563	8
9	0.889 268	0.887 624	0.885 983	0.884 346	0.882 712	0.881 081	9
10	0.877 748	0.875 945	0.874 146	0.872 351	0.870 560	0.868 774	10
11	0.866 376	0.864 419	0.862 467	0.860 519	0.858 576	0.856 638	11
12	0.855 153	0.853 045	0.850 943	0.848 847	0.846 757	0.844 672	12
13	0.844 074	0.841 821	0.839 574	0.837 334	0.835 100	0.832 873	13
14	0.833 139	0.830 744	0.828 357	0.825 977	0.823 604	0.821 239	14
15	0.822 346	0.819 814	0.817 289	0.814 774	0.812 266	0.809 767	15
16	0.811 692	0.809 026	0.806 370	0.803 722	0.801 084	0.798 455	16
17	0.801 177	0.798 381	0.795 596	0.792 821	0.790 056	0.787 302	17
18	0.790 798	0.787 876	0.784 966	0.782 068	0.779 180	0.776 304	18
19	0.780 553	0.777 510	0.774 479	0.771 460	0.768 454	0.765 460	19
20	0.770 441	0.767 279	0.764 131	0.760 996	0.757 875	0.754 768	20
21	0.760 460	0.757 183	0.753 922	0.750 675	0.747 442	0.744 225	21
22	0.750 608	0.747 220	0.743 849	0.740 493	0.737 153	0.733 829	22
23	0.740 884	0.737 389	0.733 910	0.730 449	0.727 005	0.723 578	23
24	0.731 286	0.727 686	0.724 105	0.720 542	0.716 997	0.713 471	24
25	0.721 812	0.718 111	0.714 430	0.710 769	0.707 127	0.703 504	25
26	0.712 461	0.708 662	0.704 885	0.701 128	0.697 392	0.693 677	26
27	0.703 231	0.699 338	0.695 467	0.691 618	0.687 792	0.683 987	27
28	0.694 121	0.690 136	0.686 175	0.682 238	0.678 324	0.674 433	28
29	0.685 129	0.681 055	0.677 007	0.672 984	0.668 986	0.665 012	29
30	0.676 253	0.672 094	0.667 962	0.663 856	0.659 776	0.655 722	30
31	0.667 492	0.663 251	0.659 038	0.654 852	0.650 694	0.646 563	31
32	0.658 845	0.654 524	0.650 232	0.645 970	0.641 736	0.637 531	32
33	0.650 309	0.645 912	0.641 545	0.637 208	0.632 902	0.628 626	33
34	0.641 885	0.637 413	0.632 973	0.628 565	0.624 189	0.619 844	34
35	0.633 569	0.629 026	0.624 516	0.620 040	0.615 597	0.611 186	35
36	0.625 361	0.620 749	0.616 172	0.611 630	0.607 122	0.602 648	36
37	0.617 260	0.612 581	0.607 940	0.603 334	0.598 764	0.594 230	37
38	0.609 263	0.604 521	0.599 817	0.595 151	0.590 522	0.585 930	38
39	0.601 370	0.596 567	0.591 803	0.587 079	0.582 392	0.577 745	39
40	0.593 579	0.588 717	0.583 896	0.579 116	0.574 375	0.569 674	40
41	0.585 889	0.580 971	0.576 095	0.571 261	0.566 468	0.561 717	41
42	0.578 299	0.573 327	0.568 398	0.563 513	0.558 670	0.553 870	42
43	0.570 807	0.565 783	0.560 804	0.555 869	0.550 979	0.546 133	43
44	0.563 413	0.558 338	0.553 311	0.548 330	0.543 394	0.538 505	44
45	0.556 114	0.550 992	0.545 918	0.540 893	0.535 914	0.530 982	45
46	0.548 909	0.543 742	0.538 624	0.533 556	0.528 537	0.523 565	46
47	0.541 798	0.536 587	0.531 428	0.526 319	0.521 261	0.516 252	47
YRS							
4	0.534 779	0.529 527	0.524 328	0.519 181	0.514 085	0.509 040	48
5	0.457 318	0.451 711	0.446 173	0.440 705	0.435 305	0.429 972	60
6	0.391 076	0.385 330	0.379 668	0.374 091	0.368 597	0.363 185	72
7	0.334 430	0.328 704	0.323 076	0.317 546	0.312 112	0.306 772	84
8	0.285 989	0.280 399	0.274 920	0.269 548	0.264 283	0.259 122	96
9	0.244 564	0.239 193	0.233 941	0.228 805	0.223 784	0.218 873	108
10	0.209 140	0.204 042	0.199 071	0.194 221	0.189 490	0.184 876	120
11	0.178 846	0.174 057	0.169 398	0.164 864	0.160 452	0.156 159	132
12	0.152 941	0.148 479	0.144 148	0.139 944	0.135 864	0.131 903	144
13	0.130 788	0.126 659	0.122 662	0.118 791	0.115 044	0.111 415	156
14	0.111 843	0.108 046	0.104 378	0.100 836	0.097 414	0.094 109	168
15	0.095 643	0.092 168	0.088 820	0.085 594	0.082 486	0.079 491	180
16	0.081 790	0.078 624	0.075 581	0.072 656	0.069 846	0.067 144	192
17	0.069 943	0.067 069	0.064 315	0.061 674	0.059 142	0.056 715	204
18	0.059 812	0.057 213	0.054 728	0.052 352	0.050 079	0.047 905	216
19	0.051 148	0.048 806	0.046 571	0.044 439	0.042 405	0.040 464	228
20	0.043 739	0.041 633	0.039 629	0.037 722	0.035 907	0.034 179	240
21	0.037 404	0.035 515	0.033 722	0.032 020	0.030 404	0.028 870	252
22	0.031 986	0.030 296	0.028 696	0.027 180	0.025 745	0.024 386	264
23	0.027 353	0.025 844	0.024 418	0.023 072	0.021 800	0.020 598	276
24	0.023 391	0.022 046	0.020 779	0.019 584	0.018 459	0.017 399	288
25	0.020 003	0.018 806	0.017 681	0.016 624	0.015 630	0.014 696	300
26	0.017 105	0.016 043	0.015 046	0.014 111	0.013 235	0.012 413	312
27	0.014 628	0.013 685	0.012 803	0.011 978	0.011 207	0.010 485	324
28	0.012 509	0.011 674	0.010 895	0.010 168	0.009 490	0.008 857	336
29	0.010 697	0.009 958	0.009 271	0.008 631	0.008 035	0.007 481	348
30	0.009 148	0.008 495	0.007 889	0.007 326	0.006 804	0.006 319	360

SECTION 4

MOS	17.25% ANNUAL RATE	17.50% ANNUAL RATE	17.75% ANNUAL RATE	18.00% ANNUAL RATE	18.25% ANNUAL RATE	18.50% ANNUAL RATE	MOS
1	0.985 829	0.985 626	0.985 424	0.985 222	0.985 019	0.984 817	1
2	0.971 858	0.971 459	0.971 060	0.970 662	0.970 263	0.969 865	2
3	0.958 086	0.957 496	0.956 906	0.956 317	0.955 728	0.955 140	3
4	0.944 508	0.943 733	0.942 958	0.942 184	0.941 411	0.940 639	4
5	0.931 124	0.930 168	0.929 214	0.928 260	0.927 308	0.926 357	5
6	0.917 928	0.916 798	0.915 669	0.914 542	0.913 417	0.912 293	6
7	0.904 920	0.903 620	0.902 322	0.901 027	0.899 733	0.898 442	7
8	0.892 096	0.890 632	0.889 170	0.887 711	0.886 255	0.884 801	8
9	0.879 454	0.877 830	0.876 210	0.874 592	0.872 978	0.871 368	9
10	0.866 991	0.865 212	0.863 438	0.861 667	0.859 901	0.858 138	10
11	0.854 705	0.852 776	0.850 852	0.848 933	0.847 019	0.845 109	11
12	0.842 592	0.840 519	0.838 450	0.836 387	0.834 330	0.832 278	12
13	0.830 652	0.828 437	0.826 229	0.824 027	0.821 831	0.819 642	13
14	0.818 880	0.816 529	0.814 186	0.811 849	0.809 520	0.807 198	14
15	0.807 276	0.804 793	0.802 318	0.799 852	0.797 393	0.794 942	15
16	0.795 836	0.793 225	0.790 624	0.788 031	0.785 448	0.782 873	16
17	0.784 558	0.781 823	0.779 099	0.776 385	0.773 681	0.770 987	17
18	0.773 439	0.770 586	0.767 743	0.764 912	0.762 091	0.759 282	18
19	0.762 479	0.759 510	0.756 552	0.753 607	0.750 675	0.747 754	19
20	0.751 674	0.748 593	0.745 525	0.742 470	0.739 429	0.736 401	20
21	0.741 021	0.737 833	0.734 658	0.731 498	0.728 352	0.725 220	21
22	0.730 520	0.727 227	0.723 950	0.720 688	0.717 441	0.714 210	22
23	0.720 168	0.716 774	0.713 397	0.710 037	0.706 693	0.703 366	23
24	0.709 962	0.706 471	0.702 999	0.699 544	0.696 107	0.692 687	24
25	0.699 901	0.696 317	0.692 752	0.689 206	0.685 679	0.682 170	25
26	0.689 982	0.686 308	0.682 654	0.679 021	0.675 407	0.671 813	26
27	0.680 204	0.676 443	0.672 704	0.668 986	0.665 289	0.661 613	27
28	0.670 565	0.666 720	0.662 898	0.659 099	0.655 323	0.651 568	28
29	0.661 062	0.657 137	0.653 236	0.649 359	0.645 506	0.641 676	29
30	0.651 694	0.647 692	0.643 714	0.639 762	0.635 836	0.631 933	30
31	0.642 459	0.638 382	0.634 332	0.630 308	0.626 310	0.622 339	31
32	0.633 354	0.629 206	0.625 086	0.620 993	0.616 928	0.612 890	32
33	0.624 379	0.620 162	0.615 974	0.611 816	0.607 686	0.603 585	33
34	0.615 531	0.611 248	0.606 996	0.602 774	0.598 583	0.594 421	34
35	0.606 808	0.602 462	0.598 148	0.593 866	0.589 616	0.585 396	35
36	0.598 209	0.593 802	0.589 430	0.585 090	0.580 783	0.576 508	36
37	0.589 731	0.585 267	0.580 838	0.576 443	0.572 082	0.567 756	37
38	0.581 374	0.576 855	0.572 372	0.567 924	0.563 512	0.559 136	38
39	0.573 135	0.568 563	0.564 029	0.559 531	0.555 071	0.550 646	39
40	0.565 013	0.560 391	0.555 807	0.551 262	0.546 755	0.542 286	40
41	0.557 006	0.552 336	0.547 706	0.543 116	0.538 565	0.534 053	41
42	0.549 113	0.544 397	0.539 723	0.535 089	0.530 497	0.525 945	42
43	0.541 331	0.536 572	0.531 855	0.527 182	0.522 550	0.517 959	43
44	0.533 660	0.528 859	0.524 103	0.519 391	0.514 722	0.510 095	44
45	0.526 097	0.521 258	0.516 464	0.511 715	0.507 011	0.502 351	45
46	0.518 642	0.513 765	0.508 936	0.504 153	0.499 415	0.494 724	46
47	0.511 292	0.506 381	0.501 517	0.496 702	0.491 934	0.487 213	47

YRS							
4	0.504 046	0.499 102	0.494 207	0.489 362	0.484 565	0.479 815	48
5	0.424 705	0.419 504	0.414 368	0.409 296	0.404 287	0.399 340	60
6	0.357 854	0.352 601	0.347 427	0.342 330	0.337 309	0.332 362	72
7	0.301 525	0.296 368	0.291 300	0.286 321	0.281 427	0.276 618	84
8	0.254 062	0.249 103	0.244 241	0.239 475	0.234 803	0.230 223	96
9	0.214 071	0.209 375	0.204 784	0.200 294	0.195 903	0.191 609	108
10	0.180 375	0.175 984	0.171 701	0.167 523	0.163 448	0.159 472	120
11	0.151 982	0.147 918	0.143 963	0.140 114	0.136 369	0.132 725	132
12	0.128 059	0.124 328	0.120 706	0.117 190	0.113 777	0.110 464	144
13	0.107 902	0.104 500	0.101 206	0.098 016	0.094 928	0.091 937	156
14	0.090 917	0.087 834	0.084 856	0.081 979	0.079 201	0.076 517	168
15	0.076 606	0.073 826	0.071 147	0.068 567	0.066 080	0.063 684	180
16	0.064 548	0.062 052	0.059 654	0.057 348	0.055 132	0.053 003	192
17	0.054 387	0.052 156	0.050 017	0.047 965	0.045 999	0.044 113	204
18	0.045 826	0.043 838	0.041 936	0.040 118	0.038 378	0.036 714	216
19	0.038 613	0.036 847	0.035 162	0.033 554	0.032 020	0.030 556	228
20	0.032 535	0.030 970	0.029 481	0.028 064	0.026 715	0.025 431	240
21	0.027 414	0.026 031	0.024 719	0.023 472	0.022 289	0.021 166	252
22	0.023 099	0.021 880	0.020 725	0.019 632	0.018 597	0.017 616	264
23	0.019 463	0.018 390	0.017 377	0.016 420	0.015 516	0.014 661	276
24	0.016 399	0.015 457	0.014 570	0.013 733	0.012 945	0.012 202	288
25	0.013 818	0.012 992	0.012 216	0.011 486	0.010 801	0.010 156	300
26	0.011 643	0.010 920	0.010 243	0.009 607	0.009 011	0.008 452	312
27	0.009 810	0.009 179	0.008 588	0.008 035	0.007 518	0.007 035	324
28	0.008 266	0.007 715	0.007 201	0.006 721	0.006 273	0.005 855	336
29	0.006 965	0.006 484	0.006 037	0.005 621	0.005 234	0.004 873	348
30	0.005 868	0.005 450	0.005 062	0.004 701	0.004 367	0.004 056	360

PRESENT VALUE

MONTHLY
COMPOUNDING

MOS	18.75% ANNUAL RATE	19.00% ANNUAL RATE	19.25% ANNUAL RATE	19.50% ANNUAL RATE	19.75% ANNUAL RATE	20.00% ANNUAL RATE	MOS
1	0.984 615	0.984 413	0.984 212	0.984 010	0.983 808	0.983 607	1
2	0.969 467	0.969 070	0.968 672	0.968 275	0.967 878	0.967 482	2
3	0.954 553	0.953 965	0.953 379	0.952 792	0.952 207	0.951 622	3
4	0.939 867	0.939 096	0.938 326	0.937 557	0.936 789	0.936 021	4
5	0.925 408	0.924 459	0.923 512	0.922 565	0.921 620	0.920 677	5
6	0.911 171	0.910 050	0.908 931	0.907 814	0.906 698	0.905 583	6
7	0.897 153	0.895 865	0.894 580	0.893 297	0.892 017	0.890 738	7
8	0.883 350	0.881 902	0.880 456	0.879 013	0.877 573	0.876 136	8
9	0.869 760	0.868 156	0.866 555	0.864 958	0.863 364	0.861 773	9
10	0.856 379	0.854 625	0.852 874	0.851 127	0.849 384	0.847 645	10
11	0.843 204	0.841 304	0.839 408	0.837 517	0.835 631	0.833 749	11
12	0.830 232	0.828 191	0.826 155	0.824 125	0.822 101	0.820 081	12
13	0.817 459	0.815 282	0.813 112	0.810 947	0.808 789	0.806 637	13
14	0.804 883	0.802 575	0.800 274	0.797 980	0.795 694	0.793 414	14
15	0.792 500	0.790 066	0.787 639	0.785 220	0.782 810	0.780 407	15
16	0.780 308	0.777 751	0.775 203	0.772 665	0.770 135	0.767 614	16
17	0.768 303	0.765 629	0.762 964	0.760 310	0.757 665	0.755 030	17
18	0.756 483	0.753 695	0.750 918	0.748 152	0.745 397	0.742 652	18
19	0.744 845	0.741 948	0.739 062	0.736 189	0.733 327	0.730 478	19
20	0.733 386	0.730 383	0.727 394	0.724 417	0.721 454	0.718 503	20
21	0.722 103	0.718 999	0.715 909	0.712 834	0.709 772	0.706 724	21
22	0.710 993	0.707 792	0.704 606	0.701 435	0.698 279	0.695 138	22
23	0.700 055	0.696 760	0.693 482	0.690 219	0.686 973	0.683 742	23
24	0.689 285	0.685 900	0.682 533	0.679 183	0.675 850	0.672 534	24
25	0.678 681	0.675 209	0.671 757	0.668 322	0.664 906	0.661 508	25
26	0.668 239	0.664 685	0.661 151	0.657 636	0.654 140	0.650 664	26
27	0.657 959	0.654 325	0.650 712	0.647 120	0.643 549	0.639 997	27
28	0.647 836	0.644 126	0.640 439	0.636 773	0.633 128	0.629 506	28
29	0.637 870	0.634 087	0.630 327	0.626 590	0.622 877	0.619 186	29
30	0.628 056	0.624 204	0.620 375	0.616 571	0.612 791	0.609 035	30
31	0.618 394	0.614 474	0.610 581	0.606 712	0.602 869	0.599 051	31
32	0.608 880	0.604 897	0.600 940	0.597 011	0.593 108	0.589 231	32
33	0.599 513	0.595 469	0.591 453	0.587 464	0.583 504	0.579 571	33
34	0.590 289	0.586 187	0.582 114	0.578 071	0.574 056	0.570 070	34
35	0.581 208	0.577 051	0.572 924	0.568 827	0.564 761	0.560 725	35
36	0.572 266	0.568 056	0.563 878	0.559 732	0.555 616	0.551 532	36
37	0.563 462	0.559 202	0.554 976	0.550 781	0.546 620	0.542 491	37
38	0.554 794	0.550 486	0.546 213	0.541 974	0.537 769	0.533 597	38
39	0.546 258	0.541 906	0.537 590	0.533 308	0.529 062	0.524 850	39
40	0.537 854	0.533 460	0.529 102	0.524 780	0.520 495	0.516 246	40
41	0.529 580	0.525 145	0.520 748	0.516 389	0.512 067	0.507 783	41
42	0.521 432	0.516 960	0.512 526	0.508 132	0.503 776	0.499 459	42
43	0.513 410	0.508 902	0.504 434	0.500 007	0.495 619	0.491 271	43
44	0.505 512	0.500 970	0.496 470	0.492 012	0.487 594	0.483 217	44
45	0.497 735	0.493 162	0.488 632	0.484 144	0.479 699	0.475 295	45
46	0.490 077	0.485 475	0.480 917	0.476 403	0.471 932	0.467 504	46
47	0.482 537	0.477 908	0.473 324	0.468 785	0.464 290	0.459 840	47

YRS							
4	0.475 114	0.470 459	0.465 851	0.461 289	0.456 773	0.452 301	48
5	0.394 455	0.389 630	0.384 865	0.380 160	0.375 513	0.370 924	60
6	0.327 489	0.322 688	0.317 959	0.313 300	0.308 710	0.304 188	72
7	0.271 892	0.267 247	0.262 683	0.258 198	0.253 790	0.249 459	84
8	0.225 733	0.221 332	0.217 017	0.212 788	0.208 641	0.204 577	96
9	0.187 411	0.183 305	0.179 290	0.175 364	0.171 524	0.167 769	108
10	0.155 594	0.151 812	0.148 121	0.144 522	0.141 010	0.137 585	120
11	0.129 179	0.125 729	0.122 371	0.119 104	0.115 925	0.112 831	132
12	0.107 249	0.104 128	0.101 098	0.098 157	0.095 302	0.092 530	144
13	0.089 041	0.086 238	0.083 522	0.080 893	0.078 348	0.075 882	156
14	0.073 925	0.071 421	0.069 003	0.066 666	0.064 410	0.062 230	168
15	0.061 375	0.059 150	0.057 007	0.054 941	0.052 951	0.051 033	180
16	0.050 955	0.048 988	0.047 096	0.045 279	0.043 531	0.041 852	192
17	0.042 305	0.040 571	0.038 909	0.037 315	0.035 787	0.034 322	204
18	0.035 123	0.033 601	0.032 145	0.030 752	0.029 421	0.028 147	216
19	0.029 160	0.027 828	0.026 557	0.025 344	0.024 187	0.023 082	228
20	0.024 210	0.023 047	0.021 940	0.020 887	0.019 884	0.018 930	240
21	0.020 100	0.019 087	0.018 126	0.017 213	0.016 347	0.015 524	252
22	0.016 687	0.015 808	0.014 975	0.014 186	0.013 438	0.012 731	264
23	0.013 854	0.013 092	0.012 371	0.011 691	0.011 048	0.010 440	276
24	0.011 502	0.010 843	0.010 221	0.009 635	0.009 082	0.008 562	288
25	0.009 550	0.008 980	0.008 444	0.007 940	0.007 467	0.007 021	300
26	0.007 928	0.007 437	0.006 976	0.006 544	0.006 138	0.005 758	312
27	0.006 582	0.006 159	0.005 763	0.005 393	0.005 046	0.004 722	324
28	0.005 465	0.005 101	0.004 761	0.004 444	0.004 149	0.003 873	336
29	0.004 537	0.004 225	0.003 934	0.003 663	0.003 411	0.003 176	348
30	0.003 767	0.003 499	0.003 250	0.003 019	0.002 804	0.002 604	360

MOS	20.25% ANNUAL RATE	20.50% ANNUAL RATE	20.75% ANNUAL RATE	21.00% ANNUAL RATE	21.25% ANNUAL RATE	21.50% ANNUAL RATE	MOS
1	0.983 405	0.983 204	0.983 002	0.982 801	0.982 600	0.982 399	1
2	0.967 085	0.966 689	0.966 293	0.965 898	0.965 502	0.965 107	2
3	0.951 037	0.950 452	0.949 869	0.949 285	0.948 702	0.948 120	3
4	0.935 254	0.934 488	0.933 723	0.932 959	0.932 195	0.931 432	4
5	0.919 734	0.918 792	0.917 852	0.916 913	0.915 974	0.915 037	5
6	0.904 471	0.903 360	0.902 250	0.901 143	0.900 036	0.898 932	6
7	0.889 461	0.888 187	0.886 914	0.885 644	0.884 375	0.883 109	7
8	0.874 701	0.873 268	0.871 839	0.870 412	0.868 987	0.867 565	8
9	0.860 185	0.858 601	0.857 019	0.855 441	0.853 867	0.852 295	9
10	0.845 910	0.844 179	0.842 452	0.840 729	0.839 009	0.837 294	10
11	0.831 872	0.830 000	0.828 132	0.826 269	0.824 410	0.822 556	11
12	0.818 068	0.816 059	0.814 056	0.812 058	0.810 065	0.808 078	12
13	0.804 492	0.802 352	0.800 219	0.798 091	0.795 970	0.793 855	13
14	0.791 141	0.788 876	0.786 617	0.784 365	0.782 120	0.779 882	14
15	0.778 012	0.775 625	0.773 246	0.770 875	0.768 511	0.766 155	15
16	0.765 101	0.762 598	0.760 103	0.757 616	0.755 139	0.752 670	16
17	0.752 404	0.749 789	0.747 183	0.744 586	0.741 999	0.739 422	17
18	0.739 918	0.737 195	0.734 482	0.731 780	0.729 088	0.726 407	18
19	0.727 639	0.724 813	0.721 998	0.719 194	0.716 402	0.713 621	19
20	0.715 564	0.712 638	0.709 725	0.706 825	0.703 936	0.701 060	20
21	0.703 689	0.700 669	0.697 662	0.694 668	0.691 688	0.688 721	21
22	0.692 012	0.688 900	0.685 803	0.682 720	0.679 652	0.676 599	22
23	0.680 528	0.677 329	0.674 146	0.670 978	0.667 826	0.664 690	23
24	0.669 234	0.665 952	0.662 687	0.659 438	0.656 206	0.652 990	24
25	0.658 129	0.654 767	0.651 423	0.648 096	0.644 788	0.641 497	25
26	0.647 207	0.643 769	0.640 350	0.636 950	0.633 568	0.630 205	26
27	0.636 467	0.632 956	0.629 465	0.625 995	0.622 544	0.619 113	27
28	0.625 904	0.622 325	0.618 766	0.615 228	0.611 712	0.608 216	28
29	0.615 518	0.611 872	0.608 248	0.604 647	0.601 068	0.597 510	29
30	0.605 303	0.601 595	0.597 909	0.594 248	0.590 609	0.586 993	30
31	0.595 258	0.591 490	0.587 746	0.584 027	0.580 332	0.576 662	31
32	0.585 380	0.581 555	0.577 756	0.573 982	0.570 234	0.566 512	32
33	0.575 665	0.571 787	0.567 935	0.564 111	0.560 312	0.556 540	33
34	0.566 112	0.562 183	0.558 282	0.554 408	0.550 563	0.546 744	34
35	0.556 718	0.552 740	0.548 792	0.544 873	0.540 983	0.537 121	35
36	0.547 479	0.543 456	0.539 464	0.535 502	0.531 570	0.527 667	36
37	0.538 394	0.534 328	0.530 294	0.526 292	0.522 320	0.518 379	37
38	0.529 459	0.525 353	0.521 281	0.517 240	0.513 232	0.509 255	38
39	0.520 673	0.516 529	0.512 420	0.508 344	0.504 301	0.500 292	39
40	0.512 032	0.507 854	0.503 710	0.499 601	0.495 526	0.491 486	40
41	0.503 535	0.499 323	0.495 148	0.491 008	0.486 904	0.482 835	41
42	0.495 179	0.490 937	0.486 732	0.482 563	0.478 432	0.474 336	42
43	0.486 961	0.482 691	0.478 458	0.474 264	0.470 107	0.465 988	43
44	0.478 880	0.474 583	0.470 326	0.466 107	0.461 927	0.457 786	44
45	0.470 933	0.466 612	0.462 331	0.458 090	0.453 889	0.449 728	45
46	0.463 118	0.458 774	0.454 472	0.450 212	0.445 992	0.441 812	46
47	0.455 433	0.451 069	0.446 747	0.442 469	0.438 231	0.434 036	47

YRS							
4	0.447 875	0.443 492	0.439 154	0.434 858	0.430 606	0.426 396	48
5	0.366 392	0.361 916	0.357 496	0.353 130	0.348 819	0.344 561	60
6	0.299 733	0.295 345	0.291 021	0.286 762	0.282 566	0.278 432	72
7	0.245 202	0.241 019	0.236 908	0.232 868	0.228 897	0.224 995	84
8	0.200 592	0.196 686	0.192 856	0.189 102	0.185 422	0.181 814	96
9	0.164 098	0.160 507	0.156 996	0.153 562	0.150 204	0.146 920	108
10	0.134 243	0.130 983	0.127 803	0.124 701	0.121 675	0.118 722	120
11	0.109 820	0.106 890	0.104 039	0.101 264	0.098 564	0.095 937	132
12	0.089 840	0.087 229	0.084 693	0.082 233	0.079 844	0.077 525	144
13	0.073 495	0.071 184	0.068 945	0.066 778	0.064 679	0.062 646	156
14	0.060 124	0.058 090	0.056 125	0.054 227	0.052 394	0.050 623	168
15	0.049 186	0.047 405	0.045 689	0.044 036	0.042 442	0.040 907	180
16	0.040 237	0.038 685	0.037 193	0.035 760	0.034 381	0.033 056	192
17	0.032 917	0.031 569	0.030 278	0.029 039	0.027 851	0.026 712	204
18	0.026 928	0.025 762	0.024 648	0.023 581	0.022 561	0.021 585	216
19	0.022 029	0.021 024	0.020 065	0.019 149	0.018 276	0.017 443	228
20	0.018 021	0.017 157	0.016 334	0.015 550	0.014 805	0.014 095	240
21	0.014 743	0.014 001	0.013 296	0.012 628	0.011 993	0.011 390	252
22	0.012 060	0.011 425	0.010 824	0.010 254	0.009 715	0.009 204	264
23	0.009 866	0.009 324	0.008 811	0.008 327	0.007 870	0.007 437	276
24	0.008 071	0.007 609	0.007 173	0.006 762	0.006 375	0.006 010	288
25	0.006 603	0.006 209	0.005 839	0.005 491	0.005 164	0.004 857	300
26	0.005 402	0.005 067	0.004 753	0.004 459	0.004 183	0.003 925	312
27	0.004 419	0.004 135	0.003 870	0.003 621	0.003 389	0.003 171	324
28	0.003 615	0.003 374	0.003 150	0.002 941	0.002 745	0.002 563	336
29	0.002 957	0.002 754	0.002 564	0.002 388	0.002 224	0.002 071	348
30	0.002 419	0.002 247	0.002 087	0.001 939	0.001 801	0.001 673	360

MOS	21.75% ANNUAL RATE	22.00% ANNUAL RATE	22.50% ANNUAL RATE	23.00% ANNUAL RATE	23.50% ANNUAL RATE	24.00% ANNUAL RATE	MOS
1	0.982 198	0.981 997	0.981 595	0.981 194	0.980 793	0.980 392	1
2	0.964 712	0.964 318	0.963 529	0.962 741	0.961 955	0.961 169	2
3	0.947 538	0.946 957	0.945 795	0.944 636	0.943 478	0.942 322	3
4	0.930 670	0.929 908	0.928 388	0.926 871	0.925 357	0.923 845	4
5	0.914 102	0.913 167	0.911 301	0.909 440	0.907 583	0.905 731	5
6	0.897 829	0.896 727	0.894 529	0.892 337	0.890 151	0.887 971	6
7	0.881 845	0.880 583	0.878 065	0.875 555	0.873 054	0.870 560	7
8	0.866 146	0.864 730	0.861 904	0.859 089	0.856 285	0.853 490	8
9	0.850 727	0.849 162	0.846 041	0.842 933	0.839 838	0.836 755	9
10	0.835 582	0.833 874	0.830 470	0.827 081	0.823 707	0.820 348	10
11	0.820 707	0.818 861	0.815 185	0.811 526	0.807 886	0.804 263	11
12	0.806 096	0.804 119	0.800 182	0.796 265	0.792 369	0.788 493	12
13	0.791 746	0.789 643	0.785 454	0.781 290	0.777 149	0.773 033	13
14	0.777 651	0.775 426	0.770 998	0.766 597	0.762 223	0.757 875	14
15	0.763 807	0.761 466	0.756 808	0.752 180	0.747 582	0.743 015	15
16	0.750 209	0.747 757	0.742 879	0.738 034	0.733 223	0.728 446	16
17	0.736 854	0.734 295	0.729 206	0.724 155	0.719 140	0.714 163	17
18	0.723 736	0.721 075	0.715 785	0.710 536	0.705 328	0.700 159	18
19	0.710 852	0.708 094	0.702 611	0.697 174	0.691 780	0.686 431	19
20	0.698 197	0.695 346	0.689 680	0.684 062	0.678 493	0.672 971	20
21	0.685 767	0.682 827	0.676 986	0.671 198	0.665 461	0.659 776	21
22	0.673 559	0.670 534	0.664 527	0.658 575	0.652 680	0.646 839	22
23	0.661 568	0.658 462	0.652 296	0.646 190	0.640 143	0.634 156	23
24	0.649 791	0.646 608	0.640 291	0.634 037	0.627 848	0.621 721	24
25	0.638 223	0.634 967	0.628 506	0.622 114	0.615 789	0.609 531	25
26	0.626 861	0.623 535	0.616 938	0.610 414	0.603 961	0.597 579	26
27	0.615 702	0.612 310	0.605 584	0.598 934	0.592 361	0.585 862	27
28	0.604 741	0.601 286	0.594 438	0.587 671	0.580 983	0.574 375	28
29	0.593 975	0.590 461	0.583 497	0.576 619	0.569 824	0.563 112	29
30	0.583 401	0.579 831	0.572 758	0.565 775	0.558 879	0.552 071	30
31	0.573 015	0.569 392	0.562 217	0.555 135	0.548 145	0.541 246	31
32	0.562 814	0.559 141	0.551 869	0.544 695	0.537 617	0.530 633	32
33	0.552 794	0.549 075	0.541 712	0.534 451	0.527 291	0.520 229	33
34	0.542 953	0.539 189	0.531 742	0.524 400	0.517 163	0.510 028	34
35	0.533 288	0.529 482	0.521 955	0.514 538	0.507 230	0.500 028	35
36	0.523 794	0.519 950	0.512 349	0.504 862	0.497 487	0.490 223	36
37	0.514 469	0.510 589	0.502 919	0.495 367	0.487 932	0.480 611	37
38	0.505 310	0.501 397	0.493 663	0.486 051	0.478 560	0.471 187	38
39	0.496 315	0.492 370	0.484 577	0.476 910	0.469 368	0.461 948	39
40	0.487 479	0.483 506	0.475 658	0.467 941	0.460 353	0.452 890	40
41	0.478 801	0.474 801	0.466 904	0.459 141	0.451 511	0.444 010	41
42	0.470 277	0.466 253	0.458 311	0.450 507	0.442 839	0.435 304	42
43	0.461 905	0.457 859	0.449 875	0.442 034	0.434 333	0.426 769	43
44	0.453 682	0.449 616	0.441 596	0.433 721	0.425 991	0.418 401	44
45	0.445 605	0.441 521	0.433 468	0.425 565	0.417 808	0.410 197	45
46	0.437 673	0.433 573	0.425 490	0.417 561	0.409 784	0.402 154	46
47	0.429 881	0.425 767	0.417 659	0.409 709	0.401 913	0.394 268	47

YRS							
4	0.422 228	0.418 102	0.409 972	0.402 004	0.394 193	0.386 538	48
5	0.340 356	0.336 204	0.328 052	0.320 101	0.312 346	0.304 782	60
6	0.274 360	0.270 348	0.262 501	0.254 885	0.247 493	0.240 319	72
7	0.221 160	0.217 392	0.210 049	0.202 956	0.196 106	0.189 490	84
8	0.178 277	0.174 809	0.168 077	0.161 607	0.155 388	0.149 411	96
9	0.143 708	0.140 567	0.134 492	0.128 707	0.123 125	0.117 810	108
10	0.115 842	0.113 033	0.107 618	0.102 465	0.097 560	0.092 892	120
11	0.093 380	0.090 892	0.086 114	0.081 589	0.077 304	0.073 245	132
12	0.075 273	0.073 088	0.068 907	0.064 967	0.061 253	0.057 753	144
13	0.060 678	0.058 771	0.055 138	0.051 731	0.048 535	0.045 538	156
14	0.048 912	0.047 259	0.044 120	0.041 191	0.038 458	0.035 906	168
15	0.039 428	0.038 002	0.035 304	0.032 799	0.030 473	0.028 312	180
16	0.031 783	0.030 558	0.028 250	0.026 117	0.024 146	0.022 324	192
17	0.025 620	0.024 572	0.022 605	0.020 796	0.019 132	0.017 602	204
18	0.020 652	0.019 759	0.018 088	0.016 559	0.015 160	0.013 879	216
19	0.016 647	0.015 889	0.014 474	0.013 185	0.012 012	0.010 944	228
20	0.013 419	0.012 776	0.011 582	0.010 499	0.009 518	0.008 629	240
21	0.010 817	0.010 274	0.009 267	0.008 360	0.007 542	0.006 804	252
22	0.008 720	0.008 261	0.007 416	0.006 657	0.005 976	0.005 365	264
23	0.007 029	0.006 643	0.005 934	0.005 301	0.004 735	0.004 230	276
24	0.005 666	0.005 342	0.004 748	0.004 221	0.003 752	0.003 335	288
25	0.004 567	0.004 295	0.003 799	0.003 361	0.002 973	0.002 630	300
26	0.003 682	0.003 454	0.003 040	0.002 676	0.002 356	0.002 074	312
27	0.002 968	0.002 777	0.002 433	0.002 131	0.001 867	0.001 635	324
28	0.002 392	0.002 233	0.001 947	0.001 697	0.001 479	0.001 289	336
29	0.001 928	0.001 796	0.001 558	0.001 351	0.001 172	0.001 017	348
30	0.001 555	0.001 444	0.001 246	0.001 076	0.000 929	0.000 802	360

SECTION 4

QTRS	5.25% ANNUAL RATE	5.50% ANNUAL RATE	5.75% ANNUAL RATE	6.00% ANNUAL RATE	6.25% ANNUAL RATE	6.50% ANNUAL RATE	QTRS
1	0.987 045	0.986 436	0.985 829	0.985 222	0.984 615	0.984 010	1
2	0.974 258	0.973 057	0.971 858	0.970 662	0.969 467	0.968 275	2
3	0.961 636	0.959 859	0.958 086	0.956 317	0.954 553	0.952 792	3
4	0.949 178	0.946 840	0.944 508	0.942 184	0.939 867	0.937 557	4
5	0.936 882	0.933 997	0.931 124	0.928 260	0.925 408	0.922 565	5
6	0.924 745	0.921 329	0.917 928	0.914 542	0.911 171	0.907 814	6
7	0.912 765	0.908 833	0.904 920	0.901 027	0.897 153	0.893 297	7
8	0.900 940	0.896 506	0.892 096	0.887 711	0.883 350	0.879 013	8
9	0.889 268	0.884 346	0.879 454	0.874 592	0.869 760	0.864 958	9
10	0.877 748	0.872 351	0.866 991	0.861 667	0.856 379	0.851 127	10
11	0.866 376	0.860 519	0.854 705	0.848 933	0.843 204	0.837 517	11
12	0.855 153	0.848 847	0.842 592	0.836 387	0.830 232	0.824 125	12
13	0.844 074	0.837 334	0.830 652	0.824 027	0.817 459	0.810 947	13
14	0.833 139	0.825 977	0.818 880	0.811 849	0.804 883	0.797 980	14
15	0.822 346	0.814 774	0.807 276	0.799 852	0.792 500	0.785 220	15
16	0.811 692	0.803 722	0.795 836	0.788 031	0.780 308	0.772 665	16
17	0.801 177	0.792 821	0.784 558	0.776 385	0.768 303	0.760 310	17
18	0.790 798	0.782 068	0.773 439	0.764 912	0.756 483	0.748 152	18
19	0.780 553	0.771 460	0.762 479	0.753 607	0.744 845	0.736 189	19
20	0.770 441	0.760 996	0.751 674	0.742 470	0.733 386	0.724 417	20
21	0.760 460	0.750 675	0.741 021	0.731 498	0.722 103	0.712 834	21
22	0.750 608	0.740 493	0.730 520	0.720 688	0.710 993	0.701 435	22
23	0.740 884	0.730 449	0.720 168	0.710 037	0.700 055	0.690 219	23
24	0.731 286	0.720 542	0.709 962	0.699 544	0.689 285	0.679 183	24
25	0.721 812	0.710 769	0.699 901	0.689 206	0.678 681	0.668 322	25
26	0.712 461	0.701 128	0.689 982	0.679 021	0.668 239	0.657 636	26
27	0.703 231	0.691 618	0.680 204	0.668 986	0.657 959	0.647 120	27
28	0.694 121	0.682 238	0.670 565	0.659 099	0.647 836	0.636 773	28
29	0.685 129	0.672 984	0.661 062	0.649 359	0.637 870	0.626 590	29
30	0.676 253	0.663 856	0.651 694	0.639 762	0.628 056	0.616 571	30
31	0.667 492	0.654 852	0.642 459	0.630 308	0.618 394	0.606 712	31
32	0.658 845	0.645 970	0.633 354	0.620 993	0.608 880	0.597 011	32
33	0.650 309	0.637 208	0.624 379	0.611 816	0.599 513	0.587 464	33
34	0.641 885	0.628 565	0.615 531	0.602 774	0.590 289	0.578 071	34
35	0.633 569	0.620 040	0.606 808	0.593 866	0.581 208	0.568 827	35
36	0.625 361	0.611 630	0.598 209	0.585 090	0.572 266	0.559 732	36
37	0.617 260	0.603 334	0.589 731	0.576 443	0.563 462	0.550 781	37
38	0.609 263	0.595 151	0.581 374	0.567 924	0.554 794	0.541 974	38
39	0.601 370	0.587 079	0.573 135	0.559 531	0.546 258	0.533 308	39
40	0.593 579	0.579 116	0.565 013	0.551 262	0.537 854	0.524 780	40
41	0.585 889	0.571 261	0.557 006	0.543 116	0.529 580	0.516 389	41
42	0.578 299	0.563 513	0.549 113	0.535 089	0.521 432	0.508 132	42
43	0.570 807	0.555 869	0.541 331	0.527 182	0.513 410	0.500 007	43
44	0.563 413	0.548 330	0.533 660	0.519 391	0.505 512	0.492 012	44
45	0.556 114	0.540 893	0.526 097	0.511 715	0.497 735	0.484 144	45
46	0.548 909	0.533 556	0.518 642	0.504 153	0.490 077	0.476 403	46
47	0.541 798	0.526 319	0.511 292	0.496 702	0.482 537	0.468 785	47
48	0.534 779	0.519 181	0.504 046	0.489 362	0.475 114	0.461 289	48
49	0.527 851	0.512 139	0.496 903	0.482 130	0.467 804	0.453 913	49
50	0.521 013	0.505 192	0.489 861	0.475 005	0.460 607	0.446 655	50
51	0.514 263	0.498 340	0.482 919	0.467 985	0.453 521	0.439 513	51
52	0.507 601	0.491 581	0.476 076	0.461 069	0.446 544	0.432 485	52
53	0.501 025	0.484 913	0.469 329	0.454 255	0.439 674	0.425 569	53
54	0.494 534	0.478 336	0.462 678	0.447 542	0.432 910	0.418 764	54
55	0.488 127	0.471 848	0.456 121	0.440 928	0.426 250	0.412 068	55
YRS							
14	0.481 804	0.465 448	0.449 658	0.434 412	0.419 692	0.405 479	56
15	0.457 318	0.440 705	0.424 705	0.409 296	0.394 455	0.380 160	60
16	0.434 076	0.417 277	0.401 138	0.385 632	0.370 735	0.356 422	64
17	0.412 016	0.395 095	0.378 878	0.363 337	0.348 442	0.334 166	68
18	0.391 076	0.374 091	0.357 854	0.342 330	0.327 489	0.313 300	72
19	0.371 201	0.354 205	0.337 996	0.322 538	0.307 796	0.293 736	76
20	0.352 336	0.335 375	0.319 240	0.303 890	0.289 287	0.275 395	80
21	0.334 430	0.317 546	0.301 525	0.286 321	0.271 892	0.258 198	84
22	0.317 434	0.300 666	0.284 793	0.269 767	0.255 542	0.242 076	88
23	0.301 301	0.284 682	0.268 989	0.254 170	0.240 176	0.226 960	92
24	0.285 989	0.269 548	0.254 062	0.239 475	0.225 733	0.212 788	96
25	0.271 454	0.255 219	0.239 964	0.225 629	0.212 159	0.199 501	100
26	0.257 659	0.241 652	0.226 648	0.212 585	0.199 401	0.187 043	104
27	0.244 564	0.228 805	0.214 071	0.200 294	0.187 411	0.175 364	108
28	0.232 135	0.216 642	0.202 192	0.188 714	0.176 141	0.164 413	112
29	0.220 337	0.205 125	0.190 972	0.177 803	0.165 549	0.154 147	116
30	0.209 140	0.194 221	0.180 375	0.167 523	0.155 594	0.144 522	120

PRESENT VALUE

QTRS	6.75% ANNUAL RATE	7.00% ANNUAL RATE	7.25% ANNUAL RATE	7.50% ANNUAL RATE	7.75% ANNUAL RATE	8.00% ANNUAL RATE	QTRS
1	0.983 405	0.982 801	0.982 198	0.981 595	0.980 993	0.980 392	1
2	0.967 085	0.965 898	0.964 712	0.963 529	0.962 348	0.961 169	2
3	0.951 037	0.949 285	0.947 538	0.945 795	0.944 057	0.942 322	3
4	0.935 254	0.932 959	0.930 670	0.928 388	0.926 113	0.923 845	4
5	0.919 734	0.916 913	0.914 102	0.911 301	0.908 511	0.905 731	5
6	0.904 471	0.901 143	0.897 829	0.894 529	0.891 243	0.887 971	6
7	0.889 461	0.885 644	0.881 845	0.878 065	0.874 303	0.870 560	7
8	0.874 701	0.870 412	0.866 146	0.861 904	0.857 686	0.853 490	8
9	0.860 185	0.855 441	0.850 727	0.846 041	0.841 384	0.836 755	9
10	0.845 910	0.840 729	0.835 582	0.830 470	0.825 392	0.820 348	10
11	0.831 872	0.826 269	0.820 707	0.815 185	0.809 704	0.804 263	11
12	0.818 068	0.812 058	0.806 096	0.800 182	0.794 314	0.788 493	12
13	0.804 492	0.798 091	0.791 746	0.785 454	0.779 217	0.773 033	13
14	0.791 141	0.784 365	0.777 651	0.770 998	0.764 406	0.757 875	14
15	0.778 012	0.770 875	0.763 807	0.756 808	0.749 878	0.743 015	15
16	0.765 101	0.757 616	0.750 209	0.742 879	0.735 625	0.728 446	16
17	0.752 404	0.744 586	0.736 854	0.729 206	0.721 643	0.714 163	17
18	0.739 918	0.731 780	0.723 736	0.715 785	0.707 927	0.700 159	18
19	0.727 639	0.719 194	0.710 852	0.702 611	0.694 471	0.686 431	19
20	0.715 564	0.706 825	0.698 197	0.689 680	0.681 272	0.672 971	20
21	0.703 689	0.694 668	0.685 767	0.676 986	0.668 323	0.659 776	21
22	0.692 012	0.682 720	0.673 559	0.664 527	0.655 620	0.646 839	22
23	0.680 528	0.670 978	0.661 568	0.652 296	0.643 159	0.634 156	23
24	0.669 234	0.659 438	0.649 791	0.640 291	0.630 935	0.621 721	24
25	0.658 129	0.648 096	0.638 223	0.628 506	0.618 943	0.609 531	25
26	0.647 207	0.636 950	0.626 861	0.616 938	0.607 179	0.597 579	26
27	0.636 467	0.625 995	0.615 702	0.605 584	0.595 638	0.585 862	27
28	0.625 904	0.615 228	0.604 741	0.594 438	0.584 317	0.574 375	28
29	0.615 518	0.604 647	0.593 975	0.583 497	0.573 211	0.563 112	29
30	0.605 303	0.594 248	0.583 401	0.572 758	0.562 316	0.552 071	30
31	0.595 258	0.584 027	0.573 015	0.562 217	0.551 628	0.541 246	31
32	0.585 380	0.573 982	0.562 814	0.551 869	0.541 144	0.530 633	32
33	0.575 665	0.564 111	0.552 794	0.541 712	0.530 858	0.520 229	33
34	0.566 112	0.554 408	0.542 953	0.531 742	0.520 769	0.510 028	34
35	0.556 718	0.544 873	0.533 288	0.521 955	0.510 870	0.500 028	35
36	0.547 479	0.535 502	0.523 794	0.512 349	0.501 160	0.490 223	36
37	0.538 394	0.526 292	0.514 469	0.502 919	0.491 635	0.480 611	37
38	0.529 459	0.517 240	0.505 310	0.493 663	0.482 291	0.471 187	38
39	0.520 673	0.508 344	0.496 315	0.484 577	0.473 124	0.461 948	39
40	0.512 032	0.499 601	0.487 479	0.475 658	0.464 131	0.452 890	40
41	0.503 535	0.491 008	0.478 801	0.466 904	0.455 310	0.444 010	41
42	0.495 179	0.482 563	0.470 277	0.458 311	0.446 656	0.435 304	42
43	0.486 961	0.474 264	0.461 905	0.449 875	0.438 166	0.426 769	43
44	0.478 880	0.466 107	0.453 682	0.441 596	0.429 838	0.418 401	44
45	0.470 933	0.458 090	0.445 605	0.433 468	0.421 668	0.410 197	45
46	0.463 118	0.450 212	0.437 673	0.425 490	0.413 654	0.402 154	46
47	0.455 433	0.442 469	0.429 881	0.417 659	0.405 792	0.394 268	47
48	0.447 875	0.434 858	0.422 228	0.409 972	0.398 079	0.386 538	48
49	0.440 442	0.427 379	0.414 711	0.402 426	0.390 513	0.378 958	49
50	0.433 133	0.420 029	0.407 329	0.395 020	0.383 090	0.371 528	50
51	0.425 945	0.412 805	0.400 077	0.387 750	0.375 809	0.364 243	51
52	0.418 877	0.405 705	0.392 955	0.380 613	0.368 666	0.357 101	52
53	0.411 926	0.398 727	0.385 959	0.373 608	0.361 659	0.350 099	53
54	0.405 090	0.391 869	0.379 088	0.366 732	0.354 785	0.343 234	54
55	0.398 367	0.385 130	0.372 340	0.359 982	0.348 042	0.336 504	55

YRS							QTRS
14	0.391 756	0.378 506	0.365 711	0.353 357	0.341 426	0.329 906	56
15	0.366 392	0.353 130	0.340 356	0.328 052	0.316 200	0.304 782	60
16	0.342 670	0.329 456	0.316 759	0.304 560	0.292 837	0.281 572	64
17	0.320 483	0.307 369	0.294 798	0.282 749	0.271 200	0.260 129	68
18	0.299 733	0.286 762	0.274 360	0.262 501	0.251 162	0.240 319	72
19	0.280 327	0.267 537	0.255 338	0.243 703	0.232 604	0.222 017	76
20	0.262 177	0.249 601	0.237 636	0.226 251	0.215 418	0.205 110	80
21	0.245 202	0.232 868	0.221 160	0.210 049	0.199 501	0.189 490	84
22	0.229 326	0.217 256	0.205 827	0.195 007	0.184 761	0.175 059	88
23	0.214 478	0.202 691	0.191 557	0.181 042	0.171 109	0.161 728	92
24	0.200 592	0.189 102	0.178 277	0.168 077	0.158 467	0.149 411	96
25	0.187 604	0.176 424	0.165 917	0.156 041	0.146 758	0.138 033	100
26	0.175 458	0.164 596	0.154 414	0.144 866	0.135 908	0.127 521	104
27	0.164 098	0.153 562	0.143 708	0.134 492	0.125 872	0.117 810	108
28	0.153 473	0.143 267	0.133 745	0.124 861	0.116 572	0.108 838	112
29	0.143 536	0.133 662	0.124 472	0.115 919	0.107 959	0.100 550	116
30	0.134 243	0.124 701	0.115 842	0.107 618	0.099 982	0.092 892	120

PRESENT VALUE

QUARTERLY COMPOUNDING

QTRS	8.25% ANNUAL RATE	8.50% ANNUAL RATE	8.75% ANNUAL RATE	9.00% ANNUAL RATE	9.25% ANNUAL RATE	9.50% ANNUAL RATE	QTRS
1	0.979 792	0.979 192	0.978 593	0.977 995	0.977 398	0.976 801	1
2	0.959 992	0.958 817	0.957 645	0.956 474	0.955 306	0.954 140	2
3	0.940 592	0.938 866	0.937 145	0.935 427	0.933 714	0.932 005	3
4	0.921 585	0.919 331	0.917 084	0.914 843	0.912 610	0.910 383	4
5	0.902 961	0.900 201	0.897 452	0.894 712	0.891 983	0.889 263	5
6	0.884 714	0.881 470	0.878 240	0.875 024	0.871 822	0.868 633	6
7	0.866 835	0.863 129	0.859 440	0.855 769	0.852 117	0.848 482	7
8	0.849 318	0.845 169	0.841 042	0.836 938	0.832 857	0.828 798	8
9	0.832 155	0.827 583	0.823 038	0.818 522	0.814 032	0.809 571	9
10	0.815 339	0.810 362	0.805 420	0.800 510	0.795 633	0.790 789	10
11	0.798 862	0.793 501	0.788 178	0.782 895	0.777 650	0.772 444	11
12	0.782 718	0.776 990	0.771 306	0.765 667	0.760 074	0.754 524	12
13	0.766 901	0.760 822	0.754 795	0.748 819	0.742 894	0.737 020	13
14	0.751 403	0.744 991	0.738 637	0.732 341	0.726 103	0.719 922	14
15	0.736 219	0.729 489	0.722 825	0.716 226	0.709 691	0.703 220	15
16	0.721 341	0.714 310	0.707 352	0.700 466	0.693 651	0.686 906	16
17	0.706 764	0.699 447	0.692 210	0.685 052	0.677 973	0.670 971	17
18	0.692 482	0.684 893	0.677 392	0.669 978	0.662 649	0.655 405	18
19	0.678 488	0.670 642	0.662 891	0.655 235	0.647 671	0.640 200	19
20	0.664 777	0.656 687	0.648 701	0.640 816	0.633 033	0.625 348	20
21	0.651 343	0.643 023	0.634 814	0.626 715	0.618 725	0.610 840	21
22	0.638 181	0.629 643	0.621 225	0.612 925	0.604 740	0.596 670	22
23	0.625 284	0.616 542	0.607 927	0.599 437	0.591 071	0.582 827	23
24	0.612 648	0.603 713	0.594 913	0.586 247	0.577 712	0.569 306	24
25	0.600 268	0.591 151	0.582 178	0.573 346	0.564 654	0.556 099	25
26	0.588 137	0.578 850	0.569 715	0.560 730	0.551 892	0.543 198	26
27	0.576 252	0.566 806	0.557 520	0.548 391	0.539 418	0.530 596	27
28	0.564 607	0.555 012	0.545 585	0.536 324	0.527 226	0.518 287	28
29	0.553 197	0.543 463	0.533 906	0.524 522	0.515 309	0.506 263	29
30	0.542 018	0.532 155	0.522 477	0.512 980	0.503 662	0.494 519	30
31	0.531 065	0.521 082	0.511 292	0.501 692	0.492 278	0.483 046	31
32	0.520 333	0.510 239	0.500 347	0.490 652	0.481 151	0.471 840	32
33	0.509 818	0.499 622	0.489 636	0.479 856	0.470 276	0.460 894	33
34	0.499 516	0.489 226	0.479 155	0.469 296	0.459 647	0.450 201	34
35	0.489 421	0.479 046	0.468 897	0.458 970	0.449 258	0.439 757	35
36	0.479 531	0.469 078	0.458 860	0.448 870	0.439 104	0.429 555	36
37	0.469 841	0.459 318	0.449 037	0.438 993	0.429 179	0.419 590	37
38	0.460 346	0.449 761	0.439 425	0.429 333	0.419 478	0.409 856	38
39	0.451 043	0.440 402	0.430 018	0.419 885	0.409 997	0.400 348	39
40	0.441 928	0.431 238	0.420 813	0.410 646	0.400 730	0.391 060	40
41	0.432 998	0.422 265	0.411 805	0.401 610	0.391 673	0.381 988	41
42	0.424 248	0.413 479	0.402 989	0.392 772	0.382 820	0.373 126	42
43	0.415 674	0.404 875	0.394 363	0.384 129	0.374 167	0.364 470	43
44	0.407 274	0.396 450	0.385 921	0.375 677	0.365 710	0.356 015	44
45	0.399 044	0.388 201	0.377 659	0.367 410	0.357 445	0.347 755	45
46	0.390 980	0.380 124	0.369 575	0.359 325	0.349 365	0.339 688	46
47	0.383 079	0.372 214	0.361 663	0.351 418	0.341 469	0.331 807	47
48	0.375 338	0.364 469	0.353 921	0.343 685	0.333 751	0.324 110	48
49	0.367 753	0.356 885	0.346 345	0.336 122	0.326 207	0.316 591	49
50	0.360 321	0.349 459	0.338 931	0.328 726	0.318 834	0.309 246	50
51	0.353 040	0.342 188	0.331 676	0.321 493	0.311 628	0.302 072	51
52	0.345 906	0.335 068	0.324 575	0.314 418	0.304 584	0.295 064	52
53	0.338 915	0.328 096	0.317 627	0.307 499	0.297 700	0.288 219	53
54	0.332 067	0.321 269	0.310 828	0.300 733	0.290 971	0.281 533	54
55	0.325 356	0.314 584	0.304 174	0.294 115	0.284 395	0.275 001	55

YRS

YRS	8.25%	8.50%	8.75%	9.00%	9.25%	9.50%	
14	0.318 781	0.308 038	0.297 663	0.287 643	0.277 967	0.268 622	56
15	0.293 784	0.283 189	0.272 982	0.263 149	0.253 675	0.244 549	60
16	0.270 747	0.260 344	0.250 347	0.240 740	0.231 507	0.222 633	64
17	0.249 516	0.239 342	0.229 589	0.220 239	0.211 275	0.202 681	68
18	0.229 950	0.220 035	0.210 552	0.201 484	0.192 812	0.184 518	72
19	0.211 918	0.202 285	0.193 094	0.184 327	0.175 962	0.167 982	76
20	0.195 301	0.185 966	0.177 083	0.168 630	0.160 585	0.152 928	80
21	0.179 986	0.170 965	0.162 400	0.154 270	0.146 551	0.139 223	84
22	0.165 872	0.157 173	0.148 935	0.141 133	0.133 744	0.126 746	88
23	0.152 865	0.144 494	0.136 586	0.129 114	0.122 056	0.115 388	92
24	0.140 878	0.132 838	0.125 260	0.118 119	0.111 390	0.105 047	96
25	0.129 831	0.122 122	0.114 874	0.108 061	0.101 655	0.095 633	100
26	0.119 651	0.112 270	0.105 349	0.098 859	0.092 772	0.087 063	104
27	0.110 268	0.103 213	0.096 614	0.090 440	0.084 664	0.079 261	108
28	0.101 621	0.094 887	0.088 603	0.082 739	0.077 266	0.072 158	112
29	0.093 653	0.087 233	0.081 257	0.075 693	0.070 513	0.065 691	116
30	0.086 309	0.080 196	0.074 519	0.069 247	0.064 351	0.059 804	120

PRESENT VALUE

QTRS	9.75% ANNUAL RATE	10.00% ANNUAL RATE	10.25% ANNUAL RATE	10.50% ANNUAL RATE	10.75% ANNUAL RATE	11.00% ANNUAL RATE	QTRS
1	0.976 205	0.975 610	0.975 015	0.974 421	0.973 828	0.973 236	1
2	0.952 976	0.951 814	0.950 655	0.949 497	0.948 342	0.947 188	2
3	0.930 300	0.928 599	0.926 903	0.925 210	0.923 522	0.921 838	3
4	0.908 164	0.905 951	0.903 744	0.901 545	0.899 352	0.897 166	4
5	0.886 554	0.883 854	0.881 165	0.878 485	0.875 814	0.873 154	5
6	0.865 458	0.862 297	0.859 149	0.856 014	0.852 893	0.849 785	6
7	0.844 865	0.841 265	0.837 683	0.834 119	0.830 571	0.827 041	7
8	0.824 761	0.820 747	0.816 754	0.812 783	0.808 834	0.804 906	8
9	0.805 136	0.800 728	0.796 347	0.791 993	0.787 665	0.783 364	9
10	0.785 978	0.781 198	0.776 451	0.771 735	0.767 051	0.762 398	10
11	0.767 275	0.762 145	0.757 051	0.751 995	0.746 976	0.741 993	11
12	0.749 018	0.743 556	0.738 137	0.732 760	0.727 426	0.722 134	12
13	0.731 195	0.725 420	0.719 695	0.714 017	0.708 388	0.702 807	13
14	0.713 796	0.707 727	0.701 713	0.695 754	0.689 849	0.683 997	14
15	0.696 812	0.690 466	0.684 181	0.677 957	0.671 794	0.665 691	15
16	0.680 231	0.673 625	0.667 087	0.660 616	0.654 212	0.647 874	16
17	0.664 045	0.657 195	0.650 420	0.643 719	0.637 090	0.630 535	17
18	0.648 244	0.641 166	0.634 169	0.627 253	0.620 417	0.613 659	18
19	0.632 819	0.625 528	0.618 325	0.611 209	0.604 179	0.597 235	19
20	0.617 761	0.610 271	0.602 876	0.595 575	0.588 367	0.581 251	20
21	0.603 062	0.595 386	0.587 813	0.580 341	0.572 969	0.565 694	21
22	0.588 712	0.580 865	0.573 127	0.565 497	0.557 973	0.550 554	22
23	0.574 703	0.566 697	0.558 808	0.551 032	0.543 370	0.535 819	23
24	0.561 028	0.552 875	0.544 846	0.536 938	0.529 149	0.521 478	24
25	0.547 679	0.539 391	0.531 233	0.523 204	0.515 300	0.507 521	25
26	0.534 647	0.526 235	0.517 960	0.509 821	0.501 814	0.493 938	26
27	0.521 925	0.513 400	0.505 019	0.496 780	0.488 681	0.480 718	27
28	0.509 505	0.500 878	0.492 401	0.484 073	0.475 891	0.467 852	28
29	0.497 382	0.488 661	0.480 099	0.471 692	0.463 436	0.455 331	29
30	0.485 547	0.476 743	0.468 104	0.459 626	0.451 308	0.443 144	30
31	0.473 993	0.465 115	0.456 408	0.447 870	0.439 496	0.431 284	31
32	0.462 714	0.453 771	0.445 005	0.436 414	0.427 994	0.419 741	32
33	0.451 704	0.442 703	0.433 887	0.425 251	0.416 792	0.408 507	33
34	0.440 956	0.431 905	0.423 046	0.414 374	0.405 884	0.397 574	34
35	0.430 463	0.421 371	0.412 476	0.403 775	0.395 262	0.386 933	35
36	0.420 220	0.411 094	0.402 171	0.393 447	0.384 917	0.376 577	36
37	0.410 221	0.401 067	0.392 123	0.383 383	0.374 843	0.366 499	37
38	0.400 460	0.391 285	0.382 325	0.373 576	0.365 033	0.356 690	38
39	0.390 931	0.381 741	0.372 773	0.364 021	0.355 479	0.347 143	39
40	0.381 629	0.372 431	0.363 460	0.354 710	0.346 176	0.337 852	40
41	0.372 548	0.363 347	0.354 379	0.345 637	0.337 116	0.328 810	41
42	0.363 683	0.354 485	0.345 525	0.336 796	0.328 293	0.320 010	42
43	0.355 029	0.345 839	0.336 892	0.328 181	0.319 701	0.311 445	43
44	0.346 581	0.337 404	0.328 475	0.319 787	0.311 334	0.303 109	44
45	0.338 335	0.329 174	0.320 268	0.311 607	0.303 186	0.294 997	45
46	0.330 284	0.321 146	0.312 266	0.303 637	0.295 251	0.287 102	46
47	0.322 425	0.313 313	0.304 464	0.295 870	0.287 524	0.279 418	47
48	0.314 753	0.305 671	0.296 857	0.288 302	0.279 999	0.271 939	48
49	0.307 263	0.298 216	0.289 440	0.280 928	0.272 671	0.264 661	49
50	0.299 952	0.290 942	0.282 208	0.273 742	0.265 535	0.257 578	50
51	0.292 814	0.283 846	0.275 158	0.266 740	0.258 585	0.250 684	51
52	0.285 847	0.276 923	0.268 283	0.259 917	0.251 817	0.243 975	52
53	0.279 045	0.270 169	0.261 580	0.253 269	0.245 227	0.237 445	53
54	0.272 405	0.263 579	0.255 044	0.246 791	0.238 809	0.231 090	54
55	0.265 923	0.257 151	0.248 672	0.240 478	0.232 559	0.224 905	55

YRS							
14	0.259 596	0.250 879	0.242 459	0.234 327	0.226 473	0.218 886	56
15	0.235 755	0.227 284	0.219 121	0.211 256	0.203 678	0.196 377	60
16	0.214 105	0.205 908	0.198 029	0.190 457	0.183 179	0.176 183	64
17	0.194 442	0.186 542	0.178 968	0.171 706	0.164 742	0.158 065	68
18	0.176 585	0.168 998	0.161 741	0.154 800	0.148 161	0.141 810	72
19	0.160 368	0.153 104	0.146 173	0.139 559	0.133 249	0.127 227	76
20	0.145 641	0.138 705	0.132 103	0.125 819	0.119 838	0.114 144	80
21	0.132 265	0.125 659	0.119 387	0.113 432	0.107 776	0.102 406	84
22	0.120 119	0.113 841	0.107 896	0.102 264	0.096 929	0.091 875	88
23	0.109 087	0.103 135	0.097 510	0.092 195	0.087 173	0.082 427	92
24	0.099 069	0.093 435	0.088 124	0.083 118	0.078 399	0.073 951	96
25	0.089 971	0.084 647	0.079 642	0.074 935	0.070 509	0.066 346	100
26	0.081 708	0.076 686	0.071 976	0.067 557	0.063 412	0.059 524	104
27	0.074 205	0.069 474	0.065 048	0.060 906	0.057 030	0.053 403	108
28	0.067 390	0.062 940	0.058 786	0.054 909	0.051 290	0.047 911	112
29	0.061 201	0.057 021	0.053 128	0.049 503	0.046 128	0.042 984	116
30	0.055 581	0.051 658	0.048 014	0.044 629	0.041 485	0.038 564	120

QTRS	11.25% ANNUAL RATE	11.50% ANNUAL RATE	11.75% ANNUAL RATE	12.00% ANNUAL RATE	12.25% ANNUAL RATE	12.50% ANNUAL RATE	QTRS
1	0.972 644	0.972 053	0.971 463	0.970 874	0.970 285	0.969 697	1
2	0.946 037	0.944 888	0.943 741	0.942 596	0.941 453	0.940 312	2
3	0.920 158	0.918 482	0.916 810	0.915 142	0.913 478	0.911 818	3
4	0.894 986	0.892 813	0.890 647	0.888 487	0.886 334	0.884 187	4
5	0.870 503	0.867 862	0.865 231	0.862 609	0.859 996	0.857 394	5
6	0.846 690	0.843 608	0.840 540	0.837 484	0.834 442	0.831 412	6
7	0.823 528	0.820 032	0.816 554	0.813 092	0.809 646	0.806 218	7
8	0.801 000	0.797 115	0.793 252	0.789 409	0.785 588	0.781 787	8
9	0.779 088	0.774 839	0.770 615	0.766 417	0.762 244	0.758 096	9
10	0.757 776	0.753 185	0.748 624	0.744 094	0.739 594	0.735 124	10
11	0.737 046	0.732 136	0.727 261	0.722 421	0.717 617	0.712 847	11
12	0.716 884	0.711 675	0.706 507	0.701 380	0.696 293	0.691 246	12
13	0.697 273	0.691 786	0.686 346	0.660 951	0.675 603	0.670 299	13
14	0.678 199	0.672 453	0.666 760	0.661 118	0.655 527	0.649 987	14
15	0.659 646	0.653 661	0.647 733	0.641 862	0.636 048	0.630 290	15
16	0.641 601	0.635 393	0.629 248	0.623 167	0.617 148	0.611 191	16
17	0.624 050	0.617 636	0.611 292	0.605 016	0.598 809	0.592 670	17
18	0.606 979	0.600 375	0.593 847	0.587 395	0.581 016	0.574 710	18
19	0.590 374	0.583 597	0.576 901	0.570 286	0.563 751	0.557 294	19
20	0.574 224	0.567 287	0.560 438	0.553 676	0.546 999	0.540 407	20
21	0.558 516	0.551 434	0.544 445	0.537 549	0.530 745	0.524 031	21
22	0.543 238	0.536 023	0.528 908	0.521 893	0.514 974	0.508 151	22
23	0.528 377	0.521 043	0.513 815	0.506 692	0.499 671	0.492 753	23
24	0.513 923	0.506 482	0.499 152	0.491 934	0.484 824	0.477 821	24
25	0.499 864	0.492 327	0.484 908	0.477 606	0.470 417	0.463 341	25
26	0.486 190	0.478 568	0.471 071	0.463 695	0.456 439	0.449 301	26
27	0.472 890	0.465 194	0.457 628	0.450 189	0.442 876	0.435 685	27
28	0.459 954	0.452 193	0.444 569	0.437 077	0.429 716	0.422 483	28
29	0.447 372	0.439 556	0.431 882	0.424 346	0.416 947	0.409 680	29
30	0.435 133	0.427 272	0.419 558	0.411 987	0.404 557	0.397 266	30
31	0.423 230	0.415 331	0.407 585	0.399 987	0.392 536	0.385 227	31
32	0.411 652	0.403 724	0.395 954	0.388 337	0.380 871	0.373 554	32
33	0.400 391	0.392 442	0.384 654	0.377 026	0.369 554	0.362 234	33
34	0.389 438	0.381 474	0.373 678	0.366 045	0.358 573	0.351 257	34
35	0.378 785	0.370 813	0.363 014	0.355 383	0.347 918	0.340 613	35
36	0.368 423	0.360 450	0.352 655	0.345 032	0.337 579	0.330 291	36
37	0.358 345	0.350 377	0.342 591	0.334 983	0.327 548	0.320 283	37
38	0.348 542	0.340 585	0.332 815	0.325 226	0.317 815	0.310 577	38
39	0.339 007	0.331 067	0.323 317	0.315 754	0.308 371	0.301 166	39
40	0.329 734	0.321 815	0.314 091	0.306 557	0.299 208	0.292 039	40
41	0.320 714	0.312 821	0.305 128	0.297 628	0.290 317	0.283 190	41
42	0.311 940	0.304 079	0.296 420	0.288 959	0.281 690	0.274 608	42
43	0.303 407	0.295 581	0.287 962	0.280 543	0.273 320	0.266 287	43
44	0.295 107	0.287 321	0.279 744	0.272 372	0.265 198	0.258 218	44
45	0.287 034	0.279 291	0.271 761	0.264 439	0.257 318	0.250 393	45
46	0.279 182	0.271 486	0.264 006	0.256 737	0.249 672	0.242 805	46
47	0.271 545	0.263 899	0.256 472	0.249 259	0.242 253	0.235 447	47
48	0.264 117	0.256 524	0.249 153	0.241 999	0.235 054	0.228 313	48
49	0.256 892	0.249 355	0.242 043	0.234 950	0.228 069	0.221 394	49
50	0.249 864	0.242 386	0.235 136	0.228 107	0.221 292	0.214 685	50
51	0.243 029	0.235 612	0.228 426	0.221 463	0.214 717	0.208 179	51
52	0.236 381	0.229 028	0.221 907	0.215 013	0.208 336	0.201 871	52
53	0.229 914	0.222 627	0.215 575	0.208 750	0.202 146	0.195 754	53
54	0.223 625	0.216 405	0.209 423	0.202 670	0.196 139	0.189 822	54
55	0.217 508	0.210 358	0.203 447	0.196 767	0.190 311	0.184 070	55

YRS							
14	0.211 558	0.204 479	0.197 641	0.191 036	0.184 656	0.178 492	56
15	0.189 341	0.182 561	0.176 029	0.169 733	0.163 666	0.157 820	60
16	0.169 458	0.162 993	0.156 779	0.150 806	0.145 063	0.139 542	64
17	0.151 662	0.145 523	0.139 635	0.133 989	0.128 574	0.123 382	68
18	0.135 736	0.129 924	0.124 365	0.119 047	0.113 960	0.109 092	72
19	0.121 481	0.115 998	0.110 766	0.105 772	0.101 006	0.096 458	76
20	0.108 724	0.103 565	0.098 653	0.093 977	0.089 525	0.085 287	80
21	0.097 307	0.092 464	0.087 865	0.083 497	0.079 349	0.075 410	84
22	0.087 088	0.082 553	0.078 257	0.074 186	0.070 330	0.066 676	88
23	0.077 943	0.073 704	0.069 699	0.065 914	0.062 336	0.058 954	92
24	0.069 758	0.065 804	0.062 077	0.058 563	0.055 250	0.052 127	96
25	0.062 432	0.058 751	0.055 289	0.052 033	0.048 970	0.046 090	100
26	0.055 876	0.052 454	0.049 243	0.046 231	0.043 404	0.040 752	104
27	0.050 008	0.046 831	0.043 858	0.041 075	0.038 470	0.036 032	108
28	0.044 757	0.041 812	0.039 062	0.036 495	0.034 098	0.031 859	112
29	0.040 057	0.037 330	0.034 790	0.032 425	0.030 222	0.028 170	116
30	0.035 850	0.033 329	0.030 986	0.028 809	0.026 787	0.024 907	120

162

QTRS	12.75% ANNUAL RATE	13.00% ANNUAL RATE	13.25% ANNUAL RATE	13.50% ANNUAL RATE	13.75% ANNUAL RATE	14.00% ANNUAL RATE	QTRS
1	0.969 110	0.968 523	0.967 937	0.967 352	0.966 767	0.966 184	1
2	0.939 173	0.938 037	0.936 902	0.935 770	0.934 639	0.933 511	2
3	0.910 162	0.908 510	0.906 862	0.905 219	0.903 579	0.901 943	3
4	0.882 047	0.879 913	0.877 786	0.875 665	0.873 550	0.871 442	4
5	0.854 800	0.852 216	0.849 641	0.847 076	0.844 520	0.841 973	5
6	0.828 395	0.825 391	0.822 399	0.819 421	0.816 454	0.813 501	6
7	0.802 806	0.799 410	0.796 031	0.792 668	0.789 321	0.785 991	7
8	0.778 007	0.774 247	0.770 508	0.766 789	0.763 090	0.759 412	8
9	0.753 974	0.749 876	0.745 803	0.741 755	0.737 731	0.733 731	9
10	0.730 683	0.726 272	0.721 890	0.717 538	0.713 214	0.708 919	10
11	0.708 112	0.703 411	0.698 745	0.694 112	0.689 512	0.684 946	11
12	0.686 238	0.681 270	0.676 341	0.671 450	0.666 598	0.661 783	12
13	0.665 040	0.659 826	0.654 655	0.649 528	0.644 445	0.639 404	13
14	0.644 497	0.639 056	0.633 665	0.628 323	0.623 028	0.617 782	14
15	0.624 588	0.618 941	0.613 348	0.607 809	0.602 323	0.596 891	15
16	0.605 294	0.599 458	0.593 682	0.587 965	0.582 307	0.576 706	16
17	0.586 596	0.580 589	0.574 647	0.568 769	0.562 955	0.557 204	17
18	0.568 476	0.562 314	0.556 222	0.550 200	0.544 247	0.538 361	18
19	0.550 916	0.544 614	0.538 388	0.532 237	0.526 160	0.520 156	19
20	0.533 898	0.527 471	0.521 126	0.514 860	0.508 674	0.502 566	20
21	0.517 406	0.510 868	0.504 417	0.498 051	0.491 770	0.485 571	21
22	0.501 423	0.494 787	0.488 244	0.481 791	0.475 427	0.469 151	22
23	0.485 934	0.479 213	0.472 589	0.466 061	0.459 627	0.453 286	23
24	0.470 923	0.464 129	0.457 437	0.450 845	0.444 353	0.437 957	24
25	0.456 376	0.449 519	0.442 770	0.436 126	0.429 585	0.423 147	25
26	0.442 278	0.435 370	0.428 574	0.421 887	0.415 309	0.408 838	26
27	0.428 616	0.421 666	0.414 832	0.408 113	0.401 507	0.395 012	27
28	0.415 376	0.408 393	0.401 531	0.394 789	0.388 164	0.381 654	28
29	0.402 545	0.395 538	0.388 657	0.381 900	0.375 265	0.368 748	29
30	0.390 110	0.383 088	0.376 196	0.369 432	0.362 794	0.356 278	30
31	0.378 060	0.371 029	0.364 134	0.357 371	0.350 737	0.344 230	31
32	0.366 381	0.359 350	0.352 459	0.345 703	0.339 081	0.332 590	32
33	0.355 063	0.348 039	0.341 158	0.334 417	0.327 812	0.321 343	33
34	0.344 095	0.337 084	0.330 219	0.323 498	0.316 918	0.310 476	34
35	0.333 466	0.326 473	0.319 631	0.312 937	0.306 386	0.299 977	35
36	0.323 165	0.316 197	0.309 383	0.302 720	0.296 204	0.289 833	36
37	0.313 183	0.306 244	0.299 463	0.292 837	0.286 361	0.280 032	37
38	0.303 508	0.296 604	0.289 862	0.283 276	0.276 844	0.270 562	38
39	0.294 133	0.287 268	0.280 568	0.274 028	0.267 644	0.261 413	39
40	0.285 047	0.278 226	0.271 572	0.265 081	0.258 749	0.252 572	40
41	0.276 242	0.269 468	0.262 865	0.256 427	0.250 150	0.244 031	41
42	0.267 709	0.260 986	0.254 437	0.248 055	0.241 837	0.235 779	42
43	0.259 439	0.252 771	0.246 279	0.239 957	0.233 800	0.227 806	43
44	0.251 425	0.244 815	0.238 382	0.232 122	0.226 031	0.220 102	44
45	0.243 658	0.237 109	0.230 739	0.224 544	0.218 519	0.212 659	45
46	0.236 131	0.229 645	0.223 341	0.217 213	0.211 257	0.205 468	46
47	0.228 837	0.222 417	0.216 180	0.210 121	0.204 236	0.198 520	47
48	0.221 768	0.215 416	0.209 248	0.203 261	0.197 449	0.191 806	48
49	0.214 918	0.208 635	0.202 539	0.196 625	0.190 887	0.185 320	49
50	0.208 279	0.202 068	0.196 045	0.190 206	0.184 544	0.179 053	50
51	0.201 845	0.195 707	0.189 760	0.183 996	0.178 411	0.172 998	51
52	0.195 610	0.189 547	0.183 675	0.177 989	0.172 482	0.167 148	52
53	0.189 568	0.183 581	0.177 786	0.172 178	0.166 750	0.161 496	53
54	0.183 712	0.177 802	0.172 086	0.166 557	0.161 208	0.156 035	54
55	0.178 037	0.172 205	0.166 568	0.161 119	0.155 851	0.150 758	55

YRS	12.75%	13.00%	13.25%	13.50%	13.75%	14.00%	QTRS
14	0.172 537	0.166 785	0.161 228	0.155 859	0.150 672	0.145 660	56
15	0.152 186	0.146 756	0.141 523	0.136 480	0.131 619	0.126 934	60
16	0.134 235	0.129 133	0.124 227	0.119 511	0.114 976	0.110 616	64
17	0.118 402	0.113 626	0.109 045	0.104 651	0.100 437	0.096 395	68
18	0.104 436	0.099 981	0.095 718	0.091 639	0.087 737	0.084 003	72
19	0.092 117	0.087 974	0.084 020	0.080 245	0.076 643	0.073 204	76
20	0.081 252	0.077 410	0.073 751	0.070 268	0.066 951	0.063 793	80
21	0.071 668	0.068 114	0.064 738	0.061 531	0.058 485	0.055 592	84
22	0.063 214	0.059 934	0.056 826	0.053 881	0.051 090	0.048 445	88
23	0.055 758	0.052 737	0.049 881	0.047 182	0.044 630	0.042 217	92
24	0.049 181	0.046 404	0.043 785	0.041 315	0.038 986	0.036 790	96
25	0.043 380	0.040 831	0.038 434	0.036 178	0.034 056	0.032 060	100
26	0.038 263	0.035 928	0.033 737	0.031 680	0.029 750	0.027 939	104
27	0.033 750	0.031 614	0.029 614	0.027 741	0.025 988	0.024 347	108
28	0.029 769	0.027 817	0.025 994	0.024 292	0.022 702	0.021 217	112
29	0.026 258	0.024 477	0.022 817	0.021 272	0.019 831	0.018 489	116
30	0.023 161	0.021 537	0.020 029	0.018 627	0.017 324	0.016 112	120

PRESENT VALUE

	14.25% ANNUAL RATE	14.50% ANNUAL RATE	14.75% ANNUAL RATE	15.00% ANNUAL RATE	15.25% ANNUAL RATE	15.50% ANNUAL RATE	
QTRS							QTRS
1	0.965 600	0.965 018	0.964 436	0.963 855	0.963 275	0.962 696	1
2	0.932 384	0.931 260	0.930 138	0.929 017	0.927 899	0.926 783	2
3	0.900 311	0.898 683	0.897 059	0.895 438	0.893 822	0.892 210	3
4	0.869 340	0.867 245	0.865 156	0.863 073	0.860 997	0.858 926	4
5	0.839 436	0.836 907	0.834 388	0.831 878	0.829 377	0.826 884	5
6	0.810 559	0.807 631	0.804 714	0.801 810	0.798 918	0.796 038	6
7	0.782 677	0.779 378	0.776 096	0.772 829	0.769 578	0.766 342	7
8	0.755 753	0.752 114	0.748 495	0.744 895	0.741 315	0.737 754	8
9	0.729 755	0.725 804	0.721 876	0.717 971	0.714 090	0.710 233	9
10	0.704 652	0.700 414	0.696 203	0.692 020	0.687 865	0.683 738	10
11	0.680 412	0.675 912	0.671 444	0.667 008	0.662 604	0.658 231	11
12	0.657 007	0.652 267	0.647 565	0.642 899	0.638 270	0.633 676	12
13	0.634 406	0.629 450	0.624 535	0.619 662	0.614 829	0.610 037	13
14	0.612 583	0.607 430	0.602 324	0.597 264	0.592 250	0.587 280	14
15	0.591 510	0.586 181	0.580 903	0.575 676	0.570 499	0.565 372	15
16	0.571 162	0.565 675	0.560 244	0.554 869	0.549 548	0.544 281	16
17	0.551 515	0.545 887	0.540 320	0.534 813	0.529 366	0.523 977	17
18	0.532 543	0.526 791	0.521 104	0.515 483	0.509 925	0.504 430	18
19	0.514 224	0.508 363	0.502 572	0.496 851	0.491 198	0.485 613	19
20	0.496 535	0.490 579	0.484 699	0.478 892	0.473 159	0.467 497	20
21	0.479 454	0.473 418	0.467 461	0.461 583	0.455 782	0.450 058	21
22	0.462 961	0.456 857	0.450 837	0.444 899	0.439 044	0.433 269	22
23	0.447 035	0.440 875	0.434 803	0.428 819	0.422 920	0.417 106	23
24	0.431 658	0.425 452	0.419 340	0.413 319	0.407 388	0.401 546	24
25	0.416 809	0.410 569	0.404 427	0.398 380	0.392 427	0.386 566	25
26	0.402 471	0.396 207	0.390 044	0.383 981	0.378 015	0.372 146	26
27	0.388 626	0.382 347	0.376 173	0.370 102	0.364 133	0.358 263	27
28	0.375 257	0.368 971	0.362 795	0.356 725	0.350 760	0.344 898	28
29	0.362 349	0.356 064	0.349 892	0.343 831	0.337 878	0.332 032	29
30	0.349 884	0.343 608	0.337 449	0.331 403	0.325 470	0.319 646	30
31	0.337 848	0.331 588	0.325 448	0.319 425	0.313 517	0.307 722	31
32	0.326 226	0.319 989	0.313 874	0.307 879	0.302 003	0.296 242	32
33	0.315 004	0.308 795	0.302 711	0.296 751	0.290 912	0.285 191	33
34	0.304 168	0.297 993	0.291 946	0.286 025	0.280 228	0.274 552	34
35	0.293 705	0.287 568	0.281 563	0.275 687	0.269 937	0.264 310	35
36	0.283 602	0.277 509	0.271 550	0.265 722	0.260 024	0.254 450	36
37	0.273 846	0.267 801	0.261 893	0.256 118	0.250 474	0.244 958	37
38	0.264 426	0.258 433	0.252 579	0.246 861	0.241 276	0.235 820	38
39	0.255 330	0.249 392	0.243 596	0.237 938	0.232 415	0.227 023	39
40	0.246 547	0.240 668	0.234 933	0.229 338	0.223 879	0.218 554	40
41	0.238 065	0.232 249	0.226 578	0.221 049	0.215 657	0.210 401	41
42	0.229 876	0.224 124	0.218 520	0.213 059	0.207 737	0.202 552	42
43	0.221 969	0.216 284	0.210 749	0.205 358	0.200 108	0.194 996	43
44	0.214 333	0.208 718	0.203 254	0.197 935	0.192 759	0.187 722	44
45	0.206 960	0.201 417	0.196 025	0.190 781	0.185 680	0.180 719	45
46	0.199 841	0.194 371	0.189 054	0.183 885	0.178 861	0.173 977	46
47	0.192 966	0.187 571	0.182 330	0.177 239	0.172 293	0.167 487	47
48	0.186 328	0.181 010	0.175 846	0.170 833	0.165 965	0.161 239	48
49	0.179 919	0.174 678	0.169 592	0.164 658	0.159 870	0.155 224	49
50	0.173 730	0.168 567	0.163 561	0.158 707	0.153 999	0.149 434	50
51	0.167 753	0.162 670	0.157 744	0.152 970	0.148 343	0.143 859	51
52	0.161 983	0.156 980	0.152 134	0.147 441	0.142 895	0.138 492	52
53	0.156 411	0.151 488	0.146 724	0.142 112	0.137 648	0.133 326	53
54	0.151 030	0.146 189	0.141 506	0.136 975	0.132 592	0.128 352	54
55	0.145 835	0.141 075	0.136 473	0.132 024	0.127 723	0.123 564	55
YRS							
14	0.140 818	0.136 140	0.131 620	0.127 252	0.123 032	0.118 955	56
15	0.122 419	0.118 067	0.113 872	0.109 828	0.105 930	0.102 173	60
16	0.106 424	0.102 393	0.098 517	0.094 790	0.091 206	0.087 759	64
17	0.092 518	0.088 800	0.085 232	0.081 810	0.078 528	0.075 379	68
18	0.080 430	0.077 011	0.073 739	0.070 608	0.067 612	0.064 745	72
19	0.069 921	0.066 787	0.063 796	0.060 940	0.058 214	0.055 611	76
20	0.060 785	0.057 921	0.055 193	0.052 596	0.050 122	0.047 766	80
21	0.052 843	0.050 232	0.047 751	0.045 394	0.043 155	0.041 027	84
22	0.045 939	0.043 563	0.041 312	0.039 178	0.037 156	0.035 239	88
23	0.039 936	0.037 780	0.035 741	0.033 814	0.031 991	0.030 268	92
24	0.034 718	0.032 765	0.030 922	0.029 184	0.027 544	0.025 998	96
25	0.030 182	0.028 415	0.026 752	0.025 188	0.023 716	0.022 330	100
26	0.026 238	0.024 643	0.023 145	0.021 739	0.020 419	0.019 180	104
27	0.022 810	0.021 371	0.020 024	0.018 762	0.017 581	0.016 474	108
28	0.019 830	0.018 534	0.017 324	0.016 193	0.015 137	0.014 150	112
29	0.017 239	0.016 074	0.014 988	0.013 976	0.013 033	0.012 154	116
30	0.014 986	0.013 940	0.012 967	0.012 062	0.011 221	0.010 439	120

PRESENT VALUE

QUARTERLY COMPOUNDING

QTRS	15.75% ANNUAL RATE	16.00% ANNUAL RATE	16.50% ANNUAL RATE	17.00% ANNUAL RATE	17.50% ANNUAL RATE	18.00% ANNUAL RATE	QTRS
1	0.962 117	0.961 538	0.960 384	0.959 233	0.958 084	0.956 938	1
2	0.925 668	0.924 556	0.922 338	0.920 127	0.917 925	0.915 730	2
3	0.890 601	0.888 996	0.885 799	0.882 616	0.879 449	0.876 297	3
4	0.856 862	0.854 804	0.850 707	0.846 634	0.842 586	0.838 561	4
5	0.824 401	0.821 927	0.817 005	0.812 119	0.807 268	0.802 451	5
6	0.793 170	0.790 315	0.784 639	0.779 011	0.773 430	0.767 896	6
7	0.763 122	0.759 918	0.753 555	0.747 253	0.741 011	0.734 828	7
8	0.734 213	0.730 690	0.723 702	0.716 789	0.709 951	0.703 185	8
9	0.706 398	0.702 587	0.695 032	0.687 568	0.680 192	0.672 904	9
10	0.679 638	0.675 564	0.667 498	0.659 537	0.651 681	0.643 928	10
11	0.653 891	0.649 581	0.641 054	0.632 650	0.624 365	0.616 199	11
12	0.629 119	0.624 597	0.615 658	0.606 858	0.598 194	0.589 664	12
13	0.605 286	0.600 574	0.591 269	0.582 118	0.573 120	0.564 272	13
14	0.582 356	0.577 475	0.567 845	0.558 387	0.549 097	0.539 973	14
15	0.560 294	0.555 265	0.545 349	0.535 623	0.526 081	0.516 720	15
16	0.539 068	0.533 908	0.523 745	0.513 787	0.504 030	0.494 469	16
17	0.518 647	0.513 373	0.502 996	0.492 841	0.482 903	0.473 176	17
18	0.498 998	0.493 628	0.483 070	0.472 749	0.462 661	0.452 800	18
19	0.480 095	0.474 642	0.463 932	0.453 477	0.443 268	0.433 302	19
20	0.461 907	0.456 387	0.445 553	0.434 989	0.424 688	0.414 643	20
21	0.444 409	0.438 834	0.427 902	0.417 256	0.406 887	0.396 787	21
22	0.427 573	0.421 955	0.410 951	0.400 246	0.389 832	0.379 701	22
23	0.411 375	0.405 726	0.394 671	0.383 929	0.373 492	0.363 350	23
24	0.395 791	0.390 121	0.379 035	0.368 277	0.357 836	0.347 703	24
25	0.380 797	0.375 117	0.364 019	0.353 263	0.342 837	0.332 731	25
26	0.366 371	0.360 689	0.349 599	0.338 862	0.328 467	0.318 402	26
27	0.352 492	0.346 817	0.335 749	0.325 047	0.314 699	0.304 691	27
28	0.339 138	0.333 477	0.322 448	0.311 796	0.301 508	0.291 571	28
29	0.326 290	0.320 651	0.309 674	0.299 085	0.288 870	0.279 015	29
30	0.313 929	0.308 319	0.297 406	0.286 892	0.276 761	0.267 000	30
31	0.302 037	0.296 460	0.285 624	0.275 196	0.265 161	0.255 502	31
32	0.290 595	0.285 058	0.274 309	0.263 977	0.254 046	0.244 500	32
33	0.279 586	0.274 094	0.263 442	0.253 215	0.243 397	0.233 971	33
34	0.268 994	0.263 552	0.253 005	0.242 892	0.233 195	0.223 896	34
35	0.258 804	0.253 415	0.242 982	0.232 990	0.223 420	0.214 254	35
36	0.248 999	0.243 669	0.233 356	0.223 492	0.214 056	0.205 028	36
37	0.239 567	0.234 297	0.224 112	0.214 381	0.205 083	0.196 199	37
38	0.230 491	0.225 285	0.215 233	0.205 641	0.196 487	0.187 750	38
39	0.221 759	0.216 621	0.206 707	0.197 257	0.188 251	0.179 665	39
40	0.213 358	0.208 289	0.198 518	0.189 216	0.180 360	0.171 929	40
41	0.205 275	0.200 278	0.190 653	0.181 502	0.172 800	0.164 525	41
42	0.197 499	0.192 575	0.183 100	0.174 103	0.165 557	0.157 440	42
43	0.190 017	0.185 168	0.175 847	0.167 005	0.158 617	0.150 661	43
44	0.182 819	0.178 046	0.168 880	0.160 197	0.151 961	0.144 173	44
45	0.175 893	0.171 198	0.162 190	0.153 666	0.145 599	0.137 964	45
46	0.169 229	0.164 614	0.155 765	0.147 401	0.139 496	0.132 023	46
47	0.162 818	0.158 283	0.149 594	0.141 392	0.133 649	0.126 338	47
48	0.156 650	0.152 195	0.143 668	0.135 628	0.128 047	0.120 898	48
49	0.150 716	0.146 341	0.137 976	0.130 099	0.122 680	0.115 692	49
50	0.145 006	0.140 713	0.132 510	0.124 795	0.117 537	0.110 710	50
51	0.139 513	0.135 301	0.127 261	0.119 707	0.112 611	0.105 942	51
52	0.134 228	0.130 097	0.122 219	0.114 827	0.107 890	0.101 380	52
53	0.129 143	0.125 093	0.117 377	0.110 146	0.103 368	0.097 014	53
54	0.124 250	0.120 282	0.112 727	0.105 656	0.099 035	0.092 837	54
55	0.119 543	0.115 656	0.108 262	0.101 348	0.094 884	0.088 839	55

YRS							QTRS
14	0.115 015	0.111 207	0.103 973	0.097 217	0.090 907	0.085 013	56
15	0.098 552	0.095 060	0.088 450	0.082 307	0.076 597	0.071 289	60
16	0.084 445	0.081 258	0.075 245	0.069 684	0.064 539	0.059 780	64
17	0.072 358	0.069 460	0.064 012	0.058 997	0.054 380	0.050 129	68
18	0.062 001	0.059 374	0.054 455	0.049 949	0.045 820	0.042 037	72
19	0.053 126	0.050 754	0.046 325	0.042 288	0.038 607	0.035 250	76
20	0.045 522	0.043 384	0.039 409	0.035 803	0.032 530	0.029 559	80
21	0.039 006	0.037 085	0.033 526	0.030 312	0.027 409	0.024 787	84
22	0.033 423	0.031 701	0.028 521	0.025 663	0.023 095	0.020 786	88
23	0.028 639	0.027 098	0.024 263	0.021 727	0.019 459	0.017 430	92
24	0.024 539	0.023 163	0.020 640	0.018 395	0.016 396	0.014 616	96
25	0.021 027	0.019 800	0.017 559	0.015 574	0.013 815	0.012 257	100
26	0.018 017	0.016 925	0.014 938	0.013 185	0.011 640	0.010 278	104
27	0.015 438	0.014 468	0.012 707	0.011 163	0.009 808	0.008 619	108
28	0.013 228	0.012 367	0.010 810	0.009 451	0.008 264	0.007 227	112
29	0.011 335	0.010 571	0.009 196	0.008 002	0.006 963	0.006 061	116
30	0.009 712	0.009 036	0.007 823	0.006 774	0.005 867	0.005 082	120

165

PRESENT VALUE

QTRS	18.50% ANNUAL RATE	19.00% ANNUAL RATE	19.50% ANNUAL RATE	20.00% ANNUAL RATE	20.50% ANNUAL RATE	21.00% ANNUAL RATE	QTRS
1	0.955 795	0.954 654	0.953 516	0.952 381	0.951 249	0.950 119	1
2	0.913 543	0.911 364	0.909 193	0.907 029	0.904 874	0.902 726	2
3	0.873 160	0.870 037	0.866 930	0.863 838	0.860 760	0.857 697	3
4	0.834 561	0.830 585	0.826 632	0.822 702	0.818 796	0.814 914	4
5	0.797 669	0.792 921	0.788 207	0.783 526	0.778 879	0.774 265	5
6	0.762 408	0.756 965	0.751 568	0.746 215	0.740 907	0.735 643	6
7	0.728 705	0.722 640	0.716 632	0.710 681	0.704 787	0.698 949	7
8	0.696 492	0.689 871	0.683 320	0.676 839	0.670 428	0.664 084	8
9	0.665 703	0.658 588	0.651 557	0.644 609	0.637 743	0.630 959	9
10	0.636 276	0.628 723	0.621 270	0.613 913	0.606 652	0.599 486	10
11	0.608 149	0.600 213	0.592 391	0.584 679	0.577 077	0.569 583	11
12	0.581 265	0.572 996	0.564 854	0.556 837	0.548 944	0.541 171	12
13	0.555 570	0.547 013	0.538 598	0.530 321	0.522 182	0.514 177	13
14	0.531 011	0.522 208	0.513 561	0.505 068	0.496 725	0.488 529	14
15	0.507 537	0.498 528	0.489 689	0.481 017	0.472 509	0.464 161	15
16	0.485 101	0.475 922	0.466 926	0.458 112	0.449 473	0.441 008	16
17	0.463 657	0.454 341	0.445 222	0.436 297	0.427 561	0.419 010	17
18	0.443 161	0.433 738	0.424 526	0.415 521	0.406 717	0.398 109	18
19	0.423 571	0.414 070	0.404 793	0.395 734	0.386 889	0.378 251	19
20	0.404 847	0.395 293	0.385 976	0.376 889	0.368 027	0.359 383	20
21	0.386 950	0.377 368	0.368 035	0.358 942	0.350 085	0.341 457	21
22	0.369 845	0.360 256	0.350 927	0.341 850	0.333 018	0.324 425	22
23	0.353 496	0.343 920	0.334 614	0.325 571	0.316 783	0.308 242	23
24	0.337 869	0.328 324	0.319 060	0.310 068	0.301 339	0.292 866	24
25	0.322 934	0.313 436	0.304 229	0.295 303	0.286 649	0.278 258	25
26	0.308 658	0.299 223	0.290 087	0.281 241	0.272 674	0.264 378	26
27	0.295 014	0.285 655	0.276 603	0.267 848	0.259 381	0.251 190	27
28	0.281 973	0.272 701	0.263 745	0.255 094	0.246 736	0.238 661	28
29	0.269 508	0.260 335	0.251 485	0.242 946	0.234 707	0.226 756	29
30	0.257 594	0.248 530	0.239 795	0.231 377	0.223 265	0.215 445	30
31	0.246 207	0.237 260	0.228 649	0.220 359	0.212 380	0.204 699	31
32	0.235 323	0.226 501	0.218 020	0.209 866	0.202 026	0.194 488	32
33	0.224 921	0.216 231	0.207 886	0.199 873	0.192 177	0.184 787	33
34	0.214 978	0.206 425	0.198 222	0.190 355	0.182 808	0.175 569	34
35	0.205 475	0.197 065	0.189 008	0.181 290	0.173 896	0.166 812	35
36	0.196 392	0.188 129	0.180 222	0.172 657	0.165 418	0.158 491	36
37	0.187 710	0.179 598	0.171 845	0.164 436	0.157 354	0.150 585	37
38	0.179 412	0.171 454	0.163 857	0.156 605	0.149 683	0.143 074	38
39	0.171 481	0.163 679	0.156 240	0.149 148	0.142 385	0.135 937	39
40	0.163 901	0.156 257	0.148 978	0.142 046	0.135 444	0.129 156	40
41	0.156 656	0.149 171	0.142 053	0.135 282	0.128 841	0.122 714	41
42	0.149 730	0.142 407	0.135 449	0.128 840	0.122 560	0.116 593	42
43	0.143 112	0.135 949	0.129 153	0.122 704	0.116 585	0.110 777	43
44	0.136 785	0.129 784	0.123 150	0.116 861	0.110 901	0.105 251	44
45	0.130 739	0.123 899	0.117 425	0.111 297	0.105 494	0.100 001	45
46	0.124 959	0.118 281	0.111 967	0.105 997	0.100 351	0.095 013	46
47	0.119 435	0.112 917	0.106 762	0.100 949	0.095 459	0.090 274	47
48	0.114 156	0.107 797	0.101 799	0.096 142	0.090 805	0.085 771	48
49	0.109 109	0.102 909	0.097 067	0.091 564	0.086 378	0.081 492	49
50	0.104 286	0.098 242	0.092 555	0.087 204	0.082 167	0.077 427	50
51	0.099 676	0.093 787	0.088 253	0.083 051	0.078 162	0.073 565	51
52	0.095 270	0.089 534	0.084 151	0.079 096	0.074 351	0.069 896	52
53	0.091 058	0.085 474	0.080 239	0.075 330	0.070 726	0.066 409	53
54	0.087 033	0.081 599	0.076 509	0.071 743	0.067 278	0.063 097	54
55	0.083 186	0.077 898	0.072 953	0.068 326	0.063 998	0.059 949	55

YRS							
14	0.079 509	0.074 366	0.069 562	0.065 073	0.060 878	0.056 959	56
15	0.066 355	0.061 767	0.057 502	0.053 536	0.049 847	0.046 417	60
16	0.055 377	0.051 303	0.047 533	0.044 044	0.040 815	0.037 826	64
17	0.046 216	0.042 611	0.039 292	0.036 235	0.033 419	0.030 825	68
18	0.038 570	0.035 392	0.032 480	0.029 811	0.027 363	0.025 119	72
19	0.032 189	0.029 396	0.026 849	0.024 525	0.022 405	0.020 470	76
20	0.026 863	0.024 416	0.022 194	0.020 177	0.018 345	0.016 681	80
21	0.022 419	0.020 280	0.018 347	0.016 600	0.015 021	0.013 594	84
22	0.018 710	0.016 844	0.015 166	0.013 657	0.012 299	0.011 078	88
23	0.015 615	0.013 990	0.012 537	0.011 235	0.010 070	0.009 027	92
24	0.013 032	0.011 620	0.010 363	0.009 243	0.008 246	0.007 357	96
25	0.010 876	0.009 652	0.008 566	0.007 604	0.006 751	0.005 995	100
26	0.009 076	0.008 016	0.007 081	0.006 256	0.005 528	0.004 885	104
27	0.007 575	0.006 658	0.005 854	0.005 147	0.004 526	0.003 981	108
28	0.006 322	0.005 530	0.004 839	0.004 234	0.003 706	0.003 244	112
29	0.005 276	0.004 593	0.004 000	0.003 484	0.003 035	0.002 644	116
30	0.004 403	0.003 815	0.003 306	0.002 866	0.002 485	0.002 155	120

QTRS	21.50% ANNUAL RATE	22.00% ANNUAL RATE	22.50% ANNUAL RATE	23.00% ANNUAL RATE	23.50% ANNUAL RATE	24.00% ANNUAL RATE	QTRS
1	0.948 992	0.947 867	0.946 746	0.945 626	0.944 510	0.943 396	1
2	0.900 585	0.898 452	0.896 327	0.894 209	0.892 099	0.889 996	2
3	0.854 648	0.851 614	0.848 594	0.845 588	0.842 597	0.839 619	3
4	0.811 054	0.807 217	0.803 402	0.799 611	0.795 841	0.792 094	4
5	0.769 683	0.765 134	0.760 618	0.756 133	0.751 680	0.747 258	5
6	0.730 423	0.725 246	0.720 111	0.715 019	0.709 969	0.704 961	6
7	0.693 165	0.687 437	0.681 762	0.676 141	0.670 573	0.665 057	7
8	0.657 808	0.651 599	0.645 455	0.639 377	0.633 363	0.627 412	8
9	0.624 255	0.617 629	0.611 082	0.604 612	0.598 218	0.591 898	9
10	0.592 412	0.585 431	0.578 539	0.571 737	0.565 023	0.558 395	10
11	0.562 194	0.554 911	0.547 729	0.540 650	0.533 669	0.526 788	11
12	0.533 518	0.525 982	0.518 560	0.511 253	0.504 056	0.496 969	12
13	0.506 304	0.498 561	0.490 945	0.483 454	0.476 086	0.468 839	13
14	0.480 478	0.472 569	0.464 800	0.457 167	0.449 668	0.442 301	14
15	0.455 970	0.447 933	0.440 047	0.432 309	0.424 716	0.417 265	15
16	0.432 712	0.424 581	0.416 613	0.408 803	0.401 149	0.393 646	16
17	0.410 640	0.402 447	0.394 426	0.386 575	0.378 889	0.371 364	17
18	0.389 694	0.381 466	0.373 421	0.365 555	0.357 864	0.350 344	18
19	0.369 816	0.361 579	0.353 535	0.345 679	0.338 006	0.330 513	19
20	0.350 952	0.342 729	0.334 708	0.326 883	0.319 250	0.311 805	20
21	0.333 051	0.324 862	0.316 883	0.309 109	0.301 535	0.294 155	21
22	0.316 063	0.307 926	0.300 008	0.292 302	0.284 803	0.277 505	22
23	0.299 941	0.291 873	0.284 031	0.276 408	0.268 999	0.261 797	23
24	0.284 641	0.276 657	0.268 905	0.261 379	0.254 073	0.246 979	24
25	0.270 122	0.262 234	0.254 584	0.247 167	0.239 974	0.232 999	25
26	0.256 344	0.248 563	0.241 027	0.233 728	0.226 658	0.219 810	26
27	0.243 268	0.235 605	0.228 191	0.221 016	0.214 081	0.207 368	27
28	0.230 859	0.223 322	0.216 039	0.209 002	0.202 201	0.195 630	28
29	0.219 084	0.211 679	0.204 534	0.197 637	0.190 981	0.184 557	29
30	0.207 909	0.200 644	0.193 641	0.186 891	0.180 384	0.174 110	30
31	0.197 303	0.190 184	0.183 329	0.176 729	0.170 374	0.164 255	31
32	0.187 239	0.180 269	0.173 566	0.167 120	0.160 920	0.154 957	32
33	0.177 689	0.170 871	0.164 323	0.158 033	0.151 991	0.146 186	33
34	0.168 625	0.161 963	0.155 572	0.149 440	0.143 557	0.137 912	34
35	0.160 024	0.153 520	0.147 287	0.141 315	0.135 591	0.130 105	35
36	0.151 861	0.145 516	0.139 443	0.133 631	0.128 067	0.122 741	36
37	0.144 115	0.137 930	0.132 017	0.126 365	0.120 960	0.115 793	37
38	0.136 764	0.130 739	0.124 987	0.119 494	0.114 248	0.109 239	38
39	0.129 788	0.123 924	0.118 331	0.112 997	0.107 909	0.103 056	39
40	0.123 168	0.117 463	0.112 029	0.106 853	0.101 921	0.097 222	40
41	0.116 885	0.111 339	0.106 063	0.101 043	0.096 265	0.091 719	41
42	0.110 923	0.105 535	0.100 415	0.095 549	0.090 924	0.086 527	42
43	0.105 265	0.100 033	0.095 067	0.090 353	0.085 878	0.081 630	43
44	0.099 896	0.094 818	0.090 005	0.085 440	0.081 113	0.077 009	44
45	0.094 800	0.089 875	0.085 211	0.080 795	0.076 612	0.072 650	45
46	0.089 964	0.085 190	0.080 673	0.076 402	0.072 361	0.068 538	46
47	0.085 376	0.080 748	0.076 377	0.072 247	0.068 345	0.064 658	47
48	0.081 021	0.076 539	0.072 310	0.068 319	0.064 553	0.060 998	48
49	0.076 888	0.072 549	0.068 459	0.064 604	0.060 971	0.057 546	49
50	0.072 966	0.068 767	0.064 813	0.061 092	0.057 588	0.054 288	50
51	0.069 244	0.065 182	0.061 362	0.057 770	0.054 392	0.051 215	51
52	0.065 712	0.061 783	0.058 094	0.054 629	0.051 374	0.048 316	52
53	0.062 360	0.058 563	0.055 000	0.051 658	0.048 523	0.045 582	53
54	0.059 179	0.055 509	0.052 071	0.048 849	0.045 831	0.043 001	54
55	0.056 161	0.052 616	0.049 298	0.046 193	0.043 287	0.040 567	55

YRS							
14	0.053 296	0.049 873	0.046 673	0.043 682	0.040 885	0.038 271	56
15	0.043 226	0.040 258	0.037 497	0.034 928	0.032 538	0.030 314	60
16	0.035 059	0.032 497	0.030 125	0.027 929	0.025 895	0.024 012	64
17	0.028 434	0.026 232	0.024 203	0.022 332	0.020 609	0.019 020	68
18	0.023 062	0.021 175	0.019 444	0.017 857	0.016 401	0.015 065	72
19	0.018 704	0.017 093	0.015 622	0.014 279	0.013 053	0.011 933	76
20	0.015 170	0.013 798	0.012 551	0.011 417	0.010 388	0.009 452	80
21	0.012 304	0.011 138	0.010 083	0.009 130	0.008 267	0.007 487	84
22	0.009 979	0.008 990	0.008 101	0.007 300	0.006 579	0.005 930	88
23	0.008 094	0.007 257	0.006 508	0.005 837	0.005 236	0.004 697	92
24	0.006 564	0.005 858	0.005 229	0.004 667	0.004 167	0.003 721	96
25	0.005 324	0.004 729	0.004 201	0.003 732	0.003 316	0.002 947	100
26	0.004 318	0.003 817	0.003 375	0.002 984	0.002 639	0.002 334	104
27	0.003 502	0.003 081	0.002 711	0.002 386	0.002 100	0.001 849	108
28	0.002 840	0.002 487	0.002 178	0.001 908	0.001 672	0.001 465	112
29	0.002 304	0.002 008	0.001 750	0.001 526	0.001 330	0.001 160	116
30	0.001 868	0.001 621	0.001 406	0.001 220	0.001 059	0.000 919	120

SECTION 4

HALF YRS	5.25% ANNUAL RATE	5.50% ANNUAL RATE	5.75% ANNUAL RATE	6.00% ANNUAL RATE	6.25% ANNUAL RATE	6.50% ANNUAL RATE	HALF YRS
1	0.974 421	0.973 236	0.972 053	0.970 874	0.969 697	0.968 523	1
2	0.949 497	0.947 188	0.944 888	0.942 596	0.940 312	0.938 037	2
3	0.925 210	0.921 838	0.918 482	0.915 142	0.911 818	0.908 510	3
4	0.901 545	0.897 166	0.892 813	0.888 487	0.884 187	0.879 913	4
5	0.878 485	0.873 154	0.867 862	0.862 609	0.857 394	0.852 216	5
6	0.856 014	0.849 785	0.843 608	0.837 484	0.831 412	0.825 391	6
7	0.834 119	0.827 041	0.820 032	0.813 092	0.806 218	0.799 410	7
8	0.812 783	0.804 906	0.797 115	0.789 409	0.781 787	0.774 247	8
9	0.791 993	0.783 364	0.774 839	0.766 417	0.758 096	0.749 876	9
10	0.771 735	0.762 398	0.753 185	0.744 094	0.735 124	0.726 272	10
11	0.751 995	0.741 993	0.732 136	0.722 421	0.712 847	0.703 411	11
12	0.732 760	0.722 134	0.711 675	0.701 380	0.691 246	0.681 270	12
13	0.714 017	0.702 807	0.691 786	0.680 951	0.670 299	0.659 826	13
14	0.695 754	0.683 997	0.672 453	0.661 118	0.649 987	0.639 056	14
15	0.677 957	0.665 691	0.653 661	0.641 862	0.630 290	0.618 941	15
16	0.660 616	0.647 874	0.635 393	0.623 167	0.611 191	0.599 458	16
17	0.643 719	0.630 535	0.617 636	0.605 016	0.592 670	0.580 589	17
18	0.627 253	0.613 659	0.600 375	0.587 395	0.574 710	0.562 314	18
19	0.611 209	0.597 235	0.583 597	0.570 286	0.557 294	0.544 614	19
20	0.595 575	0.581 251	0.567 287	0.553 676	0.540 407	0.527 471	20
21	0.580 341	0.565 694	0.551 434	0.537 549	0.524 031	0.510 868	21
22	0.565 497	0.550 554	0.536 023	0.521 893	0.508 151	0.494 787	22
23	0.551 032	0.535 819	0.521 043	0.506 692	0.492 753	0.479 213	23
24	0.536 938	0.521 478	0.506 482	0.491 934	0.477 821	0.464 129	24
25	0.523 204	0.507 521	0.492 327	0.477 606	0.463 341	0.449 519	25
26	0.509 821	0.493 938	0.478 568	0.463 695	0.449 301	0.435 370	26
27	0.496 780	0.480 718	0.465 194	0.450 189	0.435 685	0.421 666	27
28	0.484 073	0.467 852	0.452 193	0.437 077	0.422 483	0.408 393	28
29	0.471 692	0.455 331	0.439 556	0.424 346	0.409 680	0.395 538	29
30	0.459 626	0.443 144	0.427 272	0.411 987	0.397 266	0.383 088	30
31	0.447 870	0.431 284	0.415 331	0.399 987	0.385 227	0.371 029	31
32	0.436 414	0.419 741	0.403 724	0.388 337	0.373 554	0.359 350	32
33	0.425 251	0.408 507	0.392 442	0.377 026	0.362 234	0.348 039	33
34	0.414 374	0.397 574	0.381 474	0.366 045	0.351 257	0.337 084	34
35	0.403 775	0.386 933	0.370 813	0.355 383	0.340 613	0.326 473	35
36	0.393 447	0.376 577	0.360 450	0.345 032	0.330 291	0.316 197	36
37	0.383 383	0.366 499	0.350 377	0.334 983	0.320 283	0.306 244	37
38	0.373 576	0.356 690	0.340 585	0.325 226	0.310 577	0.296 604	38
39	0.364 021	0.347 143	0.331 067	0.315 754	0.301 166	0.287 268	39
40	0.354 710	0.337 832	0.321 815	0.306 557	0.292 039	0.278 226	40
41	0.345 637	0.328 810	0.312 821	0.297 628	0.283 190	0.269 468	41
42	0.336 796	0.320 010	0.304 079	0.288 959	0.274 608	0.260 986	42
43	0.328 181	0.311 445	0.295 581	0.280 543	0.266 287	0.252 771	43
44	0.319 787	0.303 109	0.287 321	0.272 372	0.258 218	0.244 815	44
45	0.311 607	0.294 997	0.279 291	0.264 439	0.250 393	0.237 109	45
46	0.303 607	0.287 102	0.271 486	0.256 737	0.242 805	0.229 645	46
47	0.295 870	0.279 418	0.263 899	0.249 259	0.235 447	0.222 417	47
48	0.288 302	0.271 939	0.256 524	0.241 999	0.228 313	0.215 416	48
49	0.280 928	0.264 661	0.249 355	0.234 950	0.221 394	0.208 635	49
50	0.273 742	0.257 578	0.242 386	0.228 107	0.214 685	0.202 068	50
51	0.266 740	0.250 684	0.235 612	0.221 463	0.208 179	0.195 707	51
52	0.259 917	0.243 975	0.229 028	0.215 013	0.201 871	0.189 547	52
53	0.253 269	0.237 445	0.222 627	0.208 750	0.195 754	0.183 581	53
54	0.246 791	0.231 090	0.216 405	0.202 670	0.189 822	0.177 802	54
55	0.240 478	0.224 905	0.210 358	0.196 767	0.184 070	0.172 205	55
56	0.234 327	0.218 886	0.204 479	0.191 036	0.178 492	0.166 785	56
57	0.228 333	0.213 027	0.198 764	0.185 472	0.173 083	0.161 535	57
58	0.222 493	0.207 326	0.193 210	0.180 070	0.167 838	0.156 450	58
59	0.216 802	0.201 777	0.187 810	0.174 825	0.162 752	0.151 526	59

YRS	5.25% ANNUAL RATE	5.50% ANNUAL RATE	5.75% ANNUAL RATE	6.00% ANNUAL RATE	6.25% ANNUAL RATE	6.50% ANNUAL RATE	
30	0.211 256	0.196 377	0.182 561	0.169 733	0.157 820	0.146 756	60
31	0.200 587	0.186 006	0.172 500	0.159 990	0.148 400	0.137 663	62
32	0.190 457	0.176 183	0.162 993	0.150 806	0.139 542	0.129 133	64
33	0.180 838	0.166 878	0.154 010	0.142 149	0.131 214	0.121 131	66
34	0.171 706	0.158 065	0.145 523	0.133 989	0.123 382	0.113 626	68
35	0.163 034	0.149 717	0.137 503	0.126 297	0.116 017	0.106 585	70
36	0.154 800	0.141 810	0.129 924	0.119 047	0.109 092	0.099 981	72
37	0.146 982	0.134 321	0.122 764	0.112 214	0.102 581	0.093 785	74
38	0.139 559	0.127 227	0.115 998	0.105 772	0.096 458	0.087 974	76
39	0.132 511	0.120 508	0.109 605	0.099 700	0.090 701	0.082 523	78
40	0.125 819	0.114 144	0.103 565	0.093 977	0.085 287	0.077 410	80

PRESENT VALUE

SEMIANNUAL COMPOUNDING

HALF YRS	6.75% ANNUAL RATE	7.00% ANNUAL RATE	7.25% ANNUAL RATE	7.50% ANNUAL RATE	7.75% ANNUAL RATE	8.00% ANNUAL RATE	HALF YRS
1	0.967 352	0.966 184	0.965 018	0.963 855	0.962 696	0.961 538	1
2	0.935 770	0.933 511	0.931 260	0.929 017	0.926 783	0.924 556	2
3	0.905 219	0.901 943	0.898 683	0.895 438	0.892 210	0.888 996	3
4	0.875 665	0.871 442	0.867 245	0.863 073	0.858 926	0.854 804	4
5	0.847 076	0.841 973	0.836 907	0.831 878	0.826 884	0.821 927	5
6	0.819 421	0.813 501	0.807 631	0.801 810	0.796 038	0.790 315	6
7	0.792 668	0.785 991	0.779 378	0.772 829	0.766 342	0.759 918	7
8	0.766 789	0.759 412	0.752 114	0.744 895	0.737 754	0.730 690	8
9	0.741 755	0.733 731	0.725 804	0.717 971	0.710 233	0.702 587	9
10	0.717 538	0.708 919	0.700 414	0.692 020	0.683 738	0.675 564	10
11	0.694 112	0.684 946	0.675 912	0.667 008	0.658 231	0.649 581	11
12	0.671 450	0.661 783	0.652 267	0.642 899	0.633 676	0.624 597	12
13	0.649 528	0.639 404	0.629 450	0.619 662	0.610 037	0.600 574	13
14	0.628 323	0.617 782	0.607 430	0.597 264	0.587 280	0.577 475	14
15	0.607 809	0.596 891	0.586 181	0.575 676	0.565 372	0.555 265	15
16	0.587 965	0.576 706	0.565 675	0.554 869	0.544 281	0.533 908	16
17	0.568 769	0.557 204	0.545 887	0.534 813	0.523 977	0.513 373	17
18	0.550 200	0.538 361	0.526 791	0.515 483	0.504 430	0.493 628	18
19	0.532 237	0.520 156	0.508 363	0.496 851	0.485 613	0.474 642	19
20	0.514 860	0.502 566	0.490 579	0.478 892	0.467 497	0.456 387	20
21	0.498 051	0.485 571	0.473 418	0.461 583	0.450 058	0.438 834	21
22	0.481 791	0.469 151	0.456 857	0.444 899	0.433 269	0.421 955	22
23	0.466 061	0.453 286	0.440 875	0.428 819	0.417 106	0.405 726	23
24	0.450 845	0.437 957	0.425 452	0.413 319	0.401 546	0.390 121	24
25	0.436 126	0.423 147	0.410 569	0.398 380	0.386 566	0.375 117	25
26	0.421 887	0.408 838	0.396 207	0.383 981	0.372 146	0.360 689	26
27	0.408 113	0.395 012	0.382 347	0.370 102	0.358 263	0.346 817	27
28	0.394 789	0.381 654	0.368 971	0.356 725	0.344 898	0.333 477	28
29	0.381 900	0.368 748	0.356 064	0.343 831	0.332 032	0.320 651	29
30	0.369 432	0.356 278	0.343 608	0.331 403	0.319 646	0.308 319	30
31	0.357 371	0.344 230	0.331 588	0.319 425	0.307 722	0.296 460	31
32	0.345 703	0.332 590	0.319 989	0.307 879	0.296 242	0.285 058	32
33	0.334 417	0.321 343	0.308 795	0.296 751	0.285 191	0.274 094	33
34	0.323 498	0.310 476	0.297 993	0.286 025	0.274 552	0.263 552	34
35	0.312 937	0.299 977	0.287 568	0.275 687	0.264 310	0.253 415	35
36	0.302 720	0.289 833	0.277 509	0.265 722	0.254 450	0.243 669	36
37	0.292 837	0.280 032	0.267 801	0.256 118	0.244 958	0.234 297	37
38	0.283 276	0.270 562	0.258 433	0.246 861	0.235 820	0.225 285	38
39	0.274 028	0.261 413	0.249 392	0.237 938	0.227 023	0.216 621	39
40	0.265 081	0.252 572	0.240 668	0.229 338	0.218 554	0.208 289	40
41	0.256 427	0.244 031	0.232 249	0.221 049	0.210 401	0.200 278	41
42	0.248 055	0.235 779	0.224 124	0.213 059	0.202 552	0.192 575	42
43	0.239 957	0.227 806	0.216 284	0.205 358	0.194 996	0.185 168	43
44	0.232 122	0.220 102	0.208 718	0.197 935	0.187 722	0.178 046	44
45	0.224 544	0.212 659	0.201 417	0.190 781	0.180 719	0.171 198	45
46	0.217 213	0.205 468	0.194 371	0.183 885	0.173 977	0.164 614	46
47	0.210 121	0.198 520	0.187 571	0.177 239	0.167 487	0.158 283	47
48	0.203 261	0.191 806	0.181 010	0.170 833	0.161 239	0.152 195	48
49	0.196 625	0.185 320	0.174 678	0.164 668	0.155 224	0.146 341	49
50	0.190 206	0.179 053	0.168 567	0.158 707	0.149 434	0.140 713	50
51	0.183 996	0.172 998	0.162 670	0.152 970	0.143 859	0.135 301	51
52	0.177 989	0.167 148	0.156 980	0.147 441	0.138 492	0.130 097	52
53	0.172 178	0.161 496	0.151 488	0.142 112	0.133 326	0.125 093	53
54	0.166 557	0.156 035	0.146 189	0.136 975	0.128 352	0.120 282	54
55	0.161 119	0.150 758	0.141 075	0.132 024	0.123 564	0.115 656	55
56	0.155 859	0.145 660	0.136 140	0.127 252	0.118 955	0.111 207	56
57	0.150 770	0.140 734	0.131 378	0.122 653	0.114 517	0.106 930	57
58	0.145 848	0.135 975	0.126 782	0.118 220	0.110 245	0.102 817	58
59	0.141 086	0.131 377	0.122 347	0.113 947	0.106 133	0.098 863	59
YRS							
30	0.136 480	0.126 934	0.118 067	0.109 828	0.102 173	0.095 060	60
31	0.127 714	0.118 495	0.109 951	0.102 032	0.094 693	0.087 889	62
32	0.119 511	0.110 616	0.102 393	0.094 790	0.087 759	0.081 258	64
33	0.111 834	0.103 261	0.095 354	0.088 061	0.081 334	0.075 128	66
34	0.104 651	0.096 395	0.088 800	0.081 810	0.075 379	0.069 460	68
35	0.097 929	0.089 986	0.082 696	0.076 003	0.069 860	0.064 219	70
36	0.091 639	0.084 003	0.077 011	0.070 608	0.064 745	0.059 374	72
37	0.085 753	0.078 418	0.071 717	0.065 596	0.060 004	0.054 895	74
38	0.080 245	0.073 204	0.066 787	0.060 940	0.055 611	0.050 754	76
39	0.075 091	0.068 336	0.062 196	0.056 615	0.051 539	0.046 924	78
40	0.070 268	0.063 793	0.057 921	0.052 596	0.047 766	0.043 384	80

169

SECTION 4

	8.25%	8.50%	8.75%	9.00%	9.25%	9.50%	
	ANNUAL RATE	ANNUAL RATE	ANNUAL RATE	ANNUAL RATE	ANNUAL RATE	ANNUAL RATE	
HALF YRS							**HALF YRS**
1	0.960 384	0.959 233	0.958 084	0.956 938	0.955 795	0.954 654	1
2	0.922 338	0.920 127	0.917 925	0.915 730	0.913 543	0.911 364	2
3	0.885 799	0.882 616	0.879 449	0.876 297	0.873 160	0.870 037	3
4	0.850 707	0.846 634	0.842 586	0.838 561	0.834 561	0.830 585	4
5	0.817 005	0.812 119	0.807 268	0.802 451	0.797 669	0.792 921	5
6	0.784 639	0.779 011	0.773 430	0.767 896	0.762 408	0.756 965	6
7	0.753 555	0.747 253	0.741 011	0.734 828	0.728 705	0.722 640	7
8	0.723 702	0.716 789	0.709 951	0.703 185	0.696 492	0.689 871	8
9	0.695 032	0.687 568	0.680 192	0.672 904	0.665 703	0.658 588	9
10	0.667 498	0.659 537	0.651 681	0.643 928	0.636 276	0.628 723	10
11	0.641 054	0.632 650	0.624 365	0.616 199	0.608 149	0.600 213	11
12	0.615 658	0.606 858	0.598 194	0.589 664	0.581 265	0.572 996	12
13	0.591 269	0.582 118	0.573 120	0.564 272	0.555 570	0.547 013	13
14	0.567 845	0.558 387	0.549 097	0.539 973	0.531 011	0.522 208	14
15	0.545 349	0.535 623	0.526 081	0.516 720	0.507 537	0.498 528	15
16	0.523 745	0.513 787	0.504 030	0.494 469	0.485 101	0.475 922	16
17	0.502 996	0.492 841	0.482 903	0.473 176	0.463 657	0.454 341	17
18	0.483 070	0.472 749	0.462 661	0.452 800	0.443 161	0.433 738	18
19	0.463 932	0.453 477	0.443 268	0.433 302	0.423 571	0.414 070	19
20	0.445 553	0.434 989	0.424 688	0.414 643	0.404 847	0.395 293	20
21	0.427 902	0.417 256	0.406 887	0.396 787	0.386 950	0.377 368	21
22	0.410 951	0.400 246	0.389 832	0.379 701	0.369 845	0.360 256	22
23	0.394 671	0.383 929	0.373 492	0.363 350	0.353 496	0.343 920	23
24	0.379 035	0.368 277	0.357 836	0.347 703	0.337 869	0.328 324	24
25	0.364 019	0.353 263	0.342 837	0.332 731	0.322 934	0.313 436	25
26	0.349 599	0.338 862	0.328 467	0.318 402	0.308 658	0.299 223	26
27	0.335 749	0.325 047	0.314 699	0.304 691	0.295 014	0.285 655	27
28	0.322 448	0.311 796	0.301 508	0.291 571	0.281 973	0.272 701	28
29	0.309 674	0.299 085	0.288 870	0.279 015	0.269 508	0.260 335	29
30	0.297 406	0.286 892	0.276 761	0.267 000	0.257 594	0.248 530	30
31	0.285 624	0.275 196	0.265 161	0.255 502	0.246 207	0.237 260	31
32	0.274 309	0.263 977	0.254 046	0.244 500	0.235 323	0.226 501	32
33	0.263 442	0.253 215	0.243 397	0.233 971	0.224 921	0.216 231	33
34	0.253 005	0.242 892	0.233 195	0.223 896	0.214 978	0.206 425	34
35	0.242 982	0.232 990	0.223 420	0.214 254	0.205 475	0.197 065	35
36	0.233 356	0.223 492	0.214 056	0.205 028	0.196 392	0.188 129	36
37	0.224 112	0.214 381	0.205 083	0.196 199	0.187 710	0.179 598	37
38	0.215 233	0.205 641	0.196 487	0.187 750	0.179 412	0.171 454	38
39	0.206 707	0.197 257	0.188 251	0.179 665	0.171 481	0.163 679	39
40	0.198 518	0.189 216	0.180 360	0.171 929	0.163 901	0.156 257	40
41	0.190 653	0.181 502	0.172 800	0.164 525	0.156 656	0.149 171	41
42	0.183 100	0.174 103	0.165 557	0.157 440	0.149 730	0.142 407	42
43	0.175 847	0.167 005	0.158 617	0.150 661	0.143 112	0.135 949	43
44	0.168 880	0.160 197	0.151 969	0.144 173	0.136 785	0.129 784	44
45	0.162 190	0.153 666	0.145 599	0.137 964	0.130 739	0.123 899	45
46	0.155 765	0.147 401	0.139 496	0.132 023	0.124 959	0.118 281	46
47	0.149 594	0.141 392	0.133 649	0.126 338	0.119 435	0.112 917	47
48	0.143 668	0.135 628	0.128 047	0.120 898	0.114 156	0.107 797	48
49	0.137 976	0.130 099	0.122 680	0.115 692	0.109 109	0.102 909	49
50	0.132 510	0.124 795	0.117 537	0.110 710	0.104 286	0.098 242	50
51	0.127 261	0.119 707	0.112 611	0.105 942	0.099 676	0.093 787	51
52	0.122 219	0.114 827	0.107 890	0.101 380	0.095 270	0.089 534	52
53	0.117 377	0.110 146	0.103 368	0.097 014	0.091 058	0.085 474	53
54	0.112 727	0.105 656	0.099 035	0.092 837	0.087 033	0.081 599	54
55	0.108 262	0.101 348	0.094 884	0.088 839	0.083 186	0.077 898	55
56	0.103 973	0.097 217	0.090 907	0.085 013	0.079 509	0.074 366	56
57	0.099 854	0.093 253	0.087 096	0.081 353	0.075 994	0.070 994	57
58	0.095 898	0.089 452	0.083 446	0.077 849	0.072 634	0.067 774	58
59	0.092 099	0.085 805	0.079 948	0.074 497	0.069 424	0.064 701	59
YRS							
30	0.088 450	0.082 307	0.076 597	0.071 289	0.066 355	0.061 767	60
31	0.081 581	0.075 733	0.070 310	0.065 281	0.060 618	0.056 292	62
32	0.075 245	0.069 684	0.064 539	0.059 780	0.055 377	0.051 303	64
33	0.069 402	0.064 118	0.059 242	0.054 743	0.050 589	0.046 756	66
34	0.064 012	0.058 997	0.054 380	0.050 129	0.046 216	0.042 611	68
35	0.059 040	0.054 284	0.049 917	0.045 905	0.042 220	0.038 835	70
36	0.054 455	0.049 949	0.045 820	0.042 037	0.038 570	0.035 392	72
37	0.050 226	0.045 959	0.042 059	0.038 494	0.035 235	0.032 255	74
38	0.046 325	0.042 288	0.038 607	0.035 250	0.032 189	0.029 396	76
39	0.042 728	0.038 911	0.035 438	0.032 280	0.029 406	0.026 791	78
40	0.039 409	0.035 803	0.032 530	0.029 559	0.026 863	0.024 416	80

HALF YRS	9.75% ANNUAL RATE	10.00% ANNUAL RATE	10.50% ANNUAL RATE	11.00% ANNUAL RATE	11.50% ANNUAL RATE	12.00% ANNUAL RATE	HALF YRS
1	0.953 516	0.952 381	0.950 119	0.947 867	0.945 626	0.943 396	1
2	0.909 193	0.907 029	0.902 726	0.898 452	0.894 209	0.889 996	2
3	0.866 930	0.863 838	0.857 697	0.851 614	0.845 588	0.839 619	3
4	0.826 632	0.822 702	0.814 914	0.807 217	0.799 611	0.792 094	4
5	0.788 207	0.783 526	0.774 265	0.765 134	0.756 133	0.747 258	5
6	0.751 568	0.746 215	0.735 643	0.725 246	0.715 019	0.704 961	6
7	0.716 632	0.710 681	0.698 949	0.687 437	0.676 141	0.665 057	7
8	0.683 320	0.676 839	0.664 084	0.651 599	0.639 377	0.627 412	8
9	0.651 557	0.644 609	0.630 959	0.617 629	0.604 612	0.591 898	9
10	0.621 270	0.613 913	0.599 486	0.585 431	0.571 737	0.558 395	10
11	0.592 391	0.584 679	0.569 583	0.554 911	0.540 650	0.526 788	11
12	0.564 854	0.556 837	0.541 171	0.525 982	0.511 253	0.496 969	12
13	0.538 598	0.530 321	0.514 177	0.498 561	0.483 454	0.468 839	13
14	0.513 561	0.505 068	0.488 529	0.472 569	0.457 167	0.442 301	14
15	0.489 689	0.481 017	0.464 161	0.447 933	0.432 309	0.417 265	15
16	0.466 926	0.458 112	0.441 008	0.424 581	0.408 803	0.393 646	16
17	0.445 222	0.436 297	0.419 010	0.402 447	0.386 575	0.371 364	17
18	0.424 526	0.415 521	0.398 109	0.381 466	0.365 555	0.350 344	18
19	0.404 793	0.395 734	0.378 251	0.361 579	0.345 679	0.330 513	19
20	0.385 976	0.376 889	0.359 383	0.342 729	0.326 883	0.311 805	20
21	0.368 035	0.358 942	0.341 457	0.324 862	0.309 109	0.294 155	21
22	0.350 927	0.341 850	0.324 425	0.307 926	0.292 302	0.277 505	22
23	0.334 614	0.325 571	0.308 242	0.291 873	0.276 408	0.261 797	23
24	0.319 060	0.310 068	0.292 866	0.276 657	0.261 379	0.246 979	24
25	0.304 229	0.295 303	0.278 258	0.262 234	0.247 167	0.232 999	25
26	0.290 087	0.281 241	0.264 378	0.248 563	0.233 728	0.219 810	26
27	0.276 603	0.267 848	0.251 190	0.235 605	0.221 019	0.207 368	27
28	0.263 745	0.255 094	0.238 661	0.223 322	0.209 002	0.195 630	28
29	0.251 485	0.242 946	0.226 756	0.211 679	0.197 637	0.184 557	29
30	0.239 795	0.231 377	0.215 445	0.200 644	0.186 891	0.174 110	30
31	0.228 649	0.220 359	0.204 699	0.190 184	0.176 729	0.164 255	31
32	0.218 020	0.209 866	0.194 488	0.180 269	0.167 120	0.154 957	32
33	0.207 886	0.199 873	0.184 787	0.170 871	0.158 033	0.146 186	33
34	0.198 222	0.190 355	0.175 569	0.161 963	0.149 440	0.137 912	34
35	0.189 008	0.181 290	0.166 812	0.153 520	0.141 315	0.130 105	35
36	0.180 222	0.172 657	0.158 491	0.145 516	0.133 631	0.122 741	36
37	0.171 845	0.164 436	0.150 585	0.137 930	0.126 365	0.115 793	37
38	0.163 857	0.156 605	0.143 074	0.130 739	0.119 494	0.109 239	38
39	0.156 240	0.149 148	0.135 937	0.123 924	0.112 997	0.103 056	39
40	0.148 978	0.142 046	0.129 156	0.117 463	0.106 853	0.097 222	40
41	0.142 053	0.135 282	0.122 714	0.111 339	0.101 043	0.091 719	41
42	0.135 449	0.128 840	0.116 593	0.105 535	0.095 549	0.086 527	42
43	0.129 153	0.122 704	0.110 777	0.100 033	0.090 353	0.081 630	43
44	0.123 150	0.116 861	0.105 251	0.094 818	0.085 440	0.077 009	44
45	0.117 425	0.111 297	0.100 001	0.089 875	0.080 795	0.072 650	45
46	0.111 967	0.105 997	0.095 013	0.085 190	0.076 402	0.068 538	46
47	0.106 762	0.100 949	0.090 274	0.080 748	0.072 247	0.064 658	47
48	0.101 799	0.096 142	0.085 771	0.076 539	0.068 319	0.060 998	48
49	0.097 067	0.091 564	0.081 492	0.072 549	0.064 604	0.057 546	49
50	0.092 555	0.087 204	0.077 427	0.068 767	0.061 092	0.054 288	50
51	0.088 253	0.083 051	0.073 565	0.065 182	0.057 770	0.051 215	51
52	0.084 151	0.079 096	0.069 896	0.061 783	0.054 629	0.048 316	52
53	0.080 239	0.075 330	0.066 409	0.058 563	0.051 658	0.045 582	53
54	0.076 509	0.071 743	0.063 097	0.055 509	0.048 849	0.043 001	54
55	0.072 953	0.068 326	0.059 949	0.052 616	0.046 193	0.040 567	55
56	0.069 562	0.065 073	0.056 959	0.049 873	0.043 682	0.038 271	56
57	0.066 328	0.061 974	0.054 118	0.047 273	0.041 307	0.036 105	57
58	0.063 245	0.059 023	0.051 418	0.044 808	0.039 061	0.034 061	58
59	0.060 305	0.056 212	0.048 854	0.042 472	0.036 937	0.032 133	59
YRS							
30	0.057 502	0.053 536	0.046 417	0.040 258	0.034 928	0.030 314	60
31	0.052 280	0.048 558	0.041 901	0.036 170	0.031 233	0.026 980	62
32	0.047 533	0.044 044	0.037 826	0.032 497	0.027 929	0.024 012	64
33	0.043 217	0.039 949	0.034 146	0.029 197	0.024 974	0.021 370	66
34	0.039 292	0.036 235	0.030 825	0.026 232	0.022 332	0.019 020	68
35	0.035 724	0.032 866	0.027 826	0.023 568	0.019 970	0.016 927	70
36	0.032 480	0.029 811	0.025 119	0.021 175	0.017 857	0.015 065	72
37	0.029 531	0.027 039	0.022 676	0.019 025	0.015 968	0.013 408	74
38	0.026 849	0.024 525	0.020 470	0.017 093	0.014 279	0.011 933	76
39	0.024 411	0.022 245	0.018 479	0.015 357	0.012 768	0.010 620	78
40	0.022 194	0.020 177	0.016 681	0.013 798	0.011 417	0.009 452	80

PRESENT VALUE

	12.50% ANNUAL RATE	13.00% ANNUAL RATE	13.50% ANNUAL RATE	14.00% ANNUAL RATE	14.50% ANNUAL RATE	15.00% ANNUAL RATE	
HALF YRS							HALF YRS
1	0.941 176	0.938 967	0.936 768	0.934 579	0.932 401	0.930 233	1
2	0.885 813	0.881 659	0.877 535	0.873 439	0.869 371	0.865 333	2
3	0.833 706	0.827 849	0.822 046	0.816 298	0.810 603	0.804 961	3
4	0.784 665	0.777 323	0.770 067	0.762 895	0.755 807	0.748 801	4
5	0.738 508	0.729 881	0.721 374	0.712 986	0.704 715	0.696 559	5
6	0.695 067	0.685 334	0.675 760	0.666 342	0.657 077	0.647 962	6
7	0.654 180	0.643 506	0.633 031	0.622 750	0.612 659	0.602 755	7
8	0.615 699	0.604 231	0.593 003	0.582 009	0.571 244	0.560 702	8
9	0.579 481	0.567 353	0.555 506	0.543 934	0.532 628	0.521 583	9
10	0.545 394	0.532 726	0.520 381	0.508 349	0.496 623	0.485 194	10
11	0.513 312	0.500 212	0.487 476	0.475 093	0.463 052	0.451 343	11
12	0.483 117	0.469 683	0.456 652	0.444 012	0.431 750	0.419 854	12
13	0.454 699	0.441 017	0.427 777	0.414 964	0.402 564	0.390 562	13
14	0.427 952	0.414 100	0.400 728	0.387 817	0.375 351	0.363 313	14
15	0.402 778	0.388 827	0.375 389	0.362 446	0.349 978	0.337 966	15
16	0.379 085	0.365 095	0.351 653	0.338 735	0.326 320	0.314 387	16
17	0.356 786	0.342 813	0.329 417	0.316 574	0.304 261	0.292 453	17
18	0.335 799	0.321 890	0.308 587	0.295 864	0.283 693	0.272 049	18
19	0.316 046	0.302 244	0.289 075	0.276 508	0.264 516	0.253 069	19
20	0.297 455	0.283 797	0.270 796	0.258 419	0.246 635	0.235 413	20
21	0.279 958	0.266 476	0.253 673	0.241 513	0.229 962	0.218 989	21
22	0.263 490	0.250 212	0.237 633	0.225 713	0.214 417	0.203 711	22
23	0.247 990	0.234 941	0.222 607	0.210 947	0.199 923	0.189 498	23
24	0.233 402	0.220 602	0.208 531	0.197 147	0.186 408	0.176 277	24
25	0.219 673	0.207 138	0.195 345	0.184 249	0.173 807	0.163 979	25
26	0.206 751	0.194 496	0.182 993	0.172 195	0.162 058	0.152 539	26
27	0.194 589	0.182 625	0.171 422	0.160 930	0.151 103	0.141 896	27
28	0.183 143	0.171 479	0.160 583	0.150 402	0.140 889	0.131 997	28
29	0.172 370	0.161 013	0.150 429	0.140 563	0.131 365	0.122 788	29
30	0.162 230	0.151 186	0.140 917	0.131 367	0.122 484	0.114 221	30
31	0.152 687	0.141 959	0.132 007	0.122 773	0.114 205	0.106 252	31
32	0.143 706	0.133 295	0.123 660	0.114 741	0.106 484	0.098 839	32
33	0.135 252	0.125 159	0.115 840	0.107 235	0.099 286	0.091 943	33
34	0.127 296	0.117 520	0.108 516	0.100 219	0.092 575	0.085 529	34
35	0.119 808	0.110 348	0.101 654	0.093 663	0.086 317	0.079 562	35
36	0.112 761	0.103 613	0.095 226	0.087 535	0.080 482	0.074 011	36
37	0.106 128	0.097 289	0.089 205	0.081 809	0.075 041	0.068 847	37
38	0.099 885	0.091 351	0.083 564	0.076 457	0.069 969	0.064 044	38
39	0.094 009	0.085 776	0.078 280	0.071 455	0.065 239	0.059 576	39
40	0.088 479	0.080 541	0.073 331	0.066 780	0.060 829	0.055 419	40
41	0.083 275	0.075 625	0.068 694	0.062 412	0.056 717	0.051 553	41
42	0.078 376	0.071 010	0.064 350	0.058 329	0.052 883	0.047 956	42
43	0.073 766	0.066 676	0.060 281	0.054 513	0.049 308	0.044 610	43
44	0.069 427	0.062 606	0.056 469	0.050 946	0.045 975	0.041 498	44
45	0.065 343	0.058 785	0.052 899	0.047 613	0.042 867	0.038 603	45
46	0.061 499	0.055 197	0.049 554	0.044 499	0.039 969	0.035 910	46
47	0.057 882	0.051 828	0.046 420	0.041 587	0.037 267	0.033 404	47
48	0.054 477	0.048 665	0.043 485	0.038 867	0.034 748	0.031 074	48
49	0.051 272	0.045 695	0.040 736	0.036 324	0.032 399	0.028 906	49
50	0.048 256	0.042 906	0.038 160	0.033 948	0.030 209	0.026 889	50
51	0.045 418	0.040 287	0.035 747	0.031 727	0.028 167	0.025 013	51
52	0.042 746	0.037 829	0.033 487	0.029 651	0.026 263	0.023 268	52
53	0.040 232	0.035 520	0.031 369	0.027 711	0.024 487	0.021 645	53
54	0.037 865	0.033 352	0.029 386	0.025 899	0.022 832	0.020 135	54
55	0.035 638	0.031 316	0.027 527	0.024 204	0.021 289	0.018 730	55
56	0.033 541	0.029 405	0.025 787	0.022 621	0.019 850	0.017 423	56
57	0.031 568	0.027 610	0.024 156	0.021 141	0.018 508	0.016 208	57
58	0.029 711	0.025 925	0.022 629	0.019 758	0.017 257	0.015 077	58
59	0.027 964	0.024 343	0.021 198	0.018 465	0.016 090	0.014 025	59
YRS							
30	0.026 319	0.022 857	0.019 858	0.017 257	0.015 002	0.013 046	60
31	0.023 313	0.020 152	0.017 426	0.015 073	0.013 043	0.011 290	62
32	0.020 651	0.017 767	0.015 292	0.013 166	0.011 339	0.009 769	64
33	0.018 293	0.015 665	0.013 419	0.011 499	0.009 858	0.008 454	66
34	0.016 204	0.013 811	0.011 776	0.010 044	0.008 570	0.007 315	68
35	0.014 354	0.012 177	0.010 334	0.008 773	0.007 451	0.006 330	70
36	0.012 715	0.010 736	0.009 068	0.007 662	0.006 477	0.005 478	72
37	0.011 263	0.009 465	0.007 957	0.006 693	0.005 631	0.004 740	74
38	0.009 977	0.008 345	0.006 983	0.005 846	0.004 896	0.004 102	76
39	0.008 838	0.007 358	0.006 128	0.005 106	0.004 256	0.003 549	78
40	0.007 829	0.006 487	0.005 377	0.004 460	0.003 700	0.003 071	80

	15.50%	16.00%	16.50%	17.00%	17.50%	18.00%	
	ANNUAL RATE	ANNUAL RATE	ANNUAL RATE	ANNUAL RATE	ANNUAL RATE	ANNUAL RATE	
HALF YRS							HALF YRS
1	0.928 074	0.925 926	0.923 788	0.921 659	0.919 540	0.917 431	1
2	0.861 322	0.857 339	0.853 383	0.849 455	0.845 554	0.841 680	2
3	0.799 371	0.793 832	0.788 345	0.782 908	0.777 521	0.772 183	3
4	0.741 875	0.735 030	0.728 263	0.721 574	0.714 962	0.708 425	4
5	0.688 515	0.680 583	0.672 760	0.665 045	0.657 436	0.649 931	5
6	0.638 993	0.630 170	0.621 488	0.612 945	0.604 539	0.596 267	6
7	0.593 033	0.583 490	0.574 123	0.564 926	0.555 898	0.547 034	7
8	0.550 379	0.540 269	0.530 367	0.520 669	0.511 171	0.501 866	8
9	0.510 792	0.500 249	0.489 947	0.479 880	0.470 042	0.460 428	9
10	0.474 053	0.463 193	0.452 607	0.442 285	0.432 222	0.422 411	10
11	0.439 957	0.428 883	0.418 112	0.407 636	0.397 446	0.387 533	11
12	0.408 312	0.397 114	0.386 247	0.375 702	0.365 468	0.355 535	12
13	0.378 944	0.367 698	0.356 810	0.346 269	0.336 062	0.326 179	13
14	0.351 688	0.340 461	0.329 617	0.319 142	0.309 023	0.299 246	14
15	0.326 393	0.315 242	0.304 496	0.294 140	0.284 159	0.274 538	15
16	0.302 917	0.291 890	0.281 289	0.271 097	0.261 295	0.251 870	16
17	0.281 129	0.270 269	0.259 852	0.249 859	0.240 272	0.231 073	17
18	0.260 909	0.250 249	0.240 048	0.230 285	0.220 939	0.211 994	18
19	0.242 143	0.231 712	0.221 753	0.212 244	0.203 163	0.194 490	19
20	0.224 727	0.214 548	0.204 853	0.195 616	0.186 816	0.178 431	20
21	0.208 563	0.198 656	0.189 240	0.180 292	0.171 785	0.163 698	21
22	0.193 562	0.183 941	0.174 818	0.166 167	0.157 963	0.150 182	22
23	0.179 640	0.170 315	0.161 495	0.153 150	0.145 254	0.137 781	23
24	0.166 719	0.157 699	0.149 187	0.141 152	0.133 567	0.126 405	24
25	0.154 728	0.146 018	0.137 817	0.130 094	0.122 820	0.115 968	25
26	0.143 599	0.135 202	0.127 314	0.119 902	0.112 938	0.106 393	26
27	0.133 270	0.125 187	0.117 611	0.110 509	0.103 851	0.097 608	27
28	0.123 685	0.115 914	0.108 647	0.101 851	0.095 495	0.089 548	28
29	0.114 789	0.107 328	0.100 367	0.093 872	0.087 811	0.082 155	29
30	0.106 532	0.099 377	0.092 718	0.086 518	0.080 746	0.075 371	30
31	0.098 870	0.092 016	0.085 651	0.079 740	0.074 249	0.069 148	31
32	0.091 759	0.085 200	0.079 124	0.073 493	0.068 275	0.063 438	32
33	0.085 159	0.078 889	0.073 094	0.067 736	0.062 782	0.058 200	33
34	0.079 034	0.073 045	0.067 523	0.062 429	0.057 730	0.053 395	34
35	0.073 349	0.067 635	0.062 377	0.057 539	0.053 085	0.048 986	35
36	0.068 073	0.062 625	0.057 623	0.053 031	0.048 814	0.044 941	36
37	0.063 177	0.057 986	0.053 231	0.048 876	0.044 887	0.041 231	37
38	0.058 633	0.053 690	0.049 174	0.045 047	0.041 275	0.037 826	38
39	0.054 416	0.049 713	0.045 427	0.041 518	0.037 954	0.034 703	39
40	0.050 502	0.046 031	0.041 965	0.038 266	0.034 900	0.031 838	40
41	0.046 870	0.042 621	0.038 766	0.035 268	0.032 092	0.029 209	41
42	0.043 499	0.039 464	0.035 812	0.032 505	0.029 510	0.026 797	42
43	0.040 370	0.036 541	0.033 083	0.029 959	0.027 136	0.024 584	43
44	0.037 466	0.033 834	0.030 561	0.027 612	0.024 952	0.022 555	44
45	0.034 771	0.031 328	0.028 232	0.025 448	0.022 945	0.020 692	45
46	0.032 270	0.029 007	0.026 081	0.023 455	0.021 099	0.018 984	46
47	0.029 949	0.026 859	0.024 093	0.021 617	0.019 401	0.017 416	47
48	0.027 795	0.024 869	0.022 257	0.019 924	0.017 840	0.015 978	48
49	0.025 796	0.023 027	0.020 560	0.018 363	0.016 405	0.014 659	49
50	0.023 941	0.021 321	0.018 993	0.016 924	0.015 085	0.013 449	50
51	0.022 219	0.019 742	0.017 546	0.015 599	0.013 871	0.012 338	51
52	0.020 621	0.018 280	0.016 209	0.014 377	0.012 755	0.011 319	52
53	0.019 137	0.016 925	0.014 973	0.013 250	0.011 729	0.010 385	53
54	0.017 761	0.015 672	0.013 832	0.012 212	0.010 785	0.009 527	54
55	0.016 484	0.014 511	0.012 778	0.011 255	0.009 917	0.008 741	55
56	0.015 298	0.013 436	0.011 804	0.010 374	0.009 119	0.008 019	56
57	0.014 198	0.012 441	0.010 905	0.009 561	0.008 386	0.007 357	57
58	0.013 176	0.011 519	0.010 074	0.008 812	0.007 711	0.006 749	58
59	0.012 229	0.010 666	0.009 306	0.008 122	0.007 090	0.006 192	59
YRS							
30	0.011 349	0.009 876	0.008 597	0.007 485	0.006 520	0.005 681	60
31	0.009 775	0.008 467	0.007 336	0.006 359	0.005 513	0.004 781	62
32	0.008 420	0.007 259	0.006 261	0.005 401	0.004 662	0.004 024	64
33	0.007 252	0.006 223	0.005 343	0.004 588	0.003 942	0.003 387	66
34	0.006 246	0.005 336	0.004 559	0.003 897	0.003 333	0.002 851	68
35	0.005 380	0.004 574	0.003 891	0.003 311	0.002 818	0.002 400	70
36	0.004 634	0.003 922	0.003 320	0.002 812	0.002 383	0.002 020	72
37	0.003 991	0.003 362	0.002 834	0.002 389	0.002 015	0.001 700	74
38	0.003 438	0.002 883	0.002 418	0.002 029	0.001 704	0.001 431	76
39	0.002 961	0.002 471	0.002 064	0.001 724	0.001 441	0.001 204	78
40	0.002 550	0.002 119	0.001 761	0.001 464	0.001 218	0.001 014	80

PRESENT VALUE

HALF YRS	18.50% ANNUAL RATE	19.00% ANNUAL RATE	19.50% ANNUAL RATE	20.00% ANNUAL RATE	20.50% ANNUAL RATE	21.00% ANNUAL RATE	HALF YRS
1	0.915 332	0.913 242	0.911 162	0.909 091	0.907 029	0.904 977	1
2	0.837 832	0.834 011	0.830 216	0.826 446	0.822 702	0.818 984	2
3	0.766 895	0.761 654	0.756 461	0.751 315	0.746 215	0.741 162	3
4	0.701 963	0.695 574	0.689 258	0.683 013	0.676 839	0.670 735	4
5	0.642 529	0.635 228	0.628 026	0.620 921	0.613 913	0.607 000	5
6	0.588 127	0.580 117	0.572 233	0.564 474	0.556 837	0.549 321	6
7	0.538 332	0.529 787	0.521 397	0.513 158	0.505 068	0.497 123	7
8	0.492 752	0.483 824	0.475 077	0.466 507	0.458 112	0.449 885	8
9	0.451 032	0.441 848	0.432 872	0.424 098	0.415 521	0.407 136	9
10	0.412 844	0.403 514	0.394 416	0.385 543	0.376 889	0.368 449	10
11	0.377 889	0.368 506	0.359 377	0.350 494	0.341 850	0.333 438	11
12	0.345 894	0.336 535	0.327 450	0.318 631	0.310 068	0.301 754	12
13	0.316 608	0.307 338	0.298 360	0.289 664	0.281 241	0.273 080	13
14	0.289 801	0.280 674	0.271 855	0.263 331	0.255 094	0.247 132	14
15	0.265 264	0.256 323	0.247 703	0.239 392	0.231 377	0.223 648	15
16	0.242 805	0.234 085	0.225 698	0.217 629	0.209 866	0.202 397	16
17	0.222 247	0.213 777	0.205 647	0.197 845	0.190 355	0.183 164	17
18	0.203 430	0.195 230	0.187 378	0.179 859	0.172 657	0.165 760	18
19	0.186 206	0.178 292	0.170 732	0.163 508	0.156 605	0.150 009	19
20	0.170 440	0.162 824	0.155 564	0.148 644	0.142 046	0.135 755	20
21	0.156 009	0.148 697	0.141 744	0.135 131	0.128 840	0.122 855	21
22	0.142 800	0.135 797	0.129 152	0.122 846	0.116 861	0.111 181	22
23	0.130 709	0.124 015	0.117 678	0.111 678	0.105 997	0.100 616	23
24	0.119 642	0.113 256	0.107 224	0.101 526	0.096 142	0.091 055	24
25	0.109 513	0.103 430	0.097 698	0.092 296	0.087 204	0.082 403	25
26	0.100 240	0.094 457	0.089 019	0.083 905	0.079 096	0.074 573	26
27	0.091 753	0.086 262	0.081 111	0.076 278	0.071 743	0.067 487	27
28	0.083 985	0.078 778	0.073 905	0.069 343	0.065 073	0.061 074	28
29	0.076 874	0.071 943	0.067 339	0.063 039	0.059 023	0.055 271	29
30	0.070 365	0.065 702	0.061 357	0.057 309	0.053 536	0.050 019	30
31	0.064 407	0.060 002	0.055 906	0.052 099	0.048 558	0.045 266	31
32	0.058 954	0.054 796	0.050 940	0.047 362	0.044 044	0.040 964	32
33	0.053 963	0.050 042	0.046 414	0.043 057	0.039 949	0.037 072	33
34	0.049 394	0.045 700	0.042 291	0.039 143	0.036 235	0.033 549	34
35	0.045 212	0.041 736	0.038 534	0.035 584	0.032 866	0.030 361	35
36	0.041 384	0.038 115	0.035 110	0.032 349	0.029 811	0.027 476	36
37	0.037 880	0.034 808	0.031 991	0.029 408	0.027 039	0.024 865	37
38	0.034 672	0.031 788	0.029 149	0.026 735	0.024 525	0.022 503	38
39	0.031 737	0.029 030	0.026 560	0.024 304	0.022 245	0.020 364	39
40	0.029 050	0.026 512	0.024 200	0.022 095	0.020 177	0.018 429	40
41	0.026 590	0.024 211	0.022 050	0.020 086	0.018 301	0.016 678	41
42	0.024 339	0.022 111	0.020 091	0.018 260	0.016 600	0.015 093	42
43	0.022 278	0.020 193	0.018 306	0.016 600	0.015 056	0.013 659	43
44	0.020 392	0.018 441	0.016 680	0.015 091	0.013 657	0.012 361	44
45	0.018 665	0.016 841	0.015 198	0.013 719	0.012 387	0.011 187	45
46	0.017 085	0.015 380	0.013 848	0.012 472	0.011 235	0.010 124	46
47	0.015 638	0.014 045	0.012 618	0.011 338	0.010 191	0.009 162	47
48	0.014 314	0.012 827	0.011 497	0.010 307	0.009 243	0.008 291	48
49	0.013 102	0.011 714	0.010 476	0.009 370	0.008 384	0.007 503	49
50	0.011 993	0.010 698	0.009 545	0.008 519	0.007 604	0.006 790	50
51	0.010 978	0.009 770	0.008 697	0.007 744	0.006 897	0.006 145	51
52	0.010 048	0.008 922	0.007 924	0.007 040	0.006 256	0.005 561	52
53	0.009 197	0.008 148	0.007 220	0.006 400	0.005 675	0.005 033	53
54	0.008 419	0.007 441	0.006 579	0.005 818	0.005 147	0.004 554	54
55	0.007 706	0.006 796	0.005 994	0.005 289	0.004 668	0.004 122	55
56	0.007 053	0.006 206	0.005 462	0.004 809	0.004 234	0.003 730	56
57	0.006 456	0.005 668	0.004 977	0.004 371	0.003 841	0.003 376	57
58	0.005 910	0.005 176	0.004 535	0.003 974	0.003 484	0.003 055	58
59	0.005 409	0.004 727	0.004 132	0.003 613	0.003 160	0.002 765	59
YRS							
30	0.004 951	0.004 317	0.003 765	0.003 284	0.002 866	0.002 502	60
31	0.004 148	0.003 600	0.003 125	0.002 714	0.002 358	0.002 049	62
32	0.003 476	0.003 003	0.002 595	0.002 243	0.001 940	0.001 678	64
33	0.002 912	0.002 504	0.002 154	0.001 854	0.001 596	0.001 374	66
34	0.002 440	0.002 089	0.001 789	0.001 532	0.001 313	0.001 126	68
35	0.002 044	0.001 742	0.001 485	0.001 266	0.001 080	0.000 922	70
36	0.001 713	0.001 453	0.001 233	0.001 046	0.000 889	0.000 755	72
37	0.001 435	0.001 212	0.001 023	0.000 865	0.000 731	0.000 618	74
38	0.001 202	0.001 010	0.000 850	0.000 715	0.000 601	0.000 506	76
39	0.001 007	0.000 843	0.000 705	0.000 591	0.000 495	0.000 415	78
40	0.000 844	0.000 703	0.000 586	0.000 488	0.000 407	0.000 340	80

PRESENT VALUE

HALF YRS	21.50% ANNUAL RATE	22.00% ANNUAL RATE	22.50% ANNUAL RATE	23.00% ANNUAL RATE	23.50% ANNUAL RATE	24.00% ANNUAL RATE	HALF YRS
1	0.902 935	0.900 901	0.898 876	0.896 861	0.894 855	0.892 857	1
2	0.815 291	0.811 622	0.807 979	0.804 360	0.800 765	0.797 194	2
3	0.736 154	0.731 191	0.726 273	0.721 399	0.716 568	0.711 780	3
4	0.664 699	0.658 731	0.652 830	0.646 994	0.641 224	0.635 518	4
5	0.600 180	0.593 451	0.586 813	0.580 264	0.573 802	0.567 427	5
6	0.541 923	0.534 641	0.527 473	0.520 416	0.513 470	0.506 631	6
7	0.489 321	0.481 658	0.474 133	0.466 741	0.459 481	0.452 349	7
8	0.441 825	0.433 926	0.426 187	0.418 602	0.411 168	0.403 883	8
9	0.398 939	0.390 925	0.383 089	0.375 428	0.367 936	0.360 610	9
10	0.360 216	0.352 184	0.344 350	0.336 706	0.329 249	0.321 973	10
11	0.325 251	0.317 283	0.309 528	0.301 979	0.294 630	0.287 476	11
12	0.293 681	0.285 841	0.278 227	0.270 833	0.263 651	0.256 675	12
13	0.265 174	0.257 514	0.250 092	0.242 900	0.235 929	0.229 174	13
14	0.239 435	0.231 995	0.224 802	0.217 847	0.211 123	0.204 620	14
15	0.216 194	0.209 004	0.202 069	0.195 379	0.188 924	0.182 696	15
16	0.195 209	0.188 292	0.181 635	0.175 227	0.169 059	0.163 122	16
17	0.176 261	0.169 633	0.163 267	0.157 155	0.151 284	0.145 644	17
18	0.159 152	0.152 822	0.146 757	0.140 946	0.135 377	0.130 040	18
19	0.143 704	0.137 678	0.131 917	0.126 409	0.121 143	0.116 107	19
20	0.129 755	0.124 034	0.118 577	0.113 371	0.108 405	0.103 667	20
21	0.117 161	0.111 742	0.106 586	0.101 678	0.097 007	0.092 560	21
22	0.105 788	0.100 669	0.095 808	0.091 191	0.086 807	0.082 643	22
23	0.095 520	0.090 693	0.086 119	0.081 786	0.077 680	0.073 788	23
24	0.086 248	0.081 705	0.077 410	0.073 351	0.069 512	0.065 882	24
25	0.077 877	0.073 608	0.069 582	0.065 785	0.062 203	0.058 823	25
26	0.070 317	0.066 314	0.062 546	0.059 000	0.055 663	0.052 521	26
27	0.063 492	0.059 742	0.056 221	0.052 915	0.049 810	0.046 894	27
28	0.057 329	0.053 822	0.050 536	0.047 457	0.044 573	0.041 869	28
29	0.051 764	0.048 488	0.045 425	0.042 563	0.039 886	0.037 383	29
30	0.046 740	0.043 683	0.040 832	0.038 173	0.035 692	0.033 378	30
31	0.042 203	0.039 354	0.036 703	0.034 236	0.031 939	0.029 802	31
32	0.038 107	0.035 454	0.032 991	0.030 705	0.028 581	0.026 609	32
33	0.034 408	0.031 940	0.029 655	0.027 538	0.025 576	0.023 758	33
34	0.031 068	0.028 775	0.026 656	0.024 698	0.022 887	0.021 212	34
35	0.028 052	0.025 924	0.023 961	0.022 150	0.020 480	0.018 940	35
36	0.025 329	0.023 355	0.021 538	0.019 866	0.018 327	0.016 910	36
37	0.022 871	0.021 040	0.019 360	0.017 817	0.016 400	0.015 098	37
38	0.020 651	0.018 955	0.017 402	0.015 979	0.014 676	0.013 481	38
39	0.018 646	0.017 077	0.015 642	0.014 331	0.013 132	0.012 036	39
40	0.016 836	0.015 384	0.014 060	0.012 853	0.011 752	0.010 747	40
41	0.015 202	0.013 860	0.012 639	0.011 527	0.010 516	0.009 595	41
42	0.013 727	0.012 486	0.011 361	0.010 338	0.009 410	0.008 567	42
43	0.012 394	0.011 249	0.010 212	0.009 272	0.008 421	0.007 649	43
44	0.011 191	0.010 134	0.009 179	0.008 316	0.007 535	0.006 830	44
45	0.010 105	0.009 130	0.008 251	0.007 458	0.006 743	0.006 098	45
46	0.009 124	0.008 225	0.007 417	0.006 689	0.006 034	0.005 445	46
47	0.008 238	0.007 410	0.006 667	0.005 999	0.005 400	0.004 861	47
48	0.007 439	0.006 676	0.005 992	0.005 380	0.004 832	0.004 340	48
49	0.006 717	0.006 014	0.005 386	0.004 825	0.004 324	0.003 875	49
50	0.006 065	0.005 418	0.004 842	0.004 328	0.003 869	0.003 460	50
51	0.005 476	0.004 881	0.004 352	0.003 881	0.003 462	0.003 089	51
52	0.004 945	0.004 397	0.003 912	0.003 481	0.003 098	0.002 758	52
53	0.004 465	0.003 962	0.003 516	0.003 122	0.002 773	0.002 463	53
54	0.004 031	0.003 569	0.003 161	0.002 800	0.002 481	0.002 199	54
55	0.003 640	0.003 215	0.002 841	0.002 511	0.002 220	0.001 963	55
56	0.003 287	0.002 897	0.002 554	0.002 252	0.001 987	0.001 753	56
57	0.002 968	0.002 610	0.002 296	0.002 020	0.001 778	0.001 565	57
58	0.002 680	0.002 351	0.002 063	0.001 812	0.001 591	0.001 398	58
59	0.002 419	0.002 118	0.001 855	0.001 625	0.001 424	0.001 248	59

YRS

YRS							
30	0.002 185	0.001 908	0.001 667	0.001 457	0.001 274	0.001 114	60
31	0.001 781	0.001 549	0.001 347	0.001 172	0.001 020	0.000 888	62
32	0.001 452	0.001 257	0.001 088	0.000 943	0.000 817	0.000 708	64
33	0.001 184	0.001 020	0.000 879	0.000 758	0.000 654	0.000 564	66
34	0.000 965	0.000 828	0.000 711	0.000 610	0.000 524	0.000 450	68
35	0.000 787	0.000 672	0.000 574	0.000 491	0.000 419	0.000 359	70
36	0.000 642	0.000 545	0.000 464	0.000 395	0.000 336	0.000 286	72
37	0.000 523	0.000 443	0.000 375	0.000 317	0.000 269	0.000 228	74
38	0.000 426	0.000 359	0.000 303	0.000 255	0.000 215	0.000 182	76
39	0.000 348	0.000 292	0.000 245	0.000 205	0.000 172	0.000 145	78
40	0.000 283	0.000 237	0.000 198	0.000 165	0.000 138	0.000 115	80

SECTION 4

YRS	5.25% ANNUAL RATE	5.50% ANNUAL RATE	5.75% ANNUAL RATE	6.00% ANNUAL RATE	6.25% ANNUAL RATE	6.50% ANNUAL RATE	YRS
1	0.950 119	0.947 867	0.945 626	0.943 396	0.941 176	0.938 967	1
2	0.902 726	0.898 452	0.894 209	0.889 996	0.885 813	0.881 659	2
3	0.857 697	0.851 614	0.845 588	0.839 619	0.833 706	0.827 849	3
4	0.814 914	0.807 217	0.799 611	0.792 094	0.784 665	0.777 323	4
5	0.774 265	0.765 134	0.756 133	0.747 258	0.738 508	0.729 881	5
6	0.735 643	0.725 246	0.715 019	0.704 961	0.695 067	0.685 334	6
7	0.698 949	0.687 437	0.676 141	0.665 057	0.654 180	0.643 506	7
8	0.664 084	0.651 599	0.639 377	0.627 412	0.615 699	0.604 231	8
9	0.630 959	0.617 629	0.604 612	0.591 898	0.579 481	0.567 353	9
10	0.599 486	0.585 431	0.571 737	0.558 395	0.545 394	0.532 726	10
11	0.569 583	0.554 911	0.540 650	0.526 788	0.513 312	0.500 212	11
12	0.541 171	0.525 982	0.511 253	0.496 969	0.483 117	0.469 683	12
13	0.514 177	0.498 561	0.483 454	0.468 839	0.454 699	0.441 017	13
14	0.488 529	0.472 569	0.457 167	0.442 301	0.427 952	0.414 100	14
15	0.464 161	0.447 933	0.432 309	0.417 265	0.402 778	0.388 827	15
16	0.441 008	0.424 581	0.408 803	0.393 646	0.379 085	0.365 095	16
17	0.419 010	0.402 447	0.386 575	0.371 364	0.356 786	0.342 813	17
18	0.398 109	0.381 466	0.365 555	0.350 344	0.335 799	0.321 890	18
19	0.378 251	0.361 579	0.345 679	0.330 513	0.316 046	0.302 244	19
20	0.359 383	0.342 729	0.326 883	0.311 805	0.297 455	0.283 797	20
21	0.341 457	0.324 862	0.309 109	0.294 155	0.279 958	0.266 476	21
22	0.324 425	0.307 926	0.292 302	0.277 505	0.263 490	0.250 212	22
23	0.308 242	0.291 873	0.276 408	0.261 797	0.247 990	0.234 941	23
24	0.292 866	0.276 657	0.261 379	0.246 979	0.233 402	0.220 602	24
25	0.278 258	0.262 234	0.247 167	0.232 999	0.219 673	0.207 138	25
26	0.264 378	0.248 563	0.233 728	0.219 810	0.206 751	0.194 496	26
27	0.251 190	0.235 605	0.221 019	0.207 368	0.194 589	0.182 625	27
28	0.238 661	0.223 322	0.209 002	0.195 630	0.183 143	0.171 479	28
29	0.226 756	0.211 679	0.197 637	0.184 557	0.172 370	0.161 013	29
30	0.215 445	0.200 644	0.186 891	0.174 110	0.162 230	0.151 186	30
31	0.204 699	0.190 184	0.176 729	0.164 255	0.152 687	0.141 959	31
32	0.194 488	0.180 269	0.167 120	0.154 957	0.143 706	0.133 295	32
33	0.184 787	0.170 871	0.158 033	0.146 186	0.135 252	0.125 159	33
34	0.175 569	0.161 963	0.149 440	0.137 912	0.127 296	0.117 520	34
35	0.166 812	0.153 520	0.141 315	0.130 105	0.119 808	0.110 348	35
36	0.158 491	0.145 516	0.133 631	0.122 741	0.112 761	0.103 613	36
37	0.150 585	0.137 930	0.126 365	0.115 793	0.106 128	0.097 289	37
38	0.143 074	0.130 739	0.119 494	0.109 239	0.099 885	0.091 351	38
39	0.135 937	0.123 924	0.112 997	0.103 056	0.094 009	0.085 776	39
40	0.129 156	0.117 463	0.106 853	0.097 222	0.088 479	0.080 541	40
41	0.122 714	0.111 339	0.101 043	0.091 719	0.083 275	0.075 625	41
42	0.116 593	0.105 535	0.095 549	0.086 527	0.078 376	0.071 010	42
43	0.110 777	0.100 033	0.090 353	0.081 630	0.073 766	0.066 676	43
44	0.105 251	0.094 818	0.085 440	0.077 009	0.069 427	0.062 606	44
45	0.100 001	0.089 875	0.080 795	0.072 650	0.065 343	0.058 785	45
46	0.095 013	0.085 190	0.076 402	0.068 538	0.061 499	0.055 197	46
47	0.090 274	0.080 748	0.072 247	0.064 658	0.057 882	0.051 828	47
48	0.085 771	0.076 539	0.068 319	0.060 998	0.054 477	0.048 665	48
49	0.081 492	0.072 549	0.064 604	0.057 546	0.051 272	0.045 695	49
50	0.077 427	0.068 767	0.061 092	0.054 288	0.048 256	0.042 906	50

PRESENT VALUE

YRS	6.75% ANNUAL RATE	7.00% ANNUAL RATE	7.25% ANNUAL RATE	7.50% ANNUAL RATE	7.75% ANNUAL RATE	8.00% ANNUAL RATE	YRS
1	0.936 768	0.934 579	0.932 401	0.930 233	0.928 074	0.925 926	1
2	0.877 535	0.873 439	0.869 371	0.865 333	0.861 322	0.857 339	2
3	0.822 046	0.816 298	0.810 603	0.804 961	0.799 371	0.793 832	3
4	0.770 067	0.762 895	0.755 807	0.748 801	0.741 875	0.735 030	4
5	0.721 374	0.712 986	0.704 715	0.696 559	0.688 515	0.680 583	5
6	0.675 760	0.666 342	0.657 077	0.647 962	0.638 993	0.630 170	6
7	0.633 031	0.622 750	0.612 659	0.602 755	0.593 033	0.583 490	7
8	0.593 003	0.582 009	0.571 244	0.560 702	0.550 379	0.540 269	8
9	0.555 506	0.543 934	0.532 628	0.521 583	0.510 792	0.500 249	9
10	0.520 381	0.508 349	0.496 623	0.485 194	0.474 053	0.463 193	10
11	0.487 476	0.475 093	0.463 052	0.451 343	0.439 957	0.428 883	11
12	0.456 652	0.444 012	0.431 750	0.419 854	0.408 312	0.397 114	12
13	0.427 777	0.414 964	0.402 564	0.390 562	0.378 944	0.367 698	13
14	0.400 728	0.387 817	0.375 351	0.363 313	0.351 688	0.340 461	14
15	0.375 389	0.362 446	0.349 978	0.337 966	0.326 393	0.315 242	15
16	0.351 653	0.338 735	0.326 320	0.314 387	0.302 917	0.291 890	16
17	0.329 417	0.316 574	0.304 261	0.292 453	0.281 129	0.270 269	17
18	0.308 587	0.295 864	0.283 693	0.272 049	0.260 909	0.250 249	18
19	0.289 075	0.276 508	0.264 516	0.253 069	0.242 143	0.231 712	19
20	0.270 796	0.258 419	0.246 635	0.235 413	0.224 727	0.214 548	20
21	0.253 673	0.241 513	0.229 962	0.218 989	0.208 563	0.198 656	21
22	0.237 633	0.225 713	0.214 417	0.203 711	0.193 562	0.183 941	22
23	0.222 607	0.210 947	0.199 923	0.189 498	0.179 640	0.170 315	23
24	0.208 531	0.197 147	0.186 408	0.176 277	0.166 719	0.157 699	24
25	0.195 345	0.184 249	0.173 807	0.163 979	0.154 728	0.146 018	25
26	0.182 993	0.172 195	0.162 058	0.152 539	0.143 599	0.135 202	26
27	0.171 422	0.160 930	0.151 103	0.141 896	0.133 270	0.125 187	27
28	0.160 583	0.150 402	0.140 889	0.131 997	0.123 685	0.115 914	28
29	0.150 429	0.140 563	0.131 365	0.122 788	0.114 789	0.107 328	29
30	0.140 917	0.131 367	0.122 484	0.114 221	0.106 532	0.099 377	30
31	0.132 007	0.122 773	0.114 205	0.106 252	0.098 870	0.092 016	31
32	0.123 660	0.114 741	0.106 484	0.098 839	0.091 759	0.085 200	32
33	0.115 840	0.107 235	0.099 286	0.091 943	0.085 159	0.078 889	33
34	0.108 516	0.100 219	0.092 575	0.085 529	0.079 034	0.073 045	34
35	0.101 654	0.093 663	0.086 317	0.079 562	0.073 349	0.067 635	35
36	0.095 226	0.087 535	0.080 482	0.074 011	0.068 073	0.062 625	36
37	0.089 205	0.081 809	0.075 041	0.068 847	0.063 177	0.057 986	37
38	0.083 564	0.076 457	0.069 969	0.064 044	0.058 633	0.053 690	38
39	0.078 280	0.071 455	0.065 239	0.059 576	0.054 416	0.049 713	39
40	0.073 331	0.066 780	0.060 829	0.055 419	0.050 502	0.046 031	40
41	0.068 694	0.062 412	0.056 717	0.051 553	0.046 870	0.042 621	41
42	0.064 350	0.058 329	0.052 883	0.047 956	0.043 499	0.039 464	42
43	0.060 281	0.054 513	0.049 308	0.044 610	0.040 370	0.036 541	43
44	0.056 469	0.050 946	0.045 975	0.041 498	0.037 466	0.033 834	44
45	0.052 899	0.047 613	0.042 867	0.038 603	0.034 771	0.031 328	45
46	0.049 554	0.044 499	0.039 969	0.035 910	0.032 270	0.029 007	46
47	0.046 420	0.041 587	0.037 267	0.033 404	0.029 949	0.026 859	47
48	0.043 485	0.038 867	0.034 748	0.031 074	0.027 795	0.024 869	48
49	0.040 736	0.036 324	0.032 399	0.028 906	0.025 796	0.023 027	49
50	0.038 160	0.033 948	0.030 209	0.026 889	0.023 941	0.021 321	50

SECTION 4

YRS	8.25% ANNUAL RATE	8.50% ANNUAL RATE	8.75% ANNUAL RATE	9.00% ANNUAL RATE	9.25% ANNUAL RATE	9.50% ANNUAL RATE	YRS
1	0.923 788	0.921 659	0.919 540	0.917 431	0.915 332	0.913 242	1
2	0.853 383	0.849 455	0.845 554	0.841 680	0.837 832	0.834 011	2
3	0.788 345	0.782 908	0.777 521	0.772 183	0.766 895	0.761 654	3
4	0.728 263	0.721 574	0.714 962	0.708 425	0.701 963	0.695 574	4
5	0.672 760	0.665 045	0.657 436	0.649 931	0.642 529	0.635 228	5
6	0.621 488	0.612 945	0.604 539	0.596 267	0.588 127	0.580 117	6
7	0.574 123	0.564 926	0.555 898	0.547 034	0.538 332	0.529 787	7
8	0.530 367	0.520 669	0.511 171	0.501 866	0.492 752	0.483 824	8
9	0.489 947	0.479 880	0.470 042	0.460 428	0.451 032	0.441 848	9
10	0.452 607	0.442 285	0.432 222	0.422 411	0.412 844	0.403 514	10
11	0.418 112	0.407 636	0.397 446	0.387 533	0.377 889	0.368 506	11
12	0.386 247	0.375 702	0.365 468	0.355 535	0.345 894	0.336 535	12
13	0.356 810	0.346 269	0.336 062	0.326 179	0.316 608	0.307 338	13
14	0.329 617	0.319 142	0.309 023	0.299 246	0.289 801	0.280 674	14
15	0.304 496	0.294 140	0.284 159	0.274 538	0.265 264	0.256 323	15
16	0.281 289	0.271 097	0.261 295	0.251 870	0.242 805	0.234 085	16
17	0.259 852	0.249 859	0.240 272	0.231 073	0.222 247	0.213 777	17
18	0.240 048	0.230 285	0.220 939	0.211 994	0.203 430	0.195 230	18
19	0.221 753	0.212 244	0.203 163	0.194 490	0.186 206	0.178 292	19
20	0.204 853	0.195 616	0.186 816	0.178 431	0.170 440	0.162 824	20
21	0.189 240	0.180 292	0.171 785	0.163 698	0.156 009	0.148 697	21
22	0.174 818	0.166 167	0.157 963	0.150 182	0.142 800	0.135 797	22
23	0.161 495	0.153 150	0.145 254	0.137 781	0.130 709	0.124 015	23
24	0.149 187	0.141 152	0.133 567	0.126 405	0.119 642	0.113 256	24
25	0.137 817	0.130 094	0.122 820	0.115 968	0.109 513	0.103 430	25
26	0.127 314	0.119 902	0.112 938	0.106 393	0.100 240	0.094 457	26
27	0.117 611	0.110 509	0.103 851	0.097 608	0.091 753	0.086 262	27
28	0.108 647	0.101 851	0.095 495	0.089 548	0.083 985	0.078 778	28
29	0.100 367	0.093 872	0.087 811	0.082 155	0.076 874	0.071 943	29
30	0.092 718	0.086 518	0.080 746	0.075 371	0.070 365	0.065 702	30
31	0.085 651	0.079 740	0.074 249	0.069 148	0.064 407	0.060 002	31
32	0.079 124	0.073 493	0.068 275	0.063 438	0.058 954	0.054 796	32
33	0.073 094	0.067 736	0.062 782	0.058 200	0.053 963	0.050 042	33
34	0.067 523	0.062 429	0.057 730	0.053 395	0.049 394	0.045 700	34
35	0.062 377	0.057 539	0.053 085	0.048 986	0.045 212	0.041 736	35
36	0.057 623	0.053 031	0.048 814	0.044 941	0.041 384	0.038 115	36
37	0.053 231	0.048 876	0.044 887	0.041 231	0.037 880	0.034 808	37
38	0.049 174	0.045 047	0.041 275	0.037 826	0.034 672	0.031 788	38
39	0.045 427	0.041 518	0.037 954	0.034 703	0.031 737	0.029 030	39
40	0.041 965	0.038 266	0.034 900	0.031 838	0.029 050	0.026 512	40
41	0.038 766	0.035 268	0.032 092	0.029 209	0.026 590	0.024 211	41
42	0.035 812	0.032 505	0.029 510	0.026 797	0.024 339	0.022 111	42
43	0.033 083	0.029 959	0.027 136	0.024 584	0.022 278	0.020 193	43
44	0.030 561	0.027 612	0.024 952	0.022 555	0.020 392	0.018 441	44
45	0.028 232	0.025 448	0.022 945	0.020 692	0.018 665	0.016 841	45
46	0.026 081	0.023 455	0.021 099	0.018 984	0.017 085	0.015 380	46
47	0.024 093	0.021 617	0.019 401	0.017 416	0.015 638	0.014 045	47
48	0.022 257	0.019 924	0.017 840	0.015 978	0.014 314	0.012 827	48
49	0.020 560	0.018 363	0.016 405	0.014 659	0.013 102	0.011 714	49
50	0.018 993	0.016 924	0.015 085	0.013 449	0.011 993	0.010 698	50

PRESENT VALUE

YRS	9.75% ANNUAL RATE	10.00% ANNUAL RATE	10.25% ANNUAL RATE	10.50% ANNUAL RATE	10.75% ANNUAL RATE	11.00% ANNUAL RATE	YRS
1	0.911 162	0.909 091	0.907 029	0.904 977	0.902 935	0.900 901	1
2	0.830 216	0.826 446	0.822 702	0.818 984	0.815 291	0.811 622	2
3	0.756 461	0.751 315	0.746 215	0.741 162	0.736 154	0.731 191	3
4	0.689 258	0.683 013	0.676 839	0.670 735	0.664 699	0.658 731	4
5	0.628 026	0.620 921	0.613 913	0.607 000	0.600 180	0.593 451	5
6	0.572 233	0.564 474	0.556 837	0.549 321	0.541 923	0.534 641	6
7	0.521 397	0.513 158	0.505 068	0.497 123	0.489 321	0.481 658	7
8	0.475 077	0.466 507	0.458 112	0.449 885	0.441 825	0.433 926	8
9	0.432 872	0.424 098	0.415 521	0.407 136	0.398 939	0.390 925	9
10	0.394 416	0.385 543	0.376 889	0.368 449	0.360 216	0.352 184	10
11	0.359 377	0.350 494	0.341 850	0.333 438	0.325 251	0.317 283	11
12	0.327 450	0.318 631	0.310 068	0.301 754	0.293 681	0.285 841	12
13	0.298 360	0.289 664	0.281 241	0.273 080	0.265 174	0.257 514	13
14	0.271 855	0.263 331	0.255 094	0.247 132	0.239 435	0.231 995	14
15	0.247 703	0.239 392	0.231 377	0.223 648	0.216 194	0.209 004	15
16	0.225 698	0.217 629	0.209 866	0.202 397	0.195 209	0.188 292	16
17	0.205 647	0.197 845	0.190 355	0.183 164	0.176 261	0.169 633	17
18	0.187 378	0.179 859	0.172 657	0.165 760	0.159 152	0.152 822	18
19	0.170 732	0.163 508	0.156 605	0.150 009	0.143 704	0.137 678	19
20	0.155 564	0.148 644	0.142 046	0.135 755	0.129 755	0.124 034	20
21	0.141 744	0.135 131	0.128 840	0.122 855	0.117 161	0.111 742	21
22	0.129 152	0.122 846	0.116 861	0.111 181	0.105 788	0.100 669	22
23	0.117 678	0.111 678	0.105 997	0.100 616	0.095 520	0.090 693	23
24	0.107 224	0.101 526	0.096 142	0.091 055	0.086 248	0.081 705	24
25	0.097 698	0.092 296	0.087 204	0.082 403	0.077 877	0.073 608	25
26	0.089 019	0.083 905	0.079 096	0.074 573	0.070 317	0.066 314	26
27	0.081 111	0.076 278	0.071 743	0.067 487	0.063 492	0.059 742	27
28	0.073 905	0.069 343	0.065 073	0.061 074	0.057 329	0.053 822	28
29	0.067 339	0.063 039	0.059 023	0.055 271	0.051 764	0.048 488	29
30	0.061 357	0.057 309	0.053 536	0.050 019	0.046 740	0.043 683	30
31	0.055 906	0.052 099	0.048 558	0.045 266	0.042 203	0.039 354	31
32	0.050 940	0.047 362	0.044 044	0.040 964	0.038 107	0.035 454	32
33	0.046 414	0.043 057	0.039 949	0.037 072	0.034 408	0.031 940	33
34	0.042 291	0.039 143	0.036 235	0.033 549	0.031 068	0.028 775	34
35	0.038 534	0.035 584	0.032 866	0.030 361	0.028 052	0.025 924	35
36	0.035 110	0.032 349	0.029 811	0.027 476	0.025 329	0.023 355	36
37	0.031 991	0.029 408	0.027 039	0.024 865	0.022 871	0.021 040	37
38	0.029 149	0.026 735	0.024 525	0.022 503	0.020 651	0.018 955	38
39	0.026 560	0.024 304	0.022 245	0.020 364	0.018 646	0.017 077	39
40	0.024 200	0.022 095	0.020 177	0.018 429	0.016 836	0.015 384	40
41	0.022 050	0.020 086	0.018 301	0.016 678	0.015 202	0.013 860	41
42	0.020 091	0.018 260	0.016 600	0.015 093	0.013 727	0.012 486	42
43	0.018 306	0.016 600	0.015 056	0.013 659	0.012 394	0.011 249	43
44	0.016 680	0.015 091	0.013 657	0.012 361	0.011 191	0.010 134	44
45	0.015 198	0.013 719	0.012 387	0.011 187	0.010 105	0.009 130	45
46	0.013 848	0.012 472	0.011 235	0.010 124	0.009 124	0.008 225	46
47	0.012 618	0.011 338	0.010 191	0.009 162	0.008 238	0.007 410	47
48	0.011 497	0.010 307	0.009 243	0.008 291	0.007 439	0.006 676	48
49	0.010 476	0.009 370	0.008 384	0.007 503	0.006 717	0.006 014	49
50	0.009 545	0.008 519	0.007 604	0.006 790	0.006 065	0.005 418	50

SECTION 4

YRS	11.25% ANNUAL RATE	11.50% ANNUAL RATE	11.75% ANNUAL RATE	12.00% ANNUAL RATE	12.25% ANNUAL RATE	12.50% ANNUAL RATE	YRS
1	0.898 876	0.896 861	0.894 855	0.892 857	0.890 869	0.888 889	1
2	0.807 979	0.804 360	0.800 765	0.797 194	0.793 647	0.790 123	2
3	0.726 273	0.721 399	0.716 568	0.711 780	0.707 035	0.702 332	3
4	0.652 830	0.646 994	0.641 224	0.635 518	0.629 875	0.624 295	4
5	0.586 813	0.580 264	0.573 802	0.567 427	0.561 136	0.554 929	5
6	0.527 473	0.520 416	0.513 470	0.506 631	0.499 899	0.493 270	6
7	0.474 133	0.466 741	0.459 481	0.452 349	0.445 344	0.438 462	7
8	0.426 187	0.418 602	0.411 168	0.403 883	0.396 743	0.389 744	8
9	0.383 089	0.375 428	0.367 936	0.360 610	0.353 446	0.346 439	9
10	0.344 350	0.336 706	0.329 249	0.321 973	0.314 874	0.307 946	10
11	0.309 528	0.301 979	0.294 630	0.287 476	0.280 511	0.273 730	11
12	0.278 227	0.270 833	0.263 651	0.256 675	0.249 899	0.243 315	12
13	0.250 092	0.242 900	0.235 929	0.229 174	0.222 627	0.216 280	13
14	0.224 802	0.217 847	0.211 123	0.204 620	0.198 331	0.192 249	14
15	0.202 069	0.195 379	0.188 924	0.132 696	0.176 687	0.170 888	15
16	0.181 635	0.175 227	0.169 059	0.163 122	0.157 405	0.151 901	16
17	0.163 267	0.157 155	0.151 284	0.145 644	0.140 227	0.135 023	17
18	0.146 757	0.140 946	0.135 377	0.130 040	0.124 924	0.120 020	18
19	0.131 917	0.126 409	0.121 143	0.116 107	0.111 291	0.106 685	19
20	0.118 577	0.113 371	0.108 405	0.103 667	0.099 145	0.094 831	20
21	0.106 586	0.101 678	0.097 007	0.092 560	0.088 326	0.084 294	21
22	0.095 808	0.091 191	0.086 807	0.082 643	0.078 687	0.074 928	22
23	0.086 119	0.081 786	0.077 680	0.073 788	0.070 099	0.066 603	23
24	0.077 410	0.073 351	0.069 512	0.065 882	0.062 449	0.059 202	24
25	0.069 582	0.065 785	0.062 203	0.058 823	0.055 634	0.052 624	25
26	0.062 546	0.059 000	0.055 663	0.052 521	0.049 563	0.046 777	26
27	0.056 221	0.052 915	0.049 810	0.046 894	0.044 154	0.041 580	27
28	0.050 536	0.047 457	0.044 573	0.041 869	0.039 335	0.036 960	28
29	0.045 425	0.042 563	0.039 886	0.037 383	0.035 043	0.032 853	29
30	0.040 832	0.038 173	0.035 692	0.033 378	0.031 218	0.029 203	30
31	0.036 703	0.034 236	0.031 939	0.029 802	0.027 811	0.025 958	31
32	0.032 991	0.030 705	0.028 581	0.026 609	0.024 776	0.023 074	32
33	0.029 655	0.027 538	0.025 576	0.023 758	0.022 072	0.020 510	33
34	0.026 656	0.024 698	0.022 887	0.021 212	0.019 664	0.018 231	34
35	0.023 961	0.022 150	0.020 480	0.018 940	0.017 518	0.016 205	35
36	0.021 538	0.019 866	0.018 327	0.016 910	0.015 606	0.014 405	36
37	0.019 360	0.017 817	0.016 400	0.015 098	0.013 903	0.012 804	37
38	0.017 402	0.015 979	0.014 676	0.013 481	0.012 386	0.011 382	38
39	0.015 642	0.014 331	0.013 132	0.012 036	0.011 034	0.010 117	39
40	0.014 060	0.012 853	0.011 752	0.010 747	0.009 830	0.008 993	40
41	0.012 639	0.011 527	0.010 516	0.009 595	0.008 757	0.007 994	41
42	0.011 361	0.010 338	0.009 410	0.008 567	0.007 801	0.007 105	42
43	0.010 212	0.009 272	0.008 421	0.007 649	0.006 950	0.006 316	43
44	0.009 179	0.008 316	0.007 535	0.006 830	0.006 192	0.005 614	44
45	0.008 251	0.007 458	0.006 743	0.006 098	0.005 516	0.004 990	45
46	0.007 417	0.006 689	0.006 034	0.005 445	0.004 914	0.004 436	46
47	0.006 667	0.005 999	0.005 400	0.004 861	0.004 378	0.003 943	47
48	0.005 992	0.005 380	0.004 832	0.004 340	0.003 900	0.003 505	48
49	0.005 386	0.004 825	0.004 324	0.003 875	0.003 474	0.003 115	49
50	0.004 842	0.004 328	0.003 869	0.003 460	0.003 095	0.002 769	50

PRESENT VALUE

YRS	12.75% ANNUAL RATE	13.00% ANNUAL RATE	13.25% ANNUAL RATE	13.50% ANNUAL RATE	13.75% ANNUAL RATE	14.00% ANNUAL RATE	YRS
1	0.886 918	0.884 956	0.883 002	0.881 057	0.879 121	0.877 193	1
2	0.786 623	0.783 147	0.779 693	0.776 262	0.772 854	0.769 468	2
3	0.697 670	0.693 050	0.688 471	0.683 931	0.679 432	0.674 972	3
4	0.618 776	0.613 319	0.607 921	0.602 583	0.597 303	0.592 080	4
5	0.548 804	0.542 760	0.536 796	0.530 910	0.525 101	0.519 369	5
6	0.486 744	0.480 319	0.473 992	0.467 762	0.461 627	0.455 587	6
7	0.431 702	0.425 061	0.418 536	0.412 125	0.405 826	0.399 637	7
8	0.382 884	0.376 160	0.369 568	0.363 106	0.356 770	0.350 559	8
9	0.339 587	0.332 885	0.326 329	0.319 917	0.313 644	0.307 508	9
10	0.301 186	0.294 588	0.288 150	0.281 865	0.275 731	0.269 744	10
11	0.267 127	0.260 698	0.254 437	0.248 339	0.242 401	0.236 617	11
12	0.236 920	0.230 706	0.224 668	0.218 801	0.213 100	0.207 559	12
13	0.210 128	0.204 165	0.198 382	0.192 776	0.187 341	0.182 069	13
14	0.186 367	0.180 677	0.175 172	0.169 847	0.164 695	0.159 710	14
15	0.165 292	0.159 891	0.154 677	0.149 645	0.144 787	0.140 096	15
16	0.146 600	0.141 496	0.136 580	0.131 846	0.127 285	0.122 892	16
17	0.130 023	0.125 218	0.120 601	0.116 164	0.111 899	0.107 800	17
18	0.115 319	0.110 812	0.106 491	0.102 347	0.098 373	0.094 561	18
19	0.102 279	0.098 064	0.094 032	0.090 173	0.086 482	0.082 948	19
20	0.090 713	0.086 782	0.083 030	0.079 448	0.076 028	0.072 762	20
21	0.080 455	0.076 798	0.073 316	0.069 998	0.066 838	0.063 826	21
22	0.071 357	0.067 963	0.064 738	0.061 672	0.058 758	0.055 988	22
23	0.063 288	0.060 144	0.057 164	0.054 337	0.051 656	0.049 112	23
24	0.056 131	0.053 225	0.050 476	0.047 874	0.045 412	0.043 081	24
25	0.049 784	0.047 102	0.044 570	0.042 180	0.039 922	0.037 790	25
26	0.044 154	0.041 683	0.039 356	0.037 163	0.035 096	0.033 149	26
27	0.039 161	0.036 888	0.034 751	0.032 742	0.030 854	0.029 078	27
28	0.034 733	0.032 644	0.030 685	0.028 848	0.027 124	0.025 507	28
29	0.030 805	0.028 889	0.027 095	0.025 417	0.023 846	0.022 375	29
30	0.027 321	0.025 565	0.023 925	0.022 394	0.020 963	0.019 627	30
31	0.024 232	0.022 624	0.021 126	0.019 730	0.018 429	0.017 217	31
32	0.021 492	0.020 021	0.018 654	0.017 383	0.016 201	0.015 102	32
33	0.019 061	0.017 718	0.016 472	0.015 316	0.014 243	0.013 248	33
34	0.016 906	0.015 680	0.014 545	0.013 494	0.012 521	0.011 621	34
35	0.014 994	0.013 876	0.012 843	0.011 889	0.011 008	0.010 194	35
36	0.013 299	0.012 279	0.011 340	0.010 475	0.009 677	0.008 942	36
37	0.011 795	0.010 867	0.010 014	0.009 229	0.008 507	0.007 844	37
38	0.010 461	0.009 617	0.008 842	0.008 131	0.007 479	0.006 880	38
39	0.009 278	0.008 510	0.007 807	0.007 164	0.006 575	0.006 035	39
40	0.008 229	0.007 531	0.006 894	0.006 312	0.005 780	0.005 294	40
41	0.007 298	0.006 665	0.006 087	0.005 561	0.005 082	0.004 644	41
42	0.006 473	0.005 898	0.005 375	0.004 900	0.004 467	0.004 074	42
43	0.005 741	0.005 219	0.004 746	0.004 317	0.003 927	0.003 573	43
44	0.005 092	0.004 619	0.004 191	0.003 803	0.003 453	0.003 135	44
45	0.004 516	0.004 088	0.003 701	0.003 351	0.003 035	0.002 750	45
46	0.004 005	0.003 617	0.003 268	0.002 953	0.002 668	0.002 412	46
47	0.003 552	0.003 201	0.002 885	0.002 601	0.002 346	0.002 116	47
48	0.003 151	0.002 833	0.002 548	0.002 292	0.002 062	0.001 856	48
49	0.002 794	0.002 507	0.002 250	0.002 019	0.001 813	0.001 628	49
50	0.002 478	0.002 219	0.001 987	0.001 779	0.001 594	0.001 428	50

YRS	14.25% ANNUAL RATE	14.50% ANNUAL RATE	14.75% ANNUAL RATE	15.00% ANNUAL RATE	15.25% ANNUAL RATE	15.50% ANNUAL RATE	YRS
1	0.875 274	0.873 362	0.871 460	0.869 565	0.867 679	0.865 801	1
2	0.766 104	0.762 762	0.759 442	0.756 144	0.752 867	0.749 611	2
3	0.670 550	0.666 168	0.661 823	0.657 516	0.653 247	0.649 014	3
4	0.586 915	0.581 806	0.576 752	0.571 753	0.566 808	0.561 917	4
5	0.513 711	0.508 127	0.502 616	0.497 177	0.491 808	0.486 508	5
6	0.449 638	0.443 779	0.438 010	0.432 328	0.426 731	0.421 219	6
7	0.393 556	0.387 580	0.381 708	0.375 937	0.370 266	0.364 692	7
8	0.344 469	0.338 498	0.332 643	0.326 902	0.321 272	0.315 751	8
9	0.301 505	0.295 631	0.289 885	0.284 262	0.278 761	0.273 377	9
10	0.263 899	0.258 193	0.252 623	0.247 185	0.241 875	0.236 690	10
11	0.230 984	0.225 496	0.220 151	0.214 943	0.209 870	0.204 927	11
12	0.202 174	0.196 940	0.191 853	0.186 907	0.182 100	0.177 426	12
13	0.176 958	0.172 000	0.167 192	0.162 528	0.158 004	0.153 615	13
14	0.154 886	0.150 218	0.145 701	0.141 329	0.137 097	0.133 000	14
15	0.135 568	0.131 195	0.126 972	0.122 894	0.118 956	0.115 152	15
16	0.118 659	0.114 581	0.110 651	0.106 865	0.103 216	0.099 698	16
17	0.103 859	0.100 071	0.096 428	0.092 926	0.089 558	0.086 319	17
18	0.090 905	0.087 398	0.084 033	0.080 805	0.077 708	0.074 735	18
19	0.079 567	0.076 330	0.073 232	0.070 265	0.067 425	0.064 706	19
20	0.069 643	0.066 664	0.063 818	0.061 100	0.058 503	0.056 022	20
21	0.060 956	0.058 222	0.055 615	0.053 131	0.050 762	0.048 504	21
22	0.053 354	0.050 849	0.048 466	0.046 201	0.044 045	0.041 995	22
23	0.046 699	0.044 409	0.042 237	0.040 174	0.038 217	0.036 359	23
24	0.040 874	0.038 785	0.036 807	0.034 934	0.033 160	0.031 480	24
25	0.035 776	0.033 874	0.032 076	0.030 378	0.028 772	0.027 255	25
26	0.031 314	0.029 584	0.027 953	0.026 415	0.024 965	0.023 598	26
27	0.027 408	0.025 838	0.024 360	0.022 970	0.021 662	0.020 431	27
28	0.023 990	0.022 566	0.021 229	0.019 974	0.018 795	0.017 689	28
29	0.020 998	0.019 708	0.018 500	0.017 369	0.016 308	0.015 315	29
30	0.018 379	0.017 212	0.016 122	0.015 103	0.014 151	0.013 260	30
31	0.016 086	0.015 032	0.014 050	0.013 133	0.012 278	0.011 480	31
32	0.014 080	0.013 129	0.012 244	0.011 420	0.010 653	0.009 940	32
33	0.012 324	0.011 466	0.010 670	0.009 931	0.009 244	0.008 606	33
34	0.010 787	0.010 014	0.009 298	0.008 635	0.008 021	0.007 451	34
35	0.009 441	0.008 746	0.008 103	0.007 509	0.006 959	0.006 451	35
36	0.008 264	0.007 638	0.007 062	0.006 529	0.006 038	0.005 585	36
37	0.007 233	0.006 671	0.006 154	0.005 678	0.005 239	0.004 836	37
38	0.006 331	0.005 826	0.005 363	0.004 937	0.004 546	0.004 187	38
39	0.005 541	0.005 088	0.004 674	0.004 293	0.003 945	0.003 625	39
40	0.004 850	0.004 444	0.004 073	0.003 733	0.003 423	0.003 138	40
41	0.004 245	0.003 881	0.003 549	0.003 246	0.002 970	0.002 717	41
42	0.003 716	0.003 390	0.003 093	0.002 823	0.002 577	0.002 353	42
43	0.003 252	0.002 960	0.002 695	0.002 455	0.002 236	0.002 037	43
44	0.002 847	0.002 586	0.002 349	0.002 134	0.001 940	0.001 764	44
45	0.002 492	0.002 258	0.002 047	0.001 856	0.001 683	0.001 527	45
46	0.002 181	0.001 972	0.001 784	0.001 614	0.001 461	0.001 322	46
47	0.001 909	0.001 722	0.001 555	0.001 403	0.001 267	0.001 145	47
48	0.001 671	0.001 504	0.001 355	0.001 220	0.001 100	0.000 991	48
49	0.001 462	0.001 314	0.001 181	0.001 061	0.000 954	0.000 858	49
50	0.001 280	0.001 147	0.001 029	0.000 923	0.000 828	0.000 743	50

YRS	15.75% ANNUAL RATE	16.00% ANNUAL RATE	16.25% ANNUAL RATE	16.50% ANNUAL RATE	16.75% ANNUAL RATE	17.00% ANNUAL RATE	YRS
1	0.863 931	0.862 069	0.860 215	0.858 369	0.856 531	0.854 701	1
2	0.746 377	0.743 163	0.739 970	0.736 798	0.733 645	0.730 514	2
3	0.644 818	0.640 658	0.636 533	0.632 444	0.628 390	0.624 371	3
4	0.557 078	0.552 291	0.547 556	0.542 871	0.538 236	0.533 650	4
5	0.481 277	0.476 113	0.471 015	0.465 983	0.461 016	0.456 111	5
6	0.415 790	0.410 442	0.405 175	0.399 986	0.394 874	0.389 839	6
7	0.359 214	0.353 830	0.348 537	0.343 335	0.338 222	0.333 195	7
8	0.310 336	0.305 025	0.299 817	0.294 708	0.289 698	0.284 782	8
9	0.268 109	0.262 953	0.257 907	0.252 969	0.248 135	0.243 404	9
10	0.231 627	0.226 684	0.221 856	0.217 140	0.212 535	0.208 037	10
11	0.200 110	0.195 417	0.190 844	0.186 387	0.182 043	0.177 810	11
12	0.172 881	0.168 463	0.164 166	0.159 989	0.155 926	0.151 974	12
13	0.149 357	0.145 227	0.141 218	0.137 329	0.133 555	0.129 892	13
14	0.129 035	0.125 195	0.121 478	0.117 879	0.114 394	0.111 019	14
15	0.111 477	0.107 927	0.104 497	0.101 184	0.097 982	0.094 888	15
16	0.096 308	0.093 041	0.089 890	0.086 853	0.083 925	0.081 101	16
17	0.083 204	0.080 207	0.077 325	0.074 552	0.071 884	0.069 317	17
18	0.071 882	0.069 144	0.066 516	0.063 993	0.061 571	0.059 245	18
19	0.062 101	0.059 607	0.057 218	0.054 930	0.052 737	0.050 637	19
20	0.053 651	0.051 385	0.049 220	0.047 150	0.045 171	0.043 280	20
21	0.046 351	0.044 298	0.042 340	0.040 472	0.038 691	0.036 991	21
22	0.040 044	0.038 188	0.036 421	0.034 740	0.033 140	0.031 616	22
23	0.034 595	0.032 920	0.031 330	0.029 820	0.028 385	0.027 022	23
24	0.029 888	0.028 380	0.026 951	0.025 596	0.024 313	0.023 096	24
25	0.025 821	0.024 465	0.023 183	0.021 971	0.020 825	0.019 740	25
26	0.022 308	0.021 091	0.019 943	0.018 859	0.017 837	0.016 872	26
27	0.019 272	0.018 182	0.017 155	0.016 188	0.015 278	0.014 421	27
28	0.016 650	0.015 674	0.014 757	0.013 895	0.013 086	0.012 325	28
29	0.014 384	0.013 512	0.012 694	0.011 927	0.011 209	0.010 534	29
30	0.012 427	0.011 648	0.010 920	0.010 238	0.009 600	0.009 004	30
31	0.010 736	0.010 042	0.009 393	0.008 788	0.008 223	0.007 696	31
32	0.009 275	0.008 657	0.008 080	0.007 543	0.007 043	0.006 577	32
33	0.008 013	0.007 463	0.006 951	0.006 475	0.006 033	0.005 622	33
34	0.006 923	0.006 433	0.005 979	0.005 558	0.005 167	0.004 805	34
35	0.005 981	0.005 546	0.005 143	0.004 771	0.004 426	0.004 107	35
36	0.005 167	0.004 781	0.004 424	0.004 095	0.003 791	0.003 510	36
37	0.004 464	0.004 121	0.003 806	0.003 515	0.003 247	0.003 000	37
38	0.003 857	0.003 553	0.003 274	0.003 017	0.002 781	0.002 564	38
39	0.003 332	0.003 063	0.002 816	0.002 590	0.002 382	0.002 192	39
40	0.002 878	0.002 640	0.002 423	0.002 223	0.002 040	0.001 873	40
41	0.002 487	0.002 276	0.002 084	0.001 908	0.001 748	0.001 601	41
42	0.002 148	0.001 962	0.001 793	0.001 638	0.001 497	0.001 368	42
43	0.001 856	0.001 692	0.001 542	0.001 406	0.001 282	0.001 170	43
44	0.001 604	0.001 458	0.001 327	0.001 207	0.001 098	0.001 000	44
45	0.001 385	0.001 257	0.001 141	0.001 036	0.000 941	0.000 854	45
46	0.001 197	0.001 084	0.000 982	0.000 889	0.000 806	0.000 730	46
47	0.001 034	0.000 934	0.000 844	0.000 763	0.000 690	0.000 624	47
48	0.000 893	0.000 805	0.000 726	0.000 655	0.000 591	0.000 533	48
49	0.000 772	0.000 694	0.000 625	0.000 562	0.000 506	0.000 456	49
50	0.000 667	0.000 599	0.000 537	0.000 483	0.000 434	0.000 390	50

SECTION 4

YRS	17.25% ANNUAL RATE	17.50% ANNUAL RATE	17.75% ANNUAL RATE	18.00% ANNUAL RATE	18.25% ANNUAL RATE	18.50% ANNUAL RATE	YRS
1	0.852 878	0.851 064	0.849 257	0.847 458	0.845 666	0.843 882	1
2	0.727 402	0.724 310	0.721 237	0.718 184	0.715 151	0.712 137	2
3	0.620 385	0.616 434	0.612 516	0.608 631	0.604 779	0.600 959	3
4	0.529 113	0.524 624	0.520 183	0.515 789	0.511 441	0.507 139	4
5	0.451 269	0.446 489	0.441 769	0.437 109	0.432 508	0.427 965	5
6	0.384 878	0.379 991	0.375 176	0.370 432	0.365 757	0.361 152	6
7	0.328 254	0.323 396	0.318 620	0.313 925	0.309 309	0.304 770	7
8	0.279 961	0.275 231	0.270 591	0.266 038	0.261 572	0.257 189	8
9	0.238 773	0.234 239	0.229 801	0.225 456	0.221 202	0.217 038	9
10	0.203 644	0.199 352	0.195 160	0.191 064	0.187 063	0.183 154	10
11	0.173 684	0.169 662	0.165 741	0.161 919	0.158 193	0.154 560	11
12	0.148 131	0.144 393	0.140 757	0.137 220	0.133 778	0.130 431	12
13	0.126 338	0.122 888	0.119 539	0.116 288	0.113 132	0.110 068	13
14	0.107 751	0.104 585	0.101 519	0.098 549	0.095 672	0.092 884	14
15	0.091 898	0.089 009	0.086 216	0.083 516	0.080 906	0.078 384	15
16	0.078 378	0.075 752	0.073 219	0.070 776	0.068 420	0.066 146	16
17	0.066 847	0.064 470	0.062 182	0.059 980	0.057 860	0.055 820	17
18	0.057 012	0.054 868	0.052 808	0.050 830	0.048 930	0.047 105	18
19	0.048 625	0.046 696	0.044 848	0.043 077	0.041 379	0.039 751	19
20	0.041 471	0.039 741	0.038 087	0.036 506	0.034 993	0.033 545	20
21	0.035 370	0.033 822	0.032 346	0.030 937	0.029 592	0.028 308	21
22	0.030 166	0.028 785	0.027 470	0.026 218	0.025 025	0.023 889	22
23	0.025 728	0.024 498	0.023 329	0.022 218	0.021 163	0.020 159	23
24	0.021 943	0.020 849	0.019 812	0.018 829	0.017 897	0.017 012	24
25	0.018 715	0.017 744	0.016 826	0.015 957	0.015 135	0.014 356	25
26	0.015 961	0.015 101	0.014 289	0.013 523	0.012 799	0.012 115	26
27	0.013 613	0.012 852	0.012 135	0.011 460	0.010 824	0.010 224	27
28	0.011 610	0.010 938	0.010 306	0.009 712	0.009 153	0.008 628	28
29	0.009 902	0.009 309	0.008 753	0.008 230	0.007 740	0.007 281	29
30	0.008 445	0.007 923	0.007 433	0.006 975	0.006 546	0.006 144	30
31	0.007 203	0.006 743	0.006 313	0.005 911	0.005 536	0.005 185	31
32	0.006 143	0.005 738	0.005 361	0.005 009	0.004 681	0.004 375	32
33	0.005 239	0.004 884	0.004 553	0.004 245	0.003 959	0.003 692	33
34	0.004 469	0.004 156	0.003 867	0.003 598	0.003 348	0.003 116	34
35	0.003 811	0.003 537	0.003 284	0.003 049	0.002 831	0.002 629	35
36	0.003 250	0.003 010	0.002 789	0.002 584	0.002 394	0.002 219	36
37	0.002 772	0.002 562	0.002 368	0.002 190	0.002 025	0.001 872	37
38	0.002 364	0.002 181	0.002 011	0.001 856	0.001 712	0.001 580	38
39	0.002 017	0.001 856	0.001 708	0.001 573	0.001 448	0.001 333	39
40	0.001 720	0.001 579	0.001 451	0.001 333	0.001 224	0.001 125	40
41	0.001 467	0.001 344	0.001 232	0.001 129	0.001 036	0.000 950	41
42	0.001 251	0.001 144	0.001 046	0.000 957	0.000 876	0.000 801	42
43	0.001 067	0.000 974	0.000 889	0.000 811	0.000 741	0.000 676	43
44	0.000 910	0.000 829	0.000 755	0.000 687	0.000 626	0.000 571	44
45	0.000 776	0.000 705	0.000 641	0.000 583	0.000 530	0.000 482	45
46	0.000 662	0.000 600	0.000 544	0.000 494	0.000 448	0.000 406	46
47	0.000 565	0.000 511	0.000 462	0.000 418	0.000 379	0.000 343	47
48	0.000 481	0.000 435	0.000 393	0.000 355	0.000 320	0.000 289	48
49	0.000 411	0.000 370	0.000 333	0.000 300	0.000 271	0.000 244	49
50	0.000 350	0.000 315	0.000 283	0.000 255	0.000 229	0.000 206	50

PRESENT VALUE

YRS	18.75% ANNUAL RATE	19.00% ANNUAL RATE	19.25% ANNUAL RATE	19.50% ANNUAL RATE	19.75% ANNUAL RATE	20.00% ANNUAL RATE	YRS
1	0.842 105	0.840 336	0.838 574	0.836 820	0.835 073	0.833 333	1
2	0.709 141	0.706 165	0.703 207	0.700 268	0.697 347	0.694 444	2
3	0.597 172	0.593 416	0.589 691	0.585 998	0.582 336	0.578 704	3
4	0.502 881	0.498 669	0.494 500	0.490 375	0.486 293	0.482 253	4
5	0.423 479	0.419 049	0.414 675	0.410 356	0.406 090	0.401 878	5
6	0.356 614	0.352 142	0.347 736	0.343 394	0.339 115	0.334 898	6
7	0.300 306	0.295 918	0.291 603	0.287 359	0.283 186	0.279 082	7
8	0.252 890	0.248 671	0.244 530	0.240 468	0.236 481	0.232 568	8
9	0.212 960	0.208 967	0.205 057	0.201 228	0.197 479	0.193 807	9
10	0.179 334	0.175 602	0.171 956	0.168 392	0.164 909	0.161 506	10
11	0.151 019	0.147 565	0.144 198	0.140 914	0.137 711	0.134 588	11
12	0.127 173	0.124 004	0.120 920	0.117 919	0.114 999	0.112 157	12
13	0.107 093	0.104 205	0.101 401	0.098 677	0.096 032	0.093 464	13
14	0.090 184	0.087 567	0.085 032	0.082 575	0.080 194	0.077 887	14
15	0.075 944	0.073 586	0.071 306	0.069 101	0.066 968	0.064 905	15
16	0.063 953	0.061 837	0.059 795	0.057 825	0.055 923	0.054 088	16
17	0.053 855	0.051 964	0.050 143	0.048 389	0.046 700	0.045 073	17
18	0.045 352	0.043 667	0.042 048	0.040 493	0.038 998	0.037 561	18
19	0.038 191	0.036 695	0.035 261	0.033 885	0.032 566	0.031 301	19
20	0.032 161	0.030 836	0.029 569	0.028 356	0.027 195	0.026 084	20
21	0.027 083	0.025 913	0.024 796	0.023 729	0.022 710	0.021 737	21
22	0.022 807	0.021 775	0.020 793	0.019 857	0.018 964	0.018 114	22
23	0.019 206	0.018 299	0.017 436	0.016 616	0.015 837	0.015 095	23
24	0.016 173	0.015 377	0.014 622	0.013 905	0.013 225	0.012 579	24
25	0.013 619	0.012 922	0.012 261	0.011 636	0.011 044	0.010 483	25
26	0.011 469	0.010 859	0.010 282	0.009 737	0.009 222	0.008 735	26
27	0.009 658	0.009 125	0.008 622	0.008 148	0.007 701	0.007 280	27
28	0.008 133	0.007 668	0.007 230	0.006 819	0.006 431	0.006 066	28
29	0.006 849	0.006 444	0.006 063	0.005 706	0.005 370	0.005 055	29
30	0.005 768	0.005 415	0.005 085	0.004 775	0.004 485	0.004 213	30
31	0.004 857	0.004 550	0.004 264	0.003 996	0.003 745	0.003 511	31
32	0.004 090	0.003 824	0.003 575	0.003 344	0.003 127	0.002 926	32
33	0.003 444	0.003 213	0.002 998	0.002 798	0.002 612	0.002 438	33
34	0.002 900	0.002 700	0.002 514	0.002 341	0.002 181	0.002 032	34
35	0.002 442	0.002 269	0.002 108	0.001 959	0.001 821	0.001 693	35
36	0.002 057	0.001 907	0.001 768	0.001 640	0.001 521	0.001 411	36
37	0.001 732	0.001 602	0.001 483	0.001 372	0.001 270	0.001 176	37
38	0.001 459	0.001 347	0.001 243	0.001 148	0.001 061	0.000 980	38
39	0.001 228	0.001 132	0.001 043	0.000 961	0.000 886	0.000 816	39
40	0.001 034	0.000 951	0.000 874	0.000 804	0.000 740	0.000 680	40
41	0.000 871	0.000 799	0.000 733	0.000 673	0.000 618	0.000 567	41
42	0.000 733	0.000 671	0.000 615	0.000 563	0.000 516	0.000 472	42
43	0.000 618	0.000 564	0.000 516	0.000 471	0.000 431	0.000 394	43
44	0.000 520	0.000 474	0.000 432	0.000 394	0.000 360	0.000 328	44
45	0.000 438	0.000 398	0.000 363	0.000 330	0.000 300	0.000 273	45
46	0.000 369	0.000 335	0.000 304	0.000 276	0.000 251	0.000 228	46
47	0.000 311	0.000 281	0.000 255	0.000 231	0.000 209	0.000 190	47
48	0.000 262	0.000 236	0.000 214	0.000 193	0.000 175	0.000 158	48
49	0.000 220	0.000 199	0.000 179	0.000 162	0.000 146	0.000 132	49
50	0.000 185	0.000 167	0.000 150	0.000 135	0.000 122	0.000 110	50

SECTION 4

YRS	20.25% ANNUAL RATE	20.50% ANNUAL RATE	20.75% ANNUAL RATE	21.00% ANNUAL RATE	21.25% ANNUAL RATE	21.50% ANNUAL RATE	YRS
1	0.831 601	0.829 876	0.828 157	0.826 446	0.824 742	0.823 045	1
2	0.691 560	0.688 693	0.685 845	0.683 013	0.680 200	0.677 404	2
3	0.575 102	0.571 530	0.567 987	0.564 474	0.560 990	0.557 534	3
4	0.478 255	0.474 299	0.470 383	0.466 507	0.462 672	0.458 876	4
5	0.397 717	0.393 609	0.389 551	0.385 543	0.381 585	0.377 675	5
6	0.330 742	0.326 646	0.322 610	0.318 631	0.314 709	0.310 844	6
7	0.275 045	0.271 076	0.267 171	0.263 331	0.259 554	0.255 839	7
8	0.228 728	0.224 959	0.221 260	0.217 629	0.214 065	0.210 567	8
9	0.190 210	0.186 688	0.183 238	0.179 859	0.176 549	0.173 306	9
10	0.158 179	0.154 928	0.151 750	0.148 644	0.145 607	0.142 639	10
11	0.131 542	0.128 571	0.125 673	0.122 846	0.120 088	0.117 398	11
12	0.109 390	0.106 698	0.104 077	0.101 526	0.099 042	0.096 624	12
13	0.090 969	0.088 546	0.086 192	0.083 905	0.081 684	0.079 526	13
14	0.075 650	0.073 482	0.071 381	0.069 343	0.067 368	0.065 453	14
15	0.062 911	0.060 981	0.059 114	0.057 309	0.055 561	0.053 871	15
16	0.052 316	0.050 607	0.048 956	0.047 362	0.045 824	0.044 338	16
17	0.043 506	0.041 997	0.040 543	0.039 143	0.037 793	0.036 492	17
18	0.036 180	0.034 852	0.033 576	0.032 349	0.031 169	0.030 035	18
19	0.030 087	0.028 923	0.027 806	0.026 735	0.025 707	0.024 720	19
20	0.025 021	0.024 003	0.023 028	0.022 095	0.021 201	0.020 346	20
21	0.020 807	0.019 919	0.019 071	0.018 260	0.017 486	0.016 746	21
22	0.017 303	0.016 530	0.015 794	0.015 091	0.014 421	0.013 782	22
23	0.014 389	0.013 718	0.013 080	0.012 472	0.011 894	0.011 343	23
24	0.011 966	0.011 384	0.010 832	0.010 307	0.009 809	0.009 336	24
25	0.009 951	0.009 448	0.008 971	0.008 519	0.008 090	0.007 684	25
26	0.008 275	0.007 840	0.007 429	0.007 040	0.006 672	0.006 324	26
27	0.006 882	0.006 507	0.006 152	0.005 818	0.005 503	0.005 205	27
28	0.005 723	0.005 400	0.005 095	0.004 809	0.004 538	0.004 284	28
29	0.004 759	0.004 481	0.004 220	0.003 974	0.003 743	0.003 526	29
30	0.003 958	0.003 719	0.003 495	0.003 284	0.003 087	0.002 902	30
31	0.003 291	0.003 086	0.002 894	0.002 714	0.002 546	0.002 389	31
32	0.002 737	0.002 561	0.002 397	0.002 243	0.002 100	0.001 966	32
33	0.002 276	0.002 125	0.001 985	0.001 854	0.001 732	0.001 618	33
34	0.001 893	0.001 764	0.001 644	0.001 532	0.001 428	0.001 332	34
35	0.001 574	0.001 464	0.001 361	0.001 266	0.001 178	0.001 096	35
36	0.001 309	0.001 215	0.001 127	0.001 046	0.000 972	0.000 902	36
37	0.001 089	0.001 008	0.000 934	0.000 865	0.000 801	0.000 742	37
38	0.000 905	0.000 837	0.000 773	0.000 715	0.000 661	0.000 611	38
39	0.000 753	0.000 694	0.000 640	0.000 591	0.000 545	0.000 503	39
40	0.000 626	0.000 576	0.000 530	0.000 488	0.000 450	0.000 414	40
41	0.000 521	0.000 478	0.000 439	0.000 403	0.000 371	0.000 341	41
42	0.000 433	0.000 397	0.000 364	0.000 333	0.000 306	0.000 280	42
43	0.000 360	0.000 329	0.000 301	0.000 276	0.000 252	0.000 231	43
44	0.000 299	0.000 273	0.000 249	0.000 228	0.000 208	0.000 190	44
45	0.000 249	0.000 227	0.000 207	0.000 188	0.000 172	0.000 156	45
46	0.000 207	0.000 188	0.000 171	0.000 156	0.000 141	0.000 129	46
47	0.000 172	0.000 156	0.000 142	0.000 129	0.000 117	0.000 106	47
48	0.000 143	0.000 130	0.000 117	0.000 106	0.000 096	0.000 087	48
49	0.000 119	0.000 108	0.000 097	0.000 088	0.000 079	0.000 072	49
50	0.000 099	0.000 089	0.000 080	0.000 073	0.000 065	0.000 059	50

PRESENT VALUE

ANNUAL COMPOUNDING

YRS	21.75% ANNUAL RATE	22.00% ANNUAL RATE	22.50% ANNUAL RATE	23.00% ANNUAL RATE	23.50% ANNUAL RATE	24.00% ANNUAL RATE	YRS
1	0.821 355	0.819 672	0.816 327	0.813 008	0.809 717	0.806 452	1
2	0.674 624	0.671 862	0.666 389	0.660 982	0.655 641	0.650 364	2
3	0.554 106	0.550 707	0.543 991	0.537 384	0.530 883	0.524 487	3
4	0.455 118	0.451 399	0.444 074	0.436 897	0.429 865	0.422 974	4
5	0.373 814	0.369 999	0.362 510	0.355 201	0.348 069	0.341 108	5
6	0.307 034	0.303 278	0.295 926	0.288 781	0.281 837	0.275 087	6
7	0.252 184	0.248 589	0.241 572	0.234 782	0.228 208	0.221 844	7
8	0.207 132	0.203 761	0.197 202	0.190 879	0.184 784	0.178 907	8
9	0.170 129	0.167 017	0.160 981	0.155 187	0.149 623	0.144 280	9
10	0.139 737	0.136 899	0.131 413	0.126 168	0.121 152	0.116 354	10
11	0.114 773	0.112 213	0.107 276	0.102 576	0.098 099	0.093 834	11
12	0.094 270	0.091 978	0.087 572	0.083 395	0.079 432	0.075 673	12
13	0.077 429	0.075 391	0.071 488	0.067 801	0.064 318	0.061 026	13
14	0.063 597	0.061 796	0.058 357	0.055 122	0.052 079	0.049 215	14
15	0.052 235	0.050 653	0.047 639	0.044 815	0.042 169	0.039 689	15
16	0.042 904	0.041 519	0.038 889	0.036 435	0.034 145	0.032 008	16
17	0.035 239	0.034 032	0.031 746	0.029 622	0.027 648	0.025 813	17
18	0.028 944	0.027 895	0.025 915	0.024 083	0.022 387	0.020 817	18
19	0.023 773	0.022 865	0.021 155	0.019 580	0.018 127	0.016 788	19
20	0.019 526	0.018 741	0.017 269	0.015 918	0.014 678	0.013 538	20
21	0.016 038	0.015 362	0.014 098	0.012 942	0.011 885	0.010 918	21
22	0.013 173	0.012 592	0.011 508	0.010 522	0.009 623	0.008 805	22
23	0.010 820	0.010 321	0.009 394	0.008 554	0.007 792	0.007 101	23
24	0.008 887	0.008 460	0.007 669	0.006 955	0.006 309	0.005 726	24
25	0.007 299	0.006 934	0.006 260	0.005 654	0.005 109	0.004 618	25
26	0.005 995	0.005 684	0.005 110	0.004 597	0.004 137	0.003 724	26
27	0.004 924	0.004 659	0.004 172	0.003 737	0.003 350	0.003 003	27
28	0.004 045	0.003 819	0.003 406	0.003 038	0.002 712	0.002 422	28
29	0.003 322	0.003 130	0.002 780	0.002 470	0.002 196	0.001 953	29
30	0.002 729	0.002 566	0.002 269	0.002 008	0.001 778	0.001 575	30
31	0.002 241	0.002 103	0.001 853	0.001 633	0.001 440	0.001 270	31
32	0.001 841	0.001 724	0.001 512	0.001 328	0.001 166	0.001 024	32
33	0.001 512	0.001 413	0.001 235	0.001 079	0.000 944	0.000 826	33
34	0.001 242	0.001 158	0.001 008	0.000 877	0.000 764	0.000 666	34
35	0.001 020	0.000 949	0.000 823	0.000 713	0.000 619	0.000 537	35
36	0.000 838	0.000 778	0.000 672	0.000 580	0.000 501	0.000 433	36
37	0.000 688	0.000 638	0.000 548	0.000 472	0.000 406	0.000 349	37
38	0.000 565	0.000 523	0.000 448	0.000 383	0.000 329	0.000 282	38
39	0.000 464	0.000 429	0.000 365	0.000 312	0.000 266	0.000 227	39
40	0.000 381	0.000 351	0.000 298	0.000 253	0.000 215	0.000 183	40
41	0.000 313	0.000 288	0.000 243	0.000 206	0.000 174	0.000 148	41
42	0.000 257	0.000 236	0.000 199	0.000 167	0.000 141	0.000 119	42
43	0.000 211	0.000 193	0.000 162	0.000 136	0.000 114	0.000 096	43
44	0.000 174	0.000 159	0.000 132	0.000 111	0.000 093	0.000 078	44
45	0.000 143	0.000 130	0.000 108	0.000 090	0.000 075	0.000 063	45
46	0.000 117	0.000 107	0.000 088	0.000 073	0.000 061	0.000 050	46
47	0.000 096	0.000 087	0.000 072	0.000 059	0.000 049	0.000 041	47
48	0.000 079	0.000 072	0.000 059	0.000 048	0.000 040	0.000 033	48
49	0.000 065	0.000 059	0.000 048	0.000 039	0.000 032	0.000 026	49
50	0.000 053	0.000 048	0.000 039	0.000 032	0.000 026	0.000 021	50

SECTION 5
PRESENT VALUE
OF $1 PER PERIOD

Present value per period is the basic compound interest function for a series of repeated payments or withdrawals. It is probably the most widely used function and is frequently called ordinary annuity. By convention, it is assumed that each payment is made at the end of each compounding period. If the payments are made at the beginning of each period, the function is called annuity due. Interest is earned on the remaining investment after each payment is made, and after each period interest begins to be earned on the interest.

USE OF PRESENT VALUE PER PERIOD

Present value per period is the amount you need today to be able to make a series of $1 payments or withdrawals at the end of each compounding period. The assumptions are:

- The payments are uniform and repeat at a regular interval.
- All interest earned is left in the account to begin earning interest on interest.
- The residual balance in the account after each payment is made earns interest at a uniform rate throughout the terms of the obligation.

The tables in this section are used to solve the following types of problems:

1. How much is a series of repeated future payments worth today?
2. How long will it take for a series of repeated future payments to be worth a certain amount today?
3. What rate must be paid for a series of repeated future payments to be worth a certain amount today?

EXAMPLES

Present Worth of an Annuity. An insurance company will pay you $200 each month for the next 3 years (36 months). What is this annuity worth today at 12% compounded monthly?

Turn to page 196 in the monthly compounding section and locate the column labeled 12.00%. Move down the column to the 36-month row and find the entry: 30.107505. Multiply 30.107505 by $200 to get $6,021.50, the present value of the series of payments.

The following three examples consider variations of this example.

Payments Made in Advance. What would the annuity in the preceding example be worth if the $200 payments were made at the start of each month, rather than at the end?

If you add 1 to the present value per period table entry, you make the entry equivalent to payments made at the beginning of a month, albeit one payment more. Therefore, simply look up the entry for 35 months and add 1 to get the applicable factor. Find the 35-month factor 29.408580 and add 1 to get 30.408580. Multiply 30.408580 by $200 to get $6,081.72, the present value of the series of payments made at the beginning of each month.

If there is no entry for one period less than the applicable number of payments, solve the problem as follows. Each payment made at the beginning of a month has the time to earn the recipient one month's more interest than the payment received at the end of a month. To find the growth of a single payment after one month, turn to page 12 of the future value tables and find the column labeled 12.00%. Look in the row for 1 month to find the entry: 1.01. Multiply 1.01 by the present value, $6,021.50, which you found in the preceding example, to get $6,081.72, the present value for payments made at the start of each month.

Payments More Frequent Than Compounding. What would the annuity in the preceding examples be worth if the $200 payments made at the end of the month earned 12% interest compounded quarterly rather than monthly? In this situation, the payment period is shorter than the compounding period.

To solve this problem, you must refigure the payments as equivalent payments for the compounding period. You must figure the worth of three payments of $200 per month paid at the end of a quarter. The first month's payment earns two months' interest, the second month's payment earns one month's interest, and the third month's payment earns no interest to the end of the quarter. Thus the total interest earned in one quarter for the three payments is 3 months' simple interest, or 3% on a $200 payment. This equals $6, which when combined with three $200 monthly payments gives a total equivalent quarterly payment of $606.

Next, turn to page 208 in the quarterly compounding section and locate the column labeled 12.00%. Move down the column to the 12-quarter (3-year) row and find the entry: 9.954004. Multiply 9.954004 by the equivalent quarterly payment of $606 to get $6,032.13, the present value for monthly payments compounded quarterly.

Compounding More Frequent Than Payments. What would the annuity in the preceding examples be worth if you choose to receive $600 payments at the end of every quarter but the annuity is compounded monthly? In this situation, the compounding period is shorter than the payment period.

To solve this problem, find the equivalent monthly payment that can duplicate the $600 quarterly payment. You are really providing a sinking fund of three payments compounded monthly at 12%. Turn to page 104 in the monthly compounding section of the sinking fund tables and locate the column labeled 12.00%. Move down the column to the 3-month row and find the entry: 0.330022. Multiply 0.330022 by $600 to get $198.01, the equivalent monthly payment.

Return to the present value per period tables, and on page 196 of the monthly compounding section locate the column labeled 12.00%. Move down the column to the 36-month row and find the entry: 30.107505. Multiply 30.107505 by $198.01 to get $5,961.59, the present value of the $600 quarterly payments compounded monthly.

Serial Loan: Makeham's Formula. You wish to purchase a $40,000 mortgage that pays $4,000 plus interest at the end of each year for 10 years. The interest rate on the mortgage is 10%. What should you pay for the mortgage if you wish to earn 12% compounded annually?

This mortgage is an example of a serial loan, where repayment is by a series of level payments of principal. The problem is solved using *Makeham's formula*:

$$A = K + \frac{j}{i} \times (C - K)$$

where:

A = present value of the mortgage
K = present value of the principal payments at the earnings rate i
j = interest rate per period on the mortgage
i = earnings rate (yield) per period at purchase
C = amount of the mortgage

For this example, C is $40,000, j is 10%, and i is 12%. You must find the present value of the principal payments at the desired earnings rate of 12%. Turn to page 226 in the annual compounding section and locate the column labeled 12.00%. Move down the column to the 10-year row and find the entry: 5.650223. Multiply 5.650223 by the $4,000 principal payment to get $22,600.89, the present value of the principal payments at 12%. Substitute the values into Makeham's formula:

$$A = 22,600.89 + \frac{10}{12} \times (40,000 - 22,600.89)$$
$$A = 22,600.89 + 14,499.26$$
$$A = 37,100.15$$

To earn 12%, you should purchase the mortgage for $37,100.15.

The partial payment to amortize tables (Section 6) are the reciprocal tables to present value per period. The payment and withdrawal examples presented in Section 6 are useful supplements to the examples in this section.

THE FORMULA FOR PRESENT VALUE PER PERIOD

The symbol $A_{\overline{n}|}$ is the widely accepted notation for present value per period. The formula for figuring table entries for present value per period is:

$$A_{\overline{n}|} = \frac{1 - V^n}{i}$$

where:

V^n = Present Value
i = interest rate per period
n = number of compounding periods

Note that i is the interest rate *per period*, not the nominal annual rate. You can easily find the interest rate per period by dividing the annual rate by the number of compounding periods per year. For example, a nominal annual rate of 12% compounded monthly converts to 1% per month (12% ÷ 12 months per year).

PRESENT VALUE PER PERIOD

MOS	5.25% ANNUAL RATE	5.50% ANNUAL RATE	5.75% ANNUAL RATE	6.00% ANNUAL RATE	6.25% ANNUAL RATE	6.50% ANNUAL RATE	MOS
1	0.995 644	0.995 438	0.995 231	0.995 025	0.994 819	0.994 613	1
2	1.986 951	1.986 334	1.985 716	1.985 099	1.984 483	1.983 867	2
3	2.973 940	2.972 709	2.971 478	2.970 248	2.969 019	2.967 791	3
4	3.956 630	3.954 583	3.952 539	3.950 496	3.948 454	3.946 415	4
5	4.935 039	4.931 979	4.928 921	4.925 866	4.922 815	4.919 766	5
6	5.909 186	5.904 914	5.900 647	5.896 384	5.892 126	5.887 873	6
7	6.879 090	6.873 411	6.867 739	6.862 074	6.856 416	6.850 765	7
8	7.844 770	7.837 489	7.830 219	7.822 959	7.815 709	7.808 469	8
9	8.806 242	8.797 169	8.788 110	8.779 064	8.770 032	8.761 014	9
10	9.763 527	9.752 470	9.741 432	9.730 412	9.719 410	9.708 426	10
11	10.716 641	10.703 413	10.690 208	10.677 027	10.663 869	10.650 735	11
12	11.665 604	11.650 017	11.634 460	11.618 932	11.603 434	11.587 967	12
13	12.610 434	12.592 302	12.574 208	12.556 151	12.538 132	12.520 149	13
14	13.551 148	13.530 288	13.509 475	13.488 708	13.467 986	13.447 310	14
15	14.487 764	14.463 995	14.440 282	14.416 625	14.393 022	14.369 475	15
16	15.420 300	15.393 442	15.366 650	15.339 925	15.313 266	15.286 672	16
17	16.348 774	16.318 648	16.288 601	16.258 632	16.228 741	16.198 928	17
18	17.273 204	17.239 633	17.206 155	17.172 768	17.139 473	17.106 269	18
19	18.193 607	18.156 416	18.119 333	18.082 356	18.045 486	18.008 722	19
20	19.110 000	19.069 017	19.028 156	18.987 419	18.946 805	18.906 313	20
21	20.022 402	19.977 453	19.932 646	19.887 979	19.843 453	19.799 068	21
22	20.930 830	20.881 745	20.832 822	20.784 059	20.735 456	20.687 013	22
23	21.835 301	21.781 911	21.728 705	21.675 681	21.622 837	21.570 174	23
24	22.735 831	22.677 971	22.620 316	22.562 866	22.505 621	22.448 578	24
25	23.632 439	23.569 942	23.507 675	23.445 638	23.383 830	23.322 249	25
26	24.525 142	24.457 843	24.390 802	24.324 018	24.257 489	24.191 213	26
27	25.413 956	25.341 694	25.269 745	25.198 028	25.126 621	25.055 496	27
28	26.298 898	26.221 512	26.144 443	26.067 689	25.991 250	25.915 123	28
29	27.179 986	27.097 316	27.014 996	26.933 024	26.851 399	26.770 118	29
30	28.057 235	27.969 124	27.881 398	27.794 054	27.707 091	27.620 507	30
31	28.930 664	28.836 955	28.743 668	28.650 800	28.558 350	28.466 314	31
32	29.800 287	29.700 826	29.601 826	29.503 284	29.405 197	29.307 565	32
33	30.666 123	30.560 756	30.455 891	30.351 526	30.247 658	30.144 283	33
34	31.528 187	31.416 762	31.305 884	31.195 548	31.085 753	30.976 494	34
35	32.386 496	32.268 863	32.151 823	32.035 371	31.919 505	31.804 221	35
36	33.241 067	33.117 077	32.993 728	32.871 016	32.748 938	32.627 489	36
37	34.091 915	33.961 420	33.831 618	33.702 504	33.574 073	33.446 321	37
38	34.939 056	34.801 912	34.665 513	34.529 854	34.394 933	34.260 742	38
39	35.782 508	35.638 568	35.495 430	35.353 089	35.211 539	35.070 776	39
40	36.622 285	36.471 408	36.321 390	36.172 228	36.023 915	35.876 445	40
41	37.458 405	37.300 447	37.143 411	36.987 291	36.832 081	36.677 774	41
42	38.290 882	38.125 704	37.961 513	37.798 300	37.636 060	37.474 785	42
43	39.119 733	38.947 196	38.775 712	38.605 274	38.435 873	38.267 503	43
44	39.944 974	39.764 940	39.586 029	39.408 232	39.231 542	39.055 950	44
45	40.766 620	40.578 953	40.392 482	40.207 196	40.023 088	39.840 149	45
46	41.584 687	41.389 253	41.195 089	41.002 185	40.810 533	40.620 123	46
47	42.399 191	42.195 855	41.993 868	41.793 219	41.593 899	41.395 896	47

YRS							
4	43.210 146	42.998 777	42.788 838	42.580 318	42.373 205	42.167 488	48
5	52.670 434	52.352 835	52.037 886	51.725 561	51.415 833	51.108 680	60
6	61.647 896	61.207 425	60.771 314	60.339 514	59.911 975	59.488 649	72
7	70.167 176	69.589 216	69.017 867	68.453 042	67.894 666	67.342 623	84
8	78.251 657	77.523 453	76.804 687	76.095 218	75.394 907	74.703 617	96
9	85.923 530	85.034 035	84.157 405	83.293 424	82.441 884	81.602 576	108
10	93.203 853	92.143 582	91.100 219	90.073 453	89.062 980	88.068 500	120
11	100.112 611	98.873 509	97.655 982	96.459 599	95.283 933	94.128 569	132
12	106.668 766	105.244 084	103.846 272	102.474 743	101.128 925	99.808 260	144
13	112.890 315	111.274 498	109.691 463	108.140 440	106.620 678	105.131 446	156
14	118.794 334	116.982 911	115.210 793	113.476 990	111.780 539	110.120 506	168
15	124.397 030	122.386 519	120.422 429	118.503 515	116.628 567	114.796 412	180
16	129.713 780	127.501 597	125.343 525	123.238 025	121.183 606	119.178 820	192
17	134.759 180	132.343 550	129.990 277	127.697 486	125.463 363	123.286 152	204
18	139.547 078	136.926 962	134.377 980	131.897 876	129.484 475	127.135 675	216
19	144.090 615	141.265 639	138.521 075	135.854 246	133.262 573	130.743 570	228
20	148.402 264	145.372 649	142.433 199	139.580 772	136.812 343	134.125 004	240
21	152.493 859	149.260 361	146.127 228	143.090 806	140.147 585	137.294 192	252
22	156.376 632	152.940 485	149.615 321	146.396 927	143.281 262	140.264 456	264
23	160.061 239	156.424 105	152.908 958	149.510 979	146.225 557	143.048 282	276
24	163.557 795	159.721 715	156.018 980	152.444 121	148.991 915	145.657 372	288
25	166.875 897	162.843 245	158.955 623	155.206 864	151.591 090	148.172 695	300
26	170.024 653	165.798 099	161.728 552	157.809 106	154.033 184	150.394 529	312
27	173.012 706	168.595 175	164.346 896	160.260 172	156.327 692	152.542 509	324
28	175.848 258	171.242 899	166.819 270	162.568 844	158.483 532	154.555 664	336
29	178.539 091	173.749 245	169.153 814	164.743 394	160.509 085	156.442 457	348
30	181.092 592	176.121 763	171.358 210	166.791 614	162.412 224	158.210 820	360

MOS	6.75% ANNUAL RATE	7.00% ANNUAL RATE	7.25% ANNUAL RATE	7.50% ANNUAL RATE	7.75% ANNUAL RATE	8.00% ANNUAL RATE	MOS
1	0.994 406	0.994 200	0.993 995	0.993 789	0.993 583	0.993 377	1
2	1.983 251	1.982 635	1.982 020	1.981 405	1.980 791	1.980 176	2
3	2.966 564	2.965 337	2.964 112	2.962 887	2.961 663	2.960 440	3
4	3.944 377	3.942 340	3.940 306	3.938 273	3.936 242	3.934 212	4
5	4.916 720	4.913 677	4.910 637	4.907 600	4.904 566	4.901 535	5
6	5.883 625	5.879 381	5.875 142	5.870 907	5.866 677	5.862 452	6
7	6.845 121	6.839 484	6.833 854	6.828 231	6.822 615	6.817 005	7
8	7.801 239	7.794 019	7.786 808	7.779 608	7.772 418	7.765 237	8
9	8.752 009	8.743 018	8.734 040	8.725 076	8.716 126	8.707 189	9
10	9.697 461	9.686 513	9.675 584	9.664 672	9.653 779	9.642 903	10
11	10.637 624	10.624 537	10.611 473	10.598 432	10.585 415	10.572 420	11
12	11.572 529	11.557 120	11.541 741	11.526 392	11.511 072	11.495 782	12
13	12.502 204	12.484 295	12.466 423	12.448 588	12.430 790	12.413 028	13
14	13.426 679	13.406 093	13.385 552	13.365 057	13.344 606	13.324 200	14
15	14.345 982	14.322 545	14.299 162	14.275 833	14.252 558	14.229 338	15
16	15.260 144	15.233 682	15.207 284	15.180 952	15.154 684	15.128 481	16
17	16.169 192	16.139 534	16.109 953	16.080 449	16.051 022	16.021 670	17
18	17.073 156	17.040 133	17.007 201	16.974 359	16.941 607	16.908 944	18
19	17.972 063	17.935 510	17.899 061	17.862 717	17.826 478	17.790 342	19
20	18.865 942	18.825 693	18.785 565	18.745 558	18.705 670	18.665 902	20
21	19.754 821	19.710 714	19.666 745	19.622 914	19.579 221	19.535 665	21
22	20.638 728	20.590 602	20.542 633	20.494 822	20.447 166	20.399 667	22
23	21.517 691	21.465 387	21.413 262	21.361 314	21.309 542	21.257 947	23
24	22.391 738	22.335 099	22.278 661	22.222 423	22.166 384	22.110 544	24
25	23.260 895	23.199 767	23.138 864	23.078 185	23.017 728	22.957 494	25
26	24.125 191	24.059 421	23.993 901	23.928 631	23.863 609	23.798 835	26
27	24.984 652	24.914 089	24.843 803	24.773 795	24.704 062	24.634 604	27
28	25.839 306	25.763 800	25.688 601	25.613 709	25.539 122	25.464 838	28
29	26.689 180	26.608 583	26.528 326	26.448 406	26.368 823	26.289 575	29
30	27.534 299	27.448 467	27.363 008	27.277 919	27.193 200	27.108 849	30
31	28.374 692	28.283 480	28.192 677	28.102 280	28.012 288	27.922 698	31
32	29.210 383	29.113 650	29.017 364	28.921 521	28.826 119	28.731 157	32
33	30.041 400	29.939 006	29.837 098	29.735 673	29.634 728	29.534 262	33
34	30.867 769	30.759 575	30.651 909	30.544 768	30.438 148	30.332 048	34
35	31.689 516	31.575 385	31.461 827	31.348 838	31.236 413	31.124 551	35
36	32.506 666	32.386 464	32.266 882	32.147 913	32.029 556	31.911 806	36
37	33.319 245	33.192 840	33.067 101	32.942 025	32.817 609	32.693 847	37
38	34.127 279	33.994 538	33.862 515	33.731 205	33.600 605	33.470 708	38
39	34.930 793	34.791 587	34.653 152	34.515 484	34.378 576	34.242 426	39
40	35.729 813	35.584 014	35.439 041	35.294 891	35.151 556	35.009 032	40
41	36.524 364	36.371 845	36.220 211	36.069 457	35.919 575	35.770 562	41
42	37.314 470	37.155 107	36.996 689	36.839 211	36.682 666	36.527 048	42
43	38.100 156	37.933 826	37.768 505	37.604 185	37.440 861	37.278 525	43
44	38.881 448	38.708 029	38.535 685	38.364 408	38.194 190	38.025 024	44
45	39.658 370	39.477 742	39.298 258	39.119 908	38.942 685	38.766 580	45
46	40.430 946	40.242 991	40.056 251	39.870 716	39.686 377	39.503 226	46
47	41.199 200	41.003 803	40.809 693	40.616 861	40.425 297	40.234 992	47

YRS							
4	41.963 157	41.760 201	41.558 610	41.358 371	41.159 476	40.961 913	48
5	50.804 074	50.501 994	50.202 413	49.905 308	49.610 656	49.318 433	60
6	59.069 488	58.654 444	58.243 472	57.836 524	57.433 556	57.034 522	72
7	66.796 860	66.257 285	65.723 817	65.196 376	64.674 883	64.159 261	84
8	74.021 215	73.347 569	72.682 548	72.026 024	71.377 873	70.737 970	96
9	80.775 298	79.959 850	79.156 037	78.363 665	77.582 547	76.812 497	108
10	87.089 720	86.126 354	85.178 120	84.244 743	83.325 951	82.421 481	120
11	92.993 102	91.877 134	90.780 276	89.702 148	88.642 377	87.600 600	132
12	98.512 201	97.240 216	95.991 786	94.766 401	93.563 568	92.382 800	144
13	103.672 031	102.241 738	100.839 890	99.465 827	98.118 905	96.798 498	156
14	108.495 980	106.906 074	105.349 929	103.826 706	102.335 588	100.875 784	168
15	113.005 911	111.255 958	109.545 477	107.873 427	106.238 793	104.640 592	180
16	117.222 266	115.312 587	113.448 464	111.628 623	109.851 825	108.116 871	192
17	121.164 156	119.095 732	117.079 291	115.113 294	113.196 255	111.326 733	204
18	124.849 447	122.623 831	120.456 934	118.346 930	116.292 053	114.290 596	216
19	128.294 841	125.914 077	123.599 051	121.347 615	119.157 701	117.027 313	228
20	131.515 956	128.982 506	126.522 063	124.132 131	121.810 311	119.554 292	240
21	134.527 392	131.844 073	129.241 249	126.716 051	124.265 720	121.887 606	252
22	137.342 796	134.512 723	131.770 823	129.113 825	126.538 587	124.042 099	264
23	139.974 930	137.001 461	134.124 007	131.338 863	128.642 485	126.031 475	276
24	142.435 724	139.322 418	136.313 100	133.403 610	130.589 973	127.868 388	288
25	144.736 332	141.486 903	138.349 544	135.319 613	132.392 681	129.564 523	300
26	146.887 181	143.505 467	140.243 984	137.097 587	134.061 371	131.130 668	312
27	148.898 019	145.387 946	142.006 323	138.747 475	135.606 007	132.576 786	324
28	150.777 960	147.143 515	143.645 771	140.278 506	137.035 812	133.912 076	336
29	152.535 526	148.780 729	145.170 898	141.699 242	138.359 321	135.145 031	348
30	154.178 682	150.307 568	146.589 676	143.017 627	139.584 437	136.283 494	360

193

MOS	8.25% ANNUAL RATE	8.50% ANNUAL RATE	8.75% ANNUAL RATE	9.00% ANNUAL RATE	9.25% ANNUAL RATE	9.50% ANNUAL RATE	MOS
1	0.993 172	0.992 966	0.992 761	0.992 556	0.992 351	0.992 146	1
2	1.979 562	1.978 949	1.978 336	1.977 723	1.977 110	1.976 498	2
3	2.959 218	2.957 996	2.956 776	2.955 556	2.954 337	2.953 119	3
4	3.932 184	3.930 158	3.928 133	3.926 110	3.924 089	3.922 070	4
5	4.898 507	4.895 482	4.892 459	4.889 440	4.886 423	4.883 409	5
6	5.858 231	5.854 016	5.849 804	5.845 598	5.841 396	5.837 198	6
7	6.811 403	6.805 808	6.800 219	6.794 638	6.789 063	6.783 496	7
8	7.758 066	7.750 906	7.743 754	7.736 613	7.729 482	7.722 360	8
9	8.698 266	8.689 356	8.680 459	8.671 576	8.662 707	8.653 851	9
10	9.632 045	9.621 206	9.610 384	9.599 580	9.588 793	9.578 024	10
11	10.559 449	10.546 501	10.533 576	10.520 675	10.507 796	10.494 940	11
12	11.480 521	11.465 289	11.450 086	11.434 913	11.419 768	11.404 653	12
13	12.395 303	12.377 614	12.359 961	12.342 345	12.324 765	12.307 221	13
14	13.303 839	13.283 522	13.263 250	13.243 022	13.222 839	13.202 699	14
15	14.206 172	14.183 059	14.160 000	14.136 995	14.114 043	14.091 144	15
16	15.102 343	15.076 269	15.050 259	15.024 313	14.998 430	14.972 611	16
17	15.992 395	15.963 196	15.934 073	15.905 025	15.876 052	15.847 154	17
18	16.876 370	16.843 885	16.811 489	16.779 181	16.746 961	16.714 829	18
19	17.754 309	17.718 380	17.682 554	17.646 830	17.611 208	17.575 688	19
20	18.626 254	18.586 724	18.547 313	18.508 020	18.468 844	18.429 785	20
21	19.492 245	19.448 961	19.405 812	19.362 799	19.319 920	19.277 174	21
22	20.352 323	20.305 133	20.258 097	20.211 215	20.164 485	20.117 908	22
23	21.206 528	21.155 283	21.104 212	21.053 315	21.002 590	20.952 037	23
24	22.054 900	21.999 453	21.944 202	21.889 146	21.834 284	21.779 615	24
25	22.897 480	22.837 686	22.778 112	22.718 755	22.659 616	22.600 693	25
26	23.734 307	23.670 024	23.605 985	23.542 189	23.478 635	23.415 322	26
27	24.565 419	24.496 507	24.427 865	24.359 493	24.291 389	24.223 552	27
28	25.390 857	25.317 177	25.243 796	25.170 713	25.097 926	25.025 434	28
29	26.210 659	26.132 075	26.053 820	25.975 893	25.898 293	25.821 018	29
30	27.024 863	26.941 241	26.857 981	26.775 080	26.692 538	26.610 352	30
31	27.833 508	27.744 716	27.656 320	27.568 318	27.480 708	27.393 487	31
32	28.636 631	28.542 539	28.448 880	28.355 650	28.262 848	28.170 471	32
33	29.434 270	29.334 752	29.235 703	29.137 122	29.039 006	28.941 352	33
34	30.226 463	30.121 392	30.016 830	29.912 776	29.809 226	29.706 178	34
35	31.013 247	30.902 499	30.792 303	30.682 656	30.573 555	30.464 997	35
36	31.794 659	31.678 112	31.562 162	31.446 805	31.332 037	31.217 856	36
37	32.570 735	32.448 271	32.326 449	32.205 266	32.084 718	31.964 801	37
38	33.341 512	33.213 012	33.085 202	32.958 080	32.831 641	32.705 879	38
39	34.107 026	33.972 374	33.838 464	33.705 290	33.572 850	33.441 137	39
40	34.867 314	34.726 395	34.586 272	34.446 938	34.308 389	34.170 620	40
41	35.622 410	35.475 113	35.328 667	35.183 065	35.038 302	34.894 373	41
42	36.372 350	36.218 565	36.065 688	35.913 713	35.762 632	35.612 441	42
43	37.117 169	36.956 788	36.797 374	36.638 921	36.481 421	36.324 869	43
44	37.856 903	37.689 818	37.523 763	37.358 730	37.194 712	37.031 701	44
45	38.591 586	38.417 693	38.244 894	38.073 181	37.902 546	37.732 982	45
46	39.321 252	39.140 448	38.960 805	38.782 314	38.604 967	38.428 754	46
47	40.045 936	39.858 120	39.671 533	39.486 168	39.302 014	39.119 062	47

YRS							
4	40.765 672	40.570 744	40.377 117	40.184 782	39.993 729	39.803 947	48
5	49.028 616	48.741 183	48.456 109	48.173 374	47.892 954	47.614 827	60
6	56.639 378	56.248 080	55.860 585	55.476 849	55.096 831	54.720 488	72
7	63.649 433	63.145 324	62.646 859	62.153 965	61.666 569	61.184 601	84
8	70.106 194	69.482 425	68.866 545	68.258 439	67.657 991	67.065 090	96
9	76.053 333	75.304 875	74.566 949	73.839 382	73.122 003	72.414 648	108
10	81.531 072	80.654 470	79.791 425	78.941 693	78.105 033	77.281 211	120
11	86.576 461	85.569 611	84.579 708	83.606 420	82.649 420	81.708 388	132
12	91.223 625	90.085 581	88.968 217	87.871 092	86.793 776	85.735 849	144
13	95.503 994	94.234 798	92.990 328	91.770 018	90.573 316	89.399 684	156
14	99.446 520	98.047 046	96.676 632	95.334 564	94.020 152	92.732 722	168
15	103.077 868	101.549 693	100.055 165	98.593 409	97.163 573	95.764 831	180
16	106.422 599	104.767 881	103.151 625	101.572 769	100.030 286	98.523 180	192
17	109.503 335	107.724 713	105.989 560	104.296 613	102.644 650	101.032 487	204
18	112.340 913	110.441 412	108.590 555	106.786 856	105.028 879	103.315 236	216
19	114.954 525	112.937 482	110.974 393	109.063 531	107.203 230	105.391 883	228
20	117.361 849	115.230 840	113.159 204	111.144 954	109.186 179	107.281 037	240
21	119.579 165	117.337 948	115.161 604	113.047 870	110.994 574	108.999 624	252
22	121.621 472	119.273 933	116.996 823	114.787 589	112.643 781	110.563 046	264
23	123.502 583	121.052 692	118.678 820	116.378 106	114.147 812	111.985 311	276
24	125.235 220	122.686 994	120.220 386	117.832 218	115.519 447	113.279 165	288
25	126.831 103	124.188 570	121.633 247	119.161 622	116.770 341	114.456 200	300
26	128.301 025	125.568 199	122.928 148	120.377 014	117.911 122	115.526 965	312
27	129.654 928	126.835 785	124.114 937	121.488 172	118.951 483	116.501 054	324
28	130.901 969	128.000 428	125.202 641	122.504 035	119.900 264	117.387 195	336
29	132.050 583	129.070 487	126.199 532	123.432 776	120.765 526	118.193 330	348
30	133.108 539	130.053 643	127.113 192	124.281 866	121.554 622	118.926 681	360

PRESENT VALUE PER PERIOD

MONTHLY COMPOUNDING

MOS	9.75% ANNUAL RATE	10.00% ANNUAL RATE	10.25% ANNUAL RATE	10.50% ANNUAL RATE	10.75% ANNUAL RATE	11.00% ANNUAL RATE	MOS
1	0.991 940	0.991 736	0.991 531	0.991 326	0.991 121	0.990 917	1
2	1.975 886	1.975 275	1.974 664	1.974 053	1.973 442	1.972 832	2
3	2.951 902	2.950 686	2.949 470	2.948 256	2.947 042	2.945 829	3
4	3.920 052	3.918 036	3.916 021	3.914 008	3.911 997	3.909 987	4
5	4.880 399	4.877 391	4.874 386	4.871 384	4.868 384	4.865 388	5
6	5.833 005	5.828 817	5.824 634	5.820 455	5.816 280	5.812 110	6
7	6.777 935	6.772 381	6.766 834	6.761 293	6.755 760	6.750 233	7
8	7.715 248	7.708 146	7.701 054	7.693 971	7.686 898	7.679 835	8
9	8.645 008	8.636 178	8.627 362	8.618 559	8.609 769	8.600 992	9
10	9.567 273	9.556 540	9.545 824	9.535 126	9.524 446	9.513 783	10
11	10.482 106	10.469 296	10.456 508	10.443 743	10.431 001	10.418 282	11
12	11.389 566	11.374 508	11.359 479	11.344 479	11.329 508	11.314 565	12
13	12.289 712	12.272 240	12.254 803	12.237 402	12.220 037	12.202 707	13
14	13.182 604	13.162 552	13.142 544	13.122 579	13.102 659	13.082 781	14
15	14.068 299	14.045 506	14.022 766	14.000 079	13.977 444	13.954 862	15
16	14.946 855	14.921 163	14.895 533	14.869 967	14.844 462	14.819 021	16
17	15.818 332	15.789 583	15.760 909	15.732 309	15.703 783	15.675 330	17
18	16.682 784	16.650 826	16.618 955	16.587 171	16.555 473	16.523 861	18
19	17.540 269	17.504 952	17.469 735	17.434 618	17.399 602	17.364 685	19
20	18.390 844	18.352 018	18.313 309	18.274 714	18.236 235	18.197 871	20
21	19.234 563	19.192 084	19.149 738	19.107 524	19.065 441	19.023 489	21
22	20.071 482	20.025 207	19.979 083	19.933 109	19.887 284	19.841 608	22
23	20.901 656	20.851 445	20.801 405	20.751 533	20.701 830	20.652 295	23
24	21.725 139	21.670 855	21.616 761	21.562 858	21.509 144	21.455 619	24
25	22.541 986	22.483 492	22.425 213	22.367 145	22.309 290	22.251 645	25
26	23.352 249	23.289 414	23.226 817	23.164 456	23.102 332	23.040 441	26
27	24.155 981	24.088 675	24.021 632	23.954 852	23.888 332	23.822 072	27
28	24.953 236	24.881 331	24.809 716	24.738 391	24.667 354	24.596 603	28
29	25.744 066	25.667 435	25.591 125	25.515 133	25.439 458	25.364 099	29
30	26.528 521	26.447 043	26.365 916	26.285 138	26.204 708	26.124 623	30
31	27.306 655	27.220 208	27.134 145	27.048 464	26.963 163	26.878 239	31
32	28.078 517	27.986 983	27.895 868	27.805 169	27.714 884	27.625 010	32
33	28.844 158	28.747 421	28.651 140	28.555 310	28.459 930	28.364 998	33
34	29.603 629	29.501 575	29.400 014	29.298 944	29.198 362	29.098 264	34
35	30.356 978	30.249 496	30.142 547	30.036 128	29.930 236	29.824 869	35
36	31.104 256	30.991 236	30.878 791	30.766 918	30.655 613	30.544 874	36
37	31.845 511	31.726 845	31.608 799	31.491 368	31.374 550	31.258 340	37
38	32.580 792	32.456 375	32.332 624	32.209 535	32.087 103	31.965 324	38
39	33.310 147	33.179 876	33.050 319	32.921 472	32.793 329	32.665 887	39
40	34.033 624	33.897 398	33.761 936	33.627 233	33.493 285	33.360 086	40
41	34.751 270	34.608 990	34.467 526	34.326 873	34.187 026	34.047 980	41
42	35.463 132	35.314 701	35.167 140	35.020 444	34.874 608	34.729 625	42
43	36.169 257	36.014 579	35.860 829	35.707 999	35.556 085	35.405 078	43
44	36.869 690	36.708 674	36.548 643	36.389 591	36.231 511	36.074 396	44
45	37.564 479	37.397 032	37.230 631	37.065 269	36.900 940	36.737 634	45
46	38.253 668	38.079 701	37.906 843	37.735 087	37.564 425	37.394 848	46
47	38.937 303	38.756 728	38.577 329	38.399 095	38.222 020	38.046 093	47
YRS							
4	39.615 427	39.428 160	39.242 135	39.057 344	38.873 775	38.691 421	48
5	47.338 973	47.065 369	46.793 994	46.524 827	46.257 847	45.993 034	60
6	54.347 780	53.978 665	53.613 104	53.251 057	52.892 484	52.537 346	72
7	60.707 990	60.236 667	59.770 664	59.309 613	58.853 748	58.402 903	84
8	66.479 625	65.901 488	65.330 572	64.766 771	64.209 982	63.660 103	96
9	71.717 152	71.029 355	70.351 099	69.682 229	69.022 594	68.372 043	108
10	76.469 997	75.671 163	74.884 490	74.109 758	73.346 757	72.595 275	120
11	80.783 012	79.872 986	78.978 010	78.097 792	77.232 045	76.380 487	132
12	84.696 900	83.676 528	82.674 341	81.689 957	80.723 001	79.773 109	144
13	88.248 596	87.119 542	86.012 022	84.925 549	83.859 649	82.813 859	156
14	91.471 617	90.236 201	89.025 850	87.839 962	86.677 947	85.539 231	168
15	94.396 379	93.057 439	91.747 251	90.465 078	89.210 206	87.981 937	180
16	97.050 483	95.611 259	94.204 596	92.829 614	91.485 457	90.171 293	192
17	99.458 976	97.923 008	96.423 539	94.959 437	93.529 785	92.133 576	204
18	101.644 586	100.015 633	98.427 122	96.877 844	95.366 626	93.892 337	216
19	103.627 939	101.909 902	100.236 328	98.605 822	97.017 041	95.468 685	228
20	105.427 753	103.624 619	101.869 988	100.162 274	98.499 949	96.881 539	240
21	107.061 011	105.176 801	103.345 136	101.564 226	99.832 351	98.147 856	252
22	108.543 127	106.581 856	104.677 152	102.827 014	101.029 524	99.282 835	264
23	109.888 088	107.853 730	105.879 924	103.964 453	102.105 191	100.300 098	276
24	111.108 586	109.005 045	106.965 992	104.988 985	103.071 685	101.211 853	288
25	112.216 138	110.047 230	107.946 680	105.911 817	103.940 086	102.029 044	300
26	113.221 198	110.990 629	108.832 214	106.743 045	104.720 350	102.761 478	312
27	114.133 249	111.844 605	109.631 824	107.491 762	105.421 422	103.417 947	324
28	114.960 898	112.617 635	110.353 850	108.166 158	106.051 340	104.006 328	336
29	115.711 957	113.317 392	111.005 818	108.773 611	106.617 325	104.533 685	348
30	116.393 513	113.950 820	111.594 527	109.320 766	107.125 867	105.006 346	360

PRESENT VALUE PER PERIOD

MOS	11.25% ANNUAL RATE	11.50% ANNUAL RATE	11.75% ANNUAL RATE	12.00% ANNUAL RATE	12.25% ANNUAL RATE	12.50% ANNUAL RATE	MOS
1	0.990 712	0.990 508	0.990 303	0.990 099	0.989 895	0.989 691	1
2	1.972 222	1.971 613	1.971 004	1.970 395	1.969 787	1.969 178	2
3	2.944 617	2.943 405	2.942 195	2.940 985	2.939 776	2.938 568	3
4	3.907 979	3.905 973	3.903 969	3.901 966	3.899 964	3.897 965	4
5	4.862 394	4.859 404	4.856 416	4.853 431	4.850 449	4.847 470	5
6	5.807 945	5.803 784	5.799 628	5.795 476	5.791 329	5.787 187	6
7	6.744 713	6.739 200	6.733 694	6.728 195	6.722 702	6.717 216	7
8	7.672 781	7.665 737	7.658 703	7.651 678	7.644 663	7.637 657	8
9	8.592 229	8.583 479	8.574 742	8.566 018	8.557 307	8.548 609	9
10	9.503 137	9.492 910	9.481 898	9.471 305	9.460 728	9.450 170	10
11	10.405 585	10.392 910	10.380 258	10.367 628	10.355 021	10.342 436	11
12	11.299 650	11.284 764	11.269 907	11.255 077	11.240 276	11.225 504	12
13	12.185 412	12.168 153	12.150 929	12.133 740	12.116 586	12.099 468	13
14	13.062 947	13.043 156	13.023 408	13.003 703	12.984 041	12.964 421	14
15	13.932 331	13.909 853	13.887 427	13.865 053	13.842 730	13.820 458	15
16	14.793 641	14.768 323	14.743 068	14.717 874	14.692 741	14.667 670	16
17	15.646 951	15.618 645	15.590 412	15.562 251	15.534 163	15.506 148	17
18	16.492 335	16.460 895	16.429 539	16.398 269	16.367 083	16.335 981	18
19	17.329 868	17.295 149	17.260 530	17.226 008	17.191 585	17.157 260	19
20	18.159 621	18.121 485	18.083 462	18.045 553	18.007 756	17.970 072	20
21	18.981 668	18.939 977	18.898 416	18.856 983	18.815 679	18.774 504	21
22	19.796 080	19.750 699	19.705 466	19.660 379	19.615 438	19.570 643	22
23	20.602 927	20.553 726	20.504 691	20.455 821	20.407 116	20.358 574	23
24	21.402 281	21.349 130	21.296 166	21.243 387	21.190 793	21.138 383	24
25	22.194 210	22.136 984	22.079 966	22.023 156	21.966 551	21.910 152	25
26	22.978 784	22.917 360	22.856 166	22.795 204	22.734 470	22.673 965	26
27	23.756 071	23.690 327	23.624 840	23.559 608	23.494 629	23.429 904	27
28	24.526 138	24.455 958	24.386 060	24.316 443	24.247 107	24.178 049	28
29	25.289 054	25.214 320	25.139 898	25.065 785	24.991 980	24.918 481	29
30	26.044 883	25.965 485	25.886 427	25.807 708	25.729 327	25.651 281	30
31	26.793 692	26.709 518	26.625 717	26.542 285	26.459 222	26.376 525	31
32	27.535 546	27.446 490	27.357 838	27.269 589	27.181 742	27.094 293	32
33	28.270 510	28.176 465	28.082 860	27.989 693	27.896 960	27.804 661	33
34	28.998 648	28.899 511	28.800 852	28.702 666	28.604 951	28.507 706	34
35	29.720 023	29.615 694	29.511 881	29.408 580	29.305 788	29.203 503	35
36	30.434 697	30.325 079	30.216 016	30.107 505	29.999 543	29.892 126	36
37	31.142 734	31.027 730	30.913 323	30.799 510	30.686 287	30.573 651	37
38	31.844 195	31.723 711	31.603 868	31.484 663	31.366 092	31.248 149	38
39	32.539 140	32.413 086	32.287 718	32.163 033	32.039 026	31.915 694	39
40	33.227 631	33.095 916	32.964 936	32.834 686	32.705 161	32.576 357	40
41	33.909 728	33.772 266	33.635 588	33.499 689	33.364 565	33.230 209	41
42	34.585 489	34.442 195	34.299 736	34.158 108	34.017 305	33.877 320	42
43	35.254 973	35.105 764	34.957 445	34.810 008	34.663 445	34.517 760	43
44	35.918 240	35.763 035	35.608 775	35.455 454	35.303 063	35.151 598	44
45	36.575 346	36.414 067	36.253 790	36.094 508	35.936 214	35.778 901	45
46	37.226 349	37.058 919	36.892 551	36.727 236	36.562 967	36.399 737	46
47	37.871 305	37.697 650	37.525 117	37.353 699	37.183 387	37.014 173	47
YRS							
4	38.510 272	38.330 318	38.151 550	37.973 959	37.797 537	37.622 274	48
5	45.730 366	45.469 825	45.211 389	44.955 038	44.700 755	44.448 517	60
6	52.185 606	51.837 225	51.492 166	51.150 391	50.811 866	50.476 552	72
7	57.957 015	57.516 018	57.079 852	56.648 453	56.221 761	55.799 715	84
8	63.117 034	62.580 675	62.050 930	61.527 703	61.010 900	60.500 428	96
9	67.730 430	67.097 611	66.473 444	65.857 790	65.250 512	64.651 476	108
10	71.855 110	71.126 060	70.407 928	69.700 522	69.003 652	68.317 132	120
11	75.542 845	74.718 850	73.908 238	73.110 752	72.326 139	71.554 154	132
12	78.839 923	77.923 095	77.022 284	76.137 157	75.267 390	74.412 664	144
13	81.787 728	80.780 815	79.792 692	78.822 939	77.871 148	76.936 921	156
14	84.423 259	83.329 485	82.257 381	81.206 434	80.176 140	79.166 011	168
15	86.779 597	85.602 527	84.450 090	83.321 664	82.216 646	81.134 449	180
16	88.886 318	87.629 750	86.400 830	85.198 824	84.023 015	82.872 712	192
17	90.769 865	89.437 737	88.136 304	86.864 707	85.622 114	84.407 717	204
18	92.453 881	91.050 199	89.680 267	88.343 095	87.037 725	85.763 229	216
19	93.959 501	92.488 279	91.053 851	89.655 089	88.290 902	86.960 239	228
20	95.305 625	93.770 838	92.275 859	90.819 416	89.400 284	88.017 279	240
21	96.509 148	94.914 693	93.363 017	91.852 698	90.382 370	88.950 717	252
22	97.585 177	95.934 846	94.330 205	92.769 683	91.251 768	89.775 006	264
23	98.547 217	96.844 673	95.190 663	93.583 461	92.021 407	90.502 909	276
24	99.407 345	97.656 106	95.956 169	94.305 647	92.702 734	91.145 697	288
25	100.176 355	98.379 787	96.637 200	94.946 551	93.305 883	91.713 322	300
26	100.863 902	99.025 204	97.243 079	95.515 321	93.839 823	92.214 573	312
27	101.478 613	99.600 823	97.782 098	96.020 075	94.312 497	92.657 212	324
28	102.028 205	100.114 191	98.261 636	96.468 019	94.730 934	93.048 092	336
29	102.519 577	100.572 040	98.688 256	96.865 546	95.101 358	93.393 265	348
30	102.958 896	100.980 375	99.067 798	97.218 331	95.429 278	93.698 077	360

MOS	12.75% ANNUAL RATE	13.00% ANNUAL RATE	13.25% ANNUAL RATE	13.50% ANNUAL RATE	13.75% ANNUAL RATE	14.00% ANNUAL RATE	MOS
1	0.989 487	0.989 283	0.989 079	0.988 875	0.988 671	0.988 468	1
2	1.968 571	1.967 963	1.967 356	1.966 749	1.966 143	1.965 537	2
3	2.937 361	2.936 155	2.934 949	2.933 745	2.932 541	2.931 338	3
4	3.895 967	3.893 970	3.891 975	3.889 982	3.887 991	3.886 001	4
5	4.844 494	4.841 520	4.838 550	4.835 582	4.832 617	4.829 655	5
6	5.783 049	5.778 915	5.774 786	5.770 662	5.766 542	5.762 427	6
7	6.711 737	6.706 264	6.700 798	6.695 339	6.689 887	6.684 442	7
8	7.630 661	7.623 674	7.616 697	7.609 730	7.602 772	7.595 824	8
9	8.539 924	8.531 253	8.522 594	8.513 948	8.505 315	8.496 696	9
10	9.439 628	9.429 104	9.418 597	9.408 107	9.397 634	9.387 178	10
11	10.329 873	10.317 333	10.304 814	10.292 318	10.279 844	10.267 392	11
12	11.210 759	11.196 042	11.181 354	11.166 693	11.152 060	11.137 455	12
13	12.082 384	12.065 335	12.048 320	12.031 340	12.014 395	11.997 485	13
14	12.944 845	12.925 310	12.905 818	12.886 369	12.866 961	12.847 596	14
15	13.798 238	13.776 070	13.753 952	13.731 885	13.709 869	13.687 904	15
16	14.642 660	14.617 711	14.592 823	14.567 995	14.543 228	14.518 521	16
17	15.478 204	15.450 332	15.422 532	15.394 804	15.367 146	15.339 559	17
18	16.304 964	16.274 030	16.243 181	16.212 414	16.181 730	16.151 130	18
19	17.123 032	17.088 901	17.054 866	17.020 928	16.987 087	16.953 341	19
20	17.932 499	17.895 038	17.857 688	17.820 448	17.783 319	17.746 300	20
21	18.733 456	18.692 535	18.651 741	18.611 074	18.570 532	18.530 116	21
22	19.525 992	19.481 486	19.437 123	19.392 904	19.348 827	19.304 892	22
23	20.310 196	20.261 981	20.213 928	20.166 036	20.118 305	20.070 733	23
24	21.086 156	21.034 112	20.982 249	20.930 567	20.879 065	20.827 743	24
25	21.853 958	21.797 967	21.742 179	21.686 593	21.631 208	21.576 023	25
26	22.613 687	22.553 636	22.493 810	22.434 208	22.374 829	22.315 673	26
27	23.365 430	23.301 206	23.237 232	23.173 506	23.110 027	23.046 794	27
28	24.109 269	24.040 765	23.972 535	23.904 579	23.836 896	23.769 483	28
29	24.845 287	24.772 397	24.699 808	24.627 520	24.555 531	24.483 839	29
30	25.573 568	25.496 188	25.419 139	25.342 418	25.266 024	25.189 956	30
31	26.294 193	26.212 222	26.130 613	26.049 362	25.968 469	25.887 930	31
32	27.007 241	26.920 583	26.834 317	26.748 442	26.662 956	26.577 855	32
33	27.712 792	27.621 351	27.530 337	27.439 745	27.349 575	27.259 824	33
34	28.410 926	28.314 610	28.218 755	28.123 357	28.028 416	27.933 928	34
35	29.101 720	29.000 438	28.899 654	28.799 365	28.699 567	28.600 258	35
36	29.785 252	29.678 917	29.573 118	29.467 851	29.363 115	29.258 904	36
37	30.461 598	30.350 124	30.239 226	30.128 901	30.019 145	29.909 955	37
38	31.130 832	31.014 137	30.898 060	30.782 597	30.667 744	30.553 497	38
39	31.793 031	31.671 034	31.549 699	31.429 020	31.308 995	31.189 619	39
40	32.448 269	32.320 891	32.194 221	32.068 253	31.942 982	31.818 404	40
41	33.096 617	32.963 784	32.831 704	32.700 373	32.569 786	32.439 938	41
42	33.738 149	33.599 786	33.462 226	33.325 462	33.189 490	33.054 304	42
43	34.372 937	34.228 972	34.085 861	33.943 596	33.802 173	33.661 586	43
44	35.001 051	34.851 415	34.702 685	34.554 854	34.407 916	34.261 864	44
45	35.622 561	35.467 187	35.312 773	35.159 312	35.006 797	34.855 220	45
46	36.237 537	36.076 360	35.916 199	35.757 045	35.598 893	35.441 733	46
47	36.846 048	36.679 004	36.513 034	36.348 129	36.184 281	36.021 482	47

YRS	12.75%	13.00%	13.25%	13.50%	13.75%	14.00%	
4	37.448 161	37.275 190	37.103 351	36.932 637	36.763 038	36.594 546	48
5	44.198 308	43.950 107	43.703 896	43.459 656	43.217 369	42.977 016	60
6	50.144 416	49.815 421	49.489 533	49.166 717	48.846 940	48.530 168	72
7	55.382 257	54.969 328	54.560 870	54.156 827	53.757 142	53.361 760	84
8	59.996 197	59.498 115	59.006 096	58.520 052	58.039 898	57.565 549	96
9	64.060 550	63.477 604	62.902 511	62.335 146	61.775 387	61.223 111	108
10	67.640 780	66.974 419	66.317 872	65.670 668	65.033 539	64.405 420	120
11	70.794 554	70.047 103	69.311 569	68.587 726	67.875 352	67.174 230	132
12	73.572 668	72.747 100	71.935 663	71.138 066	70.354 027	69.583 269	144
13	76.019 869	75.119 613	74.235 783	73.368 018	72.515 967	71.679 284	156
14	78.175 574	77.204 363	76.251 929	75.317 832	74.401 645	73.502 950	168
15	80.074 503	79.036 253	78.019 160	77.022 700	76.046 363	75.089 654	180
16	81.747 242	80.645 952	79.568 208	78.513 394	77.480 913	76.470 187	192
17	83.220 735	82.060 410	80.926 008	79.816 818	78.732 151	77.671 337	204
18	84.518 713	83.303 307	82.116 174	80.956 500	79.823 500	78.716 413	216
19	85.662 083	84.395 453	83.159 401	81.953 009	80.775 392	79.625 696	228
20	86.669 262	85.355 132	84.073 830	82.824 331	81.605 648	80.416 829	240
21	87.556 471	86.198 412	84.875 363	83.586 193	82.329 810	81.105 164	252
22	88.338 001	86.939 409	85.577 938	84.252 345	82.961 436	81.704 060	264
23	89.026 440	87.590 531	86.193 773	84.834 813	83.512 350	82.225 136	276
24	89.632 875	88.162 677	86.733 576	85.344 107	83.992 866	82.678 506	288
25	90.167 076	88.665 428	87.206 735	85.789 421	84.411 980	83.072 966	300
26	90.637 645	89.107 200	87.621 477	86.178 793	84.777 538	83.416 171	312
27	91.052 163	89.495 389	87.985 015	86.519 249	85.096 383	83.714 781	324
28	91.417 306	89.836 495	88.303 670	86.816 936	85.374 485	83.974 591	336
29	91.738 956	90.136 227	88.582 983	87.077 226	85.617 050	84.200 641	348
30	92.022 292	90.399 605	88.827 813	87.304 817	85.828 619	84.397 320	360

MOS	14.25% ANNUAL RATE	14.50% ANNUAL RATE	14.75% ANNUAL RATE	15.00% ANNUAL RATE	15.25% ANNUAL RATE	15.50% ANNUAL RATE	MOS
1	0.988 264	0.988 061	0.987 858	0.987 654	0.987 451	0.987 248	1
2	1.964 931	1.964 325	1.963 720	1.963 115	1.962 511	1.961 907	2
3	2.930 135	2.928 934	2.927 733	2.926 534	2.925 335	2.924 137	3
4	3.884 013	3.882 026	3.880 041	3.878 058	3.876 076	3.874 096	4
5	4.826 696	4.823 739	4.820 786	4.817 835	4.814 887	4.811 942	5
6	5.758 316	5.754 209	5.750 107	5.746 010	5.741 917	5.737 828	6
7	6.679 003	6.673 570	6.668 145	6.662 726	6.657 314	6.651 908	7
8	7.588 885	7.581 955	7.575 035	7.568 124	7.561 223	7.554 331	8
9	8.488 089	8.479 495	8.470 913	8.462 345	8.453 789	8.445 247	9
10	9.376 700	9.366 318	9.355 914	9.345 526	9.335 155	9.324 801	10
11	10.254 962	10.242 554	10.230 168	10.217 803	10.205 461	10.193 140	11
12	11.122 878	11.108 328	11.093 806	11.079 312	11.064 845	11.050 406	12
13	11.980 608	11.963 766	11.946 958	11.930 185	11.913 445	11.896 739	13
14	12.828 272	12.808 991	12.789 751	12.770 553	12.751 396	12.732 281	14
15	13.665 989	13.644 124	13.622 310	13.600 546	13.578 832	13.557 167	15
16	14.493 874	14.469 287	14.444 760	14.420 292	14.395 884	14.371 535	16
17	15.312 044	15.284 598	15.257 223	15.229 918	15.202 683	15.175 518	17
18	16.120 611	16.090 175	16.059 821	16.029 549	15.999 358	15.969 248	18
19	16.919 690	16.886 135	16.852 674	16.819 308	16.786 036	16.752 857	19
20	17.709 390	17.672 591	17.635 899	17.599 316	17.562 841	17.526 474	20
21	18.489 824	18.449 657	18.409 614	18.369 695	18.329 899	18.290 225	21
22	19.261 099	19.217 447	19.173 935	19.130 563	19.087 330	19.044 237	22
23	20.023 322	19.976 069	19.928 974	19.882 037	19.835 257	19.788 634	23
24	20.776 600	20.725 634	20.674 846	20.624 235	20.573 799	20.523 538	24
25	21.521 037	21.466 250	21.411 661	21.357 269	21.303 072	21.249 071	25
26	22.256 739	22.198 024	22.139 529	22.081 253	22.023 194	21.965 352	26
27	22.983 806	22.921 061	22.858 560	22.796 299	22.734 279	22.672 499	27
28	23.702 341	23.635 466	23.568 859	23.502 518	23.436 441	23.370 628	28
29	24.412 443	24.341 342	24.270 534	24.200 018	24.129 792	24.059 855	29
30	25.114 212	25.038 790	24.963 688	24.888 906	24.814 442	24.740 293	30
31	25.807 745	25.727 911	25.648 426	25.569 290	25.490 500	25.412 054	31
32	26.493 139	26.408 804	26.324 850	26.241 274	26.158 074	26.075 248	32
33	27.170 489	27.081 569	26.993 061	26.904 962	26.817 271	26.729 986	33
34	27.839 890	27.746 301	27.653 157	27.560 456	27.468 196	27.376 375	34
35	28.501 436	28.403 097	28.305 239	28.207 858	28.110 953	28.014 520	35
36	29.155 218	29.052 051	28.949 402	28.847 267	28.745 644	28.644 529	36
37	29.801 327	29.693 258	29.585 744	29.478 783	29.372 370	29.266 503	37
38	30.439 854	30.326 809	30.214 359	30.102 501	29.991 231	29.880 546	38
39	31.070 887	30.952 796	30.835 341	30.718 520	30.602 327	30.486 759	39
40	31.694 514	31.571 309	31.448 784	31.326 933	31.205 754	31.085 241	40
41	32.310 823	32.182 438	32.054 777	31.927 835	31.801 608	31.676 091	41
42	32.919 900	32.786 271	32.653 412	32.521 319	32.389 986	32.259 407	42
43	33.521 828	33.382 894	33.244 778	33.107 475	32.970 979	32.835 285	43
44	34.116 692	33.972 394	33.828 964	33.686 395	33.544 682	33.403 819	44
45	34.704 575	34.554 856	34.406 056	34.258 168	34.111 186	33.965 103	45
46	35.285 559	35.130 364	34.976 141	34.822 882	34.670 581	34.519 230	46
47	35.859 725	35.699 002	35.539 304	35.380 624	35.222 956	35.066 290	47

YRS							
4	36.427 153	36.260 850	36.095 628	35.931 481	35.768 399	35.606 374	48
5	42.738 580	42.502 042	42.267 385	42.034 592	41.803 644	41.574 525	60
6	48.216 368	47.905 507	47.597 553	47.292 474	46.990 239	46.690 816	72
7	52.970 627	52.583 688	52.200 892	51.822 185	51.447 517	51.076 835	84
8	57.096 923	56.633 938	56.176 513	55.724 570	55.278 031	54.836 819	96
9	60.678 201	60.140 540	59.610 013	59.086 509	58.569 915	58.060 124	108
10	63.786 449	63.176 466	62.575 317	61.982 847	61.398 908	60.823 352	120
11	66.484 146	65.804 893	65.136 267	64.478 068	63.830 100	63.192 173	132
12	68.825 521	68.080 518	67.348 003	66.627 722	65.919 429	65.222 881	144
13	70.857 636	70.050 696	69.258 143	68.479 668	67.714 965	66.963 738	156
14	72.621 342	71.756 425	70.907 814	70.075 134	69.258 020	68.456 114	168
15	74.152 090	73.233 202	72.332 534	71.449 643	70.584 097	69.735 477	180
16	75.480 650	74.511 757	73.562 977	72.633 794	71.723 707	70.832 231	192
17	76.633 729	75.618 698	74.625 635	73.653 950	72.703 070	71.772 440	204
18	77.634 504	76.577 058	75.543 388	74.532 823	73.544 719	72.578 449	216
19	78.503 092	77.406 782	76.335 994	75.289 980	74.268 019	73.269 413	228
20	79.256 954	78.125 136	77.020 520	75.942 278	74.889 612	73.861 752	240
21	79.911 242	78.747 069	77.611 703	76.504 237	75.423 799	74.369 545	252
22	80.479 110	79.285 522	78.122 271	76.988 370	75.882 871	74.804 857	264
23	80.971 971	79.751 701	78.563 217	77.405 455	76.277 390	75.178 036	276
24	81.399 733	80.155 306	78.944 036	77.764 777	76.616 433	75.497 949	288
25	81.770 994	80.504 738	79.272 925	78.074 336	76.907 802	75.772 200	300
26	82.093 218	80.807 267	79.556 967	78.341 024	77.158 200	76.007 306	312
27	82.372 881	81.069 189	79.802 276	78.570 778	77.373 387	76.208 854	324
28	82.615 605	81.295 954	80.014 135	78.768 713	77.558 316	76.381 634	336
29	82.826 269	81.492 281	80.197 104	78.939 236	77.717 241	76.529 752	348
30	83.009 107	81.662 256	80.355 124	79.086 142	77.853 819	76.656 729	360

PRESENT VALUE PER PERIOD

MOS	15.75% ANNUAL RATE	16.00% ANNUAL RATE	16.25% ANNUAL RATE	16.50% ANNUAL RATE	16.75% ANNUAL RATE	17.00% ANNUAL RATE	MOS
1	0.987 045	0.986 842	0.986 639	0.986 436	0.986 234	0.986 031	1
2	1.961 303	1.960 699	1.960 096	1.959 493	1.958 891	1.958 289	2
3	2.922 939	2.921 743	2.920 547	2.919 352	2.918 158	2.916 965	3
4	3.872 118	3.870 141	3.868 166	3.866 192	3.864 220	3.862 250	4
5	4.809 000	4.806 060	4.803 124	4.800 190	4.797 259	4.794 330	5
6	5.733 744	5.729 665	5.725 589	5.721 519	5.717 452	5.713 391	6
7	6.646 509	6.641 116	6.635 731	6.630 351	6.624 979	6.619 613	7
8	7.547 449	7.540 575	7.533 712	7.526 857	7.520 012	7.513 176	8
9	8.436 717	8.428 199	8.419 695	8.411 203	8.402 724	8.394 257	9
10	9.314 464	9.304 144	9.293 841	9.283 554	9.273 284	9.263 031	10
11	10.180 841	10.168 563	10.156 307	10.144 073	10.131 860	10.119 669	11
12	11.035 993	11.021 600	11.007 251	10.992 921	10.978 617	10.964 341	12
13	11.880 068	11.863 430	11.846 825	11.830 255	11.813 717	11.797 214	13
14	12.713 207	12.694 174	12.675 182	12.656 231	12.637 321	12.618 452	14
15	13.535 553	13.513 987	13.492 472	13.471 005	13.449 588	13.428 219	15
16	14.347 245	14.323 014	14.298 841	14.274 728	14.250 672	14.226 675	16
17	15.148 422	15.121 395	15.094 438	15.067 549	15.040 729	15.013 977	17
18	15.939 220	15.909 272	15.879 404	15.849 617	15.819 909	15.790 281	18
19	16.719 773	16.686 781	16.653 883	16.621 077	16.588 363	16.555 741	19
20	17.490 214	17.454 450	17.418 014	17.382 073	17.346 238	17.310 509	20
21	18.250 674	18.211 244	18.171 935	18.132 748	18.093 681	18.054 734	21
22	19.001 282	18.958 464	18.915 784	18.873 241	18.830 834	18.788 562	22
23	19.742 166	19.695 853	19.649 695	19.603 690	19.557 839	19.512 140	23
24	20.473 452	20.423 539	20.373 799	20.324 232	20.274 836	20.225 611	24
25	21.195 264	21.141 650	21.088 230	21.035 001	20.981 963	20.929 115	25
26	21.907 725	21.850 313	21.793 115	21.736 129	21.679 355	21.622 792	26
27	22.610 956	22.549 651	22.488 582	22.427 747	22.367 147	22.306 780	27
28	23.305 077	23.239 787	23.174 757	23.109 985	23.045 471	22.981 212	28
29	23.990 206	23.920 842	23.851 764	23.782 969	23.714 456	23.646 224	29
30	24.666 458	24.592 937	24.519 764	24.446 825	24.374 233	24.301 947	30
31	25.333 950	25.256 187	25.178 764	25.101 677	25.024 926	24.948 509	31
32	25.992 795	25.910 711	25.828 996	25.747 647	25.666 663	25.586 041	32
33	26.643 104	26.556 623	26.470 541	26.384 855	26.299 565	26.214 666	33
34	27.284 989	27.194 036	27.103 514	27.013 421	26.923 754	26.834 511	34
35	27.918 558	27.823 062	27.728 030	27.633 461	27.539 350	27.445 697	35
36	28.543 919	28.443 811	28.344 203	28.245 091	28.146 473	28.048 345	36
37	29.161 178	29.056 392	28.952 142	28.848 425	28.745 237	28.642 575	37
38	29.770 441	29.660 914	29.551 960	29.443 576	29.335 759	29.228 505	38
39	30.371 811	30.257 480	30.143 763	30.030 654	29.918 151	29.806 249	39
40	30.965 390	30.846 198	30.727 659	30.609 770	30.492 526	30.375 924	40
41	31.551 280	31.427 169	31.303 794	31.181 031	31.058 994	30.937 641	41
42	32.129 579	32.000 496	31.872 152	31.744 543	31.617 665	31.491 511	42
43	32.700 386	32.566 279	32.432 956	32.300 413	32.168 644	32.037 644	43
44	33.263 799	33.124 617	32.986 267	32.848 742	32.712 038	32.576 149	44
45	33.819 913	33.675 609	33.532 185	33.389 635	33.247 952	33.107 131	45
46	34.368 822	34.219 351	34.070 809	33.923 191	33.776 489	33.630 696	46
47	34.910 620	34.755 938	34.602 238	34.449 510	34.297 749	34.146 948	47

YRS							
4	35.445 399	35.285 465	35.126 565	34.968 691	34.811 834	34.655 988	48
5	41.347 218	41.121 706	40.897 973	40.676 001	40.455 775	40.237 278	60
6	46.394 174	46.100 283	45.809 114	45.520 636	45.234 820	44.951 636	72
7	50.710 091	50.347 235	49.988 218	49.632 991	49.281 508	48.933 722	84
8	54.400 859	53.970 077	53.544 399	53.123 753	52.708 070	52.297 278	96
9	57.557 029	57.060 524	56.570 508	56.086 877	55.609 534	55.138 379	108
10	60.256 035	59.696 816	59.145 555	58.602 117	58.066 368	57.538 177	120
11	62.564 098	61.945 692	61.336 776	60.737 172	60.146 709	59.565 218	132
12	64.537 844	63.864 085	63.201 380	62.549 508	61.908 252	61.277 403	144
13	66.225 697	65.500 561	64.788 053	64.087 904	63.399 851	62.723 638	156
14	67.669 070	66.896 549	66.138 222	65.393 767	64.662 872	63.945 231	168
15	68.903 373	68.087 390	67.287 140	66.502 246	65.732 344	64.977 077	180
16	69.958 891	69.103 231	68.264 803	67.443 176	66.637 927	65.848 648	192
17	70.861 520	69.969 789	69.096 740	68.241 881	67.404 735	66.584 839	204
18	71.633 406	70.709 003	69.804 671	68.919 860	68.054 035	67.206 679	216
19	72.293 486	71.339 585	70.407 081	69.495 360	68.603 834	67.731 930	228
20	72.857 955	71.877 501	70.919 697	69.983 873	69.069 380	68.175 595	240
21	73.340 662	72.336 367	71.355 904	70.398 545	69.463 585	68.550 346	252
22	73.753 450	72.727 801	71.727 092	70.750 538	69.797 380	68.866 887	264
23	74.106 447	73.061 711	72.042 952	71.049 327	70.080 024	69.134 261	276
24	74.408 313	73.346 552	72.311 731	71.302 953	70.319 354	69.360 104	288
25	74.666 455	73.589 534	72.540 447	71.518 243	70.522 008	69.550 868	300
26	74.887 205	73.796 809	72.735 071	71.700 991	70.693 607	69.712 000	312
27	75.075 981	73.973 623	72.900 685	71.856 116	70.838 910	69.848 104	324
28	75.237 413	74.124 454	73.041 613	71.987 794	70.961 946	69.963 067	336
29	75.375 461	74.253 120	73.161 535	72.099 568	71.066 128	70.060 174	348
30	75.493 514	74.362 878	73.263 582	72.194 447	71.154 344	70.142 196	360

MONTHLY COMPOUNDING

SECTION 5

MOS	17.25% ANNUAL RATE	17.50% ANNUAL RATE	17.75% ANNUAL RATE	18.00% ANNUAL RATE	18.25% ANNUAL RATE	18.50% ANNUAL RATE	MOS
1	0.985 829	0.985 626	0.985 424	0.985 222	0.985 019	0.984 817	1
2	1.957 687	1.957 085	1.956 484	1.955 883	1.955 283	1.954 683	2
3	2.915 773	2.914 581	2.913 390	2.912 200	2.911 011	2.909 823	3
4	3.860 281	3.858 314	3.856 349	3.854 385	3.852 422	3.850 462	4
5	4.791 405	4.788 482	4.785 562	4.782 645	4.779 731	4.776 819	5
6	5.709 333	5.705 280	5.701 231	5.697 187	5.693 147	5.689 112	6
7	6.614 253	6.608 900	6.603 554	6.598 214	6.592 881	6.587 554	7
8	7.506 349	7.499 532	7.492 724	7.485 925	7.479 135	7.472 355	8
9	8.385 803	8.377 362	8.368 933	8.360 517	8.352 114	8.343 723	9
10	9.252 795	9.242 575	9.232 371	9.222 185	9.212 014	9.201 861	10
11	10.107 499	10.095 351	10.083 224	10.071 118	10.059 033	10.046 970	11
12	10.950 092	10.935 869	10.921 674	10.907 505	10.893 363	10.879 248	12
13	11.780 744	11.764 307	11.747 903	11.731 532	11.715 195	11.698 890	13
14	12.599 624	12.580 836	12.562 089	12.543 382	12.524 715	12.506 088	14
15	13.406 900	13.385 629	13.364 407	13.343 233	13.322 108	13.301 030	15
16	14.202 735	14.178 854	14.155 030	14.131 264	14.107 555	14.083 904	16
17	14.987 293	14.960 677	14.934 130	14.907 649	14.881 236	14.854 891	17
18	15.760 733	15.731 263	15.701 873	15.672 561	15.643 327	15.614 172	18
19	16.523 211	16.490 773	16.458 425	16.426 168	16.394 002	16.361 926	19
20	17.274 885	17.239 365	17.203 950	17.168 639	17.133 431	17.098 327	20
21	18.015 906	17.977 198	17.938 608	17.900 137	17.861 783	17.823 547	21
22	18.746 426	18.704 425	18.662 558	18.620 824	18.579 224	18.537 757	22
23	19.466 594	19.421 199	19.375 955	19.330 861	19.285 917	19.241 123	23
24	20.176 556	20.127 671	20.078 954	20.030 405	19.982 024	19.933 810	24
25	20.876 457	20.823 988	20.771 706	20.719 611	20.667 703	20.615 980	25
26	21.566 439	21.510 296	21.454 360	21.398 632	21.343 110	21.287 793	26
27	22.246 644	22.186 739	22.127 064	22.067 617	22.008 399	21.949 406	27
28	22.917 209	22.853 459	22.789 962	22.726 717	22.663 721	22.600 975	28
29	23.578 271	23.510 597	23.443 198	23.376 076	23.309 227	23.242 651	29
30	24.229 966	24.158 288	24.086 913	24.015 838	23.945 062	23.874 584	30
31	24.872 425	24.796 670	24.721 244	24.646 146	24.571 373	24.496 923	31
32	25.505 779	25.425 876	25.346 330	25.267 139	25.188 301	25.109 814	32
33	26.130 158	26.046 038	25.962 304	25.878 954	25.795 987	25.713 399	33
34	26.745 689	26.657 286	26.569 300	26.481 728	26.394 569	26.307 820	34
35	27.352 497	27.259 748	27.167 448	27.075 595	26.984 185	26.893 216	35
36	27.950 705	27.853 550	27.756 878	27.660 684	27.564 967	27.469 724	36
37	28.540 436	28.438 818	28.337 716	28.237 127	28.137 050	28.037 480	37
38	29.121 810	29.015 672	28.910 087	28.805 052	28.700 562	28.596 615	38
39	29.694 946	29.584 236	29.474 116	29.364 583	29.255 633	29.147 262	39
40	30.259 959	30.144 626	30.029 923	29.915 845	29.802 388	29.689 548	40
41	30.816 965	30.696 962	30.577 629	30.458 961	30.340 953	30.223 601	41
42	31.366 077	31.241 359	31.117 352	30.994 050	30.871 449	30.749 545	42
43	31.907 408	31.777 931	31.649 207	31.521 232	31.393 999	31.267 505	43
44	32.441 068	32.306 790	32.173 310	32.040 622	31.908 721	31.777 600	44
45	32.967 165	32.828 048	32.689 774	32.552 337	32.415 731	32.279 951	45
46	33.485 807	33.341 813	33.198 710	33.056 490	32.915 147	32.774 674	46
47	33.997 098	33.848 194	33.700 227	33.553 192	33.407 081	33.261 887	47

YRS

MOS	17.25%	17.50%	17.75%	18.00%	18.25%	18.50%	MOS
4	34.501 144	34.347 296	34.194 435	34.042 554	33.891 645	33.741 702	48
5	40.020 495	39.805 409	39.592 006	39.380 269	39.170 183	38.961 733	60
6	44.671 058	44.393 055	44.117 601	43.844 667	43.574 226	43.306 252	72
7	48.589 587	48.249 057	47.912 087	47.578 633	47.248 652	46.922 100	84
8	51.891 310	51.490 098	51.093 575	50.701 675	50.314 336	49.931 492	96
9	54.673 317	54.214 253	53.761 094	53.313 690	52.872 128	52.436 143	108
10	57.017 415	56.503 956	55.997 676	55.498 454	55.006 171	54.520 710	120
11	58.992 534	58.428 493	57.872 939	57.325 714	56.786 667	56.255 650	132
12	60.656 754	60.046 103	59.445 253	58.854 011	58.272 189	57.699 602	144
13	62.059 014	61.405 734	60.763 561	60.132 260	59.511 605	58.901 372	156
14	63.240 547	62.548 529	61.868 896	61.201 371	60.545 686	59.901 580	168
15	64.236 098	63.509 070	62.795 665	62.095 562	61.408 452	60.734 031	180
16	65.074 942	64.316 422	63.572 714	62.843 452	62.128 283	61.426 861	192
17	65.781 745	64.995 017	64.224 231	63.468 978	62.728 860	62.003 489	204
18	66.377 292	65.565 388	64.770 496	63.992 160	63.229 939	62.483 404	216
19	66.879 096	66.044 796	65.228 512	64.429 743	63.648 005	62.882 827	228
20	67.301 912	66.447 747	65.612 535	64.795 732	63.996 810	63.215 258	240
21	67.658 173	66.786 434	65.934 520	65.101 841	64.287 828	63.491 933	252
22	67.958 356	67.071 108	66.204 488	65.357 866	64.530 633	63.722 203	264
23	68.211 288	67.310 381	66.430 843	65.572 002	64.733 213	63.913 852	276
24	68.424 407	67.511 495	66.620 620	65.751 103	64.902 231	64.073 358	288
25	68.603 979	67.680 535	66.779 757	65.900 901	65.043 248	64.206 111	300
26	68.755 285	67.822 616	66.913 177	66.026 190	65.160 903	64.316 598	312
27	68.882 775	67.942 037	67.025 043	66.130 980	65.259 066	64.408 554	324
28	68.990 196	68.042 414	67.118 838	66.218 625	65.340 966	64.485 088	336
29	69.080 709	68.126 782	67.197 479	66.291 930	65.409 298	64.548 785	348
30	69.156 974	68.197 695	67.263 417	66.353 242	65.466 310	64.601 798	360

	18.75% ANNUAL RATE	19.00% ANNUAL RATE	19.25% ANNUAL RATE	19.50% ANNUAL RATE	19.75% ANNUAL RATE	20.00% ANNUAL RATE	
MOS							**MOS**
1	0.984 615	0.984 413	0.984 212	0.984 010	0.983 808	0.983 607	1
2	1.954 083	1.953 483	1.952 884	1.952 285	1.951 687	1.951 088	2
3	2.908 635	2.907 449	2.906 263	2.905 078	2.903 893	2.902 710	3
4	3.848 503	3.846 545	3.844 589	3.842 635	3.840 682	3.838 731	4
5	4.773 910	4.771 004	4.768 101	4.765 200	4.762 303	4.759 408	5
6	5.685 081	5.681 054	5.677 032	5.673 014	5.669 000	5.664 991	6
7	6.582 233	6.576 920	6.571 612	6.566 311	6.561 017	6.555 729	7
8	7.465 584	7.458 822	7.452 069	7.445 325	7.438 590	7.431 865	8
9	8.335 344	8.326 978	8.318 624	8.310 283	8.301 954	8.293 637	9
10	9.191 723	9.181 602	9.171 498	9.161 410	9.151 338	9.141 283	10
11	10.034 928	10.022 906	10.010 906	9.998 927	9.986 969	9.975 032	11
12	10.865 159	10.851 097	10.837 062	10.823 053	10.809 070	10.795 113	12
13	11.682 618	11.666 380	11.650 174	11.634 000	11.617 859	11.601 751	13
14	12.487 501	12.468 955	12.450 448	12.431 980	12.413 553	12.395 165	14
15	13.280 001	13.259 020	13.238 087	13.217 201	13.196 363	13.175 572	15
16	14.060 309	14.036 771	14.013 290	13.989 866	13.966 497	13.943 186	16
17	14.828 612	14.802 400	14.776 254	14.750 175	14.724 162	14.698 215	17
18	15.585 095	15.556 095	15.527 173	15.498 327	15.469 559	15.440 868	18
19	16.329 939	16.298 043	16.266 235	16.234 517	16.202 887	16.171 345	19
20	17.063 325	17.028 426	16.993 629	16.958 934	16.924 340	16.889 848	20
21	17.785 428	17.747 425	17.709 538	17.671 768	17.634 112	17.596 571	21
22	18.496 421	18.455 217	18.414 145	18.373 203	18.332 391	18.291 710	22
23	19.196 476	19.151 978	19.107 627	19.063 422	19.019 364	18.975 452	23
24	19.885 761	19.837 878	19.790 160	19.742 605	19.695 214	19.647 986	24
25	20.564 442	20.513 087	20.461 916	20.410 928	20.360 120	20.309 494	25
26	21.232 681	21.177 773	21.123 067	21.068 563	21.014 261	20.960 158	26
27	21.890 640	21.832 098	21.773 779	21.715 684	21.657 809	21.600 156	27
28	22.538 476	22.476 224	22.414 218	22.352 456	22.290 938	22.229 661	28
29	23.176 346	23.110 311	23.044 545	22.979 047	22.913 814	22.848 847	29
30	23.804 402	23.734 515	23.664 920	23.595 618	23.526 606	23.457 882	30
31	24.422 796	24.348 989	24.275 501	24.202 330	24.129 475	24.056 933	31
32	25.031 676	24.953 886	24.876 441	24.799 341	24.722 582	24.646 164	32
33	25.631 189	25.549 354	25.467 894	25.386 805	25.306 086	25.225 735	33
34	26.221 478	26.135 542	26.050 008	25.964 876	25.880 142	25.795 805	34
35	26.802 686	26.712 592	26.622 932	26.533 703	26.444 903	26.356 530	35
36	27.374 952	27.280 649	27.186 810	27.093 435	27.000 520	26.908 062	36
37	27.938 415	27.839 851	27.741 786	27.644 216	27.547 140	27.450 553	37
38	28.493 208	28.390 337	28.287 999	28.186 191	28.084 909	27.984 150	38
39	29.039 467	28.932 243	28.825 589	28.719 499	28.613 971	28.509 000	39
40	29.577 321	29.465 703	29.354 691	29.244 279	29.134 466	29.025 246	40
41	30.106 901	29.990 848	29.875 439	29.760 669	29.646 533	29.533 029	41
42	30.628 333	30.507 808	30.387 965	30.268 801	30.150 309	30.032 487	42
43	31.141 743	31.016 710	30.892 440	30.768 807	30.645 929	30.523 758	43
44	31.647 255	31.517 680	31.388 870	31.260 819	31.133 523	31.006 975	44
45	32.144 989	32.010 842	31.877 501	31.744 963	31.613 222	31.482 271	45
46	32.635 066	32.496 317	32.358 419	32.221 366	32.085 154	31.949 774	46
47	33.117 604	32.974 225	32.831 743	32.690 151	32.549 444	32.409 614	47
YRS							
4	33.592 718	33.444 684	33.297 594	33.151 440	33.006 217	32.861 916	48
5	38.754 905	38.549 682	38.346 051	38.143 997	37.943 505	37.744 561	60
6	43.040 717	42.777 596	42.516 861	42.258 489	42.002 452	41.748 727	72
7	46.598 935	46.279 115	45.962 599	45.649 346	45.339 316	45.032 470	84
8	49.553 081	49.179 042	48.809 314	48.443 838	48.082 555	47.725 406	96
9	52.005 707	51.580 735	51.161 144	50.746 850	50.337 773	49.933 833	108
10	54.041 956	53.569 796	53.104 120	52.644 820	52.191 790	51.744 924	120
11	55.732 514	55.217 118	54.709 321	54.208 986	53.715 978	53.230 165	132
12	57.136 070	56.581 415	56.035 467	55.498 055	54.969 014	54.448 184	144
13	58.301 346	57.711 314	57.131 069	56.560 409	55.999 136	55.447 059	156
14	59.268 796	58.647 086	58.036 207	57.435 922	56.846 000	56.266 217	168
15	60.072 003	59.422 084	58.783 991	58.157 454	57.542 208	56.937 994	180
16	60.738 852	60.063 930	59.401 778	58.752 088	58.114 561	57.488 906	192
17	61.292 491	60.595 501	59.912 165	59.242 140	58.585 092	57.940 698	204
18	61.752 140	61.035 743	60.333 824	59.646 005	58.971 917	58.311 205	216
19	62.133 755	61.400 348	60.682 181	59.978 840	59.289 925	58.615 050	228
20	62.450 282	61.702 310	60.969 977	60.253 138	59.551 361	58.864 229	240
21	62.713 625	61.952 393	61.207 742	60.479 194	59.766 287	59.068 575	252
22	62.932 011	62.159 509	61.404 172	60.665 492	59.942 977	59.236 156	264
23	63.113 321	62.331 041	61.566 454	60.819 025	60.088 235	59.373 585	276
24	63.263 851	62.473 102	61.700 525	60.945 566	60.207 651	59.486 289	288
25	63.388 826	62.590 755	61.811 288	61.049 833	60.305 824	59.578 715	300
26	63.492 584	62.688 195	61.902 795	61.135 770	60.386 531	59.654 512	312
27	63.578 727	62.768 894	61.978 394	61.206 593	60.452 881	59.716 672	324
28	63.650 245	62.835 728	62.040 851	61.264 961	60.507 427	59.767 648	336
29	63.709 623	62.891 079	62.092 450	61.313 062	60.552 270	59.809 452	348
30	63.758 919	62.936 920	62.135 079	61.352 704	60.589 135	59.843 735	360

	20.25% ANNUAL RATE	20.50% ANNUAL RATE	20.75% ANNUAL RATE	21.00% ANNUAL RATE	21.25% ANNUAL RATE	21.50% ANNUAL RATE	
MOS							MOS
1	0.983 405	0.983 204	0.983 002	0.982 801	0.982 600	0.982 399	1
2	1.950 491	1.949 893	1.949 296	1.948 699	1.948 102	1.947 506	2
3	2.901 527	2.900 345	2.899 164	2.897 984	2.896 805	2.895 626	3
4	3.836 782	3.834 834	3.832 887	3.830 943	3.828 999	3.827 058	4
5	4.756 515	4.753 626	4.750 739	4.747 855	4.744 974	4.742 095	5
6	5.660 986	5.656 986	5.652 989	5.648 998	5.645 010	5.641 027	6
7	6.550 447	6.545 172	6.539 904	6.534 641	6.529 386	6.524 136	7
8	7.425 148	7.418 441	7.411 742	7.405 053	7.398 373	7.391 701	8
9	8.285 333	8.277 041	8.268 762	8.260 494	8.252 239	8.243 996	9
10	9.131 243	9.121 220	9.111 214	9.101 223	9.091 248	9.081 290	10
11	9.963 116	9.951 220	9.939 346	9.927 492	9.915 659	9.903 846	11
12	10.781 183	10.767 279	10.753 401	10.739 550	10.725 724	10.711 924	12
13	11.585 675	11.569 631	11.553 620	11.537 641	11.521 694	11.505 779	13
14	12.376 816	12.358 507	12.340 237	12.322 006	12.303 814	12.285 661	14
15	13.154 828	13.134 132	13.113 483	13.092 880	13.072 325	13.051 816	15
16	13.919 930	13.896 730	13.873 585	13.850 497	13.827 463	13.804 485	16
17	14.672 334	14.646 518	14.620 768	14.595 083	14.569 463	14.543 907	17
18	15.412 252	15.383 713	15.355 250	15.326 863	15.298 551	15.270 314	18
19	16.139 892	16.108 526	16.077 248	16.046 057	16.014 953	15.983 935	19
20	16.855 456	16.821 164	16.786 973	16.752 881	16.718 889	16.684 996	20
21	17.559 145	17.521 833	17.484 635	17.447 549	17.410 577	17.373 717	21
22	18.251 157	18.210 733	18.170 437	18.130 269	18.090 229	18.050 315	22
23	18.931 685	18.888 062	18.844 583	18.801 248	18.758 055	18.715 005	23
24	19.600 919	19.554 014	19.507 270	19.460 686	19.414 261	19.367 995	24
25	20.259 048	20.208 781	20.158 693	20.108 782	20.059 048	20.009 491	25
26	20.906 255	20.852 550	20.799 042	20.745 732	20.692 617	20.639 697	26
27	21.542 721	21.485 506	21.428 508	21.371 726	21.315 161	21.258 810	27
28	22.168 626	22.107 830	22.047 274	21.986 955	21.926 872	21.867 026	28
29	22.784 143	22.719 702	22.655 522	22.591 602	22.527 940	22.464 536	29
30	23.389 446	23.321 297	23.253 431	23.185 849	23.118 549	23.051 529	30
31	23.984 705	23.912 787	23.841 178	23.769 877	23.698 881	23.628 191	31
32	24.570 084	24.494 342	24.418 934	24.343 859	24.269 116	24.194 703	32
33	25.145 750	25.066 128	24.986 869	24.907 970	24.829 428	24.751 243	33
34	25.711 860	25.628 311	25.545 151	25.462 378	25.379 991	25.297 987	34
35	26.268 580	26.181 052	26.093 943	26.007 251	25.920 973	25.835 108	35
36	26.816 059	26.724 508	26.633 407	26.542 753	26.452 543	26.362 775	36
37	27.354 453	27.258 836	27.163 701	27.069 045	26.974 863	26.881 154	37
38	27.883 912	27.784 190	27.684 982	27.586 285	27.488 095	27.390 410	38
39	28.404 584	28.300 719	28.197 402	28.094 629	27.992 396	27.890 701	39
40	28.916 616	28.808 573	28.701 112	28.594 230	28.487 923	28.382 187	40
41	29.420 151	29.307 896	29.196 260	29.085 238	28.974 827	28.865 022	41
42	29.915 330	29.798 833	29.682 991	29.567 801	29.453 259	29.339 358	42
43	30.402 291	30.281 523	30.161 450	30.042 065	29.923 366	29.805 346	43
44	30.881 172	30.756 107	30.631 775	30.508 172	30.385 293	30.263 132	44
45	31.352 105	31.222 718	31.094 106	30.966 263	30.839 182	30.712 860	45
46	31.815 223	31.681 493	31.548 579	31.416 474	31.285 174	31.154 672	46
47	32.270 656	32.132 562	31.995 326	31.858 943	31.723 405	31.588 707	47
YRS							
4	32.718 530	32.576 054	32.434 480	32.293 801	32.154 011	32.015 103	48
5	37.547 151	37.351 261	37.156 877	36.963 986	36.772 573	36.582 626	60
6	41.497 288	41.248 111	41.001 171	40.756 445	40.513 909	40.273 540	72
7	44.728 767	44.428 171	44.130 641	43.836 142	43.544 636	43.256 087	84
8	47.372 336	47.023 287	46.678 205	46.337 035	45.999 723	45.666 217	96
9	49.534 953	49.141 055	48.752 063	48.367 904	47.988 504	47.613 791	108
10	51.304 120	50.869 278	50.440 300	50.017 087	49.599 546	49.187 582	120
11	52.751 418	52.279 611	51.814 618	51.356 319	50.904 595	50.459 329	132
12	53.935 406	53.430 525	52.933 390	52.443 854	51.961 770	51.486 999	144
13	54.903 988	54.369 739	53.844 133	53.326 994	52.818 151	52.317 436	156
14	55.696 353	55.136 193	54.585 528	54.044 156	53.511 876	52.988 495	168
15	56.344 561	55.761 665	55.189 066	54.626 532	54.073 838	53.530 763	180
16	56.874 839	56.272 086	55.680 379	55.099 456	54.529 064	53.968 957	192
17	57.308 643	56.688 621	56.080 335	55.483 497	54.897 827	54.323 052	204
18	57.663 523	57.028 537	56.405 921	55.795 361	55.196 549	54.609 189	216
19	57.953 839	57.305 929	56.670 967	56.048 612	55.438 533	54.840 410	228
20	58.191 338	57.532 297	56.886 729	56.254 267	55.634 556	55.027 254	240
21	58.385 627	57.717 027	57.062 371	56.421 270	55.793 348	55.178 239	252
22	58.544 569	57.867 777	57.205 354	56.556 887	55.921 979	55.300 247	264
23	58.674 595	57.990 799	57.321 750	56.667 015	56.026 179	55.398 838	276
24	58.780 964	58.091 191	57.416 502	56.756 446	56.110 588	55.478 508	288
25	58.867 982	58.173 117	57.493 636	56.829 069	56.178 964	55.542 887	300
26	58.939 168	58.239 974	57.556 428	56.888 043	56.234 354	55.594 911	312
27	58.997 403	58.294 533	57.607 543	56.935 933	56.279 223	55.636 950	324
28	59.045 043	58.339 056	57.649 154	56.974 823	56.315 570	55.670 921	336
29	59.084 016	58.375 390	57.683 028	57.006 404	56.345 013	55.698 372	348
30	59.115 898	58.405 041	57.710 603	57.032 049	56.368 864	55.720 555	360

PRESENT VALUE PER PERIOD

MOS	21.75% ANNUAL RATE	22.00% ANNUAL RATE	22.50% ANNUAL RATE	23.00% ANNUAL RATE	23.50% ANNUAL RATE	24.00% ANNUAL RATE	MOS
1	0.982 198	0.981 997	0.981 595	0.981 194	0.980 793	0.980 392	1
2	1.946 910	1.946 314	1.945 124	1.943 935	1.942 747	1.941 561	2
3	2.894 448	2.893 271	2.890 919	2.888 571	2.886 225	2.883 883	3
4	3.825 118	3.823 179	3.819 307	3.815 441	3.811 582	3.807 729	4
5	4.739 219	4.736 346	4.730 608	4.724 881	4.719 165	4.713 460	5
6	5.637 048	5.633 073	5.625 137	5.617 218	5.609 316	5.601 431	6
7	6.518 893	6.513 656	6.503 202	6.492 773	6.482 369	6.471 991	7
8	7.385 039	7.378 386	7.365 106	7.351 862	7.338 654	7.325 481	8
9	8.235 766	8.227 548	8.211 147	8.194 795	8.178 492	8.162 237	9
10	9.071 348	9.061 421	9.041 617	9.021 876	9.002 199	8.982 585	10
11	9.892 054	9.880 283	9.856 802	9.833 403	9.810 085	9.786 848	11
12	10.698 150	10.684 402	10.656 983	10.629 667	10.602 453	10.575 341	12
13	11.489 896	11.474 045	11.442 438	11.410 957	11.379 603	11.348 374	13
14	12.267 547	12.249 471	12.213 436	12.177 554	12.141 825	12.106 249	14
15	13.031 353	13.010 937	12.970 244	12.929 734	12.889 408	12.849 264	15
16	13.781 563	13.758 895	13.713 123	13.667 769	13.622 631	13.577 709	16
17	14.518 416	14.492 990	14.442 329	14.391 924	14.341 772	14.291 872	17
18	15.242 152	15.214 065	15.158 114	15.102 460	15.047 099	14.992 031	18
19	15.953 004	15.922 159	15.860 726	15.799 633	15.738 880	15.678 462	19
20	16.651 201	16.617 505	16.550 406	16.483 696	16.417 373	16.351 433	20
21	17.336 968	17.300 332	17.227 392	17.154 894	17.082 834	17.011 209	21
22	18.010 528	17.970 866	17.891 919	17.813 469	17.735 513	17.658 048	22
23	18.672 096	18.629 328	18.544 215	18.459 659	18.375 657	18.292 204	23
24	19.321 887	19.275 936	19.184 505	19.093 696	19.003 505	18.913 926	24
25	19.960 110	19.910 903	19.813 011	19.715 810	19.619 294	19.523 456	25
26	20.586 971	20.534 438	20.429 950	20.326 224	20.223 255	20.121 036	26
27	21.202 672	21.146 748	21.035 533	20.925 158	20.815 616	20.706 898	27
28	21.807 413	21.748 034	21.629 971	21.512 829	21.396 599	21.281 272	28
29	22.401 388	22.338 495	22.213 469	22.089 448	21.966 423	21.844 385	29
30	22.984 789	22.918 326	22.786 227	22.655 223	22.525 303	22.396 456	30
31	23.557 803	23.487 717	23.348 444	23.210 358	23.073 448	22.937 702	31
32	24.120 617	24.046 858	23.900 313	23.755 053	23.611 064	23.468 335	32
33	24.673 412	24.595 933	24.442 025	24.289 504	24.138 355	23.988 564	33
34	25.216 365	25.135 122	24.973 767	24.813 904	24.655 518	24.498 592	34
35	25.749 653	25.664 605	25.495 722	25.328 442	25.162 747	24.998 619	35
36	26.273 446	26.184 554	26.008 071	25.833 304	25.660 234	25.488 842	36
37	26.787 915	26.695 143	26.510 990	26.328 671	26.148 166	25.969 453	37
38	27.293 226	27.196 540	27.004 652	26.814 722	26.626 726	26.440 641	38
39	27.789 540	27.688 910	27.489 229	27.291 633	27.096 094	26.902 589	39
40	28.277 019	28.172 416	27.964 888	27.759 574	27.556 447	27.355 479	40
41	28.755 820	28.647 217	28.431 792	28.218 715	28.007 958	27.799 489	41
42	29.226 097	29.113 470	28.890 102	28.669 222	28.450 796	28.234 794	42
43	29.688 002	29.571 329	29.339 978	29.111 256	28.885 129	28.661 562	43
44	30.141 684	30.020 945	29.781 573	29.544 977	29.311 120	29.079 963	44
45	30.587 289	30.462 466	30.215 041	29.970 542	29.728 928	29.490 160	45
46	31.024 962	30.896 039	30.640 531	30.388 103	30.138 712	29.892 314	46
47	31.454 843	31.321 806	31.058 190	30.797 812	30.540 625	30.286 582	47
YRS							
4	31.877 071	31.739 908	31.468 162	31.199 816	30.934 818	30.673 120	48
5	36.394 131	36.207 074	35.837 226	35.472 979	35.114 232	34.760 887	60
6	40.035 314	39.799 209	39.333 271	38.875 549	38.425 869	37.984 063	72
7	42.970 458	42.687 714	42.130 742	41.584 895	41.049 906	40.525 516	84
8	45.336 466	45.010 417	44.369 226	43.742 252	43.129 111	42.529 434	96
9	47.243 695	46.878 147	46.160 420	45.460 079	44.776 608	44.109 510	108
10	48.781 105	48.380 024	47.593 700	46.827 924	46.082 032	45.355 389	120
11	50.020 405	49.587 713	48.740 585	47.917 090	47.116 410	46.337 756	132
12	51.019 400	50.558 839	49.658 301	48.784 355	47.936 018	47.112 345	144
13	51.824 686	51.339 740	50.392 640	49.474 928	48.585 450	47.723 104	156
14	52.473 824	51.967 678	50.980 245	50.024 806	49.100 039	48.204 683	168
15	52.997 091	52.472 614	51.450 435	50.462 655	49.507 784	48.584 405	180
16	53.418 895	52.878 054	51.826 673	50.811 299	49.830 868	48.883 813	192
17	53.758 909	53.205 140	52.127 732	51.088 911	50.086 869	49.119 894	204
18	54.032 993	53.467 682	52.368 633	51.309 965	50.289 717	49.306 042	216
19	54.253 931	53.678 797	52.561 398	51.485 981	50.450 447	49.452 819	228
20	54.432 029	53.848 558	52.715 645	51.626 137	50.577 805	49.568 552	240
21	54.575 592	53.985 067	52.839 070	51.737 739	50.678 719	49.659 806	252
22	54.691 318	54.094 836	52.937 833	51.826 603	50.758 680	49.731 759	264
23	54.784 605	54.183 103	53.016 861	51.897 362	50.822 039	49.788 494	276
24	54.859 802	54.254 081	53.080 098	51.953 705	50.872 242	49.833 229	288
25	54.920 419	54.311 155	53.130 699	51.998 569	50.912 022	49.868 500	300
26	54.969 282	54.357 050	53.171 189	52.034 293	50.943 542	49.896 315	312
27	55.008 670	54.393 955	53.203 589	52.062 739	50.968 517	49.918 245	324
28	55.040 421	54.423 631	53.229 514	52.085 389	50.988 307	49.935 537	336
29	55.066 015	54.447 494	53.250 259	52.103 424	51.003 988	49.949 171	348
30	55.086 646	54.466 682	53.266 859	52.117 785	51.016 413	49.959 922	360

QTRS	5.25% ANNUAL RATE	5.50% ANNUAL RATE	5.75% ANNUAL RATE	6.00% ANNUAL RATE	6.25% ANNUAL RATE	6.50% ANNUAL RATE	QTRS
1	0.987 045	0.986 436	0.985 829	0.985 222	0.984 615	0.984 010	1
2	1.961 303	1.959 493	1.957 687	1.955 883	1.954 083	1.952 285	2
3	2.922 939	2.919 352	2.915 773	2.912 200	2.908 635	2.905 078	3
4	3.872 118	3.866 192	3.860 281	3.854 385	3.848 503	3.842 635	4
5	4.809 000	4.800 190	4.791 405	4.782 645	4.773 910	4.765 200	5
6	5.733 744	5.721 519	5.709 333	5.697 187	5.685 081	5.673 014	6
7	6.646 509	6.630 351	6.614 253	6.598 214	6.582 233	6.566 311	7
8	7.547 449	7.526 857	7.506 349	7.485 925	7.465 584	7.445 325	8
9	8.436 717	8.411 203	8.385 803	8.360 517	8.335 344	8.310 283	9
10	9.314 464	9.283 554	9.252 795	9.222 185	9.191 723	9.161 410	10
11	10.180 841	10.144 073	10.107 499	10.071 118	10.034 928	9.998 927	11
12	11.035 993	10.992 921	10.950 092	10.907 505	10.865 159	10.823 053	12
13	11.880 068	11.830 255	11.780 744	11.731 532	11.682 618	11.634 000	13
14	12.713 207	12.656 231	12.599 624	12.543 382	12.487 501	12.431 980	14
15	13.535 553	13.471 005	13.406 900	13.343 233	13.280 001	13.217 201	15
16	14.347 245	14.274 728	14.202 735	14.131 264	14.060 309	13.989 866	16
17	15.148 422	15.067 549	14.987 293	14.907 649	14.828 612	14.750 175	17
18	15.939 220	15.849 617	15.760 733	15.672 561	15.585 095	15.498 327	18
19	16.719 773	16.621 077	16.523 211	16.426 168	16.329 939	16.234 517	19
20	17.490 214	17.382 073	17.274 885	17.168 639	17.063 325	16.958 934	20
21	18.250 674	18.132 748	18.015 906	17.900 137	17.785 428	17.671 768	21
22	19.001 282	18.873 241	18.746 426	18.620 824	18.496 421	18.373 203	22
23	19.742 166	19.603 690	19.466 594	19.330 861	19.196 476	19.063 422	23
24	20.473 452	20.324 232	20.176 556	20.030 405	19.885 761	19.742 605	24
25	21.195 264	21.035 001	20.876 457	20.719 611	20.564 442	20.410 928	25
26	21.907 725	21.736 129	21.566 439	21.398 632	21.232 681	21.068 563	26
27	22.610 956	22.427 747	22.246 644	22.067 617	21.890 640	21.715 684	27
28	23.305 077	23.109 985	22.917 209	22.726 717	22.538 476	22.352 456	28
29	23.990 206	23.782 969	23.578 271	23.376 076	23.176 346	22.979 047	29
30	24.666 458	24.446 825	24.229 966	24.015 838	23.804 402	23.595 618	30
31	25.333 950	25.101 677	24.872 425	24.646 146	24.422 796	24.202 330	31
32	25.992 795	25.747 647	25.505 779	25.267 139	25.031 676	24.799 341	32
33	26.643 104	26.384 855	26.130 158	25.878 954	25.631 189	25.386 805	33
34	27.284 989	27.013 421	26.745 689	26.481 728	26.221 478	25.964 876	34
35	27.918 558	27.633 461	27.352 497	27.075 595	26.802 686	26.533 703	35
36	28.543 919	28.245 091	27.950 705	27.660 684	27.374 952	27.093 435	36
37	29.161 178	28.848 425	28.540 436	28.237 127	27.938 415	27.644 216	37
38	29.770 441	29.443 576	29.121 810	28.805 052	28.493 208	28.186 191	38
39	30.371 811	30.030 654	29.694 946	29.364 583	29.039 467	28.719 499	39
40	30.965 390	30.609 770	30.259 959	29.915 845	29.577 321	29.244 279	40
41	31.551 280	31.181 031	30.816 965	30.458 961	30.106 901	29.760 669	41
42	32.129 579	31.744 543	31.366 077	30.994 050	30.628 333	30.268 801	42
43	32.700 386	32.300 413	31.907 408	31.521 232	31.141 743	30.768 807	43
44	33.263 799	32.848 742	32.441 068	32.040 622	31.647 255	31.260 819	44
45	33.819 913	33.389 635	32.967 165	32.552 337	32.144 989	31.744 963	45
46	34.368 822	33.923 191	33.485 807	33.056 490	32.635 066	32.221 366	46
47	34.910 620	34.449 510	33.997 098	33.553 192	33.117 604	32.690 151	47
48	35.445 399	34.968 691	34.501 144	34.042 554	33.592 718	33.151 440	48
49	35.973 250	35.480 829	34.998 047	34.524 683	34.060 522	33.605 353	49
50	36.494 263	35.986 022	35.487 909	34.999 688	34.521 129	34.052 008	50
51	37.008 526	36.484 362	35.970 828	35.467 673	34.974 650	34.491 521	51
52	37.516 127	36.975 942	36.446 904	35.928 742	35.421 194	34.924 006	52
53	38.017 152	37.460 856	36.916 233	36.382 997	35.860 868	35.349 575	53
54	38.511 686	37.939 192	37.378 911	36.830 539	36.293 778	35.768 340	54
55	38.999 813	38.411 040	37.835 033	37.271 467	36.720 028	36.180 408	55
YRS							
14	39.481 617	38.876 488	38.284 690	37.705 879	37.139 719	36.585 887	56
15	41.347 218	40.676 001	40.020 495	39.380 269	38.754 905	38.143 997	60
16	43.118 006	42.379 851	41.659 977	40.957 853	40.272 964	39.604 813	64
17	44.798 801	43.993 124	43.208 482	42.444 228	41.699 739	40.974 412	68
18	46.394 174	45.520 636	44.671 058	43.844 667	43.040 717	42.258 489	72
19	47.908 468	46.966 944	46.052 473	45.164 138	44.301 058	43.462 385	76
20	49.345 804	48.336 367	47.357 231	46.407 323	45.485 612	44.591 106	80
21	50.710 091	49.632 991	48.589 587	47.578 633	46.598 935	45.649 346	84
22	52.005 044	50.860 687	49.753 557	48.682 222	47.645 311	46.641 508	88
23	53.234 185	52.023 117	50.852 937	49.722 007	48.628 765	47.571 715	92
24	54.400 859	53.123 753	51.891 310	50.701 675	49.553 081	48.443 838	96
25	55.508 241	54.165 879	52.872 062	51.624 704	50.421 815	49.261 503	100
26	56.559 344	55.152 605	53.798 391	52.494 366	51.238 310	50.028 111	104
27	57.557 029	56.086 877	54.673 317	53.313 749	52.005 707	50.746 850	108
28	58.504 009	56.971 483	55.499 691	54.085 758	52.726 958	51.420 709	112
29	59.402 863	57.809 063	56.280 209	54.813 133	53.404 838	52.052 490	116
30	60.256 035	58.602 117	57.017 415	55.498 454	54.041 956	52.644 820	120

PRESENT VALUE PER PERIOD

QUARTERLY COMPOUNDING

QTRS	6.75% ANNUAL RATE	7.00% ANNUAL RATE	7.25% ANNUAL RATE	7.50% ANNUAL RATE	7.75% ANNUAL RATE	8.00% ANNUAL RATE	QTRS
1	0.983 405	0.982 801	0.982 198	0.981 595	0.980 993	0.980 392	1
2	1.950 491	1.948 699	1.946 910	1.945 124	1.943 341	1.941 561	2
3	2.901 527	2.897 984	2.894 448	2.890 919	2.887 398	2.883 883	3
4	3.836 782	3.830 943	3.825 118	3.819 307	3.813 511	3.807 729	4
5	4.756 515	4.747 855	4.739 219	4.730 608	4.722 022	4.713 460	5
6	5.660 986	5.648 998	5.637 048	5.625 137	5.613 265	5.601 431	6
7	6.550 447	6.534 641	6.518 893	6.503 202	6.487 568	6.471 991	7
8	7.425 148	7.405 053	7.385 039	7.365 106	7.345 254	7.325 481	8
9	8.285 333	8.260 494	8.235 766	8.211 147	8.186 638	8.162 237	9
10	9.131 243	9.101 223	9.071 348	9.041 617	9.012 030	8.982 585	10
11	9.963 116	9.927 492	9.892 054	9.856 802	9.821 734	9.786 848	11
12	10.781 183	10.739 550	10.698 150	10.656 983	10.616 048	10.575 341	12
13	11.585 675	11.537 641	11.489 896	11.442 438	11.395 264	11.348 374	13
14	12.376 816	12.322 006	12.267 547	12.213 436	12.159 671	12.106 249	14
15	13.154 828	13.092 880	13.031 353	12.970 244	12.909 548	12.849 264	15
16	13.919 930	13.850 497	13.781 563	13.713 123	13.645 173	13.577 709	16
17	14.672 334	14.595 083	14.518 416	14.442 329	14.366 816	14.291 872	17
18	15.412 252	15.326 863	15.242 152	15.158 114	15.074 743	14.992 031	18
19	16.139 892	16.046 057	15.953 004	15.860 726	15.769 214	15.678 462	19
20	16.855 456	16.752 881	16.651 201	16.550 406	16.450 486	16.351 433	20
21	17.559 145	17.447 549	17.336 968	17.227 392	17.118 809	17.011 209	21
22	18.251 157	18.130 269	18.010 528	17.891 919	17.774 430	17.658 048	22
23	18.931 685	18.801 248	18.672 096	18.544 215	18.417 589	18.292 204	23
24	19.600 919	19.460 686	19.321 887	19.184 505	19.048 524	18.913 926	24
25	20.259 048	20.108 782	19.960 110	19.813 011	19.667 467	19.523 456	25
26	20.906 255	20.745 732	20.586 971	20.429 950	20.274 645	20.112 036	26
27	21.542 721	21.371 726	21.202 672	21.035 533	20.870 284	20.706 898	27
28	22.168 626	21.986 955	21.807 413	21.629 971	21.454 601	21.281 272	28
29	22.784 143	22.591 602	22.401 388	22.213 469	22.027 812	21.844 385	29
30	23.389 446	23.185 849	22.984 789	22.786 227	22.590 128	22.396 456	30
31	23.984 705	23.769 877	23.557 803	23.348 444	23.141 757	22.937 702	31
32	24.570 084	24.343 859	24.120 617	23.900 313	23.682 900	23.468 335	32
33	25.145 750	24.907 970	24.673 412	24.442 025	24.213 759	23.988 564	33
34	25.711 862	25.462 378	25.216 365	24.973 767	24.734 527	24.498 592	34
35	26.268 580	26.007 251	25.749 653	25.495 722	25.245 398	24.998 619	35
36	26.816 059	26.542 753	26.273 446	26.008 071	25.746 558	25.488 842	36
37	27.354 453	27.069 045	26.787 915	26.510 990	26.238 193	25.969 453	37
38	27.883 912	27.586 285	27.293 226	27.004 652	26.720 484	26.440 641	38
39	28.404 584	28.094 629	27.789 540	27.489 229	27.193 608	26.902 589	39
40	28.916 616	28.594 230	28.277 019	27.964 888	27.657 739	27.355 479	40
41	29.420 151	29.085 238	28.755 820	28.431 792	28.113 049	27.799 489	41
42	29.915 330	29.567 801	29.226 097	28.890 102	28.559 704	28.234 794	42
43	30.402 291	30.042 065	29.688 002	29.339 978	28.997 871	28.661 562	43
44	30.881 172	30.508 172	30.141 684	29.781 573	29.427 709	29.079 963	44
45	31.352 105	30.966 263	30.587 289	30.215 041	29.849 377	29.490 160	45
46	31.815 223	31.416 474	31.024 962	30.640 531	30.263 031	29.892 314	46
47	32.270 656	31.858 943	31.454 843	31.058 190	30.668 822	30.286 582	47
48	32.718 530	32.293 801	31.877 071	31.468 162	31.066 901	30.673 120	48
49	33.158 973	32.721 181	32.291 782	31.870 589	31.457 414	31.052 078	49
50	33.592 106	33.141 209	32.699 111	32.265 608	31.840 504	31.423 606	50
51	34.018 051	33.554 014	33.099 188	32.653 358	32.216 313	31.787 849	51
52	34.436 628	33.959 719	33.492 143	33.033 971	32.584 979	32.144 950	52
53	34.848 854	34.358 446	33.878 103	33.407 579	32.946 638	32.495 049	53
54	35.253 943	34.750 316	34.257 191	33.774 311	33.301 423	32.838 283	54
55	35.652 311	35.135 445	34.629 531	34.134 293	33.649 464	33.174 788	55

YRS							QTRS
14	36.044 067	35.513 951	34.995 242	34.487 649	33.990 891	33.504 694	56
15	37.547 151	36.963 986	36.394 131	35.837 226	35.292 925	34.760 887	60
16	38.952 916	38.316 807	37.696 034	37.090 158	36.498 755	35.921 415	64
17	40.267 664	39.578 934	38.907 676	38.253 364	37.615 491	36.993 564	68
18	41.497 288	40.756 445	40.035 314	39.333 271	38.649 714	37.984 063	72
19	42.647 299	41.855 015	41.084 773	40.335 844	39.607 523	38.899 132	76
20	43.722 852	42.879 935	42.061 473	41.266 620	40.494 562	39.744 514	80
21	44.728 767	43.836 142	42.970 458	42.130 742	41.316 060	40.525 516	84
22	45.669 554	44.728 244	43.816 423	42.932 982	42.076 860	41.247 041	88
23	46.549 429	45.560 539	44.603 737	43.677 772	42.781 448	41.913 619	92
24	47.372 336	46.337 035	45.336 466	44.369 226	43.433 976	42.529 434	96
25	48.141 963	47.061 473	46.018 395	45.011 164	44.038 290	43.098 352	100
26	48.861 760	47.737 344	46.653 045	45.607 131	44.597 954	43.623 944	104
27	49.534 953	48.367 904	47.243 695	46.160 420	45.116 266	44.109 510	108
28	50.164 560	48.956 190	47.793 395	46.674 087	45.596 281	44.558 097	112
29	50.753 402	49.505 036	48.304 985	47.150 969	46.040 830	44.972 523	116
30	51.304 120	50.017 087	48.781 105	47.593 700	46.452 533	45.355 389	120

QTRS	8.25% ANNUAL RATE	8.50% ANNUAL RATE	8.75% ANNUAL RATE	9.00% ANNUAL RATE	9.25% ANNUAL RATE	9.50% ANNUAL RATE	QTRS
1	0.979 792	0.979 192	0.978 593	0.977 995	0.977 398	0.976 801	1
2	1.939 784	1.938 009	1.936 238	1.934 470	1.932 704	1.930 941	2
3	2.880 376	2.876 876	2.873 383	2.869 897	2.866 418	2.862 946	3
4	3.801 961	3.796 206	3.790 466	3.784 740	3.779 028	3.773 330	4
5	4.704 922	4.696 408	4.687 918	4.679 453	4.671 011	4.662 593	5
6	5.589 635	5.577 878	5.566 158	5.554 477	5.542 833	5.531 226	6
7	6.456 471	6.441 007	6.425 598	6.410 246	6.394 950	6.379 708	7
8	7.305 789	7.286 175	7.266 641	7.247 185	7.227 807	7.208 506	8
9	8.137 944	8.113 758	8.089 679	8.065 706	8.041 839	8.018 077	9
10	8.953 282	8.924 120	8.895 099	8.866 216	8.837 473	8.808 866	10
11	9.752 144	9.717 621	9.683 277	9.649 111	9.615 123	9.581 310	11
12	10.534 863	10.494 610	10.454 583	10.414 779	10.375 196	10.335 834	12
13	11.301 764	11.255 433	11.209 378	11.163 598	11.118 091	11.072 854	13
14	12.053 167	12.000 424	11.948 015	11.895 939	11.844 194	11.792 775	14
15	12.789 386	12.729 913	12.670 840	12.612 166	12.553 885	12.495 996	15
16	13.510 727	13.444 223	13.378 192	13.312 631	13.247 536	13.182 902	16
17	14.217 492	14.143 670	14.070 402	13.997 683	13.925 508	13.853 872	17
18	14.909 973	14.828 563	14.747 794	14.667 661	14.588 157	14.509 277	18
19	15.588 461	15.499 205	15.410 686	15.322 896	15.235 829	15.149 477	19
20	16.253 238	16.155 892	16.059 387	15.963 712	15.868 861	15.774 825	20
21	16.904 581	16.798 915	16.694 201	16.590 428	16.487 586	16.385 665	21
22	17.542 762	17.428 559	17.315 426	17.203 352	17.092 326	16.982 335	22
23	18.168 046	18.045 100	17.923 353	17.802 790	17.683 397	17.565 162	23
24	18.780 694	18.648 813	18.518 266	18.389 036	18.261 109	18.134 469	24
25	19.380 962	19.239 964	19.100 443	18.962 383	18.825 763	18.690 568	25
26	19.969 099	19.818 814	19.670 159	19.523 113	19.377 655	19.233 766	26
27	20.545 351	20.385 619	20.227 678	20.071 504	19.917 073	19.764 362	27
28	21.109 958	20.940 631	20.773 263	20.607 828	20.444 298	20.282 649	28
29	21.663 156	21.484 094	21.307 169	21.132 350	20.959 607	20.788 912	29
30	22.205 174	22.016 249	21.829 645	21.645 330	21.463 269	21.283 431	30
31	22.736 239	22.537 330	22.340 937	22.147 022	21.955 547	21.766 477	31
32	23.256 572	23.047 570	22.841 284	22.637 674	22.436 699	22.238 317	32
33	23.766 391	23.547 192	23.330 920	23.117 530	22.906 975	22.699 211	33
34	24.265 906	24.036 418	23.810 075	23.586 826	23.366 622	23.149 412	34
35	24.755 328	24.515 464	24.278 972	24.045 796	23.815 879	23.589 169	35
36	25.234 859	24.984 543	24.737 832	24.494 666	24.254 983	24.018 725	36
37	25.704 699	25.443 861	25.186 870	24.933 658	24.684 162	24.438 315	37
38	26.165 045	25.893 621	25.626 294	25.362 991	25.103 640	24.848 171	38
39	26.616 088	26.334 023	26.056 312	25.782 876	25.513 637	25.248 518	39
40	27.058 017	26.765 261	26.477 125	26.193 522	25.914 367	25.639 578	40
41	27.491 015	27.187 527	26.888 930	26.595 132	26.306 040	26.021 566	41
42	27.915 262	27.601 005	27.291 919	26.987 904	26.688 860	26.394 692	42
43	28.330 937	28.005 880	27.686 282	27.372 033	27.063 028	26.759 162	43
44	28.738 211	28.402 331	28.072 202	27.747 710	27.428 738	27.115 177	44
45	29.137 255	28.790 532	28.449 862	28.115 120	27.786 183	27.462 932	45
46	29.528 235	29.170 655	28.819 437	28.474 444	28.135 548	27.802 620	46
47	29.911 314	29.542 869	29.181 100	28.825 863	28.477 017	28.134 427	47
48	30.286 652	29.907 339	29.535 021	29.169 548	28.810 768	28.458 537	48
49	30.654 405	30.264 224	29.881 367	29.505 670	29.136 976	28.775 128	49
50	31.014 726	30.613 683	30.220 297	29.834 396	29.455 810	29.084 374	50
51	31.367 766	30.955 871	30.551 973	30.155 889	29.767 438	29.386 446	51
52	31.713 672	31.290 938	30.876 549	30.470 307	30.072 023	29.681 510	52
53	32.052 587	31.619 034	31.194 176	30.777 806	30.369 723	29.969 729	53
54	32.384 654	31.940 302	31.505 004	31.078 539	30.660 694	30.251 261	54
55	32.710 010	32.254 886	31.809 178	31.372 654	30.945 089	30.526 263	55
YRS							
14	33.028 791	32.562 924	32.106 841	31.660 298	31.223 056	30.794 884	56
15	34.240 784	33.732 299	33.235 122	32.748 953	32.273 500	31.808 482	60
16	35.357 739	34.807 342	34.269 850	33.744 902	33.232 146	32.731 244	64
17	36.387 107	35.795 661	35.218 782	34.656 039	34.107 016	33.571 311	68
18	37.335 757	36.704 254	36.089 032	35.489 587	34.905 431	34.336 095	72
19	38.210 018	37.539 551	36.887 124	36.252 153	35.634 073	35.032 341	76
20	39.015 723	38.307 464	37.619 041	36.949 781	36.299 038	35.666 192	80
21	39.758 249	39.013 431	38.290 270	37.588 001	36.905 893	36.243 240	84
22	40.442 549	39.662 448	38.905 843	38.171 873	37.459 714	36.768 574	88
23	41.073 189	40.259 109	39.470 375	38.706 024	37.965 137	37.246 830	92
24	41.654 378	40.807 638	39.988 098	39.194 689	38.426 390	37.682 226	96
25	42.189 992	41.311 917	40.462 893	39.641 741	38.847 335	38.078 604	100
26	42.683 606	41.775 517	40.898 320	40.050 723	39.231 494	38.439 459	104
27	43.138 513	42.201 718	41.297 643	40.424 877	39.582 081	38.767 976	108
28	43.557 748	42.593 538	41.663 855	40.767 170	39.902 030	39.067 052	112
29	43.944 109	42.953 749	41.999 702	41.080 315	40.194 019	39.339 326	116
30	44.300 173	43.284 903	42.307 702	41.366 793	40.460 490	39.587 200	120

PRESENT VALUE PER PERIOD
QUARTERLY COMPOUNDING

QTRS	9.75% ANNUAL RATE	10.00% ANNUAL RATE	10.25% ANNUAL RATE	10.50% ANNUAL RATE	10.75% ANNUAL RATE	11.00% ANNUAL RATE	QTRS
1	0.976 205	0.975 610	0.975 015	0.974 421	0.973 828	0.973 236	1
2	1.929 181	1.927 424	1.925 670	1.923 919	1.922 170	1.920 424	2
3	2.859 481	2.856 024	2.852 573	2.849 129	2.845 692	2.842 262	3
4	3.767 645	3.761 974	3.756 317	3.750 674	3.745 044	3.739 428	4
5	4.654 199	4.645 828	4.637 482	4.629 158	4.620 858	4.612 582	5
6	5.519 657	5.508 125	5.496 631	5.485 173	5.473 751	5.462 360	6
7	6.364 522	6.349 391	6.334 314	6.319 291	6.304 323	6.289 408	7
8	7.189 283	7.170 137	7.151 068	7.132 074	7.113 157	7.094 314	8
9	7.994 419	7.970 866	7.947 415	7.924 067	7.900 822	7.877 678	9
10	8.780 397	8.752 064	8.723 866	8.695 803	8.667 873	8.640 076	10
11	9.547 673	9.514 209	9.480 918	9.447 798	9.414 849	9.382 069	11
12	10.296 691	10.257 765	10.219 054	10.180 558	10.142 275	10.104 204	12
13	11.027 886	10.983 185	10.938 749	10.894 576	10.850 664	10.807 011	13
14	11.741 683	11.690 912	11.640 462	11.590 330	11.540 512	11.491 008	14
15	12.438 494	12.381 378	12.324 643	12.268 287	12.212 307	12.156 699	15
16	13.118 725	13.055 003	12.991 730	12.928 903	12.866 519	12.804 573	16
17	13.782 770	13.712 198	13.642 150	13.572 621	13.503 609	13.435 108	17
18	14.431 014	14.353 364	14.276 319	14.199 875	14.124 026	14.048 767	18
19	15.063 833	14.978 891	14.894 644	14.811 084	14.728 206	14.646 002	19
20	15.681 594	15.589 162	15.497 520	15.406 659	15.316 573	15.227 252	20
21	16.284 656	16.184 549	16.085 333	15.987 001	15.889 541	15.792 946	21
22	16.873 368	16.765 413	16.658 460	16.552 498	16.447 514	16.343 500	22
23	17.448 071	17.332 110	17.217 268	17.103 530	16.990 884	16.879 319	23
24	18.009 099	17.884 986	17.762 114	17.640 468	17.520 034	17.400 797	24
25	18.556 778	18.424 376	18.293 347	18.163 671	18.035 334	17.908 318	25
26	19.091 424	18.950 611	18.811 307	18.673 492	18.537 148	18.402 256	26
27	19.613 349	19.464 011	19.316 326	19.170 272	19.025 829	18.882 974	27
28	20.122 854	19.964 889	19.808 727	19.654 346	19.501 720	19.350 826	28
29	20.620 236	20.453 550	20.288 826	20.126 037	19.965 157	19.806 157	29
30	21.105 783	20.930 293	20.756 930	20.585 664	20.416 464	20.249 301	30
31	21.579 776	21.395 407	21.213 338	21.033 534	20.855 960	20.680 585	31
32	22.042 490	21.849 178	21.658 343	21.469 947	21.283 954	21.100 326	32
33	22.494 194	22.291 881	22.092 230	21.895 198	21.700 746	21.508 833	33
34	22.935 150	22.723 786	22.515 276	22.309 572	22.106 631	21.906 407	34
35	23.365 613	23.145 157	22.927 752	22.713 347	22.501 892	22.293 340	35
36	23.785 003	23.556 251	23.329 923	23.106 793	22.886 809	22.669 918	36
37	24.196 054	23.957 318	23.722 045	23.490 176	23.261 652	23.036 416	37
38	24.596 514	24.348 603	24.104 371	23.863 753	23.626 685	23.393 106	38
39	24.987 445	24.730 344	24.477 144	24.227 774	23.982 165	23.740 249	39
40	25.369 074	25.102 775	24.840 604	24.582 484	24.328 340	24.078 101	40
41	25.741 622	25.466 122	25.194 982	24.928 120	24.665 456	24.406 911	41
42	26.105 305	25.820 607	25.540 507	25.264 916	24.993 749	24.726 921	42
43	26.460 335	26.166 446	25.877 398	25.593 098	25.313 450	25.038 366	43
44	26.806 916	26.503 849	26.205 873	25.912 884	25.624 784	25.341 475	44
45	27.145 251	26.833 024	26.526 141	26.224 491	25.927 970	25.636 472	45
46	27.475 325	27.154 170	26.838 406	26.528 128	26.223 221	25.923 574	46
47	27.797 959	27.467 483	27.142 870	26.823 998	26.510 745	26.202 992	47
48	28.112 712	27.773 154	27.439 727	27.112 300	26.790 743	26.474 931	48
49	28.419 975	28.071 369	27.729 167	27.393 228	27.063 414	26.739 592	49
50	28.719 927	28.362 312	28.011 376	27.666 970	27.328 949	26.997 170	50
51	29.012 741	28.646 158	28.286 533	27.933 710	27.587 534	27.247 854	51
52	29.298 588	28.923 081	28.554 816	28.193 627	27.839 351	27.491 829	52
53	29.577 633	29.193 249	28.816 396	28.446 896	28.084 578	27.729 274	53
54	29.850 039	29.456 829	29.071 440	28.693 687	28.323 387	27.960 364	54
55	30.115 962	29.713 979	29.320 113	28.934 165	28.555 946	28.185 269	55

YRS	9.75% ANNUAL RATE	10.00% ANNUAL RATE	10.25% ANNUAL RATE	10.50% ANNUAL RATE	10.75% ANNUAL RATE	11.00% ANNUAL RATE	QTRS
14	30.375 558	29.964 858	29.562 572	29.168 492	28.782 419	28.404 155	56
15	31.353 622	30.908 656	30.473 325	30.047 377	29.630 568	29.222 662	60
16	32.241 865	31.763 691	31.296 413	30.839 730	30.393 353	29.956 999	64
17	33.048 535	32.538 311	32.040 274	31.554 073	31.079 365	30.615 821	68
18	33.781 123	33.240 078	32.712 535	32.198 084	31.696 331	31.206 893	72
19	34.446 433	33.875 844	33.320 086	32.778 690	32.251 201	31.737 183	76
20	35.050 644	34.451 817	33.869 158	33.302 132	32.750 224	32.212 941	80
21	35.599 366	34.973 620	34.365 378	33.774 038	33.199 022	32.639 775	84
22	36.097 065	35.446 348	34.813 834	34.199 482	33.602 649	33.022 715	88
23	36.550 260	35.874 616	35.219 124	34.583 040	33.965 652	33.366 276	92
24	36.961 262	36.262 606	35.585 402	34.928 834	34.292 119	33.674 508	96
25	37.334 520	36.614 105	35.916 424	35.240 583	34.585 728	33.951 042	100
26	37.673 499	36.932 546	36.215 583	35.521 638	34.849 785	34.199 140	104
27	37.981 348	37.221 039	36.485 947	35.775 023	35.087 266	34.421 724	108
28	38.260 924	37.482 398	36.730 286	36.003 460	35.300 845	34.621 419	112
29	38.514 826	37.719 177	36.951 107	36.209 406	35.492 927	34.800 579	116
30	38.745 410	37.933 687	37.150 672	36.395 076	35.665 677	34.961 315	120

PRESENT VALUE PER PERIOD

QUARTERLY COMPOUNDING

	11.25% ANNUAL RATE	11.50% ANNUAL RATE	11.75% ANNUAL RATE	12.00% ANNUAL RATE	12.25% ANNUAL RATE	12.50% ANNUAL RATE	
QTRS							QTRS
1	0.972 644	0.972 053	0.971 463	0.970 874	0.970 285	0.969 697	1
2	1.918 681	1.916 941	1.915 204	1.913 470	1.911 738	1.910 009	2
3	2.838 839	2.835 423	2.832 014	2.828 611	2.825 216	2.821 827	3
4	3.733 825	3.728 236	3.722 661	3.717 098	3.711 550	3.706 014	4
5	4.604 329	4.596 098	4.587 891	4.579 707	4.571 546	4.563 408	5
6	5.451 019	5.439 707	5.428 431	5.417 191	5.405 988	5.394 820	6
7	6.274 547	6.259 739	6.244 985	6.230 283	6.215 634	6.201 037	7
8	7.075 547	7.056 855	7.038 236	7.019 692	7.001 221	6.982 824	8
9	7.854 636	7.831 694	7.808 851	7.786 109	7.763 465	7.740 920	9
10	8.612 412	8.584 878	8.557 476	8.530 203	8.503 059	8.476 044	10
11	9.349 458	9.317 014	9.284 737	9.252 624	9.220 676	9.188 891	11
12	10.066 342	10.028 689	9.991 244	9.954 004	9.916 969	9.880 137	12
13	10.763 615	10.720 476	10.677 590	10.634 955	10.592 571	10.550 436	13
14	11.441 814	11.392 929	11.344 349	11.296 073	11.248 098	11.200 422	14
15	12.101 461	12.046 589	11.992 082	11.937 935	11.884 146	11.830 713	15
16	12.743 062	12.681 982	12.621 330	12.561 102	12.501 294	12.441 903	16
17	13.367 112	13.299 618	13.232 622	13.166 118	13.100 103	13.034 573	17
18	13.974 091	13.899 994	13.826 469	13.753 513	13.681 119	13.609 283	18
19	14.564 465	14.483 590	14.403 370	14.323 799	14.244 870	14.166 577	19
20	15.138 690	15.050 878	14.963 809	14.877 475	14.791 869	14.706 984	20
21	15.697 206	15.602 311	15.508 254	15.415 024	15.322 614	15.231 015	21
22	16.240 443	16.138 334	16.037 162	15.936 917	15.837 588	15.739 166	22
23	16.768 820	16.659 377	16.550 977	16.443 608	16.337 259	16.231 918	23
24	17.282 743	17.165 859	17.050 129	16.935 542	16.822 083	16.709 739	24
25	17.782 607	17.658 186	17.535 038	17.413 148	17.292 500	17.173 080	25
26	18.268 797	18.136 754	18.006 108	17.876 842	17.748 939	17.622 381	26
27	18.741 687	18.601 948	18.463 736	18.327 031	18.191 815	18.058 066	27
28	19.201 641	19.054 142	18.908 305	18.764 108	18.621 530	18.480 549	28
29	19.649 013	19.493 698	19.340 187	19.188 455	19.038 477	18.890 229	29
30	20.084 146	19.920 970	19.759 744	19.600 441	19.443 034	19.287 495	30
31	20.507 376	20.336 301	20.167 329	20.000 428	19.835 570	19.672 723	31
32	20.919 028	20.740 025	20.563 282	20.388 766	20.216 441	20.046 276	32
33	21.319 420	21.132 467	20.947 937	20.765 792	20.585 995	20.408 510	33
34	21.708 858	21.513 941	21.321 614	21.131 837	20.944 568	20.759 768	34
35	22.087 643	21.884 754	21.684 628	21.487 220	21.292 485	21.100 381	35
36	22.456 066	22.245 205	22.037 283	21.832 252	21.630 065	21.430 672	36
37	22.814 411	22.595 582	22.379 874	22.167 235	21.957 613	21.750 955	37
38	23.162 953	22.936 167	22.712 689	22.492 462	22.275 428	22.061 532	38
39	23.501 960	23.267 234	23.036 006	22.808 215	22.583 799	22.362 698	39
40	23.831 694	23.589 049	23.350 097	23.114 772	22.883 007	22.654 737	40
41	24.152 407	23.901 870	23.655 225	23.412 400	23.173 324	22.937 927	41
42	24.464 348	24.205 949	23.951 646	23.701 359	23.455 014	23.212 535	42
43	24.767 755	24.501 530	24.239 607	23.981 902	23.728 334	23.478 822	43
44	25.062 862	24.788 851	24.519 351	24.254 274	23.993 532	23.737 040	44
45	25.349 896	25.068 142	24.791 112	24.518 713	24.250 850	23.987 432	45
46	25.629 078	25.339 627	25.055 118	24.775 449	24.500 521	24.230 237	46
47	25.900 623	25.603 526	25.311 590	25.024 708	24.742 774	24.465 685	47
48	26.164 740	25.860 050	25.560 743	25.266 707	24.977 828	24.693 997	48
49	26.421 631	26.109 404	25.802 786	25.501 657	25.205 897	24.915 391	49
50	26.671 495	26.351 790	26.037 923	25.729 764	25.427 189	25.130 077	50
51	26.914 524	26.587 402	26.266 349	25.951 227	25.641 906	25.338 256	51
52	27.150 905	26.816 430	26.488 256	26.166 240	25.850 242	25.540 127	52
53	27.380 820	27.039 057	26.703 831	26.374 990	26.052 388	25.735 881	53
54	27.604 445	27.255 463	26.913 254	26.577 660	26.248 527	25.925 703	54
55	27.821 952	27.465 820	27.116 701	26.774 428	26.438 837	26.109 772	55
YRS							
14	28.033 510	27.670 299	27.314 342	26.965 464	26.623 493	26.288 264	56
15	28.823 429	28.432 645	28.050 093	27.675 564	27.308 851	26.949 757	60
16	29.530 395	29.113 277	28.705 388	28.306 478	27.916 307	27.534 640	64
17	30.163 120	29.720 954	29.289 024	28.867 038	28.454 716	28.051 787	68
18	30.729 401	30.263 497	29.808 837	29.365 088	28.931 926	28.509 041	72
19	31.236 214	30.747 886	30.271 807	29.807 598	29.354 893	28.913 339	76
20	31.689 804	31.180 355	30.684 150	30.200 763	29.729 784	29.270 815	80
21	32.095 762	31.566 469	31.051 402	30.550 086	30.062 061	29.586 890	84
22	32.459 088	31.911 197	31.378 494	30.860 454	30.356 571	29.866 359	88
23	32.784 260	32.218 974	31.669 817	31.136 212	30.617 604	30.113 462	92
24	33.075 284	32.493 762	31.929 283	31.381 219	30.848 967	30.331 948	96
25	33.335 747	32.739 096	32.160 376	31.598 905	31.054 031	30.525 130	100
26	33.568 858	32.958 134	32.366 198	31.792 317	31.235 787	30.695 939	104
27	33.777 488	33.153 693	32.549 513	31.964 160	31.396 883	30.846 966	108
28	33.964 210	33.328 291	32.712 782	32.116 840	31.539 668	30.980 502	112
29	34.131 323	33.484 175	32.858 196	32.252 495	31.666 223	31.098 573	116
30	34.280 887	33.623 350	32.987 709	32.373 023	31.778 393	31.202 970	120

PRESENT VALUE PER PERIOD QUARTERLY
COMPOUNDING

QTRS	12.75% ANNUAL RATE	13.00% ANNUAL RATE	13.25% ANNUAL RATE	13.50% ANNUAL RATE	13.75% ANNUAL RATE	14.00% ANNUAL RATE	QTRS
1	0.969 110	0.968 523	0.967 937	0.967 352	0.966 767	0.966 184	1
2	1.908 283	1.906 560	1.904 839	1.903 122	1.901 407	1.899 694	2
3	2.818 445	2.815 070	2.811 702	2.808 340	2.804 985	2.801 637	3
4	3.700 492	3.694 983	3.689 487	3.684 005	3.678 535	3.673 079	4
5	4.555 292	4.547 199	4.539 129	4.531 081	4.523 055	4.515 052	5
6	5.383 687	5.372 590	5.361 528	5.350 501	5.339 510	5.328 553	6
7	6.186 493	6.172 000	6.157 559	6.143 170	6.128 831	6.114 544	7
8	6.964 499	6.946 247	6.928 067	6.909 958	6.891 921	6.873 956	8
9	7.718 473	7.696 123	7.673 870	7.651 713	7.629 652	7.607 687	9
10	8.449 156	8.422 395	8.395 760	8.369 251	8.342 866	8.316 605	10
11	9.157 268	9.125 806	9.094 505	9.063 362	9.032 378	9.001 551	11
12	9.843 506	9.807 076	9.770 846	9.734 812	9.698 976	9.663 334	12
13	10.508 546	10.466 902	10.425 501	10.384 341	10.343 421	10.302 738	13
14	11.153 043	11.105 958	11.059 166	11.012 664	10.966 449	10.920 520	14
15	11.777 631	11.724 899	11.672 514	11.620 473	11.568 773	11.517 411	15
16	12.382 925	12.324 358	12.266 196	12.208 438	12.151 079	12.094 117	16
17	12.969 522	12.904 947	12.840 843	12.777 207	12.714 034	12.651 321	17
18	13.537 998	13.467 261	13.397 065	13.327 407	13.258 281	13.189 682	18
19	14.088 914	14.011 875	13.935 454	13.859 644	13.784 441	13.709 837	19
20	14.622 812	14.539 346	14.456 579	14.374 505	14.293 115	14.212 403	20
21	15.140 218	15.050 214	14.960 996	14.872 556	14.784 884	14.697 974	21
22	15.641 640	15.545 002	15.449 240	15.354 347	15.260 311	15.167 125	22
23	16.127 574	16.024 215	15.921 830	15.820 408	15.719 938	15.620 410	23
24	16.598 497	16.488 343	16.379 266	16.271 253	16.164 291	16.058 368	24
25	17.054 873	16.937 863	16.822 037	16.707 379	16.593 876	16.481 515	25
26	17.497 151	17.373 233	17.250 610	17.129 266	17.009 186	16.890 352	26
27	17.925 767	17.794 899	17.665 442	17.537 380	17.410 693	17.285 365	27
28	18.341 143	18.203 292	18.066 974	17.932 169	17.798 857	17.667 019	28
29	18.743 688	18.598 830	18.455 631	18.314 069	18.174 122	18.035 767	29
30	19.133 798	18.981 917	18.831 827	18.683 501	18.536 915	18.392 045	30
31	19.511 858	19.352 947	19.195 961	19.040 872	18.887 652	18.736 276	31
32	19.878 239	19.712 297	19.548 419	19.386 575	19.226 733	19.068 865	32
33	20.233 302	20.060 336	19.889 577	19.720 991	19.554 546	19.390 208	33
34	20.577 398	20.397 420	20.219 796	20.044 490	19.871 464	19.700 684	34
35	20.910 864	20.723 893	20.539 428	20.357 427	20.177 851	20.000 661	35
36	21.234 029	21.040 090	20.848 811	20.660 147	20.474 055	20.290 494	36
37	21.547 212	21.346 335	21.148 274	20.952 983	20.760 416	20.570 525	37
38	21.850 720	21.642 939	21.438 136	21.236 260	21.037 260	20.841 087	38
39	22.144 853	21.930 207	21.718 704	21.510 287	21.304 904	21.102 500	39
40	22.429 900	22.208 433	21.990 276	21.775 369	21.563 653	21.355 072	40
41	22.706 142	22.477 901	22.253 141	22.031 796	21.813 804	21.599 104	41
42	22.973 850	22.738 888	22.507 577	22.279 851	22.055 641	21.834 883	42
43	23.233 289	22.991 659	22.753 856	22.519 807	22.289 442	22.062 689	43
44	23.484 714	23.236 473	22.992 238	22.751 930	22.515 472	22.282 791	44
45	23.728 372	23.473 582	23.222 977	22.976 474	22.733 991	22.495 450	45
46	23.964 504	23.703 227	23.446 317	23.193 687	22.945 248	22.700 918	46
47	24.193 341	23.925 644	23.662 497	23.403 808	23.149 485	22.899 438	47
48	24.415 109	24.141 059	23.871 746	23.607 070	23.346 934	23.091 244	48
49	24.630 027	24.349 694	24.074 285	23.803 695	23.537 821	23.276 564	49
50	24.838 306	24.551 762	24.270 330	23.993 901	23.722 365	23.455 618	50
51	25.040 151	24.747 469	24.460 090	24.177 897	23.900 778	23.628 616	51
52	25.235 761	24.937 016	24.643 765	24.355 886	24.073 258	23.795 765	52
53	25.425 329	25.120 597	24.821 551	24.528 063	24.240 007	23.957 260	53
54	25.609 041	25.298 399	24.993 637	24.694 620	24.401 216	24.113 295	54
55	25.787 078	25.470 604	25.160 205	24.855 739	24.557 066	24.264 053	55

YRS							
14	25.959 615	25.637 389	25.321 433	25.011 597	24.707 738	24.409 713	56
15	26.598 088	26.253 656	25.916 280	25.585 781	25.261 988	24.944 734	60
16	27.161 251	26.795 918	26.438 428	26.088 574	25.746 154	25.410 974	64
17	27.657 987	27.273 061	26.896 762	26.528 852	26.169 097	25.817 275	68
18	28.096 131	27.692 905	27.299 081	26.914 387	26.538 559	26.171 343	72
19	28.482 595	28.062 332	27.652 231	27.251 987	26.861 303	26.479 892	76
20	28.823 474	28.387 395	27.962 222	27.547 612	27.143 236	26.748 776	80
21	29.124 146	28.673 422	28.234 326	27.806 480	27.389 519	26.983 092	84
22	29.389 352	28.925 102	28.473 176	28.033 162	27.604 659	27.187 285	88
23	29.623 277	29.146 557	28.682 835	28.231 659	27.792 595	27.365 227	92
24	29.829 609	29.341 419	28.866 871	28.405 476	27.956 766	27.520 294	96
25	30.011 603	29.512 881	29.028 415	28.557 681	28.100 178	27.655 425	100
26	30.172 131	29.663 752	29.170 216	28.690 962	28.225 456	27.773 185	104
27	30.313 724	29.796 506	29.294 686	28.807 671	28.334 892	27.875 805	108
28	30.438 616	29.913 317	29.403 945	28.909 870	28.430 490	27.965 233	112
29	30.548 777	30.016 101	29.499 851	28.999 361	28.514 000	28.043 164	116
30	30.645 943	30.106 542	29.584 035	29.077 726	28.586 950	28.111 077	120

QTRS	14.25% ANNUAL RATE	14.50% ANNUAL RATE	14.75% ANNUAL RATE	15.00% ANNUAL RATE	15.25% ANNUAL RATE	15.50% ANNUAL RATE	QTRS
1	0.965 600	0.965 018	0.964 436	0.963 855	0.963 275	0.962 696	1
2	1.897 985	1.896 278	1.894 574	1.892 873	1.891 174	1.889 478	2
3	2.798 295	2.794 961	2.791 633	2.788 311	2.784 996	2.781 688	3
4	3.667 636	3.662 206	3.656 788	3.651 384	3.645 993	3.640 614	4
5	4.507 072	4.499 113	4.491 176	4.483 262	4.475 369	4.467 498	5
6	5.317 631	5.306 743	5.295 890	5.285 072	5.274 287	5.263 536	6
7	6.100 307	6.086 122	6.071 986	6.057 900	6.043 865	6.029 879	7
8	6.856 060	6.838 235	6.820 481	6.802 796	6.785 180	6.767 633	8
9	7.585 816	7.564 039	7.542 356	7.520 767	7.499 270	7.477 866	9
10	8.290 468	8.264 453	8.238 559	8.212 787	8.187 135	8.161 603	10
11	8.970 880	8.940 364	8.910 003	8.879 795	8.849 739	8.819 835	11
12	9.627 887	9.592 632	9.557 568	9.522 694	9.488 009	9.453 511	12
13	10.262 293	10.222 081	10.182 103	10.142 356	10.102 838	10.063 549	13
14	10.874 875	10.829 511	10.784 427	10.739 620	10.695 088	10.650 829	14
15	11.466 385	11.415 692	11.365 330	11.315 296	11.265 587	11.216 201	15
16	12.037 547	11.981 968	11.925 575	11.870 165	11.815 135	11.760 483	16
17	12.589 062	12.527 255	12.465 895	12.404 978	12.344 501	12.284 460	17
18	13.121 605	13.054 046	12.986 999	12.920 461	12.854 426	12.788 890	18
19	13.635 829	13.562 408	13.489 571	13.417 312	13.345 624	13.274 503	19
20	14.132 363	14.052 988	13.974 270	13.896 204	13.818 783	13.742 001	20
21	14.611 817	14.526 405	14.441 731	14.357 787	14.274 565	14.192 059	21
22	15.074 778	14.983 262	14.892 568	14.802 686	14.713 609	14.625 327	22
23	15.521 814	15.424 137	15.327 371	15.231 505	15.136 529	15.042 433	23
24	15.953 441	15.849 590	15.746 711	15.644 824	15.543 917	15.443 979	24
25	16.370 280	16.260 159	16.151 138	16.043 204	15.936 344	15.830 545	25
26	16.772 751	16.656 366	16.541 182	16.427 185	16.314 359	16.202 690	26
27	17.161 207	17.038 712	16.917 354	16.797 286	16.678 492	16.560 954	27
28	17.536 634	17.407 684	17.280 149	17.154 011	17.029 251	16.905 852	28
29	17.898 983	17.763 748	17.630 041	17.497 842	17.367 130	17.237 884	29
30	18.248 867	18.107 356	17.967 490	17.829 245	17.692 599	17.557 530	30
31	18.586 715	18.438 944	18.292 938	18.148 670	18.006 116	17.865 251	31
32	18.912 942	18.758 933	18.606 812	18.456 549	18.308 119	18.161 493	32
33	19.227 946	19.067 728	18.909 523	18.753 301	18.599 031	18.446 684	33
34	19.532 114	19.365 721	19.201 469	19.039 326	18.879 259	18.721 236	34
35	19.825 820	19.653 289	19.483 032	19.315 013	19.149 196	18.985 547	35
36	20.109 422	19.930 797	19.754 582	19.580 735	19.409 220	19.239 997	36
37	20.383 268	20.198 598	20.016 474	19.836 853	19.659 694	19.484 955	37
38	20.647 694	20.457 031	20.269 053	20.083 714	19.900 969	19.720 775	38
39	20.903 023	20.706 423	20.512 649	20.321 652	20.133 384	19.947 798	39
40	21.149 570	20.947 091	20.747 582	20.550 990	20.357 263	20.166 351	40
41	21.387 635	21.179 340	20.974 160	20.772 039	20.572 921	20.376 752	41
42	21.617 512	21.403 464	21.192 680	20.985 097	20.780 658	20.579 304	42
43	21.839 480	21.619 749	21.403 428	21.190 455	20.980 766	20.774 300	43
44	22.053 813	21.828 467	21.606 682	21.388 391	21.173 526	20.962 022	44
45	22.260 773	22.029 883	21.802 707	21.579 172	21.359 206	21.142 741	45
46	22.460 614	22.224 254	21.991 761	21.763 057	21.538 067	21.316 718	46
47	22.653 580	22.411 825	22.174 091	21.940 296	21.710 360	21.484 205	47
48	22.839 908	22.592 835	22.349 937	22.111 129	21.876 325	21.645 444	48
49	23.019 827	22.767 513	22.519 530	22.275 787	22.036 195	21.800 668	49
50	23.193 556	22.936 080	22.683 091	22.434 493	22.190 194	21.950 102	50
51	23.361 310	23.098 750	22.840 835	22.587 463	22.338 537	22.093 961	51
52	23.523 292	23.255 730	22.992 969	22.734 904	22.481 432	22.232 453	52
53	23.679 703	23.407 218	23.139 693	22.877 016	22.619 080	22.365 779	53
54	23.830 733	23.553 407	23.281 199	23.013 992	22.751 673	22.494 131	54
55	23.976 568	23.694 482	23.417 672	23.146 016	22.879 396	22.617 696	55

YRS							
14	24.117 386	23.830 622	23.549 292	23.273 268	23.002 428	22.736 651	56
15	24.633 856	24.329 195	24.030 598	23.737 916	23.451 003	23.169 719	60
16	25.082 844	24.761 579	24.447 003	24.138 941	23.837 225	23.541 693	64
17	25.473 167	25.136 563	24.807 258	24.485 054	24.169 761	23.861 191	68
18	25.812 491	25.461 765	25.118 934	24.783 776	24.456 073	24.135 616	72
19	26.107 479	25.743 795	25.388 583	25.041 594	24.702 587	24.371 327	76
20	26.363 924	25.988 384	25.621 872	25.264 110	24.914 834	24.573 786	80
21	26.586 862	26.200 503	25.823 703	25.456 158	25.097 578	24.747 683	84
22	26.780 671	26.384 462	25.998 318	25.621 909	25.254 920	24.897 047	88
23	26.949 157	26.544 000	26.149 387	25.764 965	25.390 391	25.025 340	92
24	27.095 629	26.682 358	26.280 086	25.888 432	25.507 032	25.135 535	96
25	27.222 963	26.802 348	26.393 160	25.994 993	25.607 458	25.230 183	100
26	27.333 659	26.906 410	26.490 988	26.086 963	25.693 925	25.311 480	104
27	27.429 892	26.996 666	26.575 623	26.166 340	25.768 373	25.381 307	108
28	27.513 551	27.074 922	26.648 846	26.234 848	25.832 473	25.441 284	112
29	27.586 279	27.142 797	26.712 196	26.293 976	25.887 662	25.492 800	116
30	27.649 505	27.201 662	26.767 003	26.345 007	25.935 180	25.537 048	120

	15.75%	16.00%	16.50%	17.00%	17.50%	18.00%	
	ANNUAL RATE	ANNUAL RATE	ANNUAL RATE	ANNUAL RATE	ANNUAL RATE	ANNUAL RATE	
QTRS							QTRS
1	0.962 117	0.961 538	0.960 384	0.959 233	0.958 084	0.956 938	1
2	1.887 785	1.886 095	1.882 722	1.879 360	1.876 008	1.872 668	2
3	2.778 386	2.775 091	2.768 520	2.761 976	2.755 457	2.748 964	3
4	3.635 248	3.629 895	3.619 227	3.608 610	3.598 043	3.587 526	4
5	4.459 650	4.451 822	4.436 233	4.420 729	4.405 311	4.389 977	5
6	5.252 820	5.242 137	5.220 872	5.199 740	5.178 741	5.157 872	6
7	6.015 942	6.002 055	5.974 427	5.946 993	5.919 751	5.892 701	7
8	6.750 155	6.732 745	6.698 129	6.663 782	6.629 702	6.595 886	8
9	7.456 553	7.435 332	7.393 161	7.351 350	7.309 894	7.268 790	9
10	8.136 190	8.110 896	8.060 669	8.010 887	7.961 575	7.912 718	10
11	8.790 081	8.760 477	8.701 713	8.643 537	8.585 940	8.528 917	11
12	9.419 200	9.385 074	9.317 372	9.250 395	9.184 134	9.118 581	12
13	10.024 486	9.985 648	9.908 640	9.832 513	9.757 255	9.682 852	13
14	10.606 841	10.563 123	10.476 485	10.390 900	10.306 352	10.222 825	14
15	11.167 136	11.118 387	11.021 834	10.926 523	10.832 433	10.739 546	15
16	11.706 204	11.652 296	11.545 579	11.440 309	11.336 463	11.234 015	16
17	12.224 850	12.165 669	12.048 576	11.933 151	11.819 365	11.707 191	17
18	12.723 849	12.659 297	12.531 645	12.405 900	12.282 027	12.159 992	18
19	13.203 063	13.133 939	12.995 578	12.859 376	12.725 295	12.593 294	19
20	13.665 851	13.590 326	13.441 131	13.294 366	13.149 983	13.007 936	20
21	14.110 259	14.029 160	13.869 033	13.711 622	13.556 870	13.404 724	21
22	14.537 832	14.451 115	14.279 984	14.111 868	13.946 702	13.784 425	22
23	14.949 207	14.856 842	14.674 654	14.495 796	14.320 193	14.147 775	23
24	15.344 998	15.246 963	15.053 690	14.864 073	14.678 030	14.495 478	24
25	15.725 795	15.622 080	15.417 709	15.217 336	15.020 867	14.828 209	25
26	16.092 166	15.982 769	15.767 308	15.556 198	15.349 333	15.146 611	26
27	16.444 657	16.329 586	16.103 057	15.881 245	15.664 032	15.451 303	27
28	16.783 795	16.663 063	16.425 505	16.193 041	15.965 540	15.742 874	28
29	17.110 286	16.983 715	16.735 179	16.492 125	16.254 409	16.021 889	29
30	17.424 015	17.292 033	17.032 584	16.779 017	16.531 171	16.288 889	30
31	17.726 052	17.588 494	17.318 208	17.054 213	16.796 331	16.544 391	31
32	18.016 646	17.873 551	17.592 517	17.318 190	17.050 377	16.788 891	32
33	18.296 232	18.147 646	17.855 959	17.571 405	17.293 774	17.022 862	33
34	18.565 226	18.411 198	18.108 964	17.814 298	17.526 970	17.246 758	34
35	18.824 030	18.664 613	18.351 946	18.047 288	17.750 390	17.461 012	35
36	19.073 030	18.908 282	18.585 302	18.270 780	17.964 445	17.666 041	36
37	19.312 596	19.142 579	18.809 414	18.485 160	18.169 329	17.862 240	37
38	19.543 087	19.367 864	19.024 647	18.690 801	18.366 015	18.049 990	38
39	19.764 846	19.584 485	19.231 354	18.888 059	18.554 266	18.229 656	39
40	19.978 204	19.792 774	19.429 872	19.077 275	18.734 626	18.401 584	40
41	20.183 480	19.993 052	19.620 525	19.258 777	18.907 426	18.566 109	41
42	20.380 981	20.185 627	19.803 626	19.432 879	19.072 983	18.723 550	42
43	20.570 996	20.370 795	19.979 472	19.599 884	19.231 601	18.874 210	43
44	20.753 814	20.548 841	20.148 353	19.760 081	19.383 570	19.018 383	44
45	20.929 707	20.720 040	20.310 543	19.913 747	19.529 169	19.156 347	45
46	21.098 937	20.884 654	20.466 308	20.061 148	19.668 665	19.288 371	46
47	21.261 755	21.042 936	20.615 902	20.202 540	19.802 313	19.414 709	47
48	21.418 405	21.195 131	20.759 570	20.338 168	19.930 360	19.535 607	48
49	21.569 121	21.341 472	20.897 546	20.468 266	20.053 040	19.651 298	49
50	21.714 127	21.482 185	21.030 056	20.593 061	20.170 577	19.762 008	50
51	21.853 640	21.617 485	21.157 317	20.712 769	20.283 187	19.867 950	51
52	21.987 868	21.747 582	21.279 536	20.827 596	20.391 078	19.969 330	52
53	22.117 011	21.872 675	21.396 913	20.937 742	20.494 446	20.066 345	53
54	22.241 261	21.992 957	21.509 640	21.043 397	20.593 481	20.159 181	54
55	22.360 804	22.108 612	21.617 902	21.144 746	20.688 365	20.248 021	55
YRS							
14	22.475 819	22.219 819	21.721 875	21.241 962	20.779 272	20.333 034	56
15	22.893 926	22.623 490	22.098 175	21.592 779	21.106 359	20.638 022	60
16	23.252 186	22.968 549	22.418 297	21.889 793	21.381 957	20.893 773	64
17	23.559 145	23.263 507	22.690 627	22.141 254	21.614 173	21.108 236	68
18	23.822 204	23.515 639	22.922 299	22.354 150	21.809 834	21.288 077	72
19	24.047 592	23.731 162	23.119 385	22.534 395	21.974 695	21.438 884	76
20	24.240 718	23.915 392	23.287 047	22.686 997	22.113 605	21.565 345	80
21	24.406 201	24.072 872	23.429 678	22.816 195	22.230 649	21.671 390	84
22	24.547 997	24.207 487	23.551 016	22.925 578	22.329 268	21.760 316	88
23	24.669 496	24.322 557	23.654 238	23.018 185	22.412 363	21.834 885	92
24	24.773 605	24.420 919	23.742 050	23.096 590	22.482 378	21.897 417	96
25	24.862 811	24.504 999	23.816 753	23.162 970	22.541 371	21.949 853	100
26	24.939 249	24.576 871	23.880 303	23.219 170	22.591 078	21.993 824	104
27	25.004 745	24.638 308	23.934 365	23.266 750	22.632 961	22.030 696	108
28	25.060 867	24.690 824	23.980 356	23.307 034	22.668 250	22.061 616	112
29	25.108 955	24.735 715	24.019 481	23.341 139	22.697 985	22.087 544	116
30	25.150 160	24.774 088	24.052 765	23.370 014	22.723 038	22.109 286	120

QTRS	18.50% ANNUAL RATE	19.00% ANNUAL RATE	19.50% ANNUAL RATE	20.00% ANNUAL RATE	20.50% ANNUAL RATE	21.00% ANNUAL RATE	QTRS
1	0.955 795	0.954 654	0.953 516	0.952 381	0.951 249	0.950 119	1
2	1.869 338	1.866 018	1.862 709	1.859 410	1.856 122	1.852 844	2
3	2.742 497	2.736 055	2.729 639	2.723 248	2.716 882	2.710 541	3
4	3.577 058	3.566 640	3.556 271	3.545 951	3.535 679	3.525 455	4
5	4.374 727	4.359 561	4.344 478	4.329 477	4.314 557	4.299 719	5
6	5.137 135	5.116 526	5.096 045	5.075 692	5.055 465	5.035 363	6
7	5.865 840	5.839 166	5.812 677	5.786 373	5.760 252	5.734 311	7
8	6.562 332	6.529 036	6.495 998	6.463 213	6.430 680	6.398 396	8
9	7.228 035	7.187 624	7.147 554	7.107 822	7.068 423	7.029 355	9
10	7.864 311	7.816 348	7.768 824	7.721 735	7.675 075	7.628 840	10
11	8.472 459	8.416 561	8.361 215	8.306 414	8.252 153	8.198 423	11
12	9.053 725	8.989 557	8.926 069	8.863 252	8.801 096	8.739 595	12
13	9.609 295	9.536 570	9.464 666	9.393 573	9.323 278	9.253 772	13
14	10.140 306	10.058 778	9.978 228	9.898 641	9.820 003	9.742 301	14
15	10.647 843	10.557 306	10.467 917	10.379 658	10.292 512	10.206 462	15
16	11.132 944	11.033 228	10.934 843	10.837 770	10.741 985	10.647 469	16
17	11.596 601	11.487 568	11.380 065	11.274 066	11.169 546	11.066 479	17
18	12.039 762	11.921 306	11.804 591	11.689 587	11.576 263	11.464 588	18
19	12.463 333	12.335 376	12.209 384	12.085 321	11.963 151	11.842 839	19
20	12.868 180	12.730 669	12.595 360	12.462 210	12.331 178	12.202 223	20
21	13.255 130	13.108 037	12.963 395	12.821 153	12.681 263	12.543 679	21
22	13.624 975	13.468 293	13.314 321	13.163 003	13.014 281	12.868 104	22
23	13.978 471	13.812 213	13.648 936	13.488 574	13.331 064	13.176 346	23
24	14.316 340	14.140 538	13.967 996	13.798 642	13.632 404	13.469 212	24
25	14.639 274	14.453 974	14.272 225	14.093 945	13.919 052	13.747 470	25
26	14.947 932	14.753 197	14.562 312	14.375 185	14.191 726	14.011 848	26
27	15.242 946	15.038 852	14.838 915	14.643 034	14.451 107	14.263 038	27
28	15.524 918	15.311 553	15.102 660	14.898 127	14.697 843	14.501 699	28
29	15.794 426	15.571 888	15.354 146	15.141 074	14.932 549	14.728 455	29
30	16.052 020	15.820 418	15.593 941	15.372 451	15.155 814	14.943 901	30
31	16.298 227	16.057 679	15.822 590	15.592 811	15.368 194	15.148 599	31
32	16.533 550	16.284 180	16.040 610	15.802 677	15.570 220	15.343 087	32
33	16.758 471	16.500 410	16.248 496	16.002 549	15.762 397	15.527 874	33
34	16.973 449	16.706 836	16.446 719	16.192 904	15.945 206	15.703 443	34
35	17.178 924	16.903 901	16.635 727	16.374 194	16.119 102	15.870 255	35
36	17.375 315	17.092 029	16.815 949	16.546 852	16.284 520	16.028 745	36
37	17.563 026	17.271 627	16.987 794	16.711 287	16.441 874	16.179 331	37
38	17.742 438	17.443 081	17.151 651	16.867 893	16.591 557	16.322 404	38
39	17.913 919	17.606 759	17.307 892	17.017 041	16.733 942	16.458 341	39
40	18.077 820	17.763 016	17.456 869	17.159 086	16.869 386	16.587 498	40
41	18.234 475	17.912 187	17.598 922	17.294 368	16.998 227	16.710 212	41
42	18.384 206	18.054 594	17.734 371	17.423 208	17.120 787	16.826 804	42
43	18.527 317	18.190 543	17.863 524	17.545 912	17.237 371	16.937 581	43
44	18.664 103	18.320 328	17.986 673	17.662 773	17.348 272	17.042 833	44
45	18.794 841	18.444 227	18.104 099	17.774 070	17.453 767	17.142 834	45
46	18.919 800	18.562 508	18.216 066	17.880 066	17.554 118	17.237 847	46
47	19.039 236	18.675 425	18.322 828	17.981 016	17.649 577	17.328 121	47
48	19.153 391	18.783 222	18.424 628	18.077 158	17.740 383	17.413 891	48
49	19.262 501	18.886 131	18.521 695	18.168 722	17.826 761	17.495 384	49
50	19.366 787	18.984 373	18.614 250	18.255 925	17.908 929	17.572 811	50
51	19.466 463	19.078 160	18.702 503	18.338 977	17.987 090	17.646 376	51
52	19.561 733	19.167 695	18.786 654	18.418 073	18.061 441	17.716 272	52
53	19.652 791	19.253 169	18.866 893	18.493 403	18.132 168	17.782 681	53
54	19.739 824	19.334 768	18.943 402	18.565 146	18.199 446	17.845 778	54
55	19.823 010	19.412 666	19.016 355	18.633 472	18.263 445	17.905 727	55

YRS

	18.50% ANNUAL RATE	19.00% ANNUAL RATE	19.50% ANNUAL RATE	20.00% ANNUAL RATE	20.50% ANNUAL RATE	21.00% ANNUAL RATE	
14	19.902 519	19.487 032	19.085 916	18.698 545	18.324 323	17.962 686	56
15	20.186 925	19.752 269	19.333 296	18.929 290	18.539 570	18.163 493	60
16	20.424 280	19.972 570	19.537 788	19.119 124	18.715 813	18.327 132	64
17	20.622 367	20.155 549	19.706 828	19.275 301	18.860 120	18.460 485	68
18	20.787 682	20.307 529	19.846 561	19.403 788	18.978 278	18.569 155	72
19	20.925 649	20.433 761	19.962 069	19.509 495	19.075 026	18.657 712	76
20	21.040 790	20.538 607	20.057 552	19.596 460	19.154 243	18.729 879	80
21	21.136 882	20.625 691	20.136 481	19.668 007	19.219 105	18.788 688	84
22	21.217 077	20.698 021	20.201 726	19.726 869	19.272 214	18.836 613	88
23	21.284 004	20.758 098	20.255 660	19.775 294	19.315 699	18.875 667	92
24	21.339 859	20.807 996	20.300 244	19.815 134	19.351 305	18.907 493	96
25	21.386 474	20.849 441	20.337 098	19.847 910	19.380 459	18.933 428	100
26	21.425 376	20.883 865	20.367 562	19.874 875	19.404 330	18.954 564	104
27	21.457 843	20.912 456	20.392 746	19.897 060	19.423 876	18.971 787	108
28	21.484 938	20.936 204	20.413 563	19.915 311	19.439 879	18.985 822	112
29	21.507 551	20.955 929	20.430 771	19.930 326	19.452 983	18.997 260	116
30	21.526 423	20.972 312	20.444 996	19.942 679	19.463 713	19.006 581	120

PRESENT VALUE PER PERIOD

QTRS	21.50% ANNUAL RATE	22.00% ANNUAL RATE	22.50% ANNUAL RATE	23.00% ANNUAL RATE	23.50% ANNUAL RATE	24.00% ANNUAL RATE	QTRS
1	0.948 992	0.947 867	0.946 746	0.945 626	0.944 510	0.943 396	1
2	1.849 577	1.846 320	1.843 073	1.839 836	1.836 609	1.833 393	2
3	2.704 225	2.697 933	2.691 666	2.685 424	2.679 206	2.673 012	3
4	3.515 279	3.505 150	3.495 069	3.485 035	3.475 047	3.465 106	4
5	4.284 962	4.270 284	4.255 686	4.241 167	4.226 727	4.212 364	5
6	5.015 385	4.995 530	4.975 798	4.956 187	4.936 696	4.917 324	6
7	5.708 550	5.682 967	5.657 560	5.632 328	5.607 269	5.582 381	7
8	6.366 359	6.334 566	6.303 015	6.271 705	6.240 632	6.209 794	8
9	6.990 613	6.952 195	6.914 098	6.876 317	6.838 849	6.801 692	9
10	7.583 026	7.537 626	7.492 637	7.448 054	7.403 872	7.360 087	10
11	8.145 220	8.092 536	8.040 366	7.988 703	7.937 541	7.886 875	11
12	8.678 738	8.618 518	8.558 926	8.499 956	8.441 597	8.383 844	12
13	9.185 042	9.117 079	9.049 871	8.983 410	8.917 684	8.852 683	13
14	9.665 520	9.589 648	9.514 671	9.440 576	9.367 352	9.294 984	14
15	10.121 490	10.037 581	9.954 718	9.872 886	9.792 068	9.712 249	15
16	10.554 202	10.462 162	10.371 331	10.281 688	10.193 216	10.105 895	16
17	10.964 841	10.864 609	10.765 757	10.668 263	10.572 105	10.477 260	17
18	11.354 535	11.246 074	11.139 178	11.033 819	10.929 969	10.827 603	18
19	11.724 351	11.607 654	11.492 713	11.379 498	11.267 976	11.158 116	19
20	12.075 304	11.950 382	11.827 421	11.706 381	11.587 226	11.469 921	20
21	12.408 355	12.275 244	12.144 304	12.015 490	11.888 761	11.764 077	21
22	12.724 417	12.583 170	12.444 311	12.307 792	12.173 565	12.041 582	22
23	13.024 358	12.875 042	12.728 342	12.584 200	12.442 564	12.303 379	23
24	13.308 999	13.151 699	12.997 247	12.845 580	12.696 637	12.550 358	24
25	13.579 122	13.413 933	13.251 831	13.092 747	12.936 611	12.783 356	25
26	13.835 465	13.662 495	13.492 858	13.326 474	13.163 269	13.003 166	26
27	14.078 733	13.898 100	13.721 049	13.547 494	13.377 349	13.210 534	27
28	14.309 593	14.121 422	13.937 088	13.756 495	13.579 551	13.406 164	28
29	14.528 676	14.333 101	14.141 622	13.954 132	13.770 532	13.590 721	29
30	14.736 585	14.533 745	14.335 263	14.141 024	13.950 916	13.764 831	30
31	14.933 888	14.723 929	14.518 592	14.317 753	14.121 290	13.929 086	31
32	15.121 128	14.904 198	14.692 158	14.484 873	14.282 210	14.084 043	32
33	15.298 816	15.075 069	14.856 481	14.642 906	14.434 201	14.230 230	33
34	15.467 441	15.237 033	15.012 053	14.792 346	14.577 758	14.368 141	34
35	15.627 465	15.390 542	15.159 340	14.933 660	14.713 348	14.498 246	35
36	15.779 326	15.536 068	15.298 784	15.067 291	14.841 415	14.620 987	36
37	15.923 441	15.673 999	15.430 801	15.193 656	14.962 376	14.736 780	37
38	16.060 205	15.804 738	15.555 788	15.313 150	15.076 624	14.846 019	38
39	16.189 993	15.928 662	15.674 119	15.426 146	15.184 533	14.949 075	39
40	16.313 161	16.046 125	15.786 148	15.532 999	15.286 453	15.046 297	40
41	16.430 046	16.157 464	15.892 211	15.634 041	15.382 719	15.138 016	41
42	16.540 969	16.262 999	15.992 626	15.729 590	15.473 642	15.224 543	42
43	16.646 234	16.363 032	16.087 693	15.819 943	15.559 520	15.306 173	43
44	16.746 129	16.457 851	16.177 698	15.905 384	15.640 633	15.383 182	44
45	16.840 929	16.547 726	16.262 909	15.986 178	15.717 245	15.455 832	45
46	16.930 894	16.632 915	16.343 583	16.062 580	15.789 606	15.524 370	46
47	17.016 269	16.713 664	16.419 960	16.134 828	15.857 951	15.589 028	47
48	17.097 290	16.790 203	16.492 270	16.203 147	15.922 504	15.650 027	48
49	17.174 178	16.862 751	16.560 729	16.267 751	15.983 475	15.707 572	49
50	17.247 144	16.931 518	16.625 542	16.328 842	16.041 062	15.761 861	50
51	17.316 388	16.996 699	16.686 904	16.386 612	16.095 455	15.813 076	51
52	17.382 100	17.058 483	16.744 998	16.441 241	16.146 828	15.861 393	52
53	17.444 460	17.117 045	16.799 998	16.492 899	16.195 351	15.906 974	53
54	17.503 640	17.172 555	16.852 069	16.541 749	16.241 182	15.949 976	54
55	17.559 801	17.225 170	16.901 367	16.587 942	16.284 469	15.990 543	55

YRS							
14	17.613 097	17.275 043	16.948 040	16.631 624	16.325 355	16.028 814	56
15	17.800 447	17.449 854	17.111 164	16.783 866	16.467 434	16.161 428	60
16	17.952 398	17.590 965	17.242 219	16.905 582	16.580 506	16.266 470	64
17	18.075 639	17.704 871	17.347 508	17.002 916	16.670 493	16.349 673	68
18	18.175 594	17.796 819	17.432 098	17.080 745	16.742 109	16.415 578	72
19	18.256 663	17.871 040	17.500 058	17.142 978	16.799 103	16.467 781	76
20	18.322 414	17.930 953	17.554 657	17.192 740	16.844 462	16.509 131	80
21	18.375 741	17.979 316	17.598 522	17.232 530	16.880 560	16.541 883	84
22	18.418 993	18.018 355	17.633 763	17.264 347	16.909 289	16.567 827	88
23	18.454 072	18.049 868	17.662 076	17.289 788	16.932 152	16.588 376	92
24	18.482 524	18.075 306	17.684 823	17.310 131	16.950 348	16.604 653	96
25	18.505 599	18.095 839	17.703 098	17.326 397	16.964 828	16.617 546	100
26	18.524 315	18.112 415	17.717 780	17.339 404	16.976 353	16.627 759	104
27	18.539 494	18.125 794	17.729 575	17.349 804	16.985 524	16.635 848	108
28	18.551 805	18.136 595	17.739 052	17.358 120	16.992 824	16.642 255	112
29	18.561 790	18.145 313	17.746 665	17.364 770	16.998 632	16.647 331	116
30	18.569 889	18.152 351	17.752 782	17.370 087	17.003 255	16.651 351	120

HALF YRS	5.25% ANNUAL RATE	5.50% ANNUAL RATE	5.75% ANNUAL RATE	6.00% ANNUAL RATE	6.25% ANNUAL RATE	6.50% ANNUAL RATE	HALF YRS
1	0.974 421	0.973 236	0.972 053	0.970 874	0.969 697	0.968 523	1
2	1.923 919	1.920 424	1.916 941	1.913 470	1.910 009	1.906 560	2
3	2.849 129	2.842 262	2.835 423	2.828 611	2.821 827	2.815 070	3
4	3.750 674	3.739 428	3.728 236	3.717 098	3.706 014	3.694 980	4
5	4.629 158	4.612 582	4.596 098	4.579 707	4.563 408	4.547 199	5
6	5.485 173	5.462 367	5.439 707	5.417 191	5.394 820	5.372 590	6
7	6.319 291	6.289 408	6.259 739	6.230 283	6.201 037	6.172 000	7
8	7.132 074	7.094 314	7.056 855	7.019 692	6.982 824	6.946 247	8
9	7.924 067	7.877 678	7.831 694	7.786 109	7.740 920	7.696 123	9
10	8.695 803	8.640 076	8.584 878	8.530 203	8.476 044	8.422 395	10
11	9.447 798	9.382 069	9.317 014	9.252 624	9.188 891	9.125 806	11
12	10.180 558	10.104 204	10.028 689	9.954 004	9.880 137	9.807 076	12
13	10.894 576	10.807 011	10.720 476	10.634 955	10.550 436	10.466 902	13
14	11.590 330	11.491 008	11.392 929	11.296 073	11.200 422	11.105 958	14
15	12.268 287	12.156 699	12.046 589	11.937 935	11.830 713	11.724 899	15
16	12.928 903	12.804 573	12.681 982	12.561 102	12.441 903	12.324 358	16
17	13.572 622	13.435 108	13.299 618	13.166 118	13.034 573	12.904 947	17
18	14.199 875	14.048 767	13.899 994	13.753 513	13.609 283	13.467 261	18
19	14.811 084	14.646 002	14.483 590	14.323 799	14.166 577	14.011 875	19
20	15.406 659	15.227 252	15.050 878	14.877 475	14.706 984	14.539 346	20
21	15.987 001	15.792 946	15.602 311	15.415 024	15.231 015	15.050 214	21
22	16.552 498	16.343 500	16.138 334	15.936 917	15.739 166	15.545 002	22
23	17.103 530	16.879 319	16.659 377	16.443 608	16.231 918	16.024 215	23
24	17.640 468	17.400 797	17.165 859	16.935 542	16.709 739	16.488 343	24
25	18.163 671	17.908 318	17.658 186	17.413 148	17.173 080	16.937 863	25
26	18.673 492	18.402 256	18.136 754	17.876 842	17.622 381	17.373 233	26
27	19.170 272	18.882 974	18.601 948	18.327 031	18.058 066	17.794 899	27
28	19.654 346	19.350 826	19.054 142	18.764 108	18.480 549	18.203 292	28
29	20.126 037	19.806 157	19.493 698	19.188 455	18.890 229	18.598 830	29
30	20.585 664	20.249 301	19.920 970	19.600 441	19.287 495	18.981 917	30
31	21.033 534	20.680 585	20.336 301	20.000 428	19.672 723	19.352 947	31
32	21.469 947	21.100 326	20.740 025	20.388 766	20.046 276	19.712 297	32
33	21.895 198	21.508 833	21.132 467	20.765 792	20.408 510	20.060 336	33
34	22.309 572	21.906 407	21.513 941	21.131 837	20.759 768	20.397 420	34
35	22.713 347	22.293 340	21.884 754	21.487 220	21.100 381	20.723 893	35
36	23.106 793	22.669 918	22.245 205	21.832 252	21.430 672	21.040 090	36
37	23.490 176	23.036 416	22.595 582	22.167 235	21.750 955	21.346 335	37
38	23.863 753	23.393 106	22.936 167	22.492 462	22.061 532	21.642 939	38
39	24.227 774	23.740 249	23.267 234	22.808 215	22.362 698	21.930 207	39
40	24.582 484	24.078 101	23.589 049	23.114 772	22.654 737	22.208 433	40
41	24.928 120	24.406 911	23.901 870	23.412 400	22.937 927	22.477 901	41
42	25.264 916	24.726 921	24.205 949	23.701 359	23.212 535	22.738 888	42
43	25.593 098	25.038 366	24.501 530	23.981 902	23.478 822	22.991 659	43
44	25.912 884	25.341 475	24.788 851	24.254 274	23.737 040	23.236 473	44
45	26.224 491	25.636 472	25.068 142	24.518 713	23.987 432	23.473 582	45
46	26.528 128	25.923 574	25.339 627	24.775 449	24.230 237	23.703 227	46
47	26.823 998	26.202 992	25.603 526	25.024 708	24.465 685	23.925 644	47
48	27.112 300	26.474 931	25.860 050	25.266 707	24.693 997	24.141 059	48
49	27.393 228	26.739 592	26.109 404	25.501 657	24.915 391	24.349 694	49
50	27.666 970	26.997 170	26.351 790	25.729 764	25.130 077	24.551 762	50
51	27.933 710	27.247 854	26.587 402	25.951 227	25.338 256	24.747 469	51
52	28.193 627	27.491 829	26.816 430	26.166 240	25.540 127	24.937 016	52
53	28.446 896	27.729 274	27.039 057	26.374 990	25.735 881	25.120 597	53
54	28.693 687	27.960 364	27.255 463	26.577 660	25.925 703	25.298 399	54
55	28.934 165	28.185 269	27.465 820	26.774 428	26.109 772	25.470 604	55
56	29.168 492	28.404 155	27.670 299	26.965 464	26.288 264	25.637 389	56
57	29.396 826	28.617 182	27.869 064	27.150 936	26.461 347	25.798 924	57
58	29.619 319	28.824 508	28.062 273	27.331 005	26.629 185	25.955 374	58
59	29.836 120	29.026 285	28.250 083	27.505 831	26.791 937	26.106 900	59
YRS							
30	30.047 377	29.222 662	28.432 645	27.675 564	26.949 757	26.253 656	60
31	30.453 817	29.599 789	28.782 604	28.000 343	27.251 195	26.533 456	62
32	30.839 730	29.956 999	29.113 277	28.306 478	27.534 640	26.795 918	64
33	31.206 154	30.295 344	29.425 729	28.595 040	27.801 168	27.042 117	66
34	31.554 073	30.615 821	29.720 954	28.867 038	28.051 787	27.273 061	68
35	31.884 420	30.919 372	29.999 913	29.123 421	28.287 447	27.489 695	70
36	32.198 084	31.206 893	30.263 497	29.365 088	28.509 041	27.692 905	72
37	32.495 908	31.479 229	30.512 555	29.592 881	28.717 409	27.883 524	74
38	32.778 690	31.737 183	30.747 886	29.807 598	28.913 339	28.062 332	76
39	33.047 191	31.981 514	30.970 248	30.009 990	29.097 575	28.230 060	78
40	33.302 132	32.212 941	31.180 355	30.200 763	29.270 815	28.387 395	80

214

HALF YRS	6.75% ANNUAL RATE	7.00% ANNUAL RATE	7.25% ANNUAL RATE	7.50% ANNUAL RATE	7.75% ANNUAL RATE	8.00% ANNUAL RATE	HALF YRS
1	0.967 352	0.966 184	0.965 018	0.963 855	0.962 696	0.961 538	1
2	1.903 122	1.899 694	1.896 278	1.892 873	1.889 478	1.886 095	2
3	2.808 340	2.801 637	2.794 961	2.788 311	2.781 688	2.775 091	3
4	3.684 005	3.673 079	3.662 206	3.651 384	3.640 614	3.629 895	4
5	4.531 081	4.515 052	4.499 113	4.483 262	4.467 498	4.451 822	5
6	5.350 501	5.328 553	5.306 743	5.285 072	5.263 536	5.242 137	6
7	6.143 170	6.114 544	6.086 122	6.057 900	6.029 879	6.002 055	7
8	6.909 958	6.873 956	6.838 235	6.802 796	6.767 633	6.732 745	8
9	7.651 713	7.607 687	7.564 039	7.520 767	7.477 866	7.435 332	9
10	8.369 251	8.316 605	8.264 453	8.212 787	8.161 603	8.110 896	10
11	9.063 362	9.001 551	8.940 364	8.879 795	8.819 835	8.760 477	11
12	9.734 812	9.663 334	9.592 632	9.522 694	9.453 511	9.385 074	12
13	10.384 341	10.302 738	10.222 081	10.142 356	10.063 549	9.985 648	13
14	11.012 664	10.920 520	10.829 511	10.739 620	10.650 829	10.563 123	14
15	11.620 473	11.517 411	11.415 692	11.315 296	11.216 201	11.118 387	15
16	12.208 438	12.094 117	11.981 368	11.870 165	11.760 483	11.652 296	16
17	12.777 207	12.651 321	12.527 255	12.404 978	12.284 460	12.165 669	17
18	13.327 407	13.189 682	13.054 046	12.920 461	12.788 890	12.659 297	18
19	13.859 644	13.709 837	13.562 408	13.417 312	13.274 503	13.133 939	19
20	14.374 505	14.212 403	14.052 988	13.896 204	13.742 001	13.590 326	20
21	14.872 556	14.697 974	14.526 405	14.357 787	14.192 059	14.029 160	21
22	15.334 347	15.167 125	14.983 262	14.802 686	14.625 327	14.451 115	22
23	15.820 408	15.620 410	15.424 137	15.231 505	15.042 433	14.856 842	23
24	16.271 253	16.058 368	15.849 590	15.644 824	15.443 979	15.246 963	24
25	16.707 379	16.481 515	16.260 159	16.043 204	15.830 545	15.622 080	25
26	17.129 266	16.890 352	16.656 366	16.427 185	16.202 691	15.982 769	26
27	17.537 380	17.285 365	17.038 712	16.797 286	16.560 954	16.329 586	27
28	17.932 169	17.667 019	17.407 684	17.154 011	16.905 852	16.663 063	28
29	18.314 069	18.035 767	17.763 748	17.497 842	17.237 884	16.983 715	29
30	18.683 501	18.392 045	18.107 356	17.829 245	17.557 530	17.292 033	30
31	19.040 872	18.736 276	18.438 944	18.148 670	17.865 251	17.588 494	31
32	19.386 575	19.068 865	18.758 933	18.456 549	18.161 493	17.873 551	32
33	19.720 991	19.390 208	19.067 728	18.753 301	18.446 684	18.147 646	33
34	20.044 490	19.700 684	19.365 721	19.039 326	18.721 236	18.411 198	34
35	20.357 427	20.000 661	19.653 289	19.315 013	18.985 547	18.664 613	35
36	20.660 147	20.290 494	19.930 797	19.580 735	19.239 997	18.908 282	36
37	20.952 983	20.570 525	20.198 598	19.836 853	19.484 955	19.142 579	37
38	21.236 260	20.841 087	20.457 031	20.083 714	19.720 775	19.367 864	38
39	21.510 287	21.102 500	20.706 423	20.321 652	19.947 798	19.584 485	39
40	21.775 369	21.355 072	20.947 091	20.550 990	20.166 351	19.792 774	40
41	22.031 796	21.599 104	21.179 340	20.772 039	20.376 752	19.993 052	41
42	22.279 851	21.834 883	21.403 464	20.985 097	20.579 304	20.185 627	42
43	22.519 807	22.062 689	21.619 749	21.190 455	20.774 300	20.370 795	43
44	22.751 930	22.282 791	21.828 467	21.388 391	20.962 022	20.548 841	44
45	22.976 474	22.495 450	22.029 883	21.579 172	21.142 741	20.720 040	45
46	23.193 687	22.700 918	22.224 254	21.763 057	21.316 718	20.884 654	46
47	23.403 808	22.899 438	22.411 825	21.940 296	21.484 205	21.042 936	47
48	23.607 070	23.091 244	22.592 835	22.111 129	21.645 444	21.195 131	48
49	23.803 695	23.276 564	22.767 513	22.275 787	21.800 668	21.341 472	49
50	23.993 901	23.455 618	22.936 080	22.434 493	21.950 102	21.482 185	50
51	24.177 897	23.628 616	23.098 750	22.587 463	22.093 961	21.617 485	51
52	24.355 886	23.795 765	23.255 730	22.734 904	22.232 453	21.747 582	52
53	24.528 063	23.957 260	23.407 218	22.877 016	22.365 779	21.872 675	53
54	24.694 620	24.113 295	23.553 407	23.013 992	22.494 131	21.992 957	54
55	24.855 739	24.264 053	23.694 482	23.146 016	22.617 696	22.108 612	55
56	25.011 597	24.409 713	23.830 622	23.273 268	22.736 651	22.219 819	56
57	25.162 367	24.550 448	23.962 000	23.395 921	22.851 168	22.326 749	57
58	25.308 215	24.686 423	24.088 781	23.514 141	22.961 413	22.429 567	58
59	25.449 301	24.817 800	24.211 128	23.628 088	23.067 546	22.528 430	59
YRS							
30	25.585 781	24.944 734	24.329 195	23.737 916	23.169 719	22.623 490	60
31	25.845 519	25.185 870	24.553 082	23.945 807	23.362 773	22.802 783	62
32	26.088 574	25.410 974	24.761 579	24.138 941	23.541 693	22.968 549	64
33	26.316 017	25.621 110	24.955 744	24.318 366	23.707 512	23.121 810	66
34	26.528 852	25.817 275	25.136 563	24.485 054	23.861 191	23.263 507	68
35	26.728 016	26.000 397	25.304 951	24.639 911	24.003 618	23.394 515	70
36	26.914 387	26.171 343	25.461 765	24.783 776	24.135 616	23.515 639	72
37	27.088 788	26.330 923	25.607 799	24.917 429	24.257 950	23.627 625	74
38	27.251 987	26.479 892	25.743 795	25.041 594	24.371 327	23.731 162	76
39	27.404 704	26.618 957	25.870 443	25.156 946	24.476 403	23.826 888	78
40	27.547 612	26.748 776	25.988 384	25.264 110	24.573 786	23.915 392	80

SECTION 5

HALF YRS	8.25% ANNUAL RATE	8.50% ANNUAL RATE	8.75% ANNUAL RATE	9.00% ANNUAL RATE	9.25% ANNUAL RATE	9.50% ANNUAL RATE	HALF YRS
1	0.960 384	0.959 233	0.958 084	0.956 938	0.955 795	0.954 654	1
2	1.882 722	1.879 360	1.876 008	1.872 668	1.869 338	1.866 018	2
3	2.768 520	2.761 976	2.755 457	2.748 964	2.742 497	2.736 055	3
4	3.619 227	3.608 610	3.598 043	3.587 526	3.577 058	3.566 640	4
5	4.436 233	4.420 729	4.405 311	4.389 977	4.374 727	4.359 561	5
6	5.220 872	5.199 740	5.178 741	5.157 872	5.137 135	5.116 526	6
7	5.974 427	5.946 993	5.919 751	5.892 701	5.865 840	5.839 166	7
8	6.698 129	6.663 782	6.629 702	6.595 886	6.562 332	6.529 036	8
9	7.393 161	7.351 350	7.309 894	7.268 790	7.228 035	7.187 624	9
10	8.060 659	8.010 887	7.961 575	7.912 718	7.864 311	7.816 348	10
11	8.701 713	8.643 537	8.585 870	8.528 917	8.472 459	8.416 561	11
12	9.317 372	9.250 395	9.184 134	9.118 581	9.053 725	8.989 557	12
13	9.908 640	9.832 513	9.757 255	9.682 852	9.609 295	9.536 570	13
14	10.476 485	10.390 900	10.306 352	10.222 825	10.140 306	10.058 778	14
15	11.021 834	10.926 523	10.832 433	10.739 546	10.647 843	10.557 306	15
16	11.545 579	11.440 309	11.336 463	11.234 015	11.132 944	11.033 228	16
17	12.048 576	11.933 151	11.819 365	11.707 191	11.596 601	11.487 568	17
18	12.531 645	12.405 900	12.282 027	12.159 992	12.039 762	11.921 306	18
19	12.995 578	12.859 376	12.725 295	12.593 294	12.463 333	12.335 376	19
20	13.441 131	13.294 366	13.149 983	13.007 936	12.868 180	12.730 669	20
21	13.869 033	13.711 622	13.556 870	13.404 724	13.255 130	13.108 037	21
22	14.279 984	14.111 868	13.946 702	13.784 425	13.624 975	13.468 293	22
23	14.674 654	14.495 796	14.320 193	14.147 775	13.978 471	13.812 213	23
24	15.053 690	14.864 073	14.678 030	14.495 478	14.316 340	14.140 538	24
25	15.417 709	15.217 336	15.020 867	14.828 209	14.639 274	14.453 974	25
26	15.767 308	15.556 198	15.349 333	15.146 611	14.947 932	14.753 197	26
27	16.103 057	15.881 245	15.664 032	15.451 303	15.242 946	15.038 852	27
28	16.425 505	16.193 041	15.965 540	15.742 874	15.524 918	15.311 553	28
29	16.735 179	16.492 125	16.254 409	16.021 889	15.794 426	15.571 888	29
30	17.032 584	16.779 017	16.531 171	16.288 889	16.052 020	15.820 418	30
31	17.318 208	17.054 213	16.796 331	16.544 391	16.298 227	16.057 679	31
32	17.592 517	17.318 190	17.050 377	16.788 891	16.533 550	16.284 180	32
33	17.855 959	17.571 405	17.293 774	17.022 862	16.758 471	16.500 410	33
34	18.108 964	17.814 298	17.526 970	17.246 758	16.973 449	16.706 836	34
35	18.351 946	18.047 288	17.750 390	17.461 012	17.178 924	16.903 901	35
36	18.585 302	18.270 780	17.964 445	17.666 041	17.375 315	17.092 029	36
37	18.809 414	18.485 160	18.169 529	17.862 240	17.563 026	17.271 627	37
38	19.024 647	18.690 801	18.366 015	18.049 990	17.742 438	17.443 081	38
39	19.231 354	18.888 059	18.554 266	18.229 656	17.913 919	17.606 759	39
40	19.429 872	19.077 275	18.734 626	18.401 584	18.077 820	17.763 016	40
41	19.620 525	19.258 777	18.907 426	18.566 109	18.234 475	17.912 187	41
42	19.803 626	19.432 879	19.072 983	18.723 550	18.384 206	18.054 594	42
43	19.979 472	19.599 884	19.231 601	18.874 210	18.527 317	18.190 543	43
44	20.148 353	19.760 081	19.383 570	19.018 383	18.664 103	18.320 328	44
45	20.310 543	19.913 747	19.529 169	19.156 347	18.794 841	18.444 227	45
46	20.466 308	20.061 148	19.668 665	19.288 371	18.919 800	18.562 508	46
47	20.615 902	20.202 540	19.802 313	19.414 709	19.039 236	18.675 425	47
48	20.759 570	20.338 168	19.930 360	19.535 607	19.153 391	18.783 222	48
49	20.897 546	20.468 266	20.053 040	19.651 298	19.262 501	18.886 131	49
50	21.030 056	20.593 061	20.170 577	19.762 008	19.366 787	18.984 373	50
51	21.157 317	20.712 769	20.283 187	19.867 950	19.466 463	19.078 160	51
52	21.279 536	20.827 596	20.391 078	19.969 330	19.561 733	19.167 695	52
53	21.396 913	20.937 742	20.494 446	20.066 345	19.652 791	19.253 169	53
54	21.509 640	21.043 397	20.593 481	20.159 181	19.739 824	19.334 768	54
55	21.617 902	21.144 746	20.688 365	20.248 021	19.823 010	19.412 666	55
56	21.721 875	21.241 962	20.779 272	20.333 034	19.902 519	19.487 032	56
57	21.821 728	21.335 216	20.866 368	20.414 387	19.978 512	19.558 026	57
58	21.917 626	21.424 667	20.949 814	20.492 236	20.051 147	19.625 801	58
59	22.009 725	21.510 472	21.029 762	20.566 733	20.120 571	19.690 502	59
YRS							
30	22.098 175	21.592 779	21.106 359	20.638 022	20.186 925	19.752 269	60
31	22.264 703	21.747 463	21.250 055	20.771 523	20.310 965	19.867 528	62
32	22.418 297	21.889 793	21.381 957	20.893 773	20.424 280	19.972 570	64
33	22.559 963	22.020 754	21.503 034	21.005 722	20.527 798	20.068 303	66
34	22.690 627	22.141 254	21.614 173	21.108 236	20.622 367	20.155 549	68
35	22.811 143	22.252 130	21.716 190	21.202 112	20.708 759	20.235 063	70
36	22.922 299	22.354 150	21.809 834	21.288 077	20.787 682	20.307 529	72
37	23.024 823	22.448 022	21.895 792	21.366 797	20.859 782	20.373 572	74
38	23.119 385	22.534 395	21.974 695	21.438 884	20.925 649	20.433 761	76
39	23.206 603	22.613 870	22.047 123	21.504 896	20.985 820	20.488 615	78
40	23.287 047	22.686 997	22.113 605	21.565 345	21.040 790	20.538 607	80

HALF YRS	9.75% ANNUAL RATE	10.00% ANNUAL RATE	10.50% ANNUAL RATE	11.00% ANNUAL RATE	11.50% ANNUAL RATE	12.00% ANNUAL RATE	HALF YRS
1	0.953 516	0.952 381	0.950 119	0.947 867	0.945 626	0.943 396	1
2	1.862 709	1.859 410	1.852 844	1.846 320	1.839 836	1.833 393	2
3	2.729 639	2.723 248	2.710 541	2.697 933	2.685 424	2.673 012	3
4	3.556 271	3.545 951	3.525 455	3.505 150	3.485 035	3.465 106	4
5	4.344 478	4.329 477	4.299 719	4.270 284	4.241 167	4.212 364	5
6	5.096 045	5.075 692	5.035 363	4.995 530	4.956 187	4.917 324	6
7	5.812 677	5.786 373	5.734 311	5.682 967	5.632 328	5.582 381	7
8	6.495 998	6.463 213	6.398 396	6.334 566	6.271 705	6.209 794	8
9	7.147 554	7.107 822	7.029 355	6.952 195	6.876 317	6.801 692	9
10	7.768 824	7.721 735	7.628 840	7.537 626	7.448 054	7.360 087	10
11	8.361 215	8.306 414	8.198 423	8.092 536	7.988 703	7.886 875	11
12	8.926 069	8.863 252	8.739 595	8.618 518	8.499 956	8.383 844	12
13	9.464 666	9.393 573	9.253 772	9.117 079	8.983 410	8.852 683	13
14	9.978 228	9.898 641	9.742 301	9.589 648	9.440 576	9.294 984	14
15	10.467 917	10.379 658	10.206 462	10.037 581	9.872 886	9.712 249	15
16	10.934 843	10.837 770	10.647 469	10.462 162	10.281 688	10.105 895	16
17	11.380 065	11.274 066	11.066 479	10.864 609	10.668 263	10.477 260	17
18	11.804 591	11.689 587	11.464 588	11.246 074	11.033 819	10.827 603	18
19	12.209 384	12.085 321	11.842 839	11.607 654	11.379 498	11.158 116	19
20	12.595 360	12.462 210	12.202 223	11.950 382	11.706 381	11.469 921	20
21	12.963 395	12.821 153	12.543 679	12.275 244	12.015 490	11.764 077	21
22	13.314 321	13.163 003	12.868 104	12.583 170	12.307 792	12.041 582	22
23	13.648 936	13.488 574	13.176 346	12.875 042	12.584 200	12.303 379	23
24	13.967 996	13.798 642	13.469 212	13.151 699	12.845 580	12.550 358	24
25	14.272 225	14.093 945	13.747 470	13.413 933	13.092 747	12.783 356	25
26	14.562 312	14.375 185	14.011 848	13.662 695	13.326 474	13.003 166	26
27	14.838 915	14.643 034	14.263 038	13.898 100	13.547 494	13.210 534	27
28	15.102 660	14.898 127	14.501 699	14.121 422	13.756 495	13.406 164	28
29	15.354 146	15.141 074	14.728 455	14.333 101	13.954 132	13.590 721	29
30	15.593 941	15.372 451	14.943 901	14.533 745	14.141 024	13.764 831	30
31	15.822 590	15.592 811	15.148 599	14.723 929	14.317 753	13.929 086	31
32	16.040 610	15.802 677	15.343 087	14.904 198	14.484 873	14.084 043	32
33	16.248 496	16.002 549	15.527 874	15.075 069	14.642 906	14.230 230	33
34	16.446 719	16.192 904	15.703 443	15.237 033	14.792 346	14.368 141	34
35	16.635 727	16.374 194	15.870 255	15.390 552	14.933 660	14.498 246	35
36	16.815 949	16.546 852	16.028 745	15.536 068	15.067 291	14.620 987	36
37	16.987 794	16.711 287	16.179 331	15.673 999	15.193 656	14.736 780	37
38	17.151 651	16.867 893	16.322 404	15.804 738	15.313 150	14.846 019	38
39	17.307 892	17.017 041	16.458 341	15.928 662	15.426 146	14.949 075	39
40	17.456 869	17.159 086	16.587 498	16.046 125	15.532 999	15.046 297	40
41	17.598 922	17.294 368	16.710 212	16.157 464	15.634 041	15.138 016	41
42	17.734 371	17.423 208	16.826 804	16.262 999	15.729 590	15.224 543	42
43	17.863 524	17.545 912	16.937 581	16.363 032	15.819 943	15.306 173	43
44	17.986 674	17.662 773	17.042 833	16.457 851	15.905 384	15.383 182	44
45	18.104 099	17.774 070	17.142 834	16.547 726	15.986 178	15.455 832	45
46	18.216 066	17.880 066	17.237 847	16.632 915	16.062 580	15.524 370	46
47	18.322 828	17.981 016	17.328 121	16.713 664	16.134 828	15.589 028	47
48	18.424 628	18.077 158	17.413 891	16.790 203	16.203 147	15.650 027	48
49	18.521 695	18.168 722	17.495 384	16.862 751	16.267 751	15.707 572	49
50	18.614 250	18.255 925	17.572 811	16.931 518	16.328 842	15.761 861	50
51	18.702 503	18.338 977	17.646 376	16.996 699	16.386 612	15.813 076	51
52	18.786 654	18.418 073	17.716 272	17.058 483	16.441 241	15.861 393	52
53	18.866 893	18.493 403	17.782 681	17.117 045	16.492 899	15.906 974	53
54	18.943 402	18.565 146	17.845 778	17.172 555	16.541 749	15.949 976	54
55	19.016 355	18.633 472	17.905 727	17.225 170	16.587 942	15.990 543	55
56	19.085 916	18.698 545	17.962 686	17.275 043	16.631 624	16.028 814	56
57	19.152 244	18.760 519	18.016 804	17.322 316	16.672 930	16.064 919	57
58	19.215 489	18.819 542	18.068 222	17.367 124	16.711 991	16.098 980	58
59	19.275 794	18.875 754	18.117 076	17.409 596	16.748 927	16.131 113	59

YRS							
30	19.333 296	18.929 290	18.163 493	17.449 854	16.783 856	16.161 428	60
31	19.440 405	19.028 834	18.249 495	17.524 183	16.848 118	16.217 006	62
32	19.537 788	19.119 124	18.327 132	17.590 965	16.905 582	16.266 470	64
33	19.626 328	19.201 019	18.397 217	17.650 964	16.956 967	16.310 493	66
34	19.706 828	19.275 301	18.460 485	17.704 871	17.002 916	16.349 673	68
35	19.780 018	19.342 677	18.517 598	17.753 304	17.044 004	16.384 544	70
36	19.846 561	19.403 788	18.569 155	17.796 819	17.080 745	16.415 578	72
37	19.907 062	19.459 268	18.615 697	17.835 914	17.113 599	16.443 199	74
38	19.962 069	19.509 495	18.657 712	17.871 040	17.142 978	16.467 781	76
39	20.012 082	19.555 098	18.695 640	17.902 599	17.169 248	16.489 659	78
40	20.057 552	19.596 460	18.729 879	17.930 953	17.192 740	16.509 131	80

SEMIANNUAL COMPOUNDING

SECTION 5

HALF YRS	12.50% ANNUAL RATE	13.00% ANNUAL RATE	13.50% ANNUAL RATE	14.00% ANNUAL RATE	14.50% ANNUAL RATE	15.00% ANNUAL RATE	HALF YRS
1	0.941 176	0.938 967	0.936 768	0.934 579	0.932 401	0.930 233	1
2	1.826 990	1.820 626	1.814 303	1.808 018	1.801 772	1.795 565	2
3	2.660 696	2.648 476	2.636 349	2.624 316	2.612 375	2.600 526	3
4	3.445 361	3.425 799	3.406 416	3.387 211	3.368 182	3.349 326	4
5	4.183 869	4.155 679	4.127 790	4.100 197	4.072 897	4.045 885	5
6	4.878 936	4.841 014	4.803 551	4.766 540	4.729 974	4.693 846	6
7	5.533 116	5.484 520	5.436 581	5.389 289	5.342 633	5.296 601	7
8	6.148 815	6.088 751	6.029 584	5.971 299	5.913 877	5.857 304	8
9	6.728 297	6.656 104	6.585 091	6.515 232	6.446 505	6.378 887	9
10	7.273 691	7.188 830	7.105 471	7.023 582	6.943 128	6.864 081	10
11	7.787 003	7.689 042	7.592 947	7.498 674	7.406 180	7.315 424	11
12	8.270 121	8.158 725	8.049 600	7.942 686	7.837 930	7.735 278	12
13	8.724 819	8.599 742	8.477 377	8.357 651	8.240 495	8.125 840	13
14	9.152 771	9.013 842	8.878 105	8.745 468	8.615 846	8.489 154	14
15	9.555 549	9.402 669	9.253 494	9.107 914	8.965 824	8.827 120	15
16	9.934 635	9.767 764	9.605 146	9.446 649	9.292 143	9.141 507	16
17	10.291 421	10.110 577	9.934 563	9.763 223	9.596 404	9.433 960	17
18	10.627 220	10.432 466	10.243 151	10.059 087	9.880 097	9.706 009	18
19	10.943 266	10.734 710	10.532 225	10.335 595	10.144 612	9.959 078	19
20	11.240 721	11.018 507	10.803 021	10.594 014	10.391 247	10.194 491	20
21	11.520 678	11.284 983	11.056 695	10.835 527	10.621 209	10.413 480	21
22	11.784 168	11.535 196	11.294 327	11.061 240	10.835 626	10.617 191	22
23	12.032 158	11.770 137	11.516 934	11.272 187	11.035 549	10.806 689	23
24	12.265 560	11.990 739	11.725 465	11.469 334	11.221 957	10.982 967	24
25	12.485 233	12.197 877	11.920 811	11.653 583	11.395 764	11.146 946	25
26	12.691 984	12.392 373	12.103 804	11.825 779	11.557 822	11.299 485	26
27	12.886 573	12.574 998	12.275 226	11.986 709	11.708 925	11.441 381	27
28	13.069 716	12.746 477	12.435 809	12.137 111	11.849 814	11.573 378	28
29	13.242 086	12.907 490	12.586 238	12.277 674	11.981 178	11.696 165	29
30	13.404 316	13.058 676	12.727 155	12.409 041	12.103 663	11.810 386	30
31	13.557 003	13.200 635	12.859 162	12.531 814	12.217 867	11.916 638	31
32	13.700 709	13.333 929	12.982 821	12.646 555	12.324 352	12.015 478	32
33	13.835 961	13.459 088	13.098 662	12.753 790	12.423 638	12.107 421	33
34	13.963 258	13.576 609	13.207 177	12.854 009	12.516 213	12.192 950	34
35	14.083 066	13.686 957	13.308 831	12.947 672	12.602 529	12.272 511	35
36	14.195 827	13.790 570	13.404 057	13.035 208	12.683 011	12.346 522	36
37	14.301 955	13.887 859	13.493 262	13.117 017	12.758 052	12.415 370	37
38	14.401 840	13.979 210	13.576 826	13.193 473	12.828 021	12.479 414	38
39	14.495 849	14.064 986	13.655 107	13.264 928	12.893 259	12.538 989	39
40	14.584 329	14.145 527	13.728 437	13.331 709	12.954 088	12.594 409	40
41	14.667 603	14.221 152	13.797 131	13.394 120	13.010 805	12.645 962	41
42	14.745 980	14.292 161	13.861 481	13.452 449	13.063 687	12.693 918	42
43	14.819 746	14.358 837	13.921 762	13.506 962	13.112 995	12.738 528	43
44	14.889 172	14.421 443	13.978 231	13.557 908	13.158 970	12.780 026	44
45	14.954 515	14.480 228	14.031 130	13.605 522	13.201 837	12.818 629	45
46	15.016 014	14.535 426	14.080 684	13.650 020	13.241 806	12.854 539	46
47	15.073 896	14.587 254	14.127 104	13.691 608	13.279 073	12.887 943	47
48	15.128 372	14.635 919	14.170 589	13.730 474	13.313 821	12.919 017	48
49	15.179 645	14.681 615	14.211 325	13.766 799	13.346 220	12.947 922	49
50	15.227 901	14.724 521	14.249 485	13.800 746	13.376 429	12.974 812	50
51	15.273 318	14.764 808	14.285 232	13.832 473	13.404 596	12.999 825	51
52	15.316 064	14.802 637	14.318 718	13.862 124	13.430 858	13.023 093	52
53	15.356 296	14.838 157	14.350 087	13.889 836	13.455 346	13.044 737	53
54	15.394 161	14.871 509	14.379 473	13.915 735	13.478 178	13.064 872	54
55	15.429 799	14.902 825	14.407 000	13.939 939	13.499 467	13.083 602	55
56	15.463 340	14.932 230	14.432 787	13.962 560	13.519 316	13.101 025	56
57	15.494 908	14.959 840	14.456 944	13.983 701	13.537 824	13.117 233	57
58	15.524 619	14.985 766	14.479 572	14.003 458	13.555 081	13.132 309	58
59	15.552 583	15.010 109	14.500 770	14.021 924	13.571 171	13.146 334	59

YRS	12.50%	13.00%	13.50%	14.00%	14.50%	15.00%	YRS
30	15.578 902	15.032 966	14.520 628	14.039 181	13.586 173	13.159 381	60
31	15.626 985	15.074 580	14.556 656	14.070 383	13.613 204	13.182 806	62
32	15.669 579	15.111 270	14.588 271	14.097 635	13.636 704	13.203 078	64
33	15.707 309	15.143 618	14.616 015	14.121 439	13.657 134	13.220 619	66
34	15.740 730	15.172 138	14.640 361	14.142 230	13.674 896	13.235 798	68
35	15.770 335	15.197 282	14.661 726	14.160 389	13.690 337	13.248 933	70
36	15.796 560	15.219 452	14.680 474	14.176 251	13.703 761	13.260 299	72
37	15.819 790	15.238 997	14.696 926	14.190 104	13.715 432	13.270 134	74
38	15.840 368	15.256 230	14.711 363	14.202 205	13.725 578	13.278 645	76
39	15.858 596	15.271 423	14.724 032	14.212 774	13.734 399	13.286 010	78
40	15.874 742	15.284 818	14.735 150	14.222 005	13.742 067	13.292 383	80

PRESENT VALUE PER PERIOD

SEMIANNUAL COMPOUNDING

HALF YRS	15.50% ANNUAL RATE	16.00% ANNUAL RATE	16.50% ANNUAL RATE	17.00% ANNUAL RATE	17.50% ANNUAL RATE	18.00% ANNUAL RATE	HALF YRS
1	0.928 074	0.925 926	0.923 788	0.921 659	0.919 540	0.917 431	1
2	1.789 396	1.783 265	1.777 171	1.771 114	1.765 094	1.759 111	2
3	2.588 767	2.577 097	2.565 516	2.554 022	2.542 616	2.531 295	3
4	3.330 642	3.312 127	3.293 779	3.275 597	3.257 578	3.239 720	4
5	4.019 157	3.992 710	3.966 540	3.940 642	3.915 014	3.889 651	5
6	4.658 151	4.622 880	4.588 027	4.553 587	4.519 553	4.485 919	6
7	5.251 184	5.206 370	5.162 150	5.118 514	5.075 451	5.032 953	7
8	5.801 563	5.746 639	5.692 517	5.639 183	5.586 622	5.534 819	8
9	6.312 355	6.246 888	6.182 464	6.119 063	6.056 664	5.995 247	9
10	6.786 409	6.710 081	6.635 071	6.561 348	6.488 886	6.417 658	10
11	7.226 365	7.138 964	7.053 183	6.968 984	6.886 332	6.805 191	11
12	7.634 678	7.536 078	7.439 430	7.344 686	7.251 800	7.160 725	12
13	8.013 622	7.903 776	7.796 240	7.690 955	7.587 862	7.486 904	13
14	8.365 310	8.244 237	8.125 857	8.010 097	7.896 884	7.786 150	14
15	8.691 703	8.559 479	8.430 353	8.304 237	8.181 043	8.060 688	15
16	8.994 620	8.851 369	8.711 642	8.575 333	8.442 338	8.312 558	16
17	9.275 750	9.121 638	8.971 494	8.825 192	8.682 610	8.543 631	17
18	9.536 659	9.371 887	9.211 542	9.055 476	8.903 549	8.755 625	18
19	9.778 802	9.603 599	9.433 295	9.267 720	9.106 712	8.950 115	19
20	10.003 528	9.818 147	9.638 148	9.463 337	9.293 528	9.128 546	20
21	10.212 091	10.016 803	9.827 388	9.643 628	9.465 313	9.292 244	21
22	10.405 653	10.200 744	10.002 206	9.809 796	9.623 277	9.442 425	22
23	10.585 293	10.371 059	10.163 701	9.962 945	9.768 530	9.580 207	23
24	10.752 012	10.528 758	10.312 888	10.104 097	9.902 097	9.706 612	24
25	10.906 740	10.674 776	10.450 705	10.234 191	10.024 917	9.822 580	25
26	11.050 338	10.809 978	10.578 018	10.354 093	10.137 854	9.928 972	26
27	11.183 609	10.935 165	10.695 629	10.464 602	10.241 705	10.026 580	27
28	11.307 293	11.051 078	10.804 276	10.566 453	10.337 200	10.116 128	28
29	11.422 082	11.158 406	10.904 643	10.660 326	10.425 012	10.198 283	29
30	11.528 614	11.257 783	10.997 361	10.746 844	10.505 758	10.273 654	30
31	11.627 484	11.349 799	11.083 012	10.826 584	10.580 007	10.342 802	31
32	11.719 243	11.434 999	11.162 136	10.900 078	10.648 282	10.406 240	32
33	11.804 402	11.513 888	11.235 230	10.967 813	10.711 064	10.464 441	33
34	11.883 436	11.586 934	11.302 752	11.030 243	10.768 795	10.517 835	34
35	11.956 785	11.654 568	11.365 129	11.087 781	10.821 880	10.566 821	35
36	12.024 858	11.717 193	11.422 752	11.140 812	10.870 695	10.611 763	36
37	12.088 036	11.775 179	11.475 984	11.189 689	10.915 581	10.652 993	37
38	12.146 669	11.828 869	11.525 158	11.234 736	10.956 856	10.690 820	38
39	12.201 085	11.878 582	11.570 585	11.276 255	10.994 810	10.725 523	39
40	12.251 587	11.924 613	11.612 549	11.314 520	11.029 711	10.757 360	40
41	12.298 456	11.967 235	11.651 316	11.349 788	11.061 803	10.786 569	41
42	12.341 955	12.006 699	11.687 128	11.382 293	11.091 313	10.813 366	42
43	12.382 325	12.043 240	11.720 210	11.412 252	11.118 449	10.837 950	43
44	12.419 791	12.077 074	11.750 772	11.439 864	11.143 401	10.860 505	44
45	12.454 562	12.108 402	11.779 004	11.465 312	11.166 346	10.881 197	45
46	12.486 833	12.137 409	11.805 085	11.488 767	11.187 444	10.900 181	46
47	12.516 782	12.164 267	11.829 177	11.510 384	11.206 846	10.917 597	47
48	12.544 577	12.189 136	11.851 434	11.530 308	11.224 686	10.933 575	48
49	12.570 373	12.212 163	11.871 995	11.548 671	11.241 090	10.948 234	49
50	12.594 314	12.233 485	11.890 988	11.565 595	11.256 175	10.961 683	50
51	12.616 533	12.253 227	11.908 534	11.581 194	11.270 046	10.974 021	51
52	12.637 153	12.271 506	11.924 743	11.595 570	11.282 801	10.985 340	52
53	12.656 291	12.288 432	11.939 716	11.608 821	11.294 529	10.995 725	53
54	12.674 052	12.304 103	11.953 548	11.621 033	11.305 314	11.005 252	54
55	12.690 535	12.318 614	11.966 326	11.632 288	11.315 232	11.013 993	55
56	12.705 833	12.332 050	11.978 131	11.642 662	11.324 351	11.022 012	56
57	12.720 031	12.344 491	11.989 035	11.652 223	11.332 737	11.029 369	57
58	12.733 207	12.356 010	11.999 109	11.661 035	11.340 447	11.036 118	58
59	12.745 436	12.366 676	12.008 415	11.669 157	11.347 538	11.042 310	59
60	12.756 785	12.376 552	12.017 011	11.676 642	11.354 058	11.047 991	60
62	12.777 093	12.394 163	12.032 289	11.689 900	11.365 566	11.057 984	62
64	12.794 585	12.409 262	12.045 326	11.701 161	11.375 297	11.066 395	64
66	12.809 651	12.422 207	12.056 452	11.710 728	11.383 525	11.073 475	66
68	12.822 628	12.433 305	12.065 947	11.718 854	11.390 482	11.079 433	68
70	12.833 805	12.442 820	12.074 050	11.725 757	11.396 365	11.084 449	70
72	12.843 432	12.450 977	12.080 965	11.731 620	11.401 339	11.088 670	72
74	12.851 724	12.457 971	12.086 866	11.736 601	11.405 545	11.092 223	74
76	12.858 866	12.463 967	12.091 901	11.740 832	11.409 101	11.095 213	76
78	12.865 018	12.469 107	12.096 199	11.744 426	11.412 108	11.097 730	78
80	12.870 317	12.473 514	12.099 866	11.747 479	11.414 651	11.099 849	80

PRESENT VALUE PER PERIOD

HALF YRS	18.50% ANNUAL RATE	19.00% ANNUAL RATE	19.50% ANNUAL RATE	20.00% ANNUAL RATE	20.50% ANNUAL RATE	21.00% ANNUAL RATE
1	0.915 332	0.913 242	0.911 162	0.909 091	0.907 029	0.904 977
2	1.753 164	1.747 253	1.741 377	1.735 537	1.729 732	1.723 961
3	2.520 059	2.508 907	2.497 838	2.486 852	2.475 947	2.465 123
4	3.222 022	3.204 481	3.187 096	3.169 865	3.152 787	3.135 858
5	3.864 551	3.839 709	3.815 122	3.790 787	3.766 700	3.742 858
6	4.452 678	4.419 825	4.387 355	4.355 261	4.323 537	4.292 179
7	4.991 010	4.949 612	4.908 752	4.868 419	4.828 605	4.789 303
8	5.483 762	5.433 436	5.383 828	5.334 926	5.286 717	5.239 188
9	5.934 793	5.875 284	5.816 700	5.759 024	5.702 238	5.646 324
10	6.347 637	6.278 798	6.211 116	6.144 567	6.079 127	6.014 773
11	6.725 526	6.647 304	6.570 493	6.495 061	6.420 977	6.348 211
12	7.071 419	6.983 839	6.897 944	6.813 692	6.731 045	6.649 964
13	7.388 027	7.291 178	7.196 304	7.103 356	7.012 286	6.923 045
14	7.677 828	7.571 852	7.468 159	7.366 687	7.267 379	7.170 176
15	7.943 092	7.828 175	7.715 862	7.606 080	7.498 757	7.393 825
16	8.185 896	8.062 260	7.941 560	7.823 709	7.708 623	7.596 221
17	8.408 143	8.276 037	8.147 207	8.021 553	7.898 978	7.779 386
18	8.611 573	8.471 266	8.334 585	8.201 412	8.071 635	7.945 146
19	8.797 778	8.649 558	8.505 317	8.364 920	8.228 240	8.095 154
20	8.968 218	8.812 382	8.660 881	8.513 564	8.370 286	8.230 909
21	9.124 227	8.961 080	8.802 625	8.648 694	8.499 126	8.353 764
22	9.267 027	9.096 876	8.931 777	8.771 540	8.615 987	8.464 945
23	9.397 736	9.220 892	9.049 455	8.883 218	8.721 984	8.565 561
24	9.517 379	9.334 148	9.156 679	8.984 744	8.818 126	8.656 616
25	9.626 891	9.437 578	9.254 377	9.077 040	8.905 329	8.739 019
26	9.727 132	9.532 034	9.343 396	9.160 945	8.984 426	8.813 592
27	9.818 885	9.618 296	9.424 506	9.237 223	9.056 169	8.881 079
28	9.902 869	9.697 074	9.498 411	9.306 567	9.121 241	8.942 153
29	9.979 743	9.769 018	9.565 751	9.369 606	9.180 264	8.997 423
30	10.050 108	9.834 719	9.627 108	9.426 914	9.233 800	9.047 442
31	10.114 470	9.894 721	9.683 014	9.479 013	9.282 358	9.092 707
32	10.173 470	9.949 517	9.733 953	9.526 376	9.326 402	9.133 672
33	10.227 432	9.999 559	9.780 368	9.569 432	9.366 351	9.170 744
34	10.276 826	10.045 259	9.822 658	9.608 575	9.402 586	9.204 293
35	10.322 037	10.086 995	9.861 192	9.644 159	9.435 452	9.234 654
36	10.363 421	10.125 109	9.896 303	9.676 508	9.465 263	9.262 131
37	10.401 301	10.159 917	9.928 294	9.705 917	9.492 302	9.286 996
38	10.435 973	10.191 705	9.957 443	9.732 651	9.516 827	9.309 499
39	10.467 710	10.220 735	9.984 003	9.756 956	9.539 072	9.329 863
40	10.496 760	10.247 247	10.008 203	9.779 051	9.559 249	9.348 292
41	10.523 350	10.271 458	10.030 253	9.799 137	9.577 550	9.364 970
42	10.547 689	10.293 569	10.050 345	9.817 397	9.594 150	9.380 064
43	10.569 967	10.313 762	10.068 651	9.833 998	9.609 206	9.393 723
44	10.590 358	10.332 203	10.085 331	9.849 089	9.622 863	9.406 084
45	10.609 024	10.349 043	10.100 503	9.862 808	9.635 250	9.417 271
46	10.626 109	10.364 423	10.114 378	9.875 280	9.646 485	9.427 394
47	10.641 747	10.378 469	10.126 996	9.886 618	9.656 676	9.436 556
48	10.656 061	10.391 296	10.138 493	9.896 926	9.665 919	9.444 847
49	10.669 164	10.403 010	10.148 968	9.906 296	9.674 303	9.452 350
50	10.681 157	10.413 707	10.158 513	9.914 814	9.681 907	9.459 140
51	10.692 134	10.423 477	10.167 210	9.922 559	9.688 805	9.465 285
52	10.702 182	10.432 399	10.175 135	9.929 599	9.695 061	9.470 847
53	10.711 380	10.440 547	10.182 355	9.935 999	9.700 736	9.475 879
54	10.719 798	10.447 988	10.188 934	9.941 817	9.705 883	9.480 434
55	10.727 504	10.454 784	10.194 928	9.947 106	9.710 551	9.484 555
56	10.734 558	10.460 990	10.200 390	9.951 915	9.714 786	9.488 285
57	10.741 014	10.466 657	10.205 367	9.956 286	9.718 626	9.491 661
58	10.746 924	10.471 833	10.209 902	9.960 260	9.722 110	9.494 716
59	10.752 333	10.476 560	10.214 033	9.963 873	9.725 270	9.497 480

YRS

YRS	18.50%	19.00%	19.50%	20.00%	20.50%	21.00%
30	10.757 284	10.480 877	10.217 798	9.967 157	9.728 136	9.499 982
31	10.765 964	10.488 419	10.224 354	9.972 857	9.733 094	9.504 295
32	10.773 237	10.494 710	10.229 797	9.977 568	9.737 172	9.507 828
33	10.779 330	10.499 956	10.234 315	9.981 461	9.740 528	9.510 721
34	10.784 435	10.504 331	10.238 067	9.984 679	9.743 288	9.513 090
35	10.788 713	10.507 980	10.241 181	9.987 338	9.745 559	9.515 030
36	10.792 296	10.511 024	10.243 767	9.989 535	9.747 428	9.516 620
37	10.795 299	10.513 562	10.245 913	9.991 351	9.748 965	9.517 921
38	10.797 814	10.515 679	10.247 696	9.992 852	9.750 229	9.518 987
39	10.799 922	10.517 445	10.249 175	9.994 093	9.751 270	9.519 860
40	10.801 688	10.518 917	10.250 404	9.995 118	9.752 126	9.520 575

PRESENT VALUE PER PERIOD

SEMIANNUAL COMPOUNDING

HALF YRS	21.50% ANNUAL RATE	22.00% ANNUAL RATE	22.50% ANNUAL RATE	23.00% ANNUAL RATE	23.50% ANNUAL RATE	24.00% ANNUAL RATE	HALF YRS
1	0.902 935	0.900 901	0.898 876	0.896 861	0.894 855	0.892 857	1
2	1.718 225	1.712 523	1.706 855	1.701 221	1.695 619	1.690 051	2
3	2.454 380	2.443 715	2.433 128	2.422 619	2.412 187	2.401 831	3
4	3.119 079	3.102 446	3.085 958	3.069 614	3.053 411	3.037 349	4
5	3.719 258	3.695 897	3.672 771	3.649 878	3.627 214	3.604 776	5
6	4.261 181	4.230 538	4.200 244	4.170 294	4.140 684	4.111 407	6
7	4.750 502	4.712 196	4.674 376	4.637 035	4.600 164	4.563 757	7
8	5.192 327	5.146 123	5.100 563	5.055 637	5.011 333	4.967 640	8
9	5.591 266	5.537 048	5.483 652	5.431 064	5.379 269	5.328 250	9
10	5.951 482	5.889 232	5.828 002	5.767 771	5.708 518	5.650 223	10
11	6.276 733	6.206 515	6.137 530	6.069 750	6.003 148	5.937 699	11
12	6.570 414	6.492 356	6.415 757	6.340 583	6.266 799	6.194 374	12
13	6.835 588	6.749 870	6.665 849	6.583 482	6.502 728	6.423 548	13
14	7.075 023	6.981 865	6.890 651	6.801 329	6.713 851	6.628 168	14
15	7.291 217	7.190 870	7.092 720	6.996 708	6.902 775	6.810 864	15
16	7.486 426	7.379 162	7.274 355	7.171 935	7.071 834	6.973 986	16
17	7.662 687	7.548 794	7.437 622	7.329 090	7.223 118	7.119 630	17
18	7.821 840	7.701 617	7.584 380	7.470 036	7.358 495	7.249 670	18
19	7.965 544	7.839 294	7.716 296	7.596 445	7.479 637	7.365 777	19
20	8.095 299	7.963 328	7.834 873	7.709 816	7.588 042	7.469 444	20
21	8.212 460	8.075 070	7.941 459	7.811 494	7.685 049	7.562 003	21
22	8.318 248	8.175 739	8.037 267	7.902 685	7.771 856	7.644 646	22
23	8.413 768	8.266 432	8.123 386	7.984 471	7.849 536	7.718 434	23
24	8.500 016	8.348 137	8.200 796	8.057 822	7.919 048	7.784 316	24
25	8.577 893	8.421 745	8.270 379	8.123 607	7.981 251	7.843 139	25
26	8.648 210	8.488 058	8.332 925	8.182 607	8.036 913	7.895 660	26
27	8.711 702	8.547 800	8.389 146	8.235 522	8.086 723	7.942 554	27
28	8.769 031	8.601 622	8.439 681	8.282 979	8.131 296	7.984 423	28
29	8.820 796	8.650 110	8.485 107	8.325 542	8.171 182	8.021 806	29
30	8.867 536	8.693 793	8.525 939	8.363 715	8.206 874	8.055 184	30
31	8.909 739	8.733 146	8.562 642	8.397 951	8.238 814	8.084 986	31
32	8.947 845	8.768 600	8.595 633	8.428 655	8.267 395	8.111 594	32
33	8.982 253	8.800 541	8.625 288	8.456 193	8.292 971	8.135 352	33
34	9.013 321	8.829 316	8.651 944	8.480 891	8.315 858	8.156 564	34
35	9.041 373	8.855 240	8.675 905	8.503 041	8.336 338	8.175 504	35
36	9.066 703	8.878 594	8.697 443	8.522 907	8.354 665	8.192 414	36
37	9.089 574	8.899 635	8.716 802	8.540 723	8.371 065	8.207 513	37
38	9.110 225	8.918 590	8.734 204	8.556 703	8.385 740	8.220 993	38
39	9.128 871	8.935 666	8.749 847	8.571 034	8.398 873	8.233 030	39
40	9.145 707	8.951 051	8.763 907	8.583 887	8.410 624	8.243 777	40
41	9.160 910	8.964 911	8.776 546	8.595 414	8.421 140	8.253 372	41
42	9.174 636	8.977 397	8.787 906	8.605 753	8.430 551	8.261 939	42
43	9.187 030	8.988 646	8.798 118	8.615 025	8.438 971	8.269 589	43
44	9.198 222	8.998 780	8.807 297	8.623 341	8.446 507	8.276 418	44
45	9.208 327	9.007 910	8.815 548	8.630 799	8.453 250	8.282 516	45
46	9.217 451	9.016 135	8.822 964	8.637 488	8.459 284	8.287 961	46
47	9.225 689	9.023 545	8.829 631	8.643 487	8.464 684	8.292 822	47
48	9.233 128	9.030 221	8.835 623	8.648 867	8.469 516	8.297 163	48
49	9.239 845	9.036 235	8.841 010	8.653 692	8.473 840	8.301 038	49
50	9.245 909	9.041 653	8.845 851	8.658 020	8.477 709	8.304 498	50
51	9.251 385	9.046 534	8.850 204	8.661 901	8.481 171	8.307 588	51
52	9.256 330	9.050 932	8.854 116	8.665 382	8.484 269	8.310 346	52
53	9.260 794	9.054 894	8.857 632	8.668 504	8.487 042	8.312 809	53
54	9.264 826	9.058 463	8.860 793	8.671 304	8.489 523	8.315 008	54
55	9.268 466	9.061 678	8.863 634	8.673 816	8.491 743	8.316 972	55
56	9.271 752	9.064 575	8.866 188	8.676 068	8.493 730	8.318 725	56
57	9.274 720	9.067 185	8.868 483	8.678 088	8.495 508	8.320 290	57
58	9.277 399	9.069 536	8.870 547	8.679 899	8.497 099	8.321 687	58
59	9.279 819	9.071 654	8.872 402	8.681 524	8.498 522	8.322 935	59
YRS							
30	9.282 004	9.073 562	8.874 069	8.682 981	8.499 796	8.324 049	60
31	9.285 757	9.076 830	8.876 915	8.685 460	8.501 956	8.325 932	62
32	9.288 818	9.079 482	8.879 214	8.687 454	8.503 686	8.327 433	64
33	9.291 313	9.081 635	8.881 072	8.689 058	8.505 071	8.328 630	66
34	9.293 347	9.083 382	8.882 573	8.690 348	8.506 180	8.329 584	68
35	9.295 005	9.084 800	8.883 786	8.691 386	8.507 069	8.330 344	70
36	9.296 357	9.085 951	8.884 766	8.692 220	8.507 780	8.330 950	72
37	9.297 460	9.086 885	8.885 557	8.692 892	8.508 349	8.331 434	74
38	9.298 359	9.087 643	8.886 197	8.693 432	8.508 805	8.331 819	76
39	9.299 091	9.088 258	8.886 714	8.693 866	8.509 171	8.332 126	78
40	9.299 689	9.088 757	8.887 132	8.694 216	8.509 463	8.332 371	80

YRS	5.25% ANNUAL RATE	5.50% ANNUAL RATE	5.75% ANNUAL RATE	6.00% ANNUAL RATE	6.25% ANNUAL RATE	6.50% ANNUAL RATE	YRS
1	0.950 119	0.947 867	0.945 626	0.943 396	0.941 176	0.938 967	1
2	1.852 844	1.846 320	1.839 836	1.833 393	1.826 990	1.820 626	2
3	2.710 541	2.697 933	2.685 424	2.673 012	2.660 696	2.648 476	3
4	3.525 455	3.505 150	3.485 035	3.465 106	3.445 361	3.425 799	4
5	4.299 719	4.270 284	4.241 167	4.212 364	4.183 869	4.155 679	5
6	5.035 363	4.995 530	4.956 187	4.917 324	4.878 936	4.841 014	6
7	5.734 311	5.682 967	5.632 328	5.582 381	5.533 116	5.484 520	7
8	6.398 396	6.334 566	6.271 705	6.209 794	6.148 815	6.088 751	8
9	7.029 355	6.952 195	6.876 317	6.801 692	6.728 297	6.656 104	9
10	7.628 840	7.537 626	7.448 054	7.360 087	7.273 691	7.188 830	10
11	8.198 423	8.092 536	7.988 703	7.886 875	7.787 003	7.689 042	11
12	8.739 595	8.618 518	8.499 956	8.383 844	8.270 121	8.158 725	12
13	9.253 772	9.117 079	8.983 410	8.852 683	8.724 819	8.599 742	13
14	9.742 301	9.589 648	9.440 576	9.294 984	9.152 771	9.013 842	14
15	10.206 462	10.037 581	9.872 886	9.712 249	9.555 549	9.402 669	15
16	10.647 469	10.462 162	10.281 688	10.105 895	9.934 635	9.767 764	16
17	11.066 479	10.864 609	10.668 263	10.477 260	10.291 421	10.110 577	17
18	11.464 588	11.246 074	11.033 819	10.827 603	10.627 220	10.432 466	18
19	11.842 839	11.607 654	11.379 498	11.158 116	10.943 266	10.734 710	19
20	12.202 223	11.950 382	11.706 381	11.469 921	11.240 721	11.018 507	20
21	12.543 679	12.275 244	12.015 490	11.764 077	11.520 678	11.284 983	21
22	12.868 104	12.583 170	12.307 792	12.041 582	11.784 168	11.535 196	22
23	13.176 346	12.875 042	12.584 200	12.303 379	12.032 158	11.770 137	23
24	13.469 212	13.151 699	12.845 580	12.550 358	12.265 560	11.990 739	24
25	13.747 470	13.413 933	13.092 747	12.783 356	12.485 233	12.197 877	25
26	14.011 848	13.662 495	13.326 474	13.003 166	12.691 984	12.392 373	26
27	14.263 038	13.898 100	13.547 494	13.210 534	12.886 573	12.574 998	27
28	14.501 699	14.121 422	13.756 495	13.406 164	13.069 716	12.746 477	28
29	14.728 455	14.333 101	13.954 132	13.590 721	13.242 086	12.907 490	29
30	14.943 901	14.533 745	14.141 024	13.764 831	13.404 316	13.058 676	30
31	15.148 599	14.723 929	14.317 753	13.929 086	13.557 003	13.200 635	31
32	15.343 087	14.904 198	14.484 873	14.084 043	13.700 709	13.333 929	32
33	15.527 874	15.075 069	14.642 906	14.230 230	13.835 961	13.459 088	33
34	15.703 443	15.237 033	14.792 346	14.368 141	13.963 258	13.576 609	34
35	15.870 255	15.390 552	14.933 660	14.498 246	14.083 066	13.686 957	35
36	16.028 745	15.536 068	15.067 291	14.620 987	14.195 827	13.790 570	36
37	16.179 331	15.673 999	15.193 656	14.736 780	14.301 955	13.887 859	37
38	16.322 404	15.804 738	15.313 150	14.846 019	14.401 840	13.979 210	38
39	16.458 341	15.928 662	15.426 146	14.949 075	14.495 849	14.064 986	39
40	16.587 498	16.046 125	15.532 999	15.046 297	14.584 329	14.145 527	40
41	16.710 212	16.157 464	15.634 041	15.138 016	14.667 603	14.221 152	41
42	16.826 804	16.262 999	15.729 590	15.224 543	14.745 980	14.292 161	42
43	16.937 581	16.363 032	15.819 943	15.306 173	14.819 746	14.358 837	43
44	17.042 833	16.457 851	15.905 384	15.383 182	14.889 172	14.421 443	44
45	17.142 834	16.547 726	15.986 178	15.455 832	14.954 515	14.480 228	45
46	17.237 847	16.632 915	16.062 580	15.524 370	15.016 014	14.535 426	46
47	17.328 121	16.713 664	16.134 828	15.589 028	15.073 896	14.587 254	47
48	17.413 891	16.790 203	16.203 147	15.650 027	15.128 372	14.635 919	48
49	17.495 384	16.862 751	16.267 751	15.707 572	15.179 645	14.681 615	49
50	17.572 811	16.931 518	16.328 842	15.761 861	15.227 901	14.724 521	50

YRS	6.75% ANNUAL RATE	7.00% ANNUAL RATE	7.25% ANNUAL RATE	7.50% ANNUAL RATE	7.75% ANNUAL RATE	8.00% ANNUAL RATE	YRS
1	0.936 768	0.934 579	0.932 401	0.930 233	0.928 074	0.925 926	1
2	1.814 303	1.808 018	1.801 772	1.795 565	1.789 396	1.783 265	2
3	2.636 349	2.624 316	2.612 375	2.600 526	2.588 767	2.577 097	3
4	3.406 416	3.387 211	3.368 182	3.349 326	3.330 642	3.312 127	4
5	4.127 790	4.100 197	4.072 897	4.045 885	4.019 157	3.992 710	5
6	4.803 551	4.766 540	4.729 974	4.693 846	4.658 151	4.622 880	6
7	5.436 581	5.389 289	5.342 633	5.296 601	5.251 184	5.206 370	7
8	6.029 584	5.971 299	5.913 877	5.857 304	5.801 563	5.746 639	8
9	6.585 091	6.515 232	6.446 505	6.378 887	6.312 355	6.246 888	9
10	7.105 471	7.023 582	6.943 128	6.864 081	6.786 409	6.710 081	10
11	7.592 947	7.498 674	7.406 180	7.315 424	7.226 365	7.138 964	11
12	8.049 600	7.942 686	7.837 930	7.735 278	7.634 678	7.536 078	12
13	8.477 377	8.357 651	8.240 495	8.125 840	8.013 622	7.903 776	13
14	8.878 105	8.745 468	8.615 846	8.489 154	8.365 310	8.244 237	14
15	9.253 494	9.107 914	8.965 824	8.827 120	8.691 703	8.559 479	15
16	9.605 146	9.446 649	9.292 143	9.141 507	8.994 620	8.851 369	16
17	9.934 563	9.763 223	9.596 404	9.433 960	9.275 750	9.121 638	17
18	10.243 151	10.059 087	9.880 097	9.706 009	9.536 659	9.371 887	18
19	10.532 225	10.335 595	10.144 612	9.959 078	9.778 802	9.603 599	19
20	10.803 021	10.594 014	10.391 247	10.194 491	10.003 528	9.818 147	20
21	11.056 695	10.835 527	10.621 209	10.413 480	10.212 091	10.016 803	21
22	11.294 327	11.061 240	10.835 626	10.617 191	10.405 653	10.200 744	22
23	11.516 934	11.272 187	11.035 549	10.806 689	10.585 293	10.371 059	23
24	11.725 465	11.469 334	11.221 957	10.982 967	10.752 012	10.528 758	24
25	11.920 811	11.653 583	11.395 764	11.146 946	10.906 740	10.674 776	25
26	12.103 804	11.825 779	11.557 822	11.299 485	11.050 338	10.809 978	26
27	12.275 226	11.986 709	11.708 925	11.441 381	11.183 609	10.935 165	27
28	12.435 809	12.137 111	11.849 814	11.573 378	11.307 293	11.051 078	28
29	12.586 238	12.277 674	11.981 178	11.696 165	11.422 082	11.158 406	29
30	12.727 155	12.409 041	12.103 663	11.810 386	11.528 614	11.257 783	30
31	12.859 162	12.531 814	12.217 867	11.916 638	11.627 484	11.349 799	31
32	12.982 821	12.646 555	12.324 352	12.015 478	11.719 243	11.434 999	32
33	13.098 662	12.753 790	12.423 638	12.107 421	11.804 402	11.513 888	33
34	13.207 177	12.854 009	12.516 213	12.192 950	11.883 436	11.586 934	34
35	13.308 831	12.947 672	12.602 529	12.272 511	11.956 785	11.654 568	35
36	13.404 057	13.035 208	12.683 011	12.346 522	12.024 858	11.717 193	36
37	13.493 262	13.117 017	12.758 052	12.415 370	12.088 036	11.775 179	37
38	13.576 826	13.193 473	12.828 021	12.479 414	12.146 669	11.828 869	38
39	13.655 107	13.264 928	12.893 259	12.538 989	12.201 085	11.878 582	39
40	13.728 437	13.331 709	12.954 088	12.594 409	12.251 587	11.924 613	40
41	13.797 131	13.394 120	13.010 805	12.645 962	12.298 456	11.967 235	41
42	13.861 481	13.452 449	13.063 687	12.693 918	12.341 955	12.006 699	42
43	13.921 762	13.506 962	13.112 995	12.738 528	12.382 325	12.043 240	43
44	13.978 231	13.557 908	13.158 970	12.780 026	12.419 791	12.077 074	44
45	14.031 130	13.605 522	13.201 837	12.818 629	12.454 562	12.108 402	45
46	14.080 684	13.650 020	13.241 806	12.854 539	12.486 833	12.137 409	46
47	14.127 104	13.691 608	13.279 073	12.887 943	12.516 782	12.164 267	47
48	14.170 589	13.730 474	13.313 821	12.919 017	12.544 577	12.189 136	48
49	14.211 325	13.766 799	13.346 220	12.947 922	12.570 373	12.212 163	49
50	14.249 485	13.800 746	13.376 429	12.974 812	12.594 314	12.233 485	50

YRS	8.25% ANNUAL RATE	8.50% ANNUAL RATE	8.75% ANNUAL RATE	9.00% ANNUAL RATE	9.25% ANNUAL RATE	9.50% ANNUAL RATE	YRS
1	0.923 788	0.921 659	0.919 540	0.917 431	0.915 332	0.913 242	1
2	1.777 171	1.771 114	1.765 094	1.759 111	1.753 164	1.747 253	2
3	2.565 516	2.554 022	2.542 616	2.531 295	2.520 059	2.508 907	3
4	3.293 779	3.275 597	3.257 578	3.239 720	3.222 022	3.204 481	4
5	3.966 540	3.940 642	3.915 014	3.889 651	3.864 551	3.839 709	5
6	4.588 027	4.553 587	4.519 553	4.485 919	4.452 678	4.419 825	6
7	5.162 150	5.118 514	5.075 451	5.032 953	4.991 010	4.949 612	7
8	5.692 517	5.639 183	5.586 622	5.534 819	5.483 762	5.433 436	8
9	6.182 464	6.119 063	6.056 664	5.995 247	5.934 793	5.875 284	9
10	6.635 071	6.561 348	6.488 886	6.417 658	6.347 637	6.278 798	10
11	7.053 183	6.968 984	6.886 332	6.805 191	6.725 526	6.647 304	11
12	7.439 430	7.344 686	7.251 800	7.160 725	7.071 419	6.983 839	12
13	7.796 240	7.690 955	7.587 862	7.486 904	7.388 027	7.291 178	13
14	8.125 857	8.010 097	7.896 884	7.786 150	7.677 828	7.571 852	14
15	8.430 353	8.304 237	8.181 043	8.060 688	7.943 092	7.828 175	15
16	8.711 642	8.575 333	8.442 338	8.312 558	8.185 896	8.062 260	16
17	8.971 494	8.825 192	8.682 610	8.543 631	8.408 143	8.276 037	17
18	9.211 542	9.055 476	8.903 549	8.755 625	8.611 573	8.471 266	18
19	9.433 295	9.267 720	9.106 712	8.950 115	8.797 778	8.649 558	19
20	9.638 148	9.463 337	9.293 528	9.128 546	8.968 218	8.812 382	20
21	9.827 388	9.643 628	9.465 313	9.292 244	9.124 227	8.961 080	21
22	10.002 206	9.809 796	9.623 277	9.442 425	9.267 027	9.096 876	22
23	10.163 701	9.962 945	9.768 530	9.580 207	9.397 736	9.220 892	23
24	10.312 888	10.104 097	9.902 097	9.706 612	9.517 379	9.334 148	24
25	10.450 705	10.234 191	10.024 917	9.822 580	9.626 891	9.437 578	25
26	10.578 018	10.354 093	10.137 854	9.928 972	9.727 132	9.532 034	26
27	10.695 629	10.464 602	10.241 705	10.026 580	9.818 885	9.618 296	27
28	10.804 276	10.566 453	10.337 200	10.116 128	9.902 869	9.697 074	28
29	10.904 643	10.660 326	10.425 012	10.198 283	9.979 743	9.769 018	29
30	10.997 361	10.746 844	10.505 758	10.273 654	10.050 108	9.834 719	30
31	11.083 012	10.826 584	10.580 007	10.342 802	10.114 516	9.894 721	31
32	11.162 136	10.900 078	10.648 282	10.406 240	10.173 470	9.949 517	32
33	11.235 230	10.967 813	10.711 064	10.464 441	10.227 432	9.999 559	33
34	11.302 752	11.030 243	10.768 795	10.517 835	10.276 826	10.045 259	34
35	11.365 129	11.087 781	10.821 880	10.566 821	10.322 037	10.086 995	35
36	11.422 752	11.140 812	10.870 695	10.611 763	10.363 421	10.125 109	36
37	11.475 984	11.189 689	10.915 581	10.652 993	10.401 301	10.159 917	37
38	11.525 158	11.234 736	10.956 856	10.690 820	10.435 973	10.191 705	38
39	11.570 585	11.276 255	10.994 810	10.725 523	10.467 710	10.220 735	39
40	11.612 549	11.314 520	11.029 711	10.757 360	10.496 769	10.247 247	40
41	11.651 316	11.349 788	11.061 803	10.786 569	10.523 350	10.271 458	41
42	11.687 128	11.382 293	11.091 313	10.813 366	10.547 689	10.293 569	42
43	11.720 210	11.412 252	11.118 449	10.837 950	10.569 967	10.313 762	43
44	11.750 772	11.439 864	11.143 401	10.860 505	10.590 358	0.332 203	44
45	11.779 004	11.465 312	11.166 346	10.881 197	10.609 024	10.349 043	45
46	11.805 085	11.488 767	11.187 444	10.900 181	10.626 109	10.364 423	46
47	11.829 177	11.510 384	11.206 846	10.917 597	10.641 747	10.378 469	47
48	11.851 434	11.530 308	11.224 686	10.933 575	10.656 061	10.391 296	48
49	11.871 995	11.548 671	11.241 090	10.948 234	10.669 164	10.403 010	49
50	11.890 988	11.565 595	11.256 175	10.961 683	10.681 157	10.413 707	50

YRS	9.75% ANNUAL RATE	10.00% ANNUAL RATE	10.25% ANNUAL RATE	10.50% ANNUAL RATE	10.75% ANNUAL RATE	11.00% ANNUAL RATE	YRS
1	0.911 162	0.909 091	0.907 029	0.904 977	0.902 935	0.900 901	1
2	1.741 377	1.735 537	1.729 732	1.723 961	1.718 225	1.712 523	2
3	2.497 838	2.486 852	2.475 947	2.465 123	2.454 380	2.443 715	3
4	3.187 096	3.169 865	3.152 787	3.135 858	3.119 079	3.102 446	4
5	3.815 122	3.790 787	3.766 700	3.742 858	3.719 258	3.695 897	5
6	4.387 355	4.355 261	4.323 537	4.292 179	4.261 181	4.230 538	6
7	4.908 752	4.868 419	4.828 605	4.789 303	4.750 502	4.712 196	7
8	5.383 828	5.334 926	5.286 717	5.239 188	5.192 327	5.146 123	8
9	5.816 700	5.759 024	5.702 238	5.646 324	5.591 266	5.537 048	9
10	6.211 116	6.144 567	6.079 127	6.014 773	5.951 482	5.889 232	10
11	6.570 493	6.495 061	6.420 977	6.348 211	6.276 733	6.206 515	11
12	6.897 944	6.813 692	6.731 045	6.649 964	6.570 414	6.492 356	12
13	7.196 304	7.103 356	7.012 286	6.923 045	6.835 588	6.749 870	13
14	7.468 159	7.366 687	7.267 379	7.170 176	7.075 023	6.981 865	14
15	7.715 862	7.606 080	7.498 757	7.393 825	7.291 217	7.190 870	15
16	7.941 560	7.823 709	7.708 623	7.596 221	7.486 426	7.379 162	16
17	8.147 207	8.021 553	7.898 978	7.779 386	7.662 687	7.548 794	17
18	8.334 585	8.201 412	8.071 635	7.945 146	7.821 840	7.701 617	18
19	8.505 317	8.364 920	8.228 240	8.095 154	7.965 544	7.839 294	19
20	8.660 881	8.513 564	8.370 286	8.230 909	8.095 299	7.963 328	20
21	8.802 625	8.648 694	8.499 126	8.353 764	8.212 460	8.075 070	21
22	8.931 777	8.771 540	8.615 987	8.464 945	8.318 248	8.175 739	22
23	9.049 455	8.883 218	8.721 984	8.565 561	8.413 768	8.266 432	23
24	9.156 679	8.984 744	8.818 126	8.656 616	8.500 016	8.348 137	24
25	9.254 377	9.077 040	8.905 329	8.739 019	8.577 893	8.421 745	25
26	9.343 396	9.160 945	8.984 426	8.813 592	8.648 210	8.488 058	26
27	9.424 506	9.237 223	9.056 169	8.881 079	8.711 702	8.547 800	27
28	9.498 411	9.306 567	9.121 241	8.942 153	8.769 031	8.601 622	28
29	9.565 751	9.369 606	9.180 264	8.997 423	8.820 796	8.650 110	29
30	9.627 108	9.426 914	9.233 800	9.047 442	8.867 536	8.693 793	30
31	9.683 014	9.479 013	9.282 358	9.092 707	8.909 739	8.733 146	31
32	9.733 953	9.526 376	9.326 402	9.133 672	8.947 845	8.768 600	32
33	9.780 368	9.569 432	9.366 351	9.170 744	8.982 253	8.800 541	33
34	9.822 658	9.608 575	9.402 586	9.204 293	9.013 321	8.829 316	34
35	9.861 192	9.644 159	9.435 452	9.234 654	9.041 373	8.855 240	35
36	9.896 303	9.676 508	9.465 263	9.262 131	9.066 703	8.878 594	36
37	9.928 294	9.705 917	9.492 302	9.286 996	9.089 574	8.899 635	37
38	9.957 443	9.732 651	9.516 827	9.309 499	9.110 225	8.918 590	38
39	9.984 003	9.756 956	9.539 072	9.329 863	9.128 871	8.935 666	39
40	10.008 203	9.779 051	9.559 249	9.348 292	9.145 707	8.951 051	40
41	10.030 253	9.799 137	9.577 550	9.364 970	9.160 910	8.964 911	41
42	10.050 345	9.817 397	9.594 150	9.380 064	9.174 636	8.977 397	42
43	10.068 651	9.833 998	9.609 206	9.393 723	9.187 030	8.988 646	43
44	10.085 331	9.849 089	9.622 863	9.406 084	9.198 222	8.998 780	44
45	10.100 530	9.862 808	9.635 250	9.417 271	9.208 327	9.007 910	45
46	10.114 378	9.875 280	9.646 485	9.427 394	9.217 451	9.016 135	46
47	10.126 996	9.886 618	9.656 676	9.436 556	9.225 689	9.023 545	47
48	10.138 493	9.896 926	9.665 919	9.444 847	9.233 128	9.030 221	48
49	10.148 968	9.906 296	9.674 303	9.452 350	9.239 845	9.036 235	49
50	10.158 513	9.914 814	9.681 907	9.459 140	9.245 909	9.041 653	50

YRS	11.25% ANNUAL RATE	11.50% ANNUAL RATE	11.75% ANNUAL RATE	12.00% ANNUAL RATE	12.25% ANNUAL RATE	12.50% ANNUAL RATE	YRS
1	0.898 876	0.896 861	0.894 855	0.892 857	0.890 869	0.888 889	1
2	1.706 855	1.701 221	1.695 619	1.690 051	1.684 515	1.679 012	2
3	2.433 128	2.422 619	2.412 187	2.401 831	2.391 551	2.381 344	3
4	3.085 958	3.069 614	3.053 411	3.037 349	3.021 426	3.005 639	4
5	3.672 771	3.649 878	3.627 214	3.604 776	3.582 562	3.560 568	5
6	4.200 244	4.170 294	4.140 684	4.111 407	4.082 461	4.053 839	6
7	4.674 376	4.637 035	4.600 164	4.563 757	4.527 805	4.492 301	7
8	5.100 563	5.055 637	5.011 333	4.967 640	4.924 547	4.882 045	8
9	5.483 652	5.431 064	5.379 269	5.328 250	5.277 993	5.228 485	9
10	5.828 002	5.767 771	5.708 518	5.650 223	5.592 867	5.536 431	10
11	6.137 530	6.069 750	6.003 148	5.937 699	5.873 378	5.810 161	11
12	6.415 757	6.340 583	6.266 799	6.194 374	6.123 277	6.053 476	12
13	6.665 849	6.583 482	6.502 728	6.423 548	6.345 904	6.269 757	13
14	6.890 651	6.801 329	6.713 851	6.628 168	6.544 235	6.462 006	14
15	7.092 720	6.996 708	6.902 775	6.810 864	6.720 922	6.632 894	15
16	7.274 355	7.171 935	7.071 834	6.973 986	6.878 327	6.784 795	16
17	7.437 622	7.329 090	7.223 118	7.119 630	7.018 554	6.919 818	17
18	7.584 380	7.470 036	7.358 495	7.249 670	7.143 478	7.039 838	18
19	7.716 296	7.596 445	7.479 637	7.365 777	7.254 769	7.146 523	19
20	7.834 873	7.709 816	7.588 042	7.469 444	7.353 914	7.241 353	20
21	7.941 459	7.811 494	7.685 049	7.562 003	7.442 240	7.325 647	21
22	8.037 267	7.902 685	7.771 856	7.644 646	7.520 926	7.400 575	22
23	8.123 386	7.984 471	7.849 536	7.718 434	7.591 026	7.467 178	23
24	8.200 796	8.057 822	7.919 048	7.784 316	7.653 475	7.526 381	24
25	8.270 379	8.123 607	7.981 251	7.843 139	7.709 109	7.579 005	25
26	8.332 925	8.182 607	8.036 913	7.895 660	7.758 672	7.625 782	26
27	8.389 146	8.235 522	8.086 723	7.942 554	7.802 826	7.667 362	27
28	8.439 681	8.282 979	8.131 296	7.984 423	7.842 161	7.704 322	28
29	8.485 107	8.325 542	8.171 182	8.021 806	7.877 204	7.737 175	29
30	8.525 939	8.363 715	8.206 874	8.055 184	7.908 422	7.766 378	30
31	8.562 642	8.397 951	8.238 814	8.084 986	7.936 233	7.792 336	31
32	8.595 633	8.428 655	8.267 395	8.111 594	7.961 010	7.815 410	32
33	8.625 288	8.456 193	8.292 971	8.135 352	7.983 082	7.835 920	33
34	8.651 944	8.480 891	8.315 858	8.156 564	8.002 746	7.854 151	34
35	8.675 905	8.503 041	8.336 338	8.175 504	8.020 263	7.870 356	35
36	8.697 443	8.522 907	8.354 665	8.192 414	8.035 869	7.884 761	36
37	8.716 802	8.540 723	8.371 065	8.207 513	8.049 772	7.897 565	37
38	8.734 204	8.556 703	8.385 740	8.220 993	8.062 158	7.908 947	38
39	8.749 847	8.571 034	8.398 873	8.233 030	8.073 192	7.919 064	39
40	8.763 907	8.583 887	8.410 624	8.243 777	8.083 022	7.928 057	40
41	8.776 546	8.595 414	8.421 140	8.253 372	8.091 779	7.936 051	41
42	8.787 906	8.605 753	8.430 551	8.261 939	8.099 580	7.943 156	42
43	8.798 118	8.615 025	8.438 971	8.269 589	8.106 530	7.949 472	43
44	8.807 297	8.623 341	8.446 507	8.276 418	8.112 722	7.955 086	44
45	8.815 548	8.630 799	8.453 250	8.282 516	8.118 238	7.960 077	45
46	8.822 964	8.637 488	8.459 284	8.287 961	8.123 152	7.964 513	46
47	8.829 631	8.643 487	8.464 684	8.292 822	8.127 529	7.968 456	47
48	8.835 623	8.648 867	8.469 516	8.297 163	8.131 429	7.971 961	48
49	8.841 010	8.653 692	8.473 840	8.301 038	8.134 904	7.975 076	49
50	8.845 851	8.658 020	8.477 709	8.304 498	8.137 999	7.977 845	50

YRS	12.75% ANNUAL RATE	13.00% ANNUAL RATE	13.25% ANNUAL RATE	13.50% ANNUAL RATE	13.75% ANNUAL RATE	14.00% ANNUAL RATE	YRS
1	0.886 918	0.884 956	0.883 002	0.881 057	0.879 121	0.877 193	1
2	1.673 541	1.668 102	1.662 695	1.657 319	1.651 974	1.646 661	2
3	2.371 212	2.361 153	2.351 166	2.341 250	2.331 406	2.321 632	3
4	2.989 988	2.974 471	2.959 087	2.943 833	2.928 709	2.913 712	4
5	3.538 792	3.517 231	3.495 882	3.474 743	3.453 810	3.433 081	5
6	4.025 536	3.997 550	3.969 874	3.942 505	3.915 437	3.888 668	6
7	4.457 239	4.422 610	4.388 410	4.354 630	4.321 263	4.288 305	7
8	4.840 123	4.798 770	4.757 978	4.717 735	4.678 034	4.638 864	8
9	5.179 710	5.131 655	5.084 307	5.037 652	4.991 678	4.946 372	9
10	5.480 896	5.426 243	5.372 456	5.319 517	5.267 409	5.216 116	10
11	5.748 023	5.686 941	5.626 893	5.567 857	5.509 810	5.452 733	11
12	5.984 943	5.917 647	5.851 561	5.786 658	5.722 910	5.660 292	12
13	6.195 071	6.121 812	6.049 944	5.979 434	5.910 251	5.842 362	13
14	6.381 438	6.302 488	6.225 116	6.149 281	6.074 946	6.002 072	14
15	6.546 730	6.462 379	6.379 793	6.298 926	6.219 732	6.142 168	15
16	6.693 330	6.603 875	6.516 374	6.430 772	6.347 018	6.265 060	16
17	6.823 353	6.729 093	6.636 975	6.546 936	6.458 917	6.372 859	17
18	6.938 672	6.839 905	6.743 465	6.649 283	6.557 289	6.467 420	18
19	7.040 951	6.937 969	6.837 497	6.739 456	6.643 771	6.550 369	19
20	7.131 664	7.024 752	6.920 527	6.818 904	6.719 798	6.623 131	20
21	7.212 119	7.101 550	6.993 843	6.888 902	6.786 636	6.686 957	21
22	7.283 475	7.169 513	7.058 581	6.950 575	6.845 394	6.742 944	22
23	7.346 763	7.229 658	7.115 745	7.004 912	6.897 050	6.792 056	23
24	7.402 894	7.282 883	7.166 221	7.052 786	6.942 461	6.835 137	24
25	7.452 678	7.329 985	7.210 791	7.094 965	6.982 384	6.872 927	25
26	7.496 832	7.371 668	7.250 146	7.132 128	7.017 480	6.906 077	26
27	7.535 993	7.408 556	7.284 898	7.164 870	7.048 334	6.935 155	27
28	7.570 725	7.441 200	7.315 583	7.193 718	7.075 459	6.960 662	28
29	7.601 530	7.470 088	7.342 678	7.219 135	7.099 304	6.983 037	29
30	7.628 852	7.495 653	7.366 603	7.241 529	7.120 268	7.002 664	30
31	7.653 083	7.518 277	7.387 729	7.261 259	7.138 697	7.019 881	31
32	7.674 575	7.538 299	7.406 383	7.278 642	7.154 898	7.034 983	32
33	7.693 636	7.556 016	7.422 855	7.293 958	7.169 141	7.048 231	33
34	7.710 542	7.571 696	7.437 399	7.307 452	7.181 663	7.059 852	34
35	7.725 536	7.585 572	7.450 242	7.319 341	7.192 670	7.070 045	35
36	7.738 835	7.597 851	7.461 583	7.329 816	7.202 348	7.078 987	36
37	7.750 630	7.608 718	7.471 596	7.339 045	7.210 855	7.086 831	37
38	7.761 091	7.618 334	7.480 438	7.347 176	7.218 334	7.093 711	38
39	7.770 369	7.626 844	7.488 246	7.354 340	7.224 909	7.099 747	39
40	7.778 597	7.634 376	7.495 140	7.360 652	7.230 689	7.105 041	40
41	7.785 896	7.641 040	7.501 227	7.366 213	7.235 771	7.109 685	41
42	7.792 369	7.646 938	7.506 602	7.371 113	7.240 238	7.113 759	42
43	7.798 110	7.652 158	7.511 349	7.375 430	7.244 165	7.117 332	43
44	7.803 202	7.656 777	7.515 540	7.379 233	7.247 618	7.120 467	44
45	7.807 718	7.660 864	7.519 240	7.382 585	7.250 653	7.123 217	45
46	7.811 723	7.664 482	7.522 508	7.385 537	7.253 321	7.125 629	46
47	7.815 275	7.667 683	7.525 393	7.388 138	7.255 667	7.127 744	47
48	7.818 426	7.670 516	7.527 941	7.390 430	7.257 729	7.129 600	48
49	7.821 220	7.673 023	7.530 191	7.392 450	7.259 542	7.131 228	49
50	7.823 699	7.675 242	7.532 177	7.394 229	7.261 136	7.132 656	50

YRS	14.25% ANNUAL RATE	14.50% ANNUAL RATE	14.75% ANNUAL RATE	15.00% ANNUAL RATE	15.25% ANNUAL RATE	15.50% ANNUAL RATE	YRS
1	0.875 274	0.873 362	0.871 460	0.869 565	0.867 679	0.865 801	1
2	1.641 377	1.636 124	1.630 902	1.625 709	1.620 546	1.615 412	2
3	2.311 928	2.302 292	2.292 725	2.283 225	2.273 792	2.264 426	3
4	2.898 843	2.884 098	2.869 477	2.854 978	2.840 601	2.826 343	4
5	3.412 554	3.392 225	3.372 093	3.352 155	3.332 408	3.312 851	5
6	3.862 191	3.836 005	3.810 103	3.784 483	3.759 140	3.734 070	6
7	4.255 747	4.223 585	4.191 811	4.160 420	4.129 405	4.098 762	7
8	4.600 217	4.562 083	4.524 454	4.487 322	4.450 677	4.414 513	8
9	4.901 721	4.857 714	4.814 339	4.771 584	4.729 438	4.687 890	9
10	5.165 620	5.115 908	5.066 962	5.018 769	4.971 313	4.924 580	10
11	5.396 604	5.341 404	5.287 113	5.233 712	5.181 182	5.129 506	11
12	5.598 778	5.538 344	5.478 965	5.420 619	5.363 282	5.306 932	12
13	5.775 736	5.710 344	5.646 157	5.583 147	5.521 286	5.460 547	13
14	5.930 622	5.860 563	5.791 858	5.724 476	5.658 382	5.593 547	14
15	6.066 190	5.991 758	5.918 831	5.847 370	5.777 338	5.708 699	15
16	6.184 849	6.106 339	6.029 482	5.954 235	5.880 554	5.808 397	16
17	6.288 708	6.206 409	6.125 910	6.047 161	5.970 112	5.894 716	17
18	6.379 613	6.293 807	6.209 944	6.127 966	6.047 819	5.969 451	18
19	6.459 180	6.370 137	6.283 175	6.198 231	6.115 245	6.034 157	19
20	6.528 823	6.436 801	6.346 994	6.259 331	6.173 748	6.090 179	20
21	6.589 779	6.495 023	6.402 609	6.312 462	6.224 510	6.138 683	21
22	6.643 133	6.545 871	6.451 075	6.358 663	6.268 555	6.180 678	22
23	6.689 832	6.590 281	6.493 312	6.398 837	6.306 773	6.217 037	23
24	6.730 706	6.629 066	6.530 119	6.433 771	6.339 933	6.248 517	24
25	6.766 482	6.662 940	6.562 195	6.464 149	6.368 705	6.275 772	25
26	6.797 796	6.692 524	6.590 148	6.490 564	6.393 671	6.299 370	26
27	6.825 205	6.718 362	6.614 508	6.513 534	6.415 332	6.319 801	27
28	6.849 195	6.740 927	6.635 737	6.533 508	6.434 128	6.337 490	28
29	6.870 192	6.760 635	6.654 237	6.550 877	6.450 436	6.352 805	29
30	6.888 571	6.777 847	6.670 359	6.565 980	6.464 587	6.366 065	30
31	6.904 657	6.792 880	6.684 409	6.579 113	6.476 865	6.377 546	31
32	6.918 737	6.806 008	6.696 653	6.590 533	6.487 518	6.387 485	32
33	6.931 061	6.817 475	6.707 323	6.600 463	6.496 762	6.396 091	33
34	6.941 848	6.827 489	6.716 621	6.609 099	6.504 783	6.403 542	34
35	6.951 289	6.836 235	6.724 724	6.616 607	6.511 742	6.409 993	35
36	6.959 553	6.843 873	6.731 786	6.623 137	6.517 781	6.415 579	36
37	6.966 786	6.850 544	6.737 940	6.628 815	6.523 020	6.420 414	37
38	6.973 117	6.856 370	6.743 303	6.633 752	6.527 566	6.424 601	38
39	6.978 658	6.861 459	6.747 976	6.638 045	6.531 511	6.428 226	39
40	6.983 508	6.865 903	6.752 049	6.641 778	6.534 933	6.431 365	40
41	6.987 753	6.869 784	6.755 598	6.645 025	6.537 903	6.434 082	41
42	6.991 469	6.873 174	6.758 691	6.647 848	6.540 480	6.436 435	42
43	6.994 721	6.876 135	6.761 387	6.650 302	6.542 716	6.438 471	43
44	6.997 568	6.878 720	6.763 736	6.652 437	6.544 656	6.440 235	44
45	7.000 059	6.880 978	6.765 783	6.654 293	6.546 339	6.441 762	45
46	7.002 240	6.882 950	6.767 567	6.655 907	6.547 800	6.443 084	46
47	7.004 149	6.884 673	6.769 121	6.657 310	6.549 067	6.444 229	47
48	7.005 820	6.886 177	6.770 476	6.658 531	6.550 167	6.445 219	48
49	7.007 282	6.887 491	6.771 657	6.659 592	6.551 121	6.446 077	49
50	7.008 562	6.888 638	6.772 686	6.660 515	6.551 949	6.446 820	50

PRESENT VALUE PER PERIOD

ANNUAL COMPOUNDING

YRS	15.75% ANNUAL RATE	16.00% ANNUAL RATE	16.25% ANNUAL RATE	16.50% ANNUAL RATE	16.75% ANNUAL RATE	17.00% ANNUAL RATE	YRS
1	0.863 931	0.862 069	0.860 215	0.858 369	0.856 531	0.854 701	1
2	1.610 307	1.605 232	1.600 185	1.595 167	1.590 176	1.585 214	2
3	2.255 125	2.245 890	2.236 718	2.227 611	2.218 567	2.209 585	3
4	2.812 203	2.798 181	2.784 274	2.770 481	2.756 802	2.743 235	4
5	3.293 480	3.274 294	3.255 289	3.236 465	3.217 818	3.199 346	5
6	3.709 270	3.684 736	3.660 464	3.636 450	3.612 692	3.589 185	6
7	4.068 484	4.038 565	4.009 001	3.979 786	3.950 914	3.922 380	7
8	4.378 820	4.343 591	4.308 818	4.274 494	4.240 611	4.207 163	8
9	4.646 929	4.606 544	4.566 725	4.527 463	4.488 746	4.450 566	9
10	4.878 556	4.833 227	4.788 581	4.744 603	4.701 282	4.658 604	10
11	5.078 666	5.028 644	4.979 424	4.930 990	4.883 325	4.836 413	11
12	5.251 547	5.197 107	5.143 591	5.090 978	5.039 250	4.988 387	12
13	5.400 905	5.342 334	5.284 809	5.228 308	5.172 805	5.118 280	13
14	5.529 939	5.467 529	5.406 288	5.346 187	5.287 200	5.229 299	14
15	5.641 416	5.575 456	5.510 785	5.447 371	5.385 182	5.324 187	15
16	5.737 725	5.668 497	5.600 675	5.534 224	5.469 106	5.405 288	16
17	5.820 928	5.748 704	5.678 000	5.608 776	5.540 990	5.474 605	17
18	5.892 811	5.817 848	5.744 516	5.672 769	5.602 561	5.533 851	18
19	5.954 912	5.877 455	5.801 735	5.727 699	5.655 299	5.584 488	19
20	6.008 563	5.928 841	5.850 954	5.774 849	5.700 470	5.627 767	20
21	6.054 914	5.973 139	5.893 294	5.815 321	5.739 161	5.664 758	21
22	6.094 958	6.011 326	5.929 715	5.850 061	5.772 300	5.696 375	22
23	6.129 554	6.044 247	5.961 045	5.879 880	5.800 686	5.723 397	23
24	6.159 442	6.072 627	5.987 996	5.905 477	5.824 998	5.746 493	24
25	6.185 263	6.097 092	6.011 179	5.927 448	5.845 823	5.766 234	25
26	6.207 570	6.118 183	6.031 122	5.946 307	5.863 660	5.783 106	26
27	6.226 843	6.136 364	6.048 277	5.962 495	5.878 938	5.797 526	27
28	6.243 493	6.152 038	6.063 034	5.976 391	5.892 024	5.809 851	28
29	6.257 877	6.165 550	6.075 728	5.988 318	5.903 232	5.820 386	29
30	6.270 304	6.177 198	6.086 648	5.998 557	5.912 833	5.829 390	30
31	6.281 040	6.187 240	6.096 041	6.007 345	5.921 056	5.837 085	31
32	6.290 316	6.195 897	6.104 121	6.014 888	5.928 099	5.843 663	32
33	6.298 329	6.203 359	6.111 072	6.021 363	5.934 132	5.849 284	33
34	6.305 252	6.209 792	6.117 051	6.026 921	5.939 300	5.854 089	34
35	6.311 233	6.215 338	6.122 195	6.031 692	5.943 726	5.858 196	35
36	6.316 400	6.220 119	6.126 619	6.035 787	5.947 517	5.861 706	36
37	6.320 864	6.224 241	6.130 425	6.039 302	5.950 764	5.864 706	37
38	6.324 720	6.227 794	6.133 699	6.042 320	5.953 545	5.867 270	38
39	6.328 052	6.230 857	6.136 515	6.044 909	5.955 927	5.869 461	39
40	6.330 930	6.233 497	6.138 938	6.047 133	5.957 968	5.871 335	40
41	6.333 417	6.235 773	6.141 022	6.049 041	5.959 715	5.872 936	41
42	6.335 566	6.237 736	6.142 814	6.050 679	5.961 212	5.874 304	42
43	6.337 422	6.239 427	6.144 357	6.052 085	5.962 494	5.875 473	43
44	6.339 025	6.240 886	6.145 683	6.053 292	5.963 593	5.876 473	44
45	6.340 411	6.242 143	6.146 824	6.054 328	5.964 533	5.877 327	45
46	6.341 607	6.243 227	6.147 806	6.055 217	5.965 339	5.878 058	46
47	6.342 641	6.244 161	6.148 650	6.055 980	5.966 029	5.878 682	47
48	6.343 535	6.244 966	6.149 376	6.056 635	5.966 620	5.879 215	48
49	6.344 306	6.245 661	6.150 001	6.057 198	5.967 127	5.879 671	49
50	6.344 973	6.246 259	6.150 539	6.057 680	5.967 560	5.880 061	50

YRS	17.25% ANNUAL RATE	17.50% ANNUAL RATE	17.75% ANNUAL RATE	18.00% ANNUAL RATE	18.25% ANNUAL RATE	18.50% ANNUAL RATE	YRS
1	0.852 878	0.851 064	0.849 257	0.847 458	0.845 666	0.843 882	1
2	1.580 280	1.575 373	1.570 494	1.565 642	1.560 817	1.556 018	2
3	2.200 665	2.191 807	2.183 010	2.174 273	2.165 596	2.156 978	3
4	2.729 779	2.716 432	2.703 193	2.690 062	2.677 037	2.664 116	4
5	3.181 048	3.162 921	3.144 962	3.127 171	3.109 545	3.092 081	5
6	3.565 926	3.542 911	3.520 138	3.497 603	3.475 302	3.453 233	6
7	3.894 180	3.866 307	3.838 758	3.811 528	3.784 611	3.758 003	7
8	4.174 140	4.141 538	4.109 349	4.077 566	4.046 182	4.015 192	8
9	4.412 913	4.375 777	4.339 150	4.303 022	4.267 385	4.232 230	9
10	4.616 557	4.575 129	4.534 310	4.494 086	4.454 448	4.415 384	10
11	4.790 240	4.744 791	4.700 051	4.656 005	4.612 641	4.569 944	11
12	4.938 371	4.889 184	4.840 807	4.793 225	4.746 419	4.700 375	12
13	5.064 709	5.012 071	4.960 346	4.909 513	4.859 551	4.810 443	13
14	5.172 460	5.116 657	5.061 865	5.008 062	4.955 223	4.903 327	14
15	5.264 358	5.205 665	5.148 081	5.091 578	5.036 129	4.981 711	15
16	5.342 736	5.281 417	5.221 300	5.162 354	5.104 549	5.047 857	16
17	5.409 583	5.345 887	5.283 482	5.222 334	5.162 409	5.103 677	17
18	5.466 595	5.400 755	5.336 290	5.273 164	5.211 340	5.150 782	18
19	5.515 220	5.447 451	5.381 138	5.316 241	5.252 719	5.190 534	19
20	5.556 691	5.487 192	5.419 226	5.352 746	5.287 711	5.224 079	20
21	5.592 060	5.521 015	5.451 572	5.383 683	5.317 304	5.252 387	21
22	5.622 226	5.549 800	5.479 042	5.409 901	5.342 329	5.276 276	22
23	5.647 954	5.574 298	5.502 371	5.432 120	5.363 491	5.296 436	23
24	5.669 897	5.595 147	5.522 183	5.450 949	5.381 388	5.313 448	24
25	5.688 611	5.612 891	5.539 009	5.466 906	5.396 523	5.327 804	25
26	5.704 573	5.627 992	5.553 299	5.480 429	5.409 322	5.339 919	26
27	5.718 186	5.640 845	5.565 434	5.491 889	5.420 145	5.350 143	27
28	5.729 796	5.651 783	5.575 740	5.501 601	5.429 298	5.358 770	28
29	5.739 698	5.661 092	5.584 493	5.509 831	5.437 039	5.366 051	29
30	5.748 143	5.669 014	5.591 926	5.516 806	5.443 584	5.372 195	30
31	5.755 346	5.675 757	5.598 239	5.522 717	5.449 120	5.377 380	31
32	5.761 489	5.681 495	5.603 600	5.527 726	5.453 801	5.381 755	32
33	5.766 729	5.686 379	5.608 153	5.531 971	5.457 760	5.385 447	33
34	5.771 197	5.690 535	5.612 019	5.535 569	5.461 108	5.388 563	34
35	5.775 008	5.694 072	5.615 303	5.538 618	5.463 939	5.391 192	35
36	5.778 259	5.697 083	5.618 092	5.541 201	5.466 333	5.393 411	36
37	5.781 031	5.699 645	5.620 460	5.543 391	5.468 358	5.395 284	37
38	5.783 395	5.701 826	5.622 471	5.545 247	5.470 070	5.396 864	38
39	5.785 412	5.703 681	5.624 179	5.546 819	5.471 518	5.398 197	39
40	5.787 131	5.705 261	5.625 630	5.548 152	5.472 743	5.399 323	40
41	5.788 598	5.706 605	5.626 862	5.549 281	5.473 778	5.400 272	41
42	5.789 849	5.707 749	5.627 908	5.550 238	5.474 654	5.401 074	42
43	5.790 916	5.708 722	5.628 797	5.551 049	5.475 394	5.401 750	43
44	5.791 826	5.709 551	5.629 552	5.551 737	5.476 021	5.402 321	44
45	5.792 602	5.710 256	5.630 192	5.552 319	5.476 550	5.402 802	45
46	5.793 264	5.710 856	5.630 737	5.552 813	5.476 998	5.403 209	46
47	5.793 829	5.711 367	5.631 199	5.553 231	5.477 377	5.403 552	47
48	5.794 310	5.711 802	5.631 591	5.553 586	5.477 697	5.403 841	48
49	5.794 721	5.712 172	5.631 925	5.553 886	5.477 968	5.404 085	49
50	5.795 071	5.712 487	5.632 208	5.554 141	5.478 197	5.404 291	50

YRS	18.75% ANNUAL RATE	19.00% ANNUAL RATE	19.25% ANNUAL RATE	19.50% ANNUAL RATE	19.75% ANNUAL RATE	20.00% ANNUAL RATE	YRS
1	0.842 105	0.840 336	0.838 574	0.836 820	0.835 073	0.833 333	1
2	1.551 247	1.546 501	1.541 781	1.537 088	1.532 420	1.527 778	2
3	2.148 418	2.139 917	2.131 473	2.123 086	2.114 756	2.106 481	3
4	2.651 299	2.638 586	2.625 973	2.613 461	2.601 049	2.588 735	4
5	3.074 779	3.057 635	3.040 648	3.023 817	3.007 139	2.990 612	5
6	3.431 392	3.409 777	3.388 384	3.367 211	3.346 254	3.325 510	6
7	3.731 699	3.705 695	3.679 987	3.654 570	3.629 439	3.604 592	7
8	3.984 589	3.954 366	3.924 517	3.895 037	3.865 920	3.837 160	8
9	4.197 548	4.163 332	4.129 574	4.096 266	4.063 399	4.030 967	9
10	4.376 883	4.338 935	4.301 530	4.264 657	4.228 308	4.192 472	10
11	4.527 901	4.486 500	4.445 727	4.405 571	4.366 019	4.327 060	11
12	4.655 075	4.610 504	4.566 648	4.523 490	4.481 018	4.439 217	12
13	4.762 168	4.714 709	4.668 048	4.622 168	4.577 051	4.532 681	13
14	4.852 352	4.802 277	4.753 080	4.704 743	4.657 245	4.610 567	14
15	4.928 297	4.875 863	4.824 386	4.773 843	4.724 213	4.675 473	15
16	4.992 250	4.937 700	4.884 181	4.831 668	4.780 136	4.729 561	16
17	5.046 105	4.989 664	4.934 324	4.880 057	4.826 836	4.774 634	17
18	5.091 457	5.033 331	4.976 372	4.920 550	4.865 834	4.812 195	18
19	5.129 648	5.070 026	5.011 633	4.954 435	4.898 400	4.843 496	19
20	5.161 809	5.100 862	5.041 202	4.982 791	4.925 595	4.869 580	20
21	5.188 892	5.126 775	5.065 997	5.006 519	4.948 305	4.891 316	21
22	5.211 698	5.148 550	5.086 790	5.026 376	4.967 269	4.909 430	22
23	5.230 904	5.166 849	5.104 226	5.042 993	4.983 106	4.924 525	23
24	5.247 077	5.182 226	5.118 848	5.056 898	4.996 330	4.937 104	24
25	5.260 696	5.195 148	5.131 110	5.068 534	5.007 374	4.947 587	25
26	5.272 165	5.206 007	5.141 392	5.078 271	5.016 596	4.956 323	26
27	5.281 823	5.215 132	5.150 014	5.086 419	5.024 297	4.963 602	27
28	5.289 957	5.222 800	5.157 244	5.093 238	5.030 729	4.969 668	28
29	5.296 806	5.229 243	5.163 308	5.098 944	5.036 099	4.974 724	29
30	5.302 573	5.234 658	5.168 392	5.103 719	5.040 584	4.978 936	30
31	5.307 430	5.239 209	5.172 656	5.107 714	5.044 329	4.982 447	31
32	5.311 520	5.243 033	5.176 231	5.111 058	5.047 456	4.985 372	32
33	5.314 964	5.246 246	5.179 230	5.113 856	5.050 068	4.987 810	33
34	5.317 865	5.248 946	5.181 744	5.116 198	5.052 249	4.989 842	34
35	5.320 307	5.251 215	5.183 852	5.118 157	5.054 070	4.991 535	35
36	5.322 364	5.253 122	5.185 620	5.119 797	5.055 591	4.992 946	36
37	5.324 096	5.254 724	5.187 103	5.121 169	5.056 861	4.994 122	37
38	5.325 554	5.256 071	5.188 346	5.122 317	5.057 921	4.995 101	38
39	5.326 783	5.257 202	5.189 389	5.123 278	5.058 807	4.995 918	39
40	5.327 817	5.258 153	5.190 263	5.124 082	5.059 546	4.996 598	40
41	5.328 688	5.258 952	5.190 997	5.124 755	5.060 164	4.997 165	41
42	5.329 421	5.259 624	5.191 611	5.125 318	5.060 680	4.997 638	42
43	5.330 039	5.260 188	5.192 127	5.125 789	5.061 110	4.998 031	43
44	5.330 559	5.260 662	5.192 559	5.126 183	5.061 470	4.998 359	44
45	5.330 997	5.261 061	5.192 922	5.126 513	5.061 770	4.998 633	45
46	5.331 366	5.261 396	5.193 226	5.126 789	5.062 021	4.998 861	46
47	5.331 677	5.261 677	5.193 481	5.127 020	5.062 231	4.999 051	47
48	5.331 938	5.261 913	5.193 695	5.127 214	5.062 406	4.999 209	48
49	5.332 159	5.262 112	5.193 874	5.127 375	5.062 552	4.999 341	49
50	5.332 344	5.262 279	5.194 024	5.127 511	5.062 674	4.999 451	50

PRESENT VALUE PER PERIOD

YRS	20.25% ANNUAL RATE	20.50% ANNUAL RATE	20.75% ANNUAL RATE	21.00% ANNUAL RATE	21.25% ANNUAL RATE	21.50% ANNUAL RATE	YRS
1	0.831 601	0.829 876	0.828 157	0.826 446	0.824 742	0.823 045	1
2	1.523 161	1.518 569	1.514 002	1.509 460	1.504 942	1.500 449	2
3	2.098 263	2.090 099	2.081 989	2.073 934	2.065 932	2.057 983	3
4	2.576 518	2.564 397	2.552 372	2.540 441	2.528 603	2.516 858	4
5	2.974 235	2.958 006	2.941 923	2.925 984	2.910 188	2.894 533	5
6	3.304 977	3.284 652	3.264 532	3.244 615	3.224 898	3.205 377	6
7	3.580 023	3.555 728	3.531 704	3.507 946	3.484 452	3.461 216	7
8	3.808 751	3.780 687	3.752 964	3.725 576	3.698 517	3.671 783	8
9	3.998 961	3.967 375	3.936 202	3.905 434	3.875 065	3.845 089	9
10	4.157 140	4.122 303	4.087 952	4.054 078	4.020 673	3.987 727	10
11	4.288 682	4.250 874	4.213 625	4.176 924	4.140 761	4.105 125	11
12	4.398 072	4.357 572	4.317 702	4.278 450	4.239 803	4.201 749	12
13	4.489 041	4.446 118	4.403 894	4.362 355	4.321 487	4.281 275	13
14	4.564 691	4.519 600	4.475 274	4.431 698	4.388 855	4.346 728	14
15	4.627 602	4.580 581	4.534 389	4.489 007	4.444 417	4.400 600	15
16	4.679 919	4.631 187	4.583 345	4.536 369	4.490 240	4.444 938	16
17	4.723 425	4.673 184	4.623 888	4.575 512	4.528 033	4.481 430	17
18	4.759 605	4.708 037	4.657 464	4.607 861	4.559 203	4.511 465	18
19	4.789 692	4.736 960	4.685 270	4.634 596	4.584 910	4.536 185	19
20	4.814 713	4.760 963	4.708 299	4.656 691	4.606 111	4.556 531	20
21	4.835 520	4.780 882	4.727 369	4.674 951	4.623 597	4.573 277	21
22	4.852 823	4.797 412	4.743 163	4.690 042	4.638 018	4.587 059	22
23	4.867 213	4.811 131	4.756 243	4.702 514	4.649 912	4.598 403	23
24	4.879 179	4.822 515	4.767 075	4.712 822	4.659 721	4.607 739	24
25	4.889 130	4.831 963	4.776 045	4.721 340	4.667 811	4.615 423	25
26	4.897 406	4.839 803	4.783 474	4.728 380	4.674 483	4.621 747	26
27	4.904 287	4.846 310	4.789 627	4.734 199	4.679 986	4.626 952	27
28	4.910 010	4.851 709	4.794 722	4.739 007	4.684 525	4.631 237	28
29	4.914 769	4.856 190	4.798 942	4.742 981	4.688 268	4.634 763	29
30	4.918 727	4.859 909	4.802 436	4.746 265	4.691 355	4.637 665	30
31	4.922 018	4.862 995	4.805 330	4.748 980	4.693 901	4.640 053	31
32	4.924 755	4.865 556	4.807 727	4.751 223	4.696 001	4.642 019	32
33	4.927 032	4.867 681	4.809 712	4.753 077	4.697 733	4.643 637	33
34	4.928 924	4.869 445	4.811 355	4.754 609	4.699 161	4.644 969	34
35	4.930 498	4.870 909	4.812 717	4.755 875	4.700 339	4.646 065	35
36	4.931 807	4.872 123	4.813 844	4.756 922	4.701 310	4.646 967	36
37	4.932 896	4.873 131	4.814 778	4.757 786	4.702 112	4.647 709	37
38	4.933 801	4.873 968	4.815 551	4.758 501	4.702 773	4.648 321	38
39	4.934 554	4.874 662	4.816 191	4.759 092	4.703 318	4.648 823	39
40	4.935 180	4.875 238	4.816 721	4.759 580	4.703 767	4.649 237	40
41	4.935 701	4.875 717	4.817 161	4.759 984	4.704 138	4.649 578	41
42	4.936 134	4.876 113	4.817 524	4.760 317	4.704 444	4.649 859	42
43	4.936 494	4.876 443	4.817 826	4.760 593	4.704 696	4.650 089	43
44	4.936 793	4.876 716	4.818 075	4.760 820	4.704 904	4.650 279	44
45	4.937 042	4.876 943	4.818 282	4.761 008	4.705 075	4.650 436	45
46	4.937 249	4.877 131	4.818 453	4.761 164	4.705 217	4.650 564	46
47	4.937 421	4.877 287	4.818 594	4.761 293	4.705 333	4.650 670	47
48	4.937 564	4.877 417	4.818 712	4.761 399	4.705 430	4.650 757	48
49	4.937 684	4.877 524	4.818 809	4.761 487	4.705 509	4.650 829	49
50	4.937 783	4.877 613	4.818 889	4.761 559	4.705 574	4.650 888	50

PRESENT VALUE PER PERIOD

YRS	21.75% ANNUAL RATE	22.00% ANNUAL RATE	22.50% ANNUAL RATE	23.00% ANNUAL RATE	23.50% ANNUAL RATE	24.00% ANNUAL RATE	YRS
1	0.821 355	0.819 672	0.816 327	0.813 008	0.809 717	0.806 452	1
2	1.495 980	1.491 535	1.482 716	1.473 990	1.465 358	1.456 816	2
3	2.050 086	2.042 241	2.026 707	2.011 374	1.996 241	1.981 303	3
4	2.505 204	2.493 641	2.470 781	2.448 272	2.426 106	2.404 277	4
5	2.879 018	2.863 640	2.833 291	2.803 473	2.774 175	2.745 384	5
6	3.186 052	3.166 918	3.129 217	3.092 254	3.056 012	3.020 471	6
7	3.438 235	3.415 506	3.370 789	3.327 036	3.284 220	3.242 316	7
8	3.645 368	3.619 268	3.567 991	3.517 916	3.469 004	3.421 222	8
9	3.815 497	3.786 285	3.728 972	3.673 102	3.618 627	3.565 502	9
10	3.955 234	3.923 184	3.860 386	3.799 270	3.739 779	3.681 856	10
11	4.070 007	4.035 397	3.967 662	3.901 846	3.837 878	3.775 691	11
12	4.164 277	4.127 375	4.055 234	3.985 240	3.917 310	3.851 363	12
13	4.241 706	4.202 766	4.126 722	4.053 041	3.981 627	3.912 390	13
14	4.305 303	4.264 562	4.185 079	4.108 163	4.033 706	3.961 605	14
15	4.357 538	4.315 215	4.232 717	4.152 978	4.075 876	4.001 294	15
16	4.400 442	4.356 734	4.271 606	4.189 413	4.110 021	4.033 302	16
17	4.435 681	4.390 765	4.303 352	4.219 035	4.137 669	4.059 114	17
18	4.464 625	4.418 660	4.329 267	4.243 118	4.160 056	4.079 931	18
19	4.488 399	4.441 525	4.350 422	4.262 698	4.178 183	4.096 718	19
20	4.507 925	4.460 266	4.367 691	4.278 616	4.192 860	4.110 257	20
21	4.523 963	4.475 628	4.381 789	4.291 558	4.204 745	4.121 175	21
22	4.537 136	4.488 220	4.393 297	4.302 079	4.214 369	4.129 980	22
23	4.547 956	4.498 541	4.402 691	4.310 634	4.222 161	4.137 080	23
24	4.556 842	4.507 001	4.410 360	4.317 588	4.228 470	4.142 807	24
25	4.564 142	4.513 935	4.416 621	4.323 243	4.233 579	4.147 425	25
26	4.570 137	4.519 619	4.421 731	4.327 839	4.237 716	4.151 149	26
27	4.575 061	4.524 278	4.425 903	4.331 577	4.241 066	4.154 152	27
28	4.579 106	4.528 096	4.429 309	4.334 615	4.243 778	4.156 575	28
29	4.582 428	4.531 227	4.432 089	4.337 086	4.245 974	4.158 528	29
30	4.585 156	4.533 792	4.434 358	4.339 094	4.247 752	4.160 103	30
31	4.587 397	4.535 895	4.436 211	4.340 727	4.249 192	4.161 373	31
32	4.589 238	4.537 619	4.437 723	4.342 054	4.250 358	4.162 398	32
33	4.590 750	4.539 032	4.438 958	4.343 134	4.251 302	4.163 224	33
34	4.591 992	4.540 190	4.439 965	4.344 011	4.252 066	4.163 890	34
35	4.593 012	4.541 140	4.440 788	4.344 724	4.252 685	4.164 428	35
36	4.593 849	4.541 918	4.441 460	4.345 304	4.253 186	4.164 861	36
37	4.594 537	4.542 555	4.442 008	4.345 776	4.253 592	4.165 211	37
38	4.595 103	4.543 078	4.442 455	4.346 159	4.253 921	4.165 492	38
39	4.595 567	4.543 507	4.442 821	4.346 471	4.254 187	4.165 720	39
40	4.595 948	4.543 858	4.443 119	4.346 724	4.254 402	4.165 903	40
41	4.596 261	4.544 146	4.443 362	4.346 930	4.254 577	4.166 051	41
42	4.596 519	4.544 382	4.443 561	4.347 098	4.254 718	4.166 170	42
43	4.596 730	4.544 575	4.443 723	4.347 234	4.254 832	4.166 266	43
44	4.596 903	4.544 734	4.443 856	4.347 345	4.254 925	4.166 344	44
45	4.597 046	4.544 864	4.443 964	4.347 435	4.255 000	4.166 406	45
46	4.597 163	4.544 970	4.444 052	4.3 7 508	4.255 061	4.166 457	46
47	4.597 259	4.545 058	4.444 124	4.347 567	4.255 110	4.166 497	47
48	4.597 338	4.545 129	4.444 183	4.347 616	4.255 150	4.166 530	48
49	4.597 403	4.545 188	4.444 231	4.347 655	4.255 182	4.166 556	49
50	4.597 456	4.545 236	4.444 270	4.347 687	4.255 208	4.166 578	50

SECTION 6
PARTIAL PAYMENT
TO AMORTIZE $1

The *partial payment to amortize* is a basic compound interest function for a series of repeated payments or withdrawals. By convention, it is assumed that each payment is made at the end of each compounding period. Interest is earned on the remaining investment after each payment is made, and after each period interest begins to earn on the interest.

USE OF PARTIAL PAYMENT TO AMORTIZE

Partial payment to amortize is the amount that must be paid in a series of payments or withdrawals to be worth $1 today. The assumptions are:

- The payments are uniform and repeat at a regular interval.
- All interest earned is left in the account to begin earning interest on interest.
- The residual balance in the account after each payment is made earns interest at a uniform rate throughout the term of the obligation.

The tables in this section are used to solve the following types of problems:

234

1. What must be the size of future payments made in a series to meet a current obligation?
2. How long will it take for a series of repeated future payments to meet a current obligation?
3. What interest rate must be paid for a series of repeated future payments to meet a current obligation?

The present value per period tables (Section 5) are the reciprocal tables to partial payment to amortize. The payment and withdrawal examples presented in Section 5 are useful supplements to the examples in this section.

EXAMPLES

Size of Payments. Your retirement nest egg is $150,000. If you can earn 9% compounded monthly, what monthly withdrawals (i.e., payments to yourself) can you make for the next 15 years?

Turn to page 240 in the monthly compounding section and locate the column labeled 9.00%. Move down the column to the 15-year row and find the entry: 0.010143. Multiply $150,000 by 0.010143 to get $1,521.45, the desired monthly withdrawal.

Length of Time to Meet Obligation. You borrow $25,000 at 10.5% interest payable at $750 each month. How long will it take to pay off the loan?

Figure the factor for partial payment to amortize. Divide $750 by $25,000 to get 0.03. Turn to page 241 in the monthly compounding section and locate the column labeled 10.50%. Move down the column until you find the first entry that is less than 0.03. Find 0.029738 and read across to find 40 months (3 years and 4 months). It will take slightly less than 40 months to retire the obligation.

Interest Rate to Meet Obligation. You are making $600 payments each quarter on a loan for $15,000. Interest is compounded quarterly and the loan term is 9 years. What is the nominal annual rate?

Figure the factor for partial payment to amortize. Divide $600 by $15,000 to get 0.04. Start at the first page of the quarterly compounding section and begin to scan across the 36-quarter (9-year) row until you find the first entry that is greater than 0.04. On page 252 find 0.040025. Move up the column to find 8.50%. You have been paying slightly less than 8.5% on your loan. If you wish more precise results, use the interpolation technique discussed in the Introduction.

Monthly Payment to Partially Amortize Loan. You are getting an auto loan for $6,000 at 15% compounded monthly. You wish to reduce the balance of the loan to $2,000 at the end of 36 months. What monthly payment must you make to achieve your objective?

The required payment consists of two components: principal and interest. First figure the interest-only payment on the residual value. Interest at 15% on $2,000 is $300 per year. Therefore the monthly interest payment is $25.

Next figure the payment to amortize the $4,000 difference between the original loan balance ($6,000) and the desired residual value ($2,000). Turn to page 244 of the monthly compounding section and locate the column labeled 15.00%. Move down the column to the 36-month row and find 0.034665. Multiply 0.034665 by $4,000 to get $138.66, the portion of the payment required to pay down the loan.

The total monthly payment is the sum of $25 and $138.66, or $163.66.

Monthly Payments and Loan Balance. Your $50,000 home mortgage is written for 20 years (240 months) at 13.5% interest compounded monthly. What is the monthly payment? What will your loan balance be after 12 years (144 months)?

Turn to page 243 of the monthly compounding section and find the column labeled 13.50%. Move down the column to the 20-year row and find the entry: 0.012074. Multiply $50,000 by 0.012074 to get $603.70 as the monthly payment. After 12 years, the loan has 8 years remaining. The loan balance at that time is the present value per period of $603.70 for the remaining 96 monthly payments. You could look up this factor in Section 5, but since this section's factors are the reciprocal of Section 5's, find the partial payment to amortize factor in the 13.50% column at the 96-month row. It is 0.017088. Divide $603.70 by 0.017088 to get $35,329 as the balance remaining after 144 payments.

Length of Time to Partially Pay Off Loan. A $200,000 loan calls for $15,000 semiannual payments at 12% interest. How long will it take to pay off $120,000?

First figure the semiannual interest-only payment on the portion of the loan that is not paid off. This portion is $200,000 less $120,000, or $80,000. Annual interest at 12% on $80,000 is $9,600. The semiannual interest payment is $4,800.

Next find the remaining portion of the payment available to amortize $120,000; subtract $4,800 from $15,000 to get $10,200. Find the factor for partial payment to amortize; divide $10,200 by $120,000 to get 0.085. Turn to page 263 in the semiannual compounding section and locate the column labeled 12.00%. Move down the column until you find the entry closest to 0.085.

Find 0.085005 and read across to find 21 half-years (10 years and 6 months). It will take slightly more than 10 years and 6 months to retire $120,000 of the original debt.

THE FORMULA FOR PARTIAL PAYMENT TO AMORTIZE

The symbol $\dfrac{1}{A_{\overline{n}|}}$ is the widely accepted notation for partial payment to amortize. The formula for figuring table entries for partial payment to amortize is:

$$\frac{1}{A_{\overline{n}|}} = \frac{i}{(1 - V^n)}$$

where:

V^n = Present Value
i = interest rate per period
n = number of compounding periods

Note that i is the interest rate *per period*, not the nominal annual rate. You can easily find the interest rate per period by dividing the annual rate by the number of compounding periods per year. For example, a nominal annual rate of 12% compounded monthly converts to 1% per month (12% ÷ 12 months per year).

PARTIAL PAYMENT TO AMORTIZE

MOS	5.25% ANNUAL RATE	5.50% ANNUAL RATE	5.75% ANNUAL RATE	6.00% ANNUAL RATE	6.25% ANNUAL RATE	6.50% ANNUAL RATE	MOS
1	1.004 375	1.004 583	1.004 792	1.005 000	1.005 208	1.005 417	1
2	0.503 284	0.503 440	0.503 597	0.503 753	0.503 910	0.504 066	2
3	0.336 584	0.336 394	0.336 533	0.336 672	0.336 812	0.336 951	3
4	0.252 740	0.252 871	0.253 002	0.253 133	0.253 264	0.253 395	4
5	0.202 633	0.202 758	0.202 884	0.203 010	0.203 136	0.203 262	5
6	0.169 228	0.169 350	0.169 473	0.169 595	0.169 718	0.169 841	6
7	0.145 368	0.145 488	0.145 608	0.145 729	0.145 849	0.145 969	7
8	0.127 473	0.127 592	0.127 710	0.127 829	0.127 947	0.128 066	8
9	0.113 556	0.113 673	0.113 790	0.113 907	0.114 025	0.114 142	9
10	0.102 422	0.102 538	0.102 654	0.102 771	0.102 887	0.103 003	10
11	0.093 313	0.093 428	0.093 544	0.093 659	0.093 775	0.093 890	11
12	0.085 722	0.085 837	0.085 952	0.086 066	0.086 181	0.086 296	12
13	0.079 299	0.079 414	0.079 528	0.079 642	0.079 757	0.079 871	13
14	0.073 794	0.073 908	0.074 022	0.074 136	0.074 250	0.074 364	14
15	0.069 024	0.069 137	0.069 251	0.069 364	0.069 478	0.069 592	15
16	0.064 850	0.064 963	0.065 076	0.065 189	0.065 303	0.065 416	16
17	0.061 167	0.061 280	0.061 393	0.061 506	0.061 619	0.061 732	17
18	0.057 893	0.058 006	0.058 119	0.058 232	0.058 345	0.058 458	18
19	0.054 964	0.055 077	0.055 190	0.055 303	0.055 416	0.055 529	19
20	0.052 329	0.052 441	0.052 554	0.052 666	0.052 779	0.052 892	20
21	0.049 944	0.050 056	0.050 169	0.050 282	0.050 394	0.050 507	21
22	0.047 776	0.047 889	0.048 001	0.048 114	0.048 227	0.048 340	22
23	0.045 797	0.045 910	0.046 022	0.046 135	0.046 247	0.046 360	23
24	0.043 983	0.044 096	0.044 208	0.044 321	0.044 433	0.044 546	24
25	0.042 315	0.042 427	0.042 539	0.042 652	0.042 765	0.042 878	25
26	0.040 774	0.040 887	0.040 999	0.041 112	0.041 224	0.041 337	26
27	0.039 348	0.039 461	0.039 573	0.039 686	0.039 798	0.039 911	27
28	0.038 024	0.038 137	0.038 249	0.038 362	0.038 474	0.038 588	28
29	0.036 792	0.036 904	0.037 016	0.037 129	0.037 242	0.037 355	29
30	0.035 641	0.035 754	0.035 866	0.035 979	0.036 092	0.036 205	30
31	0.034 565	0.034 678	0.034 790	0.034 903	0.035 016	0.035 129	31
32	0.033 557	0.033 669	0.033 782	0.033 895	0.034 008	0.034 121	32
33	0.032 609	0.032 722	0.032 834	0.032 947	0.033 060	0.033 174	33
34	0.031 718	0.031 830	0.031 943	0.032 056	0.032 169	0.032 283	34
35	0.030 877	0.030 990	0.031 102	0.031 215	0.031 329	0.031 442	35
36	0.030 083	0.030 196	0.030 309	0.030 422	0.030 535	0.030 649	36
37	0.029 332	0.029 445	0.029 558	0.029 671	0.029 785	0.029 899	37
38	0.028 621	0.028 734	0.028 847	0.028 960	0.029 074	0.029 188	38
39	0.027 947	0.028 059	0.028 173	0.028 286	0.028 400	0.028 514	39
40	0.027 306	0.027 419	0.027 532	0.027 646	0.027 759	0.027 873	40
41	0.026 696	0.026 809	0.026 923	0.027 036	0.027 150	0.027 264	41
42	0.026 116	0.026 229	0.026 342	0.026 456	0.026 570	0.026 685	42
43	0.025 563	0.025 676	0.025 789	0.025 903	0.026 017	0.026 132	43
44	0.025 034	0.025 148	0.025 261	0.025 375	0.025 490	0.025 604	44
45	0.024 530	0.024 643	0.024 757	0.024 871	0.024 986	0.025 100	45
46	0.024 047	0.024 161	0.024 275	0.024 389	0.024 503	0.024 618	46
47	0.023 585	0.023 699	0.023 813	0.023 927	0.024 042	0.024 157	47
YRS							
4	0.023 143	0.023 256	0.023 371	0.023 485	0.023 600	0.023 715	48
5	0.018 986	0.019 101	0.019 217	0.019 333	0.019 449	0.019 566	60
6	0.016 221	0.016 338	0.016 455	0.016 573	0.016 691	0.016 810	72
7	0.014 252	0.014 370	0.014 489	0.014 609	0.014 729	0.014 849	84
8	0.012 779	0.012 899	0.013 020	0.013 141	0.013 263	0.013 386	96
9	0.011 638	0.011 760	0.011 882	0.012 006	0.012 130	0.012 255	108
10	0.010 729	0.010 853	0.010 977	0.011 102	0.011 228	0.011 355	120
11	0.009 989	0.010 114	0.010 240	0.010 367	0.010 495	0.010 624	132
12	0.009 375	0.009 502	0.009 630	0.009 759	0.009 888	0.010 019	144
13	0.008 858	0.008 987	0.009 116	0.009 247	0.009 379	0.009 512	156
14	0.008 418	0.008 548	0.008 680	0.008 812	0.008 946	0.009 081	168
15	0.008 039	0.008 171	0.008 304	0.008 439	0.008 574	0.008 711	180
16	0.007 709	0.007 843	0.007 978	0.008 114	0.008 252	0.008 391	192
17	0.007 421	0.007 556	0.007 693	0.007 831	0.007 970	0.008 111	204
18	0.007 166	0.007 303	0.007 442	0.007 582	0.007 723	0.007 866	216
19	0.006 940	0.007 079	0.007 219	0.007 361	0.007 504	0.007 649	228
20	0.006 738	0.006 879	0.007 021	0.007 164	0.007 309	0.007 456	240
21	0.006 558	0.006 700	0.006 843	0.006 989	0.007 135	0.007 284	252
22	0.006 395	0.006 538	0.006 684	0.006 831	0.006 979	0.007 129	264
23	0.006 248	0.006 393	0.006 540	0.006 688	0.006 839	0.006 991	276
24	0.006 114	0.006 261	0.006 409	0.006 560	0.006 712	0.006 865	288
25	0.005 992	0.006 141	0.006 291	0.006 443	0.006 597	0.006 752	300
26	0.005 882	0.006 031	0.006 183	0.006 337	0.006 492	0.006 649	312
27	0.005 780	0.005 931	0.006 085	0.006 240	0.006 397	0.006 556	324
28	0.005 687	0.005 840	0.005 995	0.006 151	0.006 310	0.006 470	336
29	0.005 601	0.005 755	0.005 912	0.006 070	0.006 230	0.006 392	348
30	0.005 522	0.005 678	0.005 836	0.005 996	0.006 157	0.006 321	360

MOS	6.75% ANNUAL RATE	7.00% ANNUAL RATE	7.25% ANNUAL RATE	7.50% ANNUAL RATE	7.75% ANNUAL RATE	8.00% ANNUAL RATE	MOS
1	1.005 625	1.005 833	1.006 042	1.006 250	1.006 458	1.006 667	1
2	0.504 223	0.504 379	0.504 536	0.504 692	0.504 849	0.505 006	2
3	0.337 090	0.337 230	0.337 369	0.337 509	0.337 648	0.337 788	3
4	0.253 525	0.253 656	0.253 787	0.253 918	0.254 049	0.254 181	4
5	0.203 388	0.203 514	0.203 640	0.203 766	0.203 892	0.204 018	5
6	0.169 963	0.170 086	0.170 209	0.170 331	0.170 454	0.170 577	6
7	0.146 089	0.146 210	0.146 330	0.146 451	0.146 571	0.146 692	7
8	0.128 185	0.128 304	0.128 422	0.128 541	0.128 660	0.128 779	8
9	0.114 259	0.114 377	0.114 495	0.114 612	0.114 730	0.114 848	9
10	0.103 120	0.103 236	0.103 353	0.103 470	0.103 586	0.103 703	10
11	0.094 006	0.094 122	0.094 238	0.094 354	0.094 470	0.094 586	11
12	0.086 412	0.086 527	0.086 642	0.086 757	0.086 873	0.086 988	12
13	0.079 986	0.080 101	0.080 215	0.080 330	0.080 445	0.080 561	13
14	0.074 479	0.074 593	0.074 707	0.074 822	0.074 937	0.075 051	14
15	0.069 706	0.069 820	0.069 934	0.070 048	0.070 163	0.070 277	15
16	0.065 530	0.065 644	0.065 758	0.065 872	0.065 986	0.066 100	16
17	0.061 846	0.061 960	0.062 073	0.062 187	0.062 301	0.062 415	17
18	0.058 571	0.058 685	0.058 799	0.058 912	0.059 026	0.059 140	18
19	0.055 642	0.055 755	0.055 869	0.055 983	0.056 096	0.056 210	19
20	0.053 006	0.053 119	0.053 232	0.053 346	0.053 460	0.053 574	20
21	0.050 621	0.050 734	0.050 847	0.050 961	0.051 075	0.051 188	21
22	0.048 453	0.048 566	0.048 679	0.048 793	0.048 907	0.049 020	22
23	0.046 473	0.046 587	0.046 700	0.046 814	0.046 927	0.047 041	23
24	0.044 659	0.044 773	0.044 886	0.045 000	0.045 113	0.045 227	24
25	0.042 991	0.043 104	0.043 217	0.043 331	0.043 445	0.043 559	25
26	0.041 450	0.041 564	0.041 677	0.041 791	0.041 905	0.042 019	26
27	0.040 025	0.040 138	0.040 251	0.040 365	0.040 479	0.040 593	27
28	0.038 701	0.038 814	0.038 928	0.039 042	0.039 156	0.039 270	28
29	0.037 468	0.037 582	0.037 696	0.037 809	0.037 924	0.038 038	29
30	0.036 318	0.036 432	0.036 546	0.036 660	0.036 774	0.036 888	30
31	0.035 243	0.035 356	0.035 470	0.035 584	0.035 699	0.035 813	31
32	0.034 234	0.034 348	0.034 462	0.034 576	0.034 691	0.034 805	32
33	0.033 287	0.033 401	0.033 515	0.033 630	0.033 744	0.033 859	33
34	0.032 396	0.032 510	0.032 624	0.032 739	0.032 854	0.032 968	34
35	0.031 556	0.031 670	0.031 785	0.031 899	0.032 014	0.032 129	35
36	0.030 763	0.030 877	0.030 992	0.031 106	0.031 221	0.031 336	36
37	0.030 013	0.030 127	0.030 242	0.030 356	0.030 471	0.030 587	37
38	0.029 302	0.029 416	0.029 531	0.029 646	0.029 761	0.029 877	38
39	0.028 628	0.028 743	0.028 857	0.028 973	0.029 088	0.029 204	39
40	0.027 988	0.028 103	0.028 217	0.028 333	0.028 448	0.028 564	40
41	0.027 379	0.027 494	0.027 609	0.027 724	0.027 840	0.027 956	41
42	0.026 799	0.026 914	0.027 029	0.027 145	0.027 261	0.027 377	42
43	0.026 247	0.026 362	0.026 477	0.026 593	0.026 709	0.026 825	43
44	0.025 719	0.025 834	0.025 950	0.026 066	0.026 182	0.026 298	44
45	0.025 215	0.025 331	0.025 446	0.025 562	0.025 679	0.025 795	45
46	0.024 734	0.024 849	0.024 965	0.025 081	0.025 198	0.025 314	46
47	0.024 272	0.024 388	0.024 504	0.024 620	0.024 737	0.024 854	47

YRS							
4	0.023 830	0.023 946	0.024 062	0.024 179	0.024 296	0.024 413	48
5	0.019 683	0.019 801	0.019 919	0.020 038	0.020 157	0.020 276	60
6	0.016 929	0.017 049	0.017 169	0.017 290	0.017 411	0.017 533	72
7	0.014 971	0.015 093	0.015 215	0.015 338	0.015 462	0.015 586	84
8	0.013 510	0.013 634	0.013 758	0.013 884	0.014 010	0.014 137	96
9	0.012 380	0.012 506	0.012 633	0.012 761	0.012 889	0.013 019	108
10	0.011 482	0.011 611	0.011 740	0.011 870	0.012 001	0.012 133	120
11	0.010 753	0.010 884	0.011 016	0.011 148	0.011 281	0.011 415	132
12	0.010 151	0.010 284	0.010 418	0.010 552	0.010 688	0.010 825	144
13	0.009 646	0.009 781	0.009 917	0.010 054	0.010 192	0.010 331	156
14	0.009 217	0.009 354	0.009 492	0.009 631	0.009 772	0.009 913	168
15	0.008 849	0.008 988	0.009 129	0.009 270	0.009 413	0.009 557	180
16	0.008 531	0.008 672	0.008 815	0.008 958	0.009 103	0.009 249	192
17	0.008 253	0.008 397	0.008 541	0.008 687	0.008 834	0.008 983	204
18	0.008 010	0.008 155	0.008 302	0.008 450	0.008 599	0.008 750	216
19	0.007 795	0.007 942	0.008 091	0.008 241	0.008 392	0.008 545	228
20	0.007 604	0.007 753	0.007 904	0.008 056	0.008 209	0.008 364	240
21	0.007 433	0.007 585	0.007 737	0.007 892	0.008 047	0.008 204	252
22	0.007 281	0.007 434	0.007 589	0.007 745	0.007 903	0.008 062	264
23	0.007 144	0.007 299	0.007 456	0.007 614	0.007 773	0.007 935	276
24	0.007 021	0.007 178	0.007 336	0.007 496	0.007 658	0.007 821	288
25	0.006 909	0.007 068	0.007 228	0.007 390	0.007 553	0.007 718	300
26	0.006 808	0.006 968	0.007 130	0.007 294	0.007 459	0.007 626	312
27	0.006 716	0.006 878	0.007 042	0.007 207	0.007 374	0.007 543	324
28	0.006 632	0.006 796	0.006 962	0.007 129	0.007 297	0.007 468	336
29	0.006 556	0.006 721	0.006 888	0.007 057	0.007 228	0.007 399	348
30	0.006 486	0.006 653	0.006 822	0.006 992	0.007 164	0.007 338	360

239

PARTIAL PAYMENT TO AMORTIZE

MOS	8.25% ANNUAL RATE	8.50% ANNUAL RATE	8.75% ANNUAL RATE	9.00% ANNUAL RATE	9.25% ANNUAL RATE	9.50% ANNUAL RATE	MOS
1	1.006 875	1.007 083	1.007 292	1.007 500	1.007 708	1.007 91	1
2	0.505 162	0.505 319	0.505 475	0.505 632	0.505 789	0.505 945	2
3	0.337 927	0.338 067	0.338 206	0.338 346	0.338 485	0.338 625	3
4	0.254 312	0.254 443	0.254 574	0.254 705	0.254 836	0.254 967	4
5	0.204 144	0.204 270	0.204 396	0.204 522	0.204 649	0.204 775	5
6	0.170 700	0.170 823	0.170 946	0.171 069	0.171 192	0.171 315	6
7	0.146 813	0.146 933	0.147 054	0.147 175	0.147 296	0.147 417	7
8	0.128 898	0.129 017	0.129 136	0.129 256	0.129 375	0.129 494	8
9	0.114 965	0.115 083	0.115 201	0.115 319	0.115 437	0.115 555	9
10	0.103 820	0.103 937	0.104 054	0.104 171	0.104 288	0.104 406	10
11	0.094 702	0.094 818	0.094 935	0.095 051	0.095 167	0.095 284	11
12	0.087 104	0.087 220	0.087 336	0.087 451	0.087 567	0.087 684	12
13	0.080 676	0.080 791	0.080 906	0.081 022	0.081 137	0.081 253	13
14	0.075 166	0.075 281	0.075 396	0.075 511	0.075 627	0.075 742	14
15	0.070 392	0.070 507	0.070 621	0.070 736	0.070 851	0.070 967	15
16	0.066 215	0.066 329	0.066 444	0.066 559	0.066 674	0.066 789	16
17	0.062 530	0.062 644	0.062 759	0.062 873	0.062 988	0.063 103	17
18	0.059 254	0.059 369	0.059 483	0.059 598	0.059 712	0.059 827	18
19	0.056 324	0.056 439	0.056 553	0.056 667	0.056 782	0.056 897	19
20	0.053 688	0.053 802	0.053 916	0.054 031	0.054 145	0.054 260	20
21	0.051 302	0.051 417	0.051 531	0.051 645	0.051 760	0.051 875	21
22	0.049 134	0.049 249	0.049 363	0.049 477	0.049 592	0.049 707	22
23	0.047 155	0.047 270	0.047 384	0.047 498	0.047 613	0.047 728	23
24	0.045 341	0.045 456	0.045 570	0.045 685	0.045 800	0.045 914	24
25	0.043 673	0.043 787	0.043 902	0.044 016	0.044 131	0.044 246	25
26	0.042 133	0.042 248	0.042 362	0.042 477	0.042 592	0.042 707	26
27	0.040 708	0.040 822	0.040 937	0.041 052	0.041 167	0.041 282	27
28	0.039 384	0.039 499	0.039 614	0.039 729	0.039 844	0.039 959	28
29	0.038 152	0.038 267	0.038 382	0.038 497	0.038 613	0.038 728	29
30	0.037 003	0.037 118	0.037 233	0.037 348	0.037 464	0.037 579	30
31	0.035 928	0.036 043	0.036 158	0.036 274	0.036 389	0.036 505	31
32	0.034 920	0.035 035	0.035 151	0.035 266	0.035 382	0.035 498	32
33	0.033 974	0.034 089	0.034 205	0.034 320	0.034 436	0.034 553	33
34	0.033 084	0.033 199	0.033 315	0.033 431	0.033 547	0.033 663	34
35	0.032 244	0.032 360	0.032 476	0.032 592	0.032 708	0.032 825	35
36	0.031 452	0.031 568	0.031 684	0.031 800	0.031 916	0.032 033	36
37	0.030 702	0.030 818	0.030 934	0.031 051	0.031 167	0.031 284	37
38	0.029 993	0.030 109	0.030 225	0.030 342	0.030 458	0.030 576	38
39	0.029 319	0.029 436	0.029 552	0.029 669	0.029 786	0.029 903	39
40	0.028 680	0.028 797	0.028 913	0.029 030	0.029 147	0.029 265	40
41	0.028 072	0.028 189	0.028 306	0.028 423	0.028 540	0.028 658	41
42	0.027 493	0.027 610	0.027 727	0.027 845	0.027 962	0.028 080	42
43	0.026 942	0.027 059	0.027 176	0.027 293	0.027 411	0.027 529	43
44	0.026 415	0.026 532	0.026 650	0.026 768	0.026 886	0.027 004	44
45	0.025 912	0.026 030	0.026 147	0.026 265	0.026 383	0.026 502	45
46	0.025 432	0.025 549	0.025 667	0.025 785	0.025 903	0.026 022	46
47	0.024 971	0.025 089	0.025 207	0.025 325	0.025 444	0.025 563	47

YRS							
4	0.024 530	0.024 648	0.024 767	0.024 885	0.025 004	0.025 123	48
5	0.020 396	0.020 517	0.020 637	0.020 758	0.020 880	0.021 002	60
6	0.017 656	0.017 778	0.017 902	0.018 026	0.018 150	0.018 275	72
7	0.015 711	0.015 836	0.015 962	0.016 089	0.016 216	0.016 344	84
8	0.014 264	0.014 392	0.014 521	0.014 650	0.014 780	0.014 911	96
9	0.013 149	0.013 279	0.013 411	0.013 543	0.013 676	0.013 809	108
10	0.012 265	0.012 399	0.012 533	0.012 668	0.012 803	0.012 940	120
11	0.011 550	0.011 686	0.011 823	0.011 961	0.012 099	0.012 239	132
12	0.010 962	0.011 101	0.011 240	0.011 380	0.011 522	0.011 664	144
13	0.010 471	0.010 612	0.010 754	0.010 897	0.011 041	0.011 186	156
14	0.010 056	0.010 199	0.010 344	0.010 489	0.010 636	0.010 784	168
15	0.009 701	0.009 847	0.009 994	0.010 143	0.010 292	0.010 442	180
16	0.009 397	0.009 545	0.009 694	0.009 845	0.009 997	0.010 150	192
17	0.009 132	0.009 283	0.009 435	0.009 588	0.009 742	0.009 898	204
18	0.008 901	0.009 055	0.009 209	0.009 364	0.009 521	0.009 679	216
19	0.008 699	0.008 854	0.009 011	0.009 169	0.009 328	0.009 488	228
20	0.008 521	0.008 678	0.008 837	0.008 997	0.009 159	0.009 321	240
21	0.008 363	0.008 522	0.008 683	0.008 846	0.009 009	0.009 174	252
22	0.008 222	0.008 384	0.008 547	0.008 712	0.008 878	0.009 045	264
23	0.008 097	0.008 261	0.008 426	0.008 593	0.008 761	0.008 930	276
24	0.007 985	0.008 151	0.008 318	0.008 487	0.008 657	0.008 828	288
25	0.007 885	0.008 052	0.008 221	0.008 392	0.008 564	0.008 737	300
26	0.007 794	0.007 964	0.008 135	0.008 307	0.008 481	0.008 656	312
27	0.007 713	0.007 884	0.008 057	0.008 231	0.008 407	0.008 584	324
28	0.007 639	0.007 812	0.007 987	0.008 163	0.008 340	0.008 519	336
29	0.007 573	0.007 748	0.007 924	0.008 102	0.008 281	0.008 461	348
30	0.007 513	0.007 689	0.007 867	0.008 046	0.008 227	0.008 409	360

SECTION 6

MOS	9.75% ANNUAL RATE	10.00% ANNUAL RATE	10.25% ANNUAL RATE	10.50% ANNUAL RATE	10.75% ANNUAL RATE	11.00% ANNUAL RATE	MOS
1	1.008 125	1.008 333	1.008 542	1.008 750	1.008 958	1.009 167	1
2	0.506 102	0.506 259	0.506 415	0.506 572	0.506 729	0.506 885	2
3	0.338 613	0.338 765	0.338 904	0.339 044	0.339 184	0.339 323	3
4	0.255 099	0.255 230	0.255 361	0.255 493	0.255 624	0.255 755	4
5	0.204 901	0.205 028	0.205 154	0.205 280	0.205 407	0.205 533	5
6	0.171 438	0.171 561	0.171 685	0.171 808	0.171 931	0.172 055	6
7	0.147 538	0.147 659	0.147 780	0.147 901	0.148 022	0.148 143	7
8	0.129 613	0.129 733	0.129 852	0.129 972	0.130 091	0.130 211	8
9	0.115 674	0.115 792	0.115 910	0.116 029	0.116 147	0.116 266	9
10	0.104 523	0.104 640	0.104 758	0.104 875	0.104 993	0.105 111	10
11	0.095 401	0.095 517	0.095 634	0.095 751	0.095 868	0.095 985	11
12	0.087 800	0.087 916	0.088 032	0.088 149	0.088 265	0.088 382	12
13	0.081 369	0.081 485	0.081 601	0.081 717	0.081 833	0.081 949	13
14	0.075 858	0.075 973	0.076 089	0.076 205	0.076 320	0.076 436	14
15	0.071 082	0.071 197	0.071 313	0.071 428	0.071 544	0.071 660	15
16	0.066 904	0.067 019	0.067 134	0.067 250	0.067 365	0.067 481	16
17	0.063 218	0.063 333	0.063 448	0.063 563	0.063 679	0.063 795	17
18	0.059 942	0.060 057	0.060 172	0.060 288	0.060 403	0.060 519	18
19	0.057 012	0.057 127	0.057 242	0.057 357	0.057 473	0.057 588	19
20	0.054 375	0.054 490	0.054 605	0.054 720	0.054 836	0.054 951	20
21	0.051 990	0.052 105	0.052 220	0.052 335	0.052 451	0.052 567	21
22	0.049 822	0.049 937	0.050 052	0.050 168	0.050 283	0.050 399	22
23	0.047 843	0.047 958	0.048 074	0.048 189	0.048 305	0.048 421	23
24	0.046 030	0.046 145	0.046 260	0.046 376	0.046 492	0.046 608	24
25	0.044 362	0.044 477	0.044 593	0.044 708	0.044 824	0.044 940	25
26	0.042 822	0.042 938	0.043 054	0.043 170	0.043 286	0.043 402	26
27	0.041 398	0.041 513	0.041 629	0.041 745	0.041 861	0.041 978	27
28	0.040 075	0.040 191	0.040 307	0.040 423	0.040 539	0.040 656	28
29	0.038 844	0.038 960	0.039 076	0.039 192	0.039 309	0.039 426	29
30	0.037 695	0.037 811	0.037 928	0.038 044	0.038 161	0.038 278	30
31	0.036 621	0.036 737	0.036 854	0.036 971	0.037 088	0.037 205	31
32	0.035 614	0.035 731	0.035 848	0.035 965	0.036 082	0.036 199	32
33	0.034 669	0.034 786	0.034 903	0.035 020	0.035 137	0.035 255	33
34	0.033 780	0.033 896	0.034 014	0.034 131	0.034 248	0.034 366	34
35	0.032 941	0.033 058	0.033 176	0.033 293	0.033 411	0.033 529	35
36	0.032 150	0.032 267	0.032 385	0.032 502	0.032 620	0.032 739	36
37	0.031 402	0.031 519	0.031 637	0.031 755	0.031 873	0.031 991	37
38	0.030 693	0.030 811	0.030 929	0.031 047	0.031 165	0.031 284	38
39	0.030 021	0.030 139	0.030 257	0.030 375	0.030 494	0.030 613	39
40	0.029 383	0.029 501	0.029 619	0.029 738	0.029 857	0.029 976	40
41	0.028 776	0.028 894	0.029 013	0.029 132	0.029 251	0.029 370	41
42	0.028 198	0.028 317	0.028 436	0.028 555	0.028 674	0.028 794	42
43	0.027 648	0.027 767	0.027 886	0.028 005	0.028 125	0.028 245	43
44	0.027 123	0.027 242	0.027 361	0.027 480	0.027 600	0.027 720	44
45	0.026 621	0.026 740	0.026 860	0.026 979	0.027 100	0.027 220	45
46	0.026 141	0.026 261	0.026 380	0.026 501	0.026 621	0.026 742	46
47	0.025 682	0.025 802	0.025 922	0.026 042	0.026 163	0.026 284	47

YRS							
4	0.025 243	0.025 363	0.025 483	0.025 603	0.025 724	0.025 846	48
5	0.021 124	0.021 247	0.021 370	0.021 494	0.021 618	0.021 742	60
6	0.018 400	0.018 526	0.018 652	0.018 779	0.018 906	0.019 034	72
7	0.016 472	0.016 601	0.016 731	0.016 861	0.016 991	0.017 122	84
8	0.015 042	0.015 174	0.015 307	0.015 440	0.015 574	0.015 708	96
9	0.013 944	0.014 079	0.014 214	0.014 351	0.014 488	0.014 626	108
10	0.013 077	0.013 215	0.013 354	0.013 493	0.013 634	0.013 775	120
11	0.012 379	0.012 520	0.012 662	0.012 804	0.012 948	0.013 092	132
12	0.011 807	0.011 951	0.012 096	0.012 241	0.012 388	0.012 536	144
13	0.011 332	0.011 478	0.011 626	0.011 775	0.011 925	0.012 075	156
14	0.010 932	0.011 082	0.011 233	0.011 384	0.011 537	0.011 691	168
15	0.010 594	0.010 746	0.010 900	0.011 054	0.011 209	0.011 366	180
16	0.010 304	0.010 459	0.010 615	0.010 772	0.010 931	0.011 090	192
17	0.010 054	0.010 212	0.010 371	0.010 531	0.010 692	0.010 854	204
18	0.009 838	0.009 998	0.010 160	0.010 322	0.010 486	0.010 650	216
19	0.009 650	0.009 813	0.009 976	0.010 141	0.010 307	0.010 475	228
20	0.009 485	0.009 650	0.009 816	0.009 984	0.010 152	0.010 322	240
21	0.009 340	0.009 508	0.009 676	0.009 846	0.010 017	0.010 189	252
22	0.009 213	0.009 382	0.009 553	0.009 725	0.009 898	0.010 072	264
23	0.009 100	0.009 272	0.009 445	0.009 619	0.009 794	0.009 970	276
24	0.009 000	0.009 174	0.009 349	0.009 525	0.009 702	0.009 880	288
25	0.008 911	0.009 087	0.009 264	0.009 442	0.009 621	0.009 801	300
26	0.008 832	0.009 010	0.009 188	0.009 368	0.009 549	0.009 731	312
27	0.008 762	0.008 941	0.009 121	0.009 303	0.009 486	0.009 670	324
28	0.008 699	0.008 880	0.009 062	0.009 245	0.009 429	0.009 615	336
29	0.008 642	0.008 825	0.009 009	0.009 193	0.009 379	0.009 566	348
30	0.008 592	0.008 776	0.008 961	0.009 147	0.009 335	0.009 523	360

PARTIAL PAYMENT TO AMORTIZE

MONTHLY COMPOUNDING

MOS	11.25% ANNUAL RATE	11.50% ANNUAL RATE	11.75% ANNUAL RATE	12.00% ANNUAL RATE	12.25% ANNUAL RATE	12.50% ANNUAL RATE	MOS
1	1.009 375	1.009 583	1.009 792	1.010 000	1.010 208	1.010 417	1
2	0.507 042	0.507 199	0.507 356	0.507 512	0.507 669	0.507 826	2
3	0.339 603	0.339 743	0.339 882	0.340 022	0.340 162	0.340 302	3
4	0.255 887	0.256 018	0.256 150	0.256 281	0.256 413	0.256 544	4
5	0.205 660	0.205 787	0.205 913	0.206 040	0.206 166	0.206 293	5
6	0.172 178	0.172 301	0.172 425	0.172 548	0.172 672	0.172 796	6
7	0.148 264	0.148 386	0.148 507	0.148 628	0.148 750	0.148 871	7
8	0.130 331	0.130 451	0.130 570	0.130 690	0.130 810	0.130 930	8
9	0.116 384	0.116 503	0.116 622	0.116 740	0.116 859	0.116 978	9
10	0.105 228	0.105 346	0.105 464	0.105 582	0.105 700	0.105 818	10
11	0.096 102	0.096 219	0.096 337	0.096 454	0.096 572	0.096 689	11
12	0.088 498	0.088 615	0.088 732	0.088 849	0.088 966	0.089 083	12
13	0.082 065	0.082 182	0.082 298	0.082 415	0.082 531	0.082 648	13
14	0.076 552	0.076 669	0.076 785	0.076 901	0.077 018	0.077 134	14
15	0.071 775	0.071 891	0.072 008	0.072 124	0.072 240	0.072 357	15
16	0.067 597	0.067 712	0.067 828	0.067 945	0.068 061	0.068 177	16
17	0.063 910	0.064 026	0.064 142	0.064 258	0.064 374	0.064 491	17
18	0.060 634	0.060 750	0.060 866	0.060 982	0.061 098	0.061 215	18
19	0.057 704	0.057 820	0.057 936	0.058 052	0.058 168	0.058 284	19
20	0.055 067	0.055 183	0.055 299	0.055 415	0.055 532	0.055 648	20
21	0.052 682	0.052 798	0.052 914	0.053 031	0.053 147	0.053 264	21
22	0.050 515	0.050 631	0.050 747	0.050 864	0.050 980	0.051 097	22
23	0.048 537	0.048 653	0.048 769	0.048 886	0.049 003	0.049 119	23
24	0.046 724	0.046 840	0.046 957	0.047 073	0.047 190	0.047 307	24
25	0.045 057	0.045 173	0.045 290	0.045 407	0.045 524	0.045 641	25
26	0.043 518	0.043 635	0.043 752	0.043 869	0.043 986	0.044 103	26
27	0.042 095	0.042 211	0.042 328	0.042 446	0.042 563	0.042 681	27
28	0.040 773	0.040 890	0.041 007	0.041 124	0.041 242	0.041 360	28
29	0.039 543	0.039 660	0.039 777	0.039 895	0.040 013	0.040 131	29
30	0.038 395	0.038 513	0.038 630	0.038 748	0.038 866	0.038 984	30
31	0.037 322	0.037 440	0.037 558	0.037 676	0.037 794	0.037 912	31
32	0.036 317	0.036 435	0.036 553	0.036 671	0.036 789	0.036 908	32
33	0.035 373	0.035 491	0.035 609	0.035 727	0.035 846	0.035 965	33
34	0.034 484	0.034 603	0.034 721	0.034 840	0.034 959	0.035 078	34
35	0.033 647	0.033 766	0.033 885	0.034 004	0.034 123	0.034 242	35
36	0.032 857	0.032 976	0.033 095	0.033 214	0.033 334	0.033 454	36
37	0.032 110	0.032 229	0.032 349	0.032 468	0.032 588	0.032 708	37
38	0.031 403	0.031 522	0.031 642	0.031 761	0.031 882	0.032 002	38
39	0.030 732	0.030 852	0.030 972	0.031 092	0.031 212	0.031 333	39
40	0.030 095	0.030 215	0.030 335	0.030 456	0.030 576	0.030 697	40
41	0.029 490	0.029 610	0.029 730	0.029 851	0.029 972	0.030 093	41
42	0.028 914	0.029 034	0.029 155	0.029 276	0.029 397	0.029 518	42
43	0.028 365	0.028 485	0.028 606	0.028 727	0.028 849	0.028 971	43
44	0.027 841	0.027 962	0.028 083	0.028 204	0.028 326	0.028 448	44
45	0.027 341	0.027 462	0.027 583	0.027 705	0.027 827	0.027 949	45
46	0.026 863	0.026 984	0.027 106	0.027 228	0.027 350	0.027 473	46
47	0.026 405	0.026 527	0.026 649	0.026 771	0.026 894	0.027 017	47

YRS							
4	0.025 967	0.026 089	0.026 211	0.026 334	0.026 457	0.026 580	48
5	0.021 867	0.021 993	0.022 118	0.022 244	0.022 371	0.022 498	60
6	0.019 162	0.019 291	0.019 420	0.019 550	0.019 680	0.019 811	72
7	0.017 254	0.017 386	0.017 519	0.017 653	0.017 787	0.017 921	84
8	0.015 844	0.015 979	0.016 116	0.016 253	0.016 391	0.016 529	96
9	0.014 764	0.014 904	0.015 044	0.015 184	0.015 326	0.015 468	108
10	0.013 917	0.014 060	0.014 203	0.014 347	0.014 492	0.014 638	120
11	0.013 238	0.013 384	0.013 530	0.013 678	0.013 826	0.013 975	132
12	0.012 684	0.012 833	0.012 983	0.013 134	0.013 286	0.013 439	144
13	0.012 227	0.012 379	0.012 532	0.012 687	0.012 842	0.012 998	156
14	0.011 845	0.012 001	0.012 157	0.012 314	0.012 473	0.012 632	168
15	0.011 523	0.011 682	0.011 841	0.012 002	0.012 163	0.012 325	180
16	0.011 250	0.011 412	0.011 574	0.011 737	0.011 902	0.012 067	192
17	0.011 017	0.011 181	0.011 346	0.011 512	0.011 679	0.011 847	204
18	0.010 816	0.010 983	0.011 151	0.011 320	0.011 489	0.011 660	216
19	0.010 643	0.010 812	0.010 983	0.011 154	0.011 326	0.011 500	228
20	0.010 493	0.010 664	0.010 837	0.011 011	0.011 186	0.011 361	240
21	0.010 362	0.010 536	0.010 711	0.010 887	0.011 064	0.011 242	252
22	0.010 247	0.010 424	0.010 601	0.010 779	0.010 959	0.011 139	264
23	0.010 147	0.010 326	0.010 505	0.010 686	0.010 867	0.011 049	276
24	0.010 060	0.010 240	0.010 421	0.010 604	0.010 787	0.010 971	288
25	0.009 982	0.010 165	0.010 348	0.010 532	0.010 717	0.010 904	300
26	0.009 914	0.010 098	0.010 284	0.010 470	0.010 656	0.010 844	312
27	0.009 854	0.010 040	0.010 227	0.010 414	0.010 603	0.010 792	324
28	0.009 801	0.009 989	0.010 177	0.010 366	0.010 556	0.010 747	336
29	0.009 754	0.009 943	0.010 133	0.010 324	0.010 515	0.010 707	348
30	0.009 713	0.009 903	0.010 094	0.010 286	0.010 479	0.010 673	360

PARTIAL PAYMENT TO AMORTIZE

MOS	12.75% ANNUAL RATE	13.00% ANNUAL RATE	13.25% ANNUAL RATE	13.50% ANNUAL RATE	13.75% ANNUAL RATE	14.00% ANNUAL RATE	MOS
1	1.010 625	1.010 833	1.011 042	1.011 250	1.011 458	1.011 667	1
2	0.507 983	0.508 140	0.508 296	0.508 453	0.508 610	0.508 767	2
3	0.340 442	0.340 581	0.340 721	0.340 861	0.341 001	0.341 141	3
4	0.256 676	0.256 807	0.256 939	0.257 071	0.257 202	0.257 334	4
5	0.206 420	0.206 547	0.206 673	0.206 800	0.206 927	0.207 054	5
6	0.172 919	0.173 043	0.173 167	0.173 290	0.173 414	0.173 538	6
7	0.148 993	0.149 114	0.149 236	0.149 358	0.149 479	0.149 601	7
8	0.131 050	0.131 170	0.131 290	0.131 411	0.131 531	0.131 651	8
9	0.117 097	0.117 216	0.117 335	0.117 454	0.117 574	0.117 693	9
10	0.105 936	0.106 055	0.106 173	0.106 291	0.106 410	0.106 528	10
11	0.096 807	0.096 924	0.097 042	0.097 160	0.097 278	0.097 396	11
12	0.089 200	0.089 317	0.089 435	0.089 552	0.089 670	0.089 787	12
13	0.082 765	0.082 882	0.082 999	0.083 116	0.083 233	0.083 351	13
14	0.077 251	0.077 368	0.077 484	0.077 601	0.077 718	0.077 836	14
15	0.072 473	0.072 590	0.072 706	0.072 823	0.072 940	0.073 057	15
16	0.068 294	0.068 410	0.068 527	0.068 644	0.068 761	0.068 878	16
17	0.064 607	0.064 724	0.064 840	0.064 957	0.065 074	0.065 191	17
18	0.061 331	0.061 448	0.061 564	0.061 681	0.061 798	0.061 915	18
19	0.058 401	0.058 518	0.058 634	0.058 751	0.058 868	0.058 985	19
20	0.055 765	0.055 881	0.055 998	0.056 115	0.056 232	0.056 350	20
21	0.053 380	0.053 497	0.053 614	0.053 731	0.053 849	0.053 966	21
22	0.051 214	0.051 331	0.051 448	0.051 565	0.051 683	0.051 800	22
23	0.049 236	0.049 354	0.049 471	0.049 588	0.049 706	0.049 824	23
24	0.047 424	0.047 542	0.047 659	0.047 777	0.047 895	0.048 013	24
25	0.045 758	0.045 876	0.045 994	0.046 111	0.046 230	0.046 348	25
26	0.044 221	0.044 339	0.044 457	0.044 575	0.044 693	0.044 812	26
27	0.042 798	0.042 916	0.043 034	0.043 153	0.043 271	0.043 390	27
28	0.041 478	0.041 596	0.041 714	0.041 833	0.041 952	0.042 071	28
29	0.040 249	0.040 368	0.040 486	0.040 605	0.040 724	0.040 843	29
30	0.039 103	0.039 222	0.039 340	0.039 460	0.039 579	0.039 698	30
31	0.038 031	0.038 150	0.038 269	0.038 389	0.038 508	0.038 628	31
32	0.037 027	0.037 146	0.037 266	0.037 385	0.037 505	0.037 625	32
33	0.036 084	0.036 204	0.036 324	0.036 443	0.036 564	0.036 684	33
34	0.035 198	0.035 317	0.035 437	0.035 558	0.035 678	0.035 799	34
35	0.034 362	0.034 482	0.034 602	0.034 723	0.034 844	0.034 965	35
36	0.033 574	0.033 694	0.033 814	0.033 935	0.034 056	0.034 178	36
37	0.032 828	0.032 949	0.033 070	0.033 191	0.033 312	0.033 434	37
38	0.032 122	0.032 243	0.032 364	0.032 486	0.032 608	0.032 729	38
39	0.031 453	0.031 575	0.031 696	0.031 818	0.031 940	0.032 062	39
40	0.030 818	0.030 940	0.031 061	0.031 183	0.031 306	0.031 428	40
41	0.030 215	0.030 336	0.030 458	0.030 581	0.030 703	0.030 826	41
42	0.029 640	0.029 762	0.029 884	0.030 007	0.030 130	0.030 253	42
43	0.029 093	0.029 215	0.029 338	0.029 461	0.029 584	0.029 707	43
44	0.028 571	0.028 693	0.028 816	0.028 939	0.029 063	0.029 187	44
45	0.028 072	0.028 195	0.028 318	0.028 442	0.028 566	0.028 690	45
46	0.027 596	0.027 719	0.027 843	0.027 967	0.028 091	0.028 215	46
47	0.027 140	0.027 264	0.027 387	0.027 512	0.027 636	0.027 761	47

YRS							
4	0.026 704	0.026 827	0.026 952	0.027 076	0.027 201	0.027 326	48
5	0.022 625	0.022 753	0.022 881	0.023 010	0.023 139	0.023 268	60
6	0.019 942	0.020 074	0.020 206	0.020 339	0.020 472	0.020 606	72
7	0.018 056	0.018 192	0.018 328	0.018 465	0.018 602	0.018 740	84
8	0.016 668	0.016 807	0.016 947	0.017 088	0.017 230	0.017 372	96
9	0.015 610	0.015 754	0.015 898	0.016 042	0.016 188	0.016 334	108
10	0.014 784	0.014 931	0.015 079	0.015 227	0.015 377	0.015 527	120
11	0.014 125	0.014 276	0.014 428	0.014 580	0.014 733	0.014 887	132
12	0.013 592	0.013 746	0.013 901	0.014 057	0.014 214	0.014 371	144
13	0.013 154	0.013 312	0.013 471	0.013 630	0.013 790	0.013 951	156
14	0.012 792	0.012 953	0.013 114	0.013 277	0.013 441	0.013 605	168
15	0.012 488	0.012 652	0.012 817	0.012 983	0.013 150	0.013 317	180
16	0.012 233	0.012 400	0.012 568	0.012 737	0.012 906	0.013 077	192
17	0.012 016	0.012 186	0.012 357	0.012 529	0.012 701	0.012 875	204
18	0.011 832	0.012 004	0.012 178	0.012 352	0.012 528	0.012 704	216
19	0.011 674	0.011 849	0.012 025	0.012 202	0.012 380	0.012 559	228
20	0.011 538	0.011 716	0.011 894	0.012 074	0.012 254	0.012 435	240
21	0.011 421	0.011 601	0.011 782	0.011 964	0.012 146	0.012 330	252
22	0.011 320	0.011 502	0.011 685	0.011 869	0.012 054	0.012 239	264
23	0.011 233	0.011 417	0.011 602	0.011 788	0.011 974	0.012 162	276
24	0.011 157	0.011 343	0.011 530	0.011 717	0.011 906	0.012 095	288
25	0.011 091	0.011 278	0.011 467	0.011 656	0.011 847	0.012 038	300
26	0.011 033	0.011 222	0.011 413	0.011 604	0.011 796	0.011 988	312
27	0.010 983	0.011 174	0.011 366	0.011 558	0.011 751	0.011 945	324
28	0.010 939	0.011 131	0.011 325	0.011 518	0.011 713	0.011 908	336
29	0.010 900	0.011 094	0.011 289	0.011 484	0.011 680	0.011 876	348
30	0.010 867	0.011 062	0.011 258	0.011 454	0.011 651	0.011 849	360

SECTION 6

MOS	14.25% ANNUAL RATE	14.50% ANNUAL RATE	14.75% ANNUAL RATE	15.00% ANNUAL RATE	15.25% ANNUAL RATE	15.50% ANNUAL RATE	MOS
1	1.011 875	1.012 083	1.012 292	1.012 500	1.012 708	1.012 917	1
2	0.508 924	0.509 081	0.509 238	0.509 394	0.509 551	0.509 708	2
3	0.341 281	0.341 421	0.341 561	0.341 701	0.341 841	0.341 981	3
4	0.257 466	0.257 597	0.257 729	0.257 861	0.257 993	0.258 125	4
5	0.207 181	0.207 308	0.207 435	0.207 562	0.207 689	0.207 816	5
6	0.173 662	0.173 786	0.173 910	0.174 034	0.174 158	0.174 282	6
7	0.149 723	0.149 845	0.149 967	0.150 089	0.150 211	0.150 333	7
8	0.131 772	0.131 892	0.132 013	0.132 133	0.132 254	0.132 374	8
9	0.117 812	0.117 932	0.118 051	0.118 171	0.118 290	0.118 410	9
10	0.106 647	0.106 766	0.106 884	0.107 003	0.107 122	0.107 241	10
11	0.097 514	0.097 632	0.097 750	0.097 868	0.097 987	0.098 105	11
12	0.089 905	0.090 023	0.090 140	0.090 258	0.090 376	0.090 494	12
13	0.083 468	0.083 586	0.083 703	0.083 821	0.083 939	0.084 057	13
14	0.077 953	0.078 070	0.078 188	0.078 305	0.078 423	0.078 541	14
15	0.073 174	0.073 292	0.073 409	0.073 526	0.073 644	0.073 762	15
16	0.068 995	0.069 112	0.069 229	0.069 347	0.069 464	0.069 582	16
17	0.065 308	0.065 425	0.065 543	0.065 660	0.065 778	0.065 896	17
18	0.062 032	0.062 150	0.062 267	0.062 385	0.062 503	0.062 620	18
19	0.059 103	0.059 220	0.059 338	0.059 455	0.059 573	0.059 691	19
20	0.056 467	0.056 585	0.056 703	0.056 820	0.056 938	0.057 057	20
21	0.054 084	0.054 202	0.054 319	0.054 437	0.054 556	0.054 674	21
22	0.051 918	0.052 036	0.052 154	0.052 272	0.052 391	0.052 509	22
23	0.049 942	0.050 060	0.050 178	0.050 297	0.050 415	0.050 534	23
24	0.048 131	0.048 249	0.048 368	0.048 487	0.048 606	0.048 725	24
25	0.046 466	0.046 585	0.046 704	0.046 822	0.046 942	0.047 061	25
26	0.044 930	0.045 049	0.045 168	0.045 287	0.045 407	0.045 526	26
27	0.043 509	0.043 628	0.043 747	0.043 867	0.043 986	0.044 106	27
28	0.042 190	0.042 309	0.042 429	0.042 549	0.042 669	0.042 789	28
29	0.040 963	0.041 082	0.041 202	0.041 322	0.041 443	0.041 563	29
30	0.039 818	0.039 938	0.040 058	0.040 179	0.040 299	0.040 420	30
31	0.038 748	0.038 868	0.038 989	0.039 109	0.039 230	0.039 351	31
32	0.037 746	0.037 866	0.037 987	0.038 108	0.038 229	0.038 351	32
33	0.036 805	0.036 925	0.037 047	0.037 168	0.037 289	0.037 411	33
34	0.035 920	0.036 041	0.036 162	0.036 284	0.036 406	0.036 528	34
35	0.035 086	0.035 207	0.035 329	0.035 451	0.035 573	0.035 696	35
36	0.034 299	0.034 421	0.034 543	0.034 665	0.034 788	0.034 911	36
37	0.033 556	0.033 678	0.033 800	0.033 923	0.034 046	0.034 169	37
38	0.032 852	0.032 974	0.033 097	0.033 220	0.033 343	0.033 467	38
39	0.032 184	0.032 307	0.032 430	0.032 554	0.032 677	0.032 801	39
40	0.031 551	0.031 674	0.031 798	0.031 921	0.032 045	0.032 170	40
41	0.030 949	0.031 073	0.031 197	0.031 321	0.031 445	0.031 570	41
42	0.030 377	0.030 501	0.030 625	0.030 749	0.030 874	0.030 999	42
43	0.029 831	0.029 955	0.030 080	0.030 205	0.030 330	0.030 455	43
44	0.029 311	0.029 436	0.029 560	0.029 686	0.029 811	0.029 937	44
45	0.028 815	0.028 939	0.029 065	0.029 190	0.029 316	0.029 442	45
46	0.028 340	0.028 465	0.028 591	0.028 717	0.028 843	0.028 969	46
47	0.027 886	0.028 012	0.028 138	0.028 264	0.028 391	0.028 517	47

YRS							
4	0.027 452	0.027 578	0.027 704	0.027 831	0.027 958	0.028 085	48
5	0.023 398	0.023 528	0.023 659	0.023 790	0.023 921	0.024 053	60
6	0.020 740	0.020 874	0.021 009	0.021 145	0.021 281	0.021 417	72
7	0.018 878	0.019 017	0.019 157	0.019 297	0.019 437	0.019 578	84
8	0.017 514	0.017 657	0.017 801	0.017 945	0.018 090	0.018 236	96
9	0.016 480	0.016 628	0.016 776	0.016 924	0.017 074	0.017 224	108
10	0.015 677	0.015 829	0.015 981	0.016 133	0.016 287	0.016 441	120
11	0.015 041	0.015 196	0.015 352	0.015 509	0.015 667	0.015 825	132
12	0.014 529	0.014 688	0.014 848	0.015 009	0.015 170	0.015 332	144
13	0.014 113	0.014 275	0.014 439	0.014 603	0.014 768	0.014 933	156
14	0.013 770	0.013 936	0.014 103	0.014 270	0.014 439	0.014 608	168
15	0.013 486	0.013 655	0.013 825	0.013 996	0.014 167	0.014 340	180
16	0.013 248	0.013 421	0.013 594	0.013 768	0.013 942	0.014 118	192
17	0.013 049	0.013 224	0.013 400	0.013 577	0.013 755	0.013 933	204
18	0.012 881	0.013 059	0.013 237	0.013 417	0.013 597	0.013 778	216
19	0.012 738	0.012 919	0.013 100	0.013 282	0.013 465	0.013 648	228
20	0.012 617	0.012 800	0.012 984	0.013 168	0.013 353	0.013 539	240
21	0.012 514	0.012 699	0.012 885	0.013 071	0.013 258	0.013 446	252
22	0.012 426	0.012 613	0.012 800	0.012 989	0.013 178	0.013 368	264
23	0.012 350	0.012 539	0.012 729	0.012 919	0.013 110	0.013 302	276
24	0.012 285	0.012 476	0.012 667	0.012 859	0.013 052	0.013 245	288
25	0.012 229	0.012 422	0.012 615	0.012 808	0.013 003	0.013 197	300
26	0.012 181	0.012 375	0.012 570	0.012 765	0.012 960	0.013 157	312
27	0.012 140	0.012 335	0.012 531	0.012 727	0.012 924	0.013 122	324
28	0.012 104	0.012 301	0.012 498	0.012 695	0.012 894	0.013 092	336
29	0.012 073	0.012 271	0.012 469	0.012 668	0.012 867	0.013 067	348
30	0.012 047	0.012 246	0.012 445	0.012 644	0.012 845	0.013 045	360

MOS	15.75% ANNUAL RATE	16.00% ANNUAL RATE	16.25% ANNUAL RATE	16.50% ANNUAL RATE	16.75% ANNUAL RATE	17.00% ANNUAL RATE	MOS
1	1.013 125	1.013 333	1.013 542	1.013 750	1.013 958	1.014 167	1
2	0.509 865	0.510 022	0.510 179	0.510 336	0.510 493	0.510 650	2
3	0.342 121	0.342 261	0.342 402	0.342 542	0.342 682	0.342 822	3
4	0.258 257	0.258 389	0.258 520	0.258 652	0.258 784	0.258 916	4
5	0.207 943	0.208 071	0.208 198	0.208 325	0.208 452	0.208 580	5
6	0.174 406	0.174 530	0.174 655	0.174 779	0.174 903	0.175 027	6
7	0.150 455	0.150 577	0.150 699	0.150 822	0.150 944	0.151 066	7
8	0.132 495	0.132 616	0.132 737	0.132 858	0.132 979	0.133 100	8
9	0.118 530	0.118 649	0.118 769	0.118 889	0.119 009	0.119 129	9
10	0.107 360	0.107 479	0.107 598	0.107 717	0.107 837	0.107 956	10
11	0.098 224	0.098 342	0.098 461	0.098 580	0.098 699	0.098 817	11
12	0.090 613	0.090 731	0.090 849	0.090 968	0.091 086	0.091 205	12
13	0.084 175	0.084 293	0.084 411	0.084 529	0.084 647	0.084 766	13
14	0.078 658	0.078 776	0.078 894	0.079 012	0.079 131	0.079 249	14
15	0.073 880	0.073 997	0.074 115	0.074 234	0.074 352	0.074 470	15
16	0.069 700	0.069 818	0.069 936	0.070 054	0.070 172	0.070 290	16
17	0.066 013	0.066 131	0.066 250	0.066 368	0.066 486	0.066 605	17
18	0.062 738	0.062 856	0.062 975	0.063 093	0.063 211	0.063 330	18
19	0.059 809	0.059 928	0.060 046	0.060 165	0.060 283	0.060 402	19
20	0.057 175	0.057 293	0.057 412	0.057 531	0.057 649	0.057 768	20
21	0.054 792	0.054 911	0.055 030	0.055 149	0.055 268	0.055 387	21
22	0.052 628	0.052 747	0.052 866	0.052 985	0.053 104	0.053 224	22
23	0.050 653	0.050 772	0.050 891	0.051 011	0.051 130	0.051 250	23
24	0.048 844	0.048 963	0.049 083	0.049 202	0.049 322	0.049 442	24
25	0.047 180	0.047 300	0.047 420	0.047 540	0.047 660	0.047 780	25
26	0.045 646	0.045 766	0.045 886	0.046 006	0.046 127	0.046 247	26
27	0.044 226	0.044 347	0.044 467	0.044 588	0.044 708	0.044 829	27
28	0.042 909	0.043 030	0.043 150	0.043 27.	0.043 392	0.043 514	28
29	0.041 684	0.041 805	0.041 926	0.042 047	0.042 168	0.042 290	29
30	0.040 541	0.040 662	0.040 783	0.040 905	0.041 027	0.041 149	30
31	0.039 473	0.039 594	0.039 716	0.039 838	0.039 960	0.040 083	31
32	0.038 472	0.038 594	0.038 716	0.038 839	0.038 961	0.039 084	32
33	0.037 533	0.037 655	0.037 778	0.037 901	0.038 023	0.038 147	33
34	0.036 650	0.036 773	0.036 896	0.037 019	0.037 142	0.037 265	34
35	0.035 818	0.035 941	0.036 065	0.036 188	0.036 312	0.036 436	35
36	0.035 034	0.035 157	0.035 281	0.035 404	0.035 528	0.035 653	36
37	0.034 292	0.034 416	0.034 540	0.034 664	0.034 788	0.034 913	37
38	0.033 590	0.033 714	0.033 839	0.033 963	0.034 088	0.034 213	38
39	0.032 925	0.033 050	0.033 174	0.033 299	0.033 425	0.033 550	39
40	0.032 294	0.032 419	0.032 544	0.032 669	0.032 795	0.032 921	40
41	0.031 694	0.031 820	0.031 945	0.032 071	0.032 197	0.032 323	41
42	0.031 124	0.031 250	0.031 375	0.031 501	0.031 628	0.031 755	42
43	0.030 581	0.030 707	0.030 833	0.030 959	0.031 086	0.031 213	43
44	0.030 063	0.030 189	0.030 316	0.030 443	0.030 570	0.030 697	44
45	0.029 568	0.029 695	0.029 822	0.029 949	0.030 077	0.030 205	45
46	0.029 096	0.029 223	0.029 351	0.029 478	0.029 606	0.029 735	46
47	0.028 645	0.028 772	0.028 900	0.029 028	0.029 156	0.029 285	47

YRS							
4	0.028 212	0.028 340	0.028 468	0.028 597	0.028 726	0.028 855	48
5	0.024 185	0.024 318	0.024 451	0.024 585	0.024 718	0.024 853	60
6	0.021 554	0.021 692	0.021 830	0.021 968	0.022 107	0.022 246	72
7	0.019 720	0.019 862	0.020 005	0.020 148	0.020 292	0.020 436	84
8	0.018 382	0.018 529	0.018 676	0.018 824	0.018 972	0.019 121	96
9	0.017 374	0.017 525	0.017 677	0.017 829	0.017 983	0.018 136	108
10	0.016 596	0.016 751	0.016 907	0.017 064	0.017 222	0.017 380	120
11	0.015 984	0.016 143	0.016 303	0.016 464	0.016 626	0.016 788	132
12	0.015 495	0.015 658	0.015 822	0.015 987	0.016 153	0.016 319	144
13	0.015 100	0.015 267	0.015 435	0.015 604	0.015 773	0.015 943	156
14	0.014 778	0.014 948	0.015 120	0.015 292	0.015 465	0.015 638	168
15	0.014 513	0.014 687	0.014 862	0.015 037	0.015 213	0.015 390	180
16	0.014 294	0.014 471	0.014 649	0.014 827	0.015 006	0.015 186	192
17	0.014 112	0.014 292	0.014 472	0.014 654	0.014 836	0.015 018	204
18	0.013 960	0.014 142	0.014 326	0.014 510	0.014 694	0.014 879	216
19	0.013 833	0.014 017	0.014 203	0.014 389	0.014 576	0.014 764	228
20	0.013 725	0.013 913	0.014 100	0.014 289	0.014 478	0.014 668	240
21	0.013 635	0.013 824	0.014 014	0.014 205	0.014 396	0.014 588	252
22	0.013 559	0.013 750	0.013 942	0.014 134	0.014 327	0.014 521	264
23	0.013 494	0.013 687	0.013 881	0.014 075	0.014 269	0.014 465	276
24	0.013 439	0.013 634	0.013 829	0.014 025	0.014 221	0.014 418	288
25	0.013 393	0.013 589	0.013 785	0.013 982	0.014 180	0.014 378	300
26	0.013 353	0.013 551	0.013 749	0.013 947	0.014 146	0.014 345	312
27	0.013 320	0.013 518	0.013 717	0.013 917	0.014 117	0.014 317	324
28	0.013 291	0.013 491	0.013 691	0.013 891	0.014 092	0.014 293	336
29	0.013 267	0.013 467	0.013 668	0.013 870	0.014 071	0.014 273	348
30	0.013 246	0.013 448	0.013 649	0.013 851	0.014 054	0.014 257	360

MOS	17.25% ANNUAL RATE	17.50% ANNUAL RATE	17.75% ANNUAL RATE	18.00% ANNUAL RATE	18.25% ANNUAL RATE	18.50% ANNUAL RATE	MOS
1	1.014 375	1.014 583	1.014 792	1.015 000	1.015 208	1.015 417	1
2	0.510 807	0.510 964	0.511 121	0.511 278	0.511 435	0.511 592	2
3	0.342 962	0.343 102	0.343 243	0.343 383	0.343 523	0.343 664	3
4	0.259 048	0.259 181	0.259 313	0.259 445	0.259 577	0.259 709	4
5	0.208 707	0.208 834	0.208 962	0.209 089	0.209 217	0.209 344	5
6	0.175 152	0.175 276	0.175 401	0.175 525	0.175 650	0.175 774	6
7	0.151 189	0.151 311	0.151 434	0.151 556	0.151 679	0.151 801	7
8	0.133 221	0.133 342	0.133 463	0.133 584	0.133 705	0.133 827	8
9	0.119 249	0.119 369	0.119 490	0.119 610	0.119 730	0.119 851	9
10	0.108 075	0.108 195	0.108 315	0.108 434	0.108 554	0.108 674	10
11	0.098 936	0.099 055	0.099 175	0.099 294	0.099 413	0.099 532	11
12	0.091 323	0.091 442	0.091 561	0.091 680	0.091 799	0.091 918	12
13	0.084 884	0.085 003	0.085 122	0.085 240	0.085 359	0.085 478	13
14	0.079 367	0.079 486	0.079 605	0.079 723	0.079 842	0.079 961	14
15	0.074 588	0.074 707	0.074 826	0.074 944	0.075 063	0.075 182	15
16	0.070 409	0.070 528	0.070 646	0.070 765	0.070 884	0.071 003	16
17	0.066 723	0.066 842	0.066 961	0.067 080	0.067 199	0.067 318	17
18	0.063 449	0.063 568	0.063 687	0.063 806	0.063 925	0.064 044	18
19	0.060 521	0.060 640	0.060 759	0.060 878	0.060 998	0.061 118	19
20	0.057 888	0.058 007	0.058 126	0.058 246	0.058 365	0.058 485	20
21	0.055 507	0.055 626	0.055 746	0.055 865	0.055 985	0.056 106	21
22	0.053 344	0.053 463	0.053 583	0.053 703	0.053 824	0.053 944	22
23	0.051 370	0.051 490	0.051 610	0.051 731	0.051 851	0.051 972	23
24	0.049 562	0.049 683	0.049 803	0.049 924	0.050 045	0.050 166	24
25	0.047 901	0.048 022	0.048 142	0.048 263	0.048 385	0.048 506	25
26	0.046 368	0.046 489	0.046 611	0.046 732	0.046 854	0.046 975	26
27	0.044 951	0.045 072	0.045 194	0.045 315	0.045 437	0.045 559	27
28	0.043 635	0.043 757	0.043 879	0.044 001	0.044 123	0.044 246	28
29	0.042 412	0.042 534	0.042 656	0.042 779	0.042 901	0.043 024	29
30	0.041 271	0.041 394	0.041 516	0.041 639	0.041 762	0.041 886	30
31	0.040 205	0.040 328	0.040 451	0.040 574	0.040 698	0.040 821	31
32	0.039 207	0.039 330	0.039 453	0.039 577	0.039 701	0.039 825	32
33	0.038 270	0.038 394	0.038 517	0.038 641	0.038 766	0.038 890	33
34	0.037 389	0.037 513	0.037 637	0.037 762	0.037 887	0.038 012	34
35	0.036 560	0.036 684	0.036 809	0.036 934	0.037 059	0.037 184	35
36	0.035 777	0.035 902	0.036 027	0.036 152	0.036 278	0.036 404	36
37	0.035 038	0.035 163	0.035 289	0.035 414	0.035 540	0.035 667	37
38	0.034 339	0.034 464	0.034 590	0.034 716	0.034 843	0.034 969	38
39	0.033 676	0.033 802	0.033 928	0.034 055	0.034 181	0.034 309	39
40	0.033 047	0.033 173	0.033 300	0.033 427	0.033 554	0.033 682	40
41	0.032 450	0.032 577	0.032 704	0.032 831	0.032 959	0.033 087	41
42	0.031 882	0.032 009	0.032 136	0.032 264	0.032 392	0.032 521	42
43	0.031 341	0.031 468	0.031 596	0.031 725	0.031 853	0.031 982	43
44	0.030 825	0.030 953	0.031 082	0.031 210	0.031 339	0.031 469	44
45	0.030 333	0.030 462	0.030 591	0.030 720	0.030 849	0.030 979	45
46	0.029 863	0.029 992	0.030 122	0.030 251	0.030 381	0.030 511	46
47	0.029 414	0.029 544	0.029 673	0.029 803	0.029 934	0.030 064	47

YRS							
4	0.028 985	0.029 114	0.029 245	0.029 375	0.029 506	0.029 637	48
5	0.024 987	0.025 122	0.025 258	0.025 393	0.025 530	0.025 666	60
6	0.022 386	0.022 526	0.022 667	0.022 808	0.022 949	0.023 091	72
7	0.020 581	0.020 726	0.020 872	0.021 018	0.021 165	0.021 312	84
8	0.019 271	0.019 421	0.019 572	0.019 723	0.019 875	0.020 027	96
9	0.018 290	0.018 445	0.018 601	0.018 757	0.018 914	0.019 071	108
10	0.017 539	0.017 698	0.017 858	0.018 019	0.018 180	0.018 342	120
11	0.016 951	0.017 115	0.017 279	0.017 444	0.017 610	0.017 776	132
12	0.016 486	0.016 654	0.016 822	0.016 991	0.017 161	0.017 331	144
13	0.016 114	0.016 285	0.016 457	0.016 630	0.016 803	0.016 978	156
14	0.015 813	0.015 988	0.016 163	0.016 340	0.016 516	0.016 694	168
15	0.015 568	0.015 746	0.015 925	0.016 104	0.016 284	0.016 465	180
16	0.015 367	0.015 548	0.015 730	0.015 913	0.016 096	0.016 280	192
17	0.015 202	0.015 386	0.015 570	0.015 756	0.015 942	0.016 128	204
18	0.015 065	0.015 252	0.015 439	0.015 627	0.015 815	0.016 004	216
19	0.014 952	0.015 141	0.015 331	0.015 521	0.015 711	0.015 903	228
20	0.014 858	0.015 049	0.015 241	0.015 433	0.015 626	0.015 819	240
21	0.014 780	0.014 973	0.015 167	0.015 361	0.015 555	0.015 750	252
22	0.014 715	0.014 910	0.015 105	0.015 300	0.015 497	0.015 693	264
23	0.014 660	0.014 857	0.015 053	0.015 250	0.015 448	0.015 646	276
24	0.014 615	0.014 812	0.015 010	0.015 209	0.015 408	0.015 607	288
25	0.014 576	0.014 775	0.014 975	0.015 174	0.015 374	0.015 575	300
26	0.014 544	0.014 744	0.014 945	0.015 146	0.015 347	0.015 548	312
27	0.014 517	0.014 718	0.014 920	0.015 122	0.015 324	0.015 526	324
28	0.014 495	0.014 697	0.014 899	0.015 101	0.015 304	0.015 507	336
29	0.014 476	0.014 679	0.014 882	0.015 085	0.015 288	0.015 492	348
30	0.014 460	0.014 663	0.014 867	0.015 071	0.015 275	0.015 479	360

MOS	18.75% ANNUAL RATE	19.00% ANNUAL RATE	19.25% ANNUAL RATE	19.50% ANNUAL RATE	19.75% ANNUAL RATE	20.00% ANNUAL RATE	MOS
1	1.015 625	1.015 833	1.016 042	1.016 250	1.016 458	1.016 667	1
2	0.511 749	0.511 906	0.512 063	0.512 220	0.512 377	0.512 534	2
3	0.343 804	0.343 944	0.344 085	0.344 225	0.344 365	0.344 506	3
4	0.259 841	0.259 974	0.260 106	0.260 238	0.260 370	0.260 503	4
5	0.209 472	0.209 599	0.209 727	0.209 855	0.209 982	0.210 110	5
6	0.175 899	0.176 024	0.176 148	0.176 273	0.176 398	0.176 523	6
7	0.151 924	0.152 047	0.152 170	0.152 293	0.152 415	0.152 538	7
8	0.133 948	0.134 069	0.134 191	0.134 312	0.134 434	0.134 556	8
9	0.119 971	0.120 092	0.120 212	0.120 333	0.120 454	0.120 574	9
10	0.108 794	0.108 913	0.109 033	0.109 154	0.109 274	0.109 394	10
11	0.099 652	0.099 771	0.099 891	0.100 011	0.100 130	0.100 250	11
12	0.092 037	0.092 157	0.092 276	0.092 395	0.092 515	0.092 635	12
13	0.085 597	0.085 716	0.085 836	0.085 955	0.086 074	0.086 194	13
14	0.080 080	0.080 199	0.080 318	0.080 438	0.080 557	0.080 677	14
15	0.075 301	0.075 420	0.075 540	0.075 659	0.075 778	0.075 898	15
16	0.071 122	0.071 241	0.071 361	0.071 480	0.071 600	0.071 720	16
17	0.067 437	0.067 557	0.067 676	0.067 796	0.067 916	0.068 035	17
18	0.064 164	0.064 283	0.064 403	0.064 523	0.064 643	0.064 763	18
19	0.061 237	0.061 357	0.061 477	0.061 597	0.061 717	0.061 838	19
20	0.058 605	0.058 725	0.058 846	0.058 966	0.059 086	0.059 207	20
21	0.056 226	0.056 346	0.056 467	0.056 587	0.056 708	0.056 829	21
22	0.054 065	0.054 185	0.054 306	0.054 427	0.054 548	0.054 670	22
23	0.052 093	0.052 214	0.052 335	0.052 456	0.052 578	0.052 700	23
24	0.050 287	0.050 409	0.050 530	0.050 652	0.050 774	0.050 896	24
25	0.048 628	0.048 749	0.048 871	0.048 993	0.049 116	0.049 238	25
26	0.047 097	0.047 219	0.047 342	0.047 464	0.047 587	0.047 710	26
27	0.045 682	0.045 804	0.045 927	0.046 050	0.046 173	0.046 296	27
28	0.044 369	0.044 491	0.044 615	0.044 738	0.044 861	0.044 985	28
29	0.043 147	0.043 271	0.043 394	0.043 518	0.043 642	0.043 766	29
30	0.042 009	0.042 133	0.042 257	0.042 381	0.042 505	0.042 630	30
31	0.040 945	0.041 069	0.041 194	0.041 318	0.041 443	0.041 568	31
32	0.039 949	0.040 074	0.040 199	0.040 324	0.040 449	0.040 574	32
33	0.039 015	0.039 140	0.039 265	0.039 391	0.039 516	0.039 642	33
34	0.038 137	0.038 262	0.038 388	0.038 514	0.038 640	0.038 766	34
35	0.037 310	0.037 436	0.037 562	0.037 688	0.037 814	0.037 941	35
36	0.036 530	0.036 656	0.036 783	0.036 909	0.037 036	0.037 164	36
37	0.035 793	0.035 920	0.036 047	0.036 174	0.036 301	0.036 429	37
38	0.035 096	0.035 223	0.035 351	0.035 478	0.035 606	0.035 735	38
39	0.034 436	0.034 564	0.034 691	0.034 820	0.034 948	0.035 077	39
40	0.033 810	0.033 938	0.034 066	0.034 195	0.034 324	0.034 453	40
41	0.033 215	0.033 344	0.033 472	0.033 601	0.033 731	0.033 860	41
42	0.032 650	0.032 778	0.032 908	0.033 037	0.033 167	0.033 297	42
43	0.032 111	0.032 241	0.032 370	0.032 500	0.032 631	0.032 761	43
44	0.031 598	0.031 728	0.031 858	0.031 989	0.032 120	0.032 251	44
45	0.031 109	0.031 239	0.031 370	0.031 501	0.031 632	0.031 764	45
46	0.030 642	0.030 773	0.030 904	0.031 035	0.031 167	0.031 299	46
47	0.030 195	0.030 327	0.030 458	0.030 590	0.030 722	0.030 855	47

YRS							
4	0.029 768	0.029 900	0.030 032	0.030 165	0.030 297	0.030 430	48
5	0.025 803	0.025 941	0.026 078	0.026 216	0.026 355	0.026 494	60
6	0.023 234	0.023 377	0.023 520	0.023 664	0.023 808	0.023 953	72
7	0.021 460	0.021 608	0.021 757	0.021 906	0.022 056	0.022 206	84
8	0.020 180	0.020 334	0.020 488	0.020 642	0.020 798	0.020 953	96
9	0.019 229	0.019 387	0.019 546	0.019 706	0.019 866	0.020 027	108
10	0.018 504	0.018 667	0.018 831	0.018 995	0.019 160	0.019 326	120
11	0.017 943	0.018 110	0.018 278	0.018 447	0.018 616	0.018 786	132
12	0.017 502	0.017 674	0.017 846	0.018 019	0.018 192	0.018 366	144
13	0.017 152	0.017 328	0.017 504	0.017 680	0.017 857	0.018 035	156
14	0.016 872	0.017 051	0.017 231	0.017 411	0.017 591	0.017 773	168
15	0.016 647	0.016 829	0.017 011	0.017 195	0.017 379	0.017 563	180
16	0.016 464	0.016 649	0.016 835	0.017 021	0.017 207	0.017 395	192
17	0.016 315	0.016 503	0.016 691	0.016 880	0.017 069	0.017 259	204
18	0.016 194	0.016 384	0.016 574	0.016 766	0.016 957	0.017 149	216
19	0.016 094	0.016 287	0.016 480	0.016 673	0.016 866	0.017 060	228
20	0.016 013	0.016 207	0.016 402	0.016 597	0.016 792	0.016 988	240
21	0.015 945	0.016 141	0.016 338	0.016 535	0.016 732	0.016 929	252
22	0.015 890	0.016 088	0.016 286	0.016 484	0.016 683	0.016 882	264
23	0.015 845	0.016 043	0.016 243	0.016 442	0.016 642	0.016 843	276
24	0.015 807	0.016 007	0.016 207	0.016 408	0.016 609	0.016 811	288
25	0.015 776	0.015 977	0.016 178	0.016 380	0.016 582	0.016 785	300
26	0.015 750	0.015 952	0.016 154	0.016 357	0.016 560	0.016 763	312
27	0.015 729	0.015 931	0.016 135	0.016 338	0.016 542	0.016 746	324
28	0.015 711	0.015 915	0.016 118	0.016 323	0.016 527	0.016 731	336
29	0.015 696	0.015 901	0.016 105	0.016 310	0.016 515	0.016 720	348
30	0.015 684	0.015 889	0.016 094	0.016 299	0.016 505	0.016 710	360

MOS	20.25% ANNUAL RATE	20.50% ANNUAL RATE	20.75% ANNUAL RATE	21.00% ANNUAL RATE	21.25% ANNUAL RATE	21.50% ANNUAL RATE	MOS
1	1.016 875	1.017 083	1.017 292	1.017 500	1.017 708	1.017 917	1
2	0.512 692	0.512 849	0.513 006	0.513 163	0.513 320	0.513 477	2
3	0.344 646	0.344 787	0.344 927	0.345 067	0.345 208	0.345 348	3
4	0.260 635	0.260 768	0.260 900	0.261 032	0.261 165	0.261 297	4
5	0.210 238	0.210 366	0.210 494	0.210 621	0.210 749	0.210 877	5
6	0.176 648	0.176 773	0.176 898	0.177 023	0.177 148	0.177 273	6
7	0.152 661	0.152 784	0.152 907	0.153 031	0.153 154	0.153 277	7
8	0.134 677	0.134 799	0.134 921	0.135 043	0.135 165	0.135 287	8
9	0.120 695	0.120 816	0.120 937	0.121 058	0.121 179	0.121 300	9
10	0.109 514	0.109 634	0.109 755	0.109 875	0.109 996	0.110 117	10
11	0.100 370	0.100 490	0.100 610	0.100 730	0.100 851	0.100 971	11
12	0.092 754	0.092 874	0.092 994	0.093 114	0.093 234	0.093 354	12
13	0.086 313	0.086 433	0.086 553	0.086 673	0.086 793	0.086 913	13
14	0.080 796	0.080 916	0.081 036	0.081 156	0.081 276	0.081 396	14
15	0.076 018	0.076 138	0.076 257	0.076 377	0.076 497	0.076 618	15
16	0.071 839	0.071 959	0.072 079	0.072 200	0.072 320	0.072 440	16
17	0.068 155	0.068 276	0.068 396	0.068 516	0.068 637	0.068 757	17
18	0.064 883	0.065 004	0.065 124	0.065 245	0.065 366	0.065 487	18
19	0.061 958	0.062 079	0.062 200	0.062 321	0.062 442	0.062 563	19
20	0.059 328	0.059 449	0.059 570	0.059 691	0.059 813	0.059 934	20
21	0.056 950	0.057 072	0.057 193	0.057 315	0.057 436	0.057 558	21
22	0.054 791	0.054 913	0.055 034	0.055 156	0.055 278	0.055 401	22
23	0.052 822	0.052 943	0.053 066	0.053 188	0.053 310	0.053 433	23
24	0.051 018	0.051 140	0.051 263	0.051 386	0.051 509	0.051 632	24
25	0.049 361	0.049 483	0.049 606	0.049 730	0.049 853	0.049 976	25
26	0.047 833	0.047 956	0.048 079	0.048 203	0.048 326	0.048 450	26
27	0.046 419	0.046 543	0.046 667	0.046 791	0.046 915	0.047 039	27
28	0.045 109	0.045 233	0.045 357	0.045 482	0.045 606	0.045 731	28
29	0.043 890	0.044 015	0.044 139	0.044 264	0.044 389	0.044 515	29
30	0.042 754	0.042 879	0.043 004	0.043 130	0.043 255	0.043 381	30
31	0.041 693	0.041 819	0.041 944	0.042 070	0.042 196	0.042 322	31
32	0.040 700	0.040 826	0.040 952	0.041 078	0.041 205	0.041 331	32
33	0.039 768	0.039 894	0.040 021	0.040 148	0.040 275	0.040 402	33
34	0.038 893	0.039 019	0.039 146	0.039 274	0.039 401	0.039 529	34
35	0.038 068	0.038 196	0.038 323	0.038 451	0.038 579	0.038 707	35
36	0.037 291	0.037 419	0.037 547	0.037 675	0.037 804	0.037 932	36
37	0.036 557	0.036 685	0.036 814	0.036 943	0.037 072	0.037 201	37
38	0.035 863	0.035 992	0.036 121	0.036 250	0.036 379	0.036 509	38
39	0.035 206	0.035 335	0.035 464	0.035 594	0.035 724	0.035 854	39
40	0.034 582	0.034 712	0.034 842	0.034 972	0.035 103	0.035 233	40
41	0.033 990	0.034 120	0.034 251	0.034 382	0.034 513	0.034 644	41
42	0.033 428	0.033 558	0.033 689	0.033 821	0.033 952	0.034 084	42
43	0.032 892	0.033 023	0.033 155	0.033 287	0.033 419	0.033 551	43
44	0.032 382	0.032 514	0.032 646	0.032 778	0.032 911	0.033 044	44
45	0.031 896	0.032 028	0.032 160	0.032 293	0.032 426	0.032 560	45
46	0.031 431	0.031 564	0.031 697	0.031 830	0.031 964	0.032 098	46
47	0.030 988	0.031 121	0.031 255	0.031 388	0.031 522	0.031 657	47
YRS							
4	0.030 564	0.030 697	0.030 831	0.030 966	0.031 100	0.031 235	48
5	0.026 633	0.026 773	0.026 913	0.027 053	0.027 194	0.027 335	60
6	0.024 098	0.024 244	0.024 390	0.024 536	0.024 683	0.024 830	72
7	0.022 357	0.022 508	0.022 660	0.022 812	0.022 965	0.023 118	84
8	0.021 109	0.021 266	0.021 423	0.021 581	0.021 739	0.021 898	96
9	0.020 188	0.020 350	0.020 512	0.020 675	0.020 838	0.021 002	108
10	0.019 492	0.019 658	0.019 825	0.019 993	0.020 161	0.020 330	120
11	0.018 957	0.019 128	0.019 300	0.019 472	0.019 645	0.019 818	132
12	0.018 541	0.018 716	0.018 892	0.019 068	0.019 245	0.019 422	144
13	0.018 214	0.018 393	0.018 572	0.018 752	0.018 933	0.019 114	156
14	0.017 954	0.018 137	0.018 320	0.018 503	0.018 687	0.018 872	168
15	0.017 748	0.017 933	0.018 120	0.018 306	0.018 493	0.018 681	180
16	0.017 582	0.017 771	0.017 960	0.018 149	0.018 339	0.018 529	192
17	0.017 449	0.017 640	0.017 832	0.018 023	0.018 216	0.018 408	204
18	0.017 342	0.017 535	0.017 729	0.017 923	0.018 117	0.018 312	216
19	0.017 255	0.017 450	0.017 646	0.017 842	0.018 038	0.018 235	228
20	0.017 185	0.017 382	0.017 579	0.017 776	0.017 974	0.018 173	240
21	0.017 128	0.017 326	0.017 525	0.017 724	0.017 923	0.018 123	252
22	0.017 081	0.017 281	0.017 481	0.017 681	0.017 882	0.018 083	264
23	0.017 043	0.017 244	0.017 445	0.017 647	0.017 849	0.018 051	276
24	0.017 012	0.017 214	0.017 417	0.017 619	0.017 822	0.018 025	288
25	0.016 987	0.017 190	0.017 393	0.017 597	0.017 800	0.018 004	300
26	0.016 967	0.017 170	0.017 374	0.017 578	0.017 783	0.017 987	312
27	0.016 950	0.017 154	0.017 359	0.017 564	0.017 769	0.017 974	324
28	0.016 936	0.017 141	0.017 346	0.017 552	0.017 757	0.017 963	336
29	0.016 925	0.017 131	0.017 336	0.017 542	0.017 748	0.017 954	348
30	0.016 916	0.017 122	0.017 328	0.017 534	0.017 740	0.017 947	360

PARTIAL PAYMENT TO AMORTIZE — MONTHLY COMPOUNDING

MOS	21.75% ANNUAL RATE	22.00% ANNUAL RATE	22.50% ANNUAL RATE	23.00% ANNUAL RATE	23.50% ANNUAL RATE	24.00% ANNUAL RATE	MOS
1	1.018 125	1.018 333	1.018 750	1.019 167	1.019 583	1.020 000	1
2	0.513 634	0.513 792	0.514 106	0.514 420	0.514 735	0.515 050	2
3	0.345 489	0.345 630	0.345 911	0.346 192	0.346 473	0.346 755	3
4	0.261 430	0.261 562	0.261 828	0.262 093	0.262 358	0.262 624	4
5	0.211 005	0.211 133	0.211 389	0.211 646	0.211 902	0.212 158	5
6	0.177 398	0.177 523	0.177 773	0.178 024	0.178 275	0.178 526	6
7	0.153 400	0.153 524	0.153 770	0.154 017	0.154 265	0.154 512	7
8	0.135 409	0.135 531	0.135 775	0.136 020	0.136 265	0.136 510	8
9	0.121 422	0.121 543	0.121 786	0.122 029	0.122 272	0.122 515	9
10	0.110 237	0.110 358	0.110 600	0.110 842	0.111 084	0.111 327	10
11	0.101 091	0.101 212	0.101 453	0.101 694	0.101 936	0.102 178	11
12	0.093 474	0.093 594	0.093 835	0.094 076	0.094 318	0.094 560	12
13	0.087 033	0.087 153	0.087 394	0.087 635	0.087 877	0.088 118	13
14	0.081 516	0.081 636	0.081 877	0.082 118	0.082 360	0.082 602	14
15	0.076 738	0.076 858	0.077 100	0.077 341	0.077 583	0.077 825	15
16	0.072 561	0.072 681	0.072 923	0.073 165	0.073 407	0.073 650	16
17	0.068 878	0.068 999	0.069 241	0.069 483	0.069 726	0.069 970	17
18	0.065 608	0.065 729	0.065 971	0.066 214	0.066 458	0.066 702	18
19	0.062 684	0.062 806	0.063 049	0.063 293	0.063 537	0.063 782	19
20	0.060 056	0.060 178	0.060 421	0.060 666	0.060 911	0.061 157	20
21	0.057 680	0.057 802	0.058 047	0.058 292	0.058 538	0.058 785	21
22	0.055 523	0.055 646	0.055 891	0.056 137	0.056 384	0.056 631	22
23	0.053 556	0.053 679	0.053 925	0.054 172	0.054 420	0.054 668	23
24	0.051 755	0.051 878	0.052 125	0.052 373	0.052 622	0.052 871	24
25	0.050 100	0.050 224	0.050 472	0.050 721	0.050 970	0.051 220	25
26	0.048 574	0.048 699	0.048 948	0.049 198	0.049 448	0.049 699	26
27	0.047 164	0.047 289	0.047 539	0.047 789	0.048 041	0.048 293	27
28	0.045 856	0.045 981	0.046 232	0.046 484	0.046 736	0.046 990	28
29	0.044 640	0.044 766	0.045 018	0.045 270	0.045 524	0.045 778	29
30	0.043 507	0.043 633	0.043 886	0.044 140	0.044 395	0.044 650	30
31	0.042 449	0.042 575	0.042 829	0.043 084	0.043 340	0.043 596	31
32	0.041 458	0.041 585	0.041 840	0.042 096	0.042 353	0.042 611	32
33	0.040 529	0.040 657	0.040 913	0.041 170	0.041 428	0.041 687	33
34	0.039 657	0.039 785	0.040 042	0.040 300	0.040 559	0.040 819	34
35	0.038 835	0.038 964	0.039 222	0.039 481	0.039 741	0.040 002	35
36	0.038 061	0.038 190	0.038 450	0.038 710	0.038 971	0.039 233	36
37	0.037 330	0.037 460	0.037 720	0.037 981	0.038 244	0.038 507	37
38	0.036 639	0.036 769	0.037 031	0.037 293	0.037 556	0.037 821	38
39	0.035 985	0.036 116	0.036 378	0.036 641	0.036 906	0.037 171	39
40	0.035 364	0.035 496	0.035 759	0.036 024	0.036 289	0.036 556	40
41	0.034 776	0.034 907	0.035 172	0.035 437	0.035 704	0.035 972	41
42	0.034 216	0.034 348	0.034 614	0.034 881	0.035 148	0.035 417	42
43	0.033 684	0.033 817	0.034 083	0.034 351	0.034 620	0.034 890	43
44	0.033 177	0.033 310	0.033 578	0.033 847	0.034 117	0.034 388	44
45	0.032 693	0.032 827	0.033 096	0.033 366	0.033 637	0.033 910	45
46	0.032 232	0.032 367	0.032 637	0.032 908	0.033 180	0.033 453	46
47	0.031 792	0.031 927	0.032 198	0.032 470	0.032 743	0.033 018	47
YRS							
4	0.031 371	0.031 506	0.031 778	0.032 051	0.032 326	0.032 602	48
5	0.027 477	0.027 619	0.027 904	0.028 190	0.028 478	0.028 768	60
6	0.024 978	0.025 126	0.025 424	0.025 723	0.026 024	0.026 327	72
7	0.023 272	0.023 426	0.023 736	0.024 047	0.024 361	0.024 676	84
8	0.022 057	0.022 217	0.022 538	0.022 861	0.023 186	0.023 513	96
9	0.021 167	0.021 332	0.021 664	0.021 997	0.022 333	0.022 671	108
10	0.020 500	0.020 670	0.021 011	0.021 355	0.021 700	0.022 048	120
11	0.019 992	0.020 166	0.020 517	0.020 869	0.021 224	0.021 581	132
12	0.019 600	0.019 779	0.020 138	0.020 498	0.020 861	0.021 226	144
13	0.019 296	0.019 478	0.019 844	0.020 212	0.020 582	0.020 954	156
14	0.019 057	0.019 243	0.019 615	0.019 990	0.020 367	0.020 745	168
15	0.018 869	0.019 058	0.019 436	0.019 817	0.020 199	0.020 583	180
16	0.018 720	0.018 911	0.019 295	0.019 681	0.020 068	0.020 457	192
17	0.018 602	0.018 795	0.019 184	0.019 574	0.019 965	0.020 358	204
18	0.018 507	0.018 703	0.019 095	0.019 489	0.019 885	0.020 281	216
19	0.018 432	0.018 629	0.019 025	0.019 423	0.019 821	0.020 221	228
20	0.018 372	0.018 571	0.018 970	0.019 370	0.019 772	0.020 174	240
21	0.018 323	0.018 524	0.018 925	0.019 328	0.019 732	0.020 137	252
22	0.018 284	0.018 486	0.018 890	0.019 295	0.019 701	0.020 108	264
23	0.018 253	0.018 456	0.018 862	0.019 269	0.019 677	0.020 085	276
24	0.018 228	0.018 432	0.018 839	0.019 248	0.019 657	0.020 067	288
25	0.018 208	0.018 412	0.018 822	0.019 231	0.019 642	0.020 053	300
26	0.018 192	0.018 397	0.018 807	0.019 218	0.019 630	0.020 042	312
27	0.018 179	0.018 384	0.018 796	0.019 208	0.019 620	0.020 033	324
28	0.018 168	0.018 374	0.018 787	0.019 199	0.019 612	0.020 026	336
29	0.018 160	0.018 366	0.018 779	0.019 193	0.019 606	0.020 020	348
30	0.018 153	0.018 360	0.018 773	0.019 187	0.019 602	0.020 016	360

PARTIAL PAYMENT TO AMORTIZE

QTRS	5.25% ANNUAL RATE	5.50% ANNUAL RATE	5.75% ANNUAL RATE	6.00% ANNUAL RATE	6.25% ANNUAL RATE	6.50% ANNUAL RATE	QTRS
1	1.013 125	1.013 750	1.014 375	1.015 000	1.015 625	1.016 250	1
2	0.509 865	0.510 336	0.510 807	0.511 278	0.511 749	0.512 220	2
3	0.342 121	0.342 542	0.342 962	0.343 383	0.343 804	0.344 225	3
4	0.258 257	0.258 652	0.259 048	0.259 445	0.259 841	0.260 238	4
5	0.207 943	0.208 325	0.208 707	0.209 089	0.209 472	0.209 855	5
6	0.174 406	0.174 779	0.175 152	0.175 525	0.175 899	0.176 273	6
7	0.150 455	0.150 822	0.151 189	0.151 556	0.151 924	0.152 293	7
8	0.132 495	0.132 858	0.133 221	0.133 584	0.133 948	0.134 312	8
9	0.118 530	0.118 889	0.119 249	0.119 610	0.119 971	0.120 333	9
10	0.107 360	0.107 717	0.108 075	0.108 434	0.108 794	0.109 154	10
11	0.098 224	0.098 580	0.098 936	0.099 294	0.099 652	0.100 011	11
12	0.090 613	0.090 968	0.091 323	0.091 680	0.092 037	0.092 395	12
13	0.084 175	0.084 529	0.084 884	0.085 240	0.085 597	0.085 955	13
14	0.078 658	0.079 012	0.079 367	0.079 723	0.080 080	0.080 438	14
15	0.073 880	0.074 234	0.074 588	0.074 944	0.075 301	0.075 659	15
16	0.069 700	0.070 054	0.070 409	0.070 765	0.071 122	0.071 480	16
17	0.066 013	0.066 368	0.066 723	0.067 080	0.067 437	0.067 796	17
18	0.062 738	0.063 093	0.063 449	0.063 806	0.064 164	0.064 523	18
19	0.059 809	0.060 165	0.060 521	0.060 878	0.061 237	0.061 597	19
20	0.057 175	0.057 531	0.057 888	0.058 246	0.058 605	0.058 966	20
21	0.054 792	0.055 149	0.055 507	0.055 865	0.056 226	0.056 587	21
22	0.052 628	0.052 985	0.053 344	0.053 703	0.054 065	0.054 427	22
23	0.050 653	0.051 011	0.051 370	0.051 731	0.052 093	0.052 456	23
24	0.048 844	0.049 202	0.049 562	0.049 924	0.050 287	0.050 652	24
25	0.047 180	0.047 540	0.047 901	0.048 263	0.048 628	0.048 993	25
26	0.045 646	0.046 006	0.046 368	0.046 732	0.047 097	0.047 464	26
27	0.044 226	0.044 588	0.044 951	0.045 315	0.045 682	0.046 050	27
28	0.042 909	0.043 271	0.043 635	0.044 001	0.044 369	0.044 738	28
29	0.041 684	0.042 047	0.042 412	0.042 779	0.043 147	0.043 518	29
30	0.040 541	0.040 905	0.041 271	0.041 639	0.042 009	0.042 381	30
31	0.039 473	0.039 838	0.040 205	0.040 574	0.040 945	0.041 318	31
32	0.038 472	0.038 839	0.039 207	0.039 577	0.039 949	0.040 324	32
33	0.037 533	0.037 901	0.038 270	0.038 641	0.039 015	0.039 391	33
34	0.036 650	0.037 019	0.037 389	0.037 762	0.038 137	0.038 514	34
35	0.035 818	0.036 188	0.036 560	0.036 934	0.037 310	0.037 688	35
36	0.035 034	0.035 404	0.035 777	0.036 152	0.036 530	0.036 909	36
37	0.034 292	0.034 664	0.035 038	0.035 414	0.035 793	0.036 174	37
38	0.033 590	0.033 963	0.034 339	0.034 716	0.035 096	0.035 478	38
39	0.032 925	0.033 299	0.033 676	0.034 055	0.034 436	0.034 820	39
40	0.032 294	0.032 669	0.033 047	0.033 427	0.033 810	0.034 195	40
41	0.031 694	0.032 071	0.032 450	0.032 831	0.033 215	0.033 601	41
42	0.031 124	0.031 501	0.031 882	0.032 264	0.032 650	0.033 037	42
43	0.030 581	0.030 959	0.031 341	0.031 725	0.032 111	0.032 500	43
44	0.030 063	0.030 443	0.030 825	0.031 210	0.031 598	0.031 989	44
45	0.029 568	0.029 949	0.030 333	0.030 720	0.031 109	0.031 501	45
46	0.029 096	0.029 478	0.029 863	0.030 251	0.030 642	0.031 035	46
47	0.028 645	0.029 028	0.029 414	0.029 803	0.030 195	0.030 590	47
48	0.028 212	0.028 597	0.028 985	0.029 375	0.029 768	0.030 165	48
49	0.027 798	0.028 184	0.028 573	0.028 965	0.029 360	0.029 757	49
50	0.027 402	0.027 789	0.028 179	0.028 572	0.028 968	0.029 367	50
51	0.027 021	0.027 409	0.027 800	0.028 195	0.028 592	0.028 993	51
52	0.026 655	0.027 045	0.027 437	0.027 833	0.028 232	0.028 634	52
53	0.026 304	0.026 695	0.027 088	0.027 485	0.027 886	0.028 289	53
54	0.025 966	0.026 358	0.026 753	0.027 151	0.027 553	0.027 958	54
55	0.025 641	0.026 034	0.026 431	0.026 830	0.027 233	0.027 639	55

YRS							QTRS
14	0.025 328	0.025 722	0.026 120	0.026 521	0.026 925	0.027 333	56
15	0.024 185	0.024 585	0.024 987	0.025 393	0.025 803	0.026 216	60
16	0.023 192	0.023 596	0.024 004	0.024 415	0.024 831	0.025 249	64
17	0.022 322	0.022 731	0.023 144	0.023 560	0.023 981	0.024 405	68
18	0.021 554	0.021 968	0.022 386	0.022 808	0.023 234	0.023 664	72
19	0.020 873	0.021 292	0.021 714	0.022 141	0.022 573	0.023 008	76
20	0.020 265	0.020 688	0.021 116	0.021 548	0.021 985	0.022 426	80
21	0.019 720	0.020 148	0.020 581	0.021 018	0.021 460	0.021 906	84
22	0.019 229	0.019 662	0.020 099	0.020 541	0.020 988	0.021 440	88
23	0.018 785	0.019 222	0.019 665	0.020 112	0.020 564	0.021 021	92
24	0.018 382	0.018 824	0.019 271	0.019 723	0.020 180	0.020 642	96
25	0.018 015	0.018 462	0.018 914	0.019 371	0.019 833	0.020 300	100
26	0.017 681	0.018 132	0.018 588	0.019 050	0.019 517	0.019 989	104
27	0.017 374	0.017 829	0.018 290	0.018 757	0.019 229	0.019 706	108
28	0.017 093	0.017 553	0.018 018	0.018 489	0.018 966	0.019 447	112
29	0.016 834	0.017 298	0.017 768	0.018 244	0.018 725	0.019 211	116
30	0.016 596	0.017 064	0.017 539	0.018 019	0.018 504	0.018 995	120

PARTIAL PAYMENT TO AMORTIZE

QTRS	6.75% ANNUAL RATE	7.00% ANNUAL RATE	7.25% ANNUAL RATE	7.50% ANNUAL RATE	7.75% ANNUAL RATE	8.00% ANNUAL RATE	QTRS
1	1.016 875	1.017 500	1.018 125	1.018 750	1.019 375	1.020 000	1
2	0.512 692	0.513 163	0.513 634	0.514 106	0.514 578	0.515 050	2
3	0.344 646	0.345 067	0.345 489	0.345 911	0.346 333	0.346 755	3
4	0.260 635	0.261 032	0.261 430	0.261 828	0.262 226	0.262 624	4
5	0.210 238	0.210 621	0.211 005	0.211 389	0.211 774	0.212 158	5
6	0.176 646	0.177 023	0.177 398	0.177 773	0.178 149	0.178 526	6
7	0.152 661	0.153 031	0.153 400	0.153 770	0.154 141	0.154 512	7
8	0.134 677	0.135 043	0.135 409	0.135 775	0.136 142	0.136 510	8
9	0.120 695	0.121 058	0.121 422	0.121 786	0.122 150	0.122 515	9
10	0.109 514	0.109 875	0.110 237	0.110 600	0.110 963	0.111 327	10
11	0.100 370	0.100 730	0.101 091	0.101 453	0.101 815	0.102 178	11
12	0.092 754	0.093 114	0.093 474	0.093 835	0.094 197	0.094 560	12
13	0.086 313	0.086 673	0.087 033	0.087 394	0.087 756	0.088 118	13
14	0.080 796	0.081 156	0.081 516	0.081 877	0.082 239	0.082 602	14
15	0.076 018	0.076 377	0.076 738	0.077 100	0.077 462	0.077 825	15
16	0.071 839	0.072 200	0.072 561	0.072 923	0.073 286	0.073 650	16
17	0.068 155	0.068 516	0.068 878	0.069 241	0.069 605	0.069 970	17
18	0.064 883	0.065 245	0.065 608	0.065 971	0.066 336	0.066 702	18
19	0.061 958	0.062 321	0.062 684	0.063 049	0.063 415	0.063 782	19
20	0.059 328	0.059 691	0.060 056	0.060 421	0.060 788	0.061 157	20
21	0.056 950	0.057 315	0.057 680	0.058 047	0.058 415	0.058 785	21
22	0.054 791	0.055 156	0.055 523	0.055 891	0.056 261	0.056 631	22
23	0.052 822	0.053 188	0.053 556	0.053 925	0.054 296	0.054 668	23
24	0.051 018	0.051 386	0.051 755	0.052 125	0.052 498	0.052 871	24
25	0.049 361	0.049 730	0.050 100	0.050 472	0.050 845	0.051 220	25
26	0.047 833	0.048 203	0.048 574	0.048 948	0.049 323	0.049 699	26
27	0.046 419	0.046 791	0.047 164	0.047 539	0.047 915	0.048 293	27
28	0.045 109	0.045 482	0.045 856	0.046 232	0.046 610	0.046 990	28
29	0.043 890	0.044 264	0.044 640	0.045 018	0.045 397	0.045 778	29
30	0.042 754	0.043 130	0.043 507	0.043 886	0.044 267	0.044 650	30
31	0.041 693	0.042 070	0.042 449	0.042 829	0.043 212	0.043 596	31
32	0.040 700	0.041 078	0.041 458	0.041 840	0.042 225	0.042 611	32
33	0.039 768	0.040 148	0.040 529	0.040 913	0.041 299	0.041 687	33
34	0.038 893	0.039 274	0.039 657	0.040 042	0.040 429	0.040 819	34
35	0.038 068	0.038 451	0.038 835	0.039 222	0.039 611	0.040 002	35
36	0.037 291	0.037 675	0.038 061	0.038 450	0.038 840	0.039 233	36
37	0.036 557	0.036 943	0.037 330	0.037 720	0.038 112	0.038 507	37
38	0.035 863	0.036 250	0.036 639	0.037 031	0.037 424	0.037 821	38
39	0.035 206	0.035 594	0.035 985	0.036 378	0.036 773	0.037 171	39
40	0.034 582	0.034 972	0.035 364	0.035 759	0.036 156	0.036 556	40
41	0.033 990	0.034 382	0.034 776	0.035 172	0.035 571	0.035 972	41
42	0.033 428	0.033 821	0.034 216	0.034 614	0.035 014	0.035 417	42
43	0.032 892	0.033 287	0.033 684	0.034 083	0.034 485	0.034 890	43
44	0.032 382	0.032 778	0.033 177	0.033 578	0.033 982	0.034 388	44
45	0.031 896	0.032 293	0.032 693	0.033 096	0.033 502	0.033 910	45
46	0.031 431	0.031 830	0.032 232	0.032 637	0.033 044	0.033 453	46
47	0.030 988	0.031 388	0.031 792	0.032 198	0.032 606	0.033 018	47
48	0.030 564	0.030 966	0.031 371	0.031 778	0.032 189	0.032 602	48
49	0.030 158	0.030 561	0.030 968	0.031 377	0.031 789	0.032 204	49
50	0.029 769	0.030 174	0.030 582	0.030 993	0.031 407	0.031 823	50
51	0.029 396	0.029 803	0.030 212	0.030 625	0.031 040	0.031 459	51
52	0.029 039	0.029 447	0.029 858	0.030 272	0.030 689	0.031 109	52
53	0.028 695	0.029 105	0.029 518	0.029 933	0.030 352	0.030 774	53
54	0.028 366	0.028 777	0.029 191	0.029 608	0.030 029	0.030 452	54
55	0.028 049	0.028 461	0.028 877	0.029 296	0.029 718	0.030 143	55

YRS							
14	0.027 744	0.028 158	0.028 575	0.028 996	0.029 420	0.029 847	56
15	0.026 633	0.027 053	0.027 477	0.027 904	0.028 334	0.028 768	60
16	0.025 672	0.026 098	0.026 528	0.026 961	0.027 398	0.027 839	64
17	0.024 834	0.025 266	0.025 702	0.026 141	0.026 585	0.027 032	68
18	0.024 098	0.024 536	0.024 978	0.025 424	0.025 873	0.026 327	72
19	0.023 448	0.023 892	0.024 340	0.024 792	0.025 248	0.025 708	76
20	0.022 871	0.023 321	0.023 775	0.024 233	0.024 695	0.025 161	80
21	0.022 357	0.022 812	0.023 272	0.023 736	0.024 204	0.024 676	84
22	0.021 896	0.022 357	0.022 822	0.023 292	0.023 766	0.024 244	88
23	0.021 483	0.021 949	0.022 420	0.022 895	0.023 375	0.023 859	92
24	0.021 109	0.021 581	0.022 057	0.022 538	0.023 023	0.023 513	96
25	0.020 772	0.021 249	0.021 730	0.022 217	0.022 708	0.023 203	100
26	0.020 466	0.020 948	0.021 435	0.021 926	0.022 423	0.022 923	104
27	0.020 188	0.020 675	0.021 167	0.021 664	0.022 165	0.022 671	108
28	0.019 934	0.020 426	0.020 923	0.021 425	0.021 932	0.022 443	112
29	0.019 703	0.020 200	0.020 702	0.021 208	0.021 720	0.022 236	116
30	0.019 492	0.019 993	0.020 500	0.021 011	0.021 527	0.022 048	120

QTRS	8.25% ANNUAL RATE	8.50% ANNUAL RATE	8.75% ANNUAL RATE	9.00% ANNUAL RATE	9.25% ANNUAL RATE	9.50% ANNUAL RATE	QTRS
1	1.020 625	1.021 250	1.021 875	1.022 500	1.023 125	1.023 750	1
2	0.515 521	0.515 993	0.516 465	0.516 938	0.517 410	0.517 882	2
3	0.347 177	0.347 599	0.348 022	0.348 445	0.348 867	0.349 291	3
4	0.263 022	0.263 421	0.263 820	0.264 219	0.264 618	0.265 018	4
5	0.212 543	0.212 929	0.213 314	0.213 700	0.214 086	0.214 473	5
6	0.178 903	0.179 289	0.179 657	0.180 035	0.180 413	0.180 792	6
7	0.154 883	0.155 255	0.155 628	0.156 000	0.156 373	0.156 747	7
8	0.136 878	0.137 246	0.137 615	0.137 985	0.138 355	0.138 725	8
9	0.122 881	0.123 247	0.123 614	0.123 982	0.124 350	0.124 718	9
10	0.111 691	0.112 056	0.112 421	0.112 788	0.113 155	0.113 522	10
11	0.102 542	0.102 906	0.103 271	0.103 636	0.104 003	0.104 370	11
12	0.094 923	0.095 287	0.095 652	0.096 017	0.096 384	0.096 751	12
13	0.088 482	0.088 846	0.089 211	0.089 577	0.089 944	0.090 311	13
14	0.082 966	0.083 330	0.083 696	0.084 062	0.084 430	0.084 798	14
15	0.078 190	0.078 555	0.078 921	0.079 289	0.079 657	0.080 026	15
16	0.074 015	0.074 381	0.074 749	0.075 117	0.075 486	0.075 856	16
17	0.070 336	0.070 703	0.071 071	0.071 440	0.071 811	0.072 182	17
18	0.067 069	0.067 437	0.067 807	0.068 177	0.068 549	0.068 921	18
19	0.064 150	0.064 519	0.064 890	0.065 262	0.065 635	0.066 009	19
20	0.061 526	0.061 897	0.062 269	0.062 642	0.063 016	0.063 392	20
21	0.059 156	0.059 528	0.059 901	0.060 276	0.060 652	0.061 029	21
22	0.057 004	0.057 377	0.057 752	0.058 128	0.058 506	0.058 885	22
23	0.055 042	0.055 417	0.055 793	0.056 171	0.056 550	0.056 931	23
24	0.053 246	0.053 623	0.054 001	0.054 380	0.054 761	0.055 144	24
25	0.051 597	0.051 975	0.052 355	0.052 736	0.053 119	0.053 503	25
26	0.050 077	0.050 457	0.050 838	0.051 221	0.051 606	0.051 992	26
27	0.048 673	0.049 054	0.049 437	0.049 822	0.050 208	0.050 596	27
28	0.047 371	0.047 754	0.048 139	0.048 525	0.048 913	0.049 303	28
29	0.046 161	0.046 546	0.046 933	0.047 321	0.047 711	0.048 103	29
30	0.045 035	0.045 421	0.045 809	0.046 199	0.046 591	0.046 985	30
31	0.043 983	0.044 371	0.044 761	0.045 153	0.045 547	0.045 942	31
32	0.042 999	0.043 389	0.043 780	0.044 174	0.044 570	0.044 967	32
33	0.042 076	0.042 468	0.042 862	0.043 257	0.043 655	0.044 054	33
34	0.041 210	0.041 604	0.041 999	0.042 397	0.042 796	0.043 198	34
35	0.040 395	0.040 791	0.041 188	0.041 587	0.041 989	0.042 392	35
36	0.039 628	0.040 025	0.040 424	0.040 825	0.041 229	0.041 634	36
37	0.038 903	0.039 302	0.039 703	0.040 106	0.040 512	0.040 919	37
38	0.038 219	0.038 620	0.039 022	0.039 428	0.039 835	0.040 244	38
39	0.037 571	0.037 974	0.038 378	0.038 785	0.039 195	0.039 606	39
40	0.036 958	0.037 362	0.037 768	0.038 177	0.038 589	0.039 002	40
41	0.036 376	0.036 782	0.037 190	0.037 601	0.038 014	0.038 430	41
42	0.035 823	0.036 231	0.036 641	0.037 054	0.037 469	0.037 886	42
43	0.035 297	0.035 707	0.036 119	0.036 534	0.036 951	0.037 370	43
44	0.034 797	0.035 208	0.035 622	0.036 039	0.036 458	0.036 880	44
45	0.034 320	0.034 734	0.035 150	0.035 568	0.035 989	0.036 413	45
46	0.033 866	0.034 281	0.034 699	0.035 119	0.035 542	0.035 968	46
47	0.033 432	0.033 849	0.034 269	0.034 691	0.035 116	0.035 544	47
48	0.033 018	0.033 437	0.033 858	0.034 282	0.034 709	0.035 139	48
49	0.032 622	0.033 042	0.033 466	0.033 892	0.034 321	0.034 752	49
50	0.032 243	0.032 665	0.033 090	0.033 518	0.033 949	0.034 383	50
51	0.031 880	0.032 304	0.032 731	0.033 161	0.033 594	0.034 029	51
52	0.031 532	0.031 958	0.032 387	0.032 819	0.033 254	0.033 691	52
53	0.031 199	0.031 627	0.032 057	0.032 491	0.032 928	0.033 367	53
54	0.030 879	0.031 308	0.031 741	0.032 177	0.032 615	0.033 056	54
55	0.030 572	0.031 003	0.031 437	0.031 875	0.032 315	0.032 759	55

YRS							
14	0.030 277	0.030 710	0.031 146	0.031 585	0.032 028	0.032 473	56
15	0.029 205	0.029 645	0.030 089	0.030 535	0.030 985	0.031 438	60
16	0.028 282	0.028 730	0.029 180	0.029 634	0.030 091	0.030 552	64
17	0.027 482	0.027 936	0.028 394	0.028 855	0.029 319	0.029 787	68
18	0.026 784	0.027 245	0.027 709	0.028 177	0.028 649	0.029 124	72
19	0.026 171	0.026 639	0.027 110	0.027 585	0.028 063	0.028 545	76
20	0.025 631	0.026 105	0.026 582	0.027 064	0.027 549	0.028 038	80
21	0.025 152	0.025 632	0.026 116	0.026 604	0.027 096	0.027 591	84
22	0.024 726	0.025 213	0.025 703	0.026 197	0.026 695	0.027 197	88
23	0.024 347	0.024 839	0.025 335	0.025 836	0.026 340	0.026 848	92
24	0.024 007	0.024 505	0.025 007	0.025 514	0.026 024	0.026 538	96
25	0.023 702	0.024 206	0.024 714	0.025 226	0.025 742	0.026 261	100
26	0.023 428	0.023 937	0.024 451	0.024 968	0.025 490	0.026 015	104
27	0.023 181	0.023 696	0.024 214	0.024 737	0.025 264	0.025 794	108
28	0.022 958	0.023 478	0.024 002	0.024 530	0.025 061	0.025 597	112
29	0.022 756	0.023 281	0.023 810	0.024 343	0.024 879	0.025 420	116
30	0.022 573	0.023 103	0.023 636	0.024 174	0.024 715	0.025 261	120

PARTIAL PAYMENT TO AMORTIZE

QUARTERLY COMPOUNDING

QTRS	9.75% ANNUAL RATE	10.00% ANNUAL RATE	10.25% ANNUAL RATE	10.50% ANNUAL RATE	10.75% ANNUAL RATE	11.00% ANNUAL RATE	QTRS
1	1.024 375	1.025 000	1.025 625	1.026 250	1.026 875	1.027 500	1
2	0.518 355	0.518 827	0.519 300	0.519 773	0.520 245	0.520 718	2
3	0.349 714	0.350 137	0.350 561	0.350 984	0.351 408	0.351 832	3
4	0.265 418	0.265 818	0.266 218	0.266 619	0.267 020	0.267 421	4
5	0.214 860	0.215 247	0.215 634	0.216 022	0.216 410	0.216 798	5
6	0.181 171	0.181 550	0.181 930	0.182 310	0.182 690	0.183 071	6
7	0.157 121	0.157 495	0.157 870	0.158 246	0.158 621	0.158 997	7
8	0.139 096	0.139 467	0.139 839	0.140 212	0.140 585	0.140 958	8
9	0.125 087	0.125 457	0.125 827	0.126 198	0.126 569	0.126 941	9
10	0.113 890	0.114 259	0.114 628	0.114 998	0.115 369	0.115 740	10
11	0.104 738	0.105 106	0.105 475	0.105 845	0.106 215	0.106 586	11
12	0.097 119	0.097 487	0.097 856	0.098 226	0.098 597	0.098 969	12
13	0.090 679	0.091 048	0.091 418	0.091 789	0.092 160	0.092 533	13
14	0.085 167	0.085 537	0.085 907	0.086 279	0.086 651	0.087 025	14
15	0.080 396	0.080 766	0.081 138	0.081 511	0.081 885	0.082 259	15
16	0.076 227	0.076 599	0.076 972	0.077 346	0.077 721	0.078 097	16
17	0.072 554	0.072 928	0.073 302	0.073 678	0.074 054	0.074 432	17
18	0.069 295	0.069 670	0.070 046	0.070 423	0.070 801	0.071 181	18
19	0.066 384	0.066 761	0.067 138	0.067 517	0.067 897	0.068 278	19
20	0.063 769	0.064 147	0.064 526	0.064 907	0.065 289	0.065 672	20
21	0.061 407	0.061 787	0.062 168	0.062 551	0.062 934	0.063 319	21
22	0.059 265	0.059 647	0.060 030	0.060 414	0.060 799	0.061 186	22
23	0.057 313	0.057 696	0.058 081	0.058 467	0.058 855	0.059 244	23
24	0.055 527	0.055 913	0.056 300	0.056 688	0.057 078	0.057 469	24
25	0.053 889	0.054 276	0.054 665	0.055 055	0.055 447	0.055 840	25
26	0.052 380	0.052 769	0.053 160	0.053 552	0.053 946	0.054 341	26
27	0.050 986	0.051 377	0.051 770	0.052 164	0.052 560	0.052 958	27
28	0.049 695	0.050 088	0.050 483	0.050 879	0.051 278	0.051 677	28
29	0.048 496	0.048 891	0.049 288	0.049 687	0.050 087	0.050 489	29
30	0.047 380	0.047 778	0.048 177	0.048 577	0.048 980	0.049 384	30
31	0.046 340	0.046 739	0.047 140	0.047 543	0.047 948	0.048 355	31
32	0.045 367	0.045 768	0.046 172	0.046 577	0.046 984	0.047 393	32
33	0.044 456	0.044 859	0.045 265	0.045 672	0.046 081	0.046 493	33
34	0.043 601	0.044 007	0.044 414	0.044 824	0.045 235	0.045 649	34
35	0.042 798	0.043 206	0.043 615	0.044 027	0.044 441	0.044 856	35
36	0.042 042	0.042 452	0.042 863	0.043 277	0.043 693	0.044 111	36
37	0.041 329	0.041 741	0.042 155	0.042 571	0.042 989	0.043 410	37
38	0.040 656	0.041 070	0.041 486	0.041 905	0.042 325	0.042 748	38
39	0.040 020	0.040 436	0.040 854	0.041 275	0.041 698	0.042 123	39
40	0.039 418	0.039 836	0.040 257	0.040 679	0.041 104	0.041 532	40
41	0.038 848	0.039 268	0.039 690	0.040 115	0.040 543	0.040 972	41
42	0.038 306	0.038 729	0.039 153	0.039 581	0.040 010	0.040 442	42
43	0.037 792	0.038 217	0.038 644	0.039 073	0.039 505	0.039 939	43
44	0.037 304	0.037 730	0.038 159	0.038 591	0.039 025	0.039 461	44
45	0.036 839	0.037 268	0.037 699	0.038 132	0.038 568	0.039 007	45
46	0.036 396	0.036 827	0.037 260	0.037 696	0.038 134	0.038 575	46
47	0.035 974	0.036 407	0.036 842	0.037 280	0.037 721	0.038 164	47
48	0.035 571	0.036 006	0.036 444	0.036 884	0.037 326	0.037 772	48
49	0.035 187	0.035 623	0.036 063	0.036 505	0.036 950	0.037 398	49
50	0.034 819	0.035 258	0.035 700	0.036 144	0.036 591	0.037 041	50
51	0.034 468	0.034 909	0.035 353	0.035 799	0.036 248	0.036 700	51
52	0.034 131	0.034 574	0.035 020	0.035 469	0.035 920	0.036 374	52
53	0.033 809	0.034 254	0.034 702	0.035 153	0.035 607	0.036 063	53
54	0.033 501	0.033 948	0.034 398	0.034 851	0.035 307	0.035 765	54
55	0.033 205	0.033 654	0.034 106	0.034 561	0.035 019	0.035 480	55

YRS	9.75%	10.00%	10.25%	10.50%	10.75%	11.00%	QTRS
14	0.032 921	0.033 372	0.033 827	0.034 284	0.034 743	0.035 206	56
15	0.031 894	0.032 353	0.032 816	0.033 281	0.033 749	0.034 220	60
16	0.031 016	0.031 482	0.031 953	0.032 426	0.032 902	0.033 381	64
17	0.030 259	0.030 733	0.031 211	0.031 692	0.032 176	0.032 663	68
18	0.029 602	0.030 084	0.030 569	0.031 058	0.031 549	0.032 044	72
19	0.029 031	0.029 520	0.030 012	0.030 508	0.031 007	0.031 509	76
20	0.028 530	0.029 026	0.029 525	0.030 028	0.030 534	0.031 043	80
21	0.028 090	0.028 593	0.029 099	0.029 609	0.030 121	0.030 637	84
22	0.027 703	0.028 212	0.028 724	0.029 240	0.029 760	0.030 282	88
23	0.027 360	0.027 875	0.028 394	0.028 916	0.029 442	0.029 970	92
24	0.027 055	0.027 577	0.028 101	0.028 630	0.029 161	0.029 696	96
25	0.026 785	0.027 312	0.027 842	0.028 376	0.028 914	0.029 454	100
26	0.026 544	0.027 076	0.027 612	0.028 152	0.028 695	0.029 241	104
27	0.026 329	0.026 867	0.027 408	0.027 952	0.028 500	0.029 051	108
28	0.026 136	0.026 679	0.027 225	0.027 775	0.028 328	0.028 884	112
29	0.025 964	0.026 512	0.027 063	0.027 617	0.028 175	0.028 735	116
30	0.025 810	0.026 362	0.026 917	0.027 476	0.028 038	0.028 603	120

QTRS	11.25% ANNUAL RATE	11.50% ANNUAL RATE	11.75% ANNUAL RATE	12.00% ANNUAL RATE	12.25% ANNUAL RATE	12.50% ANNUAL RATE	QTRS
1	1.028 125	1.028 750	1.029 375	1.030 000	1.030 625	1.031 250	1
2	0.521 191	0.521 664	0.522 138	0.522 611	0.523 084	0.523 558	2
3	0.352 257	0.352 681	0.353 106	0.353 530	0.353 955	0.354 380	3
4	0.267 822	0.268 223	0.268 625	0.269 027	0.269 429	0.269 832	4
5	0.217 187	0.217 576	0.217 965	0.218 355	0.218 744	0.219 134	5
6	0.183 452	0.183 833	0.184 215	0.184 598	0.184 980	0.185 363	6
7	0.159 374	0.159 751	0.160 128	0.160 506	0.160 885	0.161 263	7
8	0.141 332	0.141 706	0.142 081	0.142 456	0.142 832	0.143 209	8
9	0.127 313	0.127 686	0.128 060	0.128 434	0.128 808	0.129 184	9
10	0.116 111	0.116 484	0.116 857	0.117 231	0.117 605	0.117 980	10
11	0.106 958	0.107 331	0.107 704	0.108 077	0.108 452	0.108 827	11
12	0.099 341	0.099 714	0.100 088	0.100 462	0.100 837	0.101 213	12
13	0.092 906	0.093 279	0.093 654	0.094 030	0.094 406	0.094 783	13
14	0.087 399	0.087 774	0.088 150	0.088 526	0.088 904	0.089 282	14
15	0.082 635	0.083 011	0.083 388	0.083 767	0.084 146	0.084 526	15
16	0.078 474	0.078 852	0.079 231	0.079 611	0.079 992	0.080 374	16
17	0.074 810	0.075 190	0.075 571	0.075 953	0.076 335	0.076 719	17
18	0.071 561	0.071 942	0.072 325	0.072 709	0.073 093	0.073 479	18
19	0.068 660	0.069 044	0.069 428	0.069 814	0.070 201	0.070 589	19
20	0.066 056	0.066 441	0.066 828	0.067 216	0.067 605	0.067 995	20
21	0.063 706	0.064 093	0.064 482	0.064 872	0.065 263	0.065 656	21
22	0.061 575	0.061 964	0.062 355	0.062 747	0.063 141	0.063 536	22
23	0.059 634	0.060 026	0.060 419	0.060 814	0.061 210	0.061 607	23
24	0.057 861	0.058 255	0.058 651	0.059 047	0.059 446	0.059 845	24
25	0.056 235	0.056 631	0.057 029	0.057 428	0.057 829	0.058 231	25
26	0.054 738	0.055 137	0.055 537	0.055 938	0.056 341	0.056 746	26
27	0.053 357	0.053 758	0.054 160	0.054 564	0.054 970	0.055 377	27
28	0.052 079	0.052 482	0.052 887	0.053 293	0.053 701	0.054 111	28
29	0.050 893	0.051 299	0.051 706	0.052 115	0.052 525	0.052 937	29
30	0.049 791	0.050 198	0.050 608	0.051 019	0.051 432	0.051 847	30
31	0.048 763	0.049 173	0.049 585	0.049 999	0.050 414	0.050 832	31
32	0.047 803	0.048 216	0.048 630	0.049 047	0.049 465	0.049 885	32
33	0.046 906	0.047 321	0.047 737	0.048 156	0.048 577	0.048 999	33
34	0.046 064	0.046 481	0.046 901	0.047 322	0.047 745	0.048 170	34
35	0.045 274	0.045 694	0.046 116	0.046 539	0.046 965	0.047 393	35
36	0.044 531	0.044 954	0.045 378	0.045 804	0.046 232	0.046 662	36
37	0.043 832	0.044 256	0.044 683	0.045 112	0.045 542	0.045 975	37
38	0.043 172	0.043 599	0.044 028	0.044 459	0.044 893	0.045 328	38
39	0.042 550	0.042 979	0.043 410	0.043 844	0.044 280	0.044 717	39
40	0.041 961	0.042 393	0.042 826	0.043 262	0.043 701	0.044 141	40
41	0.041 404	0.041 838	0.042 274	0.042 712	0.043 153	0.043 596	41
42	0.040 876	0.041 312	0.041 751	0.042 192	0.042 635	0.043 080	42
43	0.040 375	0.040 814	0.041 255	0.041 698	0.042 144	0.042 592	43
44	0.039 900	0.040 341	0.040 784	0.041 230	0.041 678	0.042 128	44
45	0.039 448	0.039 891	0.040 337	0.040 785	0.041 236	0.041 688	45
46	0.039 018	0.039 464	0.039 912	0.040 363	0.040 815	0.041 271	46
47	0.038 609	0.039 057	0.039 508	0.039 961	0.040 416	0.040 874	47
48	0.038 219	0.038 670	0.039 122	0.039 578	0.040 036	0.040 496	48
49	0.037 848	0.038 300	0.038 756	0.039 213	0.039 673	0.040 136	49
50	0.037 493	0.037 948	0.038 406	0.038 865	0.039 328	0.039 793	50
51	0.037 155	0.037 612	0.038 072	0.038 534	0.038 999	0.039 466	51
52	0.036 831	0.037 291	0.037 753	0.038 217	0.038 684	0.039 154	52
53	0.036 522	0.036 984	0.037 448	0.037 915	0.038 384	0.038 856	53
54	0.036 226	0.036 690	0.037 156	0.037 626	0.038 097	0.038 572	54
55	0.035 943	0.036 409	0.036 878	0.037 349	0.037 823	0.038 300	55

YRS							QTRS
14	0.035 672	0.036 140	0.036 611	0.037 084	0.037 561	0.038 040	56
15	0.034 694	0.035 171	0.035 651	0.036 133	0.036 618	0.037 106	60
16	0.033 863	0.034 349	0.034 837	0.035 328	0.035 821	0.036 318	64
17	0.033 153	0.033 646	0.034 142	0.034 642	0.035 144	0.035 648	68
18	0.032 542	0.033 043	0.033 547	0.034 054	0.034 564	0.035 077	72
19	0.032 014	0.032 523	0.033 034	0.033 548	0.034 066	0.034 586	76
20	0.031 556	0.032 071	0.032 590	0.033 112	0.033 636	0.034 164	80
21	0.031 157	0.031 679	0.032 205	0.032 733	0.033 265	0.033 799	84
22	0.030 808	0.031 337	0.031 869	0.032 404	0.032 942	0.033 482	88
23	0.030 502	0.031 038	0.031 576	0.032 117	0.032 661	0.033 208	92
24	0.030 234	0.030 775	0.031 319	0.031 866	0.032 416	0.032 969	96
25	0.029 998	0.030 545	0.031 094	0.031 647	0.032 202	0.032 760	100
26	0.029 790	0.030 342	0.030 896	0.031 454	0.032 015	0.032 578	104
27	0.029 606	0.030 163	0.030 722	0.031 285	0.031 850	0.032 418	108
28	0.029 443	0.030 005	0.030 569	0.031 136	0.031 706	0.032 278	112
29	0.029 299	0.029 865	0.030 434	0.031 005	0.031 579	0.032 156	116
30	0.029 171	0.029 741	0.030 314	0.030 890	0.031 468	0.032 048	120

PARTIAL PAYMENT TO AMORTIZE

QTRS	12.75% ANNUAL RATE	13.00% ANNUAL RATE	13.25% ANNUAL RATE	13.50% ANNUAL RATE	13.75% ANNUAL RATE	14.00% ANNUAL RATE	QTRS
1	1.031 875	1.032 500	1.033 125	1.033 750	1.034 375	1.035 000	1
2	0.524 031	0.524 505	0.524 979	0.525 453	0.525 926	0.526 400	2
3	0.354 806	0.355 231	0.355 657	0.356 082	0.356 508	0.356 934	3
4	0.270 234	0.270 637	0.271 040	0.271 444	0.271 847	0.272 251	4
5	0.219 525	0.219 916	0.220 307	0.220 698	0.221 089	0.221 481	5
6	0.185 746	0.186 130	0.186 514	0.186 898	0.187 283	0.187 668	6
7	0.161 642	0.162 022	0.162 402	0.162 782	0.163 163	0.163 544	7
8	0.143 585	0.143 963	0.144 340	0.144 719	0.145 097	0.145 477	8
9	0.129 559	0.129 936	0.130 312	0.130 690	0.131 068	0.131 446	9
10	0.118 355	0.118 731	0.119 108	0.119 485	0.119 863	0.120 241	10
11	0.109 203	0.109 579	0.109 957	0.110 334	0.110 713	0.111 092	11
12	0.101 590	0.101 967	0.102 345	0.102 724	0.103 104	0.103 484	12
13	0.095 161	0.095 539	0.095 919	0.096 299	0.096 680	0.097 062	13
14	0.089 662	0.090 042	0.090 423	0.090 805	0.091 187	0.091 571	14
15	0.084 907	0.085 289	0.085 671	0.086 055	0.086 440	0.086 825	15
16	0.080 756	0.081 140	0.081 525	0.081 911	0.082 297	0.082 685	16
17	0.077 104	0.077 490	0.077 877	0.078 264	0.078 653	0.079 043	17
18	0.073 866	0.074 254	0.074 643	0.075 033	0.075 425	0.075 817	18
19	0.070 978	0.071 368	0.071 759	0.072 152	0.072 546	0.072 940	19
20	0.068 386	0.068 779	0.069 173	0.069 568	0.069 964	0.070 361	20
21	0.066 049	0.066 444	0.066 840	0.067 238	0.067 637	0.068 037	21
22	0.063 932	0.064 329	0.064 728	0.065 128	0.065 529	0.065 932	22
23	0.062 006	0.062 406	0.062 807	0.063 209	0.063 613	0.064 019	23
24	0.060 246	0.060 649	0.061 053	0.061 458	0.061 865	0.062 273	24
25	0.058 634	0.059 039	0.059 446	0.059 854	0.060 263	0.060 674	25
26	0.057 152	0.057 560	0.057 969	0.058 380	0.058 792	0.059 205	26
27	0.055 786	0.056 196	0.056 608	0.057 021	0.057 436	0.057 852	27
28	0.054 522	0.054 935	0.055 350	0.055 766	0.056 183	0.056 603	28
29	0.053 351	0.053 767	0.054 184	0.054 603	0.055 023	0.055 445	29
30	0.052 264	0.052 682	0.053 102	0.053 523	0.053 946	0.054 371	30
31	0.051 251	0.051 672	0.052 094	0.052 519	0.052 945	0.053 372	31
32	0.050 306	0.050 730	0.051 155	0.051 582	0.052 011	0.052 442	32
33	0.049 423	0.049 850	0.050 278	0.050 707	0.051 139	0.051 572	33
34	0.048 597	0.049 026	0.049 456	0.049 889	0.050 323	0.050 760	34
35	0.047 822	0.048 253	0.048 687	0.049 122	0.049 559	0.049 998	35
36	0.047 094	0.047 528	0.047 964	0.048 402	0.048 842	0.049 284	36
37	0.046 410	0.046 846	0.047 285	0.047 726	0.048 169	0.048 613	37
38	0.045 765	0.046 204	0.046 646	0.047 089	0.047 535	0.047 982	38
39	0.045 157	0.045 599	0.046 043	0.046 489	0.046 938	0.047 388	39
40	0.044 583	0.045 028	0.045 475	0.045 923	0.046 374	0.046 827	40
41	0.044 041	0.044 488	0.044 937	0.045 389	0.045 843	0.046 298	41
42	0.043 528	0.043 978	0.044 429	0.044 884	0.045 340	0.045 798	42
43	0.043 042	0.043 494	0.043 949	0.044 405	0.044 864	0.045 325	43
44	0.042 581	0.043 036	0.043 493	0.043 952	0.044 414	0.044 878	44
45	0.042 144	0.042 601	0.043 061	0.043 523	0.043 987	0.044 453	45
46	0.041 728	0.042 188	0.042 651	0.043 115	0.043 582	0.044 051	46
47	0.041 334	0.041 796	0.042 261	0.042 728	0.043 198	0.043 669	47
48	0.040 958	0.041 423	0.041 891	0.042 360	0.042 832	0.043 306	48
49	0.040 601	0.041 068	0.041 538	0.042 010	0.042 485	0.042 962	49
50	0.040 260	0.040 730	0.041 203	0.041 677	0.042 154	0.042 634	50
51	0.039 936	0.040 408	0.040 883	0.041 360	0.041 840	0.042 322	51
52	0.039 626	0.040 101	0.040 578	0.041 058	0.041 540	0.042 024	52
53	0.039 331	0.039 808	0.040 288	0.040 770	0.041 254	0.041 741	53
54	0.039 049	0.039 528	0.040 010	0.040 495	0.040 982	0.041 471	54
55	0.038 779	0.039 261	0.039 745	0.040 232	0.040 721	0.041 213	55
YRS							
14	0.038 521	0.039 006	0.039 492	0.039 981	0.040 473	0.040 967	56
15	0.037 597	0.038 090	0.038 586	0.039 084	0.039 585	0.040 089	60
16	0.036 817	0.037 319	0.037 824	0.038 331	0.038 841	0.039 353	64
17	0.036 156	0.036 666	0.037 179	0.037 695	0.038 213	0.038 734	68
18	0.035 592	0.036 110	0.036 631	0.037 155	0.037 681	0.038 210	72
19	0.035 109	0.035 635	0.036 163	0.036 695	0.037 228	0.037 765	76
20	0.034 694	0.035 227	0.035 763	0.036 301	0.036 842	0.037 385	80
21	0.034 336	0.034 876	0.035 418	0.035 963	0.036 510	0.037 060	84
22	0.034 026	0.034 572	0.035 121	0.035 672	0.036 226	0.036 782	88
23	0.033 757	0.034 309	0.034 864	0.035 421	0.035 981	0.036 543	92
24	0.033 524	0.034 082	0.034 642	0.035 204	0.035 770	0.036 337	96
25	0.033 320	0.033 884	0.034 449	0.035 017	0.035 587	0.036 159	100
26	0.033 143	0.033 711	0.034 282	0.034 854	0.035 429	0.036 006	104
27	0.032 988	0.033 561	0.034 136	0.034 713	0.035 292	0.035 873	108
28	0.032 853	0.033 430	0.034 009	0.034 590	0.035 174	0.035 759	112
29	0.032 735	0.033 315	0.033 898	0.034 484	0.035 070	0.035 659	116
30	0.032 631	0.033 215	0.033 802	0.034 391	0.034 981	0.035 573	120

	14.25%	14.50%	14.75%	15.00%	15.25%	15.50%	
	ANNUAL RATE	ANNUAL RATE	ANNUAL RATE	ANNUAL RATE	ANNUAL RATE	ANNUAL RATE	
QTRS							QTRS
1	1.035 625	1.036 250	1.036 875	1.037 500	1.038 125	1.038 750	1
2	0.526 875	0.527 349	0.527 823	0.528 298	0.528 772	0.529 247	2
3	0.357 360	0.357 787	0.358 213	0.358 640	0.359 067	0.359 494	3
4	0.272 655	0.273 059	0.273 464	0.273 869	0.274 274	0.274 679	4
5	0.221 874	0.222 266	0.222 659	0.223 052	0.223 445	0.223 839	5
6	0.188 054	0.188 439	0.188 826	0.189 212	0.189 599	0.189 986	6
7	0.163 926	0.164 308	0.164 691	0.165 074	0.165 457	0.165 841	7
8	0.145 856	0.146 237	0.146 617	0.146 998	0.147 380	0.147 762	8
9	0.131 825	0.132 204	0.132 585	0.132 965	0.133 346	0.133 728	9
10	0.120 620	0.121 000	0.121 380	0.121 761	0.122 143	0.122 525	10
11	0.111 472	0.111 852	0.112 233	0.112 615	0.112 998	0.113 381	11
12	0.103 865	0.104 247	0.104 629	0.105 012	0.105 396	0.105 781	12
13	0.097 444	0.097 827	0.098 212	0.098 596	0.098 982	0.099 369	13
14	0.091 955	0.092 340	0.092 726	0.093 113	0.093 501	0.093 889	14
15	0.087 211	0.087 599	0.087 987	0.088 376	0.088 766	0.089 157	15
16	0.083 073	0.083 463	0.083 853	0.084 245	0.084 637	0.085 031	16
17	0.079 434	0.079 826	0.080 219	0.080 613	0.081 008	0.081 404	17
18	0.076 210	0.076 605	0.077 000	0.077 397	0.077 794	0.078 193	18
19	0.073 336	0.073 733	0.074 131	0.074 531	0.074 931	0.075 332	19
20	0.070 760	0.071 159	0.071 560	0.071 962	0.072 365	0.072 770	20
21	0.068 438	0.068 840	0.069 244	0.069 649	0.070 055	0.070 462	21
22	0.066 336	0.066 741	0.067 148	0.067 555	0.067 964	0.068 375	22
23	0.064 425	0.064 833	0.065 243	0.065 653	0.066 065	0.066 479	23
24	0.062 682	0.063 093	0.063 505	0.063 919	0.064 334	0.064 750	24
25	0.061 086	0.061 500	0.061 915	0.062 332	0.062 750	0.063 169	25
26	0.059 621	0.060 037	0.060 455	0.060 875	0.061 296	0.061 718	26
27	0.058 270	0.058 690	0.059 111	0.059 533	0.059 957	0.060 383	27
28	0.057 023	0.057 446	0.057 870	0.058 295	0.058 722	0.059 151	28
29	0.055 869	0.056 294	0.056 721	0.057 150	0.057 580	0.058 012	29
30	0.054 798	0.055 226	0.055 656	0.056 088	0.056 521	0.056 956	30
31	0.053 802	0.054 233	0.054 666	0.055 100	0.055 537	0.055 975	31
32	0.052 874	0.053 308	0.053 744	0.054 181	0.054 621	0.055 062	32
33	0.052 008	0.052 445	0.052 883	0.053 324	0.053 766	0.054 210	33
34	0.051 198	0.051 638	0.052 079	0.052 523	0.052 968	0.053 415	34
35	0.050 439	0.050 882	0.051 327	0.051 773	0.052 222	0.052 672	35
36	0.049 728	0.050 174	0.050 621	0.051 071	0.051 522	0.051 975	36
37	0.049 060	0.049 508	0.049 959	0.050 411	0.050 865	0.051 322	37
38	0.048 432	0.048 883	0.049 336	0.049 792	0.050 249	0.050 708	38
39	0.047 840	0.048 294	0.048 750	0.049 209	0.049 669	0.050 131	39
40	0.047 282	0.047 739	0.048 198	0.048 659	0.049 123	0.049 588	40
41	0.046 756	0.047 216	0.047 678	0.048 142	0.048 608	0.049 076	41
42	0.046 259	0.046 721	0.047 186	0.047 653	0.048 122	0.048 593	42
43	0.045 789	0.046 254	0.046 721	0.047 191	0.047 663	0.048 136	43
44	0.045 344	0.045 812	0.046 282	0.046 754	0.047 229	0.047 705	44
45	0.044 922	0.045 393	0.045 866	0.046 341	0.046 818	0.047 298	45
46	0.044 522	0.044 996	0.045 472	0.045 949	0.046 429	0.046 912	46
47	0.044 143	0.044 619	0.045 098	0.045 578	0.046 061	0.046 546	47
48	0.043 783	0.044 262	0.044 743	0.045 226	0.045 712	0.046 199	48
49	0.043 441	0.043 922	0.044 406	0.044 892	0.045 380	0.045 870	49
50	0.043 115	0.043 599	0.044 086	0.044 574	0.045 065	0.045 558	50
51	0.042 806	0.043 292	0.043 781	0.044 272	0.044 766	0.045 261	51
52	0.042 511	0.043 000	0.043 492	0.043 985	0.044 481	0.044 979	52
53	0.042 230	0.042 722	0.043 216	0.043 712	0.044 210	0.044 711	53
54	0.041 963	0.042 457	0.042 953	0.043 452	0.043 953	0.044 456	54
55	0.041 707	0.042 204	0.042 703	0.043 204	0.043 707	0.044 213	55
YRS							
14	0.041 464	0.041 963	0.042 464	0.042 968	.043 474	0.043 982	56
15	0.040 595	0.041 103	0.041 614	0.042 127	0.042 642	0.043 160	60
16	0.039 868	0.040 385	0.040 905	0.041 427	0.041 951	0.042 478	64
17	0.039 257	0.039 783	0.040 311	0.040 841	0.041 374	0.041 909	68
18	0.038 741	0.039 275	0.039 811	0.040 349	0.040 890	0.041 433	72
19	0.038 303	0.038 844	0.039 388	0.039 934	0.040 482	0.041 032	76
20	0.037 931	0.038 479	0.039 029	0.039 582	0.040 137	0.040 694	80
21	0.037 613	0.038 167	0.038 724	0.039 283	0.039 844	0.040 408	84
22	0.037 340	0.037 901	0.038 464	0.039 029	0.039 596	0.040 165	88
23	0.037 107	0.037 673	0.038 242	0.038 812	0.039 385	0.039 959	92
24	0.036 906	0.037 478	0.038 052	0.038 627	0.039 205	0.039 784	96
25	0.036 734	0.037 310	0.037 889	0.038 469	0.039 051	0.039 635	100
26	0.036 585	0.037 166	0.037 749	0.038 333	0.038 920	0.039 508	104
27	0.036 457	0.037 042	0.037 628	0.038 217	0.038 807	0.039 399	108
28	0.036 346	0.036 935	0.037 525	0.038 117	0.038 711	0.039 306	112
29	0.036 250	0.036 842	0.037 436	0.038 032	0.038 628	0.039 227	116
30	0.036 167	0.036 762	0.037 359	0.037 958	0.038 558	0.039 159	120

PARTIAL PAYMENT TO AMORTIZE

QUARTERLY COMPOUNDING

QTRS	15.75% ANNUAL RATE	16.00% ANNUAL RATE	16.50% ANNUAL RATE	17.00% ANNUAL RATE	17.50% ANNUAL RATE	18.00% ANNUAL RATE	QTRS
1	1.039 375	1.040 000	1.041 250	1.042 500	1.043 750	1.045 000	1
2	0.529 721	0.530 196	0.531 146	0.532 096	0.533 047	0.533 998	2
3	0.359 921	0.360 349	0.361 204	0.362 060	0.362 916	0.363 773	3
4	0.275 084	0.275 490	0.276 302	0.277 115	0.277 929	0.278 744	4
5	0.224 233	0.224 627	0.225 416	0.226 207	0.226 999	0.227 792	5
6	0.190 374	0.190 762	0.191 539	0.192 317	0.193 097	0.193 878	6
7	0.166 225	0.166 610	0.167 380	0.168 152	0.168 926	0.169 701	7
8	0.148 145	0.148 528	0.149 295	0.150 065	0.150 836	0.151 610	8
9	0.134 110	0.134 493	0.135 260	0.136 029	0.136 801	0.137 574	9
10	0.122 908	0.123 291	0.124 059	0.124 830	0.125 603	0.126 379	10
11	0.113 765	0.114 149	0.114 920	0.115 693	0.116 469	0.117 248	11
12	0.106 166	0.106 552	0.107 326	0.108 103	0.108 883	0.109 666	12
13	0.099 756	0.100 144	0.100 922	0.101 703	0.102 488	0.103 275	13
14	0.094 279	0.094 669	0.095 452	0.096 238	0.097 028	0.097 820	14
15	0.089 548	0.089 941	0.090 729	0.091 520	0.092 315	0.093 114	15
16	0.085 425	0.085 820	0.086 613	0.087 410	0.088 211	0.089 015	16
17	0.081 801	0.082 199	0.082 997	0.083 800	0.084 607	0.085 418	17
18	0.078 593	0.078 993	0.079 798	0.080 607	0.081 420	0.082 237	18
19	0.075 735	0.076 139	0.076 949	0.077 764	0.078 584	0.079 407	19
20	0.073 175	0.073 582	0.074 399	0.075 220	0.076 046	0.076 876	20
21	0.070 870	0.071 280	0.072 103	0.072 931	0.073 763	0.074 601	21
22	0.068 786	0.069 199	0.070 028	0.070 862	0.071 702	0.072 546	22
23	0.066 893	0.067 309	0.068 145	0.068 986	0.069 831	0.070 682	23
24	0.065 168	0.065 587	0.066 429	0.067 276	0.068 129	0.068 987	24
25	0.063 590	0.064 012	0.064 860	0.065 715	0.066 574	0.067 439	25
26	0.062 142	0.062 567	0.063 422	0.064 283	0.065 149	0.066 021	26
27	0.060 810	0.061 239	0.062 100	0.062 967	0.063 841	0.064 719	27
28	0.059 581	0.060 013	0.060 881	0.061 755	0.062 635	0.063 521	28
29	0.058 445	0.058 880	0.059 754	0.060 635	0.061 522	0.062 415	29
30	0.057 392	0.057 830	0.058 711	0.059 598	0.060 492	0.061 392	30
31	0.056 414	0.056 855	0.057 743	0.058 637	0.059 537	0.060 443	31
32	0.055 504	0.055 949	0.056 842	0.057 743	0.058 650	0.059 563	32
33	0.054 656	0.055 104	0.056 004	0.056 911	0.057 824	0.058 745	33
34	0.053 864	0.054 315	0.055 221	0.056 135	0.057 055	0.057 982	34
35	0.053 124	0.053 577	0.054 490	0.055 410	0.056 337	0.057 270	35
36	0.052 430	0.052 887	0.053 806	0.054 732	0.055 666	0.056 606	36
37	0.051 780	0.052 240	0.053 165	0.054 097	0.055 037	0.055 984	37
38	0.051 169	0.051 632	0.052 563	0.053 502	0.054 448	0.055 402	38
39	0.050 595	0.051 061	0.051 998	0.052 944	0.053 896	0.054 856	39
40	0.050 055	0.050 523	0.051 467	0.052 418	0.053 377	0.054 343	40
41	0.049 545	0.050 017	0.050 967	0.051 924	0.052 889	0.053 862	41
42	0.049 065	0.049 540	0.050 496	0.051 459	0.052 430	0.053 409	42
43	0.048 612	0.049 090	0.050 051	0.051 021	0.051 998	0.052 982	43
44	0.048 184	0.048 665	0.049 632	0.050 607	0.051 590	0.052 581	44
45	0.047 779	0.048 262	0.049 236	0.050 217	0.051 205	0.052 202	45
46	0.047 396	0.047 882	0.048 861	0.049 848	0.050 842	0.051 845	46
47	0.047 033	0.047 522	0.048 506	0.049 499	0.050 499	0.051 507	47
48	0.046 689	0.047 181	0.048 171	0.049 169	0.050 175	0.051 189	48
49	0.046 363	0.046 857	0.047 853	0.048 856	0.049 868	0.050 887	49
50	0.046 053	0.046 550	0.047 551	0.048 560	0.049 577	0.050 602	50
51	0.045 759	0.046 259	0.047 265	0.048 279	0.049 302	0.050 332	51
52	0.045 480	0.045 982	0.046 994	0.048 013	0.049 041	0.050 077	52
53	0.045 214	0.045 719	0.046 736	0.047 761	0.048 794	0.049 835	53
54	0.044 961	0.045 469	0.046 491	0.047 521	0.048 559	0.049 605	54
55	0.044 721	0.045 231	0.046 258	0.047 293	0.048 336	0.049 388	55

YRS	15.75% ANNUAL RATE	16.00% ANNUAL RATE	16.50% ANNUAL RATE	17.00% ANNUAL RATE	17.50% ANNUAL RATE	18.00% ANNUAL RATE	QTRS
14	0.044 492	0.045 005	0.046 037	0.047 077	0.048 125	0.049 181	56
15	0.043 680	0.044 202	0.045 253	0.046 312	0.047 379	0.048 454	60
16	0.043 007	0.043 538	0.044 606	0.045 683	0.046 768	0.047 861	64
17	0.042 446	0.042 986	0.044 071	0.045 165	0.046 266	0.047 375	68
18	0.041 978	0.042 525	0.043 626	0.044 734	0.045 851	0.046 975	72
19	0.041 584	0.042 139	0.043 254	0.044 377	0.045 507	0.046 644	76
20	0.041 253	0.041 814	0.042 942	0.044 078	0.045 221	0.046 371	80
21	0.040 973	0.041 541	0.042 681	0.043 829	0.044 983	0.046 144	84
22	0.040 737	0.041 310	0.042 461	0.043 619	0.044 784	0.045 955	88
23	0.040 536	0.041 114	0.042 276	0.043 444	0.044 618	0.045 798	92
24	0.040 366	0.040 949	0.042 119	0.043 296	0.044 479	0.045 667	96
25	0.040 221	0.040 808	0.041 987	0.043 172	0.044 363	0.045 558	100
26	0.040 097	0.040 689	0.041 876	0.043 068	0.044 265	0.045 467	104
27	0.039 992	0.040 587	0.041 781	0.042 980	0.044 183	0.045 391	108
28	0.039 903	0.040 501	0.041 701	0.042 906	0.044 115	0.045 328	112
29	0.039 826	0.040 427	0.041 633	0.042 843	0.044 057	0.045 274	116
30	0.039 761	0.040 365	0.041 575	0.042 790	0.044 008	0.045 230	120

QTRS	18.50% ANNUAL RATE	19.00% ANNUAL RATE	19.50% ANNUAL RATE	20.00% ANNUAL RATE	20.50% ANNUAL RATE	21.00% ANNUAL RATE	QTRS
1	1.046 250	1.047 500	1.048 750	1.050 000	1.051 250	1.052 500	1
2	0.534 949	0.535 900	0.536 853	0.537 805	0.538 758	0.539 711	2
3	0.364 631	0.365 490	0.366 349	0.367 209	0.368 069	0.368 930	3
4	0.279 559	0.280 376	0.281 193	0.282 012	0.282 831	0.283 651	4
5	0.228 586	0.229 381	0.230 177	0.230 975	0.231 773	0.232 573	5
6	0.194 661	0.195 445	0.196 231	0.197 017	0.197 806	0.198 595	6
7	0.170 479	0.171 257	0.172 038	0.172 820	0.173 604	0.174 389	7
8	0.152 385	0.153 162	0.153 941	0.154 722	0.155 505	0.156 289	8
9	0.138 350	0.139 128	0.139 908	0.140 690	0.141 474	0.142 261	9
10	0.127 157	0.127 937	0.128 720	0.129 505	0.130 292	0.131 082	10
11	0.118 029	0.118 813	0.119 600	0.120 389	0.121 181	0.121 975	11
12	0.110 452	0.111 240	0.112 031	0.112 825	0.113 622	0.114 422	12
13	0.104 066	0.104 860	0.105 656	0.106 456	0.107 258	0.108 064	13
14	0.098 616	0.099 416	0.100 218	0.101 024	0.101 833	0.102 645	14
15	0.093 916	0.094 721	0.095 530	0.096 342	0.097 158	0.097 977	15
16	0.089 823	0.090 635	0.091 451	0.092 270	0.093 093	0.093 919	16
17	0.086 232	0.087 051	0.087 873	0.088 699	0.089 529	0.090 363	17
18	0.083 058	0.083 883	0.084 713	0.085 546	0.086 384	0.087 225	18
19	0.080 235	0.081 068	0.081 904	0.082 745	0.083 590	0.084 439	19
20	0.077 711	0.078 550	0.079 394	0.080 243	0.081 095	0.081 952	20
21	0.075 442	0.076 289	0.077 140	0.077 996	0.078 856	0.079 721	21
22	0.073 395	0.074 248	0.075 107	0.075 971	0.076 839	0.077 712	22
23	0.071 539	0.072 400	0.073 266	0.074 137	0.075 013	0.075 894	23
24	0.069 850	0.070 719	0.071 592	0.072 471	0.073 355	0.074 243	24
25	0.068 309	0.069 185	0.070 066	0.070 952	0.071 844	0.072 741	25
26	0.066 899	0.067 782	0.068 670	0.069 564	0.070 464	0.071 368	26
27	0.065 604	0.066 494	0.067 390	0.068 292	0.069 199	0.070 111	27
28	0.064 413	0.065 310	0.066 213	0.067 123	0.068 037	0.068 957	28
29	0.063 313	0.064 218	0.065 129	0.066 046	0.066 968	0.067 896	29
30	0.062 297	0.063 209	0.064 127	0.065 051	0.065 981	0.066 917	30
31	0.061 356	0.062 276	0.063 201	0.064 132	0.065 069	0.066 013	31
32	0.060 483	0.061 409	0.062 342	0.063 280	0.064 225	0.065 176	32
33	0.059 671	0.060 605	0.061 544	0.062 490	0.063 442	0.064 400	33
34	0.058 916	0.059 856	0.060 802	0.061 755	0.062 715	0.063 680	34
35	0.058 211	0.059 158	0.060 112	0.061 072	0.062 038	0.063 011	35
36	0.057 553	0.058 507	0.059 467	0.060 434	0.061 408	0.062 388	36
37	0.056 938	0.057 898	0.058 866	0.059 840	0.060 820	0.061 807	37
38	0.056 362	0.057 329	0.058 303	0.059 284	0.060 272	0.061 265	38
39	0.055 823	0.056 796	0.057 777	0.058 765	0.059 759	0.060 759	39
40	0.055 316	0.056 297	0.057 284	0.058 278	0.059 279	0.060 286	40
41	0.054 841	0.055 828	0.056 822	0.057 822	0.058 830	0.059 844	41
42	0.054 395	0.055 388	0.056 388	0.057 395	0.058 409	0.059 429	42
43	0.053 974	0.054 974	0.055 980	0.056 993	0.058 013	0.059 040	43
44	0.053 579	0.054 584	0.055 597	0.056 616	0.057 643	0.058 676	44
45	0.053 206	0.054 218	0.055 236	0.056 262	0.057 294	0.058 333	45
46	0.052 855	0.053 872	0.054 897	0.055 928	0.056 967	0.058 012	46
47	0.052 523	0.053 546	0.054 577	0.055 614	0.056 659	0.057 710	47
48	0.052 210	0.053 239	0.054 275	0.055 318	0.056 369	0.057 425	48
49	0.051 914	0.052 949	0.053 991	0.055 040	0.056 095	0.057 158	49
50	0.051 635	0.052 675	0.053 722	0.054 777	0.055 838	0.056 906	50
51	0.051 370	0.052 416	0.053 469	0.054 529	0.055 595	0.056 669	51
52	0.051 120	0.052 171	0.053 229	0.054 294	0.055 367	0.056 445	52
53	0.050 883	0.051 940	0.053 003	0.054 073	0.055 151	0.056 234	53
54	0.050 659	0.051 720	0.052 789	0.053 864	0.054 947	0.056 036	54
55	0.050 446	0.051 513	0.052 586	0.053 667	0.054 754	0.055 848	55

YRS							QTRS
14	0.050 245	0.051 316	0.052 395	0.053 480	0.054 572	0.055 671	56
15	0.049 537	0.050 627	0.051 724	0.052 828	0.053 939	0.055 055	60
16	0.048 961	0.050 069	0.051 183	0.052 304	0.053 431	0.054 564	64
17	0.048 491	0.049 614	0.050 744	0.051 880	0.053 022	0.054 170	68
18	0.048 105	0.049 243	0.050 387	0.051 536	0.052 692	0 053 853	72
19	0.047 788	0.048 939	0.050 095	0.051 257	0.052 425	053 597	76
20	0.047 527	0.048 689	0.049 857	0.051 030	0.052 208	0.053 391	80
21	0.047 311	0.048 483	0.049 661	0.050 844	0.052 032	0.053 224	84
22	0.047 132	0.048 314	0.049 501	0.050 692	0.051 888	0.053 088	88
23	0.046 984	0.048 174	0.049 369	0.050 568	0.051 771	0.052 978	92
24	0.046 861	0.048 058	0.049 260	0.050 466	0.051 676	0.052 889	96
25	0.046 759	0.047 963	0.049 171	0.050 383	0.051 598	0.052 817	100
26	0.046 674	0.047 884	0.049 098	0.050 315	0.051 535	0.052 758	104
27	0.046 603	0.047 818	0.049 037	0.050 259	0.051 483	0.052 710	108
28	0.046 544	0.047 764	0.048 987	0.050 213	0.051 441	0.052 671	112
29	0.046 495	0.047 719	0.048 946	0.050 175	0.051 406	0.052 639	116
30	0.046 455	0.047 682	0.048 912	0.050 144	0.051 378	0.052 613	120

PARTIAL PAYMENT TO AMORTIZE

QUARTERLY COMPOUNDING

QTRS	21.50% ANNUAL RATE	22.00% ANNUAL RATE	22.50% ANNUAL RATE	23.00% ANNUAL RATE	23.50% ANNUAL RATE	24.00% ANNUAL RATE	QTRS
1	1.053 750	1.055 000	1.056 250	1.057 500	1.058 750	1.060 000	1
2	0.540 664	0.541 618	0.542 572	0.543 527	0.544 482	0.545 437	2
3	0.369 792	0.370 654	0.371 517	0.372 381	0.373 245	0.374 110	3
4	0.284 472	0.285 294	0.286 117	0.286 941	0.287 766	0.288 591	4
5	0.233 374	0.234 176	0.234 980	0.235 784	0.236 590	0.237 396	5
6	0.199 386	0.200 179	0.200 973	0.201 768	0.202 565	0.203 363	6
7	0.175 176	0.175 964	0.176 755	0.177 546	0.178 340	0.179 135	7
8	0.157 076	0.157 864	0.158 654	0.159 446	0.160 240	0.161 036	8
9	0.143 049	0.143 839	0.144 632	0.145 427	0.146 223	0.147 022	9
10	0.131 873	0.132 668	0.133 464	0.134 263	0.135 064	0.135 868	10
11	0.122 771	0.123 571	0.124 372	0.125 177	0.125 984	0.126 793	11
12	0.115 224	0.116 029	0.116 837	0.117 648	0.118 461	0.119 277	12
13	0.108 873	0.109 684	0.110 499	0.111 316	0.112 137	0.112 960	13
14	0.103 461	0.104 279	0.105 101	0.105 926	0.106 754	0.107 585	14
15	0.098 800	0.099 626	0.100 455	0.101 288	0.102 123	0.102 963	15
16	0.094 749	0.095 583	0.096 420	0.097 260	0.098 104	0.098 952	16
17	0.091 201	0.092 042	0.092 887	0.093 736	0.094 589	0.095 445	17
18	0.088 071	0.088 920	0.089 773	0.090 630	0.091 492	0.092 357	18
19	0.085 293	0.086 150	0.087 012	0.087 877	0.088 747	0.089 621	19
20	0.082 814	0.083 679	0.084 549	0.085 423	0.086 302	0.087 185	20
21	0.080 591	0.081 465	0.082 343	0.083 226	0.084 113	0.085 005	21
22	0.078 589	0.079 471	0.080 358	0.081 249	0.082 145	0.083 046	22
23	0.076 779	0.077 670	0.078 565	0.079 465	0.080 369	0.081 278	23
24	0.075 137	0.076 036	0.076 939	0.077 848	0.078 761	0.079 679	24
25	0.073 642	0.074 549	0.075 461	0.076 378	0.077 300	0.078 227	25
26	0.072 278	0.073 193	0.074 113	0.075 039	0.075 969	0.076 904	26
27	0.071 029	0.071 952	0.072 881	0.073 814	0.074 753	0.075 697	27
28	0.069 883	0.070 814	0.071 751	0.072 693	0.073 640	0.074 593	28
29	0.068 829	0.069 769	0.070 713	0.071 663	0.072 619	0.073 580	29
30	0.067 858	0.068 805	0.069 758	0.070 716	0.071 680	0.072 649	30
31	0.066 962	0.067 917	0.068 877	0.069 843	0.070 815	0.071 792	31
32	0.066 133	0.067 095	0.068 064	0.069 038	0.070 017	0.071 002	32
33	0.065 365	0.066 335	0.067 311	0.068 292	0.069 280	0.070 273	33
34	0.064 652	0.065 630	0.066 613	0.067 603	0.068 598	0.069 598	34
35	0.063 990	0.064 975	0.065 966	0.066 963	0.067 965	0.068 974	35
36	0.063 374	0.064 366	0.065 365	0.066 369	0.067 379	0.068 395	36
37	0.062 800	0.063 800	0.064 805	0.065 817	0.066 834	0.067 857	37
38	0.062 266	0.063 272	0.064 285	0.065 303	0.066 328	0.067 358	38
39	0.061 767	0.062 780	0.063 799	0.064 825	0.065 856	0.066 894	39
40	0.061 300	0.062 320	0.063 347	0.064 379	0.065 417	0.066 462	40
41	0.060 864	0.061 891	0.062 924	0.063 963	0.065 008	0.066 059	41
42	0.060 456	0.061 489	0.062 529	0.063 574	0.064 626	0.065 683	42
43	0.060 074	0.061 113	0.062 159	0.063 211	0.064 269	0.065 333	43
44	0.059 715	0.060 761	0.061 813	0.062 872	0.063 936	0.065 006	44
45	0.059 379	0.060 431	0.061 490	0.062 554	0.063 624	0.064 700	45
46	0.059 064	0.060 122	0.061 186	0.062 256	0.063 333	0.064 415	46
47	0.058 767	0.059 831	0.060 901	0.061 978	0.063 060	0.064 148	47
48	0.058 489	0.059 559	0.060 634	0.061 716	0.062 804	0.063 898	48
49	0.058 227	0.059 302	0.060 384	0.061 471	0.062 565	0.063 664	49
50	0.057 981	0.059 061	0.060 148	0.061 241	0.062 340	0.063 444	50
51	0.057 749	0.058 835	0.059 927	0.061 025	0.062 129	0.063 239	51
52	0.057 530	0.058 622	0.059 719	0.060 823	0.061 932	0.063 046	52
53	0.057 325	0.058 421	0.059 524	0.060 632	0.061 746	0.062 866	53
54	0.057 131	0.058 232	0.059 340	0.060 453	0.061 572	0.062 696	54
55	0.056 948	0.058 055	0.059 167	0.060 285	0.061 408	0.062 537	55

YRS	21.50%	22.00%	22.50%	23.00%	23.50%	24.00%	QTRS
14	0.056 776	0.057 887	0.059 004	0.060 126	0.061 254	0.062 388	56
15	0.056 178	0.057 307	0.058 441	0.059 581	0.060 726	0.061 876	60
16	0.055 703	0.056 847	0.057 997	0.059 152	0.060 312	0.061 476	64
17	0.055 323	0.056 482	0.057 645	0.058 813	0.059 986	0.061 163	68
18	0.055 019	0.056 190	0.057 365	0.058 545	0.059 730	0.060 918	72
19	0.054 775	0.055 956	0.057 143	0.058 333	0.059 527	0.060 725	76
20	0.054 578	0.055 769	0.056 965	0.058 164	0.059 367	0.060 573	80
21	0.054 420	0.055 619	0.056 823	0.058 030	0.059 240	0.060 453	84
22	0.054 292	0.055 499	0.056 709	0.057 923	0.059 139	0.060 358	88
23	0.054 189	0.055 402	0.056 618	0.057 838	0.059 059	0.060 283	92
24	0.054 105	0.055 324	0.056 546	0.057 770	0.058 996	0.060 224	96
25	0.054 038	0.055 261	0.056 487	0.057 715	0.058 945	0.060 177	100
26	0.053 983	0.055 211	0.056 440	0.057 672	0.058 905	0.060 140	104
27	0.053 939	0.055 170	0.056 403	0.057 638	0.058 874	0.060 111	108
28	0.053 903	0.055 137	0.056 373	0.057 610	0.058 848	0.060 088	112
29	0.053 874	0.055 111	0.056 349	0.057 588	0.058 828	0.060 070	116
30	0.053 851	0.055 089	0.056 329	0.057 570	0.058 812	0.060 055	120

PARTIAL PAYMENT TO AMORTIZE

SEMIANNUAL COMPOUNDING

	5.25%	5.50%	5.75%	6.00%	6.25%	6.50%	
HALF YRS	ANNUAL RATE	ANNUAL RATE	ANNUAL RATE	ANNUAL RATE	ANNUAL RATE	ANNUAL RATE	HALF YRS
1	1.026 250	1.027 500	1.028 750	1.030 000	1.031 250	1.032 500	1
2	0.519 773	0.520 718	0.521 664	0.522 611	0.523 558	0.524 505	2
3	0.350 984	0.351 832	0.352 681	0.353 530	0.354 380	0.355 231	3
4	0.266 619	0.267 421	0.268 223	0.269 027	0.269 832	0.270 637	4
5	0.216 022	0.216 798	0.217 576	0.218 355	0.219 134	0.219 916	5
6	0.182 310	0.183 071	0.183 833	0.184 598	0.185 363	0.186 130	6
7	0.158 246	0.158 997	0.159 751	0.160 506	0.161 263	0.162 022	7
8	0.140 212	0.140 958	0.141 706	0.142 456	0.143 209	0.143 963	8
9	0.126 198	0.126 941	0.127 686	0.128 434	0.129 184	0.129 936	9
10	0.114 998	0.115 740	0.116 484	0.117 231	0.117 980	0.118 731	10
11	0.105 845	0.106 586	0.107 331	0.108 077	0.108 827	0.109 579	11
12	0.098 226	0.098 969	0.099 714	0.100 462	0.101 213	0.101 967	12
13	0.091 789	0.092 533	0.093 279	0.094 030	0.094 783	0.095 539	13
14	0.086 279	0.087 025	0.087 774	0.088 526	0.089 282	0.090 042	14
15	0.081 511	0.082 259	0.083 011	0.083 767	0.084 526	0.085 289	15
16	0.077 346	0.078 097	0.078 852	0.079 611	0.080 374	0.081 140	16
17	0.073 678	0.074 432	0.075 190	0.075 953	0.076 719	0.077 490	17
18	0.070 423	0.071 181	0.071 942	0.072 709	0.073 479	0.074 254	18
19	0.067 517	0.068 278	0.069 044	0.069 814	0.070 589	0.071 368	19
20	0.064 907	0.065 672	0.066 441	0.067 216	0.067 995	0.068 779	20
21	0.062 551	0.063 319	0.064 093	0.064 872	0.065 656	0.066 444	21
22	0.060 414	0.061 186	0.061 964	0.062 747	0.063 536	0.064 329	22
23	0.058 467	0.059 244	0.060 026	0.060 814	0.061 607	0.062 406	23
24	0.056 688	0.057 469	0.058 255	0.059 047	0.059 845	0.060 649	24
25	0.055 055	0.055 840	0.056 631	0.057 428	0.058 231	0.059 039	25
26	0.053 552	0.054 341	0.055 137	0.055 938	0.056 746	0.057 560	26
27	0.052 164	0.052 958	0.053 758	0.054 564	0.055 377	0.056 196	27
28	0.050 879	0.051 677	0.052 482	0.053 293	0.054 111	0.054 935	28
29	0.049 687	0.050 489	0.051 299	0.052 115	0.052 937	0.053 767	29
30	0.048 577	0.049 384	0.050 198	0.051 019	0.051 847	0.052 682	30
31	0.047 543	0.048 355	0.049 173	0.049 999	0.050 832	0.051 672	31
32	0.046 577	0.047 393	0.048 216	0.049 047	0.049 885	0.050 730	32
33	0.045 672	0.046 493	0.047 321	0.048 156	0.048 999	0.049 850	33
34	0.044 824	0.045 649	0.046 481	0.047 322	0.048 170	0.049 026	34
35	0.044 027	0.044 856	0.045 694	0.046 539	0.047 393	0.048 253	35
36	0.043 277	0.044 111	0.044 954	0.045 804	0.046 662	0.047 528	36
37	0.042 571	0.043 410	0.044 256	0.045 112	0.045 975	0.046 846	37
38	0.041 905	0.042 748	0.043 599	0.044 459	0.045 328	0.046 204	38
39	0.041 275	0.042 123	0.042 979	0.043 844	0.044 717	0.045 599	39
40	0.040 679	0.041 532	0.042 393	0.043 262	0.044 141	0.045 028	40
41	0.040 115	0.040 972	0.041 838	0.042 712	0.043 596	0.044 488	41
42	0.039 581	0.040 442	0.041 312	0.042 192	0.043 080	0.043 978	42
43	0.039 073	0.039 939	0.040 814	0.041 698	0.042 592	0.043 494	43
44	0.038 591	0.039 461	0.040 341	0.041 230	0.042 128	0.043 036	44
45	0.038 132	0.039 007	0.039 891	0.040 785	0.041 688	0.042 601	45
46	0.037 696	0.038 575	0.039 464	0.040 363	0.041 271	0.042 188	46
47	0.037 280	0.038 164	0.039 057	0.039 961	0.040 874	0.041 796	47
48	0.036 884	0.037 772	0.038 670	0.039 578	0.040 496	0.041 423	48
49	0.036 505	0.037 398	0.038 300	0.039 213	0.040 136	0.041 068	49
50	0.036 144	0.037 041	0.037 948	0.038 865	0.039 793	0.040 730	50
51	0.035 799	0.036 700	0.037 612	0.038 534	0.039 466	0.040 408	51
52	0.035 469	0.036 374	0.037 291	0.038 217	0.039 154	0.040 101	52
53	0.035 153	0.036 063	0.036 984	0.037 915	0.038 856	0.039 808	53
54	0.034 851	0.035 765	0.036 690	0.037 626	0.038 572	0.039 528	54
55	0.034 561	0.035 480	0.036 409	0.037 349	0.038 300	0.039 261	55
56	0.034 284	0.035 206	0.036 140	0.037 084	0.038 040	0.039 006	56
57	0.034 017	0.034 944	0.035 882	0.036 831	0.037 791	0.038 761	57
58	0.033 762	0.034 693	0.035 635	0.036 588	0.037 553	0.038 528	58
59	0.033 516	0.034 452	0.035 398	0.036 356	0.037 325	0.038 304	59
YRS							
30	0.033 281	0.034 220	0.035 171	0.036 133	0.037 106	0.038 090	60
31	0.032 837	0.033 784	0.034 743	0.035 714	0.036 696	0.037 688	62
32	0.032 426	0.033 381	0.034 349	0.035 328	0.036 318	0.037 319	64
33	0.032 045	0.033 008	0.033 984	0.034 971	0.035 970	0.036 979	66
34	0.031 692	0.032 663	0.033 646	0.034 642	0.035 648	0.036 666	68
35	0.031 363	0.032 342	0.033 333	0.034 337	0.035 351	0.036 377	70
36	0.031 058	0.032 044	0.033 043	0.034 054	0.035 077	0.036 110	72
37	0.030 773	0.031 767	0.032 773	0.033 792	0.034 822	0.035 863	74
38	0.030 508	0.031 509	0.032 523	0.033 548	0.034 586	0.035 634	76
39	0.030 260	0.031 268	0.032 289	0.033 322	0.034 367	0.035 423	78
40	0.030 028	0.031 043	0.032 071	0.033 112	0.034 164	0.035 227	80

PARTIAL PAYMENT TO AMORTIZE

SEMIANNUAL COMPOUNDING

HALF YRS	6.75% ANNUAL RATE	7.00% ANNUAL RATE	7.25% ANNUAL RATE	7.50% ANNUAL RATE	7.75% ANNUAL RATE	8.00% ANNUAL RATE	HALF YRS
1	1.033 750	1.035 000	1.036 250	1.037 500	1.038 750	1.040 000	1
2	0.525 453	0.526 400	0.527 349	0.528 298	0.529 247	0.530 196	2
3	0.356 082	0.356 934	0.357 787	0.358 640	0.359 494	0.360 349	3
4	0.271 444	0.272 251	0.273 059	0.273 869	0.274 679	0.275 490	4
5	0.220 698	0.221 481	0.222 266	0.223 052	0.223 839	0.224 627	5
6	0.186 898	0.187 668	0.188 439	0.189 212	0.189 986	0.190 762	6
7	0.162 782	0.163 544	0.164 308	0.165 074	0.165 841	0.166 610	7
8	0.144 719	0.145 477	0.146 237	0.146 998	0.147 762	0.148 528	8
9	0.130 690	0.131 446	0.132 204	0.132 965	0.133 728	0.134 493	9
10	0.119 485	0.120 241	0.121 000	0.121 761	0.122 525	0.123 291	10
11	0.110 334	0.111 092	0.111 852	0.112 615	0.113 381	0.114 149	11
12	0.102 724	0.103 484	0.104 247	0.105 012	0.105 781	0.106 552	12
13	0.096 299	0.097 062	0.097 827	0.098 596	0.099 369	0.100 144	13
14	0.090 805	0.091 571	0.092 340	0.093 113	0.093 889	0.094 669	14
15	0.086 055	0.086 825	0.087 599	0.088 376	0.089 157	0.089 941	15
16	0.081 911	0.082 685	0.083 463	0.084 245	0.085 031	0.085 820	16
17	0.078 264	0.079 043	0.079 826	0.080 613	0.081 404	0.082 199	17
18	0.075 033	0.075 817	0.076 605	0.077 397	0.078 193	0.078 993	18
19	0.072 152	0.072 940	0.073 733	0.074 531	0.075 332	0.076 139	19
20	0.069 568	0.070 361	0.071 159	0.071 962	0.072 770	0.073 582	20
21	0.067 238	0.068 037	0.068 840	0.069 649	0.070 462	0.071 280	21
22	0.065 128	0.065 932	0.066 741	0.067 555	0.068 375	0.069 199	22
23	0.063 209	0.064 019	0.064 833	0.065 653	0.066 479	0.067 309	23
24	0.061 458	0.062 273	0.063 093	0.063 919	0.064 750	0.065 587	24
25	0.059 854	0.060 674	0.061 500	0.062 332	0.063 169	0.064 012	25
26	0.058 380	0.059 205	0.060 037	0.060 875	0.061 718	0.062 567	26
27	0.057 021	0.057 852	0.058 690	0.059 533	0.060 383	0.061 239	27
28	0.055 766	0.056 603	0.057 446	0.058 295	0.059 151	0.060 013	28
29	0.054 603	0.055 445	0.056 294	0.057 150	0.058 012	0.058 880	29
30	0.053 523	0.054 371	0.055 226	0.056 088	0.056 956	0.057 830	30
31	0.052 519	0.053 372	0.054 233	0.055 100	0.055 975	0.056 855	31
32	0.051 582	0.052 442	0.053 308	0.054 181	0.055 062	0.055 949	32
33	0.050 707	0.051 572	0.052 445	0.053 324	0.054 210	0.055 104	33
34	0.049 889	0.050 760	0.051 638	0.052 523	0.053 415	0.054 315	34
35	0.049 122	0.049 998	0.050 882	0.051 773	0.052 672	0.053 577	35
36	0.048 402	0.049 284	0.050 174	0.051 071	0.051 975	0.052 887	36
37	0.047 726	0.048 613	0.049 508	0.050 411	0.051 322	0.052 240	37
38	0.047 089	0.047 982	0.048 883	0.049 792	0.050 708	0.051 632	38
39	0.046 489	0.047 388	0.048 294	0.049 209	0.050 131	0.051 061	39
40	0.045 923	0.046 827	0.047 739	0.048 659	0.049 588	0.050 523	40
41	0.045 389	0.046 298	0.047 216	0.048 142	0.049 076	0.050 017	41
42	0.044 884	0.045 798	0.046 721	0.047 653	0.048 593	0.049 540	42
43	0.044 405	0.045 325	0.046 254	0.047 191	0.048 136	0.049 090	43
44	0.043 952	0.044 878	0.045 812	0.046 754	0.047 705	0.048 665	44
45	0.043 523	0.044 453	0.045 393	0.046 341	0.047 298	0.048 262	45
46	0.043 115	0.044 051	0.044 996	0.045 949	0.046 912	0.047 882	46
47	0.042 728	0.043 669	0.044 619	0.045 578	0.046 546	0.047 522	47
48	0.042 360	0.043 306	0.044 262	0.045 226	0.046 199	0.047 181	48
49	0.042 010	0.042 962	0.043 922	0.044 892	0.045 870	0.046 857	49
50	0.041 677	0.042 634	0.043 599	0.044 574	0.045 558	0.046 550	50
51	0.041 360	0.042 322	0.043 292	0.044 272	0.045 261	0.046 259	51
52	0.041 058	0.042 024	0.043 000	0.043 985	0.044 979	0.045 982	52
53	0.040 770	0.041 741	0.042 722	0.043 712	0.044 711	0.045 719	53
54	0.040 495	0.041 471	0.042 457	0.043 452	0.044 456	0.045 469	54
55	0.040 232	0.041 213	0.042 204	0.043 204	0.044 213	0.045 231	55
56	0.039 981	0.040 967	0.041 963	0.042 968	0.043 982	0.045 005	56
57	0.039 742	0.040 732	0.041 733	0.042 742	0.043 761	0.044 789	57
58	0.039 513	0.040 508	0.041 513	0.042 528	0.043 551	0.044 584	58
59	0.039 294	0.040 294	0.041 303	0.042 323	0.043 351	0.044 388	59
YRS							
30	0.039 084	0.040 089	0.041 103	0.042 127	0.043 160	0.044 202	60
31	0.038 691	0.039 705	0.040 728	0.041 761	0.042 803	0.043 854	62
32	0.038 331	0.039 353	0.040 385	0.041 427	0.042 478	0.043 538	64
33	0.038 000	0.039 030	0.040 071	0.041 121	0.042 181	0.043 249	66
34	0.037 695	0.038 734	0.039 783	0.040 841	0.041 909	0.042 986	68
35	0.037 414	0.038 461	0.039 518	0.040 585	0.041 660	0.042 745	70
36	0.037 155	0.038 210	0.039 275	0.040 349	0.041 433	0.042 525	72
37	0.036 916	0.037 978	0.039 051	0.040 133	0.041 224	0.042 323	74
38	0.036 695	0.037 765	0.038 844	0.039 934	0.041 032	0.042 139	76
39	0.036 490	0.037 567	0.038 654	0.039 750	0.040 856	0.041 969	78
40	0.036 301	0.037 385	0.038 479	0.039 582	0.040 694	0.041 814	80

261

PARTIAL PAYMENT TO AMORTIZE

SEMIANNUAL COMPOUNDING

HALF YRS	8.25% ANNUAL RATE	8.50% ANNUAL RATE	8.75% ANNUAL RATE	9.00% ANNUAL RATE	9.25% ANNUAL RATE	9.50% ANNUAL RATE	HALF YRS
1	1.041 250	1.042 500	1.043 750	1.045 000	1.046 250	1.047 500	1
2	0.531 146	0.532 096	0.533 047	0.533 998	0.534 949	0.535 900	2
3	0.361 204	0.362 060	0.362 916	0.363 773	0.364 631	0.365 490	3
4	0.276 302	0.277 115	0.277 929	0.278 744	0.279 559	0.280 376	4
5	0.225 416	0.226 207	0.226 999	0.227 792	0.228 586	0.229 381	5
6	0.191 539	0.192 317	0.193 097	0.193 878	0.194 661	0.195 445	6
7	0.167 380	0.168 152	0.168 926	0.169 701	0.170 479	0.171 257	7
8	0.149 295	0.150 065	0.150 836	0.151 610	0.152 385	0.153 162	8
9	0.135 260	0.136 029	0.136 801	0.137 574	0.138 350	0.139 128	9
10	0.124 059	0.124 830	0.125 603	0.126 379	0.127 157	0.127 937	10
11	0.114 920	0.115 693	0.116 469	0.117 248	0.118 029	0.118 813	11
12	0.107 326	0.108 103	0.108 883	0.109 666	0.110 452	0.111 240	12
13	0.100 922	0.101 703	0.102 488	0.103 275	0.104 066	0.104 860	13
14	0.095 452	0.096 238	0.097 028	0.097 820	0.098 616	0.099 416	14
15	0.090 729	0.091 520	0.092 315	0.093 114	0.093 916	0.094 721	15
16	0.086 613	0.087 410	0.088 211	0.089 015	0.089 823	0.090 635	16
17	0.082 997	0.083 800	0.084 607	0.085 418	0.086 232	0.087 051	17
18	0.079 798	0.080 607	0.081 420	0.082 237	0.083 058	0.083 883	18
19	0.076 949	0.077 764	0.078 584	0.079 407	0.080 235	0.081 068	19
20	0.074 399	0.075 220	0.076 046	0.076 876	0.077 711	0.078 550	20
21	0.072 103	0.072 931	0.073 763	0.074 601	0.075 442	0.076 289	21
22	0.070 028	0.070 862	0.071 702	0.072 546	0.073 395	0.074 248	22
23	0.068 145	0.068 986	0.069 831	0.070 682	0.071 539	0.072 400	23
24	0.066 429	0.067 276	0.068 129	0.068 987	0.069 850	0.070 719	24
25	0.064 860	0.065 715	0.066 574	0.067 439	0.068 309	0.069 185	25
26	0.063 422	0.064 283	0.065 149	0.066 021	0.066 899	0.067 782	26
27	0.062 100	0.062 967	0.063 841	0.064 719	0.065 604	0.066 494	27
28	0.060 881	0.061 755	0.062 635	0.063 521	0.064 413	0.065 310	28
29	0.059 754	0.060 635	0.061 522	0.062 415	0.063 313	0.064 218	29
30	0.058 711	0.059 598	0.060 492	0.061 392	0.062 297	0.063 209	30
31	0.057 743	0.058 637	0.059 537	0.060 443	0.061 356	0.062 276	31
32	0.056 842	0.057 743	0.058 650	0.059 563	0.060 483	0.061 409	32
33	0.056 004	0.056 911	0.057 824	0.058 745	0.059 671	0.060 605	33
34	0.055 221	0.056 135	0.057 055	0.057 982	0.058 916	0.059 856	34
35	0.054 490	0.055 410	0.056 337	0.057 270	0.058 211	0.059 158	35
36	0.053 806	0.054 732	0.055 666	0.056 606	0.057 553	0.058 507	36
37	0.053 165	0.054 097	0.055 037	0.055 984	0.056 938	0.057 898	37
38	0.052 563	0.053 502	0.054 448	0.055 402	0.056 362	0.057 329	38
39	0.051 998	0.052 944	0.053 896	0.054 856	0.055 823	0.056 796	39
40	0.051 467	0.052 418	0.053 377	0.054 343	0.055 316	0.056 297	40
41	0.050 967	0.051 924	0.052 889	0.053 862	0.054 841	0.055 828	41
42	0.050 496	0.051 459	0.052 430	0.053 409	0.054 395	0.055 388	42
43	0.050 051	0.051 021	0.051 998	0.052 982	0.053 974	0.054 974	43
44	0.049 632	0.050 607	0.051 590	0.052 581	0.053 579	0.054 584	44
45	0.049 236	0.050 217	0.051 205	0.052 202	0.053 206	0.054 218	45
46	0.048 861	0.049 848	0.050 842	0.051 845	0.052 855	0.053 872	46
47	0.048 506	0.049 499	0.050 499	0.051 507	0.052 523	0.053 546	47
48	0.048 171	0.049 169	0.050 175	0.051 189	0.052 210	0.053 239	48
49	0.047 853	0.048 856	0.049 868	0.050 887	0.051 914	0.052 949	49
50	0.047 551	0.048 560	0.049 577	0.050 602	0.051 635	0.052 675	50
51	0.047 265	0.048 279	0.049 302	0.050 332	0.051 370	0.052 416	51
52	0.046 994	0.048 013	0.049 041	0.050 077	0.051 120	0.052 171	52
53	0.046 736	0.047 761	0.048 794	0.049 835	0.050 883	0.051 940	53
54	0.046 491	0.047 521	0.048 559	0.049 605	0.050 659	0.051 720	54
55	0.046 258	0.047 293	0.048 336	0.049 388	0.050 446	0.051 513	55
56	0.046 037	0.047 077	0.048 125	0.049 181	0.050 245	0.051 316	56
57	0.045 826	0.046 871	0.047 924	0.048 985	0.050 054	0.051 130	57
58	0.045 625	0.046 675	0.047 733	0.048 799	0.049 872	0.050 953	58
59	0.045 434	0.046 489	0.047 552	0.048 622	0.049 700	0.050 786	59

YRS	8.25%	8.50%	8.75%	9.00%	9.25%	9.50%	
30	0.045 253	0.046 312	0.047 379	0.048 454	0.049 537	0.050 627	60
31	0.044 914	0.045 982	0.047 059	0.048 143	0.049 234	0.050 333	62
32	0.044 606	0.045 683	0.046 768	0.047 861	0.048 961	0.050 069	64
33	0.044 326	0.045 412	0.046 505	0.047 606	0.048 714	0.049 830	66
34	0.044 071	0.045 165	0.046 266	0.047 375	0.048 491	0.049 614	68
35	0.043 838	0.044 940	0.046 049	0.047 165	0.048 289	0.049 419	70
36	0.043 626	0.044 734	0.045 851	0.046 975	0.048 105	0.049 243	72
37	0.043 431	0.044 547	0.045 671	0.046 802	0.047 939	0.049 083	74
38	0.043 254	0.044 377	0.045 507	0.046 644	0.047 788	0.048 939	76
39	0.043 091	0.044 221	0.045 357	0.046 501	0.047 651	0.048 808	78
40	0.042 942	0.044 078	0.045 221	0.046 371	0.047 527	0.048 689	80

PARTIAL PAYMENT TO AMORTIZE

HALF YRS	9.75% ANNUAL RATE	10.00% ANNUAL RATE	10.50% ANNUAL RATE	11.00% ANNUAL RATE	11.50% ANNUAL RATE	12.00% ANNUAL RATE	HALF YRS
1	1.048 750	1.050 000	1.052 500	1.055 000	1.057 500	1.060 000	1
2	0.536 853	0.537 805	0.539 711	0.541 618	0.543 527	0.545 437	2
3	0.366 349	0.367 209	0.368 930	0.370 654	0.372 381	0.374 110	3
4	0.281 193	0.282 012	0.283 651	0.285 294	0.286 941	0.288 591	4
5	0.230 177	0.230 975	0.232 573	0.234 176	0.235 784	0.237 396	5
6	0.196 231	0.197 017	0.198 595	0.200 179	0.201 768	0.203 363	6
7	0.172 038	0.172 820	0.174 389	0.175 964	0.177 546	0.179 135	7
8	0.153 941	0.154 722	0.156 289	0.157 864	0.159 446	0.161 036	8
9	0.139 908	0.140 690	0.142 261	0.143 839	0.145 427	0.147 022	9
10	0.128 720	0.129 505	0.131 082	0.132 668	0.134 263	0.135 868	10
11	0.119 600	0.120 389	0.121 975	0.123 571	0.125 177	0.126 793	11
12	0.112 031	0.112 825	0.114 422	0.116 029	0.117 648	0.119 277	12
13	0.105 656	0.106 456	0.108 064	0.109 684	0.111 316	0.112 960	13
14	0.100 218	0.101 024	0.102 645	0.104 279	0.105 926	0.107 585	14
15	0.095 530	0.096 342	0.097 977	0.099 626	0.101 288	0.102 963	15
16	0.091 451	0.092 270	0.093 919	0.095 583	0.097 260	0.098 952	16
17	0.087 873	0.088 699	0.090 363	0.092 042	0.093 736	0.095 445	17
18	0.084 713	0.085 546	0.087 225	0.088 920	0.090 630	0.092 357	18
19	0.081 904	0.082 745	0.084 439	0.086 150	0.087 877	0.089 621	19
20	0.079 394	0.080 243	0.081 952	0.083 679	0.085 423	0.087 185	20
21	0.077 140	0.077 996	0.079 721	0.081 465	0.083 226	0.085 005	21
22	0.075 107	0.075 971	0.077 712	0.079 471	0.081 249	0.083 046	22
23	0.073 266	0.074 137	0.075 894	0.077 670	0.079 465	0.081 278	23
24	0.071 592	0.072 471	0.074 243	0.076 036	0.077 848	0.079 679	24
25	0.070 066	0.070 952	0.072 741	0.074 549	0.076 378	0.078 227	25
26	0.068 670	0.069 564	0.071 368	0.073 193	0.075 039	0.076 904	26
27	0.067 390	0.068 292	0.070 111	0.071 952	0.073 814	0.075 697	27
28	0.066 213	0.067 123	0.068 957	0.070 814	0.072 693	0.074 593	28
29	0.065 129	0.066 046	0.067 896	0.069 769	0.071 663	0.073 580	29
30	0.064 127	0.065 051	0.066 917	0.068 805	0.070 716	0.072 649	30
31	0.063 201	0.064 132	0.066 013	0.067 917	0.069 843	0.071 792	31
32	0.062 342	0.063 280	0.065 176	0.067 095	0.069 038	0.071 002	32
33	0.061 544	0.062 490	0.064 400	0.066 335	0.068 292	0.070 273	33
34	0.060 802	0.061 755	0.063 680	0.065 630	0.067 603	0.069 598	34
35	0.060 112	0.061 072	0.063 011	0.064 975	0.066 963	0.068 974	35
36	0.059 467	0.060 434	0.062 388	0.064 366	0.066 369	0.068 395	36
37	0.058 866	0.059 840	0.061 807	0.063 800	0.065 817	0.067 857	37
38	0.058 303	0.059 284	0.061 265	0.063 272	0.065 303	0.067 358	38
39	0.057 777	0.058 765	0.060 759	0.062 780	0.064 825	0.066 894	39
40	0.057 284	0.058 278	0.060 286	0.062 320	0.064 379	0.066 462	40
41	0.056 822	0.057 822	0.059 844	0.061 891	0.063 963	0.066 059	41
42	0.056 388	0.057 395	0.059 429	0.061 489	0.063 574	0.065 683	42
43	0.055 980	0.056 993	0.059 040	0.061 113	0.063 211	0.065 333	43
44	0.055 597	0.056 616	0.058 676	0.060 761	0.062 872	0.065 006	44
45	0.055 236	0.056 262	0.058 333	0.060 431	0.062 554	0.064 700	45
46	0.054 897	0.055 928	0.058 012	0.060 122	0.062 256	0.064 415	46
47	0.054 577	0.055 614	0.057 710	0.059 831	0.061 978	0.064 148	47
48	0.054 275	0.055 318	0.057 425	0.059 559	0.061 716	0.063 898	48
49	0.053 991	0.055 040	0.057 158	0.059 302	0.061 471	0.063 664	49
50	0.053 722	0.054 777	0.056 906	0.059 061	0.061 241	0.063 444	50
51	0.053 469	0.054 529	0.056 669	0.058 835	0.061 025	0.063 239	51
52	0.053 229	0.054 294	0.056 445	0.058 622	0.060 823	0.063 046	52
53	0.053 003	0.054 073	0.056 234	0.058 421	0.060 632	0.062 866	53
54	0.052 789	0.053 864	0.056 036	0.058 232	0.060 453	0.062 696	54
55	0.052 586	0.053 667	0.055 848	0.058 055	0.060 285	0.062 537	55
56	0.052 395	0.053 480	0.055 671	0.057 887	0.060 126	0.062 388	56
57	0.052 213	0.053 303	0.055 504	0.057 729	0.059 977	0.062 247	57
58	0.052 041	0.053 136	0.055 346	0.057 580	0.059 837	0.062 116	58
59	0.051 879	0.052 978	0.055 197	0.057 440	0.059 705	0.061 992	59

YRS							
30	0.051 724	0.052 828	0.055 055	0.057 307	0.059 581	0.061 876	60
31	0.051 439	0.052 552	0.054 796	0.057 064	0.059 354	0.061 664	62
32	0.051 183	0.052 304	0.054 564	0.056 847	0.059 152	0.061 476	64
33	0.050 952	0.052 081	0.054 356	0.056 654	0.058 973	0.061 310	66
34	0.050 744	0.051 880	0.054 170	0.056 482	0.058 813	0.061 163	68
35	0.050 556	0.051 699	0.054 003	0.056 328	0.058 672	0.061 033	70
36	0.050 387	0.051 536	0.053 853	0.056 190	0.058 545	0.060 918	72
37	0.050 233	0.051 390	0.053 718	0.056 067	0.058 433	0.060 815	74
38	0.050 095	0.051 257	0.053 597	0.055 956	0.058 333	0.060 725	76
39	0.049 970	0.051 138	0.053 488	0.055 858	0.058 244	0.060 644	78
40	0.049 857	0.051 030	0.053 391	0.055 769	0.058 164	0.060 573	80

HALF YRS	12.50% ANNUAL RATE	13.00% ANNUAL RATE	13.50% ANNUAL RATE	14.00% ANNUAL RATE	14.50% ANNUAL RATE	15.00% ANNUAL RATE	HALF YRS
1	1.062 500	1.065 000	1.067 500	1.070 000	1.072 500	1.075 000	1
2	0.547 348	0.549 262	0.551 176	0.553 092	0.555 009	0.556 928	2
3	0.375 841	0.377 576	0.379 312	0.381 052	0.382 793	0.384 538	3
4	0.290 245	0.291 903	0.293 564	0.295 228	0.296 896	0.298 568	4
5	0.239 013	0.240 635	0.242 260	0.243 891	0.245 525	0.247 165	5
6	0.204 963	0.206 568	0.208 179	0.209 796	0.211 418	0.213 045	6
7	0.180 730	0.182 331	0.183 939	0.185 553	0.187 174	0.188 800	7
8	0.162 633	0.164 237	0.165 849	0.167 468	0.169 094	0.170 727	8
9	0.148 626	0.150 238	0.151 858	0.153 486	0.155 123	0.156 767	9
10	0.137 482	0.139 105	0.140 737	0.142 378	0.144 027	0.145 686	10
11	0.128 419	0.130 055	0.131 701	0.133 357	0.135 022	0.136 697	11
12	0.120 917	0.122 568	0.124 230	0.125 902	0.127 585	0.129 278	12
13	0.114 616	0.116 283	0.117 961	0.119 651	0.121 352	0.123 064	13
14	0.109 257	0.110 940	0.112 637	0.114 345	0.116 065	0.117 797	14
15	0.104 651	0.106 353	0.108 067	0.109 795	0.111 535	0.113 287	15
16	0.100 658	0.102 378	0.104 111	0.105 858	0.107 618	0.109 391	16
17	0.097 168	0.098 906	0.100 659	0.102 425	0.104 206	0.106 000	17
18	0.094 098	0.095 855	0.097 626	0.099 413	0.101 214	0.103 029	18
19	0.091 380	0.093 156	0.094 947	0.096 753	0.098 574	0.100 411	19
20	0.088 962	0.090 756	0.092 567	0.094 393	0.096 235	0.098 092	20
21	0.086 800	0.088 613	0.090 443	0.092 289	0.094 151	0.096 029	21
22	0.084 860	0.086 691	0.088 540	0.090 406	0.092 288	0.094 187	22
23	0.083 111	0.084 961	0.086 829	0.088 714	0.090 616	0.092 535	23
24	0.081 529	0.083 398	0.085 284	0.087 189	0.089 111	0.091 050	24
25	0.080 095	0.081 981	0.083 887	0.085 811	0.087 752	0.089 711	25
26	0.078 790	0.080 695	0.082 619	0.084 561	0.086 521	0.088 500	26
27	0.077 600	0.079 523	0.081 465	0.083 426	0.085 405	0.087 402	27
28	0.076 513	0.078 453	0.080 413	0.082 392	0.084 390	0.086 405	28
29	0.075 517	0.077 474	0.079 452	0.081 449	0.083 464	0.085 498	29
30	0.074 603	0.076 577	0.078 572	0.080 586	0.082 620	0.084 671	30
31	0.073 763	0.075 754	0.077 766	0.079 797	0.081 847	0.083 916	31
32	0.072 989	0.074 997	0.077 025	0.079 073	0.081 140	0.083 226	32
33	0.072 275	0.074 299	0.076 344	0.078 408	0.080 492	0.082 594	33
34	0.071 617	0.073 656	0.075 716	0.077 797	0.079 896	0.082 015	34
35	0.071 007	0.073 062	0.075 138	0.077 234	0.079 349	0.081 483	35
36	0.070 443	0.072 513	0.074 604	0.076 715	0.078 846	0.080 994	36
37	0.069 921	0.072 005	0.074 111	0.076 237	0.078 382	0.080 545	37
38	0.069 436	0.071 535	0.073 655	0.075 794	0.077 954	0.080 132	38
39	0.068 985	0.071 099	0.073 233	0.075 387	0.077 560	0.079 751	39
40	0.068 567	0.070 694	0.072 842	0.075 009	0.077 196	0.079 400	40
41	0.068 177	0.070 318	0.072 479	0.074 660	0.076 859	0.079 077	41
42	0.067 815	0.069 968	0.072 142	0.074 336	0.076 548	0.078 778	42
43	0.067 478	0.069 644	0.071 830	0.074 036	0.076 260	0.078 502	43
44	0.067 163	0.069 341	0.071 540	0.073 758	0.075 994	0.078 247	44
45	0.066 869	0.069 060	0.071 270	0.073 500	0.075 747	0.078 011	45
46	0.066 596	0.068 797	0.071 019	0.073 260	0.075 518	0.077 794	46
47	0.066 340	0.068 553	0.070 786	0.073 037	0.075 306	0.077 592	47
48	0.066 101	0.068 325	0.070 569	0.072 831	0.075 110	0.077 405	48
49	0.065 878	0.068 112	0.070 366	0.072 639	0.074 928	0.077 232	49
50	0.065 669	0.067 914	0.070 178	0.072 460	0.074 758	0.077 072	50
51	0.065 474	0.067 729	0.070 002	0.072 294	0.074 601	0.076 924	51
52	0.065 291	0.067 556	0.069 839	0.072 139	0.074 455	0.076 787	52
53	0.065 120	0.067 394	0.069 686	0.071 995	0.074 320	0.076 659	53
54	0.064 960	0.067 243	0.069 544	0.071 861	0.074 194	0.076 541	54
55	0.064 810	0.067 101	0.069 411	0.071 736	0.074 077	0.076 432	55
56	0.064 669	0.066 969	0.069 287	0.071 620	0.073 968	0.076 330	56
57	0.064 537	0.066 846	0.069 171	0.071 512	0.073 867	0.076 236	57
58	0.064 414	0.066 730	0.069 063	0.071 411	0.073 773	0.076 148	58
59	0.064 298	0.066 622	0.068 962	0.071 317	0.073 686	0.076 067	59

YRS

YRS	12.50%	13.00%	13.50%	14.00%	14.50%	15.00%	HALF YRS
30	0.064 189	0.066 520	0.068 868	0.071 229	0.073 604	0.075 991	60
31	0.063 992	0.066 337	0.068 697	0.071 071	0.073 458	0.075 856	62
32	0.063 818	0.066 176	0.068 548	0.070 934	0.073 332	0.075 740	64
33	0.063 665	0.066 034	0.068 418	0.070 814	0.073 222	0.075 639	66
34	0.063 529	0.065 910	0.068 304	0.070 710	0.073 127	0.075 553	68
35	0.063 410	0.065 801	0.068 205	0.070 620	0.073 044	0.075 478	70
36	0.063 305	0.065 705	0.068 118	0.070 541	0.072 973	0.075 413	72
37	0.063 212	0.065 621	0.068 041	0.070 472	0.072 911	0.075 357	74
38	0.063 130	0.065 547	0.067 975	0.070 412	0.072 857	0.075 309	76
39	0.063 057	0.065 482	0.067 916	0.070 359	0.072 810	0.075 267	78
40	0.062 993	0.065 424	0.067 865	0.070 314	0.072 769	0.075 231	80

PARTIAL PAYMENT TO AMORTIZE

HALF YRS	15.50% ANNUAL RATE	16.00% ANNUAL RATE	16.50% ANNUAL RATE	17.00% ANNUAL RATE	17.50% ANNUAL RATE	18.00% ANNUAL RATE	HALF YRS
1	1.077 500	1.080 000	1.082 500	1.085 000	1.087 500	1.090 000	1
2	0.558 848	0.560 769	0.562 692	0.564 616	0.566 542	0.568 469	2
3	0.386 284	0.388 034	0.389 785	0.391 539	0.393 296	0.395 055	3
4	0.300 242	0.301 921	0.303 603	0.305 288	0.306 977	0.308 669	4
5	0.248 808	0.250 456	0.252 109	0.253 766	0.255 427	0.257 092	5
6	0.214 677	0.216 315	0.217 959	0.219 607	0.221 261	0.222 920	6
7	0.190 433	0.192 072	0.193 718	0.195 369	0.197 027	0.198 691	7
8	0.172 367	0.174 015	0.175 669	0.177 331	0.178 999	0.180 674	8
9	0.158 419	0.160 080	0.161 748	0.163 424	0.165 107	0.166 799	9
10	0.147 353	0.149 029	0.150 714	0.152 408	0.154 110	0.155 820	10
11	0.138 382	0.140 076	0.141 780	0.143 493	0.145 215	0.146 947	11
12	0.130 981	0.132 695	0.134 419	0.136 153	0.137 897	0.139 651	12
13	0.124 788	0.126 522	0.128 267	0.130 023	0.131 789	0.133 567	13
14	0.119 541	0.121 297	0.123 064	0.124 842	0.126 632	0.128 433	14
15	0.115 052	0.116 830	0.118 619	0.120 420	0.122 234	0.124 059	15
16	0.111 178	0.112 977	0.114 789	0.116 614	0.118 451	0.120 300	16
17	0.107 808	0.109 629	0.111 464	0.113 312	0.115 173	0.117 046	17
18	0.104 859	0.106 702	0.108 559	0.110 430	0.112 315	0.114 212	18
19	0.102 262	0.104 128	0.106 007	0.107 901	0.109 809	0.111 730	19
20	0.099 965	0.101 852	0.103 754	0.105 671	0.107 602	0.109 546	20
21	0.097 923	0.099 832	0.101 756	0.103 695	0.105 649	0.107 617	21
22	0.096 102	0.098 032	0.099 978	0.101 939	0.103 915	0.105 905	22
23	0.094 471	0.096 422	0.098 389	0.100 372	0.102 370	0.104 382	23
24	0.093 006	0.094 978	0.096 966	0.098 970	0.100 989	0.103 023	24
25	0.091 686	0.093 679	0.095 687	0.097 712	0.099 751	0.101 806	25
26	0.090 495	0.092 507	0.094 536	0.096 580	0.098 640	0.100 715	26
27	0.089 417	0.091 448	0.093 496	0.095 560	0.097 640	0.099 735	27
28	0.088 438	0.090 489	0.092 556	0.094 639	0.096 738	0.098 852	28
29	0.087 550	0.089 619	0.091 704	0.093 806	0.095 923	0.098 056	29
30	0.086 741	0.088 827	0.090 931	0.093 051	0.095 186	0.097 336	30
31	0.086 003	0.088 107	0.090 228	0.092 365	0.094 518	0.096 686	31
32	0.085 330	0.087 451	0.089 589	0.091 742	0.093 912	0.096 096	32
33	0.084 714	0.086 852	0.089 006	0.091 176	0.093 361	0.095 562	33
34	0.084 151	0.086 304	0.088 474	0.090 660	0.092 861	0.095 077	34
35	0.083 635	0.085 803	0.087 988	0.090 189	0.092 405	0.094 636	35
36	0.083 161	0.085 345	0.087 545	0.089 760	0.091 990	0.094 235	36
37	0.082 726	0.084 924	0.087 139	0.089 368	0.091 612	0.093 870	37
38	0.082 327	0.084 539	0.086 767	0.089 010	0.091 267	0.093 538	38
39	0.081 960	0.084 185	0.086 426	0.088 682	0.090 952	0.093 236	39
40	0.081 622	0.083 860	0.086 114	0.088 382	0.090 664	0.092 960	40
41	0.081 311	0.083 561	0.085 827	0.088 107	0.090 401	0.092 708	41
42	0.081 024	0.083 287	0.085 564	0.087 856	0.090 161	0.092 478	42
43	0.080 760	0.083 034	0.085 323	0.087 625	0.089 941	0.092 268	43
44	0.080 517	0.082 802	0.085 101	0.087 414	0.089 739	0.092 077	44
45	0.080 292	0.082 587	0.084 897	0.087 220	0.089 555	0.091 902	45
46	0.080 084	0.082 390	0.084 709	0.087 042	0.089 386	0.091 742	46
47	0.079 893	0.082 208	0.084 537	0.086 878	0.089 231	0.091 595	47
48	0.079 716	0.082 040	0.084 378	0.086 728	0.089 089	0.091 461	48
49	0.079 552	0.081 886	0.084 232	0.086 590	0.088 959	0.091 339	49
50	0.079 401	0.081 743	0.084 097	0.086 463	0.088 840	0.091 227	50
51	0.079 261	0.081 611	0.083 973	0.086 347	0.088 731	0.091 124	51
52	0.079 132	0.081 490	0.083 859	0.086 240	0.088 630	0.091 030	52
53	0.079 012	0.081 377	0.083 754	0.086 141	0.088 538	0.090 944	53
54	0.078 901	0.081 274	0.083 657	0.086 051	0.088 454	0.090 866	54
55	0.078 799	0.081 178	0.083 568	0.085 968	0.088 376	0.090 794	55
56	0.078 704	0.081 090	0.083 485	0.085 891	0.088 305	0.090 728	56
57	0.078 616	0.081 008	0.083 410	0.085 821	0.088 240	0.090 667	57
58	0.078 535	0.080 932	0.083 340	0.085 756	0.088 180	0.090 612	58
59	0.078 459	0.080 862	0.083 275	0.085 696	0.088 125	0.090 561	59

YRS							
30	0.078 390	0.080 798	0.083 215	0.085 641	0.088 074	0.090 514	60
31	0.078 265	0.080 683	0.083 110	0.085 544	0.087 985	0.090 432	62
32	0.078 158	0.080 585	0.083 020	0.085 462	0.087 910	0.090 364	64
33	0.078 066	0.080 501	0.082 943	0.085 392	0.087 846	0.090 306	66
34	0.077 987	0.080 429	0.082 878	0.085 333	0.087 793	0.090 257	68
35	0.077 919	0.080 368	0.082 822	0.085 282	0.087 747	0.090 216	70
36	0.077 861	0.080 315	0.082 775	0.085 240	0.087 709	0.090 182	72
37	0.077 811	0.080 270	0.082 734	0.085 204	0.087 677	0.090 153	74
38	0.077 767	0.080 231	0.082 700	0.085 173	0.087 649	0.090 129	76
39	0.077 730	0.080 198	0.082 671	0.085 147	0.087 626	0.090 109	78
40	0.077 698	0.080 170	0.082 646	0.085 125	0.087 607	0.090 091	80

HALF YRS	18.50% ANNUAL RATE	19.00% ANNUAL RATE	19.50% ANNUAL RATE	20.00% ANNUAL RATE	20.50% ANNUAL RATE	21.00% ANNUAL RATE	HALF YRS
1	1.092 500	1.095 000	1.097 500	1.100 000	1.102 500	1.105 000	1
2	0.570 397	0.572 327	0.574 258	0.576 190	0.578 124	0.580 059	2
3	0.396 816	0.398 580	0.400 346	0.402 115	0.403 886	0.405 659	3
4	0.310 364	0.312 063	0.313 765	0.315 471	0.317 180	0.318 892	4
5	0.258 762	0.260 436	0.262 115	0.263 79.	0.265 484	0.267 175	5
6	0.224 584	0.226 253	0.227 928	0.229 607	0.231 292	0.232 982	6
7	0.200 360	0.202 036	0.203 718	0.205 405	0.207 099	0.208 799	7
8	0.182 357	0.184 046	0.185 741	0.187 444	0.189 153	0.190 869	8
9	0.168 498	0.170 205	0.171 919	0.173 641	0.175 370	0.177 106	9
10	0.157 539	0.159 266	0.161 002	0.162 745	0.164 497	0.166 257	10
11	0.148 687	0.150 437	0.152 196	0.153 963	0.155 740	0.157 525	11
12	0.141 414	0.143 188	0.144 971	0.146 763	0.148 565	0.150 377	12
13	0.135 354	0.137 152	0.138 960	0.140 779	0.142 607	0.144 445	13
14	0.130 245	0.132 068	0.133 902	0.135 746	0.137 601	0.139 467	14
15	0.125 896	0.127 744	0.129 603	0.131 474	0.133 355	0.135 248	15
16	0.122 161	0.124 035	0.125 920	0.127 817	0.129 725	0.131 644	16
17	0.118 932	0.120 831	0.122 741	0.124 664	0.126 599	0.128 545	17
18	0.116 123	0.118 046	0.119 982	0.121 930	0.123 891	0.125 863	18
19	0.113 665	0.115 613	0.117 574	0.119 547	0.121 533	0.123 531	19
20	0.111 505	0.113 477	0.115 462	0.117 460	0.119 470	0.121 493	20
21	0.109 598	0.111 594	0.113 602	0.115 624	0.117 659	0.119 707	21
22	0.107 909	0.109 928	0.111 960	0.114 005	0.116 063	0.118 134	22
23	0.106 409	0.108 449	0.110 504	0.112 572	0.114 653	0.116 747	23
24	0.105 071	0.107 134	0.109 210	0.111 300	0.113 403	0.115 519	24
25	0.103 876	0.105 959	0.108 057	0.110 168	0.112 292	0.114 429	25
26	0.102 805	0.104 909	0.107 027	0.109 159	0.111 304	0.113 461	26
27	0.101 845	0.103 969	0.106 106	0.108 258	0.110 422	0.112 599	27
28	0.100 981	0.103 124	0.105 281	0.107 451	0.109 634	0.111 830	28
29	0.100 203	0.102 364	0.104 540	0.106 728	0.108 929	0.111 143	29
30	0.099 501	0.101 681	0.103 873	0.106 079	0.108 298	0.110 528	30
31	0.098 868	0.101 064	0.103 274	0.105 496	0.107 731	0.109 978	31
32	0.098 295	0.100 507	0.102 733	0.104 972	0.107 222	0.109 485	32
33	0.097 776	0.100 004	0.102 246	0.104 499	0.106 765	0.109 042	33
34	0.097 306	0.099 549	0.101 805	0.104 074	0.106 354	0.108 645	34
35	0.096 880	0.099 138	0.101 408	0.103 690	0.105 983	0.108 288	35
36	0.096 493	0.098 764	0.101 048	0.103 343	0.105 649	0.107 967	36
37	0.096 142	0.098 426	0.100 722	0.103 030	0.105 349	0.107 677	37
38	0.095 822	0.098 119	0.100 427	0.102 747	0.105 077	0.107 417	38
39	0.095 532	0.097 840	0.100 160	0.102 491	0.104 832	0.107 183	39
40	0.095 267	0.097 587	0.099 918	0.102 259	0.104 611	0.106 971	40
41	0.095 027	0.097 357	0.099 698	0.102 050	0.104 411	0.106 781	41
42	0.094 808	0.097 148	0.099 499	0.101 860	0.104 230	0.106 609	42
43	0.094 608	0.096 958	0.099 318	0.101 688	0.104 067	0.106 454	43
44	0.094 426	0.096 785	0.099 154	0.101 532	0.103 919	0.106 314	44
45	0.094 259	0.096 627	0.099 005	0.101 391	0.103 786	0.106 188	45
46	0.094 108	0.096 484	0.098 869	0.101 263	0.103 665	0.106 074	46
47	0.093 970	0.096 353	0.098 746	0.101 147	0.103 555	0.105 971	47
48	0.093 843	0.096 234	0.098 634	0.101 041	0.103 456	0.105 878	48
49	0.093 728	0.096 126	0.098 532	0.100 946	0.103 367	0.105 794	49
50	0.093 623	0.096 027	0.098 440	0.100 859	0.103 285	0.105 718	50
51	0.093 527	0.095 937	0.098 355	0.100 780	0.103 212	0.105 649	51
52	0.093 439	0.095 855	0.098 279	0.100 709	0.103 145	0.105 587	52
53	0.093 359	0.095 780	0.098 209	0.100 644	0.103 085	0.105 531	53
54	0.093 285	0.095 712	0.098 146	0.100 585	0.103 030	0.105 480	54
55	0.093 218	0.095 650	0.098 088	0.100 532	0.102 981	0.105 435	55
56	0.093 157	0.095 593	0.098 035	0.100 483	0.102 936	0.105 393	56
57	0.093 101	0.095 541	0.097 988	0.100 439	0.102 895	0.105 356	57
58	0.093 050	0.095 494	0.097 944	0.100 399	0.102 858	0.105 322	58
59	0.093 003	0.095 451	0.097 905	0.100 363	0.102 825	0.105 291	59
YRS							
30	0.092 960	0.095 412	0.097 868	0.100 330	0.102 795	0.105 263	60
31	0.092 885	0.095 343	0.097 806	0.100 272	0.102 742	0.105 216	62
32	0.092 823	0.095 286	0.097 754	0.100 225	0.102 699	0.105 176	64
33	0.092 770	0.095 238	0.097 710	0.100 186	0.102 664	0.105 145	66
34	0.092 726	0.095 199	0.097 675	0.100 153	0.102 635	0.105 118	68
35	0.092 689	0.095 166	0.097 645	0.100 127	0.102 611	0.105 097	70
36	0.092 659	0.095 138	0.097 620	0.100 105	0.102 591	0.105 079	72
37	0.092 633	0.095 115	0.097 600	0.100 087	0.102 575	0.105 065	74
38	0.092 611	0.095 096	0.097 583	0.100 072	0.102 562	0.105 053	76
39	0.092 593	0.095 080	0.097 569	0.100 059	0.102 551	0.105 044	78
40	0.092 578	0.095 067	0.097 557	0.100 049	0.102 542	0.105 036	80

PARTIAL PAYMENT TO AMORTIZE — SEMIANNUAL COMPOUNDING

HALF YRS	21.50% ANNUAL RATE	22.00% ANNUAL RATE	22.50% ANNUAL RATE	23.00% ANNUAL RATE	23.50% ANNUAL RATE	24.00% ANNUAL RATE	HALF YRS
1	1.107 500	1.110 000	1.112 500	1.115 000	1.117 500	1.120 000	1
2	0.581 996	0.583 934	0.585 873	0.587 813	0.589 755	0.591 698	2
3	0.407 435	0.409 213	0.410 994	0.412 776	0.414 562	0.416 349	3
4	0.320 608	0.322 326	0.324 048	0.325 774	0.327 503	0.329 234	4
5	0.268 871	0.270 570	0.272 274	0.273 982	0.275 694	0.277 410	5
6	0.234 677	0.236 377	0.238 081	0.239 791	0.241 506	0.243 226	6
7	0.210 504	0.212 215	0.213 932	0.215 655	0.217 384	0.219 118	7
8	0.192 592	0.194 321	0.196 057	0.197 799	0.199 548	0.201 303	8
9	0.178 850	0.180 602	0.182 360	0.184 126	0.185 899	0.187 679	9
10	0.168 025	0.169 801	0.171 585	0.173 377	0.175 177	0.176 984	10
11	0.159 319	0.161 121	0.162 932	0.164 751	0.166 579	0.168 415	11
12	0.152 197	0.154 027	0.155 866	0.157 714	0.159 571	0.161 437	12
13	0.146 293	0.148 151	0.150 018	0.151 895	0.153 782	0.155 677	13
14	0.141 342	0.143 228	0.145 124	0.147 030	0.148 946	0.150 871	14
15	0.137 151	0.139 065	0.140 990	0.142 924	0.144 869	0.146 824	15
16	0.133 575	0.135 517	0.137 469	0.139 432	0.141 406	0.143 390	16
17	0.130 503	0.132 471	0.134 452	0.136 443	0.138 444	0.140 457	17
18	0.127 847	0.129 843	0.131 850	0.133 868	0.135 897	0.137 937	18
19	0.125 541	0.127 563	0.129 596	0.131 641	0.133 696	0.135 763	19
20	0.123 528	0.125 576	0.127 634	0.129 705	0.131 786	0.133 879	20
21	0.121 766	0.123 838	0.125 921	0.128 016	0.130 123	0.132 240	21
22	0.120 218	0.122 313	0.124 420	0.126 539	0.128 669	0.130 811	22
23	0.118 853	0.120 971	0.123 101	0.125 243	0.127 396	0.129 560	23
24	0.117 647	0.119 787	0.121 939	0.124 103	0.126 278	0.128 463	24
25	0.116 579	0.118 740	0.120 913	0.123 098	0.125 294	0.127 500	25
26	0.115 631	0.117 813	0.120 006	0.122 210	0.124 426	0.126 652	26
27	0.114 788	0.116 989	0.119 202	0.121 425	0.123 659	0.125 904	27
28	0.114 038	0.116 257	0.118 488	0.120 730	0.122 982	0.125 244	28
29	0.113 368	0.115 605	0.117 854	0.120 112	0.122 381	0.124 660	29
30	0.112 771	0.115 025	0.117 289	0.119 564	0.121 849	0.124 144	30
31	0.112 237	0.114 506	0.116 786	0.119 077	0.121 377	0.123 686	31
32	0.111 759	0.114 043	0.116 338	0.118 643	0.120 957	0.123 280	32
33	0.111 331	0.113 629	0.115 938	0.118 257	0.120 584	0.122 920	33
34	0.110 947	0.113 259	0.115 581	0.117 912	0.120 252	0.122 601	34
35	0.110 603	0.112 927	0.115 262	0.117 605	0.119 957	0.122 317	35
36	0.110 294	0.112 630	0.114 976	0.117 331	0.119 694	0.122 064	36
37	0.110 016	0.112 364	0.114 721	0.117 086	0.119 459	0.121 840	37
38	0.109 767	0.112 125	0.114 492	0.116 867	0.119 250	0.121 640	38
39	0.109 543	0.111 911	0.114 288	0.116 672	0.119 064	0.121 462	39
40	0.109 341	0.111 719	0.114 104	0.116 497	0.118 897	0.121 304	40
41	0.109 159	0.111 546	0.113 940	0.116 341	0.118 749	0.121 163	41
42	0.108 996	0.111 391	0.113 793	0.116 201	0.118 616	0.121 037	42
43	0.108 849	0.111 251	0.113 661	0.116 076	0.118 498	0.120 925	43
44	0.108 717	0.111 126	0.113 542	0.115 964	0.118 392	0.120 825	44
45	0.108 597	0.111 014	0.113 436	0.115 864	0.118 298	0.120 736	45
46	0.108 490	0.110 912	0.113 341	0.115 774	0.118 213	0.120 657	46
47	0.108 393	0.110 821	0.113 255	0.115 694	0.118 138	0.120 586	47
48	0.108 306	0.110 739	0.113 178	0.115 622	0.118 071	0.120 523	48
49	0.108 227	0.110 666	0.113 109	0.115 558	0.118 010	0.120 467	49
50	0.108 156	0.110 599	0.113 047	0.115 500	0.117 956	0.120 417	50
51	0.108 092	0.110 540	0.112 992	0.115 448	0.117 908	0.120 372	51
52	0.108 034	0.110 486	0.112 942	0.115 402	0.117 865	0.120 332	52
53	0.107 982	0.110 438	0.112 897	0.115 360	0.117 827	0.120 296	53
54	0.107 935	0.110 394	0.112 857	0.115 323	0.117 792	0.120 264	54
55	0.107 893	0.110 355	0.112 821	0.115 290	0.117 761	0.120 236	55
56	0.107 854	0.110 320	0.112 788	0.115 260	0.117 734	0.120 211	56
57	0.107 820	0.110 288	0.112 759	0.115 233	0.117 709	0.120 188	57
58	0.107 789	0.110 259	0.112 733	0.115 209	0.117 687	0.120 168	58
59	0.107 761	0.110 233	0.112 709	0.115 187	0.117 668	0.120 150	59

YRS

HALF YRS	21.50%	22.00%	22.50%	23.00%	23.50%	24.00%	HALF YRS
30	0.107 735	0.110 210	0.112 688	0.115 168	0.117 650	0.120 134	60
31	0.107 692	0.110 171	0.112 652	0.115 135	0.117 620	0.120 107	62
32	0.107 656	0.110 138	0.112 623	0.115 109	0.117 596	0.120 085	64
33	0.107 627	0.110 112	0.112 599	0.115 087	0.117 577	0.120 068	66
34	0.107 604	0.110 091	0.112 580	0.115 070	0.117 562	0.120 054	68
35	0.107 585	0.110 074	0.112 565	0.115 056	0.117 549	0.120 043	70
36	0.107 569	0.110 060	0.112 552	0.115 045	0.117 539	0.120 034	72
37	0.107 556	0.110 049	0.112 542	0.115 037	0.117 532	0.120 027	74
38	0.107 546	0.110 040	0.112 534	0.115 029	0.117 525	0.120 022	76
39	0.107 537	0.110 032	0.112 528	0.115 024	0.117 520	0.120 017	78
40	0.107 530	0.110 026	0.112 522	0.115 019	0.117 516	0.120 014	80

SECTION 6

YRS	5.25% ANNUAL RATE	5.50% ANNUAL RATE	5.75% ANNUAL RATE	6.00% ANNUAL RATE	6.25% ANNUAL RATE	6.50% ANNUAL RATE	YRS
1	1.052 500	1.055 000	1.057 500	1.060 000	1.062 500	1.065 000	1
2	0.539 711	0.541 618	0.543 527	0.545 437	0.547 348	0.549 262	2
3	0.368 930	0.370 654	0.372 381	0.374 110	0.375 841	0.377 576	3
4	0.283 651	0.285 294	0.286 941	0.288 591	0.290 245	0.291 903	4
5	0.232 573	0.234 176	0.235 784	0.237 396	0.239 013	0.240 635	5
6	0.198 595	0.200 179	0.201 768	0.203 363	0.204 963	0.206 568	6
7	0.174 389	0.175 964	0.177 546	0.179 135	0.180 730	0.182 331	7
8	0.156 289	0.157 864	0.159 446	0.161 036	0.162 633	0.164 237	8
9	0.142 261	0.143 839	0.145 427	0.147 022	0.148 626	0.150 238	9
10	0.131 082	0.132 668	0.134 263	0.135 868	0.137 482	0.139 105	10
11	0.121 975	0.123 571	0.125 177	0.126 793	0.128 419	0.130 055	11
12	0.114 422	0.116 029	0.117 648	0.119 277	0.120 917	0.122 568	12
13	0.108 064	0.109 684	0.111 316	0.112 960	0.114 616	0.116 283	13
14	0.102 645	0.104 279	0.105 926	0.107 585	0.109 257	0.110 940	14
15	0.097 977	0.099 626	0.101 288	0.102 963	0.104 651	0.106 353	15
16	0.093 919	0.095 583	0.097 260	0.098 952	0.100 658	0.102 378	16
17	0.090 363	0.092 042	0.093 736	0.095 445	0.097 168	0.098 906	17
18	0.087 225	0.088 920	0.090 630	0.092 357	0.094 098	0.095 855	18
19	0.084 439	0.086 150	0.087 877	0.089 621	0.091 380	0.093 156	19
20	0.081 952	0.083 679	0.085 423	0.087 185	0.088 962	0.090 756	20
21	0.079 721	0.081 465	0.083 226	0.085 005	0.086 800	0.088 613	21
22	0.077 712	0.079 471	0.081 249	0.083 046	0.084 860	0.086 691	22
23	0.075 894	0.077 670	0.079 465	0.081 278	0.083 111	0.084 961	23
24	0.074 243	0.076 036	0.077 848	0.079 679	0.081 529	0.083 398	24
25	0.072 741	0.074 549	0.076 378	0.078 227	0.080 095	0.081 981	25
26	0.071 368	0.073 193	0.075 039	0.076 904	0.078 790	0.080 695	26
27	0.070 111	0.071 952	0.073 814	0.075 697	0.077 600	0.079 523	27
28	0.068 957	0.070 814	0.072 693	0.074 593	0.076 513	0.078 453	28
29	0.067 896	0.069 769	0.071 663	0.073 580	0.075 517	0.077 474	29
30	0.066 917	0.068 805	0.070 716	0.072 649	0.074 603	0.076 577	30
31	0.066 013	0.067 917	0.069 843	0.071 792	0.073 763	0.075 754	31
32	0.065 176	0.067 095	0.069 038	0.071 002	0.072 989	0.074 997	32
33	0.064 400	0.066 335	0.068 292	0.070 273	0.072 275	0.074 299	33
34	0.063 680	0.065 630	0.067 603	0.069 598	0.071 617	0.073 656	34
35	0.063 011	0.064 975	0.066 963	0.068 974	0.071 007	0.073 062	35
36	0.062 388	0.064 366	0.066 369	0.068 395	0.070 443	0.072 513	36
37	0.061 807	0.063 800	0.065 817	0.067 857	0.069 921	0.072 005	37
38	0.061 265	0.063 272	0.065 303	0.067 358	0.069 436	0.071 535	38
39	0.060 759	0.062 780	0.064 825	0.066 894	0.068 985	0.071 099	39
40	0.060 286	0.062 320	0.064 379	0.066 462	0.068 567	0.070 694	40
41	0.059 844	0.061 891	0.063 963	0.066 059	0.068 177	0.070 318	41
42	0.059 429	0.061 489	0.063 574	0.065 683	0.067 815	0.069 968	42
43	0.059 040	0.061 113	0.063 211	0.065 333	0.067 478	0.069 644	43
44	0.058 676	0.060 761	0.062 872	0.065 006	0.067 163	0.069 341	44
45	0.058 333	0.060 431	0.062 554	0.064 700	0.066 869	0.069 060	45
46	0.058 012	0.060 122	0.062 256	0.064 415	0.066 596	0.068 797	46
47	0.057 710	0.059 831	0.061 978	0.064 148	0.066 340	0.068 553	47
48	0.057 425	0.059 559	0.061 716	0.063 898	0.066 101	0.068 325	48
49	0.057 158	0.059 302	0.061 471	0.063 664	0.065 878	0.068 112	49
50	0.056 906	0.059 061	0.061 241	0.063 444	0.065 669	0.067 914	50

SECTION 6

YRS	6.75% ANNUAL RATE	7.00% ANNUAL RATE	7.25% ANNUAL RATE	7.50% ANNUAL RATE	7.75% ANNUAL RATE	8.00% ANNUAL RATE	YRS
1	1.067 500	1.070 000	1.072 500	1.075 000	1.077 500	1.080 000	1
2	0.551 176	0.553 092	0.555 009	0.556 928	0.558 848	0.560 769	2
3	0.379 312	0.381 052	0.382 793	0.384 538	0.386 284	0.388 034	3
4	0.293 564	0.295 228	0.296 896	0.298 568	0.300 242	0.301 921	4
5	0.242 260	0.243 891	0.245 525	0.247 165	0.248 808	0.250 456	5
6	0.208 179	0.209 796	0.211 418	0.213 045	0.214 677	0.216 315	6
7	0.183 939	0.185 553	0.187 174	0.188 800	0.190 433	0.192 072	7
8	0.165 849	0.167 468	0.169 094	0.170 727	0.172 367	0.174 015	8
9	0.151 858	0.153 486	0.155 123	0.156 767	0.158 419	0.160 080	9
10	0.140 737	0.142 378	0.144 027	0.145 686	0.147 353	0.149 029	10
11	0.131 701	0.133 357	0.135 022	0.136 697	0.138 382	0.140 076	11
12	0.124 230	0.125 902	0.127 585	0.129 278	0.130 981	0.132 695	12
13	0.117 961	0.119 651	0.121 352	0.123 064	0.124 788	0.126 522	13
14	0.112 637	0.114 345	0.116 065	0.117 797	0.119 541	0.121 297	14
15	0.108 067	0.109 795	0.111 535	0.113 287	0.115 052	0.116 830	15
16	0.104 111	0.105 858	0.107 618	0.109 391	0.111 178	0.112 977	16
17	0.100 659	0.102 425	0.104 206	0.106 000	0.107 808	0.109 629	17
18	0.097 626	0.099 413	0.101 214	0.103 029	0.104 859	0.106 702	18
19	0.094 947	0.096 753	0.098 574	0.100 411	0.102 262	0.104 128	19
20	0.092 567	0.094 393	0.096 235	0.098 092	0.099 965	0.101 852	20
21	0.090 443	0.092 289	0.094 151	0.096 029	0.097 923	0.099 832	21
22	0.088 540	0.090 406	0.092 288	0.094 187	0.096 102	0.098 032	22
23	0.086 829	0.088 714	0.090 616	0.092 535	0.094 471	0.096 422	23
24	0.085 284	0.087 189	0.089 111	0.091 050	0.093 006	0.094 978	24
25	0.083 887	0.085 811	0.087 752	0.089 711	0.091 686	0.093 679	25
26	0.082 619	0.084 561	0.086 521	0.088 500	0.090 495	0.092 507	26
27	0.081 465	0.083 426	0.085 405	0.087 402	0.089 417	0.091 448	27
28	0.080 413	0.082 392	0.084 390	0.086 405	0.088 438	0.090 489	28
29	0.079 452	0.081 449	0.083 464	0.085 498	0.087 550	0.089 619	29
30	0.078 572	0.080 586	0.082 620	0.084 671	0.086 741	0.088 827	30
31	0.077 766	0.079 797	0.081 847	0.083 916	0.086 003	0.088 107	31
32	0.077 025	0.079 073	0.081 140	0.083 226	0.085 330	0.087 451	32
33	0.076 344	0.078 408	0.080 492	0.082 594	0.084 714	0.086 852	33
34	0.075 716	0.077 797	0.079 896	0.082 015	0.084 151	0.086 304	34
35	0.075 138	0.077 234	0.079 349	0.081 483	0.083 635	0.085 803	35
36	0.074 604	0.076 715	0.078 846	0.080 994	0.083 161	0.085 345	36
37	0.074 111	0.076 237	0.078 382	0.080 545	0.082 726	0.084 924	37
38	0.073 655	0.075 795	0.077 954	0.080 132	0.082 327	0.084 539	38
39	0.073 233	0.075 387	0.077 560	0.079 751	0.081 960	0.084 185	39
40	0.072 842	0.075 009	0.077 196	0.079 400	0.081 622	0.083 860	40
41	0.072 479	0.074 660	0.076 859	0.079 077	0.081 311	0.083 561	41
42	0.072 142	0.074 336	0.076 548	0.078 778	0.081 024	0.083 287	42
43	0.071 830	0.074 036	0.076 260	0.078 502	0.080 760	0.083 034	43
44	0.071 540	0.073 758	0.075 994	0.078 247	0.080 517	0.082 802	44
45	0.071 270	0.073 500	0.075 747	0.078 011	0.080 292	0.082 587	45
46	0.071 019	0.073 260	0.075 518	0.077 794	0.080 084	0.082 390	46
47	0.070 786	0.073 037	0.075 306	0.077 592	0.079 893	0.082 208	47
48	0.070 569	0.072 831	0.075 110	0.077 405	0.079 716	0.082 040	48
49	0.070 366	0.072 639	0.074 928	0.077 232	0.079 552	0.081 886	49
50	0.070 178	0.072 460	0.074 758	0.077 072	0.079 401	0.081 743	50

PARTIAL PAYMENT TO AMORTIZE

YRS	8.25% ANNUAL RATE	8.50% ANNUAL RATE	8.75% ANNUAL RATE	9.00% ANNUAL RATE	9.25% ANNUAL RATE	9.50% ANNUAL RATE	YRS
1	1.082 500	1.085 000	1.087 500	1.090 000	1.092 500	1.095 000	1
2	0.562 692	0.564 616	0.566 542	0.568 469	0.570 397	0.572 327	2
3	0.389 785	0.391 539	0.393 296	0.395 055	0.396 816	0.398 580	3
4	0.303 603	0.305 288	0.306 977	0.308 669	0.310 364	0.312 063	4
5	0.252 109	0.253 766	0.255 427	0.257 092	0.258 762	0.260 436	5
6	0.217 959	0.219 607	0.221 261	0.222 920	0.224 584	0.226 253	6
7	0.193 718	0.195 369	0.197 027	0.198 691	0.200 360	0.202 036	7
8	0.175 669	0.177 331	0.178 999	0.180 674	0.182 357	0.184 046	8
9	0.161 748	0.163 424	0.165 107	0.166 799	0.168 498	0.170 205	9
10	0.150 714	0.152 408	0.154 110	0.155 820	0.157 539	0.159 266	10
11	0.141 780	0.143 493	0.145 215	0.146 947	0.148 687	0.150 437	11
12	0.134 419	0.136 153	0.137 897	0.139 651	0.141 414	0.143 188	12
13	0.128 267	0.130 023	0.131 789	0.133 567	0.135 354	0.137 152	13
14	0.123 064	0.124 842	0.126 632	0.128 433	0.130 245	0.132 068	14
15	0.118 619	0.120 420	0.122 234	0.124 059	0.125 896	0.127 744	15
16	0.114 789	0.116 614	0.118 451	0.120 300	0.122 161	0.124 035	16
17	0.111 464	0.113 312	0.115 173	0.117 046	0.118 932	0.120 831	17
18	0.108 559	0.110 430	0.112 315	0.114 212	0.116 123	0.118 046	18
19	0.106 007	0.107 901	0.109 809	0.111 730	0.113 665	0.115 613	19
20	0.103 754	0.105 671	0.107 602	0.109 546	0.111 505	0.113 477	20
21	0.101 756	0.103 695	0.105 649	0.107 617	0.109 598	0.111 594	21
22	0.099 978	0.101 939	0.103 915	0.105 905	0.107 909	0.109 928	22
23	0.098 389	0.100 372	0.102 370	0.104 382	0.106 409	0.108 449	23
24	0.096 966	0.098 970	0.100 989	0.103 023	0.105 071	0.107 134	24
25	0.095 687	0.097 712	0.099 751	0.101 806	0.103 876	0.105 959	25
26	0.094 536	0.096 580	0.098 640	0.100 715	0.102 805	0.104 909	26
27	0.093 496	0.095 560	0.097 640	0.099 735	0.101 845	0.103 969	27
28	0.092 556	0.094 639	0.096 738	0.098 852	0.100 981	0.103 124	28
29	0.091 704	0.093 806	0.095 923	0.098 056	0.100 203	0.102 364	29
30	0.090 931	0.093 051	0.095 186	0.097 336	0.099 501	0.101 681	30
31	0.090 228	0.092 365	0.094 518	0.096 686	0.098 868	0.101 064	31
32	0.089 589	0.091 742	0.093 912	0.096 096	0.098 295	0.100 507	32
33	0.089 006	0.091 176	0.093 361	0.095 562	0.097 776	0.100 004	33
34	0.088 474	0.090 660	0.092 861	0.095 077	0.097 306	0.099 549	34
35	0.087 988	0.090 189	0.092 405	0.094 636	0.096 880	0.099 138	35
36	0.087 545	0.089 760	0.091 990	0.094 235	0.096 493	0.098 764	36
37	0.087 139	0.089 368	0.091 612	0.093 870	0.096 142	0.098 426	37
38	0.086 767	0.089 010	0.091 267	0.093 538	0.095 822	0.098 119	38
39	0.086 426	0.088 682	0.090 952	0.093 236	0.095 532	0.097 840	39
40	0.086 114	0.088 382	0.090 664	0.092 960	0.095 267	0.097 587	40
41	0.085 827	0.088 107	0.090 401	0.092 708	0.095 027	0.097 357	41
42	0.085 564	0.087 856	0.090 161	0.092 478	0.094 808	0.097 148	42
43	0.085 323	0.087 625	0.089 941	0.092 268	0.094 608	0.096 958	43
44	0.085 101	0.087 414	0.089 739	0.092 077	0.094 426	0.096 785	44
45	0.084 897	0.087 220	0.089 555	0.091 902	0.094 259	0.096 627	45
46	0.084 709	0.087 042	0.089 386	0.091 742	0.094 108	0.096 484	46
47	0.084 537	0.086 878	0.089 231	0.091 595	0.093 970	0.096 353	47
48	0.084 378	0.086 728	0.089 089	0.091 461	0.093 843	0.096 234	48
49	0.084 232	0.086 590	0.088 959	0.091 339	0.093 728	0.096 126	49
50	0.084 097	0.086 463	0.088 840	0.091 227	0.093 623	0.096 027	50

YRS	9.75% ANNUAL RATE	10.00% ANNUAL RATE	10.25% ANNUAL RATE	10.50% ANNUAL RATE	10.75% ANNUAL RATE	11.00% ANNUAL RATE	YRS
1	1.097 500	1.100 000	1.102 500	1.105 000	1.107 500	1.110 000	1
2	0.574 258	0.576 190	0.578 124	0.580 059	0.581 996	0.583 934	2
3	0.400 346	0.402 115	0.403 886	0.405 659	0.407 435	0.409 213	3
4	0.313 765	0.315 471	0.317 180	0.318 892	0.320 608	0.322 326	4
5	0.262 115	0.263 797	0.265 484	0.267 175	0.268 871	0.270 570	5
6	0.227 928	0.229 607	0.231 292	0.232 982	0.234 677	0.236 377	6
7	0.203 718	0.205 405	0.207 099	0.208 799	0.210 504	0.212 215	7
8	0.185 741	0.187 444	0.189 153	0.190 869	0.192 592	0.194 321	8
9	0.171 919	0.173 641	0.175 370	0.177 106	0.178 850	0.180 602	9
10	0.161 002	0.162 745	0.164 497	0.166 257	0.168 025	0.169 801	10
11	0.152 196	0.153 963	0.155 740	0.157 525	0.159 319	0.161 121	11
12	0.144 971	0.146 763	0.148 565	0.150 377	0.152 197	0.154 027	12
13	0.138 960	0.140 779	0.142 607	0.144 445	0.146 293	0.148 151	13
14	0.133 902	0.135 746	0.137 601	0.139 467	0.141 342	0.143 228	14
15	0.129 603	0.131 474	0.133 355	0.135 248	0.137 151	0.139 065	15
16	0.125 920	0.127 817	0.129 725	0.131 644	0.133 575	0.135 517	16
17	0.122 741	0.124 664	0.126 599	0.128 545	0.130 503	0.132 471	17
18	0.119 982	0.121 930	0.123 891	0.125 863	0.127 847	0.129 843	18
19	0.117 574	0.119 547	0.121 533	0.123 531	0.125 541	0.127 563	19
20	0.115 462	0.117 460	0.119 470	0.121 493	0.123 528	0.125 576	20
21	0.113 602	0.115 624	0.117 659	0.119 707	0.121 766	0.123 838	21
22	0.111 960	0.114 005	0.116 063	0.118 134	0.120 218	0.122 313	22
23	0.110 504	0.112 572	0.114 653	0.116 747	0.118 853	0.120 971	23
24	0.109 210	0.111 300	0.113 403	0.115 519	0.117 647	0.119 787	24
25	0.108 057	0.110 168	0.112 292	0.114 429	0.116 579	0.118 740	25
26	0.107 027	0.109 159	0.111 304	0.113 461	0.115 631	0.117 813	26
27	0.106 106	0.108 258	0.110 422	0.112 599	0.114 788	0.116 989	27
28	0.105 281	0.107 451	0.109 634	0.111 830	0.114 038	0.116 257	28
29	0.104 540	0.106 728	0.108 929	0.111 143	0.113 368	0.115 605	29
30	0.103 873	0.106 079	0.108 298	0.110 528	0.112 771	0.115 025	30
31	0.103 274	0.105 496	0.107 731	0.109 978	0.112 237	0.114 506	31
32	0.102 733	0.104 972	0.107 222	0.109 485	0.111 759	0.114 043	32
33	0.102 246	0.104 499	0.106 765	0.109 042	0.111 331	0.113 629	33
34	0.101 805	0.104 074	0.106 354	0.108 645	0.110 947	0.113 259	34
35	0.101 408	0.103 690	0.105 983	0.108 288	0.110 603	0.112 927	35
36	0.101 048	0.103 343	0.105 649	0.107 967	0.110 294	0.112 630	36
37	0.100 722	0.103 030	0.105 349	0.107 677	0.110 016	0.112 364	37
38	0.100 427	0.102 747	0.105 077	0.107 417	0.109 767	0.112 125	38
39	0.100 160	0.102 491	0.104 832	0.107 183	0.109 543	0.111 911	39
40	0.099 918	0.102 259	0.104 611	0.106 971	0.109 341	0.111 719	40
41	0.099 698	0.102 050	0.104 411	0.106 781	0.109 159	0.111 546	41
42	0.099 499	0.101 860	0.104 230	0.106 609	0.108 996	0.111 391	42
43	0.099 318	0.101 688	0.104 067	0.106 454	0.108 849	0.111 251	43
44	0.099 154	0.101 532	0.103 919	0.106 314	0.108 717	0.111 126	44
45	0.099 005	0.101 391	0.103 786	0.106 188	0.108 597	0.111 014	45
46	0.098 869	0.101 263	0.103 665	0.106 074	0.108 490	0.110 912	46
47	0.098 746	0.101 147	0.103 555	0.105 971	0.108 393	0.110 821	47
48	0.098 634	0.101 041	0.103 456	0.105 878	0.108 306	0.110 739	48
49	0.098 532	0.100 946	0.103 367	0.105 794	0.108 227	0.110 666	49
50	0.098 440	0.100 859	0.103 285	0.105 718	0.108 156	0.110 599	50

YRS	11.25% ANNUAL RATE	11.50% ANNUAL RATE	11.75% ANNUAL RATE	12.00% ANNUAL RATE	12.25% ANNUAL RATE	12.50% ANNUAL RATE	YRS
1	1.112 500	1.115 000	1.117 500	1.120 000	1.122 500	1.125 000	1
2	0.585 873	0.587 813	0.589 755	0.591 698	0.593 643	0.595 588	2
3	0.410 994	0.412 776	0.414 562	0.416 349	0.418 139	0.419 931	3
4	0.324 048	0.325 774	0.327 503	0.329 234	0.330 970	0.332 708	4
5	0.272 274	0.273 982	0.275 694	0.277 410	0.279 130	0.280 854	5
6	0.238 081	0.239 791	0.241 506	0.243 226	0.244 950	0.246 680	6
7	0.213 932	0.215 655	0.217 384	0.219 118	0.220 858	0.222 603	7
8	0.196 057	0.197 799	0.199 548	0.201 303	0.203 064	0.204 832	8
9	0.182 360	0.184 126	0.185 899	0.187 679	0.189 466	0.191 260	9
10	0.171 585	0.173 377	0.175 177	0.176 984	0.178 799	0.180 622	10
11	0.162 932	0.164 751	0.166 579	0.168 415	0.170 260	0.172 112	11
12	0.155 866	0.157 714	0.159 571	0.161 437	0.163 311	0.165 194	12
13	0.150 018	0.151 895	0.153 782	0.155 677	0.157 582	0.159 496	13
14	0.145 124	0.147 030	0.148 946	0.150 871	0.152 806	0.154 751	14
15	0.140 990	0.142 924	0.144 869	0.146 824	0.148 789	0.150 764	15
16	0.137 469	0.139 432	0.141 406	0.143 390	0.145 384	0.147 388	16
17	0.134 452	0.136 443	0.138 444	0.140 457	0.142 479	0.144 512	17
18	0.131 850	0.133 868	0.135 897	0.137 937	0.139 988	0.142 049	18
19	0.129 596	0.131 641	0.133 696	0.135 763	0.137 840	0.139 928	19
20	0.127 634	0.129 705	0.131 786	0.133 879	0.135 982	0.138 096	20
21	0.125 921	0.128 016	0.130 123	0.132 240	0.134 368	0.136 507	21
22	0.124 420	0.126 539	0.128 669	0.130 811	0.132 962	0.135 125	22
23	0.123 101	0.125 243	0.127 396	0.129 560	0.131 735	0.133 919	23
24	0.121 939	0.124 103	0.126 278	0.128 463	0.130 660	0.132 866	24
25	0.120 913	0.123 098	0.125 294	0.127 500	0.129 717	0.131 943	25
26	0.120 006	0.122 210	0.124 426	0.126 652	0.128 888	0.131 134	26
27	0.119 202	0.121 425	0.123 659	0.125 904	0.128 159	0.130 423	27
28	0.118 488	0.120 730	0.122 982	0.125 244	0.127 516	0.129 797	28
29	0.117 854	0.120 112	0.122 381	0.124 660	0.126 949	0.129 246	29
30	0.117 289	0.119 564	0.121 849	0.124 144	0.126 447	0.128 760	30
31	0.116 786	0.119 077	0.121 377	0.123 686	0.126 004	0.128 331	31
32	0.116 338	0.118 643	0.120 957	0.123 280	0.125 612	0.127 952	32
33	0.115 938	0.118 257	0.120 584	0.122 920	0.125 265	0.127 617	33
34	0.115 581	0.117 912	0.120 252	0.122 601	0.124 957	0.127 321	34
35	0.115 262	0.117 605	0.119 957	0.122 317	0.124 684	0.127 059	35
36	0.114 976	0.117 331	0.119 694	0.122 064	0.124 442	0.126 827	36
37	0.114 721	0.117 086	0.119 459	0.121 840	0.124 227	0.126 621	37
38	0.114 492	0.116 867	0.119 250	0.121 640	0.124 036	0.126 439	38
39	0.114 288	0.116 672	0.119 064	0.121 462	0.123 867	0.126 278	39
40	0.114 104	0.116 497	0.118 897	0.121 304	0.123 716	0.126 134	40
41	0.113 940	0.116 341	0.118 749	0.121 163	0.123 582	0.126 007	41
42	0.113 793	0.116 201	0.118 616	0.121 037	0.123 463	0.125 895	42
43	0.113 661	0.116 076	0.118 498	0.120 925	0.123 357	0.125 795	43
44	0.113 542	0.115 964	0.118 392	0.120 825	0.123 263	0.125 706	44
45	0.113 436	0.115 864	0.118 298	0.120 736	0.123 179	0.125 627	45
46	0.113 341	0.115 774	0.118 213	0.120 657	0.123 105	0.125 557	46
47	0.113 255	0.115 694	0.118 138	0.120 586	0.123 039	0.125 495	47
48	0.113 178	0.115 622	0.118 071	0.120 523	0.122 980	0.125 440	48
49	0.113 109	0.115 558	0.118 010	0.120 467	0.122 927	0.125 391	49
50	0.113 047	0.115 500	0.117 956	0.120 417	0.122 880	0.125 347	50

YRS	12.75% ANNUAL RATE	13.00% ANNUAL RATE	13.25% ANNUAL RATE	13.50% ANNUAL RATE	13.75% ANNUAL RATE	14.00% ANNUAL RATE	YRS
1	1.127 500	1.130 000	1.132 500	1.135 000	1.137 500	1.140 000	1
2	0.597 535	0.599 484	0.601 433	0.603 384	0.605 336	0.607 290	2
3	0.421 725	0.423 522	0.425 321	0.427 122	0.428 926	0.430 731	3
4	0.334 449	0.336 194	0.337 942	0.339 693	0.341 447	0.343 205	4
5	0.282 582	0.284 315	0.286 051	0.287 791	0.289 535	0.291 284	5
6	0.248 414	0.250 153	0.251 897	0.253 646	0.255 399	0.257 157	6
7	0.224 354	0.226 111	0.227 873	0.229 641	0.231 414	0.233 192	7
8	0.206 606	0.208 387	0.210 173	0.211 966	0.213 765	0.215 570	8
9	0.193 061	0.194 869	0.196 684	0.198 505	0.200 333	0.202 168	9
10	0.182 452	0.184 290	0.186 135	0.187 987	0.189 847	0.191 714	10
11	0.173 973	0.175 841	0.177 718	0.179 602	0.181 494	0.183 394	11
12	0.167 086	0.168 986	0.170 895	0.172 811	0.174 736	0.176 669	12
13	0.161 419	0.163 350	0.165 291	0.167 240	0.169 198	0.171 164	13
14	0.156 704	0.158 667	0.160 640	0.162 621	0.164 611	0.166 609	14
15	0.152 748	0.154 742	0.156 745	0.158 757	0.160 779	0.162 809	15
16	0.149 402	0.151 426	0.153 460	0.155 502	0.157 554	0.159 615	16
17	0.146 556	0.148 608	0.150 671	0.152 743	0.154 825	0.156 915	17
18	0.144 120	0.146 201	0.148 292	0.150 392	0.152 502	0.154 621	18
19	0.142 026	0.144 134	0.146 252	0.148 380	0.150 517	0.152 663	19
20	0.140 220	0.142 354	0.144 498	0.146 651	0.148 814	0.150 986	20
21	0.138 656	0.140 814	0.142 983	0.145 161	0.147 348	0.149 545	21
22	0.137 297	0.139 479	0.141 672	0.143 873	0.146 084	0.148 303	22
23	0.136 114	0.138 319	0.140 533	0.142 757	0.144 990	0.147 231	23
24	0.135 082	0.137 308	0.139 544	0.141 788	0.144 041	0.146 303	24
25	0.134 180	0.136 426	0.138 681	0.140 945	0.143 218	0.145 498	25
26	0.133 390	0.135 655	0.137 928	0.140 211	0.142 501	0.144 800	26
27	0.132 697	0.134 979	0.137 270	0.139 570	0.141 877	0.144 193	27
28	0.132 088	0.134 387	0.136 695	0.139 010	0.141 334	0.143 664	28
29	0.131 552	0.133 867	0.136 190	0.138 521	0.140 859	0.143 204	29
30	0.131 081	0.133 411	0.135 748	0.138 092	0.140 444	0.142 803	30
31	0.130 666	0.133 009	0.135 360	0.137 717	0.140 082	0.142 453	31
32	0.130 300	0.132 656	0.135 019	0.137 388	0.139 764	0.142 147	32
33	0.129 978	0.132 345	0.134 719	0.137 100	0.139 487	0.141 880	33
34	0.129 693	0.132 071	0.134 456	0.136 847	0.139 244	0.141 646	34
35	0.129 441	0.131 829	0.134 224	0.136 624	0.139 030	0.141 442	35
36	0.129 218	0.131 616	0.134 020	0.136 429	0.138 844	0.141 263	36
37	0.129 022	0.131 428	0.133 840	0.136 258	0.138 680	0.141 107	37
38	0.128 848	0.131 262	0.133 682	0.136 107	0.138 536	0.140 970	38
39	0.128 694	0.131 116	0.133 543	0.135 974	0.138 410	0.140 850	39
40	0.128 558	0.130 986	0.133 420	0.135 858	0.138 299	0.140 745	40
41	0.128 437	0.130 872	0.133 312	0.135 755	0.138 202	0.140 653	41
42	0.128 331	0.130 771	0.133 216	0.135 665	0.138 117	0.140 573	42
43	0.128 236	0.130 682	0.133 132	0.135 585	0.138 042	0.140 502	43
44	0.128 153	0.130 603	0.133 058	0.135 515	0.137 976	0.140 440	44
45	0.128 078	0.130 534	0.132 992	0.135 454	0.137 919	0.140 386	45
46	0.128 013	0.130 472	0.132 934	0.135 400	0.137 868	0.140 338	46
47	0.127 955	0.130 417	0.132 883	0.135 352	0.137 823	0.140 297	47
48	0.127 903	0.130 369	0.132 838	0.135 310	0.137 784	0.140 260	48
49	0.127 857	0.130 327	0.132 799	0.135 273	0.137 750	0.140 228	49
50	0.127 817	0.130 289	0.132 764	0.135 241	0.137 719	0.140 200	50

PARTIAL PAYMENT TO AMORTIZE

YRS	14.25% ANNUAL RATE	14.50% ANNUAL RATE	14.75% ANNUAL RATE	15.00% ANNUAL RATE	15.25% ANNUAL RATE	15.50% ANNUAL RATE	YRS
1	1.142 500	1.145 000	1.147 500	1.150 000	1.152 500	1.155 000	1
2	0.609 244	0.611 200	0.613 158	0.615 116	0.617 076	0.619 037	2
3	0.432 539	0.434 350	0.436 162	0.437 977	0.439 794	0.441 613	3
4	0.344 965	0.346 729	0.348 496	0.350 265	0.352 038	0.353 814	4
5	0.293 036	0.294 792	0.296 552	0.298 316	0.300 083	0.301 855	5
6	0.258 920	0.260 688	0.262 460	0.264 237	0.266 018	0.267 804	6
7	0.234 976	0.236 766	0.238 560	0.240 360	0.242 166	0.243 976	7
8	0.217 381	0.219 198	0.221 021	0.222 850	0.224 685	0.226 526	8
9	0.204 010	0.205 858	0.207 713	0.209 574	0.211 442	0.213 316	9
10	0.193 588	0.195 469	0.197 357	0.199 252	0.201 154	0.203 063	10
11	0.185 302	0.187 217	0.189 139	0.191 069	0.193 006	0.194 951	11
12	0.178 610	0.180 559	0.182 516	0.184 481	0.186 453	0.188 433	12
13	0.173 138	0.175 121	0.177 112	0.179 110	0.181 117	0.183 132	13
14	0.168 616	0.170 632	0.172 656	0.174 688	0.176 729	0.178 777	14
15	0.164 848	0.166 896	0.168 952	0.171 017	0.173 090	0.175 171	15
16	0.161 685	0.163 764	0.165 852	0.167 948	0.170 052	0.172 165	16
17	0.159 015	0.161 124	0.163 241	0.165 367	0.167 501	0.169 643	17
18	0.156 749	0.158 886	0.161 032	0.163 186	0.165 349	0.167 520	18
19	0.154 818	0.156 982	0.159 155	0.161 336	0.163 526	0.165 723	19
20	0.153 167	0.155 357	0.157 555	0.159 761	0.161 976	0.164 199	20
21	0.151 750	0.153 964	0.156 186	0.158 417	0.160 655	0.162 901	21
22	0.150 531	0.152 768	0.155 013	0.157 266	0.159 526	0.161 795	22
23	0.149 481	0.151 739	0.154 005	0.156 278	0.158 560	0.160 848	23
24	0.148 573	0.150 851	0.153 137	0.155 430	0.157 730	0.160 038	24
25	0.147 787	0.150 084	0.152 388	0.154 699	0.157 018	0.159 343	25
26	0.147 106	0.149 420	0.151 742	0.154 070	0.156 405	0.158 746	26
27	0.146 516	0.148 846	0.151 183	0.153 526	0.155 877	0.158 233	27
28	0.146 003	0.148 348	0.150 699	0.153 057	0.155 421	0.157 791	28
29	0.145 556	0.147 915	0.150 280	0.152 651	0.155 028	0.157 411	29
30	0.145 168	0.147 539	0.149 917	0.152 300	0.154 689	0.157 083	30
31	0.144 830	0.147 213	0.149 602	0.151 996	0.154 396	0.156 800	31
32	0.144 535	0.146 929	0.149 328	0.151 733	0.154 142	0.156 556	32
33	0.144 278	0.146 682	0.149 091	0.151 505	0.153 923	0.156 345	33
34	0.144 054	0.146 467	0.148 884	0.151 307	0.153 733	0.156 164	34
35	0.143 858	0.146 279	0.148 705	0.151 135	0.153 569	0.156 006	35
36	0.143 687	0.146 116	0.148 549	0.150 986	0.153 426	0.155 871	36
37	0.143 538	0.145 974	0.148 413	0.150 857	0.153 303	0.155 753	37
38	0.143 408	0.145 850	0.148 295	0.150 744	0.153 196	0.155 652	38
39	0.143 294	0.145 742	0.148 193	0.150 647	0.153 104	0.155 564	39
40	0.143 195	0.145 647	0.148 103	0.150 562	0.153 024	0.155 488	40
41	0.143 108	0.145 565	0.148 025	0.150 489	0.152 954	0.155 422	41
42	0.143 031	0.145 493	0.147 958	0.150 425	0.152 894	0.155 366	42
43	0.142 965	0.145 431	0.147 899	0.150 369	0.152 842	0.155 316	43
44	0.142 907	0.145 376	0.147 847	0.150 321	0.152 796	0.155 274	44
45	0.142 856	0.145 328	0.147 803	0.150 279	0.152 757	0.155 237	45
46	0.142 811	0.145 287	0.147 764	0.150 242	0.152 723	0.155 205	46
47	0.142 773	0.145 250	0.147 730	0.150 211	0.152 694	0.155 178	47
48	0.142 738	0.145 218	0.147 700	0.150 183	0.152 668	0.155 154	48
49	0.142 709	0.145 191	0.147 674	0.150 159	0.152 646	0.155ꞏ133	49
50	0.142 683	0.145 167	0.147 652	0.150 139	0.152 626	0.155 115	50

YRS	15.75% ANNUAL RATE	16.00% ANNUAL RATE	16.25% ANNUAL RATE	16.50% ANNUAL RATE	16.75% ANNUAL RATE	17.00% ANNUAL RATE	YRS
1	1.157 500	1.160 000	1.162 500	1.165 000	1.167 500	1.170 000	1
2	0.620 999	0.622 963	0.624 928	0.626 894	0.628 861	0.630 829	2
3	0.443 434	0.445 258	0.447 084	0.448 911	0.450 741	0.452 574	3
4	0.355 593	0.357 375	0.359 160	0.360 948	0.362 739	0.364 533	4
5	0.303 630	0.305 409	0.307 192	0.308 979	0.310 770	0.312 564	5
6	0.269 595	0.271 390	0.273 189	0.274 993	0.276 802	0.278 615	6
7	0.245 792	0.247 613	0.249 439	0.251 270	0.253 106	0.254 947	7
8	0.228 372	0.230 224	0.232 082	0.233 946	0.235 815	0.237 690	8
9	0.215 196	0.217 082	0.218 975	0.220 874	0.222 779	0.224 691	9
10	0.204 979	0.206 901	0.208 830	0.210 766	0.212 708	0.214 657	10
11	0.196 902	0.198 861	0.200 826	0.202 799	0.204 779	0.206 765	11
12	0.190 420	0.192 415	0.194 417	0.196 426	0.198 442	0.200 466	12
13	0.185 154	0.187 184	0.189 222	0.191 266	0.193 319	0.195 378	13
14	0.180 834	0.182 898	0.184 970	0.187 049	0.189 136	0.191 230	14
15	0.177 260	0.179 358	0.181 462	0.183 575	0.185 695	0.187 822	15
16	0.174 285	0.176 414	0.178 550	0.180 694	0.182 845	0.185 004	16
17	0.171 794	0.173 952	0.176 118	0.178 292	0.180 473	0.182 662	17
18	0.169 698	0.171 885	0.174 079	0.176 281	0.178 490	0.180 706	18
19	0.167 929	0.170 142	0.172 362	0.174 590	0.176 825	0.179 067	19
20	0.166 429	0.168 667	0.170 912	0.173 165	0.175 424	0.177 690	20
21	0.165 155	0.167 416	0.169 684	0.171 960	0.174 242	0.176 530	21
22	0.164 070	0.166 353	0.168 642	0.170 938	0.173 241	0.175 550	22
23	0.163 144	0.165 447	0.167 756	0.170 071	0.172 393	0.174 721	23
24	0.162 352	0.164 673	0.167 001	0.169 334	0.171 674	0.174 019	24
25	0.161 675	0.164 013	0.166 357	0.168 707	0.171 062	0.173 423	25
26	0.161 094	0.163 447	0.165 807	0.168 172	0.170 542	0.172 917	26
27	0.160 595	0.162 963	0.165 336	0.167 715	0.170 099	0.172 487	27
28	0.160 167	0.162 548	0.164 934	0.167 325	0.169 721	0.172 121	28
29	0.159 799	0.162 192	0.164 589	0.166 992	0.169 399	0.171 810	29
30	0.159 482	0.161 886	0.164 294	0.166 707	0.169 124	0.171 545	30
31	0.159 209	0.161 623	0.164 041	0.166 463	0.168 889	0.171 318	31
32	0.158 975	0.161 397	0.163 824	0.166 254	0.168 688	0.171 126	32
33	0.158 772	0.161 203	0.163 637	0.166 075	0.168 517	0.170 961	33
34	0.158 598	0.161 036	0.163 477	0.165 922	0.168 370	0.170 821	34
35	0.158 448	0.160 892	0.163 340	0.165 791	0.168 245	0.170 701	35
36	0.158 318	0.160 769	0.163 222	0.165 678	0.168 137	0.170 599	36
37	0.158 206	0.160 662	0.163 121	0.165 582	0.168 046	0.170 512	37
38	0.158 110	0.160 571	0.163 034	0.165 499	0.167 967	0.170 437	38
39	0.158 027	0.160 492	0.162 959	0.165 428	0.167 900	0.170 373	39
40	0.157 955	0.160 424	0.162 895	0.165 368	0.167 842	0.170 319	40
41	0.157 893	0.160 365	0.162 839	0.165 315	0.167 793	0.170 273	41
42	0.157 839	0.160 315	0.162 792	0.165 271	0.167 751	0.170 233	42
43	0.157 793	0.160 271	0.162 751	0.165 232	0.167 715	0.170 199	43
44	0.157 753	0.160 234	0.162 716	0.165 199	0.167 684	0.170 170	44
45	0.157 718	0.160 201	0.162 686	0.165 171	0.167 658	0.170 145	45
46	0.157 689	0.160 174	0.162 660	0.165 147	0.167 635	0.170 124	46
47	0.157 663	0.160 150	0.162 637	0.165 126	0.167 616	0.170 106	47
48	0.157 641	0.160 129	0.162 618	0.165 108	0.167 599	0.170 091	48
49	0.157 622	0.160 111	0.162 602	0.165 093	0.167 585	0.170 078	49
50	0.157 605	0.160 096	0.162 587	0.165 080	0.167 573	0.170 066	50

YRS	17.25% ANNUAL RATE	17.50% ANNUAL RATE	17.75% ANNUAL RATE	18.00% ANNUAL RATE	18.25% ANNUAL RATE	18.50% ANNUAL RATE	YRS
1	1.172 500	1.175 000	1.177 500	1.180 000	1.182 500	1.185 000	1
2	0.632 799	0.634 770	0.636 742	0.638 716	0.640 690	0.642 666	2
3	0.454 408	0.456 245	0.458 083	0.459 924	0.461 767	0.463 612	3
4	0.366 330	0.368 130	0.369 933	0.371 739	0.373 547	0.375 359	4
5	0.314 362	0.316 163	0.317 969	0.319 778	0.321 590	0.323 407	5
6	0.280 432	0.282 254	0.284 080	0.285 910	0.287 745	0.289 584	6
7	0.256 793	0.258 645	0.260 501	0.262 362	0.264 228	0.266 099	7
8	0.239 570	0.241 456	0.243 348	0.245 244	0.247 147	0.249 054	8
9	0.226 608	0.228 531	0.230 460	0.232 395	0.234 336	0.236 282	9
10	0.216 612	0.218 573	0.220 541	0.222 515	0.224 495	0.226 481	10
11	0.208 758	0.210 757	0.212 764	0.214 776	0.216 796	0.218 821	11
12	0.202 496	0.204 533	0.206 577	0.208 628	0.210 685	0.212 749	12
13	0.197 445	0.199 518	0.201 599	0.203 686	0.205 780	0.207 881	13
14	0.193 332	0.195 440	0.197 556	0.199 678	0.201 807	0.203 943	14
15	0.189 957	0.192 098	0.194 247	0.196 403	0.198 565	0.200 734	15
16	0.187 170	0.189 343	0.191 523	0.193 710	0.195 904	0.198 104	16
17	0.184 857	0.187 060	0.189 269	0.191 485	0.193 708	0.195 937	17
18	0.182 929	0.185 159	0.187 396	0.189 639	0.191 889	0.194 145	18
19	0.181 316	0.183 572	0.185 834	0.188 103	0.190 378	0.192 658	19
20	0.179 963	0.182 243	0.184 528	0.186 820	0.189 118	0.191 421	20
21	0.178 825	0.181 126	0.183 433	0.185 746	0.188 065	0.190 390	21
22	0.177 865	0.180 187	0.182 514	0.184 846	0.187 184	0.189 528	22
23	0.177 055	0.179 395	0.181 740	0.184 090	0.186 446	0.188 806	23
24	0.176 370	0.178 726	0.181 088	0.183 454	0.185 826	0.188 202	24
25	0.175 790	0.178 161	0.180 538	0.182 919	0.185 305	0.187 695	25
26	0.175 298	0.177 683	0.180 073	0.182 467	0.184 866	0.187 269	26
27	0.174 881	0.177 278	0.179 681	0.182 087	0.184 497	0.186 911	27
28	0.174 526	0.176 935	0.179 348	0.181 765	0.184 186	0.186 610	28
29	0.174 225	0.176 644	0.179 067	0.181 494	0.183 924	0.186 357	29
30	0.173 969	0.176 398	0.178 829	0.181 264	0.183 702	0.186 144	30
31	0.173 751	0.176 188	0.178 628	0.181 070	0.183 516	0.185 964	31
32	0.173 566	0.176 010	0.178 457	0.180 906	0.183 358	0.185 813	32
33	0.173 409	0.175 859	0.178 312	0.180 767	0.183 225	0.185 686	33
34	0.173 274	0.175 730	0.178 189	0.180 650	0.183 113	0.185 578	34
35	0.173 160	0.175 621	0.178 085	0.180 550	0.183 018	0.185 488	35
36	0.173 063	0.175 528	0.177 996	0.180 466	0.182 938	0.185 411	36
37	0.172 980	0.175 450	0.177 921	0.180 395	0.182 870	0.185 347	37
38	0.172 909	0.175 382	0.177 858	0.180 335	0.182 813	0.185 293	38
39	0.172 849	0.175 325	0.177 804	0.180 284	0.182 765	0.185 247	39
40	0.172 797	0.175 277	0.177 758	0.180 240	0.182 724	0.185 208	40
41	0.172 753	0.175 236	0.177 719	0.180 204	0.182 689	0.185 176	41
42	0.172 716	0.175 200	0.177 686	0.180 172	0.182 660	0.185 148	42
43	0.172 684	0.175 171	0.177 658	0.180 146	0.182 635	0.185 125	43
44	0.172 657	0.175 145	0.177 634	0.180 124	0.182 614	0.185 106	44
45	0.172 634	0.175 123	0.177 614	0.180 105	0.182 597	0.185 089	45
46	0.172 614	0.175 105	0.177 597	0.180 089	0.182 582	0.185 075	46
47	0.172 597	0.175 089	0.177 582	0.180 075	0.182 569	0.185 063	47
48	0.172 583	0.175 076	0.177 570	0.180 064	0.182 558	0.185 054	48
49	0.172 571	0.175 065	0.177 559	0.180 054	0.182 549	0.185 045	49
50	0.172 560	0.175 055	0.177 550	0.180 046	0.182 542	0.185 038	50

YRS	18.75% ANNUAL RATE	19.00% ANNUAL RATE	19.25% ANNUAL RATE	19.50% ANNUAL RATE	19.75% ANNUAL RATE	20.00% ANNUAL RATE	YRS
1	1.187 500	1.190 000	1.192 500	1.195 000	1.197 500	1.200 000	1
2	0.644 643	0.646 621	0.648 600	0.650 581	0.652 563	0.654 545	2
3	0.465 459	0.467 308	0.469 159	0.471 012	0.472 868	0.474 725	3
4	0.377 174	0.378 991	0.380 811	0.382 634	0.384 460	0.386 289	4
5	0.325 227	0.327 050	0.328 877	0.330 708	0.332 542	0.334 380	5
6	0.291 427	0.293 274	0.295 126	0.296 982	0.298 842	0.300 706	6
7	0.267 974	0.269 855	0.271 740	0.273 630	0.275 525	0.277 424	7
8	0.250 967	0.252 885	0.254 808	0.256 737	0.258 671	0.260 609	8
9	0.238 234	0.240 192	0.242 156	0.244 125	0.246 099	0.248 079	9
10	0.228 473	0.230 471	0.232 475	0.234 485	0.236 501	0.238 523	10
11	0.220 853	0.222 891	0.224 935	0.226 985	0.229 042	0.231 104	11
12	0.214 819	0.216 896	0.218 979	0.221 068	0.223 164	0.225 265	12
13	0.209 988	0.212 102	0.214 222	0.216 349	0.218 481	0.220 620	13
14	0.206 086	0.208 235	0.210 390	0.212 551	0.214 719	0.216 893	14
15	0.202 910	0.205 092	0.207 280	0.209 475	0.211 675	0.213 882	15
16	0.200 310	0.202 523	0.204 743	0.206 968	0.209 199	0.211 436	16
17	0.198 173	0.200 414	0.202 662	0.204 916	0.207 175	0.209 440	17
18	0.196 407	0.198 676	0.200 950	0.203 229	0.205 515	0.207 805	18
19	0.194 945	0.197 238	0.199 536	0.201 839	0.204 148	0.206 462	19
20	0.193 731	0.196 045	0.198 365	0.200 691	0.203 021	0.205 357	20
21	0.192 719	0.195 054	0.197 395	0.199 740	0.202 089	0.204 444	21
22	0.191 876	0.194 229	0.196 588	0.198 950	0.201 318	0.203 690	22
23	0.191 172	0.193 542	0.195 916	0.198 295	0.200 678	0.203 065	23
24	0.190 582	0.192 967	0.195 356	0.197 750	0.200 147	0.202 548	24
25	0.190 089	0.192 487	0.194 890	0.197 296	0.199 705	0.202 119	25
26	0.189 675	0.192 086	0.194 500	0.196 917	0.199 338	0.201 762	26
27	0.189 329	0.191 750	0.194 174	0.196 602	0.199 033	0.201 467	27
28	0.189 037	0.191 468	0.193 902	0.196 339	0.198 778	0.201 221	28
29	0.188 793	0.191 232	0.193 674	0.196 119	0.198 566	0.201 016	29
30	0.188 588	0.191 034	0.193 484	0.195 936	0.198 390	0.200 846	30
31	0.188 415	0.190 869	0.193 324	0.195 782	0.198 242	0.200 705	31
32	0.188 270	0.190 729	0.193 191	0.195 654	0.198 120	0.200 587	32
33	0.188 148	0.190 612	0.193 079	0.195 547	0.198 017	0.200 489	33
34	0.188 045	0.190 514	0.192 985	0.195 458	0.197 932	0.200 407	34
35	0.187 959	0.190 432	0.192 907	0.195 383	0.197 860	0.200 339	35
36	0.187 886	0.190 363	0.192 841	0.195 320	0.197 801	0.200 283	36
37	0.187 825	0.190 305	0.192 786	0.195 268	0.197 751	0.200 235	37
38	0.187 774	0.190 256	0.192 740	0.195 224	0.197 710	0.200 196	38
39	0.187 731	0.190 215	0.192 701	0.195 188	0.197 675	0.200 163	39
40	0.187 694	0.190 181	0.192 668	0.195 157	0.197 646	0.200 136	40
41	0.187 663	0.190 152	0.192 641	0.195 131	0.197 622	0.200 113	41
42	0.187 638	0.190 128	0.192 618	0.195 110	0.197 602	0.200 095	42
43	0.187 616	0.190 107	0.192 599	0.195 092	0.197 585	0.200 079	43
44	0.187 598	0.190 090	0.192 583	0.195 077	0.197 571	0.200 066	44
45	0.187 582	0.190 076	0.192 570	0.195 064	0.197 559	0.200 055	45
46	0.187 569	0.190 064	0.192 559	0.195 054	0.197 550	0.200 046	46
47	0.187 558	0.190 053	0.192 549	0.195 045	0.197 541	0.200 038	47
48	0.187 549	0.190 045	0.192 541	0.195 038	0.197 535	0.200 032	48
49	0.187 541	0.190 038	0.192 535	0.195 032	0.197 529	0.200 026	49
50	0.187 535	0.190 032	0.192 529	0.195 026	0.197 524	0.200 022	50

YRS	20.25% ANNUAL RATE	20.50% ANNUAL RATE	20.75% ANNUAL RATE	21.00% ANNUAL RATE	21.25% ANNUAL RATE	21.50% ANNUAL RATE	YRS
1	1.202 500	1.205 000	1.207 500	1.210 000	1.212 500	1.215 000	1
2	0.656 530	0.658 515	0.660 501	0.662 489	0.664 477	0.666 467	2
3	0.476 585	0.478 446	0.480 310	0.482 175	0.484 043	0.485 913	3
4	0.388 121	0.389 955	0.391 792	0.393 632	0.395 475	0.397 321	4
5	0.336 221	0.338 066	0.339 914	0.341 765	0.343 620	0.345 479	5
6	0.302 574	0.304 446	0.306 323	0.308 203	0.310 087	0.311 976	6
7	0.279 328	0.281 236	0.283 149	0.285 067	0.286 989	0.288 916	7
8	0.262 553	0.264 502	0.266 456	0.268 415	0.270 379	0.272 347	8
9	0.250 065	0.252 056	0.254 052	0.256 053	0.258 060	0.260 072	9
10	0.240 550	0.242 583	0.244 621	0.246 665	0.248 715	0.250 769	10
11	0.233 172	0.235 246	0.237 325	0.239 411	0.241 502	0.243 598	11
12	0.227 372	0.229 486	0.231 605	0.233 730	0.235 860	0.237 996	12
13	0.222 765	0.224 915	0.227 072	0.229 234	0.231 402	0.233 575	13
14	0.219 073	0.221 259	0.223 450	0.225 647	0.227 850	0.230 058	14
15	0.216 095	0.218 313	0.220 537	0.222 766	0.225 001	0.227 242	15
16	0.213 679	0.215 927	0.218 181	0.220 441	0.222 705	0.224 975	16
17	0.211 711	0.213 987	0.216 268	0.218 555	0.220 846	0.223 143	17
18	0.210 101	0.212 403	0.214 709	0.217 020	0.219 337	0.221 657	18
19	0.208 782	0.211 106	0.213 435	0.215 769	0.218 107	0.220 450	19
20	0.207 697	0.210 042	0.212 391	0.214 745	0.217 103	0.219 465	20
21	0.206 803	0.209 166	0.211 534	0.213 906	0.216 282	0.218 662	21
22	0.206 066	0.208 446	0.210 830	0.213 218	0.215 609	0.218 005	22
23	0.205 456	0.207 851	0.210 250	0.212 652	0.215 058	0.217 467	23
24	0.204 953	0.207 361	0.209 772	0.212 187	0.214 605	0.217 026	24
25	0.204 535	0.206 955	0.209 378	0.211 804	0.214 233	0.216 665	25
26	0.204 190	0.206 620	0.209 053	0.211 489	0.213 927	0.216 368	26
27	0.203 903	0.206 343	0.208 785	0.211 229	0.213 676	0.216 125	27
28	0.203 666	0.206 113	0.208 563	0.211 015	0.213 469	0.215 925	28
29	0.203 468	0.205 923	0.208 379	0.210 838	0.213 298	0.215 761	29
30	0.203 305	0.205 765	0.208 228	0.210 692	0.213 158	0.215 626	30
31	0.203 169	0.205 635	0.208 102	0.210 572	0.213 042	0.215 515	31
32	0.203 056	0.205 526	0.207 999	0.210 472	0.212 947	0.215 423	32
33	0.202 962	0.205 437	0.207 913	0.210 390	0.212 869	0.215 348	33
34	0.202 884	0.205 362	0.207 842	0.210 322	0.212 804	0.215 287	34
35	0.202 819	0.205 300	0.207 783	0.210 266	0.212 751	0.215 236	35
36	0.202 765	0.205 249	0.207 734	0.210 220	0.212 707	0.215 194	36
37	0.202 721	0.205 207	0.207 694	0.210 182	0.212 670	0.215 160	37
38	0.202 683	0.205 172	0.207 661	0.210 150	0.212 641	0.215 131	38
39	0.202 653	0.205 142	0.207 633	0.210 124	0.212 616	0.215 108	39
40	0.202 627	0.205 118	0.207 610	0.210 103	0.212 596	0.215 089	40
41	0.202 605	0.205 098	0.207 591	0.210 085	0.212 579	0.215 073	41
42	0.202 588	0.205 081	0.207 575	0.210 070	0.212 565	0.215 060	42
43	0.202 573	0.205 068	0.207 563	0.210 058	0.212 554	0.215 050	43
44	0.202 561	0.205 056	0.207 552	0.210 048	0.212 544	0.215 041	44
45	0.202 550	0.205 046	0.207 543	0.210 040	0.212 536	0.215 034	45
46	0.202 542	0.205 039	0.207 536	0.210 033	0.212 530	0.215 028	46
47	0.202 535	0.205 032	0.207 529	0.210 027	0.212 525	0.215 023	47
48	0.202 529	0.205 027	0.207 524	0.210 022	0.212 520	0.215 019	48
49	0.202 524	0.205 022	0.207 520	0.210 018	0.212 517	0.215 015	49
50	0.202 520	0.205 018	0.207 517	0.210 015	0.212 514	0.215 013	50

278

YRS	21.75% ANNUAL RATE	22.00% ANNUAL RATE	22.50% ANNUAL RATE	23.00% ANNUAL RATE	23.50% ANNUAL RATE	24.00% ANNUAL RATE	YRS
1	1.217 500	1.220 000	1.225 000	1.230 000	1.235 000	1.240 000	1
2	0.668 458	0.670 450	0.674 438	0.678 430	0.682 427	0.686 429	2
3	0.487 784	0.489 658	0.493 411	0.497 173	0.500 942	0.504 718	3
4	0.399 169	0.401 020	0.404 730	0.408 451	0.412 183	0.415 926	4
5	0.347 341	0.349 206	0.352 947	0.356 700	0.360 468	0.364 248	5
6	0.313 868	0.315 764	0.319 569	0.323 389	0.327 224	0.331 074	6
7	0.290 847	0.292 782	0.296 666	0.300 568	0.304 486	0.308 422	7
8	0.274 321	0.276 299	0.280 270	0.284 259	0.288 267	0.292 293	8
9	0.262 089	0.264 111	0.268 170	0.272 249	0.276 348	0.280 465	9
10	0.252 830	0.254 895	0.259 041	0.263 208	0.267 395	0.271 602	10
11	0.245 700	0.247 807	0.252 038	0.256 289	0.260 561	0.264 852	11
12	0.240 138	0.242 285	0.246 595	0.250 926	0.255 277	0.259 648	12
13	0.235 754	0.237 939	0.242 323	0.246 728	0.251 154	0.255 598	13
14	0.232 272	0.234 491	0.238 944	0.243 418	0.247 911	0.252 423	14
15	0.229 487	0.231 738	0.236 255	0.240 791	0.245 346	0.249 919	15
16	0.227 250	0.229 530	0.234 104	0.238 697	0.243 308	0.247 936	16
17	0.225 445	0.227 751	0.232 377	0.237 021	0.241 682	0.246 359	17
18	0.223 983	0.226 313	0.230 986	0.235 676	0.240 381	0.245 102	18
19	0.222 797	0.225 148	0.229 863	0.234 593	0.239 339	0.244 098	19
20	0.221 832	0.224 202	0.228 954	0.233 720	0.238 501	0.243 294	20
21	0.221 045	0.223 432	0.228 217	0.233 016	0.237 827	0.242 649	21
22	0.220 403	0.222 805	0.227 619	0.232 446	0.237 283	0.242 132	22
23	0.219 879	0.222 294	0.227 134	0.231 984	0.236 846	0.241 716	23
24	0.219 450	0.221 877	0.226 739	0.231 611	0.236 492	0.241 382	24
25	0.219 099	0.221 536	0.226 417	0.231 308	0.236 207	0.241 113	25
26	0.218 812	0.221 258	0.226 156	0.231 062	0.235 976	0.240 897	26
27	0.218 576	0.221 030	0.225 943	0.230 863	0.235 790	0.240 723	27
28	0.218 383	0.220 843	0.225 769	0.230 701	0.235 639	0.240 583	28
29	0.218 225	0.220 691	0.225 627	0.230 570	0.235 517	0.240 470	29
30	0.218 095	0.220 566	0.225 512	0.230 463	0.235 419	0.240 379	30
31	0.217 989	0.220 464	0.225 418	0.230 376	0.235 339	0.240 305	31
32	0.217 901	0.220 380	0.225 341	0.230 306	0.235 274	0.240 246	32
33	0.217 829	0.220 311	0.225 278	0.230 249	0.235 222	0.240 198	33
34	0.217 770	0.220 255	0.225 227	0.230 202	0.235 180	0.240 160	34
35	0.217 722	0.220 209	0.225 185	0.230 164	0.235 146	0.240 129	35
36	0.217 682	0.220 171	0.225 151	0.230 133	0.235 118	0.240 104	36
37	0.217 650	0.220 140	0.225 123	0.230 109	0.235 095	0.240 084	37
38	0.217 623	0.220 115	0.225 101	0.230 088	0.235 077	0.240 068	38
39	0.217 601	0.220 094	0.225 082	0.230 072	0.235 063	0.240 055	39
40	0.217 583	0.220 077	0.225 067	0.230 058	0.235 051	0.240 044	40
41	0.217 568	0.220 063	0.225 055	0.230 047	0.235 041	0.240 035	41
42	0.217 556	0.220 052	0.225 045	0.230 039	0.235 033	0.240 029	42
43	0.217 546	0.220 043	0.225 037	0.230 031	0.235 027	0.240 023	43
44	0.217 538	0.220 035	0.225 030	0.230 025	0.235 022	0.240 019	44
45	0.217 531	0.220 029	0.225 024	0.230 021	0.235 018	0.240 015	45
46	0.217 525	0.220 023	0.225 020	0.230 017	0.235 014	0.240 012	46
47	0.217 521	0.220 019	0.225 016	0.230 014	0.235 012	0.240 010	47
48	0.217 517	0.220 016	0.225 013	0.230 011	0.235 009	0.240 008	48
49	0.217 514	0.220 013	0.225 011	0.230 009	0.235 008	0.240 006	49
50	0.217 512	0.220 011	0.225 009	0.230 007	0.235 006	0.240 005	50

DEPRECIATION TABLES

These tables display 5 popular methods used to depreciate assets: straight line, sum of the years' digits, and three declining balance methods. The annual and cumulative depreciation factors for each method depend on the useful life of the asset.

EXAMPLE

A $150,000 piece of machinery has a useful life of 10 years and no scrap value. An accountant has chosen to depreciate this equipment using the 125% declining balance method. What is the fourth year's depreciation? What is the cumulative depreciation through the fourth year?

Turn to page 281 and find the 10-year useful life section. Read across the 4-year row to the 125% declining balance (125% S/L) columns to find 8.4% and 41.4%. Multiply $150,000 by 8.4% to get $12,600, the fourth year's depreciation. Multiply $150,000 by 41.4% to get $62,100, the cumulative depreciation through the fourth year.

DEPRECIATION

	STRAIGHT LINE		125% S/L		150% S/L		200% S/L		SUM YEARS DIGITS		
YEAR	ANN. %	CUM. %	ANN. %	CUM. %	ANN. %	CUM. %	ANN. %	CUM. %	ANN. %	CUM. %	YEAR
5 YEAR USEFUL LIFE											
1	20.0	20.0	25.0	25.0	30.0	30.0	40.0	40.0	33.3	33.3	1
2	20.0	40.0	18.8	43.8	21.0	51.0	24.0	64.0	26.7	60.0	2
3	20.0	60.0	14.1	57.8	14.7	65.7	14.4	78.4	20.0	80.0	3
4	20.0	80.0	10.5	68.4	10.3	76.0	8.6	87.0	13.3	93.3	4
5	20.0	100.0	7.9	76.3	7.2	83.2	5.2	92.2	6.7	100.0	5
10 YEAR USEFUL LIFE											
1	10.0	10.0	12.5	12.5	15.0	15.0	20.0	20.0	18.2	18.2	1
2	10.0	20.0	10.9	23.4	12.8	27.7	16.0	36.0	16.4	34.5	2
3	10.0	30.0	9.6	33.0	10.8	38.6	12.8	48.8	14.5	49.1	3
4	10.0	40.0	8.4	41.4	9.2	47.8	10.2	59.0	12.7	61.8	4
5	10.0	50.0	7.3	48.7	7.8	55.6	8.2	67.2	10.9	72.7	5
6	10.0	60.0	6.4	55.1	6.7	62.3	6.6	73.8	9.1	81.8	6
7	10.0	70.0	5.6	60.7	5.7	67.9	5.2	79.0	7.3	89.1	7
8	10.0	80.0	4.9	65.6	4.8	72.8	4.2	83.2	5.5	94.5	8
9	10.0	90.0	4.3	69.9	4.1	76.8	3.4	86.6	3.6	98.2	9
10	10.0	100.0	3.8	73.7	3.5	80.3	2.7	89.3	1.8	100.0	10
15 YEAR USEFUL LIFE											
1	6.7	6.7	8.3	8.3	10.0	10.0	13.3	13.3	12.5	12.5	1
2	6.7	13.3	7.6	16.0	9.0	19.0	11.6	24.9	11.7	24.2	2
3	6.7	20.0	7.0	23.0	8.1	27.1	10.0	34.9	10.8	35.0	3
4	6.7	26.7	6.4	29.4	7.3	34.4	8.7	43.6	10.0	45.0	4
5	6.7	33.3	5.9	35.3	6.6	41.0	7.5	51.1	9.2	54.2	5
6	6.7	40.0	5.4	40.7	5.9	46.9	6.5	57.6	8.3	62.5	6
7	6.7	46.7	4.9	45.6	5.3	52.2	5.7	63.3	7.5	70.0	7
8	6.7	53.3	4.5	50.1	4.8	57.0	4.9	68.2	6.7	76.7	8
9	6.7	60.0	4.2	54.3	4.3	61.3	4.2	72.4	5.8	82.5	9
10	6.7	66.7	3.8	58.1	3.9	65.1	3.7	76.1	5.0	87.5	10
20 YEAR USEFUL LIFE											
1	5.0	5.0	6.3	6.3	7.5	7.5	10.0	10.0	9.5	9.5	1
2	5.0	10.0	5.9	12.1	6.9	14.4	9.0	19.0	9.0	18.6	2
3	5.0	15.0	5.5	17.6	6.4	20.9	8.1	27.1	8.6	27.1	3
4	5.0	20.0	5.1	22.8	5.9	26.8	7.3	34.4	8.1	35.2	4
5	5.0	25.0	4.8	27.6	5.5	32.3	6.6	41.0	7.6	42.9	5
6	5.0	30.0	4.5	32.1	5.1	37.4	5.9	46.9	7.1	50.0	6
7	5.0	35.0	4.2	36.3	4.7	42.1	5.3	52.2	6.7	56.7	7
8	5.0	40.0	4.0	40.3	4.3	46.4	4.8	57.0	6.2	62.9	8
9	5.0	45.0	3.7	44.1	4.0	50.4	4.3	61.3	5.7	68.6	9
10	5.0	50.0	3.5	47.6	3.7	54.1	3.9	65.1	5.2	73.8	10
25 YEAR USEFUL LIFE											
1	4.0	4.0	5.0	5.0	6.0	6.0	8.0	8.0	7.7	7.7	1
2	4.0	8.0	4.7	9.7	5.6	11.6	7.4	15.4	7.4	15.1	2
3	4.0	12.0	4.5	14.3	5.3	16.9	6.8	22.1	7.1	22.2	3
4	4.0	16.0	4.3	18.5	5.0	21.9	6.2	28.4	6.8	28.9	4
5	4.0	20.0	4.1	22.6	4.7	26.6	5.7	34.1	6.5	35.4	5
6	4.0	24.0	3.9	26.5	4.4	31.0	5.3	39.4	6.2	41.5	6
7	4.0	28.0	3.7	30.2	4.1	35.2	4.9	44.2	5.8	47.4	7
8	4.0	32.0	3.5	33.7	3.9	39.0	4.5	48.7	5.5	52.9	8
9	4.0	36.0	3.3	37.0	3.7	42.7	4.1	52.8	5.2	58.2	9
10	4.0	40.0	3.2	40.1	3.4	46.1	3.8	56.6	4.9	63.1	10

DEPRECIATION

YEAR	METHOD										YEAR
	STRAIGHT LINE		125% S/L		150% S/L		200% S/L		SUM YEARS DIGITS		
	ANN. %	CUM. %	ANN. %	CUM. %	ANN. %	CUM. %	ANN. %	CUM. %	ANN. %	CUM. %	
30 YEAR USEFUL LIFE											
1	3.3	3.3	4.2	4.2	5.0	5.0	6.7	6.7	6.5	6.5	1
2	3.3	6.7	4.0	8.2	4.7	9.7	6.2	12.9	6.2	12.7	2
3	3.3	10.0	3.8	12.0	4.5	14.3	5.8	18.7	6.0	18.7	3
4	3.3	13.3	3.7	15.7	4.3	18.5	5.4	24.1	5.8	24.5	4
5	3.3	16.7	3.5	19.2	4.1	22.6	5.1	29.2	5.6	30.1	5
6	3.3	20.0	3.4	22.5	3.9	26.5	4.7	33.9	5.4	35.5	6
7	3.3	23.3	3.2	25.8	3.7	30.2	4.4	38.3	5.2	40.6	7
8	3.3	26.7	3.1	28.9	3.5	33.7	4.1	42.4	4.9	45.6	8
9	3.3	30.0	3.0	31.8	3.3	37.0	3.8	46.3	4.7	50.3	9
10	3.3	33.3	2.8	34.7	3.2	40.1	3.6	49.8	4.5	54.8	10
33 1/3 YEAR USEFUL LIFE											
1	3.0	3.0	3.8	3.7	4.5	4.5	6.0	6.0	5.8	5.8	1
2	3.0	6.0	3.6	7.4	4.3	8.8	5.6	11.6	5.7	11.5	2
3	3.0	9.0	3.5	10.8	4.1	12.9	5.3	16.9	5.5	17.0	3
4	3.0	12.0	3.3	14.2	3.9	16.8	5.0	21.9	5.3	22.3	4
5	3.0	15.0	3.2	17.4	3.7	20.6	4.7	26.6	5.1	27.4	5
6	3.0	18.0	3.1	20.5	3.6	24.1	4.4	31.0	5.0	32.3	6
7	3.0	21.0	3.0	23.5	3.4	27.6	4.1	35.2	4.8	37.1	7
8	3.0	24.0	2.9	26.3	3.3	30.8	3.9	39.0	4.6	41.7	8
9	3.0	27.0	2.8	29.1	3.1	33.9	3.7	42.7	4.4	46.1	9
10	3.0	30.0	2.7	31.8	3.0	36.9	3.4	46.1	4.3	50.4	10
35 YEAR USEFUL LIFE											
1	2.9	2.9	3.6	3.6	4.3	4.3	5.7	5.7	5.6	5.6	1
2	2.9	5.7	3.4	7.0	4.1	8.4	5.4	11.1	5.4	11.0	2
3	2.9	8.6	3.3	10.3	3.9	12.3	5.1	16.2	5.2	16.2	3
4	2.9	11.4	3.2	13.5	3.8	16.1	4.8	21.0	5.1	21.3	4
5	2.9	14.3	3.1	16.6	3.6	19.7	4.5	25.5	4.9	26.2	5
6	2.9	17.1	3.0	19.6	3.4	23.1	4.3	29.7	4.8	31.0	6
7	2.9	20.0	2.9	22.5	3.3	26.4	4.0	33.8	4.6	35.6	7
8	2.9	22.9	2.8	25.2	3.2	29.6	3.8	37.5	4.4	40.0	8
9	2.9	25.7	2.7	27.9	3.0	32.6	3.6	41.1	4.3	44.3	9
10	2.9	28.6	2.6	30.5	2.9	35.5	3.4	44.5	4.1	48.4	10
40 YEAR USEFUL LIFE											
1	2.5	2.5	3.1	3.1	3.8	3.7	5.0	5.0	4.9	4.9	1
2	2.5	5.0	3.0	6.2	3.6	7.4	4.7	9.7	4.8	9.6	2
3	2.5	7.5	2.9	9.1	3.5	10.8	4.5	14.3	4.6	14.3	3
4	2.5	10.0	2.8	11.9	3.3	14.2	4.3	18.5	4.5	18.8	4
5	2.5	12.5	2.8	14.7	3.2	17.4	4.1	22.6	4.4	23.2	5
6	2.5	15.0	2.7	17.3	3.1	20.5	3.9	26.5	4.3	27.4	6
7	2.5	17.5	2.6	19.9	3.0	23.5	3.7	30.2	4.1	31.6	7
8	2.5	20.0	2.5	22.4	2.9	26.3	3.5	33.7	4.0	35.6	8
9	2.5	22.5	2.4	24.9	2.8	29.1	3.3	37.0	3.9	39.5	9
10	2.5	25.0	2.3	27.2	2.7	31.8	3.2	40.1	3.8	43.3	10
50 YEAR USEFUL LIFE											
1	2.0	2.0	2.5	2.5	3.0	3.0	4.0	4.0	3.9	3.9	1
2	2.0	4.0	2.4	4.9	2.9	5.9	3.8	7.8	3.8	7.8	2
3	2.0	6.0	2.4	7.3	2.8	8.7	3.7	11.5	3.8	11.5	3
4	2.0	8.0	2.3	9.6	2.7	11.5	3.5	15.1	3.7	15.2	4
5	2.0	10.0	2.3	11.9	2.7	14.1	3.4	18.5	3.6	18.8	5
6	2.0	12.0	2.2	14.1	2.6	16.7	3.3	21.7	3.5	22.4	6
7	2.0	14.0	2.1	16.2	2.5	19.2	3.1	24.9	3.5	25.8	7
8	2.0	16.0	2.1	18.3	2.4	21.6	3.0	27.9	3.4	29.2	8
9	2.0	18.0	2.0	20.4	2.4	24.0	2.9	30.7	3.3	32.5	9
10	2.0	20.0	2.0	22.4	2.3	26.3	2.8	33.5	3.2	35.7	10